SUPERSEDED

THE INTERACTIVE CASEBOOK SERIES™

PROFESSIONAL RESPONSIBILITY

A Contemporary Approach

By

Russell G. Pearce

EDWARD & MARILYN BELLET PROFESSOR OF LEGAL
ETHICS, MORALITY & RELIGION
FORDHAM UNIVERSITY SCHOOL OF LAW

Daniel J. Capra

PHILIP D. REED PROFESSOR OF LAW
FORDHAM UNIVERSITY SCHOOL OF LAW

and

Bruce A. Green

LOUIS STEIN PROFESSOR OF LAW
FORDHAM UNIVERSITY SCHOOL OF LAW

WEST®

A Thomson Reuters business

Mat #40832857

Interactive Casebook Series is a trademark registered in the U.S. Patent and Trademark Office.

© 2011 Thomson Reuters
      610 Opperman Drive
      St. Paul, MN 55123
      1–800–313–9378

Printed in the United States of America

ISBN: 978–0–314–90884–1

To Anne

D.C.

To Nancy, Anna & Isaac

B.G.

To Michele, Jacob & Seth

R.P.

Preface

We believe that Professional Responsibility is the most important course in law school. We also recognize that many law professors and law students may not agree. Accordingly, we have written a textbook that reflects both our passion for the subject and our efforts to make the course both challenging and fun to those who may not – at least initially – share our passion.

Unlike traditional law books, this text provides the resources of both a traditional casebook and of the internet, including access to Westlaw and TWEN. The casebook's features include:

- Coverage of the major topics in the field, employing the Model Rules of Professional Conduct, the Restatement (Third) of the Law of Governing Lawyers, and relevant cases, ethics opinions, and statutes, together with links to the full texts of these materials.

- Cases, examples, and issues that will engage students, such as the Torture Memos and the Lynne Stewart case, the Buried Bodies and OPM cases, the payment of attorney's fees with equity, entertaining lawyer advertisements, and a film featuring R.E.M. songs that explores the connection between the lawyer's role, political philosophy, and moral counseling.

- Multiple-choice questions that introduce each section. Answering the questions requires the students to read the text materials closely and critically. Many of the questions are old or model MPRE questions. In the acknowledgments, we identify which questions these are and we thank the National Conference of Bar Examiners for granting us permission to use them. All of the questions will help you focus your reading of the texts.

- Text boxes that raise provocative questions, make connections to supplementary materials, and link to stimulating audio, video, photographic, and text content.

- For those who wish to go beyond doctrinal mastery, challenging materials regarding professionalism, the justifications for lawyers privileges and responsibilities, the competing visions of the lawyer's role, and strategies for promoting access to justice.

In the spirit of the interactive series, we intend to create a community of users of this text. We welcome comments and suggestions, including ideas for links that we should include in the next edition. To facilitate the creation of this community, we are establishing a blog under the title "Professional Responsibility: A Contemporary Approach." The blog will allow us to share comments and suggestions with all users of the book, as well as to provide current updates.

We owe a great debt to West and, in particular, to Editor in Chief Louis Higgins for his vision for the interactive casebook series, as well as his constant and unflagging confidence and encouragement. While we are grateful to many colleagues at West, we would like to mention in particular, Heidi Boe, Senior Product Developer, for her outstanding contributions. Thanks to Holly Saari, our editor at Red Line Editorial, for accommodating our demanding requests and for her excellent work and that of her team.

This book would not have been possible without the extraordinary contributions of the team of law students and law graduates who helped us. Thanks to David Snyder for his outstanding work on Chapter 5. We would like to thank the following team of extraordinary research assistants for their work on all the chapters in the book: Nadine Etienne, Lisa J. Gray, Michael A. Kitson, Elisia Klinka, Sinna Bryce Nasseri, and Shlomo Pill. While each of these research assistants made an invaluable contribution, Sinna was the leader of the team that created the first draft and Elisia took the lead in finishing numerous edits of the entire book.

RUSSELL G. PEARCE

DANIEL J. CAPRA

BRUCE A. GREEN

October 2010

Features of this Casebook

Throughout the book you will find various text boxes on either side of the page. These boxes provide information that will help you to understand a case or cause you to think more deeply about an issue.

 For More Information These boxes point you to resources to consult for more information on a subject.

 Food for Thought These boxes pose questions that prompt you to think about issues raised by the material.

 Take Note Here you will be prompted to take special notice of something that deserves further thought or attention.

 FYI A self-explanatory category that shares useful or simply interesting information relevant to material in the text.

 See It These boxes point you to visual information that is relevant to the material in the text.

 Go Online If there are relevant online resources that are worth consulting in relation to any matter being discussed, these boxes will direct you to them.

 Make the Connection When concepts or discussions that pertain to information covered in other law school courses appear in a case or elsewhere in this text, often you will find this text box to indicate the course in which you can study those topics. Here you may also be prompted to connect information in the current case to material that you have covered elsewhere in this course.

 It's Latin to Me The law is fond of Latin terms and phrases; when you encounter these for the first time, this box will explain their meaning.

 Practice Pointers Here you will find advice relevant to legal practice typically inspired by the actions (or inactions) of legal counsel in the cases or simply prompted by an important issue being discussed.

 What's That? These boxes explain the meaning of special legal terms that appear in the main text. *Black's Law Dictionary* definitions may be accessed by clicking on the hyperlinked term in the text.

Acknowledgments

We gratefully acknowledge receiving permission to reprint excerpts from the following materials:

Azizah al-Hibri, *On Being a Muslim Corporate Lawyer*, 27 Tex Tech. L. Rev. 946 (1996).

Joseph Allegretti, *Christ and the Code: The Dilemma of the Christian Attorney*, 34 Cath. Law. 131 (1991).

Ashley E. Compton, Note, *Shifting the Blame: The Dilemma of Fee-Shifting Statutes and Fee-Waiver Settlements*, 22 Geo J. Legal Ethics 761 (2009). Reprinted with permission of the publisher, Georgetown Journal of Legal Ethics® 2009.

Kristen M. Dama, Comment, *Redefining a Final Act: The Fourteenth Amendment and States' Obligation to Prevent Death Row Inmates from Volunteering To Be Put to Death*, 9 U. Pa. J. Const. L. 1083 (2007).

Suzanne Darrow-Kleinhaus, *Response to the Society of American Law Teachers Statement on the Bar Exam*, 54 J. Legal Educ. 442 (2004).

John S. Dzienkowski & Robert J. Peroni, *The Decline in Lawyer Independence: Lawyer Equity Investments in Clients*, 81 Tex. L. Rev. 405 (2002).

John S. Dzienkowski & Robert J. Peroni, *Multidisciplinary Practice and the American Legal Profession: A Market Approach to Regulating the Delivery of Legal services in the Twenty-First Century*, 69 Fordham L. Rev. 83 (2000).

Timothy W. Floyd & John Gallagher, *Legal Ethics, Narrative, and Professional Identity: The Story of David Spaulding*, 59 Mercer L. Rev. 941 (2008).

Written Remarks of Lawrence J. Fox, *You've Got the Soul of the Profession in Your Hands*, http://abanet.org/cpr/mdp/fox1.html.

Posting of Monroe H. Freedman, *On Teaching and Testing in Law School*, to Legal Ethics Forum: The Purpose of Law School Classes?, http://www.legalethicsforum.com/blog/2006/10/the_purpose_of_.html (Oct. 11, 2006).

Stephen Gillers, *"Eat Your Spinach?"*, 51 St. Louis U. L.J. 1215 (2007). Reprinted with permission of the Saint Louis University *Law Journal* © 2007. St. Louis University School of Law, St. Louis, Missouri.

Bruce A. Green & Russell G. Pearce, *"Public Service Must Begin At Home": The Lawyer as Civics Teacher in Everyday Practice*, 50 Wm. & Mary L. Rev. 1207 (2009)

Jonathan O. Hafen, *Children's Rights and Legal Representation—The Proper Roles of Children, Parents, and Attorneys*, 7 Notre Dame J.L. Ethics & Pub. Pol'y 423 (1993).

2006 Lawyer Discipline Report Card, HALT, Inc. 2006. (www.halt.org).

Neil Hamilton, *Assessing Professionalism: Measuring Progress in the Formation of an Ethical Professional Identity*, 5 U. St. Thomas L.J. 470 (2008).

Nicole Lancia, Note, *New Rule, New York: A Bifocal Approach to Discipline and Discrimination*, 22 Geo. J. Legal Ethics 949 (2009). Reprinted with permission of the publisher, Georgetown Journal of Legal Ethics® 2009.

Heather MacDonald, What *Good is Pro Bono?*, 10 City J., Spring 2000, at 14.

Carrie Menkel-Meadow, *Portia in a Different Voice: Speculations on a Women's Lawyering Process*, 1 Berkeley Women's L.J. 39 (1985). © 1985 by the Regents of the University of California. Reprinted from the Berkeley Women's Law Journal, Vol. 1, No. 1, by permission of the Regents of the University of California.

Paul D. Paton, *Multidisciplinary Practice Redux: Globalization, Core Values, and Reviving the MDP Debate in America*, 78 Fordham L. Rev. 2193 (2010).

Russell G. Pearce, *The Jewish Lawyer's Question*, 27 Tex. Tech. L. Rev. 1259 (1996).

Russell G. Pearce, *Teaching Ethics Seriously, Legal Ethics as the Most Important Subject in Law School*, 29 Loy. U. Chi. L.J. 719 (1998).

Deborah L. Rhode, *Cultures of Commitment: Pro Bono for Lawyers and Law Students*, 67 Fordham L. Rev. 2415 (1999).

Deborah L. Rhode, *Moral Character as a Professional Credential*, 94 Yale L.J. 491 (1985). Reprinted with permission of the Yale Law Journal Company, Inc..

Posting of Larry Ribstein, *Is Lawyer Licensing Really Necessary?* to Ideoblog, http://busmovie.typepad.com/ideoblog/2006/05/is_lawyer_licen.html (May 6, 2006).

Larry Ribstein, *Final Thoughts on Lawyer Licensing*, PointofLaw.com, http://www.pointoflaw.com/feature/archives/002536.php (May 25, 2006).

William G. Ross, *The Ethics of Hourly Billing by Attorneys*, 44 Rutgers L. Rev. 1 (1991).

William B. Rubenstein, On What A "Private Attorney General" Is—and Why It Matters, 57 Vand. L. Rev. 2129 (2004).

Vijay Sekhon, *Over-Education of American Lawyers: An Economic and Ethical Analysis of the Requirements for Practicing Law in the United States*, 14 Geo. Mason L. Rev. 769 (2007).

William H. Simon, *Ethical Discretion in Lawyering*, 101 Harv. L. Rev. 1083 (1988). Reprinted with permission of the Harvard Law Review Association.

Society of American Law Teachers Statement on the Bar Exam, 52 J. Legal Educ. 446 (2002).

Marcy Strauss, *Toward a Revised Model of Attorney-Client Relationship: The Argument for Autonomy*, 65 N.C. L. Rev. 315 (1987). Reprinted with permission of the North Carolina Law Review, Vol. 65, pp. 324-25.

Jeffrey D. Swett, Comment, *Determining A Reasonable Percentage in Establishing a Contingency Fee: A New Tool to Remedy an Old Problem*, 77 Tenn. L. Rev. 653 (2010). The full text of this article was published originally at 77 Tenn. L. Rev. 653 (2010) and the portion is reprinted here by permission of the author and the Tennessee Law Review Association, Inc.

Akshat Tewary, *Legal Ethics as a Means to Address the Problem of Elite Law Firm Non-Diversity*, 12 Asian L.J. 1 (2005).

Transcript -- Morning Session, Symposium: *The Opportunity for Legal Education*, 59 Mercer L. Rev. 821 (2007).

Transcript -- Afternoon Session, Symposium: *The Opportunity for Legal Education*, 59 Mercer L. Rev. 821 (2007).

Robert K. Vischer, *Heretics in the Temple of the Law: The Promise and Peril of the Religious Lawyering Movement*, 19 J.L. & Religion 427 (2004).

Michael Waterstone, *A New Vision of Public Enforcement*, 92 Minn. L. Rev. 434 (2007).

David B. Wilkins, *Identities and Roles: Race, Recognition, and Professional Responsibility*, 57 Md. L. Rev. 1502 (1998).

Jonathan B. Wilson, *Is Lawyer Licensing Really Necessary?*, PointofLaw.com, http://busmovie.typepad.com/ideoblog/2006/05/is_lawyer_licen.html (May 19, 2006).

Certain publicly disclosed questions and answers from past MPRE examinations have been included herein with the permission of the National Conference of Bar Examiners (NCBE), the copyright owner. These questions and answers are the only actual MPRE questions and answers included in these materials. Permission to use NCBE's questions does not constitute an endorsement by NCBE or otherwise signify that NCBE has reviewed or approved any aspect of these materials or the company or individuals who distribute these materials.

The following questions are subject to:

Ch. 2: p. 39, Question 4; p. 40, Question 5; p. 40, Question 6; p. 57, Question 5; p. 79, Question 3; p. 88, Question 3; p. 88, Question 4; p. 90, Question 5; p. 98, Question 7; p. 103, Question 9; p. 106, Question 11; Ch. 3: p. 200, Question 1;* p. 201, Question 2; p. 212, Question 4; p. 214, Question 6; p. 231, Question 8; p. 232, Question 1; p. 264, Question 9; p. 269, Question 10; p. 275, Question 16; p. 277, Question 17; p. 278, Question 18; p. 278, Question 19; Ch. 4: p. 356, Question 11; Ch. 5: p. 416, Question 9; p. 417, Question 10; p. 436, Question 12; p. 437, Question 13; p. 440, Question 14; p. 454, Question 17; p. 469, Question 21; p. 487, Question 24; Ch. 6: p. 515, Question 2; p. 516, Question 3; p. 518, Question 4; p. 520, Question 11;* p. 529, Question 8; p. 531, Question 10; p. 532, Question 11; p. 533, Question 12; p. 551, Question 15; p. 552, Question 16; p. 573, Question 1; p. 575, Question 3; p. 577, Question 4; p. 578, Question 5; p. 583, Question 6; p. 616, Question 1; p. 617, Question 2; Ch. 7: p. 720, Question 1; p. 720, Question 2; p. 764, Question 6.

Ch. 2: p. 77, Question 2; p. 85, Question 5; p. 86, Question 1; p. 87, Question 2; p. 87, Question 4;* p. 91, Question 6; p. 104, Question 10; p. 155, Question 7; p. 140, Question 2;* p. 157, Question 8; p. 157, Question 9; Ch. 3: page 181, Question 1; p. 211, Question 3; p. 213, Question 5;* p. 248, Question 7; p. 272, Question 11; p. 273, Question 13;* p. 273, Question 14; p. 274, Question 15; Ch. 4: p. 369, Question

14; p. 372, Question 13; Ch. 5: p. 401, Question 3; p. 404, Question 7; p. 451, Question 16; p. 454, Question 18;* p. 461, Question 20; Ch. 6: p. 513, Question 1; p. 528, Question 7; p. 530, Question 9; p. 534, Question 13; p. 534, Question 14; p. 584, Question 7; p. 619, Question 4; Ch. 7: p. 722, Question 3; p. 745, Question 4; p. 745, Question 5.

---

* Modified from the original text.

Table of Contents

CHAPTER SIX: *The Lawyer's Duties to the Legal System, the Profession, and Nonclients*

Chapter Eight: *What is the Proper Role of a Lawyer*

Chapter Nine: *Why Do Lawyers Have Special Privileges and Responsibilities*

Table of Cases

The principal cases are in bold type. Cases cited or discussed in the text are in roman type. References are to pages. Cases cited in principal cases and within other quoted materials are not included.

CHAPTER 1

Introducing Professionalism and Legal Ethics

My practice experience tells me that [legal ethics is] the most important class a law student can take. Sure, sure. I anticipate the objections: What about constitutional law? What about corporations? What about contracts? And, anyway, nearly everyone thinks that his or her class is the most important. True, but only one of us is right. My reason is simple. Legal ethics is the only class in the law school curriculum whose content is relevant to the daily professional life of all graduates who practice law, which is nearly everyone. Bankruptcy is important to bankruptcy lawyers, but most lawyers do not need to know much, if any, bankruptcy law. The same point can be made about criminal law and securities and civil procedure. And so on. But all lawyers "practice" legal ethics just by going to work.

The common denominator does not stop there. All lawyers also have clients, at least one, often hundreds or thousands across a career. Indirectly, the class is for clients too. Or to put it another way: How can a law school conscientiously certify graduates as competent professionals without making an earnest effort to ensure that they understand the responsibilities of their profession to clients? And the class is for the courts, adversaries, and the public as well, because every law graduate who practices law has obligations to each group. There's more. Many students will go on to run government law offices, corporate law departments, private law firms, and public interest organizations. In these roles and others, they will make choices that define the culture of their offices. Some students will be active in bar associations or become judges. In these roles, they will influence or decide the content of rules governing the profession. In short, no other law school subject will have as much importance across the population of each graduating class.

-- Professor Stephen Gillers[1]

---

1   Stephen Gillers, *"Eat Your Spinach?,"* 51 St. Louis U. L.J. 1215, 1220-21 (2007).

Professor Gillers uses the term Legal Ethics. We prefer the term Professional Responsibility. But whatever the term, we all refer to the same constellation of concepts -- not only to the legal ethics rules but also to laws relevant to lawyer's practice and to professional values. We agree that Professional Responsibility is the most important course you will take in law school but recognize that many of you (and many of your professors) will be skeptical of this claim. As Professor Gillers notes, Professional Responsibility is the only course that applies to the work of every practicing lawyer. Moreover, it will help you understand the importance of the work of lawyers generally, as well as of your own career as a lawyer. As a result, the American Bar Association requires law schools to teach students "the history, goals, structure, values, rules and responsibilities of the legal profession and its members."[2] This teaching "includes instruction in matters such as the law of lawyering and the Model Rules of Professional Conduct of the American Bar Association."[3]

This Chapter will briefly introduce you to the topics of ethics and professionalism, including the controversies regarding whether law is a business or a profession and whether professional responsibility is an important course. It concludes with a short overview of the sources of applicable law.

A. This Professional Responsibility Course is about You

Professional Responsibility is about the rules and values you will encounter in law practice. In other courses, you study law and policy concerning clients. In this course, you also study law and policy concerning yourself, your friends, your colleagues, and your adversaries. As you begin this course, you should take a few minutes to reflect on your views on what it means to be a lawyer and what you want from a legal career. This will help you establish a starting point for evaluating and applying what you learn in the course

[Question 1]

I came to law school:

    (A) to make money.

    (B) to make the world better.

    (C) to pursue a particular interest in law.

    (D) to improve my employment.

    (E) because I had nothing else to do.

---

2   AM. BAR ASS'N, STANDARDS AND RULES OF PROCEDURE FOR APPROVAL OF LAW SCHOOLS Standard 302 (a)(5) (2009-2010).

3   *Id.* at Interpretation 302-9. *available at* http://www.abanet.org/legaled/standards/standards.html.

[Question 2]

A lawyer is:

   (A) a hired gun.

   (B) an expert advisor.

   (C) an altruistic public servant.

   (D) a businessperson.

   (E) a fraud.

[Question 3]

As a result of law school and related work, my understanding of myself as a lawyer has:

   (A) not changed.

   (B) changed. I am more interested in public service.

   (C) changed. I have a different goal for my career.

   (D) changed. I am more happy about being a lawyer.

   (E) changed. I am less happy about being a lawyer.

[Question 4]

After I graduate, I would like to work in:

   (A) public interest law.

   (B) government.

   (C) a large firm.

   (D) a small firm or solo practice.

   (E) a business.

B. Professional Responsibility is About the Legal Profession

Professionalism requires lawyers to satisfy high ethical standards. Of course, the exact meaning of professionalism—and of high ethical standards—is often subject to debate. This section will provide you with a basic introduction to perspectives on professionalism and professional responsibility. The questions below are, of course, quite important to your career and how you will find meaning in your work as a lawyer. We will return to them in Chapters 8 and 9 but we wanted to provide you with a brief context for your academic study of professional responsibility. Please review the following readings before answering the questions. We recognize, moreover, that your answers to these questions may change throughout this course and indeed throughout your career.

[Question 1]

Your college has invited you to meet with undergraduates to describe a career in law. In no more than 30 seconds, how would you describe the meaning of professionalism?

[Question 2]

Law practice is:

   (A) a business.

   (B) a profession.

   (C) both a business and a profession.

[Question 3]

Lawyers should have high ethical standards because:

   (A) law is a profession.

   (B) lawyer's work has the potential to have a major impact on individuals, businesses and society.

   (C) all people should have high ethical standards.

[Question 4]

In your view, which of the following factors is the most significant cause of the crisis of professionalism?

   (A) Increased competition in the market for legal services

   (B) Increased diversity in the legal profession

   (C) Changes in legal education to devalue practice and legal ethics

   (D) Changes in American culture that encourage skepticism of claims of expertise and of commitment to the public good

[Question 5]

Do you agree that lawyers can make money, have fun, and do good, all at the same time?

   (A) Yes

   (B) No

AMERICAN BAR ASSOCIATION COMMISSION ON PROFESSIONALISM, ". . . IN THE SPIRIT OF PUBLIC SERVICE" A BLUEPRINT FOR THE REKINDLING OF LAWYER PROFESSIONALISM,

112 F.R.D. 243, 261-2 (1986)

'Professionalism' is an elastic concept the meaning and application of which are hard to pin down. That is perhaps as it should be. The term has a rich, long-standing heritage, and any single definition runs the risk of being too confining.

Yet the term is so important to lawyers that at least a working definition seems essential. Lawyers are proud of being part of one of the 'historic' or 'learned' professions, along with medicine and the clergy, which have been seen as professions through many centuries.

When he was asked to define a profession, Dean Roscoe Pound of Harvard Law School said:

> The term refers to a group . . . pursuing a learned art as a common call-
> ing in the spirit of public service-no less a public service because it may
> incidentally be a means of livelihood. Pursuit of the learned art in the
> spirit of a public service is the primary purpose

The rhetoric may be dated, but the Commission believes the spirit of Dean Pound's definition stands the test of time. The practice of law 'in the spirit of a public service' can and ought to be the hallmark of the legal profession.

More recently, others have identified some common elements which distinguish a profession from other occupations. Commission member Professor Eliot Freidson of New York University defines our profession as:

An occupation whose members have special privileges, such as exclusive licensing, that are justified by the following assumptions:

  1. That its practice requires substantial intellectual training and the use of complex judgments.

  2. That since clients cannot adequately evaluate the quality of the service, they must trust those they consult.

  3. That the client's trust presupposes that the practitioner's self-interest is overbalanced by devotion to serving both the client's interest and the public good, and

  4. That the occupation is self-regulating-that is, organized in such a way as to assure the public and the courts that its members are competent, do not violate their client's trust, and transcend their own self-interest.

RUSSELL G. PEARCE, BRIAN DANITZ & ROMELIA S. LEACH, *REVITALIZING THE LAWYER-POET: WHAT LAWYERS CAN LEARN FROM ROCK AND ROLL,*
14 Widener L.J. 907, 907-22 (2005)

* * *

In his 1984 report to the American Bar Association, Chief Justice Burger made it official. He announced that the practice of law had become a business and was no longer a profession. Leading lawyers, distinguished law school deans, and eminent judges joined the chorus. They proclaimed that lawyer's ethics and professionalism were "lost, betrayed, in decline, facing demise, near death, and in need of redemption."

Food for Thought

You might enjoy the 15 minute film version of this article, "Revitalizing the Lawyer-Poet: What Lawyers Can Learn From Rock and Roll," directed by Sundance-featured documentary filmmaker Brian Danitz. It includes appearances by numerous lawyers and rock musicians, including Richard Nixon and Jimi Hendrix. The DVD should be available in your law school library. If not, the library can obtain it free from lawyersrock@law.fordham.edu. Before you watch the film, you may find it helpful to review the thought-provoking questions, *available at* http://www.law.fordham.edu/lawyersrock.

I. THE BUSINESS-PROFESSION DICHOTOMY

Why does business behavior inspire such strong denunciation?

Lawyer professionalism is all about the dichotomy between a business and a profession.

Business people work to make money.

Lawyers work primarily to promote the public good.

Consumers are capable of evaluating business goods and services.

Consumers are not capable of evaluating the expertise of lawyers.

Market competition makes business goods and services available for the best quality at the lowest price with government intervention when market failures occur. In contrast, the inaccessible expertise and unique altruism of lawyers require significant limits on market competition and government regulation. Only lawyers are allowed to provide legal services. Nonlawyers cannot compete with them. Lawyers by and large regulate themselves—deciding who has the privilege to practice law, creating the rules governing lawyers, and controlling the enforcement of those rules. The public can trust the legal profession to regulate itself because lawyers work primarily to promote the public good and not their own self-interest.

This commitment to the public good also makes lawyers the governing class in American democracy. Among the formal institutions of government, lawyers play a key role in the executive and legislature and a dominant role in the judiciary. Equally—or more—important, lawyers are the key to informal governance. On a daily basis, they serve as the primary intermediaries between the law and the people. As Erwin Smigel described in his famous study of Wall Street Lawyers, lawyers remind people and businesses of their obligations to the spirit of the law and the public good, and not just the minimal requirements of the letter of the law. No wonder that Alexis de Tocqueville had described lawyers as the aristocracy of the United States.

II. THE DICHOTOMY COLLAPSES

Bar leaders like to blame the crisis of professionalism on changes in the market for legal services, increased diversity in the profession, and changes in legal education that devalued practice and ethics. But these explanations are unpersuasive. The bar had retained its faith in the Business-Profession dichotomy during previous historical periods when the legal services market

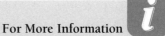

For More Information

You might want to read more about each of these arguments. *See, e.g.,* Russell G. Pearce, *Lawyers as America's Governing Class: The Formation and Dissolution of the Original Understanding of the American Lawyer's Role,* 8 U. Chi. L. Sch. Roundtable 381, 410-15 (2001) and the sources that article cites.

changed and the profession had become more diverse and law schools had never given great respect to either ethics or to practice.

What really happened was the 1960s. As with so much in America, the 1960s changed everything.

For the first time, most lawyers and nonlawyers came to believe that lawyers are just like everybody else—they're just as greedy as everybody else; they have no special relationship to the public good; and when it comes to expertise, their claim of inaccessible superiority rings false. Not only do we have books and Internet sites to help people help themselves with legal problems, but one of the leading legal advisors on the Internet has been a fifteen-year-old boy who claims to have learned everything he knows from television.

 Within the profession, the hired gun replaced the governing class as the dominant perspective. Lawyers no longer saw themselves as primarily responsible to the public good. They are responsible primarily to their client and their creed is extreme partisanship on their client's behalf without any moral accountability for any harm to the public.

The obligation for the public good shifted from ordinary lawyers to those saints who worked in the newly emerging field of public interest law or to the couple of hours a week that the ordinary lawyer devoted to the newly emerging ethical duty of pro bono.

At the same time, though, lawyers were not willing to let go of their exemptions from market competition and government regulation. They continued their allegiance to the rhetoric of professionalism at the same time as they rejected its premises.

This inconsistent approach created an insoluble problem for the bar and for individual lawyers.

No matter how much effort bar leaders devoted to reviving professionalism through commissions, mandatory continuing legal education, and strong words, they failed to make any significant change in lawyers' attitudes or in public perceptions of the legal profession. This failure should not have surprised anyone. To those who viewed lawyers as self-interested, these appeals appeared hypocritical, cynical, or just plain foolish.

Lawyers were adrift. They could no longer rely on professionalism to understand why their work was important and why they were morally accountable.

Time and time again, when a corporate or government scandal became public, we learned that lawyers had failed to counsel their clients to follow the spirit as well as the letter of the law. This was as true in the collapse of Enron as the earlier savings and loan scandals.

Not surprisingly, despite some variation in results, most studies find lawyers far less happy about their jobs than people in other occupations. Indeed, many lawyers say they would advise family members not to become lawyers and would not become lawyers if they had to make the choice again.

Studies have shown that "[o]f any occupation in the United States, lawyers have the highest incidence of depression, and are fifteen times more likely than the general population to suffer other forms of emotional distress."

Harvard Professor Mary Ann Glendon has noted that "[a]lcohol and drug abuse among lawyers is significantly higher than the population at large."

The bar's response to these problems is analogous to the way the characters in Bruce Springsteen's song "Glory Days" deal with their unhappy lives. Rather than change the present, they seek "to recapture a little of the glory" of their high school days as a high school baseball player who "could throw a speedball by you" or a girl who "turned all the boys' heads." The bar's efforts to restore an idealized past have been similarly futile.

III. ROCK AND ROLL

Perhaps it is time to look outside the box for answers.

Is it possible for lawyers to find meaning in their work without relying on the now discredited Business-Profession dichotomy?

Let me suggest that to address a problem that develops in the 1960s we look for an answer associated with that period as well, an answer that is certainly outside of the box.

Rock and roll.

One of my heroes is the rock-troubadour Jimi Hendrix. His picture sits on the wall of my office at Fordham Law School next to that of Justice Louis Brandeis. Hendrix is an exemplar of the rock and roll musician. His experimentation and creativity on the electric guitar established him, in the words of one commentator, as "perhaps the most innovative guitarist in history."

Hendrix exemplified the three aspects of rock and roll music most relevant to the practice of law.

First, rock and roll musicians play their music with a powerful and a passionate beat. It's loud; it's forceful; it gets into our heads, into our hearts, and, as Harvard University Professor Robert Coles also teaches us, even into our dreams. Hendrix, for example, maximized this effect by playing his music with incredible volume, forcing you to feel every beat.

Second, rock musicians both critique the establishment and collaborate with it. Robert Coles describes rock musicians as troubadour poets who "sp[eak] of life as it [is] being lived, and of social and political matters of significance." But rock musicians are not just social and political critics. They are trying to make lots of money and they depend on record companies, media corporations, and promoters to bring their music to their fans. A wonderful musical rendition of the tension between critique and homage to the establishment is Hendrix's version of the Star Spangled Banner. With his searing and brilliant guitar improvisation, Hendrix honors the national anthem just as he challenges us to rethink its meaning.

Third, rock and roll is democratic. Like the art of the troubadour, rock music is by regular folks, for regular folks, about regular folks. While classical musicians require years of formal training, anyone can be a rocker. They're just ordinary folks with talent who began playing in their basement or their bedroom. Hendrix, for example, learned guitar on his own by listening to his father's jazz and blues albums. By age fifteen he was sharing his talent with the public.

IV. CAN LAWYERS ROCK?

Those who want to listen to the lessons of rock and roll can find a way out of the crisis of professionalism.

Rock offers lawyers a way to find passion and importance in their work without requiring a faith that lawyers are morally superior practitioners of a mysterious art.

Rock music is made by regular folks. Lawyers are regular folks. Forget the Business-Professional dichotomy with its assumption that lawyers are morally superior. Forget as well the hired gun's assumption of amorality. We're all wrestling with what it means to be morally responsible—lawyers are just like everybody else.

Rock music is made for regular folks. Legal services are made for regular folks. Forget the Business-Profession dichotomy's assumption that legal services are beyond the capacity of consumers to evaluate. Legal services can be simple or complex just like other types of goods or services. How many of us truly understand the computer we purchase or have the capacity to judge the work of our auto mechanic?

When we jettison the Business-Profession dichotomy, what does rock provide in its stead?

Like rock, legal work is full of power and passion. Our work is about people and their stories. It's full of power and passion even, as Justice Louis Brandeis reminded us, when we represent businesses. We help people find justice, dignity, truth, riches, or maybe just a little relief.

Like rock troubadours, when we are doing our job, we are at the same time pillars of the establishment and its demanding critics. Like it or not, we do serve as intermediaries between the law and the public good on one hand, and people and businesses on the other. When rock forces us to reject the hired gun's amorality, we have no choice but to confront our governing class responsibility and incorporate moral counseling into our work.

But while a rock and roll style provides lawyers with a way to find meaning in their work, it also exacts a price.

If we apply the logic of rock, we have to give up our broad exemption from market competition and government regulation. If we're no better than folks in other occupations, why should we regulate ourselves? And if it helps bring services to low and middle income people, why not let nonlawyers and businesses provide legal services as long as government regulation and market discipline enforce the minimum standard of quality—a standard that we often don't enforce upon ourselves. The democratic vision of rock and roll is a tough one for lawyers; but if we want to rock, it's part of the package.

V. LAWYERS CAN ROCK: BUT WILL THEY?

In conclusion, lawyers can rock, but will they? I don't know. But let me end with a question for you: Would you rather yearn for Glory Days that you never had or would you rather jam with Springsteen or Hendrix?

NEIL HAMILTON, *ASSESSING PROFESSIONALISM: MEASURING PROGRESS IN THE FORMATION OF AN ETHICAL PROFESSIONAL IDENTITY,*

5 U. St. Thomas L.J. 470, 480-83 (2008)

* * *

Although professionalism is a highly useful term to describe the important elements of an ethical professional identity, legal scholars have so far been unable to construct and agree on a widely-accepted, clear and succinct definition of "professionalism." Legal scholarship regarding professionalism comes in three typical varieties. One brand discusses professionalism with no attempt to state a definition of the concept itself. In these articles, the definition of professionalism is either assumed to be self-evident or meant to be implicitly understood within the context of the article's main focus. For example, this brand of legal scholarship often asserts that "professionalism" is in decline and provides evidence of growing incivility among lawyers, increased legal malpractice actions and greater focus on profit and personal gain in the practice of law. The suggestion, then, is that professionalism itself is principally high competence and civility within the practicing bar, including also a commitment to serve the public rather than self-interest. Commonly, this type of article does not provide the legal community with a positive working definition of "professionalism;" rather, it describes problems in the profession and equates these problems with a lack of professionalism.

The second variety of scholarship on professionalism attempts to define the term by focusing on one or more characteristics that are the "core" of professionalism. Examples include a focus on professionalism as a set of core values, professional standards created by the ABA, a commitment to public service, client-oriented service, or individual morality and respect for the human beings and communities lawyers serve.

Lastly, a third brand of scholarship simply dismisses "professionalism" as a misguided concept. [Monroe] Freedman, for example, argues that professionalism's emphasis on civility and courtesy will undermine zealous advocacy, and {Rob} Atkinson believes that professionalism is a simplistic crusade based on an implicit assumption that there is one universal way to be a legal professional and categorically condemns certain conduct.

* * *

In my distillation of the major ABA reports, the Conference of Chief Justices National Action Plan and the Preamble to the Model Rules of Professional Conduct (the "Rules"), professionalism means that each lawyer:

1.   Continues to grow in personal conscience over his or her career;

2.   Agrees to comply with the ethics of duty--the minimum standards for the lawyer's professional skills and ethical conduct set by the Rules;

3.   Strives to realize, over a career, the ethics of aspiration--the core values and ideals of the profession, including internalization of the highest standards for the lawyer's professional skills and ethical conduct;

4.   Agrees to both hold other lawyers accountable for meeting the minimum standards set forth in the Rules and encourage them to realize core values and ideals of the profession; and,

5.   Agrees to act as a fiduciary, where his or her self-interest is overbalanced by devotion to serving the client and the public good in the profession's area of responsibility: justice. This includes:

a. Devoting professional time to serving the public good, particularly by representing pro bono clients; and,

b. Undertaking a continuing reflective engagement, over the course of a career, on the relative importance of income and wealth in light of the other principles of professionalism.

C. Can Professional Responsibility Be Taught?

The readings earlier in this chapter explain why the profession believes that teaching professional responsibility is important. After the questions below, you will find readings discussing how law students and professors view the course. Use all of these texts to answer the following questions. Remember that your views may very well change as the course proceeds.

[Question 1]

I expect this Professional Responsibility course to be:

(A) fun.

(B) challenging.

(C) both fun and challenging.

(D) neither fun nor challenging.

[Question 2]

I want the following from my Professional Responsibility course:

(A) Knowledge of the law and rules governing lawyers.

(B) Development of my professional identity.

(C) Development of my capacity for moral reasoning.

(D) A & B.

(E) A, B & C.

[Question 3]

I believe that a Professional Responsibility course is:

(A) the most important course in law school.

(B) the second most important course in law school.

(C) less important than my first year subject matter classes.

(D) relatively unimportant.

RUSSELL G. PEARCE, *TEACHING ETHICS SERIOUSLY: LEGAL ETHICS AS THE MOST IMPORTANT SUBJECT IN LAW SCHOOL,*

29 Loy. U. Chi. L.J. 719, 722-25 (1998)

* * *

Standing in marked contrast to the legal profession's commitment to legal ethics is the law schools' disdain for teaching legal ethics. Professor Deborah Rhode observes that "[t]hroughout the twentieth century, a wide gap has persisted between the bar's official pronouncements and educational practices concerning professional responsibility." She notes that during:

> the early twentieth century, such instruction remained quite minimal, usually consisting of lecture series by judges or prominent attorneys. For many of these series, no credit and no grade were given; sometimes, as it turned out, neither were the lectures. Those that did occur were generally short on content and long on platitudes: 'general piffle' was the description offered by one of the first serious scholars in the field.

In the 1950's, leaders of the Association of American Law Schools recommended that law schools offer both ethics courses and pervasive teaching of ethics throughout the curriculum. At the same time, the reality of law school teaching contradicted this aspiration. A survey revealed that most ethics courses "consisted of only one hour of ungraded instruction each week" and that very few, if any, non-ethics courses included pervasive ethics instruction.

The modern era of teaching legal ethics began in 1974. The notorious conduct of lawyers implicated in the Watergate scandal undermined "public confidence in the legal profession." In order to restore public confidence and bolster the integrity of lawyers, the ABA House of Delegates "mandat[ed] the teaching of professional responsibility in all ABA-accredited law schools." A late 1970s Doonesbury cartoon summarized law schools' response to this requirement. Discussing whether a legal ethics course would make a difference, a law student responds "nah—all that ethics stuff is just more Watergate fallout! Trendy lip service to our better selves." Law schools resented the "ABA's assertion of curricular authority." Although these schools may have complied with the letter of the ABA requirement, the course offerings were largely "second class."

Law students got the message. A 1975-76 American Bar Foundation ("ABF") study found that law students "perceived [professional responsibility courses] as "requiring less time, as substantially easier, as less well taught, and as a less valuable use of class time." The courses had "a low status in the latent curriculum hierarchy" because they were more likely to be taught by the discussion method rather than the socratic method and were less intellectually challenging due to the lack of doctrinal complexity. Ronald Pipkin, author of the ABF study, concluded "that the prevailing mode of [professional responsibility] instruction in fact socializes students into the belief that legal ethics are *not* important."

Since the undertaking of the Pipkin study, however, significant change has occurred. As observed by Roger Cramton and Susan Koniak, "the volume and complexity of case law dealing with the responsibilities of lawyers has exploded; new and more challenging textbooks have been published on the subject; and the subject we refer to as 'the law and ethics of lawyering' has become a halfway respectable field of academic scholarship." Deborah Rhode has provided an excellent text for making pervasive ethics a reality. Further, schools like Fordham University have developed advanced and contextual ethics courses, and a number of commentators have offered proposals for innovations in teaching ethics. Teaching ethics in a clinical setting has received more focus, and some schools have included ethics as a first year course.

Unfortunately, these developments are not representative of the current state of legal ethics teaching. Cramton and Koniak note that today, "legal ethics remains an unloved orphan of legal education." Echoing the views of a number of commentators, they find that "[i]n most law schools today legal ethics occupies a minor academic role as a one-or two-credit required course in the upper-class years, often taught by adjuncts or by a rotating group of faculty conscripts." They further observe that most schools which claim to teach ethics pervasively in fact offer "little more than tokenism designed to satisfy the [ABA] accreditation requirement." While legal ethics scholarship has advanced "half-way" to respectability, Koniak and Hazard note that "'[s]erious scholarship' in legal ethics is still considered somewhat of an oxymoron." In addition, students continue to share the faculty's low opinion of legal ethics. One observer notes that students view legal ethics as "the dog of the law school [curriculum—hard to teach, disappointing to take, and often presented to vacant seats or vacant minds."

* * *

STEPHEN GILLERS, "EAT YOUR SPINACH?,"

51 St. Louis U. L.J. 1215, 1219 (2007)

* * *

Dismissive faculty attitudes are not lost on students, who are rarely eager to take the class in any event. Mostly it's offered in the upper years, by which time in a student's career the word "required" before the word "course" is ground for indictment and summary punishment, not gratitude. Besides, students anticipate that the knowledge they gain in legal ethics—unlike excellence in (say) securities, or antitrust, or bankruptcy—is not the kind of information that will be attractive to employers. It can't be "resold" to clients. An "A" in corporations has palpable market value. An "A" in professional responsibility? Oh, that's nice. Explaining to students that they are learning rules and law that will govern their work lives for the next fifty years—ignorance of which can lead to embarrassment, anxiety, monetary sanctions, loss of status, even professional death—doesn't resonate. In the cocoon of the academy, students may view the rules governing the profession as only remotely connected to the world they are about to enter. Not true, of course, as they'll soon discover. Surely I'm not the only teacher of the subject delighted to learn that practicing lawyers are intellectually, even emotionally, invested in even the minor rules that govern how they may serve their clients.

* * *

LAUREN SOLBERG, REFORMING THE LEGAL ETHICS CURRICULUM:
A COMMENT ON EDWARD RUBIN'S "WHAT'S WRONG WITH LANGDELL'S
METHOD AND WHAT TO DO ABOUT IT,"

62 Vand. L. Rev. En Banc 12, 13-23 (2009)

* * * Despite the ABA requirement and the obvious importance of maintaining ethical behavior in legal practice, many students dislike the required professional responsibility course, in which most legal ethics is taught in law schools. Students dislike the course for many reasons, including that it is generally the only required upper-level course in law school. With this one exception, students are otherwise able to construct the remainder of their schedules based on their areas of personal and academic interest, or on the desire to learn from specific faculty members. Some students also dislike the discussion method of teaching typically used in professional responsibility courses, preferring the Socratic Method often used in core courses. * * *

* * *

The notion that students dislike the professional responsibility requirement often is attributed to the fact that, after the first year of law school, it is the only course that is required. Rubin implies as much, and other scholars have noted this fact. This dislike also can be attributed to the fact that students already think they are ethical, and do not need to learn ethics as a part of their law school curriculum. * * *

CHRISTINE PARKER, WHAT DO THEY LEARN WHEN THEY LEARN LEGAL ETHICS?,

12 Legal Educ. Rev. 175, 182 (2001)

The evidence certainly suggests that it is safe to assume that most students come into the legal ethics course cynical about whether it can teach them anything about ethics or can connect with their personal values or behaviour. Many students commented in their reflective journals (either in more or less overtly cynical terms) that ethics was a matter of personal morality and it was hard to imagine how a university course could teach ethics (this was particularly true of their first journal entries at the beginning of the course). * * *

RUSSELL G. PEARCE, TEACHING ETHICS SERIOUSLY, LEGAL ETHICS AS THE MOST IMPORTANT SUBJECT IN LAW SCHOOL,

29 Loy. U. Chi. L.J. 719, 725-35 (1998)

* * * Why Academics Wrongfully Disdain Legal Ethics

What explains the disjunction between the promise of professional aspirations and the failure of the legal academy to honor these aspirations? For years, many law professors have maintained that legal ethics need not and cannot be taught. This view is the product of three powerfully entrenched perspectives: (1) a faith in the ethical guarantees of professionalism and the methods of legal education; (2) the belief in the scientific basis of legal education; and (3) the assumption that adults lack the capacity for ethical development. While these three perspectives have an imposing pedigree, they have little persuasive force.

A. The Belief that the Profession and Education Will Ensure that Lawyers Act Ethically

Despite the diminishing faith of the general public, the faith of legal academics endures based on the belief that venerated elements of professional ideology make the teaching of legal ethics unnecessary. These elements include the professionalism's assertion of lawyer's essential goodness, the legal education's promise of character building, and the legal community's self-policing function. If any of these aspects functioned satisfactorily, law schools would not need to teach legal ethics. Unfortunately, they do not.

Professionalism maintains that lawyers will behave ethically. It presumes that most lawyers act ethically. For these lawyers, articulation of ethical standards in codes of conduct will suffice to ensure ethical conduct. There are two further mechanisms that purport to control those few practitioners who act unethically. The first of these mechanisms is the "invisible hand" of reputation. Lawyers who behave ethically earn the respect of their peers; this respect determines whether they succeed in law practice. Conversely, lawyers who behave unethically will not prosper. The second of these mechanisms are the existing formal procedures for preventing unethical people from gaining entrance to the bar and for disciplining the few rotten apples who do become lawyers. With such safeguards in place and with lawyers' success subject to the forces of reputation, the profession guarantees its own virtue, rendering ethics teaching in law school unnecessary.

The character building function of legal education serves as another reason for refusing to make special efforts to teach ethics. Oliver Wendell Holmes, for example, described how legal education imparts moral lessons, both a passion for "profounder thought" and an antipathy against "mean ideals and easy self-satisfaction." More recently, Anthony Kronman praised the case method's "function[] as an instrument for the development of moral imagination." It causes the student "to care with new intensity about the good of the legal system and the community it represents." This faith in legal instruction perhaps explains why many leaders of legal education maintain that "coverage of ethical concerns will occur naturally and pervasively throughout the curricula," even when their schools offer little or no specific instruction in legal ethics.

Unfortunately, evidence today strongly suggests that neither the promises of professionalism, nor the character building function of legal education, satisfactorily ensure lawyers' ethical conduct. In fact, the overwhelming consensus is that lawyers' ethics are declining, both in compliance with ethical codes and in commitment to the public good. At the same time, the profession has been unable to police itself adequately because its disciplinary system is underfinanced and ineffective. Whatever merit and faith in professionalism and legal education once existed, such merit and faith no longer offers credible support for academia's position that teaching legal ethics is not essential. Indeed, the mounting evidence of unethical lawyer conduct continues to prompt demands for improved ethics teaching by law schools.

B. The Mistaken Notion that Ethics and the Science of Law Do Not Mix

The belief that legal training builds character coexists with the somewhat contradictory notion that legal education is a science to which ethics is simply irrelevant. Related to this notion are the views that ethics teaching consists solely of inappropriate proselytizing and that its doctrine is too simple to merit serious consideration.

The model of legal education in today's classrooms, the case method, grew out of Harvard Dean Christopher Columbus Langdell's view of law as a science. Langdell described appellate cases as the raw materials from which to distill the principles of law. He believed that law libraries are to law professors and students as "laboratories . . . are to the chemists and physicists, the museum of natural history to the zoologists, [and] the botanical garden to the botanists."

Felix Cohen suggests that this scientific approach made legal academics hostile to teaching ethics. A science emphasizes "facts," not "moral values," and those who seek to promote the science of law believe "that law can attain the prestige of science only by showing a thorough contempt for judgments of value." After all, notes Cohen, "[t]here is no room for ethics in the oldest and most advanced science, physics. Why should those who seek to build legal science concern themselves with ethics?"

Although few law faculty today expressly identify themselves as legal scientists, Langdell's idealization of science continues to profoundly influence legal academia. While those faculty who identify themselves with a scientific perspective are more likely to draw upon a social science, such as economics, than a hard science, such as physics, these faculty still distinguish between facts and values. Legal positivists, who focus on what law is, similarly separate law from morality. Even many faculty who accept that the study of law implicates evaluative decisions do not teach about values. They commonly apply an "instrumentalist" approach that assumes that certain policy goals are worthy of pursuit, and then focuses students entirely on whether the law "provides an appropriate means for the realization of [those] policy goals."

In short, whether through old-fashioned Langdellian science, through cutting edge Law and Economics, or through policy-based instrumentalism, law professors continue to separate ethical questions from legal questions. Consequently, teachers' and students' values appear to become irrelevant. Some faculty view legal ethics as "somehow uninteresting or unworthy of fine minds." Others assert "that moral instruction will amount to moral indoctrination." As a result, legal ethics education improperly "becomes an occasion for teachers to impose their values and to penalize students with different perspectives." As David Wilkins recounts, "students who raise general ethical objections in traditional law school courses are often told that these concerns are irrelevant to the 'legal' issues being discussed."

Although these critiques persist, the ideological perspectives from which they derive their force have become an anachronism. The complexity of the law and ethics of lawyering has become undeniable. Moral reasoning has regained respect as a serious academic subject. The idea that law is a science has lost some of its hegemony, as has the distinction between facts and values. Within the academic community more broadly, the notion that science is a timeless and privileged means of discovery has become regarded as philosophically suspect

Within the scientific community, the notion that science and ethics do not mix has also lost its dominant influence. A recent National Academy of Science publication on "responsible conduct in research" discusses the ethics of "experimental techniques," the analysis of data, and "conflicts of interest," as well as "the impact [of research] on society." The publication notes that "[c]onstruction of the atomic bomb and the development of recombinant DNA—events that grew out of basic research on the nucleus of the atom and investigations of certain bacterial enzymes, respectively—are two examples of how seemingly arcane areas of science can have tremendous societal consequences." Accordingly, today little support exists for the proposition that "contempt" for ethics is necessary in order for "law [to] attain the prestige of science."

C. The Belief that Legal Ethics Cannot Make Law Students More Ethical

Many law faculty believe that law schools cannot improve the moral conduct of students through the teaching of legal ethics. They assert that students' values have been fully formed prior to law school and are not likely to change. This view, that the ethical capacity of adults is relatively static, appears to be a survival of the feudal concept of status wherein one's character and place in society was dictated by birth and family status. If birth and family circumstances dictate character, education in ethics can make little or no difference.

This view reflects two major manifestations. The first is the historical proposition that legal education and admission to practice should be limited to the "right kind of people." As one critic of required legal ethics education stated in 1930, the "'right kind' of law student already knows what constitutes moral and ethical conduct, and . . . a formal course in Legal Ethics will not supply the proper sort of character training for students who are not the 'right kind.'" Henry Drinker, perhaps the most prominent legal ethicist of the mid-twentieth century, reflected this view when he observed that "Russian Jew boys" were disproportionately "guilty of professional abuses" because their family background and education did not inculcate them in American ideals.

The second manifestation of this view, common in legal academia today, incorporates Drinker's view that family and environmental influences prior to law school determine law students' and lawyers' ethics. Rather than associate unethical conduct with particular groups, it relies on the notion that a person's capacity for moral development maximizes once a person reaches adulthood.

By their own terms, these perspectives are unpersuasive. Even if a student's moral development was generally complete before law school, that student would still have to apply this moral framework to the pursuit of law. John Mixon and Robert Schuwerk observe that "while law students have well-formed personal values stemming from family, church, and society, they nonetheless have relatively unsophisticated and unformed ideas of what it means to be a 'good lawyer.'"

Research demonstrating that values are malleable in adulthood renders these perspectives even less persuasive. Psychologists have shown that adulthood, like childhood, is a time of personal growth and development. Not surprisingly, studies reveal that moral development continues "after the age of 18." As the Committee on Professionalism of the ABA Section of Legal Education and Admissions concluded, "[t]he once widely held view that ethical precepts are fully formed before law school has been proven to be untrue."

Research further confirms that law school in particular is a time when students' values change. For example, political scientist Robert Stover documented the law school experience and its effect on students as making them less altruistic and less willing to work in a public interest job. Further underscoring the dramatic impact of a law school on a law student's personal development is an American Bar Foundation study reporting that law students' rate of significant mental health problems begins at an average rate but rises to as much as four times the average by graduation. Other studies support the specific proposition that ethics can be taught. Deborah Rhode notes that "[m]ore than a hundred studies evaluating moral education courses find that well-designed curricula can significantly improve capacities of moral reasoning . . . ."

The literature on legal ethics education, however, is less definitive. Some commentators have found ethics education to be significant, while others have not. Despite these mixed findings, Deborah Rhode observes that "[t]here is . . . more evidence on the effectiveness of professional responsibility instruction than there is on the effectiveness of most professional education."

Consequently, the contention that adults do not develop morally is a weak justification for resistance to teaching legal ethics, as is the faith in existing professional structures and the belief that law is purely a science. Whatever authority these three views once had, they possess little viability today. It is now time for law faculties to consider teaching ethics seriously.

D. The Legal Dimension of Professional Responsibility

The basic resources for exploring the lawyer's legal obligations are the ethics rules, bar opinions, the Restatement, caselaw, and statutes.

The ABA Model Rules of Professional Conduct (the "Rules") are the basic source of rules governing the conduct of lawyers. The Amerian Bar Association promulgates the Rules as a model. The ABA's Rules are not binding on governmental jurisdictions, but every State except California, as well as the District of Columbia and the Virgin Islands, has adopted some version of the Rules. http://www.abanet.org/cpr/mrpc/alpha_states.html. In each jurisdiction, the Courts promulgate the ethics rules, with the exception of California where the legislature has a major role. Restatement § 1(c) explains that "[t]he highest courts in most states have ruled as a matter of state constiutional law that their power to regulate lawyers is inherent in the judicial function. . . . The power is said to derive from the historical role of courts in the United States in regulating lawyers through admission and disbarment and from the traditional practice of courts in England." The federal courts also establish their own ethics rules for lawyers appearing before them, but they often adopt the rules of their local jurisdiction.

> **Practice Pointer**
>
> Because every jurisdiction is free to adopt its own version of the Rules, make sure to consult the applicable Rules in the jurisdiction where you are admitted or are practicing.

The Rules are the ABA's third codification of legal ethics. The first was the Canons of Professional Ethics, promulgated in 1908. The Canons were hortatory but courts and bar associations would often apply them to govern lawyers' conduct. The second was the Code of Professional Responsibility, adopted in 1970. The Code consisted of aspirational Ethical Considerations, as well as binding Disciplinary Rules. In 1983, the ABA enacted the Rules, almost all of which are binding. The ABA's Commission on Ethics 20/20 is currently considering proposed revisions to the Rules to respond to changes in law practice resulting rom technological developments and the globalization of legal practice.

In addition to their role in promulgating ethics rules for lawyers, courts interpret those rules through their review of discipline for violation of the rules, as well as in court matters, such as motions to disqualify, that require the courts to apply the rules. Another role of courts is to promulgate procedural and evidentiary rules that regulate lawyers, such as Rule 11 of the Federal Rules of Civil Procedure or the attorney-client privilege provisions of the Federal Rules of Evidence that combine common law principles with specific regulations.

Bar associations also play an important role in interpreting the rules. Many bar associations establish ethics committees to advise lawyers on whether their proposed conduct conforms to the rules. This advice can take the form of informal, telephone advice in

Go Online

Click here for the ABA Commission on Ethics 20/20's website.

urgent situations or of systematic, written opinions. Bar opinions are not binding on courts either in disciplinary or other matters. Nonetheless, courts tend to treat bar opinions with some deference and compliance with a bar opinion can help mitigate discipline even where the court disagrees with the bar committee's substantive determination of the relevant ethical question.

Both courts and bar associations rely on the American Law Institute's Restatement of the Law Governing Lawyers. The Restatement is not binding but has proven very influential.

Beyond the rules, common law and statutes also regulate lawyer conduct. The most familiar common law regulation of lawyers is the law of malpractice, but other common law doctrines, such as fraud, also apply to lawyers. In addition, legislatures regulate lawyers directly, such as through the Sarbanes-Oxley provisions governing lawyers who practice before the Securities and Exchange Commission or the Bankruptcy Reform Act that applies to bankruptcy lawyers, as well as through laws of general application, such as the criminal law. *See, e.g.*, Bruce A. Green, *The Criminal Regulation of Lawyers*, 67 Fordham L. Rev. 327 (1998).

E. Summary

You have begun your exploration of Professional Responsibility. By now, you realize that it is a course that applies to you personally, provides you with a framework for understanding and developing your career as a lawyer, and matters a great deal to the organized bar. But you are also aware that many question the importance of having a professional responsibility class and whether professional values are still significant to the practice of law. Although this book will provide you with tools for analyzing these and related issues in this course and in your career, you will have to determine your own commitments and values.

.

CHAPTER 2

The Basic Elements of Law Practice

I. Introduction

> Just after I had entered the practice at my firm, . . . one of my senior partners, perhaps sensing my frustration, approached me with a few words. He pointed out that . . . in our vocation there are three basic relationships with which we must be concerned. First and foremost, of course, is how we relate with our clients—the returned phone call, the short note providing an update, the unhurried time just to listen and a sense of loyalty and efficiency in handling our clients' business.[1]

Most lawyers represent clients, whether in private practice, public service, public interest, or in-house for a business. The representation of clients is therefore the core of the legal and ethical governance of the legal profession.

> **FYI**
>
> You might want to look at the numbers of lawyers in particular types of jobs or sizes at law firms, including numbers by gender. Clara N. Carson, The Lawyer Statistical Report: The U.S. Legal Profession in 2000 (The American Bar Foundation).

This chapter examines the building blocks of the lawyer-client relationship. For a start, lawyers provide legal services to clients. This idea sounds simple but the chapter will explain the complexity of determining who can lawfully provide such services. Recent developments have added to this complexity. One is the development of software and websites to assist consumers in solving legal problems. A second is the tension between state licensing of lawyers and the increasing national and international scope of the market for legal services.

The chapter next provides the ethical framework for the lawyer-client relationship. It describes when the lawyer's duties begin and examines whether the lawyers' obligations require an agreement to provide representation or the status of a person or business as a client. Once begun, how does the lawyer-client relation relationship end? The chapter explains the rules lawyer must follow.

---

1   C. Wendell Manning, *Words of Encouragement to New Admittees*, <u>44 La. Bar J. 374 (1996)</u>.

Last, the chapter offers two basic ground rules for the attorney-client relationship. First, the services lawyers provide must be competent. Questions of competence arise in the contexts of ethics, malprac-tice, and the constitutional right to counsel. Second, who makes what decisions in the lawyer-client relation-ship? Many lawyers and members of the public think the client is in charge, but the chapter explains some deci-sions belong to the client and others to the lawyer, and determining which is which is not always easy.

Reminder

For this Chapter and the entire case-book, when the text refers to a Rule, remember to read the entire Rule and Comment even though the text only includes excerpts.

II. Defining the Practice of Law

In the United States, courts have generally determined the qualification of those who were able to appear in court as litigators. Until the Twentieth Century, how-ever, businesses or not-for-profit organizations controlled by nonlawyers often provided transactional and litigation services, employing lawyers when necessary to appear in court on behalf of the organization or its customers. Today, most states generally prohibit the practice of law by nonlawyers, including law-yers who are not licensed in that state. Nonetheless, some exceptions exist by custom or law. For example, nonlawyers generally may represent themselves, and accountants may provide tax advice. In recent years, efforts to provide low cost legal assistance, to find ways to provide nonlawyers ownership and manage-ment roles in delivering legal services, and to accommodate the national and international legal services market, have rekindled the debate regarding the appropriate restrictions on nonlawyer practice.

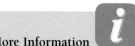

For More Information

If you want to read more about the history of the unauthorized practice restrictions, two excellent articles are Deborah L. Rhode, *Policing the Pro-fessional Monopoly: A Constitutional and Empirical Analysis of Unauthor-ized Practice Prohibitions*, 34 Stan. L. Rev. 1 (1981) and Bruce A. Green, *The Disciplinary Restrictions on Multi-disciplinary Practice: Their Derivation, Their Development, and Some Implica-tions for the Core Values Debate*, 84 Minn. L. Rev. 1115 (2000).

A. The Prohibition

The prohibition of unauthorized practice is generally a matter of Unauthorized Practice of Law ("UPL") statutes and not of ethics rules. The Comment to Rule

5.5 explains that "[t]he definition of the practice of law is established by law and varies from one jurisdiction to another."

For example, Section 6126(a) of the California Business and Professions Code provides that:

What About Your State?

For information on each state's definition of the practice of law, *see* http://www.abanet.org/cpr/model-def/model_def_statutes.pdf

> Any person advertising or holding himself or herself out as practicing or entitled to practice law or otherwise practicing law who is not an active member of the State Bar, or otherwise authorized pursuant to statute or court rule to practice law in this state at the time of doing so, is guilty of a misdemeanor punishable by up to one year in a county jail or by a fine of up to one thousand dollars ($1,000), or by both that fine and imprisonment. Upon a second or subsequent conviction, the person shall be confined in a county jail for not less than 90 days, except in an unusual case where the interests of justice would be served by imposition of a lesser sentence or a fine. If the court imposes only a fine or a sentence of less than 90 days for a second or subsequent conviction under this subdivision, the court shall state the reasons for its sentencing choice on the record.

The Los Angeles County Office of the District Attorney's, Unauthorized Practice of Law Manual for Prosecutors 6 (2004) adds:

> * * * California today defines law practice as providing *"legal advice and legal instrument and contract preparation, whether or not these subjects were rendered in the course of litigation."* Birbower, Montalban, Condo & Frank, P.C . v Superior Court. Providing legal advice or service is a violation of the State Bar Act when done by an unlicensed person, even if the advice or service does not relate to any matter pending before a court.

Make the Connection

You can find an excerpt from the *Birbower* case in Part I.D. *infra.*

As a general matter, the state Attorney General, local District Attorney, or bar association enforces unauthorized practice laws through "criminal prosecutions, civil injunctions, restitution disbarment, [and] contempt of court."[2] A private cause of action is a more recent development that is available only in some states.

B. Limits on Nonlawyers Providing Low Cost Legal Assistance

[Question 1]

What is the bar's rationale for restrictions on nonlawyer practice?

(A) Protecting the legal profession from competition

(B) Protecting consumers from incompetent and unethical practitioners

(C) Preventing innovation in the delivery of legal services

(D) None of the above

[Question 2]

As a general rule, in most jurisdictions a nonlawyer may do the all of following except:

(A) sell legal forms

(B) type in the blanks in legal forms for a customer

(C) publish books advising people on how to complete legal forms

(D) advise customers in person on how to complete legal forms

(E) no exceptions – a nonlawyer may perform all of the above.

FLORIDA BAR v. BRUMBAUGH

355 So. 2d 1186 (Fla. 1978)

PER CURIAM.

The Florida Bar has filed a petition charging Marilyn Brumbaugh with engaging in the unauthorized practice of law, and Seeking a permanent injunction pro-

---

2   Susan D. Hoppock, *Current Developments: Enforcing Unauthorized Practice of Law Prohibitions: The Emergence of the Private Cause of Action and Its Impact on Effective Enforcement,* 20 Geo. J. Legal Ethics 719, 730 (2007).

hibiting her from further engaging in these allegedly unlawful acts. Respondent, Marilyn Brumbaugh, is not and has never been a member of the Florida Bar, and is, therefore, not licensed to practice law within this state. She has advertised in various local newspapers as "Marilyn's Secretarial Service" offering to perform typing services for "Do-It-Yourself" divorces, wills, resumes, and bankruptcies. The Florida Bar charges that she performed unauthorized legal services by preparing for her customers those legal documents necessary in an uncontested dissolution of marriage proceeding and by advising her customers as to the costs involved and the procedures which should be followed in order to obtain a dissolution of marriage. For this service, Ms. Brumbaugh charges a fee of $50.

* * * In *State v. Sperry*, 140 So. 2d 587, 595 (Fla.1962), we noted:

> The reason for prohibiting the practice of law by those who have not been examined and found qualified to practice is frequently misunderstood. It is not done to aid or protect the members of the legal profession either in creating or maintaining a monopoly or closed shop. It is done to protect the public from being advised and represented in legal matters by unqualified persons over whom the judicial department can exercise little, if any, control in the matter of infractions of the code of conduct which, in the public interest, lawyers are bound to observe.

The Florida Bar as an agent of this Court, plays a large role in the enforcement of court policies and rules and has been active in regulating and disciplining unethical conduct by its members. Because of the natural tendency of all professions to act in their own self interest, however, this Court must closely scrutinize all regulations tending to limit competition in the delivery of legal services to the public, and determine whether or not such regulations are truly in the public interest.

With regard to the charges made against Marilyn Brumbaugh, this Court appointed a referee to receive evidence and to make findings of fact, conclusions of law, and recommendations as to the disposition of the case. The referee found that respondent, under the guise of a "secretarial" or "typing" service prepares, for a fee, all papers deemed by her to be needed for the pleading, filing, and securing of a dissolution of marriage, as well as detailed instructions as to how the suit should be filed, notice served, hearings set, trial conducted, and the final decree secured. The referee also found that in one instance, respondent prepared a quit claim deed in reference to the marital property of the parties. The referee determined that respondent's contention that she merely operates a typing service is rebutted by numerous facts in evidence. Ms. Brumbaugh has no blank forms either to sell or to fill out. Rather, she types up the documents for her customers after they have asked her to prepare a petition or an entire set of dissolution of marriage papers. Prior to typing up the papers, respondent asks her customers whether custody, child support, or alimony is involved. Respondent has four sets of dissolution of marriage papers, and she chooses which set is appropriate for the particular customer. She then types out those papers, filling in the blank spaces with the appropriate information. Respondent instructs her customers how the papers are to be signed, where they are to be filed, and how the customer should arrange for a final hearing.

Marilyn Brumbaugh, who is representing herself in proceedings before this Court * * * argues that she has never held herself out as an attorney, and has never professed to have legal skills. She does not give advice, but acts merely as a secretary. She is a licensed counselor, and asserts the right to talk to people and to let her customers make decisions for themselves.

This case does not arise out of a complaint by any of Ms. Brumbaugh's customers as to improper advice or unethical conduct. It has been initiated by members of The Florida Bar who believe her to be practicing law without a license. The evidence introduced at the hearing below shows that none of respondent's customers believed that she was an attorney, or that she was acting as an attorney in their behalf. Respondent's advertisements clearly addressed themselves to people who wish to do their own divorces. These customers knew that they had to have "some type of papers" to file in order to obtain their dissolution of marriage. Respondent never handled contested divorces. During the past two years respondent has assisted several hundred customers in obtaining their own divorces. The record shows that while some of her customers told respondent exactly what they wanted, generally respondent would ask her customers for the necessary information needed to fill out the divorce papers, such as the names and addresses of the parties, the place and duration of residency in this state, whether there was any property settlement to be resolved, or any determination as to custody and support of children. Finally, each petition contained the bare allegation that the marriage was irretrievably broken. Respondent would then inform the parties as to which documents needed to be signed, by whom, how many copies of each paper should be filed, where and when they should be filed, the costs involved, and what witness testimony is necessary at the court hearing. Apparently, Ms. Brumbaugh no longer informs the parties verbally as to the proper procedures for the filing of the papers, but offers to let them copy papers described as "suggested procedural education."

The Florida Bar argues that the above activities of respondent violate the rulings of this Court in *The Florida Bar v. American Legal and Business Forms, Inc.,* 274 So. 2d 225 (Fla. 1973), and *The Florida Bar v. Stupica,* 300 So. 2d 683 (Fla. 1974). In those decisions we held that it is lawful to sell to the public printed legal forms, provided they do not carry with them what purports to be instructions on how to fill out such forms or how to use them. We stated that legal advice is inextricably involved in the filling out and advice as to how to use such legal forms, and therein lies the danger of injury or damage to the public if not properly performed in accordance with law. In *Stupica, supra*, this Court rejected the rationale of the New York courts in *New York County Lawyers' Ass'n v. Dacey*, 28 A.D.2d 161, 283 N.Y.S.2d 984, *rev'd and dissenting opinion adopted* 21 N.Y.2d 694, 287 N.Y.S.2d 422, 234 N.E.2d 459 (N.Y.1967), which held that the publication of forms and instructions on their use does not constitute the unauthorized practice of law if these instructions are addressed to the public in general rather than to a specific individual legal problem. The Court in *Dacey* stated that the possibility that the principles or rules set forth in the text may be accepted by a particular reader as solution to his problem, does not mean that the publisher is practicing law. Other states have adopted the principle of law set forth in *Dacey*, holding that the sale of legal forms with instructions for their use does not constitute unauthorized practice of law. However, these courts have prohibited all personal contact between the service providing such forms and the customer, in the nature of consultation, explanation, recommendation, advice, or other assistance in selecting particular forms, in filling out any part of the forms, suggesting or advising how the forms should be used in solving the particular problems.

Although persons not licensed as attorneys are prohibited from practicing law within this state, it is somewhat difficult to define exactly what constitutes the practice of law in all instances. This Court has previously stated that:

. . . if the giving of such advice and performance of such services affect important rights of a person under the law, and if the reasonable protection of the rights and property of those advised and served requires that the persons giving such advice possess legal skill and a knowledge of the law greater than that possessed by the average citizen, then the giving of such advice and the performance of such services by one for another as a course of conduct constitute the practice of law.

This definition is broad and is given content by this Court only as it applies to specific circumstances of each case. We agree that "any attempt to formulate a lasting, all encompassing definition of 'practice of law' is doomed to failure 'for the reason that under our system of jurisprudence such practice must necessarily change with the everchanging business and social order.' "

The policy of this Court should continue to be one of encouraging persons who are unsure of their legal rights and remedies to seek legal assistance from persons licensed by us to practice law in this state. However, in order to make an intelligent decision as whether or not to engage the assistance of an attorney, a citizen must be allowed access to information which will help determine the complexity of the legal problem.

Present dissolution procedures in uncontested situations involve a very simplified method of asserting certain facts required by statute, notice to the other parties affected, and a simple hearing where the trial court may hear proof and make inquiries as to the facts asserted in those pleadings.

The legal forms necessary to obtain such an uncontested dissolution of marriage are susceptible of standardization. This Court has allowed the sale of legal forms on this and other subjects, provided that they do not carry with them what purports to be instructions on how to fill out such forms or how they are to be used. *The Florida Bar v. American Legal and Business Forms, Inc.*, supra; *The Florida Bar v. Stupica*, supra. These decisions should be reevaluated in light of those recent decisions in other states which have held that the sale of forms necessary to obtain a divorce, together with any related textual instructions directed towards the general public, does not constitute the practice of law. * * *

Although there is a danger that some published material might give false or misleading information, that is not a sufficient reason to justify its total ban. We must assume that our citizens will generally use such publications for what they are worth in the preparation of their cases, and further assume that most persons will not rely on these materials in the same way they would rely on the advice of an attorney or other persons holding themselves out as having expertise in the area. The tendency of persons seeking legal assistance to place their trust in the individual purporting to have expertise in the area necessitates this Court's regulation of such attorney-client relationships, so as to require that persons giving such advice have at least a minimal amount of legal training and experience. Although Marilyn Brumbaugh never held herself out as an attorney, it is clear that her clients placed some reliance upon her to properly prepare the necessary legal forms for their dissolution proceedings. To this extent we believe that Ms. Brumbaugh overstepped proper bounds and engaged in the unauthorized practice of law. We hold that Ms. Brumbaugh, and others in similar situations, may sell printed material purporting to explain legal practice and procedure to the public in general and she may sell sample legal forms. To this extent we limit our prior holdings in Stupica and American Legal and Business Forms, Inc. Further, we hold that it is not improper for Marilyn Brumbaugh to engage in a secretarial service, typing such forms for her clients, provided that she only copy the information given to her in writing by her clients. In addition, Ms. Brumbaugh may advertise her business activities of providing secretarial and notary services and selling legal forms and general printed information. However, Marilyn Brumbaugh must not, in conjunction with her business, engage in advising clients as to the various remedies available to them, or otherwise assist them in preparing those forms necessary for a dissolution proceeding. More specifically, Marilyn Brumbaugh may not make inquiries nor answer questions from her clients as to the particular forms which might be necessary, how best to fill out such forms, where to properly file such forms, and how to present necessary evidence at the court hearings. Our specific holding with regard to the dissolution of marriage also applies to other unauthorized legal assistance such as the preparation of wills or real estate transaction documents. While Marilyn Brumbaugh may legally sell forms in these areas, and type up instruments which have been completed by clients, she must not engage in personal legal assistance in conjunction with her business activities, including the correction of errors and omissions.

Accordingly, having defined the limits within which Ms. Brumbaugh and those engaged in similar activities may conduct their business without engaging in the unauthorized practice of law, the rule to show cause is dissolved.

Food for Thought

May a nonlawyer help a "sick friend" from church prepare papers in a worker's compensation case? Does the answer depend on whether the particular jurisdiction is one of those that allows nonlawyer advocates to represent clients in worker compensation cases? *See* Kate Howard, *Defiant Jacksonville retiree charged with practicing law without a license*, jacksonville.com, June 16, 2010.

It is so ordered.

1. Debate Regarding the Rationale for Unauthorized Practice Restrictions

The Rules share the *Brumbaugh* Court's view of the purpose of the restrictions on nonlawyer practice. The Comment to Rule 5.5 explains that the rationale for prohibitions on nonlawyer practice is to "protect[] the public against rendition of legal services by unqualified persons." But the unauthorized practice restrictions have prominent critics. Professor Deborah L. Rhode has challenged the bar's stated rationale:

> Almost from conception, the unauthorized practice movement has been dominated by the wrong people asking the wrong questions. Enforcement of sweeping prohibitions has rested with those least capable of disinterested action. Judicial involvement has been infrequent and generally unedifying. Invoking standards that are conclusory, circular, or both, courts have typically inquired only whether challenged activity calls for "legal" skills, not whether lay practitioners in fact possess them. At every level of enforcement, the consumer's need for protection has been proclaimed rather than proven. * * *

> Particularly at a time when lawyers are justifiably concerned about their public image, the bar itself has much to gain from abdicating its role as self-appointed guardian of the professional monopoly. Given mounting popular skepticism about unauthorized practice enforcement, prudential as well as policy considerations argue for greater consumer choice.

Absent evidence of significant injuries resulting from lay assistance, individuals should be entitled to determine the cost and quality of legal services that best meet their needs. Where there are demonstrable grounds for paternalism, it should emanate from institutions other than the organized bar. A profession strongly committed to maintaining both the fact and appearance of impartiality in other contexts should recognize the value of more dispassionate decisionmaking in unauthorized practice enforcement. If, as bar spokesmen repeatedly insist, the "fight to stop [lay practice] is the public's fight," it is time for the profession to relinquish the barricades.[3]

Which view do you find more persuasive? We will ask you to revisit this question after you consider the full range of questions arising under unauthorized practice of law.

2. Legal Advice Books

As the *Brumbaugh* Court notes, most jurisdictions permit the publication of books that aid people in representing themselves. In the pathbreaking case, *New York County Lawyers' Ass'n. v. Dacey*, 234 N.E.2d 459 (N.Y. 1967), the New York Court of Appeals endorsed the dissenting opinion of the lower court and held that by writing the book *How to Avoid Probate!*, Norman Dacey was simply providing information about law and not actually practicing law. In the dissent of *New York County Lawyers' Ass'n v. Dacey*, 283 N.Y.S. 2d 984 (N.Y. App. Div., 1st Dep't 1967), Justice Stevens wrote:

> Stripped of the arguments and the contentions of the various parties, the question may be briefly and baldly expressed: Does the writing, publication, advertising, sale and distribution of "How To Avoid Probate!" constitute the unauthorized practice of law * * *? It cannot be claimed that the publication of a legal text which purports to say what the law is amounts to legal practice. And the mere fact that the principles or rules stated in the text may be accepted by a particular reader as a solution to his problem does not affect this. Courts and lawyers continuously use and cite texts for this very purpose. So also with forms. The publication of a multitude of forms for all manner of legal situations is a commonplace activity and their use by the Bar and the public is general. In fact, many statutes and court rules contain the forms to be used in connection with them. Apparently it is urged that the conjoining of these two, that is, the text and the forms, with advice as to how the forms should be filled out, constitutes the unlawful practice of law. But that is the situation with many approved and accepted texts.

---

3   Deborah L. Rhode, *Policing the Professional Monopoly: A Constitutional and Empirical Analysis of Unauthorized Practice Prohibitions*, 34 Stan. L. Rev. 1, 98-99 (1981).

Dacey's book is sold to the public at large. There is no personal contact or relationship with a particular individual, Nor does there exist that relation of confidence and trust so necessary to the status of attorney and client. This is the essential of legal practice—the representation and the advising of a particular person in a particular situation. The lectures of a law school professor are not legal practice for the very reason that the principles enunciated or the procedures advised do not refer to any activity in immediate contemplation though they are intended and conceived to direct the activities of the students in situations which may arise.

* * *

At most the book assumes to offer general advice on common problems, and does not purport to give personal advice on a specific problem peculiar to a designated or readily identified person.

"How To Avoid Probate!" may be purchased by anyone willing to pay the purchase price. One is free to purchase or not as he wills. There is no personal reliance upon the selection and judgment of Dacey in the discretionary choice of a form adapted to the customer's needs.

"How To Avoid Probate!" has been published and freely sold for more than one year. There is no showing in this record that this book has exploited the public or led its members astray improperly or incorrectly. In fact there is no factual evidence submitted as to the effect of the publication and sale of the book. In order to sustain petitioner's position one has to conclude that the book by its very nature comprises the unauthorized practice of law. "How To Avoid Probate!" is, in one sense, a do-it-yourself kit. To that extent it could encroach upon the preserves of lawyers, though the present record does not give evidence of that fact.

Every individual has a right to represent himself if he chooses to do so, and to assume the risks attendant upon what could prove a precarious undertaking. Those of sufficient substance to require trusts or wills for the most part are persons of some common sense and, normally, would hardly be expected to rely completely and unquestioningly upon a mass-printed form, even with accompanying instructions. However, they have a right to do so.

See It

You can to see an original advertisement for Norman Dacey's *How to Avoid Probate!* at http://www.cover-browser.com/image/weirdest-album-covers/517-1.jpg. Today, one of the major publishers of legal self-help books is Nolo Press. To see the extensive list of legal books that Nolo Press publishes, go to http://www.nolo.com/products.

3. Legal Software

[Question 3]

Legal Software Inc. makes available to consumers a program that helps them fill out legal forms. The software asks the consumer to answer personal questions regarding the consumer's circumstances and preferences regarding the consumer's legal problem. Based on the answers, the program helps the consumer complete the appropriate form, suggesting specific provisions tailored to the consumer's needs and preferences. Has Legal Software Inc. engaged in unauthorized practice of law?

   (A) According to the traditional rule, no because software is the same as a book.

   (B) According to the traditional rule, no because the service is not personalized.

   (C) According to the traditional rule, yes because the service is personalized.

   (D) According to the traditional rule, yes, but the rule has changed to permit legal software.

Today, as a result of technological advances, the question of unauthorized practice is more complex. Many consumers use software and web sites to help them complete legal forms. In *Unauthorized Practice of Law Committee v. Parsons Technology, Inc.,* 1999 WL 47235 (N.D. Tex. 1999), the District Court enjoined the sale of Quicken Family Lawyer software finding it constituted unauthorized practice of law:

> * * * QFL offers over 100 different legal forms (such as employment agreements, real estate leases, premarital agreements, and seven different will forms) along with instructions on how to fill out these forms. QFL's packaging . . . indicates that QFL will have the user "answer a few questions to determine which estate planning and health care documents best meet [the user's] needs;" and that QFL will "interview you in a logical order, tailoring documents to your situation." Finally, the packaging reassures the user that "[h]andy hints and comprehensive legal help topics are always available."
>
> * * *
>
> QFL goes beyond merely instructing someone how to fill in a blank form. While no single one of QFL's acts, in and of itself, may constitute the practice of law, taken as a whole Parsons, through QFL, has gone

beyond publishing a sample form book with instructions, and has ventured into the unauthorized practice of law.

The Texas legislature, however, responded swiftly, amending state law in response to the court's ruling, and the Fifth Circuit Court of Appeals vacated the District Court's injunction:

Go Online

Click here to see an advertisement for $69 wills from LegalZoom. Click here to see current Quicken products and other self-help software from Nolo.

[T]he . . . Legislature enacted an amendment to § 81.101 providing that "the 'practice of law' does not include the design, creation, publication, distribution, display, or sale ... [of] computer software, or similar products if the products clearly and conspicuously state that the products are not a substitute for the advice of an attorney," effective immediately. H.B. 1507, 76th Leg., Reg. Sess. (Tex.1999). We therefore VACATE the injunction. . . .

Unauthorized Practice of Law Committee v. Parsons Tech., Inc., 179 F.3d 956 (5th Cir. 1999).

For More Information

If you want to read more about non-lawyers helping customers prepare legal documents through software or the internet, *see* Catherine J. Lanctot, *Scriveners in Cyberspace: Online Document Preparation and the Unauthorized Practice of Law*, 30 Hofstra L. Rev. 811 (2002).

C. Lawyers Working With Nonlawyers and Lawyers Providing Ancillary Nonlegal Services

Lawyers have long had nonlawyer employees. They have also provided non-legal services associated with legal services, such as **title insurance** connected to real estate transactions. In recent years, the bar has engaged in debates regarding whether to permit and regulate both **ancillary businesses** and **multidisciplinary practices**. While these debates were contentious, they did not result in significant changes. While new rules clarified lawyers' responsibilities regarding ancillary businesses – now called "law-related" businesses, the bar rejected changes to permit

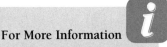

For More Information

You can find an excellent summary of both of these debates in Mary C. Daly, *What the MDP Debate Can Teach Us About Law Practice in the New Millenium and the Need for Curricular Reform*, 50 J. Legal Educ. 521 (2000).

multi-disciplinary practices. Global changes in the delivery of legal services, such as the development of Alternative Business Structures in the United Kingdom and the advent of public ownership of law firms in Australia, ensure that these debates will continue.

For More Information

For a valuable introduction to these global developments, *see* Milton C. Regan, Jr., *Lawyers, Symbols, and Money: Outside Investment in Law Firms*, 27 Penn. St. Int'l L. Rev. 407 (2008). The ABA Ethics 20/20 Commission is examining their impact and implications. *See, e.g.*, http://www.legalethicsforum.com/ blog/2010/02/excellent-summary- of-recent-ethics-2020-meeting.html.

The rules regarding lawyers working with nonlawyers and lawyers providing nonlegal services seek to ensure that the delivery of legal services fulfills lawyers' ethical standards, including their independence of judgment. The concern with regard to ancillary nonlegal services is that lawyers not take advantage of their clients' trust and that clients understand that the lawyers' ethical standards might not apply to these services.

1. Working With Nonlawyers

Lawyers may employ nonlawyers to assist them in providing legal services, but they must supervise them to ensure that they comply with the lawyer's ethical obligations. Rule 5.3 governs the lawyer's supervisory obligations toward nonlawyers. The first obligation is organizational. Rule 5.3(a) provides that "a partner and a lawyer [or lawyers with] comparable managerial authority" must "make reasonable efforts to ensure that the firm has in effect measures giving reasonable assurance that the [nonlawyer's] conduct is compatible with professional obligations of the lawyer." The second belongs to the "lawyer having direct supervisory authority over the nonlawyer." That lawyer has an obligation to "make reasonable efforts to ensure that the [nonlawyer's] conduct is compatible with the professional obligations of the lawyer[.]" Rule 5.3(b).

For More Information

The extent to which lawyers must supervise nonlawyer employees in order to avoid unauthorized practice is not always clear. Paul Tremblay observes that "[a] lawyer cannot know with confidence . . . whether the delegation of some tasks to a nonlawyer colleague might result in her assisting in the unauthorized practice of law, because the state of the law and the commentary about nonlawyer practice is so confused and incoherent. Some respected authority within the profession instructs the lawyer that she may only delegate preparatory matters and must prohibit the nonlawyer from either discussing legal matters with clients or negotiating on behalf of clients. Other authority suggests that the lawyer may delegate a wide array of tasks as long as the lawyer supervises the work of the nonlawyer and accepts responsibility for it." Paul R. Tremblay, *Shadow Lawyering: Nonlawyer Practice Within Law Firms*, 85 Ind. L.J. 653, 698 (2010).

[Question 4]

An attorney is a senior partner at a law firm in which there are 50 lawyers. The firm pays each of its lawyers a fixed annual salary. In addition, at year's end, each lawyer receives a bonus from the profits of the firm in the proportion that the annual salary of each bears to the total of the fixed annual salaries of all lawyers.

The attorney plans to introduce a new management plan under which the firm's nonlawyer office administrator would have general charge of all business matters but would not participate in any decisions involving legal judgment. The administrator would be paid a fixed annual salary and would be included as a participant in the firm's bonus plan on the same basis as the lawyers in the firm. This would usually yield a bonus of approximately one-fourth to one-third of the administrator's total annual compensation. The amount paid to the administrator will not exceed the compensation commonly paid to law office administrators within the local legal community.

Is it proper for the attorney to institute such a plan?

(A) Yes, because the amount paid to the administrator does not exceed the compensation commonly paid to the law office administrators within the local legal community.

(B) Yes, because an employee of the firm may be compensated based on the profits of the firm.

(C) No, because the administrator's bonus is computed on the same basis as those of the lawyers in the firm.

(D) No, because the administrator's compensation is derived from the legal needs of the firm's lawyers.

Rule 5.4(a) provides that:

"[a] lawyer or law firm shall not share legal fees with a nonlawyer, except that:

(1) an agreement by a lawyer with the lawyer's firm, partner, or associate may provide for the payment of money, over a reasonable period of time after the lawyer's death, to the lawyer's estate or to one or more specified persons;

(2) a lawyer who purchases the practice of a deceased, disabled, or disappeared lawyer may, pursuant to the provisions of Rule 1.17, pay to the

estate or other representative of that lawyer the agreed-upon purchase price;

(3) a lawyer or law firm may include nonlawyer employees in a compensation or retirement plan, even though the plan is based in whole or in part on a profit-sharing arrangement; and

(4) a lawyer may share court-awarded legal fees with a nonprofit organization that employed, retained or recommended employment of the lawyer in the matter.

[Question 5]

An attorney is a member of the bar and a salaried employee of a bank's trust department. As part of his duties, he prepares a monthly newsletter concerning wills, trusts, estates, and taxes that the bank sends to all of its customers. The newsletter contains a recommendation to the customer to review his or her will in light of the information contained and, if the customer has any questions to bring the will to the bank, where the attorney will review the customer's will and answer the customer's legal questions. The bank provides that attorney's services to its customers for no charge.

Is the attorney subject to discipline for the foregoing?

   (A) Yes, because by sending out the newsletter the attorney is giving legal advice to persons who are not his clients.

   (B) Yes, because the attorney is assisting the bank in the unauthorized practice of law.

   (C) No, because no charge is made for the attorney's advice.

   (D) No, because the attorney is a member of the bar.

[Question 6]

A business attorney entered into a partnership with a certified public accountant. The partnership provided legal and other assistance to clients in connection with business and tax planning, tax filings, and other personal and corporate business matters. The accountant performed only work that she was authorized to perform as a certified public accountant. The attorney made reasonable efforts to ensure that the accountant did not interfere with the attorney's compliance with his professional obligations as a lawyer.

Is the attorney subject to discipline?

(A) Yes, because some of the activities of the partnership consisted of the practice of law.

(B) Yes, because lawyers may not form partnerships with nonlawyers

(C) No, because the accountant performed only work that she was authorized to perform as a certified public accountant.

(D) No, because the attorney made reasonable efforts to ensure that the accountant did not interfere with the attorney's compliance with his professional obligations as a lawyer.

Review Rule 5.4(a) *supra*. Rule 5.5(a) provides that "a lawyer shall not practice law in violation of the regulation of the legal profession in that jurisdiction, or assist another in doing so." Rule 5.4 further provides:

(b) A lawyer shall not form a partnership with a nonlawyer if any of the activities of the partnership consist of the practice of law.

(c) A lawyer shall not permit a person who recommends, employs, or pays the lawyer to render legal services for another to direct or regulate the lawyer's professional judgment in rendering such legal services.

(d) A lawyer shall not practice with or in the form of a professional corporation or association authorized to practice law for a profit, if:

(1) a nonlawyer owns any interest therein, except that a fiduciary representative of the estate of a lawyer may hold the stock or interest of the lawyer for a reasonable time during administration;

(2) a nonlawyer is a corporate director or officer thereof or occupies the position of similar responsibility in any form of association other than a corporation ; or

(3) a nonlawyer has the right to direct or control the professional judgment of a lawyer.

Food for Thought

In-house counsel work for organizations that have nonlawyer owners, officers, or directors. Why is that permitted? The rationale is that organizations may generally represent themselves and that in-house counsel are assisting in that effort, not representing an outside client as an employee of an organization. In addition, for constitutional and policy reasons, public interest organizations are permitted to represent outside clients in pursuit of their public interest objectives.

2. Ancillary Businesses

[Question 7]

Joan Lawyer has a leading real estate practice in Small County. She is also part owner of Small County Title. She suggests to her clients who purchase real estate that they consider purchasing their title insurance from Small County Title. Joan discloses that she owns the company and recommends that her clients consider the rates and policies of competing title insurance companies. She explains that the services provided by Small County Title are not legal services and that the legal ethics rules do not apply to the purchase of title insurance. Joan suggests that clients feel free to consult another lawyer as to whether they should purchase title insurance from a company their real estate lawyer owns. The rates and policies that Small County Title offers are comparable to those of its competitors.

Which of the following is true:

- (A) Joan is not subject to discipline if the clients give informed consent in writing.

- (B) Joan is not subject to discipline because she informs clients of the opportunity to consult independent counsel.

- (C) Joan is not subject to discipline because the rates and policies of Small County Title are comparable to those of its competitors.

- (D) Joan is subject to discipline for referring clients to a business she owns.

Rule 5.7(b) defines "law-related services as services that might reasonably be performed in conjunction with and in substance are related to the provision of legal services, and that are not prohibited as unauthorized practice of law when provided by a nonlawyer." Rule 5.7(a) makes a lawyer:

> subject to the Rules of Professional Conduct with respect to the provision of law-related services * * * if the law-related services are provided:

> (1) by the lawyer in circumstances that are not distinct from the lawyer's provision of legal services to clients; or

> (2) in other circumstances by an entity controlled by the lawyer individually or with others if the lawyer fails to take reasonable measures to assure that a person obtaining the law-related services knows that the services are not legal services and that the protections of the client-lawyer relationship do not exist.

The Comments to <u>Rule 5.7</u> explain:

> [5] When a client-lawyer relationship exists with a person who is referred by a lawyer to a separate law-related service entity controlled by the lawyer, individually or with others, the lawyer must comply with Rule 1.8(a).

> [6] In taking the reasonable measures referred to in paragraph (a)(2) to assure that a person using law-related services understands the practical effect or significance of the inapplicability of the Rules of Professional Conduct, the lawyer should communicate to the person receiving the law-related services, in a manner sufficient to assure that the person understands the significance of the fact, that the relationship of the person to the business entity will not be a client-lawyer relationship. The communication should be made before entering into an agreement for provision of or providing law-related services, and preferably should be in writing.

> [7] The burden is upon the lawyer to show that the lawyer has taken reasonable measures under the circumstances to communicate the desired understanding. For instance, a sophisticated user of law-related services, such as a publicly held corporation, may require a lesser explanation than someone unaccustomed to making distinctions between legal services and law-related services, such as an individual Seeking tax advice from a lawyer-accountant or investigative services in connection with a lawsuit.

<u>Rule 1.8(a)</u> governs business transactions with a client. It forbids a lawyer from:

> enter[ing] into a business transaction with a client . . . unless:

> (1) the transaction and terms on which the lawyer acquires the interest are fair and reasonable to the client and are fully disclosed and transmitted in writing in a manner that can be reasonably understood by the client;

> (2) the client is advised in writing of the desirability of seeking and is given a reasonable opportunity to seek the advice of independent legal counsel on the transaction; and

> (3) the client gives informed consent, in a writing signed by the client, to the essential terms of the transaction and the lawyer's role in the transaction, including whether the lawyer is representing the client in the transaction.

D. Unauthorized Practice by Lawyers

[Question 8]

Giant Manufacturer wants to buy widgets from Small Producer. Both Giant and Small are headquartered in California. Small's outside counsel, John Lawyer, admitted to practice in New York, travels to California from his New York office to negotiate the deal on Small's behalf. After extensive negotiations, Giant agrees to pay Small $10 million for the widgets. John bills Small $500 thousand for legal fees. Small believes the fee is far too high and refuses to pay. It retains a California lawyer and decides to argue that it does not have to pay anything to John Lawyer because he was engaged in unauthorized practice of law. Small's argument:

(A) will fail because John is admitted to practice in New York.

(B) will fail because this was not a litigation matter.

(C) will fail because the legal services market is national and not restricted to a particular state.

(D) will succeed because John is not admitted to practice in California.

BIRBROWER, MONTALBANO, CONDON & FRANK, P.C. v. SUPERIOR COURT

949 P.2d 1 (Cal. 1998), *cert. denied*, 525 U.S. 920 (1998)

CHIN, J.

* * *

The facts with respect to the unauthorized practice of law question are essentially undisputed. [Birbrower, Montalbano, Condon & Frank, P.C. (Birbrower)] is a professional law corporation incorporated in New York. * * * During 1992 and 1993, Birbrower attorneys, defendants Kevin F. Hobbs and Thomas A. Condon (Hobbs and Condon), performed substantial work in California relating to the law firm's representation of [ESQ Business Services, Inc. (ESQ)]. Neither Hobbs nor Condon has ever been licensed to practice law in California. None of Birbrower's attorneys were licensed to practice law in California during Birbrower's ESQ representation.

ESQ is a California corporation. * * * In July 1992, the parties negotiated and executed the fee agreement in New York, providing that Birbrower would perform legal services for ESQ, including "All matters pertaining to the investigation of and prosecution of all claims and causes of action against Tandem Computers Incorporated [Tandem]." The "claims and causes of action" against Tandem, a Delaware corporation with its principal place of business in Santa Clara County, California, related to a software development and marketing contract between Tandem and ESQ dated March 16, 1990 (Tandem Agreement). The Tandem Agreement stated that "The internal laws of the State of California (irrespective of its choice of law principles) shall govern the validity of this Agreement, the construction of its terms, and the interpretation and enforcement of the rights and duties of the parties hereto." Birbrower asserts, and ESQ disputes, that ESQ knew Birbrower was not licensed to practice law in California.

While representing ESQ, Hobbs and Condon traveled to California on several occasions. In August 1992, they met in California with ESQ and its accountants. During these meetings, Hobbs and Condon discussed various matters related to ESQ's dispute with Tandem and strategy for resolving the dispute. They made recommendations and gave advice. During this California trip, Hobbs and Condon also met with Tandem representatives on four or five occasions during a two-day period. At the meetings, Hobbs and Condon spoke on ESQ's behalf. Hobbs demanded that Tandem pay ESQ $15 million. Condon told Tandem he believed that damages would exceed $15 million if the parties litigated the dispute.

Around March or April 1993, Hobbs, Condon, and another Birbrower attorney visited California to interview potential arbitrators and to meet again with ESQ and its accountants. Birbrower had previously filed a demand for arbitration against Tandem with the San Francisco offices of the American Arbitration Association (AAA). In August 1993, Hobbs returned to California to assist ESQ in settling the Tandem matter. While in California, Hobbs met with ESQ and its accountants to discuss a proposed settlement agreement Tandem authored. Hobbs also met with Tandem representatives to discuss possible changes in the proposed agreement. Hobbs gave ESQ legal advice during this trip, including his opinion that ESQ should not settle with Tandem on the terms proposed.

ESQ eventually settled the Tandem dispute, and the matter never went to arbitration. But before the settlement, ESQ and Birbrower modified the contingency fee agreement. The modification changed the fee arrangement from contingency to fixed fee, providing that ESQ would pay Birbrower over $1 million. The original contingency fee arrangement had called for Birbrower to receive "one-third (1/3) of all sums received for the benefit of the Clients ... whether obtained through settlement, motion practice, hearing, arbitration, or trial by way of judgment, award, settlement, or otherwise ...." * * *

In January 1994, ESQ sued Birbrower for legal malpractice and related claims in Santa Clara County Superior Court. * * * ESQ moved for summary judgment and/or adjudication * * * [arguing] that by practicing law without a license in California * * * Birbrower violated section 6125, rendering the fee agreement unenforceable. Based on these undisputed facts, the Santa Clara Superior Court granted ESQ's motion for summary adjudication. * * * The court concluded that: (1) Birbrower was "not admitted to the practice of law in California"; * * * (3) Birbrower "provided legal services in this state"; and (4) "The law is clear that no one may recover compensation for services as an attorney in this state unless he or she was a member of the state bar at the time those services were performed."

Although the trial court's order stated that the fee agreements were unenforceable, at the hearing on the summary adjudication motion, the trial court also observed: "It seems to me * * * if they aren't allowed to collect their attorney's fees here, I don't think that puts the attorneys in a position from being precluded from collecting all of their attorney's fees, only those fees probably that were generated by virtue of work that they performed in California and not that work that was performed in New York."

* * *

We granted review to determine whether Birbrower's actions and services performed while representing ESQ in California constituted the unauthorized practice of law under section 6125 and, if so, whether a section 6125 violation rendered the fee agreement wholly unenforceable.

II. Discussion

A. The Unauthorized Practice of Law

The California Legislature enacted section 6125 in 1927 as part of the State Bar Act (the Act), a comprehensive scheme regulating the practice of law in the state. Since the Act's passage, the general rule has been that, although persons may represent themselves and their own interests regardless of State Bar membership, no one but an active member of the State Bar may practice law for another person in California. The prohibition against unauthorized law practice * * * is designed to ensure that those performing legal services do so competently.

Although the Act did not define the term "practice law," case law explained it as " 'the doing and performing services in a court of justice in any matter depending therein throughout its various stages and in conformity with the adopted rules of procedure.' " (*People ex rel. Lawyers' Institute of San Diego v. Merchants' Protective Corp.* (1922). 209 P. 363 (*Merchants*).) *Merchants* included in its definition legal advice and legal instrument and contract preparation, whether or not these subjects were rendered in the course of litigation. * * *

In addition to not defining the term "practice law," the Act also did not define the meaning of "in California." In today's legal practice, questions often arise concerning whether the phrase refers to the nature of the legal services, or restricts the Act's application to those out-of-state attorneys who are physically present in the state.

Section 6125 has generated numerous opinions on the meaning of "practice law" but none on the meaning of "in California." In our view, the practice of law "in California" entails sufficient contact with the California client to render the nature of the legal service a clear legal representation. In addition to a quantitative analysis, we must consider the nature of the unlicensed lawyer's activities in the state. Mere fortuitous or attenuated contacts will not sustain a finding that the unlicensed lawyer practiced law "in California." The primary inquiry is whether the unlicensed lawyer engaged in sufficient activities in the state, or created a continuing relationship with the California client that included legal duties and obligations.

Our definition does not necessarily depend on or require the unlicensed lawyer's physical presence in the state. Physical presence here is one factor we may consider in deciding whether the unlicensed lawyer has violated section 6125, but it is by no means exclusive. For example, one may practice law in the state in violation of section 6125 although not physically present here by advising a California client on California law in connection with a California legal dispute by telephone, fax, computer, or other modern technological means. Conversely, although we decline to provide a comprehensive list of what activities constitute sufficient contact with the state, we do reject the notion that a person automatically practices law "in California" whenever that person practices California law anywhere, or "virtually" enters the state by telephone, fax, e-mail, or satellite. [*See e.g.*, *Baron v. City of Los Angeles*, 469 P.2d 353 (1970) (*Baron* ["practice law" does not encompass all professional activities].)] * * *

This interpretation acknowledges the tension that exists between interjurisdictional practice and the need to have a state-regulated bar. As stated in the American Bar Association Model Code of Professional Responsibility, Ethical Consideration EC 3-9, "Regulation of the practice of law is accomplished principally by the respective states. Authority to engage in the practice of law conferred in any jurisdiction is not *per se* a grant of the right to practice elsewhere, and it is improper for a lawyer to engage in practice where he is not permitted by law or by court order to do so. However, the demands of business and the mobility of our society pose distinct problems in the regulation of the practice of law by the states. In furtherance of the public interest, the legal profession should discourage regulation that unreasonably imposes territorial limitations upon the right of a lawyer to handle the legal affairs of his client or upon the opportunity of a client to obtain the services of a lawyer of his choice in all matters including the presentation of a contested matter in a tribunal before which the lawyer is not permanently admitted to practice." *Baron* implicitly agrees with this canon.

Exceptions to section 6125 do exist, but are generally limited to allowing out-of-state attorneys to make brief appearances before a state court or tribunal. They are narrowly drawn and strictly interpreted. * * *

In addition, with the permission of the California court in which a particular cause is pending, out-of-state counsel may appear before a court as counsel *pro hac vice*. A court will approve a *pro hac vice* application only if the out-of-state attorney is a member in good standing of another state bar and is eligible to practice in any United States court or the highest court in another jurisdiction. The out-of-state attorney must also associate an active member of the California Bar as attorney of record and is subject to the Rules of Professional Conduct of the State Bar. * * *

> **Non constat**
> **jus civile**
> a posteriori
>
> ### It's Latin to Me!
>
> Black's Law Dictionary defines *pro hac vice* "[f]or this occasion or a particular purpose. The phrase [usually] refers to a lawyer who has not been admitted to practice in a particular jurisdiction but who is admitted there temporarily for the purpose of conducting a particular case."

B. The Present Case

The undisputed facts here show that neither *Baron's* definition nor our "sufficient contact" definition of "practice law in California" would excuse Birbrower's extensive practice in this state. Nor would any of the limited statutory exceptions to section 6125 apply to Birbrower's California practice. As the Court of Appeal observed, Birbrower engaged in unauthorized law practice in California on more than a limited basis, and no firm attorney engaged in that practice was an active member of the California State Bar. * * *

Birbrower contends, however, that section 6125 is not meant to apply to any out-of-state attorneys. Instead, it argues that the statute is intended solely to prevent nonattorneys from practicing law. This contention is without merit because it contravenes the plain language of the statute. Section 6125 clearly states that no person shall practice law in California unless that person is a member of the State Bar. The statute does not differentiate between attorneys or nonattorneys, nor does it excuse a person who is a member of another state bar. * * *

Birbrower next argues that we do not further the statute's intent and purpose-to protect California citizens from incompetent attorneys-by enforcing it against out-of-state attorneys. Birbrower argues that because out-of-state attorneys have been licensed to practice in other jurisdictions, they have already demonstrated sufficient competence to protect California clients. But Birbrower's argument overlooks the obvious fact that other states' laws may differ substantially from California law. Competence in one jurisdiction does not necessarily guarantee competence in another. By applying section 6125 to out-of-state attorneys who engage in the extensive practice of law in California without becoming licensed in our state, we serve the statute's goal of assuring the competence of all attorneys practicing law in this state. * * *

Assuming that section 6125 does apply to out-of-state attorneys not licensed here, Birbrower alternatively asks us to create an exception to section 6125 for work incidental to private arbitration or other alternative dispute resolution proceedings. Birbrower points to fundamental differences between private arbitration and legal proceedings, including procedural differences relating to discovery, rules of evidence, compulsory process, cross-examination of witnesses, and other areas. As Birbrower observes, in light of these differences, at least one court has decided that an out-of-state attorney could recover fees for services rendered in an arbitration proceeding. * * *

We decline Birbrower's invitation to craft an arbitration exception to section 6125's prohibition of the unlicensed practice of law in this state. Any exception for arbitration is best left to the Legislature, which has the authority to determine qualifications for admission to the State Bar and to decide what constitutes the practice of law. * * * In the face of the Legislature's silence, we will not create an arbitration exception under the facts presented. * * *

Finally, Birbrower urges us to adopt an exception to section 6125 based on the unique circumstances of this case. Birbrower notes that "Multistate relationships are a common part of today's society and are to be dealt with in commonsense fashion.") In many situations, strict adherence to rules prohibiting the unauthorized practice of law by out-of-state attorneys would be " 'grossly impractical and inefficient.' " * * *

Although * * * we recognize the need to acknowledge * * * the multistate nature of law practice, the facts here show that Birbrower's extensive activities within California amounted to considerably more than any of our state's recognized exceptions to section 6125 would allow. Accordingly, we reject Birbrower's suggestion that we except the firm from section 6125's rule under the circumstances here.

* * *

Because Birbrower violated section 6125 when it engaged in the unlawful practice of law in California, the Court of Appeal found its fee agreement with ESQ unenforceable in its entirety. Without crediting Birbrower for some services performed in New York, for which fees were generated under the fee agreement, the court reasoned that the agreement was void and unenforceable because it included payment for services rendered to a California client in the state by an unlicensed out-of-state lawyer. * * * We agree with the Court of Appeal to the extent it barred Birbrower from recovering fees generated under the fee agreement for the unauthorized legal services it performed in California. We disagree with the same court to the extent it implicitly barred Birbrower from recovering fees generated under the fee agreement for the limited legal services the firm performed in New York.

It is a general rule that an attorney is barred from recovering compensation for services rendered in another state where the attorney was not admitted to the bar. The general rule, however, has some recognized exceptions.

* * *

A[n] . . . exception on which Birbrower relies to enforce its entire fee agreement relates to "Services not involving courtroom appearance." * * * California has implicitly rejected this broad exception through its comprehensive definition of what it means to "practice law." Thus, the exception Birbrower seeks for all services performed outside the courtroom in our state is too broad under section 6125.

[Another exception to the general rule of nonrecovery for in-state services s]ome jurisdictions have adopted [is] if an out-of-state attorney "makes a full disclosure to his client of his lack of local license and does not conceal or misrepresent the true facts." * * * In this case, Birbrower alleges that ESQ at all times knew that the firm was not licensed to practice law in California. Even assuming that is true, however, we reject the full disclosure exception for the same reasons we reject the argument that section 6125 is not meant to apply to nonattorneys. Recognizing these exceptions would contravene not only the plain language of section 6125 but the underlying policy of assuring the competence of those practicing law in California.

Therefore, as the Court of Appeal held, none of the exceptions to the general rule prohibiting recovery of fees generated by the unauthorized practice of law apply to Birbrower's activities in California. * * * Enforcing the fee agreement in its entirety would include payment for the unauthorized practice of law in California and would allow Birbrower to enforce an illegal contract.

Birbrower asserts that even if we agree with the Court of Appeal and find that none of the above exceptions allowing fees for unauthorized California services apply to the firm, it should be permitted to recover fees for those limited services it performed exclusively in New York under the agreement. In short, Birbrower seeks to recover under its contract for those services it performed for ESQ in New York that did not involve the practice of law in California, including fee contract negotiations and some corporate case research. Birbrower thus alternatively seeks reversal of the Court of Appeal's judgment to the extent it implicitly precluded the firm from Seeking fees generated in New York under the fee agreement.

We agree with Birbrower that it may be able to recover fees under the fee agreement for the limited legal services it performed for ESQ in New York to the extent they did not constitute practicing law in California, even though those services were performed for a California client. Because section 6125 applies to the practice of law in California, it does not, in general, regulate law practice in other states. Thus, although the general rule against compensation to out-of-state attorneys precludes Birbrower's recovery under the fee agreement for its actions in California, the severability doctrine may allow it to receive its New York fees generated under the fee agreement, if we conclude the illegal portions of the agreement pertaining to the practice of law in California may be severed from those parts regarding services Birbrower performed in New York. * * *

In this case, the parties entered into a contingency fee agreement followed by a fixed fee agreement. ESQ was to pay money to Birbrower in exchange for Birbrower's legal services. The object of their agreement may not have been entirely illegal, assuming ESQ was to pay Birbrower compensation based in part on work Birbrower performed in New York that did not amount to the practice of law in California. The illegality arises, instead, out of the amount to be paid to Birbrower, which, if paid fully, would include payment for services rendered in California in violation of section 6125.

Therefore, we conclude the Court of Appeal erred in determining that the fee agreement between the parties was entirely unenforceable because Birbrower violated section 6125's prohibition against the unauthorized practice of law in California. Birbrower's statutory violation may require exclusion of the portion of the fee attributable to the substantial illegal services, but that violation does not necessarily entirely preclude its recovery under the fee agreement for the limited services it performed outside California.

Thus, the portion of the fee agreement between Birbrower and ESQ that includes payment for services rendered in New York may be enforceable to the extent that the illegal compensation can be severed from the rest of the agreement. * * *

III. Disposition

We conclude that Birbrower violated section 6125 by practicing law in California. To the extent the fee agreement allows payment for those illegal local services, it is void, and Birbrower is not entitled to recover fees under the agreement for those services. The fee agreement is enforceable, however, to the extent it is possible to sever the portions of the consideration attributable to Birbrower's services illegally rendered in California from those attributable to Birbrower's New York services. Accordingly, we affirm the Court of Appeal judgment to the extent it concluded that Birbrower's representation of ESQ in California violated section 6125, and that Birbrower is not entitled to recover fees under the fee agreement for its local services. We reverse the judgment to the extent the court did not allow Birbrower to argue in favor of a severance of the illegal portion of the consideration (for the California fees) from the rest of the fee agreement, and remand for further proceedings consistent with this decision.

The Aftermath of Birbrower

Birbrower's ruling proved controversial and brought increased attention to the issue of extrajurisdictional practice. One result was that the California legislature modified the unauthorized practice statute to permit an out of state attorney who satisfies specific requirements set forth in the statute to represent a party in an arbitration. California Code of Civil Procedure § 1282.4. But *Birbrower* had a much broader influence as well. The case understandably caused great concern within the legal profession. The market for legal services is national and international, extending beyond the borders of any particular state. The bar realized that quite a few lawyers were engaging in unauthorized practice of law as defined by the *Birbrower* court, such as lawyers at large law firms and in-house counsel at corporations who quite often provided legal services in jurisdictions where they were not admitted. As a result, the American Bar Association amended Rules 5.5 and 8.5 to permit and regulate multijurisdictional practice under certain circumstances. Many, but not all jurisdictions, have adopted these revised rules.

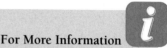

For More Information

For further discussion of the background of these rules, *see* Carol A. Needham, *Multijurisdictional Pratice Regulations Governing Attorneys Conducting a Transactional Practice*, 2003 U. Ill. L. Rev. 1331; Cynthia L. Fountaine, *Have License, Will Travel: An Analysis of the New ABA Multijurisdictional Practice Rules*, 81 Wash. U. L.Q. 737 (2003).

[Question 9]

Joan Jones is an associate at Franklin & Ignatius. She is admitted to the New York Bar. The firm sends her to the State of Sirius to appear in court in a case where the firm has been admitted *pro hac vice*. Has she committed UPL?

(A) Yes

(B) No

Rule 5.5 provides that:

(a) A lawyer shall not practice law in a jurisdiction in violation of the regulation of the legal profession in that jurisdiction, or assist another in doing so.

(b) A lawyer who is not admitted to practice in this jurisdiction shall not:

   (1) except as authorized by these Rules or other law, establish an office or other systematic and continuous presence in this jurisdiction for the practice of law; or

   (2) hold out to the public or otherwise represent that the lawyer is admitted to practice law in this jurisdiction.

(c) A lawyer admitted in another United States jurisdiction, and not disbarred or suspended from practice in any jurisdiction, may provide legal services on a temporary basis in this jurisdiction that:

* * *

(2) are in or reasonably related to a pending or potential proceeding before a tribunal in this or another jurisdiction, if the lawyer, or a person the lawyer is assisting, is authorized by law or order to appear in such proceeding or reasonably expects to be so authorized;

* * *

[Question 10]

Did Joan Jones violate UPL when she entered Sirius to investigate and prepare the case before the firm was admitted *pro hac vice*?

(A) Yes

(B) No

Refer to the provisions of Rule 5.5 above.

[Question 11]

Would she have violated UPL if the firm had brought an arbitration on behalf of its client and not a court case?

(A) Yes

(B) No

According to <u>Rule 5.5(c)</u>: A lawyer admitted in another United States jurisdiction * * * may provide legal services on a temporary basis in this jurisdiction that:

* * *

(3) are in or reasonably related to a pending or potential arbitration, mediation, or other alternative dispute resolution proceeding in this or another jurisdiction, if the services arise out of or are reasonably related to the lawyer's practice in a jurisdiction in which the lawyer is admitted to practice and are not services for which the forum requires pro hac vice admission;

[Question 12]

Does Joan violate UPL if she transfers full-time to F&I's Sirius office and works under the supervision of a Sirius admitted attorney?

(A) Yes

(B) No

Review the provisions of Rule 5.5 above. According to <u>Rule 5.5(c)</u>, A lawyer admitted in another United States jurisdiction * * * may provide legal services on a temporary basis in this jurisdiction that:

> (1) are undertaken in association with a lawyer who is admitted to practice in this jurisdiction and who actively participates in the matter; [or]

> * * *

> (4) are not within paragraphs (c)(2) or (c)(3) and arise out of or are reasonably related to the lawyer's practice in a jurisdiction in which the lawyer is admitted to practice.

[Question 13]

Does Joan commit UPL if she leaves F&I to become in-house counsel at Monolith, Inc., located in Sirius?

(A) Yes

(B) No

<u>Rule 5.5(d)</u> provides that:

> A lawyer admitted in another United States jurisdiction * * * may provide legal services in this jurisdiction that:

> (1) are provided to the lawyer's employer or its organizational affiliates and are not services for which the forum requires pro hac vice admission.

> (2) are services that the lawyer is authorized to provide by federal law or other law of this jurisdiction.

[Question 14]

Joan rejoins F&I as a partner in its New York office. As a corporate partner, she is in charge of representing ABC, Inc., based in New Jersey, in its take-over of DEF, Inc., based in New York. Her team includes Jim, a NY lawyer coordinating the NJ litigation, and Jane, a corporate associate admitted in NY and NJ. They discover ABC has made a fraudulent statement relevant to the litigation. NJ requires disclosure. NY does not. The F&I lawyers do not disclose.

Which of the following is true?

(A) If the predominant effect is in NJ, all face discipline absent contrary reasonable belief.

(B) Only Jane faces discipline because she is a NJ lawyer.

(C) Only Jim faces discipline because he is litigating the matter in NJ.

(D) None face discipline because NY does not require disclosure.

Rule 8.5

(a) Disciplinary Authority: A lawyer admitted to practice in this jurisdiction is subject to the disciplinary authority of this jurisdiction, regardless of where the lawyer's conduct occurs. A lawyer not admitted in this jurisdiction is also subject to the disciplinary authority of this jurisdiction if the lawyer provides or offers to provide any legal services in this jurisdiction. A lawyer may be subject to the disciplinary authority of both this jurisdiction and another jurisdiction for the same conduct.

(b) Choice of Law. In any exercise of the disciplinary authority of this jurisdiction, the rules of professional conduct to be applied shall be as follows:

(1) for conduct in connection with a matter pending before a tribunal, the rules of the jurisdiction in which the tribunal sits, unless the rules of the tribunal provide otherwise; and

(2) for any other conduct, the rules of the jurisdiction in which the lawyer's conduct occurred, or, if the predominant effect of the conduct is in a different jurisdiction, the rules of that jurisdiction shall be applied to the conduct. A lawyer shall not be subject to discipline if the lawyer's conduct conforms to the rules of a jurisdiction in which the lawyer reasonably believes the predominant effect of the lawyer's conduct will occur.

Food for Thought

How should the rules apply to foreign lawyers practicing in the United States? As law practice becomes increasingly globalized, this question has become more relevant. The ABA Commission on Ethics 20/20, charged with reviewing and revising the Rules, has posed the following questions:

1) Should the ABA include foreign lawyers within the scope of the ABA Model Rule for Pro Hac Vice Admssion?

2) Should the ABA adopt a policy regarding registration of foreign lawyers practicing in-house in the U.S.?

3) Should the temporary practice provisions applicable to U.S. lawyers in Rule 5.5. of the ABA Model Rules of Professional Conduct be expanded to include non-U.S. Lawyers? In 2002, the ABA adopted a Model Rule for Temporary Practice by Foreign Lawyers. Most jurisdictions that have adopted Model Rule 5.5. have not yet adopted the corollary foreign temporary practice rule.

ABA Commission on Ethics 20/20, Memoranda and Templates for comment-Inbound Foreign Lawyers, June 1, 2010, http://www.abanet.org/ethics2020/templates.pdf.

III. Creating the Lawyer-Client Relationship

Another building block of law practice is the lawyer-client relationship. In the United States, the general rule is that a lawyer has full discretion to decide whether to accept a client or not, subject to very limited exceptions. These include the lawyer's obligation to accept a court appointment and to comply with anti-discrimination laws. Nonetheless, as this Part demonstrates, the task of determining whether a lawyer has entered a lawyer-client relationship, or has obligations similar to those found in a lawyer-client relationship, can be quite complex.

[Question 1]

Your friend George finds you at a party. He explains that he is having a problem with his landlord and asks your advice. You tell him

For More Information

Should the regulation of lawyers be primarily a matter of state or federal concern? For arguments favoring federal regulation based largely on national policy considerations, *see* Ted Schneyer, *Professional Discipline in 2050: A Look Back*, 60 Fordham L. Rev. 125 (1991); Fred C. Zacharias, *Federalizing Legal Ethics*, 73 Tex. L. Rev. 335 (1994). Laurel Terry has explained that global considerations will further increase the pressure for more federal and international regulation of legal services. *See* Laurel S. Terry, *The Future Regulation of the Legal Profession: The Impact of Treating the Legal Profession as "Service Providers,"* 2008 J. Prof. Law. 189; *see also* Laurel S. Terry, *GATS' Applicability to Transnational Lawyering and its Potential Impact on U.S. State Regulation of Lawyers*, 34 Vand. J. Transnat'l L. 989 (2001), *as revised* 35 Vand. J. Transnat'l L. 1387 (2002).

what you learned about his problem in property class and explain it to him. Which of the following is correct?

(A) You have committed Unauthorized Practice of Law.

(B) If you were a lawyer, you would have created a lawyer-client relationship.

(C) Both A and B are correct.

(D) Neither A nor B is correct.

In answering the question, consider whether it matters that you never expressly agreed to represent George.

Although determination of whether a lawyer-client relationship exists is a matter of state law, Restatement § 14 provides the general rule that:

A relationship of client and lawyer arises when:

(1) a person manifests to a lawyer the person's intent that the lawyer provide legal services for the person; and either

(a) the lawyer manifests to the person consent to do so; or

(b) the lawyer fails to manifest lack of consent to do so, and the lawyer knows or reasonably should know that the person reasonably relies on the lawyer to provide the services. * * *

> **FYI**
>
> In contrast, English barristers have traditionally followed a cab-rank rule requiring that "irrespective of whether his client is paying privately or is publicly funded [a barrister must] accept any brief to appear before a Court in which he professes to practise . . . irrespective of (i) the party on whose behalf he is instructed (ii) the nature of the case and (iii) any belief or opinion which he may have formed as to the character reputation cause conduct guilt or innocence of that person." Paragraph 602 of the Code of Conduct of the English Bar. One commentator explains that "[t]he 'cab-rank rule' generally requires barristers to accept any case given by a solicitor, thereby undertaking the representation of a particular client without passing judgment on the merits or public appeal. The cab-rank rule evokes a 'patrician sense of conducting a service,' and has been praised as 'a crucial pillar of British justice, ensuring that unpopular causes or clients never go without representation.'" William C. McMahon III: *Declining Professionalism in Court: A Comparative Look at the English Barrister*, 19 Geo. J. Legal Ethics 845, 851-52 (2006).

[Question 2]

An attorney closed her law practice when she became a state senator. A bank, one of the senator's former private clients, asked her as its senator to try to persuade a state agency to grant the bank a license to open a new branch bank. While the bank's request was pending before the agency, the senator wrote a letter on her legislative letterhead to the agency's chair, asserting that the branch would satisfy a local business need and urging that the bank's application be granted. The senator neither sought nor received any compensation from the bank for her efforts. Eventually the agency granted the bank's application, in part because of the senator's efforts.

Is the senator subject to discipline?

(A) Yes, because the senator used her public position to attempt to influence the agency on behalf of the bank.

(B) Yes, because the agency granted the bank's application in part due to the senator's efforts.

(C) No, because the senator's letter to the agency's chair did not express an opinion about the law.

(D) No, because the senator acted on behalf of the bank as a constituent and not as a client.

Determining whether the Senator and the Bank have an attorney-client relationship is the key to answering the question. How would you apply Restatement § 14? Is it dispositive that the "senator neither sought nor received any compensation"?

[Question 3]

Lincoln & Fordham has represented Center Manufacturing in its transactional work. The SEC begins an investigation of Center Manufacturing. Lincoln & Fordham explains to Center that it cannot represent it in the SEC investigation. Center obtains other counsel. Nonetheless, from time to time, Center asks Lincoln & Fordham about issues that arise in the SEC matter and Lincoln & Fordham provides answers. Does Center have a lawyer-client relationship with Center for purposes of the SEC investigation?

(A) Yes, because Lincoln & Fordham has answered Center's questions.

(B) Yes, because Lincoln & Fordham represented Center in its transactional work.

(C) No, because Lincoln & Fordham made clear it was not representing Center.

(D) No, because Center has other counsel in the matter.

In answering the question, consider Restatement § 14, as well as the following case.

MORRIS v. MARGULIS & GRANT, P.C., MORRIS v. MARGULIS

718 N.E.2d 709 (Ill. App. Ct., 5th Dist. 1999),
rev'd on other grounds, 754 N.E.2d 314 (Ill. 2001)

JUSTICE MAAG delivered the opinion of the court:

* * *

This action grows out of the failure of the former Germania Bank (Germania), a St. Louis, Missouri-based savings and loan. Various civil and criminal actions flowed from Germania's failure, including actions against some officers and directors of Germania. The plaintiff in this action, Morris, was sued civilly and prosecuted criminally. Morris was convicted of various criminal charges. His conviction was affirmed on appeal. In this action, Morris alleges an attorney-client relationship existed between himself and the defendants. Morris claims that the defendants breached the fiduciary duties owing from them to him and that he was damaged as a result. With this general background, we will now address the issues raised in this case.

* * *

II. Analysis

We will now discuss the issues raised in this appeal. Unless otherwise indicated, a reference to Bryan Cave also includes the individually named partners.

Bryan Cave claimed in the trial court that it was entitled to summary judgment on several grounds. In this court its position is similar. Bryan Cave claims that (1) no attorney-client relationship existed with Morris in regard to Germania matters and thus it owed him no fiduciary duties. * * * The trial court, without specifying the basis, stated in its judgment order that it accepted "the reasoning and conclusions" of the defendants and granted summary judgment in favor of all defendants. Morris appeals. * * *

A. The Attorney-Client Relationship

Because the issues raised on appeal turn in large part on the question of whether an attorney-client relationship existed between Edward Morris and Bryan Cave with respect to Germania matters, we begin with that issue. * * *

The existence of an attorney-client relationship between Bryan Cave and Morris with respect to estate planning, domestic relations matters, and other personal matters is not contested by Bryan Cave. Bryan Cave argues, however, that no attorney-client relationship existed between Bryan Cave and Morris regarding Germania. * * *

Bryan Cave points out that Morris was represented by other counsel with respect to Germania-related matters. Bryan Cave argues that no attorney-client relationship existed between Morris and Bryan Cave because Bryan Cave formally declined representation of Morris in Germania-related matters. Bryan Cave contends further that Morris did not confide in Bryan Cave attorneys regarding Germania matters. Bryan Cave claims that it never purported to represent Morris in relation to Germania matters.

The fact that Morris was represented by counsel other than Bryan Cave with relation to Germania matters, the S.E.C. investigation, and the criminal investigation does not preclude him from having an attorney-client relationship on the same matter with Bryan Cave. A client may form an attorney-client relationship with more than one attorney or law firm on the same legal matter. * * *

The *Herbes* court, in discussing the creation of the attorney-client relationship, stated:

"Taken together, the cases teach that an attorney-client relationship need not be explicit or expressed and is not dependent on the amount of time the client spends with the attorney, the payment of fees or execution of a contract, the consent of the attorney, or the actual employment of the attorney. * * * Rather, the relationship can come into being during the initial contact between the layperson and the professional and appears to hinge on "'the client's belief that he is consulting a lawyer in that capacity and his manifested intention to Seek professional legal advice.'" * * * Like *King*, the Federal cases focus on the client's viewpoint rather than that of the attorney. If the client consults the attorney for the evident purpose of securing legal advice, an attorney-client relationship will probably be found regardless of the attorney's intent or the fact that a further relationship did not develop as a result of the primary consultation." * * *

ACTA NON VERBA! (Deeds not words!) Bryan Cave's denial of an attorney-client relationship with Morris conflicts with the admitted facts. By their own admission they aided in the preparation of a "Wells" submission. Bryan Cave admits that they met with Morris and discussed the Germania problem, and he asked them to represent him. In his deposition, Morris was asked the following question and gave the following answer.

"Q. No, sir. Here, so we get to the nub of this, I mean, you have made certain allegations here about a disclosure of confidential information, as I understand it, and the word 'confidential' is used in the lawsuit that you filed. So, I'm asking you now to give me your recollection as to what the confidential information was that you related to Bryan, Cave regarding your activities as an officer of Germania.

A. As far as I'm concerned, everything that I talked to Jack Goebel about, or other members of Bryan, Cave, with respect to Germania's activities, my activities, were [*sic*] all confidential, and those-those discussions were ongoing from the time Bryan, Cave represented the bank and Jack Goebel was a director, through, you know, we stopped talking."

It must be remembered that Morris had been represented previously by Bryan Cave on a variety of personal matters over a period of several years. Whom does a person consult on a legal problem when it arises? His attorney. Whom did Morris meet with to request representation on the Germania matter? Bryan Cave, of course.

The key to the creation of the relationship is not any belief on the part of Bryan Cave about whether an attorney-client relationship was formed. "Rather, the relationship can come into being during the initial contact," and its creation hinges on "'the client's belief that he is consulting a lawyer in that capacity[.'"] * * * Even a brief meeting, resulting in no formal retainer or payment of fees, is sufficient to create the relationship. * * *

The record fails to show what took place when Morris and Goebel met and Morris asked for representation. If in seeking counsel Morris had substantive conversations with Goebel on the Germania matter, then as a matter of law an attorney-client relationship came into being. At the very least, based on the record before us, we cannot say that no attorney-client relationship was formed. Therefore, summary judgment should not have been granted on this basis. * * *

Conclusion

Accordingly, the order of the circuit court granting summary judgment in favor of Bryan Cave, LLP, John Goebel, Daniel O'Neill, J. Thomas Archer, and Alan J. Dixon is reversed, and the cause is remanded.

Reversed and remanded.

[Question 4]

The firm of Lincoln & Fordham represents the Computer Software Association, an organization of businesses who manufacture computers or create software, in challenging proposed regulations regarding data privacy. Lincoln & Fordham has collected information on business practices from each of the businesses in the Association. Lincoln & Fordham agrees to represent one of those businesses, GoFind, in an antitrust suit against another, MacroTough. Was MacroTough a client of Lincoln & Fordham by virtue of its representation of the Computer Software Business Association?

(A) Yes, because a lawyer who represents an organization also represents its constituents.

(B) Yes, because a lawyer who represents an organization is presumed to represent its constituents absent an express agreement to the contrary.

(C) No, because a lawyer who represents an organization does not thereby represent its constituents and never has a duty to them absent an express agreement to represent the constituent in addition to the organization.

(D) No, because a lawyer who represents an organization does not thereby represent its constituents but may have a duty to them.

WESTINGHOUSE ELEC. CORP. v. KERR-MCGEE CORP.

580 F.2d 1311 (7th Cir. 1978), *cert. denied*, 439 U.S. 955 (1978)

SPRECHER, Circuit Judge.

The novel issues on this appeal are (1) whether an attorney-client relationship arises only when both parties consent to its formation or can it also occur when the lay party submits confidential information to the law party with reasonable belief that the latter is acting as the former's attorney. * * *

I

On September 8, 1975, Westinghouse, a major manufacturer of nuclear reactors, notified utility companies that 17 of its long-term uranium supply contracts had become "commercially impracticable" under § 2-615 of the Uniform Commercial Code. In response, the affected utilities filed 13 federal actions, one state action, and three foreign actions against Westinghouse, alleging breach of contract and challenging Westinghouse's invocation of § 2-615. * * *

As an outgrowth of its defense of these contract actions, Westinghouse on October 15, 1976, filed the present antitrust action against 12 foreign and 17 domestic corporations engaged in various aspects of the uranium industry.

Kirkland's representation of Westinghouse's uranium litigation has required the efforts of 8 to 14 of its attorneys and has generated some $2.5 million in legal fees.

Contemporaneously with its Westinghouse representation in the uranium cases, Kirkland represented API, using six of its lawyers in that project.

In October, 1975, Congress was presented with legislative proposals to break up the oil companies, both vertically by separating their control over production, transportation, refining and marketing entities, and horizontally by prohibiting cross-ownership of alternative energy resources in addition to oil and gas. Since this proposed legislation threatened oil companies with a potential divestiture of millions of dollars of assets, in November, 1975, the API launched a Committee on Industrial Organization to lobby against the proposals. On December 10, 1975, API's president requested that each company designate one of its senior executives to facilitate coordination of the Committee's activities with the individual companies.

The Committee was organized into five task forces. The Legal Task Force was headed by L. Bates Lea, General Counsel of Standard Oil of Indiana, assisted by Stark Ritchie, API's General Counsel.

On February 25, 1976, Ritchie wrote to Frederick M. Rowe, a partner in Kirkland's Washington office, retaining the firm to review the divestiture hearings and "prepare arguments for use in opposition to this type of legislation." On May 4, 1976, Ritchie added that the Kirkland firm's work for API "should include the preparation of possible testimony, analyzing the probable legal consequences and antitrust considerations of the proposed legislation" and "you should make an objective survey and study of the probable effects of the pending legislation, specifically including probable effects on oil companies that would have to divest assets." Ritchie noted that "(a)s a part of this study, we will arrange for interviews by your firm with a cross-section of industry personnel." The May 4 letter to Rowe concluded with:

> Your firm will, of course, act as an independent expert counsel and hold any company information learned through these interviews in strict confidence, not to be disclosed to any other company, or even to API, except in aggregated or such other form as will preclude identifying the source company with its data.

On May 25, 1976, Ritchie sent to 59 API member companies a survey questionnaire Seeking data to be used by Kirkland in connection with its engagement by API. In the introductory memorandum to the questionnaire, Ritchie advised the 59 companies that Kirkland had "ascertained that certain types of data pertinent to the pending anti-diversification legislation are not now publicly available" and the API "would appreciate your help in providing this information to Kirkland. . . ." The memorandum included the following:

> Kirkland, Ellis & Rowe is acting as an independent special counsel for API, and will hold any company information in strict confidence, not to be disclosed to any other company, or even to API, except in aggregated or such other form as will preclude identifying the source company with its data. * * *

The data sought was to assist Kirkland "in preparing positions, arguments and testimony in opposition to this type of legislative (divestiture)" and was not to be sent to API but rather to Kirkland.

Pursuant to the provision in Ritchie's May 4, 1976 letter to Rowe that interviews would be arranged with a cross-section of industry personnel, Nolan Clark, a Kirkland partner, interviewed representatives of eight oil companies between April 29 and June 15, 1976.

After going through several drafts, the final Kirkland report to API was released on October 15, 1976. The final report contains 230 pages of text and 82 pages of exhibits. References to uranium appear throughout the report and uranium is the primary subject of about 25 pages of text and 11 pages of exhibits. The report marshalls a large number of facts and arguments to show that oil company diversification does not threaten overall energy competition. In particular the report asserts that the relatively high concentration ratios in the uranium industry can be expected to decline, that current increases in uranium prices are a result of increasing demand, that oil company entry into uranium production has stimulated competition and diminished concentration, that oil companies have no incentive to act in concert to restrict coal or uranium production and that the historical record refutes any charge that oil companies have restricted uranium output. The report concludes that "the energy industries, both individually and collectively, are competitive today and are likely to remain so."

As noted at the outset of this opinion, the API report was issued on the same day as the present antitrust suit was filed against several defendants, including Gulf, Kerr-McGee and Getty.

The district court concluded that "(a) comparison of the two documents reveals a rather basic conflict in their contentions and underlying theories." The court also observed that "(p)erhaps in recognition of the diametrically opposing theories of the API report and the Westinghouse complaint, Kirkland does not attempt to rebut the oil companies' charges that it has simultaneously taken inconsistent positions on competition in the uranium industry."

Gulf, Kerr-McGee and Getty are substantial dues-paying members of API. Kerr-McGee and Getty are also represented on API's board of directors.

At Ritchie's request, the cross-section interviews were mainly arranged by Gerald Thurmond, Washington Counsel of Gulf Oil Company and a member of API's Antitrust Strategy Group. On May 11, 1976, Thurmond advised Gulf officials that Nolan Clark of Kirkland planned to visit them. Attached to Thurmond's letter were the questions "which will be covered" in the meeting.

The meeting was held on May 28, 1976 in Denver. Nolan Clark represented Kirkland. In attendance for Gulf were six vice presidents, a comptroller and a regional attorney.

Also present was a Harvard professor who "also is working with API on the same subject." The meeting lasted more than two hours followed by lunch, during which discussions continued. After the meeting and in three letters from Gulf vice president Mingee to Clark dated August 10, 11 and 13, Gulf submitted specific information sought by Clark through the questionnaire and other written questions and in each letter Mingee stressed the confidential basis upon which the information was supplied.

Nolan Clark's interview with two Kerr-McGee vice presidents took place in Oklahoma City on June 9, 1976 and lasted about three hours. Clark was given considerable background information on Kerr-McGee's uranium industry, including mining locations, uranium conversion process, and pellet fabrication. On the subject of uranium marketing and pricing, one of the Kerr-McGee vice presidents described the escalating prices and tightening supplies in the current market, and the reasons behind the trends. Kerr-McGee sent its completed questionnaire to Clark on August 25, 1976.

Kirkland did not interview any Getty personnel. However, Getty received the confidential API questionnaire which requested it to estimate the value of its assets subject to proposed divestiture and its research and development outlays in alternative energy fields. Getty completed the questionnaire and mailed its data sheets to Nolan Clark on June 4, 1976, with the understanding that the data would be held in confidence. * * *

II

The crux of the district court's determination was based upon its view that an "attorney-client relationship is one of agency to which the general rules of agency apply" and "arises only when the parties have given their consent, either express or implied, to its formation." * * *

Mr. Chief Justice (then Judge) Burger said[:]

> * * * The basic elements of the attorney-client relationship are not changed because the contract for services is expressed in a formal written contract. Indeed the very making of a formal contract and its performance impose a high duty on the attorney because he is dealing in an area in which he is expert and the client is not and as to which the client must necessarily rely on the attorney. . . . This is not to suggest that a formal contract is unimportant but rather that a formal long-term contract, superimposed on the normal attorney-client relationship, alters the relationship only by adding new dimensions of duties and obligations on the attorney.
>
> For these reasons it is obvious why an attorney-client relationship does not arise only in the agency manner such as when the parties expressly or impliedly consent to its formation as the district court erroneously concluded.

The district court first determined that there existed no explicit or express attorney-client relationship in that no oil company representative requested Kirkland to act as its attorney orally or in writing and Kirkland did not accept such employment orally or in writing. The district court found that "Kirkland sent its legal bills to the API, and was compensated only by the API." A professional relationship is not dependent upon the payment of fees nor, as we have noted, upon the execution of a formal contract.

The court then purported to determine whether the professional relationship "may be implied from the conduct of the parties." First, it found no "indicia" such as "the preparation of a legally-binding document like a contract or a will, or the attorney's appearance in a judicial or quasi-judicial proceeding." Second, the court searched for evidence of three fundamental characteristics of an agency relationship: the power to affect the legal relations of the principal and others; a fiduciary who works on behalf of his principal and primarily for his benefit; and a principal who has the right to control the conduct of the agent. Using these tests, the court concluded that "(v)iewed in its totality, we believe that the evidence shows that no attorney-client relationship has existed between Kirkland and the oil companies." As we have indicated, to apply only the agency tests is too narrow an approach for determining whether a lawyer's fiduciary obligation has arisen. * * *

III

The client is no longer simply the person who walks into a law office. A lawyer employed by a corporation represents the entity but that principle does not of itself solve the potential conflicts existing between the entity and its individual participants.

Three district courts have held that each individual member of an Unincorporated association is a client of the association's lawyer. In *Halverson v. Convenient Food Mart, Inc.*, 458 F.2d 927, 930 (7th Cir. 1972), we held that a lawyer who had represented an informal group of 75 franchisees "(b)ecause . . . (he) in effect had represented and benefited every franchisee, . . . [they] could reasonably believe that each one of them was his client."

Here we are faced with neither an ordinary commercial corporation nor with an informal or unincorporated association, but instead with a nation-wide trade association with 350 corporate and 7,500 individual members and doing business as a non-profit corporation.

We need not make any generalized pronouncements of whether an attorney for such an organization represents every member because this case can and should be decided on a much more narrow ground.

There are several fairly common situations where, although there is no express attorney-client relationship, there exists nevertheless a fiduciary obligation or an implied professional relation:

(1) The fiduciary relationship existing between lawyer and client extends to preliminary consultation by a prospective client with a view to retention of the lawyer, although actual employment does not result.

(2) When information is exchanged between co-defendants and their attorneys in a criminal case, an attorney who is the recipient of such information breaches his fiduciary duty if he later, in his representation of another client, is able to use this information to the detriment of one of the co-defendants, even though that co-defendant is not the one which he represented in the criminal case.

(3) When an insurer retains an attorney to investigate the circumstances of a claim and the insured, pursuant to a cooperation clause in the policy, cooperates with the attorney, the attorney may not thereafter represent a third party suing the insured nor indeed continue to represent the insurer once a conflict of interest surfaces.

(4) In a recent case, where an auditor's regional counsel was instrumental in hiring a second law firm to represent some plaintiffs suing the auditor and where the second firm through such relationship was in a position to receive privileged information, the second law firm, although having no direct attorney-client relationship with the auditor, was disqualified from representing the plaintiffs.

(5) In a recent case in this circuit, a law firm who represented for many years both the plaintiff in an action and also a corporation which owned 20% of the outstanding stock of the defendant corporation, was permitted to continue its representation of the plaintiff but was directed to disassociate itself from representing or advising the corporation owning 20% of defendant's stock.

In none of the above categories or situations did the disqualified or disadvantaged lawyer or law firm actually represent the "client" in the sense of a formal or even express attorney-client relation. In each of those categories either an implied relation was found or at least the lawyer was found to owe a fiduciary obligation to the laymen.

The professional relationship for purposes of the privilege for attorney-client communications "hinges upon the client's belief that he is consulting a lawyer in that capacity and his manifested intention to seek professional legal advice." The affidavits before the district court established that: the Washington counsel for Gulf "was given to believe that the Kirkland firm was representing both API and Gulf;" Kerr-McGee's vice president understood a Kirkland partner to explain that Kirkland was working on behalf of API and also its members such as Kerr-McGee; and Getty's vice president stated that in submitting data to Kirkland he "acted upon the belief and expectation that such submission was made in order to enable (Kirkland) to render legal service to Getty in furtherance of Getty's interests." * * *

[R]eversed and remanded.

Make the Connection

We will consider the *Westinghouse* case again in Chapter 5. To read more about similar situations, *see* Nancy J. Moore, *Expanding Duties of Attorneys to "Non-Clients": Reconceptualizing the Attorney-Client Relationship in Entity Representation and Other Inherently Ambiguous Situations*, 45 S.C. L. Rev. 659 (1994); John Leubsdorf, *Pluralizing the Client-Lawyer Relationship*, 77 Cornell L. Rev. 825 (1992).

Rule 1.13(a) provides the general rule that "A lawyer employed or retained by an organization represents the organization acting through its duly authorized constituents." The Comment explains that even when constituents of an organization communicate with the lawyer "[t]his does not mean * * * that the constituents of an organization are the clients of the lawyer."

Food for Thought

Lawyer Websites and the Lawyer-Client Relationship

Lawyers' use of the internet has resulted in new variations on issues relating to creation of a lawyer-client relationship.

Professor David Hricik writes:

Has a lawyer who merely opens an unsolicited e-mail done something to indicate to it's sender that the lawyer assents to receive information in confidence or is open to representing that person? Should an e-mail sent unilaterally by a prospective client through a law firm website be treated any differently than a phone call placed to a lawyer, or a meeting held between lawyer and prospective client? Is e-mail different enough from these "old-world" forms of communications so that a different rule should apply, and so these advance waivers are unnecessary?

The opinions so far conclude that by posting a website, a lawyer has manifested an intent to offer to form attorney-client relationships and to keep submitted information confidential. * * * Thus, disclaimers are necessary.

David Hricik, *The Speed of Normal: Conflicts, Competency, and Confidentiality in the Digital Age*, 10 Comp. L. Rev. & Tech. J. 73, 77-78 (2005).

[Question 5]

The court appoints a lawyer who believes that abortion is murder to represent a teenage girl Seeking court permission to obtain an abortion without the consent of her parents. The lawyer explains that he believes that abortion is murder and asks the court to withdraw the appointment. The court refuses. Under the Rules, which of the following is true?

(A) The lawyer should not have sought to avoid the appointment.

(B) The lawyer was ethically permitted to seek to avoid the appointment and can refuse the representation.

(C) The lawyer was ethically permitted to seek to avoid the appointment but must continue the representation.

(D) The lawyer must represent the client, but does not have to follow the client's instructions.

Restatement § 14(2) explains that a lawyer-client relationship arises when "a tribunal with power to do so appoints the lawyer to provide services." Rule 6.2 advises that lawyers as a matter of "public service" should generally accept court appointments and "shall not seek to avoid appointment * * * to represent a person except for good cause, such as:

(a) representing the client is likely to result in violation of the Rules of Professional Conduct or other law;

(b) representing the client is likely to result in an unreasonable financial burden on the lawyer; or

(c) the client or the cause is so repugnant to the lawyer as to be likely to impair the client-lawyer relationship or the lawyer's ability to represent the client."

BOARD OF PROFESSIONAL RESPONSIBILITY OF THE SUPREME COURT OF TENNESSEE

Formal Ethics Op. No. 96-F-140, 1996 WL 340719 (1996)

Inquiry is made as to several issues involving the ethical obligations of court-appointed counsel for minors who obtain abortions via judicial bypass of the parental consent for abortion provisions within Tennessee Code Annotated (T.C.A.) §§37-10-303 and 37-10-304.

The inquiring attorney routinely practices before the Juvenile Court in a particular county, and said attorney has been appointed to represent minors who have elected to petition the Juvenile Court for waivers of the parental consent requirement to obtain abortions. Several moral, ethical and constitutional law issues have been presented in the inquiry, [including the question of whether the attorney can] decline to accept the appointment for moral, religious or malpractice insurance reasons. * * *

[This] question is the most difficult to answer, given that legal and ethical issues are inextricably intertwined. Essentially, counsel asks whether he can ethically decline such appointments due to malpractice insurance reasons, and a deep-seated, sincere belief that appointments in such cases constitute state action violative of his free exercise of religion rights guaranteed by the First Amendment to the United States Constitution. DR 6-102(A) states that a lawyer should not attempt to exonerate himself from or limit his liability to his client for personal malpractice; thus, this reason does not appear to be a sufficient ground for declining such appointments. Counsel also alleges that he is a devout Catholic and cannot, under any circumstances, advocate a point of view ultimately resulting in what he considers to be the loss of human life. The religious beliefs are so compelling that counsel fears his own personal interests will subject him to conflicting interests and impair his independent professional judgment in violation of DR 5-101(A). In other words, counsel contends his status is akin to that of a conscientious objector, who is opposed to participation in abortion in any form.

Although counsel's religious and moral beliefs are clearly fervently held, EC 2-29 exhorts appointed counsel to refrain from withdrawal where a person is unable to retain counsel, except for compelling reasons. Compelling reasons as contemplated by this EC do not include such factors as:

> . . . the repugnance of the subject matter of the proceeding, the identity or position of a person involved in the case, the belief of the lawyer that the defendant in a criminal proceeding is guilty, or the belief of the lawyer regarding the merits of the civil case.

Several Tennessee cases addressing this issue from the perspective of contempt cast serious doubt on whether such an argument would prevail. * * * Reported federal cases are similarly pessimistic on whether one's free exercise rights are unconstitutionally burdened under analogous facts. * * * Ultimately, counsel should allow the juvenile court to determine as a matter of law the propriety of his withdrawal after motion and hearing to develop an adequate record. * * * Tennessee Formal Ethics Opinion 84-F-73 is also instructive on this issue, although this opinion specifically addresses ethical obligations of counsel in first degree murder cases. The Board opined, though, in cases involving conflicts between the moral and ethical beliefs of counsel and those of his client that:

> . . . [c]ounsel's moral beliefs and usually acceptable ethical standards and duties must yield to the moral beliefs and legal rights of the defendant... Counsel is ethically obligated to follow the law and to do nothing in opposition to the client's moral and legal choices. . . .

> Counsel should move the court to withdraw during the portion of the trial where the conflict is manifested. In the event the court fails to grant such motions, the attorney should seek an immediate review by the appellate court. . . .

* * *

This opinion is only intended to address the ethical obligations of counsel.

Approved and adopted by the Board

————————————

Do you agree with the Tennessee Board of Professional Responsibility?

> **FYI**
>
> The client has a right "to reject appointed counsel and proceed pro se." Restatement § 14, Reporter's Note to Comment g (citing *Faretta v. California*, 422 U.S. 806 (1975) (criminal); *Knox Leasing v. Turner*, 562 A.2d 168 (N.H. 1989) (civil)). Nonetheless, courts may appoint standby counsel, even where the client objects. *See, e.g., McKaskle v. Wiggins*, 465 U.S. 168 (1984).

[Question 6]

Joan Lawyer practices matrimonial law. She only represents women because she seeks to "redress the social and legal wrongs done to women." John Client asks her to represent him. She refuses on the ground that he is a man. John Client sues her for unlawful discrimination. What result?

(A) Joan is liable for violating the laws against gender discrimination.

(B) Joan is subject to discipline for violating her ethical obligation to ensure that all clients have a right to representation.

(C) Joan is not liable because she has complied with all of her obligations under the ethics rules.

(D) Joan is not liable because her freedoms of speech and association allow her to represent only women.

NATHANSON v. MCAD

2003 WL 22480688 (Mass. Super.)

ELIZABETH M. FAHEY, Justice of the Superior Court.

The plaintiff, Attorney Judith Nathanson, ("Nathanson"), seeks judicial review of a decision and order rendered by a Commissioner of the Massachusetts Commission Against Discrimination ("MCAD"), which was subsequently adopted by the full Commission. The order required Nathanson to cease and desist her discriminatory practices in refusing to represent men in her legal practice. For the reasons stated herein, the plaintiff's motion for judgment on the pleadings is denied and the MCAD decision is affirmed.

I. Facts

Joseph Stropnicky filed a complaint with MCAD against Attorney Nathanson for gender discrimination in a place of public accommodation in violation of G.L.c. 272, § 98. Specifically, Stropnicky alleged that Attorney Nathanson excluded him from her legal practice and declined to represent him in his divorce proceedings because Nathanson only represents women in her divorce practice. Although she advertises to the general public via the white and yellow pages and local newspapers, Nathanson, desiring to ameliorate the impact of divorce on females, limits her divorce practice to representing women. Nathanson is forthcoming, and candidly admits that her reason for refusing to represent Stropnicky is because his gender interferes with or precludes her ability to provide him zealous legal representation.

In 1991, Nathanson was an attorney in private practice in Lawrence, MA. She had earned a law degree with the purpose of helping to advance the status of women in the legal system, and her legal work had been devoted to that goal. In her divorce practice, she only represented wives, and not husbands. Nathanson had only a certain amount of time and energy to devote to her clients, and she felt it was essential to use her resources in the effort to redress social and legal wrongs done to women. The report from the Supreme Judicial Court's Gender Bias Study indicated that women were disadvantaged relative to men in access to the judicial system and treatment within that system. The Gender Bias Study, published in 1989, reinforced Nathanson's commitment to use her legal talents and time to promote more equal treatment of women in the judicial system. There is no evidence of Nathanson's improper animus towards men, as she has represented men in legal matters other than divorce proceedings against women.

Pursuant to G.L.c. 151B, § 5, an Investigating Commissioner found probable cause to credit the allegations, and after conciliation efforts failed, a hearing was held before Hearing Commissioner Charles Walker. On February 25, 1997, the Hearing Commissioner issued his decision that Nathanson had engaged in gender discrimination in violation of G.L.c. 272, § 98. The Full Commission of the MCAD affirmed the decision on July 26, 1999.

On August 25, 1999, Nathanson filed the instant action in Superior Court, seeking relief pursuant to G.L.c. 30A, § 14 and G.L.c. 151B, § 6. * * * G.L.c. 30A, § 14 grants any person or entity who is aggrieved by a decision of any agency in an adjudicatory proceeding the right to appeal that decision to the Superior Court. * * *

III. Discussion

A. Whether the Commission Erred in Asserting Jurisdiction

Arguing that the Commission erred in asserting jurisdiction over Stropnicky's claims, Nathanson claims that issues pertaining to her behavior as an attorney are within the exclusive jurisdiction of the Supreme Judicial Court and the Board of Bar OverSeers. In 1991, when the alleged discriminatory conduct occurred, the Massachusetts Canons of Ethics and Disciplinary Rules, as set forth in S.J.C. Rule 3:07, were in effect. The Canons were replaced by the Massachusetts Rules of Professional Conduct in 1998. See S.J.C. Rule 3:07.

The Massachusetts Canons of Ethics and Disciplinary Rules, in effect at the time of the alleged discriminatory conduct, provide that "[t]he practice of law by members of the Massachusetts Bar shall be *regulated* by the Canons of Ethics and Disciplinary Rules attached hereto and incorporated by reference herein." S.J.C. Rule 3:07 (Introduction) (emphasis added). While the Supreme Judicial Court and Board of Bar OverSeers do have jurisdiction over Nathanson's conduct as a member of the bar, this jurisdiction is not exclusive. In determining whether the SJC jurisdiction is exclusive, this court is mindful both that there is nothing in the SJC Rules' language that speaks of exclusivity of said regulation and also that there are numerous other circumstances where the SJC has at least implied that jurisdiction is not exclusive. Attorneys are subject to the same penalties and liabilities as any member of the public for failing to act in conformity with the law. For these reasons, the Commission did not err in asserting jurisdiction over Stropnicky's claim.

Nathanson makes the additional argument that, under the 1991 rules and under the rules in effect today, an attorney must represent her clients zealously, and Nathanson's commitment to representing women in divorce proceedings precludes her from advocating zealously on behalf of men. It is certainly true that Nathanson had a duty to represent her clients zealously at the time of the alleged discriminatory conduct. S.J.C. Rule 3:07, Canon 7 ("A Lawyer Should Represent a Client Zealously Within the Bounds of the Law"). While an attorney's ability to advocate zealously for a client is a relevant consideration in determining whether an attorney is legally required to provide representation, it is not permissible for an attorney to assert a discriminatory agenda as grounds that she is unable to advocate zealously for a client. This is because an attorney is required to adhere to and follow the law. Nathanson's belief, that her advocacy on behalf of women in divorce would be undermined should she take on a male client, cannot be countenanced. Nathanson's claim that she was devoting her professional expertise to "the betterment of a disadvantaged protected class," "women in divorce proceedings" cannot be supported when the male she declines to represent is similarly situated to many of Nathanson's female clients. Nathanson's ethical obligations as an attorney licensed to practice law in this Commonwealth require that she uphold the law in her practice. As an officer of the court, she, as a lawyer, is prohibited from practicing discrimination such as the discrimination at issue in the instant case.

* * *

C. Whether a Law Office Is a Place of Public Accommodation

As an additional ground why the MCAD decision should be reversed, Nathanson argues that G.L.c. 272, § 98 does not apply. Under G.L.c. 272, § 98, discrimination on the basis of gender is prohibited in any place of public accommodation. G.L.c. 272, § 92A defines a place of public accommodation as "any place, whether licensed or unlicensed, which is open to and accepts and solicits the patronage of the general public ..." The statute subsequently lists a number of establishments and places which are included in the definition, but also states that these examples are to be read "without limiting the generality of this definition." G.L.c. 272, § 92A.

Plaintiff Nathanson argues that a law office is not a place of public accommodation, because a law office has unique characteristics which distinguish it from the examples listed in the statute. Nathanson asserts that if the special character of the attorney-client relationship were intended to be included in the scope of the statute's protections, it would have been stated explicitly in the statutory list of examples. This court declines to adopt her view, as the statute, specifically nonexhaustive in its listing, lists establishments which offer services to the public, and which are easily comparable to services offered by a law office.

* * *

Based on this reasoning, the MCAD decision is correct unless affirming it would unreasonably interfere with Attorney Nathanson's First Amendment rights.

D. Whether Nathanson's First Amendment Rights Are Abridged by Application of the Statute

Nathanson's final argument against the MCAD's decision is that her exclusion of male clients in her divorce practice is constitutionally protected free speech and free association.

1. Free Association

Nathanson argues that her right to free association will be infringed if she is forced to represent Stropnicky. Rights to free association are delineated in "two distinct senses"; first, there is a right "to enter into and maintain certain intimate human relationships," and, second, there is a "right to associate for the purpose of engaging in those activities protected by the First Amendment—speech, assembly, petition for the redress of grievances, and the exercise of religion." *Roberts v. United States Jaycees,* 468 U.S. 609, 617-18 (1984). An association must be sufficiently selective or exclusive to impair Nathanson's rights to intimate association. Nathanson does not argue that she uses any particular criteria to select her clients, and in fact admits that she refused to represent Stropnicky for no reason other than his gender. The relationship between Nathanson and her clients "is not the kind of intimate or private relation that warrants constitutional protection."

A more difficult question concerns whether application of the statute infringes Nathanson's rights to expressive association. A statute infringes rights to free expressive association when it affects, in a "significant way," the ability of indi viduals to form associations that advocate public or private viewpoints. Assuming the type of associations and relationships protected by the First Amendment are applicable to the "association" that is formed when an attorney represents a client, Nathanson's duty to represent Stropnicky under the Massachusetts Public Accommodations Statute does not compromise her ability to advocate her viewpoints or her ability to accomplish her purposes. As noted above, Stropnicky represents the same interests as the women that Nathanson typically represents in divorce proceedings.

Further, assuming *arguendo* that requiring Nathanson to represent Stropnicky infringes her rights to free association, these rights are subordinate to "regulations adopted to serve compelling state interests." Statutes enacted for purposes of abating discrimination, such as the Massachusetts Public Accommodation statute, serve compelling state interests. Accordingly, Nathanson's free association rights are not outweighed by society's interest in non-discrimination in this case.

2. Free Speech

An attorney may advocate for a client and concurrently engage in constitutionally protected free speech. Nevertheless, the right to free speech is not absolute and will be forfeited to a compelling state interest. * * *

The Commonwealth's compelling interest in abating gender discrimination outweighs Nathanson's constitutionally protected right to free speech in her capacity as a private attorney. The Massachusetts Public Accommodation statute Seeks to eliminate discrimination, including discrimination on the basis of gender, and "does not, on its face, target speech or discriminate on the basis of its content, the focal point of its prohibition being rather on the act of discriminating against individuals in the provision of publicly available goods, privileges, and services on the proscribed grounds." *Hurley,* 515 U.S. at 503 (interpreting G.L.c. 272, § 98). Statutes which aim to quell discrimination against women and other groups have been upheld because they serve compelling state interests.

Further, the degree to which courts will afford protection to a speaker varies with the extent to which the speaker acts as a conduit for the expression of others.

A private attorney, when representing a client, operates more as a conduit for the speech and expression of the client, rather than as a speaker for herself. In contrast to *Hurley,* the public accommodation at issue here is the client's access to legal rights and remedies, rather than use of Nathanson's speech and her law office as a vehicle for her own expression. As a practical matter, Nathanson's legal practice aims to elevate the status of divorced women by providing them access to their legal rights and remedies, and Stropnicky sought representation for that purpose (i.e., because he wanted to have his rights vindicated). Nathanson rejected Stropnicky as a client specifically because he is a male, and not because his business would burden any particular message that her legal practice attempts to communicate. Compare *Hurley,* 515 U.S. at 573 (for homosexuals in parade, "participation as a unit in the parade was equally expressive" and the homosexual organization was "formed for the very purpose of marching in order to celebrate its members' identity as openly gay, lesbian and bisexual ..."). The defendant MCAD has sufficiently demonstrated a compelling interest in the elimination of gender discrimination, including elimination of gender discrimination against the male Stropnicky. Even if the MCAD's interest does not rise to the level of a "compelling interest" because of Stropnicky's male gender, it is sufficient to overcome the interference with private attorney Nathanson's free expression.

For these reasons, any free speech activities that Nathanson engages in are subordinate to the state's compelling interest in eliminating discrimination on the basis of gender.

* * *

Accordingly, plaintiff's motion for Judgment on the Pleadings is *DENIED,* and the MCAD decision is *AFFIRMED.*

———————————

This decision has proven quite controversial. *See, e.g.,* Martha Minow, *Symposium: A Duty to Represent? Critical Reflections on* Stropnicky v. Nathanson: *Foreword: Of Legal Ethics, Taxis, and Doing the Right Thing,* 20 W. New Eng. L. Rev. 5 (1998). What do you think?

IV. Ending the Lawyer-Client Relationship

After exploring the creation of the lawyer-client relationship, we examine the special rules governing the termination of that relationship. Lawyers do not have the freedom unilaterally to terminate the lawyer-client relationship. While the parties can of course agree to end a lawyer-client relationship, lawyers must satisfy the ethics rules if they want to terminate the relationship without the client's permission.

[Question 1]

Attorney Alpha, a sole practitioner, recently suffered a heart attack and was advised that she could not return to work for six months. Alpha delivered all of her clients' files to Attorney Beta, who is also a sole practitioner. Beta agreed to review each client's file promptly, take any action necessary to protect each client's interests, and treat the information in the files as confidential. Alpha then wrote her clients, advising each client that the client's file had been delivered to Beta for review and for any action necessary to protect the client's interest, and that the client was fee to select another lawyer.

Alpha knows that Beta is a competent attorney. Beta did not accept the file of any person whose interests were, or could be, adverse to the interests of any of Beta's own clients.

Was it proper for Alpha to deliver the files to Beta for review?

    (A) Yes, because Alpha knows that Beta is competent to protect the clients' interests.

    (B) Yes, because Beta agreed to treat the information in the files as confidential.

    (C) Yes, because given her medical condition, Alpha's delivery of the files was necessary to protect the client's interests.

    (D) No, because Alpha did not obtain the prior consent of each client whose file was delivered to Beta.

[Question 2]

Attorney is employed in the legal department of Electco, a public utility company, and represents that company in litigation. Electco has been sued by a consumer group that alleges Electco is guilty of various acts in violation of its charter. Through its general counsel, Electco has instructed Attorney not to negotiate a settlement but to go to trial under any circumstances since a precedent needs to be established. Attorney believes the case should be settled if possible. Must Attorney withdraw as counsel in the case?

(A) Yes, if Electco is controlling Attorney's judgment in settling the case.

(B) Yes, because a lawyer should endeavor to avoid litigation.

(C) No, if Electco's defense can be supported by a good faith argument.

(D) No, because as an employee, Attorney is bound by the instructions of the general counsel.

Restatement § 31

* * *

> *b. Rationale.* Just as mutual consent is usually a prerequisite to creating the client-lawyer relationship, the end of such consent usually ends the relationship. Consent might end because client or lawyer withdraws consent or becomes incapable of giving a valid consent. Alternatively, the lawyer might have completed the representation or have become incapable of providing services to completion.

Rule 1.16 governs the termination of the lawyer-client relationship. Rule 1.16(a) requires a lawyer to withdraw from representation if:

> (1) the representation will result in violation of the rules of professional conduct or other law;

> (2) the lawyer's physical or mental condition materially impairs the lawyer's ability to represent the client; or

> (3) the lawyer is discharged.

Rule 1.16(b) in addition permits a lawyer to withdraw from representation under the following circumstances:

> (1) withdrawal can be accomplished without material adverse effect on the interests of the client;

> (2) the client persists in a course of action involving the lawyer's services that the lawyer reasonably believes is criminal or fraudulent;

> (3) the client has used the lawyer's services to perpetrate a crime or fraud;

> (4) the client insists upon taking action that the lawyer considers repugnant or with which the lawyer has a fundamental disagreement;

(5) the client fails substantially to fulfill an obligation to the lawyer regarding the lawyer's services and has been given reasonable warning that the lawyer will withdraw unless the obligation is fulfilled;

(6) the representation will result in an unreasonable financial burden on the lawyer or has been rendered unreasonably difficult by the client; or

(7) other good cause for withdrawal exists.

Even where Rule 1.16(a) would require withdrawal or Rule 1.16(b) would permit it, Rule 1.16(c) provides that "[a] lawyer must comply with applicable law requiring notice to or permission of a tribunal when terminating a representation. When ordered to do so by a tribunal, a lawyer shall continue representation notwithstanding good cause for terminating the representation."

Where a lawyer satisfies the conditions for terminating the representation, Rule 1.16(d) further requires that "a lawyer shall take steps to the extent reasonably practicable to protect a client's interests, such as giving reasonable notice to the client, allowing time for employment of other counsel, surrendering papers and property to which the client is entitled and refunding any advance payment of fee or expense that has not been earned or incurred. The lawyer may retain papers relating to the client to the extent permitted by other law."

For purposes of Question 1, consider whether Rule 1.6 is relevant. Rule 1.6 is the general rule on confidentiality. It provides that "[a] lawyer shall not reveal information relating to the representation of a client unless the client gives informed consent, the disclosure is impliedly authorized in order to carry out the representation or the disclosure" falls within the exceptions in paragraph (b), none of which is relevant here. We will explore the lawyer's duty of confidentially more fully in Chapter 4.

For purposes of Question 2, consider whether Rule 3.1 is relevant. It provides that "[a] lawyer shall not bring or defend a proceeding, or assert or controvert an issue therein, unless there is a basis in law and fact for doing so that is not frivolous, which includes a good faith argument for an extension, modification or reversal of existing law." We will consider Rule 3.1 again in Chapter 6.

[Question 3]

An Attorney represents a Client in commercial litigation that is scheduled to go to trial in two months. Over the past several weeks, the Client has disagreed with almost every tactical decision that the Attorney has made. Frustrated, the Attorney finally said to the Client that if the Client didn't like the way he was handling the lawsuit, then perhaps the Client should get another lawyer. The Client was upset at the suggestion and accused the Attorney of trying to get out of the case. Reasonably believing that he could no longer work effectively with the Client, the Attorney sought the Client's

permission to withdraw from the representation, and the Client reluctantly agreed. After giving the Client sufficient notice to obtain replacement counsel, the Attorney requested the Court's permission to withdraw from the litigation, but the Court denied the request.

May the attorney withdraw from the representation?

(A) Yes, because the Client agreed, and the Attorney gave the client sufficient notice to obtain replacement counsel.

(B) Yes, because the Client had made it unreasonably difficult for the Attorney to carry out the representation effectively.

(C) No, because the Court denied the Attorney's request to withdraw.

(D) No, because the Attorney's withdrawal would cause material prejudice to the Client, and the Client's agreement was not voluntary.

Review <u>Rule 1.16</u> and consider the following case. Although decided under the provisions of the Code, and not the Rules, the court explains how to analyze a motion to withdraw.

WHITING v. *LACARA,*

<u>187 F.3d 317 (2d Cir. 1999)</u>

PER CURIAM:

Garrett R. Lacara appeals from two orders of Judge Spatt denying Lacara's motions to withdraw as counsel for plaintiff-appellee Joseph M. Whiting. Although the record before Judge Spatt justified denial of the motions, amplification of Whiting's position at oral argument persuades us to reverse.

BACKGROUND

In July 1996, appellee, a former police officer, filed a civil rights action against Nassau County, the Incorporated Village of Old Brooksville, the Old Brooksville Police Department, other villages, and various individual defendants. The action was based on the termination of his employment as an officer. He sought $9,999,000 in damages. * * *

Whiting retained Lacara in December 1997. In June 1998, the district court partially granted defendants' summary judgment motion and dismissed plaintiff's due process claims. The court scheduled the remaining claims, one free speech claim and two equal protection claims, for a jury trial on August 18, 1998. * * *

On August 6, 1998, Lacara moved to be relieved as counsel. In support, he offered an affidavit asserting that appellee "[had] failed to follow legal advice," that appellee "[wa]s not focused on his legal rights," and that appellee "demand[ed] publicity against legal advice." Lacara also asserted that appellee had failed to keep adequate contact with his office, was "not sufficiently thinking clearly to be of assistance at the time of trial," and would "be of little or no help during trial." Furthermore, Lacara stated that appellee had "demand[ed] that [Lacara] argue collateral issues which would not be allowed in evidence," demanded that Lacara continue to argue a due process claim already dismissed by the court, and drafted a Rule 68 Offer without Lacara's consent and demanded that he serve it on defendants. Finally, Lacara asserted that on July 30, 1998, Whiting had entered his office and, without permission, had "commenced to riffle [Lacara's] 'in box.' " Lacara stated that he had to call 911 when Whiting had refused to leave the office. Lacara offered to provide further information to the court in camera. Whiting's responsive affidavit essentially denied Lacara's allegations. Whiting stated that he would not be opposed to an order relieving counsel upon the condition that Lacara's firm refund the legal fees paid by Whiting.

On August 13, Judge Spatt denied Lacara's motion to withdraw as counsel. * * *

On August 13, 1998, Lacara filed a notice of appeal and moved for an emergency stay of the district court's order and to be relieved as appellee's attorney. We granted Lacara's motion for an emergency stay pending appeal but denied his request for relief on the merits at that time. At a status conference on September 23, 1998, the district court entertained another motion from Lacara to withdraw as counsel, which Judge Spatt again denied. Lacara filed a timely appeal, which was consolidated with the earlier appeal.

DISCUSSION

* * *

We review a district court's denial of a motion to withdraw only for abuse of discretion. District courts are due considerable deference in decisions not to grant a motion for an attorney's withdrawal. The trial judge is closest to the parties and the facts, and we are very reluctant to interfere with district judges' management of their very busy dockets.

Judge Spatt denied Lacara's motion pursuant to Rule 1.4 of the Civil Rules of the United States District Court for the Southern and Eastern Districts of New York, which provides that

[a]n attorney who has appeared as attorney of record for a party may be relieved or displaced only by order of the court and may not withdraw from a case without leave of the court granted by order. Such an order may be granted only upon a showing by affidavit or otherwise of satisfactory reasons for withdrawal or displacement and the posture of the case, including its position, if any, on the calendar.

In addressing motions to withdraw as counsel, district courts have typically considered whether "the prosecution of the suit is [likely to be] disrupted by the withdrawal of counsel."

Considerations of judicial economy weigh heavily in favor of our giving district judges wide latitude in these situations, but there are some instances in which an attorney representing a plaintiff in a civil case might have to withdraw even at the cost of significant interference with the trial court's management of its calendar. For example, the Code of Professional Responsibility might mandate withdrawal where "the client is bringing the legal action ... merely for the purpose of harassing or maliciously injuring" the defendant. Model Code of Professional Responsibility ("Model Code") DR 2-110(B)(1). In such a situation, by denying a counsel's motion to withdraw, even on the eve of trial, a court would be forcing an attorney to violate ethical duties and possibly to be subject to sanctions.

Lacara does not claim that he faces mandatory withdrawal. Rather, he asserts three bases for "[p]ermissive withdrawal" under the Model Code: (i) Whiting "[i]nsists upon presenting a claim or defense that is not warranted under existing law and cannot be supported by good faith argument for an extension, modification, or reversal of existing law," Model Code DR 2-110(C)(1)(a); (ii) Whiting's "conduct [has] render[ed] it unreasonably difficult for [Lacara] to carry out employment effectively," DR 2-110(C)(1)(d); and (iii) Whiting has "[d]eliberately disregard[ed] an agreement or obligation to [Lacara] as to expenses or fees," DR 2-110(C)(1)(f). Although the Model Code "was drafted solely for its use in disciplinary proceedings and cannot by itself serve as a basis for granting a [m]otion to withdraw as counsel," we continue to believe that "the Model Code provides guidance for the court as to what constitutes 'good cause' to grant leave to withdraw as counsel."   However, a district court has wide latitude to deny a counsel's motion to withdraw, as here, on the eve of trial, where the Model Code merely permits withdrawal.

In the instant matter, we would be prepared to affirm if the papers alone were our only guide. Although Lacara has alleged a nonpayment of certain disputed fees, he has not done so with sufficient particularity to satisfy us that withdrawal was justified on the eve of trial. Moreover, there is nothing in the district court record to suggest error in that court's finding that "Whiting has been very cooperative and desirous of assisting his attorney in this litigation."   To be sure, we are concerned by Lacara's allegation that appellee trespassed in his office and that appellant had to call 911 to get Whiting to leave. However, Whiting disputes Lacara's description of these events. Moreover, we strongly agree with the district court that, as the third attorney in this case, Lacara had ample notice that appellee was a difficult client.

Nevertheless, we reverse the denial of appellant's motion for withdrawal under Model Code DR 2-110(C)(1)(a). Among Lacara's allegations are that Whiting insisted upon pressing claims already dismissed by the district court and calling witnesses Lacara deemed detrimental to his case. At oral argument, Whiting confirmed Lacara's contention that Whiting intends to dictate how his action is to be pursued. Whiting was asked by a member of the panel:

> Are you under the impression that if we affirm Judge Spatt's ruling, you will be able to tell Mr. Lacara to make the arguments you want made in this case? . . . [T]hat, if Mr. Lacara says, "That witness doesn't support your case," and you don't agree with that, are you under the impression that if we affirm Judge Spatt's ruling you'll be able to force him to call that witness?

To which Whiting replied, "Yes I am."

Moreover, in his statements at oral argument, Whiting made it clear that he was as interested in using the litigation to make public his allegations of corruption within the Brookville police department as in advancing his specific legal claims. For example, Whiting thought it relevant to inform us at oral argument that police officers in the department were guilty of "illegal drug use, acceptance of gratuities, [and] ongoing extramarital affairs while they were on duty." Appellee stated that he wanted to call an officer to testify that the officer could not "bring up anything criminal about the lieutenant, the two lieutenants, or the chief, which could get them in trouble or make the department look bad." Finally, Whiting made clear that he disagreed with Lacara about the handling of his case partly because Whiting suspects that Lacara wants to cover up corruption. Appellee stated: "For some strange reason, Mr. Lacara states that he doesn't want to put certain witnesses on the stand. . . . The bottom line is he does not want to make waves and expose all of the corruption that's going on within this community."

Also, at oral argument, appellee continued to bring up the already-dismissed due process claims. He asserted: "They found me guilty of something which was investigated by their department on two separate occasions and closed as unfounded on two separate occasions." We thus have good reason to conclude that Whiting will insist that Lacara pursue the already dismissed claims at trial.

Finally, appellee indicated that he might sue Lacara if not satisfied that Lacara provided representation as Whiting dictated. After admitting that he did not consider Lacara to be the "right attorney" for him in this case, Whiting asserted that he deemed Lacara "ineffective." The following exchange also occurred:

> *Question from Panel:* If you think that Mr. Lacara is ineffective in representing you as you stand here now, doesn't Mr. Lacara face the prospect of a . . . malpractice suit, by you, against him, if he continues in the case?
>
> *Appellee's Reply:* Yes, I believe he absolutely does.
>
> *Question from Panel:* Then, isn't that all the more reason to relieve him? So that what you say is ineffective and is in effect a distortion of the attorney-client relationship, doesn't continue?
>
> *Appellee's Reply:* I believe I do have grounds to sue Mr. Lacara for misrepresentation. . . .
>
> We believe that appellee's desire both to dictate legal strategies to his counsel and to sue counsel if those strategies are not followed places Lacara in *so impossible a situation that he must be permitted to withdraw.*

(emphasis added).

Model Code DR 2-110(C)(1)(a) limits the obligations of attorneys to follow their clients' dictates in how to conduct litigation. Attorneys have a duty to the court not to make "legal contentions . . . [un]warranted by existing law or by a nonfrivolous argument for the extension, modification, or reversal of existing law. . . ." Fed.R.Civ.P. 11(b)(2) * * * In this case, appellee's belief that he can dictate to Lacara how to handle his case and sue him if Lacara declines to follow those dictates leaves Lacara in a position amounting to a functional conflict of interest. If required to continue to represent Whiting, Lacara will have to choose between exposure to a malpractice action or to potential Rule 11 or other sanctions. To be sure, such a malpractice action would have no merit. However, we have no doubt it would be actively pursued, and even frivolous malpractice claims can have substantial collateral consequences.

As previously noted, the interest of the district court in preventing counsel from withdrawing on the eve of trial is substantial. Moreover, we would normally be loath to allow an attorney to withdraw on the eve of trial when the

Make the Connection

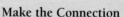

For a discussion of the rules prohibiting lawyers from making frivolous arguments, *see* Chapter 6.

attorney had as much notice as did Lacara that he was taking on a difficult client. However, the functional conflict of interest developed at oral argument causes us to conclude that the motion to withdraw should be granted.

We therefore reverse and order the district court to grant appellant's motion to withdraw as counsel. We note that Lacara agreed in this court to waive all outstanding fees and to turn over all pertinent files to Whiting.

[Question 4]

Attorney experienced several instances when clients failed to pay their fees in a timely manner, but it was too late in the representation to withdraw without prejudicing the clients. To avoid a recurrence of this situation, Attorney drafted a stipulation of consent to withdraw if fees are not paid according to the fee agreement. She proposes to have all clients sign the stipulation at the outset of the representation.

Is it proper for Attorney to use the stipulation to withdraw from representation whenever a client fails to pay fees?

(A) Yes, because a lawyer may withdraw when the financial burden of continuing the representation would be substantially greater than the parties anticipated at the time of the agreement.

(B) Yes, because the clients consented to the withdrawal in the stipulation.

(C) No, because a client's failure to pay fees when due may be insufficient in itself to justify withdrawal.

(D) No, unless clients are provided an opportunity to seek independent legal advice before signing the stipulation.

To answer this question, review Rule 1.16.

See It

Click here to see a cartoon lamenting .10 hour billing increments.

[Question 5]

Rule 1.16 implements the dominant conception that the lawyer should serve as a "neutral partisan"[4] for her client.

(A) True

(B) False

---

4   David Luban, *Legal Ethics and Human Dignity* 9 (1st ed. 2007).

According to Professor David Luban, the dominant conception "consist[s] of (1) a role obligation (the 'principle of partisanship') that identifies professionalism with extreme partisan zeal on behalf of the client and (2) the 'principle of nonaccountability,' which insists that the lawyer bears no moral responsibility for the client's goals or the means used to attain them."[5]

V. Competence

A bedrock duty of the lawyer is to provide competent representation. Although this duty may Seem simple to understand, this section will examine the complexities of the standards for competence under the Rules, malpractice law, and the Constitutional guarantee of effective assistance of counsel.

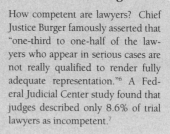

Food for Thought

How competent are lawyers? Chief Justice Burger famously asserted that "one-third to one-half of the lawyers who appear in serious cases are not really qualified to render fully adequate representation."[6] A Federal Judicial Center study found that judges described only 8.6% of trial lawyers as incompetent.[7]

A. Discipline

[Question 1]

Attorney represented Plaintiff in an action against several defendants. The retainer agreement provided that Plaintiff would pay all costs and expenses of litigation and would, on demand, reimburse Attorney for any costs or expenses advanced by Attorney. After serving process on two defendants, Attorney had difficulty locating and serving the remaining defendants. Plaintiff approved the hiring of an investigator to locate and serve the defendants, and Attorney advanced the costs for the investigator. When Attorney asked Plaintiff for reimbursement, Plaintiff refused to pay. Attorney then told Plaintiff that Attorney would do no more work on the case until Attorney was reimbursed for the amount advanced.

Thereafter, one of the defendants filed a counterclaim that required a responsive pleading within thirty days. Because Attorney had not been paid, Attorney permitted the time to respond to the counterclaim to expire without filing a responsive pleading, and a default was entered on the counterclaim. Later, Plaintiff reimbursed Attorney for the costs Attorney had advanced, and Attorney was successful in having the default on the counterclaim set

5   David Luban, Lawyers and Justice: An Ethical Study xx (1988). *See* Murray L. Schwartz, *The Professionalism and Accountability of Lawyers*, 66 Cal. L. Rev. 669, 671-73 (1978); *see also* William H. Simon, The Practice of Justice: A Theory of Lawyers' Ethics (1998).

6   Warren E. Burger, *The Special Skills of Advocacy: Are Specialized Training and Certification of Advocates Essential to Our System of Justice?*, 42 Fordham L. Rev. 227, 234 (1973).

7   Roger C. Cramton & Erik M. Jensen, *The State of Trial Advocacy and Legal Education: Three New Studies*, 30 J. Legal Educ. 253, 257 (1979).

aside. The case was tried, and Plaintiff prevailed on Plaintiff's complaint, and the counter-claimant recovered nothing.

Is Attorney subject to discipline for not initially filing a responsive pleading to the counterclaim?

(A) Yes, because Attorney neglected Plaintiff's cause.

(B) Yes, unless Attorney had asked leave of court to withdraw.

(C) No, because Plaintiff breached the agreement to reimburse Attorney.

(D) No, because Plaintiff did not sustain any prejudice as a result of Attorney's action.

[Question 2]

Witness was subpoenaed to appear and testify at a state legislative committee hearing. Witness retained Attorney to represent her at the hearing. During the hearing, Attorney, reasonably believing that it was in Witness's best interest not to answer, advised Witness not to answer certain questions on the grounds that Witness had a constitutional right not to answer. The committee chairperson directed Witness to answer and cautioned her that refusal to answer was a misdemeanor and that criminal prosecution would be instituted if she did not answer.

Upon Attorney's advice, Witness persisted in her refusal to answer. Witness was subsequently convicted for her refusal to answer.

Is Attorney subject to discipline?

(A) Yes, because Attorney's advice to Witness was not legally sound.

(B) Yes, because Witness, in acting on Attorney's advice, committed a crime.

(C) No, if the offense Witness committed did not involve moral turpitude.

(D) No, if Attorney reasonably believed Witness had a legal right to refuse to answer the questions.

In 2010, 166 Representatives and 56 Senators were lawyers.[8]

---

8   Am. Bar Ass'n Governmental Affairs Office, Lawyers in the 111th Cong. - Se. 1 (prepared for ABA Day, April 2010) (on file with authors); Am. Bar Ass'n Governmental Affairs Office, Lawyers in the 111th Cong. - H. 3 (prepared for ABA Day, April 2010) (on file with authors).

[Question 3]

A sole practitioner was appointed to represent a criminal defendant on appeal. A recently admitted lawyer who shared office space with the sole practitioner agreed to write the brief if the sole practitioner would pay him one-half of the statutory fee. The defendant agreed to the arrangement in writing, after a full consultation. The recently admitted lawyer entered an appearance as co-counsel for the defendant and, with the sole practitioner's knowledge, applied for and received several extensions of time to file the brief. Subsequently, the appellate court dismissed the appeal for failure to pursue the appeal. A third lawyer was later appointed to represent the defendant, whose conviction was affirmed after the appeal was reinstated. Is the sole practitioner subject to discipline?

(A) Yes, because the sole practioner neglected the defendant's case.

(B) Yes, because the sole practioner shared fees with the recently admitted lawyer.

(C) No, because the defendant agreed in writing to the co-counsel arrangement.

(D) No, because the affirmance by the appellate court indicated that the defendant's appeal was without merit.

To answer Questions 1, 2 and 3, apply the standard of Rule 1.1. It requires a lawyer to "provide competent representation to a client. Competent representation requires the legal knowledge, skill, thoroughness, and preparation reasonably necessary for the representation."

[Question 4]

An attorney was recently admitted to practice and was hired as a new associate of a large law firm. The attorney was working late one night when he received a telephone call from his cousin. The cousin said that he was calling from the police station because he had just been arrested for possession of cocaine with intent to distribute. He was permitted to make only one phone call, and the attorney was the only one he knew. The attorney responded that he had no criminal law experience and that his firm did not handle criminal cases. Nevertheless, the cousin pleaded with the attorney to come to the police station and see what he could do to get him out on bail. The attorney replied that he would do what he could.

The attorney went to the police station and used what information he recalled from his criminal law and procedure courses to attempt to get his cousin released on bail. However, as a result of his inexperience, the attorney was unable to secure his cousin's release that night. The next morning, the attorney found an experienced criminal lawyer for his cousin, who obtained his release within one hour.

Was the attorney's conduct proper?

   (A) Yes, because neither referral to another lawyer nor consultation with another lawyer was practical under the circumstances.

   (B) Yes, because the attorney was a close relative.

   (C) No, because the attorney had no special training or experience in criminal cases.

   (D) No, because the attorney did not have the requisite level of competence to accept representation in the case.

Review Rule 1.1.

In addition, the Comment to Rule 1.1 provides in part:

[1] In determining whether a lawyer employs the requisite knowledge and skill in a particular matter, relevant factors include the relative complexity and specialized nature of the matter, the lawyer's general experience, the lawyer's training and experience in the field in question, the preparation and study the lawyer is able to give the matter and whether it is feasible to refer the matter to, or associate or consult with, a lawyer of established competence in the field in question. In many instances, the required proficiency is that of a general practitioner. Expertise in a particular field of law may be required in some circumstances.

[2] A lawyer need not necessarily have special training or prior experience to handle legal problems of a type with which the lawyer is unfamiliar. A newly admitted lawyer can be as competent as a practitioner with long experience. Some important legal skills, such as the analysis of precedent, the evaluation of evidence and legal drafting, are required in all legal problems. Perhaps the most fundamental legal skill consists of determining what kind of legal problems a situation may involve, a skill that necessarily transcends any particular specialized knowledge. A lawyer can provide adequate representation in a wholly novel field through necessary study. Competent representation can also be provided through the association of a lawyer of established competence in the field in question.

[3] In an emergency a lawyer may give advice or assistance in a matter in which the lawyer does not have the skill ordinarily required where referral to or consultation or association with another lawyer would be impractical. Even in an emergency, however, assistance should be limited to that reasonably necessary in the circumstances, for ill-considered action under emergency conditions can jeopardize the client's interest.

[4] A lawyer may accept representation where the requisite level of competence can be achieved by reasonable preparation. * * *

[Question 5]

An attorney hired a recent law school graduate as an associate. For the first six months, the associate was assigned to draft legal documents that the attorney carefully reviewed and revised before filing. However, shortly after the associate was admitted to the bar, the attorney told the associate that he would be going on vacation the following week and was assigning her the representation of the landlord in a housing case that was going to trial while he was away. The associate had never conducted or observed a trial before and, because she had not previously worked on any housing cases, she was unfamiliar with the relevant law and procedure. She did not believe that she would have enough time to learn everything that she needed to know, but she was reluctant to decline the assignment. Before the trial began, she met with the landlord and disclosed that this would be her first trial, but the landlord did not object. Although the associate prepared diligently, the landlord lost the trial.

Is the attorney subject to discipline?

  (A) Yes, because the attorney did not ensure that the associate was competent to conduct the trial on her own.

  (B) Yes, because the landlord lost the trial.

  (C) No, because the attorney could reasonably assume that, having been admitted to the bar, the associate was capable of conducting the trial.

  (D) No, because the landlord did not object to the associate's representation.

Review Rule 1.1 and Comment.

Also consider Rule 5.1. It requires "[a] partner in a law firm, and a lawyer who individually or together with other lawyers possesses comparable managerial authority in a law firm, [to] make reasonable efforts to ensure that the firm has in effect measures giving reasonable assurance that all lawyers in the firm conform to the Rules of Professional Conduct. Rule 5.1(a). Rule 5.1(b) makes "[a] lawyer having direct supervisory authority over another lawyer" responsible for "reasonable efforts to ensure that the other lawyer conforms to the Rules of Professional Conduct." Last, Rule 5.1(c) makes a lawyer:

responsible for another lawyer's violation of the Rules of Professional Conduct if:

  (1) the lawyer orders or, with knowledge of the specific conduct, ratifies the conduct involved; or

(2) the lawyer is a partner or has comparable managerial authority in the law firm in which the other lawyer practices, or has direct supervisory authority over the other lawyer, and knows of the conduct at a time when its consequences can be avoided or mitigated but fails to take reasonable remedial action.

[Question 6]

Attorney has a highly efficient staff of paraprofessional legal assistants, all of whom are graduates of recognized legal assistant educational programs. Recently, the statute of limitations ran against a claim of a client of Attorney's when a legal assistant negligently misplaced Client's file and suit was not filed within the time permitted by law.

> **Practice Pointer**
>
> Delegating excessive caseloads to lower-level attorneys may also violate Rule 5.1(b). *See* ABA Comm. On Ethics and Prof'l Responsibility, Formal Op. 441 (2006) (stating that a supervisor must ensure subordinate's workload is not so heavy that competent and diligent representation is undermined).

Which of the following correctly states Attorney's professional responsibility?

(A) Attorney is subject to civil liability and is also subject to discipline on the theory of respondent superior.

(B) Attorney is subject to civil liability or is subject to discipline at Client's election.

(C) Attorney is subject to civil liability but is NOT subject to discipline unless Attorney failed to supervise the legal assistant adequately.

(D) Attorney is NOT subject to civil liability and is NOT subject to discipline if Attorney personally was not negligent.

Review Rule 1.1 and consider the following authorities.

Rule 5.3 explains "responsibilities regarding nonlawyer assistants." Rule 5.3(a) provides that "a partner, and a lawyer who individually or together with other lawyers possesses comparable managerial authority in a law firm shall make reasonable efforts to ensure that the firm has in effect measures giving reasonable assurance that the person's conduct is compatible with the professional obligations of the lawyer." With regard to "a lawyer having direct supervisory authority over the nonlawyer," Rule 5.3(b) requires the lawyer to "make reasonable efforts to ensure that the person's conduct is compatible with the professional obligations of the lawyer[.]" Rule 5.3(c) also makes a lawyer:

responsible for conduct of such a person that would be a violation of the Rules of Professional Conduct if engaged in by a lawyer if:

> (1) the lawyer orders or, with the knowledge of the specific conduct, ratifies the conduct involved; or

> (2) the lawyer is a partner or has comparable managerial authority in the law firm in which the person is employed, or has direct supervisory authority over the person, and knows of the conduct at a time when its consequences can be avoided or mitigated but fails to take reasonable remedial action.

In re WILKINSON

805 So. 2d 142 (La. 2002)

PER CURIAM

* * *

In August, 1996, Kimberly Saucier Emanuel approached respondent [Neal W. Wilkinson] about handling the **succession** of her father, who had passed away, leaving Mrs. Emanuel as **executrix** of his estate. Respondent advised Mrs. Emanuel that he could not take the case because he was involved in an election campaign. However, he introduced Mrs. Emanuel to Paul Doug Stewart, a Mississippi law school graduate who was working as a law clerk in respondent's office and had taken the Louisiana bar examination in July, 1996. Respondent advised Mrs. Emanuel that Mr. Stewart could handle the necessary preliminary matters in the case under respondent's supervision, and then fully assume the representation once he was admitted to the bar. Based on respondent's assertions, Mrs. Emanuel agreed to the arrangement, and gave respondent $650, which he agreed to hold in trust for Mr. Stewart's anticipated expenses. According to respondent, he cautioned Mr. Stewart not to give any legal advice to Mrs. Emanuel.

Days following the meeting, Mr. Stewart drafted a letter to Mrs. Emanuel, under both his name and respondent's name, confirming that respondent's law firm would be handling the succession matter. The letter promised to keep Mrs. Emanuel informed on a variety of issues on which she might need "further legal advice." Respondent was generally made aware of the contents of the letter by telephone, and directed his secretary to send it out under his signature. Mr. Stewart also signed the letter.

The following day, respondent sent a letter to the will's notary and witnesses asking them to execute affidavits to permit the probate of the will. After sending these letters, respondent had no further involvement in the succession. He never spoke with Mrs. Emanuel again, nor did he ever review her file. Although he discussed the fee arrangement with Mr. Stewart, respondent never specifically inquired about the details of Mr. Stewart's handling of the succession proceeding.

In early September, 1996, still prior to Mr. Stewart's bar admission, the heirs began receiving notices from one of the mortgage creditors. While Mr. Stewart attempted to resolve the matter with the mortgage company, he was unable to successfully handle the problem. Mr. Stewart never advised respondent of the problems with the mortgage company.

In October, 1996, Mr. Stewart was admitted to the practice of law in Louisiana. Approximately four months later, Mr. Stewart left respondent's firm for other employment. Mr. Stewart specifically advised respondent's secretary that he was leaving the succession file. The file sat unattended for several months in respondent's office.

DISCIPLINARY PROCEEDINGS

Subsequently, Mrs. Emanuel learned that incorrect advice given by Mr. Stewart resulted in creditors foreclosing on certain succession property. As a result, Mrs. Emanuel filed a disciplinary complaint against Mr. Stewart for mishandling the succession. The ODC ultimately closed its investigation into the complaint because Mr. Stewart was not admitted to the bar at the time of the misconduct.

However, the ODC initiated its own investigation into respondent's conduct, based on his failure to supervise Mr. Stewart during the time in question. As a result of this investigation, the ODC filed one count of formal charges against respondent alleging violations of Rules 1.1 (incompetence), 1.2 (lack of due diligence), 5.1 (failure of attorney to supervise a subordinate attorney) and 5.3 (failure to properly supervise a nonlawyer assistant) of the Rules of Professional Conduct. Subsequently, it amended the formal charges to include a violation of Rule 5.5 (assisting a nonmember of the bar to engage in the unauthorized practice of law). Respondent filed answers denying any misconduct on his part.

Formal Hearing

At the formal hearing, Mr. Stewart testified Mrs. Emanuel knew he was unlicensed and that he could not formally begin the succession proceedings until his admission to the bar. He maintained, prior to his admission, he had only gathered information and conducted research. He conceded he gave Mrs. Emanuel erroneous legal advice regarding the property, but stated respondent was unaware he had given this advice. Mr. Stewart testified respondent had instructed him not to give any legal advice, but noted that respondent did not make any attempts to determine whether he had given advice to her during their meeting, which occurred in respondent's absence.

* * *

Respondent testified Mrs. Emanuel knew he had no interest in handling her case. As to his referring the matter to Mr. Stewart, respondent asserted he never thought he placed his client at risk because he believed the case was a simple succession matter that would not require any initial legal advice. Respondent stated he had no knowledge Mr. Stewart had given erroneous legal advice, and that he was unaware there were any problems with the succession until the complaint was filed against Mr. Stewart. As to the letter of representation forwarded to Mrs. Emanuel, respondent alleged he was only generally made aware of the contents of the letter by telephone, whereupon he instructed his secretary to sign and mail the letter out. He maintained that had he known the full contents of the letter, he probably would not have sent the letter out. While he asserted he did not violate the Rules of Professional Conduct, respondent admitted if he had known about the problem earlier, he would have stepped in to do something about it.

In mitigation, respondent noted, at the time in question, his wife was suffering from a terminal illness. He traveled to New Orleans after work each day, where she was hospitalized, and returned each evening to care for his children. His wife passed away soon after.

Recommendation of the Hearing Committee

The hearing committee determined the ODC failed to sustain its burden of proving respondent's conduct rose to the level of a professional violation. In support, the committee noted respondent made it clear to all involved that he would not handle the succession. Moreover, it pointed out Mr. Stewart never informed respondent he had given advice to [Mrs. Emanuel and other] heirs, and respondent never knew, or had reason to know, that Mr. Stewart had given the legal advice. Further, it stated Mr. Stewart accepted responsibility for his actions and their consequences. Finally, the committee recognized no member of the public had made a complaint against respondent for the problems associated with the succession. Accordingly, it dismissed the charges pending against respondent.

Recommendation of the Disciplinary Board

The disciplinary board determined the hearing committee properly concluded the ODC failed to prove by clear and convincing evidence respondent violated Rules 1.1 (incompetence), 1.2 (lack of due diligence) and 5.5(a) (assisting a nonlawyer in the unauthorized practice of law). However, the board found the committee erred in failing to find violations of Rules 5.1 (failure of attorney to supervise a subordinate attorney) and 5.3 (failure to properly supervise a nonlawyer assistant).

As a threshold matter, the board determined there was an attorney-client relationship between respondent and Mrs. Emanuel. In support, it relied on the lengthy letter of representation forwarded to Mrs. Emanuel, as well as the letters directed to the notary and witnesses to the will, all of which were sent under respondent's signature. In light of this attorney-client relationship, the board determined respondent failed to supervise Mr. Stewart's work in the succession matter, in violation of Rule 5.3(b). Although the board recognized respondent advised Mr. Stewart not to give legal advice prior to his bar admission, it pointed out respondent took no measures to determine what transpired at the meeting between Mrs. Emanuel and Mr. Stewart in his absence. It found respondent's failure to supervise was further demonstrated by the fact respondent was "only generally made aware of" the contents of the letter of representation drafted by Mr. Stewart and that he testified he would not have sent it out had he known the full contents of the letter. Thus, although it recognized respondent may not have known of the erroneous legal advice given by Mr. Stewart at the time, the board found his negligent failure to supervise Mr. Stewart resulted in actual harm to his client.

The board also determined respondent violated Rule 5.1(b) when he failed to make reasonable efforts to ensure Mr. Stewart conformed to the Rules of Professional Conduct once Mr. Stewart was admitted to the bar. In support, the board stated respondent took no effort to oversee Mr. Stewart's handling of the succession matter. It noted respondent reviewed pieces of the file, but he never reviewed the file in its entirety, even after Mr. Stewart left the firm. Therefore, the board concluded respondent negligently breached duties owed to his client, causing the succession to pay $9,292.91 to redeem the seized property.

As aggravating factors, the board recognized respondent's refusal to acknowledge the wrongful nature of his misconduct, his substantial experience in the practice of law (admitted in 1975) and his indifference to making restitution. As mitigating factors, the board noted the absence of selfish motive and respondent's personal or emotional problems stemming from the illness and death of his wife, as well as his good character and reputation.

[T]he board . . . recommended a sixty-day suspension. * * *

Respondent filed an objection to the imposition of a sanction . . .

DISCUSSION

The record supports the disciplinary board's conclusion that an attorney-client relationship existed between Mrs. Emanuel and respondent. Despite respondent's assertions that he did not take the case, he authorized the sending of a letter to his client in his name assuming the representation, and sent letters to other persons in his capacity as attorney for Mrs. Emanuel.

While respondent may have not been directly responsible for the incorrect legal advice given by Mr. Stewart to Mrs. Emanuel, we find he breached his professional obligation to Mrs. Emanuel by failing to properly supervise Mr. Stewart. Respondent essentially turned the case over to Mr. Stewart, knowing at the time that Mr. Stewart was not licensed to practice law in Louisiana and was unfamiliar with Louisiana succession law. Respondent did not speak with Mrs. Emanuel after his initial meeting, nor did he review her file.

Under these circumstances, we conclude respondent breached his fundamental obligations to Mrs. Emanuel under Rules 5.1(b) and 5.3(b) to ensure the actions of his nonlawyer assistant (and later subordinate attorney) conformed to the rules of professional conduct. Although the evidence indicated respondent did not know Mr. Stewart gave the incorrect advice to Mrs. Emanuel, respondent, as the client's attorney, retains complete responsibility for the representation. As we explained [previously]:

> A lawyer often delegates tasks to clerks, secretaries, and other lay persons. Such delegation is proper if the lawyer maintains a direct relationship with his client, supervises the delegated work, and has complete professional responsibility for the work product ... A lawyer cannot delegate his professional responsibility to a law student employed in his office ... The student in all his work must act as agent for the lawyer employing him, who must supervise his work and be responsible for his good conduct.

Having found respondent violated Rules 5.1(b) and 5.3(b) in failing to supervise Mr. Stewart's handling of the matter, the sole question remaining is the appropriate sanction for this misconduct. In making a determination of the appropriate sanction, we are mindful that the purpose of lawyer disciplinary proceedings is not primarily to punish the lawyer, but rather to maintain appropriate standards of professional conduct to safeguard the public, to preserve the integrity of the legal profession, and to deter other lawyers from engaging in violations of the standards of the profession. * * *

[W]e conclude the appropriate sanction for respondent's misconduct is a sixty-day suspension from the practice of law. * * *

B. Malpractice Liability

General

State law determines malpractice liability. According to Restatement § 48, "a lawyer is civilly liable for professional negligence to a person to whom the lawyer owes a duty of care * * * if the lawyer fails to exercise care * * * and if that failure is a legal cause of injury[.]" Restatement § 52 defines the "standard of care" as "the competence and diligence normally exercised by lawyers in similar circumstances."

Standard of Care

In determining the relevant standard of care, courts look to the "practices and standards * * * of lawyers undertaking similar matters in the relevant jurisdiction (typically, a state)." Restatement § 52 Comment b. In some legal areas, such as federal securities law or federal litigation of federal law, "there exists a national practice with national standards." *Id.*

A lawyer may be held to a higher standard where a lawyer has a "special skill" or where a lawyer "represents to a client that the lawyer has greater competence or will exercise greater diligence than that normally demonstrated by lawyers * * * undertaking similar matters." Restatement § 52 (d).

Violation of a Rule or Statute

As Restatement § 52 Comment f explains, "[a] rule or statute regulating the conduct of lawyers but not providing a damages remedy does not give rise to an implied cause of action for lack of care or fiduciary breach." Nevertheless, "the trier of fact may consider the content and construction of a relevant statute or rule, for example a statute or a rule of professional conduct * * * designed for the protection of persons in the position of the claimant. Such a provision is relevant to whether a lawyer has failed to exercise * * * competence and diligence [or] has violated a fiduciary duty[.]" *Id.*

Nonclients

Restatement § 51 identifies three limited circumstances under which lawyers have a duty of care to nonclients. These are:

1. "[T]he lawyer or (with the lawyer's acquiescence) the lawyer's client invites the nonclient to rely on the lawyer's opinion or provision of other legal services, and the nonclient so relies; and * * * the nonclient is not, under applicable tort law, too remote from the lawyer to be entitled to protection[.]"

2. "[T]he lawyer knows that a client intends as one of the primary objectives of the representation that the lawyer's services benfit the nonclient; * * * such a duty would not significantly impair the lawyer's performance of obligations to the client; and * * * the absence of such a duty would make enforcement of those obligations to the client unlikely[.]"

3. "[T]he lawyer's client is a trustee, guardian, executor, or fiduciary acting primarily to perform similar functions for the nonclient; * * * the lawyer knows that appropriate action by the lawyer is necessary with respect to a matter within the scope of the representation to prevent or rectify the breach of a fiduciary duty owed by the client to the nonclient, where (i) the breach is a crime or fraud or (ii) the lawyer has assisted or is assisting the breach; * * * the nonclient is not

reasonably able to protect its rights; and * * * such a duty would not significantly impair the performance of the lawyer's obligations to the client."

Contract or Tort?

Restatement § 48, Comment d explains that:

> Ordinarily, a plaintiff may cast a legal-malpractice claim in the mold of tort or contract or both[.] * * * Whether the claim is considered in tort or in contract is usually of practical significance when it must be decided whether it is subject to a tort or a contract statute of limitations in a jurisdiction having a different limitations period for each. * * * Some jurisdictions assign all legal-malpractice claims to one category, while others treat some claims as in contract and others as in tort, depending on the facts alleged or the relief sought.

Law Firm Liability

A difference between malpractice and discipline is that, with exception of New York Rule 5.1(a), law firms are generally not vicariously liable for discipline. With regard to malpractice, Restatement § 58(1) explains that "[a] law firm is subject to civil liability for injury legally caused to a person by any wrongful act or omission of any principal or employee of the firm who was acting in the ordinary course of the firm's business or with actual or apparent authority."

[Question 7]

An attorney who is a sole practitioner limits his practice to personal injury cases. He regularly places advertisements in local newspapers, stating that his practice is limited to personal injury cases, including medical malpractice. After seeing one of the attorney's ads, a man approached the attorney for representation in a medical malpractice case. After a 30-minute interview, the attorney told the man that he was too busy to take his case because it appeared quite complicated. He further offered to refer the man to another lawyer who regularly practiced in the field. He reminded the man that he should see another lawyer promptly before the statute of limitations expired and he lost his right to sue.

Although the attorney did not charge the man for the interview, the man was upset at wasting 30 minutes of his time. The man did not contact another lawyer until eight months later, when he learned that the statute of limitations on his claim had expired six months after his interview with the attorney. In fact, the man had a meritorious medical malpractice claim.

Is the attorney subject to civil liability?

(A) Yes, because the attorney falsely advertised his availability for medical malpractice cases.

(B) Yes, because the attorney did not advise the man as to the date the statute of limitations would expire.

(C) No, because the attorney did not violate any duty owed to the man.

(D) No, because the attorney offered to refer the man to another medical malpractice lawyer.

Prospective Clients

A lawyer must "use reasonable care to the extent the lawyer provides * * * legal services" to a prospective client. Restatement § 15(1)(c). What services might a lawyer provide to a prospective client? Restatement § 15 Comment e explains that:

> When a prospective client and a lawyer discuss the possibility of representation, the lawyer might comment on such matters as whether that person has a promising claim or defense, whether the lawyer is appropriate for the matter in question, whether conflicts of interest exist and if so how they might be dealt with, the time within which action must be taken and, if the representation does not proceed, what other lawyer might represent the prospective client. * * * The lawyer must also not harm a prospective client through unreasonable delay after indicating that the lawyer might undertake the representation.

[Question 8]

Jane Lawyer represents Ron Client in settling a dispute with his employer. After Jane explained the terms of the settlement to Ron, he knowingly and voluntarily agreed to it. The terms of the settlement were fair. Ron later learns that his friend Lester had received a significantly better settlement based on a similar dispute with their mutual employer. Ron retains counsel to sue Jane Lawyer for malpractice. Ron is:

(A) not barred from suing Jane Lawyer.

(B) barred from suing Jane Lawyer because he voluntarily agreed to the settlement.

(C) barred from suing Jane Lawyer because the settlement was fair.

(D) barred from suing Jane Lawyer unless Jane intentionally mislead Ron regarding the terms of the settlement.

ZIEGELHEIM v. APOLLO

607 A.2d 1298 (N.J. 1992)

HANDLER, J.

In this case we must decide what duties an attorney owes a client when negotiating a settlement and whether a client's agreement to a negotiated settlement bars her from recovering from her attorney for the negligent handling of her case.

* * *

Like most professionals, lawyers owe a duty to their clients to provide their services with reasonable knowledge, skill, and diligence. We have consistently recited that command in rather broad terms, for lawyers' duties in specific cases vary with the circumstances presented. "What constitutes a reasonable degree of care is not to be considered in a vacuum but with reference to the type of service the attorney undertakes to perform." The lawyer must take "any steps necessary in the proper handling of the case." Those steps will include, among other things, a careful investigation of the facts of the matter, the formulation of a legal strategy, the filing of appropriate papers, and the maintenance of communication with the client.

In accepting a case, the lawyer agrees to pursue the goals of the client to the extent the law permits, even when the lawyer believes that the client's desires are unwise or ill-considered. At the same time, because the client's desires may be influenced in large measure by the advice the lawyer provides, the lawyer is obligated to give the client reasonable advice. As a legal matter progresses and circumstances change, the wishes of the client may change as well. Accordingly, the lawyer is obligated to keep the client informed of the status of the matter for which the lawyer has been retained, and is required to advise the client on the various legal and strategic issues that arise.

In this case, Mrs. Ziegelheim made several claims impugning Apollo's handling of her divorce, and the trial court dismissed all of them on Apollo's motion for summary judgment. As we explain, we believe that the trial court's rulings on several of her claims were erroneous.

In legal malpractice cases, as in other cases, summary disposition is appropriate only when there is no genuine dispute of material fact. A litigant has a right to proceed to trial "where there is the slightest doubt as to the facts." All inferences are drawn in favor of the party opposing the motion for summary judgment.

On Mrs. Ziegelheim's claim that Apollo negligently advised her with respect to her chances of winning a greater proportion of the marital estate if she proceeded to trial, we conclude, as did the Appellate Division, that there was a genuine dispute regarding the appropriate advice that an attorney should give in cases like hers. According to the expert retained by Mrs. Ziegelheim, women in her position—who are in relatively poor health, have little earning capacity, and have been wholly dependent on their husbands—often receive upwards of fifty percent of the marital estate. The expert said that Mrs. Ziegelheim's chances of winning such a large fraction of the estate had she gone to trial would have been especially good because the couple had enjoyed a high standard of living while they were together and because her husband's earning capacity was "tremendous" and would remain so for some time. Her expert's opinion was brought to the trial court's attention, as was the expert report of Mr. Ziegelheim. If plaintiff's expert's opinion were credited, as it should have been for purposes of summary judgment, then Apollo very well could have been found negligent in advising her that she could expect to win only ten to twenty percent of the marital estate.

Apollo urges us to adopt the rule enunciated by the Pennsylvania Supreme Court * * * that a dissatisfied litigant may not recover from his or her attorney for malpractice in negotiating a settlement that the litigant has accepted unless the litigant can prove actual fraud on the part of the attorney. Under that rule, no cause of action can be made based on negligence or contract principles against an attorney for malpractice in negotiating a settlement. The Pennsylvania Supreme Court rationalized its severe rule by explaining that it had a "longstanding public policy which encourages settlements."

New Jersey, too, has a longstanding policy that encourages settlements, but we reject the rule espoused by the Pennsylvania Supreme Court. Although we encourage settlements, we recognize that litigants rely heavily on the professional advice of counsel when they decide whether to accept or reject offers of settlement, and we insist that the lawyers of our state advise clients with respect to settlements with the same skill, knowledge, and diligence with which they pursue all other legal tasks. Attorneys are supposed to know the likelihood of success for the types of cases they handle and they are supposed to know the range of possible awards in those cases.

As we noted [previously,] "One who undertakes to render services in the practice of a profession or trade is required to exercise the skill and knowledge normally possessed by members of that profession in good standing in similar communities." * * * Lawyers are clearly included[.] Like most courts, we see no reason to apply a more lenient rule to lawyers who negotiate settlements. After all, the negotiation of settlements is one of the most basic and most frequently undertaken tasks that lawyers perform.* * *

Although the Appellate Division reversed the trial court on Mrs. Ziegelheim's claim relating to Apollo's advice, it affirmed the trial court on all other claims. On the issue of Apollo's alleged failure to make a proper investigation into Mr. Ziegelheim's assets, the trial court ruled that litigation on that issue was precluded by the family court's determination that the settlement was fair and equitable. We conclude that the family court's determination should not have barred Mrs. Ziegelheim from litigating that claim. * * *

The fact that a party received a settlement that was "fair and equitable" does not mean necessarily that the party's attorney was competent or that the party would not have received a more favorable settlement had the party's incompetent attorney been competent. Thus, in this case, notwithstanding the family court's decision, Mrs. Ziegelheim still may proceed against Apollo in her negligence action.

Moreover, another aspect of the alleged professional incompetence that led to the improvident acceptance of the settlement was the attorney's own failure to discover hidden marital assets. When Mrs. Ziegelheim sought to reopen her divorce settlement, the family court denied her motion with the observation that "[a] mple opportunity existed for full discovery," and that "the parties had their own accountants as well as counsel." The court did not determine definitively that Mr. Ziegelheim had hidden no assets, but stated instead that it "suspected that everything to be known was known to the parties." The earlier ruling did not implicate the competence of counsel and, indeed, was premised on the presumptive competence of counsel. Hence, defendant cannot invoke that ruling now to bar a challenge to his competence. Mrs. Ziegelheim should have been allowed to prove that Apollo negligently failed to discover certain assets concealed by her former husband.

The Appellate Division also affirmed the trial court's dismissal of Mrs. Ziegelheim's claims that Apollo negligently delayed in finalizing the settlement and that the written settlement differed from the one recited by Mr. Ziegelheim's lawyer. Again we conclude that she should have been allowed to litigate those claims on the merits. To be sure, lawyers generally cannot be held liable for their failure to persuade opposing parties to agree to terms, but Mrs. Ziegelheim alleges here that the two sides had agreed to terms and that Apollo simply failed to see to it that the terms were put into writing. Apollo may be able to refute her factual account, but he should not have prevailed on summary judgment, for there were genuine disputes concerning the accuracy of the written version and the reason for the nine-month delay in finalizing it.

Mrs. Ziegelheim's final claim is that Apollo was negligent in not writing down the terms of the settlement prior to the hearing in which the settlement was recited and approved by her and Mr. Ziegelheim. She asserts that a competent attorney would have written them down so that she could review them and make an informed and reasoned assessment of their fairness. At trial she may be able to prove that she would not have accepted the settlement offer had it been presented to her in writing for her review. She may be able to demonstrate, for example, that Apollo's oral presentation of the settlement obscured the fact that it did not include the tax and insurance provisions she desired. We cannot determine the merits of those allegations and decline to speculate on defendant's possible refutation of them. We simply observe that on this record, her final claim, too, presents genuine issues of material fact and should not have been resolved on summary judgment.

In holding as we do today, we do not open the door to malpractice suits by any and every dissatisfied party to a settlement. Many such claims could be averted if settlements were explained as a matter of record in open court in proceedings reflecting the understanding and assent of the parties. Further, plaintiffs must allege particular facts in support of their claims of attorney incompetence and may not litigate complaints containing mere generalized assertions of malpractice. We are mindful that attorneys cannot be held liable simply because they are not successful in persuading an opposing party to accept certain terms. Similarly, we acknowledge that attorneys who pursue reasonable strategies in handling their cases and who render reasonable advice to their clients cannot be held liable for the failure of their strategies or for any unprofitable outcomes that result because their clients took their advice. The law demands that attorneys handle their cases with knowledge, skill, and diligence, but it does not demand that they be perfect or infallible, and it does not demand that they always secure optimum outcomes for their clients.

* * *

The judgment of the Appellate Division is affirmed in part and reversed in part and the matter is remanded in accordance with this opinion.

[Question 9]

An attorney agreed to represent a client in a lawsuit. The attorney and the client executed the attorney's preprinted retainer form that provides, in part:

"The client agrees to pay promptly the attorney's fee for services. In addition, the client and the attorney agree to release each other from any and all liability arising from the representation. The client agrees that the attorney need not return the client's file prior to receiving the client's executed release. Upon full payment, the attorney will return the file to the client."

Although the attorney recommended that the client consult independent counsel before signing the retainer agreement, the client chose not to do so.

The attorney reasonably believes that his fee is fair and that the quality of his work will be competent.

Is the attorney's retainer agreement with the client proper?

- (A) Yes, because the attorney furnished consideration by agreeing to return the client's file.

- (B) Yes, because the attorney reasonably believes that his fee is fair and that the quality of his work will be competent.

- (C) No, because the attorney is attempting to limit his liability for malpractice.

- (D) No, because the attorney uses a preprinted form for all retainers.

[Question 10]

Attorney represented Buyer in a real estate transaction. Due to Attorney's negligence in drafting the purchase agreement, Buyer was required to pay for a survey that should have been paid by Seller, the other party to the transaction. Attorney fully disclosed this negligence to Buyer, and Buyer suggested that he would be satisfied if Attorney simply reimbursed Buyer for the entire cost of the survey.

Although Buyer might have recovered additional damages if a malpractice action were filed, Attorney reasonably believed that the proposed settlement was fair to Buyer. Accordingly, in order to forestall a malpractice action, Attorney readily agreed to make the reimbursement. Attorney drafted a settlement agreement, and it was executed by both Attorney and Buyer.

Was Attorney's conduct proper?

- (A) Yes, if Attorney advised Buyer in writing that Buyer should Seek independent representation before deciding to enter into the settlement agreement.

- (B) Yes, because Attorney reasonably believed that the proposed settlement was fair to Buyer.

- (C) No, because Attorney improperly settled a case involving liability for malpractice while the matter was still ongoing.

- (D) No, unless Buyer was separately represented in negotiating and finalizing the settlement agreement.

Rule 1.8(h) provides that "a lawyer shall not:

> (1) make an agreement prospectively limiting the lawyer's liability to a client for malpractice unless the client is independently represented in making the agreement; or

> (2) settle a claim or potential claim for such liability with an unrepresented client or former client unless that person is advised in writing of the desirability of seeking and is given a reasonable opportunity to seek the advice of independent legal counsel in connection therewith.

AM. BAR ASS'N, STANDING COMM. ON ETHICS & PROF'L RESPONSIBILITY,

Formal Op. 02-425 (2002)

Retainer Agreement Requiring the Arbitration of Fee Disputes and Malpractice Claims

Overview

The use of binding arbitration provisions in retainer agreements has increased significantly in recent years. Provisions requiring the arbitration of fee disputes have gained more willing acceptance than those involving malpractice claims. The Model Rules of Professional Conduct, in a comment to Rule 1.5, provide that when a "procedure has been established for resolution of fee disputes, such as an arbitration or mediation procedure established by the bar, the lawyer must comply with the procedure when it is mandatory, and, even when it is voluntary, the lawyer should conscientiously consider submitting to it." The greater acceptance of such provisions by lawyers also is attributable to the fact that there are ABA Model Rules for Fee Arbitration and that most bar associations have implemented fee arbitration programs that have been upheld by the courts. The Model Rules do not specifically address provisions for arbitration of disputes with clients over matters other than fees.

Because the attorney-client relationship involves professional and fiduciary duties on the part of the lawyer that generally are not present in other relationships, the retainer contract may be subject to special oversight and review. The authority for this oversight comes from the Model Rules, which impose rigorous disclosure obligations on the lawyer and expressly limit and condition the lawyer's freedom to enter into contractual arrangements with clients. We now turn to an examination of the rules implicated by the inclusion of mandatory arbitration provisions in retainer agreements.

Prospective Agreements to Limit the Lawyer's Liability

The concern most frequently expressed about provisions mandating the use of arbitration to resolve fee disputes and malpractice claims stems from Rule 1.8(h), which prohibits the lawyer from prospectively agreeing to limit the lawyer's malpractice liability unless such an agreement is permitted by law and the client is represented by independent counsel. Commentators and most state bar ethics' committees have concluded that mandatory arbitration provisions do not prospectively limit a lawyer's liability, but instead only prescribe a procedure for resolving such claims.

The Committee agrees that mandatory arbitration provisions are proper unless the retainer agreement insulates the lawyer from liability or limits the liability to which she otherwise would be exposed under common or statutory law. For example, if the law of the jurisdiction precludes an award of punitive damages in arbitration but permits punitive damages in malpractice lawsuits, the provision would violate Rule 1.8(h) unless the client is independently represented in making the agreement.

The mere fact that a client is required to submit disputes to arbitration rather than litigation does not violate Rule 1.8(h), even though the procedures implicated by various mandatory arbitration provisions can markedly differ from typical litigation procedures. The Committee believes, however, that clients must receive sufficient information about these differences and their effect on the clients' rights to permit affected clients to make an informed decision about whether to accept an agreement that includes such a provision.

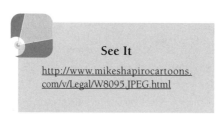

See It

http://www.mikeshapirocartoons.com/v/Legal/W8095.JPEG.html

[Question 11]

An attorney is widely regarded as an exceptionally competent practitioner in the field of criminal law. A client of the attorney became the subject of a grand jury investigation in a matter that could result in a felony indictment. The client lacked sufficient funds to pay for the attorney's services beyond the grand jury stage. He asked the attorney to provide limited representation for a flat fee. Under the arrangement he proposed, the attorney would advise the client concerning the grand jury investigation, but the representation would end when an indictment was returned or the grand jury decided not to indict. The attorney fully advised the client of the practical and legal aspects of the client's proposal.Is it proper for the attorney to accept this limited representation?

(A) Yes, because the client and not the attorney suggested this arrangement.

(B) Yes, because the attorney and the client may agree to limit the scope of the representation so long as the limitation is reasonable under the circumstances.

(C) No, because the attorney should not limit the scope of the representation based on the client's ability to pay.

(D) No, because the scope of the representation may not be limited in a criminal case.

Rule 1.2(c) provides that "[a] lawyer may limit the scope of the representation if the limitation is reasonable under the circumstances and the client gives informed consent." The Comment explains:

[6] The scope of services to be provided by a lawyer may be limited by agreement with the client or by the terms under which the lawyer's services are made available to the client. When a lawyer has been retained by an insurer to represent an insured, for example, the representation may be limited to matters related to the insurance coverage. A limited representation may be appropriate because the client has limited objectives for the representation. In addition, the terms upon which representation is undertaken may exclude specific means that might otherwise be used to accomplish the client's objectives. Such limitations may exclude actions that the client thinks are too costly or that the lawyer regards as repugnant or imprudent.

[7] Although this Rule affords the lawyer and client substantial latitude to limit the representation, the limitation must be reasonable under the circumstances. If, for example, a client's objective is limited to securing general information about the law the client needs in order to handle a common and typically uncomplicated legal problem, the lawyer and client may agree that the lawyer's services will be limited to a brief telephone consultation. Such a limitation, however, would not be reasonable if the time allotted was not sufficient to yield advice upon which the client could rely. Although an agreement for a limited representation does not exempt a lawyer from the duty to provide competent representation, the limitation is a factor to be considered when determining the legal knowledge, skill, thoroughness and preparation reasonably necessary for the representation. *See* Rule 1.1.

[8] All agreements concerning a lawyer's representation of a client must accord with the Rules of Professional Conduct and other law. *See, e.g.*, Rules 1.1, 1.8 and 5.6.

LERNER v. LAUFER

819 A.2d 471 (N.J. Super. App.Div. 2003)

WELLS, J.A.D.

We address in this appeal from a judgment dismissing a legal malpractice action, the issue of whether and to what extent, if any, an attorney may limit the scope of his representation of a matrimonial client in reviewing a mediated property settlement agreement (PSA).

The circumstances out of which the appeal arises are undisputed. The plaintiff, Lynne C. Lerner, was married to Michael H. Lerner in November 1969 and had been married to him 24 years when he filed an action for divorce in 1994. The couple had two children, a son and a daughter, born in 1974 and 1976. Michael contacted a New York lawyer, Brett Meyer, who represented him and his company in New York, but who also was a friend of the family and trusted by Lynne, to mediate a PSA. The couple had amassed a considerable fortune.

Meyer mediated over several sessions as the result of which a comprehensive, written PSA emerged. He then gave Lynne a list of New Jersey attorneys to consult prior to signing the agreement. That list, in turn, had been given to Meyer by James Andrews, a New Jersey attorney who would represent Michael in the divorce proceedings. While the record does not disclose whether Andrews alerted everyone on the list, he did alert the defendant, William Laufer, that Lynne might call, and on January 26, 1994, sent him a draft of the mediated PSA. Lynne selected Laufer of the firm of Courter, Kobert, Laufer, Purcell & Cohen, P.C. (CKLP & C) from the list. Laufer was an experienced matrimonial attorney and held himself out as a specialist in the field.

On January 28, 1994, Lynne and Laufer spoke by telephone. On February 2, 1994, the first time that Lynne and Laufer met in person, Laufer produced a two-page letter, dated that day, for Lynne to consider. While the letter is of some length, its importance to this case is such that we reproduce it in full:

> Dear Mrs. Lerner:
>
> This letter will confirm that you have retained my law firm for the purpose of reviewing a Property Settlement Agreement that was the product of divorce mediation conducted by Mr. Brett J. Meyer, an Attorney at Law of the State of New York.
>
> This letter will further confirm that I have not conducted any discovery in this matter on your behalf. I have not reviewed income tax returns

or other financial documentation to confirm or verify your husband's income for the past several years. I have no information concerning the gross and net values of the properties in Summit, Belmar, Teluride, Colorado or Short Hills, New Jersey. I have seen no information concerning the value of the stock in Marisa Christina, Inc. or the other corporations referred to on Page 10 of the Property Settlement Agreement. In addition, I have not had the opportunity to review any documentation concerning the respective incomes, assets, liabilities or other financial information in your case.

Based upon the fact that I have not had an opportunity to conduct full and complete discovery in this matter, including but not limited to appraisals of real estate and business interests, depositions and interrogatories, I am not in a position to advise you as to whether or not the Agreement is fair and equitable and whether or not you should execute the Agreement as prepared. Accordingly, it is difficult for me to make a recommendation as to whether you should accept the sum of $500,000.00 and 15% of the stock that the two of you have acquired during the marriage in consideration for waiving your right to 85% of the stock that was acquired during the marriage.

In sum, I am not in a position to make a recommendation or determination that the Property Settlement Agreement as prepared represents a fair and reasonable compromise of the issues concerning equitable distribution or whether the amount of alimony and/or child support that you will receive under the terms of the Agreement is an amount that would be awarded to you if, in fact, this matter proceeded to trial.

This letter will confirm that I have reviewed and suggested various modifications to the Property Settlement Agreement to the mediator. I have discussed the contents of the Agreement with you, and in your opinion you are satisfied that the Agreement represents a fair and reasonable compromise of all issues arising from the marital relationship. You have indicated to me that you are entering into the Agreement freely and voluntarily and that you have been satisfied with the services of the mediator in this matter. You have further indicated to me that the Agreement will be providing you with a substantial amount of assets in excess of Three Million Dollars, and that you will be receiving alimony payments as specifically set forth in Paragraph 5 of the Property Settlement Agreement.

After reviewing the Agreement with you and Mr. Meyer, I am satisfied that you understand the terms and conditions of the Agreement; that you feel that you are receiving a fair and equitable amount of the assets that were acquired during the marriage; and that the amount of support that is provided in the Agreement will, in fact, provide you with an income that will allow you to maintain a respectable lifestyle.

This letter will also confirm that you are accepting my services based upon the representations specifically set forth above and that under no circumstances will you now or in the future be asserting any claims against me or my firm arising from the negotiation or execution of your Property Settlement Agreement.

Thank you for the opportunity to be of service to you in this matter, and if I can be of any future assistance, please do not hesitate to contact me.

Lynne read and signed the letter. She and Laufer then conferenced for about an hour, during which time each term of the mediated PSA was read and discussed. In addition, they discussed the value of the couple's interest in Marisa Christina, a very valuable company doing business in New York. Thereupon, a four-way conference ensued between Lynne, Laufer, Michael and Andrews, and the PSA was executed.

Five days later, on February 7, 1994, a standard retainer agreement issued from Laufer's office to Lynne, which she signed and returned. It provided in part:

The legal services which I anticipate will be rendered to you will involve legal research and factual investigation as to (i) assets which you owned at the time you were married, assets which were acquired over the course of the marriage; (ii) income and your ability/need for support; (iii) grounds for divorce; (iv) custody and visitation, and (v) payment of counsel fees and costs.

The retainer agreement also provided that the plaintiff: "will have the benefit of my [defendants'] advice and my prediction of the likely results if the matter were not settled, and were instead submitted for judicial resolution."

* * *

The divorce was granted, and the PSA was incorporated into the final judgment dated May 6, 1994. We note that during the course of his representation of Lynne between January 28, 1994 and April 11, 1994, the date of the divorce hearing, Laufer suggested changes in the mediated PSA either to Meyer or to Andrews. Some of the changes were adopted and some were not. * * *

In September 1999, Lynne commenced the present malpractice action against Laufer through the office of Hilton Stein. * * *

I

Lynne argues that the judge * * * permitted Laufer to assume the role of a "potted plant" in representing her contrary to the general duty of a lawyer to act with reasonable knowledge, skill and diligence. She urges that Laufer had a duty to perform those duties reasonably and usually expected of a lawyer engaged by a matrimonial client, anything short of which constituted malpractice. She claims that the letter of February 2, 1994 does not constitute either a limitation on the scope of Laufer's representation or a waiver of her right to full representation.

* * * Lynne asserts that it makes no difference that she described the second amended PSA as fair and equitable in the 1999 divorce proceeding because had Laufer competently represented her at the outset, she would not have been burdened by the baggage of the mediated PSA. In the latter respect, she contends that because the judge did not vacate the mediated agreement along with the divorce, she was presented with the prospect that were she to go to trial in the second proceeding, the mediated agreement would be re-approved by the judge.

Laufer argues that Lynne ignores RPC 1.2(c), which permits an attorney to limit the scope of his representation "if the client consents after consultation." He urges that the letter of February 2, 1994 disclosed the limited purpose of his representation, the details of those services he would not perform, and that he "was not in a position to advise ... as to whether or not the agreement is fair or equitable and whether or not [Lynne] should execute the Agreement as prepared." He urges that the letter is an effective consent to limit his representation under the RPC and constitutes a waiver of full representation.

Laufer also claims that Lynne is estopped to claim in this case that the PSA was unfair because she stated under oath in the 1999 divorce proceeding that she understood that she had a right to go to trial as to all issues raised in the second divorce proceeding.

II

At the heart of this case lies a clash over two significant values to the legal community. The first is the value more recently discerned and encouraged in resolving disputes by mediation. The second is the older, more established value perceived in the resolution of conflict in adversarial proceedings by parties represented by fully independent and empowered attorneys. In the former process, it is the clients, assisted by a mediator, who arrange the disposition of their own dispute. It is largely a self-help process only tangentially informed by what the law would allow or dictate. In the latter process, it is lawyers who seek to reach ends sought by their clients under laws and rules often little understood by those clients. It is a process whereby established rights and duties are sought to be vindicated.

* * *

When a PSA reached through the mediation process must be formally incorporated in a judgment of divorce, the participation of attorneys governed by the adversarial process gives rise to a question as to the nature and extent of the duty of care imposed upon the attorneys. A mediated divorce settlement may well look substantially different on the same facts than would such a settlement hammered out in adversarial proceedings. * * *

Yet the law has never foreclosed the right of competent, informed citizens to resolve their own disputes in whatever way may suit them. "Clients have the right to make the final decision as to whether, when, and how to settle their cases and as to economic and other positions to be taken with respect to issues in the case." * * * The courts approve hundreds of such settlements in all kinds of cases without once looking into their wisdom or the adequacy of the consideration that supports them. In divorce proceedings, the court daily approves settlements upon the express finding that it does not pass upon the fairness or merits of the agreement, so long as the parties acknowledge that the agreement was reached voluntarily and is for them, at least, fair and equitable.

RPC 1.2(c) expressly permits an attorney with the consent of the client after consultation to limit the scope of representation. In *Ziegelheim*, . . . the Court stated " 'what constitutes a reasonable degree of care is not to be considered in a vacuum but with reference to the type of service the attorney undertakes to perform.' To us that means if the service is limited by consent, then the degree of care is framed by the agreed service.* * *

We hold it is not a breach of the standard of care for an attorney under a signed precisely drafted consent agreement to limit the scope of representation to not perform such services in the course of representing a matrimonial client that he or she might otherwise perform absent such a consent. Except as we hereinafter note, we are satisfied that Laufer, with Lynne's consent after consultation, properly limited the scope of his representation of her under RPC 1.2(c), to a review of the terms of the mediated agreement without going outside its four corners. We acknowledge that the letter of February 2, 1994 does not quote or cite RPC 1.2(c) nor does it expressly describe itself as a "limit to the scope of representation." It, indeed, could have been more precise in those respects. Nevertheless, we reject the argument that the content failings of the letter deprive it of its intended efficacy to limit the scope of Laufer's duties as an attorney. We are satisfied that the letter is unmistakable in its import that Laufer did not and would not perform the named services, could not render an opinion on the fairness of the agreement, and could not advise Lynne whether or not to execute it.

Armed as he was with the letter of February 2, 1994, Laufer did not, therefore, breach a proved standard of care by performing no discovery or related investigatory services necessary to evaluate the merits in fact of the mediated PSA.

Furthermore, we reject the argument that by his conduct in suggesting modifications to the PSA, some of which were adopted, Laufer stepped from under the protection of his limited scope of representation and became fully liable as if no such limitation existed. First, we harken to Laufer's own testimony that his role was to see to it that the agreement was "clear and concise," to resolve interpretation problems in the text, and to clarify the agreement. Second, we discern no evidence that in performing his role Laufer's conduct actually altered Lynne's expectations of Laufer's duty or changed her demands for the kind of service she wished.

* * *

There are several aspects of what Laufer did, of which we expressly disapprove. We mention them in answer to Lynne's contentions that they have a bearing on the issue of Laufer's alleged malpractice. Our conclusion is that while these actions were improper, they do not alter our opinion that Laufer's overall representation of Lynne did not fall below any standard of care established by Lynne's proofs.

Laufer should not have included in his letter of February 2, 1994, an undertaking not to sue him. Such a limitation violated the express terms of RPC 1.8(h). Such a provision should not be included in a consent to limit the scope of representation presented to a client for consideration or signature. We note that in the course of these proceedings Laufer did not rely on that part of his letter as a defense. He

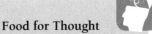

Food for Thought

Under what circumstances should a lawyer be permitted to provide legal assistance that does not meet the standard of competent representation? The legal profession is grappling with this question in responding to the reality that many low- and middle-income people cannot afford full legal services. One commentator has noted that "[t]he majority of litigants now proceed *pro* se in state courts."[6] In response, courts and bar leaders are seeking to permit unbundled legal services,

a practice in which the lawyer and client agree that the lawyer will provide some, but not all, of the work involved in traditional full service representation. Clients choose the legal assistance according to their needs and perform the remaining tasks on their own. Unbundling has been described as ordering "a la carte," rather than from the "full-service menu." A client might hire a lawyer for trial representation, but not for court filings, discovery, and negotiations. Unbundled services can take many forms, including telephone, Internet, or in-person advice; assisting clients in negotiations and litigation; assistance with discovery; or limited court appearances. For many clients, these limited engagements make a lawyer's services affordable.

Fern Fisher-Brandveen & Rochelle Klempner, *Unbundled Legal Services: Untying the Bundle in New York State*, 29 Fordham Urb. L.J. 1107, 1108 (2002).

---

6 Alicia M. Farley, *An Important Piece of the Bundle: How Limited Appearances Can Provide An Ethically Sound Way to Increase Access to Justice for Pro Se Litigants*, 20 Geo. J. Legal Ethics 563, 564 (2007).

acknowledged that the limitation was unenforceable.

Laufer should not have presented Lynne with a separate, standard form of retainer agreement. Whether or not the retainer was "boilerplate" as the motion judge thought, the point is that it conflicted with the letter of February 2, 1994. It is undisputed that that letter, not the standard retainer agreement, formed the basis of Laufer's representation. Lynne does not argue nor are there facts to support any contention that she reasonably believed the retainer supplanted the terms of the February 2 letter or that she expected from Laufer unlimited representation under the retainer. Consent to limit the scope of representation under RPC 1.2(c) should be included in a single, specifically tailored form of retainer agreement.

* * *

Affirmed.

C. Ineffective Assistance of Counsel

[Question 12]

Rascal was convicted of murder. In preparing for the sentencing phase of the case, Rascal's lawyer Matlock investigated potential mitigation evidence. Matlock spoke with Rascal and five of his family members who described Rascal's childhood and mental condition as normal. Matlock also consulted with mental health experts who did not offer helpful mitigation evidence. Matlock was aware that the prosecution was planning to introduce evidence of Rascal's previous convictions for a violent rape, as well as a juvenile record. Matlock did not examine the files of the earlier cases. If he had done so, he would have discovered mitigating evidence of schizophrenia, organic brain damage, alcoholism, and serious childhood problems. Rascal is sentenced to death. He appeals claiming ineffective assistance of counsel. What result?

(A) Not ineffective assistance. Matlock's conduct was not perfect but it was reasonable because the interviews with Racal and his family members did not indicate the existence of mitigating evidence.

(B) Not ineffective assistance. Matlock's conduct was unreasonable but it was not prejudicial.

(C) Ineffective assistance. Matlock failed to provide zealous representation.

(D) Ineffective assistance. Matlock's unreasonable conduct prejudiced Rascal.

ROMPILLA v. BEARD

545 U.S. 374 (2005)

Justice SOUTER delivered the opinion of the Court.

This case calls for specific application of the standard of reasonable competence required on the part of defense counsel by the Sixth Amendment. We hold that even when a capital defendant's family members and the defendant himself have suggested that no mitigating evidence is available, his lawyer is bound to make reasonable efforts to obtain and review material that counsel knows the prosecution will probably rely on as evidence of aggravation at the sentencing phase of trial.

* * *

Ineffective assistance under *Strickland v. Washington,* 466 U.S. 668, 104 S.Ct. 2052, 80 L.Ed.2d 674 (1984) is deficient performance by counsel resulting in prejudice, with performance being measured against an "objective standard of reasonableness," * * * "under prevailing professional norms." * * * This case, like some others recently, looks to norms of adequate investigation in preparing for the sentencing phase of a capital trial, when defense counsel's job is to counter the State's evidence of aggravated culpability with evidence in mitigation. In judging the defense's investigation, as in applying *Strickland* generally, hindsight is discounted by pegging adequacy to "counsel's perspective at the time" investigative decisions are made, and by giving a "heavy measure of deference to counsel's judgments." * * *

A

A standard of reasonableness applied as if one stood in counsel's shoes spawns few hard-edged rules, and the merits of a number of counsel's choices in this case are subject to fair debate. This is not a case in which defense counsel simply ignored their obligation to find mitigating evidence, and their workload as busy public defenders did not keep them from making a number of efforts, including interviews with Rompilla and some members of his family, and examinations of reports by three mental health experts who gave opinions at the guilt phase. None of the sources proved particularly helpful.

Rompilla's own contributions to any mitigation case were minimal. Counsel found him uninterested in helping, as on their visit to his prison to go over a proposed mitigation strategy, when Rompilla told them he was "bored being here listening" and returned to his cell. To questions about childhood and schooling, his answers indicated they had been normal, save for quitting school in the ninth grade. There were times when Rompilla was even actively obstructive by sending counsel off on false leads.

The lawyers also spoke with five members of Rompilla's family (his former wife, two brothers, a sister-in-law, and his son), and counsel testified that they developed a good relationship with the family in the course of their representation. The state postconviction court found that counsel spoke to the relatives in a "detailed manner," attempting to unearth mitigating information, although the weight of this finding is qualified by the lawyers' concession that "the overwhelming response from the family was that they didn't really feel as though they knew him all that well since he had spent the majority of his adult years and some of his childhood years in custody[.]" Defense counsel also said that because the family was "coming from the position that [Rompilla] was innocent . . . they weren't looking for reasons for why he might have done this."

The third and final source tapped for mitigating material was the cadre of three mental health witnesses who were asked to look into Rompilla's mental state as of the time of the offense and his competency to stand trial. But their reports revealed "nothing useful" to Rompilla's case, and the lawyers consequently did not go to any other historical source that might have cast light on Rompilla's mental condition.

When new counsel entered the case to raise Rompilla's postconviction claims, however, they identified a number of likely avenues the trial lawyers could fruitfully have followed in building a mitigation case. School records are one example, which trial counsel never examined in spite of the professed unfamiliarity of the several family members with Rompilla's childhood, and despite counsel's knowledge that Rompilla left school after the ninth grade. Other examples are records of Rompilla's juvenile and adult incarcerations, which counsel did not consult, although they were aware of their client's criminal record. And while counsel knew from police reports provided in pretrial discovery that Rompilla had been drinking heavily at the time of his offense, and although one of the mental health experts reported that Rompilla's troubles with alcohol merited further investigation, counsel did not look for evidence of a history of dependence on alcohol that might have extenuating significance.

Before us, trial counsel and the Commonwealth respond to these unexplored possibilities by emphasizing this Court's recognition that the duty to investigate does not force defense lawyers to scour the globe on the off chance something will turn up; reasonably diligent counsel may draw a line when they have good reason to think further investigation would be a waste. * * * The Commonwealth argues that the information trial counsel gathered from Rompilla and the other sources gave them sound reason to think it would have been pointless to spend time and money on the additional investigation espoused by postconviction counsel, and we can say that there is room for debate about trial counsel's obligation to follow at least some of those potential lines of enquiry. There is no need to say more, however, for a further point is clear and dispositive: the lawyers were deficient in failing to examine the court file on Rompilla's prior conviction.

B

There is an obvious reason that the failure to examine Rompilla's prior conviction file fell below the level of reasonable performance. Counsel knew that the Commonwealth intended to seek the death penalty by proving Rompilla had a significant history of felony convictions indicating the use or threat of violence, an aggravator under state law. Counsel further knew that the Commonwealth would attempt to establish this history by proving Rompilla's prior conviction for rape and assault, and would emphasize his violent character by introducing a transcript of the rape victim's testimony given in that earlier trial. There is no question that defense counsel were on notice, since they acknowledge that a "plea letter," written by one of them four days prior to trial, mentioned the prosecutor's plans. It is also undisputed that the prior conviction file was a public document, readily available for the asking at the very courthouse where Rompilla was to be tried.

It is clear, however, that defense counsel did not look at any part of that file, including the transcript, until warned by the prosecution a second time. In a colloquy the day before the evidentiary sentencing phase began, the prosecutor again said he would present the transcript of the victim's testimony to establish the prior conviction.

* * * At the postconviction evidentiary hearing, Rompilla's lawyer confirmed that she had not seen the transcript before the hearing in which this exchange took place, *id.*, at 506-507, and crucially, even after obtaining the transcript of the victim's testimony on the eve of the sentencing hearing, counsel apparently examined none of the other material in the file.

With every effort to view the facts as a defense lawyer would have done at the time, it is difficult to see how counsel could have failed to realize that without examining the readily available file they were seriously compromising their opportunity to respond to a case for aggravation. The prosecution was going to use the dramatic facts of a similar prior offense, and Rompilla's counsel had a duty to make all reasonable efforts to learn what they could about the offense. Reasonable efforts certainly included obtaining the Commonwealth's own readily available file on the prior conviction to learn what the Commonwealth knew about the crime, to discover any mitigating evidence the Commonwealth would downplay, and to anticipate the details of the aggravating evidence the Commonwealth would emphasize. Without making reasonable efforts to review the file, defense counsel could have had no hope of knowing whether the prosecution was quoting selectively from the transcript, or whether there were circumstances extenuating the behavior described by the victim. The obligation to get the file was particularly pressing here owing to the similarity of the violent prior offense to the crime charged and Rompilla's sentencing strategy stressing residual doubt. Without making efforts to learn the details and rebut the relevance of the earlier crime, a convincing argument for residual doubt was certainly beyond any hope.

Nor is there any merit to the United States's contention that further enquiry into the prior conviction file would have been fruitless because the sole reason the transcript was being introduced was to establish the aggravator that Rompilla had committed prior violent felonies. The Government maintains that because the transcript would incontrovertibly establish the fact that Rompilla had committed a violent felony, the defense could not have expected to rebut that aggravator through further investigation of the file. That analysis ignores the fact that the sentencing jury was required to weigh aggravating factors against mitigating factors. We may reasonably assume that the jury could give more relative weight to a prior violent felony aggravator where defense counsel missed an opportunity to argue that circumstances of the prior conviction were less damning than the prosecution's characterization of the conviction would suggest.

The notion that defense counsel must obtain information that the State has and will use against the defendant is not simply a matter of common sense. As the District Court points out, the American Bar Association Standards for Criminal Justice in circulation at the time of Rompilla's trial describes the obligation in terms no one could misunderstand in the circumstances of a case like this one:

> "It is the duty of the lawyer to conduct a prompt investigation of the circumstances of the case and to explore all avenues leading to facts relevant to the merits of the case and the penalty in the event of conviction. The investigation should always include efforts to secure information in the possession of the prosecution and law enforcement authorities. The duty to investigate exists regardless of the accused's admissions or statements to the lawyer of facts constituting guilt or the accused's stated desire to plead guilty."

1 ABA Standards for Criminal Justice 4-4.1 (2d ed. 1982 Supp.).

"[W]e long have referred [to these ABA Standards] as 'guides to determining what is reasonable.'" [Precedent] and the Commonwealth has come up with no reason to think the quoted standard impertinent here.

Later, and current, ABA Guidelines relating to death penalty defense are even more explicit:

> "Counsel must . . . investigate prior convictions . . . that could be used as aggravating circumstances or otherwise come into evidence. If a prior conviction is legally flawed, counsel should Seek to have it set aside. Counsel may also find extenuating circumstances that can be offered to lessen the weight of a conviction."

ABA Guidelines for the Appointment and Performance of Defense Counsel in Death Penalty Cases 10.7, comment. (rev. ed.2003).

Our decision in *Wiggins* made precisely the same point in citing the earlier 1989 ABA Guidelines. ("The ABA Guidelines provide that investigations into mitigating evidence 'should comprise efforts to discover *all reasonably available* mitigating evidence and evidence to rebut any aggravating evidence that may be introduced by the prosecutor' " (quoting 1989 ABA Guideline 11.4.1.C; emphasis in original)). For reasons given in the text, no such further investigation was needed to point to the reasonable duty to look in the file in question here.

At argument the most that Pennsylvania (and the United States as *amicus*) could say was that defense counsel's efforts to find mitigating evidence by other means excused them from looking at the prior conviction file. And that, of course, is the position taken by the state postconviction courts. Without specifically discussing the prior case file, they too found that defense counsel's efforts ere enough to free them from any obligation to enquire further.

We think this conclusion of the state court fails to answer the considerations we have set out, to the point of being an objectively unreasonable conclusion. It flouts prudence to deny that a defense lawyer should try to look at a file he knows the prosecution will cull for aggravating evidence, let alone when the file is sitting in the trial courthouse, open for the asking. No reasonable lawyer would forgo examination of the file thinking he could do as well by asking the defendant or family relations whether they recalled anything helpful or damaging in the prior victim's testimony. Nor would a reasonable lawyer compare possible searches for school reports, juvenile records, and evidence of drinking habits to the opportunity to take a look at a file disclosing what the prosecutor knows and even plans to read from in his case. Questioning a few more family members and searching for old records can promise less than looking for a needle in a haystack, when a lawyer truly has reason to doubt there is any needle there. E.g., *Strickland, supra*, at 699, 104 S.Ct. 2052. But looking at a file the prosecution says it will use is a sure bet: whatever may be in that file is going to tell defense counsel something about what the prosecution can produce.

The dissent thinks this analysis creates a "rigid, *per se* " rule that requires defense counsel to do a complete review of the file on any prior conviction introduced, but that is a mistake. Counsel fell short here because they failed to make reasonable efforts to review the prior conviction file, despite knowing that the prosecution intended to introduce Rompilla's prior conviction not merely by entering a notice of conviction into evidence but by quoting damaging testimony of the rape victim in that case. The unreasonableness of attempting no more than they did was heightened by the easy availability of the file at the trial courthouse, and the great risk that testimony about a similar violent crime would hamstring counsel's chosen defense of residual doubt. It is owing to these circumstances that the state courts were objectively unreasonable in concluding that counsel could reasonably decline to make any effort to review the file. Other situations, where a defense lawyer is not charged with knowledge that the prosecutor intends to use a prior conviction in this way, might well warrant a different assessment.

C

Since counsel's failure to look at the file fell below the line of reasonable practice, there is a further question about prejudice, that is, whether "there is a reasonable probability that, but for counsel's unprofessional errors, the result of the proceeding would have been different." * * * Because the state courts found the representation adequate, they never reached the issue of prejudice, and so we examine this element of the *Strickland* claim *de novo,* * * * and agree with the dissent in the Court of Appeals. We think Rompilla has shown beyond any doubt that counsel's lapse was prejudicial; Pennsylvania, indeed, does not even contest the claim of prejudice.

If the defense lawyers had looked in the file on Rompilla's prior conviction, it is uncontested they would have found a range of mitigation leads that no other source had opened up. In the same file with the transcript of the prior trial were the records of Rompilla's imprisonment on the earlier conviction, which defense counsel testified she had never seen. * * * The prison files pictured Rompilla's childhood and mental health very differently from anything defense counsel had Seen or heard. An evaluation by a corrections counselor states that Rompilla was "reared in the slum environment of Allentown, Pa. vicinity. He early came to [the] attention of juvenile authorities, quit school at 16, [and] started a series of incarcerations in and out Penna. often of assaultive nature and commonly related to over-indulgence in alcoholic beverages." The same file discloses test results that the defense's mental health experts would have viewed as pointing to schizophrenia and other disorders, and test scores showing a third grade level of cognition after nine years of schooling.

The accumulated entries would have destroyed the benign conception of Rompilla's upbringing and mental capacity defense counsel had formed from talking with Rompilla himself and some of his family members, and from the reports of the mental health experts. With this information, counsel would have become skeptical of the impression given by the five family members and would unquestionably have gone further to build a mitigation case. Further effort would presumably have unearthed much of the material postconviction counsel found, including testimony from several members of Rompilla's family, whom trial counsel did not interview. Judge Sloviter summarized this evidence:

> "Rompilla's parents were both severe alcoholics who drank constantly. His mother drank during her pregnancy with Rompilla, and he and his brothers eventually developed serious drinking problems. His father, who had a vicious temper, frequently beat Rompilla's mother, leaving her bruised

and black-eyed, and bragged about his cheating on her. His parents fought violently, and on at least one occasion his mother stabbed his father. He was abused by his father who beat him when he was young with his hands, fists, leather straps, belts and sticks. All of the children lived in terror. There were no expressions of parental love, affection or approval. Instead, he was subjected to yelling and verbal abuse. His father locked Rompilla and his brother Richard in a small wire mesh dog pen that was filthy and excrement filled. He had an isolated background, and was not allowed to visit other children or to speak to anyone on the phone. They had no indoor plumbing in the house, he slept in the attic with no heat, and the children were not given clothes and attended school in rags." * * *

The jury never heard any of this and neither did the mental health experts who examined Rompilla before trial. While they found "nothing helpful to [Rompilla's] case," their postconviction counterparts, alerted by information from school, medical, and prison records that trial counsel never saw, found plenty of "'red flags'" pointing up a need to test further. * * * When they tested, they found that Rompilla "suffers from organic brain damage, an extreme mental disturbance significantly impairing several of his cognitive functions." They also said that "Rompilla's problems relate back to his childhood, and were likely caused by fetal alcohol syndrome [and that] Rompilla's capacity to appreciate the criminality of his conduct or to conform his conduct to the law was substantially impaired at the time of the offense."

These findings in turn would probably have prompted a look at school and juvenile records, all of them easy to get, showing, for example, that when Rompilla was 16 his mother "was missing from home frequently for a period of one or several weeks at a time." * * * The same report noted that his mother "has been reported ... frequently under the influence of alcoholic beverages, with the result that the children have always been poorly kept and on the filthy side which was also the condition of the home at all times." School records showed Rompilla's IQ was in the mentally retarded range.

This evidence adds up to a mitigation case that bears no relation to the few naked pleas for mercy actually put before the jury, and although we suppose it is possible that a jury could have heard it all and still have decided on the death penalty, that is not the test. It goes without saying that the undiscovered "mitigating evidence, taken as a whole, 'might well have influenced the jury's appraisal' of [Rompilla's] culpability," * * * and the likelihood of a different result if the evidence had gone in is "sufficient to undermine confidence in the outcome" actually reached at sentencing, *Strickland,* 466 U.S., at 694, 104 S.Ct. 2052.

The judgment of the Third Circuit is reversed, and Pennsylvania must either retry the case on penalty or stipulate to a life sentence.

It is so ordered.

Note on Malpractice Suits Arising from Criminal Cases

A convicted criminal defendant faces higher hurdles than other plaintiffs in mal-practice actions. Restatement § 53(d) explains:

A convicted criminal defendant suing for malpractice must prove both that the lawyer failed to act properly and that, but for that failure, the result would have been differ-ent, for example because a double-jeopardy defense would have prevented convic-tion. Although most jurisdictions addressing the issue have stricter rules, under this Section it is not necessary to prove that the convicted defendant was in fact innocent.

D. Debating Whether The Torture Memos Represent Compt-etent Legal Work

One of the most prominent debates regarding legal ethics is the controversy regarding the "Torture Memos," the four memos from the United States Depart-ment of Justice's Office of Legal Counsel that responded to questions regarding the appropriateness of harsh interrogation techniques, such as waterboarding, in the aftermath of the 9/11 attack. Many ethical questions have arisen with regard to these memos. A February 2010 Justice Department report concluded that the memos' authors had not committed professional misconduct.[7] Following are two contrasting views as to whether the authors of the memos fulfilled their ethical duty of competence. What is your view?

WHAT WENT WRONG: TORTURE AND THE OFFICE OF LEGAL COUNSEL IN THE BUSH ADMINISTRATION: HEARING BEFORE THE S. COMM. ON THE JUDICIARY, 111TH CONG. (2009) (STATEMENT OF DAVID LUBAN, PROF. OF LAW, GEO. U.L. CENTER)

May 13, 2009

http://judiciary.senate.gov/hearings/testimony.cfm?id=3842&wit_id=7905

* * *

Thank you for inviting me to testify today. You've asked me to talk about the legal ethics of the torture and interrogation memos written by lawyers in the Office of Legal Counsel. Based on the publicly-available sources I've studied, I believe that the memos are an ethical train wreck.

---

7   Eric Lichtblau & Scott Shane, *Report Faults 2 Authors of Bush Terror Memos*, N.Y. Times, Feb. 19, 2010, *available at* http://www.nytimes.com/2010/02/20/us/politics/20justice.html (linking to report and describing it as concluding that lawyers "used flawed legal reasoning but were not guilty of professional misconduct").

* * * The rules of professional ethics forbid lawyers from counseling or assisting clients in illegal conduct; they require competence; and they demand that lawyers explain enough that the client can make an informed decision, which surely means explaining the law as it is. Lawyers must not misrepresent the law, because lawyers are prohibited from *all* "conduct involving dishonesty, fraud, deceit or misrepresentation."

* * * [I]t is likely that the torture memos were exactly what the client wanted; according to a Senate Intelligence Committee report, "On July 17, 2002, according to CIA records, the Director of Central Intelligence (DCI) met with the National Security Adviser, who advised that the CIA could proceed with its proposed interrogation of Abu Zubaydah. This advice, which authorized CIA to proceed as a policy matter, was subject to a determination of legality by OLC." In other words, the "program" had already been approved, pending legal approval by OLC.

* * *

Does that mean a client cannot come to a lawyer with the request, "Give me the best argument you can find that I can do X"? As a general proposition, nothing forbids a lawyer from doing so, but it would be deceptive to package one-sided advice as an authentic legal opinion. Emphatically this is not OLC's mission, which is to tender objective advice about matters of law, binding on the executive branch. Nor do Professor Yoo, Judge Bybee, and Mr. Bradbury claim they are simply giving, in a one-sided way, the best arguments they can find for the permissibility of the tactics. The August 1, 2002 "techniques" memo states, "We wish to emphasize that this is our best reading of the law," while Mr. Bradbury describes his May 10, 2005 "techniques" memo in similar terms: "the legal standards we apply in this memorandum... constitute our authoritative view of the legal standards applicable under [the torture statutes]."

Unfortunately, the torture memos fall far short of professional standards of candid advice and independent judgment. They involve a selective and in places deeply eccentric reading of the law. The memos cherry-pick sources of law that back their conclusions, and leave out sources of law that do not. They read as if they were reverse engineered to reach a pre-determined outcome: approval of waterboarding and the other CIA techniques.

* * *

Twenty-six years ago, President Reagan's Justice Department prosecuted law enforcement officers for waterboarding prisoners to make them confess. The case is called *United States v. Lee*. Four men were convicted and drew hefty sentences that the Court of Appeals upheld.

The Court of Appeals repeatedly referred to the technique as "torture." This is perhaps the single most relevant case in American law to the legality of waterboarding. Any lawyer can find the *Lee* case in a few seconds on a computer just by typing the words "water torture" into a database. But the authors of the torture memos never mentioned it. They had no trouble finding cases where courts *didn't* call harsh interrogation techniques "torture." It's hard to avoid the conclusion that Mr. Yoo, Judge Bybee, and Mr. Bradbury chose not to mention the *Lee* case because it casts doubt on their conclusion that waterboarding is legal.

In past discussion before this Committee, Attorney General Mukasey responded that *Lee* is not germane, because it is a civil rights denial case, not a torture case. That response misses the point, however, which was not what legal issue the court was addressing in *Lee*, but the fact that the judges had no hesitation about labeling waterboarding "torture," a label they used at least nine times. They obviously could not reference the Convention Against Torture (CAT) or the torture statutes, 18 U.S.C. §§ 2340-2340A, which did not yet exist. But there is no reason to suppose that they would have reached a different characterization of waterboarding than they did in *Lee*. That might be the case if CAT and the torture statutes had transformed the meaning of the ordinary-language word 'torture,' making it more technical, and raising the standard of harshness so that waterboarding might not be torture under the new, technical standard.

That simply did not happen. The statutes' definition of torture as severe mental or physical pain or suffering is neither unusual nor technical. Indeed, a standard pre-CAT dictionary definition of torture describes it as "severe or excruciating pain or suffering (of body or mind)..." -- a definition so similar to the language of CAT that it Seems entirely possible that CAT's drafters modeled the treaty language on the Oxford English Dictionary definition. Other *Lee*-era dictionaries use formulations that do not in any way suggest that at the time of *Lee* 'torture' meant something milder than the statutory standard--Webster's Third (1971) says "intense pain"; Webster's Second (1953) says "severe pain" and "extreme pain."

Other significant omissions include the failure of the August 1, 2002 "torture" memo to discuss or even mention the *Steel Seizure Case* in its analysis of the President's commander-in-chief power, or the highly significant early decision *Little v. Barreme*, 6 U.S. (2 Cranch) 170 (1804), which found that President Adams, as commander-in-chief during the "quasi-War" with France, could not authorize the seizure of a ship contrary to an act of Congress. In its discussion of the necessity defense, the Bybee Memo fails to mention the recently-decided *United States v. Oakland Cannabis Buyers' Co-op*, 532 U.S. 483, 490 (2001), which calls into question whether federal criminal law even contains a necessity defense if no statute specifies that there is one. Likewise, the opinion fails to mention that there is no reported case in which a federal court has accepted a necessity defense for a crime of violence--surely a crucial piece of information for a client who might be relying on the OLC's opinion in the momentous decision whether or not to waterboard detainees. In one place, the opinion may fairly be said to falsify what a source says. Discussing whether interrogators accused of torture could plead self-defense, the memo says: "Leading scholarly commentators believe that interrogation of such individuals using methods that might violate [the anti-torture statute] would be justified under the doctrine of self-defense." The opinion refers to a law review article. What the article's author actually says on the page cited is nearly the opposite: "*The literal law of self-defense is not available to justify their torture.* But the principle uncovered as the moral basis of the defense may be applicable" (emphasis added). Omitting to discuss leading contrary cases, and spinning what cited sources say, is not honest opinion writing, and violates the ethical requirements of candor and independent judgment, and communication to a client of everything reasonably necessary for the client to make an informed decision.

I would like to briefly discuss other ways that the torture memos twisted and distorted the law, even though doing so requires getting even further into technicalities that, quite frankly, only a lawyer could love. The first Bybee memo advances a startlingly broad theory of executive power, according to which the President as commander-in-chief can override criminal laws such as the torture statute. This was a theory that Jack Goldsmith, who headed the OLC after Judge Bybee's departure, described as an "extreme conclusion," reached through "cursory and one-sided legal arguments—a conclusion that "has no foundation in prior OLC opinions, or in judicial decisions, or in any other source of law." It comes very close to President Nixon's notorious statement that "when the President does it, that means it is not illegal—except that Mr. Nixon was speaking off the cuff in a high pressure interview, not a written opinion by the Office of Legal Counsel. The *Youngstown* case I mentioned previously found that President Truman could not seize steel mills during the Korean War because doing so impinged on Congress's powers. It is a case limiting the commander-in-chief power, and it is known to every law student who has taken constitutional law.

Professor Yoo has explained that he and Judge Bybee did not discuss the *Steel Seizure* case because of a long-standing OLC tradition of upholding the President's commander-in-chief powers, central among which is the power to interrogate captives. Suffice it to say, however, that nothing in either U.S. law or U.S. military tradition suggests that authority to torture captives belongs among the commander-in-chief's historical powers, any more than the authority to execute captives as a way of inducing other captives to reveal information is part of the traditional commander-in-chief power. It is perhaps for this reason that the TJAGs of the Army, Navy, Marines, and Air Force all protested the torture memos when they learned of them months after they were issued. MG Jack Rives, TJAG of the Air Force, objected that "the use of the more extreme interrogation techniques simply is not how the U.S. armed forces have operated in recent history. We have taken the legal and moral 'high ground'. . . ." And BG Kevin Sankuhler, the Marine TJAG, noted sharply that "OLC does not represent the services; thus, understandably, concern for servicemembers is not reflected in their opinion."

I believe Professor Goldsmith's view that no source of law supports the Bybee Memo's proposition that the commander-in-chief power can override the criminal law on torture is correct; surely Professor Goldsmith, a Bush appointee, a conservative, and an intellectual ally of Professor Yoo, cannot have lightly decided to withdraw the memos. The same conclusion is reached in the definitive study of the commander-in-chief's power, the nearly 300-page articles by Professors David Barron and Martin Lederman, who conclude that "[t]here is a radical disjuncture between the approach to constitutional war powers the current President [George W. Bush] has asserted and the one that prevailed at the moment of ratification and for much of our history that followed."

This is not simply a matter of scholarly disagreement; and, obviously, I am not saying that taking one side of a contested and complex constitutional issue is unethical. It is not. But omitting the leading case on the commander-in-chief power "at lowest ebb" (that is, in the face of a contrary statute) is a different matter. A lawyer writing an appellate brief on whether the torture statute encroaches on the President's constitutional authority who failed to cite or discuss *Youngstown Sheet & Tube* would be committing legal malpractice, and might face professional discipline for failing to cite directly contrary authority if, improbably, the adversary also failed to cite *Youngstown*. Briefs have more, not less leeway to present a one-sided view of the law than advisory opinions for clients, and an omission that would be malpractice in a brief is a fortiori unacceptable in an opinion.

The first Bybee memo also wrenches language from a Medicare statute to explain the legal definition of torture. The Medicare statute lists "severe pain" as a symptom that might indicate a medical emergency. Mr. Yoo flips the statute and announces that only pain equivalent in intensity to "organ failure, impairment of bodily function, or even death" can be "severe." This definition was so bizarre that the OLC itself disowned it a few months after it became public. It is unusual for one OLC opinion to disown an earlier one, and it shows just how far out of the mainstream Professor Yoo and Judge Bybee had wandered. The memo's authors were obviously looking for a standard of torture so high that none of the enhanced interrogation techniques would count. But legal ethics does not permit lawyers to make frivolous arguments merely because it gets them the results they wanted. I should note that on January 15 of this year, Mr. Bradbury found it necessary to withdraw six additional OLC opinions by Professor Yoo or Judge Bybee.

Of course, it is well-known that the 2004 Levin memorandum that replaced the Bybee Memo stated, "While we have identified various disagreements with the August 2002 Memorandum, we have reviewed this Office's prior opinions addressing issues involving treatment of detainees and do not believe that any of their conclusions would be different under the standards set forth in this memorandum." However, Mr. Levin stated in testimony to the House Judiciary Committee that he "did *not* mean, as some have interpreted—and . . . this is my fault, no doubt, in drafting--that we had concluded that we would have reached the same conclusions as those earlier opinions did. We were in fact analyzing that at the time and we never completed that analysis." Rather, he meant that his predecessors, Professor Yoo and Judge Bybee, would have reached the same conclusions based on his standards.

I have said little about the three May 2005 opinions, beyond the point I have already noted that they approve waterboarding without citing or discussing *Lee.* (Nor do they acknowledge earlier cases where the U.S. has condemned water torture—the *Glenn* court-martial from the U.S. Philippines campaign in the early twentieth century, and the *Sawada* case, in which a Japanese general was condemned for forms of cruelty that included water torture. The 2005 memos are not as conspicuously one-sided as the August 1, 2002 torture memo which—again quoting Professor Goldsmith—"lacked the tenor of detachment and caution that usually characterizes OLC work, and that is so central to the legitimacy of OLC." Mr. Bradbury's memos are more cautious, and contain repeated reminders that reasonable people could reach the opposite conclusion. But they too contain troubling features.

To take one example, the May 30, 2005 memo states twice that courts might reach the opposite conclusion in their interpretation of whether the CIA techniques "shock the conscience." This is an important warning, and I believe that it is perfectly ethical for a lawyer to offer a non-standard interpretation of the law in an advisory opinion, provided that the lawyer flags—as Mr. Bradbury does—that it may indeed be nonstandard. However, in both places he immediately adds that the interpretation is "unlikely to be subject to judicial inquiry." This is uncomfortably close to a lawyer telling the client, "it's likely to be found illegal, but don't worry—you probably won't be caught."

Other features of the memos are likewise troubling. To reach the conclusion that waterboarding does not cause "severe physical suffering," the memos rely on a specious finding from the 2004 memo, namely that to qualify as severe, suffering must be prolonged. There is no such requirement in the torture statute—and indeed, there is strong reason to believe that no such requirement was intended. Congress *did* stipulate that severe mental suffering must be "prolonged" (18 U.S.C. § 2340(2)). Ordinary canons of statutory construction would lead virtually all competent lawyers to conclude that if Congress omitted the word "prolonged" in connection with physical suffering, but included it in the definition of mental suffering in the same statute, it does not exist in connection with physical suffering. In Mr. Bradbury's memo, the requirement of duration is crucial in finding that waterboarding does not induce severe physical suffering, because it does not last long enough. But, to repeat, the law itself contains no duration requirement for severe physical suffering—and it is wildly implausible that the overwhelming sensation of drowning, which is surely a form of physical suffering, is not severe.

Equally troubling is the manner in which the May 30 memo responds to bodies of law strongly indicating that the United States Government condemns the very techniques the memo is approving, which would indicate that these techniques are not "traditional executive behavior" or "customary practice"—as, hopefully, they are not! For example, the memo notes that our own State Department's annual Country Reports routinely condemn several of the practices the CIA used: dousing people with cold water, food and sleep deprivation, waterboarding, stripping and blindfolding them. The memo responds that "The condemned conduct is often undertaken for reasons totally unlike the CIA's." But of course these countries often undertake the conduct for reasons very similar to the CIA's: learning information about terrorists. We still condemn it. In any event, the response does not even speak to the question of whether these practices represent U.S. custom or traditional executive behavior—as they surely do not. The memo goes on with an argument that is absurd on its face: the fact that the U.S. offers SERE training shows that these SERE-derived interrogation tactics are indeed traditional executive behavior. It is obvious that a method of training SEALs to resist torture and cruelty is hardly traditional executive behavior in dealing with captives. In any case, the May 10 "techniques" memo notes explicitly that SERE is quite different from the CIA's program, and that the detainees were waterboarded far more often than in SERE (dozens of times instead of two).

These arguments are so implausible that it seems clear that Mr. Bradbury was straining to reach a result. There are other difficulties with these three memos, which I do not wish to belabor here. While I find these memoranda deeply troubling—and their conclusions are even more troubling than the Bybee memos, because the 2005 memos discuss the techniques both singly and in combination and conclude that they do not violate a lower standard than the definition of torture—they do not exhibit the one-sided and manipulative use of law to the same extent as the August 1, 2002 memos. And that is where the main problems of legal ethics in these memos lie.

* * *

This morning I have called the torture memos an ethical train wreck. I believe it's impossible that lawyers of such great talent and intelligence could have written these memos in the good faith belief that they accurately state the law. * * *

LETTER FROM ATTORNEY GENERAL MICHAEL B. MUKASEY & DEPUTY ATTORNEY GENERAL MARK FILIP TO MR. H. MARSHALL JARRET, COUNSEL, OFFICE OF PROFESSIONAL RESPONSIBILITY (OPR), UNITED STATES DEPARTMENT OF JUSTICE, RE: OPR REPORT REGARDING THE OFFICE OF LEGAL COUNSEL'S MEMORANDA ON ISSUES RELATING TO THE CIA'S USE OF ENHANCED INTERROGATION TECHNIQUES ON SUSPECTED TERRORISTS, (JAN. 19, 2009)

http://judiciary.house.gov/hearings/pdf/Mukasey-Filip090119.pdf

* * *

Rule 1.1 Finding—Professional Incompetence

With respect to its proposed finding of professional incompetence under Rule 1.1, we understand that OPR is aware of no direct evidence that either Bybee or Yoo believed that they were giving inaccurate advice. Further, OPR bases its conclusions concerning putative professional incompetence on a collection of facts *and* findings, a number of which do not survive close scrutiny or are not presented in an even-handed manner, thereby calling into question the ultimate suggestion of professional misconduct.

First, in a number of instances, the Draft Report criticizes the OLC Memoranda for not discussing cases that are themselves not appropriate for citation or are inapposite. For example, with respect to Rule 1.1, the Draft Report concludes that the Bybee Memo did not meet professional standards of competence based on a combination of seven factors. One of the seven factors is the Memo's analysis of judicial opinions by United States courts. The Draft Report criticizes the Bybee Memo because it did not analyze federal case law "that has applied the [Convention Against Torture's (CAT)] definition of torture in the context of removal proceedings against aliens." The Draft Report, after previously stressing that "the analysis of precedent is an essential element of competent legal advice"], suggests that the Bybee Memo should have identified and discussed three listed cases, including *Kourteva v. INS,* 151 F. Supp. 2d 1126 (N.D. Cal. 2001), *and Khanuja v. INS, 11 Fed. Appx. 824* (9th Cir. 2001). However, under Ninth Circuit rules, it would have been improper—indeed even potentially sanctionable—for an attorney to cite *Khanuja,* which is an unpublished Ninth Circuit opinion, as the cite for it to "Fed. Appx." clearly suggests. The opinion on its face, when printed from any standard legal research service, expressly states that it was not selected for publication. It further expressly cautions, on the face of the opinion, that any reader should consult Ninth Circuit Rule 36-3 before citing it. Ninth Circuit Rule 36-3 has long prohibited citation of unpublished opinions for almost all purposes, including the purposes for which *Khanuja* is offered in the Draft Report. In addition, *Kourteva* is a district court case that discusses the relevant issue only in dictum. As such, it could not, and should not, be relied upon as precedent. OPR's conclusion that the Bybee Memo is sanctionable under Rule 1.1 in part because it failed to cite these cases, the citation of one of which would have been potentially sanctionable under the rules of the issuing court, is troubling. We expect that any final Report will omit this conclusion because it is completely unfounded.

Similarly, the Draft Report criticizes the Bybee Memo' s discussion of a potential good faith defense to a putative violation of the torture statute as "overly simplistic." Among other things, relying on a Fourth Circuit case, *United States v. Wilson,* 721 F.2d 967 (4th Cir. 1983), it faults the Bybee Memo for not advising that a court "might refuse to extend the good faith defense to a crime of violence such as torture." But *Wilson* contains no language suggesting that a good faith defense is unavailable for crimes of violence. Rather, it holds that the defendant in that particular case had not made the factual showing necessary to warrant instructing the jury on the defense. *See Wilson,* 721 F.2d at 974-75 ("The District Court properly denied appellant's requested [good faith] instruction on the ground that there was insufficient evidence to justify it.").

To be clear, we do not, of course, suggest that because of these errors OPR has engaged in misconduct or that the Draft Report reflects professional incompetence. It is a lengthy document, addressing complex issues, and we presume and believe that any errors were the product of good faith. Nonetheless, we do note the clear errors identified above to show the importance, with all respect, of context. Even after four and a half years to research, write, edit, and shepardize the Draft Report, it contains, just pages into its legal analysis, errors of the sort the Draft Report itself repeatedly identifies as being part of basic legal competence under Rule 1.1. If mistakes like this happen even in the most relaxed circumstances, some considerations should be made when they occur in the circumstances in which OLC was asked to provide its advice.

The Draft Report also faults the Bybee Memo because its "analysis began with the assertion that Congress's use of the phrase `severe pain' elsewhere in the United States Code [in a statute pertaining to health-care benefits] can shed light on its meaning" in the torture statute. The Draft Report concludes that it was "unreasonable" to rely on that language because the health care statute was unrelated to the torture statute.

While we have both stated our disagreement—rendered with the benefit of substantial subsequent legal work by OLC and others—with the Bybee Memo's conclusions about the meaning of "severe pain," the Draft Report's stated criticism ignores that the Bybee Memo's analysis actually begins not by looking to the health care statute, but by evaluating three separate dictionary definitions of the word "severe." Even more to the point, it is common practice for lawyers to look to other sources for guidance in interpretation when there is no direct precedent, which is how the Bybee Memo indicated it used the definition in the healthcare statute In Mr. Bybee's own words: "We're struggling here to try and give some meaning that we can work with because we had an application that we were also required to make at this time, and we couldn't discuss this just simply as a philosophical nicety; we had real questions before us." Furthermore, the Bybee Memo itself alluded to the remote nature of the statutory definitional analogy, which reflects that it presented the argument in guarded terms, as is best done.

Throughout its criticism of the Bybee Memorandum, the Draft Report relies on commentary from others to substantiate the Memorandum's errors, but does not contain sufficient information to allow the reader to evaluate these sources readily. For example, the Draft Report bolsters its critique at several points by quoting articles or papers written by, among others, Professor David Luban. Thus, to support its conclusion that "[a]t various points, the [Bybee] memorandum advanced novel legal theories, ignored relevant authority, failed to adequately support its conclusions, and misinterpreted case law," the Draft Report cites an article written by Professor Luban. As reflected in the Draft Report itself, and as confirmed in our meeting, the Draft Report draws substantially from Professor Luban's work. At no point, however, does the Draft Report inform the reader why Professor Luban and other critics of the OLC memoranda should be considered authoritative, or why their work was favored over other academics and commentators who have defended the work or approaches of OLC, Bybee, and Yoo during this period of time.

Even more important, given the substantial reliance of the Draft Report on this source, notwithstanding that OPR had over four years to work on the draft, the Draft Report does not sufficiently relate the background of Professor Luban so that a reader would easily appreciate his potential strengths, weaknesses, and biases. We are not personally familiar with all of Professor Luban's work, and have nothing bad to say about him, but commentators, like witnesses, typically have certain seeming biases that are conveyed so as to inform a reader or jury or decision-maker. Thus, for example, it would appear at least worth mentioning that, while Professor Luban seems to be a very thoughtful and prolific scholar, he is a trained philosopher, not an attorney; and he has not practiced law. He also appears to be a longtime—to be sure, thoughtful and sincere, but longtime—critic of the Bush Administration and of the War on Terror in general . These facts about Professor Luban do not make him wrong necessarily, of course, but they seemingly would be related in a report where his views are cited as authority for the contention that Mr. Bybee, now a federal appellate judge, and John Yoo, a tenured professor at the University of California Boalt School of Law, were professionally incompetent in their work at OLC. Of course, legal arguments should stand or fall on their own merit and not by virtue of who advances them. The Draft Report, however, appears to rely substantially on others' analyses, such that the identities and potential predispositions of the authors of these arguments are at least relevant to the reader.

The Draft Report also repeatedly quotes from interviews with Steve Bradbury and Jack Goldsmith. Often it does so in a way that suggests that Mr. Bradbury and Mr. Goldsmith would agree with the conclusion that Yoo and Bybee committed misconduct or even were professionally incompetent. To the extent that was the intent of the Draft Report, we recommend that you consider asking Bradbury and Goldsmith whether they believe either Mr. Yoo or Mr. Bybee committed professional misconduct. Since attorneys typically have an obligation to refer another attorney to relevant bar authorities where they believe another lawyer has committed an ethical failing, it would appear that neither Mr. Goldsmith nor Mr. Bradbury believes Mr. Yoo or Mr. Bybee violated ethical canons. Instead, we suspect that both would state that, despite their disagreement with aspects of the Yoo and Bybee memos, they do not believe that Mr. Yoo or Mr. Bybee committed professional misconduct.

The Draft Report also takes issue with the Bybee Memo's discussion of a potential necessity defense, a discussion with which we have also disagreed in the past. Nevertheless, several of the Draft Report's criticisms seem to us unfair in light of language in the Bybee Memo itself. For example, the Draft Report suggests that the discussion was not relevant because "it is difficult to imagine a real-world situation" where an interrogator would "reasonably anticipate[]" that his questioning would produce information that would avoid an imminent, threatening harm. Yet the Bybee Memo itself counseled that the availability and strength of the defense would depend on (1) the degree of certainty that government officials have that a "particular individual has information needed to prevent an attack" and (2) the likelihood that the terrorist attack is to occur and the amount of damage the attack would cause. It is, with all respect, therefore misleading to suggest, as the Draft Report does, that the Bybee Memo advised that a necessity defense would be available without reference to these considerations.

The Draft Report also asserts inexplicably that the Bybee Memo did not address an element of the necessity defense requiring the defendant to show that there was no available alternative to violating the law. Yet as the Draft Report itself acknowledges in a footnote on the same page, the Bybee Memo does address this point. The Bybee Memo states: "[T]he defendant *cannot* rely upon the necessity defense if a third alternative is open and known to him that will cause less harm."

Finally, at various points, the Draft Report goes beyond questioning OLC's methodology and questions the motives of attorneys Yoo and Bybee directly. For example, the Draft Report asserts expressly that the Commander-in-Chief and the affirmative defense sections of the Bybee Memo were added not to provide a more complete analysis of relevant legal authority, but rather because then-Assistant Attorney General for the Criminal Division, Michael Chertoff, properly had refused to decline prosecution of future violations of the anti-torture statute, so OLC attorneys sought to reverse the effect of that decision. To support this very serious accusation, the Draft Report seemingly relies on little more than the fact that the two sections were drafted following a White House meeting at which the Criminal Division declined to provide an advance declination. Without explanation or evidence to the contrary, the Draft Report dismisses the more innocuous possibility that discussions of these areas of law were added for the sake of completeness (as OPR was informed by attorneys Yoo and Koester), at the request of or with the support of OLC's clients (as attorney Philbin and David Addington indicated). Notably, the Draft Report presents no evidence that the OLC attorneys even opposed the Department's decision to decline prosecution; to the contrary, OLC was tasked with drafting the written notice refusing to decline prosecution of future statutory violations. Again, one may take issue with the conclusions that OLC reached in this time period—as we too have both previously done—but we see little basis for OPR's conclusion that it reached these conclusions in bad faith.

In summary, we believe there are substantial, material problems with the Draft Report's analysis of the Rule 1.1 issue. * * *

VI. Allocating Decision-Making Between Lawyer and Client

The dominant understanding that lawyers serve as partisans for their clients would seem to translate into a rule that lawyers must follow client instructions within the bounds of the law. In fact, the law and rules are more complicated. In part, this complexity results from competing understandings of the lawyer's role. The Restatement explains that:

> Traditionally, some lawyers considered that a client put affairs in the lawyer's hands, who then managed them as the lawyer thought would best advance the client's interests. So conducting the relationship can subordinate the client to the lawyer. The lawyer might not fully understand the client's best interests or might consciously or unconsciously pursue the lawyer's own interests. An opposite view of the client-lawyer relationship treats the lawyer as a servant of the client, who must do whatever the client wants limited only by the requirements of the law. That view ignores the interest of the lawyer and of society that a lawyer practices responsibly and independently.

A middle view is that the client defines the goals of the representation and the lawyer implements them, but that each consults with the other.[8]

This "middle view" is the basis for the law and the rules govern allocation of decision-making authority between lawyer and client.

[Question 1]

On appeal, the court appoints John Lawyer to represent Joan Client, an indigent criminal defendant. John Lawyer refuses to make arguments that Joan Client instructs him to make. John Lawyer considers the

> **FYI**
>
> Despite the belief that lawyers should serve as partisans for their clients, most empirical studies have found that lawyers actually seek to control clients either because the lawyers believe they know better or because they do what will protect their relationships with other lawyers or the court.[9] The exception to these findings is representation of corporate clients, where lawyers do tend to serve as client partisans.[10]

arguments non-frivolous, but believes that raising them would be bad strategy. Do the Rules require John Lawyer to make the arguments? Does the failure to follow Joan Client's instructions deprive her of her constitutional right to counsel?

(A) Neither the Rules nor the right to counsel require John Lawyer to follow the client's instructions.

(B) Both the Rules and the right to counsel require John Lawyer to follow the client's instructions.

(C) The Rules require John Lawyer to make the arguments but the right to counsel does not.

(D) The right to counsel requires John Lawyer to make the arguments but the Rules do not.

---

8 Restatement, Introductory Note: Topic 3. Authority to Make Decisions, at 168-69.

9 *See, e.g.*, Douglas E. Rosenthal, Lawyer and Client: Who's in Charge? (1974); Austin Sarat & William L.F. Felstiner, Divorce Lawyers and Their Clients: Power and Meaning in the Legal Process (1995); Abraham S. Blumberg, *The Practice of Law as a Confidence Game: Organizational Cooptation of a Profession*, 1 L. & Soc'y Rev. 15 (1967); Roy B. Flemming, *Client Games: Defense Attorney Perspectives on Their Relations with Criminal Clients*, 1986 Am. B. Found. Res. J. 253; Lyn Mather, *What do Clients Want? What do Lawyers Do?*, 52 Emory L.J. 1065 (2003); Tamara Relis, *"It's Not About the Money!": A Theory on Misconceptions of Plaintiffs' Litigation Aims*, 68 U. Pitt. L. Rev. 701 (2007); Ann Southworth, *Lawyer-Client Decisionmaking in Civil Rights and Poverty Practice: An Empirical Study of Lawyers' Norms*, 9 Geo. J. Legal Ethics 1101 (1996); Rodney J. Uphoff & Peter B. Wood, *The Allocation of Decisionmaking Between Defense Counsel and Criminal Defendant: An Empirical Study of Attorney-Client Decisionmaking*, 47 Kan. L. Rev. 1, 55-58 (1998).

10 *See* Eve Spangler, Lawyers for Hire: Salaried Professionals at Work 64 (1986); Robert L. Nelson, *Ideology, Practice, and Professional Autonomy: Social Values and Client Relationships in the Large Law Firm*, 37 Stan. L. Rev. 503, 504-05 (1985).

Rule 1.2(a) provides that:

Subject to paragraphs (c) and (d), a lawyer shall abide by a client's decisions concerning the objectives of representation and, as required by Rule 1.4, shall consult with the client as to the means by which they are to be pursued. A lawyer may take such action on behalf of the client as is impliedly authorized to carry out the representation. A lawyer shall abide by a client's decision whether to settle a matter. In a criminal case, the lawyer shall abide by the client's decision, after consultation with the lawyer, as to a plea to be entered, whether to waive jury trial and whether the client will testify.

JONES v. BARNES

463 U.S. 745 (1983)

Chief Justice BURGER delivered the opinion of the Court.

We granted certiorari to consider whether defense counsel assigned to prosecute an appeal from a criminal conviction has a constitutional duty to raise every non-frivolous issue requested by the defendant.

I

In 1976, Richard Butts was robbed at knifepoint by four men in the lobby of an apartment building; he was badly beaten and his watch and money were taken. Butts informed a Housing Authority Detective that he recognized one of his assailants as a person known to him as "Froggy," and gave a physical description of the person to the detective. The following day the detective arrested respondent David Barnes, who is known as "Froggy."

Respondent was charged with first and second degree robbery, second degree assault, and third degree larceny. The prosecution rested primarily upon Butts' testimony and his identification of respondent. During cross-examination, defense counsel asked Butts whether he had ever undergone psychiatric treatment; however, no offer of proof was made on the substance or relevance of the question after the trial judge **sua sponte** instructed Butts not to answer. At the close of trial, the trial judge declined to give an instruction on accessorial liability requested by the defense. The jury convicted respondent of first and second degree robbery and second degree assault.

It's Latin to Me!

Black's Law Dictionary explains that the term **sua sponte** refers to a court acting "[w]ithout prompting or suggestion; on its own motion."

Non constat
jus civile
a posteriori

The Appellate Division of the Supreme Court of New York, Second Department, assigned Michael Melinger to represent respondent on appeal. Respondent sent Melinger a letter listing several claims that he felt should be raised. Included were claims that Butts' identification testimony should have been suppressed, that the trial judge improperly excluded psychiatric evidence, and that respondent's trial counsel was ineffective. Respondent also enclosed a copy of a *pro se* brief he had written.

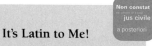

It's Latin to Me!

Black's Law Dictionary explains that the term **pro se** refers to acting "[f]or oneself; on one's own behalf; without a lawyer."

In a return letter, Melinger accepted some but rejected most of the suggested claims, stating that they would not aid respondent in obtaining a new trial and that they could not be raised on appeal because they were not based on evidence in the record. * * * [After argument, the Appellate Division affirmed the decision below.]

[O]n March 31, 1980, [Barnes] filed a petition in the New York Court of Appeals for reconsideration of that court's denial of leave to appeal. In that petition, respondent for the first time claimed that his appellate counsel, Melinger, had provided ineffective assistance. The New York Court of Appeals denied the application on April 16, 1980.

Respondent then returned to United States District Court * * * with a petition for habeas corpus based on the claim of ineffective assistance by appellate counsel. The District Court * * * dismissed the petition, holding that the record gave no support to the claim of ineffective assistance of appellate counsel on "any ... standard which could reasonably be applied." The District Court concluded:

"It is not required that an attorney argue every conceivable issue on appeal, especially when some may be without merit. Indeed, it is his professional duty to choose among potential issues, according to his judgment as to their merit and his tactical approach."

A divided panel of the Court of Appeals reversed. Laying down a new standard, the majority held that when "the appellant requests that [his attorney] raise additional colorable points [on appeal], counsel must argue the additional points to the full extent of his professional ability." In the view of the majority, this conclusion followed from *Anders v. California*, 386 U.S. 738 (1967). In *Anders*, this Court held that an appointed attorney must advocate his client's cause vigorously and may not withdraw from a nonfrivolous appeal. The Court of Appeals majority held that, since *Anders* bars counsel from abandoning a nonfrivolous appeal, it also bars counsel from abandoning a nonfrivolous issue on appeal. * * *

The court concluded that Melinger had not met the above standard in that he had failed to press at least two nonfrivolous claims: the trial judge's failure to instruct on accessory liability and ineffective assistance of trial counsel. The fact that these issues had been raised in respondent's own pro se briefs did not cure the error, since "[a] pro se brief is no substitute for the advocacy of experienced counsel." The court reversed and remanded, with instructions to grant the writ of habeas corpus unless the State assigned new counsel and granted a new appeal.

* * * We granted certiorari, and we reverse.

II

* * *

Neither *Anders* nor any other decision of this Court suggests * * * that the indigent defendant has a constitutional right to compel appointed counsel to press nonfrivolous points requested by the client, if counsel, as a matter of professional judgment, decides not to present those points.

This Court, in holding that a State must provide counsel for an indigent appellant on his first appeal as of right, recognized the superior ability of trained counsel in the "examination into the record, research of the law, and marshalling of arguments on [the appellant's] behalf." * * * Yet by promulgating a *per se* rule that the client, not the professional advocate, must be allowed to decide what issues are to be pressed, the Court of Appeals seriously undermines the ability of counsel to present the client's case in accord with counsel's professional evaluation.

Experienced advocates since time beyond memory have emphasized the importance of winnowing out weaker arguments on appeal and focusing on one central issue if possible, or at most on a few key issues. * * *

There can hardly be any question about the importance of having the appellate advocate examine the record with a view to selecting the most promising issues for review. This has assumed a greater importance in an era when oral argument is strictly limited in most courts—often to as little as 15 minutes—and when page limits on briefs are widely imposed. * * * Even in a court that imposes no time or page limits, however, the new *per se* rule laid down by the Court of Appeals is contrary to all experience and logic. A brief that raises every colorable issue runs the risk of burying good arguments—those that, in the words of the great advocate John W. Davis, "go for the jugular," in a verbal mound made up of strong and weak contentions. * * *

With the exception of these specified fundamental decisions, an attorney's duty is to take professional responsibility for the conduct of the case, after consulting with his client. * * *

Reversed.

* * *

Justice BRENNAN, with whom Justice MARSHALL joins, dissenting.

The Sixth Amendment provides that "[i]n all criminal prosecutions, the accused shall enjoy the right ... to have the *Assistance* of counsel for his defence" (emphasis added). I find myself in fundamental disagreement with the Court over what a right to "the assistance of counsel" means. The import of words like "assistance" and "counsel" seems inconsistent with a regime under which counsel appointed by the State to represent a criminal defendant can refuse to raise issues with arguable merit on appeal when his client, after hearing his assessment of the case and his advice, has directed him to raise them. I would remand for a determination whether respondent did in fact insist that his lawyer brief the issues that the Court of Appeals found were not frivolous.

* * * What is at issue here is the relationship between lawyer and client-who has ultimate authority to decide which nonfrivolous issues should be presented on appeal? I believe the right to "the assistance of counsel" carries with it a right, personal to the defendant, to make that decision, against the advice of counsel if he chooses.

If all the Sixth Amendment protected was the State's interest in substantial justice, it would not include such a right. However, in *Faretta v. California,* 422 U.S. 806, 95 S.Ct. 2525, 45 L.Ed.2d 562 (1975), we decisively rejected that view of the Constitution[.] * * *

Faretta establishes that the right to counsel is more than a right to have one's case presented competently and effectively. It is predicated on the view that the function of counsel under the Sixth Amendment is to protect the dignity and autonomy of a person on trial by *assisting* him in making choices that are his to make, not to make choices for him, although counsel may be better able to decide which tactics will be most effective for the defendant. *Anders v. California* also reflects that view. Even when appointed counsel believes an appeal has no merit, he must furnish his client a brief covering all arguable grounds for appeal so that the client may "raise any points that he chooses." * * *

The right to counsel as *Faretta* and *Anders* conceive it is not an all-or-nothing right, under which a defendant must choose between forgoing the assistance of counsel altogether or relinquishing control over every aspect of his case beyond its most basic structure (*i.e.,* how to plead, whether to present a defense, whether to appeal). A defendant's interest in his case clearly extends to other matters. * * * He may want to press the argument that he is innocent, even if other stratagems are more likely to result in the dismissal of charges or in a reduction of punishment. He may want to insist on certain arguments for political reasons. He may want to protect third parties. This is just as true on appeal as at trial, and the proper role of counsel is to *assist* him in these efforts, insofar as that is possible consistent with the lawyer's conscience, the law, and his duties to the court.

>
>
> **Take Note**
>
> Does a defendant have the right to reject appellate counsel in favor of self-representation as a way of circumventing the ruling in *Jones v. Barnes*? *See Martinez v. Court of Appeal of Cal., Fourth App. Dist.*, <u>528 U.S. 152 (2000)</u> (holding that a convicted defendant does not have the right to a pro se appeal under either the Sixth Amendment or Due Process Clause). This ruling contrasts with the right to represent oneself *pro se* under *Faretta*.

* * *

It is no secret that indigent clients often mistrust the lawyers appointed to represent them. There are many reasons for this, some perhaps unavoidable even under perfect conditions-differences in education, disposition, and socio-economic class-and some that should (but may not always) be zealously avoided. A lawyer and his client do not always have the same interests. Even with paying clients, a lawyer may have a strong interest in having judges and prosecutors think well of him, and, if he is working for a flat fee—a common arrangement for criminal defense attorneys—or if his fees for court appointments are lower than he would receive for other work, he has an obvious financial incentive to conclude cases on his criminal docket swiftly. Good lawyers undoubtedly recognize these temptations and resist them, and they endeavor to convince their clients that they will. It would be naive, however, to suggest that they always succeed in either task. A constitutional rule that encourages lawyers to disregard their clients' wishes without compelling need can only exacerbate the clients' suspicion of their lawyers. As in *Faretta,* to force a lawyer's *decisions* on a defendant "can only lead him to believe that the law conspires against him." In the end, what the Court hopes to gain in effectiveness of appellate representation by the rule it imposes today may well be lost to decreased effectiveness in other areas of representation.

* * *

Finally, today's ruling denigrates the values of individual autonomy and dignity central to many constitutional rights, especially those Fifth and Sixth Amendment rights that come into play in the criminal process. * * * The role of the defense lawyer should be above all to function as the instrument and defender of the client's autonomy and dignity in all phases of the criminal process.

* * *

The Court subtly but unmistakably adopts a different conception of the defense lawyer's role-he need do nothing beyond what the State, not his client, considers most important. In many ways, having a lawyer becomes one of the many indignities visited upon someone who has the ill fortune to run afoul of the criminal justice system.

I cannot accept the notion that lawyers are one of the punishments a person receives merely for being accused of a crime. * * *

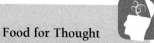

Food for Thought

Do you agree with the majority or dissent? Which best represents your view of the lawyer's role? For a more extensive discussion of perspectives on the lawyer's role, *see* Chapter 8 *infra*.

[Question 2]

During protracted pretrial proceedings, Client complained bitterly about time and expense involved and insisted that Attorney take steps to terminate pretrial proceedings. Attorney believes that the case cannot be adequately prepared for trial without further pretrial proceedings that will require an additional six months delay and further expense. The retainer states that the client has the final say on the costs of the matter. Should Attorney follow the client's instructions?

(A) Yes, because lawyers must follow client instructions.

(B) Yes, because lawyers and clients may agree to limit the scope of representation.

(C) No, because lawyers may never limit the scope of representation.

(D) No, because lawyers may not agree to limit the representation under these circumstances.

Review Rule 1.2(a).

Rule 1.2(c) provides that "A lawyer may limit the scope of the representation if the limitation is reasonable under the circumstances and the client gives informed consent.

The Comment explains:

[6] The scope of services to be provided by a lawyer may be limited by agreement with the client or by the terms under which the lawyer's services are made available to the client. When a lawyer has been retained by an insurer to represent an

insured, for example, the representation may be limited to matters related to the insurance coverage. A limited representation may be appropriate because the client has limited objectives for the representation. In addition, the terms upon which representation is undertaken may exclude specific means that might otherwise be used to accomplish the client's objectives. Such limitations may exclude actions that the client thinks are too costly or that the lawyer regards as repugnant or imprudent.

[7] Although this Rule affords the lawyer and client substantial latitude to limit the representation, the limitation must be reasonable under the circumstances. If, for example, a client's objective is limited to securing general information about the law the client needs in order to handle a common and typically uncomplicated legal problem, the lawyer and client may agree that the lawyer's services will be limited to a brief telephone consultation. Such a limitation, however, would not be reasonable if the time allotted was not sufficient to yield advice upon which the client could rely. Although an agreement for a limited representation does not exempt a lawyer from the duty to provide competent representation, the limitation is a factor to be considered when determining the legal knowledge, skill, thoroughness and preparation reasonably necessary for the representation. *See* Rule 1.1.

[8] All agreements concerning a lawyer's representation of a client must accord with the Rules of Professional Conduct and other law. *See, e.g.*, Rules 1.1, 1.8 and 5.6.

[Question 3]

A client retained an attorney to recover for a personal injury. In the retainer agreement signed by the client and the attorney, the client agreed to cooperate fully and pay the attorney a contingent fee computed as a percentage of the amount of

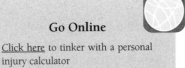

Go Online

Click here to tinker with a personal injury calculator

recovery after expenses: 25 percent if settled before trial, 30 percent if settled before verdict, 35 percent after verdict, and 40 percent after appeal.

The attorney's representation of the client in the matter extended over a three-year period during which the attorney advanced a large amount for litigation expenses. After trial, the client obtained a jury verdict for an

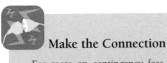

Make the Connection

For more on contingency fees, *see* Chapter 3, *infra.*

amount larger than either the attorney or the client had anticipated. However, the defendant filed an appeal based on questions of evidence and the measure of damages. Meanwhile, the defendant made an offer of settlement for approximately the amount of money the attorney had originally projected as reasonable to expect. The client, who was hard pressed financially, directed the attorney to accept the offer and settle. The attorney refused, because she was confident that there was no reversible error in the trial and that the appeal was without merit. The attorney reasonably believed that the appeal was filed solely to gain negotiating advantage in settlement negotiations.

Is the attorney subject to discipline?

   (A) Yes, because the attorney's percentage under the fee contract increased after the appeal.

   (B) Yes, because the client directed the attorney to accept the settlement offer.

   (C) No, because the decision whether to settle or defend an appeal is a tactical matter for the attorney to determine.

   (D) No, because evaluation of the merits of an appeal requires the exercise of independent professional judgment.

Review Rule 1.2(a). Is this decision one of objectives or strategy?

[Question 4]

Jane Client is seeking a divorce and wants primary custody of her children. Client instructs Susan Lawyer not to use evidence of spouse's adultery. Lawyer informs Client that the evidence of adultery will be very helpful in gaining primary custody and avoiding joint custody. Client continues to insist that Lawyer not introduce evidence of spouse's adultery. Must Susan Lawyer follow Client's instructions? If Lawyer follows Client's instructions and the court denies Client primary custody and instead awards joint custody, can Client succeed in a disciplinary and legal malpractice action against Lawyer?

   (A) The Rules and malpractice law both clearly require Lawyer to ignore the instructions.

   (B) The Rules are unclear but malpractice law makes Lawyer liable for following the instructions.

   (C) The Rules and malpractice law both clearly require Lawyer to follow instructions.

(D) The Rules are unclear but malpractice law requires Lawyer to follow instructions.

Review <u>Rule 1.2(a)</u>. The Comment adds:

[2] On occasion * * * a lawyer and a client may disagree about the means to be used to accomplish the client's objectives. Clients normally defer to the special knowledge and skill of their lawyer with respect to the means to be used to accomplish their objectives, particularly with respect to technical, legal and tactical matters. Conversely, lawyers usually defer to the client regarding such questions as the expense to be incurred and concern for third persons who might be adversely affected. Because of the varied nature of the matters about which a lawyer and client might disagree and because the actions in question may implicate the interests of a tribunal or other persons, this Rule does not prescribe how such disagreements are to be resolved. Other law, however, may be applicable and should be consulted by the lawyer. The lawyer should also consult with the client and Seek a mutually acceptable resolution of the disagreement. If such efforts are unavailing and the lawyer has a fundamental disagreement with the client, the lawyer may withdraw from the representation. *See* Rule 1.16(b)(4). Conversely, the client may resolve the disagreement by discharging the lawyer. *See* Rule 1.16(a)(3).

MARCY STRAUSS, *TOWARD A REVISED MODEL OF ATTORNEY-CLIENT RELATIONSHIP: THE ARGUMENT FOR AUTONOMY,*

<u>65 N.C. L. Rev. 315, 324-25 (1987)</u>

The current allocation of decisionmaking authority assumes that it is possible to draw a workable distinction between means and ends. Absent a clear distinction, it is difficult to understand why the client gets 'ends' decisions but not 'means,' and it is impossible to predict which decisions being to the client and which to counsel.

The means-ends distinction rests on the assumption that there exists certain determinable decisions that can be classified as means or ends. Means are merely strategic decisions that are separate and independent from the ends, or the objectives, of the lawsuit. This assumed dichotomy between means and ends does not survive close analysis. In many cases what the attorney assumes to be mere means really are part of the client's ultimate objectives. Thus, 'the client may want to win acquittal *by* asserting a certain right, because it vindicates him in a way that matters to him, or he may wish to obtain a settlement without using a certain tactic because he disapproves of the tactic.' In other words, that which is often thought to be an end might really be a means; that which is assumed to be just a means could be an end to a particular client. For instance, 'winning' is assumed to be an end of any lawsuit. As a result, criminal defendants are allowed to decide whether to plead guilty. But why assume that winning acquittal is the end? It could be that receiving the lightest possible sentence is the true end of many criminal defendants. From that perspective, pleading guilty is a means—a strategic decision—to the end of sentence reduction.

Perhaps this problem in the means—ends distinction can best be illustrated by a medical analogy. A woman diagnosed as having breast cancer obviously desires to be cured. That is the end result she wants. However, it would be difficult to accept that the only decision to be made by the woman is to choose life and that the means of a cure should be left to the discretion of others. The assumption that the woman has no legitimate interest in the type of treatment she receives—that the treatment is merely a tactical decision that can be viewed separately and independently from the end—would be repugnant to most of us.

Professor David Luban provides numerous hypothetical examples from law in which mere 'tactical' decisions matter as much, if not more, to the client than the end result. In one hypothetical, which Luban calls the 'Long Black Veil case,' an innocent client, accused of murder, forbids his attorney from calling an alibi witness, even if it means losing the case. At the time of the murder defendant was in the arms of his best friend's wife, and his personal honor requires that this incident be kept secret. Despite the fact the client clearly views protecting his lover an 'end' of the lawsuit, his attorney, under the current allocation of authority, may override the client and call the witness—in the client's own best interest. Such a decision is viewed as a means decision within the sole power of the attorney.

There are, of course, many less dramatic examples of means decisions that are difficult to distinguish from the ends. A client may not want his or her attorney to argue an insanity defense; the client's 'pride' may be more important than succeeding on this argument. Or a client may not want any more continuances in a civil case because stress from the uncertainty outweighs the possible benefits of delay. Or a client may want a certain argument raised because it might establish a long sought after legal principle, even though the chance of success is low.

In sum, the line between means and ends is imprecise at best. At a minimum, clients have a legitimate, and at times, overriding interest in what many characterize as the 'means' of the lawsuit.

Food for Thought

What do you think about the means-ends distinction? Professor Strauss mentions that the law gives patient autonomy greater deference than client autonomy. Should it?

TRUSTEES OF SCHOOLS OF TOWNSHIP 42 NORTH v. SCHROEDER

278 N.E.2d 431(Ill.App. Ct. 1971)

* * *Appellants correctly cite the obligation of an attorney to follow the instructions of his client. Whenever an attorney disobeys the lawful instructions of his client he is liable for any loss which ensues from such act. * * * Damages will not be presumed, however, and the client bears the burden of proving that damages resulted. This burden involves the task of establishing that, but for the negligence complained of, the client would have been successful in the prosecution or defense of the action in question. * * *

BOYD v. BRETT-MAJOR

449 So. 2d 952 (Fla. Dist. Ct. App. 1984)

FERGUSON, Judge.

Appeal is taken by the plaintiffs below from a judgment entered on a jury verdict for an attorney and her insurer in a legal malpractice action. * * *

The salient facts are as follows. In May 1980, plaintiffs' son was required to post a criminal appearance bond in Palm Beach County. A bonding company agreed to post the $100,000 bond and in return plaintiffs signed a mortgage and promissory note encumbering their home. The bonding company failed to file an affidavit as required by Section 903.14, Florida Statutes (1983), thereby creating an absolute defense to any subsequent foreclosure action. When plaintiffs' son failed to appear in court, the bond was estreated. The bonding company unsuccessfully sought reimbursement from plaintiffs, and ultimately filed a mortgage foreclosure action.

Plaintiffs retained the defendant-attorney to represent them in the action. Plaintiffs claim on appeal that they wished to win the suit, and that the attorney assured them of success. Defendant-attorney contends, however, that because plaintiffs wished to maintain an ongoing relationship with the bonding company, they requested only that the action be delayed so that they could raise the funds to repay the debt. In any event, the attorney filed an answer in the foreclosure action, but failed to adequately plead Section 903.14 as an affirmative defense. A final summary judgment was entered against plaintiffs on the bonding company's motion. On appeal we affirmed the judgment.

Plaintiffs thereafter filed a legal malpractice action against the attorney and her insurer. Defendants alleged as an affirmative defense to the claim:

> The Plaintiffs specifically instructed the Defendant, LIN BRETT-MAJOR, to protect their interests in an agreement which they had negotiated with

all the bondsmen, including Frank McGoey, the bondsman for International Fidelity Insurance Company, and at all times, the Defendant, LIN BRETT-MAJOR, acted in accordance with the instructions given to her by the Plaintiffs, after having explained various potential defenses to the foreclosure actions brought by the bondsmen.

At the conclusion of the evidence, the jury was instructed:

> The next issue for your consideration is that LIN BRETT-MAJOR was acting according to the specific instructions of her client and an attorney is dutibound to carry out the specific instructions of a client provided that criminal or fraudulent ends are not intended. If you find that LIN BRETT-MAJOR was carrying out the specific instructions of her client, then your verdict should be for the Defendant, LIN BRETT-MAJOR.

The proof at trial showed that the attorney was hired not to win the case but to delay the action (even though the bonding company's failure to file an affidavit created an absolute defense) because the clients intended to live up to their contractual obligation and wished to remain on good terms with the bondsman. Plaintiffs argue that to permit an affirmative defense such as that presented here, which is without legal precedence, would establish an untenable situation by which attorneys could avoid liability for their professional omissions simply by pleading that they followed a course of action desired by the client. We are not convinced that the door is opened to a parade of horribles unless we disapprove of, as a defense to a malpractice claim, that the course of action taken by counsel was at the direction of an otherwise well-advised client. The relevant inquiry is whether the attorney followed the explicit directions of his client, which presents a question of fact.

* * *

Affirmed.

1 RONALD E. MALLEN & JEFFREY M. SMITH,

Legal Malpractice § 8.9 (2009)

The client may instruct the attorney to perform certain tasks or to act in a specified manner. * * * This rule traces to the earliest American decisions and is subject to few exceptions. The instruction must be for a lawful objective. * * * The instructions must be ethically proper and not offend public policy. Of course, the client must establish that the failure to follow the instruction caused damage. On the other hand, if the attorney followed the client's instructions, there should be no liability if there was another course of action that might have been more beneficial and the lawyer explained that alternative to the client.

* * *

The client may make virtually any subject matter and any task the object of specific instructions. Thus, in litigation, the attorney may be told to file suit without delay, to file an answer, not to settle without specific authority, or how to handle distribution of a settlement. The attorney may be told to obtain a mechanic's lien, to file for a discharge in bankruptcy, to protect title, or virtually any other task involving the practice of law.

The courts have declined to extend these principles to matters of strategy or tactics.

[Question 5]

Jeff Client, who has been convicted of murder, asks Joan Lawyer to request a death sentence rather than life in prison. Must Joan Lawyer follow this instruction?

(A) Yes

(B) No

GILMORE v. UTAH

429 U.S. 1012 (1976)

On October 7, 1976, Gary Mark Gilmore was convicted of murder and sentenced to death by a judgment entered after a jury trial in a Utah court. On December 3, 1976, this Court granted an application for a stay of execution of the judgment and sentence, pending the filing here by the State of Utah of a response to the application together with transcripts of various specified hearings in the Utah courts and Board of Pardons, and until "further action of the Court on the application for stay."

The State of Utah has now filed its response and has substantially complied with the Court's request for transcripts of the specified hearings. After carefully examining the materials submitted by the State of Utah, the Court is convinced that Gary Mark Gilmore made a knowing and intelligent waiver of any and all federal rights he might have asserted after the Utah trial court's sentence was imposed, and, specifically, that the State's determinations of his competence knowingly and intelligently to waive any and all such rights were firmly grounded.

See It

Here is a picture of Gary Gilmore: http://www.apsu.edu/oconnort/images/photos/garygilmore.jpg

Accordingly, the stay of execution granted on December 3, 1976, is hereby terminated.

Mr. Chief Justice BURGER, with whom Mr. Justice POWELL, joins, concurring.

On December 2, 1976, Bessie Gilmore, claiming to act as "next friend" on behalf of her son, Gary Mark Gilmore, filed with this Court an application for stay of execution of the death sentence then scheduled for December 6, 1976. Since only a limited record was then before the Court, we granted a temporary stay of execution on December 3, 1976 in order to secure a response from the State of Utah. That response was received on December 7, 1976.[1] On December 8, 1976, a response was filed by Gary Mark Gilmore * * * challenging the standing of Bessie Gilmore to initiate any proceedings in his behalf.

When the application for a stay was initially filed on December 2, a serious question was presented as to whether Bessie Gilmore had standing to Seek the requested relief or any relief from this Court. Assuming the Court would otherwise have jurisdiction with respect to a "next friend" application, that jurisdiction would arise only if it were demonstrated that Gary Mark Gilmore is unable to seek relief in his own behalf. * * * However, in view of Gary Mark Gilmore's response on December 8, 1976, it is now clear that the "next friend" concept is wholly inapplicable to this case. Since Gary Mark Gilmore has now filed a response and appeared in his own behalf, through his retained attorneys, any basis for the standing of Bessie Gilmore to seek relief in his behalf is necessarily eliminated. The only possible exception to this conclusion would be if the record suggested, despite the representations of Gary Mark Gilmore's attorneys, that he was incompetent to waive his right of appeal under state law and was at the present time incompetent to assert rights or to challenge Bessie Gilmore's standing to assert rights in his behalf as "next friend."

After examining with care the pertinent portions of the transcripts and reports of state proceedings, and the response of Gary Mark Gilmore filed on December 8, I am in complete agreement with the conclusion expressed in the Court's order that Gary Mark Gilmore knowingly and intelligently, with full knowledge of

For More Information

A little more than a year after the Court's decision, Gary Gilmore was executed by firing squad in Utah. For an exhaustive look into his life *see* Norman Mailer's Pulitzer Prize-winning novel, *The Executioner's Song*.

---

1. This case may be unique in the annals of the Court. Not only does Gary Mark Gilmore request no relief himself; on the contrary he has expressly and repeatedly stated since his conviction in the Utah courts that he had received a fair trial and had been well treated by the Utah authorities. Nor does he claim to be innocent of the crime for which he was convicted. Indeed, his only complaint against Utah or its judicial process . . . has been with respect to the delay on the part of the State in carrying out the sentence.

his right to seek an appeal in the Utah Supreme Court, has waived that right.[4] I further agree that the State's determinations of his competence to waive his rights knowingly and intelligently were firmly grounded. * * *

KRISTEN M. DAMA, COMMENT, *REDEFINING A FINAL ACT: THE FOUR-TEENTH AMENDMENT AND STATES' OBLIGATION TO PREVENT DEATH ROW INMATES FROM VOLUNTEERING TO BE PUT TO DEATH*

9 U. Pa. J. Const. L. 1083, 1101-03 (2007)

* * *

As the foregoing discussion demonstrates, a close reading of the Supreme Court's constitutional doctrine related to defendant autonomy, competency, and the lack of standing of "next friends" who wish to prevent competent capital defendants from waiving post-conviction appeals lends itself to the conclusion that states do not

---

4. At a hearing on November 1, 1976, on a motion for a new trial, Gilmore's attorneys informed the trial court that they had been told by Gilmore not to file an appeal and not to Seek a stay of execution of sentence on his behalf. They also informed the trial court that they had advised Gilmore of his right to appeal that they believed there were substantial grounds for appeal, that the constitutionality of the Utah death penalty statute had not yet been reviewed by either the Utah Supreme Court or the United States Supreme Court, and that in their view there was a chance that the statute would eventually be held unconstitutional. The trial court itself advised Gilmore that he had a right to appeal, that the constitutional issue had not yet been resolved, and that both counsel for the State and Gilmore's own counsel would attempt to expedite an appeal to avoid unnecessary delay. Gilmore stated that he did not "care to languish in prison for another day," that the decision was his own, and that he had not made the decision as a result of the influence of drugs or alcohol or as a result of the way he was treated in prison. On November 4, the state trial court concluded that Gilmore fully understood his right to appeal and the consequences of a decision not to appeal. On November 10, the Utah Supreme Court held a hearing on the Utah Attorney General's motion to vacate a stay of execution of sentence entered two days earlier by that Court. Gilmore was present, and, in response to questions from several Justices, stated that he thought he had received a fair trial and a proper sentence, that he opposed any appeal in the case, and that he wished to withdraw an appeal previously filed without his consent by appointed trial counsel. Finally, at a hearing before the trial court on December 1, Gilmore again informed the court that he opposed all appeals that had been filed. When the record establishing a knowing and intelligent waiver of Gary Mark Gilmore's right to Seek appellate review is combined with the December 8 written response submitted to this Court, it is plain that the Court is without jurisdiction to entertain the "next friend" application filed by Bessie Gilmore. This Court has jurisdiction pursuant to Art. III of the Constitution only over "cases and controversies," and we can issue stays only in aid of our jurisdiction. There is no dispute, presently before us, between Gary Mark Gilmore and the State of Utah, and the application of Bessie Gilmore manifestly fails to meet the statutory requirements to invoke this Court's power to review the action of the Supreme Court of Utah. No authority to the contrary has been brought to our attention, and nothing suggested in dissent bears on the threshold question of jurisdiction. In his dissenting opinion, Mr. Justice WHITE suggests that Gary Mark Gilmore is "unable" as a matter of law to waive the right to state appellate review. Whatever may be said as to the merits of this suggestion, the question simply is not before us. Gilmore, duly found to be competent by the Utah courts, has had available meaningful access to this Court and has declined expressly to assert any claim here other than his explicit repudiation of Bessie Gilmore's effort to speak for him as next friend. It follows, therefore, that the Court is without jurisdiction to consider the question posed by the dissent.

have a constitutional obligation to prevent death row volunteerism. Such an inference of constitutionality is further supported by the Court's Eighth Amendment case law, while opponents of the death penalty, and even some Supreme Court Justices, argue that Eighth Amendment protections are unwaivable for the good of society, a majority of the Court has not adopted this position. Attempts to characterize death row volunteerism as suicide under the Fourteenth Amendment similarly support the right for capital defendants to waive post-conviction appeals. Death row volunteers probably are not irrational actors seeking to end their lives because of clinical depression or other mental illness—at least when states adhere to the constitutional guidelines for competency. * * * Rather, competent death row volunteers probably are more like terminally ill patients who seek to commit physician-assisted suicide or who reject lifesaving treatment—although both of these analogies have their drawbacks, either because constitutional doctrine is unsettled (in the case of physician-assisted suicide), or because the conceptual leap required by the analogy (in the case of refusal of lifesaving treatment) is a bit extreme.

Why are scholars and practitioners so eager to challenge the constitutionality of death row volunteerism despite little doctrinal support? Some are acting from a belief that states have little incentive to ensure that capital defendants who waive their appeals are competent. Others believe that the death penalty must be applied justly in all cases to preserve the public's faith in the "rightness" of the criminal justice system, and such a just application only can be attained through a rigorous appeals process. But in most cases, these members of the legal community are acting from a deeply rooted belief that the death penalty itself is inherently unjust, and that death row volunteerism undermines the abolition of capital punishment by allowing defendants to accept an unjust fate. Hugo A. Bedau, a prominent death penalty abolitionist, has been particularly outspoken against death row volunteerism. He argues that one defendant sentenced to death has no right to jeopardize the lives of his fellow death row inmates by waiving his post-conviction appeals; his theory is that execution of one defendant will make it that much easier for states to execute other defendants. Viewing the death penalty as state-sponsored murder, he argues that the death penalty becomes "no less [unjust and unconstitutional] on those occasions when a murderer welcomes his own legal execution[,]" though there is concern that states that administer capital punishment might disagree. Yet while these arguments may be compelling from a policy per-

Food for Thought

In *Jones v. Barnes, supra,* Justice Brennan asserted that the Supreme Court had decided to view lawyers as protecting substantial justice rather than the autonomy of the client. In the death volunteer cases, the Court has decided to protect the client's autonomy, without regard to the system's concern for substantive justice. What explains the Court's different approaches to these cases? Do you agree with the Court's decisions?

spective--in fact, they are viewpoints that I share--they are not rooted in constitutional doctrine. As constitutional law currently stands, to eliminate the individual right to death row volunteerism legal scholars and practitioners with abolitionist beliefs first must convince courts and/or legislatures to eliminate the death penalty itself.

[Question 6]

A county law prohibits stores from selling alcoholic beverages before noon on Sundays. Failure to comply is a misdemeanor punishable by a fine of $150.

An attorney was hired by a client who owns several liquor stores. The client asked the attorney whether any store owners had been prosecuted for violating the law and whether the fine could be imposed for every sale on a Sunday before noon or only for every Sunday on which alcohol was sold before noon. The client also asked what he could do to minimize the risk that he would be detected. The attorney accurately told the client that the fine could only be imposed for each Sunday on which he sold alcoholic beverages before noon, not for each transaction, and that no one had been prosecuted under the law as yet. She also told him that she thought it would be improper to advise him about how to avoid detection. The client thanked the attorney for the information and hung up. Several weeks later, the attorney learned that the client had begun to open his store for business on Sundays at 9 a.m.

Is the attorney subject to discipline?

(A) Yes, because the attorney reasonably should have known that the information she gave the client would encourage him to violate the law.

(B) Yes, because the attorney did not discourage her client from breaking the law.

(C) No, because the attorney merely gave the client her honest opinion about the consequences that were likely to result if he violated the law.

(D) No, because the lawyer and the client could have discussed the best way to avoid detection under the criminal law.

Rule 1.2

(d) A lawyer shall not counsel a client to engage, or assist a client, in conduct that the lawyer knows is criminal or fraudulent, but a lawyer may discuss the legal consequences of any proposed course of conduct with

a client and may counsel or assist a client to make a good faith effort to
determine the validity, scope, meaning or application of the law.

PEOPLE v. CHAPPELL

927 P.2d 829 (Colo. 1996)

PER CURIAM.

A hearing panel of the supreme court grievance committee approved the findings
and the recommendation of a hearing board that the respondent in this lawyer
discipline case be disbarred. The respondent has not excepted to the panel's
action. We accept the hearing panel's recommendation.

I.

The respondent was admitted to practice law in Colorado in 1977. Because the
respondent did not answer the complaint, a default was entered against her, and
the allegations of fact contained in the complaint were deemed admitted. Based
on the respondent's default and the evidence presented, the hearing board found
that the following had been established by clear and convincing evidence.

A man and woman were married in April 1991, and their son was born later that
year. On December 13, 1993, the husband filed a petition for dissolution of the
marriage. The wife was then pregnant with their daughter who was born on June
13, 1994. The respondent represented the wife in the dissolution proceeding.

The husband vacated the family home in January 1994. A mutual restraining
order prevented either party from removing the child from Colorado. The dissolution court granted temporary custody of the son and use of the family home
to the respondent's client. The husband was ordered to pay child support and
maintenance directly to the wife in the amount of $1,500 per month. A temporary
orders hearing was scheduled for March 11, 1994.

Dr. Jean LaCrosse was appointed to do a custody evaluation for the court. Two
days before the temporary orders hearing, the respondent and her client met with
Dr. LaCrosse who advised them that she was recommending that the husband be
granted sole custody of both the son and the unborn daughter.

Later, the respondent told her client that the court would probably accept Dr.
LaCrosse's recommendations. The wife states that the respondent advised her as
her attorney to stay, but as a mother to run. The respondent also informed her
client about a network of safehouses for people in her situation, and helped her

to liquidate her assets and empty her bank accounts. The respondent contacted a friend of her client and asked the friend to pack her client's belongings from the marital home and to put them into storage. The friend states that the respondent let her into the home with a key, and gave her money, provided to the respondent by her client, to pay for the moving and storage. The respondent kept the storage locker key according to the friend.

The respondent appeared for the temporary orders hearing on March 11, 1994 without her client. The respondent's request for a one week continuance was granted. Nevertheless, the court allowed the husband to testify concerning the temporary orders. The respondent argued against a change in the interim orders and stated that the child was doing well in his own home. When the trial judge questioned her as to the whereabouts of her client, the respondent replied that she was unable to answer because of the attorney-client privilege. The court then ordered an immediate change of custody to the husband, as well as continued support payments. The respondent asked the court to order the support payments to be made through the court's registry.

After the husband's lawyer requested it, the court rescinded the portion of the temporary restraining order that prohibited the husband from going onto the property where the child was located. The court asked the respondent to call the child's day care center and advise persons there of the change in the restraining order, and the respondent agreed to make the call. Following the hearing, the respondent notified her client of the change in the custody order.

When the husband went to the wife's residence, he discovered that she had moved. His lawyer then filed an emergency motion for custody and pick-up of the child, which was granted, and a petition for writ of habeas corpus, which was heard on March 16, 1994.

The respondent appeared in court on March 16, advised the court that she would assert the attorney-client privilege, and asked for time to hire a lawyer to represent her. The court also heard testimony from her client's friend concerning the events just prior to the March 11 hearing.

On March 21, 1994, the court ordered the return of the husband's property that was then in storage. In addition, the respondent, who was represented by counsel, testified regarding the attorney-client privilege and the exceptions to the privilege concerning a client's criminal or fraudulent acts or intentions. Upon order of the court, the respondent testified that she had notified her client of the March 11 revised custody order.

The respondent subsequently testified on March 25, 1994, that she and her client had been in contact five or six times since the March 11 hearing, and that her client was out of the state. The respondent also testified that her client had asked her to safeguard her property and that in compliance with that request, she had rented a storage facility for that purpose. The respondent then withdrew from the case.

The wife was out of Colorado for two weeks, and when she returned she and her child lived at a battered women's shelter. The husband gained physical custody of the child after the wife went to the hospital for a prenatal visit. She then retained another lawyer to represent her.

A few days after the birth of the daughter, the court entered temporary orders granting immediate custody of the infant to the husband. The court also found that the respondent had perpetrated a fraud on the court when she accepted the husband's offer to continue paying support and maintenance on March 11, despite the change in custody. The court stated that the respondent "was aware that her client was on the run with the child and yet accepted the offer of child support and maintenance." After terminating the support order, the court ordered that $1,500 held in the court's registry be returned to the husband.

A permanent orders hearing was held in March 1995. The wife testified that the respondent had explained "the underground" to her, had assisted in emptying her bank accounts, and had advised her on how to avoid being caught. The wife was charged with violation of a child custody order, contrary to section 18-3-304(2), 8B C.R.S. (1986), a class 5 felony. The wife pleaded guilty in exchange for a three-year deferred judgment.

The respondent's conduct violated R.P.C. 1.2(d) (a lawyer "shall not counsel a client to engage, or assist a client, in conduct that the lawyer knows is criminal or fraudulent"); R.P.C. 3.3(a)(2) (a lawyer shall not knowingly fail to disclose a material fact to a tribunal when disclosure is necessary to avoid assisting a criminal or fraudulent act by the client); R.P.C. 8.4(b) (it is professional misconduct for a lawyer to commit a criminal act by aiding the lawyer's client to commit a crime); and R.P.C. 8.4(c) (it is professional misconduct for a lawyer to engage in conduct involving dishonesty, fraud, deceit or misrepresentation).

II.

The hearing panel approved the board's recommendation that the respondent be disbarred, and the respondent has not excepted to that recommendation. * * *

In *People v. Bullock*, 882 P.2d 1390, 1391-92 (Colo.1994), we disbarred a lawyer following his conviction for aiding a client who was a fugitive from justice by arranging to supply the client with money. Given the seriousness of the respondent's conduct in aiding her client to violate the custody order resulting in the client being charged with a felony, the fact that the respondent has not been charged or convicted of an offense is not important for disciplinary purposes. * * *

The respondent used her license to violate the core ethical and professional standards of her profession. Disbarment is the only appropriate form of discipline. Accordingly, we accept the hearing panel's recommendation and order that the respondent be disbarred.

III.

It is hereby ordered that Lorraine A. Chappell be disbarred and that her name be stricken from the list of attorneys authorized to practice before this court, effective thirty days after the issuance of this opinion.

[Question 7]

Attorney represented Landlord in a variety of matters over several years. Plaint, an elderly widow living on public assistance, filed suit against Landlord alleging that Landlord withheld without justification the security deposit on a rental unit that Plaint vacated three years ago. She brought the action for herself, without counsel, in small claims court. Attorney investigated the claim and learned that it was legally barred by the applicable statute of limitations, although Plaint's underlying claim was meritorious. Attorney told Landlord of the legal defense, but emphasized that Plaint's claim was just and that, in all fairness, the security deposit should be returned to Plaint. Attorney told Landlord:

"I strongly recommend that you pay Plaint the full amount with interest. It is against your long-term business interests to be known in the community as a landlord who routinely withholds security deposits even though the tenant leaves the apartment in good condition. Paying the claim now will prevent future headaches for you."

Was Attorney's conduct proper?

(A) Yes, if Landlord did not object to Attorney's advice and paid Plaint's claim.

(B) Yes, because Attorney may refer to both legal and nonlegal considerations in advising a client.

(C) No, unless Attorney's engagement letter informed Landlord that Attorney's advice on the matter would include both legal and nonlegal considerations.

(D) No, because in advising Landlord to pay the full claim, Attorney failed to represent zealously Landlord's legal interests.

Rule 2.1

> In representing a client, a lawyer shall exercise independent professional judgment and render candid advice. In rendering advice, a lawyer may refer not only to law but to other considerations such as moral, economic, social and political factors, that may be relevant to the client's situation.

BOARD OF PROFESSIONAL RESPONSIBILITY OF THE SUPREME COURT OF TENNESSEE,

Op. No. 96-F-140, 1996 WL 340719 (1996)

[In Part III of this Chapter, *supra*, we excerpted the portion of this opinion discussing whether an attorney who believes abortion is murder must represent a teenage girl seeking court permission for an abortion without notifying her parents. The attorney also asked the Board of Professional Responsibility whether he could "advise the minor seeking an abortion about alternatives and/or advise her to speak with her parents or legal guardian about the potential abortion?" The Board responded that:]

 If the appointed attorney represents only the minor (as we believe), then counsel has a duty to "explain a matter to the extent reasonably necessary to permit the client to make informed decisions regarding the representation." Whether informing the minor about alternatives to abortion and suggesting that she discuss the potential procedure with her parents or legal guardian is ethically appropriate may depend on a case-by-case analysis. If the minor is truly mature and well-informed enough to go forward and make the decision on her own, then counsel's hesitation and advice for the client to consult with others could possibly implicate a lack of zealous representation under DR 7-101(A)(4)(a) and (c) (a lawyer shall not intentionally fail to Seek the client's lawful objectives, or prejudice or damage his client during the course of the professional relationship). Counsel also has a duty of undivided loyalty to his client, and should not allow any other persons or entities to regulate, direct, compromise, control or interfere with his professional judgment. To the extent that counsel strongly recommends that his client discuss the potential abortion with her parents or with other individuals or entities which are known to oppose such a choice, compliance with Canon 5 [governing conflicts of interest] is called into question.

The Board decided this matter under the provisions of the Code that preceded the Rules. What should the result be under the Rules?

[Question 8]

Attorney represents Client, the plaintiff in a civil action that was filed a year ago and is about to be set for trial. Client informed Attorney that he could be available at any time during the months of October, November, and December. In discussing possible trial dates with opposing counsel and the court clerk, Attorney was advised that a trial date on October 5 was available and that the next available trial date would be December 10. Without first consulting Client, Attorney requested the December 10 trial date because she was representing Deft, the defendant in a felony criminal trial that was set for October 20 and she wanted as much time as possible to prepare for that trial.

Was it proper for Attorney to agree to the December trial date without obtaining Client's consent?

  (A) Yes, unless Client will be prejudiced by the delay.

  (B) Yes, because a criminal trial takes precedence over a civil trial.

  (C) No, because Attorney should manage her calendar so that her cases can be tried promptly.

  (D) No, unless Attorney was court-appointed counsel in the criminal case.

[Question 9]

Plaintiff and Defendant are next-door neighbors and bitter personal enemies. Plaintiff is suing Defendant over an alleged trespass. Each party believes, in good faith, in the correctness of his position. Plaintiff is represented by Attorney Alpha, and Defendant is represented by Attorney Beta. After Plaintiff had retained Alpha, he told Alpha "I do not want you to grant any delays or courtesies to Defendant or his lawyer. I want you to insist on every technicality."

Alpha has served Beta with a demand to answer written interrogatories. Beta, because of the illness of his secretary, has asked Alpha for a five-day extension of time within which to answer them.

Is Alpha subject to discipline if she grants Beta's request for a five-day extension?

  (A) Yes, because Alpha is acting contrary to her client's instructions.

  (B) Yes, unless Alpha first informs Plaintiff of the request and obtains Plaintiff's consent to grant it.

(C) No, unless granting the extension would prejudice Plaintiff's rights

(D) No, because Beta was not at fault in causing the delay.

In answering these questions, start with Rule 1.2(a) and the Comment that:

[2] On occasion, however, a lawyer and a client may disagree about the means to be used to accomplish the client's objectives. Clients normally defer to the special knowledge and skill of their lawyer with respect to the means to be used to accomplish their objectives, particularly with respect to technical, legal and tactical matters. Conversely, lawyers usually defer to the client regarding such questions as the expense to be incurred and concern for third persons who might be adversely affected. Because of the varied nature of the matters about which a lawyer and client might disagree and because the actions in question may implicate the interests of a tribunal or other persons, this Rule does not prescribe how such disagreements are to be resolved. Other law, however, may be applicable and should be consulted by the lawyer. The lawyer should also consult with the client and Seek a mutually acceptable resolution of the disagreement. If such efforts are unavailing and the lawyer has a fundamental disagreement with the client, the lawyer may withdraw from the representation. *See* Rule 1.16(b)(4). Conversely, the client may resolve the disagreement by discharging the lawyer. *See* Rule 1.16(a)(3).

[3] At the outset of a representation, the client may authorize the lawyer to take specific action on the client's behalf without further consultation. Absent a material change in circumstances and subject to Rule 1.4, a lawyer may rely on such an advance authorization. The client may, however, revoke such authority at any time.

Rule 1.3 provides that "A lawyer shall act with reasonable diligence and promptness in representing a client."

The Comment adds:

[1] A lawyer should pursue a matter on behalf of a client despite opposition, obstruction or personal inconvenience to the lawyer, and take whatever lawful and ethical measures are required to vindicate a client's cause or endeavor. A lawyer must also act with commitment and dedication to the interests of the client and with zeal in advocacy upon the client's behalf. A lawyer is not bound, however, to press for every advantage that might be realized for a client. For example, a lawyer may have authority to exercise professional discretion in determining the means by which a matter should be pursued. *See* Rule 1.2. The lawyer's duty to act with reasonable diligence does not require the use of offensive tactics or preclude the treating of all persons involved in the legal process with courtesy and respect.

[2] A lawyer's work load must be controlled so that each matter can be handled competently.

Rule 1.4 provides that:

(a) A lawyer shall:

> (1) promptly inform the client of any decision or circumstance with re-spect to which the client's informed consent, as defined in Rule 1.0(e), is required by these Rules;

> (2) reasonably consult with the client about the means by which the cli-ent's objectives are to be accomplished;

> (3) keep the client reasonably informed about the status of the matter;

> (4) promptly comply with reasonable requests for information; and

> (5) consult with the client about any relevant limitation on the lawyer's conduct when the lawyer knows that the client expects assistance not permitted by the Rules of Professional Conduct or other law.

(b) A lawyer shall explain a matter to the extent reasonably necessary to permit the client to make informed decisions regarding the representation.

Rule 3.2

A lawyer shall make reasonable efforts to expedite litigation consistent with the interests of the client.

The Comment to Rule 3.2 adds:

The question is whether a competent lawyer acting in good faith would regard the course of action as having some substantial purpose other than delay. Real-izing financial or other benefit from otherwise improper delay in litigation is not a legitimate interest of the client.

Restatement § 21 Comment d

A lawyer is not required to carry out an instruction that the lawyer reasonably believes to be contrary to professional rules or other law or which the lawyer reasonably believes to be unethical or similarly objectionable.

Restatement § 23 Comment d

Lawyers * * * have inherent authority, not subject to alteration by contract with their clients, to act and decide for clients when the legal system requires an immediate decision without time for consultation. Whether a decision falls in that category depends on the requirements of procedural systems and orders of tribunals, as well as on such circumstances as the availability of the client for immediate consultation and the effect of interruption for consultation on the orderly and effective presentation of the client's matter. The lawyer must keep the client informed of the progress of the matter and must comply, when time permits, with the client's expressed wishes to be consulted about specified matters * * * A client may give advance instructions, which the lawyer must honor to the extent that court rules and professional obligations permit.

[Question 11]

Robin and Terry had been good friends at Roosevelt Law School. Robin is now defending a big tobacco company in lawsuits from survivors of people who died from second-hand smoke. Terry thinks this is reprehensible. Robin responds that rules specifically authorize her to represent a client she finds reprehensible. Is she correct?

  (A) Yes

  (B) No

Rule 1.2(b)

A lawyer's representation of a client, including representation by appointment, does not constitute an endorsement of the client's political, economic, social or moral views or activities.

Go Online

For a provocative discussion of Rule 1.2(b), *see* Andre A. Borgeas, Note, *Necessary Adherence to Model Rule 1.2(b): Attorneys Do Not Endorse the Acts or Views of Their Clients by Virtue of Representation*, 13 Geo. J. Legal Ethics 761 (2000).

[Question 12]

Rhonda Lawyer, a staff attorney with Fordham Legal Services, represents Thomas Tenant in a non-payment eviction case brought by Lawrence Landlord. Tenant refuses to pay rent because he believes Landlord is shooting invisible but dangerous gamma rays into his apartment. Tenant offers no scientific evidence for this contention and Lawyer finds it unbelievable. Tenant insists that Lawyer counter-claim for breach of the warranty of habitability on account of the gamma rays and states that he will refuse to pay his rent even if it means he will be evicted and become homeless. When Lawyer

suggests that Tenant seek a guardian to help him, Tenant angrily refuses. Lawyer reasonably believes the client has diminished capacity. Under the Rules, Lawyer may do all the following except:

(A) follow Tenant's instructions.

(B) seek appointment of a guardian.

(C) consult with client's daughter.

(D) ask court permission to withdraw from representing Tenant.

Review Rules 1.2(a) and 1.16(b)

Rule 1.14 Client with Diminished Capacity

(a) When a client's capacity to make adequately considered decisions in connection with a representation is diminished, whether because of minority, mental impairment or for some other reason, the lawyer shall, as far as reasonably possible, maintain a normal client-lawyer relationship with the client.

(b) When the lawyer reasonably believes that the client has diminished capacity, is at risk of substantial physical, financial or other harm unless action is taken and cannot adequately act in the client's own interest, the lawyer may take reasonably necessary protective action, including consulting with individuals or entities that have the ability to take action to protect the client and, in appropriate cases, seeking the appointment of a guardian ad litem, conservator or guardian.

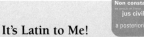

It's Latin to Me!

Black's Law Dictionary defines *guardian ad litem* as "[a] guardian, [usually] a lawyer, appointed by the court to appear in a law situation on behalf of an incompetent or minor party."

The Comment adds:

[1] The normal client-lawyer relationship is based on the assumption that the client, when properly advised and assisted, is capable of making decisions about important matters. When the client is a minor or suffers from a diminished mental capacity, however, maintaining the ordinary client-lawyer relationship may not be possible in all respects. In particular, a severely incapacitated person may have no power to make legally binding decisions. Nevertheless, a client with diminished capacity often has the ability to understand, deliberate upon, and reach conclusions about matters affecting the client's own well-being. * * *

[2] The fact that a client suffers a disability does not diminish the lawyer's obligation to treat the client with attention and respect. Even if the person has a legal representative, the lawyer should as far as possible accord the represented person the status of client, particularly in maintaining communication. * * *

[4] If a legal representative has already been appointed for the client, the lawyer should ordinarily look to the representative for decisions on behalf of the client. * * *

[5] If a lawyer reasonably believes that a client is at risk of substantial physical, financial or other harm unless action is taken, and that a normal client-lawyer relationship cannot be maintained as provided in paragraph (a) because the client lacks sufficient capacity to communicate or to make adequately considered decisions in connection with the representation, then paragraph (b) permits the lawyer to take protective measures deemed necessary. Such measures could include: consulting with family members, using a reconsideration period to permit clarification or improvement of circumstances, using voluntary surrogate decisionmaking tools such as durable powers of attorney or consulting with support groups, professional services, adult-protective agencies or other individuals or entities that have the ability to protect the client. In taking any protective action, the lawyer should be guided by such factors as the wishes and values of the client to the extent known, the client's best interests and the goals of intruding into the client's decisionmaking autonomy to the least extent feasible, maximizing client capacities and respecting the client's family and social connections.

[6] In determining the extent of the client's diminished capacity, the lawyer should consider and balance such factors as: the client's ability to articulate reasoning leading to a decision, variability of state of mind and ability to appreciate consequences of a decision; the substantive fairness of a decision; and the consistency of a decision with the known long-term commitments and values of the client. In appropriate circumstances, the lawyer may seek guidance from an appropriate diagnostician.

[7] If a legal representative has not been appointed, the lawyer should consider whether appointment of a guardian ad litem, conservator or guardian is necessary to protect the client's interests. * * * In many circumstances, however, appointment of a legal representative may be more expensive or traumatic for the client than circumstances in fact require. Evaluation of such circumstances is a matter entrusted to the professional judgment of the lawyer. In considering alternatives, however, the lawyer should be aware of any law that requires the lawyer to advocate the least restrictive action on behalf of the client. * * *

[8] Disclosure of the client's diminished capacity could adversely affect the client's interests. For example, raising the question of diminished capacity could, in some circumstances, lead to proceedings for involuntary commitment. Information relating to the representation is protected by Rule 1.6. Therefore, unless

authorized to do so, the lawyer may not disclose such information. When taking protective action pursuant to paragraph (b), the lawyer is impliedly authorized to make the necessary disclosures, even when the client directs the lawyer to the contrary. Nevertheless, given the risks of disclosure, paragraph (c) limits what the lawyer may disclose in consulting with other individuals or entities or Seeking the appointment of a legal representative. At the very least, the lawyer should determine whether it is likely that the person or entity consulted with will act adversely to the client's interests before discussing matters related to the client. The lawyer's position in such cases is an unavoidably difficult one.

Rule 3.1 provides that "[a] lawyer shall not bring or defend a proceeding, or assert or controvert an issue therein, unless there is a basis in law and fact for doing so that is not frivolous, which includes a good faith argument for an extension, modification or reversal of existing law."

Food for Thought

Michael Perlin warns of the danger of Sanism in representing persons with mental health disabilities. He argues that:

> Sanism is an irrational prejudice of the same quality and character as other irrational prejudices that cause and are reflected in prevailing social attitudes of racism, sexism, homophobia and ethnic bigotry. It permeates all aspects of mental disability law and affects all participants in the mental disability law system: litigants, fact finders, counsel, expert and lay witnesses. Its corrosive effects have warped mental disability law jurisprudence in involuntary civil commitment law, institutional law, tort law, and all aspects of the criminal process (pretrial, trial and sentencing). It reflects what civil rights lawyer Florynce Kennedy has characterized the "pathology of oppression."

> Sanist myths exert especially great power over lawyers who represent persons with mental disabilities. The use of stereotypes, typification, and deindividualization inevitably means that sanist lawyers will trivialize both their client's problems and the importance of any eventual solution to these problems. Sanist lawyers implicitly and explicitly question their clients' competence and credibility, a move that significantly impairs the lawyers' advocacy efforts.

Michael L. Perlin, *"You Have Discussed Lepers and Crooks": Sanism in Clinical Teaching*, 9 Clinical L. Rev. 683, 684 (2003) What changes in Rule 1.14 would be suggested by Perlin's argument? Professor Perlin offers the following critique:

> *First,* the commentary to the rules countenances a situation in which a lawyer can keep information from an ostensibly-mentally-disabled-but-not-incompetent client. Since incompetence cannot be presumed from mental disability, there is no principled reason offered in support of this position.

> *Second,* the rules continue to ignore some of the most important ethical problems facing counsel representing persons with mental disabilities who wish to refuse the imposition of psychotropic medications, and representing such a person who wishes to control his own funds. * * *

1 Michael L. Perlin, Mental Disability Law: Civil and Criminal §2B-10.2 (1998). What do you think of his critique of sanism? Of Rule 1.14?

Representing Children

Rule 1.14 governs the representation of children. The Comment discusses children specifically only in passing:

[c]hildren as young as five or six years of age, and certainly those of ten or twelve, are regarded as having opinions that are entitled to weight in legal proceedings concerning their custody. * * *

In matters involving a minor, whether the lawyer should look to the parents as natural guardians may depend on the type of proceeding or matter in which the lawyer is representing the minor. If the lawyer represents the guardian as distinct from the ward, and is aware that the guardian is acting adversely to the ward's interest, the lawyer may have an obligation to prevent or rectify the guardian's misconduct. *See* Rule 1.2(d).

As the following article explains, the proper representation of children has been the subject of extensive debate.

JONATHAN O. HAFEN, *CHILDREN'S RIGHTS AND LEGAL REPRESENTATION— THE PROPER ROLES OF CHILDREN, PARENTS, AND ATTORNEYS*

7 Notre Dame J.L. Ethics & Pub. Pol'y 423 (1993)

* * * [A]ttorneys representing children currently have insufficient guidance or, in some cases, experience to answer these questions themselves. Therefore, the Model Rules of Professional Conduct, as the best vehicle for defining the attorney-client relationship, should be revised to provide specific directions to attorneys representing children.

* * *

Hillary Rodham Clinton was one of the earliest and most articulate voices speaking out for children's liberation. During the early part of her legal career, she wrote several influential articles on children's rights and worked for the Children's Defense Fund.

* * *

In these early writings, Hillary Rodham Clinton advocated taking certain steps to allow children to have more control over important decisions which are made on their behalf. In one of her earliest articles, Ms. Clinton proposed a three-step plan to achieve this goal of "children's liberation." First, she advocated that "the legal status of infancy, or minority, should be abolished and the presumption of incompetency reversed;" next she urged that "all procedural rights guaranteed to adults under the Constitution should be granted to children whenever the state or a third party moves against them, judicially or administratively;" and finally, she asserted that "the presumption of identity of interests between parents and their children should be rejected whenever the child has interests demonstrably independent of those of his parents (as determined by the consequences to both of the act in question), and a competent child should be permitted to assert his or her own interests."

... Hillary Rodham Clinton asserted that "competent children" should be permitted to assert their own interests under certain circumstances. Because there would be a presumption of capacity—rather than the current presumption of incapacity — for all children, children would be able to hire and direct attorneys unless this presumption could be overcome. Logically, the existence of such a presumption makes assertion of its opposite more difficult; thus, it would be much more likely under Ms. Clinton's proposal that children would be found competent to act on their own behalf than it is under current law. Moreover, Hillary Rodham Clinton also stated that children should have the right to counsel in all types of proceedings and that the child-client should be able to control the scope and course of the litigation. She goes so far as to suggest that it should be a violation of an attorney's professional responsibility for the attorney to determine the child's best interests on behalf of the child. Therefore, under Ms. Clinton's proposal, it would be up to the child himself or herself to decide what is in his or her own long-term best interests, a difficult task for children generally and for younger children especially.

* * *

Due to the broad discretion which attorneys representing child-clients possess as to the scope and objectives of the litigation, several dangers exist. For instance, certain child advocacy organizations believe that the child should control the litigation seemingly regardless of the child's age or maturity. Such organizations have begun to operate on a local and national scale. Due to some children's inability to afford counsel, children often turn to such organizations seeking legal representation.

One national organization, The National Child's Rights Alliance (NCRA), submitted a brief amicus curiae in the Gregory K. case. Significantly, NCRA sought recognition of nearly all of the "children's rights" that Hillary Rodham Clinton articulated in her early legal writings. Thus, NCRA asserted that children should have the unlimited right to sue in their own name for termination of parental rights. * * * For example, NCRA's national coordinator recently told the New York Times that she believes that children should "have the right to be heard in court just as soon as they can talk . . . We have had experience with children as young as 3 years old saying, 'I don't want to live here anymore. . . .' We feel that all children should have the right to know what their civil rights are and have access to the people who can help them assert those rights." Such rhetoric implies that this organization fails to recognize the importance of the role of parents in a child's decisionmaking process, especially where the child's rights may be affected by litigation in which the child is involved.

* * * However, other children's organizations * * * contend that the * * * "mission to empower children at all costs can be irresponsible." * * * Cook County Public Guardian Patrick Murphy, whose office has represented over 14,000 children in various proceedings * * * welcomes additional advocates willing to represent children, [but] he points out that allowing a child to have the exclusive right to direct an attorney may be unwise: "My 10-year-old son would eat ice cream all night and watch R-rated movies, but I say 'no,' and that is my job as an adult. My job as a lawyer is not to cave in to every goofy whim of a client, particularly a child." Professor Guggenheim expresses a similar view on the general issue of absolute representation of a child's wishes:

Infants, for example, lack even the linguistic capacity to instruct counsel. Slightly older children, on the other hand, are capable of directing an attorney; nevertheless, to allow a child of age five to instruct counsel would be problematic. As attorneys experienced in this field are aware, many young children equivocate when asked about their preferences or views on a matter; thus, having an attorney take his guidance from the child may result in practice in the attorney taking whatever position he himself thinks best. More fundamentally, very young children lack the capacity to make considered and intelligent choices. While the attorney need not and should not ignore the child's wishes in the litigation, most readers would agree that the attorney ought not be bound by those wishes.

Because the Model Rules fail to give guidance on the proper course which attorneys should follow in determining whether the child-client is capable of being treated like an adult client, it is completely up to the attorney to decide whether to follow the child's wishes. As Professor Guggenheim puts it: "Lawyers are accustomed to doing their client's bidding. The lawyer who represents the young child, however, finds himself in a new, and rather intoxicating, situation. Now it is he, and not the nominal client, who has the power to control the course of the litigation." This is especially significant in light of the fact that studies have shown that judges often rely heavily on the child's counsel in making determinations concerning the child's future as well as the futures of other members of the child's family. At times this may pit the wishes of the parents against the wishes of the child's attorney, a conflict which should fall in favor of the parents under the established right of parents to raise their children as they See fit, unless the parents have forfeited their parental rights through abuse, neglect or abandonment of the child.

An example of an attorney possibly disregarding the wishes of her child-clients is found in Smith v. Organization of Foster Families for Equality and Reform (OFFER). In OFFER, foster parents and a foster parents organization sought declaratory and injunctive relief against New York State and New York City officials, claiming that the procedures used to remove foster children from foster homes violated the Due Process and Equal Protection Clauses of the Fourteenth Amendment. During the course of the proceedings before the district court, the judge appointed a lawyer to represent both the seven named foster children and the much larger class of foster children who were also parties to the litigation. In reviewing the actions of the attorney representing the children in OFFER, Professors Wald and Chambers noted that the attorney failed to ascertain the specific needs and wishes of her plaintiff class. Instead, the attorney based her actions on her own experience with the New York foster care program and substantially aligned herself with defendants, a position in direct conflict with those of the named plaintiffs she ostensibly represented. The attorney for the children also declined an invitation to divide the children into two separate classes, even though such an action could have arguably better protected her client's interests.

Such conduct suggests that where an attorney represents a "cause," such as child-welfare reform, there is a danger that the children whose cases are used as a vehicle to move the reform forward will have their individual best interests knowingly or unknowingly sacrificed by the attorney for the sake of the cause. Professor Mnookin has accurately described the attorney-client relationship itself as conducive to sacrificing the best interests of the particular client for the sake of a general cause:

The problem of ensuring that advocates work towards the best interests of the client is inherent in any system which uses counsel to represent clients. Where one party is given the authority to put forward another's interests, there is always the danger that the agent will not be faithful to the interests of his client. The agent may have misperceived something to be in the client's best interest when it actually is not. Finally, wherever power is delegated, there is always the potential and incentive for the agent to put his own interests ahead of those of his client.

* * *

One of the most difficult tasks an attorney can undertake is to represent a minor. As has been previously discussed, such representation is difficult for many reasons, among them are: the uncertainty over the proper role of the attorney in legal proceedings involving minors, potential ethical conflicts which occur when an attorney represents a minor, and questions over who has the right to control the course of the proceeding. These issues have traditionally arisen where the child is suing on his or her own behalf and where the attorney has been hired by the parents or appointed by the state. However, because children today are increasingly given the right to their own counsel in various types of proceedings, and because children might now begin to sue on their own behalf with greater frequency, more attorneys will face these problems than ever before. Thus, it is important for attorneys representing children to recognize the myriad problems which may confront them.

Surprisingly, there is a dearth of guidance available to attorneys representing children. * * * Where the client is a child lacking legal capacity to make binding decisions, the meaning of these functions certainly changes. For example, where the child is very young, it makes no sense to require the attorney to attempt to provide the child-client with an informed understanding of the child's legal rights and obligations. Instead, the lawyer should present this information to the child's parents if they are not disqualified or their interests are not in conflict with the child's, or to the guardian ad litem where the parents are not available or have lost their right to act on the child's behalf. If there is no guardian ad litem, then the attorney may view her or his role as a de facto guardian ad litem and inform the court of the options available to the child. This is the way it should be. However, under the current Model Rules, the attorney could justifiably conclude that he or she has discretion to determine what the position of the child should be and then "zealously advocate" that position. No ethical check or balance on the exercise of that discretion now exists.

Where the child is older, the attorney must then determine to what extent the child has the right to control the litigation. There is no clear guidance in the Model Rules concerning who should control the litigation in this instance. Should it be the parents unless they are unfit? What if the parents have a dispute with the child over lifestyle choices and the child takes them to court over it? What should the role of the judge be in determining the competence of the child to direct the litigation? These questions remain open to speculation under the current Model Rules.

* * *

c. Model Rule 1.14 Client Under a Disability

The section of the Model Rules which most clearly applies to the legal representation of children is Rule 1.14 "Client Under a Disability." This rule provides as follows:

> (a) When a client's ability to make adequately considered decisions in connection with the representation is impaired, whether because of minority, mental disability or for some other reason, the lawyer shall, as far as reasonably possible, maintain a normal client-lawyer relationship with the client.

(b) A lawyer may Seek the appointment of a guardian or take other protective action with respect to a client, only when the lawyer reasonably believes that the client cannot reasonably act in the client's best interest.

The Comment to this section indicates that despite the child's legal incapacity, the child should be consulted where feasible. The Comment also acknowledges the intermediate degrees of competence which exist among minors. The Comment refers only to the custody proceeding, but in so doing, suggests that children as young as five should have the opportunity to express a custody preference to the person or entity making the custody determination.

Another important aspect of the Comment to Rule 1.14 is its guidance on the appointment of a legal guardian. The Comment provides that where a legal representative has been appointed for the minor-client, the attorney should look to that legal representative for guidance on how to proceed. The Comment goes on to state that where a legal representative has not been appointed, but the attorney believes that it would be in the best interests of the client to have such a representative appointed, the attorney should seek that appointment. Despite the detail with which the Comment treats the appointment of a legal guardian, the Comment completely overlooks the parental role in a child's decisionmaking process.

A troubling entry in the Comment to Rule 1.14 is that where the attorney represents a minor or a person suffering from a disability, and the disclosure of that disability would adversely affect the client's interest, the attorney is in an "unavoidably difficult" situation regarding whether the attorney should disclose the disability. This is problematic because often the attorney is acting not as an advocate but as investigator or factfinder whose role is to provide the judge with additional information relevant to the decision at hand. If the attorney conveys the wishes of the child-client but does not disclose the fact that the attorney believes that the child is completely incapable of offering a reasonable opinion, then the attorney has fulfilled the dictates of the Model Rules but has failed to fulfill his or her proper role as an investigator. And if the attorney were to disclose the inability of the child-client to offer a reasonable opinion, then the client would be breaching Model Rule 1.14. This and other shortcomings in the Model Rules suggest that an amendment to the Model Rules is needed.

* * *

An amendment to the Model Rules would be the least expensive, most effective means of providing attorneys a standard by which to measure their conduct. This is so because nearly all states require attorneys to pass the Multistate Professional Responsibility Exam, which tests lawyers' knowledge of the Model Rules. Therefore, lawyers entering practice would quickly become familiar with the amendment. Other attorneys would likely learn about the amendment through continuing legal education courses or by word of mouth.

One possible amendment which would minimize the dangers of unrestricted representation of child-clients described above would be the following revision of Model Rule 1.14:

> (c) If the client is a minor represented by an attorney, the parent or parents have a rebuttable right to direct the course of the representation. If the interests of the parent or parents conflict with those of the child, or the parent or parents have been found "unfit" by an authorized agency or court, or the parent or parents are otherwise unable to direct the course of the representation, then this presumption is overcome.

>> (1) If this presumption is overcome, then the child's guardian ad litem shall direct the course of the representation.

>> (2) If there is no guardian ad litem, the lawyer shall seek a judicial determination of whether the child is competent to direct the attorney. If the court determines that the child is sufficiently mature to direct the attorney, the attorney shall maintain a normal attorney-client relationship with the child.

>>> (i) In making this competency determination, the court may use rebuttable presumptions concerning typical ages at which minors possess the requisite maturity to make competent decisions on various issues as reflected in current statutes.

>>> (ii) If the court determines that the minor lacks sufficient capacity to direct the attorney, the court shall appoint a neutral guardian ad litem to direct the course of representation.

Adoption of this language would ensure that parental rights in participating in important decisions over a child's future are protected where the parents have not forfeited their rights in this regard. Where parents have forfeited their rights, such as in In re A.W., attorneys would have a specific course to pursue ensuring that immature children would not be permitted to independently direct their attorney at the expense of the child's own long-term best interests. This amendment would also ensure that the attorney would have less discretion to unilaterally control the course of the litigation. Restricting the attorney's discretion in this manner would protect children from potentially unscrupulous counsel tempted to misuse the judicial process.

Food for Thought

What is your view? Do you agree with the author, Hilary Clinton, or one of the other commentators? Should Rule 1.14 be amended?

[Question 13]

The rules require a lawyer to serve as a hired gun for the client.

 (A) True

 (B) False

In answering this question, review the materials under allocation of authority between lawyer and client. Also review David Luban's description of the dominant conception of the lawyer's role, *supra*, at p. 86.

CHAPTER 3

Finding and Billing Clients

I. Introduction

To succeed in private practice, a lawyer needs to find clients and needs to get paid by those clients. Different types of lawyers will approach these tasks differently, depending in significant part on the types of legal services they provide and the size and geographic location of their practice. Whatever these differences, though, lawyers are subject to the same ethical framework. First, the ethics rules seek to protect clients as consumers. Second, they seek to protect the professional identity of lawyers. Critics of the legal profession have questioned the sincerity of these rationales and have argued that the rules instead protect lawyers from competition and from stricter regulation. Challenges to these rules have resulted in significant court decisions regarding the constitutional limitations of lawyer regulation.

While lawyers recognize the vital importance of these topics to maintaining a successful practice, they sometimes find them challenging. The traditional understanding of professionalism relies on the distinction between the behavior of professionals and the behavior of business people. The tasks of finding and billing clients are examples of professionals engaging in business behavior—behavior that blurs the dichotomy between a business and a profession.

Food for Thought

Professors Geoffrey Hazard, Russell Pearce, and Jeffrey Stempel have offered the following explanation of why many lawyers traditionally find the subject of lawyer advertising distasteful. Does their analysis apply more generally to the subject of finding and billing clients?

Perhaps the underlying anxiety about advertising stems from its tendency to portray legal services as a 'business' rather than a 'profession.' Of course, the practice of law manifestly is both a profession and a business, and a highly competitive business at that. Why the passion to deny its character as a business? The answer derives from the notion, basic to our legal ideals, that justice cannot be sold. This notion is central to the ideology of the bar. A group for which that notion is so important inevitably would find it difficult to recognize that access to justice is in any sense a question of buying and selling. Nevertheless, lawyers differ in skill, knowledge, and the time they

Food for Thought (Continued)

can devote to a case, and individuals with more resources are usually able to purchase both a superior lawyer and more of his time. Therefore, justice—actual outcomes in the legal system—is related to the quality of lawyering that a client can afford; justice at the margin can often be bought.

The legal profession is understandably reticent to acknowledge this tension between ideal and reality. One means of avoiding the unpleasant implications of this tension is to minimize overt participation by lawyers in activities, such as advertising, that suggest that effective legal assistance is bought and sold. Opposition to legal advertising, in other words, is a consequence of the inconsistency between providing legal services through the free market and realizing equal justice before the law.

Geoffrey C. Hazard, Jr., Russell G. Pearce & Jeffrey W. Stempel, *Why Lawyers Should Be Allowed to Advertise: A Market Analysis of Legal Services*, 58 N.Y.U. L. Rev. 1084, 1112-13 (1983).

II. Finding Clients

A. An Overview of Marketing Legal Services

As a law student, you are not likely to have much experience with marketing legal services. The materials in this section will provide you with samples from the voluminous literature on this topic. They will introduce you to the way lawyers discuss marketing and help provide the context for your evaluation of the relevant ethical rules.

LARRY BODINE, *WRITING YOUR PERSONAL MARKETING PLAN*

L. Prac. Today, Feb. 2007, *available at* http://www.abanet.org/lpm/lpt/articles/mkt02074.shtml

* * *

If you really want to boost the revenue you bring in to your firm * * * you must have a *written* [sales] plan to devote 100 to 200 hours per year to business development. 100 hours a year is only 2 hours a week, and any lawyer can find that time in meeting a referral source for coffee, taking a client for lunch, or attending a trade association meeting after work.

Your aim is to develop or deepen relationships, because new business comes *in person.* Your plan should be filled with *face-to-face* meetings with clients and targets. The firm's Web site, brochure, articles, newsletters, public relations, direct mail marketing, announcements and press releases will *generate leads* for your sales effort, but you have to go out and *make the sale.*

Keep several things in mind:

- A sales call is not a pitch. No one wants to hear about your credentials. A sales call is an *interview* where you are asking questions to learn about the client's business.

- Don't make any cold calls because they rarely succeed. Focus on people you already know.

- Build on your strengths. If you like to speak in front of a crowd, find a meeting of clients and do so. If instead you are more comfortable one-on-one, then plan dinner parties and private get-togethers where you can talk. Mix business development into your outside activities, hobbies, club memberships and events you enjoy.

- By making the effort, you have already succeeded. * * * Closing a sale takes months of time spent in advance. The more people you know and the more activities you undertake, the better you'll do over the long run.

* * *

STACEY CLARK, NETWORKING: IF DONE RIGHT, IT REALLY WORKS

L. Prac. Today, Dec. 2000, *available at* http://www.abanet.org/lpm/lpt/articles/ftr12093.shtml.

* * *

A guy walks into a bar (no really keep reading). He is an employment lawyer[.] * * * He is meeting an old college friend, but does not see him in the bar. So, he orders a drink and stands next to another gentlemen also seemingly by himself. He turns to the gentlemen and asks, "Have you ever had any food here?". The man says he has the chicken wings all the time, and they are terrific. The lawyer says, "Is your office nearby?" "Yes," he answers, "I work across the street at XYZ, Corp." The lawyer responds, "Oh what do you do for them?" And so the conversation begins.

The lawyer's college friend then comes in and introductions are made all around and quick stories exchanged about the bar, college and their current employers. The lawyer learns the man is about to launch his own technology firm. The lawyer and his friend retreat to a table, but not before exchanging business cards with the man at the bar. The lawyer follows up with the man in the coming months, first sending him an email telling him how great it was to meet him, and second sending him some articles from *Small Business Magazine* on cost-saving "start-up" tips. The lawyer then invites him to lunch to hear how his plans are progressing. Based on the conversation, the lawyer offers to put him in touch with a banker, a start up lawyer and a reporter who covers the trade. The lawyer then invites him to the firm's corporate update briefing for firm clients and friends. And so it goes, the man at the bar became both a friend and client. But, it took work on the part of the lawyer. He made the first move, he asked probing questions, and he followed up consistently over a period of time in a way that was meaningful and actually helpful to the business man.

* * *

BONNIE MAYFIELD, *RAINMAKING: BUSINESS DEVELOPMENT AND RETENTION TECHNIQUES,*

15 Summer Experience 24, 27 (2005)

* * *

Even if you have a mentor assigned to you by your firm or legal organization, you still have to find your own mentors. Find someone you:

- Like;

- Can befriend;

- Want to invest in and who wants to invest in you; and

- Think is on the same career or rainmaking[i] path as you or even ahead of you.

I have mentors both inside and outside of my law firm. * * * Some are lawyers. Some are not. * * * With those who are lawyers, I also refer clients to them and they refer clients to me. With all of them, I discuss rainmaking, career choices, opportunities, and a whole host of other issues * * *

How do you get a "lawyer" mentor? Without knowing that I was selecting a marketing mentor, instinctively, I asked a general counsel of a major pharmaceutical company: "How can I develop clients like you?" In short, the general counsel's answer was: Get on the dais; become a speaker; become known; and become known as an expert in your field. * * * He recommended me to his friends in the industry. * * *

A couple of years ago, an associate did something similar with me. He said he wanted me to be a mentor. * * * We have written two articles together. He attended an ABA Section * * * meeting at which I spoke. He met clients, friends, mentors, colleagues. * * * [H]e volunteered to co-chair an ABA regional meeting. It should be just a matter of time before he lands a big client and obtains referrals from the many "marketing" friends he has made. * * *

---

i   "Rainmaking" is a colloquial expression for developing business.

HELEN W. GUNNARSSON, *TWITTER AND LINKEDIN AND FACEBOOK, OH MY!*,

97 Ill. B.J. 288 (June 2009)

* * *

Networking is nothing new. The Internet simply presents us with more opportunities to interact with more people more efficiently than in person or over the phone. "In cyberspace, you're attending the world's largest cocktail party. Everyone is there," comments Chicago lawyer Sonya Olds Som. And even though the connecting may occur through electronic media, at its heart are the same human-to-human interactions that occur at in-person social functions. * * *

". . . Once you dip your toe in the online conversation, you find that blogs, Facebook, Twitter—and on and on—are all elaborations on (not replacements of) the art of one human relating to another." * * *

Ross believes you'll get out of social media what you put into it. * * *

Along with Som * * * Ross emphasizes her view of proper social networking etiquette. "The first rule is always, 'Give first.' That's something that people in professional services fields should already know, that it's about forming a relationship and not about a transaction first, but it's a good reminder for everybody."

Comments Som, "You shouldn't just be the recipient of recommendations on LinkedIn, and you shouldn't post only when you're looking for a job or to provide a service. There needs to be give and take and back and forth. To the extent that you can, stop and think of ways you can comment on what other people are doing. Interact with them. Provide advice, feedback, assistance, and positive reinforcement to others. Live by the Golden Rule."

Adds [another], "When people extend the virtual hand to you, you shake that hand. When people issue a friend request to you, it's a very good idea to accept it."

* * *

More on social networking for lawyers [Gunnarsson provides a list of resources]

* * *

> "Social Networking for Lawyers: The How, What, Why and Importance of NOW!" by lawyer blogger Carolyn Elefant, a 36-page e-book available for free download: http://www.jdsupra.com/post/documentViewer. aspx?fid=4523296c-275e-49e4-8e31-15bd6231b1c2

BURKEY BELSER ET AL, *LAW FIRM WEBSITES THAT WORK: THESE FIRMS USE THE INTERNET TO GET THE JOB DONE*,

95 A.B.A. J. 32 (Apr. 2009), *available at* http://www.abajournal.com/magazine/article/law_firm_websites_that_work/.

WEBSITES HAVE BECOME THE SHINGLES, BUSINESS cards and phone-book ads of modern lawyering. Even law firms that don't expect much interest from the Internet crowd are being pressed to put up some sort of site, including one called "the world's worst" by its Aussie firm owners.

But what makes a good website? In many ways, it depends on what the site owners want it to do. We asked several experts in Internet presence to recommend websites they feel work well within certain categories. Their choices are meant to be exemplary, not exhaustive.

Here's what our panelists recommend:

BRANDING [Burkey Belser is president of *Greenfield/Belser, a professional services marketing firm* * * *]

* * *

IT'S ALMOST IMPOSSIBLE TO FIND law firm websites that effectively succeed in the all-important job of branding the firm—creating a distinct identity based on a promise of value that is different from any other.

Sameness rules. If fact, when we looked at every one of the Am Law 250 websites * * * we discovered we could re-create the prototypical site. * * * Here's the formula:

- Logo top-left.

- Long, thin image across the top of the site featuring a skyline.

- Below that, three columns of type (news, highlights and a definition of the firm).

As if that weren't bad enough, there are those in charge of website design who demand law firm sites follow that convention because that norm has become equal to "professional site[.]" * * * Enough rant. My job was to discover an exemplar of effective branding. I'm giving the nod to Baker & Hostetler. [http://www.bakerlaw.com]

* * * Here's what I like: Baker & Hostetler follows our three rules of an effective site:

1)   Have a purpose. What do you want the reader to do?

2)   Create a dialogue with the reader.

3)   Position yourself as important, confident and a leader.

How does the firm achieve that goal? First, with a distinct market position on the home page: "counsel to market leaders." If you don't believe that, then just drop below to the proof points that rotate through ("10 of the *Fortune* 25" and other stories) plus the names of those 25 and other "dynamic leaders." Yes, the leaders are self-described as such by the firm, but there's enough proof to convince me to read on.

In any case, they're trying! Don't get me started on Wachtell and Cravath.

ALL BUSINESS [[F]ormer New York City commercial litigator Neil J. Squillante is publisher of *TechnoLawyer Blog* * * *]

       * * *

Using your website to attract clients doesn't require a degree in rocket science. But it does require an understanding of lead generation, which has three components.

1.   Develop a way to attract prospects to your site.

2.   Offer these people something of value so they will part with their contact information.

3.   Contact and qualify prospects quickly, because after visiting your site they will likely go to the sites of other law firms.

       * * *

Gerald M. Oginski [http://www.oginski-law.com] specializes in medical-malpractice cases in the New York metropolitan area. Realizing early on that YouTube essentially offers a free advertising platform for reaching millions of consumers, he began producing short videos. In each, he asks and answers a question about malpractice cases.

Using YouTube's tools, he embeds these videos on his firm's site, which now houses more than 130 videos.

Fit and affable with a slight New York accent, Oginski is an online video natural. His videos make prospects feel as if they have met him. But the videos alone are not sufficient to seal the deal, and he knows it.

That's why you'll also find a blog and dozens of articles and FAQs. This written content attracts prospects from Google searches. After reading an article and perhaps watching a video, they'll gravitate to the most important component of the site, a free, 200-page e-book, *Secrets of a New York Medical-Malpractice and Injury Attorney.*

The e-book resides behind a form. When people fill out the form to get a copy, Oginski gets a lead his team can use to contact and hopefully transform the visitor into a client.

What kind of results has the site delivered? "In April 2006, I accepted a brain-damaged-baby case that came from my website. One week ago that case settled, through trial counsel, for $5.1 million," Oginski says.

Los Angeles divorce and family lawyer Kelly Chang Rickert believes families lie at the heart of successful societies. Her website, Law Offices of Kelly Chang [http://www.purposedrivenlawyers.com], plays a key role in attracting clients. In fact, her site exemplifies the phenomenon of a virtuous cycle.

In 2007 Rickert created a slick YouTube video about her practice that depicted her as an energetic advocate for her clients. This video, which she periodically updates and embeds on her site, led to coverage in print and online media. This press resulted in a regular gig on the television show *Hollywood 411* to discuss celebrity divorce cases.

It all started with her site and has come full circle. She lists every media appearance on the site, linking to audio and video clips if available, and establishing herself as an expert.

What's the upshot? Rickert is busier than ever.

GEOFFREY C. HAZARD, JR., RUSSELL G. PEARCE & JEFFREY W. STEMPEL, WHY LAWYERS SHOULD BE ALLOWED TO ADVERTISE: A MARKET ANALYSIS OF LEGAL SERVICES

58 N.Y.U. L. Rev. 1084, 1094-1100 (1983)

Advertising has advantages and disadvantages for producers as well. Before deciding to advertise, any individual producer must carefully weigh these costs and benefits. Advertising's primary advantage is that it enables the producer to reach and recruit a large number of consumers and thereby to increase revenue; the increased volume may permit the reduction of production costs through economies of scale and thereby generate further increases in profits. Advertising, however, also has drawbacks for the producer. Its chief drawback is its high cost; moreover, efficacy normally requires repetition. Advertising also incurs the costs associated with mass marketing, such as those of preparing for levels of production sufficient to meet the demand generated by advertising promotion. This increased demand may also require some form of standardized production, both to absorb marketing costs and to increase output, and standardized production entails start-up costs such as expenditures for research and development. * * *

Because advertising may fail to alter consumer choice, the producer who advertises is subject to considerable entrepreneurial risk. If he spends a great deal of money and fails to gain the consumers' attention, he has lost much. More importantly, * * * [t]he producer who advertises runs this risk of extraordinary loss because of the general effect that advertising has on consumer behavior. Advertising tends to cause consumers to seek information about the producer's reputation and about other consumers' direct experience with him. Moreover, advertising often better enables consumers to evaluate reputation information. If reputation and experience information are unfavorable, advertising can have the ironic effect of informing a much larger group of consumers about the poor quality of the producer's goods or services. * * *

B. Solicitation

In popular usage, advertising is often understood as a form of solicitation. In the field of legal ethics, however, the word "solicitation" is generally used as a term of art that refers to "direct contact with prospective clients." Rule 7.3. As the marketing literature observes, direct contact is the most effective way to obtain business. *See, e.g.*, Part II.A. *supra*. As the ethics rules and cases explain *infra*, solicitation also creates the greatest threat of harm to consumers. This Part will familiarize you with the relatively straightforward rules you need to follow when you have direct contact with prospective clients.

[Question 1]

Attorney is a sole practitioner whose practice is largely in the areas of tax, wills, estates, and trusts. Attorney learned of a new Internal Revenue Service (IRS) regulation that probably affects the trust provisions in a will she prepared for Testatrix two years ago. Attorney has not represented Testatrix since she drew the will.

Is Attorney subject to discipline if she calls Testatrix and advises her of the new IRS ruling and the need to revise the will?

(A) Yes, if Attorney has any reason to believe that Testatrix has another lawyer.

(B) Yes, because Attorney would be soliciting legal business from a person who is not a current client.

(C) No, provided Attorney does not thereafter prepare a new will for Testatrix.

(D) No, because Testatrix is a former client of Attorney.

OHRALIK v. OHIO STATE BAR ASSOCIATION,

436 U.S. 447 (1978)

POWELL, J., delivered the opinion of the Court

* * *

II

The solicitation of business by a lawyer through direct, in-person communication with the prospective client has long been viewed as inconsistent with the profession's ideal of the attorney-client relationship and as posing a significant potential for harm to the prospective client. It has been proscribed by the organized Bar for many years. Last Term the Court ruled that the justifications for prohibiting truthful, "restrained" advertising concerning "the availability and terms of routine legal services" are insufficient to override society's interest, safeguarded by the First and Fourteenth Amendments, in assuring the free flow of commercial information. * * * The balance struck in *Bates* [434 U.S. 814] does not predetermine the outcome in this case. The entitlement of in-person solicitation of clients to the protection of the First Amendment differs from that of the kind of advertising approved in Bates, as does the strength of the State's countervailing interest in prohibition.

A

Appellant contends that his solicitation of the two young women as clients is indistinguishable, for purposes of constitutional analysis, from the advertisement in Bates. Like that advertisement, his meetings with the prospective clients apprised them of their legal rights and of the availability of a lawyer to pursue their claims. According to appellant, such conduct is "presumptively an exercise of his free speech rights" which cannot be curtailed in the absence of proof that it actually caused a specific harm that the State has a compelling interest in preventing. But in-person solicitation of professional employment by a lawyer does not stand on a par with truthful advertising about the availability and terms of routine legal services, let alone with forms of speech more traditionally within the concern of the First Amendment.

Expression concerning purely commercial transactions has come within the ambit of the Amendment's protection only recently. In rejecting the notion that such speech "is wholly outside the protection of the First Amendment," we were careful not to hold "that it is wholly undifferentiable from other forms" of speech. We have not discarded the "common-sense" distinction between speech proposing a commercial transaction, which occurs in an area traditionally subject to government regulation, and other varieties of speech. To require a parity of constitutional protection for commercial and noncommercial speech alike could invite dilution, simply by a leveling process, of the force of the Amendment's guarantee with respect to the latter kind of speech. Rather than subject the First Amendment to such a devitalization, we instead have afforded commercial speech a limited measure of protection, commensurate with its subordinate position in the scale of First Amendment values, while allowing modes of regulation that might be impermissible in the realm of noncommercial expression.

Moreover, "it has never been deemed an abridgment of freedom of speech or press to make a course of conduct illegal merely because the conduct was in part initiated, evidenced, or carried out by means of language, either spoken, written, or printed." Numerous examples could be cited of communications that are regulated without offending the First Amendment, such as the exchange of information about securities, corporate proxy statements, the exchange of price and production information among competitors, and employers' threats of retaliation for the labor activities of employees. Each of these examples illustrates that the State does not lose its power to regulate commercial activity deemed harmful to the public whenever speech is a component of that activity. Neither *Virginia Pharmacy* [425 U.S. 748] nor *Bates* purported to cast doubt on the permissibility of these kinds of commercial regulation.

In-person solicitation by a lawyer of remunerative employment is a business transaction in which speech is an essential but subordinate component. While this does not remove the speech from the protection of the First Amendment, as was held in *Bates* and *Virginia Pharmacy*, it lowers the level of appropriate judicial scrutiny.

As applied in this case, the Disciplinary Rules are said to have limited the communication of two kinds of information. First, appellant's solicitation imparted to Carol McClintock and Wanda Lou Holbert certain information about his availability and the terms of his proposed legal services. In this respect, in-person solicitation serves much the same function as the advertisement at issue in Bates. But there are significant differences as well. Unlike a public advertisement, which simply provides information and leaves the recipient free to act upon it or not, in-person solicitation may exert pressure and often demands an immediate response, without providing an opportunity for comparison or reflection. The aim and effect of in-person solicitation may be to provide a one-sided presentation and to encourage speedy and perhaps uninformed decisionmaking; there is no opportunity for intervention or counter-education by agencies of the Bar, supervisory authorities, or persons close to the solicited individual. The admonition that "the fitting remedy for evil counsels is good ones" is of little value when the circumstances provide no opportunity for any remedy at all. In-person solicitation is as likely as not to discourage persons needing counsel from engaging in a critical comparison of the "availability, nature, and prices" of legal services,it actually may disserve the individual and societal interest, identified in Bates, in facilitating "informed and reliable decisionmaking."

It also is argued that in-person solicitation may provide the solicited individual with information about his or her legal rights and remedies. In this case, appellant gave Wanda Lou a "tip" about the prospect of recovery based on the uninsured-motorist clause in the McClintocks' insurance policy, and he explained that clause and Ohio's guest statute to Carol McClintock's parents. But neither of the Disciplinary Rules here at issue prohibited appellant from communicating information to these young women about their legal rights and the prospects of obtaining a monetary recovery, or from recommending that they obtain counsel. DR 2-104(A) merely prohibited him from using the information as bait with which to obtain an agreement to represent them for a fee. The Rule does not prohibit a lawyer from giving unsolicited legal advice; it proscribes the acceptance of employment resulting from such advice.

Appellant does not contend, and on the facts of this case could not contend, that his approaches to the two young women involved political expression or an exercise of associational freedom, "employ[ing] constitutionally privileged means of expression to secure constitutionally guaranteed civil rights." A lawyer's procurement of remunerative employment is a subject only marginally affected with First Amendment concerns. It falls within the State's proper sphere of economic and professional regulation. While entitled to some constitutional protection, appellant's conduct is subject to regulation in furtherance of important state interests.

B

The state interests implicated in this case are particularly strong. In addition to its general interest in protecting consumers and regulating commercial transactions, the State bears a special responsibility for maintaining standards among members of the licensed professions. "The interest of the States in regulating lawyers is especially great since lawyers are essential to the primary governmental function of administering justice, and have historically been 'officers of the courts.'" While lawyers act in part as "self-employed businessmen," they also act "as trusted agents of their clients, and as assistants to the court in search of a just solution to disputes."

As is true with respect to advertising, it appears that the ban on solicitation by lawyers originated as a rule of professional etiquette rather than as a strictly ethical rule. "[T]he rules are based in part on deeply ingrained feelings of tradition, honor and service. Lawyers have for centuries emphasized that the promotion of justice, rather than the earning of fees, is the goal of the profession." But the fact that the original motivation behind the ban on solicitation today might be considered an insufficient justification for its perpetuation does not detract from the force of the other interests the ban continues to serve. While the Court in Bates determined that truthful, restrained advertising of the prices of "routine" legal services would not have an adverse effect on the professionalism of lawyers, this was only because it found "the postulated connection between advertising and the erosion of true professionalism to be severely strained." The *Bates* Court did not question a State's interest in maintaining high standards among licensed professionals. Indeed, to the extent that the ethical standards of lawyers are linked to the service and protection of clients, they do further the goals of "true professionalism."

The substantive evils of solicitation have been stated over the years in sweeping terms: stirring up litigation, assertion of fraudulent claims, debasing the legal profession, and potential harm to the solicited client in the form of overreaching, overcharging, underrepresentation, and misrepresentation. The American Bar Association, as amicus curiae, defends the rule against solicitation primarily on three broad grounds: It is said that the prohibitions embodied in DR2-103(A) and 2-104(A) serve to reduce the likelihood of overreaching and the exertion of undue influence on lay persons, to protect the privacy of individuals, and to avoid situations where the lawyer's exercise of judgment on behalf of the client will be clouded by his own pecuniary self-interest.

We need not discuss or evaluate each of these interests in detail as appellant has conceded that the State has a legitimate and indeed "compelling" interest in preventing those aspects of solicitation that involve fraud, undue influence, intimidation, overreaching, and other forms of "vexatious conduct." We agree that protection of the public from these aspects of solicitation is a legitimate and important state interest.

III

Appellant's concession that strong state interests justify regulation to prevent the evils he enumerates would end this case but for his insistence that none of those evils was found to be present in his acts of solicitation. He challenges what he characterizes as the "indiscriminate application" of the Rules to him and thus attacks the validity of DR 2-103(A) and DR 2-104(A) not facially, but as applied to his acts of solicitation. And because no allegations or findings were made of the specific wrongs appellant concedes would justify disciplinary action, appellant terms his solicitation "pure," meaning "soliciting and obtaining agreements from Carol McClintock and Wanda Lou Holbert to represent each of them," without more. Appellant therefore argues that we must decide whether a State may discipline him for solicitation per se without offending the First and Fourteenth Amendments.

We agree that the appropriate focus is on appellant's conduct. And, as appellant urges, we must undertake an independent review of the record to determine whether that conduct was constitutionally protected. But appellant errs in assuming that the constitutional validity of the judgment below depends on proof that his conduct constituted actual overreaching or inflicted some specific injury on Wanda Holbert or Carol McClintock. His assumption flows from the premise that nothing less than actual proved harm to the solicited individual would be a sufficiently important state interest to justify disciplining the attorney who solicits employment in person for pecuniary gain.

Appellant's argument misconceives the nature of the State's interest. The Rules prohibiting solicitation are prophylactic measures whose objective is the prevention of harm before it occurs. The Rules were applied in this case to discipline a lawyer for soliciting employment for pecuniary gain under circumstances likely to result in the adverse consequences the State seeks to avert. In such a situation, which is inherently conducive to overreaching and other forms of misconduct, the State has a strong interest in adopting and enforcing rules of conduct designed to protect the public from harmful solicitation by lawyers whom it has licensed.

The State's perception of the potential for harm in circumstances such as those presented in this case is well founded. The detrimental aspects of face-to-face selling even of ordinary consumer products have been recognized and addressed by the Federal Trade Commission, and it hardly need be said that the potential for overreaching is significantly greater when a lawyer, a professional trained in the art of persuasion, personally solicits an unsophisticated, injured, or distressed lay person. Such an individual may place his trust in a lawyer, regardless of the latter's qualifications or the individual's actual need for legal representation, simply in response to persuasion under circumstances conducive to uninformed acquiescence. Although it is argued that personal solicitation is valuable because it may apprise a victim of misfortune of his legal rights, the very plight of that person not only makes him more vulnerable to influence but also may make advice all the more intrusive. Thus, under these adverse conditions the overtures of an uninvited lawyer may distress the solicited individual simply because of their obtrusiveness and the invasion of the individual's privacy, even when no other harm materializes. Under such circumstances, it is not unreasonable for the State to presume that in-person solicitation by lawyers more often than not will be injurious to the person solicited.

The efficacy of the State's effort to prevent such harm to prospective clients would be substantially diminished if, having proved a solicitation in circumstances like those of this case, the State were required in addition to prove actual injury. Unlike the advertising in Bates, in-person solicitation is not visible or otherwise open to public scrutiny. Often there is no witness other than the lawyer and the lay person whom he has solicited, rendering it difficult or impossible to obtain reliable proof of what actually took place. This would be especially true if the lay person were so distressed at the time of the solicitation that he could not recall specific details at a later date. If appellant's view were sustained, in-person solicitation would be virtually immune to effective oversight and regulation by the State or by the legal profession, in contravention of the State's strong interest in regulating members of the Bar in an effective, objective, and self-enforcing manner. It therefore is not unreasonable, or violative of the Constitution, for a State to respond with what in effect is a prophylactic rule.

On the basis of the undisputed facts of record, we conclude that the Disciplinary Rules constitutionally could be applied to appellant. He approached two young accident victims at a time when they were especially incapable of making informed judgments or of assessing and protecting their own interests. He solicited Carol McClintock in a hospital room where she lay in traction and sought out Wanda Lou Holbert on the day she came home from the hospital, knowing from his prior inquiries that she had just been released. Appellant urged his services upon the young women and used the information he had obtained from the McClintocks, and the fact of his agreement with Carol, to induce Wanda to say "O. K." in response to his solicitation. He employed a concealed tape recorder, seemingly to insure that he would have evidence of Wanda's oral assent to the representation. He emphasized that his fee would come out of the recovery, thereby tempting the young women with what sounded like a cost-free and therefore irresistible offer. He refused to withdraw when Mrs. Holbert requested him to do so only a day after the initial meeting between appellant and Wanda Lou and continued to represent himself to the insurance company as Wanda Holbert's lawyer.

The court below did not hold that these or other facts were proof of actual harm to Wanda Holbert or Carol McClintock but rested on the conclusion that appellant had engaged in the general misconduct proscribed by the Disciplinary Rules . . . . [O]ur view of the State's interest in averting harm by prohibiting solicitation in circumstances where it is likely to occur, the absence of explicit proof or findings of harm or injury is immaterial. The facts in this case present a striking example of the potential for overreaching that is inherent in a lawyer's in-person solicitation of professional employment. They also demonstrate the need for prophylactic regulation in furtherance of the State's interest in protecting the lay public. We hold that the application of DR2-103(A) and 2-104(A) to appellant does not offend the Constitution.

Accordingly, the judgment of the Supreme Court of Ohio is

Affirmed.

Rule 7.3 Direct Contact with Prospective Clients

(a) A lawyer shall not by in-person, live telephone or real-time electronic contact solicit professional employment from a prospective client when a significant motive for the lawyer's doing so is the lawyer's pecuniary gain, unless the person contacted:

(1) is a lawyer; or

(2) has a family, close personal, or prior professional relationship with the lawyer.

(b) A lawyer should not solicit professional employment from a prospective client by written, recorded or electronic communication or by in-person, telephone or real-time electronic contact even when not otherwise prohibited by paragraph (a), if:

(1) the prospective client has made known to the lawyer a desire not to be solicited by the lawyer; or

(2) the solicitation involves coercion, duress or harassment.

> **Food for Thought**
>
> The Bodine, Clark, Gunnarson, Belser, and Squillante contributing excerpts in Part II.A, *supra,* urge lawyers to engage in "direct contact with prospective clients" either in-person or by "telephone or real-time electronic contact." Do their recommendations satisfy the requirements of Rule 7.3?

[Question 2]

Alpha, an associate at Lincoln & Center, working on a pro bono case for the ACLU, solicits clients for litigation to challenge the requirement of sterilization for pregnant mothers in order to continue receiving Medicaid. Has Alpha committed a disciplinary violation?

(A) Yes

(B) No

Review Rule 7.3(a), *supra.*

The following case was decided on the same day as *Ohralik, supra.*

In re PRIMUS,

436 U.S. 412 (1978)

Mr. Justice POWELL delivered the opinion of the Court.

We consider on this appeal whether a State may punish a member of its Bar who, seeking to further political and ideological goals through associational activity, including litigation, advises a lay person of her legal rights and discloses in a subsequent letter that free legal assistance is available from a nonprofit organization with which the lawyer and her associates are affiliated. Appellant, a member of the Bar of South Carolina, received a public reprimand for writing such a letter. The appeal is opposed by the State Attorney General, on behalf of the Board of Commissioners on Grievances and Discipline of the Supreme Court of South Carolina. As this appeal presents a substantial question under the First and Fourteenth Amendments, as interpreted in *NAACP v. Button*, we noted probable jurisdiction.

I

Appellant, Edna Smith Primus, is a lawyer practicing in Columbia, S. C. During the period in question, she was associated with the "Carolina Community Law Firm," and was an officer of and cooperating lawyer with the Columbia branch of the American Civil Liberties Union (ACLU). She received no compensation for her work on behalf of the ACLU, but was paid a retainer as a legal consultant for the South Carolina Council on Human Relations (Council), a nonprofit organization with offices in Columbia.

During the summer of 1973, local and national newspapers reported that pregnant mothers on public assistance in Aiken County, S. C., were being sterilized or threatened with sterilization as a condition of the continued receipt of medical assistance under the Medicaid program. Concerned by this development, Gary Allen, an Aiken businessman and officer of a local organization serving indigents, called the Council requesting that one of its representatives come to Aiken to address some of the women who had been sterilized. At the Council's behest, appellant, who had not known Allen previously, called him and arranged a meeting in his office in July 1973. Among those attending was Mary Etta Williams, who had been sterilized by Dr. Clovis H. Pierce after the birth of her third child. Williams and her grandmother attended the meeting because Allen, an old family friend, had invited them and because Williams wanted "[t]o see what it was all about. . . ." At the meeting, appellant advised those present, including Williams and the other women who had been sterilized by Dr. Pierce, of their legal rights and suggested the possibility of a lawsuit.

Early in August 1973 the ACLU informed appellant that it was willing to provide representation for Aiken mothers who had been sterilized. Appellant testified that after being advised by Allen that Williams wished to institute suit against Dr. Pierce, she decided to inform Williams of the ACLU's offer of free legal representation. Shortly after receiving appellant's letter, dated August 30, 1973 the centerpiece of this litigation—Williams visited Dr. Pierce to discuss the progress of her third child who was ill. At the doctor's office, she encountered his lawyer and at the latter's request signed a release of liability in the doctor's favor. Williams showed appellant's letter to the doctor and his lawyer, and they retained a copy. She then called appellant from the doctor's office and announced her intention not to sue. There was no further communication between appellant and Williams.

On October 9, 1974, the Secretary of the Board of Commissioners on Grievances and Discipline of the Supreme Court of South Carolina (Board) filed a formal complaint with the Board, charging that appellant had engaged in "solicitation in violation of the Canons of Ethics" by sending the August 30, 1973, letter to Williams. Appellant denied any unethical solicitation and asserted, *inter alia,* that her conduct was protected by the First and Fourteenth Amendments and by Canon 2 of the Code of Professional Responsibility of the American Bar Association (ABA). The complaint was heard by a panel of the Board on March 20, 1975. The State's evidence consisted of the letter, the testimony of Williams, and a copy of the summons and complaint in the action instituted against Dr. Pierce and various state officials[.] Following denial of appellant's motion to dismiss, she testified in her own behalf and called Allen, a number of ACLU representatives, and several character witnesses.

The panel filed a report recommending that appellant be found guilty of soliciting a client on behalf of the ACLU, in violation of Disciplinary Rules (DR) 2-103(D)(5)(a) and (c) and 2-104(A)(5) of the Supreme Court of South Carolina, and that a private reprimand be issued. It noted that "[t]he evidence is inconclusive as to whether [appellant] solicited Mrs. Williams on her own behalf, but she did solicit Mrs. Williams on behalf of the ACLU, which would benefit financially in the event of successful prosecution of the suit for money damages." The panel determined that appellant violated DR 2-103(D)(5) "by attempting to solicit a client for a non-profit organization which, as its primary purpose, renders legal services, where respondent's associate is a staff counsel for the non-profit organization." Appellant also was found to have violated DR 2-104(A)(5) because she solicited Williams, after providing unsolicited legal advice, to join in a prospective class action for damages and other relief that was to be brought by the ACLU.

After a hearing on January 9, 1976, the full Board approved the panel report and administered a private reprimand. On March 17, 1977, the Supreme Court of South Carolina entered an order which adopted verbatim the findings and conclusions of the panel report and increased the sanction, *sua sponte,* to a public reprimand.

On July 9, 1977, appellant filed a jurisdictional statement and this appeal was docketed. * * * We now reverse.

II

This appeal concerns the tension between contending values of considerable moment to the legal profession and to society. Relying upon *NAACP v. Button,* and its progeny, appellant maintains that her activity involved constitutionally protected expression and association. In her view, South Carolina has not shown that the discipline meted out to her advances a subordinating state interest in a manner that avoids unnecessary abridgment of First Amendment freedoms. Appellee counters that appellant's letter to Williams falls outside of the protection of *Button,* and that South Carolina acted lawfully in punishing a member of its Bar for solicitation.

The States enjoy broad power to regulate "the practice of professions within their boundaries," and "[t]he interest of the States in regulating lawyers is especially great since lawyers are essential to the primary governmental function of administering justice, and have historically been 'officers of the courts.' " *Goldfarb v. Virginia State Bar,* 421 U.S. 773, 792. For example, we decide today in *Ohralik v. Ohio State Bar Assn.* that the States may vindicate legitimate regulatory interests through proscription, in certain circumstances, of in-person solicitation by lawyers who seek to communicate purely commercial offers of legal assistance to lay persons.

Unlike the situation in *Ohralik,* however, appellant's act of solicitation took the form of a letter to a woman with whom appellant had discussed the possibility of seeking redress for an allegedly unconstitutional sterilization. This was not in-person solicitation for pecuniary gain. Appellant was communicating an offer of free assistance by attorneys associated with the ACLU, not an offer predicated on entitlement to a share of any monetary recovery. And her actions were undertaken to express personal political beliefs and to advance the civil-liberties objectives of the ACLU, rather than to derive financial gain. The question presented in this case is whether, in light of the values protected by the First and Fourteenth Amendments, these differences materially affect the scope of state regulation of the conduct of lawyers.

III

In *Button, supra,* the Supreme Court of Appeals of Virginia had held that the activities of members and staff attorneys of the National Association for the Advancement of Colored People (NAACP) and its affiliate, the Virginia State Conference of NAACP Branches (Conference), constituted "solicitation of legal business" in violation of state law. Although the NAACP representatives and staff attorneys had "a right to peaceably assemble with the members of the branches and other groups to discuss with them and advise them relative to their legal rights in matters concerning racial segregation," the court found no constitutional protection for efforts to "solicit prospective litigants to authorize the filing of suits" by NAACP-compensated attorneys.

This Court reversed: "We hold that the activities of the NAACP, its affiliates and legal staff shown on this record are modes of expression and association protected by the First and Fourteenth Amendments which Virginia may not prohibit, under its power to regulate the legal profession, as improper solicitation of legal business violative of [state law] and the Canons of Professional Ethics." The solicitation of prospective litigants, many of whom were not members of the NAACP or the Conference, for the purpose of furthering the civil-rights objectives of the organization and its members was held to come within the right "'to engage in association for the advancement of beliefs and ideas.'"

Since the Virginia statute sought to regulate expressive and associational conduct at the core of the First Amendment's protective ambit, the *Button* Court insisted that "government may regulate in the area only with narrow specificity." The Attorney General of Virginia had argued that the law merely (i) proscribed control of the actual litigation by the NAACP after it was instituted, *ibid.,* and (ii) sought to prevent the evils traditionally associated with common-law **maintenance**, **champerty**, and **barratry**, The Court found inadequate the first justification because of an absence of evidence of NAACP interference with the actual conduct of litigation, or neglect or harassment of clients, and because the statute, as construed, was not drawn narrowly to advance the asserted goal. It rejected the analogy to the common-law offenses because of an absence of proof that malicious intent or the prospect of pecuniary gain inspired the NAACP-sponsored litigation. It also found a lack of proof that a serious danger of conflict of interest marked the relationship between the NAACP and its member and nonmember Negro litigants. The Court concluded that "although the [NAACP] has amply shown that its activities fall within the First Amendment's protections, the State has failed to advance any substantial regulatory interest in the form of substantive evils flowing from [the NAACP's] activities, which can justify the broad prohibitions which it has imposed."

Subsequent decisions have interpreted *Button* as establishing the principle that "collective activity undertaken to obtain meaningful access to the courts is a fundamental right within the protection of the First Amendment." The Court has held that the First and Fourteenth Amendments prevent state proscription of a range of solicitation activities by labor unions seeking to provide low-cost, effective legal representation to their members.

IV

We turn now to the question whether appellant's conduct implicates interests of free expression and association sufficient to justify the level of protection recognized in *Button* and subsequent cases. The Supreme Court of South Carolina found appellant to have engaged in unethical conduct because she "'solicit[ed] a client for a non-profit organization, which, as its primary purpose, renders legal services, where respondent's associate is a staff counsel for the non-profit organization.'" It rejected appellant's First Amendment defenses by distinguishing *Button* from the case before it. Whereas the NAACP in that case was primarily a "'political'" organization that used "'litigation as an adjunct to the overriding political aims of the organization,'" the ACLU "'has as one of its primary purposes the rendition of legal services.'" The court also intimated that the ACLU's policy of requesting an award of counsel fees indicated that the organization might "'benefit financially in the event of successful prosecution of the suit for money damages.'"

Although the disciplinary panel did not permit full factual development of the aims and practices of the ACLU, the record does not support the state court's effort to draw a meaningful distinction between the ACLU and the NAACP. From all that appears, the ACLU and its local chapters, much like the NAACP and its local affiliates in *Button,* "[engage] in extensive educational and lobbying activities" and "also [devote] much of [their] funds and energies to an extensive program of assisting certain kinds of litigation on behalf of [their] declared purposes." * * * The court below acknowledged that "'the ACLU has only entered cases in which substantial civil liberties questions are involved . . .'" It has engaged in the defense of unpopular causes and unpopular defendants and has represented individuals in litigation that has defined the scope of constitutional protection in areas such as political dissent, juvenile rights, prisoners' rights, military law, amnesty, and privacy. * * * For the ACLU, as for the NAACP, "litigation is not a technique of resolving private differences"; it is "a form of political expression" and "political association." * * *

We find equally unpersuasive any suggestion that the level of constitutional scrutiny in this case should be lowered because of a possible benefit to the ACLU. The discipline administered to appellant was premised solely on the possibility of financial benefit to the organization, rather than any possibility of pecuniary gain to herself, her associates, or the lawyers representing the plaintiffs in the *Walker v. Pierce* litigation. It is conceded that appellant received no compensation for any of the activities in question. It is also undisputed that neither the ACLU nor any lawyer associated with it would have shared in any monetary recovery by the plaintiffs in *Walker v. Pierce.* If Williams had elected to bring suit, and had been represented by staff lawyers for the ACLU, the situation would have been similar to that in *Button,* where the lawyers for the NAACP were "organized as a staff and paid by" that organization.

Contrary to appellee's suggestion, the ACLU's policy of requesting an award of counsel fees does not take this case outside the protection of *Button.* Although the Court in *Button* did not consider whether the NAACP seeks counsel fees, such requests are often made both by that organization, * * * and by the NAACP Legal Defense Fund, Inc. * * * In any event, in a case of this kind there are differences between counsel fees awarded by a court and traditional fee-paying arrangements which militate against a presumption that ACLU sponsorship of litigation is motivated by considerations of pecuniary gain rather than by its widely recognized goal of vindicating civil liberties. Counsel fees are awarded in the discretion of the court; awards are not drawn from the plaintiff's recovery, and are usually premised on a successful outcome; and the amounts awarded often may not correspond to fees generally obtainable in private litigation. Moreover, under prevailing law during the events in question, an award of counsel fees in federal litigation was available only in limited circumstances. And even if there had been an award during the period in question, it would have gone to the central fund of the ACLU. Although such benefit to the organization may increase with the maintenance of successful litigation, the same situation obtains with voluntary contributions and foundation support, which also may rise with ACLU victories in important areas of the law. That possibility, standing alone, offers no basis for equating the work of lawyers associated with the ACLU or the NAACP with that of a group that exists for the primary purpose of financial gain through the recovery of counsel fees.

Appellant's letter of August 30, 1973, to Mrs. Williams thus comes within the generous zone of First Amendment protection reserved for associational freedoms. The ACLU engages in litigation as a vehicle for effective political expression and association, as well as a means of communicating useful information to the public. * * * As *Button* indicates, and as appellant offered to prove at the disciplinary hearing, * * * the efficacy of litigation as a means of advancing the cause of civil liberties often depends on the ability to make legal assistance available to suitable litigants. "'Free trade in ideas' means free trade in the opportunity to persuade to action, not merely to describe facts." * * * The First and Fourteenth Amendments require a measure of protection for "advocating lawful means of vindicating legal rights," including "advis[ing] another that his legal rights have been infringed and refer[ring] him to a particular attorney or group of attorneys . . . for assistance[.]"

V

South Carolina's action in punishing appellant for soliciting a prospective litigant by mail, on behalf of the ACLU, must withstand the "exacting scrutiny applicable to limitations on core First Amendment rights . . . ." South Carolina must demonstrate "a subordinating interest which is compelling," and that the means employed in furtherance of that interest are "closely drawn to avoid unnecessary abridgment of associational freedoms."

Appellee contends that the disciplinary action taken in this case is part of a regulatory program aimed at the prevention of undue influence, overreaching, misrepresentation, invasion of privacy, conflict of interest, lay interference, and other evils that are thought to inhere generally in solicitation by lawyers of prospective clients, and to be present on the record before us. * * * We do not dispute the importance of these interests. This Court's decision in *Button* makes clear, however, that "[b] road prophylactic rules in the area of free expression are suspect," and that "[p] recision of regulation must be the touchstone in an area so closely touching our most precious freedoms." Because of the danger of censorship through selective enforcement of broad prohibitions, and "[b]ecause First Amendment freedoms need breathing space to survive, government may regulate in [this] area only with narrow specificity."

A

The Disciplinary Rules in question sweep broadly. Under DR 2-103(D)(5), a lawyer employed by the ACLU or a similar organization may never give unsolicited advice to a lay person that he retain the organization's free services, and it would seem that one who merely assists or maintains a cooperative relationship with the organization also must suppress the giving of such advice if he or anyone associated with the organization will be involved in the ultimate litigation. * * * Notwithstanding appellee's concession in this Court, it is far from clear that a lawyer may communicate the organization's offer of legal assistance at an informational gathering such as the July 1973 meeting in Aiken without breaching the literal terms of the Rule. * * * Moreover, the Disciplinary Rules in question permit punishment for mere solicitation unaccompanied by proof of any of the substantive evils that appellee maintains were present in this case. In sum, the Rules in their present form have a distinct potential for dampening the kind of "cooperative activity that would make advocacy of litigation meaningful," as well as for permitting discretionary enforcement against unpopular causes.

B

Even if we ignore the breadth of the Disciplinary Rules and the absence of findings in the decision below that support the justifications advanced by appellee in this Court, we think it clear from the record—which appellee does not suggest is inadequately developed—that findings compatible with the First Amendment could not have been made in this case. As in *New York Times Co. v. Sullivan*, 376 U.S. 254, 284-285, "considerations of effective judicial administration require us to review the evidence in the present record to determine whether it could constitutionally support a judgment [against appellant]. This Court's duty is not limited to the elaboration of constitutional principles; we must also in proper cases review the evidence to make certain that those principles [can be] constitutionally applied." * * *

Where political expression or association is at issue, this Court has not tolerated the degree of imprecision that often characterizes government regulation of the conduct of commercial affairs. The approach we adopt today in *Ohralik*, 436 U.S. 447, that the State may proscribe in-person solicitation for pecuniary gain under circumstances likely to result in adverse consequences, cannot be applied to appellant's activity on behalf of the ACLU. Although a showing of potential danger may suffice in the former context, appellant may not be disciplined unless her activity in fact involved the type of misconduct at which South Carolina's broad prohibition is said to be directed.

The record does not support appellee's contention that undue influence, overreaching, misrepresentation, or invasion of privacy actually occurred in this case. Appellant's letter of August 30, 1973, followed up the earlier meeting—one concededly protected by the First and Fourteenth Amendments—by notifying Williams that the ACLU would be interested in supporting possible litigation. The letter imparted additional information material to making an informed decision about whether to authorize litigation, and permitted Williams an opportunity, which she exercised, for arriving at a deliberate decision. The letter was not facially misleading; indeed, it offered "to explain what is involved so you can understand what is going on." The transmittal of this letter-as contrasted with in-person solicitation-involved no appreciable invasion of privacy; nor did it afford any significant opportunity for overreaching or coercion. Moreover, the fact that there was a written communication lessens substantially the difficulty of policing solicitation practices that do offend valid rules of professional conduct. See *Ohralik*, 436 U.S., at 466-467. The manner of solicitation in this case certainly was no more likely to cause harmful consequences than the activity considered in *Button*. * * *

Nor does the record permit a finding of a serious likelihood of conflict of interest or injurious lay interference with the attorney-client relationship. Admittedly, there is some potential for such conflict or interference whenever a lay organization supports any litigation. That potential was present in *Button*, in the NAACP's solicitation of nonmembers and its disavowal of any relief short of full integration. But the Court found that potential insufficient in the absence of proof of a "serious danger" of conflict of interest, or of organizational interference with the actual conduct of the litigation. As in *Button*, "[n]othing that this record shows as to the nature and purpose of [ACLU] activities permits an inference of any injurious intervention in or control of litigation which would constitutionally authorize the application," of the Disciplinary Rules to appellant's activity. A "very distant possibility of harm," cannot justify proscription of the activity of appellant revealed by this record.

The State's interests in preventing the "stirring up" of frivolous or vexatious litigation and minimizing commercialization of the legal profession offer no further justification for the discipline administered in this case. The *Button* Court declined to accept the proffered analogy to the common-law offenses of **maintenance**, **champerty**, and **barratry**, where the record would not support a finding that the litigant was solicited for a malicious purpose or "for private gain, serving no public interest[.]" The same result follows from the facts of this case. And considerations of undue commercialization of the legal profession are of marginal force where, as here, a nonprofit organization offers its services free of charge to individuals who may be in need of legal assistance and may lack the financial means and sophistication necessary to tap alternative sources of such aid.

At bottom, the case against appellant rests on the proposition that a State may regulate in a prophylactic fashion all solicitation activities of lawyers because there may be some potential for overreaching, conflict of interest, or other substantive evils whenever a lawyer gives unsolicited advice and communicates an offer of representation to a layman. Under certain circumstances, that approach is appropriate in the case of speech that simply "propose[s] a commercial transaction[.]" In the context of political expression and association, however, a State must regulate with significantly greater precision.

VI

The State is free to fashion reasonable restrictions with respect to the time, place, and manner of solicitation by members of its Bar. The State's special interest in regulating members whose profession it licenses, and who serve as officers of its courts, amply justifies the application of narrowly drawn rules to proscribe solicitation that in fact is misleading, overbearing, or involves other features of deception or improper influence. As we decide today in *Ohralik*, a State also may forbid in-person solicitation for pecuniary gain under circumstances likely to result in these evils. And a State may insist that lawyers not solicit on behalf of lay organizations that exert control over the actual conduct of any ensuing litigation. Accordingly, nothing in this opinion should be read to foreclose carefully tailored regulation that does not abridge unnecessarily the associational freedom of nonprofit organizations, or their members, having characteristics like those of the NAACP or the ACLU.

We conclude that South Carolina's application of its DR2-103(D)(5)(a) and (c) and 2-104(A)(5) to appellant's solicitation by letter on behalf of the ACLU violates the First and Fourteenth Amendments. The judgment of the Supreme Court of South Carolina is

Reversed.

* * *

Mr. Justice REHNQUIST, dissenting.

* * *

Neither *Button* nor any other decision of this Court compels a State to permit an attorney to engage in uninvited solicitation on an individual basis. Further, I agree with the Court's statement in the companion case that the State has a strong interest in forestalling the evils that result "when a lawyer, a professional trained in the art of persuasion, personally solicits an unsophisticated, injured, or distressed lay person." The reversal of the judgment of the Supreme Court of South Carolina thus seems to me quite unsupported by previous decisions or by any principle which may be abstracted from them.

* * *

I cannot share the Court's confidence that the danger of such consequences is minimized simply because a lawyer proceeds from political conviction rather than for pecuniary gain. A State may reasonably fear that a lawyer's desire to resolve "substantial civil liberties questions," may occasionally take precedence over his duty to advance the interests of his client. It is even more reasonable to fear that a lawyer in such circumstances will be inclined to pursue both culpable and blameless defendants to the last ditch in order to achieve his ideological goals. Although individual litigants, including the ACLU, may be free to use the courts for such purposes, South Carolina is likewise free to restrict the activities of the members of its Bar who attempt to persuade them to do so.

I can only conclude that the discipline imposed upon Primus does not violate the Constitution, and I would affirm the judgment of the Supreme Court of South Carolina.

C. Advertising

If the term "solicitation" refers to "direct contact with prospective clients," the term "advertising" applies to indirect contacts. Indirect Contacts vary widely. They include broadcast and print advertisements that are commonly understood as "advertising." But they also include websites or blogs, which are probably understood more commonly as information resources that might include advertisements but are not themselves advertising, as well as targeted mailings and brochures distributed at a shopping center, both which may be commonly described as "solicitation." All these indirect marketing efforts fall within the advertising rules.

The current advertising rules reflect a balance between the bar's ambivalence toward advertising and the commercial speech rights of lawyers. For most of the Twentieth Century, the bar considered lawyer advertising unprofessional and prohibited it. The Supreme Court struck down these bans in *Bates v. State Bar of Arizona*, 433 U.S. 350 (1977). Although the Rules generally permit lawyer advertising, States continue to push the boundaries of permissible restrictions.

Before the Twentieth Century, lawyers were generally able to advertise. David Hoffman was the first American legal ethics scholar. In 1835, he placed the following advertisement:

AMERICAN LAW AGENCY.

THE American and British Public are informed that the undersigned have established Law Agencies in each of the United States, and that claims of every description will be carefully attended to through the medium of eminent and responsible counsel in each State, and personally by the undersigned in the State of Maryland, and at Washington, in the District of Columbia.

Please address them under the firm of Hoffman & Dobbin, Counsellors at Law, Baltimore, Maryland.

DAVID HOFFMAN,
GEORGE W. DOBBIN.

Baltimore, Jan. 1, 1833.

REFERENCES :

We are of opinion that entire confidence may be placed in David Hoffman, Esq. LL. D. Counsellor-at-law in the Supreme Court of the United States, and in his associate George W. Dobbin, Esq. and that claims entrusted to them will be attended to with 'ability, integrity, and promptitude.

John Marshall, Chief Justice U. S. Richmond.
Edward Livingston, Secretary of State, S. Washington.
N. Biddle, President Bank U. S. Philadelphia.
Prime, Ward, King & Co. New York.
Thomas H. Perkins & Sons, Boston.
Robert Gilmor & Sons, } Baltimore.
Hoffman, Bend & Co. }
Baring, Brothers & Co. } London.
Thos. Wilson & Co. }
Bolton, Ogden & Co. } Liverpool.
W. & G. Brown & Co. }

Baltimore, Jan. 10—eo1m2am5m

Daily National Intelligencer, July 11, 1835, at 4, col. 2. Notice the first "reference" to vouch for Hoffman's "ability, integrity, and promptitude." Would Chief Justice Marshall's reference be considered ethical today? For examples of Abraham Lincoln's lawyer advertisements, click here.

[Question 1]

An attorney served two four-year terms as the state's governor immediately prior to reopening his law office in the state. The attorney printed and mailed an announcement of his return to private practice to members of the bar, previous clients, and personal friends whom he had never represented. The printed announcement stated that the attorney had reopened his law office, gave his address and telephone number, and added that he had been the state's governor for the past eight years. The outside envelope for the mailing displayed the phrase "Advertising Material."

Is the attorney subject to discipline for the announcement?

   (A) Yes, because the mailing included persons who had not been his clients.

   (B) Yes, because his service as governor is unrelated to his ability as a lawyer.

   (C) No, because the information in the announcement was true.

   (D) No, because the announcement does not display the words "Advertising Material."

The basic rule governing "communication concerning a lawyer's services," including both advertising and solicitation, is Rule 7.1. It provides that "[a] lawyer shall not make a false or misleading communication about the lawyer or the lawyer's services." It then explains that "[a] communication is false or misleading if it contains a material misrepresentation of fact or law, or omits a fact necessary to make the statement considered as a whole not materially misleading."

Rule 7.2(a) explains that "a lawyer may advertise services through written, recorded or electronic communication, including public media." Rule 7.2(c) requires that "[a]ny communication made pursuant to this rule shall include the name and office address of at least one lawyer or law firm responsible for its content."

Rule 7.3(c) requires that "[e]very written, recorded or electronic communication from a lawyer soliciting professional employment from a prospective client known to be in need of legal services in a particular matter shall include the words 'Advertising Material' on the outside envelope, if any, and at the beginning and ending of any recorded or electronic communication, unless the recipient of the communication is a "['lawyer [or] has a family, close personal, or prior professional relationship with the lawyer."]

[Question 2]

A recently graduated attorney began a plaintiff's personal injury practice, but was having a difficult time attracting clients. The attorney hired an advertising agency to prepare a television commercial in which the attorney appeared to be arguing a case before a jury. In the commercial, the jury brought back a large award for the attorney's client. The voice-over stated that results would vary depending upon the particular legal and factual circumstances. The attorney's only experience at the time the commercial was filmed was in moot court in law school. As a result of airing the commercial, the attorney received several significant cases.

Is the attorney subject to discipline?

(A) Yes, because the commercial created an unjustified expectation about the results that could be achieved in court.

(B) Yes, because the commercial implied that the attorney had successfully argued a case to a jury.

(C) No, because commercial speech is protected under the First Amendment.

(D) No, because the commercial contained an express disclaimer about the results a client could expect.

Review Rule 7.1 and Comment. Also consult the following case:

MATTER of ZANG

741 P.2d 267 (Ariz. 1987), *cert. denied,* 484 U.S. 1067 (1988)

FELDMAN, Vice Chief Justice.

* * *

II. False and Misleading Advertising

A. Background

Zang and Whitmer are charged with false and misleading advertising[.] * * * This charge is based on four print and nine video advertisements that appeared in Phoenix-area newspapers and on Phoenix-area television stations during 1982 and 1983.

All four print advertisements contained the bold-faced caption **"Law is Civilized Warfare!"** above a picture of Zang and Whitmer and to the left of the following language:

We're the [or "a"] personal injury law firm:

*with the medical experience to understand complicated injuries

*with investigators to find witnesses and hidden evidence

*with computers for speed, accuracy and research

Free Consultation

No recovery-no attorneys' fee

Each print advertisement also contained a photograph and a statement emphasizing some aspect of respondents' practice. The photographs featured either a judge in a courtroom, a computer circuit board leaning against several books about accident cases and medicine, a large reproduction of a fingerprint, or a woman sitting in a witness box. Beneath one of these photographs, each advertisement featured one of the following statements:

If you're in an accident ... You need a lawyer with facts and know-how, not just words.

Detailed Preparation

is part of Zang & Whitmer, Chtd. because: the better your case is *prepared for trial*, the more likely your case will settle out of court without delay or hassles.

(emphasis added).

If you're in an accident ... You need more than a lawyers' [sic] words!

Medicine and Law

> are combined at Zang & Whitmer, Chtd. because: to prove serious injury and future suffering, your lawyer must have the knowledge to *make complicated medical facts clear for the jury.*

> (emphasis added).

> If you're hurt in an accident . . . You need more than a lawyer's words!

Licensed Investigators

> are part of Zang & Whitmer, Chtd. because: an investigator searches out witnesses, examines evidence at the accident scene, and discovers the facts *essential for victory in the courtroom.*

> (emphasis added).

> If you're hurt in an accident. . . . You need a lawyer with facts and know-how, not just words.

Evidence

> is part of Zang & Whitmer, Chtd. because: *the defense* will use words and opinions to minimize their fault and your injuries. Only proof of facts will stop them.

> (emphasis added).

Like the print advertisements, respondents' television advertisements emphasized the advantages of investigators and medical knowledge. The television advertisements also were very dramatic. They featured an authoritative-sounding narrator and either frenetic or peaceful music as a backdrop for pictures of an automobile accident, a worried couple in a hospital waiting room, or a father kissing his daughter goodbye, apparently for the last time. Each of the television advertisements ended with a climactic scene showing Mr. Zang arguing before a jury in a courtroom, with the viewer visually located behind the jury box.

The [State Bar] Committee and the [Disciplinary] Commission [of the Supreme Court of Arizona] concluded that respondents' advertisements portrayed respondents as willing and able to take, and as actually taking, personal injury cases to trial. The Committee and the Commission concluded that the advertisements were false and misleading because, in fact, respondents "scrupulously avoided" taking cases to trial.

B. Discussion

1. Constitutional Protection

We note at the outset that respondents' advertisements are "commercial speech" protected by the First Amendment. As respondents candidly acknowledge, however, the proscription of false and misleading advertising in DR 2-101 is constitutionally unobjectionable.

"[T]he extension of First Amendment protection to commercial speech is justified principally by the value to consumers of the information such speech provides. . . ." Consequently, false or misleading commercial speech has little or no constitutional value and may be "prohibited entirely." "Indeed, the elimination of false and deceptive claims serves to promote the one facet of commercial . . . advertising that warrants First Amendment protection-its contribution to the flow of accurate and reliable information relevant to public and private decision making."

In short, the constitution does not prevent discipline in this case if respondents' advertisements were false and misleading. We therefore must determine (1) what message respondents' advertisements conveyed, and (2) whether that message was false or inherently misleading.

2. The Message

The Committee and the Commission found that at least one of the messages conveyed by respondents' advertisements was that the law firm of Zang & Whitmer was willing and able to try, and actually did try, personal injury cases. The Commission concluded that respondents' print advertisements plainly suggest that attorneys at Zang & Whitmer "prepare cases for trial, combine medicine and law to present facts clearly to the jury, do presentations to juries, use investigators to aid in obtaining victory in the courtroom, and prove facts and defeat defenses in court." In like manner, it found that respondents' television advertisements suggest "that Zang and Whitmer take cases to court and argue before juries." After reviewing the record, we agree that respondents' advertisements would "be interpreted by a reasonable person as representations that Respondents have an unusually high level of expertise and experience in personal injury law, specifically including trial experience."

Both the bar and the respondents called advertising and advertising law experts. The experts gave their opinions regarding the message conveyed by respondents' advertisements. With all deference to the experts, and without deprecating or passing upon the admissibility of their opinions, we find no need to rely upon expert testimony to interpret the messages conveyed by the advertisements in evidence. As a matter of common sense, we find that depicting a lawyer trying a case conveys the idea that the lawyer tries cases. When Zang is shown arguing a case to a jury, the message is that Zang argues cases to juries. Accordingly, we hold that one message conveyed by respondents' advertisements was that Zang &

Whitmer had tried personal injury cases in the past and were ready and able to prepare future cases for trial and to try them.

3. Were Respondents' Advertisements Misleading?

The Committee and the Commission found that respondents' advertisements were false and misleading because they did not accurately portray respondents' practice. Zang & Whitmer was formed in 1979. From that time until the advertisements at issue appeared in 1982 and 1983, no attorney at Zang & Whitmer had tried a personal injury case to a conclusion. Zang and Whitmer personally started only one trial, but a mistrial was declared after the first witness testified.

Zang, who holds a medical as well as a legal degree, has experience as a medical trial consultant, but has never tried a personal injury case. He conceded that although he felt fully capable of preparing personal injury cases for trial, he is not competent to try a personal injury case. Whitmer has criminal trial experience, having spent several years with the county attorney's office shortly after he graduated from law school. His only personal injury trial experience, however, consists of three or four trials that occurred more than ten years ago.

Most importantly, Zang & Whitmer consciously followed a firm policy of not taking cases to trial. Respondents believed that pretrial settlements invariably obtained better results for their clients. They settled cases before trial whenever possible. In the few cases where a trial was necessary, respondents' policy was to refer cases to trial lawyers in other firms. Thus, as the Commission concluded, "while [respondents] represented themselves as having the willingness to try cases, they in fact scrupulously avoided" litigation or trial work of any kind.

The evidence clearly demonstrates that respondents did not offer the trial services portrayed in their advertisements. Contrary to their print advertisements, respondents had not and did not prepare cases for trial, "make complicated medical facts clear for the jury," or strive for "victory in the courtroom." Nor did they argue cases in front of juries as their television advertisements suggested. Their intention was to settle all cases. Even if a settlement could not be reached, respondents had no intention of personally taking their clients' cases to trial.

We agree with the Committee and the Commission that respondents' advertisements were false and misleading. When consumers "choose[ ] a lawyer through the advertising process, [they] ha[ve] a right to expect that [their] lawyer will be able and willing to act in the manner represented. In this case, it is clear that respondents had no intention of taking a case personally to trial, and that express and implied representations of their courtroom abilities were false, misleading, and untruthful."

4. Respondents' Objections

Respondents argue that their advertisements were not false because they accurately suggest only that Zang & Whitmer has an unusually high level of expertise in personal injury law, which occasionally includes trial work. Respondents support this assertion with two pieces of evidence: the expert testimony of Professor Gerald Thain and statistics about the frequency of litigation in personal injury cases.

According to Professor Thain, a law professor specializing in advertising law, respondents' advertisements suggest that Zang & Whitmer will do what is necessary to get the best possible result for its clients, including going to court, if necessary. This suggestion is not misleading, according to Professor Thain, because the references to trial work add little to the public's preexisting perception that all lawyers appear in court. Because the public already incorrectly believes that all lawyers appear in court, consumers will not be misled further by respondents' references to trial work.

Professor Thain's testimony does not aid respondents' cause. As Professor Thain conceded, because respondents personally were unwilling and unable to take cases to court, their advertisements technically were false. Furthermore, that some consumers incorrectly believe that all lawyers routinely appear in court, does not give respondents license to present their practice in a false light. Disciplinary Rule 2-101(A) prohibits false and misleading claims, even if those claims serve only to reinforce consumers' prior misconceptions.

Respondents' second argument is that their advertisements were not misleading because respondents "litigated" as many cases as most other personal injury attorneys and also referred cases to outside trial counsel when necessary. The evidence fails to support these assertions. Expert testimony established that approximately five percent of the personal injury cases that have been filed go to trial. Zang testified that Zang & Whitmer filed complaints in only approximately five percent of their cases in 1980. None of those cases actually was tried by anyone from Zang & Whitmer. Indeed, Zang was unable to remember even taking depositions in more than a handful of cases.

There was no expert testimony on the percentage of cases in which lawyers file complaints. However, because most personal injury attorneys actually take five percent of their cases to trial and most cases settle before trial, it is fair to assume that most lawyers file complaints in far more than five percent of their personal injury cases. In this context, Zang's assertion that five percent of respondents' cases were "in litigation" in 1980 does not establish that Zang & Whitmer actually maintained the type of trial practice portrayed in its advertisements. Because ninety-five percent of respondents' cases were not filed, there could have been no discovery, no production of documents, none of the usual preparation for the "civilized warfare" of courtroom confrontation which was the theme of respondents' advertising campaign.

The evidence regarding respondents' referral practice is similarly inadequate. According to Zang, Zang & Whitmer has handled between 1,420 and 1,650 personal injury cases since its formation in 1979. Approximately twenty of those cases were referred to outside trial counsel and approximately nine actually proceeded to trial. We agree that "[a] practice which refers roughly one percent of all cases to trial counsel [in other firms] is simply too scarce to justify public claims that Zang [and] Whitmer are trial lawyers." Furthermore, even if respondents' referral practice adequately protected their clients' interests, it did not justify respondents' implicit claims that they would personally represent their clients in court. Indeed, respondents did not even inform new clients that their case would be referred to outside counsel if trial became necessary.

Respondents' final argument is that their advertisements never actually harmed anyone. This argument, inherently difficult to prove or disprove, also is unpersuasive. Although there may be little specific evidence of consumer injury or dissatisfaction, we think it self-evident that the message conveyed by respondents' advertisements was inherently misleading and potentially dangerous.

Presumably, respondents included dramatic symbols of conflict—courtrooms, judges, confrontation, and oral argument to a jury—in their advertisements because they believed such symbols would attract clients. Those clients had a right to expect that their attorneys were prepared to take their cases to court and to try them to a judge or jury if necessary. Not having been told that the firm lacked trial ability, and that it actually prepared cases for settlement, not litigation, a client may have accepted settlement recommendations without determining whether such recommendations were prompted, at least in part, by the firm's lack of in-house trial capacity.

Even if no client has yet been damaged, discipline is appropriate to protect consumers from misleading advertising. The rules governing attorneys are designed to prevent harm and protect consumers. * * * Advertisements falsely suggesting a willingness and ability to do trial work necessarily create a danger that consumers will turn to respondents for help with matters that may need to be litigated. This danger alone is sufficient justification for enforcing DR 2-101(A) without requiring proof of actual harm in the past.

Our conclusion that respondents' advertisements were false and misleading should not be read too broadly. Although it seems unlikely that personal injury lawyers can achieve the best results for their clients without earning and maintaining a proven willingness and competence to take cases to trial when necessary, we do not criticize respondents' practice of settling most cases or of referring trial work to outside counsel. Respondents were not charged with providing incomplete or incompetent legal services, nor was evidence adduced on this point. Thus, it may be, as the evidence at the disciplinary hearing suggested, that respondents' use of computers, investigators, and medical knowledge secured a fair settlement for many of their clients. The same, perhaps, could be said of a competent firm of public adjusters. The fact remains, however, that respondents' advertisements painted a false picture, portraying Zang and Whitmer as trial lawyers who prepared cases for trial, who were willing and able to try, and who actually tried, personal injury cases. That portrait was flattering past the point of deception.

C. Directions for the Future

As our prior discussion indicates, we intend strict enforcement of the rule against false and misleading advertising. As a guide for the future, we take this opportunity to outline some principles that may prove helpful in determining whether a particular advertisement is false or misleading. Although the comments that follow pertain to our present rules and are truly dicta in an adjudicatory sense (we cannot fairly evaluate respondents' conduct by standards announced today), they should provide some future direction for the bar.

The Rules of Professional Conduct regulate various aspects of commercial advertisements about a lawyer and his or her services. The only truly substantive regulation, however, is ER 7.1's prohibition of "false or misleading communication[s] about the lawyer or the lawyer's services." According to ER 7.1, an advertisement is false or misleading if it misrepresents or omits a material fact, creates an unjustified expectation about the results a lawyer can achieve, or makes unsubstantiated comparisons of legal services.

Lawyers who choose to advertise should remember that they are professionals charged with an important public trust: preserving and protecting the public's commercial, civil, and constitutional rights. Advertising that informs consumers about their rights and about the availability and cost of legal services is a valuable method of increasing access to legal representation and of furthering the rule of law. This type of advertising is fully deserving of constitutional protection, and is apparently what the Supreme Court had in mind when it extended first amendment protection to lawyer advertising.

We recognize, of course, that another primary purpose of advertising is to convince consumers to call a particular lawyer. While this focus is not objectionable standing alone, it often leads attorneys to stretch the truth or to focus on dramatic, "sophisticated" sales techniques that all too often provide little helpful information and consequently have a greater tendency to mislead consumers. While no doubt effective in attracting clients, dramatic, nonfactual advertisements are more likely to misrepresent or omit material facts, or to create unjustified expectations about the results a lawyer can achieve than are advertisements that primarily convey factual information that will help consumers make rational decisions about whether to seek legal services.

Thus, attorneys attempting to produce advertisements that are neither false nor misleading should keep in mind that the sale and use of legal services is fundamentally different than the sale and use of ordinary consumer products. It matters less which brand of beer or soap consumers choose than what kind of lawyer they choose. Legal representation may affect the consumer's basic rights and may have long-term consequences; consumers easily can discard a disappointing beer or bar of soap and try a different brand next time. Furthermore, consumers are less likely to be "taken in" by advertisements for consumer products than by advertisements for legal services. People usually have much more experience with consumer products than they have with legal services. Consequently, the Rules of Professional Conduct do not tolerate the same sort of sales pitch for legal services that the Federal Trade Commission tolerates for most consumer products.

The dramatic sales pitch is especially troublesome when it is broadcast on radio or television, which leave little time for reflection and rational deliberation. The Iowa and New Jersey Supreme Courts have responded to this potential danger by expanding their rules of professional conduct to require that television advertisements be "predominately informational." Reasoning that dramatic television advertisements are inherently misleading, both courts have severely limited the use of music, pictures, and dramatic presentations in television advertisements by attorneys. Although the Supreme Court has not reviewed either Iowa's or New Jersey's rules, its consistent refusal to explicitly extend its prior holdings to "the electronic broadcast media," and its dismissal of the appeal in Humphrey for want of a substantial federal question, suggest that even such stringent rules may be constitutional.

Our own rules do not yet place any special restrictions on television or radio broadcasts, nor do we think it necessary to take that step today. Some music or drama may help convey the attorney's message. We believe, however, that lawyer advertising, particularly on the electronic media, should be predominately informational in nature. This is consistent with the rationale for extending first amendment protection to lawyer advertising and with the public's interest in access to and knowledge about lawyers and legal services.

Advertisements are likely to minimize the danger of violating ER 7.1 if they are designed to inform consumers of their rights and of the methods available to meet legal problems and crises; to inform the public of the availability and costs of services; or to convey accurate information relevant to making informed, rational choices of counsel, including information about counsel's availability and areas of practice. In the future, the bar should examine lawyers' advertisements to determine whether, taken as a whole, they are predominately informational or are simply emotional, irrational sales pitches. While the latter may not be prohibited by ER 7.1, they should be examined carefully to assure that they are neither false nor misleading.

* * *

VII. Discipline to be Imposed

* * *

B. Suspension

1. False and Misleading Advertising

The Commission recommended a ninety-day suspension for each of the respondents on the charges of false and misleading advertising. In weighing that recommendation, and in determining the proper sanctions to be imposed for the advertising violations, we are mindful that no actual harm to the public was proved. It is our intuitive sense that the type of false and misleading advertising at issue here is likely to damage the public. Our experience leads us to conclude that those who advertise for a high volume, fast turnover litigation clientele, but who have little or no experience or competency in actually trying cases, may do a great deal of damage. First, such practitioners may lack the experience necessary for a proper evaluation of their clients' claims. Next, they may lack the standing and reputation with adverse counsel or insurers that would enable them to realize the full value of their clients' cases in settlement negotiations. Finally, because they lack trial ability, they may be tempted to settle cases that should be tried or, at the very least, to settle them early when settlement at or during trial might produce better results. We do not accept the apocryphal adage that "any settlement is better than trial." Good settlements or reasonable settlements may be better than trial, but one who holds himself out as a specialist in handling cases whose ultimate value can only be determined by trial, ought either to have trial ability or to inform his clients that he lacks it.

These thoughts, however, are products of experience and intuition, and cannot substitute for evidence. The State Bar did not attempt to prove any case in which respondents settled a claim for significantly less than the value which would have been realized by attorneys who properly hold themselves out as specialists in personal injury litigation. Lacking such evidence, and in the absence of any client complaint, we must assume that no harm was done to any client. The record also fails to establish that respondents intended to harm their clients or acted with the knowledge that their conduct would result in harm. We also note that this is a case of first impression. No Arizona lawyers have been disciplined since display and television advertising first were permitted. All of these factors militate in favor of discipline by censure rather than by suspension.

Censure, however, may not be sufficient to deter others in the future. We wish to stress that lawyers will not be permitted to knowingly engage in false advertising or to destroy the ideals of the profession by attempting to snare clients as if they were selling soap rather than providing legal services. Balancing these considerations, we deem it appropriate to suspend each of the respondents for thirty days for engaging in false and misleading advertising.

We believe that given the serious dislocation of their practice, the significant amount of costs that will be charged against them, see section VIII, post, and the time expended on this case, a thirty-day suspension is sufficient both to ensure that there will be no repetition by respondents and to deter future misconduct by others. Hopefully, there will not be a next time, but if there is, it will not be a case of first impression.

* * *

VIII. CONCLUSION

We hold that respondents received a fair hearing before an impartial tribunal. In our view, the due process standards articulated in Withrow and Davis were satisfied in this case. Even if they were not satisfied, however, any violation was cured by the de novo review conducted by the Commission and this court.

For the reasons discussed in this opinion, Stephen M. Zang is suspended from the practice of law for one year, commencing on the date of the mandate in this case. As a condition of reinstatement, he is required to make restitution to State Farm and to Rebecca Drummond as specified in section VII-A. Pursuant to former Rule 37(g), Mr. Zang is ordered to pay the State Bar of Arizona $15,441.06 for costs and expenses incurred in prosecuting this action.

C. Peter Whitmer is suspended for thirty days, commencing on the date of the mandate in this case, for engaging in false and misleading advertising. As a condition of reinstatement, he is ordered to make restitution to Rebecca Drummond as provided in section VII-A. Pursuant to former Rule 37(g), Mr. Whitmer is ordered to pay the State Bar $11,166.97 for costs and expenses.

———————

Keep this case in mind when you read the following two questions. Also consult the additional materials provided below.

[Question 3]

Attorney advertises on the local television station. In the advertisements, a professional actor says:

"Do you need a lawyer? Call Attorney-her telephone number is area code (555) 555-5555. Her fees might be lower than you think."

Attorney approved the prerecorded advertisement and is keeping in her office files a copy of the recording of the actual transmission and a record of when each transmission was made.

Is the advertisement proper?

(A) Yes, if the phrase "Advertising Material" appears at the beginning and the end of the advertisement.

(B) No, unless Attorney's fees are lower than those generally charged in the area where she practices.

(C) No, because she used a professional actor for the television advertisement.

(D) No, if she makes a charge for the initial consultation.

[Question 4]

An attorney represented a plaintiff in an action against a manufacturer of a drain cleaner. The plaintiff's complaint alleged that the manufacturer's product exploded in use and caused her serious and permanent injuries. The jury agreed and awarded the plaintiff $5,000,000 in actual damages and an additional $5,000,000 in punitive damages. The manufacturer paid the judgment.

The attorney made this recovery the cornerstone of an aggressive television advertising campaign for his law practice. In those ads, a voice-over discussed the $10,000,000 recovery obtained in the plaintiff's case. The plaintiff praised the attorney's legal skills in an on-camera statement, saying that no one would work harder on a case than the attorney.

The plaintiff prepared her on-camera statement in response to the attorney's request, but without any further involvement by the attorney, and she believed it to be entirely true.

Is the attorney subject to discipline for using the television advertisement described above?

(A) Yes, because the advertisement is likely to create an unjustified expectation about the results the attorney will be able to achieve and is therefore misleading.

(B) Yes, because the attorney's advertisement contains a client testimonial.

(C) No, because the plaintiff prepared the entire statement without any involvement by the attorney.

(D) No, because the result obtained in the plaintiff's case was reported accurately, and the plaintiff believed that everything she said about the attorney was true.

In answering questions 3 and 4, review <u>Rules 7.1</u>, <u>7.2</u> and <u>7.3</u>. The Comment to Rule 7.1 provides:

[2] Truthful statements that are misleading are also prohibited by this Rule. A truthful statement is misleading if it omits a fact necessary to make the lawyer's communication considered as a whole not materially misleading. A truthful statement is also misleading if there is a substantial likelihood that it will lead a reasonable person to formulate a specific conclusion about the lawyer or the lawyer's services for which there is no reasonable factual foundation.

[3] An advertisement that truthfully reports a lawyer's achievements on behalf of clients or former clients may be misleading if presented so as to lead a reasonable person to form an unjustified expectation that the same results could be obtained for other clients in similar matters without reference to the specific factual and legal circumstances of each client's case. Similarly, an unsubstantiated comparison of the lawyer's services or fees with the services or fees of other lawyers may be misleading if presented with such specificity as would lead a reasonable person to conclude that the comparison can be substantiated. The inclusion of an appropriate disclaimer or qualifying language may preclude a finding that a statement is likely to create unjustified expectations or otherwise mislead a prospective client.

[Question 5]

Attorney Alpha, a member of the bar, placed a printed flyer in the booth of each artist exhibiting works at a county fair. The face of the flyer contained the following information: "I, Alpha, am an attorney, with offices in 800 Bank Building, telephone (555) 555-5555. I have a J.D. degree from State Law School and an M.A. degree in fine arts from State University. My practice includes representing artists in negotiating contracts between artists and dealers and protecting artists' interests. You can find me in the van parked at the fair entrance." All factual information on the face of the flyer was correct. There was a retainer agreement on the back of the flyer. At the entrance to the fair, Alpha parked a van with a sign that read "Alpha-Attorney at Law." For which, if any, of the following is Alpha subject to discipline?

(A) Placing copies of the flyer in the booth of each artist.

(B) Including a retainer agreement on the back of the flyer.

(C) Parking the van with the sign on it at the fair entrance.

(D) A & B.

(E) **All of the above.**

(F) **None of the above.**

Review Rules 7.1 – 7.3.

Rule 7.4

(a) A lawyer may communicate the fact that the lawyer does or does not practice in particular fields of law.

* * *

(d) A lawyer shall not state or imply that a lawyer is certified as a specialist in a particular field of law, unless:

(1) the lawyer has been certified as a specialist by an organization that has been approved by an appropriate state authority or that has been accredited by the American Bar Association; and

(2) the name of the certifying organization is clearly identified in the communication.

Go Online

For an article detailing some of the more interesting and controversial marketing strategies employed by lawyers click here. One ill-advised campaign sent out paperweights that looked like grenades with the firm's name on the pin.

[Question 6]

Alpha and Beta practiced law under the firm name of Alpha & Beta. When Beta died, Alpha did not change the firm name. Thereafter, Alpha entered into an arrangement with another attorney, Gamma. Gamma pays Alpha a certain sum each month for office space, for use of Alpha's law library, and for secretarial services. Alpha and Gamma each have their own clients, and neither participates in the representation of the other's clients or shares in fees paid. On the entrance to the suite of offices shared by Alpha and Gamma are the words "Law Firm of Alpha, Beta & Gamma."

Is Alpha subject to discipline?

(A) Yes, because Beta was deceased when Alpha made the arrangement with Gamma.

(B) Yes, because Gamma is not a partner of Alpha.

(C) No, because Alpha and Beta were partners at the time of Beta's death.

(D) No, because Gamma is paying a share of the rent and office expenses.

<u>Rule 7.5</u> governs firm names and letterheads. Rule 7.5(a) prohibits firm names or letterheads that violate Rule 7.1, but it permits use of "[a] trade name in private practice if it does not imply a connection with a government agency or with a public or charitable legal services organization[.]" Similarly, Rule 7.5(c) provides that a firm may not use the name of a "lawyer holding public office . . . during any substantial period in which the lawyer is not actively and regularly practicing with the firm."

Rule 7.5 also takes into account the multi-jurisdictional nature of some practices. Rule 7.5(b) permits the use of the "same name or other professional designation in each jurisdiction, but identification of the lawyers in an office of the firm shall indicate the jurisdictional limitations on those not licensed to practice in the jurisdiction where the office is located."

Rule 7.5(d) allows lawyers to "state or imply that they practice in a partnership or other organization only when that is the fact."

[Question 7]

The State of Fordham decides to restrict lawyer advertisements in order to protect the reputation of lawyers and to prevent lawyers from misleading potential clients. Fordham enacts content restrictions prohibiting lawyers from using client testimonials, attention-getting techniques that are clearly unrelated to criteria for selecting a lawyer, or "a nickname, moniker, motto or trade name that implies an ability to obtain results in a matter." It also establishes a thirty-day moratorium on targeted advertising following a particular personal injury event. Plaintiffs sue to enjoin these restrictions. What result?

(A) The Court upholds both the content restrictions and the moratorium.

(B) The Court upholds the content restrictions, but not the moratorium.

(C) The Court upholds the moratorium, but not the content restrictions.

(D) The Court enjoins both the content restrictions and the moratorium.

Go Online

Here are examples of advertisements illustrating the strategies at issue in the question:

1. Client Testimonials. Click <u>here</u>, <u>here</u>, and <u>here</u>.

2. Attention-Getting Techniques Unrelated to Criteria for Selecting a Lawyer. Click <u>here</u>, <u>here</u>, and <u>here</u>.

3. Trade Name or Motto Implying Ability to Obtain Results. Click <u>here</u>, <u>here</u>, and <u>here</u>.

ALEXANDER v. CAHILL

598 F.3d 79 (2d Cir. 2010)

CALABRESI, Circuit Judge:

* * *

In June 2006, the presiding justices of the four departments of the Appellate Division approved for comment draft amendments to the then-existing rules. A press release explained that the new rules were designed to protect consumers "against inappropriate solicitations or potentially misleading ads, as well as overly aggressive marketing," and to "benefit the bar by ensuring that the image of the legal profession is maintained at the highest possible level." Following a comment period, the presiding justices issued final rules. These rules were set to take effect on February 1, 2007.

We consider below a subset of these final rules, which we subdivide into two categories. The first group of amendments imposes a series of content-based restrictions:

N.Y. Comp. Codes R. & Regs., tit. 22, § 1200.50(c):

(c) An advertisement shall not:

(1) include an endorsement of, or testimonial about, a lawyer or law firm from a client with respect to a matter that is still pending . . .

(3) include the portrayal of a judge, the portrayal of a fictitious law firm, the use of a fictitious name to refer to lawyers not associated together in a law firm, or otherwise imply that lawyers are associated in a law firm if that is not the case . . .

(5) rely on techniques to obtain attention that demonstrate a clear and intentional lack of relevance to the selection of counsel, including the portrayal of lawyers exhibiting characteristics clearly unrelated to legal competence . . .

(7) utilize a nickname, moniker, motto or trade name that implies an ability to obtain results in a matter.

* * *

The second group of amendments imposes a thirty-day moratorium on certain communications following a personal injury or wrongful death event:

N.Y. Comp. Codes R. & Regs., tit. 22, § 1200.52: Solicitation and Recommendation of Professional Employment

> (b) For purposes of this Rule, "solicitation" means any advertisement initiated by or on behalf of a lawyer or law firm that is directed to, or targeted at, a specific recipient or group of recipients, or their family members or legal representatives, the primary purpose of which is the retention of the lawyer or law firm, and a significant motive for which is pecuniary gain. It does not include a proposal or other writing prepared and delivered in response to a specific request of a prospective client.

> (e) No solicitation relating to a specific incident involving potential claims for personal injury or wrongful death shall be disseminated before the 30th day after the date of the incident, unless a filing must be made within 30 days of the incident as a legal prerequisite to the particular claim, in which case no unsolicited communication shall be made before the 15th day after the date of the incident.

N.Y. Comp.Codes R. & Regs., tit. 22 § 1200.36: Communication after Incidents Involving Personal Injury or Wrongful Death

> (a) In the event of a specific incident involving potential claims for personal injury or wrongful death, no unsolicited communication shall be made to an individual injured in the incident or to a family member or legal representative of such an individual, by a lawyer or law firm, or by any associate, agent, employee or other representative of a lawyer or law firm representing actual or potential defendants or entities that may defend and/or indemnify said defendants, before the 30th day after the date of the incident, unless a filing must be made within 30 days of the incident as a legal prerequisite to the particular claim, in which case no unsolicited communication shall be made before the 15th day after the date of the incident.

> (b) An unsolicited communication by a lawyer or law firm, seeking to represent an injured individual or the legal representative thereof under the circumstance described in paragraph (a) shall comply with [§ 1200.52(e)].

    * * *

C. The Present Action and District Court Decision

Plaintiffs filed their complaint on February 1, 2007, the date on which the new rules were to take effect. They sought declaratory and injunctive relief from several of the new rules, including all those set forth above. Plaintiffs contended that these rules infringed their First Amendment rights because the rules prohibited "truthful, non-misleading communications that the state has no legitimate interest in regulating." * * *   On July 23, 2007, the District Court filed its Memorandum-Decision and Order granting partial summary judgment to Plaintiffs and partial summary judgment to Defendants. Principally, the District Court found unconstitutional the disputed provisions of § 1200.50(c) set forth above, while concluding that the thirty-day moratorium provisions survived constitutional scrutiny. * * *

DISCUSSION

This case calls on us once again to assess the scope of First Amendment protection accorded to commercial speech, and the measure of evidence a state must present in regulating such speech. * * *

The Supreme Court has established a four-part inquiry for determining whether regulations of commercial speech are consistent with the First Amendment:

> [1] whether the expression is protected by the First Amendment. For commercial speech to come within that provision, it at least must concern lawful activity and not be misleading. Next, we ask [2] whether the asserted governmental interest is substantial. If both inquiries yield positive answers, we must determine [3] whether the regulation directly advances the governmental interest asserted, and [4] whether it is not more extensive than is necessary to serve that interest.

* * *

Central Hudson Gas & Elec. Corp. v. Public Serv. Comm'n of N.Y., <u>447 U.S. 557, 566, 100 S.Ct. 2343, 65 L. Ed. 2d 341</u>

A. The Disputed Provisions Regulate Commercial Speech Protected by the First Amendment

Defendants' appeal challenges the District Court's threshold conclusion as to the first prong of this inquiry—that the First Amendment protects advertising that is irrelevant, unverifiable, and non-informational. Although they do not dispute that New York's thirty-day moratorium provisions regulate protected commercial speech, Defendants argue strenuously to us that New York's content-based restrictions regulate speech that is not entitled to First Amendment protection at all.

The Supreme Court first recognized attorney advertising as within the scope of protected speech in, in which the Court invalidated a ban on price advertising for what the Court deemed "routine" legal services. In so doing, the Court reserved the question of whether similar protection would extend to "advertising claims as to the quality of services [that] are not susceptible of measurement or verification."

In the years since *Bates,* the Supreme Court has offered differing, and not always fully consistent, descriptions as to what constitutes protected commercial speech, particularly with respect to attorney advertising. Speaking generally, the Supreme Court has said that states may impose regulations to ensure that "the stream of commercial information flow[s] cleanly as well as freely." But this Court has nonetheless observed that there are "doctrinal uncertainties left in the wake of Supreme Court decisions from which the modern commercial speech doctrine has evolved. In particular, these decisions have created some uncertainty as to the degree of protection for commercial advertising that lacks precise informational content."

In the end, we agree with the District Court that, with one exception discussed below, the content-based restrictions in the disputed provisions of § 1200.50(c) regulate commercial speech protected by the First Amendment. In almost every instance, descriptions of the first prong of the Central Hudson test are phrased in the negative, and the only categories that Central Hudson, and its sequellae, clearly excludes from protection are speech that is false, deceptive, or misleading, and speech that concerns unlawful activities. * * *

There is one exception to this conclusion. Subsection 1200.50(c)(3) prohibits "the portrayal of a fictitious law firm, the use of a fictitious name to refer to lawyers not associated together in a law firm, or otherwise imply that lawyers are associated in a law firm if that is not the case." N.Y. Comp.Codes R. & Regs., tit. 22, § 1200.50(c)(3). The District Court invalidated § 1200.50(c)(3) in its entirety. *Alexander,* 634 F.Supp.2d at 249. Plaintiffs acknowledge, however, that they intended to challenge only the first clause of this subsection—prohibiting portrayals of judges—and they do not oppose Defendants' appeal seeking reinstatement of the prohibition on fictitious firms.

The provision prohibiting advertisements including fictitious firms is susceptible to more than one interpretation. But we need not decide whether it would be constitutional to prohibit dramatizations in which an advertising law firm portrays itself arguing against a fictitious opposing counsel. At oral argument, the Attorney General, representing the Defendants, suggested a narrower interpretation of this regulation. He asked that we construe this language as applying only to situations in which lawyers from different firms give the misleading impression that they are from the same firm (i.e., "The Dream Team"). * * * (We accept this interpretation. So read, this portion of § 1200.50(c)(3) addresses only attorney advertising techniques that are actually misleading (as to the existence or membership of a firm), and such advertising is not entitled to First Amendment protection. Accordingly, and subject to the above-mentioned construction, we reverse the District Court's invalidation of that portion of § 1200.50(c)(3) that prohibits advertisements that include fictitious firms.

Having concluded that the remainder of the disputed regulations falls within the zone of protected commercial speech, we turn to the rest of the *Central Hudson* test. The Supreme Court has explained that "[c]ommercial speech that is not false or deceptive and does not concern unlawful activities may be restricted only in the service of a substantial governmental interest, and only through means that directly advance that interest." "The party seeking to uphold a restriction on commercial speech carries the burden of justifying it." We apply the three remaining prongs of *Central Hudson*, in turn, to each of the two categories of regulations set forth above.

B. Central Hudson and the Content-Based Regulations

1. Substantial Interest

Under the second prong of *Central Hudson*, the State must identify "a substantial interest in support of its regulation[s]." "[T]he *Central Hudson* standard does not permit us to supplant the precise interests put forward by the State with other suppositions." Before the District Court and again on appeal, Defendants proffered a state interest in "prohibiting attorney advertisements from containing deceptive or misleading content."* * * The report by the New York State Bar Association's Task Force on Lawyer Advertising (hereinafter, the "Task Force Report" or "Report"), which the State considered in formulating its new rules and which constitutes the bulk of the record on appeal, indicates that this is a proper and genuinely asserted interest. The Task Force Report identified protecting the public "by prohibiting advertising and solicitation practices that disseminate false or misleading information" as one of its key concerns. * * * This state interest is substantial-indeed, states have a generally unfettered right to prohibit inherently or actually misleading commercial speech. * * * The disputed regulations codified at § 1200.50(c) therefore survive the second prong of the *Central Hudson* analysis.

Defendants also assert an interest in "protecting the legal profession's image and reputation." * * * In *Florida Bar,* the Supreme Court recognized a substantial interest "in preventing the erosion of confidence in the [legal] profession." Defendants explain that their interest in preventing misleading attorney advertising is "inextricably linked to its overarching interest" in maintaining attorney professionalism and respect for the bar. * * * This interest also supports the disputed regulations.

2. Materially Advanced

The penultimate prong of the *Central Hudson* test requires that a regulation impinging upon commercial expression "'directly advance the state interest involved; the regulation may not be sustained if it provides only ineffective or remote support for the government's purpose.'" The state's burden with respect to this prong "is not satisfied by mere speculation or conjecture; rather, a governmental body seeking to sustain a restriction on commercial speech must demonstrate that the harms it recites are real and that its restrictions will in fact alleviate them to a material degree." Moreover, "[i]f the protections afforded commercial speech are to retain their force, we cannot allow rote invocation of the words 'potentially misleading' to supplant" this burden.

Invalidating a regulation of commercial speech for lack of sufficient evidence under this prong of *Central Hudson* does not foreclose a similar regulation being enacted validly in the future. Rather, such invalidation returns the matter to the applicable legislating body and "forces [that body] to take a 'second look' with the eyes of the people on it." * * *

In defending the disputed § 1200.50(c) provisions, Defendants rely on three sources of evidence: (1) "history, consensus, and simple common sense," including regulations of attorney advertising in other states; (2) existing and unchallenged rules already in New York's Code of Professional Responsibility targeting advertising similar to that targeted by the new amendments; and (3) the New York State Bar Association's Task Force Report. Defendants have not submitted any statistical or anecdotal evidence of consumer problems with or complaints of the sort they seek to prohibit. Nor have they specifically identified any studies from other jurisdictions on which the state relied in implementing the amendments. Against this background, we test each of the disputed § 1200.50(c) provisions.

a. * * * Client Testimonials

This subsection prohibits advertisements that include "an endorsement of, or testimonial about, a lawyer or law firm from a client with respect to a matter that is still pending." * * * The Task Force Report observed that testimonials can be misleading because they may suggest that past results indicate future performance. * * * The Task Force Report, however, did not recommend outright prohibitions of all testimonials on this basis. Instead, as the District Court observed, the Task Force Report "recommended a different approach." * * * The Report suggested "strengthening the rules governing testimonials to prohibit the use of an actor or spokesperson who is not a member or employee of the advertising lawyer or law firm *absent disclosure thereof.*" * * * The Task Force noted, moreover, that "it would be an improper restriction on a client's free speech rights to prohibit client testimonials outright." The Task Force Report therefore does not support Defendants' assertion that prohibiting testimonials from current clients will materially advance an interest in preventing misleading advertising. Indeed, the Report "contradicts, rather than strengthens, the Board's submissions."

Nor does consensus or common sense support the conclusion that client testimonials are inherently misleading. Testimonials may, for example, mislead if they suggest that past results indicate future performance-but not all testimonials will do so, especially if they include a disclaimer. The District Court properly concluded that Defendants failed to satisfy this prong of *Central Hudson* with respect to client testimonials.

b. * * * Portrayal of a Judge

This subsection prohibits "the portrayal of a judge." * * * The Task Force Report observes that "a communication that states or implies that the lawyer has the ability to influence improperly a court" is "likely to be false, deceptive, or misleading." * * * The District Court found this comment to be persuasive evidence that a ban on portrayals of judges would materially advance the State's interest in preventing misleading advertising. We disagree. Although it seems plainly true that implying an ability to influence a court is likely to be misleading, Defendants have failed to draw the requisite connection between that common sense observation and portrayals of judges in advertisements generally. The advertisement in which Alexander & Catalano use the portrayal of a judge, for instance, depicts a judge in the courtroom and states that the judge is there "to make sure [the trial] is fair." This sort of advertisement does not imply an ability to influence a court improperly. It is not misleading; an advertisement of this sort may, instead, be informative. We believe the Task Force Report fails to support Defendants' prohibition on portrayals of judges and conclude that Defendants have not met their burden with respect to the wholesale prohibition of portrayals of judges. This prohibition consequently must fall.

c. * * * Irrelevant Techniques

This subsection prohibits advertisements that "rely on techniques to obtain attention that demonstrate a clear and intentional lack of relevance to the selection of counsel, including the portrayal of lawyers exhibiting characteristics clearly unrelated to legal competence." * * * Defendants note that the New York Code of Professional Responsibility has long declared that the purpose of attorney advertising is to "educate the public to an awareness of legal needs and to provide information relevant to the selection of the most appropriate counsel." * * * Defendants contend that their rule excluding attention-getting techniques unrelated to attorney competence reflects this principle and so materially advances "New York's interest in factual, relevant attorney advertisements." * * *

A rule barring irrelevant advertising components certainly advances an interest in keeping attorney advertising factual and relevant. But this interest is quite different from an interest in preventing misleading advertising. Like Defendants' claim that the First Amendment does not protect irrelevant and unverifiable components in advertising, Defendants here appear to conflate *irrelevant* components of advertising with *misleading* advertising. These are not one and the same. Questions of taste or effectiveness in advertising are generally matters of subjective judgment. Moreover, as the Task Force Report acknowledged, "Limiting the information that may be advertised . . . assumes that the bar can accurately forecast the kind of information that the public would regard as relevant." * * *

Defendants have introduced no evidence that the sorts of irrelevant advertising components proscribed by subsection 1200.50(c)(5) are, in fact, misleading and so subject to proscription. Significantly, the Task Force Report expressly recognized that "communications involving puffery and claims that cannot be measured or verified" were not specifically addressed in its proposed rules, although such communications would already be prohibited "to the extent that they are false, deceptive or misleading." * * * Insofar as the Task Force Report touched on style and advertising gimmicks designed to draw attention, its recommendations were hortatory only. * * *

Moreover, the sorts of gimmicks that this rule appears designed to reach—such as Alexander & Catalano's wisps of smoke, blue electrical currents, and special effects-do not actually seem likely to mislead. It is true that Alexander and his partner are not giants towering above local buildings; they cannot run to a client's house so quickly that they appear as blurs; and they do not actually provide legal assistance to space aliens. But given the prevalence of these and other kinds of special effects in advertising and entertainment, we cannot seriously believe-purely as a matter of "common sense"—that ordinary individuals are likely to be misled into thinking that these advertisements depict true characteristics. Indeed, some of these gimmicks, while seemingly irrelevant, may actually serve "important communicative functions: [they] attract[] the attention of the audience to the advertiser's message, and [they] may also serve to impart information directly." Plaintiffs assert that they use attention-getting techniques to "communicate ideas in an easy-to-understand form, to attract viewer interest, to give emphasis, and to make information more memorable." Defendants provide no evidence to the contrary; nor do they provide evidence that consumers have, in fact, been misled by these or similar advertisements. Absent such, or similar, evidence, Defendants cannot meet their burden for sustaining subsection 1200.50(c)(5)'s prohibition under *Central Hudson.*

d. * * * Nicknames, Mottos, and Trade Names

This subsection bars advertisements "utiliz[ing] a nickname, moniker, motto or trade name that implies an ability to obtain results in a matter." N.Y. Comp.Codes R. & Regs., tit. 22, § 1200.50(c)(7). We conclude, once again, that the evidence on which Defendants rely fails to support this regulation.

There is a compelling, commonsense argument that, given the uncertainties of litigation, names that imply an ability to obtain results are usually misleading. The Task Force Report made precisely this observation, stating in its recommendations that "the use of dollar signs, the terms 'most cash' or 'maximum dollars,' or like terms that suggest the outcome of the legal matter" is "likely to be false, deceptive or misleading." * * * Like its recommendations on irrelevant advertising techniques, however, the Task Force Report did not recommend outright prohibition of all such trade names or mottos-it simply acknowledged that such names are often misleading. Defendants' rule, by contrast, goes further and prohibits such descriptors-including, according to the Attorney General, Alexander & Catalano's own "Heavy Hitters" motto-even when they are not actually misleading. The Task

Force Report therefore fails to support Defendants' considerably broader rule.

Nor are we persuaded as to this rule's constitutionality by reference to *Friedman v. Rogers,* 440 U.S. 1 (1979), in which the Supreme Court upheld a prohibition on optometrist trade names. There is doubt as to *Friedman's* continued vitality. *Friedman* preceded *Central Hudson* by nine years and did not employ *Central Hudson's* multi-factor First Amendment analysis. As this Court previously observed in *Bad Frog Brewery,* subsequent Supreme Court precedent has undermined *Friedman* and moved in the direction of greater First Amendment protection for "a logo or a slogan that conveys no information, other than identifying the source of the product, but that serves, to some degree, to 'propose a commercial transaction.' " * * * Accordingly, we decline to rely solely on *Friedman* to uphold § 1200.50(c)(7) given the subsequent precedential developments establishing more specific and demanding burdens of evidence on the state.

Moreover, in *Friedman* itself, the state marshaled substantially stronger and more specific evidence supporting its prohibition on trade names than was done in this case. * * * There is a dearth of evidence in the present record supporting the need for § 1200.50(c)(7)'s prohibition on names that imply an ability to get results when the names are akin to, and no more than, the kind of puffery that is commonly seen, and indeed expected, in commercial advertisements generally. Defendants have once again failed to provide evidence that consumers have, in fact, been misled by the sorts of names and promotional devices targeted by § 1200.50(c)(7), and so have failed to meet their burden for sustaining this prohibition under *Central Hudson.*

3. Narrowly Tailored

The final prong of *Central Hudson* asks whether the "fit" between the goals identified (the state's interests) and the means chosen to advance these goals is reasonable; the fit need not be perfect. As this Court has explained, "'laws restricting commercial speech . . . need only be tailored in a *reasonable manner* to serve a substantial state interest in order to survive First Amendment scrutiny.'" Nonetheless, "restrictions upon [potentially deceptive speech] may be no broader than reasonably necessary to prevent the deception." "[T]he existence of numerous and obvious less-burdensome alternatives to the restriction on commercial speech is certainly a relevant consideration in determining whether the 'fit' between ends and means is reasonable." More precisely, the Supreme Court has emphasized that "States may not place an absolute prohibition on certain types of potentially misleading information . . . if the information also may be presented in a way that is not deceptive." And the Supreme Court has also affirmed that a state may not impose a prophylactic ban on potentially misleading speech merely to spare itself the trouble of "distinguishing the truthful from the false, the helpful from the misleading, and the harmless from the harmful."

On this basis, even if we were to find that all of the disputed Section 1200.50(c) restrictions survived scrutiny under *Central Hudson*'s third prong, each would fail the final inquiry because each wholly prohibits a category of advertising speech that is *potentially* misleading, but is not inherently or actually misleading in all cases. Contrary to Defendants' assertions, the fact that New York's rules do also permit substantial information in attorney advertising does not render the disputed provisions any less categorical. Significantly, *Zauderer* deemed a rule barring illustrations a "blanket ban." And New York's rules prohibiting, *inter alia,* all testimonials by current clients, all portrayals of judges, and all depictions of lawyers exhibiting characteristics unrelated to legal competence are similarly categorical. Because these advertising techniques are no more than potentially misleading, the categorical nature of New York's prohibitions would alone be enough to render the prohibitions invalid.

Moreover, "nowhere does the State cite any evidence or authority of any kind for its contention that the potential abuses associated with the [disputed provisions] cannot be combated by any means short of a blanket ban." As the District Court observed, the State could have, for example, required disclaimers similar to the one already required for fictional scenes. * * * Nothing in the record suggests that such disclaimers would have been ineffective.

The materials in the record show, instead, that disclaimers and other regulations short of content-based bans were in fact suggested. The Task Force "agreed at the outset to deal in practical solutions (*i.e.,* generally strengthening existing disclaimers and requiring further disclosures) without adding content-based restrictions." (Task Force Report 2) Nearly all of the Report's recommendations followed this general rule. And in comments responding to New York's draft rules, the Federal Trade Commission, "which has a long history of reviewing claims of deceptive advertising," similarly stated its belief that New York could adequately protect consumers "using less restrictive means such as requiring clear and prominent disclosure of certain information." (Letter from the FTC's Office of Policy Planning, Bureau of Consumer Protection, and Bureau of Economics to Michael Colodner, Office of Court Administration (Sept. 14, 2006)).

Defendants have failed to carry their burden with respect to *Central Hudson*'s final prong. We therefore conclude, like the District Court, that the disputed portions of subsections 1200.50(c)(1), (3), (5), and (7) are unconstitutional. In so doing, we return this matter to the Appellate Division, where that body may "take a 'second look' with the eyes of the people on it."

C. Central Hudson and the Moratorium Provisions

Plaintiffs' cross-appeal challenges the District Court's decision upholding New

York's time-limited moratorium on solicitation of accident victims or their families. "In cases where a legal filing is required within thirty days, the moratorium is limited to a fifteen-day cooling off period." * * * New York's moratorium provisions apply to all media through which an attorney might initiate communication "directed to, or targeted at, a specific recipient or group of recipients." * * *

Consistent with the regulations as written and with counsel's concessions at oral argument, we construe the moratorium provision as inapplicable to (a) broad, generalized mailings; (b) general advertisements conveying an attorney's experience in handling personal-injury suits, even when these advertisements appear near news stories in a newspaper that the attorney knows will be filled with coverage of a particular accident; or (c) advertisements informing readers of an attorney's past experience with a particular product where that product has caused repeated personal-injury problems (as with the Dalkon Shield advertisement at issue in *Zauderer*).

We turn now to the remaining *Central Hudson* inquiries relevant to the moratorium provision.

1. State Interest

In *Florida Bar,* the Supreme Court recognized as a substantial state interest "protecting the privacy and tranquility of personal injury victims and their loved ones against intrusive, unsolicited contact by lawyers." That case considered a thirty-day moratorium on direct-mail solicitation of accident victims (or their families). This case similarly involves a moratorium on contacting accident victims (and their families). The Task Force Report, which Defendants considered, recommended a limited moratorium because "the cooling off requirement would be beneficial in removing a source of annoyance and offense to those already troubled by an accident or similar occurrence." * * * *Florida Bar* makes clear that Defendants' stated interest is substantial, and the Task Force Report indicates that that interest is genuinely asserted. The moratorium provisions thus meet the requirements of *Central Hudson's* substantial interest prong.

2. Materially Advanced

Florida Bar upheld Florida's moratorium rule, which is similar to the New York provisions before us. Several other states have since adopted analogous regulations prohibiting targeted solicitation of accident victims for specific periods of time. The Task Force Report, based in part on the practices of these states, recommended a fifteen-day "cooling-off period" during which direct-mail solicitation of accident victims would be prohibited. (Task Force Report, App. I, 4) New York's moratorium provisions seek to address the same harms that the *Florida Bar* Court recognized in upholding a thirty-day ban on direct-mail solicitations. And the New York provisions seek to address those harms through similar means-a time-limited moratorium on targeted solicitation of potential clients. *Florida Bar* makes clear that such means materially advance the state's interest. We conclude, therefore, that Defendants have met their burden under this prong of *Central Hudson.* * * *

3. Narrowly Tailored

Were New York's moratorium provisions limited to direct-mail solicitation, there would be little question as to their constitutionality. * * *. But New York's moratorium is not so limited. As the District Court recognized, "The moratorium provisions in this case extend by their plain language to television, radio, newspaper, and website solicitations that are directed to or targeted at a specific recipient or group of recipients."

The Supreme Court has in some circumstances favored a technology-specific approach to the First Amendment. * * * But the differences among media may or may not be relevant to the First Amendment analysis depending on the challenged restrictions. * * *

In the context before us, we eschew a technology-specific approach to the First Amendment and conclude that New York's moratorium provisions-as we construe them-survive constitutional scrutiny notwithstanding their applicability across the technological spectrum. We focus first on the potential differences among media as to the degree of affirmative action needed to be taken by the targeted recipient to receive the material Plaintiffs seek to send. For many media forms, it is about the same. Thus, to us, the affirmative act of walking to one's mailbox and tearing open a letter seems no greater than walking to one's front step and picking up the paper or turning on a knob on a television or radio.

It is true that the Internet may appear to require more affirmative acts on the part of the user in order to recover content (and is therefore perhaps entitled to greater First Amendment protection insofar as users are soliciting information, rather than being solicited). But regardless of whether this characterization was once accurate, it no longer is so. E-mail has replaced letters; newspapers are often read online; radio streams online; television programming is broadcast on the Web; and the Internet can be connected to television. *See* Christopher S. Yoo, *The Rise and Demise of the Technology-Specific Approach to the First Amendment,* 91 Geo. L.J. 245, 248 (2003) * * * . Furthermore, Internet searches do not bring a user immediately to the desired result without distractions. Advertisements may appear with the user's search results; pop-up ads appear on web pages; and Gmail (Google's e-mail service) creates targeted advertising based on the keywords used in one's e-mail. In such a context, an accident victim who describes her experience in an e-mail might very well find an attorney advertisement targeting victims of the specific accident on her computer screen.

States are increasingly responding to these expanded and expanding roles of the Internet. Several already apply existing attorney professional responsibility rules to electronic and Internet advertisements and solicitations. *See* Amy Haywood & Melissa Jones, *Navigating a Sea of Uncertainty: How Existing Ethical Guidelines Pertain to the Marketing of Legal Services Over the Internet,* 14 Geo. J. Legal Ethics, 1099, 1113 (2001). * * * Texas and Florida have also added language to their disciplinary rules specifically to address attorney solicitation via the Internet. The New York Task Force Report reached the same conclusion. The Report repeatedly stated that "on-line advertisements and websites are not materially different than typical" printed advertisements, and that the rules should be enforced equally across media. * * * In so doing, the Report "demonstrate[d] that the harms it recites are real and its restriction will in fact alleviate them to a degree."

Accordingly, we conclude that even acknowledging that differences among media may be significant in some First Amendment analyses, they are not so in this case. Three aspects of the Supreme Court's analysis in *Florida Bar* are of particular relevance to our determination that the harms identified in that case, and put forth by Defendants in this case, are just as compelling with respect to targeted attorney advertisements on television, radio, newspapers, and the Internet as they are in justifying a ban on targeted mailings of attorney advertisements.

a. Porcelain Hearts

The Supreme Court has recognized the particular sensitivity of people to targeted (plaintiff's) attorney advertisements during periods of trauma. To the extent that the attorney advertisements, regardless of the media through which they are communicated, are directed toward the same sensitive people, there is no reason to distinguish among the mode of communication. Depending on the individual recipient, the printed word may be a likely to offend as images on a screen or in newspapers.

In *Florida Bar,* the Court recognized the state's "substantial interest . . . in protecting injured Floridians from invasive conduct by lawyers." As the dissent in *Florida Bar* pointed out, the primary distinction between the targeted letters at issue in *Florida Bar* and the untargeted letters at issue in *Shapero v. Kentucky Bar Association,* 486 U.S. 466 (1988), was that "victims or their families will be offended by receiving a [targeted] solicitation during their grief and trauma." The dissent argued that the majority should not "allow restrictions on speech to be justified on the ground that the expression might offend the listener."

But the majority of the Supreme Court in *Florida Bar* held otherwise. It focused on a subset of the public in analyzing the First Amendment: essentially, a First Amendment analogue to tort law's thin-skull plaintiffs, those who have a "porcelain heart." Some accident victims and their families might welcome targeted solicitations that inform them of their legal rights immediately after the accident (particularly when insurance companies may already be knocking on their doors). Other accident victims and their families might be perturbed—but not outraged—by the targeted solicitations. The Supreme Court, however, tailored First Amendment law, in the context of attorney solicitations, to the most sensitive members of the public. It is with these porcelain hearts in mind that we must evaluate New York's moratorium.

b. Wemmick's Castle

In Charles Dickens' "Great Expectations," the character of Mr. Wemmick has a home that is literally his castle, complete with a drawbridge and moat that are used to separate his lives inside and outside the home.

In addition to a heightened concern for public sensitivity to potentially offensive attorney communications, the Court in *Florida Bar* upheld the moratorium in part because of its belief that people should be given more of an option to avoid offensive speech in the privacy of their homes. *See Florida Bar,* 515 U.S. at 625, ("[W]e have consistently recognized that the State's interest in protecting the well-being, tranquility, and privacy of the home is certainly of the highest order in a free and civilized society.").

In this respect, the Court was adhering to a long-held position:

> One important aspect of residential privacy is protection of the unwilling listener. Although in many locations, we expect individuals simply to avoid speech they do not want to hear, the home is different. "That we are often 'captives' outside the sanctuary of the home and subject to objectionable speech ... does not mean we must be captives everywhere." Instead, a special benefit of the privacy all citizens enjoy within their own walls, which the State may legislate to protect, is an ability to avoid intrusions. Thus, we have repeatedly held that individuals are not required to welcome unwanted speech into their own homes and that the government may protect this freedom. * * *

Yet, a letter in a mailbox is no more intrusive than the newspaper in the mailbox, the e-mail in one's inbox, the television in the living room, the radio in the kitchen, or the Internet in the study. Arguably, mail is directly targeted at a residence, whereas television, radio, and the Internet may be viewed outside the home. But the Court has seemingly not focused on this distinction, and, instead, has held that the home should be protected from offensive language that disturbs domestic tranquility through the airwaves:

Patently offensive, indecent material presented over the airwaves confronts the citizen, not only in public, but also in the privacy of the home, where the individual's right to be left alone plainly outweighs the First Amendment rights of an intruder. Because the broadcast audience is constantly tuning in and out, prior warnings cannot completely protect the listener or viewer from unexpected program content. To say that one may avoid further offense by turning off the radio when he hears indecent language is like saying that the remedy for an assault is to run away after the first blow. One may hang up on an indecent phone call, but that option does not give the caller a constitutional immunity or avoid a harm that has already taken place. * * * Once again, we find no reason to distinguish among these media for our First Amendment analysis.

c. Lawyers' Reputations

Finally, *Florida Bar* recognized the state's "substantial interest . . . in preventing the erosion of confidence in the [legal] profession that . . . repeated invasions [of privacy by lawyers] have engendered." The *Florida Bar* court distinguished between two kinds of direct-mail advertisements: (1) those that cause offense to the recipient and whose harm can "be eliminated by a brief journey to the trash can," A solicitation that offends is not likely to be any less detrimental to the reputation of lawyers when spoken aloud, displayed on a computer screen, or conveyed by television.

Accordingly, we conclude that ads targeting certain accident victims that are sent by television, radio, newspapers, or the Internet are more similar to direct-mail solicitations, which can properly be prohibited within a limited time frame, than to "an untargeted letter mailed to society at large," which "involves no willful or knowing affront to or invasion of the tranquility of bereaved or injured individuals and simply does not cause the same kind of reputational harm to the profession" as direct mail solicitations.

Moreover, we do not find constitutional fault with the 30-day time period during which attorneys may not solicit potential clients in a targeted fashion. As with *Florida Bar*'s "short temporal ban," New York's moratorium permits attorneys to advertise to the general public their expertise with personal injury or wrongful death claims. It thereby fosters reaching the accident victims, so long as these victims are not specifically targeted. It further allows accident victims to initiate contact with attorneys even during the thirty days following an accident. In fact, as *amici* New York State Bar Association point out, New York's moratorium is more narrowly tailored than that of *Florida Bar* insofar as it incorporates the Task Force Report's fifteen-day black-out period, which shortens the moratorium period to fifteen days where an attorney or law firm must make a filing within thirty days of an incident as a legal prerequisite to a particular claim. No doubt the statute could have been more precisely drawn, but it need not be "perfect" or "the least restrictive means" to pass constitutional muster.

New York's moratorium provisions prohibit targeted communications by lawyers to victims, their families, or their representatives as to a specific personal injury or wrongful death event, where such communications occur within thirty days of the incident in question. Where a legal filing is required within thirty days, the moratorium is limited to fifteen days. These provisions, although they reach a broader range of advertisements than those proscribed by the moratorium in *Florida Bar,* do not impose barriers inconsistent with the First Amendment. We conclude that the moratorium provisions, as construed, are sufficiently narrowly tailored to survive constitutional scrutiny.

CONCLUSION

The thorough and well-reasoned opinion of the District Court is AFFIRMED, except as to N.Y. Comp. Codes R. & Regs., tit. 22, § 1200.50(c)(3)'s ban on "the portrayal of a fictitious law firm, the use of a fictitious name to refer to lawyers not associated together in a law firm, or otherwise imply[ing] that lawyers are associated in a law firm if that is not the case." With respect to this portion of § 1200.50(c)(3) only, the judgment of the District Court is REVERSED.

[Question 8]

An attorney and a restaurant owner entered into a reciprocal referral arrangement. The attorney agreed to prominently display ads for the restaurant in her office, and to mention the restaurant to all her clients who requested a recommendation of a nearby place to eat. In return, the owner agreed to prominently display ads for the attorney's firm in the restaurant and to recommend the attorney to any of his customers who indicated a need for the services provided by the attorney. The reciprocal referral agreement was not exclusive, and the clients and customers would be informed of the existence and nature of the agreement.

Is the attorney subject to discipline for entering into this agreement?

Food for Thought

The regulations in *Alexander v. Cahill,* like those at issue in *Florida Bar v. Went for It, Inc.,* 515 U.S. 618 (1995), create a moratorium on lawyers contacting injured persons to offer representation but do not impose a similar moratorium on insurance companies seeking to resolve the injured party's claims. Professors Monroe Freedman and Abbe Smith argue that:

> Discouraging victims and their survivors from retaining lawyers is a familiar practice of insurance companies. * * * Clearly, this is a controversy of public importance—whether an accident victim should retain a lawyer to assert her First Amendment right of petition, and whether a particular settlement is in the interest of a particular victim. Just as clearly, one side of that controversy is being permitted to speak, while the other is being gagged.

Monroe H. Freedman & Abbe Smith, Understanding Lawyers' Ethics 355 (3d ed. 2004) (note that a new edition of Understanding Lawyers' Ethics is available Oct. 2010). What do you think of their argument in light of the policy concerns discussed in *Alexander v. Cahill?*

(A) Yes, because she asked the owner to place ads for the firm in the restaurant.

(B) Yes, because the agreement provided something of value to the restaurant owner in return for recommending the attorney's services.

(C) No, because she did not pay the restaurant owner for the referrals.

(D) No, because the agreement is not exclusive, and the clients and customers will be informed of the existence and nature of the agreement.

Rule 7.2(b) provides, in relevant part, that:

A lawyer shall not give anything of value to a person for recommending the lawyer's services except that a lawyer may

(1) pay the reasonable costs of advertisements or communications permitted by this Rule; * * *

(4) refer clients to another lawyer or a nonlawyer professional pursuant to an agreement not otherwise prohibited under these Rules that provides for the other person to refer clients or customers to the lawyer, if

(i) the reciprocal referral agreement is not exclusive, and

(ii) the client is informed of the existence and nature of the agreement.

III. Fees and Billing

Today, the two most common billing strategies are hourly billing and contingent fees. Hourly billing is especially dominant in large firm practices. Contingent fees are most commonly employed for representation of plaintiffs in litigation,[2] although some lawyers have created contingent arrange-

> **For More Information**
>
> Considering that internet conduct crosses state, national, and international boundaries, how do the advertising and solicitations rules govern attorney conduct on the internet? Many ethics experts have considered their application to blogs, web advertising, social networking, on-line referral services, chat rooms, and other internet activities. *See, e.g.*, J.T. Westermeier, *Ethics and the Internet*, 17 Geo. J. Legal Ethics 267 (2004). One of the leading blogs on these issues is http://www.legalethics.com.

---

2   Herbert M. Kritzer, *Holding Back the Floodtide: The Role of Contingent Fee Lawyers*, 70 Wis. Law., March 1997, at 10 (describing author's research "reporting that relatively few individual litigants use fee structures other than contingent fees for nondivorce cases; even in practice areas such as contracts, contingent fees are the most common type of fees for individuals").

ments for defense representation.[3] Lawyers can always charge a flat fee for their services, and many do, especially for relatively routine services. Probably due to the extensive use of the venture capital model to finance high tech businesses, many lawyers for high tech businesses have accepted an equity interest in their client as payment for services. Lawyers can use any of these approaches consistent with their ethical obligations. This Chapter will explain how to do so.

As a general matter, the rationale for the fee rules is consumer protection—ensuring that fees are reasonable and that lawyers do not take advantage of clients. In some respects, though, the rules retain a historical concern with maintaining lawyer independence and prohibiting lawyers from encouraging litigation. These concerns shape the modern restrictions on holding a proprietary interest in the subject matter of a litigation, and on contingent fees in matrimonial and criminal matters, as well as the special rules preventing a third-party who is paying the client's fees from influencing the representation.

Lawyer's fees are a controversial topic today. An American Bar Association study recently found that "[c]onsumers complain about the fees charged by all types of lawyers."[4] At the same time, lawyers have debated the propriety of each method of billing. They question whether particular approaches are more or less likely to align the lawyer's interests with those of the client. This Chapter will introduce you to these controversies.

Food for Thought

Historically, leading lawyers believed that professional excellence alone would result in lawyers earning a good living. George Sharswood, the nineteenth century scholar whose 1854 essay would become the basis of our modern legal ethics codes,[5] advised:

> [L]et business seek the young attorney; and though it may come in slowly, and at intervals, and promise in its character neither fame nor profit, still, if he bears in mind that it is an important part of his training that he should understand the business he does thoroughly, that he should especially cultivate, in transacting it, habits of neatness, accuracy, punctuality, and dispatch, candor toward his client, and strict honor toward his adversary, it may be safely prophesied that his business will grow as fast as it is good for him that it should grow[.]

George Sharswood, An Essay on Professional Ethics, 32 American Bar Association Reports 131-32 (5th ed. 1907).

---

3   *See, e.g.*, Angela Wennihan, Comment, *Lets Put the Contingency Back in the Contingency Fee*, 49 S.M.U. L. Rev. 1639, 1646 (1996).

4   Am. Bar Ass'n Sec. of Lit., Public Perceptions of Lawyers: Consumer Research Findings 15 (Leo J. Shapiro & Assoc. 2002).

5   For biographical background on Sharswood and his influence on the legal ethics codes, *see* Russell G. Pearce, Rediscovering the Republican Origins of the Legal Ethics Codes, 6 Geo. J. Legal Ethics 241 (1992).

[Question 1]

A company's president telephoned his city's best-known employment attorney and asked her to represent the company in a dispute that had just arisen with the company's chief financial officer. The attorney, who had never previously represented the company, agreed. At the president's insistence, she immediately commenced the representation. A few days later, during a meeting with the president, the attorney first revealed the amount of her customary hourly fee and then explained that the company would also be responsible for reimbursing her expenses. The president responded that her fee was higher than he had expected but that he would be happy for the company to pay it, given her excellent work to date. Although the attorney intended to follow up with a confirming letter, she never did so. For several more months, she assisted the company in resolving its employment dispute. Afterward, she sent the company a bill accurately reflecting her hourly fee and expenses, which were reasonable.

Is the attorney subject to discipline?

(A) Yes, because she did not disclose the basis of her fee before commencing the representation.

(B) Yes, because she did not confirm her fee agreement in writing.

- (C) No, because she disclosed the basis of her fee within a reasonable time after commencing the representation.

(D) No, because she was not required to advise the client of her customary hourly fee, unless requested to do so.

Rule 1.5 provides in part:

(a) A lawyer shall not make an agreement for, charge, or collect an unreasonable fee or an unreasonable amount for expenses. The factors to be considered in determining the reasonableness of a fee include the following:

(1) the time and labor required, the novelty and difficulty of the questions involved, and the skill requisite to perform the legal service properly;

(2) the likelihood, if apparent to the client, that the acceptance of the particular employment will preclude other employment by the lawyer;

(3) the fee customarily charged in the locality for similar legal services;

(4) the amount involved and the results obtained;

(5) the time limitations imposed by the client or by the circumstances;

(6) the nature and length of the professional relationship with the client;

(7) the experience, reputation, and ability of the lawyer or lawyers performing the services; and

(8) whether the fee is fixed or contingent.

(b) The scope of the representation and the basis or rate of the fee and expenses for which the client will be responsible shall be communicated to the client, preferably in writing, before or within a reasonable time after commencing the representation, except when the lawyer will charge a regularly represented client on the same basis or rate. Any changes in the basis or rate of the fee or expenses shall also be communicated to the client.

* * *

[Question 2]

Is it ethical for an attorney to bill two clients the hourly fees for work performed at the same time (e.g. billing one client for reviewing a contract while traveling for another client)?

(A) Yes

– **(B) No**

[Question 3]

Three of your clients have asked you to analyze the same proposed legislation. Any work you perform for the clients is billed on an hourly basis. If you spend one hour analyzing the legislation, is it ethical to bill each client for one hour?

(A) Yes

– **(B) No**

[Question 4]

When an attorney revises and recycles a document originally prepared for another client, is it ethical for the attorney to bill the current client for more

than the revision time? The attorney is billing the current client on an hourly basis.

(A) Yes

— (B) No

[Question 5]

If a fee agreement or engagement letter states that "the client agrees to pay expenses including photocopy and facsimile charges," is it ethical for the attorney to make a profit by charging the client fifty cents per page for photocopying that costs the attorney five cents per page?

(A) Yes

— (B) No

[Question 6]

In defending a major securities fund case, a law firm uses attorneys who receive an hourly salary. If the salaried attorneys are paid $100 per hour, is it ethical for the firm to bill the client $150 per hour?

(A) Yes

— (B) No

(C) It depends on whether the attorneys are employees of the firm or whether the law firm purchases their services from an outside agency.

Review Rules 1.5 and 7.1. Read Rule 1.4(b).

AM. BAR ASS'N, STANDING COMM. ON ETHICS & PROF'L RESPONSIBILITY, BILLING FOR PROFESSIONAL FEES, DISBURSEMENTS AND OTHER EXPENSES

Formal Op. 93-379 (1993)

> *Consistent with the Model Rules of Professional Conduct, a lawyer must disclose to a client the basis on which the client is to be billed for both professional time and any other charges. Absent a contrary understanding, any invoice for professional services should fairly reflect the basis on which the client's charges*

have been determined. In matters where the client has agreed to have the fee determined with reference to the time expended by the lawyer, a lawyer may not bill more time than she actually spends on a matter, except to the extent that she rounds up to minimum time periods (such as one-quarter or one-tenth of an hour). A lawyer may not charge a client for overhead expenses generally associated with properly maintaining, staffing and equipping an office; however, the lawyer may recoup expenses reasonably incurred in connection with the client's matter for services performed in-house, such as photocopying, long distance telephone calls, computer research, special deliveries, secretarial overtime, and other similar services, so long as the charge reasonably reflects the lawyer's actual cost for the services rendered. A lawyer may not charge a client more than her disbursements for services provided by third parties like court reporters, travel agents or expert witnesses, except to the extent that the lawyer incurs costs additional to the direct cost of the third-party services.

* * * It is a common perception that pressure on lawyers to bill a minimum number of hours and on law firms to maintain or improve profits may have led some lawyers to engage in problematic billing practices. These include charges to more than one client for the same work or the same hours, surcharges on services contracted with outside vendors, and charges beyond reasonable costs for in-house services like photocopying and computer searches. Moreover, the bases on which these charges are to be assessed often are not disclosed in advance or are disguised in cryptic invoices so that the client does not fully understand exactly what costs are being charged to him.

The Model Rules of Professional Conduct provide important principles applicable to the billing of clients, principles which, if followed, would ameliorate many of the problems noted above. The Committee has decided to address several practices that are the subject of frequent inquiry, with the goal of helping the profession adhere to its ethical obligations to its clients despite economic pressures.

The first set of practices involves billing more than one client for the same hours spent. In one illustrative situation, a lawyer finds it possible to schedule court appearances for three clients on the same day. He spends a total of four hours at the courthouse, the amount of time he would have spent on behalf of each client had it not been for the fortuitous circumstance that all three cases were scheduled on the same day. May he bill each of the three clients, who otherwise understand that they will be billed on the basis of time spent, for the four hours he spent on them collectively? In another scenario, a lawyer is flying cross-country to attend a deposition on behalf of one client, expending travel time she would ordinarily bill to that client. If she decides not to watch the movie or read her novel, but to work instead on drafting a motion for another client, may she charge both clients, each of whom agreed to hourly billing, for the time during which she was traveling on behalf of one and drafting a document on behalf of the other? A third situation involves research on a particular topic for one client that later turns out to be relevant to an inquiry from a second client. May the firm bill the second client, who agreed to be charged on the basis of time spent on his case, the same amount for the recycled work product that it charged the first client?

The second set of practices involves billing for expenses and disbursements, and is exemplified by the situation in which a firm contracts for the expert witness services of an economist at an hourly rate of $200. May the firm bill the client for the expert's time at the rate of $250 per hour? Similarly, may the firm add a surcharge to the cost of computer-assisted research if the per-minute total charged by the computer company does not include the cost of purchasing the computers or staffing their operation?

The questions presented to the Committee require us to determine what constitute reasonable billing procedures; that is, what are the services and costs for which a lawyer may legitimately charge, both generally and with regard to the specific scenarios? This inquiry requires an elucidation of the Rule of Professional Conduct 1.5, and the Model Code of Professional Responsibility DR 2-106.

Disclosure of the Bases of the Amounts to Be Charged

At the outset of the representation the lawyer should make disclosure of the basis for the fee and any other charges to the client. This is a two-fold duty, including not only an explanation at the beginning of engagement of the basis on which fees and other charges will be billed, but also a sufficient explanation in the statement so that the client may reasonably be expected to understand what fees and other charges the client is actually being billed.

Authority for the obligation to make disclosure at the beginning of a representation is found in the interplay among a number of rules. Rule 1.5(b) provides that

When the lawyer has not regularly represented the client, the basis or rate of the fee shall be communicated to the client, preferably in writing, before or within a reasonable time after commencing the representation.

The Comment to Rule 1.5 gives guidance on how to execute the duty to communicate the basis of the fee:

In a new client-lawyer relationship . . . an understanding as to the fee should be promptly established. It is not necessary to recite all the factors that underlie the basis of the fee, but only those that are directly involved in its computation. It is sufficient, for example, to state that the basic rate is an hourly charge or a fixed amount or an estimated amount, or to identify the factors that may be taken into account in finally fixing the fee. When developments occur during the representation that render an earlier estimate substantially inaccurate, a revised estimate should be provided to the client. A written statement concerning the fee reduces the possibility of misunderstanding. Furnishing the client with a simple memorandum or a copy of the lawyer's customary fee schedule is sufficient if the basis or rate of the fee is set forth.

This obligation is reinforced by reference to Model Rule 1.4(b) which provides that

A lawyer shall explain a matter to the extent reasonably necessary to permit the client to make informed decisions regarding the representation.

While the Comment to this Rule suggests its obvious applicability to negotiations or litigation with adverse parties, its important principle should be equally applicable to the lawyer's obligation to explain the basis on which the lawyer expects to be compensated, so the client can make one of the more important decisions "regarding the representation."

An obligation of disclosure is also supported by Model Rule 7.1, which addresses communications concerning a lawyer's services, including the basis on which fees would be charged. The rule provides:

A lawyer shall not make a false or misleading communication about the lawyer or the lawyer's services. A communication is false or misleading if it:

> (a) contains a material misrepresentation of fact or law, or omits a fact necessary to make the statement considered as a whole not materially misleading.

It is clear under Model Rule 7.1 that in offering to perform services for prospective clients it is critical that lawyers avoid making any statements about fees that are not complete. If it is true that a lawyer when advertising for new clients must disclose, for example, that costs are the responsibility of the client * * * it necessarily follows that in entering into an actual client relationship a lawyer must make fair disclosure of the basis on which fees will be assessed.

A corollary of the obligation to disclose the basis for future billing is a duty to render statements to the client that adequately apprise the client as to how that basis for billing has been applied. In an engagement in which the client has agreed to compensate the lawyer on the basis of time expended at regular hourly rates, a bill setting out no more than a total dollar figure for unidentified professional services will often be insufficient to tell the client what he or she needs to know in order to understand how the amount was determined. By the same token, billing other charges without breaking the charges down by type would not provide the client with the information the client needs to understand the basis for the charges.

Initial disclosure of the basis for the fee arrangement fosters communication that will promote the attorney-client relationship. The relationship will be similarly benefitted if the statement for services explicitly reflects the basis for the charges so that the client understands how the fee bill was determined.

Professional Obligations Regarding the Reasonableness of Fees

Implicit in the Model Rules and their antecedents is the notion that the attorney-client relationship is not necessarily one of equals, that it is built on trust, and that the client is encouraged to be dependent on the lawyer, who is dealing with matters of great moment to the client. The client should only be charged a reasonable fee for the legal services performed. Rule 1.5 explicitly addresses the reasonableness of legal fees. The rule deals not only with the determination of a reasonable hourly rate, but also with total cost to the client. The Comment to the rule states, for example, that "[a] lawyer should not exploit a fee arrangement based primarily on hourly charges by using wasteful procedures." The goal should be solely to compensate the lawyer fully for time reasonably expended, an approach that if followed will not take advantage of the client.

Ethical Consideration 2-17 of the Model Code of Professional Responsibility provides a framework for balancing the interests between the lawyer and client in determining the reasonableness of a fee arrangement:

> The determination of a proper fee requires consideration of the interests of both client and lawyer. A lawyer should not charge more than a reasonable fee, for excessive cost of legal service would deter laymen from utilizing the legal system in protection of their rights. Furthermore, an excessive charge abuses the professional relationship between lawyer and client. On the other hand, adequate compensation is necessary in order to enable the lawyer to serve his client effectively and to preserve the integrity and independence of the profession.

The lawyer's conduct should be such as to promote the client's trust of the lawyer and of the legal profession. This means acting as the advocate for the client to the extent necessary to complete a project thoroughly. Only through careful attention to detail is the lawyer able to manage a client's case properly. An unreasonable limitation on the hours a lawyer may spend on a client should be avoided as a threat to the lawyer's ability to fulfill her obligation under Model Rule 1.1 to "provide competent representation to a client." Competent representation requires the legal knowledge, skill, thoroughness and preparation necessary for the representation." Model Rule 1.1. Certainly either a willingness on the part of the lawyer, or a demand by the client, to circumscribe the lawyer's efforts, to compromise the lawyer's ability to be as thorough and as prepared as necessary, is not in the best interests of the client and may lead to a violation of Model Rule 1.1 if it means the lawyer is unable to provide competent representation. The Comment to Model Rule 1.2, while observing that "the scope of services provided by a lawyer may be limited by agreement," also notes that an agreement "concerning the scope of representation must accord with the Rules. . . . Thus, the client may not be asked to agree to representation so limited in scope as to violate Rule 1.1. . . ."

On the other hand, the lawyer who has agreed to bill on the basis of hours expended does not fulfill her ethical duty if she bills the client for more time than she actually spent on the client's behalf. In addressing the hypotheticals regarding (a) simultaneous appearance on behalf of three clients, (b) the airplane flight on behalf of one client while working on another client's matters and (c) recycled work product, it is helpful to consider these questions, not from the perspective of what a client could be forced to pay, but rather from the perspective of what the lawyer actually earned. A lawyer who spends four hours of time on behalf of three clients has not earned twelve billable hours. A lawyer who flies for six hours for one client, while working for five hours on behalf of another, has not earned eleven billable hours. A lawyer who is able to reuse old work product has not re-earned the hours previously billed and compensated when the work product was first generated. Rather than looking to profit from the fortuity of coincidental scheduling, the desire to get work done rather than watch a movie, or the luck of being asked the identical question twice, the lawyer who has agreed to bill solely on the basis of time spent is obliged to pass the benefits of these economies on to the client. The practice of billing several clients for the same time or work product, since it results in the earning of an unreasonable fee, therefore is contrary to the mandate of the Model Rules. Model Rule 1.5.

Moreover, continuous toil on or overstaffing a project for the purpose of churning out hours is also not properly considered "earning" one's fees. * * * A lawyer should take as much time as is reasonably required to complete a project, and should certainly never be motivated by anything other than the best interests of the client when determining how to staff or how much time to spend on any particular project.

It goes without saying that a lawyer who has undertaken to bill on an hourly basis is never justified in charging a client for hours not actually expended. If a lawyer has agreed to charge the client on this basis and it turns out that the lawyer is particularly efficient in accomplishing a given result, it nonetheless will not be permissible to charge the client for more hours than were actually expended on the matter. When that basis for billing the client has been agreed to, the econo-mies associated with the result must inure to the benefit of the client, not give rise to an opportunity to bill a client phantom hours. This is not to say that the lawyer who agreed to hourly compensation is not free, with full disclosure, to suggest additional compensation because of a particularly efficient or outstanding result, or because the lawyer was able to reuse prior work product on the client's behalf. The point here is that fee enhancement cannot be accomplished simply by presenting the client with a statement reflecting more billable hours than were actually expended. On the other hand, if a matter turns out to be more difficult to accomplish than first anticipated and more hours are required than were originally estimated, the lawyer is fully entitled (though not required) to bill those hours unless the client agreement turned the original estimate into a cap on the fees to be charged.

Charges Other Than Professional Fees

In addition to charging clients fees for professional services, lawyers typically charge their clients for certain additional items which are often referred to variously as disbursements, out-of-pocket expenses or additional charges. Inquiries to the Committee demonstrate that the profession has encountered difficulties in conforming to the ethical standards in this area as well. The Rules provide no specific guidance on the issue of how much a lawyer may charge a client for costs incurred over and above her own fee. However, we believe that the reasonableness standard explicitly applicable to fees under Rule 1.5(a) should be applicable to these charges as well.

The Committee, in trying to sort out the issues related to these charges, has identified three different questions which must be addressed. First, which items are properly subject to additional charges? Second, to what extent, if at all, may clients be charged for more than actual out-of-pocket disbursements? Third, on what basis may clients be charged for the provision of in-house services? We shall address these one at a time.

A. General Overhead

When a client has engaged a lawyer to provide professional services for a fee (whether calculated on the basis of the number of hours expended, a flat fee, a contingent percentage of the amount recovered or otherwise) the client would be justifiably disturbed if the lawyer submitted a bill to the client which included, beyond the professional fee, additional charges for general office overhead. In the absence of disclosure to the client in advance of the engagement to the contrary, the client should reasonably expect that the lawyer's cost in maintaining a library, securing malpractice insurance, renting of office space, purchasing utilities and the like would be subsumed within the charges the lawyer is making for professional services.

B. Disbursements

At the beginning of the engagement lawyers typically tell their clients that they will be charged for disbursements. When that term is used clients justifiably should expect that the lawyer will be passing on to the client those actual payments of funds made by the lawyer on the client's behalf. Thus, if the lawyer hires a court stenographer to transcribe a deposition, the client can reasonably expect to be billed as a disbursement the amount the lawyer pays to the court reporting service. Similarly, if the lawyer flies to Los Angeles for the client, the client can reasonably expect to be billed as a disbursement the amount of the airfare, taxicabs, meals and hotel room.

It is the view of the Committee that, in the absence of disclosure to the contrary, it would be improper if the lawyer assessed a surcharge on these disbursements over and above the amount actually incurred unless the lawyer herself incurred additional expenses beyond the actual cost of the disbursement item. In the same regard, if a lawyer receives a discounted rate from a third-party provider, it would be improper if she did not pass along the benefit of the discount to her client rather than charge the client the full rate and reserve the profit to herself. Clients quite properly could view these practices as an attempt to create additional undisclosed profit centers when the client had been told he would be billed for disbursements.

C. In-House Provision of Services

Perhaps the most difficult issue is the handling of charges to clients for the provision of in-house services. In this connection the Committee has in view charges for photocopying, computer research, on-site meals, deliveries and other similar items. Like professional fees, it seems clear that lawyers may pass on reasonable charges for these services. Thus, in the view of the Committee, the lawyer and the client may agree in advance that, for example, photocopying will be charged at $.15 per page, or messenger services will be provided at $5.00 per mile. However, the question arises what may be charged to the client, in the absence of a specific agreement to the contrary, when the client has simply been told that costs for these items will be charged to the client. We conclude that under those circumstances the lawyer is obliged to charge the client no more than the direct cost associated with the service (i.e., the actual cost of making a copy on the photocopy machine) plus a reasonable allocation of overhead expenses directly associated with the provision of the service (e.g., the salary of a photocopy machine operator).

It is not appropriate for the Committee, in addressing ethical standards, to opine on the various accounting issues as to how one calculates direct cost and what may or may not be included in allocated overhead. These are questions which properly should be reserved for our colleagues in the accounting profession. Rather, it is the responsibility of the Committee to explain the principles it draws from the mandate of Model Rule 1.5's injunction that fees be reasonable. Any reasonable calculation of direct costs as well as any reasonable allocation of related overhead should pass ethical muster. On the other hand, in the absence of an agreement to the contrary, it is impermissible for a lawyer to create an additional source of profit for the law firm beyond that which is contained in the provision of professional services themselves. The lawyer's stock in trade is the sale of legal services, not photocopy paper, tuna fish sandwiches, computer time or messenger services.

Conclusion

As the foregoing demonstrates, the subject of fees for professional services and other charges is one that is fraught with tension between the lawyer and the client. Nonetheless, if the principles outlined in this opinion are followed, the ethical resolution of these issues can be achieved.

A. The Hourly Billing Controversy

WILLIAM G. ROSS, *THE ETHICS OF HOURLY BILLING BY ATTORNEYS*

44 Rutgers L. Rev. 1, 8-12, 88-90 (1991)

* * *

During early years of the Republic, many states followed the colonial practice of fee schedules by enacting fee regulations and providing penalties for lawyers who charged more than the prescribed amounts. * * * Similar to the fee schedules enacted prior to the Revolution, the fee regulations of the early Republic generally provided that the losing party would pay the fees of the prevailing party. * * * As the nineteenth century progressed, the courts gradually recognized the right of lawyers to collect fees that were larger than anything that was recoverable under the fee statutes. * * * The abolition of fee schedules also may have reflected the hostility of conservative middle class attorneys toward incipient trade unionism. For example, the fee schedules and other regulations that were established by the Massachusetts bar associations notably were similar to the restrictive rules of the early trade associations. * * *

As a result of the repeal of fee schedules, law firms began to use time, as well as the difficulty of the work and the results achieved, in assessing client bills. The repeal of the fee schedules also encouraged the use of contingent fees. * * * The American Bar Association reluctantly approved the use of contingent fees in 1908. Until the 1960s, few lawyers kept time records and most fees were based upon uniform schedules approved by bar associations or the courts, or upon the evaluation of various factors discussed in the canons of ethics.

During the 1960s, management experts concluded from various studies that lawyers who kept time records earned more than attorneys who did not. As one member of a legal consulting firm has explained, hourly billing appealed to clients because it was "based on something tangible that they could understand rather than on a 'value of services' concept." Similarly, hourly billing enabled business clients to "correlate the 'product' that they were buying to the products that they themselves produced and sold," and made it easier for corporate managers of outside counsel to justify to their superiors the payment of legal bills. * * * However, during the 1970s bills increasingly came to be based solely upon time. * * *

Time-based billing creates serious abuses and raises difficult ethical questions. Although the most obvious abuses are the temptation of attorneys to exaggerate the number of their billable hours or perform patently unnecessary work, "padding" and "churning" are so obviously wrong that these practices raise no ambiguous ethical questions. * * *

Far more troublesome than simple "padding" or "churning" are more complex practices that ultimately may amount to no more than sophisticated versions of those same two abuses. Through liberal methods of time recordation, attorneys may unduly inflate their hours without actually padding any entries. Similarly, over-zealous attorneys may perform tasks that yield a benefit to the client that is disproportionately small compared to the expense. These situations present the more profound ethical difficulties, because clear ethical standards often are difficult to formulate in these instances.

Perhaps the greatest danger is that some attorneys have become so accustomed to rationalizing their liberal time recordation techniques or their decisions to perform endless services for their clients regardless of cost that they may not even recognize that their actions are ethically questionable. How else, aside from preternatural stamina or lying, does one account for the views of one respondent to the author's survey who stated that he and most other attorneys who regularly bill more than 3,600 hours each year do not perform unnecessary work or exaggerate their hours?

* * *

Attorneys need to recognize that unethical time-based billing practices harm not only the client but also the legal profession, the courts, and the public. The fetish for accumulation of billable hours which increasingly pervades many law firms has eroded standards of professionalism by breeding a clock-punching mentality that until recently was the hallmark only of certain forms of industrial labor. Moreover, excessively clever strategies for accumulation of hours and the protraction of litigation for the conscious or unconscious purpose of generating more billable hours have aggravated a widespread cynicism about the legal profession that ultimately calls into question the integrity of the judicial system and weakens public faith in the quality of the nation's justice.

Since alternatives to time-based billing create their own ethical difficulties and lawyers seem loath to abandon hourly billing, both private practitioners and clients must try to purge the time-based billing system of unethical practices. Ethical billing requires constant sensitivity to the inherent conflict between the economic interests of the attorney and the real needs of the client. Ethical billing also requires a vigilant awareness of the potentials for abuse that are endemic to a system of time-based billing. It is encouraging that an increasing number of attorneys, clients, and commentators are admitting that hourly billing has encouraged a considerable measure of inefficiency and fraud and are beginning to call for more scrupulous billing practices.

DOUGLAS R. RICHMOND, *IN DEFENSE OF THE BILLABLE HOUR*

14 Prof. Law. 1 (Winter 2003)

* * *

Of the many criticisms leveled at hourly billing, the most common is that it encourages and rewards inefficiency, and encourages billing fraud. This is nonsense for several reasons.

First, at least in the litigation context, billing by the hour forces clients and their counsel to think carefully about strategy and the need to perform particular tasks when budgeting a project, thereby controlling costs and preventing needless expenditures. * * * [A]re the alternatives any better? So-called "flat fees" have their own problems. Among other things, they are a potential disincentive to zealous advocacy. Flat fees encourage attorneys to do as little work as possible. * * *

Contingent fees are not necessarily the solution. Like all forms of compensation they can be abused by lawyers who are so inclined. * * *

Even were the billable hour the source of the problems that its critics contend, lawyers' duties * * * under various ethics rules and their common law fiduciary duties, protect clients against the abuses chiefly alleged. Indeed, to believe that hourly billing causes all of

Make the Connection

For further discussion of contingent fees, *see infra*.

the problems attributed to it is to also believe that as a general rule lawyers who bill by the hour are either incompetent, inefficient or unethical. Because such a position defies logic, it must be that the problem is not the billable hour, but the few dishonest, misguided, and incompetent attorneys who misuse it. * * *

Billing pressure has been identified as the key culprit responsible for attorney dissatisfaction. Although billable hour pressure is reported to have negatively affected law firm partners, associates are thought to be "the most disenchanted casualties of the billable hour derby." In Professor Susan Saab Fortney's recent survey of 1,000 young lawyers working for Texas law firms, 74 percent of the respondents working in law firms of 100 or more lawyers indicated that billable hour pressures had taken a toll on their personal lives. * * * There is no doubt that professional success requires hard work, and that hard work sometimes takes a personal toll. * * * But, again, the problem is not the billable hour. The problem, if there is one, appears to be lawyers' income expectations or career aspirations. * * *

JONATHAN D. GLATER, *BILLABLE HOURS GIVING GROUND AT LAW FIRMS*

<u>N.Y. Times, January 30, 2009, at A1</u>

* * *

Clients have complained for years that the practice of billing for each hour worked can encourage law firms to prolong a client's problem rather than solve it. But the rough economic climate is making clients more demanding, leading many law firms to rethink their business model.

"This is the time to get rid of the billable hour," said Evan R. Chesler, presiding partner at Cravath, Swaine & Moore in New York, one of a number of large firms whose most senior lawyers bill more than $800 an hour.

"Clients are concerned about the budgets, more so than perhaps a year or two ago," he added, with a lawyer's gift for understatement.

* * *

With a sigh that is simultaneously proud and pained, lawyers will talk about charging clients for 3,000 or more hours in a year—a figure that means a lawyer spent about 12 hours a day of every weekday drafting motions or contracts and reviewing other lawyers' motions and contracts.

"Does this make any sense?" said David B. Wilkins, professor of legal ethics and director of the program on the legal profession at Harvard. "It makes as much sense as any other kind of effort to measure your value by some kind of objective, extrinsic measure. Which is not much."* * *

Food for Thought

What do you think of the controversy regarding hourly billing hours? Do you agree with Evan Chesler that "This is the time to get rid of the billable hour?"

[Question 7]

Client was an experienced oil and gas developer. Client asked Attorney for representation in a suit to establish Client's ownership of certain oil and gas royalties. Client did not have available the necessary funds to pay Attorney's reasonable hourly rate for undertaking the case. Client proposed instead to pay Attorney an amount in cash equal to 20% of the value of the proceeds received from the first year royalties Client might recover as a result of the suit. Attorney accepted the proposal and put these terms into the written fee agreement. Is Attorney subject to discipline?

(A) Yes, because the agreement gave Attorney a proprietary interest in Client's cause of action.

(B) Yes, unless the fee Attorney receives does not exceed that which Attorney would have received by charging a reasonable hourly rate.

(C) No, because Client, rather than Attorney, proposed the fee arrangement.

(D) No, because Attorney may contract with Client for a reasonable contingent fee.

Rule 1.8(i)

A lawyer shall not acquire a **proprietary interest** in the cause of action or subject matter of litigation the lawyer is conducting for a client, except that the lawyer may:

(1) acquire a lien authorized by law to secure the lawyer's fee or expenses; and

(2) contract with a client for a reasonable contingent fee in a civil case.

Comment to Rule 1.8

[16] Paragraph (i) states the traditional general rule that lawyers are prohibited from acquiring a proprietary interest in litigation. Like paragraph (e), the general rule has its basis in common law **champerty** and **maintenance** and is designed to avoid giving the lawyer too great an interest in the representation. In addition, when the lawyer acquires an ownership interest in the subject of the representation, it will be more difficult for a client to discharge the lawyer if the client so desires. The Rule is subject to specific exceptions developed in decisional law and continued in these Rules. The exception for certain advances of the costs of litigation is set forth in paragraph (e). In addition, paragraph (i) sets forth exceptions for liens authorized by law to secure the lawyer's fees or expenses and contracts for reasonable contingent fees. The law of each jurisdiction determines which liens are authorized by law. These may include liens granted by statute, liens originating in common law

and liens acquired by contract with the client. When a lawyer acquires by contract a security interest in property other than that recovered through the lawyer's efforts in the litigation, such an acquisition is a business or financial transaction with a client and is governed by the requirements of paragraph (a). Contracts for contingent fees in civil cases are governed by Rule 1.5.

Rule 1.5

(c) A fee may be contingent on the outcome of the matter for which the service is rendered, except in a matter in which a contingent fee is prohibited by paragraph (d) or other law. A contingent fee agreement shall be in a writing signed by the client and shall state the method by which the fee is to be determined, including the percentage or percentages that shall accrue to the lawyer in the event of settlement, trial or appeal; litigation and other expenses to be deducted from the recovery; and whether such expenses are to be deducted before or after the contingent fee is calculated. The agreement must clearly notify the client of any expenses for which the client will be liable whether or not the client is the prevailing party. Upon conclusion of a contingent fee matter, the lawyer shall provide the client with a written statement stating the outcome of the matter and, if there is a recovery, showing the remittance to the client and the method of its determination.

B. The Controversy Regarding Contingent Fees

Restatement § 35 Comment b:

First, [contingent fees] enable persons who could not otherwise afford counsel to assert their rights, paying their lawyers only if the assertion succeeds. Second, contingent fees give lawyers an additional incentive to seek their clients' success and to encourage only those clients with claims having a substantial likelihood of succeeding. Third, such fees enable a client to share the risk of losing with a lawyer, who is usually better able to assess the risk and to bear it by undertaking similar arrangements in other cases.

Food for Thought

In contrast to the American practice of generally permitting contingent fees, the Code of Conduct for European Lawyers (2006) prohibits contingent fees unless a jurisdiction specifically permits them. It provides as follows:

3.3. Pactum de Quota Litis

3.3.1. A lawyer shall not be entitled to make a pactum de quota litis.

3.3.2. By "pactum de quota litis" is meant an agreement between a lawyer and the client entered into prior to final conclusion of a matter to which the client is a party, by virtue of which the client undertakes to pay the lawyer a share of the result regardless of whether this is represented by a sum of money or by any other benefit achieved by the client upon the conclusion of the matter.

Food for Thought (Continued)

3.3.3. "Pactum de quota litis" does not include an agreement that fees be charged in proportion to the value of a matter handled by the lawyer if this is in accordance with an officially approved fee scale or under the control of the Competent Authority having jurisdiction over the lawyer.

Commentary on Article 3.3 – Pactum de Quota Litis

These provisions reflect the common position in all Member States that an unregulated agreement for contingency fees (pactum de quota litis) is contrary to the proper administration of justice because it encourages speculative litigation and is liable to be abused. The provisions are not, however, intended to prevent the maintenance or introduction of arrangements under which lawyers are paid according to results or only if the action or matter is successful, provided that these arrangements are under sufficient regulation and control for the protection of the client and the proper administration of justice.

Professor Laurel Terry explains that "pure contingency fees are virtually, if not universally, prohibited in Europe, [although] Rule 3.3.3." permits the use of bar-approved schedules which add a premium to the lawyer's fee if successful and which therefore are a form of contingency fee." A number of European countries ban contingent fees altogether. Laurel S. Terry, *An Introduction to the European Community's Legal Ethics Code Part I: An Analysis of the CCBE Code of Conduct,* 7 Geo. J. Legal Ethics 1, 32 n.127 & 33 n.130 (1993).

JEFFREY D. SWETT, COMMENT, *DETERMINING A REASONABLE PERCENTAGE IN ESTABLISHING A CONTINGENCY FEE: A NEW TOOL TO REMEDY AN OLD PROBLEM*

77 Tenn. L. Rev. 653, 654, 657-58, 661-665, 670-72 (2010)

* * *

Generally, the one-third contingency fee is the industry standard when determining a contingency fee percentage. However, in certain circumstances, the traditional one-third contingency fee may over-compensate the lawyer for his services, and in other situations the traditional fee may under-compensate the lawyer. * * *

Since the 1960s, the effective hourly rate of tort lawyers has increased dramatically, while the risk of non-recovery has remained relatively constant. Professor Brickman asserts that part of this problem is that when a client hires a lawyer on a contingent fee basis, the lawyer initially assigns the case a value of zero. This occurs even if the lawsuit already has significant value because a large settlement is virtually certain. Therefore, the standard contingency fee applied not only to the value that the lawyer added but also to the substantial value that the claim already possessed. Furthermore, "contingency fee lawyers not only charge fees against settlement offers previously obtained, but also routinely charge standard contingency fees in cases where they know at the outset that there is no meaningful litigation risk and that little work will need to be required to produce a settlement." Overall, "'[f]or every case in which a one-third fee is justified, there are dozens where that amount is excessive by any standard of reasonableness.'"

On the other hand, numerous advocates argue that contingency fees are not unreasonable. Professor Charles Silver maintains that there is no empirical evidence to show that attorneys are overpaid in contingency fee representations. He further asserts that "there is some evidence that attorneys who handle class actions are often underpaid." He points out that there are many instances when the lawyer receives nothing after losing at trial, despite doing extensive legal work. According to Lawrence Fox, a contingency fee expert, an evaluation of the contingency fee system must include instances where the plaintiff is unsuccessful. Fox contends that you will never hear a client offer more money in the wake of an unexpectedly low recovery when the lawyer deserved more for the time spent on the lawsuit. He states, "[T]he question is whether the reasonableness of the fee should be measured by time or by result. I favor result." In regards to the risk contingent fee lawyers assume, Robert Peck, the senior director of legal affairs for the Association of Trial Lawyers of America, reasons that by opting for a contingency fee arrangement, the client is, in effect, subsidizing other cases where the recovery is not sufficient, "much like the concept of insurance." When taken as a whole, Peck states that contingency fee lawyers "do not earn excessive returns, particularly when this risk is taken into account." * * *

Many states have enacted tort reform legislation. Most of the legislation focuses on placing different limits on a lawyer's contingency fee recovery based on the amount a plaintiff recovers in medical liability cases. * * *

Four proposals for improving the current contingency fee system have received considerable discussion in the United States, including: the early offer proposal, the New American rule, the abolishment of contingency fees, and more effective enforcement of the current ethical mandates.

A. Early Offer Proposal

In conjunction with Professor Jeffrey O'Connell and Michael Horowitz, Professor Lester Brickman designed the early offer proposal to help protect "from fee-gouging lawyers." The proposal attempts "to confine [the lawyer's] fee percentage to the value that [the lawyer] added to the claim." The proposal provides five mandates. First, a contingency fee may not be levied against settlement offers made before counsel was obtained. Second, "all defendants are given an opportunity to make settlement offers covered by the proposal, but no later than 60 days from the receipt of a notice of claim from plaintiffs' counsel." Third, the "[n]otices of claim submitted by plaintiffs' counsel are required to include basic, routinely discoverable information designed to assist defendants in evaluating plaintiff claims," and similar information in possession of the defendant must be made available to the plaintiff. Fourth, if the "plaintiff[] reject[s the] defendants' early offers, contingency fees may only be charged against net recoveries in excess of such offers." Finally, if no settlement offer is made, the contingency fee is unaffected. Therefore, "the proposal would prohibit plaintiff lawyers in personal injury cases from charging standard contingency fees where alleged responsible parties made early settlement offers before the lawyer added any significant value to the claim."

* * *

B. New American Rule

In cooperation with Jim Wooton, Professor [Richard] Painter drafted the New American rule. Generally, the New American rule "requires the lawyer charging a contingent fee to say to the client in advance that 'my fee will be X% of any judgment or settlement in this case but will be no higher than Y dollars per hour.'" The lawyer and the client would be able to freely agree on the numbers X and Y. This proposal is not tied to whether there is a settlement offer or any other action by the defendant. X and Y are determined by the price the plaintiff would pay for services in an unregulated market except for the fact that the lawyer, instead of the market, must specify both X and Y. At the conclusion of the lawsuit, the client can choose to pay either X or Y.

* * *

C. Abolishment

In response to unreasonable fees, John Barry and Bert Rein propose that "[t]he only appropriate solution is to prohibit lawyers from entering into any arrangement" in which they may obtain a financial interest in a client's claim. Barry and Rein believe that "a better approach would be to undertake a fundamental restructuring of the manner in which legal services are delivered to claim holders, preserving the societal benefits of the contingent fee system while getting attorneys out of the contingent fee business altogether." Under this plan, "parties could obtain legal representation by marketing their claims to 'claim brokers'" who would act as intermediaries between plaintiffs and lawyers This market would preserve the current efficiencies of scale, introduce healthy competition, and may "make compensation available to many holders of low-dollar claims" who would not otherwise receive representation because some lawyers refuse to pursue small claims. Finally, since the brokers would be "purchasers rather than providers," they would have the incentive to purchase the claims that reflect their value rather than just charging a standard fee.

* * *

V. Another Way to Approach Unreasonable Contingency Fees

The biggest problem with the current method of determining a contingency fee is that the lawyer does not evaluate each case on an individual basis. The standard fee is applied to most cases without regard to whether this fee under-or over-compensates the lawyer for his or her services. I believe the first step in reform is for the lawyer to evaluate each individual lawsuit on its merits and offer a reasonable contingency fee percentage based off of this evaluation. * * *

To begin evaluating an individual case, there are a number of factors that a lawyer should consider. Basically, when a lawyer takes a case on a contingency fee basis, he or she must be compensated for the time spent on the case and the risk of no payment. This compensation for time and risk will be a percentage of the recovery obtained in the lawsuit. Therefore, an estimate of a proper contingency fee percentage must take on a similar form.

A starting point in determining a proper contingency fee percentage would be to estimate the probable hours spent, the hourly wage, the costs fronted, and the probable recovery. Using this simple formula:

$$\frac{(\text{Estimated Hours x Estimated Hourly Wage}) + (\text{Estimated Costs Fronted x Risk Multiplier})}{\text{Estimated Recovery}}$$

a better estimate of a contingency fee can be determined. Rather than just blindly guessing at a proper percentage (or worse blindly assigning the standard percentage to every case), this formula will force the lawyer to evaluate each case individually.

However, I propose that the lawyer needs to expand on this simple formula. To determine a better contingency fee, the lawyer should perform a much more in-depth analysis of each phase of the lawsuit. Experienced litigators can project the tasks that will need to be performed and estimate how many hours will be required to complete each task. An in-depth analysis of each phase of the lawsuit will yield a more precise fee tied to the particular risks associated with the lawsuit. To help lawyers calculate a more accurate and individualized contingency fee, I have expanded on the formula outlined above and developed a mathematical program that helps perform an in-depth analysis of the client's case. * * *

Food for Thought

Now that you have read a variety of perspectives regarding contingent fees, what is your view? Should they be permitted? Should they be modified? Should we retain the existing rules?

[Question 8]

Software Start-up, Inc. seeks legal representation with regard to its initial public offering. Software wants to hire High Tech Law, but believes it cannot afford High Tech's hourly billing rate. Software also believes that payment of an equity interest will best ensure High Tech's devotion to the matter. Software offers High Tech an equity interest in exchange for representation. High Tech agrees to represent Software in exchange for a 2% equity interest. High Tech provides Software with a written fee agreement explaining that High Tech will take a 2% equity interest in Software and advising Software to consult outside counsel on the propriety of the fee agreement. High Tech explains verbally, but not in the written agreement, that potential conflicts might arise as a result of High Tech obtaining an equity interest but that no significant risk of a conflict exists under the circumstances. Software decides not to consult outside counsel and signs the agreement. The initial public offering is far more successful than expected and raises the total equity value of Software to $500 million. Software decides that the $10 million in stock that High Tech gains as a result of the initial public offering is an excessive fee and files a disciplinary complaint against High Tech. What result?

(A) Discipline, because lawyers cannot take a proprietary interest in their client.

(B) Discipline, because the fee was much higher than if High Tech had charged Software an hourly fee.

(C) Discipline, because High Tech failed to ensure that Software consulted an outside counsel before signing the fee agreement.

(D) No discipline, because High Tech complied with the ethics rules.

Rule 1.8(i) A lawyer shall not acquire a proprietary interest in the cause of action or subject matter of litigation the lawyer is conducting for a client, except that the lawyer may:

(1) acquire a lien authorized by law to secure the lawyer's fee or expenses; and

(2) contract with a client for a reasonable contingent fee in a civil case.

Review Rule 1.5. Comment [4] provides that:

A lawyer may accept property in payment for services, such as an ownership interest in an enterprise, providing this does not involve acquisition of a proprietary interest in the cause of action or subject matter of the litigation contrary to

Rule 1.8(i). However, a fee paid in property instead of money may be subject to the requirements of Rule 1.8(a) because such fees often have the essential qualities of a business transaction with the client.

Rule 1.8(a) provides that:

A lawyer shall not enter into a business transaction with a client or knowingly acquire an ownership, possessory, security or other pecuniary interest adverse to a client unless:

> (1) the transaction and terms on which the lawyer acquires the interest are fair and reasonable to the client and are fully disclosed and transmitted in writing in a manner that can be reasonably understood by the client;

> (2) the client is advised in writing of the desirability of seeking and is given a reasonable opportunity to seek the advice of independent legal counsel on the transaction; and

> (3) the client gives informed consent, in a writing signed by the client, to the essential terms of the transaction and the lawyer's role in the transaction, including whether the lawyer is representing the client in the transaction.

The Comment to Rule 1.8 provides in part:

[1] A lawyer's legal skill and training, together with the relationship of trust and confidence between lawyer and client, create the possibility of overreaching when the lawyer participates in a business, property or financial transaction with a client, for example, a loan or sales transaction or a lawyer investment on behalf of a client. * * * It does not apply to ordinary fee arrangements between client and lawyer, which are governed by Rule 1.5, although its requirements must be met when the lawyer accepts an interest in the client's business or other nonmonetary property as payment of all or part of a fee. In addition, the Rule does not apply to standard commercial transactions between the lawyer and the client for products or services that the client generally markets to others, for example, banking or brokerage services, medical services, products manufactured or distributed by the client, and utilities' services. In such transactions, the lawyer has no advantage in dealing with the client, and the restrictions in paragraph (a) are unnecessary and impracticable.

[2] Paragraph (a)(1) requires that the transaction itself be fair to the client and that its essential terms be communicated to the client, in writing, in a manner that can be reasonably understood. Paragraph (a)(2) requires that the client also be advised, in writing, of the desirability of seeking the advice of independent legal counsel. It also requires that the client be given a reasonable opportunity to obtain such advice. Paragraph (a)(3) requires that the lawyer obtain the client's informed con-

sent, in a writing signed by the client, both to the essential terms of the transaction and to the lawyer's role. When necessary, the lawyer should discuss both the material risks of the proposed transaction, including any risk presented by the lawyer's involvement, and the existence of reasonably available alternatives and should explain why the advice of independent legal counsel is desirable. *See* Rule 1.0(e) (definition of informed consent).

[3] The risk to a client is greatest when the client expects the lawyer to represent the client in the transaction itself or when the lawyer's financial interest otherwise poses a significant risk that the lawyer's representation of the client will be materially limited by the lawyer's financial interest in the transaction. Here the lawyer's role requires that the lawyer must comply, not only with the requirements of paragraph (a), but also with the requirements of Rule 1.7. Under that Rule, the lawyer must disclose the risks associated with the lawyer's dual role as both legal adviser and participant in the transaction, such as the risk that the lawyer will structure the transaction or give legal advice in a way that favors the lawyer's interests at the expense of the client. Moreover, the lawyer must obtain the client's informed consent. In some cases, the lawyer's interest may be such that Rule 1.7 will preclude the lawyer from seeking the client's consent to the transaction.

> **Make the Connection**
>
> Rule 1.7 is the general rule governing conflicts of interest. For an in-depth analysis of Rule 1.7, *see* Chapter 5

[4] If the client is independently represented in the transaction, paragraph (a)(2) of this Rule is inapplicable, and the paragraph (a)(1) requirement for full disclosure is satisfied either by a written disclosure by the lawyer involved in the transaction or by the client's independent counsel. The fact that the client was independently represented in the transaction is relevant in determining whether the agreement was fair and reasonable to the client as paragraph (a)(1) further requires.

* * *

DEBRA BAKER, *WHO WANTS TO BE A MILLIONAIRE?*

A.B.A. J., Feb. 2000, at 36

* * *

There's nothing unusual about law firms investing in clients; firms have done so for years. But in today's highly charged IPO market even a modest investment—generally considered to be an ownership share of no more than 1 percent—can net millions overnight.

"The values are so significant that 1 percent or less is still worth a lot," says Donald Bradley, Wilson Sonsini's general counsel. * * *

In the new high-tech culture, cash-poor clients consider a lawyer's investment as a sign of loyalty. Likewise, law firms see the ability to offer stock to their lawyers as a way to keep many of those same clients from luring away their top legal talent.

Not surprising, the law firms investing most heavily in clients are based in or near California's Silicon Valley, the Eden for young technology companies and Internet start-ups. Client investment is also becoming increasingly common in other technology-driven locales such as Texas, North Carolina and northern Virginia. * * *

The legal profession historically has taken a dim view of lawyers holding equity interests in clients, fearing conflicts between a lawyer's own interests and those of the client. But the massive growth of Internet technology and related start-up ventures over the last decade is forcing some changes in that thinking. Lawyers, particularly those practicing in technology-heavy regions, see the profits being made and want to get in on it.

Am. Bar Ass'n, Standing Comm. on Ethics & Prof'l Responsibility, *Acquiring Ownership in a Client in Connection with Performing Legal Services*

Formal Op. 00-418 (2000)

* * *

Background

With growing frequency, lawyers who provide legal services to start-up businesses are investing in their clients, sometimes accepting an ownership interest as a part or all of the fee. Some representatives of the organized bar have questioned this practice. Many lawyers nevertheless believe that acquiring ownership interests in start-up business clients is desirable in order to satisfy client needs and also, because of growing competition with higher paying venture capital and investment firms, to attract and retain partners and associates. From the client's perspective, the lawyer's willingness to invest with entrepreneurs in a start-up company frequently is viewed as a vote of confidence in the enterprise's prospects. Moreover, a lawyer's willingness to accept stock instead of a cash fee may be the only way for a cash-poor client to obtain competent legal advice. Frequently, this may be the determining factor in the client's selection of a lawyer.

The Committee in this Opinion examines the issues that must be addressed under the ABA Model Rules of Professional Conduct when a lawyer or law firm acquires an ownership interest in a client in connection with performing legal services. A typical situation might be one in which the client business is a corporation that the law firm is organizing at the request of the founding entrepreneurs. The latter already have a few friends and family members who are eager to invest funds to start up the corporation. The founders may allow the lawyer working with them to invest the firm's fee for legal services in stock of the corporation. The organizers expect the law firm to introduce them to the firm's venture capital contacts and to continue representing the corporation, eventually performing the services necessary to take it public.

A. Compliance with Rules 1.8(a) and 1.5(a) When Acquiring Ownership in a Client

In our opinion, a lawyer who acquires stock in her client corporation in lieu of or in addition to a cash fee for her services enters into a business transaction with a client, such that the requirements of Model Rule 1.8(a) must be satisfied. In determining whether Rule 1.8(a)'s first requirement of fairness and reasonableness to the client is satisfied, the general standard of Rule 1.5(a) that "[a] lawyer's fee shall be reasonable" and the factors enumerated under that Rule are relevant.

For purposes of judging the fairness and reasonableness of the transaction and its terms, the Committee's opinion is that, as when assessing the reasonableness of a contingent fee, only the circumstances reasonably ascertainable at the time of the transaction should be considered. It seems clear that "[i]n a discipline case, once proof has been introduced that the lawyer entered into a business transaction with a client, the burden of persuasion is on the lawyer to show that the transaction was fair and reasonable and that the client was adequately informed." Accordingly, it is incumbent upon the lawyer to take account of all information reasonably ascertainable at the time when the agreement for stock acquisition is made.

Determining that the fee is reasonable in terms of the enumerated factors under Rule 1.5(a) does not resolve whether the requirement of Rule 1.8(a) that the transaction and terms be "fair and reasonable to the client" has been met. Determining "reasonableness" under both rules also involves making the often difficult determination of the market value of the stock at the time of the transaction. As Professors Hazard and Hodes state, "[o]ne danger [to the lawyer who accepts stock as a fee] is that the business will so prosper that the fee will later appear unreasonably high." Of course, instead of increasing in value, the stock may become worthless, as occurs frequently with start-up enterprises. The risk of failure and the stock's nonmarketability are important factors that the lawyer must consider, along with all other information bearing on value that is reasonably ascertainable at the time when the agreement is made.

One way for the lawyer to minimize the risk noted by Professors Hazard and Hodes is to establish a reasonable fee for her services based on the factors enumerated under Rule 1.5(a) and then accept stock that at the time of the transaction is worth the reasonable fee. Of course, the stock should, if feasible, be valued at the amount per share that cash investors, knowledgeable about its value, have agreed to pay for their stock about the same time.

A reasonable fee also may include an agreed percentage of the stock issued or to be issued when the value of the shares is not reasonably ascertainable. For example, if the lawyer is engaged by two founders who are contributing intellectual property for their stock, it may not be possible to establish with reasonable certainty the cash value of their contribution. If so, it also would not be possible to establish with reasonable certainty the value of the shares to be issued to the lawyer retained to perform initial services for the corporation. In such cases, the percentage of stock agreed upon should reflect the value, as perceived by the client and the lawyer at the time of the transaction, that the legal services will contribute to the potential success of the enterprise. The value of the stock received by the lawyer will, like a contingent fee permitted under Rule 1.5(c), depend upon the success of the undertaking.

In addition to assuring that the stock transaction and its terms are fair and reasonable to the client, compliance with Rule 1.8(a) also requires that the transaction and its terms must be fully disclosed and transmitted in writing in a manner that can be reasonably understood by the client. Thus, the lawyer must be careful not only to set forth the terms in writing, but also to explain the transaction and its potential effects on the client-lawyer relationship in a way that the client can understand it. For example, if the acquisition of stock by the lawyer will create rights under corporate by-laws or other agreements that will limit the client's control of the corporation, the lawyer should discuss with the client the possible consequences of such an arrangement.

At the outset, the lawyer also should inform the client that events following the stock acquisition could create a conflict between the lawyer's exercise of her independent professional judgment as a lawyer on behalf of the corporation and her desire to protect the value of her stock. She also should advise the client that as a consequence of such a conflict, she might feel constrained to withdraw as counsel for the corporation, or at least to recommend that another lawyer advise the client on the matter regarding which she has a personal conflict of interest.

Full disclosure also includes specifying in writing the scope of the services to be performed in return for receipt of the stock or the opportunity to invest. The scope of services should be covered in the written transmission to the client even though the stock is acquired by the firm's investment partnership as an opportunity rather than by the firm directly as a part of the fee in lieu of cash. If the client's understanding is that the lawyer keeps the stock interest regardless of the amount of legal services performed by the lawyer and solely to assure the lawyer's availability, it is important to set forth this aspect of the transaction in clear terms. Otherwise, a court might regard the stock acquisition as being in the nature of an advance fee for services and require part of the stock to be returned if all the work originally contemplated as part of the services for which the stock was given has not been performed.

Although it is better practice to set forth all the salient features of the transaction in a written document, compliance with Rule 1.8(a) does not require reiteration of details that the client already knows from other sources. Indeed, too much detail may tend to distract attention from the material terms. Nonetheless, the lawyer bears the risk of omitting a term that seems unimportant at the time, but later becomes significant because she has the burden of showing reasonable compliance with Rule 1.8(a)(1). A good faith effort to explain in understandable language the important features of the particular arrangement and its material consequences as far as reasonably can be ascertained at the time of the stock acquisition should satisfy the full disclosure requirements of Rule 1.8(a).

The client also must have a reasonable opportunity to seek the advice of independent counsel in the transaction and must consent in writing to the transaction and its terms. In addition, although not required by the Model Rules, the written documentation of the transaction should include the lawyer's recommendation to obtain such advice. This serves to emphasize the importance to the client of obtaining independent advice. The client's failure to do so then is his own deliberate choice. The lawyer has complied with Rule 1.8(a) in this respect because actual consultation is not required.

The best way to comply with the requirements of Rule 1.8(a) is to set forth the salient terms of the transaction in a document written in language that the client can understand and, after the client has had an opportunity to consult with independent counsel, to have the document signed by both client and lawyer.

B. Conflicts Between the Lawyer's Interests and Those of the Client

On rare occasions the acquisition of stock in a client corporation will amount to acquiring, in the language of Rule 1.8(j), "a proprietary interest in the cause of action or subject matter of litigation the lawyer is conducting." As Comment [7] under Rule 1.8 explains, the prohibition "has its basis in common law champerty and maintenance [and] is subject to specific exceptions developed in decisional law and continued in these Rules, such as the exception for reasonable contingent fees set forth in Rule 1.5 . . . ." The modern rationale for the rule is the concern that a lawyer acquiring less than all of a client's cause of action creates so severe a conflict between the lawyer's interest and the client's interest that it is nonconsentable.

In our view, when the corporation has as its only substantial asset a claim or property right (such as a license), title to which is contested in a pending or impending lawsuit in which the lawyer represents the corporation, Rule 1.8(j) might be applicable to the acquisition of the corporation's stock in connection with the provision of legal services. If the acquisition of the stock constitutes a reasonable contingent fee, however, Rule 1.8(j) would not prohibit acquisition of the stock.

Rule 1.7(b) prohibits representation of a client if the representation "may be materially limited ... by the lawyer's own interests," unless two requirements are met. The lawyer must reasonably believe that "the representation will not be adversely affected," and the client must consent to the representation after consultation.

A lawyer's representation of a corporation in which she owns stock creates no inherent conflict of interest under Rule 1.7. Indeed, management's role primarily is to enhance the business's value for the stockholders. Thus, the lawyer's legal services in assisting management usually will be consistent

Make the Connection

For further analysis of Rule 1.7 and conflicts of interest, *see* Chapter 5 *infra.*

with the lawyer's stock ownership. In some circumstances, such as the merger of one corporation in which the lawyer owns stock into a larger entity, the lawyer's economic incentive to complete the transaction may even be enhanced.

There may, however, be other circumstances in which the lawyer's ownership of stock in her corporate client conflicts with her responsibilities as the corporation's lawyer. For example, the lawyer might have a duty when rendering an opinion on behalf of the corporation in a venture capital transaction to call upon corporate management to reveal material adverse financial information that is being withheld, even though the revelation might cause the venture capital investor to withdraw. In that circumstance, the lawyer must evaluate her ability to maintain the requisite professional independence as a lawyer in the corporate client's best interest by subordinating any economic incentive arising from her stock ownership. The lawyer also must consider whether her stock ownership might create questions concerning the objectivity of her opinion. She must consult with her client and obtain consent if the representation may be materially limited by her stock ownership.

The conflict could be more severe. For example, the stock of the client might be the lawyer's major asset so that the failure of the venture capital opportunity could create a serious financial loss to her. The lawyer's self-interest in such a case probably justifies a reasonable belief that her representation of the corporation would be affected adversely. This would disqualify her under Rule 1.7(b) from providing the opinion even were the client to consent.

In order to minimize conflicts with the interests of the clients such as those described, some law firms have adopted policies governing investments in clients. These policies may include limiting the investment to an insubstantial percentage of stock and the amount invested in any single client to a nonmaterial sum. The policies also may require that decisions regarding a firm lawyer's potential client conflict be made by someone other than the lawyer with the principal client contact (who also may have a larger stock interest in the corporate client) and may also transfer billing or supervisory responsibility to a partner with no stock ownership in the client.

Even though a lawyer owns stock in a corporation, she, of course, has no right to continue to represent it as a lawyer if the corporate client discharges her. Were the lawyer to challenge the decision duly made by the authorized corporate constituents to discharge her, she would violate Rule 1.7(b) because it is clear that her own interests adversely affect the representation of the corporation.

* * *

John S. Dzienkowski & Robert J. Peroni, The Decline in Lawyer Independence: Lawyer Equity Investments in Clients

81 Tex. L. Rev. 405, 546-49 (2002)

* * *

We believe that the rush to accept equity investments as proper vehicles for law firm compensation is misplaced. First, we expressly take issue with the ABA and state and city bar ethics opinions as downplaying the risks arising from these equity investments. As we have argued, the opinions are not consistent with the extensive body of case law examining the obligations of lawyers engaging in client business transactions, including, in particular, making investments in clients. The legal profession should return to the time when equity investments in clients were viewed with great caution and undertaken in rare circumstances. Firms that do invest in client equity should implement an extensive client consent process and an understandable form for memorializing the consent, as well as strict procedures to limit the actual and potential conflicts of interests. Second, we challenge the view that most lawyers are only involved in direct investment in a client rather than receiving equity as part of the fee. In the vast majority of cases, lawyers receive client equity at an offering price not available to most public investors. In each of these circumstances, the lawyers must comply with both the business transaction rule and the reasonable fee rule. Third, we strongly disagree with the practice of demanding equity in exchange for performing legal work for a client. The requirement of client consent necessitates that a lawyer allow a client to decline to bring lawyers into the ownership circle. Fourth, firms that accept equity investments should monitor possible conflicts of interest from the continuing representation and should consider withdrawing from future representations because of the ongoing investment. This is particularly true in the down round venture capital financing context when the client's business venture experiences financial pressures. Fifth, we urge courts and disciplinary committees to strictly construe the ethics requirements and to place the burden on the lawyer to demonstrate compliance with all of the rules.

* * *

Clients hire lawyers to provide legal advice and independent judgment. It is unrealistic to believe that lawyers who have an interest in the venture do not consider their personal financial well-being while advising the client. The disparity between the lawyer's goals and the client's goals exists in virtually every circumstance. The lawyer's personal financial goals, which may be tied almost exclusively to the short-run performance of the client's stock, will inevitably color the lawyer's judgment in advising the client. Lawyers cannot simultaneously discharge their duty of loyalty to clients and be venture capitalists. The business and legal relationships between the founding entrepreneurs and the venture capitalists must be negotiated at arm's length in every representation. The terms of the agreement have potentially dire consequences to the entrepreneur if the venture is not successful. How can the lawyers for the entrepreneurs provide independent advice when the lawyers have aligned themselves economically with the venture capitalists? Lawyer investments in client equity have been driven by lawyer greed and receive client "consent" because of a perceived value of being associated with a major Silicon Valley law firm. As long as the clients were successful in the marketplace and stock prices were dramatically rising, the negative effect of the equity investment on the independence of the lawyers (including the many actual and potential conflicts of interest) stayed below the surface. But financial and market pressures resulting from equity investment in clients in Silicon Valley have fundamentally altered the dynamics of the lawyer-client relationship and threaten to undermine the attorney's role as an independent legal adviser.

Food for Thought

You have now read arguments for and against lawyers' accepting an equity interest in their clients as payment for services. What is your view? What will you do when you are a lawyer? Should the ethics rules permit this practice?

[Question 9]

An attorney agreed to represent a plaintiff in a personal injury matter. The original agreement between the attorney and the plaintiff specified a 30% contingent fee, which was a reasonable fee for the type of cases the attorney handled. One year into the litigation, the attorney noted that he was extremely busy and that many potential clients sought his services. As a result, the attorney raised his standard fee to a 35% contingent fee, which was also a reasonable fee. The attorney's agreement with the plaintiff was silent on the possibility of a fee increase. He approached the plaintiff and proposed that she agree to modify the contingent fee percentage from 30% to 35%. The attorney informed the plaintiff that if she did not agree, the attorney would find her another experienced personal injury lawyer at the original fee, but that the attorney was unwilling to continue the representation unless the fee was modified. The plaintiff reluctantly agreed to modify the fee agreement as the attorney proposed.

Subsequently, the plaintiff's case was settled. The plaintiff, however, refused to pay the attorney more than a 30% contingent fee, and the attorney sued the plaintiff to recover under the modified fee agreement.

Is the attorney likely to prevail?

   (A) Yes, because the attorney offered to find the plaintiff another experienced personal injury lawyer at the original rate.

   (B) Yes, because a contingent fee of 35% constituted a reasonable fee.

   (C) No, because the attorney did not suggest that the plaintiff seek the advice of independent counsel before accepting the increased fee.

   (D) No, because there were no special circumstances justifying the attorney's insistence on a fee increase.

Review Rule 1.5.

Restatement § 18 Comment e:

Client-lawyer fee contracts entered into after the matter in question is under way are subject to special scrutiny. * * *

The lawyer may enforce the contract by persuading the tribunal that the contract was fair and reasonable to the client under the circumstances in which it was entered. The showing of fairness and reasonableness must encompass two elements.

First, the lawyer must show that the client was adequately aware of the effects and any material disadvantages of the proposed contract, including, if applicable, circumstances concerning the need for modification. The more experienced the client is in such dealings with lawyers, the less the lawyer need inform the client. Likewise, less disclosure is required when an independent lawyer is advising the client about the proposed contract. It will also be relevant to sustaining the contract if the client initiated the request for the modification, such as when a client who is facing unexpected financial difficulty requests that the lawyer change an hourly fee contract to one involving a contingent fee.

Second, the lawyer must show that the client was not pressured to accede in order to avoid the problems of changing counsel, alienating the lawyer, missing a deadline or losing a significant opportunity in the matter, or because a new lawyer would have to repeat significant work for which the client owed or had paid the first lawyer. * * * In general, the lawyer must show that a reasonable client might have chosen to accept the late contract, typically because it benefited the client in some substantial way (other than by relieving the client from having to find a new lawyer). Although fairness and reasonableness to the client is the issue, the strength and legitimacy of the lawyer's need for the terms of the late contract are relevant to that issue.

If the client and lawyer made an initial contract and the postinception contract in question is a modification of that contract, the client may avoid the contract unless the lawyer makes the showings indicated in Subsection (1)(a). Postinception modification beneficial to a lawyer, although justifiable in some instances, raises questions why the original contract was not itself sufficiently fair and reasonable. Yet, the scope of the representation and the relationship between client and lawyer cannot always be foreseen at the time of an initial contract. Both client and lawyer might sometimes benefit from adjusting their terms of dealing. Sometimes, indeed, a new contract may be unavoidable, as when a client asks a lawyer to expand the scope of the representation.* * *

LAWRENCE v. MILLER,

901 N.E.2d 1268 (N.Y. 2008)

JONES, J.

Sylvan Lawrence died testate in 1981, leaving his estate to his wife, Alice Lawrence, and three children. In 1982, decedent's will was admitted to probate and decedent's brother, Seymour Cohn, was named executor. In 1983, Mrs. Lawrence retained the law firm of Graubard Miller, on an hourly basis, to represent her in matters related to decedent's estate, including her lawsuit regarding Mr. Cohn's administration of decedent's estate. Mrs. Lawrence's retention of Graubard was confirmed in a letter dated August 4, 1983. Over the next 21 years, more than $350 million in distributions were made to the beneficiaries of the estate, and the firm billed Mrs. Lawrence over $18 million in legal fees. Mrs. Lawrence also paid, unbeknownst to the firm, over $5 million in "bonuses" or "gifts" to three of the firm's partners and approximately $2.7 million in taxes on those bonuses or gifts.

In November 2004, Mrs. Lawrence, facing legal bills which, according to her, had increased to almost $1 million per quarter, asked the firm about the possibility of entering a new fee arrangement. By letter dated January 14, 2005, shortly before commencement of trial in connection with decedent's estate, Mrs. Lawrence and Graubard entered a revised retainer agreement, providing that (1) for one year commencing January 1, 2005, Mrs. Lawrence would pay the firm a flat fee not exceeding $300,000 per quarter, (2) hourly billings would be capped at $1.2 million and (3) if additional monies were distributed to beneficiaries of decedent's estate, or if Mrs. Lawrence settled her case against Mr. Cohn's estate, Mrs. Lawrence was to pay from her share 40% of the total distributed to the beneficiaries, minus any amount she had already paid the firm under the revised retainer agreement.

On May 18, 2005, five months after the revised retainer agreement became effective, the firm, on behalf of Mrs. Lawrence, reached a settlement by which Mr. Cohn's estate agreed to pay decedent's estate approximately $104.8 million. Under the terms of the revised retainer agreement, Mrs. Lawrence was required to pay legal fees in excess of $40 million. She refused to pay and on August 5, 2005, Graubard commenced a proceeding in Surrogate's Court to compel payment of its legal fees. Four days later, the firm amended its petition, which further alleged that appellant Richard Lawrence is liable to Graubard for its legal fees both individually, under a theory of tortious interference with contractual relationship, and as successor executor * * *. By order dated September 12, 2005, Surrogate Renee R. Roth referred Graubard's contract enforcement proceeding to the Honorable Howard A. Levine (the Referee) to hear and report.

On September 13, 2005, Mrs. Lawrence brought suit in Supreme Court against the Graubard firm and three individual partners who had received over $5 million in bonuses or gifts from Mrs. Lawrence. This suit seeks rescission of the revised retainer agreement, return of all fees paid to Graubard Miller during the entire 22-year period it represented Mrs. Lawrence, as well as the monies she paid separately to the three partners, on the ground that the revised retainer agreement is unconscionable as a matter of law. By order of Supreme Court dated December 14, 2005, Justice Helen E. Freedman directed that Mrs. Lawrence's rescission action be removed to Surrogate's Court * * *. Thereafter, Surrogate Roth referred this action to the Referee, who also had before him the firm's contract enforcement proceeding.

Meanwhile, on or about October 24, 2005, Alice Lawrence and Richard Lawrence, individually and as successor executor to decedent's estate, each moved before the Referee to dismiss Graubard's petition * * *. The firm countered by cross-moving for partial summary judgment dismissing Mrs. Lawrence's counterclaim for a refund of all fees previously paid to Graubard and three of its partners.

Taking into account the standard of review applicable to CPLR 3211 motions to dismiss, the Referee recommended denying the motions to dismiss the petition. In support of this recommendation, the Referee, noting the general rule that retainer agreements must be fair and reasonable to the client, explained that determining whether the revised retainer agreement is unconscionable "will require evidence concerning all factors relevant to Mrs. Lawrence's capacity, her understanding of the terms of the revised agreement, the completeness of the attorneys' disclosure and whether they exploited their preexisting confidential relationship with her to obtain the favorable terms of the agreement," and that an "excessive fee" determination pursuant to Code of Professional Responsibility DR 2-106 * * * shall be made "after a review of the facts." The Referee further noted the presence of numerous questions of fact, which cannot be resolved on a pre-answer motion to dismiss. By decision dated July 10, 2006, Surrogate Roth granted motions to confirm the Referee's report and adopted his recommendations in their entirety.

By decision and order entered November 27, 2007, the Appellate Division, in a 4-1 decision, affirmed * * *. The majority, noting that unconscionability determinations require a showing of both procedural and substantive unconscionability, found that

> "while at first blush [the revised retainer] agreement might arguably seem excessive and invite skepticism, before any determination regarding unconscionability can be made, the circumstances underlying the agreement must be fully developed, including any discussions leading to the agreement, as well as the prospects at that time of successfully concluding the litigation in favor of Mrs. Lawrence." * * *

Similarly, the majority found that

> "Mrs. Lawrence's claims that the so-called 'bonuses' or 'gifts,' as well as the agreement itself, violated attorney disciplinary rules against self dealing, etc., cannot be resolved without determining [certain factual issues, i.e.,] Mrs. Lawrence's capacity . . . ; what she was advised; and whether she understood the ramifications of the revised agreement" * * *.

The dissenting Justice, noting that prior to the revised retainer agreement, Mrs. Lawrence had declined a $60 million settlement offer from Mr. Cohn's estate, concluded that a court "may find a provision of a contract so outrageous as to warrant holding it unenforceable on the grounds of substantive unconscionability alone." * * * He would have ruled that the firm is not entitled to any legal fees under the revised retainer agreement, and further, that it would be appropriate to refer Mrs. Lawrence's complaints regarding the three partners to the Departmental Disciplinary Committee.

The Appellate Division granted the Lawrences leave to appeal from its order and certified the following question to this Court: "Was the decision and order of this Court, to the extent that it affirmed the orders of the Surrogate's Court, properly made?" We now affirm and answer the certified question in the affirmative.

Whether the revised retainer agreement is unenforceable because it was unconscionable when entered into, or became so in retrospect, is the issue before us on appellants' motions to dismiss the firm's petition to compel payment of legal fees. On a motion to dismiss a petition we, of course, must accept the facts alleged in the petition as true, petitioner must be afforded every possible favorable inference, and we must determine whether the facts alleged by petitioner fit within any cognizable legal theory. * * *

It is well settled that an unconscionable contract is generally defined

> "as one which is so grossly unreasonable as to be [unenforceable according to its literal terms] because of an absence of meaningful choice on the part of one of the parties ['procedural unconscionability'] together with contract terms which are unreasonably favorable to the other party ['substantive unconscionability']" * * * .

As noted above, a fee arrangement can be deemed unconscionable when entered into or in retrospect.

In light of the applicable standard of review in resolving a motion to dismiss a petition, we conclude that the facts and circumstances surrounding the revised retainer agreement have not, at this time, been sufficiently developed to determine whether or not the agreement was unconscionable at the time it was made. Petitioner Graubard Miller has not had the opportunity to lay bare admissible proof as to, among other things, whether the revised retainer agreement was fair, reasonable, and fully known and understood by Mrs. Lawrence. Further, appellants have not submitted admissible, conclusive proof that the firm's petition is somehow deficient and/or that dismissal is otherwise warranted.

Given the courts' role in closely scrutinizing contingent fee agreements between attorneys and their clients * * *. [E]ven if such an agreement is not determined to be unconscionable as of its inception, that is not the end of a court's analysis. Our case law clearly provides that circumstances arising after contract formation can render a contingent fee agreement not unconscionable when entered into-unenforceable where the amount of the fee, combined with the large percentage of the recovery it represents, seems disproportionate to the value of the services rendered. * * *

In general, agreements entered into between competent adults, where there is no deception or overreaching in their making, should be enforced as written. Accordingly, the power to invalidate fee agreements with hindsight should be exercised only with great caution. It is not unconscionable for an attorney to recover much more than he or she could possibly have earned at an hourly rate. Indeed, the contingency system cannot work if lawyers do not sometimes get very lucrative fees, for that is what makes them willing to take the risk-a risk that often becomes reality-that they will do much work and earn nothing. If courts become too preoccupied with the ratio of fees to hours, contingency fee lawyers may run up hours just to justify their fees, or may lose interest in getting the largest possible recoveries for their clients.

Here, the firm and Mrs. Lawrence—after a long professional relationship, and $18 million in fees—entered the revised retainer agreement which provided for a 40% contingent fee. Five months later, Graubard secured a settlement with the Cohn estate exceeding $100 million and, pursuant to the agreement, the firm sought to collect legal fees exceeding $40 million from Mrs. Lawrence. On its face, the amount of the fee seems disproportionate to the five months of work since the agreement's revision. However, we have not been presented with facts to refute or support this hypothesis, or to evaluate the agreement's unconscionability.

Because questions which cannot be resolved on a motion to dismiss are present and because a full record has not been developed, dismissal of the petition is not warranted at this time. Moreover, until a determination regarding the validity of the agreement is made, appellants' claims concerning the excessiveness of the contingent fee, the partners' acceptance of the bonuses or gifts and the alleged violation of certain disciplinary rules, as well as Mr. Lawrence's motion to dismiss Graubard's tortious interference with contract claim, cannot be resolved.

Accordingly, the order of the Appellate Division should be affirmed, without costs, and the certified question answered in the affirmative.

[Question 10]

An attorney entered into a written retainer agreement with a defendant in a criminal case. The defendant agreed in writing to transfer title to her automobile to the attorney if the attorney successfully prevented her from going to prison. Later, the charges against the defendant were dismissed.

Is the attorney subject to discipline for entering into this retainer agreement?

    (A) Yes, because the attorney agreed to a fee contingent on the outcome of a criminal case.

    (B) Yes, because a lawyer may not acquire a proprietary interest in a client's property.

    (C) No, because the charges against the defendant were dismissed.

    (D) No, because the retainer agreement was in writing.

<u>Rule 1.5</u>

(c) A fee may be contingent on the outcome of the matter for which the service is rendered, except in a matter in which a contingent fee is prohibited by paragraph (d) or other law. A contingent fee agreement shall be in a writing signed by the client and shall state the method by which the fee is to be determined, including the percentage or percentages that shall accrue to the lawyer in the event of settlement, trial or appeal; litigation and other expenses to be deducted from the recovery; and whether such expenses are to be deducted before or after the contingent fee is calculated. The agreement must clearly notify the client of any expenses for which the client will be liable whether or not the client is the prevailing party. Upon conclusion of a contingent fee matter, the lawyer shall provide the client with a written statement stating the outcome of the matter and, if there is a recovery, showing the remittance to the client and the method of its determination.

(d) A lawyer shall not enter into an arrangement for, charge, or collect:

    (1) any fee in a domestic relations matter, the payment or amount of which is contingent upon the securing of a divorce or upon the amount of alimony or support, or property settlement in lieu thereof; or

    (2) a contingent fee for representing a defendant in a criminal case.

Comment

[6] This provision does not preclude a contract for a contingent fee for legal representation in connection with the recovery of post-judgment balances due under support, alimony or other financial orders because such contracts do not implicate the same policy concerns.

Food for Thought

The restriction on contingent fees in criminal cases include the absence of a res, conflicts of interest that might weigh against the lawyer seeking a plea bargain or ask for an instruction on a lesser included offense, as well as the availability of court appointed counsel for indigent defendants. Pamela S. Karlan, *Contingent Fees and Criminal Cases*, 93 Colum. L. Rev. 595, 602-06 (1993); Peter Lushing, *The Fall and Rise of the Criminal Contingent Fee*, 82 J. Crim. L. & Criminology 498 (1992). Professor Peter Lushing argues that:

> The prohibition on criminal contingent fees springs from irrelevant conceptual thinking, unverified concerns regarding conflict of interest, and prejudice against criminal attorneys and what they do. These concerns do not provide sufficient reason to bar lawyers and clients from entering into beneficial agreements. Repeal of the ban on criminal contingent fees would be of particular benefit to the middle class, who will be eager to pay for results instead of services.

Lushing, *supra*, at 546.

Do you agree or disagree with restriction on contingent fees in criminal cases?

With regard to the restriction on contingent fees in domestic relations matters, Restatement § 35(g) explains that "[t]he traditional grounds of the prohibition in divorce cases are that such a fee creates incentives inducing lawyers to discourage reconciliation and encourages bitter and wounding court battles." The Restatement acknowledges that this rationale has less force where "no-fault divorce legislation" indicates that "public policy does not clearly favor the continuation of a marriage that one spouse wishes to end." Another argument "is that such a fee arrangement is usually unnecessary in order to secure an attorney in a divorce proceeding or custody dispute [because if the opposing spouse] has assets, the courts will usually require that spouse to pay the first spouse reasonable attorney fees."

Do you agree or disagree with the restriction on contingent fees in domestic relations matters?

[Question 11]

Attorney is representing Client, the plaintiff in a personal injury case, on a contingent fee basis. Client is without resources to pay for the expenses of the investigation and the medical examinations necessary to prepare for trial. Client asked Attorney to pay for these expenses. Attorney declined to advance the funds but offered to guarantee Client's promissory note to a local bank in order to secure the funds needed to cover those expenses. Client has agreed to reimburse Attorney in the event Attorney incurs liability on the guaranty. Is Attorney subject to discipline if she guarantees Client's promissory note?

(A) Yes, because Attorney is lending her credit to Client.

(B) Yes, because Attorney is helping to finance litigation.

(C) No, because the funds will be used for trial preparation.

(D) No, because Attorney took the case on a contingent fee basis.

<u>Rule 1.8(e)</u> A lawyer shall not provide financial assistance to a client in connection with pending or contemplated litigation, except that:

> (1) a lawyer may advance court costs and expenses of litigation, the re-payment of which may be contingent on the outcome of the matter; and

> (2) a lawyer representing an indigent client may pay court costs and expenses of litigation on behalf of the client.

The limitation on financial assistance to clients results both from a concern for lawyer independence and for removing the incentive for stirring up litigation. The Comment to Rule 1.8 explains:

[10] Lawyers may not subsidize lawsuits or administrative proceedings brought on behalf of their clients, including making or guaranteeing loans to their clients for living expenses, because to do so would encourage clients to pursue lawsuits that might not otherwise be brought and because such assistance gives lawyers too great a financial stake in the litigation. These dangers do not warrant a prohibition on a lawyer lending a client court costs and litigation expenses, including the expenses of medical examination and the costs of obtaining and presenting evidence, because these advances are virtually indistinguishable from contingent fees and help ensure access to the courts. Similarly, an exception allowing lawyers representing indigent clients to pay court costs and litigation expenses regardless of whether these funds will be repaid is warranted.

[Question 12]

Gamma is a legal services lawyer. She is representing Client in eviction proceedings. Client needs to buy new shoes for his child to go to school. Which of the following actions is proper?

(A) Gamma buys the shoes for the child.

(B) Gamma gives Client money to buy the shoes for the child.

(C) All of the above

(D) None of the above

Review Rule 1.8(e) and Comment, *supra.*

[Question 13]

Attorney wants to make it easier for her clients to pay their bills for her fees.

Which of the following would be proper for Attorney?

    (A) Accept bank credit cards in payment of Attorney's fees.

    (B) Arrange for clients to obtain bank loans for the purpose of paying Attorney's fees.

    (C) If a case is interesting, suggest that the client give Attorney publication rights concerning the case as partial payment of the fee.

    (D) A & B

    (E) All of the above

    (F) None of the above

Review Rule 1.5 and Rule 1.8(e).

Rule 1.8:

(d) Prior to the conclusion of representation of a client, a lawyer shall not make or negotiate an agreement giving the lawyer literary or media rights to a portrayal or account based in substantial part on information relating to the representation.

Comment:

Literary Rights

[9] An agreement by which a lawyer acquires literary or media rights concerning the conduct of the representation creates a conflict between the interests of the client and the personal interests of the lawyer. Measures suitable in the representation of the client may detract from the publication value of an account of the representation. Paragraph (d) does not prohibit a lawyer representing a client in a transaction concerning literary property from agreeing that the lawyer's fee shall consist of a share in ownership in the property, if the arrangement conforms to Rule 1.5 and paragraphs (a) and (i).

[Question 14]

In a medical malpractice case, Attorney Alpha's contract with Client provides for a contingent fee of 20% of the recovery by settlement and 30% if the case

is tried, with a total fee not to exceed $50,000. Alpha associated Attorney Beta, a sole practitioner, in the case, with Client's written consent and after full disclosure of the fee agreement between Alpha and Beta. Beta is both a medical doctor and a lawyer and is well qualified by experience and training to try medical malpractice cases. The fee agreement between Alpha and Beta reads as follows: "The total fee in this case is 20% of recovery by settlement and 30%, if tried, with a maximum fee of $50,000. Alpha will help with discovery and will be the liaison person with Client. Beta will prepare the case and try it if it is not settled. Alpha and Beta will divide the fee, 40% to Alpha and 60% to Beta."

Are Alpha and Beta subject to discipline for their agreement for division of the fee?

(A) Yes, unless Client's consent is in writing.

(B) Yes, because Alpha will not try the case.

(C) No, if the division of the fee between Alpha and Beta is in proportion to actual work done by each.

(D) No, because the total fee does not differ from that contracted for by Alpha with Client.

Rule 1.5

(e) A division of a fee between lawyers who are not in the same firm may be made only if:

(1) the division is in proportion to the services performed by each lawyer or each lawyer assumes joint responsibility for the representation;

(2) the client agrees to the arrangement, including the share each lawyer will receive, and the agreement is confirmed in writing; and

(3) the total fee is reasonable.

[Question 15]

Attorney was retained by Defendant to represent him in a paternity suit. Aunt, Defendant's aunt, believed the suit was unfounded and motivated by malice. Aunt sent Attorney a check for $1,000 and asked Attorney to apply it to the payment of Defendant's fee. Aunt told Attorney not to tell Defendant of the payment because "Defendant is too proud to accept gifts, but I know he really needs the money:"

Is it proper for Attorney to accept Aunt's check?

(A) Yes, if Aunt does not attempt to influence Attorney's conduct of the case.

(B) Yes, if Attorney's charges to Defendant are reduced accordingly.

(C) No, because Aunt is attempting to finance litigation to which she is not a party.

(D) No, unless Attorney first informs Defendant and obtains Defendant's consent to retain the payment.

Rule 1.8

(f) A lawyer shall not accept compensation for representing a client from one other than the client unless:

(1) the client gives informed consent;

(2) there is no interference with the lawyer's independence of professional judgment or with the client-lawyer relationship; and

(3) information relating to representation of a client is protected as required by Rule 1.6.

Rule 5.4

(c) A lawyer shall not permit a person who recommends, employs, or pays the lawyer to render legal services for another to direct or regulate the lawyer's professional judgment in rendering such legal services.

For More Information

Insurance defense often raises ethical issues relating to the insurance company as a third-party payor. *See, e.g.,* Stephen L. Pepper, *Applying the Fundamentals of Lawyers' Ethics to Insurance Defense Practice*, 4 Conn. Insurance L.J. 27 (1997).

[Question 16]

An attorney represented a client as a plaintiff in a personal injury matter under a standard contingent fee contract. The client agreed to settle the case for $1,000,000, from which funds the attorney would receive $250,000. The client informed the attorney that she planned to take $25,000 of the settlement funds and spend the money purchasing lottery tickets. The attorney told the client that he disagreed with this plan and encouraged the client to take some classes on investing money. The client agreed to take the classes, but still insisted on playing the lottery.

The attorney received the check for $1,000,000 three days before the client was to attend the investing classes. The attorney held the check for one week, giving the client at least a few days of classes. The attorney then informed the client of the receipt of the funds, disbursed the funds according to the agreement, and also furnished the client with an accounting. The attorney told the client that he had delayed notice to allow time for the client to come to her senses. The client laughed and said, "I guess your plan worked, because these classes have convinced me to invest my money in the stock market instead of playing the lottery."

Is the attorney subject to discipline?

(A) Yes, because the attorney had a duty to promptly notify the client of the receipt of the $1,000,000.

(B) Yes, because the attorney gave unsolicited advice about nonlegal matters.

(C) No, because the client did not object to the withholding of the notice and funds.

(D) No, because the attorney acted in the client's best interest.

Rule 2.1

In representing a client, a lawyer shall exercise independent professional judgment and render candid advice. In rendering advice, a lawyer may refer not only to law but to other considerations such as moral, economic, social and political factors, that may be relevant to the client's situation.

Rule 1.15

(a) A lawyer shall hold property of clients or third persons that is in a lawyer's possession in connection with a representation separate from the lawyer's own property. Funds shall be kept in a separate account maintained in the state where the lawyer's office is situated, or elsewhere with the consent of the client or third person. Other property shall be identified as such and appropriately safeguarded. Complete records of such account funds and other property shall be kept by the lawyer and shall be preserved for a period of [five years] after termination of the representation.

* * *

(d) Upon receiving funds or other property in which a client or third person has an interest, a lawyer shall promptly notify the client or third person. Except as stated in this rule or otherwise permitted by law or by agreement with the client, a lawyer shall promptly deliver to the client or third person any funds or other property that the client or third person is entitled to receive and, upon request by the client or third person, shall promptly render a full accounting regarding such property.

(e) When in the course of representation a lawyer is in possession of property in which two or more persons (one of whom may be the lawyer) claim interests, the property shall be kept separate by the lawyer until the dispute is resolved. The lawyer shall promptly distribute all portions of the property as to which the interests are not in dispute.

[Question 17]

An attorney regularly represents a certain client. When the client planned to leave on a world tour, she delivered to the attorney sufficient money to pay her property taxes when they became due. The attorney placed the money in his clients' trust account. When the tax payment date arrived, the attorney was in need of a temporary loan to close the purchase of a new personal residence. Because the penalty for late payment of taxes was only 2 percent while the rate for a personal loan was 6 percent, the attorney withdrew the client's funds from the clients' trust account to cover his personal check for the closing. The attorney was confident that the client would not object. Ten days later, after the receipt of a large fee previously earned, the attorney paid the client's property taxes and the 2 percent penalty, fully satisfying the client's tax obligation. After the client returned, the attorney told her what he had done, and the client approved the attorney's conduct.

Is the attorney subject to discipline?

(A) Yes, because the attorney failed to pay the client the 10 days of interest at the fair market rate.

(B) Yes, because the attorney used the client's funds for a personal purpose.

(C) No, because the client was not harmed and the attorney reasonably believed at the time he withdrew the money that the client would not object.

(D) No, because when the attorney told the client what he had done, the client approved his conduct.

Review Rule 1.15, *supra.*

[Question 18]

A client retained an attorney to appeal his criminal conviction and to seek bail pending appeal. The agreed-upon fee for the appearance on the bail hearing was $100 per hour. The attorney received $1,600 from the client, of which $600 was a deposit to secure the attorney's fee and $1,000 was for bail costs in the event that bail was obtained. The attorney maintained two office bank accounts: a fee account, in which all fees collected from clients were deposited and from which all office expenses were paid, and a clients' trust account. The attorney deposited the $1,600 in the clients' trust account the week before the bail hearing. She expended six hours of her time preparing for and appearing at the hearing. The effort to obtain bail was unsuccessful. Dissatisfied, the client immediately demanded return of the $1,600.

What should the attorney do with the $1,600?

(A) Transfer the $1,600 to the fee account.

(B) Transfer the $600 to the fee account and leave $1,000 in the clients' trust account until the attorney's fee for the final appeal is determined.

(C) Transfer $600 to the fee account and send the client a $1,000 check on the clients' trust account.

(D) Send the client a $1,000 check and leave $600 in the clients' trust account until the matter is resolved with the client.

Review Rule 1.15, *supra.*

[Question 19]

A client telephoned an attorney who had previously represented him. The client described a problem on which he needed advice and made an appointment for the following week to discuss the matter with the attorney. Prior to the appointment, the attorney performed five hours of preliminary research on the client's problem. At the end of the appointment the client agreed that the attorney should pursue the matter and agreed to a fee of $100 per hour. The client then gave the attorney a check for $5,000 to cover the five hours already worked and as an advance on additional fees and expenses.

The attorney gave the check to the office bookkeeper with directions to deposit the check into the client trust account and immediately transfer $3,000 to the general office account to cover the five hours of research already conducted plus the 25 additional hours she would spend on the matter the following week. At that time, the attorney reasonably believed that she would spend 25 additional hours on the case.

The bookkeeper followed these directions. The next week, the attorney worked diligently on the matter for 23 hours. Reasonably believing that no significant work remained to be done on the matter, the attorney directed the bookkeeper to transfer $200 from the general office account to the client trust account. The attorney then called the client and made an appointment to discuss the status of the matter.

Is the attorney subject to discipline?

(A) Yes, because the attorney accepted legal fees in advance of performing the work.

(B) Yes, because the attorney transferred funds for unearned fees to the general office account.

(C) No, because the attorney transferred the $200 owed to the client from the general office account to the client trust account.

(D) No, because the attorney reasonably believed that she would spend 25 additional hours on the case.

Review Rule 1.15, *supra.*

C. Court-awarded Attorney's Fees

Another source of fees is court-awarded fees. As the Restatement notes, "[p]revailing litigants in some types of litigation are entitled to recover attorney fees from an opposing party." § 38(f). These cases can range from matrimonial and contempt matters to federal and state statutes providing court-awarded attorney's fees in an effort to provide an incentive to enforce particular laws. These latter provisions exist in a variety of areas of law, including securities, anti-trust, civil rights, and **qui tam** actions.

It's Latin to Me!

Black's Law Dictionary defines **qui tam action** as "[a]n action brought under a statute that allows a private person to sue for a penalty, part of which the government or some specified public institution will receive."

WILLIAM B. RUBENSTEIN, *ON WHAT A "PRIVATE ATTORNEY GENERAL" IS—AND WHY IT MATTERS*

57 Vand. L. Rev. 2129, 2133-37 (2004)

* * *

Private attorney general is an awkward expression, qualifying the public lawyer, the attorney general, with the contradictory appellation, private. * * * [T]he private attorney general, made its first appearance in the legal literature in a 1943 decision by Judge Jerome Frank for the U.S. Court of Appeals for the Second Circuit. In that time period, courts were working out the jurisdictional issues triggered by Congress' expansion of the administrative state during the New Deal. The issues posed in Frank's case were paradigmatic: who, exactly, did Congress mean to empower when in the Bituminous Coal Act of 1937 it authorized "any person aggrieved by an order issued by the [Bituminous Coal Commission] in a proceeding to which such person is a party" to seek review in a United States Court of Appeals--and how did the Constitution constrain such an authorization? In the decision's key passage, Judge Frank concluded that Congress could authorize a private citizen to file suit even if the sole purpose of the case were to vindicate the public interest as opposed to some private interest of the litigant: "Such persons, so authorized, are, so to speak, private Attorney Generals." * * *

What seems more surprising is the slow expansion of the private attorney general concept. The phrase appears but seven times in the legal literature of the 1940s, only another eleven times in the 1950s, and but seventy times during the entire 1960s. Finally, in the 1970s, use of the phrase skyrockets: it appears 759 times in those ten years and its use increases steadily each decade to the present. There are two explanations for the limited early use of the phrase. First, the private attorney general concept, when introduced, was resisted by New Deal jurists who considered these so-called litigants mere rent-seekers challenging the new administrative state. The typical early private attorney general was a losing licensee or a consortium of corporations unhappy with New Deal rate-setting; Justices Frankfurter and Douglas scorned the prospect of giving special status to these interests via the private attorney general concept—Justice Douglas's initial use of the phrase came in a dissent in which he (concurring with a similar assessment reached in a companion dissent by Justice Frankfurter) objected to the notion and called for its use to be limited. A second reason that the private attorney general phrase was rarely used before the 1970s is that it existed solely as a matter of party status. As such, it was never destined to blossom into a household word. Even in the 1960s and 1970s, when judges used the phrase more frequently as party status doctrines were expanded by public law litigation, these changes contributed to only minor increases in the phrase's appearance. The phrase explodes in the 1970s not because of public law litigation but because it takes root in new attorney's fees statutes and doctrines.

Once loosed as a matter of money, the private attorney general concept's diffusion was limited only by the imagination of lawyers seeking attorneys' fees.

Hence the present state of affairs: the widespread use of the phrase in a multitude of different situations, to refer to a plethora of discrete actors, carrying on a range of diverse functions—a muddle with but one common denominator: the mix of public and private features. Can this mess be organized? The primary attempts to do so to date have focused on the singular distinction between the ideological plaintiffs' attorney and the fees-driven plaintiffs' attorney. Professor Coffee introduced this distinction in his seminal work on plaintiffs' attorneys * * * .[5] For Professor Coffee, who brought a novel law and economics perspective to the field, the distinction is important because it is speaks to the incentives that drive the two types of private attorneys general. The distinction caught on, though, because it also makes good sense: the NAACP attorney, paid a small salary for her intense efforts, is generally driven by different incentives than those that motivate the plaintiffs' attorney subsisting on the fees she can draw from her portfolio of class action lawsuits. What's more, as Professor Coffee has demonstrated over the past quarter century, focusing on attorney incentives explains a lot about what cases get filed, how they are handled, and whether and how they settle. This organizing distinction helps explain a lot of things, a lot of the time--but not everything and not always.

* * *

ASHLEY E. COMPTON, NOTE, *SHIFTING THE BLAME: THE DILEMMA OF FEE-SHIFTING STATUES AND FEE-WAIVER SETTLEMENTS*

22 Geo. J. Legal Ethics 761, 763-64 (2009)

* * *

Most federal civil rights are not self-executing; the law depends on government enforcement and private litigation in which plaintiff's counsel acts as a private attorney general. As a general rule of American common law, litigants pay their own legal fees. Congress, however, created fee-shifting statutes to support the private litigation of federal rights by giving the prevailing party the right to seek attorney's fees and costs.

Illustrating the importance of fee-shifting statutes for the enforcement of a federal civil right, Supreme Court Associate Justice Thomas Clark stated that not

---

5   [*Ed.'s Note—See, e.g.,* John C. Coffee, Jr., *Rescuing The Private Attorney General: Why The Model of the Lawyer as Bounty Hunter is Not Working,* 42 Md. L. Rev. 215(1983); John C. Coffee, Jr., *Understanding the Plaintiff's Attorney: The Implications of Economic Theory for Private Enforcement of Law Through Class and Derivative Actions,* 86 Colum. L. Rev. 669 (1986); John C. Coffee, Jr., *The Unfaithful Champion: The Plaintiff as Monitor in Shareholder Litigation,* 48 L. & Contemp. Probs. 5 (Summer 1985).]

awarding attorney's fees in civil rights cases would be "tantamount to repealing the [Civil Rights] Act itself." Between 1870 and 1976, Congress passed over fifty fee-shifting statutes. Fee-shifting provisions are common "in laws under which 'private attorneys general' play a significant role in enforcing [Congressional civil rights] policies." In 1976, to close irregular gaps in civil rights laws caused by a Supreme Court holding, Congress passed the Civil Rights Attorney's Fees Award Act (the Fees Act), which provides that "the court, in its discretion, may allow the prevailing party . . . a reasonable attorney's fee as part of the costs." State civil rights statutes include similar fee-shifting provisions.

Fee-shifting statues generally have at least four common characteristics. First, the statutes attempt to promote private enforcement of individual rights in cases too discrete to ordinarily warrant Department of Justice enforcement. Recognizing the danger of relying on private enforcement, Congress feared that "if the cost of private enforcement becomes too great, there will be no private enforcement." Second, the statues often implicate civil rights cases in which "the citizen who must sue to enforce the law has little or no money with which to hire a lawyer." Therefore, Congress wanted these plaintiffs to "recover what it costs them to vindicate these rights in court." Third, the sought-after relief in civil rights suits is often injunctive and non-monetary. Thus, plaintiffs' attorneys cannot utilize traditional contingency fee agreements. Finally, Congress hoped the fee-shifting statutes would "deter[] frivolous suits" which would be "litigated in 'bad faith' under the guise of attempting to enforce" federal rights.

As out-of-court settlements became more popular than disposition by trial, the Supreme Court held that prevailing through settlement rather than litigation did not weaken a plaintiff's claim to fees. The Court also clarified that the statutory language "prevailing party" required that the attorney's fees are the right of the client, not the attorney.

MICHAEL WATERSTONE, *A NEW VISION OF PUBLIC ENFORCEMENT*

92 Minn. L. Rev. 434, 443-47 (2007)

* * *

To the extent that [the 1960s and 1970s] was a golden or even classic era, it did not last very long. The private attorney general as enforcer of civil rights soon faced a multilevel assault by the courts and Congress. In *Buckhannon Board & Care Home, Inc. v. West Virginia Department of Health and Human Resources*, the Court dramatically changed the ways that plaintiffs could recover attorneys' fees in civil rights cases. Rather than qualifying as "prevailing parties" by showing that their lawsuit was a catalyst for voluntary change by the defendant (the previously accepted "catalyst theory"), the Court held that plaintiffs must achieve a "material alteration of the legal relationship of the parties," such as a favorable judgment on the merits or a consent decree. This judicially imposed limitation has undermined the ability of the private attorney general to bring cases for injunctive relief. In other cases the Court has curtailed Congress's ability to authorize private damage suits against states and restricted private rights of action to enforce the disparate impact regulations promulgated under Title VI of the Civil Rights Act of 1964.

Perhaps unintentionally, statutory developments have also been unkind to the private attorney general. In 1991, Congress amended Title VII to allow plaintiffs claiming intentional discrimination to seek compensatory and punitive damages and to request jury trials. These changes were intended to bolster the private enforcement scheme. Ironically, however, by complicating the class certification inquiry, they have stymied the ability of the private parties and their lawyers to bring civil rights class actions.

The political capital and popularity of the civil rights plaintiffs' bar has also faded. The first step was the dismantling of the Legal Services Corporation (LSC). Organizations that had been effective private attorneys general in civil rights cases had their funds cut. Then, in 1996, Congress enacted a series of restrictions on the LSC, including prohibiting organizations that receive funding from the Corporation from bringing class actions. This was devastating to the LSC's ability to prosecute large cases on the public's behalf.

The civil rights private attorney general came to be viewed less as a social advocate and more akin to his mass tort or securities counterpart. The recent passage of the Class Action Fairness Act (CAFA) demonstrates the decreased political power of the plaintiffs' civil rights bar. Amongst other things, CAFA moves certain class action cases from state to federal court on the stated rationale that the civil litigation system had been abused by plaintiffs' class action lawyers. Various civil rights groups argued that CAFA was unnecessary in civil rights cases because there was no history of civil rights class action abuses in state court. Despite vehement pursuit, the civil rights community was unable to get a carve-out for civil rights class actions.

Commentators also soured on the private attorney general. In a series of articles in the 1980s, Professor John Coffee started questioning the extent to which we could "sensibly rely on private litigation as a method of law enforcement." In criticizing the private attorney general as a legal institution that had not lived up to its early promise to promote the public interest, Coffee noted that private lawyers may have different incentives than their clients, which leads to either poor representation (where plaintiffs' lawyers sell out their clients) or excessive litigation (because the parties to the litigation do not bear its costs). Although Professor

Coffee's work focused on securities litigation, his basic criticisms have recently been extended to the civil rights private attorney general. Professor Michael Selmi conducted a recent study of high-profile employment class action cases with large settlements, all of which were brought by the private bar. Professor Selmi found, quite discouragingly, that these cases have little or no effect on stock price, create little or no meaningful substantive change within corporations, and produce only modest financial benefits for class members, despite the fact that the remedial focus of these cases was monetary relief. He concludes that one of the few things these cases actually accomplished was enriching the lawyers that were involved.

* * *

PERDUE v. KENNY A. *ex rel.* WINN

130 S.Ct. 1662 (2010)

ALITO, J. delivered the opinion of the Court.

This case presents the question whether the calculation of an attorney's fee, under federal fee-shifting statutes, based on the "lodestar," i.e., the number of hours worked multiplied by the prevailing hourly rates, may be increased due to superior performance and results. We have stated in previous cases that such an increase is permitted in extraordinary circumstances, and we reaffirm that rule. But as we have also said in prior cases, there is a strong presumption that the lodestar is sufficient; factors subsumed in the lodestar calculation cannot be used as a ground for increasing an award above the lodestar; and a party seeking fees has the burden of identifying a factor that the lodestar does not adequately take into account and proving with specificity that an enhanced fee is justified. Because the District Court did not apply these standards, we reverse the decision below and remand for further proceedings consistent with this opinion.

* * * Respondents (plaintiffs below) are children in the Georgia foster-care system and their next friends. They filed this class action on behalf of 3,000 children in foster care and named as defendants the Governor of Georgia and various state officials (petitioners in this case). Claiming that deficiencies in the foster-care system in two counties near Atlanta violated their federal and state constitutional and statutory rights, respondents sought injunctive and declaratory relief, as well as attorney's fees and expenses.

The United States District Court for the Northern District of Georgia eventually referred the case to mediation, where the parties entered into a consent decree, which the District Court approved. The consent decree resolved all pending issues other than the fees that respondents' attorneys were entitled to receive under 42

U.S.C. § 1988. * * *

Respondents submitted a request for more than $14 million in attorney's fees. Half of that amount was based on their calculation of the lodestar-roughly 30,000 hours multiplied by hourly rates of $200 to $495 for attorneys and $75 to $150 for non-attorneys. In support of their fee request, respondents submitted affidavits asserting that these rates were within the range of prevailing market rates for legal services in the relevant market.

The other half of the amount that respondents sought represented a fee enhancement for superior work and results. Affidavits submitted in support of this request claimed that the lodestar amount "would be generally insufficient to induce lawyers of comparable skill, judgment, professional representation and experience" to litigate this case. * * * Petitioners objected to the fee request, contending that some of the proposed hourly rates were too high, that the hours claimed were excessive, and that the enhancement would duplicate factors that were reflected in the lodestar amount.

The District Court awarded fees of approximately $10.5 million. * * * The District Court found that the hourly rates proposed by respondents were "fair and reasonable," * * * but that some of the entries on counsel's billing records were vague and that the hours claimed for many of the billing categories were excessive. The court therefore cut the non-travel hours by 15% and halved the hourly rate for travel hours. This resulted in a lodestar calculation of approximately $6 million.

The court then enhanced this award by 75%, concluding that the lodestar calculation did not take into account "(1) the fact that class counsel were required to advance case expenses of $1.7 million over a three-year period with no on[-]going reimbursement, (2) the fact that class counsel were not paid on an on-going basis as the work was being performed, and (3) the fact that class counsel's ability to recover a fee and expense reimbursement were completely contingent on the outcome of the case." * * * The court stated that respondents' attorneys had exhibited "a higher degree of skill, commitment, dedication, and professionalism ... than the Court has seen displayed by the attorneys in any other case during its 27 years on the bench." * * * The court also commented that the results obtained were " 'extraordinary' " and added that "[a]fter 58 years as a practicing attorney and federal judge, the Court is unaware of any other case in which a plaintiff class has achieved such a favorable result on such a comprehensive scale." * * * The enhancement resulted in an additional $4.5 million fee award.

Relying on prior Circuit precedent, a panel of the Eleventh Circuit affirmed. * * * The panel held that the District Court had not abused its discretion by failing to make a larger reduction in the number of hours for which respondents' attorneys sought reimbursement, but the panel commented that it "would have cut the billable hours more if we were deciding the matter in the first instance" and added that the hourly rates approved by the District Court also "appear[ed] to be on the generous side." * * * On the question of the enhancement, however, the panel splintered, with each judge writing a separate opinion.

Judge Carnes concluded that binding Eleventh Circuit precedent required that the decision of the District Court be affirmed, but he opined that the reasoning in our opinions suggested that no enhancement should be allowed in this case. He concluded that the quality of the attorneys' performance was "adequately accounted for 'either in determining the reasonable number of hours expended on the litigation or in setting the reasonable hourly rates.' " * * * He found that an enhancement could not be justified based on delay in the recovery of attorney's fees and reimbursable expenses because such delay is a routine feature of cases brought under 42 U.S.C. § 1983. * * * The Eleventh Circuit denied rehearing en banc over the dissent of three judges. * * *

We granted certiorari.

* * *

The general rule in our legal system is that each party must pay its own attorney's fees and expenses,* * * but Congress enacted 42 U.S.C. § 1988 in order to ensure that federal rights are adequately enforced. Section 1988 provides that a prevailing party in certain civil rights actions may recover "a reasonable attorney's fee as part of the costs."[3] Unfortunately, the statute does not explain what Congress meant by a "reasonable" fee, and therefore the task of identifying an appropriate methodology for determining a "reasonable" fee was left for the courts.

* * *

Our prior decisions concerning the federal fee-shifting statutes have established six important rules that lead to our decision in this case.

First, a "reasonable" fee is a fee that is sufficient to induce a capable attorney to undertake the representation of a meritorious civil rights case. * * * Section 1988's aim is to enforce the covered civil rights statutes, not to provide "a form of economic relief to improve the financial lot of attorneys." * * *

Second, the lodestar method yields a fee that is presumptively sufficient to achieve this objective. * * *

Third, although we have never sustained an enhancement of a lodestar amount for performance, * * * we have repeatedly said that enhancements may be awarded in "'rare'" and "'exceptional'" circumstances. * * *

---

3   Virtually identical language appears in many of the federal fee-shifting statutes. * * *

Fourth, we have noted that "the lodestar figure includes most, if not all, of the relevant factors constituting a 'reasonable' attorney's fee," * * * and have held that an enhancement may not be awarded based on a factor that is subsumed in the lodestar calculation * * * . We have thus held that the novelty and complexity of a case generally may not be used as a ground for an enhancement because these factors "presumably [are] fully reflected in the number of billable hours recorded by counsel." We have also held that the quality of an attorney's performance generally should not be used to adjust the lodestar "[b]ecause considerations concerning the quality of a prevailing party's counsel's representation normally are reflected in the reasonable hourly rate." * * *

Fifth, the burden of proving that an enhancement is necessary must be borne by the fee applicant. * * *

Finally, a fee applicant seeking an enhancement must produce "specific evidence" that supports the award. * * * This requirement is essential if the lodestar method is to realize one of its chief virtues, *i.e.,* providing a calculation that is objective and capable of being reviewed on appeal.

* * *

In light of what we have said in prior cases, we reject any contention that a fee determined by the lodestar method may not be enhanced in any situation. The lodestar method was never intended to be conclusive in all circumstances. Instead, there is a "strong presumption" that the lodestar figure is reasonable, but that presumption may be overcome in those rare circumstances in which the lodestar does not adequately take into account a factor that may properly be considered in determining a reasonable fee.

* * *

In this case, we are asked to decide whether either the quality of an attorney's performance or the results obtained are factors that may properly provide a basis for an enhancement. We treat these two factors as one. When a plaintiff's attorney achieves results that are more favorable than would have been predicted based on the governing law and the available evidence, the outcome may be attributable to superior performance and commitment of resources by plaintiff's counsel. Or the outcome may result from inferior performance by defense counsel, unanticipated defense concessions, unexpectedly favorable rulings by the court, an unexpectedly sympathetic jury, or simple luck. Since none of these latter causes can justify an enhanced award, superior results are relevant only to the extent it can be shown that they are the result of superior attorney performance. Thus, we need only consider whether superior attorney performance can justify an enhancement. And in light of the principles derived from our prior cases, we inquire whether there are circumstances in which superior attorney performance is not adequately taken into account in the lodestar calculation. We conclude that there are a few such circumstances but that these circumstances are indeed "rare" and "exceptional," and require specific evidence that the lodestar fee would not have been "adequate to attract competent counsel[.]"

First, an enhancement may be appropriate where the method used in determining the hourly rate employed in the lodestar calculation does not adequately measure the attorney's true market value, as demonstrated in part during the litigation. This may occur if the hourly rate is determined by a formula that takes into account only a single factor (such as years since admission to the bar) or perhaps only a few similar factors. In such a case, an enhancement may be appropriate so that an attorney is compensated at the rate that the attorney would receive in cases not governed by the federal fee-shifting statutes. But in order to provide a calculation that is objective and reviewable, the trial judge should adjust the attorney's hourly rate in accordance with specific proof linking the attorney's ability to a prevailing market rate.

Second, an enhancement may be appropriate if the attorney's performance includes an extraordinary outlay of expenses and the litigation is exceptionally protracted. As Judge Carnes noted below, when an attorney agrees to represent a civil rights plaintiff who cannot afford to pay the attorney, the attorney presumably understands that no reimbursement is likely to be received until the successful resolution of the case, * * * and therefore enhancements to compensate for delay in reimbursement for expenses must be reserved for unusual cases. In such exceptional cases, however, an enhancement may be allowed, but the amount of the enhancement must be calculated using a method that is reasonable, objective, and capable of being reviewed on appeal, such as by applying a standard rate of interest to the qualifying outlays of expenses.

Third, there may be extraordinary circumstances in which an attorney's performance involves exceptional delay in the payment of fees. An attorney who expects to be compensated under § 1988 presumably understands that payment of fees will generally not come until the end of the case, if at all. * * * Compensation for this delay is generally made "either by basing the award on current rates or by adjusting the fee based on historical rates to reflect its present value." * * * But we do not rule out the possibility that an enhancement may be appropriate where an attorney assumes these costs in the face of unanticipated delay, particularly where the delay is unjustifiably caused by the defense. In such a case, however, the enhancement should be calculated by applying a method similar to that described above in connection with exceptional delay in obtaining reimbursement for expenses.

We reject the suggestion that it is appropriate to grant performance enhancements on the ground that departures from hourly billing are becoming more common.

As we have noted, the lodestar was adopted in part because it provides a rough approximation of general billing practices, and accordingly, if hourly billing becomes unusual, an alternative to the lodestar method may have to be found. However, neither respondents nor their *amici* contend that that day has arrived. Nor have they shown that permitting the award of enhancements on top of the lodestar figure corresponds to prevailing practice in the general run of cases.

We are told that, under an increasingly popular arrangement, attorneys are paid at a reduced hourly rate but receive a bonus if certain specified results are obtained, and this practice is analogized to the award of an enhancement such as the one in this case. The analogy, however, is flawed. An attorney who agrees, at the outset of the representation, to a *reduced hourly rate* in exchange for the opportunity to earn a performance bonus is in a position far different from an attorney in a § 1988 case who is compensated at the *full prevailing rate* and then seeks a performance enhancement in addition to the lodestar amount after the litigation has concluded. Reliance on these comparisons for the purposes of administering enhancements, therefore, is not appropriate.

* * *

In the present case, the District Court did not provide proper justification for the large enhancement that it awarded. The court increased the lodestar award by 75% but, as far as the court's opinion reveals, this figure appears to have been essentially arbitrary. Why, for example, did the court grant a 75% enhancement instead of the 100% increase that respondents sought? And why 75% rather than 50% or 25% or 10%?

The District Court commented that the enhancement was the "minimum enhancement of the lodestar necessary to reasonably compensate [respondents'] counsel." * * * But the effect of the enhancement was to increase the top rate for the attorneys to more than $866 per hour, and the District Court did not point to anything in the record that shows that this is an appropriate figure for the relevant market.

The District Court pointed to the fact that respondents' counsel had to make extraordinary outlays for expenses and had to wait for reimbursement, * * * but the court did not calculate the amount of the enhancement that is attributable to this factor. Similarly, the District Court noted that respondents' counsel did not receive fees on an ongoing basis while the case was pending, but the court did not sufficiently link this factor to proof in the record that the delay here was outside the normal range expected by attorneys who rely on § 1988 for the payment of their fees or quantify the disparity. Nor did the court provide a calculation of the cost to counsel of any extraordinary and unwarranted delay. And the court's reliance on the contingency of the outcome contravenes our holding in *Dague.* * * *

Finally, insofar as the District Court relied on a comparison of the performance of counsel in this case with the performance of counsel in unnamed prior cases, the District Court did not employ a methodology that permitted meaningful appellate review. Needless to say, we do not question the sincerity of the District Court's observations, and we are in no position to assess their accuracy. But when a trial judge awards an enhancement on an impressionistic basis, a major purpose of the lodestar method-providing an objective and reviewable basis for fees * * * is undermined.

Determining a "reasonable attorney's fee" is a matter that is committed to the sound discretion of a trial judge, see 42 U.S.C. § 1988 (permitting court, "in its discretion," to award fees), but the judge's discretion is not unlimited. It is essential that the judge provide a reasonably specific explanation for all aspects of a fee determination, including any award of an enhancement. Unless such an explanation is given, adequate appellate review is not feasible, and without such review, widely disparate awards may be made, and awards may be influenced (or at least, may appear to be influenced) by a judge's subjective opinion regarding particular attorneys or the importance of the case. In addition, in future cases, defendants contemplating the possibility of settlement will have no way to estimate the likelihood of having to pay a potentially huge enhancement. * * *

Section 1988 serves an important public purpose by making it possible for persons without means to bring suit to vindicate their rights. But unjustified enhancements that serve only to enrich attorneys are not consistent with the statute's aim. In many cases, attorney's fees *awarded under § 1988 are not paid by the individuals responsible for the constitutional or statutory violations on which the judgment is based. Instead, the fees are paid in effect by state and local taxpayers, and because state and local governments have limited budgets, money that is used to pay attorney's fees is money that cannot be used for programs that provide vital public services. * * *

* * *

For all these reasons, the judgment of the Court of Appeals is reversed, and the case is remanded for proceedings consistent with this opinion.

It is so ordered.

* * *

[Question 20]

Joan Lawyer represents a class of plaintiffs in a civil rights case against the State of Fordham. Fordham's counsel agrees to provide substantially all the relief plaintiffs seek so long as Joan Lawyer agrees to waive court-awarded attorney's fees under the applicable statute. The parties agree to the settlement. Plaintiffs then appeal the settlement on the ground that Fordham's demand for a waiver of court-awarded attorney's fees undermines the goal of the relevant statute in encouraging private attorneys general. What result?

— (A) The settlement is upheld.

(B) The settlement is reversed with regard to the waiver of attorney's fees.

EVANS v. JEFF D.

475 U.S. 717 (1986)

Justice <u>STEVENS</u> delivered the opinion of the Court.

* * *

In March 1983, one week before trial, petitioners presented respondents with a new settlement proposal. As respondents themselves characterize it, the proposal "offered virtually all of the injunctive relief [they] had sought in their complaint." * * * [H[owever, petitioners' offer included a provision for a waiver by respondents of any claim to fees or costs. Originally, this waiver was unacceptable to the Idaho Legal Aid Society, which had instructed Johnson to reject any settlement offer conditioned upon a waiver of fees, but Johnson ultimately determined that his ethical obligation to his clients mandated acceptance of the proposal. The parties conditioned the waiver on approval by the District Court. * * * After the stipulation was signed, Johnson filed a written motion requesting the District Court to approve the settlement "except for the provision on costs and attorney's fees," and to allow respondents to present a bill of costs and fees for consideration by the court. At the oral argument on that motion, Johnson contended that petitioners' offer had exploited his ethical duty to his clients-that he was "forced," by an offer giving his clients "the best result [they] could have gotten in this court or any other court," to waive his attorney's fees. The District Court, however, evaluated the waiver in the context of the entire settlement and rejected the ethical underpinnings of Johnson's argument. Explaining that although petitioners were "not willing to concede that they were obligated to [make the changes in their practices required by the stipulation], . . . they were willing to do them as long as their costs were outlined and they didn't face additional costs," it concluded that "it doesn't violate any ethical considerations for an attorney to give up his attorney fees in the interest of getting a better bargain for his client[s] ." Accordingly, the District Court approved the settlement and denied the motion to submit a costs bill.

When respondents appealed from the order denying attorney's fees and costs, petitioners filed a motion requesting the District Court to suspend or stay their obligation to comply with the substantive terms of the settlement. Because the District Court regarded the fee waiver as a material term of the complete settlement, it granted the motion.   The Court of Appeals however, granted two emergency motions for stays requiring enforcement of the substantive terms of the consent decree pending the appeal. More dramatically, after ordering preliminary relief, it invalidated the fee waiver and left standing the remainder of the settlement; it then instructed the District Court to "make its own determination of the fees that are reasonable" and remanded for that limited purpose. * * *

The question this case presents, then, is whether the Fees Act requires a district court to disapprove a stipulation seeking to settle a civil rights class action under Rule 23 when the offered relief equals or exceeds the probable outcome at trial but is expressly conditioned on waiver of statutory eligibility for attorney's fees. For reasons set out below, we are not persuaded that Congress has commanded that all such settlements must be rejected by the District Court. Moreover, on the facts of record in this case, we are satisfied that the District Court did not abuse its discretion by approving the fee waiver.

* * *

The text of the Fees Act provides no support for the proposition that Congress intended to ban all fee waivers offered in connection with substantial relief on the merits. On the contrary, the language of the Act, as well as its legislative history, indicates that Congress bestowed on the "prevailing *party* " (generally plaintiffs) a statutory eligibility for a discretionary award of attorney's fees in specified civil rights actions. It did not prevent the party from waiving this eligibility anymore than it legislated against assignment of this right to an attorney, such as effectively occurred here. Instead, Congress enacted the fee-shifting provision as "an integral part of the remedies necessary to obtain" compliance with civil rights laws, * * * to further the same general purpose-promotion of respect for civil rights-that led it to provide damages and injunctive relief. The statute and its legislative history nowhere suggest that Congress intended to forbid *all* waivers of attorney's fees-even those insisted upon by a civil rights plaintiff in exchange for some other relief to which he is indisputably not entitled -anymore than it intended to bar a concession on damages to secure broader injunctive relief. Thus, while it is undoubtedly true that Congress expected fee shifting to attract competent counsel to represent citizens deprived of their civil rights, it neither bestowed fee awards upon attorneys nor rendered them nonwaivable or nonnegotiable; instead, it added them to the arsenal of remedies available to combat violations of civil rights, a goal not invariably inconsistent with conditioning settlement on the merits on a waiver of statutory attorney's fees.

In fact, we believe that a general proscription against negotiated waiver of attorney's fees in exchange for a settlement on the merits would itself impede vindication of civil rights, at least in some cases, by reducing the attractiveness of settlement. Of particular relevance in this regard is our recent decision in *Marek v. Chesny,* 473 U.S. 1, 105 S.Ct. 3012, 87 L.Ed.2d 1 (1985). In that case, which admittedly was not a class action and therefore did not implicate the court's approval power under Rule 23(e), we specifically considered and rejected the contention that civil rights actions should be treated differently from other civil actions for purposes of settlement. As THE CHIEF JUSTICE explained in his opinion for the Court, the settlement of litigation provides benefits for civil rights plaintiffsas *well as defendants and is consistent with the purposes of the Fees Act:

"There is no evidence, however, that Congress, in considering § 1988, had any thought that civil rights claims were to be on any different footing from other civil claims insofar as settlement is concerned. Indeed, Congress made clear its concern that civil rights plaintiffs not be penalized for 'helping to lessen docket congestion' by settling their cases out of court. * * *

". . . Some plaintiffs will receive compensation in settlement where, on trial, they might not have recovered, or would have recovered less than what was offered. And, even for those who would prevail at trial, settlement will provide them with compensation at an earlier date without the burdens, stress, and time of litigation. In short, settlements rather than litigation will serve the interests of plaintiffs as well as defendants." * * *

To promote both settlement and civil rights, we implicitly acknowledged in *Marek v. Chesny* the possibility of a tradeoff between merits relief and attorney's fees when we upheld the defendant's lump-sum offer to settle the entire civil rights action, including any liability for fees and costs.

In approving the package offer in *Marek v. Chesny* we recognized that a rule prohibiting the comprehensive negotiation of all outstanding issues in a pending case might well preclude the settlement of a substantial number of cases:

"If defendants are not allowed to make lump-sum offers that would, if accepted, represent their total liability, they would understandably be reluctant to make settlement offers. As the Court of Appeals observed, 'many a defendant would be unwilling to make a binding settlement offer on terms that left it exposed to liability for attorney's fees in whatever amount the court might fix on motion of the plaintiff.' * * *

Most defendants are unlikely to settle unless the cost of the predicted judgment, discounted by its probability, plus the transaction costs of further litigation, are greater than the cost of the settlement package. If fee waivers cannot be negotiated, the settlement package must either contain an attorney's fee component of potentially large and typically uncertain magnitude, or else the parties must agree to have the fee fixed by the court. Although either of these alternatives may well be acceptable in many cases, there surely is a significant number in which neither alternative will be as satisfactory as a decision to try the entire case.

The adverse impact of removing attorney's fees and costs from bargaining might be tolerable if the uncertainty introduced into settlement negotiations were small. But it is not. The defendants' potential liability for fees in this kind of litigation can be as significant as, and sometimes even more significant than, their potential liability on the merits. This proposition is most dramatically illustrated by the fee awards of district courts in actions seeking only monetary relief. Although it is more difficult to compare fee awards with the cost of injunctive relief, in part because the cost of such relief is seldom reported in written opinions, here too attorney's fees awarded by district courts have "frequently outrun the economic benefits ultimately obtained by successful litigants." * * * Undoubtedly there are many other civil rights actions in which potential liability for attorney's fees may overshadow the potential cost of relief on the merits and darken prospects for settlement if fees cannot be negotiated.

The unpredictability of attorney's fees may be just as important as their magnitude when a defendant is striving to fix its liability. Unlike a determination of costs, which ordinarily involve smaller outlays and are more susceptible of calculation, * * * "[t]here is no precise rule or formula" for determining attorney's fees * * * . Among other considerations, the district court must determine what hours were reasonably expended on what claims, whether that expenditure was reasonable in light of the success obtained, * * * and what is an appropriate hourly rate for the services rendered. Some District Courts have also considered whether a "multiplier" or other adjustment is appropriate. The consequence of this succession of necessarily judgmental decisions for the ultimate fee award is inescapable: a defendant's liability for his opponent's attorney's fees in a civil rights action cannot be fixed with a sufficient degree of confidence to make defendants indifferent to their exclusion from negotiation. is therefore not implausible to anticipate that parties to a significant number of civil rights cases will refuse to settle if liability for attorney's fees remains open, thereby forcing more cases to trial, unnecessarily burdening the judicial system, and disserving civil rights litigants. Respondents' own waiver of attorney's fees and costs to obtain settlement of their educational claims is eloquent testimony to the utility of fee waivers in vindicating civil rights claims. We conclude, therefore, that it is not necessary to construe the Fees Act as embodying a general rule prohibiting settlements conditioned on the waiver of fees in order to be faithful to the purposes of that Act.

* * *

The question remains whether the District Court abused its discretion in this case by approving a settlement which included a complete fee waiver. As noted earlier, Rule 23(e) wisely requires court approval of the terms of any settlement of a class action. The potential conflict among members of the class-in this case, for example, the possible conflict between children primarily interested in better educational programs and those primarily interested in improved health care-fully justifies the requirement of court approval.

The Court of Appeals, respondents, and various *amici* supporting their position, however, suggest that the court's authority to pass on settlements, typically invoked to ensure fair treatment of class members, must be exercised in accordance with the Fees Act to promote the availability of attorneys in civil rights cases. Specifically, respondents assert that the State of Idaho could not pass a valid statute precluding the payment of attorney's fees in settlements of civil rights cases to which the Fees Act applies. * * * From this they reason that the Fees Act must equally preclude the adoption of a uniform state-wide policy that serves the same end, and accordingly contend that a consistent practice of insisting on a fee waiver as a condition of settlement in civil rights litigation is in conflict with the federal statute authorizing fees for prevailing parties, including those who prevail by way of settlement. Remarkably, there seems little disagreement on these points. Petitioners and the *amici* who support them never suggest that the district court is obligated to place its stamp of approval on every settlement in which the plaintiffs' attorneys have agreed to a fee waiver. The Solicitor General, for example, has suggested that a fee waiver need not be approved when the defendant had "no realistic defense on the merits," * * * or if the waiver was part of a "vindictive effort . . . to teach counsel that they had better not bring such cases[.]" * * *

We find it unnecessary to evaluate this argument, however, because the record in this case does not indicate that Idaho has adopted such a statute, policy, or practice. Nor does the record support the narrower proposition that petitioners' request to waive fees was a vindictive effort to deter attorneys from representing plaintiffs in civil rights suits against Idaho. It is true that a fee waiver was requested and obtained as a part of the early settlement of the education claims, but we do not understand respondents to be challenging that waiver, * * * and they have not offered to prove that petitioners' tactics in this case merely implemented a routine state policy designed to frustrate the objectives of the Fees Act. Our own examination of the record reveals no such policy.

In light of the record, respondents must-to sustain the judgment in their favor-confront the District Court's finding that the extensive structural relief they obtained constituted an adequate *quid pro quo* for their waiver of attorney's fees. The Court of Appeals did not overturn this finding. Indeed, even that court did not suggest that the option of rejecting the entire settlement and requiring the parties either to try the case or to attempt to negotiate a different settlement would have served the interests of justice. Only by making the unsupported assumption that the respondent class was entitled to retain the favorable portions of the settlement while rejecting the fee waiver could the Court of Appeals conclude that the District Court had acted unwisely.

What the outcome of this settlement illustrates is that the Fees Act has given the victims of civil rights violations a powerful weapon that improves their ability to employ counsel, to obtain access to the courts, and thereafter to vindicate their rights by means of settlement or trial. For aught that appears, it was the "coercive" effect of respondents' statutory right to seek a fee award that motivated petitioners' exceptionally generous offer. Whether this weapon might be even more powerful if fee waivers were prohibited in cases like this is another question, but it is in any event a question that Congress is best equipped to answer. Thus far, the Legislature has not commanded that fees be paid whenever a case is settled. Unless it issues such a command, we shall rely primarily on the sound discretion of the district courts to appraise the reasonableness of particular class-action settlements on a case-by-case basis, in the light of all the relevant circumstances. In this case, the District Court did not abuse its discretion in upholding a fee waiver which secured broad injunctive relief, relief greater than that which plaintiffs could reasonably have expected to achieve at trial.

The judgment of the Court of Appeals is reversed.

It is so ordered.

CHAPTER 4

The Lawyer's Duty of Confidentiality

I. Introduction

The lawyer's duty of confidentiality is set forth in Rule 1.6, which provides that a lawyer "shall not reveal information relating to the representation of a client unless the client gives informed consent, the disclosure is impliedly authorized in order to carry out the representation or the disclosure is permitted by" some designated exceptions, as discussed later in this Chapter.

As seen later in this Chapter, there are a number of exceptional situations in which a lawyer may disclose information that is "confidential" within the Rule 1.6 definition. For introductory purposes, the point is that the lawyer must keep secret a broad range of information that she learns when representing a client.

II. The Relationship Between the Duty of Confidentiality and the Attorney-Client Privilege

As seen from the Rule 1.6 definition above, the lawyer's duty to maintain information as secret covers more than that information protected by the attorney-client privilege. Privileged information is only one part of the definition --- it also covers information likely to be embarrassing or detrimental to the client and information that the client requests be kept secret.

[Question 1]

Lawyer represents a client who suffered injuries when he was run down by a car in a crosswalk. The lawyer investigates the matter and comes upon a surveillance tape indicating that his client, one minute before the accident, had exited from an XXX rated adult theater with a woman who was not his wife. At a dinner party, the lawyer tells everyone the "ironic" story of his client, who got run down after being so "naughty."

What is the proper finding for the disciplinary committee?

(A) The lawyer violated no duties because the information about the client's whereabouts was not protected by the attorney-client privilege.

(B) The lawyer violated the duty of confidentiality because the information was privileged.

(C) The lawyer violated the duty of confidentiality because the information was embarrassing to the client.

(D) The lawyer violated no duties because the information was not secret— it was known by the woman who was with his client at the time.

So what difference does it make whether information is protected by the attorney-client privilege or the broader duty of confidentiality? *See* Rule 1.6(b)(6) (information that is confidential—not privileged—is subject to disclosure under legal authority).

[Question 2]

Lawyer represents a client who suffered injuries when he was run down by a car in a crosswalk. The lawyer investigates the matter and comes upon a surveillance tape indicating that his client, one minute before the accident, had exited from an XXX rated adult theater with a woman who was not his wife. Before trial, the lawyer receives a discovery request from defense counsel, demanding production of any surveillance tapes that are or may be relevant to the action. The lawyer refuses to produce the surveillance tape he found.

Must the lawyer produce the surveillance tape?

(A) No, because it is privileged.

(B) No, because to do so would violate Lawyer's duty of confidentiality.

(C) Yes, because the information is not privileged and the lawyer must turn over non-privileged information if a lawful demand is made.

(D) Yes, because even though the information is privileged, the Lawyer must comply with a discovery request.

III. Basics of the Attorney-Client Privilege

While the duty of confidentiality covers more information than that protected by the attorney-client privilege, it is important to determine the scope of the privilege. While the privilege is a rule of evidence and the duty of confidentiality is a rule of professional responsibility, the lawyer's duty to invoke and protect the privilege is a critical part of the lawyer's duty of confidentiality under Rule 1.6.

A. Rationale for the Attorney-Client Privilege.

The Supreme Court set forth the commonly-accepted rationale for the attorney-client privilege in *Upjohn Co. v. United States,* 449 U.S. 383 (1981):

Make the Connection

The attorney-client privilege is an important subject in most evidence courses—the privilege is after all a rule of evidence and not a rule of ethics. But covering the privilege is important in a professional responsibility course because a lawyer needs to know how to maximize the client's claims of privilege. Privilege arguments are won and lost by proper lawyering in advance of any disclosure between a client and a lawyer.

> The attorney-client privilege is the oldest of the privileges for confidential communications known to the common law. 8 J. Wigmore, Evidence § 2290 (McNaughton rev. 1961). Its purpose is to encourage full and frank communication between attorneys and their clients and thereby promote broader public interests in the observance of law and administration of justice. The privilege recognizes that sound legal advice or advocacy serves public ends and that such advice or advocacy depends upon the lawyer's being fully informed by the client. As we stated last Term in *Trammel v. United States,* 445 U.S. 40, 51 (1980): "The lawyer-client privilege rests on the need for the advocate and counselor to know all that relates to the client's reasons for seeking representation if the professional mission is to be carried out." And in *Fisher v. United States,* 425 U.S. 391, 403 (1976), we recognized the purpose of the privilege to be "to encourage clients to make full disclosure to their attorneys." This rationale for the privilege has long been recognized by the Court, see *Hunt v. Blackburn,* 128 U.S. 464, 470 (1888) (privilege "is founded upon the necessity, in the interest and administration of justice, of the aid of persons having knowledge of the law and skilled in its practice, which assistance can only be safely and readily availed of when free from the consequences or the apprehension of disclosure").

Make the Connection

So you can see that while the privilege is a rule of evidence, it bears directly on the lawyer's ethical duty to effectively represent the client—as well as the duty to preserve secret information to the extent allowed by law.

So without the privilege, clients would not be truthful, and the lawyer would be operating under an informational deficit and would thereby be less effective as an advocate for the client.

Can you see any other reason for the privilege, which, after all, deprives the court of relevant and reliable evidence and so is contrary to the search for truth? If there were no privilege, how would the now-unprotected communication between lawyer and client be proven in court?

The attorney-client privilege is not without its detractors. *See, e.g., Developments in the Law: Privileged Communications,* 98 Harv. L. Rev. 1450 (1985) (arguing that privileges are established by lawyers, so that it is not surprising that there is an aggressively enforced attorney-client privilege, but no accountant-client privilege); *See* Elizabeth G. Thornburg, *Sanctifying Secrecy: The Mythology of the Corporate Attorney-Client Privilege,* 69 Notre Dame L. Rev. 157 (1993) (arguing that the attorney-client privilege gives unjustified protection to entrenched interests); Fred C. Zacharias, *Rethinking Confidentiality,* 74 Iowa L. Rev. 351 (1989) (criticizing the attorney-client privilege as a means of driving up lawyer fees, because clients pay a premium so that they can obtain a privilege for their communications, even though nonlawyers may be able to provide similar services more cheaply).

B. Criteria for Attorney-Client Privilege

The Judicial Conference Advisory Committee on Evidence Rules has developed a draft attempting to codify the federal law on attorney-client privilege. The draft has not yet been proposed as an amendment to the Federal Rules. The draft attempts to codify the Federal common law developed under Federal Rule of Evidence 501 (providing that rules of privilege in cases arising under federal law are to be determined by federal common law as developed in the light of reason and experience). The Rules Committee's draft is as follows:

LAWYER-CLIENT PRIVILEGE (Draft, March 1, 2010)

(a) Definitions. As used in this rule:

(1) A "communication" is any expression through which a privileged person intends to convey information to another privileged person or any record containing such an expression;

(2) A "client" is a person who or an organization that consults a lawyer to obtain professional legal services.

(3) An "organization" is a corporation, unincorporated association, partnership, trust, estate, sole proprietorship, governmental entity, or other for-profit or not-for-profit association.

(4) A "lawyer" is a person who is authorized to practice law in any domestic or foreign jurisdiction or whom a client reasonably believes to be a lawyer;

(5) A "privileged person" is a client, that client's lawyer, or an agent of either who is reasonably necessary to facilitate communications between the client and the lawyer.

(6) A communication is "in confidence" if, at the time and in the circumstances of the communication, the communicating person reasonably believes that no one except a privileged person will learn the contents of the communication.

(b) General Rule of Privilege.

A client has a privilege to refuse to disclose and to prevent any other person from disclosing a communication made in confidence between or among privileged persons for the purpose of obtaining or providing legal assistance for the client.

(c) Who May Claim the Privilege.

A client, a personal representative of an incompetent or deceased client, or a person succeeding to the interest of a client may invoke the privilege. A lawyer, agent of the lawyer, or an agent of a client from whom a privileged communication is sought may invoke the privilege on behalf of the client if implicitly or explicitly authorized by the client.

(d) Standards for Organizational Clients.

With respect to an organizational client, the lawyer-client privilege extends to a communication that

(1) is otherwise privileged;

(2) is between an organization's agent and a privileged person where the communication concerns a legal matter of interest to the organization within the scope of the agent's agency or employment; and

(3) is disclosed only to privileged persons and other agents of the organization who reasonably need to know of the communication in order to act for the organization.

(e) Privilege of Co-Clients and Common-Interest Arrangements.

If two or more clients are jointly represented by the same lawyer in a matter or if two or more clients with a common interest in a matter are represented by separate lawyers and they agree to pursue a common interest and to exchange information concerning the matter, a communication of any such client that is otherwise privileged and relates to matters of common interest is privileged as against third persons. Any such client may invoke the privilege unless the client making the communication has waived the privilege. Unless the clients agree otherwise, such a communication is not privileged as between the clients. Communications between clients or agents of clients outside the presence of a lawyer or agent of a lawyer representing at least one of the clients are not privileged.

(f) Exceptions.

The lawyer-client privilege does not apply to a communication

(1) from or to a deceased client if the communication is relevant to an issue between parties who claim an interest through the same deceased client, either by testate or intestate succession or by an inter vivos transaction;

(2) that occurs when a client consults a lawyer to obtain assistance to engage in a crime or fraud or aiding a third person to do so. Regardless of the client's purpose at the time of consultation, the communication is not privileged if the client uses the lawyer's advice or other services to engage in or assist in committing a crime or fraud.

(3) that is waived by the client;

(4) between a trustee of an express trust or a similar fiduciary and a lawyer or other privileged person retained to advise the trustee concerning the administration of the trust that is relevant to a beneficiary's claim of breach of fiduciary duties;

(5) between an organizational client and a lawyer or other privileged person, if offered in a proceeding that involves a dispute between the client and shareholders, members, or other constituents of the organization toward whom the directors, officers, or similar persons managing the organization bear fiduciary responsibilities, provided the court finds

(A) those managing the organization are charged with breach of their obligations toward the shareholders, members, or other constituents or toward the organization itself;

(B) the communication occurred prior to the assertion of the charges and relates directly to those charges; and

(C) the need of the requesting party to discover or introduce the communication is sufficiently compelling and the threat to confidentiality sufficiently confined to justify setting the privilege aside."

1. *Client Must Be Seeking Legal Advice*

A client may not "buy" a privilege by retaining an attorney to do something that a nonlawyer could do just as well. *See, e.g., In re Feldberg,* 862 F.2d 622, 626 (7th Cir. 1988) ("A business that gets marketing advice from a lawyer does not acquire a privilege in the bargain; so too a business that obtains the services of a records custodian from a member of the bar."). The client must be seeking legal advice and assistance from the lawyer. *See, e.g., In re Grand Jury Subpoena, Peek,* 682 F. Supp. 1552, 1556 (M.D. Ga. 1987) (personal loan transaction between attorney and another person is not privileged: "Otherwise, everything that a lawyer does for himself or herself would be cloaked with a privilege just because he or she is a lawyer."); *SCM Corp. v. Xerox Corp.,* 70 F.R.D. 508, 515 (D. Conn. 1976) ("Legal departments are not citadels in which public, business or technical information may be placed to defeat discovery and thereby ensure confidentiality.").

[Question 3]

Client retains lawyer for his assistance in a real estate transaction. Client asks the lawyer in confidence whether the lawyer thinks it is "a good and workable deal." How is this communication to be treated?

   (A) **As privileged, because the client was speaking in confidence to the lawyer.**

   (B) **Not privileged, because the client was not seeking legal advice, and therefore not within the duty of confidentiality secret under Model Rule 1.6.**

   (C) **Privileged, if the dominant intent is to seek legal advice, and within the duty of confidentiality.**

   (D) **Privileged, if there was any intent to seek legal advice, but not protected by the duty of confidentiality as its disclosure would not injure the client.**

Food for Thought

If you hire a lawyer to prepare your tax return, are your private communications to the lawyer privileged? *See, e.g., United States v. Frederick,* 182 F.3d 496 (7th Cir. 1999) ("There is no common law accountant's or tax preparer's privilege, and a taxpayer must not be allowed, by hiring a lawyer to do the work that an accountant, or other tax preparer, or the taxpayer himself or herself, normally would do, to obtain greater protection from government investigators than a taxpayer who did not use a lawyer as his tax preparer would be entitled to do. To rule otherwise would be to impede tax investigations, reward lawyers for doing nonlawyers' work, and create a privileged position for lawyers in competition with other tax preparers—and to do all this without promoting the legitimate aims" of the privilege). *In re Schroeder,* 842 F.2d 1223, 1224 (11th Cir. 1987) ("Courts generally have held that the preparation of tax returns does not constitute legal advice within the scope of the privilege.").

If you hire a lawyer to prepare your tax return, are your private communications to the lawyer protected by the lawyer's duty of confidentiality? *See* Model Rule 1.6, above. If it is so protected, what difference does it make that it is not privileged?

Sometimes a client seeks both legal and non-legal advice from the attorney. Should the privilege apply in these circumstances? The following case provides guidance on the subject.

In re COUNTY OF ERIE

473 F.3d 413 (2d Cir. 2007)

JACOBS, Chief Judge:

In the course of a lawsuit by a class of arrested persons against Erie County (and certain of its officials) alleging that they were subjected to unconstitutional strip searches, the United States District Court for the Western District of New York (Curtin, J.) ordered the discovery of e-mails (and other documents) between an Assistant Erie County Attorney and County officials that solicit, contain and discuss advice from attorney to client. The County defendants petition for a writ of mandamus directing the district court to vacate that order. The writ is available because: important issues of first impression are raised; the privilege will be irreversibly lost if review awaits final judgment; and immediate resolution of this dispute will promote sound discovery practices and doctrine. Upon consideration of the circumstances, we issue the writ ordering the district court: to vacate its order, to determine whether the privilege was otherwise waived, and to enter an interim order to protect the confidentiality of the disputed communications.

I

On July 21, 2004, plaintiffs-respondents Adam Pritchard, Edward Robinson and Julenne Tucker commenced suit under 42 U.S.C. § 1983, individually and on behalf of a class of others similarly situated, alleging that, pursuant to a written policy of the Erie County Sheriff's Office and promulgated by County officials, every detainee who entered the Erie County Holding Center or Erie County Correctional Facility (including plaintiffs) was subjected to an invasive strip search, without regard to individualized suspicion or the offense alleged, and that this policy violates the Fourth Amendment. They sued the County of Erie, New York, as well as Erie County Sheriff Patrick Gallivan; Undersheriff Timothy Howard; the acting Superintendent of the Erie County Correctional Facility, Donald Livingston; the Deputy Superintendent, Robert Huggins; and the Superintendent of the Erie County Holding Center, H. McCarthy Gibson (collectively, the "County").

During the course of discovery, the County withheld production of certain documents as privileged attorney-client communications; a privilege log was produced instead * * * . In August 2005, plaintiffs moved to compel production of the logged documents, almost all of which were e-mails. The County submitted the documents to Magistrate Judge Hugh B. Scott for inspection in camera. In January 2006, Judge Scott ordered production of ten of the withheld e-mails, which (variously) reviewed the law concerning strip searches of detainees, assessed the County's current search policy, recommended alternative policies, and monitored the implementation of these policy changes.

Judge Scott reasoned that:

- These communications "go beyond rendering 'legal analysis' [by] propos[ing] changes to existing policy to make it constitutional, including drafting of policy regulations";

  The "drafting and subsequent oversight of implementation of the new strip search policy ventured beyond merely rendering legal advice and analysis into the realm of policy making and administration"; and

  "[N]o legal advice is rendered apart from policy recommendations."

Judge Scott ordered the County to deliver these ten e-mails to the plaintiffs.

After considering the County's objections to this order, the district court independently reviewed the disputed e-mails in camera and, applying a "clearly erroneous" standard, overruled the objections, and directed production. This petition for a writ of mandamus followed.

II

[The Court held that mandamus was appropriate because "[t]o await resolution of this issue pending final judgment risks the development of discovery practices and doctrine that unsettle and undermine the governmental attorney-client privilege."]

III

The attorney-client privilege protects confidential communications between client and counsel made for the purpose of obtaining or providing legal assistance. Its purpose is to encourage attorneys and their clients to communicate fully and frankly and thereby to promote broader public interests in the observance of law and administration of justice. "The availability of sound legal advice inures to the benefit not only of the client who wishes to know his options and responsibilities in given circumstances, but also of the public which is entitled to compliance with the ever growing and increasingly complex body of public law." *In re Grand Jury Subpoena Duces Tecum Dated Sept. 15,* <u>1983, 731 F.2d 1032, 1036-37 (2d Cir. 1984)</u>.

At the same time, we construe the privilege narrowly because it renders relevant information undiscoverable; we apply it "only where necessary to achieve its purpose." *Fisher v. United States*, 425 U.S. 391, 403. The burden of establishing the applicability of the privilege rests with the party invoking it. *In re Grand Jury Proceedings*, 219 F.3d 175, 182 (2d Cir. 2000); *United States v. Int'l Bhd. of Teamsters, Chauffeurs, Warehousemen and Helpers of Am., AFL-CIO*, 119 F.3d 210, 214 (2d. Cir 1997).

In civil suits between private litigants and government agencies, the attorney-client privilege protects most confidential communications between government counsel and their clients that are made for the purpose of obtaining or providing legal assistance. *See, e.g., Ross v. City of Memphis*, 423 F.3d 596, 601 (6th Cir. 2005) ("[A] government entity can assert attorney-client privilege in the civil context.").

The attorney-client privilege accommodates competing values; the competition is sharpened when the privilege is asserted by a government. On the one hand, non-disclosure impinges on open and accessible government. On the other hand, public officials are duty-bound to understand and respect constitutional, judicial and statutory limitations on their authority; thus, their access to candid legal advice directly and significantly serves the public interest.

We believe that, if anything, the traditional rationale for the [attorney-client] privilege applies with special force in the government context. It is crucial that government officials, who are expected to uphold and execute the law and who may face criminal prosecution for failing to do so, be encouraged to seek out and receive fully informed legal advice. Upholding the privilege furthers a culture in which consultation with government lawyers is accepted as a normal, desirable, and even indispensable part of conducting public business. Abrogating the privilege undermines that culture and thereby impairs the public interest. * * * At least in civil litigation between a government agency and private litigants, the government's claim to the protections of the attorney-client privilege is on a par with the claim of an individual or a corporate entity.

IV

A party invoking the attorney-client privilege must show (1) a communication between client and counsel that (2) was intended to be and was in fact kept confidential, and (3) was made for the purpose of obtaining or providing legal advice. At issue here is the third consideration: whether the communications were made for the purpose of obtaining or providing legal advice, as opposed to advice on policy.

The rule that a confidential communication between client and counsel is privileged only if it is generated for the purpose of obtaining or providing legal assistance is often recited. The issue usually arises in the context of communications to and from corporate in-house lawyers who also serve as business executives. So the question usually is whether the communication was generated for the purpose of obtaining or providing legal advice as opposed to business advice.

Fundamentally, legal advice involves the interpretation and application of legal principles to guide future conduct or to assess past conduct. It requires a lawyer to rely on legal education and experience to inform judgment. But it is broader, and is not demarcated by a bright line. * * *

The complete lawyer may well promote and reinforce the legal advice given, weigh it, and lay out its ramifications by explaining: how the advice is feasible and can be implemented; the legal downsides, risks and costs of taking the advice or doing otherwise; what alternatives exist to present measures or the measures advised; what other persons are doing or thinking about the matter; or the collateral benefits, risks or costs in terms of expense, politics, insurance, commerce, morals, and appearances. So long as the predominant purpose of the communication is legal advice, these considerations and caveats are not other than legal advice or severable from it. The predominant purpose of a communication cannot be ascertained by quantification or classification of one passage or another; it should be assessed dynamically and in light of the advice being sought or rendered, as well as the relationship between advice that can be rendered only by consulting the legal authorities and advice that can be given by a nonlawyer. The more careful the lawyer, the more likely it is that the legal advice will entail follow-through by facilitation, encouragement and monitoring.

V

The County asserts that the Assistant County Attorney whose advice was solicited could not have been conveying non-legal policy advice because the Erie County Charter (§ 602) confines her authority to that of a "legal advisor," and because "only the County Sheriff and his direct appointees ha[ve] policy-making authority for the [Sheriff's] department." This argument does not assist the analysis much. A lawyer's lack of formal authority to formulate, approve or enact policy does not actually prevent the rendering of policy advice to officials who do possess that authority. A similar consideration may be useful in different circumstances. When an attorney is consulted in a capacity other than as a lawyer, as (for example) a policy advisor, media expert, business consultant, banker, referee or friend, that consultation is not privileged. *In re Lindsey,* 148 F.3d at 1106 (citing 1 McCormick on Evidence § 88, at 322-24 (4th ed. 1992); Restatement (Third) of the Law Governing Lawyers § 122 (Proposed Final Draft No. 1, 1996)).

In the government context, one court considered relevant the fact that the attorney seeking to invoke the privilege held two formal positions: Assistant to the President (ostensibly non-legal) and Deputy White House Counsel (ostensibly legal). *In re Lindsey,* 148 F.3d at 1103, 1106-07. The same is true in the private sector where "in-house attorneys are more likely to mix legal and business functions." *Bank Brussels Lambert,* 220 F. Supp. 2d at 286. In short, an attorney's dual legal and non-legal responsibilities may bear on whether a particular communication was generated for the purpose of soliciting or rendering legal advice; but here, the Assistant County Attorney's lack of formal policymaking authority is not a compelling circumstance.

The predominant purpose of a particular document--legal advice, or not--may also be informed by the overall needs and objectives that animate the client's request for advice. For example, Erie County's objective was to ascertain its obligations under the Fourth Amendment and how those requirements may be fulfilled, rather than to save money or please the electorate (even though these latter objectives would not be beyond the lawyer's consideration).

VI

After reviewing in camera the documents listed on the County's privilege log, Judge Scott determined that the ten e-mails at issue here are not privileged. These e-mails, dated between December 23, 2002 and December 11, 2003, passed between the Assistant County Attorney and various officials in the Sheriff's Office (primarily petitioners). The ten e-mails are an amalgam of the following six broad issues:

> (i) The compliance of the County's search policy with the Fourth Amendment;

> (ii) Any possible liability of the County and its officials stemming from the existing policy;

> (iii) Alternative search policies, including the availability of equipment to assist in conducting searches that comply with constitutional requirements;

> (iv) Guidance for implementing and funding these alternative policies;

> (v) Maintenance of records concerning the original search policy; and

> (vi) Evaluations of the County's progress implementing the alternative search policy.

* * * Because the e-mails "go beyond rendering legal analysis," the judge concluded that they were not privileged. We disagree.

It is to be hoped that legal considerations will play a role in governmental policy-making. When a lawyer has been asked to assess compliance with a legal obligation, the lawyer's recommendation of a policy that complies (or better complies) with the legal obligation—or that advocates and promotes compliance, or oversees implementation of compliance measures—is legal advice. Public officials who craft policies that may directly implicate the legal rights or responsibilities of the public should be encouraged to seek out and receive fully informed legal advice in the course of formulating such policies. * * *

We conclude that each of the ten disputed e-mails was sent for the predominant purpose of soliciting or rendering legal advice. They convey to the public officials responsible for formulating, implementing and monitoring Erie County's corrections policies, a lawyer's assessment of Fourth Amendment requirements, and provide guidance in crafting and implementing alternative policies for compliance. This advice—particularly when viewed in the context in which it was solicited and rendered—does not constitute general policy or political advice unprotected by the privilege.

Although the e-mails at issue were generated for the predominant purpose of legal advice, we remand for the district court to determine whether the distribution of some of the disputed e-mail communications to others within the Erie County Sheriff's Department constituted a waiver of the attorney-client privilege.

* * *

Food for Thought

Even if information is not privileged because the lawyer is being retained predominately for non-legal services, the information may still be subject to Rule 1.6—meaning the lawyer cannot disclose it voluntarily. This is only to say that the information covered by the duty of confidentiality is broader than that covered by the attorney-client privilege.

2. The Communications Requirement

[Question 4]

An attorney represents a plaintiff in a personal injury action. The plaintiff is in a bodycast and claims extensive injuries after a car accident. About a month before the trial date, the attorney goes on a skiing vacation. As he is swooshing down the slopes he sees his client—bodycast-free—swooshing down ahead of him. The defendant now subpoenas the lawyer to provide any information he has about the plaintiff's medical condition. The attorney—who has since withdrawn from the representation—refuses to supply any information and invokes both the attorney-client privilege and his duty of confidentiality.

Does the attorney have a valid claim for refusing to testify to what he knows about the former client's condition?

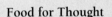

(A) No, because the information is not a communication and therefore is not protected by the privilege.

(B) No, because the attorney no longer represents the client.

(C) Yes, because turning over the information could subject the lawyer to discipline for violating Model Rule 1.6.

(D) Yes, because the privilege means that the lawyer cannot be forced to testify against his client.

See also United States v. Sayan, <u>968 F.2d 55 (D.C. Cir. 1992)</u> (statement that a client was a "sly fox," did not breach the privilege because it was merely based on observations, not the content of any communications).

Food for Thought

Did the lawyer in the above question *have to withdraw? See* Rule 1.16.

Because the privilege protects only communications, it does not protect the underlying facts pertinent to the representation. Thus, in *In re Six Grand Jury Witnesses,* <u>979 F.2d 939 (2d Cir. 1992)</u>, corporate employees were instructed by counsel to analyze certain contracts in anticipation of litigation. The Court held that the "underlying factual information" obtained by these employees was not protected by the privilege. They were not communications to an attorney. However, questions such as "With whom did you discuss this analysis?" were impermissible because the employee, in responding, "might be understood to be implying … that he had conveyed privileged information to the lawyer."

But if a lawyer discovers underlying facts, does she have any duty to *try* to keep them secret? At least until there is a lawful demand for the information? Where can that duty be found?

3. Communication Between Client and Lawyer

a. Who is the Client?

UPJOHN CO. v. UNITED STATES

449 U.S. 383 (1981)

JUSTICE REHNQUIST delivered the opinion of the Court.

We granted certiorari in this case to address important questions concerning the scope of the attorney-client privilege in the corporate context and the applicability of the work-product doctrine in proceedings to enforce tax summonses. * * *

I

Petitioner Upjohn Co. manufactures and sells pharmaceuticals here and abroad. In January 1976 independent accountants conducting an audit of one of Upjohn's foreign subsidiaries discovered that the subsidiary made payments to or for the benefit of foreign government officials in order to secure government business. The accountants so informed petitioner, Mr. Gerard Thomas, Upjohn's Vice President, Secretary, and General Counsel. Thomas is a member of the Michigan and New York Bars, and has been Upjohn's General Counsel for 20 years. He consulted with outside counsel and R. T. Parfet, Jr., Upjohn's Chairman of the Board. It was decided that the company would conduct an internal investigation of what were termed "questionable payments." As part of this investigation the attorneys prepared a letter containing a questionnaire which was sent to "All Foreign General and Area Managers" over the Chairman's signature. The letter began by noting recent disclosures that several American companies made "possibly illegal" payments to foreign government officials and emphasized that the management needed full information concerning any such payments made by Upjohn. The letter indicated that the Chairman had asked Thomas, identified as "the company's General Counsel," "to conduct an investigation for the purpose of determining the nature and magnitude of any payments made by the Upjohn Company or any of its subsidiaries to any employee or official of a foreign government." The questionnaire sought detailed information concerning such payments. Managers were instructed to treat the investigation as "highly confidential" and not to discuss it with anyone other than Upjohn employees who might be helpful in providing the requested information. Responses were to be sent directly to Thomas. Thomas and outside counsel also interviewed the recipients of the questionnaire and some 33 other Upjohn officers or employees as part of the investigation.

On March 26, 1976, the company voluntarily submitted a preliminary report to the Securities and Exchange Commission on Form 8-K disclosing certain questionable payments. A copy of the report was simultaneously submitted to the Internal Revenue Service, which immediately began an investigation to determine the tax consequences of the payments. Special agents conducting the investigation were given lists by Upjohn of all those interviewed and all who had responded to the questionnaire. On November 23, 1976, the Service issued a summons pursuant to 26 U.S.C. § 7602 demanding production of:

> "All files relative to the investigation conducted under the supervision of Gerard Thomas to identify payments to employees of foreign governments and any political contributions made by the Upjohn Company or any of its affiliates since January 1, 1971 and to determine whether any funds of the Upjohn Company had been improperly accounted for on the corporate books during the same period.

> The records should include but not be limited to written questionnaires sent to managers of the Upjohn Company's foreign affiliates, and memorandums or notes of the interviews conducted in the United States and abroad with officers and employees of the Upjohn Company and its subsidiaries."

The company declined to produce the documents specified in the second paragraph on the grounds that they were protected from disclosure by the attorney-client privilege and constituted the work product of attorneys prepared in anticipation of litigation. On August 31, 1977, the United States filed a petition seeking enforcement of the summons * * *.

* * *

II

* * * The attorney-client privilege is the oldest of the privileges for confidential communications known to the common law. 8 J. Wigmore, Evidence § 2290 (McNaughton rev. 1961). Its purpose is to encourage full and frank communication between attorneys and their clients and thereby promote broader public interests in the observance of law and administration of justice. The privilege recognizes that sound legal advice or advocacy serves public ends and that such advice or advocacy depends upon the lawyer's being fully informed by the client. * * * Admittedly complications in the application of the privilege arise when the client is a corporation, which in theory is an artificial creature of the law, and not an individual; but this Court has assumed that the privilege applies when the client is a corporation, and the Government does not contest the general proposition.

The Court of Appeals, however, considered the application of the privilege in the corporate context to present a "different problem," since the client was an inanimate entity and "only the senior management, guiding and integrating the several operations, ... can be said to possess an identity analogous to the corporation as a whole." The first case to articulate the so-called "control group test" adopted by the court below, *Philadelphia v. Westinghouse Electric Corp.*, 210 F. Supp. 483, 485 (E.D. Pa. 1962):

Keeping in mind that the question is, Is it the corporation which is seeking the lawyer's advice when the asserted privileged communication is made?, the most satisfactory solution, I think, is that if the employee making the communication, of whatever rank he may be, is in a position to control or even to take a substantial part in a decision about any action which the corporation may take upon the advice of the attorney, ... then, in effect, *he is (or personifies) the corporation* when he makes his disclosure to the lawyer and the privilege would apply." (Emphasis supplied.)

Such a view, we think, overlooks the fact that the privilege exists to protect not only the giving of professional advice to those who can act on it but also the giving of information to the lawyer to enable him to give sound and informed advice. The first step in the resolution of any legal problem is ascertaining the factual background and sifting through the facts with an eye to the legally relevant. See ABA Code of Professional Responsibility, Ethical Consideration 4-1:

> "A lawyer should be fully informed of all the facts of the matter he is handling in order for his client to obtain the full advantage of our legal system. It is for the lawyer in the exercise of his independent professional judgment to separate the relevant and important from the irrelevant and unimportant. The observance of the ethical obligation of a lawyer to hold inviolate the confidences and secrets of his client not only facilitates the full development of facts essential to proper representation of the client but also encourages laymen to seek early legal assistance."

* * *

In the case of the individual client the provider of information and the person who acts on the lawyer's advice are one and the same. In the corporate context, however, it will frequently be employees beyond the control group as defined by the court below—"officers and agents ... responsible for directing [the company's] actions in response to legal advice"—who will possess the information needed by the corporation's lawyers. Middle-level-and indeed lower-level-employees can, by actions within the scope of their employment, embroil the corporation in serious legal difficulties, and it is only natural that these employees would have the relevant information needed by corporate counsel if he is adequately to advise the client with respect to such actual or potential difficulties.

* * *

The control group test adopted by the court below thus frustrates the very purpose of the privilege by discouraging the communication of relevant information by employees of the client to attorneys seeking to render legal advice to the client corporation. The attorney's advice will also frequently be more significant to non-control group members than to those who officially sanction the advice, and the control group test makes it more difficult to convey full and frank legal advice to the employees who will put into effect the client corporation's policy. * * *

The narrow scope given the attorney-client privilege by the court below not only makes it difficult for corporate attorneys to formulate sound advice when their client is faced with a specific legal problem but also threatens to limit the valuable efforts of corporate counsel to ensure their client's compliance with the law. In light of the vast and complicated array of regulatory legislation confronting the modern corporation, corporations, unlike most individuals, "constantly go to lawyers to find out how to obey the law," Burnham, *The Attorney-Client Privilege in the Corporate Arena,* 24 Bus. Law. 901, 913 (1969), particularly since compliance with the law in this area is hardly an instinctive matter. * * * The test adopted by the court below is difficult to apply in practice, though no abstractly formulated and unvarying "test" will necessarily enable courts to decide questions such as this with mathematical precision. But if the purpose of the attorney-client privilege is to be served, the attorney and client must be able to predict with some degree of certainty whether particular discussions will be protected. An uncertain privilege, or one which purports to be certain but results in widely varying applications by the courts, is little better than no privilege at all. The very terms of the test adopted by the court below suggest the unpredictability of its application. The test restricts the availability of the privilege to those officers who play a "substantial role" in deciding and directing a corporation's legal response. Disparate decisions in cases applying this test illustrate its unpredictability. * * *

The communications at issue were made by Upjohn employees to counsel for Upjohn acting as such, at the direction of corporate superiors in order to secure legal advice from counsel. As the Magistrate found, "Mr. Thomas consulted with the Chairman of the Board and outside counsel and thereafter conducted a factual investigation to determine the nature and extent of the questionable payments *and to be in a position to give legal advice to the company with respect to the payments.*" * * * Information, not available from upper-echelon management, was needed to supply a basis for legal advice concerning compliance with securities and tax laws, foreign laws, currency regulations, duties to shareholders, and potential litigation in each of these areas. The communications concerned matters within the scope of the employees' corporate duties, and the employees themselves were sufficiently aware that they were being questioned in order that the corporation could obtain legal advice. The questionnaire identified Thomas as "the company's General Counsel" and referred in its opening sentence to the possible illegality of payments such as the ones on which information was sought. A statement of policy accompanying the questionnaire clearly indicated the legal implications of the investigation. The policy statement was issued "in order that there be no uncertainty in the future as to the policy with respect to the practices which are the subject of this investigation." * * * This statement was issued to Upjohn employees worldwide, so that even those interviewees not receiving a questionnaire were aware of the legal implications of the interviews. Pursuant to explicit instructions from the Chairman of the Board, the communications were considered "highly confidential" when made, and have been kept confidential by the company. Consistent with the underlying purposes of the attorney-client privilege, these communications must be protected against compelled disclosure.

The Court of Appeals declined to extend the attorney-client privilege beyond the limits of the control group test for fear that doing so would entail severe burdens on discovery and create a broad "zone of silence" over corporate affairs. Application of the attorney-client privilege to communications such as those involved here, however, puts the adversary in no worse position than if the communications had never taken place. The privilege only protects disclosure of communications; it does not protect disclosure of the underlying facts by those who communicated with the attorney:

> "[T]he protection of the privilege extends only to *communications* and not to facts. A fact is one thing and a communication concerning that fact is an entirely different thing. The client cannot be compelled to answer the question, `What did you say or write to the attorney?' but may not refuse to disclose any relevant fact within his knowledge merely because he incorporated a statement of such fact into his communication to his attorney." *Philadelphia v. Westinghouse Electric Corp.*, 205 F. Supp. 830, 831 (E.D. Pa. 1962).

Here the Government was free to question the employees who communicated with Thomas and outside counsel. Upjohn has provided the IRS with a list of such employees, and the IRS has already interviewed some 25 of them. While it would probably be more convenient for the Government to secure the results of petitioner's internal investigation by simply subpoenaing the questionnaires and notes taken by petitioner's attorneys, such considerations of convenience do not overcome the policies served by the attorney-client privilege. * * *

Food for Thought

If the government had questioned the employees—who were suspected of violations of federal criminal law—wouldn't they have invoked their Fifth Amendment privilege? In which case does the Court's argument that the government didn't need the communications to the corporate attorney hold water?

Needless to say, we decide only the case before us, and do not undertake to draft a set of rules which should govern challenges to investigatory subpoenas. Any such approach would violate the spirit of Federal Rule of Evidence 501. See S.Rep. No. 93-1277, p. 13 (1974) ("the recognition of a privilege based on a confidential relationship ... should be determined on a case-by-case basis"). * * * While such a "case-by-case" basis may to some slight extent undermine desirable certainty in the boundaries of the attorney-client privilege, it obeys the spirit of the Rules. At the same time we conclude that the narrow "control group test" sanctioned by the Court of Appeals, in this case cannot, consistent with "the principles of the common law as ... interpreted ... in the light of reason and experience," Fed. Rule Evid. 501, govern the development of the law in this area.

III

Our decision that the communications by Upjohn employees to counsel are covered by the attorney-client privilege disposes of the case so far as the responses to the questionnaires and any notes reflecting responses to interview questions are concerned. The summons reaches further, however, and Thomas has testified that his notes and memoranda of interviews go beyond recording responses to his questions. * * * To the extent that the material subject to the summons is not protected by the attorney-client privilege as disclosing communications between an employee and counsel, we must reach the ruling by the Court of Appeals that the work-product doctrine does not apply to summonses issued under 26 U.S.C. § 7602.

The Government concedes, wisely, that the Court of Appeals erred and that the work-product doctrine does apply to IRS summonses. * * * This doctrine was announced by the Court over 30 years ago in *Hickman v. Taylor*. * * * In that case the Court rejected "an attempt, without purported necessity or justification, to secure written statements, private memoranda and personal recollections prepared or formed by an adverse party's counsel in the course of his legal duties." * * * The Court noted that "it is essential that a lawyer work with a certain degree of privacy" and reasoned that if discovery of the material sought were permitted "much of what is now put down in writing would remain unwritten. An attorney's thoughts, heretofore inviolate, would not be his own. Inefficiency, unfairness and sharp practices would inevitably develop in the giving of legal advice and in the preparation of cases for trial. The effect on the legal profession would be demoralizing. And the interests of the clients and the cause of justice would be poorly served." * * *

The "strong public policy" underlying the work-product doctrine was reaffirmed recently in *United States v. Nobles*, 422 U.S. 225, 236-240, 95 S.Ct. 2160, 2169-

2171, 45 L.Ed.2d 141 (1975), and has been substantially incorporated in Federal Rule of Civil Procedure 26(b)(3).

* * * While conceding the applicability of the work-product doctrine, the Government asserts that it has made a sufficient showing of necessity to overcome its protections. The Magistrate apparently so found. * * *

Rule 26 accords special protection to work product revealing the attorney's mental processes. The Rule permits disclosure of documents and tangible things constituting attorney work product upon a showing of substantial need and inability to obtain the equivalent without undue hardship. This was the standard applied by the Magistrate * * *. Rule 26 goes on, however, to state that "[i]n ordering discovery of such materials when the required showing has been made, the court shall protect against disclosure of the mental impressions, conclusions, opinions or legal theories of an attorney or other representative of a party concerning the litigation." Although this language does not specifically refer to memoranda based on oral statements of witnesses, the *Hickman* court stressed the danger that compelled disclosure of such memoranda would reveal the attorney's mental processes. It is clear that this is the sort of material the draftsmen of the Rule had in mind as deserving special protection. * * *

Based on the foregoing, some courts have concluded that *no* showing of necessity can overcome protection of work product which is based on oral statements from witnesses. * * * Those courts declining to adopt an absolute rule have nonetheless recognized that such material is entitled to special protection. * * * *See, e. g., In re Grand Jury Investigation,* 599 F.2d 1224, 1231 (3rd Cir. 1979) ("special considerations ... must shape any ruling on the discoverability of interview memoranda ...; such documents will be discoverable only in a `rare situation'") * * *.

We do not decide the issue at this time. It is clear that the Magistrate applied the wrong standard when he concluded that the Government had made a sufficient showing of necessity to overcome the protections of the work-product doctrine. The Magistrate applied the "substantial need" and "without undue hardship" standard articulated in the first part of Rule 26(b)(3). The notes and memoranda sought by the Government here, however, are work product based on oral statements. If they reveal communications, they are, in this case, protected by the attorney-client privilege. To the extent they do not reveal communications, they reveal the attorneys' mental processes in evaluating the communications. As Rule 26 and *Hickman* make clear, such work product cannot be disclosed simply on a showing of substantial need and inability to obtain the equivalent without undue hardship.

While we are not prepared at this juncture to say that such material is always protected by the work-product rule, we think a far stronger showing of necessity and unavailability by other means than was made by the Government or applied by the Magistrate in this case would be necessary to compel disclosure.

Take Note

If the Upjohn agent is the client when communicating to the Upjohn lawyer, does that mean the agent can invoke the privilege and prevent the Upjohn lawyer from disclosing the information? The answer is no—because while he is speaking as part of the client, it is Upjohn's privilege, not his. What does this mean for the agent? See the next case.

* * *

Accordingly, the judgment of the Court of Appeals is reversed, and the case remanded for further proceedings.

[The concurring opinion of Chief Justice Burger is omitted].

In re GRAND JURY SUBPOENA: UNDER SEAL

415 F.3d 333 (4th Cir. 2005)

WILSON, District Judge.

This is an appeal by three former employees of AOL Time Warner ("AOL") from the decision of the district court denying their motions to quash a grand jury subpoena for documents related to an internal investigation by AOL. Appellants argued in the district court that the subpoenaed documents were protected by the attorney-client privilege. Because the district court concluded that the privilege was AOL's alone and because AOL had expressly waived its privilege, the court denied the appellants' motion. We affirm.

I.

In March of 2001, AOL began an internal investigation into its relationship with PurchasePro, Inc. AOL retained the law firm of Wilmer, Cutler & Pickering ("Wilmer Cutler") to assist in the investigation. Over the next several months, AOL's general counsel and counsel from Wilmer Cutler * * * interviewed appellants, AOL employees Kent Wakeford, John Doe 1, and John Doe 2.[1]

The investigating attorneys interviewed Wakeford, a manager in the company's Business Affairs division, on six occasions. At their third interview, and the first one in which Wilmer Cutler attorneys were present, Randall Boe, AOL's General Counsel, informed Wakeford, "We represent the company. These conversations

---

1   Because Wakeford has been indicted by the grand jury, we refer to him by name.

are privileged, but the privilege belongs to the company and the company decides whether to waive it. If there is a conflict, the attorney-client privilege belongs to the company." Memoranda from that meeting also indicate that the attorneys explained to Wakeford that they represented AOL but that they "could" represent him as well, "as long as no conflict appear[ed]." The attorneys interviewed Wakeford again three days later and, at the beginning of the interview, reiterated that they represented AOL, that the privilege belonged to AOL, and that Wakeford could retain personal counsel at company expense.

The investigating attorneys interviewed John Doe 1 three times. Before the first interview, Boe told him, "We represent the company. These conversations are privileged, but the privilege belongs to the company and the company decides whether to waive it. You are free to consult with your own lawyer at any time." Memoranda from that interview indicate that the attorneys also told him, "We can represent [you] until such time as there appears to be a conflict of interest, [but] ... the attorney-client privilege belongs to AOL and AOL can decide whether to keep it or waive it." At the end of the interview, John Doe 1 asked if he needed personal counsel. A Wilmer Cutler attorney responded that he did not recommend it, but that he would tell the company not to be concerned if Doe retained counsel.

AOL's attorneys interviewed John Doe 2 twice and followed essentially the same protocol they had followed with the other appellants. They noted, "We represent AOL, and can represent [you] too if there is not a conflict." In addition, the attorneys told him that, "the attorney-client privilege is AOL's and AOL can choose to waive it."

In November, 2001, the Securities and Exchange Commission ("SEC") began to investigate AOL's relationship with PurchasePro. In December 2001, AOL and Wakeford, through counsel, entered into an oral "common interest agreement," which they memorialized in writing in January 2002. The attorneys acknowledged that, "representation of [their] respective clients raise[d] issues of common interest to [their] respective clients and that the sharing of certain documents, information, ... and communications with clients" would be mutually beneficial. As a result, the attorneys agreed to share access to information relating to their representation of Wakeford and AOL, noting that "the oral or written disclosure of Common Interest Materials ... [would] not diminish in any way the confidentiality of such Materials and [would] not constitute a waiver of any applicable privilege."

Wakeford testified before the SEC on February 14, 2002, represented by his personal counsel. Laura Jehl, AOL's general counsel, and F. Whitten Peters of Williams & Connolly, whom AOL had retained in November 2001 in connection with the PurchasePro investigation, were also present, and both stated that they represented Wakeford "for purposes of [the] deposition." During the deposition, the SEC investigators questioned Wakeford about his discussions with AOL's attorneys. When Wakeford's attorney asserted the attorney-client privilege, the SEC investigators followed up with several questions to determine whether the privilege was applicable to the investigating attorneys' March-June 2001 interviews with Wakeford. Wakeford told them he believed, at the time of the interviews, that the investigating attorneys represented him and the company.

John Doe 1 testified before the SEC on February 27, 2002, represented by personal counsel. No representatives of AOL were present. When SEC investigators questioned Doe about the March-June 2001 internal investigation, his counsel asserted that the information was protected and directed Doe not to answer any questions about the internal investigation "in respect to the company's privilege." He stated that Doe's response could be considered a waiver of the privilege and that, "if the AOL lawyers were [present], they could make a judgment, with respect to the company's privilege, about whether or not the answer would constitute a waiver."

On February 26, 2004, a grand jury in the Eastern District of Virginia issued a subpoena commanding AOL to provide "written memoranda and other written records reflecting interviews conducted by attorneys for [AOL]" of the appellants between March 15 and June 30, 2001. While AOL agreed to waive the attorney-client privilege and produce the subpoenaed documents, counsel for the appellants moved to quash the subpoena on the grounds that each appellant had an individual attorney-client relationship with the investigating attorneys, that his interviews were individually privileged, and that he had not waived the privilege. Wakeford also claimed that the information he disclosed to the investigating attorneys was privileged under the common interest doctrine.

The district court denied John Doe 1's and John Doe 2's motions because it found they failed to prove they were clients of the investigating attorneys who interviewed them. The court based its conclusion on its findings that: (1) the investigating attorneys told them that they represented the company; (2) the investigating attorneys told them, "we *can* represent you," which is distinct from "we *do* represent you"; (3) they could not show that the investigating attorneys agreed to represent them; and (4) the investigating attorneys told them that the attorney-client privilege belonged to the company and the company could choose to waive it.

The court initially granted Wakeford's motion to quash because it found that his communications with the investigating attorneys were privileged under the common interest agreement between counsel for Wakeford and counsel for AOL. Following a motion for reconsideration, the court reversed its earlier ruling and held that the subpoenaed documents relating to Wakeford's interviews were not privileged because it found that Wakeford's common interest agreement with AOL postdated the March-June 2001 interviews. In addition, the court held that Wakeford failed to prove that he was a client of the investigating attorneys at the time the interviews took place. The court based its conclusion on its findings that: (1) none of the investigating attorneys understood that Wakeford was seeking personal legal advice; (2) the investigating attorneys did not provide any personal legal advice to him; and (3) the investigating attorneys believed they represented AOL and not Wakeford. This appeal followed.

II.

Appellants argue that because they believed that the investigating attorneys who conducted the interviews were representing them personally, their communications are privileged. However, we agree with the district court that essential touchstones for the formation of an attorney-client relationship between the investigating attorneys and the appellants were missing at the time of the interviews. There is no evidence of an objectively reasonable, mutual understanding that the appellants were seeking legal advice from the investigating attorneys or that the investigating attorneys were rendering personal legal advice. Nor, in light of the investigating attorneys' disclosure that they represented AOL and that the privilege and the right to waive it were AOL's alone, do we find investigating counsel's hypothetical pronouncement that they *could* represent appellants sufficient to establish the reasonable understanding that they *were* representing appellants. Accordingly, we find no fault with the district court's opinion that no individual attorney-client privilege attached to the appellants' communications with AOL's attorneys.

* * *

The person seeking to invoke the attorney-client privilege must prove that he is a client or that he affirmatively sought to become a client. "The professional relationship ... hinges upon the client's belief that he is consulting a lawyer in that capacity and his manifested intention to seek professional legal advice." *United States v. Evans,* 113 F.3d 1457, 1465 (7th Cir. 1997). An individual's subjective belief that he is represented is not alone sufficient to create an attorney-client relationship. *See United States v. Keplinger,* 776 F.2d 678, 701 (7th Cir. 1985)("We think no individual attorney-client relationship can be inferred without some finding that the potential client's subjective belief is minimally reasonable". Rather, the putative client must show that his subjective belief that an attorney-client relationship existed was reasonable under the circumstances.

With these precepts in mind, we conclude that appellants could not have reasonably believed that the investigating attorneys represented them personally during the time frame covered by the subpoena. First, there is no evidence that the investigating attorneys told the appellants that they represented them, nor is there evidence that the appellants asked the investigating attorneys to represent them. To the contrary, there is evidence that the investigating attorneys relayed to Wakeford the company's offer to retain personal counsel for him at the company's expense, and that they told John Doe 1 that he was free to retain personal counsel. Second, there is no evidence that the appellants ever sought personal legal advice from the investigating attorneys, nor is there any evidence that the investigating attorneys rendered personal legal advice. Third, when the appellants spoke with the investigating attorneys, they were fully apprised that the information they were giving could be disclosed at the company's discretion. Under these circumstances, appellants could not have reasonably believed that the investigating attorneys represented them personally. Therefore, the district court's finding that appellants had no attorney-client relationship with the investigating attorneys is not clearly erroneous.

The appellants argue that the phrase "we *can* represent you as long as no conflict appears," manifested an agreement by the investigating attorneys to represent them. They claim that, "it is hard to imagine a more straightforward assurance of an attorney-client relationship than 'we can represent you.' " We disagree. As the district court noted, "we *can* represent you" is distinct from "we *do* represent you." If there was any evidence that the investigating attorneys had said, "we *do* represent you," then the outcome of this appeal might be different. Furthermore, the statement actually made, "we *can* represent you," must be interpreted within the context of the entire warning. The investigating attorneys' statements to the appellants, read in their entirety, demonstrate that the attorneys' loyalty was to the company. That loyalty was never implicitly or explicitly divided. In addition to noting at the outset that they had been retained to represent AOL, the investigating attorneys warned the appellants that the content of their communications during the interview "belonged" to AOL. This protocol put the appellants on notice that, while their communications with the attorneys were considered confidential, the company could choose to reveal the content of those communications at any time, without the appellants' consent.

We note, however, that our opinion should not be read as an implicit acceptance of the watered-down "*Upjohn* warnings" the investigating attorneys gave the appellants. It is a potential legal and ethical mine field. Had the investigating attorneys, in fact, entered into an attorney-client relationship with appellants, as their statements to the appellants professed they could, they would not have been free to waive the appellants' privilege when a conflict arose. It should have seemed obvious that they could not have jettisoned one client in favor of another. Rather, they would have had to withdraw from all representation and to maintain all confidences. Indeed, the court would be hard pressed to identify how investigating counsel could robustly investigate and report to management or the board of directors of a publicly-traded corporation with the necessary candor if counsel were constrained by ethical obligations to individual employees. However, because we agree with the district court that the appellants never entered into an attorney-client relationship with the investigating attorneys, they averted these troubling issues.

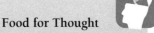

Food for Thought

The court is saying the lawyer would be operating under a conflict of interest by representing both the corporation and the corporate agents. Why? Wasn't the basic idea for everyone to try to defend against an investigation into suspected corporate misconduct?

III.

Wakeford also claims that the documents in question are protected by the joint defense privilege because of his common interest agreement with AOL. However, the district court found that no common interest agreement existed at the time of the interviews in March-June 2001. This finding was not clearly erroneous.

The joint defense privilege, an extension of the attorney-client privilege, protects communications between parties who share a common interest in litigation. *United States v. Schwimmer,* 892 F.2d 237, 243-44 (2d Cir.1989). The purpose of the privilege is to allow persons with a common interest to "communicate with their respective attorneys and with each other to more effectively prosecute or defend their claims." *In re Grand Jury Subpoenas 89-3 and 89-4, John Doe 89-129,* 902 F.2d 244, 249 (4th Cir.1990). For the privilege to apply, the proponent must establish that the parties had "some common interest about a legal matter." *Sheet Metal Workers Int'l Assoc. v. Sweeney,* 29 F.3d 120, 124 (4th Cir.1994). An employee's cooperation in an internal investigation alone is not sufficient to establish a common interest; rather "some form of joint strategy is necessary." *United States v. Weissman,* 195 F.3d 96, 100 (2d Cir.1999).

The district court found that "an agreement to share information pursuant to a common interest did not exist prior to December 2001." Uncontradicted affidavits submitted by counsel for AOL, including Randall Boe, who participated in the March-June 2001 interviews, support the court's finding. Boe stated that, at the time of the interviews, AOL had not entered into an agreement with Wakeford regarding their joint defense. There is no evidence showing that AOL and Wakeford were pursuing a common legal strategy before December 2001. During the March-June 2001 interviews, AOL was in the early stages of its internal investigation; there is no evidence that the investigating attorneys' interviews with Wakeford were for the purpose of formulating a joint defense. Indeed, the stated purpose of the interviews was to gather information regarding AOL's relationship with

PurchasePro; it would have been difficult for AOL to know at that time whether its interests were consistent with or adverse to Wakeford's personal interests. The court's finding was therefore not clearly erroneous.

Because there is no evidence that Wakeford and AOL shared a common interest before December 2001, we find no error in the district court's conclusion that Wakeford had no joint defense privilege before that time.

IV.

After review of the district court's factual findings and legal conclusions, we find no clear error. We find no error in the district court's conclusion that the appellants were not clients of the investigating attorneys and therefore could not assert the attorney-client privilege to prevent disclosure of the subpoenaed documents. Further, we agree with the district court's finding that, because Wakeford failed to establish that he and AOL were cooperating in a common defense before December 2001, he has no joint defense privilege before that time. The district court therefore properly denied the appellants' motions.

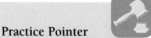

Practice Pointer

A common interest agreement allows multiple clients to pool information without waiving the privilege, at least to anyone outside the common interest unit. But a common interest agreement will not be enforceable if the parties are pursuing fundamentally different interests. Note that if the parties to a common interest arrangement end up adverse to each other in a subsequent litigation, the communications they made during their common interest arrangement can be used by each against the other—the reason being that there was no expectation of confidentiality with respect to members of the common interest arrangement. Also, in that later lawsuit, lawyers for the former common interest parties are ordinarily disqualified under Rule 1.9(c)(1), because cross-examining a member of the former common interest unit is the equivalent of using a former client's communications against them. *See United States v. Anderson,* 790 F. Supp. 231 (W.D. Wash. 1992) ("an attorney who acquires information from a potential witness pursuant to a joint defense agreement is in no different position that would be an attorney who acquires such information from a prior or jointly represented client."). For more on common interest arrangements, *see* 2 Saltzburg, Martin & Capra, Federal Rules of Evidence Manual at ¶501.02[5][e].

Lawyer's Ethical Duty to Notify Corporate Agent That There Is No Attorney-Client Relationship:

Rule 1.13 provides as follows:

> (f) In dealing with an organization's directors, officers, employees, members, shareholders or other constituents, a lawyer shall explain the identity of the client when the lawyer knows or reasonably should know that the organization's interests are adverse to those of the constituents with whom the lawyer is dealing.

Rule 1.13(f) provides the ethical grounding for what the *AOL* court, *supra*, refers to as the *Upjohn* warning. But as the court notes, the warning must be more than "I represent the corporation." It must also include "and I cannot represent you."

b. Communications to Nonlawyer Agents of the Representation

In re NEW YORK RENU WITH MOISTURELOC PRODUCT LIABILITY LITIGATION

2008 WL 2338552 (D.S.C.)

DANIEL J. CAPRA, SPECIAL MASTER:

In this litigation, Defendant Bausch & Lomb has refused to produce a number of otherwise responsive documents on the ground that they are protected by the attorney-client privilege * * * . The documents that are subject to this Order have been set forth in exhibits to an affidavit by Robert Bailey, Esq., Vice President and General Counsel for Bausch & Lomb. [This is a federal-state multi-district litigation involving thousands of claims against Bausch & Lomb for alleged contamination of its contact lens solution. The emails reviewed concerned steps considered and taken after the contamination came to light.]

* * *

In evaluating the privilege claims, I applied four fundamental legal principles:

> 1) Defendant, as the party invoking the privilege, has the burden of showing that the requirements of the privilege are met. *See, e.g., United States v. Landof,* 591 F.2d 36 (9th Cir.1978) (as the privilege is in derogation of the search for truth, the party who seeks to invoke it has the burden of establishing it).

2) Intra-corporate communications to counsel may fall within the privilege if the predominant intent is to seek legal advice. *United States v. IBM,* 66 F.R.D. 206, 212-13 (S.D.N.Y. 1974) (applying the test of predominant intent).

3) Intra-corporate communications to and from counsel can retain a privilege if disclosure is limited to those who have a "need to know" the advice of counsel; the company's burden "is to show that it limited its dissemination of the documents in keeping with their asserted confidentiality, not to justify each determination that a particular employee should have access to the information therein." *Federal Trade Comm'n v. GlaxoSmithKline,* 294 F.3d 141, 147-48 (D.C.Cir. 2002).

4) As this case is in diversity, the applicable privilege law is state law. See Fed. R. Evid. 501. And of course state privilege law applies to the actions in New York state court. Choice of law principles appear to point to New York privilege law as determinative, as that is the location of defendant's principal place of business. Federal courts have recognized that the New York law of privilege is substantially similar to federal common law. *See, e.g., Bank of Am., N.A. v. Terra Nova Ins. Co. Ltd.,* 211 F. Supp. 2d 493 (S.D.N.Y. 2002) ("New York law governing attorney-client privilege is generally similar to accepted federal doctrine."). This statement is helpful when the federal common law is itself clear and undisputed. But a difficulty arises where the federal courts are in dispute about the federal common law, and there appears to be no clear state law on the subject. Where such a situation arises, I have chosen the result that appears most consistent with the approach to privilege questions undertaken by the New York Court of Appeals; that approach is to use a utilitarian analysis to provide protection to communications to and from counsel that would not be made in absence of the privilege. *See generally* Martin & Capra, New York Evidence Handbook § 5.2 (2d ed.2003).

* * *

Exhibit 3

This exhibit consists of two-email strings regarding a contact with the FDA about a planned public statement about MoistureLoc [the contaminated contact lens solution]. The first email is from Barbara Kelley [corporate executive] to Ron Zarella [CEO of Bausch & Lomb], Bob Bailey [General Counsel], and others, including two public relations consultants from Hill & Knowlton, a public relations firm employed by Bausch & Lomb. Plaintiffs contend that any privilege is lost because of the disclosure to Hill & Knowlton. For the reasons discussed below, I agree with plaintiffs and accordingly find that this email is not privileged and must be produced in its entirety.

Communications to nonlawyers can be brought within the privilege under the so-called *Kovel* doctrine. The court in *United States v. Kovel*, 296 F.2d 918, 921 (2d Cir.1961) held that confidential communications to nonlawyers could be protected by the privilege if the nonlawyer's services are *necessary to the legal representation*. But the *Kovel* protection is applicable only if the services performed by the nonlawyer are necessary to promote the lawyer's effectiveness; it is not enough that the services are beneficial to the client in some way unrelated to the legal services of the lawyer. Id. at 922 (the "communication must be made in confidence for the purpose of obtaining legal advice from the lawyer.... If what is sought is not legal advice but only accounting services ... or if the advice sought is the accountant's rather than the lawyer's, no privilege exists."). *See also United States v. Ackert*, 169 F.3d 136, 139 (2d Cir.1999) (ruling that the communication "between an attorney and a third party does not become shielded by the attorney-client privilege solely because the communication proves important to the attorney's ability to represent the client").

Courts are in some dispute on whether public relations firms are "necessary to the representation" so as to fall within the *Kovel* protection. Most courts agree, however, that basic public relations advice, from a consultant hired by the corporate client, is not within the privilege. * * *

Judge Cote in *Haugh v. Schroder Inv. Mgmt. North Am. Inc.*, 2003 WL 21998674, at *8 (S.D.N.Y.2003) summed up the basic law, and held that disclosure to a public relations firm lost the privilege, in the following passage:

> Plaintiff has not shown that Murray [the p.r. consultant] performed anything other than standard public relations services for Haugh, and more importantly, she has not shown that her communications with Murray or Murray's with Arkin [the lawyer] were necessary so that Arkin could provide Haugh with legal advice. The conclusory descriptions of Murray's role supplied by plaintiff fail to bring the sixteen documents within the ambit of the attorney-client privilege. The documents transmitted from plaintiff to Murray and the one document from Murray to Arkin are consistent with the design of a public relations campaign. Plaintiff has not shown that Murray was "performing functions materially different from those that any ordinary public relations" advisor would perform. *Calvin Klein Trademark Trust v. Wachner et al.*, 198 F.R.D. 53, 55 (S.D.N.Y.2000). As such, Haugh's transmission of documents to Murray, even simultaneously with disclosure to former counsel, and Murray's transmission of a meeting agenda to Arkin, vitiates the application of the attorney-client privilege to these documents.

Judge Cote relied on the compelling point that "[a] media campaign is not a litigation strategy. Some attorneys may feel it is desirable at times to conduct a media campaign, but that decision does not transform their coordination of a campaign into legal advice."

It is true that a few cases have found communications to public relations consultants to be within the attorney-client privilege. But those cases arise from unusual and extreme facts and do not involve the basic provision of public relations advice by a company retained by the client, as in the instant case. For example, in *In re Copper Market Antitrust Litig.*, 200 F.R.D. 13 (S.D.N.Y. 2001), a foreign company found itself in the midst of a high profile scandal involving both regulatory and civil litigation aspects, and hired a public relations firm because it lacked experience both in English-speaking and in dealing with Western media. The public relations firm acted as the corporation's spokesperson when dealing with the Western press and conferred with the company's U.S. litigation counsel. Judge Swain upheld the attorney-client privilege claim, reasoning that the public relations firm, in the extreme circumstances of the case, was the functional equivalent of an in-house department of the corporation and thus part of the "client." Obviously the facts of *Copper Market* do not approach those of this case, in which a public relations consulting firm provides basic consulting advice.

Likewise, the facts of *In re Grand Jury Subpoenas*, 265 F. Supp. 2d 321 (S.D.N.Y. 2003) are vastly different from the instant case. Judge Kaplan held that the privilege applied to a public relations consulting firm hired to assist counsel to create a climate in which prosecutors might feel freer not to indict the client. He concluded that this was an area in which counsel were presumably unskilled and that the task constituted "legal advice." As Judge Cote stated in *Haugh:* "There is no need here to determine whether *In re Grand Jury Subpoenas* was correctly decided." Bausch & Lomb has not identified with particularity any legal advice that required the assistance of a public relations consultant; Bailey's affidavit simply states, in conclusory fashion, that Hill & Knowlton's presence was "necessary." Bausch & Lomb has not, for example, identified any nexus between the consultant's work and the attorney's role in defending against possible litigation or a regulatory action or proceeding.

I am most reluctant to rely on the broad applications in *Copper Market* and *In re Grand Jury Subpoenas* in light of the well-reasoned case law indicating that the privilege is lost when the corporate client communicates to an outside consultant, hired by the corporation, and providing nothing more than basic public relations advice. *See, e.g.,* Ann M. Murphy, *Spin Control and the High-Profile Client-Should the Attorney-Client Privilege Extend to Communications With Public Relations Consultants?*, 55 Syracuse L.Rev. 545 (2005) (concluding that "expanding the attorney-client privilege to communications with public relations consultants is inadvisable and against the interests of justice"). A conservative approach is, indeed, mandated by New York law, which appears to recognize the *Kovel* doctrine only in narrow circumstances in which the nonlawyer's services are absolutely necessary to effectuate the lawyer's legal services. *See, e.g., People v. Edney,* <u>39 N.Y.2d 620, 385 N.Y.S.2d 23, 350 N.E.2d 400 (1976)</u>.

Accordingly, the email from Barbara Kelley dated May 11, 2006 is not privileged because it was routed to employees of Hill & Knowlton. (If not for that routing, the email would be privileged because it was implicitly seeking Bob Bailey's legal advice on discussions with the FDA).

In contrast, the second email in the string, dated May 11, 2006 at 11:07 p.m., is privileged. It discusses the need to seek legal advice from Bob Bailey, and this email was *not* sent or routed to Hill & Knowlton.

Privilege claim sustained in part and denied in part.

> **FYI**
>
> In a subsequent opinion involving other emails withheld by Bausch & Lomb, the Special Master found that emails sent to non-lawyer experts on regulatory matters were protected under the *Kovel* doctrine, because the experts were necessary to the legal representation. Outside counsel hired the experts to help prepare a response to the FDA on technical regulatory issues. *See* <u>2009 WL 2842745 (D.S.C. 2009)</u>.

* * *

Exhibit 11

Exhibit 11 contains four email chains discussing the arrangement for handling consumer returns of ReNu products. All of these emails were sent to employees of Hill & Knowlton and for reasons discussed above under Exhibit 3, these documents are not privileged.

Investigation of Hill & Knowlton's contributions on these emails only fortifies the determination that Hill & Knowlton was not involved in furthering (much less necessary to providing) legal advice. In one email, Christina Cheang, an employee of Hill & Knowlton, suggests that optical shops should be used for redemptions, as a means of establishing good business relations with these shops. She has to be told, later on in the email string * * * that Bausch & Lomb cannot legally use optical shops for redemption. Clearly she is not necessary to providing legal advice—indeed she is providing business advice that is contrary to legal advice.

Privilege claim denied.

> **Practice Pointer**
>
> The *Kovel* doctrine protects confidential communications to non-lawyers—but only if they are necessary to the legal representation. In close cases, what can the lawyer do in advance of a communication to help assure that a court will find that the non-lawyer was necessary to the legal representation?

4. Expectation of Confidentiality

[Question 5]

The board of directors of a corporation votes to do a public offering of stock. The corporation hires an outside law firm to prepare the necessary documentation. The law firm communicates with corporate personnel and obtains factual information that would put the corporation in a negative light. Upon review of this information, the lawyer recommends that the corporation terminate its plan to do a public offering. The board agrees.

Is the negative information obtained by the law firm protected by the attorney-client privilege?

(A) Yes

(B) No

UNITED STATES v. HATCHER

323 F.3d 666 (8th Cir. 2003)

RICHARD S. ARNOLD, Circuit Judge.

This case involves the convictions of Michael Hatcher, Angelo Porrello, and Joseph Anthony Porrello on charges stemming from the armed robberies of jewelry stores in the Kansas City area. Appellants were convicted of charges including conspiracy, interference with interstate commerce by armed robbery, the use of a firearm during a crime of violence, attempted money laundering, and criminal forfeiture. On appeal, appellants raise numerous claims. We reject all but one of appellants' claims as without merit. As to that one claim—having to do with taped recordings of certain conversations in prison—further proceedings in the District Court will be necessary.

I.

A career criminal by the name of Clarence Burnett organized a group of robbers who successfully robbed numerous jewelry stores. * * * In each robbery, a group of men entered the jewelry store with at least one gun drawn and proceeded to ransack the jewelry cases. * * * In each case, Mr. Burnett took the jewels to J's Pawnshop, operated by Angelo and Joseph Porrello, to fence the jewels to the Porrellos. According to the evidence at trial—which came primarily through the testimony of Clarence Burnett himself—the Porrellos were involved not only in the fencing of the jewelry but also in the planning of the robberies themselves, by, for instance, providing guns, bulletproof vests, and jewelry-store floor plans for the robberies.

* * *

At trial, the majority of the evidence came from cooperating co-conspirators in exchange for reduced sentences. * * * [The defendants were convicted].

Angelo Porrello argues that the District Court erred in refusing to order the government to turn over tapes of conversations between the cooperating co-conspirators and their attorneys. These conversations took place while the co-conspirators were incarcerated, and the parties to these conversations were aware that they were being recorded by the prison. The District Court ruled that these tapes were protected by the attorney-client privilege and therefore would not order their disclosure to the defendants. The government defends the District Court's decision on the ground that the defendants failed to establish a factual record to support the argument that the attorney-client privilege had been waived.

We respectfully disagree. The presence of the prison recording device destroyed the attorney-client privilege. Because the inmates and their lawyers were aware that their conversations were being recorded, they could not reasonably expect that their conversations would remain private. The presence of the recording device was the functional equivalent of the presence of a third party. These conversations were not privileged. *See e.g., Fisher v. Mr. Harold's Hair Lab, Inc.,* <u>215 Kan. 515, 519, 527 P.2d 1026, 1030 (1974)</u> (stating that conversations are privileged only when made outside the presence of third parties); *Lipton Realty, Inc. v. St. Louis Housing Authority,* <u>705 S.W.2d 565, 570 (Mo. App.1986)</u> (stating that the attorney-client privilege is waived when the client voluntarily shares the communications with third parties). The very existence of the tapes, which were made by and are now in the custody of the United States, was factually sufficient to demonstrate that the co-conspirators waived the attorney-client privilege.

We conclude that the District Court erred in refusing to order the disclosure of the taped conversations on the ground that they were privileged. Because the tapes were never disclosed to the Court or to the defendants, we do not know what was said. We therefore cannot assess whether defendants were prejudiced by the non-disclosure. Thus, we remand the case to the District Court to consider what effect, if any, the disclosure would have had on this prosecution. This will provide the government with the opportunity to argue that the non-disclosure of the tapes was harmless error.

* * *

In general, the attorney-client privilege is personal and cannot be asserted by anyone other than the client. In this case, the United States is asserting the co-defendants' attorney-client privilege as a defense to the request for disclosure of the tapes. On remand, if the District Court deems it appropriate, it may allow the parties to pursue the issue of the government's standing by supplemental briefs, evidence, or otherwise.

BYE, Circuit Judge, concurring.

* * *

We have previously held that inmates impliedly consent to having their telephone conversations taped when they know a policy of recording all inmate telephone calls exists. *See United States v. Eggleston,* 165 F.3d 624, 626 (8th Cir.1999); *United States v. Horr,* 963 F.2d 1124, 1126 (8th Cir.1992). These same cases, however, recognize that such policies specifically exempt telephone calls made to attorneys. *Eggleston,* 165 F.3d at 626 (referencing a county jail policy excepting calls made to inmates' attorneys from the jail's monitoring policy); *Horr,* 963 F.2d at 1125 (referencing the Bureau of Prison's policy of recording all inmate telephone calls, except those between inmates and their attorneys). Because the record in this case does not show whether a similar policy existed or whether the co-conspirators knew of its existence, we have insufficient information to conclude the privilege was waived.

I recognize the attorney/client telephone calls at issue may have been placed without following the procedures necessary to protect their confidentiality. If so, the co-conspirators

Practice Pointer

If a client tells his attorney confidentially about the location of evidence that would hurt a client's case, should/must the attorney remove that evidence so that nobody finds it?

In *People v. Meredith,* 631 P.2d 46 (Cal. 1981), the court held that statements between the defendant and his attorney concerning the location of a piece of evidence, a partially burned wallet, were confidential communications protected by the attorney-client privilege. However, when the defense team removed the wallet from the trash bin where the defendant had left it, the privilege disappeared with regard to the location and condition of the wallet. "When defense counsel alters or removes physical evidence, he necessarily deprives the prosecution of the opportunity to observe that evidence in its original condition or location. * * * To extend the attorney-client privilege to a case in which the defense removed evidence might encourage defense counsel to race the police to seize critical evidence. * * * We therefore conclude that whenever defense counsel removes or alters evidence, the statutory privilege does not bar revelation of the original location or condition of the evidence in question. We thus view the defense decision to remove evidence as a tactical choice. If defense counsel leaves the evidence where he discovers it, his observations derived from privileged communications are insulated from revelation. If, however, counsel chooses to remove evidence to examine or test it, the original location and condition of that evidence loses the protection of the privilege."

See also Rule 3.4(a)(1): A lawyer may not "suppress any evidence that the lawyer or the client has a legal obligation to produce."

may well have waived any protections afforded by the privilege. There is, however, insufficient information in this record to satisfy me such was the case. Therefore, I cannot agree with the majority's conclusion that the privilege was waived simply because the conversations were taped.

Despite these concerns with the majority holding, I agree the district court should have allowed the defendants access to the tapes because the government lacks standing to lay claim to the co-conspirators' attorney/client privilege. The attorney/client privilege is personal in nature and cannot be asserted vicariously. Because the government failed to establish any basis for asserting the co-conspirators' attorney/client privilege, the district court should have ordered disclosure of the taped conversations.

* * *

C. Waiver of Attorney-Client Privilege

1. Introduction

Even where all the elements of the privilege are otherwise present, the privilege will not be recognized if it has been waived. The term "waiver" as used by the courts actually encompasses more than the traditional definition of a knowing and voluntary waiver of a right. Courts often find a "waiver" that is really more appropriately considered a "forfeiture." Judge Posner has stated that many of the waiver doctrines — such as the doctrine finding a waiver of the privilege in some circumstances when the party has mistakenly disclosed the privileged information — are not "waiver in the standard sense in which the word is used in the law: the deliberate relinquishment of a right." Rather, a "waiver" of the privilege is sometimes found "in order to punish the person claiming the privilege for a mistake." *International Oil, Chem. & Atomic Workers Local 7-517 v. Uno-Ven Co.*, 170 F.3d 779 (7th Cir. 1999).

"Waiver" in this broad sense includes the concept of forfeiture and follows from any conduct by the client that would make it unfair for the client thereafter to assert the privilege. *See United States v. Yerardi*, 192 F.3d 14 (1st Cir. 1999) ("The concept of waiver by conduct exists, but often amounts simply to a determination that the privilege holder's conduct makes it unfair to allow subsequent assertion of the privilege.").

2. Authority to Waive the Privilege

The client holds the privilege and the power to waive it. The lawyer generally has implicit authority to waive the privilege as well in the course of the representation.

The identity of the client for purposes of waiver is a problematic issue in the corporate context. The Supreme Court held in *CFTC v. Weintraub*, 471 U.S. 343, 349 (1985), that "the power to waive the corporate attorney-client privilege rests with the corporation's management and is normally exercised by its officers and directors." Therefore, in *Weintraub*, a person who had resigned as an officer no longer had authority to exercise or waive the privilege. The *Weintraub* Court further stated that "when control of a corporation passes to new management, the authority to assert and waive the corporation's attorney-client privilege passes as well." Applying this rule, the *Weintraub* Court held that a trustee in bankruptcy succeeded to management's authority to waive the corporate privilege, over the objection of former and present corporate officers. *See also United States v. Campbell*, 73 F.3d 44 (5th Cir. 1996) (a partnership, like a corporation, is an artificial person that can act only through its agents: "Accordingly, the same rule that applies to corporations in bankruptcy should apply to a bankrupt limited partnership."); *Odmark v. Westside Bancorp., Inc.*, 636 F. Supp. 552 (W.D. Wash. 1986) (after a bank's failure, the FSLIC was held to control the privilege).

3. "Selective" Waiver

[Question 6]

A corporation is being investigated by the Environmental Division of the Department of Justice on suspicion that it had illegally dumped toxic chemicals for a number of years. Before the DOJ investigation began, the corporation had hired a law firm to investigate how the company was disposing of the chemicals. Lawyers interviewed corporate agents and filed a report with the corporation. The Department of Justice requests this report from the corporation. The corporation agrees to turn over the report "in the spirit of cooperation" but only if the Department of Justice signs a confidentiality agreement under which the Department will not turn over the report to any private parties.

After receiving the report, the Department of Justice concludes its investigation of the corporation. But private parties allegedly injured by the corporation's activities bring a lawsuit against the corporation. They serve a discovery demand for the report. The corporation refuses to turn over the report, citing the attorney-client privilege.

Which of the following is correct?

(A) The report is not privileged, because the law firm was acting as a factual investigator, and so the "legal advice" requirement of the privilege is not met.

(B) The corporation waived any privilege by disclosing the report to the Department of Justice.

(C) There was no waiver, because the corporation was forced to turn over the report to the Department of Justice, in order to avoid a criminal prosecution.

(D) The private parties cannot take advantage of the waiver, because it was not a general waiver, and the Department agreed to keep the disclosure confidential.

An example of the selective waiver problem arose in *Westinghouse Elec. Corp. v. Republic of the Philippines*, 951 F.2d 1414 (3d Cir. 1991), where Westinghouse received a report from outside counsel who had conducted an internal corporate investigation. The internal investigation was in response to an inquiry by the SEC into allegations that Westinghouse had obtained certain contracts by bribing officials of the Philippine Government. Westinghouse cooperated with the SEC inquiry by turning over outside counsel's report. Later, the Department of Justice began to investigate whether Westinghouse obtained contracts from the Philippines through bribery. Again, Westinghouse cooperated by turning over the investigative report prepared by counsel. Thereafter, the Republic brought suit against Westinghouse for damages stemming from the alleged bribery of Philippine officials by agents of Westinghouse. The Republic sought access to counsel's investigative report.

The Court rejected the Westinghouse argument that the attorney-client privilege could be *selectively* waived—that is, it rejected the concept that a party who voluntarily discloses privileged material to the government nonetheless retains the privilege as to private parties. In rejecting selective waiver the *Westinghouse* Court sided with the clear majority of circuits. *See, e.g., In re Quest Communications Int'l, Inc.*, 450 F.3d 1179 (10th Cir. 2006) (concluding that the case has not been made that selective waiver protection is required to assure cooperation with law enforcement); *United States v. Billmyer*, 57 F.3d 31 (1st Cir. 1995) (corporation's disclosure of report to the government constituted a waiver of the privilege: "A risk of unfairness is evident where information is provided to one side in a case (here, the United States) and then an inquiry into its origin is shielded by a claim of privilege."); *In re Columbia/HCA Healthcare Corp. Billing Practices Litigation*, 293 F.3d 289 (6th Cir. 2002) (rejecting the concept of selective waiver, even in the face of an express confidentiality agreement). *But see Diversified Industries v. Meredith*, 572 F.2d 596 (8th Cir. 1977) (*en banc*) (adopting selective waiver).

The argument in favor of selective waiver is that it is necessary to assure cooperation with government investigations—corporations are less likely to cooperate if the consequence of disclosure is that privileged reports can be used by plaintiffs in private litigation. And if corporations don't cooperate, this will increase the costs of government investigations—the regulator will have to investigate from the ground up, rather than being able to work off the report that was prepared by corporate counsel. But the courts have countered that selective waiver is not required to encourage cooperation with government investigations, as the corporation is already fully incentivized to cooperate, given the risks of fines, indictments, and general regulatory obligations. As the Court in *Westinghouse* noted, Westinghouse disclosed the investigative report to the government even though the selective waiver rule was far from clearly established at the time.

It could be argued that *Westinghouse* places the client in a dilemma: If the client wants to cooperate with the government, it can do so but only at the expense of completely waiving the privilege. However, this supposed "tough choice" is one that attorneys and clients routinely make in a variety of contexts. Waiver of the privilege often has advantages and disadvantages. For example, in *In re John Doe Corp.*, 675 F.2d 482 (2d Cir. 1982), a corporation conducted through counsel an internal investigation of its business practices. The resulting investigative report was shown to a lawyer representing an underwriter in connection with a public offering of the corporation's securities, so that underwriter's counsel could complete a due diligence review. The corporation argued that disclosure to underwriter counsel should not be considered a waiver because disclosure was "required" by the legal duty of due diligence and the millions of dollars riding on the public offering of registered securities. Hence the waiver, according to the corporation, was not voluntary. The Second Circuit responded:

> We view this argument with no sympathy whatsoever. A claim that a need for confidentiality must be respected in order to facilitate the seeking and rendering of informed legal advice is not consistent with selective disclosure when the claimant decides that the confidential materials can be put to other beneficial purposes. Once a corporate decision is made to disclose them for commercial purposes, no matter what the economic imperatives, the privilege is lost. * * * We hold that the calculated use of otherwise privileged materials for commercial purposes will waive the privilege.

4. Mistaken Disclosures

One of the most difficult problems of waiver occurs when the disclosure of confidential information is a mistake. For example, the lawyer hits the wrong speed dial on the fax machine, and privileged information is thereby sent to the adversary. A more common example arises where the lawyer painstakingly complies with a voluminous discovery request for thousands of e-mails, and a privileged e-mail is mistakenly included in the CD sent to the adversary. Again, the loss of privilege that might occur here is really grounded in a theory of forfeiture rather than traditional waiver, which speaks in terms of intentional relinquishment of a known right. The question is, what sort of conduct should be subject to the sanction of the loss of a privilege.

The risks of mistaken disclosure are obviously profound, and these risks increase in complex cases with voluminous discovery of electronic information. The costs of privilege review, in order to avoid the consequences of waiver, can rise to the millions of dollars. Lawyers, especially in complex litigation, often enter into arrangements to control the risks of waiver when privileged electronic data is disclosed during discovery. These arrangements can cover inadvertent disclosure, or can more broadly cover even intentional disclosures. Generally speaking there are two kinds of agreements: "claw back" and "quick peek." The 2006 Advisory Committee Note to Rule 26 discusses the costs of preproduction privilege review of electronic data, as well as the use of "claw back and "quick peek" agreements:

> Parties may attempt to minimize these costs and delays by agreeing to protocols that minimize the risk of waiver. They may agree that the responding party will provide certain requested materials for initial examination without waiving any privilege or protection – sometimes known as a "quick peek." The requesting party then designates the documents it wishes to have actually produced. This designation is the Rule 34 request. The responding party then responds in the usual course, screening only those documents actually requested for formal production and asserting privilege claims as provided in Rule 26(b)(5)(A). On other occasions, parties enter agreements—sometimes called "clawback agreements"—that production without intent to waive privilege or protection should not be a waiver so long as the responding party identifies the documents mistakenly produced, and that the documents should be returned under those circumstances. Other voluntary arrangements may be appropriate depending on the circumstances of each litigation. In most circumstances, a party who receives information under such an arrangement cannot assert that production of the information waived a claim of privilege or of protection as trial-preparation material.

Although these agreements may not be appropriate for all cases, in certain cases they can facilitate prompt and economical discovery by reducing delay for the discovering party in obtaining access to documents, and by reducing the cost and burden of review by the producing party.

Practice Pointer

The way these agreements often work in practice is that the disclosing party takes a "first cut" of the material and removes all the data that is clearly privileged upon a cursory review — for example, emails from or to counsel. The rest of the material is then produced and if it turns out on further review that it is privileged, it is returned. Such agreements limit the multiple levels of intensive review of all the electronic data that would otherwise be required for preproduction privilege review. If a party has signed such an agreement, it waives any argument that a mistaken disclosure of privileged information by the other side is a waiver. *See, e.g., Prescient Partners, L.P. v. Fieldcrest Cannon, Inc.,* No. 96 Civ. 7590, 1997 WL 736726 (S.D.N.Y. Nov. 26, 1997) (enforcing a confidentiality agreement and refusing to find a waiver from an inadvertent disclosure of privileged information).

There are a number of factors that limit the utility of "claw back" and "quick peek" agreements. Most important, *they provide protection only in the proceeding in which they are entered.* An agreement between two parties in another litigation does not estop a third party, in a subsequent litigation, from arguing that a waiver occurred by disclosing the privileged information in the previous matter. Because enforceability of such agreements is uncertain, they may do little to limit the costs of pre-production privilege review. Lawyers have to be certain that mistaken disclosures of privileged information will not result in a waiver—otherwise they have no choice but to engage in the multiple levels of privilege review of all the electronic data.

Another limitation on such agreements is obvious—the parties must agree. Where the discoverable electronic data on both sides is relatively equal, then all parties have an incentive to enter such an agreement. But where one side has most of the data—*e.g.,* an employment discrimination case brought by a fired employee, where all the emails are on the employer's server—then the party with few (if any) documents to produce may not be inclined to limit the costs of the adversary's pre-production privilege review. (One factor that may still provide an incentive is if the party has an interest in *expedited* discovery; if there is no non-waiver agreement in effect, then the court is very likely to allow the party with custody of the data greater time to conduct a full pre-production privilege review).

Concerned about the rising costs of electronic discovery and privilege review, the House Judiciary Committee asked the Advisory Committee on Evidence Rules to prepare a rule that would provide some protection against these costs, by providing a more liberal, and a uniform, rule on waiver. The rule as prepared by the Advisory Committee (drafted by the Reporter to that Committee, who is a co-author of this Casebook) was enacted by Congress in September, 2010 as Rule 502 of the Federal Rules of Evidence. Among other things, the Rule provides for the possibility of a court order that will protect against the consequences of waiver.

Text of Federal Rule of Evidence 502

Rule 502. Attorney-Client Privilege and Work Product; Limitations on Waiver

The following provisions apply, in the circumstances set out, to disclosure of a communication or information covered by the attorney-client privilege or work-product protection.

(a)　Disclosure made in a federal proceeding or to a federal office or agency; scope of a waiver. — When the disclosure is made in a federal proceeding or to a federal office or agency and waives the attorney-client privilege or work-product protection, the waiver extends to an undisclosed communication or information in a federal or state proceeding only if:

(1) the waiver is intentional;

(2) the disclosed and undisclosed communications or information concern the same subject matter; and

(3) they ought in fairness to be considered together.

(b) Inadvertent disclosure. — When made in a federal proceeding or to a federal office or agency, the disclosure does not operate as a waiver in a federal or state proceeding if:

(1) the disclosure is inadvertent;

(2) the holder of the privilege or protection took reasonable steps to prevent disclosure; and

(3) the holder promptly took reasonable steps to rectify the error, i n - cluding (if applicable) following <u>Fed. R. Civ. P. 26(b)(5)(B)</u>.

(c) Disclosure made in a state proceeding. — When the disclosure is made in a state proceeding and is not the subject of a state-court order concerning waiver, the disclosure does not operate as a waiver in a federal proceeding if the disclosure:

(1) would not be a waiver under this rule if it had been made in a federal proceeding; or

(2) is not a waiver under the law of the state where the disclosure o c - curred.

(d) Controlling effect of a court order. — A federal court may order that the privilege or protection is not waived by disclosure connected with the litigation pending before the court – in which event the disclosure is also not a waiver in any other federal or state proceeding.

(e) Controlling effect of a party agreement. — An agreement on the effect of disclosure in a federal proceeding is binding only on the parties to the agreement, unless it is incorporated into a court order.

(f) Controlling effect of this rule. — Notwithstanding Rules 101 and 1101, this rule applies to state proceedings and to federal court-annexed and federal court-mandated arbitration proceedings, in the circumstances set out in the rule. And notwithstanding Rule 501, this rule applies even if state law provides the rule of decision.

(g) Definitions. — In this rule:

1) "attorney-client privilege" means the protection that applicable law provides for confidential attorney-client communications; and

2) "work-product protection" means the protection that applicable law provides for tangible material (or its intangible equivalent) prepared in anticipation of litigation or for trial.

Explanatory Note on Rule 502

Prepared by the Judicial Conference Advisory Committee on Evidence Rules

This new rule has two major purposes:

1) It resolves some longstanding disputes in the courts about the effect of certain disclosures of communications or information protected by the attorney-client privilege or as work product—specifically those disputes involving inadvertent disclosure and subject matter waiver.

2) It responds to the widespread complaint that litigation costs necessary to protect against waiver of attorney-client privilege or work product have become prohibitive due to the concern that any disclosure (however innocent or minimal) will operate as a subject matter waiver of all protected communications or information. This concern is especially troubling in cases involving electronic discovery. *See, e.g., Hopson v. City of Baltimore,* 232 F.R.D. 228, 244 (D. Md. 2005) (electronic discovery may encompass "millions of documents" and to insist upon "record-by-record pre-production privilege review, on pain of subject matter waiver, would impose upon parties costs of production that bear no proportionality to what is at stake in the litigation").

The rule seeks to provide a predictable, uniform set of standards under which parties can determine the consequences of a disclosure of a communication or information covered by the attorney-client privilege or work product protection. Parties to litigation need to know, for example, that if they exchange privileged information pursuant to a confidentiality order, the court's order will be enforceable. Moreover, if a federal court's confidentiality order is not enforceable in a state court then the burdensome costs of privilege review and retention are unlikely to be reduced.

The rule makes no attempt to alter federal or state law on whether a communication or information is protected under the attorney-client privilege or work product immunity as an initial matter. Moreover, while establishing some exceptions to waiver, the rule does not purport to supplant applicable waiver doctrine generally.

The rule governs only certain waivers by disclosure. Other common-law waiver doctrines may result in a finding of waiver even where there is no disclosure of privileged information or work product. *See, e.g., Nguyen v. Excel Corp.,* 197 F.3d 200 (5th Cir. 1999) (reliance on an advice of counsel defense waives the privilege with respect to attorney-client communications pertinent to that defense); *Byers v. Burleson,* 100 F.R.D. 436 (D.D.C. 1983) (allegation of lawyer malpractice constituted a waiver of confidential communications under the circumstances). The rule is not intended to displace or modify federal common law concerning waiver of privilege or work product where no disclosure has been made.

* * *

Subdivision (b). Courts are in conflict over whether an inadvertent disclosure of a communication or information protected as privileged or work product constitutes a waiver. A few courts find that a disclosure must be intentional to be a waiver. Most courts find a waiver only if the disclosing party acted carelessly in disclosing the communication or information and failed to request its return in a timely manner. And a few courts hold that any inadvertent disclosure of a communication or information protected under the attorney-client privilege or as work product constitutes a waiver without regard to the protections taken to avoid such a disclosure. *See generally Hopson v. City of Baltimore,* 232 F.R.D. 228 (D. Md. 2005), for a discussion of this case law.

The rule opts for the middle ground: inadvertent disclosure of protected communications or information in connection with a federal proceeding or to a federal office or agency does not constitute a waiver if the holder took reasonable steps to prevent disclosure and also promptly took reasonable steps to rectify the error. This position is in accord with the majority view on whether inadvertent disclosure is a waiver.

Cases such as *Lois Sportswear, U.S.A., Inc. v. Levi Strauss & Co.,* 104 F.R.D. 103, 105 (S.D.N.Y. 1985) and *Hartford Fire Ins. Co. v. Garvey,* 109 F.R.D. 323, 332 (N.D. Cal. 1985), set out a multi-factor test for determining whether inadvertent disclosure is a waiver. The stated factors (none of which are dispositive) are the reasonableness of precautions taken, the time taken to rectify the error, the scope of discovery, the extent of disclosure and the overriding issue of fairness. The rule does not explicitly codify that test, because it is really a set of non-determinative guidelines that vary from case to case. The rule is flexible enough to accommodate any of those listed factors. Other considerations bearing on the reasonableness of a producing party's efforts include the number of documents to be reviewed and the time constraints for production. Depending on the circumstances, a party that uses advanced analytical software applications and linguistic tools in screening for privilege and work product may be found to have taken "reasonable steps" to prevent inadvertent disclosure. The implementation of an efficient system of records management before litigation may also be relevant.

The rule does not require the producing party to engage in a post-production review to determine whether any protected communication or information has been produced by mistake. But the rule does require the producing party to follow up on any obvious indications that a protected communication or information has been produced inadvertently.

The rule applies to inadvertent disclosures made to a federal office or agency, including but not limited to an office or agency that is acting in the course of its regulatory, investigative or enforcement authority. The consequences of waiver, and the concomitant costs of pre-production privilege review, can be as great with respect to disclosures to offices and agencies as they are in litigation.

* * *

Subdivision (d). Confidentiality orders are becoming increasingly important in limiting the costs of privilege review and retention, especially in cases involving electronic discovery. But the utility of a confidentiality order in reducing discovery costs is substantially diminished if it provides no protection outside the particular litigation in which the order is entered. Parties are unlikely to be able to reduce the costs of pre-production review for privilege and work product if the consequence of disclosure is that the communications or information could be used by non-parties to the litigation.

There is some dispute on whether a confidentiality order entered in one case is enforceable in other proceedings. *See generally Hopson v. City of Baltimore,* 232 F.R.D. 228 (D. Md. 2005), for a discussion of this case law. The rule provides that when a confidentiality order governing the consequences of disclosure in that case is entered in a federal proceeding, its terms are enforceable against non-parties in any federal or state proceeding. For example, the court order may provide for return of documents without waiver irrespective of the care taken by the disclosing party; the rule contemplates enforcement of "claw-back" and "quick peek" arrangements as a way to avoid the excessive costs of pre-production review for privilege and work product. *See Zubulake v. UBS Warburg LLC,* 216 F.R.D. 280, 290 (S.D.N.Y. 2003) (noting that parties may enter into "so-called 'claw-back' agreements that allow the parties to forego privilege review altogether in favor of an agreement to return inadvertently produced privilege documents"). The rule provides a party with a predictable protection from a court order—predictability that is needed to allow the party to plan in advance to limit the prohibitive costs of privilege and work product review and retention.

Under the rule, a confidentiality order is enforceable whether or not it memorializes an agreement among the parties to the litigation. Party agreement should not be a condition of enforceability of a federal court's order.

* * *

[Question 7]

One big corporation sued another for fraud after a deal went sour. Each sought discovery of thousands of emails that were relevant to the case. At the defendant's request, and over the plaintiff's objection, the court entered an order providing that any disclosure of information protected by the attorney-client privilege during discovery would not constitute a waiver of the privilege. After the order was entered, the defendant produced 650,000 emails; 1000 emails involved confidential attorney-client communications. Subsequently the defendant was sued for fraud by another corporation that was involved in the deal that went bad. The plaintiff in this second case sought to use as evidence the 1000 privileged emails that the defendant produced in the previous litigation — arguing that the defendant waived the privilege by producing them in that litigation.

Has the defendant waived the privilege by producing the emails in the prior litigation?

   (A) No, because there has been no showing that any waiver was intentional.

   (B) No, because the court order protects against a waiver in any subsequent litigation.

   (C) Yes, because the order in the previous case cannot bind a person who was not a party in that case.

   (D) Yes, because the order was entered in the absence of agreement between the parties in the case.

5. Duties of the Party Receiving Privileged Information

AM. BAR ASS'N, STANDING COMM. ON ETHICS & PROF'L RESPONSIBILITY,
Formal Op. 06-442 (2006)

The Model Rules of Professional Conduct do not contain any specific prohibition against a lawyer's reviewing and using embedded information in electronic documents, whether received from opposing counsel, an adverse party, or an agent of an adverse party. A lawyer who is concerned about the possibility of sending, producing, or providing to opposing counsel a document that contains or might contain metadata, or who wishes to take some action to reduce or remove the potentially harmful consequences of its dissemination, may be able to limit the likelihood of its transmission by "scrubbing" metadata from documents or by sending a different version of the document without the embedded information.

* * *

E-mail and other electronic documents often contain "embedded" information. Such embedded information is commonly referred to as "metadata." This opinion addresses whether the ABA Model Rules of Professional Conduct permit a lawyer to review and use embedded information contained in e-mail and other electronic documents, whether received from opposing counsel, an adverse party or an agent of an adverse party. The Committee concludes that the Rules generally permit a lawyer to do so.

Metadata is ubiquitous in electronic documents. For example:

> • Electronic documents routinely contain as embedded information the last date and time that a document was saved, and data on when it last was accessed. Anyone who has an electronic copy of such a document usually can "right click" on it with a computer mouse (or equivalent) to see that information.

> • Many computer programs automatically embed in an electronic document the name of the owner of the computer that created the document, the date and time of its creation, and the name of the person who last saved the document. Again, that information might simply be a "right click" away.

> • Some word processing programs allow users, when they review and edit a document, to "redline" the changes they make in the document to identify what they added and deleted. The redlined changes might be readily visible, or they might be hidden, but even in the latter case, they often will be revealed simply by clicking on a software icon in the program.

> • Some programs also allow users to embed comments in a document. The comments may or may not be flagged in some manner, and they may or may not "pop up" as a cursor is moved over their locations.

Other types of metadata may or may not be as well known and easily understandable as the foregoing examples. Moreover, more thorough or extraordinary investigative measures sometimes might permit the retrieval of embedded information that the provider of electronic documents either did not know existed, or thought was deleted.

Not all metadata, it should be noted, is of any consequence; most is probably of no import. In ordinary day-to-day circumstances, the embedded information that is found in most documents, such as when they were saved, or who the authors were, is unlikely to be of any interest, much less material to a matter. In some instances, however, such as when a party to a lawsuit is attempting to establish "who knew what when," the date and time that a critical document was created or who drafted it may be a critical piece of information. If a payment amount is being negotiated, then a redlined change or a comment in a draft agreement that suggests how much more the opposing party is willing to pay or how much less they might take likely is of the highest importance.

The Committee first notes that the Rules do not contain any specific prohibition against a lawyer's reviewing and using embedded information in electronic documents. The most closely applicable rule, Rule 4.4(b), relates to a lawyer's receipt of inadvertently sent information [and] is silent as to the ethical propriety of a lawyer's review or use of such information. The Rule provides only that "[a] lawyer who receives a document relating to the representation of the lawyer's client and knows or reasonably should know that the document was inadvertently sent shall promptly notify the sender." * * *

Some authorities have addressed questions related to a lawyer's search for, or use of, metadata under the rubric of a lawyer's honesty, and have found such conduct ethically impermissible. The Committee does not share such a view, but instead reads the recent addition of Rule 4.4(b) identifying the sole requirement of providing notice to the sender of the receipt of inadvertently sent information, as evidence of the intention to set no other specific restrictions on the receiving lawyer's conduct found in other Rules.

* * * The Committee observes that counsel sending or producing electronic documents may be able to limit the likelihood of transmitting metadata in electronic documents. Computer users can avoid creating some kinds of metadata in electronic documents in the first place. For example, they often can choose not to use the redlining function of a word processing program or not to embed comments in a document. * * * Methods to avoid or eliminate embedded information have been, and no doubt will continue to be, discussed in many legal programs, practice guides, and articles, as well as in general office software publications and support web sites. The specifics of any such software are beyond the scope of this opinion.

A lawyer who is concerned about the possibility of sending, producing, or providing to opposing counsel a document that contains or might contain metadata also may be able to send a different version of the document without the embedded information. For example, she might send it in hard copy, create an image of the document and send only the image (this can be done by printing and scanning), or print it out and send it via facsimile.

Finally, if a lawyer is concerned about risks relating to metadata and wishes to take some action to reduce or remove the potentially harmful consequences of its dissemination, then before sending, producing, or otherwise making available any electronic documents, she may seek to negotiate a confidentiality agreement or, if in litigation, a protective order, that will allow her or her client to "pull back," or prevent the introduction of evidence based upon, the document that contains that embedded information or the information itself. Of course, if the embedded information is on a subject such as her client's willingness to settle at a particular price, then there might be no way to "pull back" that information.

Make the Connection

Rule 4.4(b) governs inadvertent receipt of a document. *See* Chapter 6.

* * *

In re NITLA S.A. DE C.V.

92 S.W.3d 419 (Tex. 2002)

PER CURIAM

The issue here is whether the trial court abused its discretion when it refused to disqualify Nitla's counsel, who had reviewed privileged documents that the trial court ordered the opposing party to produce. * * *

Nitla, a Mexican pharmaceutical company, sued Bank of America (BOA) in 1996. Nitla claimed that BOA misappropriated over $24 million of Nitla's funds on deposit. During discovery, Nitla asked BOA to produce certain documents. BOA resisted and asserted the attorney-client and work-product privileges. After an in camera inspection and a hearing, the trial court identified numerous documents that it determined BOA should produce. BOA asked the trial court to stay production until BOA decided whether to seek emergency relief in the court of appeals. Rather than issue an order, the trial court requested additional briefing and scheduled another hearing. The trial court also indicated it would order BOA to produce any nonprivileged documents at that time.

At the second hearing, after considering the additional briefing and oral arguments, the trial court ordered BOA to produce the previously identified documents. BOA again asked the trial court to stay production, arguing that if Nitla's counsel reviewed the documents, BOA would be irreparably harmed. Moreover, BOA argued that if Nitla's counsel reviewed the documents and the court of appeals determined them privileged, Nitla's counsel could be disqualified. Nevertheless, the trial court granted, in part, Nitla's motion to compel production. The trial court next handed the documents, which were under the trial court's control, directly to Nitla's counsel. This enabled Nitla's counsel to review the documents before BOA could seek mandamus relief.

Later that same day, BOA notified Nitla by fax that it still believed all the tendered documents were privileged. BOA also asked Nitla not to review or distribute the documents, because BOA would seek mandamus relief. However, Nitla's counsel relied on the trial court's order and reviewed the documents.

After BOA filed for mandamus relief, the court of appeals abated the proceeding to allow the trial court's new judge to reconsider his predecessor's decision. After another hearing, the trial court again overruled BOA's objection that the documents were privileged. However, the trial court ordered Nitla to return the documents to BOA pending appellate review. Nitla complied with this order. BOA then reurged its mandamus petition in the court of appeals, and the court of appeals held that most of the documents were privileged.

BOA then moved to disqualify Nitla's counsel, alleging that Nitla's counsel "disregarded their ethical and professional obligations to gain an unfair advantage" when they reviewed the privileged documents. BOA also argued that the *Meador* factors support disqualification. *See In re Meador*, 968 S.W.2d 346, 351-52 (Tex.1998) (discussing six factors a trial court should consider when deciding whether to disqualify an attorney who receives privileged information outside the normal course of discovery).

After a hearing, the trial court denied BOA's motion to disqualify. Even though the trial court found that Nitla had extensively reviewed the documents and that BOA had "clean hands," the trial court denied the disqualification motion because it found: (1) Nitla's counsel did not act unprofessionally or violate any disciplinary rules; (2) Nitla's counsel did not obtain the documents wrongfully, but rather, after a judicial proceeding; and (3) no competent evidence showed that Nitla's counsel had developed its trial strategy based on the documents. Moreover, the trial court determined that it had less severe measures available to prevent Nitla from using the privileged information to gain unfair advantage.

* * * Nitla contends that the trial court correctly refused to disqualify Nitla's counsel, because BOA did not prove the disqualification grounds with specificity and did not prove it would suffer actual harm. * * * In response, BOA claims that * * * Nitla improperly reviewed the documents when it knew BOA intended to seek appellate relief; Nitla's actions irreparably harmed BOA; and there is no evidence that disqualification would harm Nitla.

* * *

"Disqualification is a severe remedy." It can result in immediate and palpable harm, disrupt trial court proceedings, and deprive a party of the right to have counsel of choice. In considering a motion to disqualify, the trial court must strictly adhere to an exacting standard to discourage a party from using the motion as a dilatory trial tactic. This Court often looks to the disciplinary rules to decide disqualification issues. However, the disciplinary rules are merely guidelines—not controlling standards—for disqualification motions. Even if a lawyer violates a disciplinary rule, the party requesting disqualification must demonstrate that the opposing lawyer's conduct caused actual prejudice that requires disqualification. And, under appropriate circumstances, a trial court has the power to disqualify a lawyer even if he has not violated a specific disciplinary rule.

In *Meador*, we acknowledged that there are undoubtedly some situations when a party's lawyer who reviews another party's privileged information must be disqualified, even though the lawyer did not participate in obtaining the information. However, we did not articulate a bright-line standard for disqualification in such situations. Instead, we determined that a trial court must consider the importance of our discovery privileges along with all the facts and circumstances to decide "whether the interests of justice require disqualification." We then identified six factors a trial court should consider when a lawyer receives an opponent's privileged materials. However, we emphasized that "these factors apply only when a lawyer receives an opponent's privileged materials outside the normal course of discovery."

Here, the trial court determined that Nitla's counsel did not violate a disciplinary rule. Consequently, the disciplinary rules provide no guidance. Moreover, Nitla's counsel received the documents directly from the trial court in a discovery hearing. Thus, the six *Meador* factors do not apply. We have not defined a precise standard for disqualification in such circumstances. Nevertheless, the trial court referred to the appropriate guiding principles when it denied BOA's motion to disqualify.

In disqualification cases, our analysis begins with the premise that disqualification is a severe measure that can result in immediate harm, because it deprives a party of its chosen counsel and can disrupt court proceedings. Consequently, when a party receives documents from a trial court, and a reviewing court later deems the documents privileged, the party moving to disqualify opposing counsel must show that: (1) opposing counsel's reviewing the privileged documents caused actual harm to the moving party; and (2) disqualification is necessary, because the trial court lacks any lesser means to remedy the moving party's harm.

We conclude that the trial court correctly applied these principles. Thus, we hold that the trial court did not abuse its discretion when it denied BOA's motion to disqualify Nitla's counsel. At the disqualification hearing, the trial court focused on whether BOA proved it suffered actual prejudice. BOA argued that the mere fact that Nitla had extensively reviewed the privileged documents demonstrated prejudice to BOA. However, BOA could not show that Nitla's trial strategy had significantly changed after reviewing the documents. Indeed, BOA could only demonstrate that reviewing the documents might have enabled Nitla's counsel to identify four new witnesses to depose, and that this additional testimony could potentially harm BOA. Recognizing that disqualification is a severe measure, the trial court determined that less severe measures, such as quashing depositions, could cure BOA's alleged harm. Accordingly, the trial court [properly] concluded that disqualification was neither a necessary nor an appropriate remedy.

Food for Thought

If you receive privileged information that you weren't supposed to get, are you content to rely on the authorities above and exploit the information as much as a court will allow? Or would you be concerned about getting a reputation as a "Rambo" lawyer?

* * *

D. The Crime-Fraud Exception to the Attorney-Client Privilege

[Question 8]

Joe is a used car salesman. He has been sued by a buyer who claims she bought a car with a turned-back odometer. Joe retains Lawyer to defend the case. When Lawyer asks Joe to describe the background of the dispute, Joe makes two statements to the Lawyer in confidence:

1) "I've destroyed a number of documents that could be used to prove the buyer's case."

2) "I still think there might be some documents in the files that could be relevant to her case. Could you look through the files and let me know what you think she might ask for in discovery?"

Are these statements privileged?

(A) Neither is privileged, because each can be used to prove that Joe engaged in crime or fraud.

(B) Both are privileged, because they sought advice on a legal matter and were made in confidence.

(C) The first statement is privileged and the second is not --- the second was made to further a crime or fraud, the first was not.

(D) The second statement is privileged, so long as Joe abandoned his plan to destroy more records.

Statements made by the client to the attorney, even though in confidence, are not privileged if the purpose of the communication is to further crime or fraud. The crime-fraud exception is triggered when the party seeking the information provides *prima facie* evidence that the client was seeking the attorney's advice and services in furtherance of a preconceived plan of wrongdoing. The Court in *In re Grand Jury*, 845 F.2d 896 (11th Cir. 1988) set forth the standards for applying the crime-fraud exception:

> First, there must be a prima facie showing that the client was engaged in criminal or fraudulent conduct when he sought the advice of counsel, that he was planning such conduct when he sought the advice of counsel, or that he committed a crime of fraud subsequent to receiving the benefit of counsel's advice. Second, there must be a showing that the attorney's assistance was obtained in furtherance of the criminal or fraudulent activity or was closely related to it.

Note that the exception can apply even if the client never actually committed a fraudulent or criminal act. The exception is triggered when the client communicates with the attorney with the intent to further a plan of crime or fraud. See *In re Grand Jury Proceedings*, 87 F.3d 377 (9th Cir. 1996) (government is not required to show that the client's plan succeeded, nor that the attorney's advice in fact helped the client in his plan).

The crime-fraud exception can apply even if the attorney is an unwitting instrument in the crime or fraud. The basis of the exception is that the client may not in bad faith exploit the privilege by using the attorney as an instrument of crime or fraud. Therefore it does not matter whether the attorney was knowingly involved in the client's scheme. The Court in *In re Grand Jury Proceedings*, 87 F.3d 377 (9th Cir. 1996) explained this result as follows:

> Inasmuch as today's privilege exists for the benefit of the client, not the attorney, it is the client's knowledge and intentions that are of paramount concern to the application of the crime-fraud exception; the attorney need know nothing about the client's ongoing or planned illicit activity for the exception to apply."

The crime-fraud exception applies only when the attorney is being used to further a *future or ongoing* scheme of misconduct. It does not apply to communications seeking legal representation with respect to a past act of crime or fraud; such statements are at the heart of the protection provided by the privilege. *See, e.g., Coleman v. American Broadcasting Co.*, 106 F.R.D. 201 (D.D.C. 1985) ("Only communications in regard to ongoing or future misconduct fall outside the scope of the privilege. This distinction goes to the very core of the policies underlying the privilege."). Moreover, the exception will not apply if the client consulted with an attorney *in order to determine whether a prospective course of conduct was lawful.* As one Court put it:

> The crime-fraud exception has a precise focus: It applies only when the communications between the client and his lawyer further a crime, fraud or other misconduct. * * * [The exception should not be applied to deny a client] the privilege where even its stern critics acknowledge that the justification for the shield is strongest—where a client seeks counsel's advice to determine the legality of conduct *before* the client takes any action.

United States v. White, 887 F.2d 267 (D.C. Cir. 1989); *see In re Grand Jury Proceedings,* 87 F.3d 377 (9th Cir. 1996) (crime-fraud exception should not be applied in such a way as to "discourage many would-be clients from consulting an attorney about entirely legitimate legal dilemmas").

On the other hand, the crime-fraud exception will apply if the client already knows that a prospective course of conduct is impermissible and is simply using counsel in an attempt to effectuate the plan. *See, e.g., United States v. Reeder,* 170 F.3d 93 (1st Cir. 1999) (client conferred with counsel in order to obtain "some ideas" on how to cover up a series of questionable loans, and proposed that the loans could be backdated; these communications were within the crime-fraud exception and not privileged); *United States v. Jacobs,* 117 F.3d 82 (2d Cir. 1997) (crime-fraud exception was found where "the wrong-doer had set upon a criminal course *before* consulting counsel").

Likewise, any communications made with a view to covering up past acts of misconduct are in fact made with the purpose of perpetrating a crime or fraud, and hence are not privileged. *See United States v. Edwards,* 303 F.3d 606 (5th Cir. 2002) (crime-fraud exception applied where the legal services sought by the defendant were "to conceal and cover up the crimes committed"; "[r]ather than merely defending himself from wrongdoing, [the client] was actively continuing the cover-up of extortion and perpetuating his tax fraud.").

The fact that a communication with counsel can be used to *prove* a crime or fraud is not sufficient to trigger the exception. Timing is critical, and unless the scheme of crime or fraud was afoot at the time of the communication, the statements remain privileged. For example, assume that a corporation seeks legal advice to determine whether a large account receivable is, in fact, legally collectible. Counsel investigates and informs the corporation that the receivable is not legally collectible. A few months later, the corporation sells the receivable without informing the buyer about the advice received from counsel. Of course, counsel's report would be relevant to prove that the seller-client acted fraudulently. But in order for the crime-fraud exception to apply, the seller must establish a *prima facie* case that the seller had a fraudulent intent at the time that counsel's advice was sought. If not, the privilege will apply even though the client acted fraudulently subsequent to receiving the legal advice. *See, e.g., Pritchard-Keang Nam Corp. v. Jaworski,* 751 F.2d 277 (8th Cir. 1984):

> That the report may help *prove* that a fraud occurred does not mean that it was *used* in perpetrating the fraud. … Timing is critical, for the prima facie showing requires that the client was engaged in or planning a criminal or fraudulent scheme when he sought the advice of counsel to further the scheme.

See also In re Sealed Case, 107 F.3d 46 (D.C. Cir. 1997) (the mere fact that a person commits a fraud after consulting with counsel does not establish a *prima facie* case that the consultation was in furtherance of the fraud).

IV. The Basics of the Duty of Confidentiality Under Rule 1.6

As discussed above, the lawyer's duty of confidentiality covers more information than protected by the evidentiary privilege. As to non-privileged information, the lawyer must make all reasonable efforts to keep it secret. But if the lawyer is subject to a lawful demand for the information, she must disclose it—whereas the very point of the evidentiary privilege is that there can be no lawful demand for it.

A. Triggering the Duty of Confidentiality

The duty of confidentiality certainly applies once an attorney-client relationship has been formed. But it can also apply when a lawyer and prospective client have preliminary discussions about *whether* to form an attorney-client relationship.

[Question 9]

Smith meets with Lawyer to discuss a possible property claim against Rich. After Smith explains his claim, Lawyer determines that Smith cannot afford her services and refuses the case. Rich then meets with Lawyer and offers to meet all of Lawyer's financial terms. In representing Rich, Lawyer uses the information Smith provided, reasoning that because they never had an attorney-client relationship, Lawyer owed Smith no duty of confidentiality. Is she subject to discipline?

(A) Yes, because Smith was a client.

(B) Yes, because Smith was a prospective client.

(C) No, because Smith was not a client.

(D) No, because the information was not dispositive.

Rule 1.18: Duties to Prospective Clients

(a) A person who discusses with a lawyer the possibility of forming a client-lawyer relationship with respect to a matter is a prospective client.

(b) Even when no client-lawyer relationship ensues, a lawyer who has had discussions with a prospective client shall not use or reveal information learned in the consultation, except as Rule 1.9 would permit with respect to information of a former client.

(c) A lawyer subject to paragraph (b) shall not represent a client with interests materially adverse to those of a prospective client in the same or a substantially related matter if the lawyer received information from the prospective client that could be significantly harmful to that person in the matter, except as provided in paragraph (d). If a lawyer is disqualified from representation under this paragraph, no lawyer in a firm with which that lawyer is associated may knowingly undertake or continue representation in such a matter, except as provided in paragraph (d).

(d) When the lawyer has received disqualifying information as defined in paragraph (c), representation is permissible if:

(1) both the affected client and the prospective client have given informed consent, confirmed in writing, or:

(2) the lawyer who received the information took reasonable measures to avoid exposure to more disqualifying information than was reasonably necessary to determine whether to represent the prospective client; and

(i) the disqualified lawyer is timely screened from any participation in the matter and is apportioned no part of the fee therefrom; and

(ii) written notice is promptly given to the prospective client.

B. Scope of Information Within the Duty of Confidentiality

[Question 10]

An attorney represented a client in an action against the client's former partner to recover damages for breach of contract. During the representation, the client presented the attorney with incontrovertible proof that the former partner had committed perjury in a prior action which was resolved in the partner's favor. Neither the attorney nor the client was involved in any way in the prior action. The attorney believes that it would be detrimental to the client's best interests to reveal the perjury because of the implication that might be drawn from the former close personal and business relationship between the client and the former partner.

Would it be proper for the attorney to fail to disclose the perjury to the tribunal?

  (A) No, because the information is not protected by the attorney-client privilege.

  (B) No, because the attorney has knowledge that the former partner perpetrated a fraud on the tribunal.

  (C) Yes, because neither the client nor the attorney was involved in the prior action.

  (D) Yes, because the attorney believes that disclosure would be detrimental to the client's interests.

1. Information Known to the Public

LAWYERS MUST THINK TWICE BEFORE REVEALING ANYTHING RELATING TO CLIENT'S REPRESENTATION

25 ABABNA Lawyers' Manual of Professional Conduct 449

The ethics rule on lawyer-client confidentiality constrains a lawyer from revealing any information relating to a client's representation, even if the information is generally known and not adverse to the client, and the client doesn't consider it confidential, the Nevada bar's ethics committee advised June 24 (Nevada State Bar Standing Comm. on Ethics and Professional Responsibility, Formal Op. 41, 6/24/09).

The opinion urges lawyers to pause and think twice before disclosing anything about a client's representation. To drive the point home, the committee listed numerous examples of common situations that potentially involve a breach of confidentiality.

All Information Is Protected

Nevada Rule of Professional Conduct 1.6(a) forbids a lawyer to reveal information relating to representation of a client unless the client gives informed consent, the disclosure is implicitly authorized to carry out the representation, or an exception in the rule applies.

* * *

The committee noted that Rule 1.6(a) operates automatically, whether or not the client has asked that the information be kept confidential or considers it confidential. Also, the rule applies even if the information is not covered by the attorney-client privilege, even if the information is not embarrassing and detrimental to the client, regardless of when the lawyer learned of the information, and whatever the source of the information, the committee said.

* * *

As "food for thought" before disclosing any information about a client's representation, the committee listed 13 examples of common situations which it said raise issues under Rule 1.6(a) in the absence of client consent:

- Phoning the client and leaving a message about the representation on the answering machine or discussing the matter with the client's roommate or spouse.

- Submitting a copy of the client's billing statements to support an application for fees.

- Submitting a client list that reveals the identity of clients to a bank to support the lawyer's loan application.

- Identifying clients in a law firm brochure.

- Revealing the identity of a client by processing a credit card payment.

- Telling a story to friends about a recent trial without revealing the client's identity or any other fact not contained in the public record.

• Taking a client file or discovery documents to the local photocopy shop.

• Employing an outside computer tech support person to troubleshoot the firm's computer system.

• Providing insurance defense bills for auditing by an insurance company auditor.

• Providing a homeowner with billing statements for legal services rendered to the homeowner's association.

• Providing billing statements for representing a corporation in litigation to a disgruntled shareholder.

• Providing billing statements under an open records act for representing a public entity as outside counsel.

Practice Pointer

Under <u>Rule 1.6</u>, it does not appear to matter that information held by the lawyer is in fact widely known. It is still subject to the lawyer's duty of confidentiality. Compare New York Rule 1.6, which provides that confidential information "does not ordinarily include * * * information that is generally known in the local community or in the trade, field or profession to which the witness relates." As a practical matter, it is unlikely that a lawyer would be disciplined for disclosing client information that is widely known. But it will always be prudent to get client consent in advance of any disclosure.

• Listing "best" clients in Martindale-Hubbell.

2. Information Unrelated to the Representation

[Question 11]

An attorney represents a client who is under indictment for homicide. In the course of the representation, the client told the attorney that she had previously killed two other people. These murders are completely unrelated to the murder indictment for which the attorney is providing representation. With the client's consent, the attorney made a tape recording of the client's confession regarding the unrelated homicides. At the attorney's request, the client also drew a map of the remote locations of the victims' graves from the unrelated killings. Those bodies have not been found by the police, and the client is not a suspect in either crime, both of which remain unsolved.

Is the attorney subject to discipline if he fails to voluntarily disclose to the authorities his knowledge of the two prior murders and the locations of the victims' bodies?

(A) Yes, because as an officer of the court, the attorney must disclose any knowledge that he has, whether privileged or not, concerning the commission of the prior crimes by his client.

(B) Yes, because the attorney is impeding the state's access to significant evidence.

(C) No, because the attorney did not represent or advise his client with respect to the prior crimes.

(D) No, because the information was obtained by the attorney in the course of the representation.

Rule 1.6 specifically covers only that information "relating to the representation of the client." But of course "relating to" can be broad and depending on the matter it could cover all types of background and personal information about the client. Some states have defined confidential information even more broadly than the *Rule. See, e.g.*, New York Rule 1.6 (confidential information defined as that gained "during or relating to" the representation of a client).

3. Information on Matters of Public Interest

PEOPLE v. BELGE

372 N.Y.S.2d 798 (Sup. Ct. Onandaga Cty 1975)

ORMAND N. GALE, Judge.

In the summer of 1973 Robert F. Garrow, Jr. stood charged in Hamilton County with the crime of MURDER. The Defendant was assigned two attorneys, Frank H. Armani and Francis R. Belge. A defense of insanity had been interposed by counsel for Mr. Garrow. During the course of the discussions between Garrow and his two counsel, three other murders were admitted by Garrow, one being in Onondaga County. On or about September of 1973 Mr. Belge conducted his own investigation based upon what his client had told him and with the assistance of a friend the location of the body of Alicia Hauck was found in Oakwood Cemetery in Syracuse. Mr. Belge personally inspected the body and was satisfied, presumably, that this was the Alicia Hauck that his client had told him that he murdered.

This discovery was not disclosed to the authorities, but became public during the trial of Mr. Garrow in June of 1974, when to affirmatively establish the defense of insanity, these three other murders were brought before the jury by the defense in the Hamilton County trial. Public indignation reached the fever pitch; statements were made by the District Attorney of Onondaga County relative to the situation and he caused the Grand Jury of Onondaga County, then sitting, to conduct a thorough investigation. As a result of this investigation Frank Armani was No Billed by the Grand Jury but Indictment No. 75-55 was returned as against Francis R. Belge, Esq., accusing him of having violated section 4200(1) of the Public Health Law, which, in essence, requires that a decent burial be accorded the dead, and section 4143 of the Public Health Law, which, in essence, requires anyone knowing of the death of a person without medical attendance, to report the same to the proper authorities. Defense counsel moves for a dismissal of the Indictment on the grounds that a confidential, privileged communication existed between him and Mr. Garrow, which should excuse the attorney from making full disclosure to the authorities.

* * *

In the most recent issue of the New York State Bar Journal (June 1975) there is an article by Jack B. Weinstein, entitled "Educating Ethical Lawyers." In a sub-caption to this article is the following language which is pertinent:

> "The most difficult ethical dilemmas result from the frequent conflicts between the obligation to one's client and those to the legal system and to society. It is in this area that legal education has its greatest responsibility, and can have its greatest effects."

In the course of his article Mr. Weinstein states that there are three major types of pressure facing a practicing lawyer. He uses the following language to describe these:

> "First, there are those that originate in the attorney's search for his own well-being. Second, pressures arise from the attorney's obligation to his client. Third, the lawyer has certain obligations to the courts, the legal system, and society in general."

Our system of criminal justice is an adversary system and the interests of the state are not absolute, or even paramount.

* * *

The effectiveness of counsel is only as great as the confidentiality of its client-attorney relationship. If the lawyer cannot get all the facts about the case, he can only give his client half of a defense. This, of necessity, involves the client telling his attorney everything remotely connected with the crime.

Apparently, in the instant case, after analyzing all the evidence, and after hearing of the bizarre episodes in the life of their client, they decided that the only possibility of salvation was in a defense of insanity. For the client to disclose not only everything about this particular crime but also everything about other crimes which might have a bearing upon his defense, requires the strictest confidence in, and on the part of, the attorney.

When the facts of the other homicides became public, as a result of the defendant's testimony to substantiate his claim of insanity, members of the public were shocked at the apparent callousness of these lawyers, whose conduct was seen as typifying the unhealthy lack of concern of most lawyers with the public interest and with simple decency. A hue and cry went up from the press and other news media suggesting that the attorneys should be found guilty of such crimes as obstruction of justice or becoming an accomplice after the fact. From a layman's standpoint, this certainly was a logical conclusion. However, the constitution of the United States of America attempts to preserve the dignity of the individual and to do that guarantees him the services of an attorney who will bring to the bar and to the bench every conceivable protection from the inroads of the state against such rights as are vested in the constitution for one accused of crime. Among those substantial constitutional rights is that a defendant does not have to incriminate himself. His attorneys were bound to uphold that concept and maintain what has been called a sacred trust of confidentiality.

* * *

Garrow was constitutionally exempt from any statutory requirement to disclose the location of the body. And Attorney Belge, as Garrow's attorney, was not only equally exempt, but under a positive stricture precluding such disclosure. Garrow, although constitutionally privileged against a requirement of compulsory disclosure, was free to make such a revelation if he chose to do so. Attorney Belge was affirmatively required to withhold disclosure. The criminal defendant's self-incrimination rights become completely nugatory if compulsory disclosure can be exacted through his attorney.'

* * *

In the case at bar we must weigh the importance of the general privilege of confidentiality in the performance of the defendant's duties as an attorney, against the inroads of such a privilege, on the fair administration of criminal justice as well as the heart tearing that went on in the victim's family by reason of their uncertainty as to the whereabouts of Alicia Hauck. In this type situation the Court must balance the rights of the individual against the rights of society as a whole. There is no question but Attorney Belge's failure to bring to the attention of the authorities the whereabouts of Alicia Hauck when he first verified it, prevented bringing Garrow to the immediate bar of justice for this particular murder. This was in a sense, obstruction of justice. This duty, I am sure, loomed large in the mind of Attorney Belge. However, against this was the Fifth Amendment right of his client, Garrow, not to incriminate himself. * * *

It is the decision of this Court that Francis R. Belge conducted himself as an officer of the Court with all the zeal at his command to protect the constitutional rights of his client. Both on the grounds of a privileged communication and in the interests of justice the Indictment is dismissed.

C. Exceptions to the Duty of Confidentiality

<u>Rule 1.6(b)</u> provides a number of exceptions under which a lawyer is permitted to disclose the client's confidential information:

> (b) A lawyer may reveal information relating to the representation of a client to the extent the lawyer reasonably believes necessary:

Practice Pointer

After Garrow was convicted and incarcerated, he escaped. When officers searched his cell, they found a list of names. Belge was on that list, as was his daughter, and a number of other people against whom Garrow held a grudge. (During Garrow's trial, Garrow had made several inappropriate comments about Belge's daughter, who was in the courtroom.) When police informed Belge that Garrow had escaped and about the list in his cell, Belge volunteered information concerning where he thought Garrow might be hiding. He learned this information—Garrow's favorite haunts—during the representation. Should Belge have been disciplined for disclosing these locations? *See* Chapter 8 for further discussion.

> (1) to prevent reasonably certain death or substantial bodily harm;

> (2) to prevent the client from committing a crime or fraud that is reasonably certain to result in substantial injury to the financial interests or property of another and in furtherance of which the client has used or is using the lawyer's services;

> (3) to prevent, mitigate or rectify substantial injury to the financial interests or property of another that is reasonably certain to result or has resulted from the client's commission of a crime or fraud in furtherance of which the client has used the lawyer's services;

(4) to secure legal advice about the lawyer's compliance with these Rules;

(5) to establish a claim or defense on behalf of the lawyer in a controversy between the lawyer and the client, to establish a defense to a criminal charge or civil claim against the lawyer based upon conduct in which the client was involved, or to respond to allegations in any proceeding concerning the lawyer's representation of the client; or

(6) to comply with other law or a court order.

The remainder of this Chapter discusses some of the problems of applying these exceptions. Note that these exceptions do not *require* disclosure of confidential information. They *permit* it—so the lawyer cannot be disciplined for disclosing or not disclosing.

1. To Prevent Death or Serious Bodily Harm:

[Question 12]

A lawyer represents a client charged with murder. When interviewing the client about what happened, the client says "I hope they don't find out about that other murder I did in Virginia. If they do, they'll put me on death row if they find me guilty now." At the lawyer's request, the client then gives the details about the other murder. The lawyer does some surfing on the internet and finds out that another person has been convicted of that murder in Virginia, and is awaiting execution for the crime. The lawyer discloses the information to the authorities. Eventually the person convicted of that murder is released and the lawyer's client is convicted and sentenced to death.

Is the lawyer subject to discipline?

(A) No, because he had to disclose to prevent a death.

(B) No, because he was permitted to disclose to prevent a death.

(C) Yes, because he caused death.

(D) Yes, because death was not reasonably certain.

For more on the ethical dilemma of disclosing a confidence to protect against reasonably certain death or bodily harm, see the Symposium in Volume 29 of the Loyola L.A. Law Review (1996): *Executing the Wrong Person: The Professionals' Ethical Dilemma.*

[Question 13]

A lawyer is representing a client who has been charged with murder. The murder weapon, a gun, has never been found. In a conference with the lawyer, the client says: "I'm worried about them finding that gun. I can't see any way out other than to get rid of it. I'm going to throw it in the swamp tonight, they'll never find it there." After the client leaves, the lawyer calls the police and tells them about the client's plan. The police then follow the client and arrest him just before he is going to throw the gun away.

Is the lawyer subject to discipline?

    (A) No, because the lawyer should not have to sit silently while the client commits a future crime.

    (B) No, because the information was not privileged because the client was not seeking legal advice.

    (C) No, because disposing of a weapon could lead to death or serious bodily harm.

    (D) Yes, because there is no exception to the duty of confidentiality under these circumstances.

[Question 14]

[MPRE Question]

Attorney has been hired by Client to represent Client in a civil commitment proceeding initiated by the state. Client is now undergoing psychiatric evaluation to determine whether civil commitment should be ordered. Client told Attorney that Client intends to commit suicide as soon as the tests are completed, and Attorney believes that Client will carry out this threat. Suicide and attempted suicide are crimes in the state.

    (A) Yes, because the information concerns a future crime and is not protected by the attorney-client evidentiary privilege.

    (B) Yes, because disclosure of the information might prevent the Client's death.

    (C) No, unless Attorney knows that client has attempted suicide in the past.

(D) No, because disclosure would aid the state in its civil commitment case against Client.

Rule 1.6, Comment 6

[6] Although the public interest is usually best served by a strict rule requiring lawyers to preserve the confidentiality of information relating to the representation of their clients, the confidentiality rule is subject to limited exceptions. Paragraph (b)(1) recognizes the overriding value of life and physical integrity and permits disclosure reasonably necessary to prevent reasonably certain death or substantial bodily harm. Such harm is reasonably certain to occur if it will be suffered imminently or if there is a present and substantial threat that a person will suffer such harm at a later date if the lawyer fails to take action necessary to eliminate the threat. Thus, a lawyer who knows that a client has accidentally discharged toxic waste into a town's water supply may reveal this information to the authorities if there is a present and substantial risk that a person who drinks the water will contract a life- threatening or debilitating disease and the lawyer's disclosure is necessary to eliminate the threat or reduce the number of victims.

Food for Thought

The exception in Rule 1.6(b) permitting disclosure to prevent reasonably certain death or bodily harm did not exist at the time of *People v. Belge, supra.* If it had, could Belge have used it to disclose the location of the body? Could Belge have used it to disclose Garrow's whereabouts after Garrow escaped from prison?

2. To Protect Victims When the Client has Misused the Lawyer's Services:

STUART TAYLOR, JR., ETHICS AND THE LAW: A CASE HISTORY

N.Y. Times Mag., Jan. 9, 1983 at 33

In a third-floor corridor of the Federal District Court on Manhattan's Foley Square, one afternoon last month, a tall, bespectacled man looking no more than his 36 years stood talking with friends, nervously drawing on a cigarette. Myron S. Goodman had, over the course of the 1970's, been the mastermind behind the meteoric growth of the multimillion-dollar O.P.M. Leasing Services Inc. He had become a leading figure in the computer-leasing field and an extravagant philanthropist. Now, together with his partner and brother-in-law, Mordecai Weissman, Goodman was to appear before Judge Charles S. Haight Jr. for sentencing in one of the most massive corporate frauds in American history. Goodman and Weissman had pleaded guilty to defrauding banks and other lenders of more than $210 million [in 1983 dollars] before their company went bankrupt in 1981. * * * . [W]hen the sentences were pronounced, they were tough: 12 years in prison for Goodman, 10 years for Weissman. The judge had not been moved by Goodman's promise [of reform], which had a familiar ring for some in the court-room.

Over his years as O.P.M.'s executive vice president, Goodman had made the same promise again and again, sometimes in tears, to the group of men who served as the company's attorneys. And over the years, they had believed him * * * while they carried out his directions. As a result, their firm, Singer Hutner Levine & Seeman, has been accused by some lenders of complicity in the leasing company's fraud.

> **FYI**
>
> It is important to note that this article covers an event that oc-curred *before* the ethics rules were amended to allow a lawyer to dis-close confidences to protect victims if the lawyer's services have been misused. The ABA had rejected such an exception on at least three differ-ent occasions. But in the wake of the Enron scandal, Rule 1.6 was amend-ed to add the exception.
>
> Also note that the ethics rules re-ferred to here are from the Code of Professional Responsibility, a precur-sor of the Model Rules, but the prin-ciples discussed are the same.

Because of the special nature of the case, the details of the O.P.M. fraud and of the relationship between the company and its law firm have become publicly avail-able to an extraordinary extent. The following article is largely based upon the many thousands of pages of depositions taken in a sweeping bankruptcy investi-gation. In them, Myron Goodman is portrayed as a volatile, ingenious manipula-tor of men and money - purloining a letter that contained incriminating evidence, threatening to hurl himself from his ninth-floor office window.

Singer Hutner is shown confronting a painful dilemma. Warned that it might be in the midst of a massive fraud orchestrated by its most important client, the law firm sought the advice of respected legal experts, and with their approval proceeded to close new loans for O.P.M. Even after learning that more than $60 million of these new loans was fraudulent, Singer Hutner kept its silence while bowing out of the picture. Thus Goodman was able to use new lawyers to swindle lenders out of another $15 million before his house of cards collapsed early in 1981.

* * *

In practice, [the] line between what a lawyer must do to discharge his ethical obligation to his client and what he may not do without becoming his client's accomplice in crime is sometimes so thin it seems invisible. Should a divorce lawyer go along when his clients conceal some of their assets to keep down the size of their alimony payments? Should a personal injury lawyer go along when his clients fake or exaggerate their pain and suffering? Should a criminal-defense lawyer go along when his clients lie on the witness stand about their whereabouts on the night of the murder? On the face of it, the answer to all three questions may seem to most laymen to be a resounding "no." But to many lawyers it is not so clear. Suppose, for example, the attorney only suspects the truth. At what point should he stop giving his client the benefit of the doubt? What obligation does he have to investigate the facts? Under what circumstances should he resign from the case? At what point does he become responsible for preventing a client from performing criminal acts?

* * *

As children, Mordecai Weissman and Myron Goodman went to the same yeshiva in Brooklyn. They attended Brooklyn College together. In 1969, Goodman ended up marrying Lydia Ganz, whose sister had recently married Weissman. It seemed logical that the two men would become business partners, and so they did. Weissman started the company in 1970 in a small office on Church Avenue in Brooklyn, and Goodman joined him a few months later. Weissman handled the marketing end, Goodman was the inside man, in charge of finances; they each owned half of the business. O.P.M. was Weissman's name for the company - short for "other people's money." The company would borrow money to purchase computers and other business equipment and then lease the equipment to corporate customers. In theory, the lease payments to O.P.M. would be large enough to allow the company to service its loans with enough left over to provide a handsome profit.

The formula seemed to work magically. By the late 1970's, O.P.M. had become one of the nation's five largest computer-leasing companies, with 250 employees in 11 offices across the country, including plush headquarters on Broadway in Manhattan. It was buying multimillion-dollar computers from the likes of I.B.M. and leasing them to such corporations as American Telephone and Telegraph, Revlon and Polaroid. Prestigious banks, insurance companies and other financial institutions were glad to lend O.P.M. money, secured as it was by the obligations of the lessees to make lease payments and by the value of the computers themselves. Many of these lenders were recruited by Lehman Brothers, the company's investment banker. O.P.M. also raised cash by selling legal title to the computers to individual investors seeking tax shelters.

* * *

Almost from the start, the company was basically insolvent and survived by means of fraud and bribery. A single computer would be used as collateral for two or three loans with different banks; the value of a given piece of equipment would be inflated to obtain larger loans. * * * To win a place in the competitive computer-leasing market, Weissman bribed employees of potential customers, and the company offered lease rates far below those of its competitors. Moreover, the company offered lessors a risky bonus. In return for granting O.P.M. a long lease of, say, seven years, customers were promised that they could cancel the contract in the event a technological breakthrough made the computers obsolete.

Goodman was pushing the company toward ever bigger loans, building the shaky pyramid ever higher, when I.B.M. announced in 1977 a forthcoming new line of computers that would revolutionize the business. O.P.M. customers soon started lining up to cancel their leases. To avoid bankruptcy, Goodman resorted to fraud on a much grander scale than ever before, as Weissman's role in the illegal actions diminished. He relied almost totally on leases supposedly entered into by Rockwell International, the huge California aerospace company. He used forged signatures, documents falsified to overstate the value of leases and computers, and loans obtained upon equipment that did not exist. Between 1978 and 1981, O.P.M. obtained from 19 banks, pension funds and other lenders more than $196 million in loans secured by phony Rockwell leases. These new loans went to meet payments on old loans until the company finally came crashing down in March 1981.

Andrew B. Reinhard was 26 years old, an honors graduate of Harvard Law School, when he joined a small New York law firm in 1969. When the newly created O.P.M. Leasing Services Inc. started casting about for a law firm, Myron Goodman remembered Reinhard, older brother of a boyhood friend. That was the start of the long, tumultuous relationship between the company and Singer Hutner. All through the decade of fraud at O.P.M., Singer Hutner handled the company's legal work. That included closing loans and supplying the legal opinions that lenders relied on as to O.P.M.'s title to computers and as to the legality of O.P.M. leases. * * *

Today, looking back on that time, Singer Hutner lawyers who have testified insist that up until June 1980, they had no inkling that their chief client was engaged in large-scale fraud; they thought O.P.M. a booming, legitimate business. * * * The relationship between Singer Hutner and O.P.M. took a dramatic turn on June 12, 1980, when Joseph L. Hutner, a senior partner in the law firm, received an extraordinary visit from Myron Goodman. The O.P.M. executive indicated that he was troubled, that he might have done something wrong in his stewardship of the company - something he could not set right because it involved millions of dollars more than he could raise. But during the meeting with Hutner, which lasted for several hours as Reinhard and others shuttled in and out of the room, Goodman indicated he had no intention of telling Hutner any details unless he could be sure the attorney would not tell them to anyone else. Hutner could not give him such an assurance since the law firm also represented O.P.M. itself and thus might have to inform Weissman.

One of the matters troubling Goodman was a letter that John A. Clifton, O.P.M.'s chief in-house accountant, had told Goodman he was preparing to send to Reinhard. Clifton had discovered evidence of the Rockwell lease fraud. After consulting his own lawyer, William J. Davis, Clifton decided to turn the information over to Singer Hutner and then resign. He hoped thereby to avoid criminal prosecution while putting the onus on Singer Hutner to decide whether to blow the whistle on O.P.M.

Goodman was worried that Clifton might go to the authorities. He said he promised Clifton $50,000 to $100,000 in severance pay that, Goodman testified, was "meant to induce him to keep his mouth shut." * * *

According to a memorandum prepared by Singer Hutner at the time, Davis said Clifton had evidence that O.P.M. had perpetrated a multimillion-dollar fraud and that the opinion letters Singer Hutner had drawn up to obtain loans for O.P.M. had been based upon false documents. And Davis also passed along, Mattioli recalled, an ominous opinion from Clifton - that O.P.M., "in order to survive, would probably have to continue the same type of wrongful activity."

* * *

The seriousness of the situation was not lost on Singer Hutner, which decided it needed some outside legal advice of its own. On June 18, the firm made an appointment with Joseph M. McLaughlin [now a senior judge on the Second Circuit Court of Appeals]. * * * [I]t soon became clear to McLaughlin that, given the apparent scope of the fraud and the law-firm's close relationship with O.P.M., the central problem was one of "ethics, professional responsibility." He * * * proceeded to bring into the case a legal-ethics expert, Henry Putzel 3d * * * .

The next day, at a two-and-a-half-hour meeting in Hutner's office, Hutner, Mattioli and Rubino gave McLaughlin and Putzel a detailed report on what they had learned from Goodman and Davis. The Singer Hutner lawyers stressed two major points * * * : they wanted to do the ethical thing, and they wanted to continue representing O.P.M. unless they were ethically and legally obliged to quit.

[McLaughlin and Putzel advised that] Singer Hutner could ethically continue to represent O.P.M., giving the benefit of the doubt to Goodman's assurances that there was no ongoing fraud. The firm could continue to close new loans for O.P.M. pending efforts to find out the details of Goodman's past wrongdoing; such information would help them guard against any continuing fraud. Singer Hutner was bound to keep everything it had already learned secret, except from Weissman.

* * * As to the possibly false opinion letters and documents the firm had unwittingly provided to banks to obtain loans for O.P.M., Putzel [opined that] Singer

Hutner had no legal duty to withdraw them. He reasoned that leaving the victims of a past fraud in the dark was not an ongoing fraud.

McLaughlin and Putzel did recommend some steps aimed at stopping any efforts to commit new fraud. They said, for example, that O.P.M. should be required to certify in writing the legitimacy of each new transaction. Goodman was unfazed; he simply signed certifications he knew to be false. And he found ways to put off giving the law firm the kind of detailed description of his crimes that would have made the attorneys better able to judge the dangers of their position.

* * *

Meanwhile, the lawyers were becoming increasingly upset at Goodman's continuing refusal to disclose the details of his wrongdoing. Late on the afternoon of July 22 * * * Hutner telephoned Goodman and set a deadline for him to tell Weissman what he had done. Goodman responded with threats to hurl himself out the window of his huge, luxuriously appointed office.

* * *

All through this summer of nondisclosure, Singer Hutner continued closing loans for O.P.M. without checking the legitimacy of underlying Rockwell leases. Some were legitimate, but leases securing loans of $22 million in June, $17 million in July and $22 million in August proved to be fraudulent.

In the first week of September, Goodman finally told Hutner some of the details of the fraud he had first hinted at in June, and Hutner explained it all to Putzel over lunch at the Yale Club in New York. * * * The two men tentatively agreed that the law firm should quit as O.P.M.'s counsel * * * . "What struck me as so, frankly, evil about this," Putzel said in his deposition, "was that the lawyers had been manipulated in this fashion." It was now apparent, he said, that "the attorneys were the instruments, the unwitting instruments, of the fraud by Goodman."

* * *

Singer Hutner voted formally to resign as O.P.M.'s general counsel on Sept. 23 in a daylong series of meetings punctuated by expressions of concern about the effect of a possible O.P.M. bankruptcy on the law firm's fees. Goodman was in the firm's offices that day and bitterly accused the lawyers of disloyalty, seemingly unabashed by their knowledge that he had used them to swindle banks out of tens of millions of dollars. He * * * warned the Singer Hutner lawyers to "keep their mouths shut." * * * Singer Hutner quit O.P.M. gradually, completing the process in December 1980. The lawyers assumed that an abrupt withdrawal would cause O.P.M. to collapse; they would handle legal business until Goodman, who had vowed that he would eventually pay back the victims of the fraud, could find new counsel. * * * Still, Singer Hutner had cause to worry about its own potential liability during the withdrawal period, and the firm took steps to prevent new fraud. Its lawyers refused to proceed with new loans unless Goodman authorized them to check out the collateral with third parties such as Rockwell. * * *

Once the decision to quit O.P.M. was made, Singer Hutner had to determine what to do with its knowledge that it had been part of a giant fraud. On Putzel's advice, the law firm kept the facts to itself, telling nothing to the corporations and bankers who had been defrauded. * * * The law firm responded to inquiries from lenders and other interested parties by saying that Singer Hutner and O.P.M. had "agreed" to part ways. * * * This stance played right into the hands of Goodman. He was able to continue obtaining fraudulent loans while spreading the suggestion that he had dismissed Singer Hutner and assuring business contacts that there was nothing wrong with the loans.

The close-mouthed stance was also called for by Putzel as the appropriate way of dealing with the lawyers who would fill Singer Hutner's shoes - in spite of the considerable risk that Goodman would simply lie to the new attorneys. Thus he advised Singer Hutner that it must honor Goodman's demand that Gary R. Simon, the O.P.M. inhouse lawyer who was preparing to handle new loan closings, be kept in the dark.

* * *

A similar series of events was played out with Kaye, Scholer, Fierman, Hays & Handler, one of New York's largest law firms, which Goodman invited to step into Singer Hutner's place and close new loans for O.P.M. Hutner wanted to warn Peter M. Fishbein, a Kaye Scholer partner and an old friend, to stay away from O.P.M. * * * Fishbein phoned Hutner in October 1980 asking "if there was anything he should be aware of" in considering Goodman's invitation. Hutner told him only that "the decision to terminate was mutual and that there was mutual agreement that the circumstances of termination would not be discussed." Two years later, Hutner testified that "this specific thing caused me more personal pain than anything I can recall during the course of the entire O.P.M. thing, including learning that Myron was a thief."

The end result of Singer Hutner's close-mouthed policy: Goodman was able to use the unwitting Gary Simon and Kaye Scholer to close more than $15 million in loans for O.P.M. in December 1980 and early 1981 that were secured by fraudulent Rockwell leases.

* * *

After O.P.M. came tumbling down, Singer Hutner, and four codefendants including Rockwell and Lehman Brothers, became the targets of a spate of multimillion-dollar lawsuits. The suits, brought by lenders, accused the law firm of being an accomplice in the O.P.M. crimes, on the ground that the attorneys knew or should have known they were part of an ongoing fraud. A tentative settlement of the lawsuits has been reached whereby the five defendants would pay $65 million; Singer Hutner's share would be about $10 million. But the law firm still maintains that it acted in conformity with the ethics code * * *. And Putzel said in a recent interview, "I am in my own conscience absolutely convinced that the advice we gave was correct advice based on what we knew at the time."

* * *

Whether or not Singer Hutner violated the ethical code, a basic question remains: Is there not something wrong with a code that can plausibly be used to justify the extreme lengths to which Singer Hutner went to protect its criminal client? Indeed, there is growing concern both inside and outside the legal profession that the current rules make it too easy for lawyers to condone or even actively assist their clients' ongoing crimes, frauds and cover-up conspiracies.

This concern has found expression in some of the reforms contained in the proposed new American Bar Association model ethics code * * *. [C]ontroversy centers on provisions dealing with the kinds of dilemmas that confronted Singer Hutner. The new proposals are designed to make it clearer that lawyers' customary vows of loyalty to their clients and silence about their guilty secrets must sometimes give way to a higher duty to keep their own hands clean --- even to the point of blowing the whistle.

The current ethics code, in its tilt toward the client, reflects in part the economic self-interest of its authors. The code was written by lawyers and for lawyers who get paid to help clients do what they want to do. Lawyers are not paid to place restraints on their clients. * * *

The whistle-blowing provisions of the proposed new code are not universally admired. John C. Elam, a past president of the prestigious American College of Trial Lawyers, is the leader of that group's opposition. He denounces the proposals as "a tremendous assault on the traditional role of the lawyer." If clients cannot be sure that their lawyers' lips are sealed, he reasons, they will not disclose plans that might be illegal, and lawyers will not have any opportunity to persuade them to obey the law.

* * *

If the new code had been in effect in the fall of 1980, Putzel's advice that Singer Hutner could not alert the victims of the O.P.M. fraud, or even the lawyers whom Goodman used after Singer Hutner had quit, might have been different. One proposed rule says that lawyers may blow the whistle if necessary "to rectify the consequences of a client's criminal or fraudulent act in the furtherance of which the lawyer's services had been used." * * * Joseph Hutner, for one, says that [the change] might not be such a bad idea: "I would have been much happier protecting the other lawyers, and in particular my close personal friend Peter Fishbein, from getting in bed with a criminal."

Comment 7 and 8 to Rule 1.6

[7] Paragraph (b)(2) is a limited exception to the rule of confidentiality that permits the lawyer to reveal information to the extent necessary to enable affected persons or appropriate authorities to prevent the client from committing a crime or fraud, as defined in Rule 1.0(d), that is reasonably certain to result in substantial injury to the financial or property interests of another and in furtherance of which the client has used or is using the lawyer's services. Such a serious abuse of the client-lawyer relationship by the client forfeits the protection of this Rule. The client can, of course, prevent such disclosure by refraining from the wrongful conduct. Although paragraph (b)(2) does not require the lawyer to reveal the client's misconduct, the lawyer may not counsel or assist the client in conduct the lawyer knows is criminal or fraudulent. *See* Rule 1.2(d). See also Rule 1.16 with respect to the lawyer's obligation or right to withdraw from the representation of the cli-

Food for Thought

If the exception to confidentiality for situations in which the lawyers services have been misused had been applicable at the time of OPM, would Singer Hutner have been subject to discipline for refusing to inform victims of the fraud?

Note that there are two things going on in OPM—informing the victims of fraud with regard to past and existing leases, and helping OPM with new leases that appear to be fraudulent. Rule 1.6 governs the former situation. Rule 1.2(d) governs the latter situation:

(d) A lawyer shall not counsel a client to engage, or assist a client, in conduct that the lawyer knows is criminal or fraudulent, but a lawyer may discuss the legal consequences of any proposed course of conduct with a client and may counsel or assist a client to make a good faith effort to determine the validity, scope, meaning or application of the law.

Did Singer Hutner violate Rule 1.2(d) by continuing to assist OPM in its transactions? Did it "know" at the time that OPM was up to no good?

ent in such circumstances, and Rule 1.13(c), which permits the lawyer, where the client is an organization, to reveal information relating to the representation in limited circumstances.

[8] Paragraph (b)(3) addresses the situation in which the lawyer does not learn of the client's crime or fraud until after it has been consummated. Although the client no longer has the option of preventing disclosure by refraining from the wrongful conduct, there will be situations in which the loss suffered by the affected person can be prevented, rectified or mitigated. In such situations, the lawyer may disclose information relating to the representation to the extent necessary to enable the affected persons to prevent or mitigate reasonably certain losses or to attempt to recoup their losses. Paragraph (b)(3) does not apply when a person who has committed a crime or fraud thereafter employs a lawyer for representation concerning that offense.

3. Self-Protection:

[Question 13]

Attorney represented Client in negotiating a large real estate transaction. Buyer, who purchased the real estate from Client, has filed suit against both Client and Attorney, alleging fraud and violation of the state unfair trade practices statute. Attorney had advised Client by letter against making the statements relied on by Buyer as the basis for Buyer's claim. Attorney and Client are each represented by separate counsel. In responding to a deposition under subpoena, Attorney wishes to reveal, to the extent Attorney reasonably believes necessary to defend herself, confidential information imparted to Attorney by Client that will be favorable to Attorney but damaging to Client.

Is it proper for Attorney to reveal such information?

(A) Yes, unless Client objects to the disclosure.

(B) Yes, because Attorney may reveal such information to defend herself against a civil claim.

(C) No, unless criminal charges have also been brought against Attorney.

(D) No, because the disclosure will be detrimental to Client.

Comment 10 and 11 to Rule 1.6

[10] Where a legal claim or disciplinary charge alleges complicity of the lawyer in a client's conduct or other misconduct of the lawyer involving representation of the client, the lawyer may respond to the extent the lawyer reasonably believes necessary to establish a defense. The same is true with respect to a claim involving the conduct or representation of a former client. Such a charge can arise in a civil, criminal, disciplinary or other proceeding and can be based on a wrong allegedly committed by the lawyer against the client or on a wrong alleged by a third person, for example, a person claiming to have been defrauded by the lawyer and client acting together. The lawyer's right to respond arises when an assertion of such complicity has been made. Paragraph (b)(5) does not require the lawyer to await the commencement of an action or proceeding that charges such complicity, so that the defense may be established by responding directly to a third party who has made such an assertion. The right to defend also applies, of course, where a proceeding has been commenced.

[11] A lawyer entitled to a fee is permitted by paragraph (b)(5) to prove the services rendered in an action to collect it. This aspect of the rule expresses the principle that the beneficiary of a fiduciary relationship may not exploit it to the detriment of the fiduciary.

V. Corporate Counsel and the Duty of Confidentiality Under Sarbanes-Oxley

[Question 14]

Attorney is outside counsel for Refcon Corp., a securities trading firm. Attorney is asked by the CFO of Refcon to prepare papers for a "round-trip loan" transaction that is designed to hide a large, unrecoverable debt to the company by a paper transaction conducted just before a reporting period. That transaction will then be "un-wound" just after the reporting period. Attorney believes that this transaction may be fraudulent and refuses to participate. A few weeks later, Attorney learns that the CFO retained a different outside counsel to complete the round-trip loan transaction.

Is the refusal to participate sufficient?

(A) Yes, because to do anything more would risk disclosure of confidences from the CFO.

(B) **Yes, because business judgment is for the client, not the lawyer.**

(C) **No, because the lawyer must report this misconduct to the authorities.**

(D) **No, because the lawyer must report the misconduct "up the ladder" in the corporate structure.**

Model Rule 1.13

(a) A lawyer employed or retained by an organization represents the organization acting through its duly authorized constituents.

(b) If a lawyer for an organization knows that an officer, employee or other person associated with the organization is engaged in action, intends to act or refuses to act in a matter related to the representation that is a violation of a legal obligation to the organization, or a violation of law that reasonably might be imputed to the organization, and that is likely to result in substantial injury to the organization, then the lawyer shall proceed as is reasonably necessary in the best interest of the organization. Unless the lawyer reasonably believes that it is not necessary in the best interest of the organization to do so, the lawyer shall refer the matter to higher authority in the organization, including, if warranted by the circumstances, to the highest authority that can act on behalf of the organization as determined by applicable law.

(c) Except as provided in paragraph (d), if

(1) despite the lawyer's efforts in accordance with paragraph (b) the highest authority that can act on behalf of the organization insists upon or fails to address in a timely and appropriate manner an action or a refusal to act, that is clearly a violation of law and

(2) the lawyer reasonably believes that the violation is reasonably certain to result in substantial injury to the organization,

then the lawyer may reveal information relating to the representation whether or not Rule 1.6 permits such disclosure, but only if and to the extent the lawyer reasonably believes necessary to prevent substantial injury to the organization.

(d) Paragraph (c) shall not apply with respect to information relating to a lawyer's representation of an organization to investigate an alleged violation of law, or to defend the organization or other constituent associated with the organization against a claim arising out of an alleged violation of law.

(e) A lawyer who reasonably believes that he or she has been discharged because of the lawyer's actions taken pursuant to paragraphs (b) or (c), or who withdraws under circumstances that require or permit the lawyer to take action under either of those paragraphs, shall proceed as the lawyer reasonably believes necessary to assure that the organization's highest authority is informed of the lawyer's discharge or withdrawal.

(f) In dealing with an organization's directors, officers, employees, members, shareholders or other constituents, a lawyer shall explain the identity of the client when the lawyer knows or reasonably should know that the organization's interests are adverse to those of the constituents with whom the lawyer is dealing.

(g) A lawyer representing an organization may also represent any of its directors, officers, employees, members, shareholders or other constituents, subject to the provisions of Rule 1.7. If the organization's consent to the dual representation is required by Rule 1.7, the consent shall be given by an appropriate official of the organization other than the individual who is to be represented, or by the shareholders.

Comment 3-6 to Rule 1.13

[3] When constituents of the organization make decisions for it, the decisions ordinarily must be accepted by the lawyer even if their utility or prudence is doubtful. Decisions concerning policy and operations, including ones entailing serious risk, are not as such in the lawyer's province. Paragraph (b) makes clear, however, that when the lawyer knows that the organization is likely to be substantially injured by action of an officer or other constituent that violates a legal obligation to the organization or is in violation of law that might be imputed to the organization, the lawyer must proceed as is reasonably necessary in the best interest of the organization. As defined in Rule 1.0(f), knowledge can be inferred from circumstances, and a lawyer cannot ignore the obvious.

[4] In determining how to proceed under paragraph (b), the lawyer should give due consideration to the seriousness of the violation and its consequences, the responsibility in the organization and the apparent motivation of the person involved, the policies of the organization concerning such matters, and any other relevant considerations. Ordinarily, referral to

a higher authority would be necessary. In some circumstances, however, it may be appropriate for the lawyer to ask the constituent to reconsider the matter; for example, if the circumstances involve a constituent's innocent misunderstanding of law and subsequent acceptance of the lawyer's advice, the lawyer may reasonably conclude that the best interest of the organization does not require that the matter be referred to a higher authority. If a constituent persists in conduct contrary to the lawyer's advice, it will be necessary for the lawyer to take steps to have the matter reviewed by a higher authority in the organization. If the matter is of sufficient seriousness and importance or urgency to the organization, referral to higher authority in the organization may be necessary even if the lawyer has not communicated with the constituent. Any measures taken should, to the extent practicable, minimize the risk of revealing information relating to the representation to persons outside the organization. Even in circumstances where a lawyer is not obligated by Rule 1.13 to proceed, a lawyer may bring to the attention of an organizational client, including its highest authority, matters that the lawyer reasonably believes to be of sufficient importance to warrant doing so in the best interest of the organization.

[5] Paragraph (b) also makes clear that when it is reasonably necessary to enable the organization to address the matter in a timely and appropriate manner, the lawyer must refer the matter to higher authority, including, if warranted by the circumstances, the highest authority that can act on behalf of the organization under applicable law. The organization's highest authority to whom a matter may be referred ordinarily will be the board of directors or similar governing body. However, applicable law may prescribe that under certain conditions the highest authority reposes elsewhere, for example, in the independent directors of a corporation.

[6] * * * Paragraph (c) of this Rule supplements Rule 1.6(b) by providing an additional basis upon which the lawyer may reveal information relating to the representation, but does not modify, restrict, or limit the provisions of Rule 1.6(b)(1)-(6). Under paragraph (c) the lawyer may reveal such information only when the organization's highest authority insists upon or fails to address threatened or ongoing action that is clearly a violation of law, and then only to the extent the lawyer reasonably believes necessary to prevent reasonably certain substantial injury to the organization. It is not necessary that the lawyer's services be used in furtherance of the violation, but it is required that the matter be related to the lawyer's representation of the organization. If the lawyer's services are being used by an organization to further a crime or fraud by the organization, Rules 1.6(b)(2) and 1.6(b)(3) may permit the lawyer to disclose confidential information. In such circumstances Rule 1.2(d) may also be applicable, in which event, withdrawal from the representation under Rule 1.16(a)(1) may be required.

Description of SEC Regulations Enacted Under the Authority of the Sarbanes-Oxley Act

17 CFR Part 205 applies to attorneys communicating with the SEC, representing an issuer, or providing securities law advice in connection with a document, whether or not the document is to be filed. This Rule does not prevent jurisdictions from requiring additional obligations of attorneys, but preempts conflicting standards.

Pursuant to Part 205, an attorney representing an issuer before the SEC who becomes aware of a potential material violation of securities laws, fiduciary duty, or something similar that a reasonably prudent investor would want to know must follow an up-the-ladder reporting requirement. Namely, the attorney must report to the Chief Legal Officer (CLO) (or the equivalent thereof) or to the CLO and Chief Executive Officer (CEO) (or the equivalent thereof). Then, the CLO (or the equivalent thereof) must inquire into the evidence to determine the existence of a violation and respond accordingly.

The CLO (or the equivalent thereof) must do one of two things:

> 1) conduct a reasonably appropriate investigation. If, after performing the investigation, the CLO finds no material violation, then the CLO must notify the reporting attorney and provide the basis for reaching this conclusion. If a material violation exists, the CLO must take all reasonable steps to cause the issuer to act appropriately and advise the reporting attorney.

> 2) refer the matter to the Qualified Legal Compliance Committee ("QLCC"), assuming this Committee exists. Unless the reporting attorney believes the response of the Chief Legal Officer (or the equivalent thereof) is timely and appropriate, the attorney must report to an audit committee, other independent committee, or the board of directors.

The expectation is that in the majority of cases of such reports, the potential violation will be addressed and remedied before significantly harming investors. As punishment for violating the securities laws, the SEC may impose civil penalties and remedies and may censure or temporarily or permanently bar violating attorneys from practicing before the SEC. No private right of action exists.

But what if the attorney with information of wrongdoing determines that the internal processes of review are inadequate? That question is answered by 17 CFR 205.3, set forth immediately below.

17 CFR 205.3

(d) Issuer confidences.

* * *

(2) An attorney appearing and practicing before the Commission in the representation of an issuer may reveal to the Commission, without the issuer's consent, confidential information related to the representation to the extent the attorney reasonably believes necessary:

> (i) To prevent the issuer from committing a material violation that is likely to cause substantial injury to the financial interest or property of the issuer or investors;

> (ii) To prevent the issuer, in a Commission investigation or administrative proceeding from committing perjury, proscribed in 18 U.S.C. 1621; suborning perjury, proscribed in 18 U.S.C. 1622; or committing any act proscribed in 18 U.S.C. 1001 that is likely to perpetrate a fraud upon the Commission; or

> (iii) To rectify the consequences of a material violation by the issuer that caused, or may cause, substantial injury to the financial interest or property of the issuer or investors in the furtherance of which the attorney's services were used.

FYI

Note that the Sarbanes-Oxley regulations apply only to lawyers representing issuers—so they do not apply to lawyers representing privately-held corporations. However, Rule 1.13 provides similar authority to permit—but not require—disclosure of confidential information to prevent harm to the corporation from internal wrongdoing.

CAROLINE HARRINGTON, *ATTORNEY GATEKEEPER IN AN INCREASINGLY COMPLEX WORLD: REVISITING THE "NOISY WITHDRAWAL" PROPOSAL OF SEC RULE 205*

22 Geo. J. Legal Ethics 893 (2009)

* * * The Enron experience directly called into question the ethical standards of everyone involved, including the attorneys. * * * The ramifications of the last wave of regulatory reform, culminating in the Public Company Accounting Reform and Investor Protection Act of 2002 (commonly, the Sarbanes-Oxley

Act, hereinafter "SOX"), provide a starting point for this analysis. The passage of SOX initiated developments in the legal community on two principal fronts. First, more aggressive enforcement measures implicated the attorney-client relationship, arguably interfering with the role of the attorney as zealous advocate in defending against government accusations and investigations. Secondly, SOX spurred reassessment of the role of transactional lawyers, assigning to them the role of "gatekeeper" with respect to the organizations they serve. In doing so, it prompted the legal community to reconsider what the ethical canons of client loyalty and confidentiality entail in the transactional context.

Recent developments suggest that a consensus has begun to emerge with respect to the deleterious impact visited on the attorney-client privilege by post-SOX investigative and enforcement tactics. Briefly stated, the prevailing argument has been that vigorous protection of attorney-client communications is necessary to promote effective lawyering and protect the rights of accused individuals. This argument is premised on the notion that the lawyer's predominant role is as zealous advocate for her client. By contrast, the debate about the relative merits of the "gatekeeper" concept as applied to transactional lawyers has attracted greater divergence of opinion. Those who emphasize its disadvantages tend to adopt the same "zealous advocate" argument that has carried the day in the enforcement context. However, as proponents of the "gatekeeper" model have pointed out, invoking that argument in the transactional context ignores the distinctive features of litigation that justify such zeal, features that are absent in the transactional context.

* * *

The corporate scandals of 2001, most notably those implicating Enron and World-Com, resulted in the most significant changes to the federal securities laws since the 1930s. SOX imposed more exacting compliance obligations on public corporations and set out to redefine the role of corporate and securities attorneys. Specifically, SOX imposed more comprehensive requirements for public disclosure of financial information and tighter regulation of insider conflicts, clarified obligations with respect to the structure and duties of boards of directors and other corporate governance matters, created new responsibilities for ancillary gatekeepers such as auditors, analysts, and ratings agencies, and outlined new rules for attorneys practicing before the Securities Exchange Commission ("SEC"). The underlying policy goal of SOX was to prevent corporate fraud by strengthening the ability of independent boards of directors to provide a check against the type of opportunistic management that led to the demise of Enron, WorldCom, and the like.

* * *

Following the fallout from Enron and WorldCom, Congress was not only outraged at the flagrant misconduct by corporate management, but was also deeply troubled by the ancillary question, "[w]here were the lawyers?" In response, the Senate added Section 307 to SOX to empower the SEC to enact "minimum standards of professional conduct" for securities lawyers. The purpose was to impose an explicit mandate requiring securities attorneys to take specific action when they become aware of a legal violation being committed by a corporate agent. In essence, Congress embraced a "gatekeeper" function for securities lawyers. The gatekeeper thesis is premised on the notion that transactional lawyers have a duty to provide detached and independent judgment to promote compliance with the law. In contrast to the zealous advocate model * * * , which places singular emphasis on loyalty to the client, the gatekeeper model posits that the transactional context demands a detached, unbiased approach from the lawyer. This concept of a "duty of independence" suggests that the transactional lawyer has an affirmative obligation to promote the spirit of the law, taking into account all potentially affected interests.

* * * Because securities lawyers are necessary to achieve the consummation of a transaction and are in a position to detect wrong-doing, they fit the bill to perform gatekeeping duties. This model, of course, presupposes that transactional lawyers are also *willing* to obstruct a client's objective when it is of questionable legality. * * *

In accordance with Section 307 of SOX, after extensive notice and comment, the SEC promulgated Rule 205, Standards of Professional Conduct for Attorneys. Meanwhile, the ABA, compelled to respond to the perception that attorneys' complicity contributed to the scandals, created a Task Force on Corporate Responsibility. In early 2003 the ABA House of Delegates adopted, by a slim margin, amendments to Model Rules 1.6 (Confidentiality of Information) and 1.13 (Organization as Client) recommended by the Task Force. The amendments emphasize that lawyers' primary allegiances are to their clients, but recognize that lawyers must also be accountable to third parties that have a legitimate claim to protection against harm from client misconduct.

The 2003 amendments to the Model Rules were symbolically significant, given the organized bars' pre-SOX reluctance to assign any duties of preventing or rectifying client fraud * * * . Similarly significant, the SEC's implementation of "minimum standards of professional conduct" under Section 307 represented an unprecedented shift toward federalization of legal ethics standards. Nevertheless, * * * the gatekeeper functions ultimately adopted were not as extensive as they might have been.

The SEC promulgated Rule 205 pursuant to Section 307 of SOX. The rule applies to any attorney "appearing and practicing before the Commission." It imposes on such attorneys the "duty to report evidence of a material violation" by any officer, manager, or employee of the issuer client to the chief legal officer ("CLO") of the organization (or equivalent), who is then charged with investigating the reporting attorney's evidence of material violation, and undertaking all "reasonable steps" to rectify the situation. If the reporting attorney is not satisfied that the CLO has made "an appropriate response within a reasonable time," the attorney is required to report the material violation to the board of directors or appropriate committee of the board.

During the notice and comment stage for SEC Rule 205, the debate over the appropriate role for lawyers ultimately settled on this framework of "loyal disclosure" obligations. The SEC refrained from imposing more controversial adverse disclosure requirements, tabling and eventually abandoning a mandatory "noisy withdrawal" provision for Rule 205. Instead, the rule contains a permissive adverse disclosure provision, which allows an attorney to report to the SEC confidential information without the issuer's consent to prevent or rectify a material violation. * * *

Model Rule 1.13 provides that a corporate attorney represents the entity, not the constituents of the corporation. Accordingly, if a lawyer knows that a constituent of the organization is committing, or intends to engage in, a violation of law that is likely to result in substantial injury to the organization, the lawyer shall report the matter to a "higher authority" in the organization, unless the lawyer "reasonably believes it is not necessary in the best interest of the organization to do so." Model Rule 1.13 thus echoes the policy embodied by Rule 205 that violations of law by senior management will be prevented, or at least mitigated, by clarifying the attorney's duty to "report up" within the organization. Both Rule 205 and Model Rule 1.13 make clear that such an obligation does not impinge the ethical duty of client confidentiality because that duty extends to the entity, rather than to any individual constituent.

Model Rule 1.6 addresses a situation not covered by Rule 1.13—where client misconduct will harm the interests of someone other than the organizational client. Rule 1.6 allows for disclosure of client confidences *to a third party* when necessary to prevent substantial harm to the financial interests of another that is likely to result from a client's crime or fraud, which the lawyer's services have been used to advance. As noted above, SEC Rule 205 contains a similar provision, allowing but not requiring disclosure of information to the SEC.

In form, both SEC Rule 205 and the Model Rules support a conception of lawyers as gatekeepers. For example, Model Rule 1.13 requires an attorney to report up to a "higher authority" when confronted with unlawful conduct by a corporate constituent. However, the rule qualifies the obligation in a number of ways, thus making the effectiveness of the gatekeeper role a function of the individual lawyer's discretion. If the dominant paradigm motivating the rules was the duty of independence, this would perhaps be an optimal framework. However, the rule relies heavily on the zealous advocate paradigm, purporting to reach the ethical optimum by stressing the duty of loyalty to the organization, rather than recognizing any overarching ethical obligation to promote the integrity of the law. This emphasis may be problematic where, despite the rule's reliance on the entity theory of representation, the lawyer conflates the organizational client with senior management. Because most lawyers are directly accountable to management, the framing of the rule improperly suggests that the lawyer still owes a duty to a wrongdoing co-agent.

Similarly, while SEC Rule 205 clearly mandates up-the-ladder reporting of misconduct, it does so through vague and imprecise standards. Again, much turns on the discretion of the individual attorney to determine what constitutes a "material violation," or what an "appropriate response" from senior management might be. Of course, reliance on attorney discretion is an unavoidable, and indeed integral, element of the gatekeeper thesis. Still, skeptics argue that the vague terms of Rule 205 make the rule virtually impossible to enforce, and thus ineffective in encouraging lawyers to serve a gatekeeper function. For example, the triggering standard is formulated in a double negative: the attorney must determine whether it would be "*unreasonable* ... for a prudent and competent attorney *not to conclude* that it is reasonably likely that a material violation has occurred ..." As is the case with Model Rule 1.13, such hedging effectively disavows any notion of a transactional lawyer's duty of independence. Furthermore, as noted above, the rule permits but does not require reporting *out* when the lawyer reasonably believes that disclosure of confidential information is necessary to prevent a material violation likely to cause substantial injury to the organization or to investors. Such a permissive standard arguably fails to provide a sufficient counterbalance to the alignment of interests that exists between the lawyers for the organization and the other agents.

Model Rule 1.6's allowance of disclosure of client confidences to third parties is likewise discretionary, and applies *only if* the lawyer's services were being used in furtherance of the crime or fraud. This latter limitation is consistent with the general ethical duty not to assist in conduct that the lawyer knows is criminal or fraudulent. However, the combination of this limitation with the discretionary aspect of disclosure, suggests that Rule 1.6, like Rule 1.13, does not contemplate an extensive gatekeeper function. Thus, neither SEC Rule 205 nor the 2003 amendments to the Model Rules go as far as they could in sponsoring the concept of attorney-as-gatekeeper.

* * *

In the modern financial system markets are constantly evolving to develop more intricate and complex instruments and transactions. In this context, there is arguably now a greater need than ever for lawyers to ensure that such innovation does not undermine the spirit of the law by outpacing the letter of the law. The premise of the gatekeeper thesis is that attorneys have less incentive than other actors in an organization to go along with a fraudulent or criminal scheme because the gains will be small whereas the costs will be significant. Attorneys make significant investments in "reputational" capital, i.e. they earn credibility from serving many clients over many years in a lawful and effective manner. This investment deters them from risking that reputation on any particular client.

* * *

Opposition to the idea of attorneys as gatekeepers in the aftermath of the corporate scandals was strong enough to cause the SEC to table its "noisy withdrawal" proposal to Rule 205. During the Notice and Comment stage, supporters of the proposal argued that such a rule would be necessary to effectuate the policy behind Section 307. Without the provision, these commentators argued, an attorney would lack the leverage necessary to induce an intractable issuer to undertake appropriate remedial measures. Critics, however, countered that the rule would simply result in the exclusion of attorneys from situations where information was being exchanged that might cause an attorney to believe a material violation had been committed. In this situation, attorneys would not be capable of counseling compliance because they would not have access to critical information or the decision-making processes of the client constituents.

Furthermore, some commentators feared that the rule would impede compliance by encouraging lawyers to withdraw their representation for fear of liability, rather than provide legal advice when the issuer client needs it most. * * * These critics feared that an obligatory reporting-out requirement would convert lawyers from "advisers and advocates" for their clients into "quasi-regulators and judges" of them. Again, the argument relies heavily on the zealous advocate paradigm and reveals a reluctance to assign any ethical duty of independence to transactional lawyers.

For many commentators, then, the proffered justification was simply too attenuated to justify the costs to client confidentiality that it would entail. However, the critics may overstate the problem. The argument that a noisy withdrawal provision would result in unwarranted disclosures that adversely affect the client ignores the incentive structures that inhere in transactional legal work. Under the current business framework, even after the changes implemented by SOX, the attorney faces pressures to acquiesce in the decisions and conduct of managers and officers. * * *

Because the natural balance weighs in favor of accommodating the desires and decisions of the organizational client's constituents, the likelihood that a noisy withdrawal rule would result in a higher than optimal level of disclosures is low. Only after forming a reasonable belief based on credible evidence that a material violation is occurring, reporting that concern up the ladder, and receiving the report from the CLO or other higher authority investigating the possible violation, would an attorney have to consider reporting out. At that point, an attorney will likely have a sufficient understanding of the situation to determine whether, in fact, a material violation of the securities laws is ongoing or likely to occur. Given lawyers' general duties and incentives to accommodate the organization's decision-making process, unwarranted noisy withdrawals causing adverse effects on the company's stock value, are not likely.

The concern that too much emphasis on gatekeeping duties will discourage client constituents from consulting and communicating fully with lawyers, thus undermining the attorney's ability to effectively counsel and represent the client, is similarly overstated. As a practical matter, most senior managers and officers, while certainly eager to create innovative investment vehicles and execute value-maximizing transactions, do not want to do so at the risk of incurring liability for violating the securities laws. These people generally *want* to comply with the law, and they seek the advice of attorneys to do that. Thus, a reporting-out requirement is not likely to affect their decision to communicate with counsel because their goal is not only to execute transactions, but to do so in a way that is lawful.

For those officers and managers who may be willing to break the law, the reporting-out requirement could deter bad conduct. Because attorneys' knowledge and skill are frequently necessary to facilitate transactions, the manager or employee will be forced to seek counsel even if he realizes the legality of his objective is questionable. In these scenarios, a reporting-out requirement could help maintain the integrity of the system by one of two routes. First, such a requirement would increase the costs to the attorney who might be tempted to stretch the letter of the law to accommodate the manager in order to keep his job. Second, a noisy withdrawal requirement would provide an attorney the necessary leverage to talk the officer into compliance. If the manager continues on his course of bad conduct, the reporting up and out requirements will be triggered, and the manager will be subject to inquiries from upper

FYI

For other articles on the effect of SOX on lawyering in general and the duty of confidentiality in particular, *see, e.g.*, Schaefer, *Protecting a Business Entity from Itself Through Loyal Disclosure*, 118 Yale L.J. Pocket Part 152 (2009); Long, *Whistleblowing Attorneys and Ethical Infrastructures*, 68 Md. L. Rev. 786 (2009); Mahat, *A Carrot for the Lawyer: Providing Economic Incentives for In-House Lawyers in a Sarbanes-Oxley Regime*, 21 Geo. J. Legal Ethics 913 (2008).

management, the board, and ultimately enforcement agencies. This outcome is entirely consistent with an attorney's duty to counsel compliance with the law.

The above discussion illustrates that the purported negative consequences of the noisy withdrawal provision are not a foregone conclusion. Rather, if one takes as a starting point the proposition that transactional lawyers have an ethical duty of independence, the noisy withdrawal proposal may have significant merit. By requiring attorneys to withdraw from representation when faced with an intransigent client insistent on non-compliance, a noisy withdrawal provision would reinforce the attorney's duty to assess situations critically and render advice that is not only in the best interests of her client, but also is consistent with the spirit of the law.

Make the Connection

We will revisit the Sarbanes-Oxley regulations in Chapter 6.

CHAPTER 5

Conflicts of Interest

I. Introduction

From a client's perspective, the lawyer's duty of loyalty signifies more than a mere ethical obligation. For clients whose civil or criminal liability hangs in the balance, or for those whose business interests depend upon the successful completion of a transaction, the retention of counsel carries with it an implied expectation that the attorney will advocate devotedly and diligently, and will spurn conduct inimical to the clients' interests. In other words, clients often come to the lawyer-client relationship in a position of vulnerability, and as a practical imperative, are entitled to demand of their counsel undivided loyalty during and after the culmination of the representation. Of course, the lawyer's duty of loyalty is independent of the relative strength or weakness of the client's position. As the U.S. Supreme Court noted long ago:

> There are few business relations of life involving a higher trust and confidence than those of attorney and client, or generally speaking one more honorably and faithfully discharged, few more anxiously guarded by the law or governed by sterner principles of morality and justice; and it is the duty of the court to administer them in a corresponding spirit, and to be watchful and industrious, to see that confidence thus reposed shall not be used to the detriment of prejudice of the rights of the party bestowing it.

Stockton v. Ford, 52 U.S. (11 How.) 232, 247 (1850).

In the following materials, notice the many scenarios in which attorneys use confidence reposed "to the detriment of . . . the party bestowing it," and the ways in which contemporary ethical guidelines "anxiously guard" the attorney-client relationship.

II. Simultaneous Representations of Multiple Clients

A. Is There a Current Attorney-Client Relationship?

E. F. HUTTON & CO. v. *BROWN*

305 F. Supp. 371 (S.D. Tex. 1969)

NOEL, District Judge.

[Plaintiff E. F. Hutton & Company, Inc. ("Hutton"), a national brokerage firm, sued defendant John D. Brown, its former Houston regional vice president, for negligence and breach of fiduciary duty to the corporation. Hutton was represented by a Houston law firm ("the Houston firm"), and by Cahill, Gordon ("the New York firm"). Brown moved to disqualify both firms from continuing to represent or to advise Hutton in connection with the litigation, and to enjoin them from disclosing certain information to Hutton.]

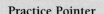

Practice Pointer

Prior to analyzing an alleged conflict of interest, courts may need to resolve the threshold question of whether an attorney-client relationship in fact came into existence. What factors are dispositive to the courts' determinations in the following decisions?

* * *

In part, this litigation is an outgrowth of the collapse of Westec Corporation in August, 1966. In late July or early August, a man named John Hurbrough approached Brown seeking a substantial loan from Hutton to be secured by Westec common stock. After negotiations, Brown authorized and made a loan to Hurbrough in the amount of $650,000, and caused Hutton to lend that sum to Hurbrough upon receipt of the collateral. Shortly after the loan was completed, however, the American Stock Exchange and the Securities and Exchange Commission (SEC) suspended trading in Westec stock. In due course, Brown and other Hutton personnel were asked by the SEC to testify in a formal investigation into the internal affairs of Westec and into trading in Westec stock. Subsequently, these same personnel were asked to testify at public hearings instituted by Westec's trustee in bankruptcy. In accordance with its usual practice in such cases, the New York firm dispatched one of its members (hereinafter called "the New York partner") to accompany Brown to each hearing. A member of the Houston firm (hereinafter called "the Houston partner") also accompanied Brown to the bankruptcy hearing.

* * *

Several months [later], Hutton terminated Brown's employment on the advice of counsel and commenced this action. The complaint alleges that Brown was negligent in authorizing and making the Hurbrough loan, and that he also breached his fiduciary duty to the corporation by failing to supervise an account executive adequately, a failure which allegedly resulted in the embezzlement of substantial sums of money from Hutton.

In this litigation, the Houston partner is counsel of record for Hutton. As more fully appears hereafter, the New York partner and other members of the New York firm have cooperated with the Houston partner in the preparation and presentation of Hutton's case. Shortly after suit was filed, Brown's present attorney requested the Houston partner and his firm to withdraw from further representation of Hutton in this litigation. The Houston partner refused, whereupon Brown filed the pending motion.

In support of his motion to disqualify, Brown asserts that the New York and Houston partners represented him individually when he appeared at the SEC and bankruptcy hearings and testified about the Hurbrough loan transaction. He asserts that the instant lawsuit may well turn in substantial part on his understanding of that transaction, and contends that counsel's continued representation of Hutton violates their subsisting duty to him as their former client. In opposition, Hutton denies that the partners ever represented Brown individually, and contends that even if they did, Brown is not now entitled to insist on their disqualification.

* * *

II. WHETHER COUNSEL REPRESENTED HUTTON ONLY

* * *

B. The SEC Investigative Hearing

The formal SEC investigation into trading in Westec stock was commenced shortly after trading was suspended. Proceedings were conducted by an investigating officer of the SEC, who examined witnesses under oath. Pursuant to regulation, the hearings were non-public: only the witness, his attorney, and representatives of the Texas State Securities Board and the SEC were allowed in the hearing room. Witnesses called by the investigating officer included the former officers and directors of Westec and parties to business transactions involving transfers of Westec stock.

Early in April 1967, the SEC requested Hutton to produce Brown to testify. Hutton so informed Brown. On the day before the hearing the New York partner and associate flew from New York to Houston. On arrival, they went directly to Brown's office. They and Brown discussed the Westec situation generally, and the Hurbrough loan transaction in particular. Brown was handed copies of the reports the associate had prepared for Hutton after his previous visits to Houston, and asked to study them. Both lawyers urged Brown to give responsive, truthful, and candid answers to all questions the SEC examiner might ask. In the course of the meeting, the partner informed Brown that he would accompany him to the hearing.

The next morning, both lawyers again met briefly with Brown, after which the partner accompanied him to the hearing. There the SEC's examining attorney informed Brown that the hearing was a non-public, formal investigative proceeding * * * . He then said to Brown, "I see you are accompanied by (the partner) here this morning. Is he your counsel in this proceeding?" Brown answered, "Yes."

Brown's answer was unexpected, if affidavits filed by the New York partner and the associate are to be believed. In those affidavits, both the partner and the associate claim that during their conference the evening before the hearing, Brown was specifically informed of the New York firm's position as counsel only for Hutton. They also allege that Brown agreed to explain their firm's position to the examining officer if he was asked whether the partner represented him individually.

Brown submitted his supplemental affidavit to deny these allegations. Neither he nor Hutton, however, has offered to present testimony or any other evidence to assist the Court in resolving the conflict between his affidavit and those of counsel. * * *

Food for Thought

Why are both sides reluctant to put on evidence on what went on between them? Could it be something about the private nature of those discussions?

The ensuing questioning focused primarily on the Hurbrough loan transaction, with particular reference to the scope of Brown's inquiry into the purpose of the loan, and Brown's knowledge of factual circumstances which might have caused him to doubt the loan's nonpurpose nature. Near the end of the examination, the partner declined the opportunity to ask Brown questions, although he did make one statement for the record. During Brown's testimony, the partner observed, took notes, and at two points caused Brown to clarify his answers.

The official transcript of the SEC hearing states that the New York partner appeared as "Counsel for John D. Brown."

C. The Bankruptcy Hearing

Shortly after the suspension of trading, Westec experienced severe financial difficulties, and corporate reorganization proceedings were begun under Chapter X of the Bankruptcy Act. Counsel for Westec's court-appointed trustee immediately began to investigate the affairs of the debtor, and soon instituted public hearings. One of the transactions which came under his scrutiny was the Hurbrough loan. Aware that the Houston firm represented Hutton locally, counsel for the trustee approached the Houston partner in August 1967 and requested that Hutton produce Brown and two other Hutton employees for examination. This request was reported to Brown and to Hutton's New York office. The latter requested the New York partner to be present in Houston during the examinations. On the day before Brown was due to testify, the New York partner flew to Houston. On arrival, he met briefly with the Houston partner and Brown. The next morning, the New York partner and the Houston partner accompanied Brown to the hearing.

As soon as Brown had been sworn, the Special Master informed him that the SEC was participating, and warned him that the facts developed at the hearing could constitute violations of the securities laws. [Then] the following colloquy took place:

The Master: "Do I understand correctly that you are represented by counsel of your choice here this morning?"

The Witness: "Yes, sir."

The Master: "Namely (the Houston partner) and (the New York partner)?"

The Witness: "Correct."

The Master: "Thank you, sir."

After this exchange, and following a discussion among counsel concerning documents which counsel for the trustee had subpoenaed from Hutton, counsel for the trustee questioned Brown briefly about his background and experience in the securities field, and then conducted a searching examination with emphasis on the Hurbrough loan transaction.

At the conclusion of the hearing, the New York partner returned to New York and reported to Hutton there with respect to Brown's testimony. Subsequently, when the transcript of Brown's testimony became available, the partner furnished a copy to Hutton in New York. On the transcript, the official court reporter listed the Houston partner and the New York partner as having appeared "on behalf of the witness, John D. Brown."

D. Findings and Conclusions

* * *

An attorney's appearance in a judicial or semi-judicial proceeding creates a presumption that an attorney-client relationship exists between the attorney and the person with whom he appears. This presumption shifts to Hutton, the party denying the existence of the relationship, the burden of persuasion. When the relationship is also evidenced by the entry of a formal appearance by the attorney on behalf of the person with whom he appears, the presumption becomes almost irrebuttable, for the entry of a formal appearance has quite properly been called record evidence of the highest character. In this case the Court finds that Hutton's opposition has failed to overcome the presumption that the New York and Houston partners represented Brown when he testified in the SEC and bankruptcy investigations.

Hutton's briefs and affidavits collect and cite a great number of facts to show that counsel represented only Hutton at the SEC and bankruptcy hearings. Several merely evidence Hutton's longstanding relationship with the New York and Houston firms. These are inapposite, for Brown does not assert that counsel did not represent Hutton at the two hearings. His motion is based on the proposition that counsel represented him as well. Hutton and its counsel are in error if they believe that an attorney cannot ever represent two clients with respect to a single matter. Attorneys frequently represent more than one party to a single transaction. Ordinarily there is nothing improper in such a practice so long as the attorney discloses the consequences of the joint representation to all of his clients, and all parties as well as the attorney consent.

The remaining evidence marshaled by Hutton is also insufficient to overcome the presumption. Brown admits that he cannot recall ever conversing with either firm about representing him personally, or paying either firm a fee. But, the relation of attorney and client may be implied from the conduct of the parties. It is not dependent on the payment of a fee, nor upon the execution of a formal contract. The Court takes judicial notice that it is not uncommon for corporate counsel to represent an individual corporate officer when he is sued as a result of actions he has taken within the ambit of his official duties. When this occurs, corporate counsel becomes counsel for the individual officer as well, even if the corporation pays all of his fee. If the officer is a party to a proceeding, and corporate counsel appear on his behalf, an implied relationship between them arises.

* * *

In asking the Court to consider all the circumstances when determining whether Brown believed counsel to be his attorneys, Hutton has proposed a proper inquiry. Brown's reasonable understanding of his relation with the attorneys is the controlling factor here. But when all circumstances are considered, it becomes clear that the transcripts of the two hearings reflect Brown's understanding of his relation with counsel accurately.

The formal SEC investigation had been convened to ascertain whether the securities laws or regulations had been violated. * * * When Brown was requested to appear, his conduct as an officer of Hutton had come under official scrutiny. Although Brown may not have known before the hearing that the focus of the inquiry would be on his approval of the Hurbrough loan, and particularly on his knowledge of its purpose, he was aware that the hearing was part of an SEC investigation into the trading in Westec stock. Brown and Hutton must have known, but if they did not actually know they were charged with knowledge by virtue of the securities laws which regulated them in the conduct of their business, that if criminal violations were discovered in the course of Brown's examination, his freedom, but not Hutton's, would be in jeopardy; and additionally, that each could be fined. Since he, as well as Hutton, was in potential criminal jeopardy from what might be discovered from his testimony, both were entitled to and under the circumstances needed, the assistance of counsel.

Similarly, when Brown appeared at the bankruptcy hearing he knew that counsel for the trustee had been conducting a through investigation of transactions involving Westec stock, including the Hurbrough loan. He knew that the trustee's announced intention was to bring a civil action against all persons and companies suspected of violating securities laws and regulations in dealings with Westec stock. He knew that no criminal indictments had yet been returned. At the hearing he was told that the SEC was a party to the proceeding, although it was not conducting the investigation. Brown was told that any evidence developed at the hearing could be used against him. Most certainly, he knew that such evidence would be available to the trustee or any other person in a subsequent civil action and to the Department of Justice in criminal prosecutions if either should be brought. When he appeared to testify, therefore, he faced potential civil liability as well as the possibility of criminal charges. Again he was entitled to and in need of counsel.

In this atmosphere it would seem reasonable and natural for Brown to have assumed that the New York partner represented him as well as Hutton when the partner accompanied him to the hearing before the SEC examiner; and, that the New York and Houston partners represented him as well as Hutton when they accompanied him to his examination by counsel for the Westec trustee. * * *

The reasonableness of Brown's assumption is not destroyed by the coincidence that Hutton, for some of the same reasons as he, needed to be represented by counsel at the hearings. Hutton and Brown agree that at the time of the two hearings, both they and counsel believed their interests to be identical. Certainly in these circumstances, Brown's awareness that counsel were representing Hutton could not have caused him to doubt that they were representing him as well.

The only other event urged by Hutton as establishing that Brown could not have understood counsel's appearances as appearances for him is the conversation alleged by the New York partner and associate to have occurred the evening before the SEC appearance. Counsel allege in their affidavits to have told Brown what to say the next day when he was asked of the attorney appearing with him was his attorney, and that Brown agreed to say that the attorney represented Hutton only. Brown, of course, denies that this discussion occurred.

In pondering this conflict in the affidavits, the Court has discovered that the record in this case provides many more questions than answers. If the conversation occurred as counsel allege, why did Brown not keep his promise when asked the expected question at the hearing? If so, why did the New York partner not cause Brown to clarify his answer, as he caused him to clarify other answers later in the examination? Why did the partner enter an appearance as counsel for Brown, not for Hutton? Why did he not speak to Brown after the hearing or take any steps to correct the transcript, if it was incorrect? Why did he again enter an appearance as counsel for Brown, not for Hutton, when Brown was called four months later to testify in the bankruptcy proceeding? Why did the Houston partner enter an appearance for Brown, not for Hutton, on the same occasion? Why did not the New York and Houston partners explain their firms' position with regard to representing Brown individually immediately before the bankruptcy hearing? Why did they not speak up when Brown described them as his attorneys, not as Hutton's? Why did they fail to correct the transcript of the bankruptcy hearing when it was received, if it was incorrect? Why did Hutton's New York management not correct the transcript on receipt, if it was incorrect? Why did Hutton and its counsel wait until after Brown's present counsel raised the issue—a year after the bankruptcy hearing and sixteen months after the alleged evening conversation—to deny that counsel had represented Brown at the SEC and bankruptcy hearings and to attack the accuracy of Brown's testimony?

* * * [T]he Court is impressed by the fact that after hearing Brown testify they were his counsel at the SEC hearing, New York counsel did not attempt to correct the record; and, that Brown gave the same answer as to his being represented by New York counsel when asked at the bankruptcy hearing four months later, although he had conferred further with the counsel after they had had a full opportunity to reflect on his testimony at the SEC hearing and to be certain that he not make the same mistake at the bankruptcy hearing, indeed if such a mistake had been made at the SEC hearing. Therefore, the Court is not persuaded that Brown agreed with New York counsel at a conference held in Houston on the evening before his appearance at the SEC hearing, to testify that New York counsel represented Hutton only. The Court will assume arguendo but not find that the conference transpired precisely as New York counsel now contend; but nevertheless, the Court finds from Brown's reply given to the SEC examiner the day follow-

ing the alleged conference and from his testimony before the Special Master in bankruptcy four months later, that Brown did not then appreciate the distinction between his individual and his representative capacity. He continued to believe that counsel would represent his interests, as well as Hutton's.

The Court thus finds that nothing advanced by Hutton has rebutted the presumption raised by counsel's appearances with Brown at the SEC and bankruptcy hearings. Nothing establishes that Brown believed or should have believed that the New York and Houston partners were appearing only for Hutton—in fact, the record has persuaded this Court to the contrary. Not until after Brown had moved to disqualify the New York and Houston partners and firms from continuing to represent Hutton in this case did Hutton or either partner attempt to disclaim the partners' appearances for Brown individually as they are revealed in Brown's statements at the hearings and in the official transcripts. Their belated disclaimers in opposition to Brown's motion to disqualify now come too late. An attorney may not wait to contradict the record until it is in the interest of himself of his client to do so.

* * *

Practice Pointer

It's clear that if a lawyer does not want to be saddled with the obligation of an attorney-client relationship, she must clarify any ambiguity on the subject. What would you have done in your discussion with Brown—and during the two proceedings—to clarify that you had not entered into an attorney-client relationship with Brown?

Food for Thought

Would it make any difference if, at the time of the representation, Brown's and Hutton's interests were clearly in conflict? With respect to whether there was an attorney-client relationship with Brown, the answer is no. The question of the existence of an attorney-client relationship is answered from the *client's* perspective. It's not up to the client to figure out that the person he thinks is his lawyer is operating under a conflict of interest.

ROHM AND HAAS CO. v. DOW CHEMICAL CO.

2009 WL 445609 (Del. Ch. 2009)

WILLIAM B. CHANDLER, III, Chancellor.

Dear Counsel:

Before me is defendants' motion to disqualify Wachtell, Lipton, Rosen & Katz ("Wachtell") from conducting discovery against The Dow Chemical Company and examining Dow witnesses. I have considered the parties' briefs, and oral argument was presented to the Court on February 11, 2009. For the reasons set forth briefly below, the motion to disqualify is denied.

Dow argues that Wachtell should be disqualified because the firm's representation of Rohm and Haas Company in this matter presents a conflict of interest as a result of Wachtell's representation of Dow. Dow alleges that Wachtell is in violation of the Delaware Rules of Professional Conduct because Dow is both a current client of Wachtell and a client whom Wachtell has previously represented in matters substantially related to the instant proceedings. Dow alleges that it is prejudiced in this action because Wachtell was privy to sensitive information in its capacity as Dow's counsel.

Dow argues that it is a current client of Wachtell because the firm never took steps to inform Dow that it was no longer a client following Wachtell's representation of Dow in 2007 and 2008 in connection with the termination of two Dow executives and potential defensive measures in response to rumors of a takeover bid. * * *

Plaintiff Rohm and Haas counters that there is not a concurrent conflict of interest because Dow is no longer a Wachtell client. According to Rohm and Haas, it should have been clear to Dow that Dow was no longer a Wachtell client when the firm appeared opposite Dow in its representation of Rohm and Haas in the negotiations of the initial confidentiality agreement and the merger agreement in mid-2008. * * *

After careful consideration of the parties' arguments, * * * I am not convinced by the argument that Dow reasonably believes it is a current client of Wachtell or that Dow relied on such a belief. Dow knew that Wachtell was representing Rohm and Hass during the negotiations of the merger agreement and did not object. Rather, Dow obtained its own separate counsel to represent Dow in the merger negotiations. Wachtell sent its final bill to Dow in June 2008, and there is no convincing evidence that Wachtell continued to perform services for Dow that would justify a reasonable belief by Dow that it is a current Wachtell client. I am also not convinced by Dow's argument that there was an implicit promise by Wachtell that they would represent Rohm and Haas in the negotiations but would discontinue the representation if litigation arose. In short, if Dow truly felt that they were a current client of Wachtell and that they should not be "across the table" from their own lawyers, then Dow should have objected at the outset of the negotiations of the merger agreement that eventually led to this litigation rather than waiting until this expedited litigation was commenced to attempt to make Rohm and Haas obtain new counsel.

* * *

For the foregoing reasons, the motion to disqualify is denied.

Very truly yours,

William B. Chandler III

MURRAY v. METROPOLITAN LIFE INS. CO.

583 F.3d 173 (2d Cir. 2009)

DENNIS JACOBS, Chief Judge:

Plaintiffs in this class action were policyholders of Metropolitan Life Insurance Company when it was a mutual insurance company. They complain that they were misled and shortchanged in the transaction by which the company demutualized in 2000. Nine years after the action was commenced and five weeks before trial was scheduled to begin, plaintiffs moved to disqualify the lead counsel for Metropolitan Life Insurance Company and MetLife, Inc. ("MetLife"), Debevoise & Plimpton LLP ("Debevoise"). The grounds alleged related to that firm's representation of MetLife in the underlying demutualization. * * *

The district court disqualified Debevoise on the ground that its representation of MetLife in the 2000 demutualization made it counsel to the policyholders as well. On appeal, plaintiffs urge affirmance on that ground * * *.

We conclude that * * * Debevoise did not have an attorney-client relationship with the policyholders by virtue of its representation of MetLife * * *. Accordingly, we reverse.

I

In 1915, MetLife converted from a stock life insurance company to a mutual insurance company. On April 7, 2000, MetLife completed a months-long process of demutualization back to a stock insurance company. Debevoise served as MetLife's corporate counsel in that transaction.

On April 18, 2000, plaintiffs filed this class action lawsuit in the Eastern District of New York, alleging that MetLife violated federal securities laws by misrepresenting or altogether omitting certain information from the materials provided to its policyholders during the demutualization process. In June 2007, MetLife invoked the attorney-client privilege to prevent plaintiffs' discovery of particular communications between MetLife and its in-house and outside counsel. The district court denied a protective order on the ground that the plaintiff policyholders were the owners of the mutual company and were therefore clients of Debevoise during the demutualization.

Following discovery and the usual preliminaries, the trial was set to begin on September 8, 2009. When last-minute settlement negotiations failed, plaintiffs moved to disqualify Debevoise on July 31, 2009—more than nine years after the action was commenced, more than two years after the court ruled that plaintiffs were clients of Debevoise, and five weeks before trial.

Plaintiffs argued that disqualification was appropriate for the same reason articulated by the district court to support its 2007 discovery ruling: Debevoise had been counsel to plaintiffs in the demutualization and cannot now jump sides to become adverse to plaintiffs at trial. * * *

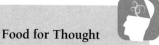

Food for Thought

Why does the Court make so much about the timing of the disqualification motion?

MetLife's response invoked the doctrine of laches; argued that as a matter of law the policyholders of a mutual insurance company are not *a priori* the clients of that company's corporate counsel; * * * and charged that the motion was made for improper tactical purposes.

* * *

III

We conclude that plaintiffs were not clients of Debevoise. It is well-settled that outside counsel to a corporation represents the corporation, not its shareholders or other constituents. This rule is entirely consonant with Rule 1.13 of the New York Rules of Professional Conduct, N.Y. R. Prof'l Conduct § 1.13(a) ("[A] lawyer employed or retained by an organization . . . is the lawyer for the organization and not for any of the constituents."), and with the Restatement (Third) of the Rule Governing Lawyers, § 96 cmt. b (explaining that a lawyer retained by a corporation has an attorney-client relationship with the corporation, but the lawyer "does not thereby also form a client-lawyer relationship with all or any individuals employed by it or who direct its operations or who have an ownership or other beneficial interest in it, such as shareholders").

These principles apply as well to a mutual insurance company. Under New York law, "[a] mutual insurance company is a cooperative enterprise in which the policyholders constitute the members for whose benefit the company is organized, maintained and operated." But a policyholder, "even in a mutual company, [is] in no sense a partner of the corporation which issued the policy, and . . . the relation between the policy-holder and the company [is] one of contract, measured by the terms of the policy."

The district court's 2007 decision reasoned that plaintiffs were clients of Debevoise during the demutualization "because they were MetLife's beneficiaries and the beneficiaries of MetLife counsel's advice." But this does not distinguish a mutual insurance company from any other corporation.

Not every beneficiary of a lawyer's advice is deemed a client. *See* N.Y. R. Prof'l Conduct 2.3(a) ("A lawyer may provide an evaluation of a matter affecting a client for the use of *someone other than the client* if the lawyer reasonably believes that making the evaluation is compatible with other aspects of the lawyer's relationship with the client.") (emphasis added); *see also Fiala v. Metro. Life Ins. Co.,* 6 A.D.3d 320, 322, 776 N.Y.S.2d 29, 32 (1st Dep't 2004) ("[A]n insurance company does not owe its policyholder a common-law fiduciary duty except when it is called upon to defend its insured."); N.Y. State Bar Ass'n, Comm. on Prof'l Ethics, Op. No. 477 (1977) (explaining that the lawyer for the executor of an estate need not provide substantive legal advice to potential beneficiaries because doing so would violate the lawyer's duty to provide undivided loyalty to his client, the executor).

In light of these principles, and without any extraordinary circumstances raised by the parties, we conclude that the policyholders in this case were not clients of Debevoise.

* * *

For More Information

The RESTATEMENT is an excellent starting point for further reading on issues relating to the formation of an attorney-client relationship. Section 14 of the RESTATEMENT may provide some clarity with respect to when an attorney-client relationship has been created:

A relationship of client and lawyer arises when:
(1) a person manifests to a lawyer the person's intent that the lawyer provide legal services for the person; and either
(a) the lawyer manifests to the person consent to do so; or
(b) the lawyer fails to manifest lack of consent to do so, and the lawyer knows or reasonably should know that the person reasonably relies on the lawyer to provide the services; or
(2) a tribunal with power to do so appoints the lawyer to provide the services.

See the Comment and Reporter's Note accompanying § 14 for further applications of the general rule.

B. Simultaneous Representation Standards

Rule 1.7—Conflict of Interest: Current Clients

(a) Except as provided in paragraph (b), a lawyer shall not represent a client if the representation involves a concurrent conflict of interest. A concurrent conflict of interest exists if:

(1) the representation of one client will be directly adverse to another client; or

(2) there is a significant risk that the representation of one or more clients will be materially limited by the lawyer's responsibilities to another client, a former client or a third person or by a personal interest of the lawyer.

Take Note

Assuming the formation of an attorney-client relationship, the next inquiry focuses on whether an interest of the lawyer, another client or third party is in conflict with that relationship. Rule 1.7 provides guidance for whether a concurrent conflict exists and establishes the requirements for continuing the representation despite the conflict.

(b) Notwithstanding the existence of a concurrent conflict of interest under paragraph (a), a lawyer may represent a client if:

(1) the lawyer reasonably believes that the lawyer will be able to provide competent and diligent representation to each affected client;

(2) the representation is not prohibited by law;

(3) the representation does not involve the assertion of a claim by one client against another client represented by the lawyer in the same litigation or other proceeding before a tribunal; and

(4) each affected client gives informed consent, confirmed in writing.

1. *"Directly Adverse" Under Rule 1.7(a)(1):*

Litigation Conflicts

[Question 1]

Tilley's equipment and crew were involved in an accident where Starkey lost an arm. Two years later, Tilley asks Insurance Co. to retain Lawyer when Starkey sues. Unknown to Tilley, Lawyer helps Insurance Co. develop a claim that the Insurance Co. had no obligation to provide coverage because Tilley had notice at the time of the accident and failed to comply with the policy requirement of informing the insurer. Insurance Co. seeks declaratory judgment relieving it of responsibility to Tilley.

Did the Lawyer operated under a conflict of interest?

(A) No, because Tilley failed to comply with the terms of the policy.

→ (B) No, because Insurance Co. paid for Lawyer's services.

(C) No, because a Lawyer can represent two clients at the same time.

→ (D) Yes, because the Insurance Co. and Tilley were adverse as to whether Tilley had rights under the insurance policy.

[Question 2]

L&C represents Intel for immigration matters related to its plant in Israel. Chipper, Inc. asks L&C to represent it in a billion dollar patent infringement claim against Intel.

Must L&C obtain Intel's informed consent before agreeing to represent Chipper, Inc.?

(A) Yes, because representing Chipper, Inc. would result in L&C being directly adverse to Intel.

(B) Yes, because L&C would be representing one client against another in the same litigation.

(C) No, because L&C can represent both Intel and Chipper, Inc. competently.

(D) No, because there would be no direct adversity or material limitation.

[Question 3]

Attorney Alpha currently represents Builder, a building contractor who is the plaintiff in a suit to recover for breach of a contract to build a house. Builder also has pending before the zoning commission a petition to rezone property Builder owns. Builder is represented by Attorney Beta in the zoning matter.

Neighbor, who owns property adjoining that of Builder, has asked Alpha to represent Neighbor in opposing Builder's petition for rezoning. Neighbor knows that Alpha represents Builder in the contract action.

May Alpha represent Neighbor in the zoning matter?

(A) Yes, if there is no common issue of law or fact between the two matters.

(B) Yes, because one matter is a judicial proceeding and the other is an
administrative proceeding.

(C) No, because Alpha is currently representing Builder in the contract
action.

(D) No, if there is a possibility that both matters will be appealed to the
same court.

Non-Litigation Conflicts

[Question 4]

L represents Ballet Dancer ("BD") in an employment negotiation with Ballet. Ballet asks L to represent it in real estate negotiations with the Lincoln
Center. Does L need BD's consent in order to represent Ballet in the real
estate negotiation?

(A) Yes, because they are directly adverse.

(B) Yes, because L does not know of the Ballet's plans for the negotiations
with BD.

(C) No, because no significant risk of material limitation exists.

(D) No, because the two matters are unrelated.

[Question 5]

Same facts as Question 4, *supra*. With informed consent from both BD and
Ballet, L agrees to represent Ballet in the real estate negotiation with the
Lincoln Center. L knows confidential financial information about both BD
and Ballet. The BD-Ballet negotiation subsequently becomes hostile.

**Is there any problem with continued representation? Can BD or Ballet revoke
consent?**

Comment to Rule 1.7

Loyalty to a current client prohibits undertaking representation directly adverse to
that client without that client's informed consent. Thus, absent consent, a lawyer
may not act as an advocate in one matter against a person the lawyer represents

in some other matter, even when the matters are wholly unrelated. The client as to whom the representation is directly adverse is likely to feel betrayed, and the resulting damage to the client-lawyer relationship is likely to impair the lawyer's ability to represent the client effectively. In addition, the client on whose behalf the adverse representation is undertaken reasonably may fear that the lawyer will pursue that client's case less effectively out of deference to the other client,

Take Note

Directly adverse conflicts from simultaneous representation of multiple clients are not limited to litigation; such conflicts arise also in transactional matters. For example, many courts have held that a lawyer cannot represent both sides of a commercial real estate transaction. Why not?

i.e., that the representation may be materially limited by the lawyer's interest in retaining the current client. Similarly, a directly adverse conflict may arise when a lawyer is required to cross-examine a client who appears as a witness in a lawsuit involving another client, as when the testimony will be damaging to the client who is represented in the lawsuit. On the other hand, simultaneous representation in unrelated matters of clients whose interests are only economically adverse, such as representation of competing economic enterprises in unrelated litigation, does not ordinarily constitute a conflict of interest and thus may not require consent of the respective clients.

REPRESENTATION OF LENDER AND BORROWERS VIOLATED DUTIES FOR RESIDENTIAL HOME LOANS

25 ABA Lawyers' Manual on Professional Conduct 566

An attorney's pattern of representing both lender and borrower in real estate transactions without obtaining their informed written consent warrants a suspension from practice of three months followed by a one-year probationary period, the Delaware Supreme Court decided Sept. 24 (In re Katz, Del., No. 442, 2009, 9/24/09).

* * *

In the course of his solo tax and estate practice, lawyer I. Jay Katz started handling private loan transactions in which one of his clients, Robert Lubach, loaned money to people in dire financial trouble in return for a mortgage on their homes.

* * *

Katz represented both the lender and the borrowers in these transactions. For one of the clients, who received four loans from the lender, Katz did not have the borrower sign a consent to the dual representation.

The court found that Katz violated Rule 1.7 by representing that borrower in loan transactions in which another client was the lender, without having obtained the borrower's informed consent, confirmed in writing, to the concurrent representation.

* * *

Katz never tried to obtain the lender's written informed consent, and his attempts to obtain the borrower's consent for each loan transaction "were all untimely and uninformed," the court said.

In several of the transactions, Katz provided the borrower—on the very day of the closing—with a "statement of representation and disclosure" that made certain disclosures required by the "Interpretive Guideline Re: Residential real estate transactions" that accompanies Rule 1.16 in Delaware.

The court concluded that Katz violated the interpretative guideline by failing to notify borrowers of their absolute right to retain an attorney of their choice, and by failing to advise them of his concurrent representation of the lender in the loan transactions—including a statement that the other representation might be "possibly conflicting" and might adversely affect the exercise of his professional judgment on their behalf.

* * *

The court emphasized that * * * a lawyer is supposed to make timely written disclosure of a concurrent conflict before the representation is commenced.

* * *

Finding that Katz's misconduct was knowing and caused potential and actual injury to all of his clients, the court decided that the discipline recommended by the Board on Professional Responsibility—a public reprimand—was not a sufficient sanction.

Applying Standard 4.32 of the ABA Standards for Imposing Lawyer Sanctions, the court concluded that a suspension was more appropriate. It suspended Katz for three months, followed by a one-year period of probation on specified conditions.

2. *"Materially Limited" Under Rule 1.7(a)(2)*

[Question 6]

Father, Son, and Daughter use attorney Alpha for family and business purposes. In front of Son and Daughter, Father executes a will with Alpha in the morning. In the afternoon, Father subsequently changes his will to be more favorable to Son, and asks Alpha to keep it confidential from his daughter. Daughter consults Alpha regarding her estate plan and asks him to explain her father's will. Alpha describes only the morning will. Is Alpha's conduct problematic?

(A) No, because Alpha was not representing Daughter with regard to Father's will.

(B) No, because Alpha did not tell Daughter about the later will.

(C) No, because Daughter had no legal right to a greater share under the will.

(D) Yes, because Alpha had a conflict of interest.

3. *"Reasonably Believes" and "Competent and Diligent Representation" Under Rule 1.7(b) (1):*

[Question 7]

Four years ago, Attorney represented Husband and Wife, both high school teachers, in the purchase of a new home. Since then, Attorney prepared their tax returns and drafted their wills.

Recently, Husband called Attorney and told her that he and Wife had decided to divorce, but wanted the

> FYI
>
> As the Comment to Rule 1.7 notes, a conflict of interest may exist if there is a significant risk that a lawyer's ability "to consider, recommend or carry out an appropriate course of action" will be materially limited due to the lawyer's other interests. This result obtains even where there is no direct adverseness. An example cited in the Comment may prove instructive:
>
> > [A] lawyer asked to represent several individuals seeking to form a joint venture is likely to be materially limited in the lawyer's ability to recommend or advocate all possible positions that each might take because of the lawyer's duty of loyalty to the others. The conflict in effect forecloses alternatives that would otherwise be available to the client. The mere possibility of subsequent harm does not itself require disclosure and consent. The critical questions are the likelihood that a difference in interests will eventuate and, if it does, whether it will materially interfere with the lawyer's independent professional judgment in considering alternatives or foreclose courses of action that reasonably should be pursued on behalf of the client.

matter to be resolved amicably. Husband stated that they were planning to file and process their own divorce case, utilizing the state's new streamlined divorce procedure, applicable in "no-fault" cases where there are no minor children. Husband asked if Attorney would agree to work with them to prepare a financial settlement agreement that could be presented to the divorce court, reminding Attorney that the couple's assets were modest and that they wanted to "split it all down the middle."

After considering the risks of a conflict of interest arising in this limited representation, Attorney wrote to the couple separately, and advised each that he or she might be better off with separate lawyers, but that Attorney would assist with the financial settlement agreement, charging an hourly fee of $140 per hour, provided that they were in complete agreement and remained so.

Attorney advised that if a conflict developed, or if either party was dissatisfied or uncomfortable about continuing with the joint representation, Attorney would withdraw and would not represent either party from that point forward, forcing them to start all over again with separate lawyers. Finally, Attorney cautioned Husband and Wife that Attorney would be representing both of them equally, would not and could not favor one or the other, and that their separate communications to her could not be kept confidential from the other party. Both Husband and Wife signed their individual copy of the letter, consenting to the joint representation, and returned them to Attorney.

Was it proper for Attorney to accept the representation on these terms?

(A) Yes, because there was little risk that the interests of either Husband or Wife would be materially prejudiced if no settlement was reached.

Make the Connection

Paragraph (b)(1) of Rule 1.7 provides that, despite the existence of a current conflict, representation is permissible so long as the lawyer "reasonably believes" that the lawyer will be able to provide "competent" and "diligent" representation to each client. In other words, clients may not consent to a conflicted representation unless the lawyer can first reasonably conclude that the lawyer will be able to provide the clients with competent and diligent representation.

"Competent" representation requires that a lawyer employ the legal knowledge, skill, thoroughness and preparation that are reasonably necessary for the representation. Rule 1.1. "Diligent" representation requires that the lawyer act with "reasonable diligence and promptness in representing a client." Rule 1.3. The Comment to Rule 1.3 advises that lawyers should take whatever lawful and ethical measures are required to vindicate their clients' causes. Diligence further requires that the lawyer "act with commitment and dedication to the interests of the client and with zeal in advocacy upon the client's behalf."

(B) Yes, because Attorney had previously represented Husband and Wife in their joint affairs.

(C) No, because Attorney conditioned representation upon receiving a waiver of client confidentiality.

(D) No, unless Attorney advised both Husband and Wife, in writing, that they should seek independent counsel before agreeing to enter into the financial settlement on the terms proposed.

SANFORD v. COMMONWEALTH OF VIRGINIA

2009 WL 4430295 (E.D. Va. 2009)

ROBERT E. PAYNE, Senior District Judge.

[Plaintiff's decedent, John Sanford, had been admitted to a Virginia-run hospital for the removal of his kidney. Sanford was mentally and physically disabled due to a neurological condition. His head and body shook almost continuously; he was able to walk only with the assistance of a walker, and wore leg braces from knee to foot. Two days after his surgery, Sanford's brother found Sanford naked, delirious and hallucinating in the hallway of the hospital, struggling to hold himself upright without the assistance of his walker. The medical staff were aware of Sanford's condition and summoned police officers (the "VCUPD") to restrain him. The next day, other family members found Sanford partially disrobed on the floor in his hospital room cleaning imaginary blood. Sanford became delirious again the following day, allegedly as a result of medications he had been prescribed by the hospital's staff. The nurses summoned the VCUPD, who allegedly seized Sanford, wrestled him to the ground, handcuffed him and held him "prone." Sanford remained in this position for approximately thirty minutes, during which time he was injected with Haldol, a sedative. When the VCUPD finally turned Sanford over, they discovered that he was dead.

Sanford's family sued the VCUPD and the hospital staff (the "MCV defendants") on claims including gross negligence, battery, false imprisonment, intentional infliction of emotional distress and a violation of Sanford's rights under the Fourth and Four-

Food for Thought

Assuming there is a conflict of interest on the part of defense counsel, why should the plaintiffs be able to complain about it? Wouldn't the conflict of interest actually help them? If the plaintiffs are just trying to make the defendants' lives miserable by making them find their own counsel, should that motivation be considered by the court in determining whether to disqualify the defense lawyers?

teenth Amendments. The same lawyer represented all of the VCUPD defendants. Another lawyer represented the MCV defendants. The plaintiffs have moved to disqualify the lawyers for operating under a conflict of interest.]

DISCUSSION

[*Ed.'s Note*—The court recites Virginia State Bar Rule of Professional Conduct 1.7, which tracks the Model Rule.]

* * *

A. VCUPD Officer Defendants

First, there is, according to the Plaintiffs, the conflict between Colonel Fuller and all of the subordinate VCU police officers respecting the adequacy of training for dealing with hospital patients. * * * In sum, it is the position of Colonel Fuller that his officers are adequately trained to deal with hospital patients because their general training about how to deal with handcuffed persons includes instruction to check for signs of physical distress and for difficulty in breathing.

The testimony of Officer LaVigne is that subordinate officers received no training for handling patients in a health care setting and Officer Carter testifies that she is not trained to look for signs of distress or difficulty in breathing. * * *

Thus, on this topic, the adequacy of training, there appears to be a substantial discrepancy in the testimony of the VCUPD officer defendants and an incompatibility in positions that the VCUPD officer defendants occupy vis-à-vis Colonel Fuller. The possibilities for settlement also appear to be substantially different on the claims and liabilities in question as to Colonel Fuller, on one hand, and the VCUPD officer defendants, on the other.

It is also asserted by the Plaintiffs that there is conflict between the VCUPD officer defendants who initially responded to the summons to Sanford's room and effectuated the seizure by handcuffing Sanford and keeping him facedown on the floor, and those officers who arrived on the scene later. This conflict arises out of the undisputed evidence that the accepted protocol for the VCUPD in situations such as the one here at issue is that the first responding officer provides the lead and that subsequently responding officers follow the instructions of the lead officer. * * *

[The subsequently responding officers] would be able to assert that their conduct was governed by protocol, which had been set in place when they arrived upon the scene and by the instructions of [first responder] Officer Bailey. Thus, they could argue that the reasonableness of their conduct, which lies at the heart of their ability to defend a number of the claims against them, must be assessed differently than the conduct of Officer Bailey who was the one who first laid hands on Sanford and who also dictated that Sanford be kept in handcuffs and be kept facedown in the prone position. The positional incompatibility in presenting a defense is obvious. * * *

* * *

B. VCU Medical Defendants

The motion asserts several conflicts among the VCU medical defendants. First, Dr. Meguid diagnosed Sanford's condition as opium withdrawal rather than delirium, a condition which Dr. Meguid stated might be present in Sanford only in its waning stages. Several defense experts (a pharmacist, a toxicologist, and a psychiatrist) have expressed the opinion that Sanford's symptoms were consistent with delirium, not with opium withdrawal. The Plaintiffs intend to offer evidence that Dr. Meguid's diagnosis was erroneous and that, as a consequence of the misdiagnosis, certain of Sanford's medications were resumed without the necessary, precedent tests. As a consequence, it will be said by other expert witnesses that certain drug levels reached toxic levels and created episodes of delirium which led to the decision to restrain Sanford and hence to his death.

In other words, the expert opinions of the defense experts will support the conclusion that Dr. Meguid misdiagnosed Sanford. There is a medical malpractice claim against Dr. Meguid and an attorney representing Dr. Meguid would certainly want to present expert testimony that Dr. Meguid's diagnosis was correct. However, there appears to be no such evidence offered on his behalf and, indeed, the defense experts render opinions which make it quite difficult for Dr. Meguid to assert that his diagnosis was a correct one. On this record, there is a significant incompatibility in position between Dr. Meguid and the other medical professionals on this issue. * * *

Second, it is undisputed that Dr. Meguid made a medical note that Haldol should be avoided for Sanford, if possible. Further, Dr. Meguid recognized that Haldol might not be appropriate for a patient with Biemond's Syndrome and that the drug could have adverse cardiac side effects. Dr. Maiberger, however, prescribed Haldol and Nurse Brown or Nurse Ferguson administered Haldol. Neither of the three were aware of Dr. Meguid's cautions respecting the use of Haldol for Sanford. At oral argument on the disqualification motion, counsel for the medical defendants asserted that it was the position of Dr. Maiberger and Nurse Brown that they had no reason to be aware of Dr. Meguid's caution because Dr. Meguid had not entered his note in the computerized system which, in turn, would have alerted the nurses to Dr. Meguid's cautionary advice. That failure is a further indictment of Dr. Meguid.

Quite clearly there are conflicting positions presented by the testimony. Dr. Meguid certainly is entitled to present, as part of his defense, that he cautioned against the use of Haldol. At the same time, Dr. Maiberger and the nurses intend to say that they had no reason to know of this caution because Dr. Meguid did not act in accord with established procedure at the Hospital to take the necessary actions to alert them to his caution. Counsel for Dr. Maiberger and the nurses, therefore, would certainly want to point the finger of fault toward Dr. Meguid as part of the means of defending Dr. Maiberger and the nurses.

* * *

C. The Legal Principles

* * * Rule 1.7 of the Virginia Rules of Professional Conduct governs conflicts of interest. * * * Rule 1.7 prohibits a lawyer from representing a client if the representation involves a concurrent conflict of interest, which exists if "there is a significant risk that the representation of one or more clients will be materially limited by the lawyer's responsibilities to another client." The notes to Rule 1.7 make clear that "[l]oyalty and independent judgment are essential elements in the lawyer's relationship to a client." This assessment ought to be undertaken at the beginning of the representation of multiple clients in the same action, but the rules make clear that if the conflict arises after the representation has been undertaken, it is the obligation of the lawyer to withdraw from the representation.

* * * It is also important to note that "[s]imultaneous representation of parties whose interests in litigation may conflict, such as co-plaintiffs or co-defendants, is governed by paragraph (a)(2)" of Rule 1.7. "An impermissible conflict may exist by reason of substantial discrepancy in the parties' testimony, incompatibility in positions in relation to an opposing party or the fact that there are substantially different possibilities of settlement of the claims or liabilities in question."

* * *

It is, of course, important in our system of justice that parties be free to retain counsel of their choice. However, this Court has held that the right of one to retain counsel of his choosing is secondary in importance to the Court's duty to maintain the highest ethical standards of professional conduct to insure and preserve trust in the integrity of the bar. Accordingly, there must be a balance between the client's free choice of counsel and the maintenance of the highest and ethical and professional standards in the legal community. Moreover, the party seeking disqualification has a high standard of proof to show that disqualification is warranted. These principles are well settled.

The rules of professional responsibility make clear that the resolution of conflict of interest questions is principally the responsibility of the lawyer undertaking the litigation. However, those rules also make equally clear that, during litigation, it is appropriate for a court to raise the question in certain circumstances, or the conflict can be raised properly by opposing counsel. Such an objection should be viewed with caution, however, for it can be misused as a technique of harassment. * * *

[T]he asserted conflict must be a real one and not a hypothetical one or a fanciful one. Put another way, disqualification simply cannot be based on mere speculation that a chain of events whose occurrence theoretically could lead counsel to act counter to his client's interests might in fact occur. The applicable rule requires disqualification when the independent professional judgment of the lawyer is likely to be affected. Accordingly, some stronger indicator than judicial intuition or surmise on the part of opposing counsel is necessary to warrant the drastic step of disqualification of counsel.

* * *

It is obvious from reviewing the motions for summary judgment and the expert opinions that counsel, both for the VCUPD officers and the VCU medical defendants, have staked out defensive positions that they think are the best positions for the defense side of the case considered as a whole. It does not appear, however, that counsel have considered, or that they appreciate, how the assertion of those positions could affect the ability of each individual defendant to defend herself or himself by presenting arguments that other defendants are really responsible for Sanford's tragic death even though another defendant may have had some involvement in the circumstances leading up to that death. * * *

* * * [T]he Court must conclude that the conflicts alleged here are real ones that are currently in existence. The conflicts also present very real risks of serious, adverse consequences for the rights of the litigants, mostly the defendants, but also those of the plaintiffs.

Moreover, the nature of the conflicts is such that disqualification is necessary to ensure and preserve trust in the integrity of the bar. The present record contains testimony that tends to inculpate the VCUPD officers in different degrees. That same testimony would permit some VCUPD officer defendants to urge their exoneration by arguing that other VCUPD officer defendants are the cause of Sanford's death. The same is true respecting the VCU medical defendants.

Each defendant is entitled to use the record to exonerate himself or herself even if to do so inculpates another defendant in the same category of defendants (*i.e.*, the same group of clients).

The pleadings, motions and briefs filed thus far afford no indication that such a course in being pursued on behalf of any defendant who, from the record evidence, could take it. * * * The option can be exercised by the asking of questions, or by refraining from asking questions and by asking for instructions. And, most importantly, it can be pursued in closing argument. Of course, a lawyer who represents all defendants is not free to pursue such a course on behalf of any defendant because to do so would be to act adversely to one or more of his other clients. On the other hand, the failure to pursue such a course compromises the interest of any defendant on whose behalf that approach could be taken at trial.

* * *

Counsel for each group of defendants asserts that disqualification is not required because all of the defendants have consented to multiple representations. It is true that Rule 1.7(b) provides that the written consent of the client may allow counsel to represent clients who otherwise would not be representable under Rule 1.7(a)(2). However, there are four conditions to a representation under the consent process: (1) the lawyer must reasonably believe that he will be able to provide competent representation to each affected client; (2) the representation must not be prohibited by law; (3) the representation does not involve the assertion of a claim by one client against another; and (4) the waiver of conflict must be in writing. Rule 1.7(b). The second and third conditions above do not present any problems for the counsel in this case. As will be explained below, the fourth condition, for purposes of the Plaintiff's motion, is not dispositive, and the Court will assume compliance therewith. However, the Court cannot conclude that any lawyer reasonably could believe, as the first condition requires, that he would be able to provide competent and diligent representation to each of the affected clients identified in the foregoing discussion of conflicts.

* * *

For consent to be effective under Rule 1.7(b), it must be meaningful and that, in turn, necessitates that the clients be advised clearly about the conflicts that might very well arise.

The record shows that each of the VCUPD defendants, including the legal guardian for the now incompetent Colonel Fuller, signed documents stating the following:

> I, [Defendant's name], hereby declare that, notwithstanding the existence of any possible conflicts of interest, I knowingly and voluntarily consent to the continued representation by [counsel for the VCUPD Defendants] in this matter. This informed consent is made after consultation with my attorney.

Although counsel for these defendants asserts that the consent was provided knowingly and voluntarily, there is no basis in the record to conclude that the affected defendants had the very real conflicts described to them thoroughly and accurately.

And, such a showing is essential especially where, as here, the conflicts are so patent and so numerous and have such potentially adverse consequences for many of the defendant clients. The absence of that showing alone renders the record on consent here insufficient to animate the exception permitted by Rule 1.7(b).

* * *

Setting aside the importance of obtaining properly executed written consent, to focus on the particularities of the conflict waivers is to miss the key point. As provided in Note [19] to Rule 1.7, "when a disinterested lawyer would conclude that the client should not agree to the representation under the circumstances, the lawyer involved cannot properly ask for such agreement or provide representation on the basis of the client's consent." In this case, neither of these counsel were in position to request a waiver because, for the reasons set forth fully above, neither reasonably could have believed that, under the circumstances of this case, they could represent all of the defendants whom they undertook to represent.

CONCLUSION

For the foregoing reasons, the [plaintiff's motion to disqualify] is granted. The question arises whether the grant of this motion to disqualify permits existing counsel to remain in the case for any of the defendants. The approach taken in the Virginia Rules of Professional Responsibility is that "[o]rdinarily, the lawyer would be forced to withdraw from representing all of the clients if the common representation fails." This commentary leaves open the possibility that a lawyer might remain as counsel to one or more defendants even if he is disqualified from representing all defendants. Considering the complex issues presented in this record and the rather significant nature of the conflict, it appears that this case ought to be one in which counsel, having been disqualified, should not further remain in the case. However, it is appropriate to leave that prospect open and to allow for discussion and further assessment of that issue after each defendant is separately advised by counsel not laboring under conflicts.

AM. BAR ASS'N, STANDING COMM. ON ETHICS & PROF'L RESPONSIBILITY,

Formal Op. 05-434, Dec. 8, 2004

Lawyer Retained by Testator to Disinherit Beneficiary that Lawyer Represents on Unrelated Matters

This opinion addresses whether, under the Model Rules of Professional Conduct, there is a conflict of interest if a lawyer is retained by a testator to prepare instruments disinheriting a beneficiary whom the lawyer represents on unrelated matters.

* * *

[A] testator is, unless limited by contractual or quasi-contractual obligations or by state law, free to dispose of his estate as he chooses, or to consume his entire estate during his lifetime or give it all away, leaving nothing to pass under his will.

A potential beneficiary * * * has no legal right to that bequest but has, instead, merely an expectancy. Thus, except where the testator has a legal duty to make the bequest that is to be revoked or altered, there is no conflict of legal rights and duties as between the testator and the beneficiary and there is no direct adversity.

* * *

The preparation of an instrument disinheriting a beneficiary ordinarily is a simple, straightforward, almost ministerial task, without call for the lawyer to consider alternative courses of action, and it is difficult to imagine a circumstance in which a responsibility of the lawyer to her other client * * * would pose a significant risk of limiting the lawyer's ability to discharge her professional obligations to the testator. The lawyer's representation of a testator does not, of itself, create responsibilities owed by the lawyer to prospective beneficiaries * * * other than the duty to effect the testator's intent as expressed explicitly or implicitly in the instrument. If, however, because of her relationship with the other client, the lawyer finds it repugnant or distasteful to carry out the assignment, or has good faith doubts as to whether there is a significant risk that she will be able to exercise independent professional judgment on behalf of the testator, then the lawyer may decline the engagement.[14]

The issue becomes more complicated if the testator asks for the lawyer's advice as to whether the beneficiary should be disinherited, or if the lawyer initiates such advice, either as a matter of the lawyer's usual practice in dealing with such matters, or because the lawyer believes that such advice is, in the circumstances, in the testator's interest. By advising the testator whether, rather than how, to disinherit the beneficiary, the lawyer has raised the level of the engagement from the purely ministerial to a situation in which the lawyer must exercise judgment and discretion on behalf of the testator. In such circumstances, there is a heightened risk that the lawyer may, perhaps without consciously intending to do so, seek to influence the testator to change his objectives in favor of her other client, thus permitting her representation of the testator to be materially limited by her responsibilities to the beneficiary or by a personal interest arising out of her relationship with the beneficiary.

---

14 See Rule 1.16(a)(1) (lawyer must withdraw if representation will result in violation of rules of professional conduct), and Rule 1.16(b)(4) (lawyer may withdraw if client insists upon taking action that lawyer considers repugnant or with which lawyer has a fundamental disagreement).

Problems also can arise in situations where the lawyer has represented both the testator and other family members in connection with family estate planning. If proceeding as the testator has directed violates previously agreed-upon family estate planning objectives, the lawyer must consider her responsibilities to other family members who have been her clients for family estate planning. If, for instance, a family has made its estate plans on the shared assumption (never reduced to an enforceable agreement) that the testator has provided for a disabled family member, thus relieving the others of that burden, then the lawyer may conclude that, in light of her responsibilities to her other clients, she cannot in good conscience implement the testator's intended disinheritance of that disabled family member, especially if the testator refuses to permit the lawyer to reveal the disinheritance.

In summary, ordinarily there is no conflict of interest when a lawyer undertakes an engagement by a testator to disinherit a beneficiary whom the lawyer represents on unrelated matters. However, this may not be the case if the testator is restricted by a contractual or quasi-contractual legal obligation from disinheriting the beneficiary, or if there is a significant risk that the lawyer's responsibilities to the testator will be materially limited by the lawyer's responsibilities to the beneficiary, as may be the case if the lawyer finds herself advising the testator whether to proceed with the disinheritance.

> **FYI**
>
> What type of representation might be precluded under substantive law? As the Comment to Rule 1.7 notes, some states bar a lawyer from representing more than one defendant in a capital case, regardless of whether the defendants would consent to the representation. Because such a representation is barred under state law, it is also non-consentable under Rule 1.7.

4. *"Not Prohibited by Law" Under Rule 1.7(b)(2):*

Rule 1.7(b)(2) precludes clients from consenting to conflicted representations that are prohibited under the applicable substantive law.

5. *"Assertion of a Claim by One Client against Another" Under Rule 1.7(b)(3):*

[Question 8]

Same facts as in Question 7, *supra*. If Husband and Wife reach an amicable agreement, can attorney represent both in court?

Rule 1.7 (b)(3) prevents lawyers from representing opposing parties in the same litigation, regardless of the parties' consent. The Comment to Rule 1.7 explains that the "institutional interest in vigorous development of each client's position" renders consent ineffective when the clients are "aligned directly against each other in the same litigation or other proceeding before a tribunal."

6. "Informed Consent, Confirmed in Writing" Under Rule 1.7(b)(4):

Clients must consent in writing to allow the lawyer to represent multiple clients with adverse interests. But it is important to remember that while informed consent is *required*, it is not always *sufficient* to permit representation.

[Question 9]

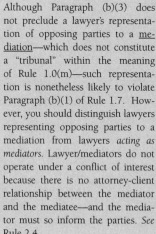

Take Note

Although Paragraph (b)(3) does not preclude a lawyer's representation of opposing parties to a <u>mediation</u>—which does not constitute a "tribunal" within the meaning of Rule 1.0(m)—such representation is nonetheless likely to violate Paragraph (b)(1) of Rule 1.7. However, you should distinguish lawyers representing opposing parties to a mediation from lawyers *acting as mediators*. Lawyer/mediators do not operate under a conflict of interest because there is no attorney-client relationship between the mediator and the mediatee—and the mediator must so inform the parties. *See* Rule 2.4.

A corporation has applied to a bank for a $900,000 loan to be secured by a lien on the corporation's inventory. The inventory, consisting of small items, constantly turns over. The security documents are complex and if improperly drawn they could result in an invalid lien. The bank has approved the loan on the condition that the corporation and the bank jointly retain an attorney to prepare the necessary security instruments and that the corporation pay the attorney's fees. Both the corporation and the bank gave informed consent in writing to the attorney's representation of both parties. This arrangement is customary in the city in which the attorney's law office and the bank are located. It is obvious to the attorney that he can adequately represent the interests of both the corporation and the bank.

Is it proper for the attorney to prepare the security documents under these circumstances?

(A) Yes, because both the bank and the corporation have given their informed consent to the arrangement.

(B) Yes, because the arrangement is customary in the community.

(C) No, because the attorney's fees are being paid by the corporation, not the bank.

(D) No, because the corporation and the bank have differing interests.

[Question 10]

An attorney was approached by a husband and a wife who had decided to dissolve their marriage. They had no children and had worked out a tentative mutual property settlement. They did not want to retain separate lawyers because they hoped to save money and believed that working with one attorney was more likely to result in a reasonably amicable dissolution. Before coming to the attorney, they had drafted and each had signed a written agreement not to run up the costs and increase the adversarial nature of the dissolution by retaining separate lawyers.

The attorney believed that he was able to ~~proved~~ *provide* competent and diligent representation to both the husband and wife. The attorney consulted with both independently concerning the implications of the common representation, including the advantages and risks involved and the effect on their respective attorney-client privileges. The attorney reduced the disclosures to writing in the form of a written retainer agreement and gave them each several days to consult independent legal counsel if they so desired. The husband and wife each chose not to consult independent counsel.

After six months of reasonably amicable negotiations, the wife announced that she had changed her mind about the representation and had decided to retain her own lawyer. However, after the husband and the attorney insisted that she was obligated to adhere to her prior written agreement, she reluctantly agreed to abide by it. The attorney was then able to draft a property settlement agreement satisfactory to both parties.

Is the attorney subject to discipline for his conduct in the representation?

(A) Yes, because the attorney should not have undertaken to represent both the husband and the wife in the first place.

(B) Yes, because the attorney insisted that the wife not hire another lawyer.

(C) No, because both the husband and the wife initially consented to all aspects of the representation.

(D) No, because the husband and the wife independently made the agreement that neither would retain separate counsel.

Comment to Rule 1.7(b)(4)

Informed Consent

Informed consent requires that each affected client be aware of the relevant circumstances and of the material and reasonably foreseeable ways that the conflict could have adverse effects on the interests of that client. * * * The information required depends on the nature of the conflict and the nature of the risks involved. When representation of multiple clients in a single matter is undertaken, the information must include the implications of the common representation, including possible effects on loyalty, confidentiality and the attorney-client privilege and the advantages and risks involved. * * *

Under some circumstances it may be impossible to make the disclosure necessary to obtain consent. For example, when the lawyer represents different clients in related matters and one of the clients refuses to consent to the disclosure necessary to permit the other client to make an informed decision, the lawyer cannot properly ask the latter to consent. In some cases the alternative to common representation can be that each party may have to obtain separate representation with the possibility of incurring additional costs. These costs, along with the benefits of securing separate representation, are factors that may be considered by the affected client in determining whether common representation is in the client's interests.

Consent Confirmed in Writing

Paragraph (b) requires the lawyer to obtain the informed consent of the client, confirmed in writing. * * * The requirement of a writing does not supplant the need in most cases for the lawyer to talk with the client, to explain the risks and advantages, if any, of representation burdened with a conflict of interest, as well as reasonably available alternatives, and to afford the client a reasonable opportunity to consider the risks and alternatives and to raise questions and concerns. Rather, the writing is required in order to impress upon clients the seriousness of the decision the client is being asked to make and to avoid disputes or ambiguities that might later occur in the absence of a writing.

Revoking Consent

A client who has given consent to a conflict may revoke the consent and, like any other client, may terminate the lawyer's representation at any time. Whether revoking consent to the client's own representation precludes the lawyer from continuing to represent other clients depends on the circumstances, including the nature of the conflict, whether the client revoked consent because of a material change in circumstances, the reasonable expectations of the other client and whether material detriment to the other clients or the lawyer would result.

7. Waiving Future Conflicts Under Rule 1.7(b)

[Question 11]

Recall the facts of Question 2, *supra*. L&C represents Intel for immigration matters related to its plant in Israel. Chipper, Inc. has asked L&C to represent it in a billion dollar patent infringement claim against Intel. In its retainer, Intel waived its right to object to future conflicts. Is that waiver effective here?

(A) Yes, because sophisticated clients can waive their right to object to future conflicts.

(B) Yes, unless the conflict is non-consentable.

(C) No, because clients cannot waive their right to object to future conflicts.

(D) No, because the conflict results in direct adversity or the attorney's material limitation.

Comment to Rule 1.7

Consent to Future Conflict

The effectiveness of waivers [of future conflicts] is generally determined by the extent to which the client reasonably understands the material risks that the waiver entails. The more comprehensive the explanation of the types of future representations that might arise and the actual and reasonably foreseeable adverse consequences of those representations, the greater the likelihood that the client will have the requisite understanding. Thus, if the client agrees to consent to a particular type of conflict with which the client is already familiar, then the consent ordinarily will be effective with regard to that type of conflict. If the consent is general and open-ended, then the consent ordinarily will be ineffective, because it is not reasonably likely that the client will have understood the material risks involved. On the other hand, if the client is an experienced user of the legal services involved and is reasonably informed regarding the risk that a conflict may arise, such consent is more likely to be effective, particularly if, *e.g.*, the client is independently represented by other counsel in giving consent and the consent is limited to future conflicts unrelated to the subject of the representation. In any case, advance consent cannot be effective if the circumstances that materialize in the future are such as would make the conflict nonconsentable under paragraph (b).

Practice Pointer

Advance waivers might be particularly useful in a globalized law practice. This is because, first, clients often insist on a regime of "conflicts by contract." Under an advance waiver system, clients can require the firm to agree that conflicts limitations of Rules 1.7 (and 1.9) apply to all of the client's corporate affiliates, rather than only to the entity immediately involved in the engagement. Second, advance waivers respond to the modern reality of large, international firms offering specialized services. As one commentator explains,

> The contract regime in international trade allows parties to put together transactions and relationships that are attractive in part because they transcend the limits of parochial national laws. So also with client-lawyer transactions. * * * [N]o one imagines that Lawyer A in Law Firm A will represent Client X Corporation in litigation in New York or London, and that Lawyer A will also at the same time represent some other client against Client X in an arbitration in Zurich. Rather, what the conflicts contract will permit is, for example, that representation by Lawyer A in Law Firm A of Corporation X will not prevent Lawyer B in Law Firm A from representing another company in a licensing negotiation with Corporation X.

Geoffrey C. Hazard, Jr., *Imputed Conflicts of Interest in International Law Practice*, 30 Okla. City U. L. Rev. 489, 510-12 (2005).

8. Protecting Against Conflicts Resulting from Multiple Representation

CARNEGIE COMPANIES, INC. v. SUMMIT PROPERTIES, INC.

918 N.E.2d 1052 (Ohio App.9 Dist. 2009)

DICKINSON, J:

INTRODUCTION

After a land deal went south, the would-be buyer, Carnegie Companies, Inc., sued the would-be seller, Summit Properties Ltd., seeking return of its deposit. Summit responded with counterclaims, including one for fraud. Carnegie later moved to disqualify the law firm representing Summit because, according to Carnegie, that firm was [at the same time] representing Carnegie in an unrelated transaction. After a hearing, the trial court granted the motion, disqualifying the firm and determining that Carnegie was entitled to an award of attorney fees and expenses associated with the motion. * * * Summit has appealed, arguing that the trial court incorrectly disqualified its lawyers * * *. This court affirms the trial court's disqualification of the law firm of Ulmer & Berne, L.L.P. because the firm's simultaneous representation of two clients with directly adverse interests violates [Ohio] Prof. Cond. R. 1.7.

BACKGROUND

In August 2007, Carnegie became interested in buying an office building in Twinsburg, Ohio, from Summit. Toward that end, Carnegie's President, Paul Pesses, began negotiating directly with Summit's lawyer, Stuart Laven, of the law firm of Ulmer & Berne, L.L.P. The parties entered into a contract and, consistent with that contract, Carnegie deposited $50,000 in earnest money with an escrow company. Later, Carnegie rescinded the contract and sought return of the earnest money. Summit refused to release the escrowed funds, and, in February 2008, Carnegie sued Summit, seeking a declaratory judgment that Summit had breached the purchase agreement and that Carnegie was entitled to return of its deposit.

Summit answered the complaint and counterclaimed for breach of contract and fraud in the inducement. * * * Summit was represented in the litigation by Stuart Laven of Ulmer & Berne.

In July 2008, Carnegie moved the trial court to disqualify Ulmer & Berne from representing Summit in this matter. Carnegie argued that it was a client of Ulmer & Berne at the time the litigation began and, therefore, lawyers from that firm could not ethically represent its opponent in this litigation without its consent. Specifically, Carnegie argued that Ulmer & Berne attorney Robert J. Karl, of the [Columbus, Ohio] office, was representing it in an unrelated matter regarding its contemplated acquisition of property in Marietta, Ohio.

* * *

CURRENT CLIENTS

The first step in the analysis under Prof. Cond. R. 1.7 is to identify the clients. Prof. Cond. R. 1.7, Comment 2. In this case, the clients' identities are clear, but Carnegie's status with Ulmer & Berne is disputed.

* * *

The law does not look to the reasonable expectations of the lawyer in order to determine whether an attorney-client relationship has been established by implication. The law focuses on the "reasonable expectations of the person seeking representation." Following [a] telephone conference of June 21, 2007, [a Carnegie official] reasonably believed that [the law firm] was representing Carnegie's interests in the Marietta deal. Nobody at Ulmer & Berne did anything to dispel that belief * * * .

* * *

CONFLICT OF INTEREST

The second step in the analysis under [Rule 1.7] is to determine whether a conflict of interest exists. Prof. Cond. R. 1.7(a)(1) provides that a conflict of interest is created if "the representation of [a] client will be directly adverse to another current client." Comment 10 to [Ohio] Prof. Cond. R. 1.7 provides that "[t]he concurrent representation of clients whose interests are directly adverse always creates a conflict of interest." Comment 11 [to Ohio Prof. Cond. R. 1.7] describes various ways that clients' interests may be directly adverse in litigation. In addition to the situation in which one client asserts claims against another, clients' interests may also be directly adverse when effective representation of one client in a lawsuit requires a lawyer to cross-examine another client, who he represents in a separate matter, but who appears as a witness in a different lawsuit. Comment 13 to [Ohio] Prof. Cond. R. 1.7 addresses directly adverse interests in the transactional setting. Comment 13 [to Ohio Prof. Cond. R. 1.7] provides that absent informed, written consent, a lawyer cannot undertake to represent a seller's interests in negotiations with a buyer whom the lawyer represents in another, unrelated matter.

* * *

The rules charge lawyers with the responsibility of detecting and avoiding potential conflicts of interest. A large law firm like Ulmer & Berne must adhere to policies and procedures designed to detect potential conflicts of interest that may arise. When a firm employs hundreds of lawyers in offices located in different cities, it must be particularly cautious in this regard. The official comment to [Ohio] Prof. Cond. R. 1.7 unequivocally provides that "[i]gnorance caused by a failure to institute or follow" reasonable procedures for detecting potential conflicts of interest "will not excuse a lawyer's violation of [Prof. Cond. R. 1.7]." [Ohio] Prof. Cond. R. 1.7, Comment 3.

Ulmer & Berne had many opportunities to avoid this situation. For instance, Laven could have run a conflict check when Summit first asked him to become involved in the Twinsburg deal. * * * He also testified that Ulmer & Berne does not have a formal procedure for disclosing to clients when their representation has terminated. Had Karl sent a termination letter to Carnegie after the June telephone conference, the conflict might have been avoided.

Even after Laven ran the conflict check in December 2007 and discovered a billing to Carnegie for services recently rendered, he and Karl failed to ascertain that a conflict existed. And Laven failed to open a file for the Twinsburg representation at that time, ensuring that no new business report was circulated to the other lawyers in the firm. Laven testified, in response to questions from the trial court, that Ulmer & Berne's policy allowed the lawyer opening the file to independently determine whether a potential opponent is a "current client" of the firm. *See* Prof. Cond. R. 1.7. The firm's ethics specialist would not be consulted unless two lawyers disagreed.

* * *

VIOLATION OF PROF. COND. R. 1.7

* * *

* * * Prof. Cond. R. 1.7 provides that multiple representation creates a conflict of interest if the representation of one client is "directly adverse to another current client." [Ohio] Prof. Cond. R. 1.7(a)(1). In this case, one of Ulmer & Berne's current clients sued another current client, and Ulmer & Berne answered and counterclaimed on behalf of one client against another client. Thus, the trial court correctly held that Ulmer & Berne's representation of the second client in this case created a conflict of interest under Prof. Cond. R. 1.7.

* * *

IMPACT OF A VIOLATION OF PROF. COND. R. 1.7

* * *

This court is aware of the delicate balance to be struck between the right to proceed with counsel of one's choice and the need to ensure that attorneys act ethically. A party does not, however, have an absolute right to be represented by a particular lawyer or law firm. * * * It is appropriate for the net of disqualification to be cast at least as wide as that of attorney discipline for conduct that not only violates an ethical rule but also undermines the basic duty of undivided loyalty to one's clients.

This court holds that a violation of Prof. Cond. R. 1.7 requires disqualification of the offending lawyer. The language of the rule prohibiting concurrent adverse representation is mandatory. * * *

C. Applications of Rule 1.7

1. Marital Issues

WARE v. WARE

687 S.E.2d 382 (W. Va. 2009)

WORKMAN, Justice.

* * *

I.

FACTS AND PROCEDURAL HISTORY

After living together for nearly two years, the parties married in February 1993, when Mrs. Ware was twenty-three years old and Mr. Ware was twenty-eight. At that time, Mrs. Ware, then known as Brenda Diane Ayers, was working as an X-ray technologist. Mr. Ware was working at a pizza restaurant at the Meadowbrook Mall in Bridgeport, West Virginia, called "The Pizza Place of Bridgeport, Inc." (hereinafter "the Pizza Place"), of which he owned a 49% share.

Several months before their wedding, Mr. Ware asked an attorney, Keith Skeen, to draft a prenuptial agreement to protect his interest in the Pizza Place. On February 10, 1993, approximately ten days before their wedding date, Attorney Skeen met with the parties at the Pizza Place and presented them with a draft agreement. Although Mr. Ware contends that he had previously discussed entering into such an agreement with his bride-to-be, Mrs. Ware denies having had any knowledge of the agreement prior to that day.

At that meeting, both parties read the proposed agreement for the first time. Mrs. Ware objected to a provision relating to a waiver of alimony and Mr. Ware agreed to remove it. Attorney Skeen revised the agreement and, on the following day, the parties signed the "Ante-Nuptial Agreement" (hereinafter "the Agreement") at Attorney Skeen's office. Among other things, it provides that

> The Pizza Place franchise located at the Meadowbrook Mall, Bridgeport, Harrison County, West Virginia, owned by DAVID GARY WARE and John Geraffo as co-owners will remain the property of DAVID GARY WARE. BRENDA DIANE AYERS releases all rights that she could or might have, by reason of marriage, in the Pizza Place franchise located at Meadow-

brook Mall, Bridgeport, Harrison County, West Virginia as well as any future acquisitions of Pizza Place franchises.

At the same meeting in which they signed the Agreement, both parties also signed two documents entitled "Certification of Attorney." In those documents, of which one pertains to Mr. Ware and one to Mrs. Ware, Attorney Skeen certified that he had consulted with each of the parties and advised each of his or her legal rights.

* * *

Shortly after they married, Mr. Ware and his business partner purchased, as a subsidiary of the Pizza Place, a candy store called "Sweets and Treats." Mrs. Ware quit her X-ray technician job to run the store, and Mr. Ware later testified that he considered it to be "Brenda's business." After five years, however, the Wares decided not to renew the lease for Sweets and Treats so that Mrs. Ware could stay home to raise their children.

Throughout the marriage, which lasted approximately twelve years, Mr. Ware acquired interests in a number of additional businesses. He and his business partner from the Pizza Place started several additional pizza corporations in other locations, most of which dissolved within a few years. In 2001, Mr. Ware "bought out" his partner's 51% interest in the Pizza Place using his share of stock in two of the other pizza corporations, as well as $18,500.00 cash.

On July 21, 2005, Mrs. Ware filed for divorce alleging cruelty and abandonment. The parties entered into a Mediated Agreement on October 15, 2005, dividing all the marital property. A dispute arose, however, over the division of the Pizza Place. Mr. Ware asserted that, pursuant to the Agreement, the business was his separate property, while Mrs. Ware argued that the Agreement was invalid, and thus the business should be considered marital property.

On December 16, 2005, the family court conducted a hearing on the validity of the Agreement, at which time Mr. Ware testified that he had obtained the Agreement in order to protect his and his business partner's interests in the Pizza Place. At the same hearing, Mrs. Ware testified that she signed the Agreement because Mr. Ware told her that he would not marry her unless she signed it, a statement disputed by Mr. Ware. She stated that she did not know anything about the Agreement until ten days before her wedding, by which time she had already purchased her wedding dress and the couple had purchased tickets for a cruise to the U.S. Virgin Islands, where the wedding was to take place. She further contended that, after being presented with the Agreement, she asked Mr. Ware if she should get her own attorney, and he told her that there was no need because Attorney Skeen would represent them both.

Attorney Skeen also testified at the hearing. With regard to Mrs. Ware's lack of independent counsel, Attorney Skeen stated that he could not specifically recall what he had told the parties at the time the Agreement was signed, but that his common practice at that time was to advise parties of their right to seek independent counsel. Nevertheless, he further indicated that he believed he could properly counsel both Mr. and Mrs. Ware in this circumstance, because the parties were not involved in a divorce and, therefore, did not have conflicting interests.

At the conclusion of the hearing, the family court ruled that the Agreement was "void and invalid" because Attorney Skeen had attempted to represent both parties, Mrs. Ware had not had an opportunity to consult with independent counsel, and because the parties had not disclosed to each other the value of their respective assets and debts.

* * *

III.

DISCUSSION

Initially, the Court must consider whether the prenuptial agreement signed by the Wares is valid and enforceable. * * * In its decision, the family court struck down the Agreement on three grounds: (1) one attorney cannot represent two parties with conflicting interests; (2) Mrs. Ware did not have the opportunity to consult with independent counsel; and (3) no disclosure of assets and debts had been made between the parties.

* * *

* * * Because the Court finds that Attorney Skeen inappropriately purported to represent both Mrs. Ware and Mr. Ware in the formation of the Agreement, thereby interfering with Mrs. Ware's opportunity to consult with independent counsel, we hold that the Agreement is invalid.

1.

* * *

In this case, Mrs. Ware did not consult with independent counsel before entering into the Agreement. At issue is whether she had such opportunity. Mrs. Ware contends that, after being presented with the Agreement, she asked Mr. Ware if she should retain her own counsel and he told her it was not necessary, because Attorney Skeen was representing them both. Mr. Ware denies that they had such conversation, and instead contends that Attorney Skeen informed Mrs. Ware of her right to obtain independent counsel.

Attorney Skeen cannot remember what was said at the time. The two "Certification of Representation" forms signed by Attorney Skeen and the parties, however, indicates that Attorney Skeen consulted with each party and "fully advised" each of their "property rights and of the legal significance of the foregoing Agreement." Nothing in the Certification indicates that Attorney Skeen advised each party of their right to independent counsel or that he advised Mrs. Ware that he was representing Mr. Ware's interests, rather than her interests. To the contrary, it appears that Attorney Skeen led both parties to believe that he could represent each of their interests sufficiently.

It is well established that one attorney may not represent two parties with conflicting interests without a knowing and voluntary waiver of rights. Rule 1.7(a) of the West Virginia Rules of Professional Conduct provides that "[a] lawyer shall not represent a client if the representation of that client will be directly adverse to another client." Similarly, Rule 1.7(b) provides that "[a] lawyer shall not represent a client if the representation of that client may be materially limited by the lawyer's responsibilities to another client. . . ." If, however, the attorney reasonably believes that such representation would not adversely affect either client, and if each client consents after consultation, then dual representation is permissible.

* * *

Food for Thought

In order to detect the existence of conflicts of interest among new associates or partners, law firms generally conduct thorough conflicts screening—that is, they solicit information from new hires regarding past representations. At the same time, new attorneys owe their former clients a duty of confidentiality. How might attorneys resolve this apparent conflict? For an in-depth examination of this interesting quandary, see Paul R. Tremblay, *Migrating Lawyers and the Ethics of Conflict Checking,* 19 GEO. J. LEGAL ETHICS 489 (2006). Note that one of the ways to protect the former client is by screening the incoming lawyer. *See* Rule 1.10.

This Court has previously recognized that, in certain instances, dual representation is never appropriate, even if both parties are willing to consent.

It is improper for a lawyer to represent both the husband and the wife at any stage of the separation and divorce proceeding, even with full disclosure and informed consent. The likelihood of prejudice is so great with dual representation so as to make adequate representation of both spouses impossible, even where the separation is "friendly" and the divorce uncontested. * * * Thus, in the context of a divorce, one attorney can never represent both parties.

Like divorce actions, the nature of prenuptial agreements is such that the parties' interests are fundamentally antagonistic to one another. Indeed, the purpose of a prenuptial agreement is to preserve the property of one spouse, thereby preventing the other from obtaining that to which he or she might otherwise be legally entitled. * * * Accordingly, the Court holds that one attorney may not represent, nor purport to counsel, both parties to a prenuptial agreement.

In the instant case, because Attorney Skeen led Mrs. Ware to believe that he could represent her interests as well as those of Mr. Ware, the Court finds that Mrs. Ware was divested of her opportunity to consult with independent counsel. * * * The Agreement, therefore, was procured in an invalid manner and, thus, is unenforceable.

* * *

2. *Positional Conflicts*

AM. BAR ASS'N, STANDING COMM. ON ETHICS & PROF'L RESPONSIBILITY,
Formal Op. 93-377 (1993)

The Committee has been asked to address the question whether a lawyer can represent a client with respect to a substantive legal issue when the lawyer knows that the client's position on that issue is directly contrary to the position being urged by the lawyer (or the lawyer's firm) on behalf of another client in a different, and unrelated, pending matter.

* * * [A]rguing a position on behalf of one client that is adverse to a position that the lawyer, or her firm, is arguing on behalf of another current client raises a number of concerns. For

> **Practice Pointer**
>
> Positional conflicts may arise where a lawyer advocates contrary positions with respect to the same substantive legal issue on behalf of separate clients. For example, a lawyer who represents clients seeking to enforce an environmental rule against a manufacturer may have a positional conflict if she represents a different manufacturer who will be subject to the legal ruling the lawyer seeks.

example, if both cases are being argued in the same court, will the impact of the lawyer's advocacy be diluted in the eyes of the judge(s)? Will the first decision rendered be persuasive (or even binding) precedent with respect to the other case, thus impairing the lawyer's effectiveness—and, if so, can the lawyer (or firm) avoid favoring one client over the other in the "race" to be first? And will one or the other of the clients become concerned that the law firm it has employed may have divided loyalties?

What, then, should a lawyer do when confronted with such a "positional conflict"?

[The Committee quotes the terms of Model Rule 1.7]

These provisions are supplemented by a Comment that recognizes (but does not resolve) the issue addressed here:

> A lawyer may represent parties having antagonistic positions on a legal question that has arisen in different cases, unless representation of either client would be adversely affected. Thus, it is ordinarily not improper to assert such positions in cases pending in different trial courts, but it may be improper to do so in cases pending at the same time in an appellate court.

The rationale of the last clause is not clear, but it may stem from the view that a ruling in one of the two appellate cases would in all likelihood constitute binding precedent with respect to the second case, under the doctrine of *stare decisis*, and it would therefore be highly unlikely that the lawyer would be able to win both cases. Conversely, if there is a likelihood that the lawyer can win both cases—as, for example, where the two cases are "pending in different trial courts" or before different trial judges in the same judicial district—there is no ethical reason why the lawyer should not proceed.

Whether this be the rationale or not, the Committee does not believe that a distinction should be drawn between appellate and trial courts in this regard. After all, the impact of an appellate court decision on the second case would be the same even if the second case were still before the trial court in that particular jurisdiction. Moreover, even if both cases were in the trial court, but assigned to different judges, the decision in the first-decided case would, in all likelihood, carry at least some precedential or persuasive weight in the second case. And if both cases should happen to end up before the same judge, the situation would be even worse. For although judges well understand that lawyers, at various stages of their careers, can find themselves arguing different sides of the same issue, the persuasiveness and credibility of the lawyer's arguments in at least one of the two pending matters would quite possibly be lessened, consciously or subconsciously, in the mind of the judge.

The Committee is therefore of the opinion that if the two matters are being litigated in the same jurisdiction, and there is a substantial risk that the law firm's representation of one client will create a legal precedent, even if not binding, which is likely materially to undercut the legal position being urged on behalf of the other client, the lawyer should either refuse to accept the second representation or (if otherwise permissible) withdraw from the first, unless both clients consent after full disclosure of the potential ramifications of the lawyer continuing to handle both matters.

If, on the other hand, the two matters will not be litigated in the same jurisdiction, the lawyer should nevertheless attempt to determine fairly and objectively whether the effectiveness of her representation of either client will be materially limited by the lawyer's (or her firm's) representation of the other. In addressing that key issue, the lawyer may usefully consider the following questions:

(a) Is the issue one of such importance that its determination is likely to affect the ultimate outcome of at least one of the cases?

(b) Is the determination of the issue in one case likely to have a significant impact on the determination of that issue in the other case? (For example, does the issue involve a new or evolving area of the law, where the first case decided may be regarded as persuasive authority by other courts, regardless of their geographical location? Or: is the issue one of federal law, where the decision by one federal judge will be given respectful consideration by another federal judge, even though they are not in the same district or state?)

(c) Will there be any inclination by the lawyer, or her firm, to "soft-pedal" or de-emphasize certain arguments or issues—which otherwise would be vigorously   pursued—so as to avoid impacting the other case?

(d) Will there be any inclination within the firm to alter any arguments for one, or both clients, so that the firm's position in the two cases can be reconciled—and, if so, could that redound to the detriment of one of the clients?

If the lawyer concludes that the issue is of such importance and that its determination in one case is likely to have a significant impact on its determination in the second case, thus impairing the lawyer's effectiveness—or if the lawyer concludes that, because of the dual representation, there will be an inclination by the firm either to "soft-pedal" the issue or to alter the firm's arguments on behalf of one or both clients, thus again impairing the lawyer's effectiveness—the lawyer should not accept the second representation. The reason is that, in such a situation, the representation of at least one client would be adversely affected if the firm were to proceed with both.

If, on the other hand, even though there is a significant potential for the representation of one client to be limited by the representation of the other, the lawyer nonetheless reasonably believes that the determination in one case will not have a significant impact on the determination of that issue in the second case and that continuing to handle both matters will not cause her, or her firm, to "soft-pedal" the issue or to alter any arguments that otherwise would have been made, the lawyer may proceed with both representations, provided that both clients consent after full disclosure has been made to them of the potential ramifications (including the possibility that the law firm's adversary in one case might become aware, and be able to make advantageous use, of the briefs filed by the law firm in the other case).

Although the foregoing discussion is predicated on the assumption that the existence of the positional conflict is immediately apparent to the lawyer at the time she is asked to represent the second client, the Committee is of the opinion that the same analysis should be followed if such a conflict emerges after the second representation has been accepted and pursued. If that analysis leads to the conclusion that the law firm should not proceed with both representations, then the law firm must withdraw from one of them.

* * *

WILLIAMS v. STATE OF DELAWARE

805 A.2d 880 (Del. 2002)

HOLLAND, Justice:

The appellant Joseph Williams filed these consolidated appeals from his conviction and death sentence for first-degree murder. Williams' lawyer, Bernard J. O'Donnell, has filed a motion to withdraw. The motion also requests that substitute counsel be appointed by this Court to represent Williams on appeal.

O'Donnell asserts that, on appeal, Williams could raise an arguable issue that the Superior Court erred when it concluded it was required to give "great weight" to the jury's 10-2 recommendation in favor of the death penalty for Williams. O'Donnell contends, however, that he may have a conflict in presenting this argument because he

> **Practice Pointer**
>
> If the rule is that positional conflicts are disabling, consider the difficulty of running conflicts checks, especially in a big firm. Typically if a new client comes to the firm with a matter, a conflicts check is run to determine if anyone in the firm has represented the new client's adversary. But this would not work with a positional conflict, because it is not the adversary that is the problem, it is current clients in a similar position as the adversary. What might be required is some kind of checklist of interests in the existing client base—e.g., pro-or-anti NAFTA? pro-or-anti environmental protection? Would this conflicts check nightmare be enough to conclude that positional conflicts should not be subject to regulation?

has advocated a contrary position on behalf of a different client in another capital murder appeal pending before this Court. In *Garden v. State*, O'Donnell argued in his opening brief that the Superior Court erred when it failed to give great weight to the jury's 2-10 vote rejecting the imposition of the death penalty for Garden.

O'Donnell is concerned that his representation of both clients on this issue will create the risk that an unfavorable precedent will be created for one client or the other. O'Donnell also is concerned that it may invite questions about his credibility with this Court and his clients' perception of his loyalty to each of them. The State agrees that O'Donnell has a conflict of interest that disqualifies him from representing Williams in this appeal.

Positional Conflict

The potential conflict identified by O'Donnell is termed a "positional" conflict of interest. It arises when two or more clients have opposing interests in unrelated matters. * * *

In determining whether a positional conflict requires a lawyer's disqualification, the question is whether the lawyer can effectively argue both sides of the same legal question without compromising the interests of one client or the other. The lawyer must attempt to strike a balance between the duty to advocate any viable interpretation of the law for one client's benefit versus the other client's right to insist on counsel's fidelity to their legal position.

Under the circumstances presented in Williams' case, we find that O'Donnell has identified and demonstrated the existence of a disqualifying positional conflict. It would be a violation of the Delaware Rules of Professional Conduct for O'Donnell to advocate conflicting legal positions in two capital murder appeals that are pending simultaneously in this Court. Both the United States Constitution and the Delaware Constitution guarantee each of O'Donnell's clients a right to the effective assistance of counsel in a direct appeal following a capital murder conviction. Given his clients' disparate legal arguments, O'Donnell's independent obligations to his clients may compromise the effectiveness of his assistance as appellate counsel for one or both clients, unless his motion to withdraw is granted.

Conclusion

Accordingly, O'Donnell's motion to withdraw must be granted and substitute counsel will be appointed. O'Donnell and the State are both commended for their recognition of and adherence to the highest standards of professional conduct.

THE STATE BAR OF CAL., STANDING COMM. ON PROF'L RESPONSIBILITY & CONDUCT

Formal Op. No. 1989-108 (1989)

ISSUE

Is it unethical for an attorney to represent two clients who are not directly adverse to one another where the attorney will be arguing opposite sides of the same legal question before the same judge?

* * *

STATEMENT OF FACTS

An attorney represents a major manufacturer in mass tort litigation arising out of past and prospective injuries allegedly resulting from the client's products. The matter is in litigation, and after two years of discovery, the attorney has filed a motion for summary judgment which will turn on how the trial judge determines an issue of law. While the above matter is pending, in an unrelated case being handled by the same attorney for a different client, the very same legal issue is involved. However, the attorney finds that they will have to argue the opposite position with respect to the legal issue than that being taken on behalf of the product manufacturer. The manufacturer is not a party to this other litigation, and the other client is not involved in the manufacturer's litigation. Both cases are pending in federal court, and have been assigned to the same judge.

The attorney realizes that it would be in the best interests of the second client to file a motion based upon this legal issue.

DISCUSSION

The above facts represent the "worst case" scenario presented by the so-called "issues conflict" conundrum. These and other similar fact situations result in a collision of countervailing ethical and jurisprudential principles. Not surprisingly, there exists little precedent to assist the practitioner in resolving this dilemma.

Conflict of Interest

The most obvious issue presented is whether a conflict of interest can occur where two clients who have adverse interests are not directly adverse to each other in the same legal matter. Most authorities speak of conflicts of interests only where the representation involves the same case or transaction. * * *

* * * By continued representation the member will be doing his or her best to establish precedent which may be used against the other client.

Furthermore, as to both clients, the credibility of the attorney before this tribunal may be seriously at risk, as the member attempts to persuade the judge to rule first one way than the other way on the same issue. Clearly the interests of each client would be better served without the existence of the other representation.

On the other hand, there are other jurisprudential and practical reasons which argue against finding a disciplinable conflict under even these most egregious facts. Stepping back from the hypothetical which burdens our present consideration of this issue, "issues conflicts" are common and prolific in our adversarial system of justice. Almost daily the litigator or transactional attorney finds himself or herself taking positions on behalf of clients which are antithetical to another client. For example, if one finds the attorney in our hypothetical to have committed a disciplinable offense, by what reasoning would a conflict not similarly exist if an attorney arguing in favor of the discovery of medical records of an adverse party did not disclose to the client that a contrary position had been taken in another court? Or would business counsel be remiss in not advising a real estate client that he or she had argued against the inclusion of the same lease provision in another negotiation with the same adverse party?

While the facts here are extreme, to find a conflict employing a test which could be imposed uniformly to "issues conflicts" of all stripes threatens the ability of attorneys to carry out their roles in the legal system. In practice areas like family law and in small communities, the practical problems stemming from such an expansive rule would be insurmountable. Indeed, every time an attorney argues a point of law it is probable that other clients will then or later be adversely affected. In accepting an engagement, would the attorney be required to advise the client and seek consent every time an issue arises where the attorney has taken the other side?

Such a finding will also interfere with the strong social policy favoring one's right to counsel of choice. The pool of available attorneys will of necessity be diminished if withdrawal results from "issues conflicts" situations. The right to counsel of choice has been referred to by courts on several cases to support decisions finding the absence of a conflict of interest. Conflict of issue detection within a firm of even several attorneys using even the most sophisticated automated conflict of interest check system would be virtually impossible. There is simply no practical way that attorneys can track the legal issues that evolve during the course of an engagement in a system which will enable the attorney to later retrieve the information before a contrary position is taken for another client.

There are a host of circumstances in the legal profession where conflicts of interest would otherwise arise but, because of strong public policy considerations, or practical concerns, the conduct does not subject the member to discipline. * * * [C]onsider the well-recognized exceptions from the conflict rules pertaining to contingent fee agreements * * * . * * *

* * * While we recognize the potential for harm arising from such matters, we feel that countervailing policy considerations, plus the impossible practical limitations of conflict detection, justify limiting the conflict of interest rules to traditional concepts.

* * *

Despite our opinion, the prudent attorney would be well-advised to disclose "issues conflicts" where the attorney has reason to believe clients might be harmed by the continued undisclosed dual representation, thereby providing the clients an opportunity to retain other counsel. This Committee is unable to provide a definitive test as to when disclosure should be made.

There are a wide array of circumstances under which the issues conflict is likely to occur, and the risk of harm to the client will differ accordingly. Client sensitivities to this dilemma will also vary significantly by individual and the client's level of sophistication. Thus, the member necessarily must make the determination on a case by case basis. Beyond client relations considerations, the attorney must keep in mind the potential for civil liability if harm to the clients does occur which might have been avoided by timely disclosure.

* * *

For More Information

Comment (f) to § 128 of the Restatement provides further tools and illustrations helpful to the positional conflicts analysis:

* * * Factors relevant in determining the risk of such an effect include whether the issue is before a trial court or an appellate court; whether the issue is substantive or procedural; the temporal relationship between the matters; the practical significance of the issue to the immediate and long-run interests of the clients involved; and the clients' reasonable expectations in retaining the lawyer. If a conflict of interest exists, absent informed consent of the affected clients under § 122, the lawyer must withdraw from one or both of the matters. Informed client consent is provided for in § 122. On circumstances in which informed client consent would not allow the lawyer to proceed with representation of both clients, *see* § 122(2)(c) and Comment g(iv) thereto.

> **For More Information (Continued)**
>
> Illustrations:
>
> 5. Lawyer represents two clients in damage actions pending in different United States District Courts. In one case, representing the plaintiff, Lawyer will attempt to introduce certain evidence at trial and argue there for its admissibility. In the other case, representing a defendant, Lawyer will object to an anticipated attempt by the plaintiff to introduce similar evidence. Even if there is some possibility that one court's ruling might be published and cited as authority in the other proceeding, Lawyer may proceed with both representations without obtaining the consent of the clients involved.
>
> 6. The same facts as in Illustration 5, except that the cases have proceeded to the point where certiorari has been granted in each by the United States Supreme Court to consider the common evidentiary question. Any position that Lawyer would assert on behalf of either client on the legal issue common to each case would have a material and adverse impact on the interests of the other client. Thus, a conflict of interest is presented. Even the informed consent of both Client A and Client B would be insufficient to permit Lawyer to represent each before the Supreme Court.

3. Aggregate Settlements

[Question 12]

Attorney represents ten plaintiffs who were injured when a train operated by Railroad was derailed. Railroad has offered Attorney a $500,000 lump sum settlement for the ten plaintiffs. Attorney has determined a division of the $500,000 among the ten plaintiffs with the amount paid each plaintiff dependent on the nature and extent of that person's injuries. Attorney believes the division is fair to each plaintiff.

Railroad will not settle any of the claims unless all are settled. Attorney has told each plaintiff the total amount Railroad is prepared to pay, the amount that the individual will receive, and the basis on which that amount was calculated. Attorney has not told any plaintiff the amount to be received by any other plaintiff. Attorney believes that if Attorney reveals to each plaintiff the amount of each settlement, there is danger that some plaintiffs will think that they are not getting enough in relation to the amounts others will receive and the entire settlement will be upset. Each of the plaintiffs has agreed to his or her settlement.

Is Attorney subject to discipline if Attorney effects such a settlement?

   (A) Yes, because Attorney is aiding the lawyer for Railroad in making a lump sum settlement.

(B) Yes, because no individual plaintiff knows the amount to be received by any other plaintiff.

(C) No, if to disclose all settlements to each plaintiff might jeopardize the entire settlement.

(D) No, if the amount received by each plaintiff is fair and each plaintiff is satisfied.

Rule 1.8(g)

A lawyer who represents two or more clients shall not participate in making an aggregate settlement of the claims of or against the clients * * * unless each client gives informed consent, in a writing signed by the client. The lawyer's disclosure shall include the existence and nature of all the claims or pleas involved and of the participation of each person in the settlement.

Comment to Rule 1.8(g)

Differences in willingness to make or accept an offer of settlement are among the risks of common representation of multiple clients by a single lawyer. Under Rule 1.7, this is one of the risks that should be discussed before undertaking the representation, as part of the process of obtaining the clients' informed consent. In addition, Rule 1.2(a) protects each client's right to have the final say in deciding whether to accept or reject an offer of settlement * * *. * * * Lawyers representing a class of plaintiffs or defendants, or those proceeding derivatively, may not have a full client-lawyer relationship with each member of the class; nevertheless, such lawyers must comply with applicable rules regulating notification of class members and other procedural requirements designed to ensure adequate protection of the entire class.

III. Conflicts Between Client's Interests and Personal or Financial Interests of the Lawyer

A. Business Transactions Between Lawyer and Client

[Question 13]

An attorney decided to obtain a master's degree in taxation, but lacked the funds required for tuition and expenses. The attorney consulted one of his clients, a wealthy banker, for advice about obtaining a loan. To the attorney's surprise, the client offered the attorney a personal loan of $10,000. The attorney told the client that he would prepare the required note without charge.

Without further consultation with the client, the attorney prepared and signed a promissory note bearing interest at the current bank rate. The note provided for repayment in the form of legal services to be rendered by the attorney to the client without charge until the value of the attorney's services equaled the principal and interest due. The note further provided that if the client died before the note was fully repaid, any remaining principal and interest would be forgiven as a gift.

The attorney mailed the executed note to the client with a transmittal letter encouraging the client to look it over and call with any questions. The client accepted the note and sent the attorney a personal check for $10,000, which the attorney used to obtain his master's degree. A month after the degree was awarded, the client was killed in a car accident. The attorney had not rendered any legal services to the client from the date of the note's execution to the date of the client's death. Thereafter, in an action brought by the client's estate to recover on the note, the court ruled that the note was discharged as a gift.

Was the attorney's conduct proper?

- (A) Yes, because the client, without having been requested by the attorney to do so, voluntarily made the loan.

- (B) Yes, because the court ruled that the note had been discharged as a gift.

- (C) No, because a lawyer may never accept a loan from a client.

- (D) No, because the attorney did not comply with the requirements for entering into a business transaction with a client.

Rule 1.8—Conflict of Interest: Business Transactions Between Client and Lawyer

(a) A lawyer shall not enter into a business transaction with a client or knowingly acquire an ownership, possessory, security or other pecuniary interest adverse to a client unless:

> (1) the transaction and terms on which the lawyer acquires the interest are fair and reasonable to the client and are fully disclosed and transmitted in writing in a manner that can be reasonably understood by the client;

(2) the client is advised in writing of the desirability of seeking and is given a reasonable opportunity to seek the advice of independent legal counsel on the transaction; and

(3) the client gives informed consent, in a writing signed by the client, to the essential terms of the transaction and the lawyer's role in the transaction, including whether the lawyer is representing the client in the transaction.

* * *

Comment to Rule 1.8

A lawyer's legal skill and training, together with the relationship of trust and confidence between lawyer and client, create the possibility of overreaching when the lawyer participates in a business, property or financial transaction with a client, for example, a loan or sales transaction or a lawyer investment on behalf of a client. The requirements of paragraph (a) must be met even when the transaction is not closely related to the subject matter of the representation, as when a lawyer drafting a will for a client learns that the client needs money for unrelated expenses and offers to make a loan to the client. The Rule applies to lawyers engaged in the sale of goods or services related to the practice of law, for example, the sale of title insurance or investment services to existing clients of the lawyer's legal practice. * * * [T]he Rule does not apply to standard commercial transactions between the lawyer and the client for products or services that the client generally markets to others, for example, banking or brokerage services, medical services, products manufactured or distributed by the client, and utilities' services. In such transactions, the lawyer has no advantage in dealing with the client, and the restrictions in paragraph (a) are unnecessary and impracticable.

Make the Connection

To review conflicts that arise when clients pay fees with equity, *see* Chapter 3, Part III. *supra.*

Conflicts that may arise with regard to contingent fees are also discussed in Chapter 3, Part III. *supra.*

To review conflicts regarding prospective limits on malpractice liability, *see* Chapter 2, Part IV *supra.*

* * *

B. Literary Rights Issues

[Question 14]

An attorney represents the plaintiff in a defamation lawsuit. Both the plaintiff and the defendant are well-known public figures, and the lawsuit has attracted much publicity. The attorney has been billing the plaintiff at an agreed-upon hourly fee for his services. Recently the plaintiff suggested that, rather than paying hourly, she would like to assign the attorney the media rights to a book and movie based on her lawsuit as full payment of services rendered from that point until the end of the litigation. The attorney responded that he would consider it, but that the plaintiff should first seek independent advice as to whether such an arrangement would be in her best interest. The attorney knew that, in the unlikely event that the lawsuit was settled quickly, the media rights might be worth more than he would have earned on an hourly fee basis.

Is the attorney subject to discipline if he agrees to the plaintiff's offer?

(A) Yes, because the attorney knew that, in the unlikely event that the lawsuit was settled quickly, the media rights might be worth more than he would have earned on an hourly fee basis.

(B) Yes, because the attorney has not concluded the representation of the plaintiff.

(C) No, because the defamation lawsuit is a civil and not a criminal matter.

(D) No, because the attorney recommended that the plaintiff first seek independent advice before entering into the arrangement.

<u>Rule 1.8</u>—Conflict of Interest: Business Transactions Between Client and Lawyer

(d) Prior to the conclusion of representation of a client, a lawyer shall not make or negotiate an agreement giving the lawyer literary or media rights to a portrayal or account based in substantial part on information relating to the representation.

Food for Thought

Assume a lawyer is paid through an assignment of media rights. What decisions might that lawyer make to benefit himself that would not be in the client's best interest? Wouldn't the ability of a client to assign media rights actually benefit the client—by allowing him to hire an attorney that he could not otherwise afford?

BEETS v. COLLINS

986 F.2d 1478 (5th Cir. 1993)

EDITH H. JONES, Circuit Judge:

* * *

I.

BACKGROUND

* * * Beets's fifth husband, Jimmy Don, disappeared on August 6, 1983. His fishing boat was found drifting on Lake Athens, Texas, suggesting that he had drowned. More than a year later, a trailer home that was Jimmy Don's separate property before his death was destroyed by fire. When the insurer refused Beets's claim for the loss, Beets sought the counsel of E. Ray Andrews, an attorney who had represented Beets since 1981 or '82. During their discussions, they also decided that Andrews would pursue any insurance or pension benefits to which Beets might be entitled.

Beets and Andrews entered into a contingent fee arrangement whereby Andrews would pursue collection on both Beets's fire insurance claim and any death benefits to which she might have been entitled in connection with Jimmy Don's disappearance. Andrews determined that certain benefits existed and so informed Beets. * * * Jimmy Don's former employer, the City of Dallas Fire Department, agreed to provide benefits to Beets.

Before Beets received the first check from the Fire Department, she was arrested on June 8, 1985, and was charged with the capital murder of Jimmy Don. Beets was charged with shooting and killing her husband and, with the assistance of her son, Robbie Branson, burying him under a planter in her front yard. Beets allegedly disposed of her fourth husband, Doyle Wayne Barker, in a similar fashion. Barker's body was found buried in the back yard underneath a patio upon which a storage shed had been erected. Beets had also shot another former husband, Bill Lane, although he survived.

Andrews agreed to extend his representation of Beets to the capital murder charge. The case generated significant media interest on both a local and national level. On October 8, just after Beets's trial commenced, she signed a contract transferring all literary and media rights in her case to Andrews's son, E. Ray Andrews, Jr. The trial judge never became aware of the media rights contract during trial, although he did learn of it three months later during a hearing on Beets's motion to appoint counsel for appeal when the prosecutor asked Beets if she had signed over the book rights to her case to Andrews's son. The judge did not inquire whether Beets was willing to waive her Sixth Amendment right to conflict-free counsel.

Beets was convicted of murder for remuneration and the promise of remuneration on the theory that she killed her husband in order to obtain his insurance and pension benefits.

* * *

II.

DISCUSSION

* * *

C. Media Rights Conflict

The contract granting E. Ray Andrews, Jr., full literary and motion picture rights to Beets's story represented full satisfaction of the fee arrangement between Beets and Andrews. * * *

Courts, scholars, and the bar have not hesitated to denounce these types of fee arrangements. Virtually every court to consider a conflict of interest arising from a media rights contract executed in favor of trial counsel has unequivocally condemned the practice. * * * Particularly in a capital murder case, it is odious to think that counsel hopes to gain his fee by marketing the tragedy and misery of his client, her family and, worst, the victim and his loved ones.

Notwithstanding Andrews's apparent breach of his ethical obligations, this court sits not to discipline counsel, but to determine whether Andrews's ethical breach violated Beets's Sixth Amendment rights. The state has the duty to punish an attorney for unethical behavior. (Why the State Bar of Texas did not discipline Andrews is not revealed in the record.) This court will not succumb to Beets's invitation to punish her attorney by granting relief to his client.

The media rights contract posed a serious potential conflict of interest, but Beets failed to show how it ripened into an actual conflict of interest. The media rights contract was almost surely unethical, but on the facts before us, it did not by itself create an actual conflict or adversely affect Andrews's performance.

* * *

C. Client-Lawyer Sexual Relationships

[Question 15]

Jim, an associate at a large law firm, is working on a deal for client Lincoln Enterprises. He works regularly with Pam, an Assistant General Counsel at Lincoln, who is supervising the deal. Their close working relationship becomes a close personal relationship and they begin to date and are thinking about moving in together.

What are the implications under the Model Rules?

(A) Jim can't work on the matter.

(B) Pam can't work on the matter.

(C) The firm can't work on the matter.

(D) No problem under the rules.

Rule 1.8(j)

A lawyer shall not have sexual relations with a client unless a consensual sexual relationship existed between them when the client-lawyer relationship commenced.

Comment to Rule 1.8(j)

The relationship between lawyer and client is a fiduciary one in which the lawyer occupies the highest position of trust and confidence. The relationship is almost always unequal; thus, a sexual relationship between lawyer and client can involve unfair exploitation of the lawyer's fiduciary role, in violation of the lawyer's basic ethical obligation not to use the trust of the client to the client's disadvantage. In addition, such a relationship presents a significant danger that, because of the lawyer's emotional involvement, the lawyer will be unable to represent the client without impairment of the exercise of independent professional judgment. Moreover, a blurred line between the professional and personal relationships may make it difficult to predict to what extent client confidences will be protected by the attorney-client evidentiary privilege, since client confidences are protected by privilege only when they are imparted in the context of the client-lawyer relationship. Because of the significant danger of harm to client interests and because the client's own emotional involvement renders it unlikely that the client could give adequate informed consent, this Rule prohibits the lawyer from having sexual relations with a client regardless of whether the relationship is consensual and regardless of the absence of prejudice to the client.

* * *

When the client is an organization, paragraph (j) of this Rule prohibits a lawyer for the organization (whether inside counsel or outside counsel) from having a sexual relationship with a constituent of the organization who supervises, directs or regularly consults with that lawyer concerning the organization's legal matters.

In re DISCIPLINARY PROCEEDINGS AGAINST INGLIMO

740 N.W.2d 125 (Wis. 2007)

PER CURIAM.

In this disciplinary proceeding, the referee concluded that the OLR had proven violations on 10 of the 15 counts contained in the complaint filed by the Office of Lawyer Regulation (OLR). * * *

Counts 1 and 2 relate to Attorney Inglimo's representation of L.K. in a criminal case between April 2000 and January 2001. During this representation in October 2000, Attorney Inglimo had sexual relations with L.K.'s girlfriend in L.K.'s presence and with L.K. also engaging in sexual relations with his girlfriend during the sexual encounter. The referee further found, however, that there was no evidence that during the encounter there was any intimate physical contact between Attorney Inglimo and L.K.

Count 1 of the OLR's complaint alleged that by having sexual relations with L.K.'s girlfriend in L.K.'s presence and with L.K. participating in the encounter, Attorney Inglimo had violated SCR 20:1.8(k)(2). Although the referee found that there had been a three-way sexual encounter involving L.K., his girlfriend and Attorney Inglimo, he concluded that there was no violation of SCR 20:1.8(k)(2) because there was no evidence that Attorney Inglimo and his client, L.K., had "sexual relations" as that term is defined in the rule. Specifically, there was no evidence that Attorney Inglimo and L.K. engaged in sexual intercourse or intentionally touched each other's intimate parts.

* * *

The OLR * * * asserts that the referee erred in concluding that there was no violation of SCR 20:1.8(k)(2) for Attorney Inglimo engaging in a three-way sexual encounter with client L.K. and his girlfriend. The OLR does not challenge the referee's factual findings. Rather, it argues that the facts as found by the referee provide clear and convincing evidence of a violation of SCR 20:1.8(k)(2).

The relevant language of SCR 20:1.8(k) is as follows:

(k)(1) In this paragraph:

> (i) "Sexual relations" means sexual intercourse or any other intentional touching of the intimate parts of a person or causing the person to touch the intimate parts of the lawyer.

. . .

> (2) A lawyer shall not have sexual relations with a current client unless a consensual sexual relationship existed between them when the lawyer-client relationship commenced.

The referee found that Attorney Inglimo engaged in sexual relations with L.K.'s girlfriend while she was doing the same with L.K. The OLR essentially argues that the word "with" in SCR 20:1.8(k)(2) connotes a temporal and spatial connection. According to the OLR, as long as the lawyer and the client are both participating in a sexual act at the same time in the same place, they are having sexual relations "with" each other. In response, Attorney Inglimo relies on the plain language of the rule and argues that the OLR's interpretation would expand the rule beyond its terms.

On this issue, we concur with the referee's conclusion. The definition of sexual relations in SCR 20:1.8(k)(1) connotes conduct directly between the lawyer and the client. When the definition refers to touching, the rule speaks of the lawyer intentionally touching the intimate parts of "a person," but the subsequent alternative definitional phrase uses the more definitive "the person" when referring to a situation in which the lawyer causes the touching to be done to him/her. In addition, to the extent that sexual intercourse also qualifies as "sexual relations" under the definition, such conduct is likewise done intentionally (i.e., not by accident). Further, SCR 20:1.8(k)(2) prohibits a lawyer from having "sexual relations" "with a current client." Thus, the definitional language of SCR 20:1.8(k)(1) and the prohibition of SCR 20:1.8(k)(2) together clearly indicate that the prohibited "sexual relations," whether intercourse or touching, must be intentionally done between the lawyer and one particular person, namely the client.

* * * There was no testimony as to precisely what occurred during Attorney Inglimo's encounter with L.K. and his girlfriend. There was no testimony that Attorney Inglimo ever intentionally touched L.K.'s intimate parts or caused L.K. to touch his intimate parts. Moreover, there was no testimony that Attorney Inglimo engaged in any form of sexual intercourse with L.K. Thus, because it does not appear that the definitional elements of "sexual relations" have been satisfied, the

simple term "with" in the prohibitional phrase in SCR 20:1.8(k)(2) cannot transform this situation into a violation of the rule.

* * *

AM. BAR ASS'N, STANDING COMM. ON ETHICS & PROF'L RESPONSIBILITY,

Formal Op. 92-364 (July 6, 1992)

Sexual Relations With Clients

[*Ed.'s Note*—This opinion predated the adoption of Rule 1.8(j).]

A sexual relationship between lawyer and client may involve unfair exploitation of the lawyer's fiduciary position, and/or significantly impair a lawyer's ability to represent the client competently * * * .

* * * The roles of lover and lawyer are potentially conflicting ones as the emotional involvement that is fostered by a sexual relationship has the potential to undercut the objective detachment that is often demanded for adequate representation. Although no detailed statistics are presently available to document the incidence of sexual relations between clients and their lawyers, there is information enough to substantiate both the existence and the seriousness of problems in this area.

* * *

The existence of a sexual relationship between lawyer and client may make it impossible for the attorney to provide the competent representation of the client that is ethically required. This may be so for several different reasons.

* * *

Emotional detachment is essential to the lawyer's ability to render competent legal services. One of the most important aspects of the attorney-client relationship is the attorney's duty to exercise independent professional judgment. * * *

It can be difficult, however, to separate sound judgment from the emotion or bias that may result from a sexual relationship. * * * Because of a desire to preserve the relationship, the lawyer may be deterred from giving candid advice by the prospect that the advice will be unpalatable to the client. Thus, a lawyer who engages in a sexual relationship with a client during the course of representation risks losing the objectivity and reasonableness that form the basis of the lawyer's independent professional judgment.

* * *

While it may be argued that such a conflict only arises in the special situations presented, for example, by divorce proceedings, the fact is that these conflicting interests can arise even in seemingly benign settings. For instance, although it is generally thought that the ethical concerns raised by a sexual relationship are not present in the commercial corporate setting, a sexual relationship with a corporate client's representative can be just as problematic as in other contexts.

In the corporate setting the lawyer's client is the corporation, not any individual employee. Model Rule 1.13(a). And even in less extreme situations than those contemplated by Rule 1.13, as a result of instructions from the client the lawyer may be obliged to follow the established corporate chain of command in fulfilling counsel's obligation to report to the entity client. A potential conflict of interest arises if the lawyer, engaging in a sexual relationship with a corporate client's representative, learns information which may redound to the detriment of the sexual partner, but which should be reported to a higher authority.

Lawyers recognize how difficult it is to deal with such a situation in a representation free from a sexual relationship. When the corporate employee shares information with the company's lawyer and asks the lawyer either not to pass it on or pass it on anonymously, the corporate lawyer is conflicted enough in reconciling the lawyer's duty to the corporate client with the trust the corporate employee has reposed. Such a conflict can only be compounded when a sexual relationship is also involved.

A related danger resulting from the blurring of relationships and one where the lover becomes a participant adverse to the client is presented in divorce cases where the attorney engaging in a sexual relationship with a client may risk becoming an adverse witness to the client on issues of adultery and child custody.

* * *

A sexual relationship between the parties may also have the potential to blur the contours of the attorney-client relationship. Client confidences are protected by privilege only when they are imparted in the context of the attorney-client relationship. The courts will not protect confidences given as part of a personal relationship; except for that of husband and wife, there is no privilege for lovers. A blurred line between any professional and personal relationship may make it difficult to predict to what extent client confidences will be protected. Expectations of confidences will be forced to rest on ever shifting sands.

* * *

MATTER OF GRIMM

674 N.E.2d 551 (Ind. 1996)

PER CURIAM.

The Disciplinary Commission charged the respondent, Edgar A. Grimm, with violations of the Rules of Professional Conduct for Attorneys at Law arising from allegations that he maintained a sexual relationship with a client during that client's divorce proceedings. A hearing officer appointed by this Court * * * heard evidence and concluded that the respondent engaged in misconduct as charged. This matter is now before us for final resolution.

* * *

The respondent was admitted to this state's bar in 1959. We now find that in May of 1987, a client (the "client") retained the respondent to represent her in the dissolution of her marriage. The respondent and the client agreed that she would pay him $75 per hour for legal services and reimburse him for any reasonable cost advances he made on her behalf. At the outset, the respondent told her that he did not believe that his legal fees and expenses for the contemplated dissolution would exceed $2,500.

The respondent filed a dissolution action in Allen Circuit Court; it was later venued to Noble Circuit Court. Thereafter, the client received from the respondent several written invoices for legal services rendered. * * *

During the ensuing months while the dissolution and post-dissolution matters pended, the client confided various personal matters to the respondent. For example, she informed him that she had been a victim in her marriage of both physical and emotional abuse, as a result of which she experienced depression, low self-esteem, and suicidal thoughts. Beginning in late 1987, the respondent began to bestow a good deal of attention on the client. He telephoned her frequently, invited her to lunch, and complimented her on her attractiveness. His attentions continued to grow, and by January 1988 he began to take interest in her children, her social activities, and other personal matters.

On Valentine's Day, 1988, the respondent visited the client at her home and gave her flowers and candy. They drank wine together, held hands, and kissed. Approximately one or two weeks later, the respondent again visited the client's home, and they engaged in sexual activity.

At some time during February 1988, the client asked the respondent why she had not received any invoices for legal services since December 10, 1987. He informed her that he was "taking care" of the legal bills for the time being and that there was "nothing for [her] to worry about," or words to similar effect. Two months later, when the client again asked about invoices, the respondent made similar assurances. Sexual relations continued between the respondent and the client until at least August 1988. During the course of this intimate relationship, the respondent gave the client various gifts, including cash and a Mexican 50 pesos gold coin attached to a gold necklace.

Trial of the dissolution occurred on February 23, February 24, March 8, April 13, and April 26, 1988. Many issues were involved, including matters of child custody, child support, child visitation, ownership of certain real estate and real property and a substantial amount of personal property, the nature and value of the husband's business, dissipation of marital assets by the husband, and allocation of the parties' obligations. The respondent knew that the marriage had produced a child, then six years old, and that the client had custody of the child during the dissolution.

Around August of 1988, the client told the respondent that she no longer felt "right" about their relationship and that it was neither healthy nor appropriate. She then terminated their personal relationship, although the respondent's professional representation of her continued. The Noble Circuit Court entered findings and judgment in the dissolution on September 30, 1988.

On November 29, 1988, the respondent filed a "Notice of Intention to File and Hold Attorney Lien" (the "notice") against the client without having sent or presented invoices for legal services to the client since December 10, 1987. The notice indicated that the respondent sought $12,718.18 in attorney fees and targeted certain real estate that had been set off to the client in the dissolution for satisfaction of his claim. * * *

Trial was held on January 29, 30, and 31, 1992. The respondent testified under oath in support of the amount he claimed the client owed to him. He further testified that he had not had sexual relations with the client and that he had never given her gifts. On October 16, 1992, the DeKalb Circuit Court entered findings and judgment, therein ordering the client to pay to the respondent $9,916.94 plus prejudgment interest for services rendered in the dissolution, but found that he was not entitled to costs in the form of additional attorney fees * * *. On November 20, 1992, the client paid the respondent, prompting the respondent to release the money judgment while preserving his right to appeal on other issues. In his appeal to the Indiana Court of Appeals, the respondent contended, *inter alia*, that the trial court erroneously heard evidence about the personal relationship that he had had with the client. The Court of Appeals ultimately stated that such allegations "were relevant to an inquiry on the amount of damages . . ." and affirmed the trial court.

In his response to the Commission's notice of grievance, the respondent referred to the client as an "unmitigated liar," and, in denying the allegations in her grievance, characterized them as "nothing more than the raving of a lazy, promiscuous, greedy, psychotic bitch."

The hearing officer concluded that the respondent's sexual involvement with his client violated Ind. Professional Conduct Rules 1.7(b), which provides in relevant part:

> A lawyer shall not represent a client if the representation of that client may be materially limited by the lawyer's responsibilities to another client or to a third person, or by the lawyer's own interests, unless:
>
> > (1) the lawyer reasonably believes the representation will not be adversely affected; and
> >
> > (2) the client consents after consultation.

* * *

The respondent's sexual relationship with his client during the pendency of dissolution and post-dissolution matters materially limited his representation of her in those matters. Specifically, the hearing officer found that the respondent ceased informing the client of the status of her attorney fees account during the period of their personal involvement, thus depriving her of notice that his legal bill was growing beyond his initial communicated estimation. Ultimately, their failed personal relationship resulted in time-consuming and costly litigation over the nature and value of the services he had provided. We therefore find that the respondent violated Prof.Cond.R. 1.7(b) by representing a client when that representation was materially limited by his own interests.

* * *

Having found that the respondent engaged in professional misconduct, we must now determine an appropriate discipline. * * *

It is clear that the respondent's ability to attend objectively to the financial aspects of his professional relationship with the client was destroyed by his intimate involvement with her. As a result, she was forced to litigate the issue of fees owed and placed in an openly adversarial position with former trusted counsel. The respondent's apparent continued emotional involvement after termination of the personal relationship caused him purposely to mislead the Commission and to provide deceptive testimony to a tribunal. It is perhaps somewhat extenuating that there is no evidence of harm to the respondent's ability to litigate effectively the substantive issues of dissolution. We do note, however, that he should have been aware that his relationship could have negatively impacted issues of child custody. The respondent's intimate involvement with his client ultimately damaged his professional objectivity, poisoned their professional relationship, and led him to other professional misconduct.

In light of the foregoing, we are convinced that the respondent should be suspended from the practice of law for a period of one year. * * *

IV. Lawyer Advocate as Witness

[Question 16]

Attorney, who had represented Testator for many years, prepared Testator's will and acted as one of the two subscribing witnesses to its execution. Testator's sister and brother were his sole heirs. The will left Testator's entire estate to his sister and nothing to his brother. Upon Testator's death two years later, Executor, the executor named in the will, asked Attorney to act as his lawyer in the probate of the will and the administration of the estate. At that time, Executor informed Attorney that Testator's brother would concede that the will was properly executed but intended to contest the will on the ground that he had been excluded because of fraud previously practiced on Testator by Testator's sister. The other subscribing witness to the will predeceased Testator, and Attorney will be called as a witness solely for the purpose of establishing the due execution of the will.

Is it proper for Attorney to accept the representation?

  (A) Yes, if there is no contested issue of fact with respect to the formal execution of the will.

  (B) Yes, because Executor has no beneficial interest under the will.

  (C) No, unless Attorney's services are necessary to avoid substantial hardship to Executor.

  (D) No, because Attorney will be called as a witness in the case.

<u>Rule 3.7</u>—Lawyer As Witness

(a) A lawyer shall not act as advocate at a trial in which the lawyer is likely to be a necessary witness unless:

(1) the testimony relates to an uncontested issue;

(2) the testimony relates to the nature and value of legal services rendered in the case; or

(3) disqualification of the lawyer would work substantial hardship on the client.

(b) A lawyer may act as advocate in a trial in which another lawyer in the lawyer's firm is likely to be called as a witness unless precluded from doing so by Rule 1.7 or Rule 1.9.

Comment to Rule 3.7

Combining the roles of advocate and witness can prejudice the tribunal and the opposing party and can also involve a conflict of interest between the lawyer and client.

Advocate-Witness Rule

The tribunal has proper objection when the trier of fact may be confused or misled by a lawyer serving as both advocate and witness. The opposing party has proper objection where the combination of roles may prejudice that party's rights in the litigation. A witness is required to testify on the basis of personal knowledge, while an advocate is expected to explain and comment on evidence given by others. It may not be clear whether a statement by an advocate-witness should be taken as proof or as an analysis of the proof.

To protect the tribunal, paragraph (a) prohibits a lawyer from simultaneously serving as advocate and necessary witness except in those circumstances specified in paragraphs (a)(1) through (a)(3). Paragraph (a)(1) recognizes that if the testimony will be uncontested, the ambiguities in the dual role are purely theoretical. Paragraph (a)(2) recognizes that where the testimony concerns the extent and value of legal services rendered in the action in which the testimony is offered, permitting the lawyers to testify avoids the need for a second trial with new counsel to resolve that issue. Moreover, in such a situation the judge has firsthand knowledge of the matter in issue; hence, there is less dependence on the adversary process to test the credibility of the testimony.

Apart from these two exceptions, paragraph (a)(3) recognizes that a balancing is required between the interests of the client and those of the tribunal and the opposing party. Whether the tribunal is likely to be misled or the opposing party is likely to suffer prejudice depends on the nature of the case, the importance and probable tenor of the lawyer's testimony, and the probability that the lawyer's testimony will conflict with that of other witnesses. Even if there is risk of such prejudice, in determining whether the lawyer should be disqualified, due regard must be given to the effect of disqualification on the lawyer's client. It is relevant that one or both parties could reasonably foresee that the lawyer would probably be a witness. The conflict of interest principles stated in Rules 1.7, 1.9 and 1.10 have no application to this aspect of the problem.

Because the tribunal is not likely to be misled when a lawyer acts as advocate in a trial in which another lawyer in the lawyer's firm will testify as a necessary witness, paragraph (b) permits the lawyer to do so except in situations involving a conflict of interest.

Conflict of Interest

In determining if it is permissible to act as advocate in a trial in which the lawyer will be a necessary witness, the lawyer must also consider that the dual role may give rise to a conflict of interest that will require compliance with Rules 1.7 or 1.9. For example, if there is likely to be substantial conflict between the testimony of the client and that of the lawyer the representation involves a conflict of interest that requires compliance with Rule 1.7. * * * Determining whether or not such a conflict exists is primarily the responsibility of the lawyer involved. If there is a conflict of interest, the lawyer must secure the client's informed consent, confirmed in writing. In some cases, the lawyer will be precluded from seeking the client's consent. * * *

Paragraph (b) provides that a lawyer is not disqualified from serving as an advocate because a lawyer with whom the lawyer is associated in a firm is precluded from doing so by paragraph (a). If, however, the testifying lawyer would also be disqualified by Rule 1.7 or Rule 1.9 from representing the client in the matter, other lawyers in the firm will be precluded from representing the client by Rule 1.10 unless the client gives informed consent under the conditions stated in Rule 1.7.

For More Information

For an early analysis of the policies at work in the lawyer-as-advocate rule, *see* John F. Sutton, Jr., *The Testifying Advocate*, 41 Tex. L. Rev. 477 (1963); *see also* 2 Geoffrey C. Hazard et al., The Law of Lawyering § 33 (3d ed. 2004) for a thorough explanation of the rule and its operation in practice.

V. Representation Adverse to a Former Client

A. The General Rules

[Question 17]

Two years ago, Attorney was employed by State's Department of Transportation (DOT) to search title to several tracts of land. Attorney has not been employed by DOT during the last year. Recently, DOT instituted proceedings to condemn a tract, owned by Owner, for a new highway route. Owner asked Attorney to represent her in obtaining the highest amount of compensation for the condemnation. Owner's tract is one of the tracts on which Attorney searched title two years ago. Attorney remembers that Engineer, a DOT engineer, once drafted a confidential memorandum advising against running a new highway across Owner's land because of potential adverse environmental impact. Because of this information, Attorney believes it is possible to prevent the condemnation of Owner's land or to increase the settlement amount.

It is proper for Attorney to:

(A) represent Owner on the issue of damages only and not disclose the information that might prevent the condemnation.

(B) represent Owner and attempt to prevent the condemnation by using the information about the adverse environmental impact.

(C) refuse to represent Owner, but disclose to Owner the information about the adverse environmental impact.

(D) refuse to represent Owner and not disclose the information about the adverse environmental impact.

[Question 18]

Attorney was formerly employed by Insurance Company as a lawyer solely to handle fire insurance claims. While so employed she investigated a fire loss claim of Claimant against Insurance Company. Attorney is now in private practice.

Assume that the original claim was settled. One year after Attorney left the employ of Insurance Company, Claimant slipped and fell in Insurance Company's office. Claimant now asks Attorney to represent him or refer him to another lawyer for suit on the "slip and fall" claim.

Which of the following would be proper for Attorney to do?

I. Refuse to discuss the matter with Claimant.

II. Represent Claimant.

III. Give Claimant a list of lawyers who Attorney knows are competent and specialize in such claims.

  (A) I only.

  (B) I and II, but not III.

  (C) I and III, but not II.

  (D) I, II, and III.

[Question 19]

K& E's Washington, D.C. office prepared a report for client API, arguing that the market for uranium was competitive. API members shared confidential info with K&E, but are not clients—only API is the client. K&E's Chicago office later represents Westinghouse in a suit alleging price fixing in uranium by API members Kerr-McGee, Gulf and Getty. They move to disqualify K&E. What result?

  (A) No disqualification, because they are not former clients.

  (B) No disqualification, because two different offices worked on the matters.

  (C) Disqualification, because a member of the organization is former client.

  (D) Disqualification, because the relationship was client-like.

Rule 1.9—Duties to Former Clients

(a) A lawyer who has formerly represented a client in a matter shall not thereafter represent another person in the same or a substantially related matter in which that person's interests are materially adverse to the interests of the former client unless the former client gives informed consent, confirmed in writing.

(b) A lawyer shall not knowingly represent a person in the same or a substantially related matter in which a firm with which the lawyer formerly was associated had previously represented a client

  (1) whose interests are materially adverse to that person; and

(2) about whom the lawyer had acquired information protected by Rules 1.6 and 1.9(c) that is material to the matter;

unless the former client gives informed consent, confirmed in writing.

(c) A lawyer who has formerly represented a client in a matter or whose present or former firm has formerly represented a client in a matter shall not thereafter:

(1) use information relating to the representation to the disadvantage of the former client except as these Rules would permit or require with respect to a client, or when the information has become generally known; or

(2) reveal information relating to the representation except as these Rules would permit or require with respect to a client.

Comment to Rule 1.9

* * *

Matters are "substantially related" for purposes of this Rule if they involve the same transaction or legal dispute or if there otherwise is a substantial risk that confidential factual information as would normally have been obtained in the prior representation would materially advance the client's position in the subsequent matter. For example, * * * a lawyer who has previously represented a client in securing environmental permits to build a shopping center would be precluded from representing neighbors seeking to oppose rezoning of the property on the basis of environmental considerations; however, the lawyer would not be precluded, on the grounds of substantial relationship, from defending a tenant of the completed shopping center in resisting eviction for nonpayment of rent. Information that has been disclosed to the public or to other parties adverse to the former client ordinarily will not be disqualifying. Information acquired in a prior representation may have been rendered obsolete by the passage of time, a circumstance that may be relevant in determining whether two representations are substantially related. In the case of an organizational client, general knowledge of the client's policies and practices ordinarily will not preclude a subsequent representation; on the other hand, knowledge of specific facts gained in a prior representation that are relevant to the matter in question ordinarily will preclude such a representation. A former client is not required to reveal the confidential information learned by the lawyer in order to establish a substantial risk that the lawyer has confidential information to use in the subsequent matter. A conclusion about the possession of such information may be based on the nature of the services the lawyer provided the former client and information that would in ordinary practice be learned by a lawyer providing such services.

WESTINGHOUSE ELEC. CORP. v. GULF OIL CORP.

588 F.2d 221 (7th Cir. 1978)

SPRECHER, Circuit Judge.

In this case we review the propriety of a district court's refusal to grant a motion to disqualify opposing counsel. The issues presented are whether there is a sufficient relationship between matters presented by the pending litigation and matters which the lawyers in question worked on in behalf of the party now seeking disqualification and whether the party seeking disqualification has given legally sufficient consent to the dual representation.

I

This case arises as one aspect of the complex litigation filed by Westinghouse against a number of parties engaged in, or having interests in, the mining of uranium. That suit alleged that increases in the price of uranium, which had encouraged Westinghouse to default on long-term uranium supply contracts, resulted from an international cartel which was alleged to have "fixed and increased the price of uranium to purchasers within the United States; * * * [and] otherwise eliminated competition among defendants. . . ." The movant here, Gulf Oil Corporation (Gulf), and the respondent, United Nuclear Corporation (UNC) are two of the named defendants in this action. UNC is being represented by the Santa Fe, New Mexico firm of Bigbee, Stephenson, Carpenter & Crout (Bigbee), which had previously performed legal work on behalf of Gulf. Gulf, accordingly, moved to disqualify the Bigbee firm.

The history of the relationship between Gulf and Bigbee had its origin in 1968, when substantial reserves of uranium ore were discovered on tracts of land located near Grants, New Mexico. By 1971 Gulf owned a substantial majority interest in a joint venture which had acquired a portion, designated as the Mt. Taylor properties, of these uranium reserves. After having acquired its interests, Gulf retained the Bigbee firm to represent it on legal matters relating to Gulf's uranium operations in New Mexico. During a five year period of representation from 1971 through 1976, the Bigbee firm through nine of its twelve attorneys performed numerous services for Gulf including the patenting of fifty-nine mining claims, drafting leases required for uranium exploration, representing Gulf in litigation involving title disputes, counseling Gulf in relation to the resolution of certain problems relating to mine waters, and lobbying on behalf of Gulf in front of the New Mexico state legislature on tax and environmental matters. One of Bigbee's name partners, G. Stanley Crout, alone spent over 2,000 hours working on behalf of Gulf.

Gulf argued before the district court that these matters on which Bigbee represented Gulf were substantially related to the matters raised in the Westinghouse
litigation. Gulf delineated this relationship by arguing that since the Mt. Taylor
properties constituted Gulf's largest supply of uranium and was not currently in
production, the reasons for Gulf's failure to produce from this property would be
material to the allegation of the Westinghouse suit that Gulf, as well as the other
defendants, withheld uranium supplies from the market. Further, Gulf argued, in
relation to Bigbee's prior representation of Gulf, Gulf had entrusted Bigbee with
confidential information relating to the quantity and quality of uranium reserves
in the Mt. Taylor properties. Finally, even though Bigbee represented UNC, a co-
defendant in Westinghouse, the position between the two parties was adverse
because UNC was attempting to exculpate itself by inculpating Gulf.

The district court accepted Gulf's argument of actual adverseness but nonetheless
declined to disqualify the Bigbee firm. The court concluded that Bigbee "certainly
did gain knowledge of Gulf's uranium properties during its work" but reasoned
that nevertheless there was not a substantial relationship between the matters
encompassed by the prior representation and those of the Westinghouse litigation, because the prior representation "focused on real estate transactions connected with Gulf's untapped and undeveloped uranium reserves," whereas the
"heart of the complaint" details a price-fixing conspiracy, the evidence of which
"will focus on meetings and communications among the alleged co-conspirators,
as well as evidence on uranium prices, terms and conditions of sale, and market
availability." Thus, the court concluded that there was no substantial relationship
between the matters.

II

The district court set out and attempted to apply what is clearly settled as the
relevant test in disqualification matters: where an attorney represents a party in a
matter in which the adverse party is that attorney's former client, the attorney will
be disqualified if the subject matter of the two representations are "substantially
related."

* * *

[I]t is clear that the determination of whether there is a substantial relationship
turns on the possibility, or appearance thereof, that confidential information might
have been given to the attorney in relation to the subsequent matter in which
disqualification is sought. The rule thus does not necessarily involve any inquiry
into the imponderables involved in the degree of relationship between the two
matters but instead involves a realistic appraisal of the possibility that confidences
had been disclosed in the one matter which will be harmful to the client in the
other. * * * [I]t is not appropriate for the court to inquire into whether actual
confidences were disclosed.

The substantial relationship test is not a rule of substantive law but a measure of the quantum of evidence required for proof of the existence of the professional obligation. The evidence need only establish the scope of the legal representation and not the actual receipt of the allegedly relevant confidential information. * * * Doubts as to the existence of an asserted conflict of interest should be resolved in favor of disqualification.

The substantial relationship is determined by asking whether it could reasonably be said that during the former representation that attorney might have acquired information related to the subject matter of the subsequent representation. * * * Essentially then, disqualification questions require three levels of inquiry. Initially, the trial judge must make a factual reconstruction of the scope of the prior legal representation. Second, it must be determined whether it is reasonable to infer that the confidential information allegedly given would have been given to a lawyer representing a client in those matters. Finally, it must be determined whether that information is relevant to the issues raised in the litigation pending against the former client.

Although the district court properly identified this rule of law, it erred in its application. * * * It was established that Bigbee prepared numerous mining patents and handled real estate transactions relating to Gulf uranium properties. Given this reconstruction, the second step in the analysis is to inquire whether it is reasonable to presume that Gulf would have transmitted to the Bigbee firm the class of confidential information allegedly given.

Gulf alleges that three types of confidential information were imparted: 1) that relating to the quantity and quality of uranium reserves at Mt. Taylor, 2) the reasons for delaying the production of those reserves, and 3) information detailing Gulf's relationship with one of the joint owners of the properties. Regardless of the reasonableness of inferring knowledge of the reasons for production delay from the scope of the former representation, we think it is clearly reasonable to presume that the information regarding quantity and quality of uranium was given. Indeed, it seems difficult to believe that Bigbee would not have acquired rather detailed information relating to the quantity and quality of the uranium reserves in the course of its filing of mining patents and resolution of conflicting claims. * * *

Having established the presumption that this information was given, disqualification must result if that information is relevant to the issues in the suit pending against Gulf. Relevance must be gauged by the violations alleged in the complaint and assessment of the evidence useful in establishing those allegations. Judge Marshall did not consider the information allegedly given to Bigbee to be relevant to the cartel litigation. He reasoned that the violation charged was essentially price fixing, not conspiratorial control of uranium production. * * *

The lower court erred, both in identifying the issues raised by an allegation of price fixing, and in assessing the relevance of circumstantial economic evidence to proof of a price fixing conspiracy. The lower court found that the "heart of the (Westinghouse) complaint is directed at alleged price-fixing arrangements." However, an agreement to restrict the production of uranium unquestionably is a price fixing arrangement. * * * Thus, the lower court's view that conspiracy to fix prices and conspiracy to restrict output are distinct offenses is in error. * * *

The lower court also erred in its determination of what evidence was relevant to proof of the alleged price fixing conspiracy. * * * Proof that Gulf was restricting its output of uranium would be highly relevant circumstantial evidence if its competitors were behaving in a parallel fashion. Although evidence of parallel behavior alone may not be sufficient to establish conspiracy, it is given great weight. Furthermore, it has been suggested that proof that an individual competitor has un-utilized productive capacity in excess of demand may in itself suggest collusive behavior within an industry. Information possibly demonstrating that Gulf had uranium reserves available for production which were not brought on to the market would be central to this mode of proof. Thus, even though Westinghouse could prove its claim of price fixing solely through direct evidence of collusive agreements, evidence of Gulf's quantity and quality of uranium reserves could serve as a central element in an alternative method of proof of the Section One Sherman Act violation alleged. * * * Therefore the incentives to disclose and abuse the confidential information are present, and disqualification is required.

In one of the most recent Second Circuit cases, a lawyer upon graduation from law school became associated with a firm representing Cook Industries, which was being sued in connection with a shipment of soybeans from Louisiana to Taiwan which was 254 tons short of the amount stated on the bills of lading and weight certificates. After putting in more than 100 hours over three years on behalf of Cook, the young lawyer left his firm and became associated with another firm where he was assigned to represent the government of India which was suing Cook Industries for delivery of grain of inferior quality and grade and of short weight. Although the two representations involved different shipments at different times to different parties, they shared similar loading and weighing procedures of Cook to which the lawyer had become privy in his first representation. The Second Circuit concluded that "(i)t would be difficult to think of a closer nexus between issues."

Here it could reasonably be said that during the former representation the attorneys might have acquired information related to the subject matter of the subsequent representation, that the former representation was lengthy and pervasive, that the former representation was more than peripheral, and that the relationship between the two matters is sufficiently close to bring the later representation within the prohibition of the canons. Therefore there was clearly a substantial relationship between the two representations.

* * *

REVERSED AND REMANDED.

B. Former and Current Government Lawyers

[Question 20]

While an assistant district attorney, Attorney Alpha was in charge of the presentation before a grand jury of evidence that led to an indictment charging thirty-two defendants with conspiracy to sell controlled drugs. Shortly after the grand jury returned the indictments, Alpha resigned as assistant district attorney and became an associate in the law office of Attorney Beta, a sole practitioner. At the time of such association, Beta was the attorney for Deft, one of the indicted codefendants. Is it proper for Attorney Beta to continue to represent Deft?

(A) Yes, if Alpha does not reveal to Beta any confidence or secret learned while an assistant district attorney.

(B) Yes, because a public prosecutor must make timely disclosure to the defense attorney of any exculpatory evidence.

(C) No, unless Alpha agrees not to participate in the representation of Deft.

(D) No, because Alpha had substantial responsibility for the indictment of Deft.

<u>Rule 1.11</u>—Special Conflicts of Interest for Former and Current Government Officers and Employees

Former Government Officers and Employees

(a) Except as law may otherwise expressly permit, a lawyer who has formerly served as a public officer or employee of the government:

(1) is subject to Rule 1.9(c); and

(2) shall not otherwise represent a client in connection with a matter in which the lawyer participated personally and substantially as a public officer or employee, unless the appropriate government agency gives its informed consent, confirmed in writing, to the representation.

(b) When a lawyer is disqualified from representation under paragraph (a), no lawyer in a firm with which that lawyer is associated may knowingly undertake or continue representation in such a matter unless:

(1) the disqualified lawyer is timely screened from any participation in the matter and is apportioned no part of the fee therefrom; and

(2) written notice is promptly given to the appropriate government agency to enable it to ascertain compliance with the provisions of this rule.

(c) Except as law may otherwise expressly permit, a lawyer having information that the lawyer knows is confidential government information about a person acquired when the lawyer was a public officer or employee, may not represent a private client whose interests are adverse to that person in a matter in which the information could be used to the material disadvantage of that person. As used in this Rule, the term "confidential government information" means information that has been obtained under governmental authority and which, at the time this Rule is applied, the government is prohibited by law from disclosing to the public or has a legal privilege not to disclose and which is not otherwise available to the public. A firm with which that lawyer is associated may undertake or continue representation in the matter only if the disqualified lawyer is timely screened from any participation in the matter and is apportioned no part of the fee therefrom.

Current Government Officers and Employees

(d) Except as law may otherwise expressly permit, a lawyer currently serving as a public officer or employee:

(1) is subject to Rules 1.7 and 1.9; and

(2) shall not:

(i) participate in a matter in which the lawyer participated personally and substantially while in private practice or nongovernmental employment, unless the appropriate government agency gives its informed consent, confirmed in writing; or

(ii) negotiate for private employment with any person who is involved as a party or as lawyer for a party in a matter in which the lawyer is participating personally and substantially, except that a lawyer serving as a law clerk to a judge, other adjudicative officer or arbitrator may negotiate for private employment as permitted by Rule 1.12(b) and subject to the conditions stated in Rule 1.12(b).

(e) As used in this Rule, the term "matter" includes:

(1) any judicial or other proceeding, application, request for a ruling or other determination, contract, claim, controversy, investigation, charge, accusation, arrest or other particular matter involving a specific party or parties, and

(2) any other matter covered by the conflict of interest rules of the appropriate government agency.

Take Note

The term "matter" for purposes of <u>Rule 1.11</u> has a specific definition and scope. ABA Formal Opinion 342 (1975) explains that, under Rule 1.11, a "matter" is a

Discrete and isolatable transaction or set of transactions between identifiable parties. * * * The same lawsuit or litigation is the same matter. By contrast, work as a government employee in drafting, enforcing or interpreting government or agency procedures, regulations, or laws, or in briefing abstract principles of law, does not disqualify the lawyer from subsequent private employment involving the same regulations, procedures, or points of law; the same "matter" is not involved because there is lacking the discrete, identifiable transactions or conduct involving a particular situation and specific parties.

BABINEAUX v. FOSTER

<u>2005 WL 711604 (E.D. La. 2005)</u>

AFRICK, J.

Before the Court is a motion to disqualify plaintiff's counsel filed on behalf of defendants, the City of Hammond and Mayor Mayson Foster. Defendants argue that plaintiff's counsel, Douglas D. Brown, should be disqualified because his previous employment as an Assistant City Attorney for the City of Hammond creates a conflict of interest. After considering the law, the arguments of the parties, and the record, defendants' motion to disqualify is DENIED.

Make the Connection

How does the concept of "matter" for purposes of Rule 1.11 compare to "matter" as defined in Rule 1.12? See below for further discussion on this point.

Background

Plaintiff, Tysonia Babineaux ("Babineaux"), was the City of Hammond's Recreation Director until she was dismissed in July 2003. In connection with her dismissal, she has sued the City of Hammond and Mayor Foster (collectively "the City") for violations of Title VII of the 1964 Civil Rights Act and Louisiana's anti-employment discrimination statute.

Babineaux retained attorney Douglas D. Brown to represent her in her employment discrimination lawsuit. Brown was an Assistant City Attorney for the City of Hammond during the administration of former Mayor Louis J. Tallo which ended on December 31, 2002, when the City's current mayor, defendant Mayson Foster, took office. Since leaving the Hammond City Attorney's office, Brown has entered private practice, representing a number of individuals in lawsuits against the City of Hammond.

The thrust of the City's motion to disqualify centers around an employment grievance filed by Babineaux in 2001, while Brown was an Assistant City Attorney for the City of Hammond. Specifically, the City alleges that (1) the subject matter of Babineaux's 2001 grievance is "similar in all material respects" to plaintiff's current allegations and (2) Brown presumably has knowledge of confidential information relating to the prior complaint. Therefore, the City argues that Louisiana law and the Louisiana Rules of Professional Conduct require Brown to withdraw from the case.

Brown argues, on behalf of the plaintiff, that no conflict of interest exists because all of the events giving rise to the current allegations occurred after he left the Hammond City Attorney's office. Further, Brown claims that the City and the Mayor hold a grudge against him for "making a living suing his former client," and, that the defendants are only bringing this motion to disqualify him because of "secondary motives." Brown also points out that he has offered to amend Paragraph 35 of plaintiff's complaint to limit the temporal reach of the action to events occurring after he left the City Attorney's office. Finally, Brown argues that Babineaux's right to counsel of her choice should outweigh any relationship between this case and Babineaux's 2001 complaint.

Law and Analysis

* * *

II. Inapplicability of Louisiana Rule of Professional Conduct 1.9

The City bases much of this motion to disqualify on Louisiana Rule of Professional Conduct 1.9(a). [Identical to Model Rule 1.9(a), supra] * * * Brown responds that Rule 1.9 is inapplicable to this case because he never "represented" the City of Hammond in relation to Babineaux's 2001 grievance.

Brown is correct that subsection (a) of Rule 1.9 is inapplicable to this case, but not because he did not represent the City of Hammond in 2001. Rather, because Brown is a former government attorney, any conflict with his former employer is governed by Rule 1.11. [Identical to Model Rule 1.11, supra].

* * *

Because Rule 1.9 would require disqualification of former non-government attorneys who have formerly represented a client in any "substantially related" matter, regardless of the attorney's involvement, it imposes a higher ethical duty on attorneys exclusively engaged in private practice. On the other hand, Rule 1.11 requires a former government attorney to have "personally and substantially" participated in a previous "matter" which, therefore, requires a higher threshold for disqualification. If parties seeking to disqualify any opposing attorney (even former government counsel) could rely on Rule 1.9(a), it would render 1.11(a) surplusage in adverse representations. In other words, if the City is correct that 1.9(a) applies in cases like this one, no party seeking disqualification of a former government attorney would ever rely on Rule 1.11(a), considering that it provides a former government attorney substantially less chance of disqualification.

* * *

ABA Model Rule 1.11 was intended to "deal with the problems peculiar to government service." ABA Formal Op. 409. Although the Louisiana version of Rule 1.11 does not include official comments, this Court finds the ABA comments to Model Rule 1.11 persuasive. In particular, comment 4 to Rule 1.11 states the reasons behind the more lenient standard for former government lawyers:

> [T]he rules governing lawyers presently or formerly employed by a government agency should not be so restrictive as to inhibit transfer of employment to and from the government. The government has a legitimate need to attract qualified lawyers as well as to maintain high ethical standards. Thus a former government lawyer is disqualified only from particular matters in which the lawyer participated personally and substantially.

Governments need and want good young lawyers to devote some time to public service without depriving themselves of the ability to obtain employment thereafter.

For the above reasons, this Court finds that Rule 1.11, and not Rule 1.9(a) or (c), applies to this case. The City, however, does not solely rely on Rule 1.9 in its motion to disqualify Brown. It also argues that Rule 1.11 requires disqualification because Brown was "personally and arguably substantially involved as counsel for Mayor Tallo" in connection with the 2001 grievance.

III. Applying Rule 1.11

The current version of Louisiana Rule of Professional Conduct 1.11(a) and (c) requires the party moving for disqualification to show either that the former government attorney participated "personally and substantially" in a previous "matter" or that the attorney actually possesses confidential government information.

A. Personal and Substantial Involvement

Neither the Fifth Circuit nor the Louisiana Supreme Court has clearly defined what constitutes "personal and substantial" participation in a previous matter. However, the Fifth Circuit has suggested that if a lawyer is only "tenuously and nominally" connected to the prior case, the personal and substantial requirement is not met. *See Hernandez v. Johnson,* 108 F.3d 554, 560 (5th Cir. 1997). * * * In a Formal Ethics Opinion addressing Rule 1.11's predecessor, DR 9-101(B), the ABA stated that:

> "substantial responsibility" envisages a much closer and more direct relationship than that of a mere perfunctory approval or disapproval of the matter in question. It contemplates a responsibility requiring the official to become personally involved to an important, material degree, in the investigative or deliberative processes regarding the transactions or facts in question.

With these guidelines in mind, the Court turns to the City's arguments.

The City contends that Brown should be disqualified pursuant to Rule 1.11 for two reasons. First, the City argues that Brown was "personally and substantially" involved in Babineaux's 2001 grievance. Second, the City argues that Brown was privy to confidential information in connection with the 2001 grievance. Specifically, the City claims that Mayor Tallo copied Brown on a "confidential" response to Babineaux's complaint. The City also argues that, based on Brown's receipt of this response letter, "it can be presumed that other confidential information transpired during Brown's representation of the City of Hammond."

In *United States v. Clark,* 333 F. Supp. 2d 789, 794 (E.D. Wis. 2004) the district court disqualified a former Assistant United States Attorney from representing a criminal defendant where the attorney (1) was currently defending a client on the same charge that he was previously assigned to prosecute; (2) had received and reviewed investigative reports in connection with the prosecution; and (3) had previously discussed the matter with the head law enforcement agent in charge of the investigation and arrest. In *United States v. Phillip Morris, Inc.,* 312 F. Supp. 2d 27 (D.D.C. 2004) the district court disqualified a former Food and Drug

Administration attorney from representing a tobacco company after the government produced timesheets indicating that the attorney had logged 382 hours on substantially-related litigation.

Neither *Clark* nor *Phillip Morris* is analogous to this case. There is no evidence that Brown conducted any investigation in connection with the 2001 complaint. There is also no evidence that Brown spent any substantial amount of time on the matter. While Brown does not dispute receiving the two letters in connection with the 2001 matter, he has submitted a declaration that he does not recall receiving the letters. Further, Brown has stated, under penalty of perjury, that any involvement he did have in the 2001 matter was limited to being copied on those two letters. * * * The City has not submitted any evidence that questions the validity of these statements.

"Professional ethics are self-enforcing, and lawyers are entitled to the presumption of being ethical, until the contrary is shown in specific instances." Therefore, this Court finds that Brown's cursory involvement in the 2001 matter does not rise to the level of "personal and substantial" participation in a matter which would require his disqualification pursuant to Rule 1.11.

B. Possession of Confidential Information

Even if Brown did not "personally and substantially participate" in the 2001 matter, Rule 1.11(c) requires disqualification if he possesses information he knows to be confidential and that information could be used to the material disadvantage of his former client. "Confidential government information" is defined * * * as "information that has been obtained under governmental authority and which, at the time [the] Rule is applied, the government is prohibited by law from disclosing to the public or has a legal privilege not to disclose and which is not otherwise available to the public." La. R. Prof. Cond. 1.11(c). * * *

The City does not contend that Brown possesses any specific confidential information beyond the information contained in the two letters on which Brown was copied. Rather, the City contends that "it can be presumed that other confidential communications transpired" during Brown's 2001 representation of the City of Hammond. Considering all of the evidence submitted, this Court finds that Brown does not possess confidential government information that could be used to the material disadvantage of the City. Consequently, the Court finds that the City has not carried its burden in showing that Brown personally and substantially participated in the 2001 grievance or possesses confidential information, and, therefore, Brown should not be disqualified pursuant to Rule 1.11.

* * *

VI. Third Party Neutrals and the Mediation Alternative—Model Rules 2.4 and 1.12

Rule 2.4—Lawyer Serving As Third-Party Neutral

(a) A lawyer serves as a third-party neutral when the lawyer assists two or more persons who are not clients of the lawyer to reach a resolution of a dispute or other matter that has arisen between them. Service as a third-party neutral may include service as an arbitrator, a mediator or in such other capacity as will enable the lawyer to assist the parties to resolve the matter.

(b) A lawyer serving as a third-party neutral shall inform unrepresented parties that the lawyer is not representing them. When the lawyer knows or reasonably should know that a party does not understand the lawyer's role in the matter, the lawyer shall explain the difference between the lawyer's role as a third-party neutral and a lawyer's role as one who represents a client.

Comment to Rule 2.4

* * *

Unlike nonlawyers who serve as third-party neutrals, lawyers serving in this role may experience unique problems as a result of differences between the role of a third-party neutral and a lawyer's service as a client representative. The potential for confusion is significant when the parties are unrepresented in the process. Thus, paragraph (b) requires a lawyer-neutral to inform unrepresented parties that the lawyer is not representing them. For some parties, particularly parties who frequently use dispute-resolution processes, this information will be sufficient. For others, particularly those who are using the process for the first time, more information will be required. Where appropriate, the lawyer should inform unrepresented parties of the important differences between the lawyer's role as third-party neutral and a lawyer's role as a client representative, including the inapplicability of the attorney-client evidentiary privilege. * * *

A lawyer who serves as a third-party neutral subsequently may be asked to serve as a lawyer representing a client in the same matter. The conflicts of interest that arise for both the individual lawyer and the lawyer's law firm are addressed in Rule 1.12.

* * *

Rule 1.12—Former Judge, Arbitrator, Mediator Or Other Third-Party Neutral

(a) Except as stated in paragraph (d), a lawyer shall not represent anyone in connection with a matter in which the lawyer participated personally and substantially as a judge or other adjudicative officer or law clerk to such a person or as an arbitrator, mediator or other third-party neutral, unless all parties to the proceeding give informed consent, confirmed in writing.

* * *

(c) If a lawyer is disqualified by paragraph (a), no lawyer in a firm with which that lawyer is associated may knowingly undertake or continue representation in the matter unless:

> (1) the disqualified lawyer is timely screened from any participation in the matter and is apportioned no part of the fee therefrom; and

> (2) written notice is promptly given to the parties and any appropriate tribunal to enable them to ascertain compliance with the provisions of this rule.

(d) An arbitrator selected as a partisan of a party in a multimember arbitration panel is not prohibited from subsequently representing that party.

Comment to Rule 1.12

* * *

Like former judges, lawyers who have served as arbitrators, mediators or other third-party neutrals may be asked to represent a client in a matter in which the lawyer participated personally and substantially. This Rule forbids such representation unless all of the parties to the proceedings give their informed consent, confirmed in writing. Other law or codes of ethics governing third-party neutrals may impose more stringent standards of personal or imputed disqualification. *See* Rule 2.4.

Although lawyers who serve as third-party neutrals do not have information concerning the parties that is protected under Rule 1.6, they typically owe the parties an obligation of confidentiality under law or codes of ethics governing third-party neutrals. Thus, paragraph (c) provides that conflicts of the personally disqualified lawyer will be imputed to other lawyers in a law firm unless the conditions of this paragraph are met.

* * *

[Question 21]

An attorney's law firm regularly represented a large company in its international business transactions. The company became involved in a contractual

dispute with a foreign government. The company invoked a mandatory arbitration procedure contained in the contract. Under the arbitration clause, each party was allowed to choose a partisan arbitrator and the partisan arbitrators were to choose an additional arbitrator to sit on the panel. The company selected the attorney to be on the arbitration panel. Neither the attorney nor his law firm had represented the company in connection with the contract with the foreign government. The arbitration was completed, and the company was awarded the sum of $100,000. The company then hired the attorney to enforce the award. The attorney obtained the consent of the other arbitrators before accepting the representation. He was successful in enforcing the award.

Is the attorney subject to discipline?

(A) Yes, because the attorney should not have represented the company in a matter in which the attorney had been an arbitrator.

(B) Yes, because the attorney should have declined the arbitration assignment in view of his law firm's regular representation of the company.

(C) No, because the attorney obtained the consent of the other arbitrators before accepting the representation.

(D) No, because the attorney was appointed to the arbitration panel as a partisan arbitrator.

Take Note

Policy Underlying the Rules: Fields-D'Arpino v. Restaurant Associates, Inc., <u>39 F. Supp. 2d</u> <u>412 (S.D.N.Y. 1999)</u>

The plaintiff in *Restaurant Associates* filed suit against her employer alleging gender and pregnancy discrimination, and sought an order disqualifying the Dornbush firm as counsel for Defendants. Plaintiff argued that the Dornbush firm's earlier involvement as a "neutral, third-party" in attempting to resolve her discrimination claim prior to litigation precluded the firm's later representation of Defendant in the same dispute. According to Plaintiff, the firm lured her into disclosing certain confidences because it held itself out as a "neutral" mediator.

Judge Pauley found that, although the Dornbush firm did not conceal or misrepresent its relationship with Defendant, the firm—through its attorney-mediator—purported to be an impartial mediator for Plaintiff's grievance. The firm failed to implement screening procedures that would have prevented the attorney-mediator from sharing with other attorneys in the firm the confidential information disclosed by Plaintiff during the mediation. Rather, the firm attempted to exploit what the attorney-mediator learned during the mediation, and even intended to call the attorney-mediator as a witness at trial.

Take Note (Continued)

In disqualifying the Dornbush firm, the court emphasized the "strong public policy favoring mediation":

> With the heavy caseloads shouldered today by federal and State courts alike, mediation provides a vital alternative to litigation. The benefits of mediation include its cost-effectiveness, speed and adaptability. Successful mediation, however, depends upon the perception and existence of mutual fairness throughout the mediation process. In this regard, courts have implicitly recognized that maintaining expectations of confidentiality is critical.

* * *

> In light of the * * * strong public policy favoring mediation, the Court finds that the appropriate remedial action to be taken here is disqualification of the Dornbush firm. Accordingly, plaintiff's motion is granted and the Dornbush firm is disqualified from representing the defendants in this action.

VII. Vicarious Disqualification Under Rule 1.10: Disqualification of an Entire Firm Because of a Tainted Lawyer

[Question 22]

Pat is a member of a 100 person firm specializing in products liability. In 2003, Pat represented a motorcycle manufacturer sued by a purchaser who was seriously injured by an alleged defective design. The case was settled in 2005 after extensive discovery. In 2010, Pat is approached by a person injured on the same model of motorcycle. The victim asked Pat to represent him.

(A) Can Pat represent the victim?

(B) Can Pat refer the victim to another member of the firm to handle the matter?

(C) What if Pat had left the firm in 2006, and the victim asks Pat's former firm to represent him?

(D) What if the victim retains a different firm and, once the action is brought against the manufacturer, that other firm hires Pat?

Rule 1.10—Imputation of Conflicts of Interest

(a) While lawyers are associated in a firm, none of them shall knowingly represent a client when any one of them practicing alone would be prohibited from doing so by Rules 1.7 or 1.9, unless

(1) the prohibition is based on a personal interest of the disqualified lawyer and does not present a significant risk of materially limiting the representation of the client by the remaining lawyers in the firm; or

(2) the prohibition is based upon Rule 1.9(a) or (b) and arises out of the disqualified lawyer's association with a prior firm, and

> (i) the disqualified lawyer is timely screened from any participation in the matter and is apportioned no part of the fee therefrom;

> (ii) written notice is promptly given to any affected former client to enable the former client to ascertain compliance with the provisions of this Rule, which shall include a description of the screening procedures employed; a statement of the firm's and of the screened lawyer's compliance with these Rules; a statement that review may be available before a tribunal; and an agreement by the firm to respond promptly to any written inquiries or objections by the former client about the screening procedures; and

> (iii) certifications of compliance with these Rules and with the screening procedures are provided to the former client by the screened lawyer and by a partner of the firm, at reasonable intervals upon the former client's written request and upon termination of the screening procedures.

(b) When a lawyer has terminated an association with a firm, the firm is not prohibited from thereafter representing a person with interests materially adverse to those of a client represented by the formerly associated lawyer and not currently represented by the firm, unless:

(1) the matter is the same or substantially related to that in which the formerly associated lawyer represented the client; and

(2) any lawyer remaining in the firm has information protected by Rules 1.6 and 1.9(c) that is material to the matter.

Take Note

The provision for screening was enacted in 2009. The rationale for allowing screening was that most courts were already allowing it anyway, and so the Rules should keep up with what the courts are doing. Another rationale was that screening was important for allowing lawyer mobility—especially in a difficult market for lawyers.

(c) A disqualification prescribed by this rule may be waived by the affected client under the conditions stated in Rule 1.7.

(d) The disqualification of lawyers associated in a firm with former or current government lawyers is governed by Rule 1.11.

LASALLE NAT'L BANK v. COUNTY OF LAKE

703 F.2d 252 (7th Cir. 1983)

CUDAHY, Circuit Judge.

* * * Lake County, Illinois, one of the parties to this appeal, is the former employer of an attorney now practicing law with the firm representing the plaintiffs-appellants. Lake County moved to disqualify the plaintiffs' law firm because of the County's former relationship with one of the firm's associates. The district court granted the motion, finding that the past association gave rise to an appearance of impropriety and holding that both the attorney and the entire law firm must be disqualified. * * * We affirm the order of the district court.

I.

Marc Seidler, the attorney upon whose career our attention must focus in this case, served as an Assistant State's Attorney in Lake County from 1976 until January 31, 1981. On December 1, 1976, Mr. Seidler was appointed Chief of the Civil Division of the Lake County State's Attorney's office, and in September 1979, he was appointed First Assistant State's Attorney. As such, he had general supervisory responsibility with respect to all civil cases handled by the State's Attorney's office. On February 2, 1981, Mr. Seidler joined the Chicago law firm of Rudnick & Wolfe as an associate, working in the firm's Northbrook, Illinois office. * * *

On June 5, 1981, Rudnick & Wolfe filed suit against the County of Lake and the Village of Grayslake, on behalf of its clients, the LaSalle National Bank as Trustee ("LaSalle National") and Lake Properties Venture ("Lake Properties"). * * *

[The Court finds that Seidler represented the defendant County on a substantially related matter, and therefore that Seidler would be personally disqualified from this action.]

IV.

Having found that Mr. Seidler was properly disqualified from representation of the plaintiffs in this case, we must now address whether this disqualification should be extended to the entire law firm of Rudnick & Wolfe. Although the knowledge possessed by one attorney in a law firm is presumed to be shared with the other attorneys in the firm, this court has held that this presumption may be rebutted. The question arises here whether this presumption may be effectively rebutted by establishing that the "infected" attorney was "screened," or insulated, from all participation in and information about a case, thus avoiding disqualification of an entire law firm based on the prior employment of one member.

* * * If past employment in government results in the disqualification of future employers from representing some of their long-term clients, it seems clearly possible that government attorneys will be regarded as "Typhoid Marys." Many talented lawyers, in turn, may be unwilling to spend a period in government service, if that service makes them unattractive or risky for large law firms to hire. In recognition of this problem, several other circuits have begun either explicitly or implicitly to approve the use of screening as a means to avoid disqualification of an entire law firm by "infection." * * *

* * *

Scholarly commentary has also generally approved screening as a device to avoid the wholesale disqualification of law firms with which former government attorneys are associated.

The screening arrangements which courts and commentators have approved, however, contain certain common characteristics. [In one case permitting screening, the screened attorney was] denied access to relevant files and did not share in the profits or fees derived from the representation in question; discussion of the suit was prohibited in his presence and no members of the firm were permitted to show him any documents relating to the case; and both the disqualified attorney and others in his firm affirmed these facts under oath. [Another] case was similarly specific: all other attorneys in the firm were forbidden to discuss the case with the disqualified attorney and instructed to prevent any documents from reaching him; the files were kept in a locked file cabinet, with the keys controlled by two partners and issued to others only on a "need to know" basis. In both cases, moreover, * * *, the screening arrangement was set up at the time when the potentially disqualifying event occurred, either when the attorney first joined the firm or when the firm accepted a case presenting an ethical problem.

In the case at hand, by contrast, Mr. Seidler joined the firm of Rudnick & Wolfe on February 2, 1981; yet screening arrangements were not established until the disqualification motion was filed in August 1981. * * * Although Mr. Seidler states in his affidavit that he did not disclose to any person associated with the firm any [confidential] information * * * on any matter relevant to this litigation, no specific institutional mechanisms were in place to insure that that information was not shared, even if inadvertently, between the months of February and

August.[3] Recognizing that this is an area in which the relevant information is singularly within the ken of the party defending against the motion to disqualify and in which the reputation of the bar as a whole is implicated, we hold that the district court did not abuse its discretion in extending the disqualification of Marc Seidler to the entire firm of Rudnick & Wolfe. The district court order is therefore

Affirmed.

HEMPSTEAD VIDEO, INC. v. INCORPORATED VILLAGE OF VALLEY STREAM

409 F.3d 127 (2d Cir. 2005)

LEVAL, Circuit Judge.

Plaintiff-appellant Hempstead Video, Inc. ("HV") appeals from a judgment of the United States District Court for the Eastern District of New York in favor of the defendant, the Incorporated Village of Valley Stream, and related officials and entities (collectively "Valley Stream" or the "Village"). The magistrate judge ruled that HV breached its settlement agreement with Valley Stream, and that Valley Stream was therefore released from its obligations of forbearance under the agreement. The judge also denied HV's motion to disqualify Valley Stream's counsel. We affirm.

BACKGROUND

HV, a corporation owned by James Alessandria, operates an adult video store in the Village of Valley Stream. Shortly after the store opened in 1994, HV became involved in a permit and zoning dispute with the Village. HV filed suit under 42 U.S.C. § 1983 in the United States District Court for the Eastern District of New York, alleging principally that Valley Stream was selectively enforcing its mercantile permit requirement in violation of the Equal Protection Clause of the Fourteenth Amendment.

The parties reached a settlement agreement on April 30, 1996[.] * * * The portion of the settlement agreement that is crucial to this dispute states:

> * * * It is specifically understood that [HV] shall not have *enclosed* viewing rooms, live peep shows or live performances or similar type activities at the premises.

* * *

I. The Present Dispute

In January 2003, Valley Stream received an anonymous tip that HV had installed several booths for viewing pornographic videos. * * *

The parties thereafter engaged in sporadic negotiations. HV suggested fitting the booths with Dutch doors or with curtains. The Village rejected the proposals * * * .

II. The Motion to Disqualify Valley Stream's Counsel

On November 12, 2003, while the case was still under consideration by the magistrate judge, HV moved to disqualify the Village's attorney, Stanley A. Camhi, and his firm of Jaspan Schlesinger Hoffmann, LLP ("Jaspan"). HV based its motion primarily on the fact that its counsel for labor matters, William Englander, had become "of counsel" to the Jaspan firm in July 2003. HV also contended the Jaspan firm should be disqualified because one of Jaspan's lawyers, Jon Santemma, had a ten-minute telephone conversation with Alessandria, the owner of HV, about a condemnation proceeding in a neighboring town.

Englander's connection with the Jaspan firm had come about as follows. Prior to July 2003, Englander was a solo practitioner, renting office space from the Jaspan firm. He had periodically represented Alessandria and his businesses on labor matters for more than twenty years. In April 2003, he began assisting HV's present counsel in defending against a complaint Elena Winter had filed with the Equal Employment Opportunity Commission (EEOC), alleging that she was fired on account of her pregnancy.

Englander, who was in his mid-70s, decided to "semi-retire" and work fewer hours. He proposed to turn the representation of several of his clients, particularly a local school district, over to the Jaspan firm. He agreed to become "of counsel" to Jaspan effective July 1, 2003 "[i]n order to effect an orderly transition of those matters." As for the Englander clients not being transferred to Jaspan, which included Alessandria and HV, Englander continued to represent them in his individual capacity. Jaspan had no access to those clients' files.

At the time Jaspan called Winter as a witness against HV in this case, Jaspan was unaware of Englander's representation of HV in the EEOC proceedings initiated by Winter, and Englander was unaware of Jaspan's representation of Valley Stream in this proceeding against HV. There had been no communication between Englander and the Jaspan lawyers about either case.

The potential conflict came to light on September 18, 2003, when Englander, in connection with Winter's EEOC proceeding against HV, sent a letter to the EEOC written on Jaspan letterhead and faxed a copy to his co-counsel in that matter, who also represents HV in this suit. Englander asserted in his affidavit that his use of the Jaspan letterhead for that letter was "an inadvertent error" as Jaspan had no involvement in the matter. In a separate incident additionally cited by HV to support its disqualification motion, a woman, who identified herself as being from the Jaspan firm, later telephoned Alessandria to ask for his fax number on Englander's behalf.

The alleged conflict involving Jon Santemma arose as follows. Santemma, who specializes in tax certiorari and condemnation proceedings, joined the Jaspan partnership in June 2003. Calls made to his number at his prior firm were automatically transferred to his phone at Jaspan. Alessandria phoned Santemma in July 2003, seeking advice about a condemnation proceeding being initiated by another town against another of Alessandria's stores. Alessandria and Santemma spoke for approximately ten minutes. Santemma was not retained and never opened a file on the matter. There is no suggestion in the record that HV owned or operated the business which was the subject of the condemnation proceeding or had any connection with that business beyond the fact that the owner of its stock also owned the other business.

III. The Magistrate Judge's Decisions

[The magistrate judge denied HV's motion to disqualify the Jaspan firm, concluding that Englander had represented HV in his capacity as a solo practitioner and was affiliated with Jaspan in a manner "too attenuated to merit imputation of the conflict of interest." He also concluded that the phone conversation between Alessandria and Santemma was insufficient to support disqualification. HV appealed.]

DISCUSSION

* * *

II. The Disqualification Motion

The authority of federal courts to disqualify attorneys derives from their inherent power to "preserve the integrity of the adversary process." In exercising this power, we have attempted to balance "a client's right freely to choose his counsel" against "the need to maintain the highest standards of the profession." Although our decisions on disqualification motions often benefit from guidance offered by the American Bar Association (ABA) and state disciplinary rules, such rules merely provide general guidance and not every violation of a disciplinary rule will necessarily lead to disqualification, because other ethical violations can be left to federal and state disciplinary mechanisms.

One recognized form of taint arises when an attorney places himself in a position where he could use a client's privileged information against that client. The standard for disqualification varies depending on whether the representation is concurrent or successive. In cases of concurrent representation, we have ruled it is "prima facie improper" for an attorney to simultaneously represent a client and another party with interests directly adverse to that client. The attorney "must be prepared to show, at the very least, that there will be no actual or apparent conflict in loyalties or diminution in the vigor of his representation." In cases of successive representation, we have held that an attorney may be disqualified if:

(1) the moving party is a former client of the adverse party's counsel;

(2) there is a substantial relationship between the subject matter of the counsel's prior representation of the moving party and the issues in the present lawsuit; and

(3) the attorney whose disqualification is sought had access to, or was likely to have had access to, relevant privileged information in the course of his prior representation of the client.

An attorney's conflicts are ordinarily imputed to his firm based on the presumption that "associated" attorneys share client confidences. * * * As discussed below, however, attorneys with limited links to a firm are not always considered to be "associated" with the firm for purposes of conflict imputation.

Although some courts have treated the presumption that confidences are shared within a firm as irrebuttable, there is a "strong trend," which we join, toward allowing the presumption of confidence sharing within a firm to be rebutted.

Prior to July 2003, Englander operated an entirely independent law firm, which leased space from Jaspan. He maintained separate files for his clients and there is no reason to believe he shared client confidences with Jaspan. Jaspan would not have been disqualified during this period by reason of Englander's representation of the adversary of one of its clients.

In July 2003, the relationship between Englander and Jaspan changed, but only to a limited degree. Englander was given the title "of counsel" and began to share a limited number of clients with Jaspan. In all other respects, Englander continued to operate a separate firm in the same manner he had before acquiring the new title. The question is whether this relationship requires disqualification of the Jaspan firm in this case.

The case before us does not fit easily within the existing framework for analyzing conflict imputation from an attorney to his firm. The first step in that framework is to determine whether an attorney is "associated" with the firm. If he is, a rebuttable presumption arises that the attorney and the firm share client confidences, and the court then proceeds to the second step, which involves determining whether that presumption has been rebutted. If the attorney is not "associated" with the firm, no presumption of confidence sharing arises, and, in the absence of other evidence demonstrating taint of the proceedings, the firm will not be disqualified. This framework functions most smoothly in cases where the relationship between the attorney and the firm is clear.

It is not altogether clear whether Englander should be deemed, for purposes of this binary rule, to be "associated" or "not associated" with the Jaspan firm. The magistrate judge placed Englander in the latter category, holding that his relationship with Jaspan was sufficiently limited that conflicts arising from his private representation of HV should not be imputed to the firm. In reaching this conclusion, however, the magistrate judge emphasized that "the Jaspan firm has been effectively screened from any knowledge that Mr. Englander may have regarding plaintiff and the danger of any unintentional transmission of client confidences is rather minuscule." The magistrate judge thus blended the first step in the traditional framework (whether the attorney is "associated" with the firm) with the second (whether the presumption of shared confidences has been rebutted). On the facts of this case, we find no error.

Whether an attorney is associated with a firm for purposes of conflict imputation depends in part on the existence and extent of screening between the attorney and the firm. An "of counsel" attorney, who handles matters independent of his firm and scrupulously maintains files for his private clients separate from the files of the firm, is less likely to be considered associated with the firm with respect to those clients than another attorney in the same position whose client files are not effectively segregated from those of the firm. Similarly, whether the screening between an attorney and his firm is considered adequate to rebut the presumption of shared confidences depends in part on the closeness and extent of the relationship between the attorney and the firm.

With these considerations in mind, we examine Englander's situation under both the first and second steps of the traditional framework, cognizant of the interrelationship between the two in the case before us.

A. Imputation of the Conflicts of an "Of Counsel" Attorney to a Firm

Englander, of course, could not have represented Valley Stream against HV while simultaneously representing HV before the EEOC, in the absence of client consent. But Englander did not represent Valley Stream against HV. Valley Stream was represented by the Jaspan firm, with which Englander had an "of counsel" relationship. We must consider whether Englander's potential conflict should be attributed to Jaspan by reason of his "of counsel" relationship.

At least two federal courts have adopted a per se rule imputing conflicts between all "of counsel" attorneys and their firms. Ethics opinions issued by the New York State Bar Association and the ABA have also recommended imputing conflicts from "of counsel" attorneys to their firms.

A *per se* rule has the virtue of clarity, but in achieving clarity, it ignores the caution that when dealing with ethical principles, we cannot paint with broad strokes. The lines are fine and must be so marked. Given the wide variation in the nature and substance of relationships lumped together under the title "of counsel," a per se approach is ill-equipped to respect appropriately "both the individual's right to be represented by counsel of his or her choice and the public's interest in maintaining the highest standards of professional conduct." It also risks elevating the label assigned to a relationship over the substance of that relationship.

We believe the better approach for deciding whether to impute an "of counsel" attorney's conflict to his firm for purposes of ordering disqualification in a suit in federal court is to examine the substance of the relationship under review and the procedures in place. The closer and broader the affiliation of an "of counsel" attorney with the firm, and the greater the likelihood that operating procedures adopted may permit one to become privy, whether intentionally or unintentionally, to the pertinent client confidences of the other, the more appropriate will be a rebuttable imputation of the conflict of one to the other. Conversely, the more narrowly limited the relationship between the "of counsel" attorney and the firm, and the more secure and effective the isolation of nonshared matters, the less appropriate imputation will be. Imputation is not always necessary to preserve high standards of professional conduct. Furthermore, imputation might well interfere with a party's entitlement to choose counsel and create opportunities for abusive disqualification motions.

* * *

We agree with the magistrate judge that Englander's relationship with Jaspan was too attenuated and too remote from the matter in question to attribute Englander's potential conflict to the firm. Englander became "of counsel" for the limited purpose of providing transitional services for several selected clients. He continued representing all his other clients, including HV and Alessandria, in his independent capacity. Moreover, the Jaspan firm had no access to the confidences of Englander's private clients. Englander maintained separate files for those clients in his private office, and Jaspan did not have access to the files. It is undisputed that Alessandria never discussed the present case with Englander, and Englander never discussed the details of either the present case or the EEOC case with anyone at Jaspan. As soon as Jaspan learned of the potential conflict, it instructed Englander not to discuss the EEOC case with anyone at the firm and to continue maintaining a separate file. We conclude on the basis of the foregoing facts that the magistrate judge correctly ruled that, for purposes of this dispute, Englander is not "associated" with the Jaspan firm and thus his conflict should not be attributed to it.

B. Rebutting the Presumption of Shared Confidences

Even assuming, in the alternative, that Englander's potential conflict should be imputed, subject to rebuttal, to Jaspan by reason of his association with the firm, Englander's limited relationship with Jaspan, the screens put in place, and the uncontroverted affidavits filed by Englander and Camhi successfully rebut the presumption that Englander shared HV's confidences with the firm. This court has adopted no categorical rule against considering practices and structures that protect client confidences within a firm in determining whether an attorney or firm should be disqualified. Courts should inquire on the facts of the case before them whether the practices and structures in place are sufficient to avoid disqualifying taint.

What's That?

"Chinese Walls" refer to physical or electronic barriers erected to safeguard attorneys in a firm from having access to information held by an attorney who is disqualified due to a conflict. *See* Rule 1.10, *supra*, which sets forth the procedural requirements for proper screening.

Responding to two opinions of this Circuit discussing procedures that may screen and safeguard client confidences (sometimes referred to as "Chinese Walls"), a few district courts have drawn a tentative inference that our Circuit may categorically reject the efficacy of isolation efforts as protection against taint. This would be a mistaken reading of our precedents.

* * *

We see no reason why, in appropriate cases and on convincing facts, isolation—whether it results from the intentional construction of a "Chinese Wall," or from de facto separation that effectively protects against any sharing of confidential information—cannot adequately protect against taint. * * *

On the particular facts of this case, with special focus on Englander's double role—of counsel to the Jaspan firm only with regard to the cases he was turning over, while independent of the Jaspan firm as to the matters he retained—coupled with the district court's finding that Englander maintained separate files and shared no confidences relating to his representation of HV with Jaspan, and that Englander and Jaspan adopted measures in September 2003 upon becoming aware of the potential conflict to protect against any breach, we are satisfied that any presumption of shared confidences that may arise by operation of law has been sufficiently rebutted, and conclude the Jaspan firm's continued representation of Valley Stream should be viewed as free of disqualifying taint.

C. Contact with a Prospective Client

HV also seeks disqualification of the Jaspan firm on the basis of the ten-minute phone conversation between Alessandria and Santemma. It forthrightly acknowledges the weakness of this argument, and an affidavit filed by its attorney explains that she would not have made the motion to disqualify Jaspan based solely on this call. HV nevertheless continues to argue on appeal that Alessandria's contact with Santemma made it a current client of the Jaspan firm during the course of Jaspan's representation of Valley Stream.

* * * Alessandria's call was not made in his capacity as the owner of HV and did not relate to the subject of this litigation. Disqualification of Camhi and Jaspan is not warranted on the basis of Alessandria's call, whether considered alone or in conjunction with the other facts advanced by HV.

Practice Pointer

There is no uniform rule on whether screening will protect a law firm from disqualification, when one of the lawyers in the firm is personally disqualified. Lawyers need to be aware of the case law in the particular court. And the uncertainty of the efficacy of screening means that law firms will be cautious about hiring lawyers who carry with them the taint of conflict with respect to matters the firm is currently pursuing.

* * *

KASSIS v. TEACHER'S INS. AND ANNUITY ASS'N

93 N.Y.2d 611, 695 N.Y.S.2d 515 (1999)

Smith, J.

Plaintiffs Henry Kassis and North River Insurance Company retained the law firm of Weg & Myers to represent them in an action premised upon property damage to a building owned by Kassis in New York City. Thurm & Heller, a firm of approximately 26 attorneys, is counsel for defendants and third-party plaintiffs, Teacher's Insurance and Annuity Association and Cauldwell-Wingate Company, Inc. The decisive issue on this appeal is whether Thurm & Heller should be disqualified from continued representation of defendants on the basis that it hired Charles Arnold, a former associate of Weg & Myers who participated in the Kassis litigation while employed there. For the reasons that follow, we hold that Thurm & Heller should be disqualified, and we reverse the order of the Appellate Division that permitted the continued representation.

In 1994, two years after commencement of the underlying action, Weg & Myers was substituted as counsel for plaintiffs. Joshua Mallin, a partner at Weg & Myers, was in charge of the case, conducting most of the discovery and planning the litigation strategy. Charles Arnold, a first-year associate, assisted Mallin. Specifically, Arnold conducted five depositions of nonparties and co-plaintiff North River, attended two court-ordered mediation sessions as sole counsel for the client, appeared as Kassis' attorney at a physical examination of the subject building, and conversed with Kassis on a regular basis. Moreover, the record indicates that Weg & Myers conducted weekly staff meetings where all associates were privy to discussions of law and strategy regarding litigation the firm handled. In addition, Arnold reviewed certain portions of the litigation file in order to conduct the depositions, but allegedly "never read the overwhelming majority of the documents contained within the file."

In February 1997, following a deposition in the Kassis matter, Arnold informed Roula Theofanis, the partner at Thurm & Heller who was primarily in charge of the Kassis litigation, that he was leaving Weg & Myers. At the suggestion of Theofanis, Arnold was interviewed by Thurm & Heller, and began working there in March 1997. During the interview and upon commencement of his employment, Thurm & Heller cautioned Arnold that he would not be permitted to participate in the Kassis litigation and that he was not to discuss that matter with anyone at the firm.

Upon learning of Arnold's employment, Mallin requested that Theofanis detail the precautionary measures that the firm planned to take in order to prevent Arnold's inadvertent disclosure of confidential information he had obtained while at Weg & Myers. By written response, Theofanis detailed the following safeguards:

> "1. The entire file which presently consists of 15 redwells will be kept in my office in lieu of our general filing area.

> "2. Mr. Arnold's office will be at a substantial distance from my office.

> "3. Mr. Arnold upon commencement of his employment with the firm on March 3, 1997 will be instructed not to touch the Kassis file nor to discuss the Kassis matter with any partner, associate or staff member of the firm.

> "4. There will be no meetings, conferences or discussions in the presence of Mr. Arnold concerning the Kassis' litigation.

> "5. All future associates who may work on the Kassis matter with me in preparation for trial will be instructed not to discuss this file with Mr. Arnold."

On March 6, 1997, three days after Arnold began working at Thurm & Heller, Mallin moved on behalf of plaintiffs to disqualify the firm from further participation in the Kassis litigation. Supreme Court denied plaintiffs' motion, finding Arnold's involvement in the Kassis litigation while employed at Weg & Myers limited. The Appellate Division affirmed, holding that the safeguards employed by Thurm & Heller eliminated the danger of Arnold inadvertently transmitting information he might have gained from his previous employment at Weg & Myers. * * *

Attorneys owe a continuing duty to former clients not to reveal confidences learned in the course of their professional relationship. It is this duty that provides the foundation for the well-established rule that a lawyer may not represent a client in a matter and thereafter represent another client with interests materially adverse to interests of the former client in the same or a substantially related matter. Indeed, such "side switching" clearly implicates the policies both of maintaining loyalty to the first client and of protecting that client's confidences. These same principles give rise to the general rule that, where an attorney working in a law firm is disqualified from undertaking a subsequent representation opposing a former client, all the attorneys in that firm are likewise precluded from such representation.

In addition to ensuring that attorneys remain faithful to the fiduciary duties of loyalty and confidentiality owed by attorneys to their clients, the rule of imputed disqualification reinforces an attorney's ethical obligation to avoid the appearance of impropriety.

* * *

[I]mputed disqualification is not an irrebuttable presumption. A per se rule of disqualification * * * is unnecessarily preclusive because it disqualifies all members of a law firm indiscriminately, whether or not they share knowledge of former client's

> ### What's That?
>
> Many professional responsibility scholars argue that the "appearance of impropriety" is a meaningless, indeed dangerous term that allows courts to disqualify lawyers on completely subjective grounds.

confidences and secrets. Such a rule also imposes significant hardships on the current client and is subject to abusive invocation purely to seek tactical advantages in a lawsuit. Additionally, a per se disqualification rule conflicts with public policies favoring client choice and restricts an attorney's ability to practice.

* * *

Thus, where one attorney is disqualified as a result of having acquired confidential client information at a former law firm, the presumption that the entirety of the attorney's current firm must be disqualified may be rebutted. Of course, no presumption of disqualification will arise if either the moving party fails to make any showing of a risk that the attorney changing firms acquired any client confidences in the prior employment or the nonmoving party disproves that the attorney had any opportunity to acquire confidential information in the former employment. In either case, it would not have been established that the side-switching attorney actually "represented the former client in a matter," and neither the attorney nor the firm would need to be disqualified.

Where the presumption does arise, however, the party seeking to avoid disqualification must prove that any information acquired by the disqualified lawyer is unlikely to be significant or material in the litigation. In that factual scenario, with the presumption rebutted, a "Chinese Wall" around the disqualified lawyer would be sufficient to avoid firm disqualification.

To determine whether the presumption of shared confidences and disqualification has been rebutted, consideration must be given to the particular facts of each case. Where, for example, a disqualified attorney formerly worked in a small law firm characterized by a certain informality and conducive to "constant cross-pollination" and a "cross current of discussion and ideas' among all attorneys on all matters which the firm handled," there will be a greater likelihood of acquiring material client confidences. Similarly, where offices are not physically isolated and files are made open and available to all lawyers, the probability that an attorney gained significant confidential information increases.

Other factors also weigh in the balance. In *Solow v. W.R. Grace & Co.*, <u>83 N.Y.2d 303, 610 N.Y.S.2d 128 (1994)</u>, for example, this Court declined to disqualify the law firm of Stroock & Stroock & Lavan, a 372-lawyer firm which represented plaintiff in a suit against defendant W.R. Grace & Co. Members of Stroock had previously defended Grace in another action, and Grace moved to disqualify the firm from participating in the action. While recognizing the importance of the presumption of shared confidences, the Court nevertheless permitted Stroock to continue as counsel against Grace, its former client. Aside from being a very large firm, the Stroock partner, associate and paralegals who actively participated in the litigation involving the former client had all left the firm long before the current litigation. Sworn affidavits by the remaining partner and associate at Stroock established that their involvement in the prior Grace litigation had been negligible.

Food for Thought

Note the difference between *Kassis* and *Hempstead Video*. *Hempstead Video*, like Rule 1.10, provides that if proper screening is in place before the tainted attorney comes into the firm, it doesn't matter *how tainted* that attorney may be. He could have been the lead counsel on the case. In contrast, *Kassis* says screening works only if the tainted lawyer had access to insignificant confidential information. In other words, it only works if the lawyer is a little bit tainted. But how do you determine when the tainted lawyer has crossed the line from significant to insignificant taint? Because of that uncertainty, in New York, screening cannot be relied on as a means of avoiding disqualification. Doesn't this put a damper on the mobility of lawyers?

Demonstrating that no significant client confidences were acquired by the disqualified attorney, however, does not wholly remove the imputation of disqualification from a law firm. Because even the appearance of impropriety must be eliminated, it follows that even where it is demonstrated that the disqualified attorney possesses no material confidential information, a firm must nonetheless erect adequate screening measures to separate the disqualified lawyer and eliminate any involvement by that lawyer in the representation.

Here, the undisputed facts in the record evidence that Arnold played an appreciable role as counsel for plaintiff in the Kassis litigation while at Weg & Myers. He was sufficiently knowledgeable and steeped in the files of this case to conduct several depositions that resulted in extensive transcripts; he appeared as sole counsel for the client in two court-ordered mediation sessions; and he conversed regularly with the client. Given Arnold's extensive participation in the Kassis litigation and Thurm & Heller's representation of the adversary in the same matter, defendants' burden in rebutting the presumption that Arnold acquired material confidences is especially heavy. Defendants' conclusory averments that Arnold did not acquire such confidences during the prior representation failed to rebut that presumption as a matter of law. The erection of a "Chinese Wall" in this case, therefore, was inconsequential. Thus, we hold, as a matter of law, that disqualification is required.

VIII. Conflicts of Interest in Criminal Cases

[Question 23]

A, B, and C are charged with the murders of D and E. Attorneys Alpha and Beta represent A, B and C, who are tried separately. A is convicted. B & C are acquitted. A claims he was denied effective assistance of counsel because his lawyers had a conflict of interest. He further argues that they did not call particular defense witnesses because those witnesses would have become less effective as witnesses for B and C.

Did A receive ineffective assistance?

(A) Yes, because his lawyers had a potential conflict of interest.

(B) Yes, if his lawyers had an actual conflict of interest.

(C) Yes, if his lawyers had an actual conflict of interest that adversely affected their performance.

(D) No, because he did not object to the conflict at trial.

[Question 24]

Able, Baker and Carter had been indicted for the armed robbery of a cashier at a grocery store. Together, Able and Baker met with an attorney and asked her to represent them. The attorney then interviewed Able and Baker separately. Each told the attorney that the robbery had been committed by Carter while Able and Baker sat in Carter's car outside the store. They each said that Carter had said he needed some cigarettes and that they knew nothing of his plan to rob the cashier. The attorney agreed to represent both Able and Baker. One week before the trial, Able told the attorney that he wanted to plea bargain and that he was prepared to testify that Baker had loaned Carter the gun Carter used in the robbery. Able also said that he and Baker had shared in the proceeds of the robbery with Carter.

What is the proper course of action for the attorney to take?

(A) Request court approval to withdraw as the attorney for both Able and Baker.

(B) Continue to represent Baker and, with Able's consent and court approval, withdraw as Able's lawyer.

(C) Continue to represent Able and, with Baker's consent and court approval, withdraw as Baker's lawyer.

(D) Continue to represent Able and Baker, but not call Able as a witness.

A. The Right to Conflict–Free Representation

The right to effective assistance of counsel may be denied because defense counsel has a conflict of interest, and cannot or does not properly protect her client's interests. One situation of potential conflict arises when counsel represents multiple defendants. Codefendants may have divergent interests at all stages of a prosecution. A plea bargain advantageous to one defendant may produce testimony adverse to another defendant. Defendants may have inconsistent defenses, or wish to testify in ways that incriminate codefendants. *See, e.g.,* United States v. Hall, 200 F.3d 962 (6th Cir. 2000) (conflict of interest where defense counsel represents two brothers, and one has a public authority defense while the other does not). Evidence inculpating one defendant might exculpate another, forcing counsel to make unsatisfactory choices in response to offered testimony. Separate counsel also might choose differing approaches to closing argument that a counsel to multiple defendants might not be able to choose.

Conflicts also might arise because defense counsel has a personal interest that could be negatively affected by aggressive representation of the defendant. For example, in one notorious case, a defense counsel was representing the defendant in a felony prosecution and simultaneously having a sexual relationship with the defendant's wife. Counsel's ardor for the wife may well have dampened his ardor to have the defendant set free. *Hernandez v. State,* 750 So. 2d 50 (Fla. App. 1999).

Another possibility is that the interests of the defendant may be in conflict with the interests of defense counsel's client in another matter, or with the interests of a former client. For example, if counsel represents two defendants charged with the same crime in separate matters, the decision whether to call one defendant to testify in the other's trial may be impacted by counsel's conflicting loyalties. *See, e.g., United States v. Elliot,* 463 F.3d 858 (9th Cir. 2006) (conflict where two clients are separately tried for the same crime and their best defense is to shift blame to each other: "To represent Elliot adequately, Gordon needed to interview, aggressively examine, and possibly place blame on Hevia, all of which clashed with his attorney-client relationship with Hevia."). And the lawyer's duty to preserve the confidences and secrets of a former client may impair a current client's representation if the former client is called as a witness for the prosecution.

For More Information

See Bruce A. Green, *"Through a Glass, Darkly": How the Court Sees Motions to Disqualify Criminal Defense Lawyers,* 89 Colum. L. Rev. 1202 (1989), for an extensive discussion of conflicts of interest that can arise in the course of representation of criminal defendants.

The rules adopted by the Supreme Court for assessing claims of defense counsel conflict of interest have been helpfully summarized by the court in *United States v. Kliti,* 156 F.3d 150 (2d Cir. 1998):

> A defendant's right to counsel under the Sixth Amendment includes the right to be represented by an attorney who is free from conflicts of interest. When the trial court knows or reasonably should know of the possibility of a conflict of interest, it has a threshold obligation to determine whether the attorney has an actual conflict, a potential conflict, or no conflict. In fulfilling this initial obligation to inquire into the existence of a conflict of interest, the trial court may rely on counsel's representations. If a district court ignores a possible conflict and does not conduct this initial inquiry, reversal of a defendant's conviction is automatic. If, through this inquiry, the court determines that the attorney suffers from an actual or potential conflict of interest, the court has a "disqualification/waiver" obligation. (An attorney has an actual, as opposed to a po-

tential, conflict of interest when during the course of the representation, the defendants' interests diverge with respect to a material fact or legal issue or to a course of action. A potential conflict of interest exists if the interests of the defendant may place the attorney under inconsistent duties at some time in the future.) If the conflict is so severe that no rational defendant would waive it, the court must disqualify the attorney. If it is a lesser conflict, the court must conduct a * * * hearing to determine whether the defendant will knowingly and intelligently waive

The Sixth Amendment provides as follows:

In all criminal prosecutions, the accused shall enjoy the right to a speedy and public trial, by an impartial jury of the State and district where in the crime shall have been committed, which district shall have been previously ascertained by law, and to be informed of the nature and cause of the accusation; to be confronted with the witnesses against him; to have compulsory process for obtaining witnesses in his favor, and to have the Assistance of Counsel for his defence.

U.S. Const. amend. VI.

his right to conflict-free representation. (Before a defendant can knowingly and intelligently waive a conflict, the court must: (1) advise the defendant about potential conflicts; (2) determine whether the defendant understands the risks of those conflicts; and (3) give the defendant time to digest and contemplate the risks, with the aid of independent counsel if desired.)

1. The Duty of Court Inquiry

Per Se Reversal: Holloway v. Arkansas

In *Holloway v. Arkansas*, <u>435 U.S. 475 (1978)</u>, the Court made it clear that joint representation of codefendants by a single attorney is not a per se violation of the right to effective assistance of counsel. The Court noted that a common defense often gives strength against a common attack. Under some circumstances, however, joint representation may create a conflict that can deny a defendant effective assistance of counsel. In *Holloway*, the defense counsel made pretrial motions for appointment of separate counsel for each defendant because of possible conflicts of interest. The trial court denied the motion, and refused defense counsel's renewed request, during the trial, for separate counsel when the three codefendants each wished to testify. Counsel felt that he would be unable to examine or cross-examine any defendant to protect the interests of the others.

Without ever reaching the issue of whether there was an actual conflict of interest, the Supreme Court reversed the defendants' convictions. Reversal was required because the judge, after timely motions, erred in failing to "either appoint separate counsel, or to take adequate steps to ascertain whether the risk was too remote to warrant separate counsel." The Court held that in these circumstances, prejudice to the defendants must be presumed:

> Joint representation of conflicting interests is suspect because of what it tends to prevent the attorney from doing. For example, in this case it may well have precluded defense counsel for [one of the codefendants] from exploring possible plea negotiations and the possibility of an agreement to testify for the prosecution, provided a lesser charge or a favorable sentencing recommendation would be acceptable. Generally speaking a conflict may also prevent an attorney from challenging the admission of evidence prejudicial to one client but perhaps favorable to another, or from arguing at the sentencing hearing the relative involvement and culpability of his clients in order to minimize the culpability of one by emphasizing that of another. Examples can be readily multiplied. * * *

> [A] rule requiring a defendant to show that a conflict of interests—which he and his counsel tried to avoid by timely objections to the joint representation—prejudiced him in some specific fashion would not be susceptible to intelligent, evenhanded application. In the normal case where a harmless error rule is applied, the error occurs at trial and its scope is readily identifiable. Accordingly, the reviewing court can undertake with some confidence its relatively narrow task of assessing the likelihood that the error materially affected the deliberations of the jury. But in a case of joint representation of conflicting interests the evil—it bears repeating—is in what the advocate finds himself compelled to *refrain* from doing, not only at trial but also as to possible pretrial plea negotiations and in the sentencing process. * * * Thus, an inquiry into a claim of harmless error here would require, unlike most cases, unguided speculation.

Go Online

For an argument in favor of a per se rule against joint representation, *see* Gary T. Lowenthal, *Joint Representation in Criminal Cases: A Critical Appraisal*, 64 Va. L. Rev. 939 (1978). For an argument against such a rule *see* Ephraim Margolin & Sandra Coliver, *Pretrial Disqualification of Criminal Defense Counsel*, 20 Am. Crim. L. Rev. 227 (1982).

Federal Rule 44

Fed. R. Crim. P. 44 attempts to address the problem of joint representation, and the need for a hearing, that the Court was concerned with in *Holloway*:

Rule 44. Right to and assignment of counsel

* * *

(c)(2) Court's Responsibilities in Cases of Joint representation.–The court must promptly inquire about the propriety of joint representation and must personally advise each defendant of the right to the effective assistance of counsel, including separate representation. Unless there is good cause to believe that no conflict of interest is likely to arise, the court must take appropriate measure to protect each defendant's right to counsel.

It should be apparent that Rule 44 does not address all the conflict situations that can arise in a criminal case. Rule 44 addresses only questions of multiple representation in the same criminal proceeding. It does not apply if defense counsel has previously represented a person who is now a government witness in the case against the defendant. It does not apply if the lawyer has a personal conflict, such as that he is suspected of being the defendant's coconspirator. It doesn't apply if the lawyer has accepted the case on a contingent fee. It does not apply if the lawyer is representing two related defendants in separate proceedings.

But these less obvious conflicts are often reviewed by the court at a hearing when they are raised to the court. Usually it is the government that raises such conflicts for the court to consider. Why would the prosecution raise these conflicts?

2. Active Conflict Impairing the Representation

A Different Kind of Prejudice Test: Cuyler v. Sullivan

In *Cuyler v. Sullivan*, 446 U.S. 335 (1980), the Court considered the propriety of relief where defense counsel operated under a conflict of interest that was not brought to the attention of the trial judge. Justice Powell's opinion for the Court rejected the petitioner's claim that *Holloway* requires a trial judge to inquire in every case into the propriety of joint representation, even in the absence of the defendant's timely motion. He reasoned as follows:

> Defense counsel have an ethical obligation to avoid conflicting representations and to advise the court promptly when a conflict of interest arises during the course of a trial. Absent special circumstances, therefore, trial courts may assume that multiple representation entails no conflict or that the lawyer and his clients knowingly accept such risk of conflict as may exist.

The opinion reiterated the suggestion in *Holloway* that multiple representation does give rise to a possibility of an improper conflict of interest and that a defendant "must have the opportunity to show that potential conflicts impermissibly imperil his right to a fair trial." But, said the Court, "a defendant who raised no objection at trial must demonstrate that an actual conflict of interest adversely affected his lawyer's performance." Thus, the Court created a limited presumption of prejudice in cases where a defendant fails to make a timely objection to conflicted simultaneous representation: prejudice is presumed, but only if the defendant demonstrates that counsel "actively represented conflicting interests" and that "an actual conflict of interest adversely affected his lawyer's performance."

The *Cuyler* prejudice standard applies when a defendant fails to bring a potential conflict to the trial court's attention. But it also applies when the defendant notifies the trial court of a potential conflict and the trial court, after a full hearing, finds that there is no actual or potential conflict and orders the multiple representation to continue. *See Freund v. Butterworth*, 165 F.3d 839 (11th Cir. 1999) (en banc). *Holloway* applies when the court refuses to hold a hearing after the defense counsel brings a potential conflict to its attention.

Application of the Cuyler Standard: Burger v. Kemp

The Supreme Court found no ineffective assistance of counsel under the *Cuyler* standards in *Burger v. Kemp*, 483 U.S. 776 (1987), a capital case in which Burger and a codefendant were represented by law partners. The defendants were soldiers charged with the murder of a fellow soldier who worked part-time driving a taxi. Each defendant confessed, and Burger took military police to the place where the victim had been drowned. Leaphart, an experienced lawyer, was appointed to represent Burger, and he insisted that his law partner represent the codefendant. The two defendants were tried separately, and at their trials each defendant sought to avoid the death penalty by emphasizing the other's culpability. Burger was sentenced to death, and attacked his representation in a habeas corpus proceeding on the ground that Leaphart's partnership relationship with counsel for the other defendant created a conflict of interest for him. A federal district court denied relief, and the court of appeals affirmed.

Justice Stevens wrote for the Court as it affirmed the denial of relief. He conceded that "[t]here is certainly much substance to petitioner's argument that the appointment of two partners to represent coindictees in their respective trials creates a possible conflict of interest that could prejudice either or both clients," and that "the risk of prejudice is increased when the two lawyers cooperate with one another in planning and conduct of trial strategy." He observed, however, that the Court's decisions do not presume prejudice in all cases, and he concluded that "the overlap of counsel, if any, did not so infect Leaphart's representation as to constitute an active representation of competing interests." Justice Stevens added that "[p]articularly in smaller communities where the supply of qualified lawyers willing to accept the demanding and unrewarding work of representing capital prisoners is extremely limited, the two defendants may actually benefit from the joint efforts of two partners who supplement one another in their preparation." He noted that "we generally presume that the lawyer is fully conscious of the overarching duty of complete loyalty to his or her client," and that trial courts "appropriately and necessarily rely in large measure upon the good faith and good judgment of defense counsel." Justice Stevens also emphasized that each defendant was tried separately, and that separate trials significantly reduce the risk of a conflict of interest. The Court declined to disturb the lower courts' findings that there was no actual conflict of interest.

Justice Stevens added that, even if an actual conflict had been established, counsel's advocacy was unaffected by it. He concluded that there was no evidence that the prosecutor would have been receptive to a plea bargain, there was no reason to believe that Leaphart attempted to protect the other defendant who was not on trial with Burger, and the decision not to offer mitigating evidence and open the door to cross-examination about Burger's background was not unreasonable even if it was erroneous. Although Justice Stevens stated that the evidence at the habeas corpus hearing "does suggest that Leaphart could well have made a more thorough investigation than he did," he added that "counsel's decision not to mount an all-out investigation into petitioner's background in search of mitigating circumstances was supported by reasonable professional judgment." Counsel had interviewed all potential witnesses who were called to his attention, and "there was a reasonable basis for his strategic decision that an explanation of petitioner's history would not have minimized the risk of the death penalty."

> **Go Online**
>
> A comprehensive discussion of the problems that can result when one lawyer, firm, or public agency represents successive criminal defendants is found in Gary T. Lowenthal, *Successive Representation By Criminal Lawyers*, 93 Yale L.J. 1 (1983).

[Question 25]

Public Defender ("PD") represented A on a burglary charge. After A's murder, the court appoints PD to represent B, who is charged with murdering A. Neither PD nor the court informs B that PD previously represented A. After trial, B is sentenced to death. The death sentence was predicated on B forcing sodomy on A. At trial, B's theory was that he did not know A. He did not argue that he knew A, knew that he was a prostitute, and that the sex was consensual, which would have mitigated the death sentence. After conviction, B argues ineffective assistance because PD did not pursue this strategy because of his conflict. What result?

(A) Ineffective assistance of counsel, because of PD's conflict and the court's failure to inquire.

(B) Ineffective assistance of counsel, because A's failure to share and use relevant info prejudiced B.

(C) Not ineffective assistance of counsel, because not a concurrent conflict.

(D) Not ineffective assistance of counsel, because did not adversely affect counsel's performance.

[Question 26]

L is appointed to represent C in an assault case, and meets once with C before C is murdered. L is then appointed to represent D, C's alleged murderer.

D is later convicted and sentenced to death, and seeks habeas relief alleging ineffective assistance of counsel due to L's conflict. What result?

3. Conflict With the Attorney's Personal Interests

In some cases counsel's personal interests may be in conflict with the duty of loyalty owed the client. *United States v. Cancilla,* 725 F.2d 867 (2d Cir. 1984), is an example. It turned out that the defendant's counsel was engaged in criminal conduct with the defendant's coconspirators. The court reasoned that "with the similarity of counsel's criminal activities to Cancilla's schemes and the link between them, it must have occurred to counsel that a vigorous defense might uncover evidence or prompt testimony revealing his own crimes." *See also United States ex rel. Duncan v. O'Leary,* 806 F.2d 1307 (7th Cir. 1986) (reversal where defense counsel is the prosecutor's campaign manager and the prosecutor is running on a "law and order" ticket).

In *Winkler v. Keane,* 7 F.3d 304 (2d Cir. 1993), the court found an actual conflict of interest where counsel represented a criminal defendant on a contingent fee basis; under the agreement, defense counsel would receive a fee of $25,000, but only if the defendant was found not guilty. The court reasoned that counsel had "a disincentive to seek a plea agreement, or to put forth mitigating defenses that would result in conviction of a lesser included offense." But the court held that the conflict of interest did not adversely affect the defense, because the defendant steadfastly maintained his innocence throughout, rejected all attempts to plea bargain, and vetoed any attempt of defense counsel to argue the partial defense of intoxication. Thus, there was no reason to believe that defense counsel's representation would have been any different "if a proper fee arrangement had been utilized."

Make the Connection

The field of behavioral economics, an outgrowth of cognitive psychology, generally attempts to form predictive models of human behavior. Can behavioral economics enhance our understanding of the conduct of attorneys who are involved in conflicts situations in criminal cases? In Tiger W. Eldred, *The Psychology of Conflicts of Interest in Criminal Cases,* 58 U. Kan. L. Rev. 43 (2009), Professor Tigran W. Eldred finds that psychological biases make it "extremely difficult," even for attorneys who act in good faith, to appreciate the "deleterious consequences" of conflicts of interest. In light of the empirical research on conflicts of interest, Professor Eldred analyzes a number of options to protect defendants from conflicts, including mandating greater disclosure in conflicts cases; limiting trial courts' discretion to grant disqualification motions; and prohibiting certain types of representations. The recommended approach, however, focuses on altering the Supreme Court's adverse effects test, which "erects too high a barrier in conflicts cases, meaning that many conflicts are never identified because of problems of proof, not because they do not exist." Under a "substantial risk" test, a defendant who is seeking a new trial based on a conflict of interest must establish that,

> based on the information that was known to defense counsel at the time, there was "a substantial risk that the lawyer's representation" of the defendant "would be materially and adversely affected by the lawyer's own interests or by the lawyer's duties to another current client, a former client, or a third person." If the defendant can prove that such risk existed, then a conflict has been established and the defendant's conviction should be reversed without requiring the defendant to prove also that the conflict had an adverse effect on the representation provided.

Would the substantial risk test better protect criminal defendants from conflicts of interest?

B. Waiver of the Right to Conflict–Free Counsel

The premise of Federal Rule 44 is that if the defendant is properly warned of the possible conflicts that could arise, then he can knowingly and voluntarily waive the right to conflict-free representation. Generally speaking, a knowing and voluntary waiver of conflict-free representation can be found if the trial court informs the defendant about the ways in which conflicted counsel can impair the representation—particularly that one client could shift blame to another, or testify against another, and defense counsel would be impaired in representing the multiple interests. The trial court must assure itself that the defendant understands the consequences, and has made a rational decision to proceed with counsel despite the conflict. An example of a typical colloquy is found in *United States v. Flores,* 5 F.3d 1070 (7th Cir. 1993). In Flores, three defendants charged with major narcotics transactions had used a group of lawyers in previous brushes with the law. According to the court,

> like sick patients who call up longtime family doctors, they contacted attorneys who represented them before. Potential conflicts of interest arose, however, as the three defendants and their attorneys played a virtual musical chairs game of attorney-client relationships. The lawyers chosen to represent Flores and Fontanez, respectively Michael Green and Roberta Samotny, represented Rodriguez in prior, unrelated criminal proceedings. Further, Rodriguez's counsel, Glenn Seiden, initially represented Fontanez in the current case then switched to Rodriguez.

The government in *Flores* moved to disqualify all counsel, and the trial court held a Rule 44 hearing, at which the following took place, according to the court:

> At the hearing, the district court asked the defendants and their respective attorneys about the alleged conflicts. The court questioned each attorney to make sure he or she had explained the problem to their respective clients. The court then asked each defendant if he wanted to continue with his current counsel. The court's questioning of Flores went as follows:
>
>> THE COURT: I want you to understand that under the Constitution, you have the right to have an attorney that represents your own personal best interests, nobody else's. Do you understand that?
>>
>> MR. FLORES: Yes, yes.
>>
>> THE COURT: And my concern is that your present attorney, having represented Mr. Rodriguez, that you understand that it is your best interests you must consider and your attorney must consider and not Mr. Rodriguez's best interests. His attorney must consider his best interests, and I want you to understand that fully. And I'd like to mention to you some of the potential—and I don't know that this would ever happen, but I want you to understand why I'm concerned. In the event Mr. Rodriguez decided to take the witness stand and cooperate with the government and testify against you, your attorney might be in the position of cross-examining somebody he once had an attorney-client relationship with. And that presents two types of problems. One is will he zealously and conscientiously represent your interests against his former client's interests; or, on the

other hand, from Mr. Rodriguez's point of view, will he, because he knows Mr. Rodriguez, be at an unfair advantage because of that prior relationship.

So I want you to be aware of this situation. Have you thought about, under these circumstances, have you though about whether you wish Mr. Green to continue representing you in this case?

MR. GREEN: [The judge] is asking if you've thought about whether you want me to continue being your lawyer. You have to answer her.

MR. FLORES: Yes, your Honor.

THE COURT: . . . You must be free to get the kind of objective legal advice on [the issue of cooperation with the government] if you're at all concerned or wish to consider any advantage to you. . . . That's another matter that you should consider in deciding whether or not you wish Mr. Green to represent you. Do you understand what I'm talking about?

MR. FLORES: Yes, your Honor.

THE COURT: Does it make sense to you? All right. Well, having considered these matters, what do you wish to do?

MR. GREEN: Do you want me to be your lawyer or not?

MR. FLORES: Yes, I would like him.

THE COURT: You wish to continue with Mr. Green's representation?

MR. FLORES: Yes, your Honor.

Next, the court questioned Samotny and Fontanez. That exchange went as follows:

THE COURT: All right. Mr. Fontanez—well, let me ask you, Miss Samotny. Have you gone over with Mr. Fontanez his right to counsel and the implications involved in that?

MS. SAMOTNY: Certainly I have, Judge.

THE COURT: And Mr. Flores, I myself—I'm sorry, Mr. Fontanez, I myself must advise you of your right to counsel, and that means an attorney who will act in your own personal best interests and no one else's. Do you understand what I'm saying?

MR. FONTANEZ: Yes.

THE COURT: . . . I want you to understand that your attorney and your relationship is a confidential matter. It's not something I want to get into in terms of anything said between you, but I want you to also understand that the person who represents you must represent only you and do what would be best for you, particularly in view of the fact you have no prior felony conviction, that you may wish to testify on your own behalf because you have no prior felony conviction, and it might be in your best interests to do so. I don't know what the facts that go into that decision are in this case, but it might be in your best interest. It might be in your best interest to cooperate with the government because it might, in effect, reduce your potential sentence. Are you aware of these things?

MR. FONTANEZ: Yes, I do.

THE COURT: And have you given some thought as to whether or not you wish Miss Samotny to continue representing you in this case?

MR. FONTANEZ: Yes, I would like for her to represent me.

THE COURT: All right. Thank you.

Finally, the court questioned Seiden and Rodriguez:

THE COURT: Have you advised Mr. Rodriguez about the potential problem of your having appeared on behalf of Mr. Fontanez?

MR. SEIDEN: * * * I found it necessary to have individual, of course, individual meetings with my client wherein I had to advise him that I was interested in him, only him, and that we would not be meeting with attorneys or other family members. Yes, we have discussed this in some detail, Judge.

THE COURT: All right. I would like to address Mr. Rodriguez directly—

MR. SEIDEN: Please.

THE COURT: Mr. Rodriguez, I wish to tell you that under the Constitution of the United States, you have the right to have a lawyer represent you that represents you, only you, in your own personal best interests. Do you understand that?

MR. RODRIGUEZ: (Through interpreter:) Yes.

THE COURT: Do you understand that you must make your own decisions in this case with the assistance of an attorney—

MR. RODRIGUEZ: (Through interpreter:) Yes.

THE COURT:—who will consider your interests, rather than those of your co-defendants? Even though they're family members, and I understand you're concerned what happens to your family, your attorney must be your own loyal spokesman here in the court and no one else's. Do you understand that?

MR. RODRIGUEZ: (Through interpreter:) Yes, yes.

THE COURT: Have you thought about this matter?

MR. RODRIGUEZ: (Through interpreter:) Yes.

THE COURT: What do you wish to do?

THE COURT: Do you wish Mr. Seiden to continue to represent you in this matter?

MR. RODRIGUEZ: (Through interpreter:) Yes.

THE COURT: All right, thank you.

The trial court in *Flores* respected the expressed preferences of each defendant and declined the government's invitation to intrude into the defendant's counsel of choice. Each defendant subsequently appealed on the ground that they had not knowingly waived their right to conflict-free counsel. They argued that the district court failed to make a detailed inquiry into how the conflict of interest might relate to the individual defendants and noted that the defendants' answers were usually only one or two words. The court of appeals rejected these arguments and found that the colloquies were sufficient to establish a knowing waiver of conflict-free counsel. The court provided the following analysis:

> First of all there is no requirement that the district court follow some pre-ordained, detailed script when eliciting a criminal defendant's waiver of the Sixth Amendment right to conflict-free counsel. We do not ask whether a defendant's decision to waive is foolish. Rather, we ask only whether the defendant made an informed decision. A waiver is sufficient if it was made knowingly and intelligently, that is to say, if it was made with sufficient awareness of the relevant circumstances and likely consequences. The district court need not conduct a long-winded dialogue with counsel and defendants when inquiring about a waiver. It is enough that the district court inform each defendant of the nature and importance of the right to conflict-free counsel and ensure that the defendant understands something of the consequences of a conflict.

> The district court in this case satisfied these standards. The transcript of the Rule 44(c) hearing reveals that the district court carefully questioned each attorney and each defendant about potential and actual conflicts created by the prior representation of co-defendants. After the district court explained the right to conflict-free counsel, each defendant made clear that he wanted to stick with his current attorney.

* * *

> The defendants' other argument—that their waivers are not valid because most of their answers at the Rule 44(c) hearing consisted of only one or two words—is also without merit. * * * The defendants answers at the Rule 44(c) hearing adequately expressed their preferences. We respect the defendants' choice of trial counsel and hold that the defendants waived their Sixth Amendment right to conflict-free counsel.

It should be noted as a matter of practice that some judges require the defendant to articulate, in his own words, what counsel's conflict is, and how it could impair his representation. While the court in *Flores* finds that this is not required, such a practice does help to assure that the defendant is making a knowing and intelligent waiver, or, to the contrary, could indicate that the defendant doesn't really know what he is giving up.

C. Conflicted Representation and The Right to Counsel of Choice

The Sixth Amendment provides a right to counsel of one's own choosing. But that right is not absolute. The following case indicates that the right to counsel of choice is qualified by the trial court's authority to disqualify a defense lawyer operating under a conflict of interest

WHEAT v. UNITED STATES

486 U.S. 153 (1988)

CHIEF JUSTICE REHNQUIST **delivered the opinion of the Court.**

The issue in this case is whether the District Court erred in declining petitioner's waiver of his right to conflict-free counsel and by refusing to permit petitioner's proposed substitution of attorneys.

I

Petitioner Mark Wheat, along with numerous codefendants, was charged with participating in a farflung drug distribution conspiracy. * * *

Also charged in the conspiracy were Juvenal Gomez–Barajas and Javier Bravo, who were represented in their criminal proceedings by attorney Eugene Iredale. Gomez–Barajas was tried first and was acquitted on drug charges overlapping with those against petitioner. To avoid a second trial on other charges, however, Gomez–Barajas offered to plead guilty to tax evasion and illegal importation of merchandise. At the commencement of petitioner's trial, the District Court had not accepted the plea; Gomez–Barajas was thus free to withdraw his guilty plea and proceed to trial.

Bravo, evidently a lesser player in the conspiracy, decided to forgo trial and plead guilty to one count of transporting approximately 2,400 pounds of marijuana from Los Angeles to a residence controlled by Victor Vidal. At the conclusion of Bravo's guilty plea proceedings on August 22, 1985, Iredale notified the District Court that he had been contacted by petitioner and had been asked to try petitioner's case as well. In response, the Government registered substantial concern about the possibility of conflict in the representation. * * *

* * * The Government's position was premised on two possible conflicts. First, the District Court had not yet accepted the plea and sentencing arrangement negotiated between Gomez–Barajas and the Government; in the event that arrangement were rejected by the court, Gomez–Barajas would be free to withdraw the plea and stand trial. He would then be faced with the prospect of representation by Iredale, who in the meantime would have acted as petitioner's attorney. Petitioner, through his participation in the drug distribution scheme, was familiar with the sources and size of Gomez–Barajas' income, and was thus likely to be called as a witness for the Government at any subsequent trial of Gomez–Barajas. This scenario would pose a conflict of interest for Iredale, who would be prevented from cross-examining petitioner and thereby from effectively representing Gomez–Barajas.

Second, and of more immediate concern, Iredale's representation of Bravo would directly affect his ability to act as counsel for petitioner. The Government believed that a portion of the marijuana delivered by Bravo to Vidal's residence eventually was transferred to petitioner. In this regard, the Government contacted Iredale and asked that Bravo be made available as a witness to testify against petitioner, and agreed in exchange to modify its position at the time of Bravo's sentencing. In the likely event that Bravo were called to testify, Iredale's position in representing both men would become untenable, for ethical proscriptions would forbid him to cross-examine Bravo in any meaningful way. By failing to do so, he would also fail to provide petitioner with effective assistance of counsel. Thus because of Iredale's prior representation of Gomez–Barajas and Bravo and the potential for serious conflict of interest, the Government urged the District Court to reject the substitution of attorneys.

In response, petitioner emphasized his right to have counsel of his own choosing and the willingness of Gomez–Barajas, Bravo, and petitioner to waive the right to conflict-free counsel. Petitioner argued that the circumstances posited by the Government that would create a conflict for Iredale were highly speculative and bore no connection to the true relationship between the co-conspirators. If called to testify, Bravo would simply say that he did not know petitioner and had no dealings with him; no attempt by Iredale to impeach Bravo would be necessary. Further, in the unlikely event that Gomez–Barajas went to trial on the charges of tax evasion and illegal importation, petitioner's lack of involvement in those alleged crimes made his appearance as a witness highly improbable. Finally, and most importantly, all three defendants agreed to allow Iredale to represent petitioner and to waive any future claims of conflict of interest. In petitioner's view, the Government was manufacturing implausible conflicts in an attempt to disqualify Iredale, who had already proved extremely effective in representing Gomez–Barajas and Bravo.

[The District Court found for the Government and rejected the substitution of Iredale. Wheat was convicted and the court of appeals affirmed the conviction.]

II

* * * We have * * * recognized that the purpose of providing assistance of counsel "is simply to ensure that criminal defendants receive a fair trial," and that in evaluating Sixth Amendment claims, "the appropriate inquiry focuses on the adversarial process, not on the accused's relationship with his lawyer as such." Thus, while the right to select and be represented by one's preferred attorney is comprehended by the Sixth Amendment, the essential aim of the Amendment is to guarantee an effective advocate for each criminal defendant rather than to ensure that a defendant will inexorably be represented by the lawyer whom he prefers.

The Sixth Amendment right to choose one's own counsel is circumscribed in several important respects. Regardless of his persuasive powers, an advocate who is not a member of the bar may not represent clients (other than himself) in court. Similarly, a defendant may not insist on representation by an attorney he cannot afford or who for other reasons declines to represent the defendant. Nor may a defendant insist on the counsel of an attorney who has a previous or ongoing relationship with an opposing party, even when the opposing party is the Government. The question raised in this case is the extent to which a criminal defendant's right under the Sixth Amendment to his chosen attorney is qualified by the fact that the attorney has represented other defendants charged in the same criminal conspiracy.

* * *

Petitioner insists that the provision of waivers by all affected defendants cures any problems created by the multiple representation. But no such flat rule can be deduced from the Sixth Amendment presumption in favor of counsel of choice. Federal courts have an independent interest in ensuring that criminal trials are conducted within the ethical standards of the profession and that legal proceedings appear fair to all who observe them. * * * Not only the interest of a criminal defendant but the institutional interest in the rendition of just verdicts in criminal cases may be jeopardized by unregulated multiple representation.

* * *

Thus, where a court justifiably finds an actual conflict of interest, there can be no doubt that it may decline a proffer of waiver, and insist that defendants be separately represented.

* * *

Unfortunately for all concerned, a district court must pass on the issue of whether or not to allow a waiver of a conflict of interest by a criminal defendant not with the wisdom of hindsight after the trial has taken place, but in the murkier pre-trial context when relationships between parties are seen through a glass, darkly. The likelihood and dimensions of nascent conflicts of interest are notoriously hard to predict, even for those thoroughly familiar with criminal trials. It is a rare attorney who will be fortunate enough to learn the entire truth from his own client, much less be fully apprised before trial of what each of the Government's witnesses will say on the stand. A few bits of unforeseen testimony or a single previously unknown or unnoticed document may significantly shift the relationship between multiple defendants. These imponderables are difficult enough for a lawyer to assess, and even more difficult to convey by way of explanation to a criminal defendant untutored in the niceties of legal ethics. Nor is it amiss to observe that the willingness of an attorney to obtain such waivers from his clients may bear an inverse relation to the care with which he conveys all the necessary information to them.

For these reasons we think the district court must be allowed substantial latitude in refusing waivers of conflicts of interest not only in those rare cases where an actual conflict may be demonstrated before trial, but in the more common cases where a potential for conflict exists which may or may not burgeon into an actual conflict as the trial progresses. In the circumstances of this case, with the motion for substitution of counsel made so close to the time of trial the District Court relied on instinct and judgment based on experience in making its decision. We do not think it can be said that the court exceeded the broad latitude which must be accorded it in making this decision. Petitioner of course rightly points out that the Government may seek to "manufacture" a conflict in order to prevent a defendant from having a particularly able defense counsel at his side; but trial courts are undoubtedly aware of this possibility, and must take it into consideration along with all of the other factors which inform this sort of a decision.

Here the District Court was confronted not simply with an attorney who wished to represent two coequal defendants in a straightforward criminal prosecution; rather, Iredale proposed to defend three conspirators of varying stature in a complex drug distribution scheme. The Government intended to call Bravo as a witness for the prosecution at petitioner's trial. [Bravo was in fact called as a witness at petitioner's trial. His testimony was elicited to demonstrate the transportation of drugs that the prosecution hoped to link to petitioner.] The Government might readily have tied certain deliveries of marijuana by Bravo to petitioner, necessitating vigorous cross-examination of Bravo by petitioner's counsel. Iredale, because of his prior representation of Bravo, would have been unable ethically to provide that cross-examination.

Iredale had also represented Gomez–Barajas, one of the alleged kingpins of the distribution ring, and had succeeded in obtaining a verdict of acquittal for him. Gomez–Barajas had agreed with the Government to plead guilty to other charges, but the District Court had not yet accepted the plea arrangement. If the agreement were rejected, petitioner's probable testimony at the resulting trial of Gomez–Barajas would create an ethical dilemma for Iredale from which one or the other of his clients would likely suffer.

Viewing the situation as it did before trial, we hold that the District Court's refusal to permit the substitution of counsel in this case was within its discretion and did not violate petitioner's Sixth Amendment rights. Other district courts might have reached differing or opposite conclusions with equal justification, but that does not mean that one conclusion was "right" and the other "wrong." The District Court must recognize a presumption in favor of petitioner's counsel of choice, but that presumption may be overcome not only by a demonstration of actual conflict but by a showing of a serious potential for conflict. The evaluation of the facts and circumstances of each case under this standard must be left primarily to the informed judgment of the trial court.

The judgment of the Court of Appeals is accordingly affirmed.

Justice Marshall, with whom Justice Brennan joins, dissenting.

* * *

At the time of petitioner's trial, Iredale's representation of Gomez–Barajas was effectively completed. * * * Gomez–Barajas was not scheduled to appear as a witness at petitioner's trial; thus, Iredale's conduct of that trial would not require him to question his former client. The only possible conflict this Court can divine from Iredale's representation of both petitioner and Gomez–Barajas rests on the premise that the trial court would reject the negotiated plea agreement and that Gomez–Barajas then would decide to go to trial. In this event, the Court tells us, "petitioner's probable testimony at the resulting trial of Gomez–Barajas would create an ethical dilemma for Iredale."

This argument rests on speculation of the most dubious kind. * * * The most likely occurrence at the time petitioner moved to retain Iredale as his defense counsel was that the trial court would accept Gomez–Barajas' plea agreement, as the court in fact later did. Moreover, even if Gomez–Barajas had gone to trial, petitioner probably would not have testified. The record contains no indication that petitioner had any involvement in or information about crimes for which Gomez–Barajas might yet have stood trial. * * * It is therefore disingenuous to say that representation of both petitioner and Gomez–Barajas posed a serious potential for a conflict of interest.

Similarly, Iredale's prior representation of Bravo was not a cause for concern. * * * As all parties were aware at the time, Bravo did not know and could not identify petitioner; indeed, prior to the commencement of legal proceedings, the two men never had heard of each other. Bravo's eventual testimony at petitioner's trial related to a shipment of marijuana in which petitioner was not involved; the testimony contained not a single reference to petitioner. Petitioner's counsel did not cross-examine Bravo, and neither petitioner's counsel nor the prosecutor mentioned Bravo's testimony in closing argument. All of these developments were predictable when the District Court ruled on petitioner's request that Iredale serve as trial counsel; the contours of Bravo's testimony were clear at that time. Given the insignificance of this testimony to any matter that petitioner's counsel would dispute, the proposed joint representation of petitioner and Bravo did not threaten a conflict of interest. The very insignificance of Bravo's testimony, combined with the timing of the prosecutor's decision to call Bravo as a witness, raises a serious concern that the prosecutor attempted to manufacture a conflict in this case. The prosecutor's decision to use Bravo as a witness was an 11th–hour development. * * * Only after the prosecutor learned of the substitution motion and decided to oppose it did he arrange for Bravo's testimony by agreeing to recommend to the trial court a reduction in Bravo's sentence. Especially in light of the scarce value of Bravo's testimony, this prosecutorial behavior very plausibly may be viewed as a maneuver to prevent Iredale from representing petitioner at trial. Iredale had proved to be a formidable adversary; he previously had gained an acquittal for the alleged kingpin of the marijuana distribution scheme. * * *

Moreover, even assuming that Bravo's testimony might have "necessitat[ed] vigorous cross-examination," the District Court could have insured against the possibility of any conflict of interest without wholly depriving petitioner of his constitutional right to the counsel of his choice. Petitioner's motion requested that Iredale either be substituted for petitioner's current counsel or be added to petitioner's defense team. Had the District Court allowed the addition of Iredale and then ordered that he take no part in the cross-examination of Bravo, any possibility of a conflict would have been removed. Especially in light of the availability of this precautionary measure, the notion that Iredale's prior representation of Bravo might well have caused a conflict of interest at petitioner's trial is nothing short of ludicrous.

* * *

[The dissenting opinion of Justice Stevens, joined by Justice Blackmun, is omitted.]

Analysis of Wheat

Wheat is criticized in Bruce A. Green, *"Through a Glass, Darkly": How the Court Sees Motions to Disqualify Criminal Defense Lawyers,* 89 Colum. L. Rev. 1201 (1989). Among other criticisms, Professor Green notes that "the Court relied on an unwarranted assumption that if the defendant is willing to waive potential conflict of interest claims his attorney probably has not complied with the ethical standards governing the investigation and disclosure of potential conflicts." Professor Green also contends that the Court in *Wheat* "inexplicably retreated from the concern expressed in previous cases for the attorney-client relationship and for the defendant's autonomy," and that it "exaggerated the significance of judicial interests" which justify disqualification of counsel despite a client's waiver.

Wheat is defended in William J. Stuntz, *Waiving Rights in Criminal Procedure,* 75 Va. L. Rev. 761 (1989). Professor Stuntz argues that clients jointly represented by a single counsel may or may not have improper motives. It may be that joint counsel is retained to deter conspirators from cutting an individual deal and cooperating with the government. Thus, some defendants may be coerced into accepting a joint counsel relationship. On the other hand, it may be that the clients have proper motives—they all want the same lawyer because that lawyer is excellent. Stuntz argues that the capability of the lawyer is likely to be known by the trial judge; if the lawyer is known to be merely average, bad motives for the multiple representation can be inferred, and disqualification should be ordered because the client's waiver of conflict-free counsel is not really voluntary. Therefore a broad grant of discretion to the trial judge is necessary to allow the judge to separate good from bad motives in joint representation. Professor Stuntz's arguments are not borne out by the facts in *Wheat,* however, where it appeared that a number of the defendants came to Iredale fairly far along in the proceedings, because he had been so successful in defending other defendants. The trial judge specifically noted that Iredale was an excellent and highly successful defense attorney, and disqualified him nonetheless.

Another concern that might have animated the result in *Wheat* is that it is trial judges who see the defendant who is purporting to waive the right to conflict-free counsel. Conflicts of interest are complicated. How is the court to be sure that the defendant really understands what he is giving up? Especially with unsophisticated defendants, a trial judge might conclude that the defendant who says he wants to waive is in fact not making a truly knowing waiver. And because it is the trial judge who sees what is going on, appellate courts should be deferent to the trial judge's assessment and decision to override the defendant's "waiver."

Why must a lawyer be disqualified if he has represented one client who is now testifying against another? Of course, the lawyer cannot cross-examine the witness-client with confidential information without client consent. But if the lawyer cross-examines the witness-client with only non-confidential information, as she must, who does the cross-examination hurt? How is that cross-examination different from that would be conducted by substitute counsel, who would not have access to the confidential information in the first place? And if there is some limited impairment in the cross-examination, why can't the defendant consent to it? And what was wrong with Justice Marshall's point that Wheat was asking for Iredale to be *cocounsel,* thus permitting his other attorney to conduct the cross-examination of Iredale's former client? Professor Green asserts that "the Court in *Wheat* upheld the denial of Wheat's choice of counsel in a case where the ethical rules plainly would have permitted that choice." *See United States v. Cunningham,* 672 F.2d 1064 (2d Cir. 1982) (no disqualification required where defense attorney would need to use only public information in cross-examining the witness).

Practice Pointer

If the trial judge allows a defendant to keep his conflicted counsel, there is a risk that the defendant once convicted will appeal on the ground that he did not knowingly and voluntarily waive his right. Thus, trial judges have to be especially vigilant in determining that the defendant knows what the projected conflict is and how his lawyer may not be able to defend in a certain way or make a certain argument. This undoubtedly causes some judges to err on the side of disqualification.

Cases Applying Wheat

After *Wheat,* appellate courts have usually upheld trial court disqualifications of defense counsel. For example, in *United States v. Stites,* 56 F.3d 1020 (9th Cir. 1995), Stites and his sister Cheryl Dark were charged with RICO violations resulting from a scheme of insurance fraud. Stites fled the state, and Cheryl was represented by Juanita Brooks. Cheryl pleaded guilty and at the sentencing hearing, Brooks argued that Cheryl was a pawn of Stites; that Stites was "the mastermind," "a thief and a fraud," and a "cheap con artist." She added for good measure that "as an officer of the court and attorney myself, it makes me angry to see that people are able to so pervert our system of justice." Brooks won a light sentence for Dark. Two years later, Stites finally turned up for trial—and retained Brooks. When the prosecution objected, both Stites and Dark waived any conflict. But the trial judge—who happened to be the same judge who sentenced Dark—disqualified Brooks. The court of appeals upheld the disqualification. The court noted that Dark would be a witness at Stites' trial, and that the trial court was right to question the voluntariness of Dark's waiver. Most importantly, though, the court found that Brooks was properly disqualified because "[s]he could not, in the very same criminal prosecution, tell the court that Stites was a liar, a thief, and the mastermind of the massive fraud charged by the government and then represent the same person contending that he was innocent of the crimes charged." The court concluded as follows:

> Students of the classics may recall Cicero's comment that speeches at trials are for "the case and the occasion," they do not disclose "the man himself." But even if a certain insincerity may accompany the filling of an advocate's role, nothing in our professional ethics permits an advocate to tell a court one set of facts today and a contradictory set of facts tomorrow.

Aren't lawyers expected to represent a client, clean the slate, and then represent another? Do hired guns act unethically? Was Brooks supposed to have a conscience when she represented Stites?

One of the more notable disqualifications of counsel occurred in the prosecution of former Mafia boss John Gotti. *United States v. Locascio*, 6 F.3d 924 (2d Cir. 1993). The trial court disqualified Gotti's long-time counsel, Bruce Cutler, on two grounds: (1) The government had proof that Cutler served as house counsel to the Mafia, representing various conspirators who had not personally retained him—thus his representation would actually be proof of conspiratorial activity at trial; and (2) The government had tapes in which Cutler was present while criminal activity was being discussed—thus, in challenging the government's interpretation of the tapes, Cutler would be acting as an unsworn witness. The court of appeals upheld the disqualification, and noted in particular with respect to Cutler's status as an unsworn witness, that Gotti's waiver of conflict was irrelevant:

> When an attorney is an unsworn witness * * * the detriment is to the government, since the defendant gains an unfair advantage, and to the court, since the factfinding process is impaired. Waiver by the defendant is ineffective in such situations, since he is not the party prejudiced.

> * * * The government was legitimately concerned that, when Cutler argued before the jury for a particular interpretation of the tapes, his interpretation would be given added credibility due to his presence in the room when the statements were made. This would have given Gotti an unfair advantage, since Cutler would not have had to take an oath in presenting his interpretation, but could merely frame it in the form of legal argument.

See also United States v. Register, 182 F.3d 820 (11th Cir. 1999) (no error in disqualifying counsel over the defendant's objections, where a government informant might testify that the defendant paid the attorney with drugs from the conspiracy: "It would have been virtually impossible for the attorney to question the informant without being concerned to a significant degree about his own interests rather than those of his client").

CHAPTER 6

The Lawyer's Duties to the Legal System, the Profession, and Nonclients

In this chapter, we turn from the lawyer's duties to clients to the lawyer's responsibilities as an officer of the court, a member of an organized profession, and a citizen. Professor Eugene Gaetke contrasts the lawyer's obligation to clients with the lawyer's obligations as an officer of a court. He explains that:

> Two antagonistic models describe the role of lawyers in our legal system. More familiar to the public, and more comfortable to lawyers, is the model of the lawyer as a 'zealous advocate,' the devoted champion of the client's cause. Indeed, the image of the lawyer as loyal advocate for the beleaguered client is perpetuated by the bar itself and reinforced by the media, in literature, and in common lore.
>
> In its public assertions, the legal profession promotes a different model: lawyers are officers of the court in the conduct of their professional, and even their personal, affairs. The organized bar has expressly emphasized this obligation in each of its major codifications of the ethical obligations of the profession[.]* * * The very words 'officer of the court' connote a mandatory public interest role for lawyers and suggest that lawyers sometimes must act in a quasi-judicial or quasi-official capacity despite duties owed to their clients. The primary distinguishing characteristic of the duties making up the officer of the court obligation, therefore, must be their subordination of the interests of the client and the lawyer to those of the judicial system and the public.[1]

As Professor Gaetke observes, the ethics rules confront the apparent conflict between these models. The Rules state that "[v]irtually all difficult ethical problems arise from conflict between a lawyer's responsibilities to clients, to the legal system and to the lawyer's own interest in remaining an ethical person while earning a satisfactory living." How does a lawyer resolve these "difficult, ethi-

---

1   Eugene R. Gaetke, *Lawyers as Officers of the Court*, 42 Vand. L. Rev. 39, 40-41, 48 (1989).

cal problems"? The Rules suggest that these "issues must be resolved through the exercise of sensitive professional and moral judgment guided by the basic principles underlying the Rules. These principles include the lawyer's obligation zealously to protect and pursue a client's legitimate interests, within the bounds of the law, while maintaining a professional, courteous and civil attitude toward all persons." The ABA Commission on Professionalism proposed a somewhat different emphasis:

> The profession's view has long been that the lawyer best serves the system of justice when he or she represents a client honestly and effectively, whether in court or in the office. Nothing that we say should be understood as inconsistent with that general observation. However, there are limitations on such representation.

> First, lawyers must avoid identifying too closely with their clients. Unless the advice provided by a lawyer is truly objective and independent, the client's own interests will not be well served.

Second, lawyers must communicate openly and fully with their clients about limitations on their ability to serve. Where necessary, they should explain to their clients what their duties are to the court or to the system of justice in a given case, beginning with the obvious prohibition against participating in any way in the giving of perjured testimony.[3]

Part I of the chapter explores the lawyer's role as officer of the court. Part II examines the lawyer's duties to third parties and the law and Part III discusses the lawyer's responsibilities to other lawyers and the bar.

Food for Thought

These analyses assume that conflicts arise when the lawyer's perception of the client's interests differs from the lawyer's perceptions of her duties to the legal system, the profession, and nonclients. Professors Russell Pearce and Eli Wald argue that this perspective presumes that people live as autonomous individuals, rather than as participants in a web of interconnected relationships.[2] They suggest that under the latter view these differences do not inevitably result in conflicts. Rather, the lawyer may be able to resolve these differences through dialogue with the client regarding how to find a mutually acceptable resolution of the lawyer's and client's obligations given that they both live their lives in a web of relationships.

---

2   Russell G. Pearce & Eli Wald, *Law as a Morally Responsible Business: Reintegrating Ethics into Economics and Law* (draft on file with authors).

3   112 F.R.D. 243, 278 (1986). The Commission also noted that "Third, the lawyer in litigation is obliged to bring to the court's attention any authority from the controlling jurisdiction which is directly in opposition to his position, if it was not raised by an adverse party. In discussions with judges around the country, we gained the clear impression that the candid citation by counsel of opposing case precedent is rare." *Id.*

I. Duties to the Court and other Tribunals

This section examines the "duties of lawyers as officers of the court to avoid conduct that undermines the integrity of the adjudicative process."[4] The particular obligations range from avoiding frivolous claims to remedying client perjury and limiting trial publicity.

A. Meritorious Claims

[Question 1]

Client hired Attorney Alpha to file a lawsuit against Client's former employer, Corp, for wrongful discharge. Alpha filed the suit in federal district court based upon three grounds. It turned out that a unanimous U.S. Supreme Court decision had recently eliminated the third ground as a theory available to plaintiffs in wrongful discharge cases. Attorney Beta, who represents Corp, filed a motion alleging that the complaint was based upon a theory (the third ground) that is no longer supported by existing law and cited the new decision. Within ten days after the filing of the complaint, Alpha withdrew the third ground and continued with the litigation. Is Alpha subject to litigation sanction?

(A) Yes, unless Alpha discussed the adverse legal authority with Client before filing the complaint.

(B) Yes, because Alpha should have cited the U.S. Supreme Court decision in the complaint.

(C) No, because Alpha withdrew the third ground within ten days after filing the complaint.

(D) No, unless Alpha knew or should have known of the recent decision when the complaint was filed.

Federal Rules of Civil Procedure Rule 11

(a) Signature.

Every pleading, written motion, and other paper must be signed by at least one attorney of record in the attorney's name—or by a party personally if the party is unrepresented. * * *

(b) Representations to the Court.

By presenting to the court a pleading, written motion, or other paper—whether by signing, filing, submitting, or later advocating it—an attorney or unrepresented

---

4   R. 3.3, Cmt. ¶ 1.

party certifies that to the best of the person's knowledge, information, and belief, formed after an inquiry reasonable under the circumstances:

(1) it is not being presented for any improper purpose, such as to harass, cause unnecessary delay, or needlessly increase the cost of litigation;

(2) the claims, defenses, and other legal contentions are warranted by existing law or by a nonfrivolous argument for extending, modifying, or reversing existing law or for establishing new law;

(3) the factual contentions have evidentiary support or, if specifically so identified, will likely have evidentiary support after a reasonable opportunity for further investigation or discovery; and

(4) the denials of factual contentions are warranted on the evidence or, if specifically so identified, are reasonably based on belief or a lack of information.

(c) Sanctions.

(1) In General.

If, after notice and a reasonable opportunity to respond, the court determines that Rule 11(b) has been violated, the court may impose an appropriate sanction on any attorney, law firm, or party that violated the rule or is responsible for the violation. Absent exceptional circumstances, a law firm must be held jointly responsible for a violation committed by its partner, associate, or employee.

(2) Motion for Sanctions. A motion for sanctions must be made separately from any other motion and must describe the specific conduct that allegedly violates Rule 11(b). The motion must be served under Rule 5, but it must not be filed or be presented to the court if the challenged paper, claim, defense, contention, or denial is withdrawn or appropriately corrected within 21 days after service or within another time the court sets. If warranted, the court may award to the prevailing party the reasonable expenses, including attorney's fees, incurred for the motion.

(3) On the Court's Initiative.

On its own, the court may order an attorney, law firm, or party to show cause why conduct specifically described in the order has not violated Rule 11(b).

(4) Nature of a Sanction.

A sanction imposed under this rule must be limited to what suffices to deter repetition of the conduct or comparable conduct by others similarly situated. The sanction may include nonmonetary directives; an order to pay a penalty into court; or, if imposed on motion and warranted for effective deterrence, an order directing payment to the movant of part or all of the reasonable attorney's fees and other expenses directly resulting from the violation.

(5) Limitations on Monetary Sanctions.

The court must not impose a monetary sanction:

(A) against a represented party for violating Rule 11(b)(2); or

(B) on its own, unless it issued the show-cause order under Rule 11(c)(3) before voluntary dismissal or settlement of the claims made by or against the party that is, or whose attorneys are, to be sanctioned.

* * *

(d) Inapplicability to Discovery.

This rule does not apply to disclosures and discovery requests, responses, objections, and motions under <u>Rules 26 through 37</u>.

[Question 2]

An attorney is employed in the legal department of a public utility and represents that company in litigation. The company has been sued by a consumer group that has accused the company of various acts in violation of its charter. Through its general counsel, the company has instructed the attorney not to negotiate a settlement but to go to trial under any circumstances because a precedent needs to be established. The attorney believes the defense can be supported by a good faith argument, but also believes the case should be settled if possible.

Must the attorney withdraw as counsel in this case?

(A) Yes, because the company is controlling the attorney's judgment in refusing to settle the case.

(B) Yes, because a lawyer should endeavor to avoid litigation.

(C) No, because the company's defense can be supported by a good faith argument.

(D) No, because, as an employee, the attorney is bound by the instructions of the general counsel.

Review Rules <u>1.2</u> and <u>1.16</u>. <u>Rule 3.1</u> governs "Meritorious Claims and Contentions." It provides that:

A lawyer shall not bring or defend a proceeding, or assert or controvert an issue therein, unless there is a basis in law and fact for doing so that is not frivolous, which includes a good faith argument for an extension, modification or reversal of existing law. A lawyer for the defendant in a criminal proceeding, or the respondent in a proceeding that could result in incarceration, may nevertheless so defend the proceeding as to require that every element of the case be established.

In addition, <u>Rule 3.3(a)</u> provides that "[a] lawyer shall not knowingly:

(1) make a false statement of fact or law to a tribunal or fail to correct a false statement of material fact or law previously made to the tribunal by the lawyer;

(2) fail to disclose to the tribunal legal authority in the controlling jurisdiction known to the lawyer to be directly adverse to the position of the client and not disclosed by opposing counsel[.]"

Food for Thought

Is the conduct in Question 1 a violation of the Rules?

B. False Testimony and Evidence

[Question 3]

An attorney represented a client in an action against the client's former partner to recover damages for breach of contract. During the representation, the client presented the attorney with incontrovertible proof that the former partner had committed perjury in a prior action which was resolved in the partner's favor. Neither the attorney nor the client was involved in any way in the prior action. The attorney believes that it would be detrimental to the client's best interests to reveal the perjury because of the implication that might be drawn from the former close personal and business relationship between the client and the former partner.

Would it be proper for the attorney to fail to disclose the perjury to the tribunal?

(A) No, because the information is unprivileged.

(B) No, because the attorney has knowledge that the former partner perpetrated a fraud on the tribunal.

C) Yes, because neither the client nor the attorney was involved in the prior action.

(D) Yes, because the attorney believes that the disclosure would be detrimental to the client's best interests.

Review <u>Rule 1.6</u>. <u>Rule 3.3</u> governs "candor to the tribunal." <u>Rule 3.3(a)</u> provides the general rule with regard to false statements and false evidence. It provides that:

(a) A lawyer shall not knowingly:

> (1) make a false statement of fact or law to a tribunal or fail to correct a false statement of material fact or law previously made to the tribunal by the lawyer;

> * * *

> (3) offer evidence that the lawyer knows to be false. If a lawyer, the lawyer's client, or a witness called by the lawyer, has offered material evidence and the lawyer comes to know of its falsity, the lawyer shall take reasonable remedial measures, including, if necessary, disclosure to the tribunal. A lawyer may refuse to offer evidence, other than the testimony of a defendant in a criminal matter, that the lawyer reasonably believes is false.

<u>Rule 3.3(b)</u> and <u>(c)</u> identify the proceedings to which these duties apply. They provide that:

(b) A lawyer who represents a client in an adjudicative proceeding and who knows that a person intends to engage, is engaging or has engaged in criminal or fraudulent conduct related to the proceeding shall take reasonable remedial measures, including, if necessary, disclosure to the tribunal.

(c) The duties stated in paragraphs (a) and (b) continue to the conclusion of the proceeding, and apply even if compliance requires disclosure of information otherwise protected by Rule 1.6.

* * *

The Comment to Rule 3.3 further explains:

Preserving Integrity of Adjudicative Process

[12] Lawyers have a special obligation to protect a tribunal against criminal or fraudulent conduct that undermines the integrity of the adjudicative process, such as bribing, intimidating or otherwise unlawfully communicating with a witness, juror, court official or other participant in the proceeding, unlawfully destroying or concealing documents or other evidence or failing to disclose information to the tribunal when required by law to do so. Thus, paragraph (b) requires a lawyer to take reasonable remedial measures, including disclosure if necessary, whenever the lawyer knows that a person, including the lawyer's client, intends to engage, is engaging or has engaged in criminal or fraudulent conduct related to the proceeding.

[Question 4]

An attorney represented a client who was injured when the television antenna he was attempting to erect in his yard came in contact with a power line. As part of its defense, the manufacturer of the antenna claimed that the antenna came with a warning label advising against erecting the antenna near power lines. The client told the attorney that he had not seen a warning label. The client's wife told the attorney that she had kept the antenna and the box it came in and that she saw no warning label anywhere.

When called by the attorney as witnesses, both the client and his wife testified that they had never seen a warning label. After their testimony, but while the trial was still in progress, the attorney learned from the wife's sister that there indeed had been a warning label on the box, but that the wife had removed and destroyed it. When the attorney confronted the wife with her sister's statement, the wife admitted destroying the label but insisted that her husband knew nothing about it. The attorney continued the trial, but made no reference to the absence of a warning label in his summation to the jury. Instead, the attorney argued that the warning label, even if seen, was insufficient to advise his client of the serious consequences that would ensure if the warning was not heeded. The jury found in favor of the manufacturer.

Is the attorney subject to discipline?

(A) Yes, because the attorney called the wife as a witness and she gave perjured testimony.

(B) Yes, because the attorney failed to take reasonable remedial action after he realized that the wife had given perjured testimony.

(C) No, because the jury apparently disbelieved the wife's testimony.

> **(D) No, because the attorney did not rely on the wife's testimony once he discovered the perjury.**

Review the provisions of <u>Rule 3.3</u> above. In addition, the Comment to <u>Rule 3.3</u> elaborates:

Offering Evidence

[5] Paragraph (a)(3) requires that the lawyer refuse to offer evidence that the lawyer knows to be false, regardless of the client's wishes. This duty is premised on the lawyer's obligation as an officer of the court to prevent the trier of fact from being misled by false evidence. * * *

[6] If a lawyer knows that the client intends to testify falsely or wants the lawyer to introduce false evidence, the lawyer should seek to persuade the client that the evidence should not be offered. If the persuasion is ineffective and the lawyer continues to represent the client, the lawyer must refuse to offer the false evidence. If only a portion of a witness's testimony will be false, the lawyer may call the witness to testify but may not elicit or otherwise permit the witness to present the testimony that the lawyer knows is false.

[7] The duties stated in paragraphs (a) and (b) apply to all lawyers, including defense counsel in criminal cases. In some jurisdictions, however, courts have required counsel to present the accused as a witness or to give a narrative statement if the accused so desires, even if counsel knows that the testimony or statement will be false. The obligation of the advocate under the Rules of Professional Conduct is subordinate to such requirements. *See also* Comment [9].

[8] The prohibition against offering false evidence only applies if the lawyer knows that the evidence is false. A lawyer's reasonable belief that evidence is false does not preclude its presentation to the trier of fact. A lawyer's knowledge that evidence is false, however, can be inferred from the circumstances. *See* Rule 1.0(f). Thus, although a lawyer should resolve doubts about the veracity of testimony or other evidence in favor of the client, the lawyer cannot ignore an obvious falsehood.

[9] Although paragraph (a)(3) only prohibits a lawyer from offering evidence the lawyer knows to be false, it permits the lawyer to refuse to offer testimony or other proof that the lawyer reasonably believes is false. Offering such proof may reflect adversely on the lawyer's ability to discriminate in the quality of evidence and thus impair the lawyer's effectiveness as an advocate. Because of the special protections historically provided criminal defendants, however, this Rule does not permit a lawyer to refuse to offer the testimony of such a client where the lawyer reasonably believes but does not know that the testimony will be false. Unless the lawyer knows the testimony will be false, the lawyer must honor the client's decision to testify. *See also* Comment [7].

Remedial Measures

[10] Having offered material evidence in the belief that it was true, a lawyer may subsequently come to know that the evidence is false. Or, a lawyer may be surprised when the lawyer's client, or another witness called by the lawyer, offers testimony the lawyer knows to be false, either during the lawyer's direct examination or in response to cross-examination by the opposing lawyer. In such situations or if the lawyer knows of the falsity of testimony elicited from the client during a deposition, the lawyer must take reasonable remedial measures. In such situations, the advocate's proper course is to remonstrate with the client confidentially, advise the client of the lawyer's duty of candor to the tribunal and seek the client's cooperation with respect to the withdrawal or correction of the false statements or evidence. If that fails, the advocate must take further remedial action. If withdrawal from the representation is not permitted or will not undo the effect of the false evidence, the advocate must make such disclosure to the tribunal as is reasonably necessary to remedy the situation, even if doing so requires the lawyer to reveal information that otherwise would be protected by Rule 1.6. It is for the tribunal then to determine what should be done—making a statement about the matter to the trier of fact, ordering a mistrial or perhaps nothing.

[11] The disclosure of a client's false testimony can result in grave consequences to the client, including not only a sense of betrayal but also loss of the case and perhaps a prosecution for perjury. But the alternative is that the lawyer cooperate in deceiving the court, thereby subverting the truth-finding process which the adversary system is designed to implement. *See* Rule 1.2(d). Furthermore, unless it is clearly understood that the lawyer will act upon the duty to disclose the existence of false evidence, the client can simply reject the lawyer's advice to reveal the false evidence and insist that the lawyer keep silent. Thus the client could in effect coerce the lawyer into being a party to fraud on the court.

[Question 5]

Attorney Alpha represents Def in a murder prosecution. Def admits to Alpha that he killed the victim but claims that he acted in self-defense. Based on other conversations with Def, Alpha reasonably believes that Alpha committed the murder but is lying about acting in self-defense. Def wants to testify at trial to explain his claim of self-defense. Under the Rules, Alpha:

(A) **must permit Def to testify.**

(B) **must refuse to allow Def to testify.**

(C) **has discretion to permit Def to testify.**

(D) **has discretion to permit Def to testify but only if he limits Def's testimony to a narrative statement.**

Review <u>Rule 3.3</u>, including the excerpts provided earlier in this section.

[Question 6]

**Assume the facts of Question 5 above. Alpha tells Def that if Def testifies
that he acted in self-defense Alpha will inform the judge the Def has committed perjury. Def decides not to testify because of Alpha's threat. Does Def
have a claim of ineffective assistance of counsel?**

(A) Yes

(B) No

Review Rule 3.3 and the following materials before answering this question.

When a defense attorney believes that her client is about to commit perjury, she
faces a particularly difficult dilemma that bears on the right to effective assistance
of counsel.

Applying Strickland to Client Perjury: Nix v. Whiteside

In a highly publicized case, *Nix v. Whiteside*, <u>475 U.S. 157 (1986)</u>, the defendant
pleaded self-defense, but in his initial statement to defense counsel, he did not mention that the victim had a gun. In a later interview, the defendant stated that he now
remembered that he saw the victim with "something metallic" in his hand. When
challenged about the discrepancy by defense counsel, the defendant referred to a
case in which an acquaintance was acquitted after testifying that his victim wielded
a gun. In apparent comparison with that case, the defendant concluded: "If I don't
say I saw a gun, I'm dead." The defense counsel told the client that any statement
about a gun would be perjury; that if the defendant testified about a gun at trial, the
lawyer would advise the court of the perjury, would probably be permitted to
impeach the testimony, and would seek to withdraw. The client succumbed to the
threats. He testified at trial that he believed the victim was reaching for a gun, but he
had not seen one. The client challenged his second degree murder conviction on an
ineffective assistance of counsel ground. Although the state courts commended the
lawyer's integrity, a federal court of appeals granted habeas corpus relief.

The Supreme Court unanimously
reversed in an opinion by Chief Justice
Burger. He reasoned that no defendant
has a right to commit perjury, so that
no defendant has a right to rely upon
counsel to assist in the development of
false testimony. The Court noted that

Make the Connection

For further discussion of *Strickland*,
see Chapter 3 *supra*.

under *Strickland v. Washington*, <u>466 U.S. 668 (1984)</u> the defendant alleging ineffective assistance must prove prejudice, and Whiteside "has no valid claim that

confidence in the result of his trial has been diminished by his desisting from the contemplated perjury."

Even if the jury would have been persuaded by the perjury, the Court concluded that under *Strickland,* "a defendant has no entitlement to the luck of a lawless decisionmaker." The Chief Justice also rejected Whiteside's argument that the *Cuyler v. Sullivan* limited presumption of prejudice should apply. Whatever conflict existed between Whiteside and his counsel "was imposed on the attorney by the client's proposal to commit the crime of fabricating testimony." The Chief Justice reasoned that "if a 'conflict' between a client's proposal and counsel's ethical obligation gives rise to a presumption that counsel's assistance was prejudicially ineffective, every guilty criminal's conviction would be suspect if the defendant had sought to obtain an acquittal by illegal means."

Make the Connection

For analysis of *Cuyler v. Sullivan, see* Chapter 5 *supra.*

Although lack of cognizable prejudice was enough to decide the case, the Chief Justice went further and held that Whiteside's counsel had not been ineffective in discouraging his client from committing perjury. He concluded that for the purposes of this case, effectiveness could be determined by reference to the prevailing rules of professional responsibility governing the conduct of lawyers. He noted that Disciplinary Rule 7–102(A)(4) of the ABA Code of Professional Responsibility (then in effect in Iowa and in a small minority of states) provided that a lawyer shall not "knowingly use perjured testimony or false evidence;" and that Rule 3.3 of the Model Rules requires disclosure of client perjury to the tribunal as a last resort. The Chief Justice found that the prevailing ethical standards "confirm that the legal profession has accepted that an attorney's ethical duty to advance the interests of his client is limited by an equally solemn duty to comply with the law and standards of professional conduct." He concluded as follows:

> [U]nder no circumstances may a lawyer either advocate or passively tolerate a client's giving false testimony. * * * The rule adopted by the Court of Appeals, which seemingly would require an attorney to remain silent while his client committed perjury, is wholly incompatible with the established standards of ethical conduct and the laws of Iowa and contrary to professional standards promulgated by that State. The position advanced by the [Government], on the contrary, is wholly consistent with the Iowa standards of professional conduct and law, with the overwhelming majority of courts, and with codes of professional ethics. Since there has been no breach of any recognized professional duty, it follows that there can be no deprivation of the right to assistance of counsel under the *Strickland* standard.

Justice Brennan wrote an opinion concurring in the judgment. He agreed with the majority's analysis on the prejudice prong of *Strickland*. As to the performance prong, however, he argued that the Court "has no constitutional authority to establish rules of ethical conduct for lawyers practicing in the state courts," and that "the Court's essay regarding what constitutes the correct response to a criminal client's suggestion that he will perjure himself is pure discourse without force of law." Justice Blackmun wrote an opinion concurring in the judgment, joined by Justices Brennan, Marshall, and Stevens. He agreed that Whiteside had not shown prejudice from his lawyer's conduct, and saw no need to "grade counsel's performance." He argued, however, that the client perjury problem could not be solved by a simple reference to lawyers' ethics codes:

> Whether an attorney's response to what he sees as a client's command to commit perjury violates a defendant's Sixth Amendment rights may depend on many factors: how certain the attorney is that the proposed testimony is false, the stage of the proceedings at which the attorney discovers the plan, or the ways in which the attorney may be able to dissuade his client, to name just three. The complex interaction of factors, which is likely to vary from case to case, makes inappropriate a blanket rule that defense attorneys must reveal, or threaten to reveal, a client's anticipated perjury to the court. Except in the rarest of cases, attorneys who adopt the role of the judge or jury to determine the facts, pose a danger of depriving their clients of the zealous and loyal advocacy required by the Sixth Amendment.

Justice Stevens also wrote an opinion concurring in the judgment, emphasizing that it is often difficult to determine whether the client's proposed testimony is perjurious.

> From the perspective of an appellate judge, after a case has been tried and the evidence has been sifted by another judge, a particular fact may be as clear and certain as a piece of crystal or a small diamond. A trial lawyer, however, must often deal with mixtures of sand and clay. Even a pebble that seems clear enough at first glance may take on a different hue in a handful of gravel. * * *

> A lawyer's certainty that a change in his client's recollection is a harbinger of intended perjury—as well as judicial review of such apparent certainty—should be tempered by the realization that, after reflection, the most honest witness may recall (or sincerely believe he recalls) details that he previously overlooked.

Whiteside Was Too Easy

Even if the propriety of counsel's performance is considered, *Whiteside* is an easy case. Most lawyers would think it entirely appropriate to try to discourage the client from a planned course of perjury. Indeed, discouragement of perjury is effective advocacy, because the jury may disbelieve the lie, the prosecutor may easily tear it apart on cross-examination, and obviously the client may subject himself to a perjury charge. Moreover, if the trial judge believes that a defendant lied on the stand, this will be taken into account at sentencing. So it certainly makes sense to do everything reasonable to discourage a client from committing perjury on the witness stand.

Harder Questions

The difficult questions, not presented by *Whiteside*, are three. First, what if the client refuses to be dissuaded from a course of perjury and demands to testify? Second, what if the client appears to have been dissuaded from testifying falsely, but then commits perjury after taking the stand? Third, what if the lawyer discovers after the testimony that the client has perjured himself? *See* Monroe H. Freedman, *Client Confidences and Client Perjury: Some Unanswered Questions*, 136 U. Pa. L. Rev. 1939 (1988) (arguing that all of these problems should be left to the adversary system and to cross-examination by the prosecutor). After *Whiteside*, the A.B.A. Standing Committee on Ethics issued Formal Opinion 87–353 (1987). That opinion provides that if the lawyer is convinced that a witness is going to commit perjury, and all discussions with the client fail, then the lawyer should inform the court. And if the lawyer discovers perjury after the fact but before the proceedings are terminated, the lawyer must inform the court as well. The opinion justifies this result as follows:

> Without doubt, the vitality of the adversary system, certainly in criminal cases, depends upon the ability of the lawyer to give loyal and zealous service to the client. And this, in turn, requires that the lawyer have the complete confidence of the client and be able to assure the client that the confidence will be protected and honored. However, the ethical rules of the bar which have supported these basic requirements of the adversary system have emphasized from the time they were first reduced to written form that the lawyer's duties to the client in this regard must be performed within the bounds of law.

> For example, these ethical rules clearly recognize that a lawyer representing a client who admits guilt in fact, but wants to plead not guilty and put the state to its proof, may assist the client in entering such a plea and vigorously challenge the state's case at trial through cross-examination, legal motions and argument to the jury. However, neither the adversary system nor the ethical rules permit the lawyer to participate in the corruption of the judicial process by assisting the client in the introduction of evidence the lawyer knows is false. * * *

> On the contrary, the lawyer, as an officer of the court, has a duty to prevent the perjury, and if the perjury has already been committed, to

prevent its playing any part in the judgment of the court. This duty the lawyer owes the court is not inconsistent with any duty owed to the client. More particularly, it is not inconsistent with the lawyer's duty to preserve the client's confidences. For that duty is based on the lawyer's need for information from the client to obtain for the client all that the law and lawful process provide. Implicit in the promise of confidentiality is its nonapplicability where the client seeks the unlawful end of corrupting the judicial process by false evidence.

The ABA opinion emphasizes, however (as did the concurring opinions in *Whiteside*), that it is not for defense counsel to judge the client, and that the lawyer should not presume that the client is going to present perjured testimony simply because it is inconsistent with a previous statement:

> It must be emphasized that this opinion does not change the professional relationship the lawyer has with the client and require the lawyer now to judge, rather than represent, the client. The lawyer's obligation to disclose client perjury to the tribunal, discussed in this opinion, is strictly limited by Rule 3.3 to the situation where the lawyer *knows* that the client has committed perjury, ordinarily based on admissions the client has made to the lawyer. (The Committee notes that some trial lawyers report that they have avoided the ethical dilemma posed by Rule 3.3 because they follow a practice of not questioning the client about the facts in the case and, therefore, never "know" that a client has given false testimony. Lawyers who engage in such practice may be violating their duties under Rule 3.3 and their obligation to provide competent representation under Rule 1.1.) * * *.

Food for Thought

What about the lawyers who "follow a practice of not questioning the client about the facts in the case"? ABA Formal Opinion 87-353, *supra.* According to Professor Stephen Ellmann, "this sort of denial of knowledge has two tremendous, and in our view fatal, disadvantages. The first is that it requires lawyers, who like everyone else no doubt believe that they "know" many things about many subjects, to profess utter lack of knowledge about matters they should be studying especially carefully, namely the facts of their cases. In other words, it requires lawyers to disclaim common sense. The second disadvantage to disclaiming knowledge in this fashion is that it requires lawyers to assert that the many provisions in the professional codes of ethics which forbid lawyers from using or uttering knowing falsehoods are actually mere pretense, because they will never, ever have any bearing on lawyers' actual duties. * * *

We worry, also, that a relationship marked at its inception by avoidance of truth may grow worse rather than better over time. Clients who have avoided one truth with the lawyer's aid may avoid other truths as well, even against the lawyer's wishes. Lawyers who might seek, for example, to counsel their clients about ethical matters may find that their standing to do so has been impaired." Stephen Ellman, *Truth and Consequences*, <u>69 Fordham L. Rev. 895, 902-06 (2000)</u>.

One problem with the ABA solution is that criminal defendants have a constitutional right to testify. They do not of course, have a constitutional right to commit perjury; but perjury occurs only when the defendant actually testifies. A common scenario proceeds like this: defense counsel believes that the client is adamant about committing perjury, even after counsel gives the defendant *Whiteside* warnings. According to the ABA, counsel must now inform the trial judge that her client intends to commit perjury. The trial judge cannot at this point, on defense counsel's word alone, prevent the defendant from testifying. To do so would risk almost certain reversal for violating the defendant's constitutional right to testify (because perjury has not been shown to a reviewing court's satisfaction). So the trial judge would have to hold some kind of hearing. At that hearing, the defendant will not admit that he is going to commit perjury if he is permitted to testify. The trial judge will be most reluctant to get into a quagmire of confidential communications between client and counsel in determining who is right about whether perjury is planned. It is very likely in most cases that a trial judge will be uncertain as to whether the defendant is going to commit perjury. The judge will not in these circumstances risk violating the constitutional right to testify by keeping the defendant off the stand. So in the vast majority of cases, defense counsel will have accomplished nothing by informing the tribunal of the client's planned perjury—the defendant will be permitted to testify anyway. The only thing accomplished is the destruction of the attorney-client relationship.

Compare the solution proposed by the ABA Ethics Committee with that proposed by Professor Monroe Freedman, who addressed the perjury problem in *Lawyer's Ethics in an Adversary System* 31–37 (1985):

> In my opinion, the attorney's obligation in such a situation would be to advise the client that the proposed testimony is unlawful, but to proceed in the normal fashion in presenting the testimony and arguing the case to the jury if the client makes the decision to go forward. Any other course would be a betrayal of the assurances of confidentiality given by the attorney in order to induce the client to reveal everything, however damaging it might appear.

Food for Thought

Can you think of anything more destructive to the attorney-client relationship than the lawyer ratting out her client? Why can't the perjury problem instead be handled through cross-examination by the prosecutor? When a District Attorney was asked what the defense lawyer should do when a client intends to commit perjury, he responded "Do me a favor. Let him try it." (quoting Monroe H. Freedman, *Client Confidences and Client Perjury: Some Unanswered Questions*, 136 U. Pa. L. Rev. 1939 (1988)). Would most prosecutors respond the same way? Is the existence of a lawyer-client relationship a sufficient reason to permit defense lawyers but not prosecutors to offer perjured testimony? *See* Stephen A. Saltzburg, *Lawyers, Clients, and the Adversary System*, 37 Mercer L. Rev. 647 (1986).

Professor Freedman argues that none of the other alternatives are workable:

> The most obvious way to avoid the ethical difficulty is for the lawyer to withdraw from the case, at least if there is sufficient time before trial for the client to retain another attorney. The client will then go to the nearest law office, realizing that the obligation of confidentiality is not what it has been represented to be, and withhold incriminating information or the fact of guilt from the new attorney. In terms of professional ethics, the practice of withdrawing from a case under such circumstances is difficult to defend, since the identical perjured testimony will ultimately be presented. Moreover, the new attorney will be ignorant of the perjury and therefore will be in no position to attempt to discourage the client from presenting it. Only the original attorney, who knows the truth, has that opportunity, but loses it in the very act of evading the ethical problem.

* * *

Professor Freedman describes the "Free Narrative" proposal, in which defense counsel lets the defendant tell his story on the stand, without asking questions and without referring to the statement in closing argument. He finds the free narrative solution unworkable:

> There are at least two critical flaws in that proposal. The first is purely practical: The prosecutor might well object to testimony from the defendant in narrative form rather than in the conventional manner, because it would give the prosecutor no opportunity to object to inadmissible evidence prior to the jury's hearing it. * * *
>
> More importantly, experienced trial attorneys have often noted that jurors assume that the defendant's lawyer knows the truth about the case, and that the jury will frequently judge the defendant by drawing inferences from the attorney's conduct in the case. There is, of course, only one inference that can be drawn if the defendant's own attorney turns his or her back on the defendant at the most critical point in the trial, and then, in closing argument, sums up the case with no reference to the fact that the defendant has given exculpatory testimony.

Despite the rejection of the "Free Narrative" solution by the ABA, the Court in *Whiteside,* and Professor Freedman, the narrative "continues to be a commonly accepted method of dealing with client perjury." *See Shockley v. State,* 565 A.2d 1373 (Del. 1989) (holding that use of free narrative was ethically permissible and did not constitute ineffective assistance of counsel); *see also The Florida Bar v. Rubin,* 549 So. 2d 1000 (Fla. 1989) (lawyer jailed for thirty days for refusing to defend client who intended to commit perjury; proper solution would have been to use a free narrative). Can the free narrative be prohibited in practice?

The National Association of Criminal Defense Lawyers has issued an ethics opinion in support of Professor Freedman's view that client perjury should be treated by defense counsel as a non-event. *See The Champion*, March, 1993, p. 23:

> In the relatively small number of cases in which the client who has contemplated perjury rejects the lawyer's advice and decides to proceed to trial, to take the stand, and to give false testimony, the lawyer should go forward at trial in the ordinary way. That is, the lawyer should examine the client in the normal professional manner and should argue the client's testimony to the jury in summation to the extent that sound tactics justify doing so.

The NACDL also emphasizes that the "perjury dilemma" does not arise unless the lawyer *knows* that the client committed perjury, and concludes that counsel in *Whiteside* did not have actual knowledge.

In the end, though, it should be noted that a lawyer who follows the Freedman/NACDL suggestion risks discipline in a jurisdiction following Rule 3.3, which *requires* the lawyer to notify the court as a last resort.

C. Argument

[Question 7]

Deft was on trial for the murder of Victim, who was killed during a barroom brawl. In the course of closing arguments to the jury, Prosecutor said, "Deft's whole defense is based on the testimony of Wit, who said that Victim attacked Deft with a knife before Deft struck him. No other witness testified to such an attack by Victim. I don't believe Wit was telling the truth, and I don't think you believe him either."

Was Prosecutor's statement proper?

(A) Yes, if Prosecutor accurately stated the testimony in the case.

(B) Yes, if Prosecutor, in fact, believed Wit was lying.

(C) No, because Prosecutor alluded to the beliefs of the jurors.

(D) No, because Prosecutor asserted his personal opinion about Wit's credibility.

Rule 3.4(e) states that "a lawyer shall not . . . in trial, allude to any matter that the lawyer does not reasonably believe is relevant or that will not be supported by admissible evidence, assert personal knowledge of facts in issue except when testifying as a witness, or state a personal opinion as to the justness of a cause, the credibility of a witness, the culpability of a civil litigant or the guilt or innocence of an accused."

Rules 3.1 and 3.3 are also relevant to a lawyer's arguments.

D. Witnesses

[Question 8]

An attorney represented the plaintiff in an automobile accident case. Two weeks before the date set for trial, the attorney discovered that there was an eyewitness to the accident. The attorney interviewed the witness. Her version of the accident was contrary to that of the plaintiff and, if believed by the trier of fact, would establish that the plaintiff was at fault. The witness told the attorney that she had not been interviewed by defense counsel.

The witness also told the attorney that she was uncomfortable with testifying and that she had been thinking about taking a vacation to Europe the following week. The attorney told the witness that, since no one had subpoenaed her yet, she had no obligation to appear. He told her that trials were very difficult for witnesses and suggested that she take the vacation so that she would be unavailable to testify.

Is the attorney subject to discipline?

(A) Yes, because the attorney asked the witness to leave the jurisdiction.

(B) Yes, because the attorney did not subpoena the witness knowing she was an eyewitness.

(C) No, because the witness had not been subpoenaed by the defense.

(D) No, because the attorney did not offer the witness any inducement not to appear at the trial.

Rule 3.4, relating to "fairness to opposing party and counsel," includes a number of provisions relating to evidence and witnesses. It states that:

[a] lawyer shall not:

(a) unlawfully obstruct another party' s access to evidence or unlawfully alter, destroy or conceal a document or other material having potential evidentiary value. A lawyer shall not counsel or assist another person to do any such act;

(b) falsify evidence, counsel or assist a witness to testify falsely, or offer an inducement to a witness that is prohibited by law;

* * *

(f) request a person other than a client to refrain from voluntarily giving relevant information to another party unless:

> (1) the person is a relative or an employee or other agent of a client; and

> (2) the lawyer reasonably believes that the person's interests will not be adversely affected by refraining from giving such information.

The Comment explains that "[t]he procedure of the adversary system contemplates that the evidence in a case is to be marshalled competitively by the contending parties. Fair competition in the adversary system is secured by prohibitions against destruction or concealment of evidence, improperly influencing witnesses, obstructive tactics in discovery procedure, and the like."

[Question 9]

Attorney represents Client, a plaintiff in a personal injury action. Wit was an eyewitness to the accident. Wit lives about 500 miles distant from the city where the case will be tried. Attorney interviewed Wit and determined that Wit's testimony would be favorable for Client. Wit asked Attorney to pay Wit, in addition to the statutory witness fees while attending the trial, the following:

I.   **Reimbursement for actual travel expenses while attending the trial.**

II. **Reimbursement for lost wages while present at the trial.**

III. **An amount equal to 5% of any recovery in the matter.**

If Attorney agrees to pay Wit the above, for which, if any, is Attorney subject to discipline?

   (A) **III only**

   (B) **II and III, but not I**

   (C) **I, II, and III**

   (D) **Neither I, II, nor III**

Review the provisions of Rule 3.4 above. In addition, Restatement § 117 provides that

[a] lawyer ay not offer or pay to a witness any consideration:

(1) in excess of the reasonable expenses of the witness incurred and the reasonable value of the witness's time spent in providing evidence, except that an expert witness may be offered and paid a noncontingent fee;

(2) contingent on the content of the witness's testimony or the outcome of the litigation; or

(3) otherwise prohibited by law.

E. Improper Communications With Judges and Jurors

[Question 10]

After both parties had completed the presentation of evidence and arguments, the judge took under advisement a case tried without a jury. The case involved a difficult fact issue of causation and a difficult issue of law.

After the case was under advisement for several weeks, the plaintiff's attorney heard rumors that the judge was having difficulty determining the issue of factual causation and was uncertain about the applicable law. Immediately after hearing these rumors, the attorney telephoned the judge, told her of the rumors he had heard, and asked the judge if she would like to reopen the case for additional evidence and briefing from both parties. Thereafter the judge reopened the case for further testimony and requested supplementary briefs from both parties.

Was it proper for the attorney to communicate with the judge?

(A) Yes, because both parties were given full opportunity to present their views on the issues in the case.

(B) Yes, because the attorney did not make any suggestion as to how the judge should decide the matter.

(C) No, because the attorney communicated with the judge on a pending matter without advising opposing counsel.

(D) No, because the attorney caused the judge to reopen a case that had been taken under advisement.

Rule 3.5 governs "impartiality and decorum of the tribunal." Rule 3.5(b) provides that "[a] lawyer shall not * * * communicate ex parte with [a judge, juror, prospective juror or other official] during the proceeding unless authorized to do so by law or court order[.]"

Restatement § 113 Comment (c) explains that the prohibition on ex parte communications "does not apply to routine and customary communications for the purpose of scheduling a hearing or similar communications[.]" As Comment (d) notes, the law generally permits ex parte communications for purposes of obtaining a temporary restraining order, but that in such circumstances a "special duty of candor" arises. Rule 3.3(d) codifies this duty by requiring a lawyer "[i]n an ex parte proceeding [to] inform the tribunal of all material facts known to the lawyer that will enable the tribunal to make an informed decision, whether or not the facts are adverse."

[Question 11]

An attorney represented a man in a case set for a jury trial. After the list of potential jurors was made available, the attorney hired a private investigator to interview the potential jurors and their family members concerning their relevant past experiences related to the subject matter of the action. The investigator did not inform the jurors or their family members that he was working on behalf of the attorney. The interviews were entirely voluntary and were not harassing.

The attorney did not provide the report of the interviews to opposing counsel. He used the report to make decisions regarding jury selection.

Is the attorney subject to discipline?

   (A) Yes, because the attorney did not provide the report of the interviews to opposing counsel.

   (B) Yes, because the investigator, at the attorney's direction, communicated with potential jurors prior to trial.

   (C) Yes, because the investigator did not inform the jurors or their family members that he was working on behalf of the attorney.

   (D) No, because the interviews were entirely voluntary and not harassing.

Rule 3.5(c) provides that

a lawyer shall not * * * communicate with a juror or prospective juror after discharge of the jury if:

(1) the communication is prohibited by law or court order;

(2) the juror has made known to the lawyer a desire not to communicate; or

(3) the communication involves misrepresentation, coercion, duress or harassment[.]

Review the provisions of <u>Rule 3.5</u>. Also consider the potential relevance of Rule 8.4(a) which states that "[i]t is professional misconduct for a lawyer to . . . violate or attempt to violate the Rules of Professional Conduct, knowingly assist or induce another to do so, or do so through the acts of another[.]"

F. Non-Adjudicative Proceeding

[Question 12]

An attorney is a well-known tax lawyer and author. During congressional hearings on tax reform, the attorney testified to her personal belief and expert opinion on the pending reform package. She failed to disclose in her testimony that she was being compensated by a private client for her appearance. In her testimony, the attorney took the position favored by her client, but the position was also one that the attorney believed was in the public interest.

Was it proper for the attorney to present this testimony without identifying her private client?

(A) Yes, because the attorney believed that the position she advocated was in the public interest.

(B) Yes, because Congress is interested in the content of the testimony and not who is paying the witness.

(C) No, because a lawyer may not accept a fee for trying to influence legislative action.

⁓ **(D) No, because a lawyer who appears in a legislative hearing should identify the capacity in which the lawyer appears.**

<u>Rule 3.9</u> provides that "[a] lawyer representing a client before a legislative body or administrative agency in a nonadjudicative proceeding shall disclose that the appearance is in a representative capacity[.]" The Rule also requires lawyers in non-adjudicative proceedings "to conform to the provisions of Rules 3.3(a) through (c), 3.4(a) through (c), and 3.5."

G. State or Imply Improper Influence

[Question 13]

Attorney is a well-known, highly skilled litigator. Attorney's practice is in an area of law in which the trial proceedings are heard by the court without a jury.

In an interview with a prospective client, Attorney said, "I make certain that I give the campaign committee of every candidate for elective judicial office more money than any other lawyer gives, whether it's $500 or $5,000. Judges know who helped them get elected." The prospective client did not retain Attorney.

Is Attorney subject to discipline?

(A) Yes, if Attorney's contributions are made without consideration of candidates' merits.

(B) Yes, because Attorney implied that Attorney receives favored treatment by judges.

(C) No, if Attorney's statements were true.

(D) No, because the prospective client did not retain Attorney.

Rule 8.4(e) defines it as "professional misconduct [to] state or imply an ability to influence improperly a government agency or official or to achieve results by means that violate the Rules of Professional Conduct or other law."

H. Trial Publicity

[Question 14]

Attorney represents Defendant, a prominent businessman, in a civil paternity suit brought by Plaintiff, who was formerly Defendant's employee. Blood tests did not exclude Defendant's paternity, and the case is being tried before a jury. The result turns on questions of fact. Defendant has steadfastly denied that he had sexual relations with Plaintiff, while Plaintiff has testified that they had sexual relations while on business trips and in her home. The trial has generated great public interest and is closely followed by the news media.

When Plaintiff completed her testimony, Attorney was interviewed by a newspaper reporter.

Which of the following statements, if believed by Attorney to be true, would be proper for Attorney to make?

I. "As stated in our pleadings, we expect to prove that other men could be the father of Plaintiff's child."

II. "We have scientific medical tests proving that Defendant is sterile."

III. "We have been unable to locate several people whose testimony will be helpful to us, and I implore them to contact me immediately."

(A) II only

(B) III only

(C) I and III, but not II

(D) I, II, and III

Rule 3.6 governs "trial publicity." It forbids "[a] lawyer who is participating or has participated in the investigation or litigation of matter" from "mak[ing] an extrajudicial statement that the lawyer knows or reasonably should know will be disseminated by means of public communication and will have a substantial likelihood of materially prejudicing an adjudicative proceeding in the matter." Rule 3.6(b) sets forth a series of statements that a lawyer is expressly permitted to make. These "safe harbors" are:

(1) the claim, offense or defense involved and, except when prohibited by law, the identity of the persons involved;

(2) information contained in a public record;

(3) that an investigation of a matter is in progress;

(4) the scheduling or result of any step in litigation;

(5) a request for assistance in obtaining evidence and information necessary thereto;

(6) a warning of danger concerning the behavior of a person involved, when there is reason to believe that there exists the likelihood of substantial harm to an individual or to the public interest; and

(7) in a criminal case, in addition to subparagraphs (1) through (6):

(i) the identity, residence, occupation and family status of the accused;

(ii) if the accused has not been apprehended, information necessary to aid in apprehension of that person;

(iii) the fact, time and place of arrest; and

(iv) the identity of investigating and arresting officers or agencies and the length of the investigation.

Rule 3.6(c) further provides that "a lawyer may make a statement that a reasonable lawyer would believe is required to protect a client from the substantial undue prejudicial effect of recent publicity not initiated by the lawyer or the lawyer's client." Rule 3.6(c) limits such a statement to "such information as is necessary to mitigate the recent adverse publicity."

Rule 3.6(d) applies the provisions of Rule 3.6 to the colleagues in a firm or the government of a lawyer covered by Rule 3.6(a).

GENTILE v. STATE BAR OF NEVADA

501 U.S. 1030 (1991)

Justice KENNEDY announced the judgment of the Court and delivered the opinion of the Court with respect to Parts III and IV, and an opinion with respect to Parts I, II, IV, and V in which Justice Marshall, Justice Blackmun, and Justice Stevens join.

Hours after his client was indicted on criminal charges, petitioner Gentile, who is a member of the Bar of the State of Nevada, held a press conference. He made a prepared statement * * * and then he responded to questions. We refer to most of those questions and responses in the course of our opinion.

Some six months later, the criminal case was tried to a jury and the client was acquitted on all counts. The State Bar of Nevada then filed a complaint against petitioner, alleging a violation of Nevada Supreme Court Rule 177, a rule governing pretrial publicity almost identical to ABA Model Rule of Professional Conduct 3.6. * * * Rule 177(1) prohibits an attorney from making "an extrajudicial statement that a reasonable person would expect to be disseminated by means of public communication if the lawyer knows or reasonably should know that it will have a substantial likelihood of materially prejudicing an adjudicative proceeding." Rule 177(2) lists a number of statements that are "ordinarily . . . likely" to result in material prejudice. Rule 177(3) provides a safe harbor for the attorney, listing a number of statements that can be made without fear of discipline notwithstanding the other parts of the Rule.

Following a hearing, the Southern Nevada Disciplinary Board of the State Bar found that Gentile had made the statements in question and concluded that he violated Rule 177. The board recommended a private reprimand. Petitioner appealed to the Nevada Supreme Court, waiving the confidentiality of the disciplinary proceeding, and the Nevada court affirmed the decision of the board.

Nevada's application of Rule 177 in this case violates the First Amendment. Petitioner spoke at a time and in a manner that neither in law nor in fact created any threat of real prejudice to his client's right to a fair trial or to the State's interest in the enforcement of its criminal laws. Furthermore, the Rule's safe harbor provision, Rule 177(3), appears to permit the speech in question, and Nevada's decision to discipline petitioner in spite of that provision raises concerns of vagueness and selective enforcement.

I

The matter before us does not call into question the constitutionality of other States' prohibitions upon an attorney's speech that will have a "substantial likelihood of materially prejudicing an adjudicative proceeding," but is limited to Nevada's interpretation of that standard. On the other hand, one central point must dominate the analysis: this case involves classic political speech. The State Bar of Nevada reprimanded petitioner for his assertion, supported by a brief sketch of his client's defense, that the State sought the indictment and conviction of an innocent man as a "scapegoat" and had not "been honest enough to indict the people who did it; the police department, crooked cops." * * * At issue here is the constitutionality of a ban on political speech critical of the government and its officials.

A

Unlike other First Amendment cases this Term in which speech is not the direct target of the regulation or statute in question, * * * this case involves punishment of pure speech in the political forum. Petitioner engaged not in solicitation of clients or advertising for his practice, as in our precedents from which some of our colleagues would discern a standard of diminished First Amendment protection. His words were directed at public officials and their conduct in office.

There is no question that speech critical of the exercise of the State's power lies at the very center of the First Amendment. Nevada seeks to punish the dissemination of information relating to alleged governmental misconduct, which only last Term we described as "speech which has traditionally been recognized as lying at the core of the First Amendment." * * *

The judicial system, and in particular our criminal justice courts, play a vital part in a democratic state, and the public has a legitimate interest in their operations. * * * Public vigilance serves us well, for "[t]he knowledge that every criminal trial is subject to contemporaneous review in the forum of public opinion is an effective restraint on possible abuse of judicial power. . . . Without publicity, all other checks are insufficient: in comparison of publicity, all other checks are of small account." * * * In *Sheppard v. Maxwell*, 384 U.S. 333, 350, 86 S.Ct. 1507, 1515, 16 L.Ed.2d 600 (1966), we reminded that "[t]he press . . . guards against the miscarriage of justice by subjecting the police, prosecutors, and judicial processes to extensive public scrutiny and criticism."

Public awareness and criticism have even greater importance where, as here, they concern allegations of police corruption * * * , or where, as is also the present circumstance, the criticism questions the judgment of an elected public prosecutor. Our system grants prosecutors vast discretion at all stages of the criminal process[.] * * * The public has an interest in its responsible exercise.

B.

We are not called upon to determine the constitutionality of the ABA Model Rule of Professional Conduct 3.6 (1981), but only Rule 177 as it has been interpreted and applied by the State of Nevada. Model Rule 3.6's requirement of substantial likelihood of material prejudice is not necessarily flawed. Interpreted in a proper and narrow manner, for instance, to prevent an attorney of record from releasing information of grave prejudice on the eve of jury selection, the phrase substantial likelihood of material prejudice might punish only speech that creates a danger of imminent and substantial harm. A rule governing speech, even speech entitled to full constitutional protection, need not use the words "clear and present danger" in order to pass constitutional muster.

"Mr. Justice Holmes' test was never intended 'to express a technical legal doctrine or to convey a formula for adjudicating cases.' * * * Properly applied, the test requires a court to make its own inquiry into the imminence and magnitude of the danger said to flow from the particular utterance and then to balance the character of the evil, as well as its likelihood, against the need for free and unfettered expression. The possibility that other measures will serve the State's interests should also be weighed." * * *

The drafters of Model Rule 3.6 apparently thought the substantial likelihood of material prejudice formulation approximated the clear and present danger test. *See* ABA Annotated Model Rules of Professional Conduct 243 (1984) ("formulation in Model Rule 3.6 incorporates a standard approximating clear and present danger by focusing on the likelihood of injury and its substantiality" citing *Landmark Communications, supra,* at 844, 98 S.Ct., at 1544; *Wood v. Georgia,* 370 U.S. 375, 82 S.Ct. 1364, 8 L.Ed.2d 569 (1962); and *Bridges v. California, supra,* 314 U.S., at 273, 62 S.Ct., at 198, for guidance in determining whether statement "poses a sufficiently serious and imminent threat to the fair administration of justice"); G. Hazard & W. Hodes, The Law of Lawyering: A Handbook on the Model Rules of Professional Conduct 397 (1985) ("To use traditional terminology, the danger of prejudice to a proceeding must be both clear (material) and present (substantially likely)"); *In re Hinds,* 90 N.J. 604, 622, 419 A.2d 483, 493 (1982) (substantial likelihood of material prejudice standard is a linguistic equivalent of clear and present danger).

The difference between the requirement of serious and imminent threat found in the disciplinary rules of some States and the more common formulation of substantial likelihood of material prejudice could prove mere semantics. Each standard requires an assessment of proximity and degree of harm. Each may be capable of valid application. Under those principles, nothing inherent in Nevada's formulation fails First Amendment review; but as this case demonstrates, Rule 177 has not been interpreted in conformance with those principles by the Nevada Supreme Court.

II

Even if one were to accept respondent's argument that lawyers participating in judicial proceedings may be subjected, consistent with the First Amendment, to speech restrictions that could not be imposed on the press or general public, the judgment should not be upheld. The record does not support the conclusion that petitioner knew or reasonably should have known his remarks created a substantial likelihood of material prejudice, if the Rule's terms are given any meaningful content.

We have held that "in cases raising First Amendment issues . . . an appellate court has an obligation to 'make an independent examination of the whole record' in order to make sure that 'the judgment does not constitute a forbidden intrusion on the field of free expression.' " * * *

Neither the disciplinary board nor the reviewing court explains any sense in which petitioner's statements had a substantial likelihood of causing material prejudice. The only evidence against Gentile was the videotape of his statements and his own testimony at the disciplinary hearing. The Bar's whole case rests on the fact of the statements, the time they were made, and petitioner's own justifications. Full deference to these factual findings does not justify abdication of our responsibility to determine whether petitioner's statements can be punished consistent with First Amendment standards.

Rather, this Court is

> "compelled to examine for [itself] the statements in issue and the circumstances under which they were made to see whether or not they do carry a threat of clear and present danger to the impartiality and good order of the courts or whether they are of a character which the principles of the First Amendment, as adopted by the Due Process Clause of the Fourteenth Amendment, protect." * * *

> " 'Whenever the fundamental rights of free speech . . . are alleged to have been invaded, it must remain open to a defendant to present the issue whether there actually did exist at the time a clear danger; whether the danger, if any, was imminent; and whether the evil apprehended was one so substantial as to justify the stringent restriction interposed by the legislature.' " *Landmark Communications, Inc. v. Virginia*, 435 U.S., at 844, 98 S.Ct., at 1544 (quoting *Whitney v. California*, 274 U.S. 357, 378-379, 47 S.Ct. 641, 649-650, 71 L.Ed. 1095 (1927) (Brandeis, J., concurring)).

Whether one applies the standard set out in *Landmark Communications* or the lower standard our colleagues find permissible, an examination of the record reveals no basis for the Nevada court's conclusion that the speech presented a substantial likelihood of material prejudice.

* * *

A.

Pre-Indictment Publicity. On January 31, 1987, undercover police officers with the Las Vegas Metropolitan Police Department (Metro) reported large amounts of cocaine (four kilograms) and travelers' checks (almost $300,000) missing from a safety deposit vault at Western Vault Corporation. The drugs and money had been used as part of an undercover operation conducted by Metro's Intelligence Bureau. Petitioner's client, Grady Sanders, owned Western Vault. John Moran, the Las Vegas sheriff, reported the theft at a press conference on February 2, 1987, naming the police and Western Vault employees as suspects.

Although two police officers, Detective Steve Scholl and Sergeant Ed Schaub, enjoyed free access to the deposit box throughout the period of the theft, and no log reported comings and goings at the vault, a series of press reports over the following year indicated that investigators did not consider these officers responsible. Instead, investigators focused upon Western Vault and its owner. Newspaper reports quoted the sheriff and other high police officials as saying that they had not lost confidence in the "elite" Intelligence Bureau. From the beginning, Sheriff Moran had "complete faith and trust" in his officers. * * *

The media reported that, following announcement of the cocaine theft, others with deposit boxes at Western Vault had come forward to claim missing items. One man claimed the theft of his life savings of $90,000. *Id.*, at 89. Western Vault suffered heavy losses as customers terminated their box rentals, and the company soon went out of business. The police opened other boxes in search of the missing items, and it was reported they seized $264,900 in United States currency from a box listed as unrented.

Initial press reports stated that Sanders and Western Vault were being cooperative; but as time went on, the press noted that the police investigation had failed to identify the culprit and through a process of elimination was beginning to point toward Sanders. Reports quoted the affidavit of a detective that the theft was part of an effort to discredit the undercover operation and that business records suggested the existence of a business relation between Sanders and the targets of a Metro undercover probe. * * *

The deputy police chief announced the two detectives with access to the vault had been "cleared" as possible suspects. According to an unnamed "source close to the investigation," the police shifted from the idea that the thief had planned to discredit the undercover operation to the theory that the thief had unwittingly stolen from the police. The stories noted that Sanders "could not be reached for comment." * * *

The story took a more sensational turn with reports that the two police suspects had been cleared by police investigators after passing lie detector tests. The tests were administered by one Ray Slaughter. But later, the Federal Bureau of Investigation (FBI) arrested Slaughter for distributing cocaine to an FBI informant, Belinda Antal. It was also reported that the $264,900 seized from the unrented safety deposit box at Western Vault had been stored there in a suitcase owned by one Tammy Sue Markham. Markham was "facing a number of federal drug-related charges" in Tucson, Arizona. Markham reported items missing from three boxes she rented at Western Vault, as did one Beatrice Connick, who, according to press reports, was a Colombian national living in San Diego and "not facing any drug related charges." (As it turned out, petitioner impeached Connick's credibility at trial with the existence of a money laundering conviction.) Connick also was reported to have taken and passed a lie detector test to substantiate her charges. * * * Finally, press reports indicated that Sanders had refused to take a police polygraph examination. * * * The press suggested that the FBI suspected Metro officers were responsible for the theft, and reported that the theft had severely damaged relations between the FBI and Metro.

B.

The Press Conference. Petitioner is a Las Vegas criminal defense attorney, an author of articles about criminal law and procedure, and a former associate dean of the National College for Criminal Defense Lawyers and Public Defenders. * * * Through leaks from the police department, he had some advance notice of the date an indictment would be returned and the nature of the charges against Sanders. Petitioner had monitored the publicity surrounding the case, and, prior to the indictment, was personally aware of at least 17 articles in the major local newspapers, the Las Vegas Sun and Las Vegas Review-Journal, and numerous local television news stories which reported on the Western Vault theft and ensuing investigation. * * * Petitioner determined, for the first time in his career, that he would call a formal press conference. He did not blunder into a press conference, but acted with considerable deliberation.

1.

Petitioner's Motivation. As petitioner explained to the disciplinary board, his primary motivation was the concern that, unless some of the weaknesses in the State's case were made public, a potential jury venire would be poisoned by repetition in the press of information being released by the police and prosecutors, in particular the repeated press reports about polygraph tests and the fact that the two police officers were no longer suspects. * * * Respondent distorts Rule 177 when it suggests this explanation admits a purpose to prejudice the venire and so proves a violation of the Rule. Rule 177 only prohibits the dissemination of information that one knows or reasonably should know has a "substantial likelihood of materially prejudicing an adjudicative proceeding." Petitioner did not indicate he thought he could sway the pool of potential jurors to form an opinion in advance of the trial, nor did he seek to discuss evidence that would be inadmissible at trial. He sought only to counter publicity already deemed prejudicial. The Southern Nevada Disciplinary Board so found. It said petitioner attempted

> "(i) to counter public opinion which he perceived as adverse to Mr. Sanders, (ii) . . . to refute certain matters regarding his client which had appeared in the media, (iii) to fight back against the perceived efforts of the prosecution to poison the prospective juror pool, and (iv) to publicly present Sanders' side of the case." * * *

Far from an admission that he sought to "materially prejudic[e] an adjudicative proceeding," petitioner sought only to stop a wave of publicity he perceived as prejudicing potential jurors against his client and injuring his client's reputation in the community.

Petitioner gave a second reason for holding the press conference, which demonstrates the additional value of his speech. Petitioner acted in part because the investigation had taken a serious toll on his client. Sanders was "not a man in good health," having suffered multiple open-heart surgeries prior to these events. * * * And prior to indictment, the mere suspicion of wrongdoing had caused the closure of Western Vault and the loss of Sanders' ground lease on an Atlantic City, New Jersey, property. * * *

An attorney's duties do not begin inside the courtroom door. He or she cannot ignore the practical implications of a legal proceeding for the client. Just as an attorney may recommend a plea bargain or civil settlement to avoid the adverse consequences of a possible loss after trial, so too an attorney may take reasonable steps to defend a client's reputation and reduce the adverse consequences of indictment, especially in the face of a prosecution deemed unjust or commenced with improper motives. A defense attorney may pursue lawful strategies to obtain dismissal of an indictment or reduction of charges, including an attempt to demonstrate in the court of public opinion that the client does not deserve to be tried.

2.

Petitioner's Investigation of Rule 177. Rule 177 is phrased in terms of what an attorney "knows or reasonably should know." On the evening before the press conference, petitioner and two colleagues spent several hours researching the extent of an attorney's obligations under Rule 177. He decided, as we have held, * * * that the timing of a statement was crucial in the assessment of possible prejudice and the Rule's application[.]* * *

Upon return of the indictment, the court set a trial date for August 1988, some six months in the future. Petitioner knew, at the time of his statement, that a jury would not be empaneled (sic) for six months at the earliest, if ever. He recalled reported cases finding no prejudice resulting from juror exposure to "far worse" information two and four months before trial, and concluded that his proposed statement was not substantially likely to result in material prejudice. * * *

A statement which reaches the attention of the venire on the eve of *voir dire* might require a continuance or cause difficulties in securing an impartial jury, and at the very least could complicate the jury selection process. * * * As turned out to be the case here, exposure to the same statement six months prior to trial would not result in prejudice, the content fading from memory long before the trial date.

In 1988, Clark County, Nevada, had population in excess of 600,000 persons. Given the size of the community from which any potential jury venire would be drawn and the length of time before trial, only the most damaging of information could give rise to any likelihood of prejudice. The innocuous content of petitioner's statements reinforces my conclusion.

3.

The Content of Petitioner's Statements. Petitioner was disciplined for statements to the effect that (1) the evidence demonstrated his client's innocence, (2) the likely thief was a police detective, Steve Scholl, and (3) the other victims were not credible, as most were drug dealers or convicted money launderers, all but one of whom had only accused Sanders in response to police pressure, in the process of "trying to work themselves out of something." * * * He also strongly implied that Steve Scholl could be observed in a videotape suffering from symptoms of cocaine use. Of course, only a small fraction of petitioner's remarks were disseminated to the public, in two newspaper stories and two television news broadcasts.

The stories mentioned not only Gentile's press conference but also a prosecution response and police press conference. * * * The chief deputy district attorney was quoted as saying that this was a legitimate indictment, and that prosecutors cannot bring an indictment to court unless they can prove the charges in it beyond a reasonable doubt. * * * Deputy Police Chief Sullivan stated for the police department: "'We in Metro are very satisfied our officers (Scholl and Sgt. Ed Schaub) had nothing to do with this theft or any other. They are both above reproach. Both are veteran police officers who are dedicated to honest law enforcement.'" * * * In the context of general public awareness, these police and prosecution statements were no more likely to result in prejudice than were petitioner's statements, but given the repetitive publicity from the police investigation, it is difficult to come to any conclusion but that the balance remained in favor of the prosecution.

Much of the information provided by petitioner had been published in one form or another, obviating any potential for prejudice. * * * The remainder, and details petitioner refused to provide, were available to any journalist willing to do a little bit of investigative work.

Petitioner's statements lack any of the more obvious bases for a finding of prejudice. Unlike the police, he refused to comment on polygraph tests except to confirm earlier reports that Sanders had not submitted to the police polygraph; he mentioned no confessions and no evidence from searches or test results; he refused to elaborate upon his charge that the other so-called victims were not credible, except to explain his general theory that they were pressured to testify in an attempt to avoid drug-related legal trouble, and that some of them may have asserted claims in an attempt to collect insurance money.

C.

Events Following the Press Conference. Petitioner's judgment that no likelihood of material prejudice would result from his comments was vindicated by events at trial. While it is true that Rule 177's standard for controlling pretrial publicity must be judged at the time a statement is made, *ex post* evidence can have probative value in some cases. Here, where the Rule purports to demand, and the Constitution requires, consideration of the character of the harm and its heightened likelihood of occurrence, the record is altogether devoid of facts one would expect to follow upon any statement that created a real likelihood of material prejudice to a criminal jury trial.

The trial took place on schedule in August 1988, with no request by either party for a venue change or continuance. The jury was empaneled with no apparent difficulty. The trial judge questioned the jury venire about publicity. Although many had vague recollections of reports that cocaine stored at Western Vault had been stolen from a police undercover operation, and, as petitioner had feared, one remembered that the police had been cleared of suspicion, not a single juror indicated any recollection of petitioner or his press conference. * * *

At trial, all material information disseminated during petitioner's press conference was admitted in evidence before the jury, including information questioning the motives and credibility of supposed victims who testified against Sanders, and Detective Scholl's ingestion of drugs in the course of * * * undercover operations (in order, he testified, to gain the confidence of suspects). * * * The jury acquitted petitioner's client, and, as petitioner explained before the disciplinary board, "when the trial was over with and the man was acquitted the next week the foreman of the jury phoned me and said to me that if they would have had a verdict form before them with respect to the guilt of Steve Scholl they would have found the man proven guilty beyond a reasonable doubt." * * *

There is no support for the conclusion that petitioner's statements created a likelihood of material prejudice, or indeed of any harm of sufficient magnitude or imminence to support a punishment for speech.

III.

As interpreted by the Nevada Supreme Court, the Rule is void for vagueness, in any event, for its safe harbor provision, Rule 177(3), misled petitioner into thinking that he could give his press conference without fear of discipline. Rule 177(3)(a) provides that a lawyer "may state without elaboration . . . the general nature of the . . . defense." Statements under this provision are protected "[n]otwithstanding subsection 1 and 2(a-f)." By necessary operation of the word "notwithstanding," the Rule contemplates that a lawyer describing the "general nature of the . . . defense" "without elaboration" need fear no discipline, even if he comments on "[t]he character, credibility, reputation or criminal record of a . . . witness," and even if he "knows or reasonably should know that [the statement] will have a substantial likelihood of materially prejudicing an adjudicative proceeding."

Given this grammatical structure, and absent any clarifying interpretation by the state court, the Rule fails to provide "'fair notice to those to whom [it] is directed.'" * * * A lawyer seeking to avail himself of Rule 177(3)'s protection must guess at its contours. The right to explain the "general" nature of the defense without "elaboration" provides insufficient guidance because "general" and "elaboration" are both classic terms of degree. In the context before us, these terms have no settled usage or tradition of interpretation in law. The lawyer has no principle for determining when his remarks pass from the safe harbor of the general to the forbidden sea of the elaborated.

Petitioner testified he thought his statements were protected by Rule 177(3) * * *. A review of the press conference supports that claim. He gave only a brief opening statement * * * , and on numerous occasions declined to answer reporters' questions seeking more detailed comments. One illustrative exchange shows petitioner's attempt to obey the rule:

> "QUESTION FROM THE FLOOR: Dominick, you mention you question the credibility of some of the witnesses, some of the people named as victims in the government indictment.
>
> "Can we go through it and *elaborate* on their backgrounds, interests-
>
> "MR. GENTILE: *I can't because ethics prohibit me from doing so.*
>
> "Last night before I decided I was going to make a statement, I took a good close look at the rules of professional responsibility. There are things that I can say and there are things that I can't. Okay?
>
> "I can't name which of the people have the drug backgrounds. I'm sure you guys can find that by doing just a little bit of investigative work." * * *

Nevertheless, the disciplinary board said only that petitioner's comments "went beyond the scope of the statements permitted by SCR 177(3)," * * * and the Nevada Supreme Court's rejection of petitioner's defense based on Rule 177(3) was just as terse * * *. The fact that Gentile was found in violation of the Rules after studying them and making a conscious effort at compliance demonstrates that Rule 177 creates a trap for the wary as well as the unwary.

The prohibition against vague regulations of speech is based in part on the need to eliminate the impermissible risk of discriminatory enforcement * * *, for history shows that speech is suppressed when either the speaker or the message is critical of those who enforce the law. The question is not whether discriminatory enforcement occurred here, and we assume it did not, but whether the Rule is so imprecise that discriminatory enforcement is a real possibility. The inquiry is of particular relevance when one of the classes most affected by the regulation is the criminal defense bar, which has the professional mission to challenge actions of the State. Petitioner, for instance, succeeded in preventing the conviction of his client, and the speech in issue involved criticism of the government.

IV.

The analysis to this point resolves the case, and in the usual order of things the discussion should end here. Five Members of the Court, however, endorse an extended discussion which concludes that Nevada may interpret its requirement of substantial likelihood of material prejudice under a standard more deferential than is the usual rule where speech is concerned. It appears necessary, therefore, to set forth my objections to that conclusion and to the reasoning which underlies it.

Respondent argues that speech by an attorney is subject to greater regulation than speech by others, and restrictions on an attorney's speech should be assessed under a balancing test that weighs the State's interest in the regulation of a specialized profession against the lawyer's First Amendment interest in the kind of speech that was at issue. The cases cited by our colleagues to support this balancing * * * involved either commercial speech by attorneys or restrictions upon release of information that the attorney could gain only by use of the court's discovery process. Neither of those categories, nor the underlying interests which justified their creation, were implicated here. Petitioner was disciplined because he proclaimed to the community what he thought to be a misuse of the prosecutorial and police powers. Wide-open balancing of interests is not appropriate in this context.

A.

Respondent would justify a substantial limitation on speech by attorneys because "lawyers have special access to information, including confidential statements from clients and information obtained through pretrial discovery or plea negotiations," and so lawyers' statements "are likely to be received as especially authoritative." * * * Rule 177, however, does not reflect concern for the attorney's special access to client confidences, material gained through discovery, or other proprietary or confidential information. We have upheld restrictions upon the release of information gained "only by virtue of the trial court's discovery processes." *Seattle Times Co. v. Rhinehart, supra,* 467 U.S., at 32, 104 S.Ct., at 2207. And *Seattle Times* would prohibit release of discovery information by the attorney as well as the client. Similar rules require an attorney to maintain client confidences. *See, e.g.,* ABA Model Rule of Professional Conduct 1.6 (1981).

This case involves no speech subject to a restriction under the rationale of *Seattle Times*. Much of the information in petitioner's remarks was included by explicit reference or fair inference in earlier press reports. Petitioner could not have learned what he revealed at the press conference through the discovery process or other special access afforded to attorneys, for he spoke to the press on the day of indictment, at the outset of his formal participation in the criminal proceeding. We have before us no complaint from the prosecutors, police, or presiding judge that petitioner misused information to which he had special access. And there is no claim that petitioner revealed client confidences, which may be waived in any event. Rule 177, on its face and as applied here, is neither limited to nor even directed at preventing release of information received through court proceedings or special access afforded attorneys. * * * It goes far beyond this.

B.

Respondent relies upon *obiter dicta* * * * for the proposition that an attorney's speech about ongoing proceedings must be subject to pervasive regulation in order to ensure the impartial adjudication of criminal proceedings. * * * In *Sheppard v. Maxwell,* we overturned a conviction after a trial that can only be described as a circus, with the courtroom taken over by the press and jurors turned into media stars. The prejudice to Dr. Sheppard's fair trial right can be traced in principal part to police and prosecutorial irresponsibility and the trial court's failure to control the proceedings and the courthouse environment. Each case suggests restrictions upon information release, but none confronted their permitted scope.

At the very least, our cases recognize that disciplinary rules governing the legal profession cannot punish activity protected by the First Amendment, and that First Amendment protection survives even when the attorney violates a disciplinary rule he swore to obey when admitted to the practice of law. * * * We have not in recent years accepted our colleagues' apparent theory that the practice of law brings with it comprehensive restrictions, or that we will defer to professional bodies when those restrictions impinge upon First Amendment freedoms. And none of the justifications put forward by respondent suffice to sanction abandonment of our normal First Amendment principles in the case of speech by an attorney regarding pending cases.

V.

Even if respondent is correct, and as in *Seattle Times* we must balance "whether the 'practice in question [furthers] an important or substantial governmental interest unrelated to the suppression of expression' and whether 'the limitation of First Amendment freedoms [is] no greater than is necessary or essential to the protection of the particular governmental interest involved,'" * * * the Rule as interpreted by Nevada fails the searching inquiry required by those precedents.

A.

Only the occasional case presents a danger of prejudice from pretrial publicity. Empirical research suggests that in the few instances when jurors have been exposed to extensive and prejudicial publicity, they are able to disregard it and base their verdict upon the evidence presented in court. * * * *Voir dire* can play an important role in reminding jurors to set aside out-of-court information and to decide the case upon the evidence presented at trial. All of these factors weigh in favor of affording an attorney's speech about ongoing proceedings our traditional First Amendment protections. Our colleagues' historical survey notwithstanding, respondent has not demonstrated any sufficient state interest in restricting the speech of attorneys to justify a lower standard of First Amendment scrutiny.

Still less justification exists for a lower standard of scrutiny here, as this speech involved not the prosecutor or police, but a criminal defense attorney. Respondent and its *amici* present not a single example where a defense attorney has managed by public statements to prejudice the prosecution of the State's case. Even discounting the obvious reason for a lack of appellate decisions on the topic-the difficulty of appealing a verdict of acquittal-the absence of anecdotal or survey evidence in a much-studied area of the law is remarkable.

The various bar association and advisory commission reports which resulted in promulgation of ABA Model Rule of Professional Conduct 3.6 (1981), and other regulations of attorney speech, and sources they cite, present no convincing case for restrictions upon the speech of defense attorneys. *See* Swift, *Model Rule 3.6: An Unconstitutional Regulation of Defense Attorney Trial Publicity*, 64 B.U.L.Rev. 1003, 1031-1049 (1984) (summarizing studies and concluding there is no empirical or anecdotal evidence of a need for restrictions on defense publicity); see also Drechsel, *supra*, at 35 ("[D]ata showing the heavy reliance of journalists on law enforcement sources and prosecutors confirms the appropriateness of focusing attention on those sources when attempting to control pre-trial publicity"). The police, the prosecution, other government officials, and the community at large hold innumerable avenues for the dissemination of information adverse to a criminal defendant, many of which are not within the scope of Rule 177 or any other regulation. By contrast, a defendant cannot speak without fear of incriminating himself and prejudicing his defense, and most criminal defendants have insufficient means to retain a public relations team apart from defense counsel for the sole purpose of countering prosecution statements. These factors underscore my conclusion that blanket rules restricting speech of defense attorneys should not be accepted without careful First Amendment scrutiny.

B.

Respondent uses the "officer of the court" label to imply that attorney contact with the press somehow is inimical to the attorney's proper role. Rule 177 posits no such inconsistency between an attorney's role and discussions with the press. It permits all comment to the press absent "a substantial likelihood of materially prejudicing an adjudicative proceeding." Respondent does not articulate the principle that contact with the press cannot be reconciled with the attorney's role or explain how this might be so.

Because attorneys participate in the criminal justice system and are trained in its complexities, they hold unique qualifications as a source of information about pending cases. "Since lawyers are considered credible in regard to pending litigation in which they are engaged and are in one of the most knowledgeable positions, they are a crucial source of information and opinion." * * * To the extent the press and public rely upon attorneys for information because attorneys are well informed, this may prove the value to the public of speech by members of the bar. If the dangers of their speech arise from its persuasiveness, from their ability to explain judicial proceedings, or from the likelihood the speech will be believed, these are not the sort of dangers that can validate restrictions. The First Amendment does not permit suppression of speech because of its power to command assent.

One may concede the proposition that an attorney's speech about pending cases may present dangers that could not arise from statements by a nonparticipant, and that an attorney's duty to cooperate in the judicial process may prevent him or her from taking actions with an intent to frustrate that process. The role of attorneys in the criminal justice system subjects them to fiduciary obligations to the court and the parties. An attorney's position may result in some added ability to obstruct the proceedings through well-timed statements to the press, though one can debate the extent of an attorney's ability to do so without violating other established duties. A court can require an attorney's cooperation to an extent not possible of nonparticipants. A proper weighing of dangers might consider the harm that occurs when speech about ongoing proceedings forces the court to take burdensome steps such as sequestration, continuance, or change of venue.

If as a regular matter speech by an attorney about pending cases raised real dangers of this kind, then a substantial governmental interest might support additional regulation of speech. But this case involves the sanction of speech so innocuous, and an application of Rule 177(3)'s safe harbor provision so begrudging, that it is difficult to determine the force these arguments would carry in a different setting. The instant case is a poor vehicle for defining with precision the outer limits under the Constitution of a court's ability to regulate an attorney's statements about ongoing adjudicative proceedings. At the very least, however, we can say that the Rule which punished petitioner's statements represents a limitation of

First Amendment freedoms greater than is necessary or essential to the protection of the particular governmental interest, and does not protect against a danger of the necessary gravity, imminence, or likelihood.

The vigorous advocacy we demand of the legal profession is accepted because it takes place under the neutral, dispassionate control of the judicial system. Though cost and delays undermine it in all too many cases, the American judicial trial remains one of the purest, most rational forums for the lawful determination of disputes. A profession which takes just pride in these traditions may consider them disserved if lawyers use their skills and insight to make untested allegations in the press instead of in the courtroom. But constraints of professional responsibility and societal disapproval will act as sufficient safeguards in most cases. And in some circumstances press comment is necessary to protect the rights of the client and prevent abuse of the courts. It cannot be said that petitioner's conduct demonstrated any real or specific threat to the legal process, and his statements have the full protection of the First Amendment.

VI

The judgment of the Supreme Court of Nevada is

Reversed.

I. Criticism of Judges

[Question 15]

An attorney regularly appears before a trial court judge who is running for reelection in six months. Over the past year, the attorney had noticed that the judge has become increasingly ill tempered on the bench. Not only is the judge abrupt and critical of lawyers appearing before him, he is also rude and abusive to litigants. On more than one occasion, the judge has thrown his gavel across the courtroom in a fit of temper. The judge's conduct on the bench is often the subject of discussion whenever a group of lawyers meets. Some lawyers are automatically filing requests for judicial substitution whenever a case in which they are to appear is assigned to the judge.

The attorney discussed the matter with her law partners, who rarely make court appearances. The attorney's law partners suggested that she, too, file a request for judicial substitution whenever one of her cases is assigned to the judge. In addition, the attorney and her law partners discussed the possibility of reporting to the judge to the appropriate disciplinary authority but are concerned that this would alienate the other judges to whom their cases are assigned. The attorney has reluctantly started filing for substitution of the judge in every one of her cases to which the judge is assigned but she has taken no further action.

Is the attorney subject to discipline?

(A) Yes, because the attorney failed to inform the appropriate authorities about the judge's conduct.

(B) Yes, because, by filing automatic requests for substitution of the judge, the attorney undermined public confidence in the administration of justice.

(C) No, because the attorney has a duty to represent her clients zealously.

(D) No, because the judge is running for reelection and may not be reelected.

Rule 8.3(b) states that: "[a] lawyer who knows that a judge has committed a violation of applicable rules of judicial conduct that raises a substantial question as to the judge's fitness for office shall inform the appropriate authority."

[Question 16]

Make the Connection

Part III of this Chapter discusses the lawyer's obligation to report misconduct by lawyers.

An attorney practices law in the same community as a lawyer who is running for election as a state judge. The attorney has frequently observed the judicial candidate's courtroom demeanor in litigated cases. Based on those experiences, the attorney believes that the judicial candidate does not have a proper judicial temperament. A local news reporter asked the attorney how he would rate the candidate, and the attorney responded in good faith that he believed the candidate was unsuited for the bench and lacked the proper judicial temperament for a judge. A local newspaper with a wide circulation quoted the attorney's remarks.

Were the attorney's remarks proper?

(A) Yes, because the attorney was not seeking judicial office.

(B) Yes, because the attorney believed the candidate was unsuited for the bench.

(C) No, because the remarks serve to bring the judiciary into disrepute.

(D) No, because a lawyer should not publicly comment on candidates for judicial office.

<u>Rule 8.2(a)</u> provides the general rule governing lawyers' statements regarding "judicial and legal officials." It states that:

A lawyer shall not make a statement that the lawyer knows to be false or with reckless disregard as to its truth or falsity concerning the qualifications or integrity of a judge, adjudicatory officer or public legal officer, or of a candidate for election or appointment to judicial or legal office.

The Comment to Rule 8.2 explains:

[1] Assessments by lawyers are relied on in evaluating the professional or personal fitness of persons being considered for election or appointment to judicial office and to public legal offices, such as attorney general, prosecuting attorney and public defender. Expressing honest and candid opinions on such matters contributes to improving the administration of justice. Conversely, false statements by a lawyer can unfairly undermine public confidence in the administration of justice. * * *

In re HOLTZMAN,

<u>577 N.E.2d 30 (N.Y. 1991)</u>

PER CURIAM.

Petitioner brought this proceeding * * * to vacate a Letter of Reprimand issued by the Grievance Committee for the Tenth Judicial District.

The charge of misconduct that is relevant to this appeal was based on the public release by petitioner, then District Attorney of Kings County,* of a letter charging Judge Irving Levine with judicial misconduct in relation to an incident that allegedly occurred in the course of a trial on criminal charges of sexual misconduct * * * and was reported to her some six weeks later. Specifically, petitioner's letter stated that:

> "Judge Levine asked the Assistant District Attorney, defense counsel, defendant, court officer and court reporter to join him in the robing room, where the judge then asked the victim to get down on the floor and show

---

* Although all proceedings conducted by the Grievance Committee were kept confidential and the decision of the Appellate Division was not published * * *, petitioner has expressly waived any right to confidentiality on this appeal.

the position she was in when she was being sexually assaulted. * * * [T]he victim reluctantly got down on her hands and knees as everyone stood and watched. In making the victim assume the position she was forced to take when she was sexually assaulted, Judge Levine profoundly degraded, humiliated and demeaned her."

The letter, addressed to Judge Kathryn McDonald as Chair of the Committee to Implement Recommendations of the New York State Task Force on Women in the Courts, was publicly disseminated after petitioner's office issued a "news alert" to the media.

Following a dispute over the truth of the accusations, Robert Keating, as Administrative Judge of the New York City Criminal Court, conducted an investigation into the allegations of judicial misconduct. His report, dated December 22, 1987, concluded that petitioner's accusations were not supported by the evidence. Upon receipt of the report, Albert M. Rosenblatt, then Chief Administrative Judge, referred the matter to the Grievance Committee for inquiry as to whether petitioner had violated the Code of Professional Responsibility.

Go Online

For press coverage of Judge Keating's report, click here.

Some six months later, the Grievance Committee sent petitioner a private Letter of Admonition in which it stated that "the totality of the circumstances presented by this matter require that you be admonished for your conduct." Petitioner's misconduct, the Committee concluded, violated DR 8-102(B), DR 1-102(A)(5), (6) and EC 8-6 of the Code of Professional Responsibility.

In July 1988, after petitioner requested a subcommittee hearing * * *, she was served with three formal charges of misconduct under DR 8-102(B) and 1-102(A)(5) and (6). Charge 1 alleged that petitioner had engaged in conduct that adversely reflected on her fitness to practice law in releasing a false accusation of misconduct against Judge Levine. Charge 2 related to petitioner's subsequent videotaping of the complaining witness's statement under oath, and release of the audio portion of the tape to the media, despite her knowledge that the complainant would be a necessary witness in other investigations. Charge 3 related to a later press release in which petitioner stated that she had knowledge of other allegations of misconduct involving the Judge, thereby further demeaning him. Only Charge 1 is in issue on this appeal.

The conduct set forth in Charge 1, allegedly demonstrating petitioner's unfitness to practice law, included release of the letter to the media (1) prior to obtaining the minutes of the criminal trial, (2) without making any effort to speak with court officers, the court reporter, defense counsel or any other person present during the alleged misconduct, (3) without meeting with or discussing the incident with the trial assistant who reported it, and (4) with the knowledge that Judge Levine was being transferred out of the Criminal Court, and the matter would be investigated by the Court's Administrative Judge as well as the Commission on Judicial Conduct (to which the petitioner had complained).

After hearings, the subcommittee submitted its findings to the full Grievance Committee. The Committee sustained the first and third charges and issued petitioner a Letter of Reprimand, which was also private. * * * The letter, dated October 19, 1989, stated that the Committee sustained Charges 1 and 3, and concluded that petitioner's conduct was "prejudicial to the administration of justice and adversely reflects on [her] fitness to practice law in violation of DR 1-102(A)(5) and (6) of the Code of Professional Responsibility." No mention was made of DR 8-102(B).

Petitioner then brought this proceeding seeking to vacate the Letter of Reprimand. The Appellate Division concluded that the record supported the Committee's findings as to Charge 1, more specifically that petitioner's conduct violated DR 8-102 and 1-102(A)(6). We now affirm, agreeing with both the Grievance Committee and the Appellate Division that petitioner's conduct violated DR 1-102(A)(6), and we reach no other question.

Petitioner relies primarily on two arguments. First, she asserts that the allegations concerning Judge Levine's conduct were true or at least not demonstrably false. Second, petitioner asserts that her conduct violates no specific disciplinary rule and further that DR 1-102(A)(6), if applicable, is unconstitutionally vague. These contentions are without merit.

The factual basis of Charge 1 is that petitioner made false accusations against the Judge. This charge was sustained by * * * the Committee and upheld by the Appellate Division, and the factual finding of falsity (which is supported by the record) is therefore binding on us.

As for the contention that petitioner's conduct did not violate any provision of the Code, DR 1-102(A)(6) (now DR 1-102[A][7]) provides that a lawyer shall not "[e]ngage in any other conduct that adversely reflects on [the lawyer's] fitness to practice law." * * *

Applying this standard, petitioner was plainly on notice that her conduct in this case, involving public dissemination of a specific accusation of improper judicial conduct under the circumstances described, could be held to reflect adversely on her fitness to practice law. Indeed, her staff, including the person assigned the task of looking into the ethical implications of release to the press, counseled her to delay publication until the trial minutes were received.

Petitioner's act was not generalized criticism but rather release to the media of a false allegation of specific wrongdoing, made without any support other than the interoffice memoranda of a newly admitted trial assistant, aimed at a named Judge who had presided over a number of cases prosecuted by her office. * * * Petitioner knew or should have known that such attacks are unwarranted and unprofessional, serve to bring the Bench and Bar into disrepute, and tend to undermine public confidence in the judicial system. * * *

Therefore, petitioner's conduct was properly the subject of disciplinary action under DR 1-102(A)(6), and it is of no consequence that she might be charged with violating DR 8-102(B) based on this same course of conduct * * * Indeed, in the present case there are factors that distinguish petitioner's conduct from that prohibited under DR 8-102(B)-most notably, release of the false charges to the media-and make it particularly relevant to her fitness to practice law.

Petitioner contends that her conduct would not be actionable under the "constitutional malice" standard enunciated by the Supreme Court in *New York Times Co. v. Sullivan*, 376 U.S. 254, 84 S.Ct. 710, 11 L.Ed.2d 686. Neither this Court nor the Supreme Court has ever extended the *Sullivan* standard to lawyer discipline and we decline to do so here.

Accepting petitioner's argument would immunize all accusations, however reckless or irresponsible, from censure as long as the attorney uttering them did not actually entertain serious doubts as to their truth * * *. Such a standard would be wholly at odds with the policy underlying the rules governing professional responsibility, which seeks to establish a "minimum level of conduct below which no lawyer can fall without being subject to disciplinary action." * * *

Unlike defamation cases, "[p]rofessional misconduct, although it may directly affect an individual, is not punished for the benefit of the affected person; the wrong is against society as a whole, the preservation of a fair, impartial judicial system, and the system of justice as it has evolved for

Food for Thought

District Attorney Holtzman relied on the representation of an Assistant District Attorney but did not conduct an independent investigation of the allegations. Do you believe that the District Attorney's reliance on the representation of her Assistant District Attorney constituted objective "reckless disregard" as to the "truth or falsity" of the allegation against Judge Levine under Rule 8.2? In reaching your conclusion, keep in mind that the federal courts and most, but not all states, agree with the *Holtzman* court that the standard for reckless disregard applicable to lawyer criticism of courts is objective, rather than subjective. *See, e.g., Standing Committee on Discipline v. Yagman*, 55 F.3d 1430, 1437 & n.12 (9th Cir. 1995).

generations." * * * It follows that the issue raised when an attorney makes public a false accusation of wrongdoing by a Judge is not whether the target of the false attack has been harmed in reputation; the issue is whether that criticism adversely affects the administration of justice and adversely reflects on the attorney's judgment and, consequentially, her ability to practice law * * *.

In order to adequately protect the public interest and maintain the integrity of the judicial system, there must be an objective standard of what a reasonable attorney would do in similar circumstances * * * . It is the reasonableness of the belief, not the state of mind of the attorney, that is determinative.

Petitioner's course of conduct satisfies any standard other than "constitutional malice," and therefore Charge 1 must be sustained.

We have examined petitioner's remaining contentions and conclude that they are without merit.

Accordingly, the order of the Appellate Division should be affirmed, without costs.

STANDING COMMITTEE ON DISCIPLINE v. YAGMAN

55 F.3d 1430 (9th Cir. 1995)

KOZINSKI, Circuit Judge:

Never far from the center of controversy, outspoken civil rights lawyer Stephen Yagman was suspended from practice before the United States District Court for the Central District of California for impugning the integrity of the court and interfering with the random selection of judges by making disparaging remarks about a judge of that court. We confront several new issues in reviewing this suspension order.

I

The convoluted history of this case begins in 1991 when Yagman filed a lawsuit pro se against several insurance companies. The case was assigned to Judge Manuel Real, then Chief Judge of the Central District. Yagman promptly sought to disqualify Judge Real on grounds of bias.[1] The disqualification motion was randomly assigned to Judge William Keller, who denied it * * * and sanctioned Yagman for pursuing the matter in an "improper and frivolous manner[.]" * * * [2]

A few days after Judge Keller's sanctions order, Yagman was quoted as saying that Judge Keller "has a penchant for sanctioning Jewish lawyers: me, David Kenner and Hugh Manes. I find this to be evidence of anti-semitism." Susan Seager, *Judge Sanctions Yagman, Refers Case to State Bar,* L.A. Daily J., June 6, 1991, at 1. The district court found that Yagman also told the Daily Journal reporter that Judge Keller was "drunk on the bench," although this accusation wasn't published in the article. * * *

Around this time, Yagman received a request from Prentice Hall, publisher of the much-fretted-about Almanac of the Federal Judiciary, for comments in connection with a profile of Judge Keller. Yagman's response was less than complimentary.[4] * * * There's

> **FYI**
>
> As Judge Kozinski observes, Stephen Yagman is an "outspoken civil rights litigator." In particular, he was one of pioneers of civil lawsuits charging the Los Angeles police with misconduct. This case was far from his only personal brush with the law. In 2007, he was sentenced to "three years in federal prison for tax evasion, money laundering and bankruptcy fraud." *See* Scott Glover, *Yagman Sentenced to Three Years,* L.A. Times, Nov. 28, 2007, *available at* http://articles.latimes.com/2007/nov/28/local/me-yagman28; *see also Whatcha Gonna Do When They Come For You?*, Taxgirl blog, June 26, 2007, *available at* http://www.taxgirl.com/whatcha-gonna-do-when-they-come-for-you/.

no doubt that Yagman wrote this intemperate letter, though the parties disagree about what Yagman did with it. The district court found that Yagman mailed

---

1. As the basis for this claim, Yagman cited an earlier case where Judge Real had granted a directed verdict against Yagman's clients and thereafter sanctioned Yagman personally in the amount of $250,000. We reversed the sanctions and remanded for reassignment to another judge. *In re Yagman,* 796 F.2d 1165, 1188 (9th Cir. 1986). Though we found no evidence that Judge Real harbored any personal animosity toward Yagman, we concluded that reassignment was necessary "to preserve the appearance of justice." *Id.* On remand, Judge Real challenged our authority to reassign the case, and Yagman successfully petitioned for a writ of mandamus. * * * The matter came to rest when the Supreme Court denied Judge Real's petition for certiorari. * * *

2. The sanctions order harshly reprimanded Yagman, stating that "neither monetary sanctions nor suspension appear to be effective in deterring Yagman's pestiferous conduct," * * * and recommended that he be "disciplined appropriately" by the California State Bar * * * . On appeal, we affirmed as to disqualification but reversed as to sanctions. * * *

4. The portion of the letter relevant here reads as follows:

    It is outrageous that the Judge wants his profile redone because he thinks it to be inaccurately harsh in portraying him in a poor light. It is an understatement to characterize the Judge as "the worst judge in the central district." It would be fairer to say that he is ignorant, dishonest, ill-tempered, and a bully, and probably is one of the worst judges in the United States. If television cameras ever were permitted in his courtroom, the other federal judges in the Country would be so embarrassed by this buffoon that they would run for cover. One might believe that some of the reason for this sub-standard human is the recent acrimonious divorce through which he recently went: but talking to attorneys who knew him years ago indicates that, if anything, he has mellowed. One other comment: his girlfriend . . . , like the Judge, is a right-wing fanatic.

copies both to Prentice Hall and to Judge Keller, * * * and we have no basis for rejecting this finding.

A few weeks later, Yagman placed an advertisement (on the stationary of his law firm) in the L.A. Daily Journal, asking lawyers who had been sanctioned by Judge Keller to contact Yagman's office.

Soon after these events, Yagman ran into Robert Steinberg, another attorney who practices in the Central District. According to Steinberg, Yagman told him that, by levelling [sic] public criticism at Judge Keller, Yagman hoped to get the judge to recuse himself in future cases. Believing that Yagman was committing misconduct, Steinberg described his conversation with Yagman in a letter to the Standing Committee on Discipline of the U.S. District Court for the Central District of California * * * .

A few weeks later, the Standing Committee received a letter from Judge Keller describing Yagman's anti-Semitism charge, his inflammatory statements to Prentice Hall and the newspaper advertisement placed by Yagman's law firm. Judge Keller stated that "Mr. Yagman's campaign of harassment and intimidation challenges the integrity of the judicial system. Moreover, there is clear evidence that Mr. Yagman's attacks upon me are motivated by his desire to create a basis for recusing me in any future proceeding." * * * Judge Keller suggested that "[t]he Standing Committee on Discipline should take action to protect the Court from further abuse." * * *

After investigating the charges in the two letters, the Standing Committee issued a Petition for Issuance of an Order to Show Cause why Yagman should not be suspended from practice or otherwise disciplined. Pursuant to Central District Local Rule 2.6.4, the matter was then assigned to a panel of three Central District judges, which issued an Order to Show Cause and scheduled a hearing. Prior to the hearing, Yagman raised serious First Amendment objections to being disciplined for criticizing Judge Keller. Both sides requested an opportunity to brief the difficult free speech issues presented, but the district court never acted on these requests. The parties thus proceeded at the hearing without knowing the allocation of the burden of proof or the legal standard the court intended to apply

During the two-day hearing, the Standing Committee and Yagman put on witnesses and introduced exhibits. In a published opinion issued several months after the hearing, the district court held that Yagman had committed sanctionable misconduct, and suspended him from practice in the Central District for two years.

III

* * *

Local Rule 2.5.2 contains two separate prohibitions. First, it enjoins attorneys from engaging in any conduct that "degrades or impugns the integrity of the Court." Second, it provides that "[n]o attorney shall engage in any conduct which . . . interferes with the administration of justice." The district court concluded that Yagman violated both prongs of the rule. Because different First Amendment standards apply to these two provisions, we discuss the propriety of the sanction under each of them separately.

A

1. We begin with the portion of Local Rule 2.5.2 prohibiting any conduct that "impugns the integrity of the Court." As the district court recognized, this provision is overbroad because it purports to punish a great deal of constitutionally protected speech, including all true statements reflecting adversely on the reputation or character of federal judges. A substantially overbroad restriction on protected speech will be declared facially invalid unless it is "fairly subject to a limiting construction." * * *

To save the "impugn the integrity" portion of Rule 2.5.2, the district court read into it an "objective" version of the malice standard enunciated in *New York Times Co. v. Sullivan,* 376 U.S. 254, 84 S.Ct. 710, 11 L.Ed.2d 686 (1964). Relying on *United States Dist. Ct. v. Sandlin,* 12 F.3d 861 (9th Cir. 1993), the court limited Rule 2.5.2 to prohibit only false statements made with either knowledge of their falsity or with reckless disregard as to their truth or falsity, judged from the standpoint of a "reasonable attorney." * * *

Sandlin involved a First Amendment challenge to Washington Rule of Professional Conduct 8.2(a), which provided in part: "A lawyer shall not make a statement that the lawyer knows to be false or with reckless disregard as to its truth or falsity concerning the qualifications, integrity, or record of a judge." * * * Though the language of the rule closely tracked the *New York Times* malice standard, we held that the purely subjective standard applicable in defamation cases is not suited to attorney disciplinary proceedings. * * * Instead, we held that such proceedings are governed by an objective standard, pursuant to which the court must determine "what the reasonable attorney, considered in light of all his professional functions, would do in the same or similar circumstances The inquiry focuses on whether the attorney had a reasonable factual basis for making the statements, considering their nature and the context in which they were made.

Yagman nonetheless urges application of the *New York Times* subjective malice standard in attorney disciplinary proceedings. *Sandlin* stands firmly in the way. In

Sandlin, we held that there are significant differences between the interests served by defamation law and those served by rules of professional ethics. Defamation actions seek to remedy an essentially private wrong by compensating individuals for harm caused to their reputation and standing in the community. Ethical rules that prohibit false statements impugning the integrity of judges, by contrast, are not designed to shield judges from unpleasant or offensive criticism, but to preserve public confidence in the fairness and impartiality of our system of justice. * * *

Though attorneys can play an important role in exposing problems with the judicial system, * * * *false* statements impugning the integrity of a judge erode public confidence without serving to publicize problems that justifiably deserve attention. *Sandlin* held that an objective malice standard strikes a constitutionally permissible balance between an attorney's right to criticize the judiciary and the public's interest in preserving confidence in the judicial system: Lawyers may freely voice criticisms supported by a reasonable factual basis even if they turn out to be mistaken.

Attorneys who make statements impugning the integrity of a judge are, however, entitled to other First Amendment protections applicable in the defamation context. To begin with, attorneys may be sanctioned for impugning the integrity of a judge or the court only if their statements are false; truth is an absolute defense. * * * Moreover, the disciplinary body bears the burden of proving falsity. * * *

It follows that statements impugning the integrity of a judge may not be punished unless they are capable of being proved true or false; statements of opinion are protected by the First Amendment unless they "imply a false assertion of fact." * * * Even statements that at first blush appear to be factual are protected by the First Amendment if they cannot reasonably be interpreted as stating actual facts about their target. * * * Thus, statements of "rhetorical hyperbole" aren't sanctionable, nor are statements that use language in a "loose, figurative sense." * * *

With these principles in mind, we examine the statements for which Yagman was disciplined.

2. We first consider Yagman's statement in the Daily Journal that Judge Keller "has a penchant for sanctioning Jewish lawyers: me, David Kenner and Hugh Manes. I find this to be evidence of anti-semitism." Though the district court viewed this entirely as an assertion of fact, * * * we conclude that the statement contains both an assertion of fact and an expression of opinion.

Yagman's claim that he, Kenner and Manes are all Jewish and were sanctioned by Judge Keller is clearly a factual assertion: The words have specific, well-defined meanings and describe objectively verifiable matters. Nothing about the context in which the words appear suggests the use of loose, figurative language or "rhetorical hyperbole." Thus, had the Standing Committee proved that Yagman, Kenner or Manes were not sanctioned by Judge Keller, or were not Jewish, this assertion might have formed the basis for discipline. The committee, however, didn't claim that Yagman's factual assertion was false, and the district court made no finding to that effect. We proceed, therefore, on the assumption that this portion of Yagman's statement is true.

The remaining portion of Yagman's Daily Journal statement is best characterized as opinion; it conveys Yagman's personal belief that Judge Keller is anti-Semitic. As such, it may be the basis for sanctions only if it could reasonably be understood as declaring or implying actual facts capable of being proved true or false. * * *

In applying this principle, we are guided by section 566 of the Restatement (Second) of Torts, which distinguishes between two kinds of opinion statements: those based on assumed or expressly stated facts, and those based on implied, undisclosed facts. * * * The statement, "I think Jones is an alcoholic," for example, is an expression of opinion based on implied facts, because the statement "gives rise to the inference that there are undisclosed facts that justify the forming of the opinion". Readers of this statement will reasonably understand the author to be implying he knows facts supporting his view- *e.g.,* that Jones stops at a bar every night after work and has three martinis. If the speaker has no such factual basis for his assertion, the statement is actionable, even though phrased in terms of the author's personal belief.

A statement of opinion based on expressly stated facts, on the other hand, might take the following form: "[Jones] moved in six months ago. He works downtown, and I have seen him during that time only twice, in his backyard around 5:30 seated in a deck chair . . . with a drink in his hand. I think he must be an alcoholic." This expression of opinion appears to disclose all the facts on which it is based, and does not imply that there are other, unstated facts supporting the belief that Jones is an alcoholic.

A statement of opinion based on fully disclosed facts can be punished only if the stated facts are themselves false and demeaning. * * * Restatement (Second) of Torts § 566, cmt. c ("A simple expression of opinion based on disclosed . . . nondefamatory facts is not itself sufficient for an action of defamation, no matter how unjustified and unreasonable the opinion may be or how derogatory it is."). The rationale behind this rule is straightforward: When the facts underlying a statement of opinion are disclosed, readers will understand they are getting the author's interpretation of the facts presented; they are therefore unlikely to construe the statement as insinuating the existence of additional, undisclosed facts. * * *, "an opinion which is unfounded reveals its lack of merit when the opinion-holder discloses the factual basis for the idea"; readers are free to accept or reject the author's opinion based on their own independent evaluation of the facts. * * * . A statement of opinion of this sort doesn't "imply a false assertion of fact," * * * and is thus entitled to full constitutional protection.

We applied this principle in *Lewis v. Time, Inc.,* 710 F.2d 549 (9th Cir. 1983), where an attorney claimed he had been defamed by an article calling him a "shady practitioner." We held that this expression of opinion was protected by the First Amendment because the article set forth the facts on which the opinion was based: a judgment entered against the attorney for defrauding his clients, and another judgment holding him liable for malpractice. Because the article's factual assertions were accurate, we concluded that the plaintiff's claim was barred: "[W]here a publication sets forth the facts underlying its statement of opinion and those facts are true, the Constitution protects that opinion from liability for defamation."

Yagman's Daily Journal remark is protected by the First Amendment as an expression of opinion based on stated facts. Like the defendant in *Lewis,* Yagman disclosed the basis for his view that Judge Keller is anti-Semitic and has a penchant for sanctioning Jewish lawyers: that he, Kenner and Manes are all Jewish and had been sanctioned by Judge Keller. The statement did not imply the existence of additional, undisclosed facts; it was carefully phrased in terms of an inference drawn from the facts specified rather than a bald accusation of bias against Jews.[17] Readers were "free to form another, perhaps contradictory opinion from the same facts," as no doubt they did.

3. The district court also disciplined Yagman for alleging that Judge Keller was "dishonest." This remark appears in the letter Yagman sent to Prentice Hall in connection with the profile of Judge Keller in the Almanac of the Federal Judiciary. *See* n. 4 *supra.* The court concluded that this allegation was sanctionable because it "plainly impl[ies] past improprieties." Had Yagman accused Judge Keller of taking bribes, we would agree with the district court. Statements that "could reasonably be understood as imputing specific criminal or other wrongful acts" are not entitled to constitutional protection merely because they are phrased in the form of an opinion. * * *

When considered in context, however, Yagman's statement cannot reasonably be interpreted as accusing Judge Keller of criminal misconduct. The term "dishonest" was one in a string of colorful adjectives Yagman used to convey the low esteem in which he held Judge Keller. The other terms he used-"ignorant," "ill-tempered," "buffoon," "sub-standard human," "right-wing fanatic," "a bully," "one of the worst judges in the United States"—all speak to competence and temperament rather than corruption; together they convey nothing more substantive than Yagman's

---

17 Even if Yagman's statement were viewed as a bare allegation of anti-Semitism, it might well qualify for protection under the First Amendment as mere "name-calling." *Cf. Stevens v. Tillman,* 855 F.2d 394, 402 (7th Cir. 1988) (allegation that plaintiff was a "racist" held not actionable); *Buckley v. Littell,* 539 F.2d 882, 894 (2d Cir. 1976) (allegation that plaintiff was a "fascist" held not actionable); *Ward v. Zelikovsky,* 136 N.J. 516, 643 A.2d 972, 983 (1994) (allegation that plaintiffs "hate Jews" held not actionable).

contempt for Judge Keller. Viewed in context of these "lusty and imaginative expression[s]," * * * the word "dishonest" cannot reasonably be construed as suggesting that Judge Keller had committed specific illegal acts.[18] * * * Yagman's remarks are thus statements of rhetorical hyperbole, incapable of being proved true or false. *Cf. In re Erdmann,* <u>33 N.Y.2d 559, 347 N.Y.S.2d 441, 441, 301 N.E.2d 426, 427 (1973)</u> (reversing sanction against attorney who criticized trial judges for not following the law, and appellate judges for being "the whores who became madams"); *State Bar v. Semaan,* <u>508 S.W.2d 429, 431-32 (Tex.Civ. App.1974)</u> (attorney's observation that judge was "a midget among giants" not sanctionable because it wasn't subject to being proved true or false).

Were we to find any substantive content in Yagman's use of the term "dishonest," we would, at most, construe it to mean "intellectually dishonest"-an accusation that Judge Keller's rulings were overly result-oriented. Intellectual dishonesty is a label lawyers frequently attach to decisions with which they disagree.[19] An allegation that a judge is intellectually dishonest, however, cannot be proved true or false by reference to a "core of objective evidence." * * * Because Yagman's allegation of "dishonesty" does not imply facts capable of objective verification, it is constitutionally immune from sanctions.

4. Finally, the district court found sanctionable Yagman's allegation that Judge Keller was "drunk on the bench." Yagman contends that, like many of the terms he used in his letter to Prentice Hall, this phrase should be viewed as mere "rhetorical hyperbole." The statement wasn't a part of the string of invective in the Prentice Hall letter, however; it was a remark Yagman allegedly made to a newspaper reporter. Yagman identifies nothing relating to the context in which this statement was made that tends to negate the literal meaning of the words he used. We therefore conclude that Yagman's "drunk on the bench" statement could reasonably be interpreted as suggesting that Judge Keller had actually, on at least one occasion, taken the bench while intoxicated. Unlike Yagman's remarks in his letter to Prentice Hall, this statement implies actual facts that are capable of objective verification. For this reason, the statement isn't protected under *Falwell, Bresler* or *Letter Carriers.*

For Yagman's "drunk on the bench" allegation to serve as the basis for sanctions, however, the Standing Committee had to prove that the statement was false. * *

18 A lawyer accusing a judge of criminal misconduct would use a more pointed term such as "crooked" or "corrupt." *See Rinaldi,* 397 N.Y.S.2d at 951, 366 N.E.2d at 1307 (accusation that judge was "corrupt" not protected because it implied the judge had committed illegal acts).

19 *See, e.g., The Comeback Kids,* The Recorder, Dec. 29, 1994, at 1 ("[Apple Computer's attorney] call[ed] the Ninth Circuit ruling [in *Apple Computer, Inc. v. Microsoft Corp.*] 'intellectually dishonest' and 'extremely detrimental to the business of the United States.' "); Philip Shenon, *Convictions Reversed in Island Slaying,* N.Y. Times, July 21, 1987, at A1 ("[T]he chief prosecutor in the case[ ] said he would challenge the appeals court's decision, which he described as 'intellectually dishonest.' "); Dawn Weyrich, *Affirmative Action Win Surprises Many,* Wash. Times, June 28, 1990, at A1 ("William Bradford Reynolds ... called the ruling [in *Metro Broadcasting, Inc. v. FCC*] 'intellectually dishonest.' 'There is no legal reasoning to justify this decision. Judicial activism has run rampant again,' Mr. Reynolds said.").

* This it failed to do; indeed, the committee introduced no evidence at all on the point. While we share the district court's inclination to presume, "[i]n the absence of supporting evidence," that the allegation is untrue * * * the fact remains that the Standing Committee bore the burden of proving Yagman had made a statement that falsely impugned the integrity of the court. By presuming falsity, the district court unconstitutionally relieved the Standing Committee of its duty to produce evidence on an element of its case. Without proof of falsity Yagman's "drunk on the bench" allegation, like the statements discussed above, cannot support the imposition of sanctions for impugning the integrity of the court.

B

As an alternative basis for sanctioning Yagman, the district court concluded that Yagman's statements violated Local Rule 2.5.2's prohibition against engaging in conduct that "interferes with the administration of justice." The court found that Yagman made the statements discussed above in an attempt to "judge-shop"— *i.e.,* to cause Judge Keller to recuse himself in cases where Yagman appeared as counsel.

The Supreme Court has held that speech otherwise entitled to full constitutional protection may nonetheless be sanctioned if it obstructs or prejudices the administration of justice. * * * Given the significant burden this rule places on otherwise protected speech, however, the Court has held that prejudice to the administration of justice must be highly likely before speech may be punished.

In a trio of cases involving contempt sanctions imposed against newspapers, the Court articulated the constitutional standard to be applied in this context. Press statements relating to judicial matters may not be restricted, the Court held, unless they pose a "clear and present danger" to the administration of justice. * * * The standard announced in these cases is a demanding one: Statements may be punished only if they "constitute an imminent, not merely a likely, threat to the administration of justice. The danger must not be remote or even probable; it must immediately imperil." * * * There was no clear and present danger in these cases, the Court concluded, because any prospect that press criticism might influence a judge's decision was far too remote. In an oft-quoted passage, the Court noted that "the law of contempt is not made for the protection of judges who may be sensitive to the winds of public opinion. Judges are supposed to be men of fortitude, able to thrive in a hardy climate." * * *

More recently, the Court held that the "clear and present danger" standard does not apply to statements made by lawyers participating in pending cases. In *Gentile,* the Court concluded that lawyers involved in pending cases may be punished if their out-of-court statements pose merely a "substantial likelihood" of materially prejudicing the fairness of the proceeding. The Court gave two principal reasons for adopting this lower threshold, one concerned with the identity of the speaker, the other with the timing of the speech. First, the Court noted, lawyers participating in pending cases have "special access to information through discovery and client communications." * * * As a result, their statements pose a heightened threat to the fair administration of justice, "since [they] are likely to be received as especially authoritative." * * * Second, statements made during the pendency of a case are "likely to influence the actual outcome of the trial" or "prejudice the jury venire, even if an untainted panel can ultimately be found." * * * The Court also noted that restricting the speech of lawyers while they are involved in pending cases does not prohibit speech altogether but "merely postpones the attorneys' comments until after trial." * * *

The special considerations identified by *Gentile* are of limited concern when no case is pending before the court. When lawyers speak out on matters unconnected to a pending case, there is no direct and immediate impact on the fair trial rights of litigants. Information the lawyers impart will not be viewed as coming from confidential sources, and will not have a direct impact on a particular jury venire. Moreover, a speech restriction that is not bounded by a particular trial or other judicial proceeding does far more than merely postpone speech; it permanently inhibits what lawyers may say about the court and its judges—whether their statements are true or false. Much speech of public importance—such as testimony at congressional hearings regarding the temperament and competence of judicial nominees-would be permanently chilled if the rule in *Gentile* were extended beyond the confines of a pending matter. We conclude, therefore, that lawyers' statements unrelated to a matter pending before the court may be sanctioned only if they pose a clear and present danger to the administration of justice. * * *

The district court found that Yagman's statements interfered with the administration of justice because they were aimed at forcing Judge Keller to recuse himself in cases where Yagman appears as counsel. Judge-shopping doubtless disrupts the proper functioning of the judicial system and may be disciplined. But after conducting an independent examination of the record to ensure that the district court's ruling "does not constitute a forbidden intrusion on the field of free expression[.]"

Yagman's criticism of Judge Keller was harsh and intemperate, and in no way to be condoned. It has long been established, however, that a party cannot force a judge to recuse himself by engaging in personal attacks on the judge: "Nor can that artifice prevail, which insinuates that the decision of this court will be the effect of personal resentment; for, if it could, every man could evade the punishment due to his offences, by first pouring a torrent of abuse upon his judges, and then asserting that they act from passion. . . . " Modern courts continue to adhere to this view, and with good reason. * * *

Criticism from a party's attorney creates an even remoter danger that a judge will disqualify himself because the federal recusal statutes, in all but the most extreme circumstances, require a showing that the judge is (or appears to be) biased or prejudiced against a party, not counsel. * * * Were it otherwise, courts have cautioned, "[l]awyers, once in a controversy with a judge, would have a license under which the judge would serve at their will," * * * any "party wishing to rid himself of the assigned judge would need only hire a lawyer with a certified record of abusive criticisms of that judge[.]" * * *

Notwithstanding this well-settled rule, judges occasionally do remove themselves voluntarily from cases as a result of harsh criticism from attorneys. As the district court recognized, then, a lawyer's vociferous criticism of a judge could interfere with the random assignment of judges. But a mere possibility—or even the probability—of harm does not amount to a clear and present danger: "The danger must not be remote or even probable; it must immediately imperil." * * * The "substantive evil must be extremely serious and the degree of imminence must be extremely high before utterances can be punished" under the First Amendment. * * *

We conclude that "the danger under this record to fair judicial administration has not the clearness and immediacy necessary to close the door of permissible public comment." * * * As noted above, firm and long-standing precedent establishes that unflattering remarks like Yagman's cannot force the disqualification of the judge at whom they are aimed. The question remains whether the possibility of voluntary recusal is so great as to amount to a clear and present danger. We believe it is not. Public criticism of judges and the decisions they make is not unusual, * * * yet this seldom leads to judicial recusal. Judge Real, for example, despite receiving harsh

criticism from Yagman, did not recuse himself in *Yagman v. Republic Ins.*, where Yagman was not merely the lawyer but also a party to the proceedings. Federal judges are well aware that "[s]ervice as a public official means that one may not be viewed favorably by every member of the public," and that they've been granted "the extraordinary protections of life tenure to shield them from such pressures." * * * Because Yagman's statements do not pose a clear and present danger to the proper functioning of the courts, we conclude that the district court erred in sanctioning Yagman for interfering with the administration of justice.

> **FYI**
>
> Even though the *Yagman* decision has not been over-ruled, it has proven controversial. For example, the Seventh Circuit noted that "[t]o the extent [the *Yagman* decision] may hold that attorneys are entitled to excoriate judges in the same way, and with the same lack of investigation, as persons may attack political officeholders, it is inconsistent with *Gentile* and our own precedents." *Matter of Palmisano,* 70 F.3d 483, 487 (7th Cir. 1995). Other courts have rejected the *Yagman* court's assertion that "prejudice to the administration of justice must be highly likely before speech may be published." *In re Comfort,* 159 P.3d 1011 (Kan. 2007).

Conclusion

We can't improve on the words of Justice Black * * * :

The assumption that respect for the judiciary can be won by shielding judges from published criticism wrongly appraises the character of American public opinion. For it is a prized American privilege to speak one's mind, although not always with perfect good taste, on all public institutions. And an enforced silence, however limited, solely in the name of preserving the dignity of the bench, would probably engender resentment, suspicion, and contempt much more than it would enhance respect.

REVERSED.

KUNSTLER v. GALLIGAN

168 A.D.2d 146 (App. Div. 1991), *aff'd*, 79 N.Y.2d 775 (1991)

Before Sullivan, J.P., and Wallach, Kupferman, Ross and Smith, JJ

Per Curiam.

On August 18, 1990, Mr. Yusef Salaam was convicted, after a jury trial, of the crimes of rape in the first degree * * *, robbery in the first degree * * *, riot in the first degree * * * , and assault in the second degree * * *, in the Supreme Court, New York County (Thomas B. Galligan, J.). Subsequently, on September 11, 1990, Justice Galligan sentenced Mr. Salaam, consecutively on the designated felonies as a juvenile offender, to an indeterminate prison term of five to ten years. All of the crimes of which Mr. Salaam was convicted arose out of a series of attacks, on April 19, 1989, in Central Park, upon a female jogger, several male joggers, and other persons.

Thereafter, in November 1990, William M. Kunstler, Esq., moved * * * to vacate Mr. Salaam's conviction, on the ground that, during his trial, a juror read press accounts of that trial and informed his fellow jurors about them. * * *

FYI

William Kunstler was one of the most famous civil rights, civil liberties, and criminal defense lawyers of the second half of the twentieth century. A leader of both the ACLU and the Center for Constitutional Rights, his clients included the Chicago 7, the American Indian Movement, and El-Sayyid Nosair. To learn more about his fascinating life, read David Langum, *William Kunstler: The Most Hated Lawyer in America* (2000). To hear William Kunstler explain his commitment to civil liberties, go to the website for the documentary on his life, Disturbing the Universe, which premiered at the 2009 Sundance Film Festival.

The subject motion was one of a number of matters to be disposed of, on December 20, 1990, in, Criminal Term, Part 59 courtroom, by Justice Galligan.

After the Clerk of Part 59 called the Mr. Salaam matter, Mr. Kunstler and the Assistant District Attorney noted their appearances, and Justice Galligan promptly informed Mr. Kunstler that the motion was denied, no hearing would be directed on same, and a copy of the motion decision would be available at the end of the day.

This colloquy then took place between Mr. Kunstler and Justice Galligan * * *:

> "MR. KUNSTLER: It is outrageous. You will not have an evidentiary hearing despite all the law that calls for it?
>
> THE COURT: I will not hear oral argument. Call the next case.
>
> MR. KUNSTLER: You have exhibited what your partisanship is. You shouldn't be sitting in court. You are a disgrace to the bench.
>
> THE COURT: Sir, I hold you in contempt of court."

After being held in contempt, Mr. Kunstler continued to argue, as follows * * *:

> "MR. KUNSTLER: You can hold me in anything you wish. I am outraged.
>
> THE COURT: I am giving you an opportunity to be heard right now.
>
> MR. KUNSTLER: I am saying this, judge. Every case in the world says you should hold a hearing in order to determine whether outside influences affected a juror. Every case there is. I submitted them to you.
>
> > Even when a juror falls asleep, the Second Department has held there should be a hearing. And for you to deny it without a hearing. I think it is outrageous. You are violating every standard of fair play.
>
> THE COURT: I am holding you in contempt of court. You are fined $250 or 30 days in jail . . . ".

Subsequently, on December 20th, Justice Galligan issued a written decision denying the * * * motion, as well as the request that he recuse himself from deciding that motion, and a written decision detailing the reasons for holding Mr. Kunstler in summary criminal contempt.

In March 1991, Mr. Kunstler (petitioner), by counsel, instituted, pursuant to Civil Practice Law and Rules Article 78, a petition to annul the summary criminal contempt order of Justice Galligan (respondent Justice). Thereafter, a Justice of this Court granted a stay, not on the merits, pending determination of the petition, and granted permission to argue orally.

The petitioner contends, in substance, that the order should be annulled, since his conduct did not justify a finding of contempt, and if it did, he was not given an opportunity to be heard in defense or extenuation, before the respondent Justice imposed punishment.

Pursuant to [the] Judiciary Law * * *, a Justice or Judge of a Court of Record, such as respondent Justice, is given the power to punish a person for criminal contempt, who commits certain acts, including:

> "1. Disorderly, contemptuous, or insolent behavior, committed during its sitting, in its immediate view and presence, and directly tending to interrupt its proceedings, or to impair the respect due to its authority.

> * * *

> 3. Wilful disobedience to its lawful mandate.

> 4. Resistance wilfully offered to its lawful mandate . . .".

Further, * * * contempts, such as those specified in the Judiciary Law * * *, "committed in the immediate view and presence of the court, may be punished summarily," by a fine of $1,000.00 or 30 days in jail or both, at the discretion of the Court.

Additionally, Judiciary Law § 755 provides that "[w]here the offense is committed in the immediate view and presence of the court, ... it may be punished summarily. For that purpose, an order must be made by the court ... stating the facts which constitute the offense and which bring the case within the provisions of this section, and plainly and specifically prescribing the punishment to be inflicted therefor . . ." [material in brackets added].

Part 604 of the Rules of this Court, deals with COURT DECORUM, and states * * * in pertinent part:

"(a) Exercise of the summary contempt power.

(1) The power of the court to punish summarily contempt committed in its immediate view and presence shall be exercised only in exceptional and necessitous circumstances, as follows:

(i) Where the offending conduct either

(a) disrupts or threatens to disrupt proceedings actually in progress; or

(b) destroys or undermines or tends seriously to destroy or undermine the dignity and authority of the court in a manner and to the extent that it appears unlikely that the court will be able to continue to conduct its normal business in an appropriate way; and

(ii) The court reasonably believes that a prompt summary adjudication of contempt may aid in maintaining or restoring and maintaining proper order and decorum.

(2) Whenever practical punishment should be determined and imposed at the time of the adjudication of contempt . . .

(3) Before summary adjudication of contempt the accused shall be given a reasonable opportunity to make a statement in his defense or in extenuation of his conduct."

It is well established law that justification for a Court's power to summarily punish a contempt, committed in its immediate view and presence, is based upon the need to preserve order in the courtroom, so that the Court can conduct its normal business. * * * [T]he United States Supreme Court stated "the court must act instantly to suppress disturbance or violence or physical obstruction or disrespect to the court when occurring in open court . . . ". Further, the Court of Appeals * * * stated "[i]t is the need for the preservation of the immediate order in the courtroom which justifies the summary procedure-one so summary that the right and need for an evidentiary hearing, counsel, opportunity for adjournment, reference to another Judge, and the like, are not allowable because it would be entirely frustrative of the maintenance of order . . .".

Our examination of the transcript of the December 20, 1990 proceeding, in the Part 59 courtroom, unequivocally indicates that petitioner, although informed by the respondent Justice that there would be neither oral argument nor an evidentiary hearing concerning the motion, and that the Clerk had been directed to "Call the next case" * * * , wilfully disobeyed that Court order, by exclaiming to the respondent Justice "You have exhibited what your partisanship is. You shouldn't be sitting in court. You are a disgrace to the bench".

Based upon the legal authority, *supra,* we find respondent Justice was justified in instantly responding to restore "proper order and decorum" in the courtroom, since the petitioner's disorderly, contemptuous, and insolent behavior, displayed in open Court, in the immediate view and presence of respondent Justice, resulted in disrupting a calendar call, and tended to seriously "undermine the dignity and authority of the court in a manner and to the extent that it . . . [appeared] unlikely that the court . . . [would] be able to continue to conduct its normal business in an appropriate way . . ." * * *

Further, we find that, after holding petitioner in summary criminal contempt, respondent Justice, in accordance with the Rules of this Court, prior to imposing punishment "at the time of the adjudication of contempt", gave the petitioner "a reasonable opportunity to make a statement in his defense or in extenuation of his conduct" * * *. However, instead of explaining his conduct, petitioner chose to continue to disobey respondent Justice's order, and to contemptuously and insolently argue the motion.

* * *

The dissent seems to argue that since the length of time involved in the contemptuous conduct was brief, it should be significant to our consideration. Here, although the nature and content of petitioner's contemptuous language may have been brief in duration, it clearly was contumacious, and clearly violated both [the] Judiciary Law * * *, as well as * * * the Rules of this Court.

Based upon our analysis, *supra,* we confirm the order of summary contempt.

* * *

All concur except WALLACH, J., who dissents in an Opinion:

* * *

I respectfully dissent, not on the ground that counsel's conduct fell short of contumacious behavior, but because the record lacks proof of what we have held to be an additional essential element of the crime of criminal contempt: namely that * * * the conduct complained of either "disrupts or threatens to disrupt proceedings actually in progress" or that the conduct undermines the dignity of the court to the extent "it appears unlikely that the court will be able to continue to conduct its normal business in an appropriate way". This provided the fundamental rationale of our decision in *Matter of Breitbart v. Galligan,* 135 A.D.2d 323, 525 N.Y.S.2d 219, where we vacated a contempt conviction citing a similar failure of proof, despite the equally egregious character of the attorney's attack on the court there. The mere fact that in *Breitbart* the trial court deferred the imposition of sentence to the end of the case provides a distinction without a difference in addressing the instant issue. Neither in *Breitbart,* nor in this matter, were we asked to review the penalty imposed, nor the manner of its imposition. In any event, the contempt ruling before us now was likewise imposed at the "end" of the * * * motion proceedings, and indeed may be said to have decisively ended them.

Long standing jurisprudence establishes that "[a]n obstruction to the performance of judicial duty resulting from an act done in the presence of the court is, then, the characteristic upon which the power to punish for contempt must rest." * * *

The **locus in quo** of the alleged crime was at the call of a motion calendar at Criminal Term. The transcript of the entire transaction consists of three pages and could have consumed no more than the same number of minutes. Two-thirds of the colloquy was routine and unexceptional; the contemptuous remark appears at page 3. Just before it the Judge issued a direction to "call the next case." There is no showing of any obstruction in the hearing of the next case, or, for that matter, in the disposition of the pending motion in this case. On this record it would appear that the good ship Justice sailed serenely on, without a one-degree compass point deviation from its appointed course. Additional evidence is required to support any finding to the contrary.

For the reasons stated, I would grant the petition and vacate the adjudication of summary contempt, without prejudice to renewal of contempt proceedings at a plenary hearing before another Justice.

> **FYI**
>
> After the finding of contempt, William Kunstler received a public censure for committing a "serious crime" in violation of the disciplinary rules. *Matter of Kunstler*, 194 A.D. 2d 233 (1993). Which other Rules could also provide the basis for discipline of Kunstler under these circumstances?

II. Duties to Third Parties and to the Law

As a general rule, the law and the rules do not make a lawyer responsible for the impact on others resulting from the lawyer's representation of a client. Indeed, Rule 1.2(b) expressly states that "a lawyer's representation of a client * * * does not constitute an endorsement of the client's political, economic, social or moral views or activities." This section describes significant exceptions to the general approach. With regard to third parties, a lawyer has duties of truthfulness, of fairness to unrepresented parties, and of obedience to the law.

> **Make the Connection**
>
> This section deals with legal responsibility. Chapter 8 examines whether lawyers have a moral responsibility for their clients' conduct.

A. Unrepresented Persons

[Question 1]

An attorney represented a respondent in proceedings instituted by a child protection services agency to establish the paternity of a child and to recover past-due child support. The mother of the child had refused to file a complaint, had refused to retain a lawyer, and in fact had asked that the agency not file any action whatsoever. However, state law permitted the agency to commence paternity and support proceedings in its own name in such circumstances.

The attorney contacted the mother without the knowledge or consent of the agency or its lawyers. The attorney identified himself to the mother as "an officer of the court" and told the mother that he was investigating the matter. Based upon what she told him, the attorney prepared and the mother signed an affidavit truthfully stating that the respondent was not the father of the child.

Is the attorney subject to discipline?

   (A) Yes, because the attorney acted without the knowledge or consent of the agency or its lawyers.

   (B) Yes, because the attorney implied that he was disinterested in the matter.

   (C) No, because all of the attorney's statements to the mother were true.

   (D) No, because the attorney did not give the mother legal advice.

Rule 4.3 governs communications "with unrepresented persons * * * on behalf of a client with a person who is not represented by counsel[.]" It provides that "a lawyer shall not state or imply that the lawyer is disinterested." The lawyer's duty is even greater "[w]hen the lawyer knows or reasonably should know that the unrepresented person misunderstands the lawyer's role in the matter[.]" In that situation, "the lawyer shall make reasonable efforts to correct the misunderstanding." The lawyer has a further obligation "if the lawyer knows or reasonably should know that the interests of such a person are or have a reasonable possibility of being in conflict with the interests of the client." Where that occurs, "[t]he lawyer shall not give legal advice to an unrepresented person, other than the advice to secure counsel."

The Comment explains that:

[1]An unrepresented person, particularly one not experienced in dealing with legal matters, might assume that a lawyer is disinterested in loyalties or is a disinterested authority on the law even when the lawyer represents a client. In order to avoid a misunder-

Familiarity with Rule 1.13(f) is essential to representation of organizations. For more information regarding Rule 1.13(f), *see generally* D.C. Ethics Op. 269 (1997); Mary C. Daly, *Avoiding the Ethical Pitfall of Misidentifying the Organizational Client*, 574 PLI/Lit 399 (1997).

standing, a lawyer will typically need to identify the lawyer's client and, where necessary, explain that the client has interests opposed to those of the unrepresented person. For misunderstandings that sometimes arise when a lawyer for an organization deals with an unrepresented constituent, *see* Rule 1.13(f).

Rule 1.13(f) provides that "[i]n dealing with an organization's directors, officers, employees, members, shareholders or other constituents, a lawyer shall explain the identity of the client when the lawyer knows or reasonably should know that the organization's interests are adverse to those of the constituents with whom the lawyer is dealing."

[Question 2]

John Lawyer represents Larry Landlord in a nonpayment eviction suit against Thomas Tenant. At court, the case is called and Lawyer asks Tenant to step outside to talk. Tenant tells Lawyer he would like to pay his rent to Landlord but that for two months Landlord has refused to repair his broken refrigerator. Lawyer tells Tenant that he has a legal obligation to pay his rent and will be evicted if he doesn't do so. Lawyer does not advise Tenant that Tenant may have potential claims against Landlord under the warranty of habitability. Lawyer suggests that if Tenant signs a stipulation agreeing to pay the back rent, Landlord will look into the repair.

Has John Lawyer committed a disciplinary violation?

(A) Yes

(B) No

Review <u>Rule 4.3</u> *supra*.

Food for Thought

Professor Russell Engler reports that lawyers for landlords frequently violate the provisions of Rule 4.3 in housing court. He suggests a number of remedies, including amending the Rules to "impose a duty of fairness on a lawyer negotiating with an unrepresented adversary, prohibit a lawyer from obtaining an unconscionable agreement from an unrepresented party, or impose on the lawyer duties toward the tribunal and/or the unrepresented adversary different from those where the adverse party is represented." Russell Engler, *Out of Sight and Out of Line: The Need For Regulation of Lawyers' Negotiation With Unrepresented Poor Persons*, <u>85 Cal. L. Rev. 79, 138 (1997)</u>. Do you think his proposal properly calibrates the interests of the parties and the legal system's need for efficient resolution of cases?

B. Truthfulness

[Question 3]

A seller was engaged in negotiations to sell his interest in a large tact of land to a buyer who was unrepresented in the transaction. Before the seller went out of town for a few days, he told the buyer to call his attorney if the buyer had any questions about the property. The buyer called the seller's attorney, responded that, based on his experience handling real estate transactions in the neighborhood, the buyer would be getting a lot of property for the price. At the time the attorney spoke to the buyer, the attorney knew that there was a defect in the title and that the buyer's attempt to purchase the seller's interest in the tract would not result in the buyer's acquisition of any interest in the property.

Relying on the attorney's assurance, the buyer agreed to make the purchase. Shortly after the sale closed, the buyer discovered that his acquisition was worthless.

Is the attorney subject to civil liability to the buyer?

    (A) Yes, because the attorney knowingly made false representations of fact to the buyer.

    (B) Yes, because the attorney implied that his opinion regarding the value of the property was a disinterested opinion.

    (C) No, because the attorney's statement that the buyer would be getting a lot of property for the money was a statement of opinion regarding the value of the property.

    (D) No, because the buyer was not a client of the attorney.

Rule 4.1 is the general rule governing "truthfulness in statements" to non-clients. It provides that "[i]n In the course of representing a client a lawyer shall not knowingly:

    (a) make a false statement of material fact or law to a third person; or

    (b) fail to disclose a material fact to a third person when disclosure is necessary to avoid assisting a criminal or fraudulent act by a client, unless disclosure is prohibited by Rule 1.6.

The Comment to Rule 4.1 explains that:

Misrepresentation

[1] A lawyer is required to be truthful when dealing with others on a client's behalf, but generally has no affirmative duty to inform an opposing party of relevant facts. A misrepresentation can occur if the lawyer incorporates or affirms a statement of another person that the lawyer knows is false. Misrepresentations can also occur by partially true but misleading statements or omissions that are the equivalent of affirmative false statements. For dishonest conduct that does not amount to a false statement or for misrepresentations by a lawyer other than in the course of representing a client, *see* Rule 8.4.

Statements of Fact

[2] This Rule refers to statements of fact. Whether a particular statement should be regarded as one of fact can depend on the circumstances. Under generally accepted conventions in negotiation, certain types of statements ordinarily are not taken as statements of material fact. Estimates of price or value placed on the subject of a transaction and a party's intentions as to an acceptable settlement of a claim are ordinarily in this category, and so is the existence of an undisclosed principal except where nondisclosure of the principal would constitute fraud. Lawyers should be mindful of their obligations under applicable law to avoid criminal and tortious misrepresentation.

* * *

[Question 4]

An attorney represented a seller in negotiating the sale of his ice cream parlor. The seller told the attorney in confidence that, although the business had once been very profitable, recent profits had been stable but modest. As the negotiations proceeded, the buyer appeared to be losing interest in the deal. Hoping to restore the buyer's interest, the attorney stated, "The ice cream business is every American's dream: happy kids, steady profits, and a clear conscience." The buyer bought the ice cream parlor but was disappointed when his own profits proved to be modest.

Is the attorney subject to discipline?

(A) Yes, because the attorney made a false statement of fact to the buyer.

(B) Yes, because the attorney exaggerated the profitability of the business.

(C) No, because the attorney represented the seller, not the buyer.

(D) No, because the attorney's statement constitutes acceptable puffing in negotiations.

Review Rule 4.1 *supra.*

C. Obedience to Law

The lawyer's obligation to compliance with law is a matter both of rules and of law. The Rules forbid a lawyer from assisting a client in a crime or fraud. The lawyer's legal obligations are more complex. The Restatement explains that as a general matter "a lawyer is subject to liability to a client or nonclient when a nonlawyer would be in similar circumstances." § 56. The Restatement explains that "[a] lawyer, like other agents, is not as such liable for acts of a client that make the client liable." But, "[o]n the other hand, a lawyer is not always free of liability to a nonclient for assisting a client's act solely because the lawyer acting in the course of representation." *Id.* at (c). Although the lawyer's potential liability varies under particular laws, Professor Geoffrey C. Hazard, Jr. has offered a helpful test that should alert a lawyer to investigate further her potential liability:

> This analysis indicates the dimensions of the lawyer's duty under criminal and civil law to refrain from "assisting" a client in conduct that is "illegal." A lawyer violates that duty if:
>
> > (1) The client is engaged in a course of conduct that violates the criminal law or is an intentional violation of a civil obligation, other than failure to perform a contract or failure to sustain a good faith claim to property;
> >
> > (2) The lawyer has knowledge of the facts sufficient to reasonably discern that the client's course of conduct is such a violation; and
> >
> > (3) The lawyer facilitates the client's course of conduct either by giving advice that encourages the client to pursue the conduct or indicates how to reduce the risks of detection, or by performing an act that substantially furthers the course of conduct.

Geoffrey C. Hazard, Jr., *How Far May a Lawyer Go in Assisting a Client in Legally Wrongful Conduct?*, 35 U. Miami L. Rev. 669, 682-83 (1981). We will refer to this test later in the section as the "Hazard Test."

[Question 5]

An attorney represented a plaintiff in a civil lawsuit against a defendant who was represented by other counsel. In the course of developing the plaintiff's case, the attorney discovered evidence that she reasonably believed showed that the defendant had committed a crime. The attorney felt that the defendant's crime should be reported to local prosecutorial authorities. After full

disclosure, the plaintiff consented to the attorney's doing so. Without advising the defendant's counsel, the attorney informed the local prosecutor of her findings, but she sought no advantage in the civil suit from her actions. The defendant was subsequently indicted, tried, and acquitted of the offense.

Was the attorney's disclosure to prosecutorial authorities proper?

(A) Yes, because the attorney reasonably believed the defendant was guilty of a crime.

(B) Yes, because the attorney was required to report knowledge of criminal conduct when that knowledge was obtained through unprivileged sources.

(C) No, because the attorney did not advise the other counsel of her disclosure before making it.

(D) No, because the plaintiff's civil suit against the defendant was still pending.

<u>Rule 4.4(a)</u> provides that "[i]n representing a client, a lawyer shall not use means that have no substantial purpose other than to embarrass, delay, or burden a third person, or use methods of obtaining evidence that violate the legal rights of such a person."

AM. BAR ASS'N COMM. ON ETHICS & PROF'L RESPONSIBILITY, *USE OF THREATS OF PROSECUTION IN CONNECTION WITH A CIVIL MATTER*

<u>Formal Op. 92-363 (1992)</u>

In this opinion the Committee reconsiders the propriety of the use or threat of criminal prosecution to gain an advantage for a client in a private civil matter. * * *

There has never been any doubt that a lawyer may represent a client in seeking to enforce a civil claim stemming from a matter that may also involve criminal activity by the opposing party. The closer questions, addressed here, are (1) whether it is proper under the Model Rules for a lawyer to inform the opposing party that the criminal activity will be brought to the attention of the prosecuting authorities if her client's civil claim is not satisfied; and (2) since such a contingent threat necessarily implies an offer to refrain from reporting such conduct in return for satisfaction of the civil claim, whether it is proper for the lawyer to agree, or have the client agree, as part of the settlement of a civil claim, to refrain from reporting the potentially criminal conduct.

The Committee concludes, for reasons to be explained, that the Model Rules do not prohibit a lawyer from using the possibility of presenting criminal charges against the opposing party in a civil matter to gain relief for her client, provided that the criminal matter is related to the civil claim, the lawyer has a well founded belief that both the civil claim and the possible criminal charges are warranted by the law and the facts, and the lawyer does not attempt to exert or suggest improper influence over the criminal process. It follows also that the Model Rules do not prohibit a lawyer from agreeing, or having the lawyer's client agree, in return for satisfaction of the client's civil claim for relief, to refrain from pursuing criminal charges against the opposing party as part of a settlement agreement, so long as such agreement is not itself in violation of law.

In addressing these issues, we will first review the predecessor Model Code's prohibition against threats to present criminal charges and the rationale for that prohibition; then examine the new Model Rules of Professional Conduct, with particular attention to the intention of the drafters in omitting the language of DR 7-105(A) or any counterpart from the Rules; then focus on the limits imposed by the Model Rules on threats to bring criminal charges.

The Express Prohibition of DR 7-105(A)

Disciplinary Rule 7-105(A) of the Model Code expressly prohibited a lawyer from threatening to use, or using, the criminal process solely to enforce a private civil claim: "A lawyer shall not present, participate in presenting, or threaten to present criminal charges solely to obtain an advantage in a civil matter." * * *

The Model Rules * * * omitted both the specific language of DR 7-105(A) and any express counterpart to its prohibition. * * * as redundant or overbroad or both. * * *

The Limitations Imposed by the Model Rules on the Use of Threats of Criminal Prosecution

Model Rule 8.4(b) provides that it is professional misconduct for a lawyer to "commit a criminal act that reflects adversely on the lawyer's honesty, trustworthiness or fitness as a lawyer in other respects." If a lawyer's conduct is extortionate or compounds a crime under the criminal law of a given jurisdiction, that conduct also violates Rule 8.4(b). It is beyond the scope of the Committee's jurisdiction to define extortionate conduct, but we note that the Model Penal Code does not criminalize threats of prosecution where the "property obtained by threat of accusation, exposure, lawsuit or other invocation of official action was honestly claimed as restitution for harm done in the circumstances to which such accusation, exposure, lawsuit or other official action relates, or as compensation for property or lawful services." Model Penal Code, § 223.4 (emphasis added); *see also* § 223.2(3) (threats are not criminally punishable if they are based on a claim of right, or if there is an honest belief that the charges are well founded.) As to the crime of compounding, we also note that the Model Penal Code, § 242.5, in defining that crime, provides that:

> A person commits a misdemeanor if he accepts any pecuniary benefit in consideration of refraining from reporting to law enforcement authorities the commission of any offense or information relating to an offense. It is an affirmative defense to prosecution under this Section that the pecuniary benefit did not exceed an amount which the actor believed to be due as restitution or indemnification for harm caused by the offense. * * *

Rule 8.4(d) and (e) provide that it is professional misconduct for a lawyer to engage in conduct prejudicial to the administration of justice and to state or imply an ability improperly to influence a government official or agency.

Rule 4.4 (Respect for Rights of Third Persons) prohibits a lawyer from using means that "have no substantial purpose other than to embarrass, delay, or burden a third person...." A lawyer who uses even a well-founded threat of criminal charges merely to harass a third person violates Rule 4.4. *See also* Hazard & Hodes, *supra*, § 4.4:104.

Rule 4.1 (Truthfulness in Statements to Others) imposes a duty on lawyers to be truthful when dealing with others on a client's behalf. A lawyer who threatens criminal prosecution, without any actual intent to so proceed, violates Rule 4.1.

Finally, Rule 3.1 (Meritorious Claims and Contentions) prohibits an advocate from asserting frivolous claims. A lawyer who threatens criminal prosecution that is not well founded in fact and in law, or threatens such prosecution in furtherance of a civil claim that is not well founded, violates Rule 3.1.

While the Model Rules contain no provision expressly requiring that the criminal offense be related to the civil action, it is only in this circumstance that a lawyer can defend against charges of compounding a crime (or similar crimes). A relatedness requirement avoids exposure to the charge of compounding, which would violate Rule 8.4(b)'s prohibition against "criminal act[s] that reflect adversely on the lawyer's honesty, trustworthiness or fitness as a lawyer in other respects." It also tends to ensure that negotiations will be focused on the true value of the civil claim, which presumably includes any criminal liability arising from the same facts or transaction, and discourages exploitation of extraneous matters that have nothing to do with evaluating that claim. Introducing into civil negotiations an unrelated criminal issue solely to gain leverage in settling a civil claim furthers no legitimate interest of the justice system, and tends to prejudice its administration. *See* Rule 8.4(c).

Accordingly, it is the opinion of the Committee that a threat to bring criminal charges for the purpose of advancing a civil claim would violate the Model Rules if the criminal wrongdoing were unrelated to the client's civil claim, if the lawyer did not believe both the civil claim and the potential criminal charges to be well-founded, or if the threat constituted an attempt to exert or suggest improper influence over the criminal process. If none of these circumstances was present, however, the threat would be ethically permissible under the Model Rules.

Implicit in the view of the drafters of the Model Rules that no general prohibition on threats of prosecution is justified is the proposition that such a prohibition would be overbroad, excessively restricting a lawyer from carrying out his or her responsibility to "zealously" assert the client's position under the adversary system. *See* Model Rules Preamble: A Lawyer's Responsibilities. Such a limitation on the lawyer's duty to the client is not justified when the criminal charges are well founded in fact and law, stem from the same matter as the civil claim, and are used to gain legitimate relief for the client. When the criminal charges are well founded in fact and law, their use by a lawyer does not result in the subversion of the criminal justice system that DR 7-105 sought to prevent.

Agreeing to Refrain from Pressing Criminal Charges as Part of the Settlement of a Client's Civil Claim

A threat of criminal prosecution is likely to be of use in advancing a civil claim only if it is accompanied by an offer, explicit or implied, to refrain from instigating the prosecution. Thus it is necessary to address the ethical propriety of a lawyer's offering to refrain from pressing criminal charges in return for favors in a civil matter. Neither the Model Rules nor the predecessor Code expressly prohibits a lawyer from agreeing to refrain from reporting an opposing party's criminal violations as a part of the settlement of a client's civil claim. Although there is no express prohibition against such an agreement, a lawyer must be careful to avoid the criminal offense of compounding a crime, which in turn would violate Rule 8.4(b)'s prohibition against "criminal act[s] that reflect adversely on the lawyer's honesty, trustworthiness or fitness as a lawyer in other respects." As noted above, however, it is an affirmative defense to the crime of compounding that "the pecuniary benefit did not exceed an amount which the actor believed to be due as restitution or indemnification for harm caused by the offense."

The Committee notes that some jurisdictions adopting the Model Rules have chosen to include language almost identical to that of DR 7-105(A). * * * In addition, ethics committees in some states have interpreted the Model Rules as continuing DR 7-105(A)'s explicit prohibition, despite the omission of DR 7-105(A)'s language, or any counterpart, from the Rules. * * *

[Question 6]

An attorney is employed by a client who is a fugitive from justice under indictment for armed robbery. The attorney, after thorough legal research and investigation of the facts furnished by the client, reasonably believes the indictment is fatally defective and should be dismissed as a matter of law. The attorney advised the client of his opinion and urged the client to surrender. The client told the attorney that she would not surrender.

The attorney informed the district attorney that he represented the client and that he had counseled her to surrender but that she refused to follow his advice. The attorney has not advised his client on how to avoid arrest and prosecution and does not know where she is hiding.

Is the attorney subject to discipline if he continues to represent the client?

(A) Yes, because the client is engaging in continuing illegal conduct.

(B) Yes, because the client refused to accept the attorney's advice and surrender.

(C) No, because the attorney is not counseling the client to avoid arrest and prosecution.

(D) No, because the attorney believes the indictment is defective.

Rule 1.2(d) provides that "[a] lawyer shall not counsel a client to engage, or assist a client, in conduct that the lawyer knows is criminal or fraudulent, but a lawyer may discuss the legal consequences of any proposed course of conduct with a client and may counsel or assist a client to make a good faith effort to determine the validity, scope, meaning or application of the law."

The Comment to the Rule explains:

* * *

[9] Paragraph (d) prohibits a lawyer from knowingly counseling or assisting a client to commit a crime or fraud. This prohibition, however, does not preclude the lawyer from giving an honest opinion about the actual consequences that appear likely to result from a client's conduct. Nor does the fact that a client uses advice in a course of action that is criminal or fraudulent of itself make a lawyer a party to the course of action. There is a critical distinction between presenting an analysis of legal aspects of questionable conduct and recommending the means by which a crime or fraud might be committed with impunity.

[10] When the client's course of action has already begun and is continuing, the lawyer's responsibility is especially delicate. The lawyer is required to avoid assisting the client, for example, by drafting or delivering documents that the lawyer knows are fraudulent or by suggesting how the wrongdoing might be concealed. A lawyer may not continue assisting a client in conduct that the lawyer originally supposed was legally proper but then discovers is criminal or fraudulent. The lawyer must, therefore, withdraw from the representation of the client in the matter. *See* Rule 1.16(a). In some cases, withdrawal alone might be insufficient. It may be necessary for the lawyer to give notice of the fact of withdrawal and to disaffirm any opinion, document, affirmation or the like. *See* Rule 4.1.

* * *

[12] Paragraph (d) applies whether or not the defrauded party is a party to the transaction. Hence, a lawyer must not participate in a transaction to effectuate criminal or fraudulent avoidance of tax liability. Paragraph (d) does not preclude undertaking a criminal defense incident to a general retainer for legal services to a lawful enterprise. The last clause of paragraph (d) recognizes that determining the validity or interpretation of a statute or regulation may require a course of action involving disobedience of the statute or regulation or of the interpretation placed upon it by governmental authorities.

* * *

[Question 7]

For many years, Attorney has served as outside counsel to Corp, a corporation. Shortly after a change in management, Attorney discovered what she reasonably believed to be a material misstatement in a document she had drafted that Attorney was about to file on Corp's behalf with a government agency. Attorney advised Corp's Board of Directors that filing the document was probably criminal. However, the Board disagreed that there was any material misstatement and directed Attorney to proceed with the filing. Attorney did so. It later becomes known that the document did indeed include a material misstatement.

Attorney faces:

  (A) no liability.

  (B) discipline.

  (C) potential civil and criminal liability.

  (D) discipline, as well as potential civil and criminal liability.

Review Rules 1.2(d), 1.6(b), and 1.16. Rule 1.13 provides specific guidance for organizational wrongdoing. Rule 1.13(b) explains the general standard:

If a lawyer for an organization knows that an officer, employee or other person associated with the organization is engaged in action, intends to act or refuses to act in a matter related to the representation that is a violation of a legal obligation to the organization, or a violation of law that reasonably might be imputed to the organization, and that is likely to result in substantial injury to the organization, then the lawyer shall proceed as is reasonably necessary in the best interest of the organization. Unless the lawyer reasonably believes that it is not necessary in the best interest of the organization to do so, the lawyer shall refer the matter to higher authority in the organization, including, if warranted by the circumstances to the highest authority that can act on behalf of the organization as determined by applicable law.

Rule 1.13(c) permits disclosure when the lawyer does not succeed in efforts under Rule 1.13(b). It states that "[e]xcept as provided in paragraph (d), if

(1) despite the lawyer's efforts in accordance with paragraph (b) the highest authority that can act on behalf of the organization insists upon or fails to address in a timely and appropriate manner an action, or a refusal to act, that is clearly a violation of law, and

(2) the lawyer reasonably believes that the violation is reasonably certain to result in substantial injury to the organization,

then the lawyer may reveal information relating to the representation whether or not Rule 1.6 permits such disclosure, but only if and to the extent the lawyer reasonably believes necessary to prevent substantial injury to the organization.

Rule 1.13(d) explains that the disclosure allowed under Rule 1.13(c) "shall not apply with respect to information relating to a lawyer's representation of an organization to investigate an alleged violation of law, or to defend the organization or an officer, employee or other constituent associated with the organization against a claim arising out of an alleged violation of law."

Rule 1.13(e) provides that "[a] lawyer who reasonably believes that he or she has been discharged because of the lawyer's actions taken pursuant to paragraphs (b) or (c), or who withdraws under circumstances that require or permit the lawyer to take action under either of those paragraphs, shall proceed as the lawyer reasonably believes necessary to assure that the organization's highest authority is informed of the lawyer's discharge or withdrawal."

Use the Hazard Test on p. 578, *supra*, as the standard for civil and criminal liability. Consider also the following case.

In re AMERICAN CONTINENTAL CORPORATION/LINCOLN SAVINGS AND LOAN SECURITIES LITIGATION

794 F. Supp. 1424 (D. Ariz. 1992)

BILBY, District Judge.

This Opinion describes the basis of this court's rulings by Order of February 14, 1992, on motions for summary judgment filed by parties to these consolidated actions.

* * *

Five separate actions are consolidated before this court. *Sarah B. Shields v. Charles H. Keating, Jr.* (" *Shields* "), a class action on behalf "all persons who purchased securities, stock or debentures, of American Continental Corporation ("ACC") between January 1, 1986 and April 14, 1989," *Shields v. Keating,* No. CV 89-2052 SVW (C.D.Cal.1989) (Order re Class Certification), was transferred to this court by the Judicial Panel on Multidistrict Litigation. The *Shields* Plaintiffs fall into two categories. The majority purchased unsecured subordinated debentures through branch offices of Lincoln Savings & Loan Association ("Lincoln" or "Lincoln Savings"), a wholly owned subsidiary of ACC. Others purchased stock or debentures through broker/dealers. *Shields* alleges the following violations: Section 10(b) of the Securities Exchange Act of 1934 ("Exchange Act") and Rule 10b-5, 15 U.S.C. § 78j(b), 17 C.F.R. 240.10b-5; Section 18 of the Exchange Act, 15 U.S.C. § 78r; the Racketeer Influenced and Corrupt Organizations Act ("RICO"), 18 U.S.C. § 1961; the Arizona Racketeering Act ("AZRAC"), 13 A.R.S. § 13-2301, and; Sections 11 and 12 of the Securities Act of 1933 ("Securities Act"), 15 U.S.C. §§ 77k, 77 l.

Charles Roble v. Arthur Young & Co. (" *Roble* "), a state action on behalf of the same class of securities purchasers, states claims for fraud, negligent misrepresentation, breach of fiduciary duty, and violations of California Corporations Code Sections 1507 and 25401.

Also before the court are federal and state actions on behalf of approximately 100 individual ACC securities purchasers. *Alan H. Yahr v. Lincoln Sav. & Loan Ass'n* (" *Yahr* "). The *Yahr* plaintiffs allege violations of Section 10(b), RICO, negligent misrepresentation, breach of fiduciary duty, conspiracy to breach fiduciary duty, California Corporations Code Section 25401, Sections 11 and 12(2) of the Securities Act, professional negligence, and negligent infliction of emotional distress.

In *Resolution Trust Corp. v. Charles H. Keating, Jr.* (" *RTC v. Keating* "), the Resolution Trust Corporation ("RTC"), as receiver for Lincoln, brings claims under RICO, AZRAC, and various state and common law theories of liability.

Finally, this opinion addresses claims made in *Frey v. Hotel Pontchartrain Ltd. Partnership* ("*Frey*"), in which investors in an ACC-related limited partnership brought claims for securities fraud, RICO, unjust enrichment, and negligent misrepresentation.

* * *

These actions originate from the business dealings of Charles H. Keating, Jr. ("Keating"), former chairman of [American Continental Corporation]. The claims at issue here were brought principally against professionals who provided services to ACC and/or Lincoln Savings. These include * * * Jones, Day, Reavis & Pogue ("Jones Day"), a Cleveland-based law firm and two of its individual partners[.]

* * *

Jones Day, a defendant in *Shields, Roble, RTC v. Keating,* and *Yahr,* focuses its summary judgment motion on an individual opinion letter given in connection with a 1986 registration statement. Jones Day claims this opinion letter was neither false, nor was it written in an expert capacity. Jones Day generally claims that it has not engaged in conduct for which it could be held liable because lawyers are obligated to keep their clients' confidence and to act in a ways that do not discourage their clients from undergoing regulatory compliance reviews.

1. The Record

The record reveals the following facts concerning Jones Day's involvement with ACC and Keating.

Prior to joining Jones Day, defendant William Schilling was director of the FHLBB Office of Examinations and Supervision. In that capacity, he was directly involved in the supervision of Lincoln Savings. During the summer of 1985, he wrote at least one memorandum and concurred in another, expressing serious regulatory concerns about numerous aspects of Lincoln's operations. For example, he wrote:

> [U]nder new management, Lincoln has engaged in several serious regulatory violations. Some of these violations, such as the overvaluation of real estate and failure to comply with Memorandum R-41(b), are the same type of violations that have lead to some of the worst failures in FSLIC's history.

Later in 1985, Schilling was hired by Jones Day to augment its expertise in thrift representation. On January 31, 1986, Schilling and Jones Day's Ron Kneipper flew to Phoenix to solicit ACC's business. ACC retained Jones Day to perform "a major internal audit of Lincoln's FHLBB compliance and a major project to help Lincoln deal with the FHLBB's direct investment regulations."

During the regulatory compliance audit, which Jones Day understood to be a pre-FHLBB examination compliance review, the law firm found multiple regulatory violations. There is evidence that Jones Day knew that Lincoln had backdated files, destroyed appraisals, removed appraisals from files, told appraisers not to issue written reports when their oral valuations were too low, and violated affiliated transaction regulations. Jones Day found that Lincoln did no loan underwriting and no post-closure loan followup to ensure that Lincoln's interests were being protected. Jones Day learned Lincoln had multiple "loans" which were, in fact, joint ventures which violated FHLBB regulations, made real estate loans in violation of regulations, and backdated corporate resolutions which were not signed by corporate officers and did not reflect actual meetings. There is evidence that Jones Day may have tacitly consented to removal of harmful documents from Lincoln files. For example, one handwritten notation on a memorandum memorializing Jones Day's advice not to remove documents from files reads, "If something is devastating, consider it individually." * * *

There is evidence that Jones Day instructed ACC in how to rectify deficiencies so that they would not be apparent to FHLBB examiners. Jones Day attorneys, including Schilling, testified that they told ACC/Lincoln personnel to provide the Jones Day-generated "to do" lists only to the attorneys responsible for rectifying the deficiencies, and to destroy the lists so that FHLB-SF would not find them in the files. For the same reason, Jones Day's regulatory compliance reports to ACC/Lincoln were oral. Jones Day paralegals testified that responsibilities for carrying out the "to do" lists were divided among Jones Day and ACC staff. Jones Day continued this work into the summer of 1986.

The evidence indicates that Jones Day may have been aware that ACC/Lincoln did not follow its compliance advice with respect to ongoing activities. There are material questions of fact concerning the procedures Jones Day used-if any-to ascertain whether their compliance advice was being heeded. The testimony suggests that Jones Day partners knew ACC/Lincoln personnel were preparing loan underwriting summaries contemporaneously with Jones Day's regulatory compliance review, even though the loan transactions had already been closed. Moreover, the evidence reveals that Jones Day attorneys participated in creating corporate resolutions to ratify forged and backdated corporate records.

On April 23, 1986, Jones Day partner Fohrman wrote:

> I received Neal Millard's memo on ACC. In looking at the long list of people involved, it occurred to me that there will be times when individuals may be called upon to render legal services that might require the issuance of opinion letters from Jones, Day. As we all know, we now possess information that could affect the way we write our opinion letters and our actual ability to give a particular opinion may be severely restricted.

However, this large list of individuals may not be aware of knowledge that is held by Messrs. Fein and Schilling. I would suggest that a follow up memo be issued by Ron Fein indicating that any work involving ACC which requires the issuance of opinions, must be cleared by Ron. . . .

Also in April 1986, ACC's Jim Grogan wrote to Jones Day's Kneipper, soliciting a strategy to "sunset" the FHLBB direct investment regulation. Jones Day subsequently made multiple Freedom of Information Act requests to FHLBB in furtherance of a direct investment rule strategy, for which Lincoln was billed. In a September 12, 1986 telephone conversation, Grogan allegedly told Kneipper: "[C]omment letters were great success—FHLBB picked it up 'hook, line and sinker' . . . Charlie wants to do again. . . ."

The record indicates that the concept of selling ACC debentures in Lincoln Savings branches may have originated at an April 9, 1986 real estate syndicate seminar given by Jones Day Defendant Ron Fein. There is evidence that Fein may have contributed to the detailed bond sales program outline, attending to details such as explaining how the sales would work, and insuring that the marketing table was far enough from the teller windows to distinguish between ACC and Lincoln Savings employees. The evidence indicates that Jones Day reviewed the debenture registration statement and prospectus, which is corroborated by Jones Day's billing records. As a result, in January 1987, ACC was able to assure the California Department of Savings & Loan that:

> The process of structuring the bond sales program was reviewed by Kaye, Scholer and Jones Day to assure compliance not only with securities laws and regulations, but also with banking and FSLIC laws and regulations.

Moreover, there is evidence which suggests that political contributions were made on behalf of ACC, in exchange for ACC's consent that Jones Day could "bill liberally." On June 23, 1986, Kneipper memorialized a phone conversation:

> (1) 1:15 p.m. Ron Kessler—in past, firm has given $ amt. to PAC, has premium billed, & PAC contri. to candidate; concern that we're an out of state law firm and that a $# in excess of $5,000.00 would look like an unusual move; Barnett and Kessler have done before; question re whether and how we can get some busi. from GOV. for this.

> (2) 3:40 p.m. Jim Grogan

> Ten tickets at $1,000.00 equals $10,000.00

> Barr wants limits of $5,000.00/contribution

> Agreed that we could bill liberally in future in recognition of this.

At deposition, Kneipper testified that his note—"agreed could bill liberally in recognition for this,"—"is what it appears to be." Jones Day set up an Arizona Political Action Committee ("PAC") specifically for the purpose of making a contribution to an Arizona gubernatorial candidate. The PAC was opened on September 4, 1986 and closed in December, 1986, after the contribution was made.

In June 1986, Jones Day solicited additional work from ACC. Jones Day attorney Caulkins wrote, in part:

> Rick Kneipper reports that ACC is very explicit that it does not care how much its legal services cost, as long as it gets the best. He states that Keating gave him an unsolicited $250,000 retainer to start the thrift work, and sent another similar check also unsolicited in two weeks. On the down side, he reports that he has never encountered a more demanding and difficult client, . . .
>
> It appears to Rick and to me that American Continental is made for us and we for them.

On October 28, 1986, Jones Day provided an opinion letter, required by Item 601(b) of SEC regulation S-K, for inclusion in an ACC bond registration statement. Jones Day's opinion letter stated that the indenture was a valid and binding obligation under California law.

2. Section 10(b), RICO, and Common Law Fraud

Jones Day seeks summary judgment on Plaintiffs' claims under Section 10(b), RICO and common law fraud.

Jones Day contends that it may not be held liable for counseling its client. The line between maintaining a client's confidence and violating the securities law is brighter than Jones Day suggests, however. Attorneys must inform a client in a clear and direct manner when its conduct violates the law. If the client continues the objectionable activity, the lawyer must withdraw "if the representation will result in violation of the rules of professional conduct or other law." Ethical <u>Rule 1.16</u> ("ER"). Under such circumstances, an attorney's ethical responsibilities do not conflict with the securities laws. An attorney may not continue to provide services to corporate clients when the attorney knows the client is engaged in a course of conduct designed to deceive others, and where it is obvious that the attorney's compliant legal services may be a substantial factor in permitting the deceit to continue. * * *

The record raises material questions about whether Jones Day knew of ACC/Lincoln's fraud, but nevertheless provided hands-on assistance in hiding loan file deficiencies from the regulators, offered detailed advice about setting up the bond sales program, carried out a lobbying strategy with respect to the direct investment rule, made political contributions on ACC's behalf, reviewed SEC registration statements and prospectuses, and lent its name to a misleading legal opinion. This evidence raises material questions concerning Section 10(b), RICO, AZRAC, common law fraud and deceit, and violations of Cal.Corp.Code §§ 25401 and 25504.1.

3. Section 11 Liability

Section 11 imposes liability for misleading statements made in connection with registration statements. Jones Day offers two arguments.

a. Statute of Limitations

Actions under Section 11 must be brought within one year from inquiry notice, with a repose of three years. U.S.C. § 77m. The shelf registration containing Jones Day's opinion became effective on November 12, 1986, and the sale of bonds subsequently began on December 2, 1986. Item 512(a)(2) of Regulation S-K provides that a post-effective date amendment to a registration statement is deemed a new registration statement for purposes of Section 11 liability. This court concludes that securities offered by post-effective date amendments are deemed initial bona fide offerings, triggering new limitations periods.

ACC filed post-effective date amendments to the shelf registration in March 1987, May 1987, and April 1988. Thus, the three-year limitations period ended (by respective offerings) in December 1989, March 1990, May 1990, and April 1991. Therefore, only actions based on the first offering are potentially barred. The court holds, however, that because Jones Day knew that it was a potential defendant at least as early as November 1989, these claims may proceed.

b. Expert Status

Jones Day further contends that it cannot be held liable under Section 11 because it did not issue an "expert" opinion. Section 11 applies to misleading statements made by one "whose profession gives authority to statements made by him." 15 U.S.C. § 77 k. Jones Day concedes that its October 28, 1986 opinion letter was required by SEC Regulation S-K, which provides in part:

> (5) *Opinion Re Legality*-(i) An opinion of counsel as to the legality of
> the securities being registered, indicating whether they will, when sold,
> be legally issued, fully paid and non-assessable, and, if debt securities,
> whether they will be binding obligations of the registrant.

SEC Regulation S-K, Item 601( )(5).

The court holds that an attorney who provides a legal opinion used in connection with an SEC registration statement is an expert within the meaning of <u>Section 11</u>. * * *

4. Breach of Fiduciary Duty to Lincoln

a. Statute of Limitations

Jones Day contends that claims for breach of fiduciary duty, brought by the RTC, are time-barred. RTC contends that its claims were preserved until the conservatorship was imposed.

Under the theory of adverse domination, the limitations period on a corporation's cause of action is tolled while wrongdoers control the corporation. * * * In this instance, ACC/Lincoln management would not have brought claims on behalf of ACC/Lincoln, for it would have brought their own misconduct to light. Furthermore, the court finds material questions as to whether Jones Day knowingly assisted in ACC's alleged fraud. Accordingly, it is equitable to toll the statute of limitations on Lincoln's behalf.

b. Validity of Claims

An attorney who represents a corporation has a duty to act in the corporation's best interest when confronted by adverse interests of directors, officers, or corporate affiliates. It is not a defense that corporate representation often involves the distinct interests of affiliated entities. Attorneys are bound to act when those interests conflict. There are genuine questions as to whether Jones Day should have sought independent representation for Lincoln. * * *

Moreover, where a law firm believes the management of a corporate client is committing serious regulatory violations, the firm has an obligation to actively discuss the violative conduct, urge cessation of the activity, and withdraw from representation where the firm's legal services may contribute to the continuation of such conduct. Jones Day contends that it would have been futile to act on these fiduciary obligations because those controlling ACC/Lincoln would not have responded. Client wrongdoing, however, cannot negate an attorney's fiduciary duty. Moreover, the evidence reveals that attorney advice influenced ACC/Lincoln's conduct in a variety of ways. Accordingly, summary judgment as to this claim is denied.

5. Professional Negligence Claims

Jones Day issued an opinion letter that was included with ACC's 1986 shelf registration statement. California authority provides that independent public accountants have a duty to those who are foreseeably injured from representations made in connection with publicly held corporations. While this duty does not extend to confidential advice which an attorney gives to its clients, it would apply where an attorney issues an SEC opinion letter to the public. * * *

Accordingly, a question of fact remains as to whether the *Yahr* Plaintiffs, who purchased bonds issued pursuant to the November, 1986 shelf registration and amendments, were injured by the Jones Day opinion letter.

* * *

CONCLUSION

Accordingly, this Memorandum Opinion affirms the court's Order of February 14, 1992 granting and denying summary judgment. * * *

> **FYI**
>
> Jones Day settled the case for $24 million. *See* Alison Leigh Cowan, *Big Law and Auditing Firms to Pay Millions in S.&L. Suit*, N.Y. Times, Mar. 31, 1992, at A1.

After the decision in American Continental Corporation, *supra*, the United States Supreme Court held that private plaintiffs could not sue for aiding and abetting liability under Section 10(b). *Central Bank v. First Interstate Bank*, 511 U.S. 164 (1994). Such liability may still be available under state tort and regulatory causes of action. *See, e.g., Oster v. Kirschner*, 2010 WL 2650532 (N.Y.A.D.) (holding that plaintiffs had properly pleaded claims against law firm for aiding and abetting client engaged in Ponzi scheme under both tort law and state regulatory law).

[Question 8]

L&C represents S&L, a savings and loan, in defending against Government Regulator's investigation. Associate brings to Partner's attention that a board resolution previously filed with Government Regulator had been back-dated to give the appearance of contemporaneous board approval of a particular transaction. Associate urges disclosure. Based upon review of the relevant law and rules, which are not clear, Partner decides against disclosure and instructs Associate not to disclose. Partner and Associate make arguments to Government Regulator predicated on the veracity of the particular board resolution. It is later determined that both the law and rules required disclosure of the back-dating to the government. Which one of the following is true:

(A) Partner and Associate face discipline but not liability.

(B) Partner and Associate face liability but not discipline.

(C) Partner and Associate face both discipline and liability.

(D) **Partner faces discipline and liability; Associate faces liability only.**

(E) **Partner faces liability only; Associate faces discipline and liability.**

Review the materials provided following Question 7 *supra*.

Under Rule 5.2, all lawyers are "bound by the Rules of Professional Conduct notwithstanding that the lawyer acted at the direction of another person." Nonetheless, Rule 5.2(b) provides that "[a] subordinate lawyer does not violate the Rules of Professional Conduct if that lawyer acts in accordance with a supervisory lawyer's reasonable resolution of an arguable question of professional duty."

Under Rule 5.1(b), a supervising lawyer "shall make reasonable efforts to ensure that the [supervised] lawyer conforms to the Rules[.]"

Rule 5.1(c) makes a lawyer:

responsible for another lawyer's violation of the Rules * * * if:

(1) the lawyer orders or, with knowledge of the specific conduct, ratifies the conduct involved; or

(2) the lawyer is a partner or has comparable managerial authority in the law firm in which the other lawyer practices, or has direct supervisory authority over the other lawyer, and knows of the conduct at a time when its consequences can be avoided or mitigated but fails to take reasonable remedial action.

[Question 9]

Lincoln & Center ("L&C") wrote an opinion letter for a transaction between Ronen Corp & Serenity, a partnership. A key issue was whether Serenity was independent of Ronen, which required that at least 3% of its equity was independent of Ronen. L&C did not investigate the independent investors, but if it had it would have discovered that they were paper entities lacking in capital. The deal is later found to be unlawful.

L&C potentially faces:

(A) **sanctions under the Sarbanes-Oxley regulations.**

(B) **sanctions under Sarbanes Oxley regulations and discipline under the Rules.**

(C) **discipline under the Rules.**

(D) **none of the above.**

Review the rules and materials for Question 8, *supra*, as well as Rule 1.1. and the Sarbanes-Oxley regulations *infra*.

Remember that Rule 1.1 requires a lawyer to "provide competent representation to a client. Competent representation requires the legal knowledge, skill, thoroughness and preparation reasonably necessary for the representation."

The Comment explains that:

[5] Competent handling of a particular matter includes inquiry into and analysis of the factual and legal elements of the problem, and use of methods and procedures meeting the standards of competent practitioners. It also includes adequate preparation. The required attention and preparation are determined in part by what is at stake; major litigation and complex transactions ordinarily require more extensive treatment than matters of lesser complexity and consequence. * * *

Professor Thomas D. Morgan has noted that "[r]egulatory solutions to problems thought to exist at Enron—and problems thought to have contributed to contemporaneous collapses of companies such as WorldCom and Global Crossing—are found in the Sarbanes-Oxley Act of 2002 (the "Act") and the Final Rules that the statute required the SEC to promulgate." Thomas D. Morgan, *Sarbanes-Oxley: A Complication, Not A Contribution, In the Effort to Improve Corporate Lawyers' Professional Conduct*, 17 Geo. J. Legal Ethics 1, 1-2 (2003). Following are lawyer regulations promulgated pursuant to the Act.

SARBANES-OXLEY REGULATIONS,

17 C.F.R. § 205.3

(a) Representing an issuer. An attorney appearing and practicing before the Commission in the representation of an issuer owes his or her professional and ethical duties to the issuer as an organization. That the attorney may work with and advise the issuer's officers, directors, or employees in the course of representing the issuer does not make such individuals the attorney's clients.

(b) Duty to report evidence of a material violation.

(1) If an attorney, appearing and practicing before the Commission in the representation of an issuer, becomes aware of evidence of a material violation by the issuer or by any officer, director, employee, or agent of the issuer, the attorney shall report such evidence to the issuer's chief legal officer (or the equivalent thereof) or to both the issuer's chief legal officer and its chief executive officer (or the equivalents thereof) forthwith. By communicating such information to the issuer's officers or directors, an attor-

ney does not reveal client confidences or secrets or privileged or otherwise protected information related to the attorney's representation of an issuer.

(2) The chief legal officer (or the equivalent thereof) shall cause such inquiry into the evidence of a material violation as he or she reasonably believes is appropriate to determine whether the material violation described in the report has occurred, is ongoing, or is about to occur. If the chief legal officer (or the equivalent thereof) determines no material violation has occurred, is ongoing, or is about to occur, he or she shall notify the reporting attorney and advise the reporting attorney of the basis for such determination. Unless the chief legal officer (or the equivalent thereof) reasonably believes that no material violation has occurred, is ongoing, or is about to occur, he or she shall take all reasonable steps to cause the issuer to adopt an appropriate response, and shall advise the reporting attorney thereof. In lieu of causing an inquiry under this paragraph (b), a chief legal officer (or the equivalent thereof) may refer a report of evidence of a material violation to a qualified legal compliance committee under paragraph (c)(2) of this section if the issuer has duly established a qualified legal compliance committee prior to the report of evidence of a material violation.

(3) Unless an attorney who has made a report under paragraph (b)(1) of this section reasonably believes that the chief legal officer or the chief executive officer of the issuer (or the equivalent thereof) has provided an appropriate response within a reasonable time, the attorney shall report the evidence of a material violation to:

(i) The audit committee of the issuer's board of directors;

(ii) Another committee of the issuer's board of directors consisting solely of directors who are not employed, directly or indirectly, by the issuer and are not, in the case of a registered investment company, "interested persons" as defined in section 2(a)(19) of the Investment Company Act of 1940 (15 U.S.C. 80a-2(a)(19) (if the issuer's board of directors has no audit committee); or

(iii) The issuer's board of directors (if the issuer's board of directors has no committee consisting solely of directors who are not employed, directly or indirectly, by the issuer and are not, in the case of a registered investment company, "interested persons" as defined in section 2(a)(19) of the Investment Company Act of 1940 (15 U.S.C. 80a-2(a)(19)).

(4) If an attorney reasonably believes that it would be futile to report evidence of a material violation to the issuer's chief legal officer and chief executive officer (or the equivalents thereof) under paragraph (b)(1) of

this section, the attorney may report such evidence as provided under paragraph (b)(3) of this section.

(5) An attorney retained or directed by an issuer to investigate evidence of a material violation reported under paragraph (b)(1), (b)(3), or (b)(4) of this section shall be deemed to be appearing and practicing before the Commission. Directing or retaining an attorney to investigate reported evidence of a material violation does not relieve an officer or director of the issuer to whom such evidence has been reported under paragraph (b)(1), (b)(3), or (b)(4) of this section from a duty to respond to the reporting attorney.

(6) An attorney shall not have any obligation to report evidence of a material violation under this paragraph (b) if:

(i) The attorney was retained or directed by the issuer's chief legal officer (or the equivalent thereof) to investigate such evidence of a material violation and:

(A) The attorney reports the results of such investigation to the chief legal officer (or the equivalent thereof); and

(B) Except where the attorney and the chief legal officer (or the equivalent thereof) each reasonably believes that no material violation has occurred, is ongoing, or is about to occur, the chief legal officer (or the equivalent thereof) reports the results of the investigation to the issuer's board of directors, a committee thereof to whom a report could be made pursuant to paragraph (b)(3) of this section, or a qualified legal compliance committee; or

(ii) The attorney was retained or directed by the chief legal officer (or the equivalent thereof) to assert, consistent with his or her professional obligations, a colorable defense on behalf of the issuer (or the issuer's officer, director, employee, or agent, as the case may be) in any investigation or judicial or administrative proceeding relating to such evidence of a material violation, and the chief legal officer (or the equivalent thereof) provides reasonable and timely reports on the progress and outcome of such proceeding to the issuer's board of directors, a committee thereof to whom a report could be made pursuant to paragraph (b)(3) of this section, or a qualified legal compliance committee.

(7) An attorney shall not have any obligation to report evidence of a material violation under this paragraph (b) if such attorney was retained or directed by a qualified legal compliance committee:

(i) To investigate such evidence of a material violation; or

(ii) To assert, consistent with his or her professional obligations, a colorable defense on behalf of the issuer (or the issuer's officer, director, employee, or agent, as the case may be) in any investigation or judicial or administrative proceeding relating to such evidence of a material violation.

(8) An attorney who receives what he or she reasonably believes is an appropriate and timely response to a report he or she has made pursuant to paragraph (b)(1), (b)(3), or (b)(4) of this section need do nothing more under this section with respect to his or her report.

(9) An attorney who does not reasonably believe that the issuer has made an appropriate response within a reasonable time to the report or reports made pursuant to paragraph (b)(1), (b)(3), or (b)(4) of this section shall explain his or her reasons therefor to the chief legal officer (or the equivalent thereof), the chief executive officer (or the equivalent thereof), and directors to whom the attorney reported the evidence of a material violation pursuant to paragraph (b)(1), (b)(3), or (b)(4) of this section.

(10) An attorney formerly employed or retained by an issuer who has reported evidence of a material violation under this part and reasonably believes that he or she has been discharged for so doing may notify the issuer's board of directors or any committee thereof that he or she believes that he or she has been discharged for reporting evidence of a material violation under this section.

(c) Alternative reporting procedures for attorneys retained or employed by an issuer that has established a qualified legal compliance committee.

(1) If an attorney, appearing and practicing before the Commission in the representation of an issuer, becomes aware of evidence of a material violation by the issuer or by any officer, director, employee, or agent of the issuer, the attorney may, as an alternative to the reporting requirements of paragraph (b) of this section, report such evidence to a qualified legal compliance committee, if the issuer has previously formed such a committee. An attorney who reports evidence of a material violation to such a qualified legal compliance committee has satisfied his or her obligation to report such evidence and is not required to assess the issuer's response to the reported evidence of a material violation.

(2) A chief legal officer (or the equivalent thereof) may refer a report of evidence of a material violation to a previously established qualified legal

compliance committee in lieu of causing an inquiry to be conducted under paragraph (b)(2) of this section. The chief legal officer (or the equivalent thereof) shall inform the reporting attorney that the report has been referred to a qualified legal compliance committee. Thereafter, pursuant to the requirements under § 205.2(k), the qualified legal compliance committee shall be responsible for responding to the evidence of a material violation reported to it under this paragraph (c).

(d) Issuer confidences.

(1) Any report under this section (or the contemporaneous record thereof) or any response thereto (or the contemporaneous record thereof) may be used by an attorney in connection with any investigation, proceeding, or litigation in which the attorney's compliance with this part is in issue.

(2) An attorney appearing and practicing before the Commission in the representation of an issuer may reveal to the Commission, without the issuer's consent, confidential information related to the representation to the extent the attorney reasonably believes necessary:

(i) To prevent the issuer from committing a material violation that is likely to cause substantial injury to the financial interest or property of the issuer or investors;

Practice Pointer

Remember that you can comply with the Rules and still face potential liability under law. In the Savings and Loan scandals, for example, the disciplinary authorities expressly cleared the lawyers at Kaye Scholer of any disciplinary violations. William H. Simon, *The Kaye Scholer Affair: The Lawyer's Duty of Candor and the Bar's Temptations of Evasion and Apology*, 23 Law & Soc. Inquiry 243, 265 (1998). Nonetheless, the firm paid $41 million to the government and $20 million to plaintiffs to settle legal claims arising from the same conduct. Alison Leigh Cowan, *Big Law and Auditing Firms to Pay Millions in S.&L. Suit*, N.Y. Times, Mar. 31, 1992, at A1.

(ii) To prevent the issuer, in a Commission investigation or administrative proceeding from committing perjury, proscribed in 18 U.S.C. 1621; suborning perjury, proscribed in 18 U.S.C. 1622; or committing any act proscribed in 18 U.S.C. 1001 that is likely to perpetrate a fraud upon the Commission; or

(iii) To rectify the consequences of a material violation by the issuer that caused, or may cause, substantial injury to the financial interest or property of the issuer or investors in the furtherance of which the attorney's services were used.

D. National Security and Obedience to Law

After the 9/11 attack, national security concerns became more significant to the practice of law. The criminal conviction of Lynne Stewart is perhaps the most famous case of a lawyer punished for violating the criminal law while representing a client convicted of terrorism.

UNITED STATES v. STEWART

590 F.3d 93 (2009)

SACK, Circuit Judge:

Defendants Lynne Stewart, Mohammed Yousry, and Ahmed Abdel Sattar appeal from judgments of conviction of the United States District Court for the Southern District of New York (John G. Koeltl, Judge) for various crimes arising from their contacts with and behavior relating to government restrictions on communications and other contacts with Sheikh Omar Ahmad Ali Abdel Rahman. Rahman is serving a life sentence in a maximum security prison for terrorism-related crimes of seditious conspiracy, solicitation of murder, solicitation of an attack on American military installations, conspiracy to murder, and a conspiracy to bomb. He is subject to "Special Administrative Measures" ("SAMs") restricting his ability to communicate with persons outside of the prison in which he is incarcerated so as to prevent him from continuing to lead terrorist organizations and their members. The government cross-appeals from the defendants' sentences.

* * *

We affirm the judgments of conviction. We also affirm the sentences of Yousry and Sattar. We remand the case, however, with respect to the sentence of Stewart, and also with respect to the sentences of Yousry and Sattar in light of the resentencing of Stewart. * * *

The SAMs

In October 1995, Sheikh Omar Ahmad Ali Abdel Rahman was convicted of a variety of terrorism-related crimes in the United States District Court for the Southern District of New York. * * * The crimes of conviction included soliciting the murder of Egyptian President Hosni Mubarak while he was visiting New York City; attacking American military installations; conspiring to murder President Mubarak; conspiring to bomb the World Trade Center in 1993, which succeeded; conspiring subsequently to bomb various structures in New York City, including bridges, tunnels, and the federal building containing the New York office of the Federal Bureau of Investigation ("FBI"), which did not succeed; and conspiring to commit crimes of sedition. * * * For these crimes, Abdel Rahman was sentenced to be incarcerated for the remainder of his life. * * * Following his conviction and appeal therefrom,

Abdel Rahman's legal team focused on two goals: improving his conditions of confinement, and obtaining his transfer from prison in the United States to Egypt.

* * * The Bureau of Prisons, following Abdel Rahman's remand to its custody in August 1997, imposed severely restrictive SAMs upon him. They were designed to prevent him from directing or facilitating yet more violent acts of terrorism from his prison cell. The SAMs have been renewed, and sometimes modified, every 120 days since they were first imposed.

The May 11, 1998, SAMs applicable to Abdel Rahman "prohibited [him] from having contact with ... others (except as noted in this document) that could foreseeably result in [his] communicating information (sending or receiving) that could circumvent the SAM intent of significantly limiting [his] ability to communicate (send or receive) terrorist information." * * * To enforce this general prohibition, the measures * * * limited his telephone contacts solely to his attorneys of record and his wife * * * and prevented matters discussed in those calls from being "divulged in any manner to any third party[.]"* * * On the condition that his attorneys would not divulge any information to third parties, Abdel Rahman was permitted to communicate with his legal team by telephone, * * * mail, * * * and in person, * * * with fewer restrictions than with other persons. * * *

Subsequent versions of the SAMs retained similar prohibitions and screening mechanisms including the prohibition against communications with the news media. * * * They retained similar provisions regarding legal communications, and incorporated provisions requiring Abdel Rahman's attorneys to sign affirmations acknowledging their receipt of the version of the SAMs in effect. * * * By virtue of those affirmations, counsel agreed to abide by the terms of SAMs then in effect. * * *

Stewart repeatedly executed such statements. * * *

The Visits to Abdel Rahman

Sometime in 1997, more than three years after Abdel Rahman was taken into federal custody, a faction of al-Gama'a declared a unilateral "cease-fire," i.e., a halting of violent operations, in Egypt. When the cease-fire was first announced, Abdel Rahman was understood to support it.

In November 1997, despite the cease-fire, a group associated with al-Gama'a attacked, killed, and mutilated the bodies of more than sixty tourists, guides, and guards at the Hatshepsut Temple in Luxor, Egypt. Rifa'i Taha Musa ("Taha")-a military leader of al-Gama'a, a follower of Abdel Rahman, and an unindicted co-conspirator herein-was involved in the incident. Alaa Abdul Raziq Atia ("Atia"), later a leader of al-Gama'a's military wing in Egypt, was also involved in the killings. Al-Gama'a later claimed responsibility for the attack and demanded Abdel Rahman's release from prison in the United States.

In January 1998, Abdel Rahman was assigned by the Bureau of Prisons to the Federal Medical Center in Rochester, Minnesota ("FMC Rochester"). In March 1999, Stewart and Yousry visited him there. Prior to the visit, Stewart signed and delivered to the United States Attorney's Office for the Southern District of New York a document in which she affirmed, under penalty of perjury, that she would abide by the SAMs imposed by the Bureau of Prisons on Abdel Rahman.

At about this time, defendant Sattar was in contact with members of al-Gama'a, who were divided over their support for what remained of the cease-fire. Pro-cease-fire and anti-cease-fire factions developed, and members of the organization wanted Abdel Rahman to take a position on the matter. To that end, several wrote messages addressed to Abdel Rahman, which they sent to Sattar for delivery to Abdel Rahman. Sattar gave the messages to Stewart and Yousry, who surreptitiously brought the messages with them to Abdel Rahman during a subsequent visit in May 2000.

Yousry read the messages to Abdel Rahman during the visit, and Abdel Rahman dictated to Yousry responses to some of them. Yousry and Stewart then smuggled the responses out of FMC Rochester among their legal papers, and sent them to Sattar. As directed by Abdel Rahman, Sattar informed various members of al-Gama'a that Abdel Rahman was willing to reconsider the effectiveness of the cease-fire and had rejected the associated idea that al-Gama'a should form a political party in Egypt.

News of Abdel Rahman's purported position spread. But some members of the media in the Middle East expressed skepticism about the veracity of Sattar's representations, questioning whether they in fact came from Abdel Rahman or whether Sattar had fabricated them himself. To refute those reports, Sattar and Yousry asked one of Abdel Rahman's lawyers, former United States Attorney General Ramsey Clark, to tell a reporter for an Arabic-language newspaper that Abdel Rahman opposed al-Gama'a's formation of a political party. Clark, they thought, would be perceived as more authoritative than Sattar. Clark eventually agreed to talk to the reporter. He told the reporter that "[t]he Sheikh has said he believes that the formation of a new political party to engage in politics in Egypt at this time is ... not correct and should not be done." * * *

In September 1999, Farid Kidwani, the then-leader of al-Gama'a's military wing, was killed along with three other members of the group in a shootout with Egyptian police. Kidwani's death precipitated further tension and debate within al-Gama'a regarding the advisability and efficacy of the cease-fire.

Taha sent another message to Sattar to be relayed to Abdel Rahman urging Abdel Rahman to support the termination of the cease-fire and noting that Taha and his associates needed a "powerful word" from Abdel Rahman to achieve this goal.

Taha told Sattar that such support from Abdel Rahman would "strengthen me among the brothers." Sattar agreed to send the message to Abdel Rahman and prepared a letter to Abdel Rahman for that purpose. In mid-September 1999, Clark and Yousry surreptitiously took the letter, along with newspaper articles relating to the killing of Kidwani in Egypt, with them during a visit to Abdel Rahman in FMC Rochester. Yousry read the letter and newspaper clippings aloud to Abdel Rahman. From these documents, Abdel Rahman first learned of Kidwani's death.

Abdel Rahman dictated a letter to Yousry in response.

To those against whom war is made, permission is given to fight, because they are wronged (oppressed)-and verily God is most powerful for their aid. . . . The latest thing published in the newspapers was about the Egyptian regime's killing of four members of the Group. This is . . . enough proof that the Egyptian regime does not have the intention to interact with this peaceful Initiative [i.e., the cease-fire] which aims at unification. I therefore demand that my brothers, the sons of [al-Gama'a] do a comprehensive review of the Initiative and its results. I also demand that they consider themselves absolved from it.

* * *

On February 18 and 19, 2000, Yousry and Abdeen Jabara, an Arabic-speaking lawyer and member of Abdel Rahman's legal team, visited Abdel Rahman at FMC Rochester. They brought with them another letter which included another message from Taha, again asking for Abdel Rahman's support for ending the cease-fire. But Jabara would not permit Abdel Rahman to dictate a letter to Yousry in response. And, notwithstanding pressure from Sattar and Taha, Jabara, like Clark before him, refused to issue any public statement regarding Abdel Rahman's position on the matter.

On May 16, 2000, defendant Stewart signed another affirmation that she and her staff would abide by the SAMs. She did not submit that affirmation to the United States Attorney's Office until May 26.

On May 18, 2000, Stewart met with Sattar, who gave her more letters for Abdel Rahman, including another message from Taha yet again seeking Abdel Rahman's approval of an end to the cease-fire. Taha asked Abdel Rahman to take a "more forceful position" regarding the end of the cease-fire and to "dictate some points we can announce in a press conference with Lynne." * * *

On May 19 and 20, 2000, Stewart and Yousry visited Abdel Rahman, taking Sattar's most recent letters with them, including the letter containing the message from Taha. Unbeknownst to them, the government, pursuant to a warrant, videotaped the meetings. Yousry told Abdel Rahman that Abu Sayyaf-an Islamic terrorist group in the Philippines-had taken hostages to be used in bargaining for the release of Abdel Rahman and others. When Yousry explained to Stewart that he was "telling the Sheikh about the Abu Sayyaf group in the Philippines" and how "they took hostages," Stewart replied, "Good for them." * * *

From the beginning of the visit, Stewart was aware of the prison guards' presence. For example, she asked Yousry, "Do they usually sit like this and watch us?" * * * And during this meeting, Stewart and Yousry took overt steps to ensure that the nature of their communication with Abdel Rahman would be concealed from the prison guards. As she suggested to Yousry, they "should give them [i.e., the guards] something to watch." * * * When the guards were standing close to the window of the conference room in which Abdel Rahman, Stewart, and Yousry, were meeting Yousry told Stewart to "look at me and talk a little bit because they are watching us closely." * * * While Yousry read the message to Abdel Rahman, Stewart uttered a meaningless series of phrases to Yousry so that it would appear to an observer as though she was taking part in a three-way conversation: "I am talking to you about . . . him going to have a, uh, chocolate eh . . . heart attack here. . . . Why don't you stop a minute now. And ([Unintelligible "UI"]) say to him that, you know, 'You understood what we are saying, (UI).' " *Id.* As Stewart spoke, Yousry said to Abdel Rahman, "I don't know, Sir, they are standing very close by the glass. . . . Lynne says, (UI) when they look, you look at me a little, talk, then look at the Sheikh." *Id.*

Stewart continued to talk while Yousry read aloud Taha's statement in Sattar's letter. Yousry explained to Abdel Rahman that "Lynne just says anything, [laughing] (UI) Sir." * * * Stewart remarked, "I can get an academy award for it." *Id.*

Stewart and Yousry then had this exchange:

YOUSRY: . . . Lynne, I think you should talk to him because they are looking at me.

STEWART: (UI) there (UI), they, uh, (UI) . . . [she taps Yousry's pad with her pen] uhm, if he finds out what this is, then we're . . . [Laughs.]

YOUSRY: [Laughs] In trouble.

STEWART: [Laughing] Yeah, that's right.

* * *

Stewart and Yousry also took evasive action when a guard appeared to take interest in their conversation. At one point, while Yousry was conversing with Abdel Rahman, Stewart touched Yousry's hand and said "Why don't you stop there and we'll talk a minute urn, the, uh. . . . Ahmed's youngest son needs glasses, did you know that?" * * * Yousry then explained to Abdel Rahman, "Lynne says, stop a little because they are by the glass." * * * Not long afterwards, Stewart tapped with the pen on the paper in front of Yousry and told him to "continue reading this 'cause this is setting up the organizational system around his conditions.'" * * * Yousry continued reading. Stewart then made a series of statements unrelated to the substance of the conversation between Yousry and Abdel Rahman. Yousry kept Abdel Rahman informed of what Yousry and Stewart were doing, noting that "Lynne continues to eh, she's watching them, she's watching them," to which Abdel Rahman replied, "[v]ery good, very good." * * * After Yousry finished reading Taha's message to Abdel Rahman, he returned it to a notebook that he had brought with him and with which he left.

On the second day of the same visit, Abdel Rahman dictated to Yousry, among other things, a letter to an al-Gama'a lawyer who favored the cease-fire, asking him to allow others in al-Gama'a to criticize it, and another to Taha asking him to "escalate the language" of criticism of the cease-fire. * * *

Meanwhile, Stewart and Yousry continued to engage in what Stewart later called "[c]overing noises," * * *, and other tactics designed to obscure the nature of what they were doing. After one such incident, Yousry explained to Abdel Rahman, "[S]he just has to say that in order to break the . . . The people are looking." * * * Stewart told Yousry, "I am making allowances for them looking in at us and seeing me never speaking and writing away here while you talk Arabic." * * * She then directed Yousry to "talk back to me now, because otherwise it doesn't make any sense.... So say something in English. . . ." * * * As Yousry explained to Abdel Rahman, "We are now acting, I talk to her in Arabic, and she responds in English, and they don't understand what is going on." * * *

At the end of the visit, Stewart and Yousry took the Yousry-transcribed responses from Abdel Rahman with them from the prison, and later gave them to Sattar. Sattar then passed them along to Taha and another member of al-Gama'a. Sattar also spoke to various members of al-Gama'a, informing them that Abdel Rahman would have "no objection" to a return to violence. Transcript of Audio Recording of Ahmed Abdel Sattar, Rifa'i Ahmad Taha Musa, and Salah Hashim, May 29, 2000, at 3.

At about this time, Sattar told members of al-Gama'a that Stewart would be making a public statement about Abdel Rahman's views on the cease-fire. Sattar and Stewart first discussed what Stewart would say to the press. Then, on June 13, 2000, Sattar and Stewart spoke to Esmat Salaheddin, a Reuters reporter based in Cairo. Stewart told Salaheddin that Abdel Rahman "is withdrawing his support for the ceasefire that currently exists." Trial Transcript ("Trial Tr.") at 5574, 5617, testimony of Salaheddin. She explained that Abdel Rahman had made the statement from prison two weeks before.

The next day, other Middle Eastern press outlets carried the news that Abdel Rahman had withdrawn his support for the cease-fire. Many noted that for the cease-fire to hold, Abdel Rahman's support was essential.

On June 20, 2000, Stewart participated in a telephone conference with Abdel Rahman. She then sent another statement on Abdel Rahman's behalf via facsimile to Salaheddin, the Reuters reporter in Cairo. The telecopy said, "Everything said in the previous statements is correct" and quoted Abdel Rahman as saying, "I do withdraw my support to the [cease-fire] initiative." Statement for Release, Abdel Rahman, June 20, 2000. Following Stewart's statements on Abdel Rahman's behalf, several members of al-Gama'a began preparations to engage anew in acts of violence.

On October 4, 2000, Sattar and Taha completed a *fatwa* on Abdel Rahman's behalf, imitating his style, "mandating the killing of the Israelis everywhere" and "the killing [of] the Jews wherever they are (UI) and wherever they are found." * * * Sattar sent the *fatwa* to, among others, Atia, who had in the meantime become the military leader of al-Gama'a. Upon receiving the message, Atia began preparing for an attack. But, on October 19, 2000, before Atia could act, the Egyptian authorities raided his hideout, killing him and killing or arresting other al-Gama'a members.

On July 13 and 14, 2001, Stewart again paid a visit to Abdel Rahman at FMC Rochester, having signed a revised affirmation agreeing to abide by the SAMs and having sent the affirmation by facsimile to the United States Attorney's Office for the Southern District of New York on May 7, 2001. Stewart again, with Yousry's assistance and contrary to provisions of the SAMs, surreptitiously brought messages to and from Abdel Rahman.

Procedural History

On April 8, 2002, the defendants were indicted in connection with these and related acts; a superseding indictment was filed on November 19, 2003. On February 10, 2005, a jury found the defendants guilty on all counts in the superseding indictment. Specifically, all three defendants were convicted of conspiring to defraud the United States in violation of 18 U.S.C. § 371 (Count One) by violating SAMs imposed upon Abdel Rahman, and various related offenses. Sattar was convicted of conspiring with Taha, Abdel Rahman, and others to murder persons in a foreign country in violation of 18 U.S.C. § 956 (Count Two), and with soliciting persons to commit crimes of violence-murder and conspiracy to commit murder-in violation of 18 U.S.C. § 373 (Count Three). Stewart and Yousry were convicted of providing and concealing material support to the Count-Two conspiracy, in violation of 18 U.S.C. § 2339A and 18 U.S.C. § 2 (Count Five), and with conspiracy to provide and conceal such support, in violation of 18 U.S.C. § 371 (Count Four). Stewart was also convicted of making false statements in violation of 18 U.S.C. § 1001 (Counts Six and Seven).

On October 16, 2006, * * * the district court sentenced the defendants. *See* Sentencing Transcript of Oct. 16, 2006 * * * Stewart was sentenced to a 28-month term of incarceration to be followed by a two-year term of supervised release and a $500 special assessment [9] * * * .

II. Count One

Each defendant asserts that the evidence admitted at trial was insufficient to support his or her conviction under 18 U.S.C. § 371 for defrauding the United States and obstructing the Department of Justice and the Bureau of Prisons in the administration and enforcement of the SAMs in force with respect to Abdel Rahman. Stewart also argues that the SAMs do not apply to lawyers, and that the district court improperly prevented her from challenging the underlying validity of the SAMs.

A. Sufficiency of the Evidence

In order to establish a conspiracy-to-defraud offense under 18 U.S.C. § 371 as charged in Count One of the indictment, a reasonable jury must have been able to conclude beyond a reasonable doubt "(1) [that the defendants] entered into an agreement (2) to obstruct a lawful function of the government [in this case, the administration and enforcement of the SAMs] (3) by deceitful or dishonest means and (4) at least one overt act in furtherance of the conspiracy." * * * Both the existence of a conspiracy and a given defendant's participation in it with the requisite knowledge and criminal intent may be established through circumstantial evidence.' " * * *

1. Evidence as to Stewart. Stewart argues that her defiance of the SAMs was open, not deceitful. One aspect of her defiance was undoubtedly public-the conveyance of Abdel Rahman's statements regarding the cease-fire and related matters to the Reuters journalist. But we agree with the district court that "[a] reasonable jury could certainly [have found] that Stewart gained access to Abdel Rahman [and thereby the information that she conveyed to the journalist] by deceit and dishonest means." * * * "Without [Stewart's] agreement to abide by the SAMs and the other representations contained in her affirmations, she knew that she would not have been allowed to visit Abdel Rahman," * * * and therefore would not later have been able to defy the regulations openly by publicizing messages on his behalf.

---

9. We are aware of a statement famously attributed to Stewart by, *inter alia,* the *Los Angeles Times,* immediately following her sentencing: "I can do that [time] standing on my head." Ellen Barry, *Terrorist's Lawyer Gets Two-Year Term,* L.A. Times, Oct. 17, 2006, at A12. A fuller purported quotation in the article reads, "I don't think anybody would say that to go to jail for two years is anything to look forward to. But-as some of my clients once put it-I can do that standing on my head." *Id.* Whether Stewart made this statement in full, in part, or not at all, is obviously entirely irrelevant to any of the issues before us.

Stewart insists that she acted with the intent, not to defraud the government, but to "zealously" represent her client. But the jury had a reasonable basis on which to disbelieve this, and to "disbelieve that zealous representation included filing false affirmations, hiding from prison guards the delivery of messages to Abdel Rahman, and the dissemination of responses by him that were obtained through dishonesty." * * * Moreover, even if Stewart acted with an intent to represent her client zealously, a rational jury could nonetheless have concluded that Stewart simultaneously acted with an intent to defraud the government. A genuinely held intent to represent a client "zealously" is not necessarily inconsistent with criminal intent. * * *

B. Propriety of the SAMs

1. Stewart's Argument. Stewart contends that the district court erred by preventing her from challenging the validity of the SAMs as part of her defense. * * *

Stewart might have effectively challenged the SAMs by refusing to sign the affirmations in which she said she would abide by them. She might then have invoked the jurisdiction of the courts by bringing suit on Abdel Rahman's or her own behalf to challenge their validity. She might have argued-as she forcefully does here-that the SAMs interfered with her capacity to effectively represent Rahman. But she did not. Instead, she signed the affirmations. Having chosen that path, she cannot be heard to attack the validity of those measures when called to account for violating them, especially where, as here, her fraudulent and deceptive conduct endangered people's lives.

The district court did not err in preventing Stewart from challenging the validity of the SAMs as part of her defense, and the jury acted within its province when it found that Stewart intentionally and fraudulently subverted them.

* * *

IV. Counts Four and Five

Stewart and Yousry challenge their Count Five convictions for violating 18 U.S.C. § 2339A and 18 U.S.C. § 2 by providing and concealing material support for the Count-Two conspiracy for which Sattar was convicted and their Count Four convictions for conspiracy to provide and conceal such support, in violation of 18 U.S.C. § 371. They argue that the evidencevwas insufficient to support their conviction on either count, and contend that their conduct was constitutionally protected in any event.

* * *

Proof of Material Support to the Conspiracy. Stewart and Yousry * * * assert that they did not provide material support in the form of "personnel" to the Count-

Two conspiracy. A reasonable jury could have concluded otherwise. There was evidence introduced at trial sufficient to support a reasonable juror's inference that Stewart and Yousry helped Abdel Rahman participate covertly in the conspiracy to engage in violence abroad by communicating to members of al-Gama'a and others his withdrawal of support for the cease-fire. Abdel Rahman's instrumental participation-indeed, his leadership-would, as the district court observed, have been unavailable to the Count-Two conspiracy "without the active participation of Stewart and Yousry[.]" * * *

The defendants argue that the government established only that they provided the underlying conspiracy with Abdel Rahman's "pure speech" and therefore did not provide "personnel" within any constitutional interpretation of section 2339A. The government does not deny that section 2339A may not be used to prosecute mere advocacy or other protected speech, but contends that the defendants were prosecuted for criminal actions that did not amount to protected speech.

The dissemination of some of the speech introduced at trial might be viewed as nothing more than the expression of views on the broad political situation in Egypt. For example, in reaffirming that he was withdrawing his support for the cease-fire, Abdel Rahman said that he had "expressed [his] opinion and left the matters to [his] brothers to examine it and study it." * * *

But a reasonable jury could have found, in light of Abdel Rahman's role as "spiritual" leader of al-Gama'a, that his messages were ultimately intended to sway al-Gama'a members to end the cease-fire, and by implication to commit criminal acts of violence. Abdel Rahman's statements were therefore not an expression of opinion, but a call to arms.

The evidence establishes, moreover, more than a one-way broadcast of Abdel Rahman's views. Abdel Rahman's comments were made in direct response to solicitations of his views from other al-Gama'a members who were seeking to effect an end to the cease-fire and to resume violence. In light of the information available to Abdel Rahman at the time, a reasonable jury could have read his statements as tailored to and necessary for al-Gama'a's operations and increased use of violence. Viewed through this lens, Abdel Rahman's statements were not materially different in substance from a crime boss making decisions about his criminal enterprise from prison and ordering a "hit."

* * * *Proof Regarding Knowing or Intentional Provision of Material Support.* Stewart and Yousry argue that the prosecution did not prove the requisite mental state to sustain their convictions. They contend that they were not aware of the existence of the conspiracy charged in Count Two and therefore could not have intended to aid it.

These arguments are unavailing. From the evidence at trial, a reasonable factfinder could have concluded that Stewart and Yousry knew (1) that an active group of people within al-Gama'a including, most notably, Taha, sought to commit violent crimes but were hindered by the cease-fire and by those members of al-Gama'a who sought to adhere to it; (2) that the support of Abdel Rahman-a key leader of the group-was critical to the continued maintenance of the cease-fire; and (3) that, in light of the letters and messages from Taha and Sattar that Yousry read to Abdel Rahman in prison, Abdel Rahman's particular opinion regarding the cease-fire-and not the view of any other person-would be dispositive on the question of whether al-Gama'a members would continue to abide by the cease-fire. A reasonable factfinder could thus have concluded that Yousry and Stewart actively and intentionally facilitated communications between Abdel Rahman and al-Gama'a, in part by engaging in various ruses during the course of their visits to Abdel Rahman, and thereby effectively delivered Abdel Rahman's order to commit violence. Stewart also did so by reaffirming to the press Abdel Rahman's stated withdrawal of support for the cease-fire, thereby dispelling any notion that the message came not from Abdel Rahman himself, but was instead fabricated by members of the pro-violence faction of al-Gama'a.

* * *

V. Counts Six and Seven

Stewart challenges her convictions on Counts Six and Seven for violating the blanket provisions of 18 U.S.C. § 1001, which subjects to criminal sanctions

whoever, in any matter within the jurisdiction of the executive, legislative, or judicial branch of the Government of the United States, knowingly and willfully—

> (1) falsifies, conceals, or covers up by any trick, scheme, or device a material fact;

> (2) makes any materially false, fictitious, or fraudulent statement or representation; or

> (3) makes or uses any false writing or document knowing the same to contain any materially false, fictitious, or fraudulent statement or entry. . . .

18 U.S.C. § 1001(a). Stewart argues that, at worst, she broke a promise, and that the statute criminalizes false statements, not false promises.

We conclude otherwise. On May 16, 2000, Stewart signed an affirmation stating that she would ("shall") abide by the SAMs. On May 26, 2000, Stewart submitted the affirmation to the United States Attorney's Office for the Southern District of New York. On May 7, 2001, Stewart signed a revised affirmation to the same effect and telecopied it to the same office. Before, after, and between executing these affirmations, she helped smuggle messages to and from Abdel Rahman in violation of the SAMs.

Stewart at least thrice affirmed "under the penalties of perjury the truth" of certain statements. The May 16, 2000, statement reads in pertinent part:

> I . . . understand that neither I nor any member of my office shall forward any mail received from inmate Abdel Rahman to a third person. Nor shall I use my meetings, correspondence or phone calls with Abdel Rahman to pass messages between third parties (including, but not limited to, the media) and Abdel Rahman.

* * * In the May 7, 2001, statement, Stewart affirmed:

> I . . . specifically understand that the meetings shall not be for the purpose of presenting statements to the defense team for further dissemination to third parties, including the media. I will only allow the meetings to be used for legal discussion between Abdel Rahman and me. * * *

A reasonable factfinder was entitled to conclude that Stewart affirmed under penalty of perjury that she had the then-present intent to have her actions conform to the terms of the SAMs. From Stewart's smuggling messages to and from Abdel Rahman, the factfinder could conclude that the assertion about her intent was knowingly and willfully false when it was made.

* * *

VII. Propriety of the Sentences

* * * The government's principal argument on appeal is that in light of the crimes of which Stewart stands convicted, her sentence was substantively unreasonable. * * *

Like the district court, we are impressed by the factors that figured in Stewart's modest sentence—particularly her admirable history of providing, at no little personal cost to herself, proficient legal services in difficult cases to those who could not otherwise afford them. We think it noteworthy, moreover, that the last of the acts for which Stewart is being punished occurred a short time before the September 11 attacks on the United States. That carnage might have raised in her, as it surely has in many or most of us, a heightened awareness of and sensitivity to the imminent dangers of terrorism and the possible scope of the deadly capabilities of the terrorists with whom she was dealing.

We also recognize, as did the district court, that the terrorism enhancement may apply to persons who are culpable in substantially different degrees; that Stewart's culpability may well be understood to be less than Sattar's; and that the district court may differentiate between different levels of culpable conduct that nonetheless trigger the same substantial enhancement. Yet Stewart's sentence is strikingly low in light of what the district court correctly described as the "irreducible core of [her] extraordinarily severe criminal conduct," * * * "which was committed over an extended period of time, involved repeated acts of deception, and involve[d] significant planning." * * *

While we will not lightly deem unreasonable a sentence imposed by the judge who has "access to, and greater familiarity with, the individual case and the individual defendant before him than the [Sentencing] Commission or the appeals court," * * * we think that in light of the fact Stewart used her privileged status as a lawyer to facilitate her serious violation of the law, and possibly committed perjury at trial in an attempt to avoid punishment for her conduct, her sentence at least tests those "boundaries."

* * * Stewart argues that she did no more than serve as a zealous advocate for her client. That belief, if indeed she harbored it, gave her no license to violate the law. Stewart's actions tended ultimately and ironically to subvert the same fundamental right of which she took advantage—the constitutional right to counsel—by making it less likely that other incarcerated persons will have the same level of access to counsel that her client was given.

The district court seemed to appreciate that fact, noting that Stewart "abused her position as a lawyer" in committing her crimes. * * * The court did not, however, explain how and to what extent the sentence reflected the seriousness of the crimes of conviction in light of the fact that Stewart was engaged as a member of the bar when she committed them.

The question therefore remains whether, because she was an experienced and dedicated lawyer acting as such when she broke the law in the manner that she did, her punishment should have been greater than it was.

* * * A comparison of Stewart's and Yousry's offense conduct serves to highlight the seriousness of Stewart's crimes and the seemingly modest sentence she received for it. Unlike Yousry, Stewart publicly disseminated "potentially lethal" statements on Abdel Rahman's behalf. Unlike Yousry, Stewart was convicted of making false statements to the government when she agreed to abide by the terms of the SAMs. Unlike Yousry, Stewart was a member of the bar and therefore acting as an officer of the court. * * * She was legally knowledgeable, highly experienced, and politically sophisticated, a lawyer acting in her professional capacity; he was a student working for her and Abdel Rahman as a translator.

Yet Yousry's sentence was 20 months; Stewart's only eight months longer.

* * * Also unlike Yousry, Stewart may well have obstructed justice at trial. The government, supported by substantial evidence, argued that Stewart committed perjury at trial. The district court summarized the argument as follows:

First, the government contends that Ms. Stewart knowingly gave false testimony when she testified that she understood that there was a bubble built into the SAMs whereby the attorneys could issue press releases containing Abdel Rahman's statements as part of their representation of him.

The government also contends that Ms. Stewart testified falsely when she denied knowing who Taha was until learning about him in the course of the trial except for an article that she came across in her representation of Yasir Ahmed.

* * * The court, having thus recited the allegations at sentencing, declined to decide the issue.

As noted, the district court gave two reasons for not making such a finding. First, it concluded that because Stewart's Guidelines calculations had reached the statutory maximum of 360 months, a finding of obstruction of justice would not have changed the calculation. This would be true if the terrorism enhancement had been applied in Stewart's case, but the district court, after determining that Stewart's conduct was in the enhancement's "heartland," may not have applied it. * * * And even were it true, the question of Stewart's perjury is nonetheless relevant to her sentence pursuant to section 3553. Section 3553(a) requires the district court to impose a sentence "sufficient, but not greater than necessary" to, among other things, promote respect for the law. * * * Whether Stewart lied to the jury under oath or upon affirmation at her trial is relevant to whether her sentence was "sufficient" under the circumstances.

The district court's second reason for declining to determine whether Stewart committed perjury during the course of her testimony was that it had determined that a non-Guidelines sentence was "reasonable and most consistent with the factors set forth in Section 3553(a)." * * * But as noted, we think that whether Stewart lied under oath at her trial is directly relevant to whether her sentence was appropriate in light of Section 3553(a). Her willingness as a lawyer knowingly and falsely to affirm her intention to obey the SAMs and then to seek to cover up this knowing violation of the law with perjurious testimony might well, if proven, influence our conclusion as to the propriety of her sentence. Any cover-up or attempt to evade responsibility by a failure to tell the truth upon oath or affirmation at her trial would compound the gravity of her crime.

We conclude that by declining to decide whether Stewart committed perjury or otherwise obstructed justice, the district court procedurally erred.

* * * Noting particularly that the absence of harm was fortuitous and not the result of efforts by Stewart to prevent harm, Judge Walker argues that it was error both procedural and substantive for the district court to use that factor as a basis for downward variance, especially such a large one. The issue is discussed also in Judge Calabresi's opinion. This Court makes no ruling on that issue now, in the circumstances of Stewart's case. We note simply that it is a serious issue to be given consideration by the district court upon reevaluating Stewart's sentence. In view of the fact that the court must resentence, we think it preferable to defer this issue until after it has been reconsidered by the court, upon its consideration of the commentary in the opinions of Judges Walker and Calabresi.

* * * The terrorism enhancement is set forth in section 3A1.4 of the Guidelines.

Terrorism

> (a) If the offense is a felony that involved, or was intended to promote, a federal crime of terrorism, increase by 12 levels; but if the resulting offense level is less than level 32, increase to level 32.

> (b) In each such case, the defendant's criminal history category from Chapter Four (Criminal History and Criminal Livelihood) shall be Category VI.

U.S.S.G. § 3A1.4.

Whether or not the district court applied the terrorism enhancement to Stewart in its Guidelines calculation may be subject to disagreement. Without reaching that issue, we nonetheless note that in light of the facts of this case and the judgments of conviction, which we affirm, the terrorism enhancement plainly applies as a matter of law to the district court's calculation of the applicable Guidelines range, irrespective of whether Stewart's behavior was "atypical" and whether it resulted in death or injury, factors that may (or may not) be employed in rendering the ultimate sentence.

* * *

We therefore remand this matter to the district court for resentencing, in the course of which we direct the court to determine the issue of perjury and if it finds such perjury, to resentence Stewart so as to reflect that finding. The district court should also consider whether Stewart's conduct as a lawyer triggers the special-skill/abuse-of-trust enhancement under the Guidelines, see U.S.S.G. § 3B1.3, and reconsider the extent to which Stewart's status as a lawyer affects the appropriate sentence. Finally, the district court should further consider the overall question whether the sentence to be given is appropriate in view of the magnitude of the offense, which the court itself has explicitly recognized. Although we do not preclude the district court's election to continue to impose a non-Guidelines sentence, we do require that such a sentence, selected after the reconsideration we have directed, begin with the terrorism enhancement and take that enhancement into account. We have serious doubts that the sentence given was reasonable, but think it appropriate to hear from the district court further before deciding the issue.

* * *

CONCLUSION

For the foregoing reasons, we affirm the conviction of Stewart, but remand this cause to the district court for resentencing of Stewart, * * * and resentencing of Sattar or Yousry or both if the district court determines that they should receive different sentences in light of the sentence imposed on Stewart. Inasmuch as the current sentences will remain in effect as to Stewart and Yousry until the district court resentences Stewart-and Sattar or Yousry if it decides to do so-and in light of the fact that we affirm on all issues related to the guilt of all defendants, the district court is directed to order Stewart and Yousry to surrender forthwith to begin serving their terms of incarceration.

Following the Court of Appeals decision, Lynne Stewart gave interviews justifying her actions. To listen to one of those interviews, click here. On remand, Judge Koetl sentenced Stewart to 10 years in prison. He "said postsentencing comments by Ms. Stewart in 2006, including a statement in a television interview that she would do 'it' again and would not 'do anything differently' influenced his decision to give a higher sentence than the one rejected as too light last year by the U.S. Court of Appeals for the Second Circuit." Mark Hamblett, *Stewart Gets a New 10-Year Prison Sentence*, N.Y. L.J. 1, July 16, 2010, at 1.

Food for Thought

Can lawyers legally provide pro bono legal services to an accused terrorist? It depends. Recently, lawyers from the Center for Constitutional Rights and the A.C.L.U. sought to challenge the legality of a reported government order authorizing the assassination of Anwar Al-Awlaki, a Yemeni cleric and United States citizen, whom the United States government has designated as a terrorist. When Al-Awalaki's father asked the civil liberties groups to represent him in contesting the reported assassination order, the groups were "in a Catch-22-like bind: because the government has designated Mr. Awlaki a terrorist, it would be a crime for the lawyers to file a lawsuit challenging the government's attempts to kill him." Charlie Savage, *Lawyers Seeking Terror Suspect's Case Sue U.S.*, N.Y. Times, Aug. 3, 2010, *available at* http://www.nytimes.com/2010/08/04/world/asia/04terror.html?_r=1. The lawyers applied for permission to represent Mr. Al-Awlaki. When they did not receive a response, they "filed a lawsuit challenging a Treasury Department regulation that requires them to obtain permission to provide uncompensated legal service benefiting Mr. Awlaki[.]" *Id.* The Treasury Department then stated that "it would 'work with the A.C.L.U. to ensure that the legal services can be delivered.'" *Id.* One of the lead lawyers in this case is Professor Bill Quigley. He explains his position in *Why We Sued to Represent Muslim Cleric Aulaqi*, Dissident Voice, August 3, 2010, *available at* http://dissidentvoice.org/2010/08/why-we-sued-to-represent-muslim-cleric-aulaqi/.

III. Duties to Lawyers and to the Bar

A lawyer has duties to lawyers and the bar that can trump those owed to the client. These range from limits on communications with a represented party to the obligation to report judge and lawyer misconduct. Some of these duties are absolute trumps, such as the prohibition of agreements restricting the lawyer's practice even when the agreement would benefit the client. Other duties are bounded by duties to the client, such as the reporting duty, which is subject to the lawyer's confidentiality obligations.

A. Represented Party

Before answering Questions 1 and 2, review the material that follows.

[Question 1]

An attorney represented a real estate developer who was trying to buy several properties. The attorney arranged a meeting with an owner of two large parcels of land, hoping to arrange a sale to the developer. When the attorney scheduled this meeting, he neither knew nor asked whether the owner was represented by counsel in the matter. Shortly after the meeting began, the owner disclosed that he had retained counsel to assist in the sale of the two parcels of land, but that his lawyer could not be present that day. He further stated that he would be meeting with his lawyer the next day. The attorney asked the owner if they could talk anyway, and stated that he wouldn't ask the owner to sign anything until his lawyer had a chance to look over anything they discussed.

The owner, an experienced businessman and negotiator, agreed to continue as suggested, and a tentative agreement was soon worked out.

Was the attorney's conduct proper?

(A) Yes, because the owner knowingly agreed to continue the discussions without his own lawyer being present.

(B) Yes, because the attorney did not present the owner with any documents to sign during the meeting.

(C) No, because the attorney negotiated with the owner after learning that the owner was represented by a lawyer in the matter.

(D) No, because the attorney failed to ascertain whether the owner was represented by a lawyer before beginning the negotiation session.

[Question 2]

An attorney represented the plaintiff in a personal injury matter. The attorney had heard that the defendant in the matter was anxious to settle the case and reasonably believed that the defendant's lawyer had not informed the defendant about the attorney's recent offer of settlement. The attorney instructed her nonlawyer investigator to tell the defendant about the settlement offer so that the attorney could be sure that the defendant's lawyer did not force the case to trial merely to increase the defendant's lawyer's fee.

Is the attorney subject to discipline?

(A) Yes, because the defendant was represented by counsel.

(B) Yes, because the attorney was assisting the investigator in the unauthorized practice of law.

(C) No, because the investigator is not a lawyer.

(D) No, because the attorney reasonably believed that the defendant's lawyer was not keeping the defendant informed.

Rule 4.2 governs "communication with person[s] represented by counsel." It states that:

"In representing a client, a lawyer shall not communicate about the subject of the representation with a person the lawyer knows to be represented by another lawyer in the matter, unless the lawyer has the consent of the other lawyer or is authorized to do so by law or a court order."

The Comment explains that Rule 4.2 "contributes to the proper functioning of the legal system by protecting a person who has chosen to be represented by a lawyer in a matter against possible overreaching by other lawyers who are participating in the matter, interference by those lawyers with the client-lawyer relationship and the uncounselled disclosure of information relating to the representation."

Rule 8.4(a) makes it "professional misconduct" for a lawyer to * * * violate or attempt to violate the Rules of Professional Conduct, knowingly assist or induce another to do so, or do so through the acts of another[.]"

Make the Connection

To explore the exception to Rule 4.2 pursuant to "law or a court order," *see* Chapter 7, Part I.E. *infra*.

B. Inadvertent Disclosures

[Question 3]

Lawrence Lawyer receives a fax from Anne Adversary Attorney. Lawrence quickly realizes that Anne has mistakenly sent him a document containing confidential client information. Under the Rules, Lawrence must:

    (A) notify Anne.

    (B) notify Anne and return the document without keeping a copy.

    (C) notify Anne and refuse to read the document.

    (D) read the document without notifying Anne.

<u>Rule 4.4(b)</u> provides that "[a] lawyer who receives a document relating to the representation of the lawyer's client and knows or reasonably should know that the document was inadvertently sent shall promptly notify the sender."

The Comment to Rule 4.4 states:

[2] Paragraph (b) recognizes that lawyers sometimes receive documents that were mistakenly sent or produced by opposing parties or their lawyers. If a lawyer knows or reasonably should know that such a document was sent inadvertently, then this Rule requires the lawyer to promptly notify the sender in order to permit that person to take protective measures. Whether the lawyer is required to take additional steps, such as returning the original document, is a matter of law beyond the scope of these Rules, as is the question of whether the privileged status of a document has been waived. Similarly, this Rule does not address the legal duties of a lawyer who receives a document that the lawyer knows or reasonably should know may have been wrongfully obtained by the sending person. For purposes of this Rule, "document" includes e-mail or other electronic modes of transmission subject to being read or put into readable form.

[3] Some lawyers may choose to return a document unread, for example, when the lawyer learns before receiving the document that it was inadvertently sent to the wrong address. Where a lawyer is not required by applicable law to do so, the decision to voluntarily return such a document is a matter of professional judgment ordinarily reserved to the lawyer. *See* Rules 1.2 and 1.4.

Make the Connection

For further discussion of the mistaken disclosure of confidential information, *see* Chapter 4 *supra*.

Food for Thought

What are the lawyer's ethical duties with regard to metadata? Professor David Hricik and Robert Jueneman explain that "[m]any documents created by software contain far more than the visible text." David Hricik & Robert Jueneman, *The Transmission and Receipt of Invisible Confidential Information*, 15 Prof'l Law., Spring 2004, at 18. This metadata may identify the authors of the document or disclose deleted material. Hricik and Jueneman offer suggestions for minimizing the amount of metadata that lawyers share with their adversaries. But what happens when a lawyer receives a document that includes metadata. Are lawyers required to uncover the metadata or to avoid searching for it? The New York State Bar Professional Ethics Committee has opined that lawyers have a duty to avoid investigating metadata. N.Y. State Bar Ass'n Comm. on Prof'l Ethics, NY Ethical Op. 749, 2001 WL 1890308.

C. Restrictions on Practice

[Question 4]

Attorney Alpha represents Wife in a marriage dissolution proceeding that involves bitterly contested issues of property division and child custody. Husband is represented by Attorney Beta. After one day of trial, Husband, through Beta, made a settlement offer. Because of Husband's intense dislike for Alpha, the proposed settlement requires that Alpha agree not to represent Wife in any subsequent proceeding, brought by either party, to modify or enforce the provisions of the decree. Wife wants to accept the offer, and Alpha believes that the settlement offer made by Husband is better than any award Wife would get if the case went to judgment.

Is it <u>proper</u> for Alpha to agree that Alpha will not represent Wife in any subsequent proceeding?

(A) Yes, because the restriction on Alpha is limited to subsequent proceedings in the same matter.

(B) Yes, if Alpha believes that it is in Wife's best interests to accept the proposed settlement.

(C) No, because the proposed settlement would restrict Alpha's right to represent Wife in the future.

(D) No, unless Alpha believes that Wife's interests can be adequately protected by another lawyer in the future.

Rule 5.6 governs restrictions on a lawyer's practice. Rule 5.6(a) provides that "[a] lawyer cannot agree with other lawyers or a an employer to "restrict[] the right of a lawyer to practice after termination of the relationship, except an agreement concerning benefits upon retirement." Rule 5.6(b) prohibits a lawyer from making "an agreement in which a restriction on the lawyer's right to practice is part of the settlement of a client controversy."

The comment describes the rationale for Rule 5.6(a) as protecting both lawyers' "professional autonomy" and "the freedom of clients to choose a lawyer." This rationale would seem to be the basis for Rule 5.6(b) as well.

D. Reporting Lawyer and Judge Misconduct

The duty to report lawyer misconduct could have been included in the previous section as well as this one. It implicates the lawyer's duties to the legal system, as well as to other lawyers. We include it here because while the duty is helpful to the legal system, it is essential to self-regulation. The Comment to Rule 8.3 explains that "[s]elf-regulation of the legal profession requires that members of the profession initiate disciplinary investigation when they know of a violation of the Rules[.]" Self-regulation is predicated both upon lawyers having expertise that is inaccessible to lay persons and upon lawyers being trustworthy. If lawyers have inaccessible expertise, then only they—and not laypeople—have the ability to identify many instances of professional conduct. If lawyers are trustworthy, then the public can rely on them to enforce their own rules.

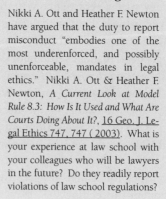

Food for Thought

Nikki A. Ott and Heather F. Newton have argued that the duty to report misconduct "embodies one of the most underenforced, and possibly unenforceable, mandates in legal ethics." Nikki A. Ott & Heather F. Newton, *A Current Look at Model Rule 8.3: How Is It Used and What Are Courts Doing About It?*, 16 Geo. J. Legal Ethics 747, 747 (2003). What is your experience at law school with your colleagues who will be lawyers in the future? Do they readily report violations of law school regulations?

[Question 5]

Anne Attorney and Lawrence Lawyer have been friends since their days at law school classmates. Recently, when she has met with him during the work day, she has smelled alcohol on his breath. She has noticed him being nasty and abusive to colleagues, adversary lawyers, and even, on occasion, to clients. She recently litigated a case against him where his performance failed to meet even minimum standards as a matter of competence. Anne then recommended to Larry that he seek help from the bar's lawyer assistance program for his alcohol problem. Larry angrily refused. Worried that any further action might jeopardize her longstanding friendship with Larry, Anne does nothing. Is Anne subject to discipline?

(A) Yes, because Anne failed to inform the appropriate authorities about Larry's conduct.

(B) Yes, unless because Anne did not ask the client in her recent case whether the client wanted her to inform the appropriate authorities.

(C) No, because Anne suggested Larry seek help from a lawyer assistance program.

(D) No, because Anne reasonably feared that Larry would end their friendship if she reported him.

As noted above, Rule 8.3 governs the lawyer's duty to report misconduct. Rule 8.3(a) requires a lawyer to "inform the appropriate professional authority" when the lawyer "knows that another lawyer has committed a violation of the Rules of Professional Conduct that raises a substantial question as to that lawyer's honesty, trustworthiness or fitness as a lawyer in other respects[.]" Rule 8.3(c) makes clear that "[t]his Rule does not require disclosure of information otherwise protected by Rule 1.6 or information gained by a lawyer or judge while participating in an approved lawyers assistance program."

In re HIMMEL

533 N.E.2d 790 (Ill. 1988)

Justice STAMOS delivered the opinion of the court:

This is a disciplinary proceeding against respondent, James H. Himmel. On January 22, 1986, the Administrator of the Attorney Registration and Disciplinary Commission (the Commission) filed a complaint with the Hearing Board, alleging that respondent violated Rule 1-103(a) of the Code of Professional Responsibility (the Code) * * * by failing to disclose to the Commission information concerning attorney misconduct. On October 15, 1986, the Hearing Board found that respondent had violated the rule and recommended that respondent be reprimanded. The Administrator filed exceptions with the Review Board. The Review Board issued its report on July 9, 1987, finding that respondent had not violated a disciplinary rule and recommending dismissal of the complaint. We granted the Administrator's petition for leave to file exceptions to the Review Board's report and recommendation. * * *

We will briefly review the facts, which essentially involve three individuals: respondent, James H. Himmel, licensed to practice law in Illinois on November 6, 1975; his client, Tammy Forsberg, formerly known as Tammy McEathron; and her former attorney, John R. Casey.

The complaint alleges that respondent had knowledge of John Casey's conversion of Forsberg's funds and respondent failed to inform the Commission of this misconduct. The facts are as follows.

In October 1978, Tammy Forsberg was injured in a motorcycle accident. In June 1980, she retained John R. Casey to represent her in any personal injury or property damage claim resulting from the accident. Sometime in 1981, Casey negotiated a settlement of $35,000 on Forsberg's behalf. Pursuant to an agreement between Forsberg and Casey, one-third of any monies received would be paid to Casey as his attorney fee.

In March 1981, Casey received the $35,000 settlement check, endorsed it, and deposited the check into his client trust fund account. Subsequently, Casey converted the funds.

Between 1981 and 1983, Forsberg unsuccessfully attempted to collect her $23,233.34 share of the settlement proceeds. In March 1983, Forsberg retained respondent to collect her money and agreed to pay him one-third of any funds recovered above $23,233.34.

Respondent investigated the matter and discovered that Casey had misappropriated the settlement funds. In April 1983, respondent drafted an agreement in which Casey would pay Forsberg $75,000 in settlement of any claim she might have against him for the misappropriated funds. By the terms of the agreement, Forsberg agreed not to initiate any criminal, civil, or attorney disciplinary action against Casey. This agreement was executed on April 11, 1983. Respondent stood to gain $17,000 or more if Casey honored the agreement. In February 1985, respondent filed suit against Casey for breaching the agreement, and a $100,000 judgment was entered against Casey. If Casey had satisfied the judgment, respondent's share would have been approximately $25,588.

The complaint stated that at no time did respondent inform the Commission of Casey's misconduct. According to the Administrator, respondent's first contact with the Commission was in response to the Commission's inquiry regarding the lawsuit against Casey.

In April 1985, the Administrator filed a petition to have Casey suspended from practicing law because of his conversion of client funds and his conduct involving moral turpitude in matters unrelated to Forsberg's claim. Casey was subsequently disbarred on consent on November 5, 1985.

A hearing on the complaint against the present respondent was held before the Hearing Board of the Commission on June 3, 1986. In its report, the Hearing Board noted that the evidence was not in dispute. The evidence supported the allegations in the complaint and provided additional facts as follows.

Before retaining respondent, Forsberg collected $5,000 from Casey. After being retained, respondent made inquiries regarding Casey's conversion, contacting the insurance company that issued the settlement check, its attorney, Forsberg, her mother, her fiance and Casey. Forsberg told respondent that she simply wanted her money back and specifically instructed respondent to take no other action. Because of respondent's efforts, Forsberg collected another $10,400 from Casey. Respondent received no fee in this case.

The Hearing Board found that respondent received unprivileged information that Casey converted Forsberg's funds, and that respondent failed to relate the information to the Commission in violation of Rule 1-103(a) of the Code. The Hearing Board noted, however, that respondent had been practicing law for 11 years, had no prior record of any complaints, obtained as good a result as could be expected in the case, and requested no fee for recovering the $23,233.34. Accordingly, the Hearing Board recommended a private reprimand.

Upon the Administrator's exceptions to the Hearing Board's recommendation, the Review Board reviewed the matter. The Review Board's report stated that the client had contacted the Commission prior to retaining respondent and, therefore, the Commission did have knowledge of the alleged misconduct. Further, the Review Board noted that respondent respected the client's wishes regarding not pursuing a claim with the Commission. Accordingly, the Review Board recommended that the complaint be dismissed.

The Administrator now raises three issues for review: (1) whether the Review Board erred in concluding that respondent's client had informed the Commission of misconduct by her former attorney; (2) whether the Review Board erred in concluding that respondent had not violated Rule 1-103(a); and (3) whether the proven misconduct warrants at least a censure.

As to the first issue, the Administrator contends that the Review Board erred in finding that Forsberg informed the Commission of Casey's misconduct prior to retaining respondent. In support of this contention, the Administrator cites to testimony in the record showing that while Forsberg contacted the Commission and received a complaint form, she did not fill out the form, return it, advise the Commission of the facts, or name whom she wished to complain about. The Administrator further contends that even if Forsberg had reported Casey's misconduct to the Commission, such an action would not have relieved respondent of his duty to report under Rule 1-103(a). Additionally, the Administrator argues that no evidence exists to prove that respondent failed to report because he assumed that Forsberg had already reported the matter.

Respondent argues that the record shows that Forsberg did contact the Commission and was forwarded a complaint form, and that the record is not clear that Forsberg failed to disclose Casey's name to the Commission. Respondent also argues that Forsberg directed respondent not to pursue the claim against Casey, a claim she had already begun to pursue.

We begin our analysis by examining whether a client's complaint of attorney misconduct to the Commission can be a defense to an attorney's failure to report the same misconduct. Respondent offers no authority for such a defense and our research has disclosed none. Common sense would dictate that if a lawyer has a duty under the Code, the actions of a client would not relieve the attorney of his own duty. Accordingly, while the parties dispute whether or not respondent's client informed the Commission, that question is irrelevant to our inquiry in this case. We have held that the canons of ethics in the Code constitute a safe guide for professional conduct, and attorneys may be disciplined for not observing them. * * * The question is, then, whether or not respondent violated the Code, not whether Forsberg informed the Commission of Casey's misconduct.

As to respondent's argument that he did not report Casey's misconduct because his client directed him not to do so, we again note respondent's failure to suggest any legal support for such a defense. A lawyer, as an officer of the court, is duty-bound to uphold the rules in the Code. The title of Canon 1 * * * reflects this obligation: "A lawyer should assist in maintaining the integrity and competence of the legal profession." A lawyer may not choose to circumvent the rules by simply asserting that his client asked him to do so.

As to the second issue, the Administrator argues that the Review Board erred in concluding that respondent did not violate Rule 1-103(a). The Administrator urges acceptance of the Hearing Board's finding that respondent had unprivileged knowledge of Casey's conversion of client funds, and that respondent failed to disclose that information to the Commission. The Administrator states that respondent's knowledge of Casey's conversion of client funds was knowledge of illegal conduct involving moral turpitude * * * . Further, the Administrator argues that the information respondent received was not privileged under the definition of privileged information articulated by this court * * * . Therefore, the Administrator concludes, respondent violated his ethical duty to report misconduct under Rule 1-103(a). According to the Administrator, failure to disclose the information deprived the Commission of evidence of serious misconduct, evidence that would have assisted in the Commission's investigation of Casey.

Respondent contends that the information was privileged information received from his client, Forsberg, and therefore he was under no obligation to disclose the matter to the Commission. Respondent argues that his failure to report Casey's misconduct was motivated by his respect for his client's wishes, not by his desire for financial gain. To support this assertion, respondent notes that his fee agreement with Forsberg was contingent upon her first receiving all the money Casey originally owed her. Further, respondent states that he has received no fee for his representation of Forsberg.

Our analysis of this issue begins with a reading of the applicable disciplinary rules. Rule 1-103(a) of the Code states:

> "(a) A lawyer possessing unprivileged knowledge of a violation of Rule 1-102(a)(3) or (4) shall report such knowledge to a tribunal or other authority empowered to investigate or act upon such violation." 107 Ill.2d R. 1-103(a).

Rule 1-102 of the Code states:

> "(a) A lawyer shall not
>
> (1) violate a disciplinary rule;
>
> (2) circumvent a disciplinary rule through actions of another;
>
> (3) engage in illegal conduct involving moral turpitude;
>
> (4) engage in conduct involving dishonesty, fraud, deceit, or misrepresentation; or
>
> (5) engage in conduct that is prejudicial to the administration of justice." 107 Ill.2d R. 1-102.

These rules essentially track the language of the American Bar Association Model Code of Professional Responsibility, upon which the Illinois Code was modeled. * * * . Therefore, we find instructive the opinion of the American Bar Association's Committee on Ethics and Professional Responsibility that discusses the Model Code's Disciplinary Rule 1-103 * * * [ABA Committee on Ethics & Professional Responsibility] Informal Opinion 1210 states that under DR 1-103(a) it is the duty of a lawyer to report to the proper tribunal or authority any unprivileged knowledge of a lawyer's perpetration of any misconduct listed in Disciplinary Rule 1-102. * * * The opinion states that "the Code of Professional Responsibility through its Disciplinary Rules necessarily deals directly with reporting of lawyer misconduct or misconduct of others directly observed in the legal practice or the administration of justice." * * *

This court has also emphasized the importance of a lawyer's duty to report misconduct. * * * Thus, if the present respondent's conduct did violate the rule on reporting misconduct, imposition of discipline for such a breach of duty is mandated.

626 PROFESSIONAL RESPONSIBILITY A Contemporary Approach

The question whether the information that respondent possessed was protected by the attorney-client privilege, and thus exempt from the reporting rule, requires application of this court's definition of the privilege. We have stated that "'(1) [w]here legal advice of any kind is sought (2) from a professional legal adviser in his capacity as such, (3) the communications relating to that purpose, (4) made in confidence (5) by the client, (6) are at his instance permanently protected (7) from disclosure by himself or by the legal adviser, (8) except the protection be waived.'" * * * We agree with the Administrator's argument that the communication regarding Casey's conduct does not meet this definition. The record does not suggest that this information was communicated by Forsberg to the respondent in confidence. We have held that information voluntarily disclosed by a client to an attorney, in the presence of third parties who are not agents of the client or attorney, is not privileged information. * * *

Though respondent repeatedly asserts that his failure to report was motivated not by financial gain but by the request of his client, we do not deem such an argument relevant in this case. This court has stated that discipline may be appropriate even if no dishonest motive for the misconduct exists. * * * We have already dealt with, and dismissed, respondent's assertion that his conduct is acceptable because he was acting pursuant to his client's directions.

Respondent does not argue that Casey's conversion of Forsberg's funds was not illegal conduct involving moral turpitude under Rule 1-102(a)(3) or conduct involving dishonesty, fraud, deceit, or misrepresentation under Rule 1-102(a)(4). (107 Ill.2d Rules 1-102(a)(3), (a)(4).) It is clear that conversion of client funds is, indeed, conduct involving moral turpitude. * * * We conclude, then, that respondent possessed unprivileged knowledge of Casey's conversion of client funds, which is illegal conduct involving moral turpitude, and that respondent failed in his duty to report such misconduct to the Commission. Because no defense exists, we agree with the Hearing Board's finding that respondent has violated Rule 1-103(a) and must be disciplined.

The third issue concerns the appropriate quantum of discipline to be imposed in this case. The Administrator contends that respondent's misconduct warrants at least a censure, although the Hearing Board recommended a private reprimand and the Review Board recommended dismissal of the matter entirely. In support of the request for a greater quantum of discipline, the Administrator cites to the purposes of attorney discipline, which include maintaining the integrity of the legal profession and safeguarding the administration of justice. The Administrator argues that these purposes will not be served unless respondent is publicly disciplined so that the profession will be on notice that a violation of Rule 1-103(a) will not be tolerated. The Administrator argues that a more severe sanction is necessary because respondent deprived the Commission of evidence of another attorney's conversion and thereby interfered with the Commission's investigative function * * * . [T]he Administrator notes that Casey converted many clients' funds after respondent's duty to report Casey arose. The Administrator also argues that both respondent and his client behaved in contravention of the Criminal Code's prohibition against compounding a crime by agreeing with Casey not to report him, in exchange for settlement funds.

In his defense, respondent reiterates his arguments that he was not motivated by desire for financial gain. He also states that Forsberg was pleased with his performance on her behalf. According to respondent, his failure to report was a "judgment call" which resulted positively in Forsberg's regaining some of her funds from Casey.

In evaluating the proper quantum of discipline to impose, we note that it is this court's responsibility to determine appropriate sanctions in attorney disciplinary cases. * * * We have stated that while recommendations of the Boards are to be considered, this court ultimately bears responsibility for deciding an appropriate sanction. * * * We reiterate our statement that "'[w]hen determining the nature and extent of discipline to be imposed, the respondent's actions must be viewed in relationship "to the underlying purposes of our disciplinary process, which purposes are to maintain the integrity of the legal profession, to protect the administration of justice from reproach, and to safeguard the public." * * *

Bearing these principles in mind, we agree with the Administrator that public discipline is necessary in this case to carry out the purposes of attorney discipline. While we have considered the Boards' recommendations in this matter, we cannot agree with the Review Board that respondent's conduct served to rectify a wrong and did not injure the bar, the public, or the administration of justice. Though we agree with the Hearing Board's assessment that respondent violated Rule 1-103 of the Code, we do not agree that the facts warrant only a private reprimand. As previously stated, the evidence proved that respondent possessed unprivileged knowledge of Casey's conversion of client funds, yet respondent did not report Casey's misconduct.

This failure to report resulted in interference with the Commission's investigation of Casey, and thus with the administration of justice. Perhaps some members of the public would have been spared from Casey's misconduct had respondent reported the information as soon as he knew of Casey's conversions of client funds. We are particularly disturbed by the fact that respondent chose to draft a settlement agreement with Casey rather than report his misconduct. As the Administrator has stated, by this conduct, both respondent and his client ran afoul of the Criminal Code's prohibition against compounding a crime[.] * * *

Both respondent and his client stood to gain financially by agreeing not to prosecute or report Casey for conversion. According to the settlement agreement, respondent would have received $17,000 or more as his fee. If Casey had satisfied the judgment entered against him for failure to honor the settlement agreement, respondent would have collected approximately $25,588.

We have held that fairness dictates consideration of mitigating factors in disciplinary cases. * * * Therefore, we do consider the fact that Forsberg recovered $10,400 through respondent's services, that respondent has practiced law for 11 years with no record of complaints, and that he requested no fee for minimum collection of Forsberg's funds.

However, these considerations do not outweigh the serious nature of respondent's failure to report Casey, the resulting interference with the Commission's investigation of Casey, and respondent's ill-advised choice to settle with Casey rather than report his misconduct.

Food for Thought

The court decided *Himmel* under provisions based on the Model Code. As the Restatement notes, the *Himmel* "court limited the confidentiality exception to only such information as was protected * * * under the attorney-client privilege." Restatement § 5 Comment i. Is the *Himmel* court's reading of the confidentiality exception consistent with Rule 8.3?

Accordingly, it is ordered that respondent be suspended from the practice of law for one year.

Respondent suspended.

CHAPTER 7

Special Ethical Rules: Prosecutors and Judges

In the previous chapter, we explored the lawyer's duties to the legal system and the public. Most, but not all, of that analysis related to representation of private clients. In this chapter, we explore two special roles for lawyers that diverge altogether from the paradigm of representing private clients—work as a prosecutor or a judge. But although prosecutors and judges share a primary obligation to the legal system and the public, their particular ethical duties differ in significant ways. Moreover, prosecutors are subject to the Rules like other lawyers, while judges are governed by the Code of Judicial Conduct.

I. Prosecutors

The prosecutor's basic job is to enforce violations of criminal law. Prosecutors decide whether to initiate criminal charges against individuals and, on occasion, entities believed to have violated the criminal law and prosecute the cases against them in court. In doing so, prosecutors wield the state's or federal government's vast criminal law enforcement power. In the process, prosecutors are governed by ethical rules and law and have broad discretion within the bounds of the law.

In most cases, a prosecutor's office is comprised of a chief prosecutor, such as a United States Attorney, a state Attorney General, or a District or County Attorney. On the federal level, the U.S. Attorney General and the United States Attorneys for each of the 94 federal districts are appointed by the President and confirmed by the Senate (although acting or interim U.S. Attorneys may be appointed by the Attorney General or by the federal district court). State attorneys general are usually elected or appointed by the Governor. Most local chief prosecutors—e.g., District or County Attorneys—are elected. Some, as in Alaska and New Jersey, are appointed.

Most prosecutors serve under the authority of the elected or appointed chief prosecutor. In a small rural community, an elected County Attorney may have no lawyers on staff, or only one or two full-time or part-time lawyers. In a large city or county, such as Manhattan or Los Angeles, the prosecutors' office may be staffed by several hundred prosecutors. While a newly elected or appointed chief prosecutor may bring in new lawyers to serve on the senior staff, lower level prosecutors in most jurisdictions are free to stay from one administration to the next. In some jurisdictions, prosecutors can be replaced "at will" by the chief prosecutor, but in others, prosecutors have civil service protection and can be fired only for good cause.

The nature of an office's legal personnel may vary in other respects as well. The junior or "line" prosecutors in a large urban office may mostly be made up of recent law school graduates and lawyers with less than five years of experience. A smaller number of senior lawyers may staff senior trial units such as homicide units and serve in supervisory positions. Few of the prosecutors may regard themselves as "career prosecutors." Most may view the job of prosecutor as a stepping stone to private employment, including as private criminal defense lawyer, that draws on trial experience. Or they may move to the private sector after several years to make more money. Elsewhere, many lawyers make a career in the prosecutor's office, because they are committed to the work, the pay and hours are relatively good compared to the other opportunities available in professional community, and the office's ethos and tradition do not encourage lawyers to leave after a short time.

Collectively, prosecutors in an office make a host of decisions and engage in a variety of conduct that substantially affects the lives of individuals—including importantly the lives of victims, witnesses and those suspected of committing crimes—as well as the lives of members of the community in general. Much of their work takes place outside the courtroom and is administrative in nature. State prosecutors work closely with the police department, sheriff's office, or other state office with investigative authority; federal prosecutors work with the F.B.I. and other federal investigative agencies. Prosecutors sometimes do not become involved in a case until the police arrest a suspect. But prosecutors often work with the police, who may need prosecutors' help to obtain search warrants, and prosecutors in some jurisdictions use the grand jury not only to approve of indictments but as an investigative tool. Prosecutors may interview or question witnesses, suspects and arrested individuals informally or question them in the grand jury.

Besides deciding in many cases whom to investigate and by what means to conduct the investigation, prosecutors decide whether to initiate criminal charges in cases where they believe a suspect committed a crime, decide what charges to bring, offer plea bargains and conduct plea negotiations, and take positions at sentencing hearings. Often, though believing an individual to be guilty, prosecutors decline to bring charges for any of a host of reasons, such as that: the crime was a low-level and first offense so that a criminal conviction would be disproportionately harsh; the policies of the office encourage alternatives to a criminal conviction; a prosecution would require excessive resources; or the case is too weak for prosecutors to be confident of securing a conviction.

Approximately 95% of the cases that prosecutors bring are resolved by a plea of guilty rather than a trial. But the most visible and media-worthy work of prosecutors involves presenting cases against defendants charged with a crime who choose to exercise their right to trial. In the trial setting, the prosecutor is much like a civil litigator representing a private party. Although the procedural rules differ—for example, the prosecutor has the burden of proving guilt beyond a reasonable doubt—the prosecutor's basic task is to present the prosecution's proof and to argue the prosecution's positions as convincingly as possible.

As to any individual prosecutor, the daily work can vary. In some large, urban offices, prosecutors' work is compartmentalized based on particular tasks or phases of work. Prosecutors may be divided into units that arraign defendants, investigate cases and present them to the grand jury, prepare for and conduct trials, and handle appeals. Some offices have different units in which prosecutors focus on particular kinds of cases—e.g., homicide, narcotics, white collar—or are divided between misdemeanor and felony units. Typically, more senior prosecutors handle the more important tasks (e.g., trials) or types of cases (e.g., homicides). Different units of a large office may develop different practices and cultures.

The fact that a chief prosecutor has broad discretion does not mean that each individual prosecutor has the same level of discretion. Where offices are divided into units along one or more lines, the units are generally supervised by an experienced prosecutor. Besides having a teaching role and serving as a source of guidance, supervisory lawyers typically have responsibility to make or approve certain decisions, such as whether to initiate an indictment, offer a particular plea bargain, grant immunity to a defendant in exchange for testifying against others, or take a particular position at a defendant's sentencing. Further, particularly in large offices, frequently recurring decisions may be governed by written or oral policies developed and approved by senior supervisory prosecutors or by the chief prosecutor. The policies may or may not be publicized. For example, an office may decide to bring misdemeanor rather than felony charges for first-offenders in narcotics possession cases or to seek at least a year's imprisonment when a defendant possesses a firearm in the course of criminal conduct. The policies may or may not be subject to exception.

> **FYI**
>
> On the allocation of decision making within a prosecutor's office, *see* Bruce A. Green & Fred C. Zacharias, *"The U.S. Attorneys Scandal" and the Allocation of Prosecutorial Power*, 69 Ohio St. L.J. 187 (2008).

In conducting their work, prosecutors have no need to pursue business or please clients. But their personal motivations may include advancing within the office or, in the case of those who are not career prosecutors, obtaining future outside employment. In any case, prosecutors are ordinarily interested in developing and preserving a favorable reputation within and/or outside the office. But this can be a double-edged sword, because the values of the relevant community may differ from prosecutors' perception of their role. The prosecutor's job prospects in or outside the office may be enhanced, on one hand, by a reputation for even-handedness, balance, fairness and candor or, on the other hand, by a reputation for zealousness, fearlessness, and a willingness to go up to the limits of the law, and even to test the law where it is ambiguous, in order to win a case.

One of the distinctive aspects of prosecutors' work is that prosecutors do not answer to a client. Chief prosecutors may have to be accountable to the public in an abstract sense, but they do not take direction from the public. Prosecutors bring cases in the name of "the United States" or "the Commonwealth of Virginia" or the "People of the State of the New York," but they make decisions on behalf of the entity that they represent. Unlike lawyers for private clients, there is no other individual or entity who hires the prosecutor to bring a particular matter, who defines the objectives of the representation, who decides whether to bring or resolve a case, or with whom the prosecutor must confer. Although a prosecutor may work closely with the police department or other investigative agency, the investigators are not clients. Further, because prosecutors do not seek or represent private clients, professional conduct rules such as those governing the protection of client funds and the solicitation of business have no relevance to their work.

To be sure, a prosecutor has some of the professional obligations that historically grow out of the lawyer's obligation as agent of a client, but these do not pose the same kinds of difficulties that they often pose for privately retained lawyers. For example, prosecutors must maintain the confidentiality of information learned in

FYI: Professors Green and Zacharias discuss the importance of identifying internal principles and policies to guide the work of prosecutors in Bruce A. Green & Fred C. Zacharias, *Prosecutorial Neutrality*, 2004 Wis. L. Rev. 837. The best example of such guidelines is the U.S. Attorney's Manual, available here. The U.S. Attorney's Manual provides guidance to federal prosecutors, who may be subject to internal discipline for violating its provisions. The U.S. Department of Justice has an office, the Office of Professional Responsibility, which investigates alleged violations of ethics rules and internal guidelines by federal prosecutors and recommends sanctions when it finds wrongdoing. Another office, the Professional Responsibility Advisory Office, gives advice to federal prosecutors about their compliance with ethics rules.

a representation. But they also generally have authority to use or disclose the information for legitimate law-enforcement purposes. Prosecutors must avoid conflicts of interest. But because they represent only one client, conflicts of interest are rare.

For More Information

For State ethics opinions relating to prosecutorial ethics, visit The National Center for Prosecution Ethics, available at http://www.ethicsfor-prosecutors.com/links.html.

More significant are the ethical rules governing trial lawyers generally, such as the rules against offering false testimony and false evidence; communicating ex parte with judges and jurors; trying the case in the press; and making jury arguments that refer to facts not in evidence, that play on the jury's sympathies or prejudices, or that are otherwise out of bounds.

Prosecutors are also subject to Rule 3.8, which identifies "Special Responsibilities of a Prosecutor." The rule is predicated on the understanding that prosecutors have an ethically exceptional status that carries with it special responsibilities. This understanding is captured by Comment 1 to Rule 3.8, which begins: "A prosecutor has the responsibility of a minister of justice and not simply that of an advocate. This responsibility carries with it specific obligations to see that the defendant is accorded procedural justice, that guilt is decided upon the basis of sufficient evidence, and that special precautions are taken to rectify the convictions of innocent persons." The prosecutor's special responsibilities have sometimes been summed up by the "duty to seek justice."

Rule 3.8 does not set forth all of a prosecutor's special responsibilities. Other responsibilities are reflected in judicial decisions.

Commentators have disagreed to some extent about the reason why prosecutors are said to have a special "duty to seek justice." Fred Zacharias argued that this duty is explained by prosecutors' special power, and that prosecutors should therefore have special duties only when they exercise power that is different from that of ordinary trial advocates. Fred C. Zacharias, *Structuring the Ethics of Prosecutorial Trial Practice: Can Prosecutors Do Justice*, 44 Vand. L. Rev. 45 (1991). In response, Bruce Green suggested that the special duty comes primarily from the prosecutor's role in representing the government, whose objectives, which are implicit in the constitution and statutes, include avoiding punishment of those who are innocent, affording the accused, and others, a lawful, fair process, treating individuals with proportionality, and treating lawbreakers with rough equality. Bruce A. Green, *Why Should Prosecutors "Seek Justice,"* 26 Fordham Urb. L.J. 607 (1999).

Prosecutorial discretion is central to the operation of all state and federal criminal justice systems. It pervades every aspect of a prosecutor's work and daily life including investigating, charging, bail and plea bargaining decisions as well as decisions in trial, sentencing and post conviction motions. Prosecutorial decision making may be guided by case law, statutes, procedural rules, and ethics provisions. Law and rules typically provide boundaries but insufficient guidance for the exercise of discretion. There are few enforceable laws that provide legal limitations on the exercise of discretion. Standards applicable to criminal cases may include informal constraints that courts can impose

> For a discussion of the reasons for the ABA's failure to make the rule more complete, and the types of additional issues that the rule might address, *see* Bruce A. Green, *Prosecutorial Ethics as Usual*, <u>2003 U. Ill. L. Rev. 1573</u>. One of the suggestions in the article was adopted around five years later when the ABA amended the rule to add Rules 3.8(g) and (h) to address prosecutors' post-conviction obligations.

upon prosecutors to establish some norms of conduct for the exercise of discretion. But mostly, discretionary choices are guided by a potential range of other factors including norms within prosecutors' offices, and individual commitment to fairness. These choices may be guided by the internal and external supervisory and accountability systems. They may be guided by political realities. These norms are rarely explicit.

Commentators have long questioned whether there are sufficient standards, principles or policies to guide discretionary decision making and have sought to delineate the boundaries of legitimate discretionary decision making. Some of the literature on this subject is normative, identifying principles or standards that should exist to exercise discretion in certain areas. Other writings describe how prosecutors have made discretionary decisions, such as those regarding charging and plea bargaining.

A. The Decision to Charge

Discretion

[Question 1]

A county prosecutor believes that Bill is a criminal mastermind who is responsible for most of the illegal drugs that are coming into the county and who is also responsible for at least ten murders. The prosecutor does not have enough evidence to obtain an indictment on those charges. But in his investigation, the prosecutor discovers that Bill lied on a form he filed with the government to obtain a zoning variance for his mansion. Lying to the government on a form is a felony, but it is a common activity and very rarely prosecuted. In fact, Bill would be the first person ever charged for this crime in the county.

Can the prosecutor ethically bring charges against Bill for lying on a government form?

(A) No, because the prosecutor is acting pretextually.

(B) No, because the prosecutor is acting selectively.

(C) Yes, because the prosecutor has probable cause to believe that Bill committed the crime.

(D) Yes, because the prosecutor's discretion to charge or not to charge is an executive decision that is not subject to regulation by lawyers' ethics rules.

Rule 3.8

The prosecutor in a criminal case shall:

> (a) refrain from prosecuting a charge that the prosecutor knows is not supported by probable cause;

STATE ex rel. MCKITTRICK v. WALLACH

182 S.W.2d 313 (Mo. 1944)

HYDE, Judge.

This case, recently coming to the writer by reassignment, is an original proceeding in quo warranto to declare forfeiture of the office of prosecuting attorney of St. Louis County, and to oust respondent therefrom. * * *

Respondent was elected to the office of prosecuting attorney in 1938, 1940 and 1942. The Commissioner's report summarizes relator's charges (which

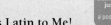

It's Latin to Me!

"Quo warranto" is translated to mean "by what authority." Quo warranto is a common-law writ used to challenge the authority by which a public office is held. Here, Petitioner brings this action questioning the Respondent's authority as County prosecutor.

were limited to the years 1941 and 1942, respondent's second term) placing them in four general classifications, as follows:

'(1) That respondent willfully, knowingly, continuously, corruptly and unlawfully neglected, failed and refused to investigate, commence prosecutions of and prosecute various persons (95 persons named in the Information) for violations of the Liquor Control Act and Non-Intoxicating Beer Laws of Missouri;

'(2) That without any reason, cause or justification therefor the respondent dismissed and caused to be dismissed various criminal cases (none designated by name or number in the Information) pending against persons charged in said county with felonies and misdemeanors;

'(3) That although respondent was advised of the evidence thereof, he has failed and refused to commence and prosecute criminal actions against persons (none designated by name in the Information) who set up, kept and operated certain named gambling machines and devices;

'(4) That respondent has failed and refused to commence and prosecute criminal actions against persons (none designated by name in the Information) who established, openly advertised and conducted lotteries:'

* * *

The duty of a prosecuting officer necessarily requires that he investigate, i.e., inquire into the matter with care and accuracy, that in each case he examine the available evidence, the law and the facts, and the applicability of each to the other; that his duties further require that he intelligently weigh the chances of successful termination of the prosecution, having always in mind the relative importance to the county he serves of the different prosecutions which he might initiate. Such duties of necessity involve a good faith exercise of the sound discretion of the prosecuting attorney. 'Discretion' in that sense means power or right conferred by law upon the prosecuting officer of acting officially in such circumstances, and upon each separate case, according to the dictates of his own judgment and conscience uncontrolled by the judgment and conscience of any other person. Such discretion must be exercised in accordance with established principles of law, fairly, wisely, and with skill and reason. It includes the right to choose a course of action or non-action, chosen not willfully or in bad faith, but chosen with regard to what is right under the circumstances. Discretion denotes the absence of a hard and fast rule or a mandatory procedure regardless of varying circumstances. That discretion may, in good faith (but not arbitrarily), be exercised with respect to when, how and against whom to initiate criminal proceedings. * * * Such discretion exercised in good faith authorizes the prosecuting officer to personally determine, in conference and in collaboration with peace officers and liquor enforcement officers, that a certain plan of action or a certain policy of enforcement will be best productive of law enforcement, and will best result in general law observance. * * *

It appearing in the record that respondent did at all times and in each instance in good faith exercise his discretion, and it further not appearing anywhere in this record that respondent's discretion was at any time arbitrarily exercised, or that his discretion was corruptly exercised, or exercised in bad faith, the Special Commissioner concludes that in those cases wherein he exercised his discretion and did not prosecute * * * the respondent had the legal right to reach the conclusion he did reach with respect to prosecution or no prosecution. * * * And that respondent has not been guilty of any act, or conduct, or of any omission, meriting the forfeiture of his right to occupy the office of prosecuting attorney. * * *

PUGACH v. KLEIN

193 F. Supp. 630 (S.D.N.Y 1961)

MacMAHON, District Judge.

These applications by Pugach for habeas corpus, mandamus, and warrants for arrest and search raise once again the vexing question of whether a federal court ought to interfere at the preliminary stage of a state criminal prosecution allegedly resulting from wire tap evidence obtained in violation of the Federal Communications Act, but in compliance with the clashing law of the State of New York.

* * *

Mandamus

Petitioner seeks, by original petition for a writ of mandamus, to compel the United States Attorney to prosecute an officer of the New York City Police Department, an Assistant District Attorney, and a County Judge.

> **Non constat**
> de non apparentibus
> **jus civile**
> a posteriori
>
> ### It's Latin to Me!
>
> Mandamus n. [Latin "we command"]
> A writ issued by a superior court to compel a lower court or a government officer to perform mandatory or purely ministerial duties correctly.

The petition, largely by resort to conclusions, purports to allege violations of, and conspiracy to violate, Sections 501 and 605 of the Communications Act of 1934, in that agents of the Bronx County District Attorney and the New York police obtained an order from the State Supreme Court authorizing them to intercept petitioner's telephone conversations, used information resulting from such interceptions, caused tapes to be made and divulged their contents and meaning both to newspapers and to the Bronx County Grand Jury, thereby causing his arrest, indictment and detention. The Judge is accused of aiding and abetting, resisting arrest, withholding evidence and remaining a fugitive.

Asserting the imminence of the trial, open defiance by New York of the wire tap prohibitions of the Communications Act, and failure of the District Attorney and the United States Attorney to enforce violations, notwithstanding admonitions by Judge Waterman of the Court of Appeals for this circuit, Pugach contends that there is no existing state process to protect his rights. He specifically alleges refusal of the United States Attorney to act on his complaints * * *. * * *

With all deference to the concern of some over the lack of prosecutions against state officers for wire tapping in accordance with state law, it is, nevertheless, clear beyond question that it is not the business of the Courts to tell the United States Attorney to perform what they conceive to be his duties.

Article II, Section 3 of the Constitution, provides that "(the President) shall take Care that the Laws (shall) be faithfully executed." The prerogative of enforcing the criminal law was vested by the Constitution, therefore, not in the Courts, nor in private citizens, but squarely in the executive arm of the government. Congress has implemented the powers of the President by conferring the power and the duty to institute prosecution for federal offenses upon the United States Attorney for each district. In exercising his power, the United States Attorney acts in an administrative capacity as the representative of the public. * * *

It by no means follows, however, that the duty to prosecute follows automatically from the presentation of a complaint. The United States Attorney is not a rubber stamp. His problems are not solved by the strict application of an inflexible formula. Rather, their solution calls for the exercise of judgment. Judgment reached primarily by balancing the public interest in effective law enforcement against the growing rights of the accused.

There are a number of elements in the equation, and all of them must be carefully considered. Paramount among them is a determination that a prosecution will promote the ends of justice, instill respect for the law, and advance the cause of ordered liberty. Here, respect for, and cooperative relations with, state law enforcement agencies weigh heavily in the scale.

Surely it is for the United States Attorney to decide whether the public interest is better served by prosecuting or declining to prosecute state law enforcement agencies and besmirch a Judge on the eve of a trial on the feeble complaint of an accuser infected with self-interest in escaping trial on a grave charge. The reason for leaving the choice with the United States Attorney is all the more compelling in an area such as this, riven with controversy, frought with friction, and confused by clashing law.

Other considerations are the likelihood of conviction, turning on choice of a strong case to test uncertain law, the degree of criminality, the weight of the evidence, the credibility of witnesses, precedent, policy, the climate of public opinion, timing, and the relative gravity of the offense. In weighing these factors, the prosecutor must apply responsible standards, based, not on loose assumptions, but, on solid evidence balanced in a scale demanding proof beyond a reasonable doubt to overcome the presumption of innocence. Just how thoroughly cases are screened to meet these basic criteria is reflected in the fact that 97% of all prosecutions commenced in this district end either in a plea of guilty or conviction after trial.

Still other factors are the relative importance of the offense compared with the competing demands of other cases on the time and resources of investigation, prosecution and trial. All of these and numerous other intangible and imponderable factors must be carefully weighed and considered by the conscientious United States Attorney in deciding whether or not to prosecute.

All of these considerations point up the wisdom of vesting broad discretion in the United States Attorney. The federal courts are powerless to interfere with his discretionary power. The Court cannot compel him to prosecute a complaint, or even an indictment, whatever his reasons for not acting. The remedy for any dereliction of his duty lies, not with the courts, but, with the executive branch of our government and ultimately with the people.

* * *

Accordingly, all of the applications are denied. It is so ordered.

1. Refusing to Prosecute a Certain Type of Crime

In some situations, a prosecutor might decide that a certain kind of crime will not be prosecuted. A prosecutor's decision not to prosecute a certain type of crime is often based on a judgment that prosecuting the conduct in question is simply not worth the resources that would have to be expended in a prosecution. Prosecutors might also be concerned about a public backlash in prosecuting certain crimes. Local and cultural conditions might be involved as well.

An example of the non-prosecution of a class of crime arose in Utah, as reported in an article in the <u>National Law Journal, Aug. 10, 1998, A10</u>:

> Facing criticism for suggesting that polygamy may fall under religious freedoms, Gov. Mike Leavitt turned to Utah's attorney general for advice on why the state fails to prosecute polygamists when the practice is widespread. * * * The Tapestry of Polygamy, a self-help group for former polygamist wives and children, held a news conference outside the governor's office July 27 and presented his chief of staff, Vicky Varela, a letter urging that the state constitutional ban on polygamy be enforced.

* * *

Ms. Varela drew a distinction between prosecuting the act of polygamy itself and prosecuting crimes that may occur within plural marriages. "Polygamy is against the law in Utah," she said. "We do not know why prosecutors do not choose to prosecute it."

There has not been a prosecution of anyone solely for practicing polygamy in Utah since 1952, when federal and state agents raided the border community of Short Creek * * *. The raid turned into a public-relations debacle as children were pulled from their parents' arms and husbands were jailed.

Ms. Varela said the governor will ask Utah Attorney General Jan Graham for a "policy statement" on polygamy prosecutions. But Ms. Graham's chief deputy, Reed Richards, said the policy is simple: "Crimes are prosecuted when we know about them, and the vast majority of these relationships are consenting adults."

Does the explanation given by Chief Deputy Graham make any sense? If crimes are prosecuted when the prosecutor knows about them, and consent is no defense to polygamy, then why is the fact of consent an answer to non-prosecution?

2. Suspected of Serious Crime, Charged with a Less Serious Crime

Daniel Richman and William Stuntz, in *Al Capone's Revenge: An Essay on the Political Economy of Pretextual Prosecution*, 105 Colum. L. Rev. 583 (2005), recall the government's prosecution of Chicago mobster Al Capone for income tax evasion after it was unable to prove far more serious crimes, such as "running illegal breweries" and "even slaughtering rival mobsters." They argue that pretextual decisions to charge create social costs:

> There is a strong social interest in non-pretextual prosecution, and that interest is much more important than the "fairness to defendants" argument that has preoccupied the literature on this subject. Criminal charges are not only a means of identifying and punishing criminal conduct. They are also a means by which prosecutors send signals to their superiors, including the voters to whom they are ultimately responsible. When a murderer is brought to justice for murder rather than for tax evasion, voters learn some important things about their community and about the justice system: that a given homicide has been committed in a particular way (if a criminal organization is involved, they may learn things about how the organization works and what kind of people comprise

it); that the crime has been solved; that the police and prosecution have done a good job of assembling evidence against the killer, and so forth. If there is a legislative body that oversees the relevant law enforcement agencies, those same signals are sent to the legislative overseers. When a prosecutor gets a conviction—usually by inducing a guilty plea—for an unrelated lesser crime than the one that motivated the investigation, the signals are muddied. They may disappear altogether. * * *

Another audience also gets a muddied signal: would-be criminals. Instead of sending the message that running illegal breweries and bribing local cops would lead to a term in a federal penitentiary, the Capone prosecution sent a much more complicated and much less helpful message: If you run a criminal enterprise, you should keep your name out of the newspapers and at least pretend to pay your taxes. * * * [T]he political economy of criminal law enforcement depends on a reasonably good match between the charges that motivate prosecution and the charges that appear on defendants' rap sheets. When crimes and charges do not coincide, no one can tell whether law enforcers are doing their jobs. The justice system loses the credibility it needs, and voters lose the trust they need to have in the justice system. Individual agents and prosecutors pay only a tiny fraction of that price, which is why they continue to follow the Capone strategy. The larger price is paid only over time—by crime victims, by law enforcement agencies, and (not least) by the voting public.

B. Factors Bearing on Prosecutor's Discretion to Charge

ABA Standards, The Prosecution Function, Standard 3-3.9 Discretion in the Charging Decision

(a) A prosecutor should not institute, or cause to be instituted, or permit the continued pendency of criminal charges when the prosecutor knows that the charges are not supported by probable cause. A prosecutor should not institute, cause to be instituted, or permit the continued pendency of criminal charges in the absence of sufficient admissible evidence to support a conviction.

(b) The prosecutor is not obliged to present all charges which the evidence might support. The prosecutor may in some circumstances and for good cause consistent with the public interest decline to prosecute, notwithstanding that sufficient evidence may exist which would support a conviction. Illustrative or the factors which the prosecutor may properly consider in exercising his or her discretion are:

(i) the prosecutor's reasonable doubt that the accused is in fact guilty;

(ii) the extent of the harm caused by the offense;

(iii) the disproportion of the authorized punishment in relation to the particular offense or the offender;

(iv) possible improper motives of a complainant;

(v) reluctance of the victim to testify;

(vi) cooperation of the accused in the apprehension or conviction of others; and

(vii) availability and likelihood of prosecution by another jurisdiction.

(c) A prosecutor should not be compelled by his or her supervisor to prosecute a case in which he or she has a reasonable doubt about the guilt of the accused.

(d) In making the decision to prosecute, the prosecutor should give no weight to the personal or political advantages or disadvantages which might be involved or to a desire to enhance his or her record of convictions.

(e) In cases which involve a serious threat to the community, the prosecutor should not be deterred from prosecution by the fact that in the jurisdiction juries have tended to acquit persons accused of the particular kind of criminal act in question.

(f) The prosecutor should not bring or seek charges greater in number of degree than can reasonably be supported with evidence at trial or than are necessary to fairly reflect the gravity of the offense.

(g) The prosecutor should not condition a dismissal of charges, nolle prosequi, or similar action on the accused's relinquishment of the right to seek civil redress unless the accused has agreed to the action knowingly and intelligently, freely and voluntarily, and where such waiver is approved by the court.

C. Selective Prosecution

UNITED STATES v. ARMSTRONG

517 U.S. 456 (1996)

CHIEF JUSTICE REHNQUIST delivered the opinion of the Court.

In this case, we consider the showing necessary for a defendant to be entitled to discovery on a claim that the prosecuting attorney singled him out for prosecution on the basis of his race. We conclude that respondents failed to satisfy the threshold showing: They failed to show that the Government declined to prosecute similarly situated suspects of other races.

In April 1992, respondents were indicted in the United States District Court for the Central District of California on charges of conspiring to possess with intent to distribute more than 50 grams of cocaine base (crack) and conspiring to distribute the same, in violation of 21 U.S.C. §§ 841 and 846, and federal firearms offenses. * * * On seven separate occasions * * * informants had bought a total of 124.3 grams of crack from respondents and witnessed respondents carrying firearms during the sales. * * *

> **FYI**
>
> Professor Fairfax discusses a number of nonevidentiary factors that the prosecutor may consider in a charging decision, including:
>
> > whether the defendant is a recidivist or is likely to offend again, whether the prosecutor has a heavy caseload at the time, whether the type of case is career-advancing, whether the investigating law enforcement agency is pleasant to work with, whether the case has jury appeal, whether a matter is more appropriately prosecuted by a different sovereign or handled as a civil matter, and whether the criminal conduct is a priority area for the prosecutor's superiors.
>
> Roger A. Fairfax, Jr., *Grand Jury Discretion and Constitutional Design*, 93 Cornell L. Rev. 705, 735 (2008); *see also* Bruce A. Green & Fred C. Zacharias, *Prosecutorial Neutrality*, 2004 Wis. L. Rev. 837 (discussing criteria for a charging decision and the difficulty of crafting clear standards given the need for prosecutorial discretion in charging).

[R]espondents filed a motion for discovery or for dismissal of the indictment, alleging that they were selected for federal prosecution because they are black. In support of their motion, they offered only an affidavit [alleging] that, in every one of the 24 §§ 841 or 846 cases closed by the office during 1991, the defendant was black. Accompanying the affidavit was a "study" listing the 24 defendants, their race, whether they were prosecuted for dealing cocaine as well as crack, and the status of each case.

The Government opposed the discovery motion, arguing, among other things, that there was no evidence or allegation "that the Government has acted unfairly or has prosecuted non-black defendants or failed to prosecute them." The District Court granted the motion. It ordered the Government (1) to provide a list of all cases from the last three years in which the Government charged both cocaine and firearms offenses, (2) to identify the race of the defendants in those cases, (3) to identify what levels of law enforcement were involved in the investigations of those cases, and (4) to explain its criteria for deciding to prosecute those defendants for federal cocaine offenses.

The Government moved for reconsideration of the District Court's discovery order. With this motion it submitted affidavits and other evidence to explain why it had chosen to prosecute respondents and why respondents' study did not support the inference that the Government was singling out blacks for cocaine prosecution. The federal and local agents participating in the case alleged in affidavits that race played no role in their investigation. An Assistant United States Attorney explained in an affidavit that the decision to prosecute met the general criteria for prosecution, because

> "there was over 100 grams of cocaine base involved, over twice the threshold necessary for a ten year mandatory minimum sentence; there were multiple sales involving multiple defendants, thereby indicating a fairly substantial crack cocaine ring; . . . there were multiple federal firearms violations intertwined with the narcotics trafficking; the overall evidence in the case was extremely strong, including audio and videotapes of defendants; . . . and several of the defendants had criminal histories including narcotics and firearms violations."

The Government also submitted sections of a published 1989 Drug Enforcement Administration report which concluded that "large-scale, interstate trafficking networks controlled by Jamaicans, Haitians and Black street gangs dominate the manufacture and distribution of crack."

In response, one of respondents' attorneys submitted an affidavit alleging that an intake coordinator at a drug treatment center had told her that there are "an equal number of caucasian users and dealers to minority users and dealers." Respondents also submitted an affidavit from a criminal defense attorney alleging that in his experience many nonblacks are prosecuted in state court for crack offenses, and a newspaper article reporting that Federal "crack criminals . . . are being punished far more severely than if they had been caught with powder cocaine, and almost every single one of them is black," Newton, *Harsher Crack Sentences Criticized as Racial Inequity*, Los Angeles Times, Nov. 23, 1992, p. 1.

The District Court denied the motion for reconsideration. When the Government indicated it would not comply with the court's discovery order, the court dismissed the case.

A divided three-judge panel of the Court of Appeals for the Ninth Circuit reversed, holding that, because of the proof requirements for a selective-prosecution claim, defendants must "provide a colorable basis for believing that 'others similarly situated have not been prosecuted' " to obtain discovery. The Court of Appeals voted to rehear the case en banc, and the en banc panel affirmed the District Court's order of dismissal, holding that "a defendant is not required to demonstrate that the government has failed to prosecute others who are similarly situated." We granted certiorari to determine the appropriate standard for discovery for a selective-prosecution claim.

[*Ed.'s Note*—The Court held that Federal Rule of Criminal Procedure 16 did not mandate disclosure of material supporting a selective prosecution claim. That Rule requires disclosure of documents "material to the preparation of the defendant's defense" and the Court construed that phrase to refer to a defense that was responsive to the government's case-in-chief (e.g., that the defendant is not guilty). A selective prosecution attack was not material to the "defense" in this sense. See the discussion of this aspect of the opinion in Chapter Eight, *infra*.]

* * *

A selective-prosecution claim is not a defense on the merits to the criminal charge itself, but an independent assertion that the prosecutor has brought the charge for reasons forbidden by the Constitution. Our cases delineating the necessary elements to prove a claim of selective prosecution have taken great pains to explain that the standard is a demanding one.* * *

A selective-prosecution claim asks a court to exercise judicial power over a "special province" of the Executive. The Attorney General and United States Attorneys retain broad discretion to enforce the Nation's criminal laws. * * * In the ordinary case, "so long as the prosecutor has probable cause to believe that the accused committed an offense defined by statute, the decision whether or not to prosecute, and what charge to file or bring before a grand jury, generally rests entirely in his discretion."

Of course, a prosecutor's discretion is "subject to constitutional constraints." One of these constraints, imposed by the equal protection component of the Due Process Clause of the Fifth Amendment, is that the decision whether to prosecute may not be based on "an unjustifiable standard such as race, religion, or other arbitrary classification." A defendant may demonstrate that the administration of a criminal law is "directed so exclusively against a particular class of persons . . . with a mind so unequal and oppressive" that the system of prosecution amounts to "a practical denial" of equal protection of the law.

In order to dispel the presumption that a prosecutor has not violated equal protection, a criminal defendant must present "clear evidence to the contrary." We explained in *Wayte* why courts are "properly hesitant to examine the decision whether to prosecute." Judicial deference to the decisions of these executive officers rests in part on an assessment of the relative competence of prosecutors and courts. "Such factors as the strength of the case, the prosecution's general deterrence value, the Government's enforcement priorities, and the case's relationship to the Government's overall enforcement plan are not readily susceptible to the kind of analysis the courts are competent to undertake." It also stems from a concern not to unnecessarily impair the performance of a core executive constitutional function. "Examining the basis of a prosecution delays the criminal proceeding, threatens to chill law enforcement by subjecting the prosecutor's motives and decisionmaking to outside inquiry, and may undermine prosecutorial effectiveness by revealing the Government's enforcement policy."

The requirements for a selective-prosecution claim draw on ordinary equal protection standards. The claimant must demonstrate that the federal prosecutorial policy had a discriminatory effect and that it was motivated by a discriminatory purpose. To establish a discriminatory effect in a race case, the claimant must show that similarly situated individuals of a different race were not prosecuted.
* * *

The similarly situated requirement does not make a selective-prosecution claim impossible to prove. [In *Yick Wo v. Hopkins*], we invalidated an ordinance, * * * adopted by San Francisco, that prohibited the operation of laundries in wooden buildings. The plaintiff in error successfully demonstrated that the ordinance was applied against Chinese nationals but not against other laundry-shop operators. The authorities had denied the applications of 200 Chinese subjects for permits to operate shops in wooden buildings, but granted the applications of 80 individuals who were not Chinese subjects to operate laundries in wooden buildings "under similar conditions."

* * *

Having reviewed the requirements to prove a selective-prosecution claim, we turn to the showing necessary to obtain discovery in support of such a claim. If discovery is ordered, the Government must assemble from its own files documents which might corroborate or refute the defendant's claim. Discovery thus imposes many of the costs present when the Government must respond to a prima facie case of selective prosecution. It will divert prosecutors' resources and may disclose the Government's prosecutorial strategy. The justifications for a rigorous standard for the elements of a selective-prosecution claim thus require a correspondingly rigorous standard for discovery in aid of such a claim.

The parties, and the Courts of Appeals which have considered the requisite showing to establish entitlement to discovery, describe this showing with a variety of phrases, like "colorable basis," "substantial threshold showing," "substantial and concrete basis," or "reasonable likelihood". However, the many labels for this showing conceal the degree of consensus about the evidence necessary to meet it. The Courts of Appeals "require some evidence tending to show the existence of the essential elements of the defense," discriminatory effect and discriminatory intent.

In this case we consider what evidence constitutes "some evidence tending to show the existence" of the discriminatory effect element. The Court of Appeals held that a defendant may establish a colorable basis for discriminatory effect without evidence that the Government has failed to prosecute others who are similarly situated to the defendant. We think it was mistaken in this view. The vast majority of the Courts of Appeals require the defendant to produce some evidence that similarly situated defendants of other races could have been prosecuted, but were not, and this requirement is consistent with our equal protection case law. As the three-judge panel explained, "selective prosecution implies that a selection has taken place."

The Court of Appeals reached its decision in part because it started "with the presumption that people of all races commit all types of crimes—not with the premise that any type of crime is the exclusive province of any particular racial or ethnic group." It cited no authority for this proposition, which seems contradicted by the most recent statistics of the United States Sentencing Commission. Those statistics show that: More than 90% of the persons sentenced in 1994 for crack cocaine trafficking were black; 93.4% of convicted LSD dealers were white; and 91% of those convicted for pornography or prostitution were white. Presumptions at war with presumably reliable statistics have no proper place in the analysis of this issue.

The Court of Appeals also expressed concern about the "evidentiary obstacles defendants face." But all of its sister Circuits that have confronted the issue have required that defendants produce some evidence of differential treatment of similarly situated members of other races or protected classes. In the present case, if the claim of selective prosecution were well founded, it should not have been an insuperable task to prove that persons of other races were being treated differently than respondents. For instance, respondents could have investigated whether similarly situated persons of other races were prosecuted by the State of California, were known to federal law enforcement officers, but were not prosecuted in federal court. We think the required threshold—a credible showing of different treatment of similarly situated persons—adequately balances the Government's interest in vigorous prosecution and the defendant's interest in avoiding selective prosecution.

In the case before us, respondents' "study" did not constitute "some evidence tending to show the existence of the essential elements of" a selective-prosecution claim. The study failed to identify individuals who were not black, could have been prosecuted for the offenses for which respondents were charged, but were not so prosecuted. This omission was not remedied by respondents' evidence in opposition to the Government's motion for reconsideration. The newspaper article, which discussed the discriminatory effect of federal drug sentencing laws, was not relevant to an allegation of discrimination in decisions to prosecute. Respondents' affidavits, which recounted one attorney's conversation with a drug treatment center employee and the experience of another attorney defending drug prosecutions in state court, recounted hearsay and reported personal conclusions based on anecdotal evidence. The judgment of the Court of Appeals is therefore reversed, and the case is remanded for proceedings consistent with this opinion.

[The concurring opinions of Justices Souter, Ginsburg and Breyer are omitted.]

JUSTICE STEVENS, **dissenting.**

* * *

[I]t is undisputed that the brunt of the elevated federal penalties [for crack cocaine] falls heavily on blacks. While 65% of the persons who have used crack are white, in 1993 they represented only 4% of the federal offenders convicted of trafficking in crack. Eighty-eight percent of such defendants were black. During the first 18 months of full guideline implementation, the sentencing disparity between black and white defendants grew from preguideline levels: blacks on average received sentences over 40% longer than whites. * * *

The extraordinary severity of the imposed penalties and the troubling racial patterns of enforcement give rise to a special concern about the fairness of charging practices for crack offenses. Evidence tending to prove that black defendants charged with distribution of crack in the Central District of California are prosecuted in federal court, whereas members of other races charged with similar offenses are prosecuted in state court, warrants close scrutiny by the federal judges in that District. In my view, the District Judge, who has sat on both the federal and the state benches in Los Angeles, acted well within her discretion to call for the development of facts that would demonstrate what standards, if any, governed the choice of forum where similarly situated offenders are prosecuted.

1. *Critique of* Armstrong

Professor Davis, in *Prosecution and Race: The Power and Privilege of Discretion*, <u>67 Fordham L. Rev. 13 (1998)</u>, provides the following critique on the intent-based test of selective prosecution set forth by the Court in *Armstrong*:

> Like police officers, prosecutors often make decisions that discriminate against African American victims and defendants. These decisions may

or may not be intentional or conscious. Although it may be difficult to prove intentional discrimination when it exists, unintentional discrimination poses even greater challenges. Prosecutors may not be aware that the seemingly harmless, reasonable, race-neutral decisions they make every day may have a racially discriminatory impact. This discriminatory impact may occur because of unconscious racism—a phenomenon that plays a powerful role in so many discretionary decisions in the criminal process—and because the lack of power and disadvantaged circumstances of so many African American defendants and victims make it more likely that prosecutors will treat them less well than whites.

* * * Instead of focusing on the harm experienced by African Americans as a result of actions by state actors, the Court has focused on whether the act itself is inherently invidious and whether the actor intended to cause the harm. In addition, the Court has placed the burden of proving intent on the shoulders of the victim. If the victim is unable to prove the actor's bad intent or, in certain contexts, if the actor can establish a non-discriminatory explanation for his behavior, the Court offers no remedy for the harm experienced by the victim.

The main problem with this intent-focused analysis is that it is backward-looking. Although perhaps adequate in combating straightforward and explicit discrimination as it existed in the past, it is totally deficient as a remedy for the more complex and systemic discrimination that African Americans currently experience. When state actors openly expressed their racist views, it was easy to identify and label the invidious nature of their actions. But today, with some notable exceptions, most racist behavior is not openly expressed. More significantly, some racist behavior is committed unconsciously, and many who engage in this behavior are well-intentioned people who would be appalled by the notion that they would be seen as behaving in a racist or discriminatory manner.

Unconscious racism, although arguably less offensive than purposeful discrimination, is no less harmful. In fact, in many ways it is more perilous because it is often unrecognizable to the victim as well as the perpetrator. And the Court, by focusing on intent rather than harm, has refused to recognize, much less provide a remedy for, this most common and widespread form of racism. * * *

For another critique of the *Armstrong* standards, *see* Richard H. McAdams, *Race and Selective Prosecution: Discovering the Pitfalls of* Armstrong, 73 Chic.-Kent L. Rev. 605 (1998).

650   Professional Responsibility *A Contemporary Approach*

2. Unprosecuted Similar Conduct

In *United States v. Parham*, 16 F.3d 844 (8th Cir. 1994), the defendants were African–Americans who were convicted of voting more than once in the same Arkansas election. The defendants, pursuing selective prosecution claims, proffered evidence of numerous voter irregularities attributable to whites that went unprosecuted. These included episodes where African–American disabled or elderly voters were refused assistance while whites were helped, and cases of intimidation of African–American voters by whites brandishing guns. While the court found that these acts by whites warranted prosecution, they were held irrelevant to the defendants' selective prosecution claims. This is because the acts by whites were

> not sufficiently similar to the acts of voter fraud for which Parham and Johnson were prosecuted to constitute a prima facie case of selective prosecution. Parham and Johnson were in effect charged with forging names on absentee ballots. They presented no evidence that other's acts of absentee ballot forgery or fraud were tolerated without prosecution. Where a defendant cannot show anyone in a similar situation who was not prosecuted, he has not met the threshold point of showing that there has been selectivity in prosecution.

Judge Heaney dissented in *Parham*, reasoning that the defendant need only establish that unprosecuted crimes are *similar*, not that they are identical. Isn't armed intimidation of voters even a more serious crime than voting more than once? Shouldn't the former crime be prosecuted before the latter?

3. Example of a Case in Which Discovery Was Ordered on a Selective Prosecution Claim

United States v. Jones, 159 F.3d 969 (6th Cir. 1998), is one of the rare cases in which discovery was ordered to permit investigation of a selective prosecution claim, after the defendant was convicted of drugs and weapons offenses. The shocking facts were related by the court as follows:

> Jones argues on appeal that he was prosecuted based on his race, citing to the Government's decision to prosecute him in federal court instead of state court and the egregious and unprofessional conduct of the arresting local law enforcement officers, Kerry Nelson and Terry Spence.
>
> The conduct of officers Nelson and Spence was undeniably shameful. Prior to the planned arrest of Jones and his wife, the two officers had t-shirts made with Jones's picture emblazoned on the front accompanied by the printed words, "See ya, wouldn't want to be ya" above the picture, and below, "going back to prison." On the back of the t-shirts appeared

a picture of Jones's wife, a co-defendant, with the words, "wait on me, Slow [Jones's nickname was "Slow Motion"], I am coming, too." The two officers were wearing the t-shirts when they arrested Jones in August of 1995. Over one year later, while on a Caribbean cruise, Officer Spence mailed a postcard purchased in Jamaica to Jones while he was in custody awaiting trial. Jones regards Spence's mailing of the postcard, that pictured a black woman with a basket of bananas on her head, as a racial insult. On the postcard, postmarked from Cozumel, Mexico on October 24, 1996, appeared the following handwritten message:

> Slow Motion. What's up? Haven't talked to you since you were in court and lost all your motions. Sorry, but life goes on. Just wanted to drop you a line and let you know that Cozumel, Mexico is beautiful. I'm on vacation and I'll be back Monday for trial, and chances are good you're going to jail for a long time. See ya, Officer Spence.

Spence testified that he sent the postcard to relieve "stress I was feeling while I was on the cruise." Regarding the t-shirts, Spence explained that "It was just—I took pride in arresting [Jones]." Nelson also testified that he wore the t-shirt to demonstrate "a great deal of pride in Mr. Jones's arrest."

In addition, there was testimony at the hearing with respect to Jones's claim that local law enforcement agents improperly referred his case for federal prosecution based on his race. The testimony showed that the Murfreesboro Police Department had referred fourteen defendants, including Jones and his Caucasian co-defendant, Donnie Billings, for federal prosecution in the preceding five years. Of those fourteen defendants, four were African–American, two were Columbian, two were Lebanese, one was Israeli and five were Caucasian. Of the cases referred for federal prosecution in the preceding five years, however, only Jones's and Billings's prosecutions involved crack cocaine. Further, Jones presented evidence of eight non-African–American defendants prosecuted for crack cocaine offenses who were not referred for federal prosecution.

The court found that Jones had established a prima facie case of discriminatory intent, which is the first part of the intent/impact test imposed by *Armstrong*. The court explained as follows:

> The conduct of Officers Spence and Nelson was not only outrageous and unprofessional, but also racially motivated. Although there were three individuals involved in this case (Jones, his wife and co-defendant Don-

nie Billings), only Jones and his wife were African–American. The officers made t-shirts for only those two. Moreover, any argument premised on the fact that Billings was not as involved in the crime as Jones fails, because Jones's wife was no more involved than Billings and yet a t-shirt was made with her picture. We also reject the officers' purported reason for making the t-shirts—that they took pride in the arrests. For some reason, this pride manifested itself in a way that the department had never done before, because this was the first time that such t-shirts were present at an arrest or a search scene.

Additionally, Spence's mailing of the postcard evidences racial animus. Even if we were to discount the obvious impropriety of mailing a postcard, any postcard, to a criminal defendant awaiting trial, we could not so easily disregard the nature of the postcard mailed to Jones. The officer sent to an African–American man a postcard of an African–American woman with bananas on her head, and did not choose any other available postcards such as the sunset or the beach. * * * Given the history of racial stereotypes against African–Americans and the prevalent one of African–Americans as animals or monkeys, it is a reasonable—perhaps even an obvious—conclusion that Spence intended the racial insult that Jones perceived in receiving the postcard. In addition, Officer Spence's testimony that he sent the postcard to relieve stress is irrational, if not incredulous. It is far more likely that Spence sent the postcard to disparage Jones and his wife on the basis of their race. Accordingly, we believe that Jones has made the requisite showing of discriminatory intent.

The court found, however, that there was not enough evidence of discriminatory impact to require dismissal of the indictment. Yet there was enough to justify further discovery.

The second prong of a selective prosecution claim—discriminatory effect—creates a greater challenge for Jones. As we have stated, to establish discriminatory effect, a defendant must show that similarly situated individuals of a different race were not similarly prosecuted. The evidence that Jones has presented to this point does not establish that law enforcement failed to refer similarly situated non-African–Americans for federal prosecution. Accordingly, Jones thus far has not established a prima facie case of discriminatory effect.

In *Armstrong*, the Supreme Court stated that in order for a defendant to obtain discovery in a selective prosecution case, there must be a showing of "some evidence tending to show the existence of the essential elements of the defense, discriminatory effect and discriminatory intent."

As we have stated, Jones has established a showing of discriminatory intent. With respect to discriminatory effect, we believe that Jones has set forth some evidence "tending to show the existence of discriminatory effect," despite the fact that Jones was unable to establish a prima facie case of discriminatory effect on the merits of his selective prosecution claim. Obviously, a defendant need not prove his case in order to justify discovery on an issue.

Jones has presented evidence that law enforcement referred only him and his co-defendant Billings for a federal prosecution that involved crack cocaine, and failed to refer for federal prosecution eight non-African–Americans who were arrested and prosecuted for crack cocaine. The harshness of the crack cocaine guidelines in federal court is certainly a factor that may have been considered in referring defendants for federal prosecution. The fact that law enforcement never considered foregoing the prosecution of Billings, Jones's white co-defendant, in federal court does not change our analysis. It would have been beyond foolish for law enforcement to have done such a thing, considering that Jones's and Billings's cases involved the same events.

Accordingly, Jones has set forth "some evidence" tending to show the existence of discriminatory effect that warrants discovery on his selective prosecution claim. Thus, the district court abused its discretion in denying Jones's request for discovery. We therefore remand the case to the district court to compel discovery on Jones's selective prosecution claim. If Jones is able to obtain evidence that establishes a prima facie case of discriminatory effect, Jones may renew his motion to dismiss the indictment.

See also United States v. Bass, 266 F.3d 532 (6th Cir. 2001) (the stark discriminatory effect of the federal death penalty protocol, when coupled with official statements of members of the Department of Justice recognizing the possibility of intentional discrimination, constituted at least "some evidence" tending to show that race played a role in deciding which defendants to charge with death-eligible offenses; district court's order for discovery on the African–American defendant's selective prosecution claim in a death penalty case was therefore a proper exercise of discretion).

4. Choice of Forum

In the American system of dual sovereignty, the same criminal conduct is often prosecutable under either federal or state law. It is also possible for the choice of forum to be outcome-determinative. For example, in federal drug cases, the relevant sentencing laws generally provide for much harsher sentences than could be given for the same conduct in a state prosecution. Suppose that the defendant can show that a federal prosecution was brought in order to trigger the harsher federal sentences—but unlike in *Jones, supra,* there is no allegation that the decision was based on racial or other discriminatory grounds. Is the defendant entitled to relief?

A typical response to a challenge to the prosecutor's choice of forum is found in *United States v. Jacobs,* 4 F.3d 603 (8th Cir. 1993), a case in which the defendant would have received probation had he been convicted on state charges, but instead received a five-year prison sentence after being convicted in federal court. As the court noted:

> Prosecutors have broad discretion in making prosecutive decisions. So long as the prosecutor has probable cause to believe that the accused committed an offense defined by statute, the decision whether or not to prosecute, and what charge to file, generally rests entirely in his discretion. In exercising this discretion, the prosecutor may take into account the penalties available upon conviction. The prosecutor may not, of course, base the decision to prosecute upon impermissible factors such as race, religion, or other arbitrary and unjustifiable classifications. Likewise the prosecutor may not file charges out of vindictiveness nor in retaliation for a defendant's exercise of legal rights.
>
> The fact that the federal government prosecutes a federal crime in a federal court that could have been or has been prosecuted as a state crime in a state court does not itself violate due process. Choice of forum lies within the realm of prosecutorial discretion.

See also United States v. Dockery, 965 F.2d 1112 (D.C.Cir. 1992) (it was permissible for the U.S. Attorney in the District of Columbia to terminate prosecutions in the D.C. Superior Court and reinstitute them in the U.S. District Court a block away to take advantage of the sterner penalties set by the federal sentencing law; defendant received a ten-year minimum sentence, which would have been 1–5 years in the Superior Court); *United States v. Williams,* 963 F.2d 1337 (10th Cir. 1992) (defendant received 20 years under federal law, and would have received 5 years under state law: "prosecution in a federal rather than a state court does not violate due process despite the absence of guidelines for such referral"); *United States v. Ucciferri,* 960 F.2d 953 (11th Cir. 1992) (it was irrelevant that a federal prosecution was motivated by a desire to avoid more rigorous state constitutional protections).

D. Vindictive Prosecution

BLACKLEDGE v. PERRY

417 U.S. 21 (1974)

Justice Stewart delivered the opinion of the Court.

While serving a term of imprisonment in a North Carolina penitentiary, the respondent Perry became involved in an altercation with another inmate. A warrant issued, charging Perry with the misdemeanor of assault with a deadly weapon. Under North Carolina law, the District Court Division of the General Court of Justice has exclusive jurisdiction for the trial of misdemeanors. Following a trial without a jury in the District Court of Northampton County, Perry was convicted of this misdemeanor and given a six-month sentence, to be served after completion of the prison term he was then serving.

Perry then filed a notice of appeal to the Northampton County Superior Court. Under North Carolina law, a person convicted in the District Court has a right to a trial de novo in the Superior Court. The right to trial de novo is absolute, there being no need for the appellant to allege error in the original proceeding. When an appeal is taken, the statutory scheme provides that the slate is wiped clean; the prior conviction is annulled, and the prosecution and the defense begin anew in the Superior Court.

After the filing of the notice of appeal, but prior to the respondent's appearance for trial de novo in the Superior Court, the prosecutor obtained an indictment from a grand jury, charging Perry with the felony of assault with a deadly weapon with intent to kill and inflict serious bodily injury. The indictment covered the same conduct for which Perry had been tried and convicted in the District Court. Perry entered a plea of guilty to the indictment in the Superior Court, and was sentenced to a term of five to seven years in the penitentiary, to be served concurrently with the identical prison sentence he was then serving.

A number of months later, the respondent filed an application for a writ of habeas corpus in the United States District Court for the Eastern District of North Carolina. * * *

I

* * * Perry * * * urges that the indictment on the felony charge constituted a penalty for his exercising his statutory right to appeal, and thus contravened the Due Process Clause of the Fourteenth Amendment.

Perry's due process arguments are derived substantially from *North Carolina v. Pearce*, 395 U.S. 711, and its progeny. In *Pearce*, the Court considered the constitutional problems presented when, following a successful appeal and reconviction, a criminal defendant was subjected to a greater punishment than that imposed at the first trial. While we concluded that such a harsher sentence was not absolutely precluded by either the Double Jeopardy or Due Process Clause, we emphasized that "imposition of a penalty upon the defendant for having successfully pursued a statutory right of appeal or collateral remedy would be . . . a violation of due process of law." Because vindictiveness against a defendant for having successfully attacked his first conviction must play no part in the sentence he receives after a new trial, we held that an increased sentence could not be imposed upon retrial unless the sentencing judge placed certain specified findings on the record.

* * *

[T]he Due Process Clause is not offended by all possibilities of increased punishment upon retrial after appeal, but only by those that pose a realistic likelihood of "vindictiveness." Unlike the circumstances presented by [*Pearce*], however, in the situation here the central figure is not the judge or the jury, but the prosecutor. The question is whether the opportunities for vindictiveness in this situation are such as to impel the conclusion that due process of law requires a rule analogous to that of the *Pearce* case. We conclude that the answer must be in the affirmative.

A prosecutor clearly has a considerable stake in discouraging convicted misdemeanants from appealing and thus obtaining a trial de novo in the Superior Court, since such an appeal will clearly require increased expenditures of prosecutorial resources before the defendant's conviction becomes final, and may even result in a formerly convicted defendant's going free. And, if the prosecutor has the means readily at hand to discourage such appeals—by "upping the ante" through a felony indictment whenever a convicted misdemeanant pursues his statutory appellate remedy—the State can insure that only the most hardy defendants will brave the hazards of a de novo trial.

There is, of course, no evidence that the prosecutor in this case acted in bad faith or maliciously in seeking a felony indictment against Perry. The rationale of our judgment in the *Pearce* case, however, was not grounded upon the proposition that actual retaliatory motivation must inevitably exist. Rather, we emphasized that "since the fear of such vindictiveness may unconstitutionally deter a defendant's exercise of the right to appeal or collaterally attack his first conviction, due process also requires that a defendant be freed of apprehension of such a retaliatory motivation on the part of the sentencing judge." We think it clear that the same considerations apply here. A person convicted of an offense is entitled to pursue his statutory right to a trial de novo, without apprehension that the State will retaliate by substituting a more serious charge for the original one, thus subjecting him to a significantly increased potential period of incarceration.

Due process of law requires that such a potential for vindictiveness must not enter into North Carolina's two-tiered appellate process. We hold, therefore, that it was not constitutionally permissible for the State to respond to Perry's invocation of his statutory right to appeal by bringing a more serious charge against him prior to the trial de novo.

* * *

Accordingly, the judgment of the Court of Appeals for the Fourth Circuit is affirmed.

It is so ordered.

[The dissenting opinion of Justice Rehnquist is omitted.]

Take Note

In footnote 7, the Court differentiates this case from one in which the State had shown that it was impossible to proceed on the more serious charge at the outset, as was the case in *Diaz v. United States*, 223 U.S. 442 (1912) In *Diaz,* case the defendant was originally convicted for assault and battery. After the original trial, the victim died, and the defendant was then convicted for homicide. "Obviously, it would not have been possible for the authorities in *Diaz* to have originally proceeded against the defendant on the more serious charge, since the crime of homicide was not complete until after the victim's death."

1. Prosecutor's Conduct After the Defendant Invokes a Trial Right: United States v. Goodwin

In *United States v. Goodwin*, 454 U.S. 1138 (1982), the Court distinguished *Blackledge* and refused to apply a presumption of vindictiveness to a prosecutor's decisions in the pretrial setting. Goodwin was charged with several misdemeanors, including assault, following an incident in which a police officer stopped his car for speeding. After he invoked his right to a jury trial, an Assistant United States Attorney obtained a four count indictment against Goodwin that included a felony charge of forcibly assaulting a federal officer. Goodwin was convicted on the felony count and one misdemeanor count. The Supreme Court, in an opinion by Justice Stevens, held that the Due Process Clause does not prohibit the government from bringing more serious charges against a defendant after he has exercised his right to a jury trial. Distinguishing *Pearce* and *Blackledge* as decisions reflecting "a recognition by the Court of the institutional bias inherent in the judicial system against the retrial of issues that have already been decided," Justice Stevens's opinion reasoned as follows:

> There is good reason to be cautious before adopting an inflexible presumption of prosecutorial vindictiveness in a pre-trial setting. In the

course of preparing for trial, the prosecutor may uncover additional information that suggests a basis for further prosecution or he simply may come to realize that information possessed by the State has a broader significance. At this stage of the proceedings, the prosecutor's assessment of the proper extent of prosecution may not have crystallized. In contrast, once a trial begins—and certainly by the time a conviction has been obtained—it is much more likely that the State has discovered and assessed all of the information against an accused and has made a determination, on the basis of that information, of the extent to which he should be prosecuted. Thus, a change in the charging decision made after an initial trial is completed is much more likely to be improperly motivated than is a pretrial decision.

Although Justice Stevens declined to adopt a presumption of vindictiveness in the circumstances presented, he stated that "we of course do not foreclose the possibility that a defendant in an appropriate case might prove objectively that the prosecutor's decision was motivated by a desire to punish him for doing something that the law plainly allowed him to do." Justice Blackmun would have presumed vindictiveness but found that the prosecutor's reasons for seeking a felony indictment adequately rebutted the presumption. Justice Brennan, joined by Justice Marshall, dissented.[1]

2. *Applications of* Goodwin

The lower courts have rarely found prosecutorial vindictiveness. For example, in *United States v. Sinigaglio*, 942 F.2d 581 (9th Cir. 1991), the court stated that "when increased charges are filed in the routine course of prosecutorial review or as a result of continuing investigation, there is no realistic likelihood of prosecutorial abuse, and therefore no appearance of vindictive prosecution arises merely because the prosecutor's action was taken after a defense right was exercised." It has also been held that the increase in charges due to the prosecutor's discovery of a new law does not warrant a presumption of vindictiveness. *United States v. Austin*, 902 F.2d 743 (9th Cir. 1990). In *United States v. Muldoon*, 931 F.2d 282 (4th Cir. 1991), the court held that a presumption of vindictiveness "does not arise from plea negotiations when the prosecutor threatens to bring additional charges if the accused refuses to plead guilty to pending charges. The Due Process Clause does not bar the prosecutor from carrying out his threat." *See also United States v. Williams*, 47 F.3d 658 (4th Cir. 1995) (no presumption of vindictiveness where prosecutor increases the charges when the defendant refuses to become a cooperating witness and undercover informant).

---

1   Recognizing that *Goodwin* prohibits a presumption of vindictiveness for pretrial activity, *State v. Halling*, 672 P.2d 1386 (Or. Ct. App. 1983), nevertheless upheld a trial judge who found *actual* vindictiveness in the filing of two indictments against a defendant who refused to plead guilty to attempted murder. The prosecutor had not mentioned additional offenses during a pretrial conference and had phoned defense counsel to say that she had found a way "to cause further evil" to the defendant.

3. Vindictiveness in Bringing Related Charges After an Acquittal?

If a defendant is acquitted, should a presumption of vindictiveness apply if the prosecutor then charges the defendant with a related crime on the basis of the same conduct? Of course, the prosecutor cannot charge the "same offence". But under the *Blockburger* test, the prosecutor may be able to prosecute on the same conduct by charging a crime with somewhat different elements than the crime first charged. While this is permissible under the Double Jeopardy Clause, does it raise a presumption of vindictiveness?

Consider *United States v. Johnson*, <u>171 F.3d 139 (2d Cir. 1999)</u>. Johnson was arrested by officers of the New York City Police Department for possession of a loaded handgun, and indicted by a state grand jury on two weapons possession charges. While the state weapons prosecution was pending, a federal grand jury indicted Johnson on RICO charges. After a jury trial in federal court, Johnson was acquitted of all outstanding RICO charges. Two months later, a federal prosecutor obtained an indictment against Johnson for possession of a firearm and ammunition by a felon, and for obliteration or alteration of a firearm's serial number. Shortly thereafter, the state weapons charges were dismissed. Johnson filed a pretrial motion seeking dismissal of the federal weapons charges due to vindictive prosecution. The trial judge granted the dismissal on the ground that "nothing had occurred that would have prompted the government to submit the instant charges to the grand jury EXCEPT that Johnson had been acquitted of the RICO charges after having demanded a jury trial on those charges." The judge reasoned that the prosecution obviously knew about the weapons offenses before the RICO case arose, could have included them as part of the RICO case, and only decided to bring the weapons charges after Johnson had been acquitted.

The court of appeals reversed and reinstated the weapons charges. It analyzed the question of vindictiveness as follows:

> Because the Government did not assert any reason why the prosecution of Johnson on federal weapons charges could not, as a practical matter, have been initiated at an earlier time, the district court assumed (appropriately, in our view) that the new charges were attributable to the acquittal on the RICO charges, which followed Johnson's exercise of his right to a jury trial. In these circumstances, it is conceivable that the weapons charges were brought in retaliation for Johnson's exercise of his rights. However, the Government also might have decided from the outset that it was unnecessary for Johnson to be convicted and sentenced for both sets of charges; under this line of thinking, the weapons prosecution was superfluous unless the RICO prosecution proved unsuccessful. This rationale does not eliminate the "but for" causal connection between Johnson's exercise of his right to a jury trial and the weapons prosecution, but

it nevertheless is entirely legitimate, and certainly cannot be considered vindictive. The relevant question, therefore, is whether there is a "realistic likelihood" that the Government acted out of a vindictive motivation, rather than a legitimate one such as that described above.

* * * [W]e join the other courts of appeals that have held that a new federal prosecution following an acquittal on separate federal charges does not, without more, give rise to a presumption of vindictiveness. Simply put, when a State brings another indictment supported by evidence against a defendant after an acquittal, the acquittal is a legitimate prosecutorial consideration because the State is not levying punishment for a right exercised but rather for the crimes the defendant committed. Accordingly, those circumstances do not present a "realistic likelihood" of prosecutorial vindictiveness.

The court noted the adverse consequences that might flow if a presumption of vindictiveness arose whenever charges on separate offenses were brought after a defendant's acquittal:

Furthermore, adoption of a presumption of vindictiveness in these circumstances would encourage prosecutors to overcharge defendants, a result we do not wish to promote.

The court rejected "a new constitutional rule that requires prosecutors to bring all possible charges in an indictment or forever hold their peace."

E. Respecting the Right to Counsel

Rule 3.8

The prosecutor in a criminal case shall:

* * *

(b) make reasonable efforts to assure that the accused has been advised of the right to, and the procedure for obtaining, counsel and has been given reasonable opportunity to obtain counsel;

(c) not seek to obtain from an unrepresented accused a waiver of important pretrial rights, such as the right to a preliminary hearing;

* * *

UNITED STATES v. HAMMAD

<u>858 F.2d 834 (2d Cir. 1988)</u>

IRVING R. KAUFMAN, Circuit Judge

On November 30, 1985, the Hammad Department Store in Brooklyn, New York, caught fire under circumstances suggesting arson. The Bureau of Alcohol, Tobacco and Firearms was assigned to investigate in conjunction with the United States Attorney for the Eastern District of New York.

During the course of his investigation, an Assistant United States Attorney ("AUSA") discovered that the store's owners, Taiseer and Eid Hammad, had been audited by the New York State Department of Social Services for Medicaid fraud. The audit revealed that the Hammad brothers had bilked Medicaid out of $400,000; they claimed reimbursement for special orthopedic footwear but supplied customers with ordinary, non-therapeutic shoes. Consequently, the Department revoked the Hammads' eligibility for Medicaid reimbursement and demanded return of the $400,000 overpayment. The Hammads challenged the Department's determination and submitted invoices purporting to document their sales of orthopedic shoes. The invoices were received from Wallace Goldstein of the Crystal Shoe Company, a supplier to the Hammads' store.

On September 22, 1986, however, Goldstein informed the AUSA that he had provided the Hammads with false invoices. Government investigators, therefore, suspected the fire had been intended to destroy actual sales records, thereby concealing the fraudulent Medicaid claims. Goldstein agreed to cooperate with the government's investigation. Accordingly, the prosecutor directed Goldstein to arrange and record a meeting with the Hammads.

Some three weeks later, on October 9, Goldstein telephoned the Hammads. He spoke briefly with Eid, who referred him to Taiseer. Goldstein falsely told Taiseer he had been subpoenaed to appear before the grand jury investigating the Hammads' Medicaid fraud. He added that the grand jury had requested records of Crystal's sales to the Hammad Department Store to compare them with the invoices the Hammads had submitted. Taiseer did not deny defrauding Medicaid, but instead urged Goldstein to conceal the fraud by lying to the grand jury and by refusing to produce Crystal's true sales records. * * *

Goldstein and Hammad saw each other five days later. The meeting was recorded and videotaped. Goldstein showed Hammad a sham subpoena supplied by the prosecutor. The subpoena instructed Goldstein to appear before the grand jury and to provide any records reflecting shoe sales from Crystal to the Hammad Department Store. Hammad apparently accepted the subpoena as genuine because he spent much of the remainder of the meeting devising strategies for Goldstein to avoid compliance. The two held no further meetings.

On April 15, 1987, after considering the recordings, videotapes and other evidence, the grand jury returned a forty-five count indictment against the Hammad brothers, including thirty-eight counts of mail fraud for filing false Medicaid invoices. Eid was also indicted for arson and for fraudulently attempting to collect fire insurance. Taiseer faced the additional charge of obstructing justice for attempting to influence Goldstein's grand jury testimony. * * *

Before trial, Taiseer Hammad moved to suppress the recordings and videotapes, alleging the prosecutor had violated DR 7-104(A)(1) of the American Bar Association's Code of Professional Responsibility. The rule prohibits a lawyer from communicating with a "party" he knows to be represented by counsel regarding the subject matter of that representation. In short, Taiseer alleged that the prosecutor—through his "alter ego" Goldstein—had violated ethical obligations by communicating directly with him after learning that he had retained counsel.

> **FYI**
>
> The Rule is 4.2, and for the purposes of this case it is substantially identical to DR 7-104.

* * *

The government vigorously disputed Hammad's assertion that the prosecutor had violated ethical standards by authorizing Goldstein to approach the defendant. It argued that DR 7-104(A)(1) was irrelevant to criminal investigations. Alternatively, it claimed the rule did not apply to investigations prior to the commencement of adversarial proceedings against a defendant. * * *

In an order dated September 21, 1987, Judge Glasser granted Taiseer's motion to suppress the recordings and videotapes. The government, he found, "was clearly aware, by at least as early as September 9, 1986, that [Taiseer] had retained counsel in connection with this case." He also determined that Goldstein was the prosecutor's "alter ego" during his discussions with Hammad. Accordingly, the court held that the prosecutor had violated DR 7-104(A)(1) and suppressed the recordings and videotapes secured as a result of the violation.

* * *

We decline to hold, as the government suggests, either that DR 7-104(A)(1) is limited in application to civil disputes or that it is coextensive with the sixth amendment. Nor has the government provided an adequate basis for reversing the able district judge's determination, after the suppression hearing, that the prosecutor knew Hammad had legal representation or that Goldstein was his "alter ego." We are mindful, however, that suppression of evidence is an extreme remedy that may impede legitimate investigatory activities. Accordingly, we find, in this case, that suppression of the recordings and videotapes constituted an abuse of the district court's discretion.

* * * The federal courts enforce professional responsibility standards pursuant to their general supervisory authority over members of the bar. In addition, the Eastern District of New York, where this action arose, has adopted the Code of Professional Responsibility through Local Rule 2 of its General Rules.

This circuit conclusively established the applicability of DR 7-104(A)(1) to criminal prosecutions in *United States v. Jamil,* 707 F.2d 638 (2d Cir. 1983). In *Jamil,* we held that "DR 7-104(A)(1) may be found to apply in criminal cases, . . . to government attorneys . . . [and] to non-attorney government law enforcement officers when they act as the alter ego of government prosecutors." Even those courts restricting the rule's ambit have suggested that, in appropriate circumstances, DR 7-104(A)(1) would apply to criminal prosecutions. * * * Thus, the government's contention that DR 7-104(A)(1) is "inapplicable to criminal investigations" is mistaken.

The applicability of DR 7-104(A)(1) to the investigatory stages of a criminal prosecution presents a closer question. The government asserts the rule is coextensive with the sixth amendment, and hence, that it remains inoperative until the onset of adversarial proceedings. The appellee responds that several courts have enforced DR 7-104(A)(1) prior to attachment of sixth amendment protections. We find no principled basis in the rule to constrain its reach as the government proposes * * * . Nonetheless, we urge restraint in applying the rule to criminal investigations to avoid handcuffing law enforcement officers in their efforts to develop evidence.

> **FYI**
>
> The Sixth Amendment right to Counsel does not apply until the defendant has been formally charged with a crime. *See, e.g., Moran v. Burbine,* 475 U.S. 412 (1986).

* * *

The Constitution defines only the "minimal historic safeguards" which defendants must receive rather than the outer bounds of those we may afford them. In other words, the Constitution prescribes a floor below which protections may not fall, rather than a ceiling beyond which they may not rise. The Model Code of Professional Responsibility, on the other hand, encompasses the attorney's duty "to maintain the highest standards of ethical conduct." The Code is designed to safeguard the integrity of the profession and preserve public confidence in our system of justice. It not only delineates an attorney's duties to the court, but defines his relationship with his client and adverse parties. Hence, the Code secures protections not contemplated by the Constitution.

Moreover, we resist binding the Code's applicability to the moment of indictment. The timing of an indictment's return lies substantially within the control of the prosecutor. Therefore, were we to construe the rule as dependent upon indictment, a government attorney could manipulate grand jury proceedings to avoid its encumbrances.

The government contends that a broad reading of DR 7-104(A)(1) would impede legitimate investigatory practices. In particular, the government fears career criminals with permanent "house counsel" could immunize themselves from infiltration by informants. We share this concern and would not interpret the disciplinary rule as precluding undercover investigations. Our task, accordingly, is imposing adequate safeguards without crippling law enforcement.

The principal question presented to us herein is: to what extent does DR 7-104(A)(1) restrict the use of informants by government prosecutors prior to indictment, but after a suspect has retained counsel in connection with the subject matter of a criminal investigation? In an attempt to avoid hampering legitimate criminal investigations by government prosecutors, Judge Glasser resolved this dilemma by limiting the rule's applicability "to instances in which a suspect has retained counsel specifically for representation in conjunction with the criminal matter in which he is held suspect, and the government has knowledge of that fact." Thus, he reasoned, the rule exempts the vast majority of cases where suspects are unaware they are being investigated.

While it may be true that this limitation will not unduly hamper the government's ability to conduct effective criminal investigations in a majority of instances, we nevertheless believe that it *is* unduly restrictive in that small but persistent number of cases where a career criminal has retained "house counsel" to represent him in connection with an ongoing fraud or criminal enterprise. This Court has recognized that prosecutors have a responsibility to perform investigative as well as courtroom-related duties in criminal matters. As we see it, under DR 7-104(A)(1), a prosecutor is "authorized by law" to employ legitimate investigative techniques in conducting or supervising criminal investigations, and the use of informants to gather evidence against a suspect will frequently fall within the ambit of such authorization.

Notwithstanding this holding, however, we recognize that in some instances a government prosecutor may overstep the already broad powers of his office, and in so doing, violate the ethical precepts of DR 7-104(A)(1). In the present case, the prosecutor issued a subpoena for the informant, not to secure his attendance before the grand jury, but to create a pretense that might help the informant elicit admissions from a represented suspect. Though we have no occasion to consider the use of this technique in relation to unrepresented suspects, we believe that use of the technique under the circumstances of this case contributed to the informant's becoming that alter ego of the prosecutor. Consequently, the informant was engaging in communications proscribed by DR 7-104(A)(1). Therefore, we agree with Judge Glasser that the prosecution violated the disciplinary rule in this case.

Notwithstanding requests for a bright-line rule, we decline to list all possible situations that may violate DR 7-104(A)(1). This delineation is best accomplished by case-by-case adjudication, particularly when ethical standards are involved. As our holding above makes clear, however, the use of informants by government prosecutors in a preindictment, non-custodial situation, absent the type of misconduct that occurred in this case, will generally fall within the "authorized by law" exception to DR 7-104(A)(1) and therefore will not be subject to sanctions.

On appeal, the government also claims that even if there was a violation of the disciplinary rule, exclusion is inappropriate to remedy an ethical breach. We have not heretofore decided whether suppression is warranted for a DR 7-104(A)(1) violation. We now hold that, in light of the underlying purposes of the Professional Responsibility Code and the exclusionary rule, suppression may be ordered in the district court's discretion.

The exclusionary rule mandates suppression of evidence garnered in contravention of a defendant's constitutional rights and protections. The rule is thus intended to: deter improper conduct by law enforcement officials; preserve judicial integrity by insulating the courts from tainted evidence; and maintain popular trust in the integrity of the judicial process. Anything short of exclusion, the Supreme Court reasoned, would be "worthless and futile" in securing the rule's goals.

These same needs arise outside the context of constitutional violations. "The principles governing the admissibility of evidence in federal criminal trials have not been restricted . . . to those derived solely from the Constitution." Hence, the exclusionary rule has application to governmental misconduct which falls short of a constitutional transgression.

Some statutes require exclusion by their own terms. For example, the government is precluded from introducing into evidence any wire or oral communication intercepted contrary to authorized procedures. Other statutes have been interpreted to permit exclusion when contravention of the statute interferes with a substantial right, such as prompt execution of a warrant. Indeed, suppression may even be ordered for violations of administrative regulations. In the instant case, we consider the exclusionary rule's applicability to yet another category of non-constitutional transgressions—breaches of ethical precepts enforced pursuant to the federal courts' supervisory authority.

* * * [W]e reject the government's effort to remove suppression from the arsenal of remedies available to district judges confronted with ethical violations. We have confidence that district courts will exercise their discretion cautiously and with clear cognizance that suppression imposes a barrier between the finder of fact and the discovery of truth.

Judge Glasser apparently assumed * * * that suppression is a necessary consequence of a DR 7-104(A)(1) violation. Exclusion, however, is not required in every case. Here, the government should not have its case prejudiced by suppression of its evidence when the law was previously unsettled in this area. Therefore, in light of the prior uncertainty regarding the reach of DR 7-104(A)(1), an exclusionary remedy is inappropriate in this case.

Accordingly, we find the district court abused its discretion in suppressing the recordings and videotapes, and its decision is reversed.

F. Plea Bargaining

[Question 2]

Walker was arrested for violently robbing a man on the street, but the victim was unwilling to testify at trial. The prosecutor entered into plea bargaining discussions with Walker and his counsel. Walker was unwilling to accept a plea with jail time. He was previously convicted of rape, and so pleading guilty to theft would demand incarceration under applicable law. The prosecutor then offered a deal: if Walker would plead guilty to illegally recording music, the robbery charg-

Courts have rarely suppressed evidence based on prosecutors' violation of Rule 4.2. However, out of concern that federal courts might interpret and apply the rule in a manner that interferes with federal criminal investigations, the Department of Justice adopted an internal policy in 1989 known as the "Thornburgh Memorandum" after then-Attorney General Richard Thornburg. The policy purported to authorize federal prosecutors to use investigative methods that might otherwise have been barred by Rule 4.2. When courts questioned the legitimacy of the policy, the Department used the federal administrative rule-making process to adopt an administrative regulation that was meant to achieve the same result in a more legally effective manner. This regulation, adopted in 1994 after a two-year process, was sometimes called the "Reno Rule" after the new Attorney General, Janet Reno. Courts looked skeptically on the rule. It was effectively repealed in 1998 by a federal statute, known as the McDade Amendment after Joseph McDade, its sponsor in the House of Representatives, who proposed the provision soon after being acquitted of bribery-related offenses and shortly before leaving office. The McDade Amendment requires federal prosecutors to comply with the ethical rules of the states in which they practice. For articles discussing these events, *see* Fred C. Zacharias & Bruce A. Green, *The Uniqueness of Federal Prosecutors*, 88 Geo. L.J. 207 (2000); Bruce A. Green, *Whose Rules of Professional Conduct Should Govern Lawyers in Federal Court and How Should the Rules Be Created?*, 64 Geo. Wash. L. Rev. 460 (1996).

es would be dropped. Walker would receive a fine and would be credited with time served since his arrest.

May the prosecutor ethically offer this plea arrangement when all agree that Walker would be pleading guilty to a crime he did not commit?

(A) Yes

(B) No

State courts in many parts of the country routinely enter judgments based on similar agreements. For more on the practice, and on legal ethics arguments made in support of and against the practice, *see* Mari Byrne, Note, *Baseless Pleas: A Mockery of Justice*, 78 Fordham L. Rev. 2961 (2010).

BORDENKIRCHER v. HAYES

434 U.S. 357 (1978)

Mr. Justice STEWART delivered the opinion of the Court.

The question in this case is whether the Due Process Clause of the Fourteenth Amendment is violated when a state prosecutor carries out a threat made during plea negotiations to reindict the accused on more serious charges if he does not plead guilty to the offense with which he was originally charged.

I

The respondent, Paul Lewis Hayes, was indicted by a Fayette County, Ky., grand jury on a charge of uttering a forged instrument in the amount of $88.30, an offense then punishable by a term of 2 to 10 years in prison. After arraignment, Hayes, his retained counsel, and the Commonwealth's Attorney met in the presence of the Clerk of the Court to discuss a possible plea agreement. During these conferences the prosecutor offered to recommend a sentence of five years in prison if Hayes would plead guilty to the indictment. He also said that if Hayes did not plead guilty and "save[d] the court the inconvenience and necessity of a trial," he would return to the grand jury to seek an indictment under the Kentucky Habitual Criminal Act, which would subject Hayes to a mandatory sentence of life imprisonment by reason of his two prior felony convictions. Hayes chose not to plead guilty, and the prosecutor did obtain an indictment charging him under the Habitual Criminal Act. It is not disputed that the recidivist charge was fully justified by the evidence, that the prosecutor was in possession of this evidence at the time of the original indictment, and that Hayes' refusal to plead guilty to the original charge was what led to his indictment under the habitual criminal statute.

A jury found Hayes guilty on the principal charge of uttering a forged instrument and, in a separate proceeding, further found that he had twice before been convicted of felonies. As required by the habitual offender statute, he was sentenced to a life term in the penitentiary. The Kentucky Court of Appeals [held] that the prosecutor's decision to indict him as a habitual offender was a legitimate use of available leverage in the plea-bargaining process.

* * *

II

It may be helpful to clarify at the outset the nature of the issue in this case. While the prosecutor did not actually obtain the recidivist indictment until after the plea conferences had ended, his intention to do so was clearly expressed at the outset of the plea negotiations. Hayes was thus fully informed of the true terms of the offer when he made his decision to plead not guilty. This is not a situation, therefore, where the prosecutor without notice brought an additional and more serious charge after plea negotiations relating only to the original indictment had ended with the defendant's insistence on pleading not guilty. As a practical matter, in short, this case would be no different if the grand jury had indicted Hayes as a recidivist from the outset, and the prosecutor had offered to drop that charge as part of the plea bargain.

* * *

III

We have recently had occasion to observe: "[W]hatever might be the situation in an ideal world, the fact is that the guilty plea and the often concomitant plea bargain are important components of this country's criminal justice system. Properly administered, they can benefit all concerned." The open acknowledgment of this previously clandestine practice has led this Court to recognize the importance of counsel during plea negotiations, * * * the need for a public record indicating that a plea was knowingly and voluntarily made, * * * and the requirement that a prosecutor's plea-bargaining promise must be kept* * * . * * *

IV

This Court held in *North Carolina v. Pearce*, 395 U.S. 711, 725, that the Due Process Clause of the Fourteenth Amendment "requires that vindictiveness against a defendant for having successfully attacked his first conviction must play no part in the sentence he receives after a new trial." The same principle was later applied to prohibit a prosecutor from reindicting a convicted misdemeanant on a felony charge after the defendant had invoked an appellate remedy, since in this situation there was also a "realistic likelihood of 'vindictiveness.' "

In those cases the Court was dealing with the State's unilateral imposition of a penalty upon a defendant who had chosen to exercise a legal right to attack his original conviction-a situation "very different from the give-and-take negotiation common in plea bargaining between the prosecution and defense, which arguably possess relatively equal bargaining power." The Court has emphasized that the due process violation in cases such as *Pearce* and *Perry* lay not in the possibility that a defendant might be deterred from the exercise of a legal right, but rather in the danger that the State might be retaliating against the accused for lawfully attacking his conviction.

To punish a person because he has done what the law plainly allows him to do is a due process violation of the most basic sort * * * . But in the "give-and-take" of plea bargaining, there is no such element of punishment or retaliation so long as the accused is free to accept or reject the prosecution's offer.

Plea bargaining flows from "the mutuality of advantage" to defendants and prosecutors, each with his own reasons for wanting to avoid trial. Defendants advised by competent counsel and protected by other procedural safeguards are presumptively capable of intelligent choice in response to prosecutorial persuasion, and unlikely to be driven to false self-condemnation. Indeed, acceptance of the basic legitimacy of plea bargaining necessarily implies rejection of any notion that a guilty plea is involuntary in a constitutional sense simply because it is the end result of the bargaining process. By hypothesis, the plea may have been induced by promises of a recommendation of a lenient sentence or a reduction of charges, and thus by fear of the possibility of a greater penalty upon conviction after a trial. * * *

While confronting a defendant with the risk of more severe punishment clearly may have a discouraging effect on the defendant's assertion of his trial rights, the imposition of these difficult choices is an inevitable—and permissible—attribute of any legitimate system which tolerates and encourages the negotiation of pleas. It follows that, by encouraging the negotiation of pleas, this Court has necessarily accepted as constitutionally legitimate the simple reality that the prosecutor's interest at the bargaining table is to persuade the defendant to forgo his right to plead not guilty.

It is not disputed here that Hayes was properly chargeable under the recidivist statute, since he had in fact been convicted of two previous felonies. In our system, so long as the prosecutor has probable cause to believe that the accused committed an offense defined by statute, the decision whether or not to prosecute, and what charge to file or bring before a grand jury, generally rests entirely in his discretion. Within the limits set by the legislature's constitutionally valid definition of chargeable offenses, the conscious exercise of some selectivity in enforcement is not in itself a federal constitutional violation so long as the selection was not deliberately based upon an unjustifiable standard such as race, religion, or other arbitrary classification. To hold that the prosecutor's desire to induce a guilty plea is an "unjustifiable standard," which, like race or religion, may play no part in his charging decision, would contradict the very premises that underlie the concept of plea bargaining itself. Moreover, a rigid constitutional rule that would prohibit a prosecutor from acting forthrightly in his dealings with the defense could only invite unhealthy subterfuge that would drive the practice of plea bargaining back into the shadows from which it has so recently emerged.

There is no doubt that the breadth of discretion that our country's legal system vests in prosecuting attorneys carries with it the potential for both individual and institutional abuse. And broad though that discretion may be, there are undoubtedly constitutional limits upon its exercise. We hold only that the course of conduct engaged in by the prosecutor in this case, which no more than openly presented the defendant with the unpleasant alternatives of forgoing trial or facing charges on which he was plainly subject to prosecution, did not violate the Due Process Clause of the Fourteenth Amendment.

Accordingly, the judgment of the Court of Appeals is

Reversed.

Mr. Justice BLACKMUN, with whom Mr. Justice BRENNAN and Mr. Justice MARSHALL join, dissenting.

* * *

It might be argued that it really makes little difference how this case * * * is decided. The Court's holding gives plea bargaining full sway despite vindictiveness. A contrary result, however, merely would prompt the aggressive prosecutor to bring the greater charge initially in every case, and only thereafter to bargain. The consequences to the accused would still be adverse, for then he would bargain against a greater charge, face the likelihood of increased bail, and run the risk that the court would be less inclined to accept a bargained plea. Nonetheless, it is far preferable to hold the prosecution to the charge it was originally content to bring and to justify in the eyes of its public.[2]

Mr. Justice POWELL, dissenting.

---

2   That prosecutors, without saying so, may sometimes bring charges more serious than they think appropriate for the ultimate disposition of a case, in order to gain bargaining leverage with a defendant, does not add support to today's decision, for this Court, in its approval of the advantages to be gained from plea negotiations, has never openly sanctioned such deliberate overcharging or taken such a cynical view of the bargaining process. Normally, of course, it is impossible to show that this is what the prosecutor is doing, and the courts necessarily have deferred to the prosecutor's exercise of discretion in initial charging decisions. * * *

Although I agree with much of the Court's opinion, I am not satisfied that the result in this case is just or that the conduct of the plea bargaining met the requirements of due process.

* * *

The plea-bargaining process, as recognized by this Court, is essential to the functioning of the criminal-justice system. It normally affords genuine benefits to defendants as well as to society. And if the system is to work effectively, prosecutors must be accorded the widest discretion, within constitutional limits, in conducting bargaining. This is especially true when a defendant is represented by counsel and presumably is fully advised of his rights. Only in the most exceptional case should a court conclude that the scales of the bargaining are so unevenly balanced as to arouse suspicion. In this case, the prosecutor's actions denied respondent due process because their admitted purpose was to discourage and then to penalize with unique severity his exercise of constitutional rights. Implementation of a strategy calculated solely to deter the exercise of constitutional rights is not a constitutionally permissible exercise of discretion. I would affirm the opinion of the Court of Appeals on the facts of this case.

1. Inverted Sentencing

As a practical matter in multi-defendant cases, those who are more culpable sometimes have a chance to receive a lighter sentence than those who are less culpable. That is because prosecutors often need cooperation from some criminals in order to convict others, and plea bargaining is about the only tool that the prosecutor can legitimately employ to encourage cooperation. The incentives result in what Professor Richman terms "inverted sentencing": "The more serious the defendant's crimes, the lower the sentence—because the greater his wrongs, the more information and assistance he has to offer a prosecutor." Daniel C. Richman, *Cooperating Clients*, 56 Ohio St. L.J. 69 (1995). Judge Bright, dissenting in *United States v. Griffin*, 17 F.3d 269 (8th Cir. 1994), had this to ask about the phenomenon of inverted sentencing:

> What kind of a criminal justice system rewards the drug kingpin or near-kingpin who informs on all the criminal colleagues he or she has recruited, but sends to prison for years and years the least knowledgeable or culpable conspirator, one who knows very little about the conspiracy and is without information for the prosecution?

Is inverted sentencing an indictment of the plea bargaining system? Or is it an inevitable consequence of the prosecutor's need for cooperation from criminals? If plea bargaining were abolished, what incentive would a criminal have to cooperate with the government by giving away information about his confederates?

2. Package Deals

Suppose a prosecutor in a multi-defendant case proposes a global settlement: all the defendants can plead to specified crimes, but they must plead guilty as a group; if all the defendants do not agree, the deal is off. Does a "wired" plea or "package deal" present a greater risk of coercion than an individual plea? In *United States v. Pollard*, 959 F.2d 1011 (D.C.Cir. 1992), the defendant pled guilty to one count of conspiracy to deliver national defense information to the Government of Israel. He later claimed that the government coerced his guilty plea by linking his wife's plea to his own, especially as his wife was seriously ill at the time. But the court rejected his argument:

> **FYI**
>
> The practice is discussed in Jonathan Liebman & Orin S. Snyder, *Joint Guilty Pleas: "Group Justice" In Federal Plea Bargaining*, N.Y. L.J., Sept. 8, 1994, at p.1, col.1 (noting that for the government, "group pleas dispose of cases in one fell swoop and thereby conserve scarce prosecutorial resources and, in some cases, avoid lengthy, costly or potentially embarrassing trials").

> To say that a practice is "coercive" or renders a plea "involuntary" means only that it creates improper pressure that would be likely to overbear the will of some innocent persons and cause them to plead guilty. Only physical harm, threats of harassment, misrepresentation, or promises that are by their nature improper as having no proper relationship to the prosecutor's business (e.g., bribes) render a guilty plea legally involuntary. * * *

> * * * We must be mindful * * * that if the judiciary were to declare wired pleas unconstitutional, the consequences would not be altogether foreseeable and perhaps would not be beneficial to defendants. Would Pollard, for instance, have been better off had he not been able to bargain to aid his wife? Would his wife have been better off? Would the bargaining take place in any event, but with winks and nods rather than in writing?

> Nor do we believe that Mrs. Pollard's medical condition makes an otherwise acceptable linkage of their pleas unconstitutional. The appropriate dividing line between acceptable and unconstitutional plea wiring does not depend upon the physical condition or personal circumstances of the defendant; rather, it depends upon the conduct of the government. Where, as here, the government had probable cause to arrest and prosecute both defendants in a related crime, and there is no suggestion that the government conducted itself in bad faith in an effort to generate additional leverage over the defendant, we think a wired plea is constitutional.

Pollard considered the problem of a defendant "pressured" because of feelings toward the person to whom his plea is linked. The court in *United States v. Caro*, <u>997 F.2d 657 (9th Cir. 1993)</u>, considered a different problem that might be created by wired pleas—the possibility of coercion by other defendants. Caro moved to set aside his guilty plea on the ground that he was pressured by his codefendants into going along with the package deal. At the hearing in which his plea was entered, the judge was never informed that Caro's plea was part of a group settlement. Judge Kozinski analyzed the problem as follows:

> Though package deal plea agreements are not per se impermissible, they pose an additional risk of coercion not present when the defendant is dealing with the government alone. Quite possibly, one defendant will be happier with the package deal than his codefendants; looking out for his own interests, the lucky one may try to force his codefendants into going along with the deal. * * * We * * * have recognized that the trial court should make a more careful examination of the voluntariness of a plea when it might have been induced by threats or promises from a third party. We make it clear today that, in describing a plea agreement * * * the prosecutor must alert the district court to the fact that codefendants are entering into a package deal.

The court held that the trial court's error—really the prosecutor's error in failing to tell the judge that the pleas were "wired"—was not harmless. It vacated Caro's guilty plea and remanded. *Compare United States v. Carr*, <u>80 F.3d 413 (10th Cir. 1996)</u> (pressures of cohorts to accept a package deal "might have been palpable" to the defendant, but they did not vitiate the voluntariness of his plea because "it was still his choice to make").

> **FYI**
>
> Professor Green, in *"Package" Plea Bargaining and the Prosecutor's Duty of Good Faith*, <u>25 Crim. L. Bull. 507 (1989)</u>, argues that prosecutors who offer multi-defendant deals have an ethical responsibility to avoid overreaching.

G. Discovery

1. Constitutional Obligation

Prosecutors have an ethical obligation to make timely disclosure to the defense of all evidence or information known to the prosecutor that negates the guilt of the accused or mitigates the seriousness of the offense. This is known as the *Brady* Rule, based on the holding of the Supreme Court in *Brady v. Maryland*, <u>373 U.S. 83 (1963)</u>. Brady and a companion, Boblit, were charged with first degree murder, a capital offense. Brady was tried first; he admitted participation in the crime, but claimed that Boblit did the actual killing. Prior to trial Brady's lawyer asked the prosecutor to allow him to see Boblit's statements. Several statements were shown to counsel, but one in which Boblit admitted the homicide was not revealed. The defense did not learn about that statement until after Brady's conviction and death sentence were affirmed. The Supreme Court found that the prosecutor has an obligation to disclose all materially exculpatory evidence, and that Boblit's admission would have had a material effect on Brady's death sentence. The Court declared that "[a] prosecution that withholds evidence on demand of an accused which, if made available, would tend to exculpate him or reduce the penalty helps shape a trial that bears heavily on the defendant. That casts the prosecutor in the role of an architect of a proceeding that does not comport with standards of justice * * *." The Court concluded as follows:

> We now hold that the suppression by the prosecution of evidence favorable to an accused upon request violates due process where the evidence is material either to guilt or to punishment, irrespective of the good faith or bad faith of the prosecution.

In *Brady,* the Court extended their holding in *Mooney v. Holohan*, 294 U.S. 103, 112 (1935), in which the Court held that the prosecutor's deliberate use of perjured testimony violates the defendant's due process rights and is a denial of a fair trial.

> It is a requirement that cannot be deemed to be satisfied by mere notice and hearing if a state has contrived a conviction through the pretense of a trial which in truth is but used as a means of depriving a defendant of liberty through a deliberate deception of court and jury by the presentation of testimony known to be perjured. Such a contrivance by a state to procure the conviction and imprisonment of a defendant is as inconsistent with the rudimentary demands of justice as is the obtaining of a like result by intimidation.

UNITED STATES v. AGURS

427 U.S. 97 (1976)

Mr. Justice Stevens **delivered the opinion of the Court.**

After a brief interlude in an inexpensive motel room, respondent repeatedly stabbed James Sewell, causing his death. She was convicted of second-degree murder. The question before us is whether the prosecutor's failure to provide defense counsel with certain background information about Sewell, which would have tended to support the argument that respondent acted in self-defense, deprived her of a fair trial under the rule of Brady v. Maryland.

* * *

I

At about 4:30 p.m. on September 24, 1971, respondent, who had been there before, and Sewell, registered in a motel as man and wife. They were assigned a room without a bath. Sewell was wearing a bowie knife in a sheath, and carried another knife in his pocket. Less than two hours earlier, according to the testimony of his estranged wife, he had had $360 in cash on his person.

About 15 minutes later three motel employees heard respondent screaming for help. A forced entry into their room disclosed Sewell on top of respondent struggling for possession of the bowie knife. She was holding the knife; his bleeding hand grasped the blade; according to one witness he was trying to jam the blade into her chest. The employees separated the two and summoned the authorities. Respondent departed without comment before they arrived. Sewell was dead on arrival at the hospital.

Circumstantial evidence indicated that the parties had completed an act of intercourse, that Sewell had then gone to the bathroom down the hall, and that the struggle occurred upon his return. The contents of his pockets were in disarray on the dresser and no money was found; the jury may have inferred that respondent took Sewell's money and that the fight started when Sewell re-entered the room and saw what she was doing.

On the following morning respondent surrendered to the police. She was given a physical examination which revealed no cuts or bruises of any kind, except needle marks on her upper arm. An autopsy of Sewell disclosed that he had several deep stab wounds in his chest and abdomen, and a number of slashes on his arms and hands, characterized by the pathologist as "defensive wounds."

Respondent offered no evidence. Her sole defense was the argument made by her attorney that Sewell had initially attacked her with the knife, and that her actions had all been directed toward saving her own life. The support for this self-defense theory was based on the fact that she had screamed for help. Sewell was on top of her when help arrived, and his possession of two knives indicated that he was a violence-prone person. It took the jury about 25 minutes to elect a foreman and return a verdict.

Three months later defense counsel filed a motion for a new trial asserting that he had discovered (1) that Sewell had a prior criminal record that would have further evidenced his violent character; (2) that the prosecutor had failed to disclose this information to the defense; and (3) that a recent opinion of the United States Court of Appeals for the District of Columbia Circuit made it clear that such evidence was admissible even if not known to the defendant. Sewell's prior record included a plea of guilty to a charge of assault and carrying a deadly weapon in 1963, and another guilty plea to a charge of carrying a deadly weapon in 1971. Apparently both weapons were knives.

The Government opposed the motion, arguing that there was no duty to tender Sewell's prior record to the defense in the absence of an appropriate request; that the evidence was readily discoverable in advance of trial and hence was not the kind of "newly discovered" evidence justifying a new trial; and that, in all events, it was not material.

The District Court denied the motion. * * *

The Court of Appeals reversed. The court found no lack of diligence on the part of the defense and no misconduct by the prosecutor in this case. It held, however, that the evidence was material, and that its nondisclosure required a new trial because the jury might have returned a different verdict if the evidence had been received.

The decision of the Court of Appeals represents a significant departure from this Court's prior holding; because we believe that that court has incorrectly interpreted the constitutional requirement of due process, we reverse.

II

The rule of *Brady v. Maryland* arguably applies in three quite different situations. Each involves the discovery, after trial, of information which had been known to the prosecution but unknown to the defense.

In the first situation, typified by *Mooney v. Holohan*, the undisclosed evidence demonstrates that the prosecution's case includes perjured testimony and that the prosecution knew, or should have known, of the perjury. In a series of subsequent cases, the Court has consistently held that a conviction obtained by the knowing use of perjured testimony is fundamentally unfair, and must be set aside if there is any reasonable likelihood that the false testimony could have affected the judgment of the jury. It is this line of cases on which the Court of Appeals placed primary reliance. In those cases the Court has applied a strict standard of materiality, not just because they involve prosecutorial misconduct, but more importantly because they involve a corruption of the truth-seeking function of the trial process. Since this case involves no misconduct, and since there is no reason to question the veracity of any of the prosecution witnesses, the test of materiality followed in the *Mooney* line of cases is not necessarily applicable to this case.

The second situation, illustrated by the *Brady* case itself, is characterized by a pretrial request for specific evidence. In that case defense counsel had requested the extrajudicial statements made by Brady's accomplice, one Boblit. This Court held that the suppression of one of Boblit's statements deprived Brady of due process, noting specifically that the statement had been requested and that it was "material." A fair analysis of the holding in *Brady* indicates that implicit in the requirement of materiality is a concern that the suppressed evidence might have affected the outcome of the trial.

* * *

In *Brady* the request was specific. It gave the prosecutor notice of exactly what the defense desired. Although there is, of course, no duty to provide defense counsel with unlimited discovery of everything known by the prosecutor, if the subject matter of such a request is material, or indeed if a substantial basis for claiming materiality exists, it is reasonable to require the prosecutor to respond either by furnishing the information or by submitting the problem to the trial judge. When the prosecutor receives a specific and relevant request, the failure to make any response is seldom, if ever, excusable.

In many cases, however, exculpatory information in the possession of the prosecutor may be unknown to defense counsel. In such a situation he may make no request at all, or possibly ask for "all *Brady* material" or for "anything exculpatory." Such a request really gives the prosecutor no better notice than if no request is made. If there is a duty to respond to a general request of that kind, it must derive from the obviously exculpatory character of certain evidence in the hands of the prosecutor. But if the evidence is so clearly supportive of a claim of innocence that it gives the prosecution notice of a duty to produce, that duty should equally arise even if no request is made. Whether we focus on the desirability of a precise definition of the prosecutor's duty or on the potential harm to the defendant, we conclude that there is no significant difference between cases in which there has been merely a general request for exculpatory matter and cases, like the one we must now decide, in which there has been no request at all. The third situation in which the *Brady* rule arguably applies, typified by this case, therefore embraces the case in which only a general request for "*Brady*" material has been made.

We now consider whether the prosecutor has any constitutional duty to volunteer exculpatory matter to the defense, and if so, what standard of materiality gives rise to that duty.

III

* * *

The Court of Appeals appears to have assumed that the prosecutor has a constitutional obligation to disclose any information that might affect the jury's verdict. That statement of a constitutional standard of materiality approaches the "sporting theory of justice" which the Court expressly rejected in *Brady*. For a jury's appraisal of a case "might" be affected by an improper or trivial consideration as well as by evidence giving rise to a legitimate doubt on the issue of guilt. If everything that might influence a jury must be disclosed, the only way a prosecutor could discharge his constitutional duty would be to allow complete discovery of his files as a matter of routine practice.

Whether or not procedural rules authorizing such broad discovery might be desirable, the Constitution surely does not demand that much. * * * The mere possibility that an item of undisclosed information might have helped the defense, or might have affected the outcome of the trial, does not establish "materiality" in the constitutional sense.

Nor do we believe the constitutional obligation is measured by the moral culpability, or the willfulness, of the prosecutor. If evidence highly probative of innocence is in his file, he should be presumed to recognize its significance even if he has actually overlooked it. Conversely, if evidence actually has no probative significance at all, no purpose would be served by requiring a new trial simply because an inept prosecutor incorrectly believed he was suppressing a fact that would be vital to the defense. If the suppression of evidence results in constitutional error, it is because of the character of the evidence, not the character of the prosecutor.

* * * [T]here are situations in which evidence is obviously of such substantial value to the defense that elementary fairness requires it to be disclosed even without a specific request. For though the attorney for the sovereign must prosecute the accused with earnestness and vigor, he must always be faithful to his client's overriding interest that "justice shall be done." He is the "servant of the law, the twofold aim of which is that guilt shall not escape or innocence suffer." *Berger v. United States*, <u>295 U.S. 78, 88</u>. This description of the prosecutor's duty illuminates the standard of materiality that governs his obligation to disclose exculpatory evidence.

* * *

The proper standard of materiality must reflect our overriding concern with the justice of the finding of guilt. Such a finding is permissible only if supported by evidence establishing guilt beyond a reasonable doubt. It necessarily follows that if the omitted evidence creates a reasonable doubt that did not otherwise exist, constitutional error has been committed. This means that the omission must be evaluated in the context of the entire record. If there is no reasonable doubt about guilt whether or not the additional evidence is considered, there is no justification for a new trial. On the other hand, if the verdict is already of questionable validity, additional evidence of relatively minor importance might be sufficient to create a reasonable doubt.

This statement of the standard of materiality describes the test which courts appear to have applied in actual cases although the standard has been phrased in different language. It is also the standard which the trial judge applied in this case. He evaluated the significance of Sewell's prior criminal record in the context of the full trial which he recalled in detail. Stressing in particular the incongruity of a claim that Sewell was the aggressor with the evidence of his multiple wounds and respondent's unscathed condition, the trial judge indicated his unqualified opinion that respondent was guilty. He noted that Sewell's prior record did not contradict any evidence offered by the prosecutor, and was largely cumulative of the evidence that Sewell was wearing a bowie knife in a sheath and carrying a second knife in his pocket when he registered at the motel.

Since the arrest record was not requested and did not even arguably give rise to any inference of perjury, since after considering it in the context of the entire record the trial judge remained convinced of respondent's guilt beyond a reasonable doubt, and since we are satisfied that his firsthand appraisal of the record was thorough and entirely reasonable, we hold that the prosecutor's failure to tender Sewell's record to the defense did not deprive respondent of a fair trial as guaranteed by the Due Process Clause of the Fifth Amendment. * * *

MR. JUSTICE MARSHALL with whom MR. JUSTICE BRENNAN joins, dissenting.

* * *

* * * [The majority's] rule creates little, if any, incentive for the prosecutor conscientiously to determine whether his files contain evidence helpful to the defense. Indeed, the rule reinforces the natural tendency of the prosecutor to overlook evidence favorable to the defense, and creates an incentive for the prosecutor to resolve close questions of disclosure in favor of concealment.

* * * I would hold that the defendant in this case had the burden of demonstrating that there is a significant chance that the withheld evidence, developed by skilled counsel, would have induced a reasonable doubt in the minds of enough jurors to avoid a conviction. * * *

2. *Refining the Test of Materiality:* United States v. Bagley

Justice Blackmun wrote for the Court in *United States v. Bagley*, <u>473 U.S. 667 (1985)</u>, in which the Court declined to overturn a conviction because of nondisclosure of exculpatory evidence. Bagley was charged with narcotics and firearms offenses and convicted in a bench trial only on the narcotics charges. Thereafter he learned that, despite his motion to discover any deals or promises between the government and its witnesses, the government had not disclosed that its two principal witnesses had signed contracts with the Bureau of Alcohol, Tobacco and Firearms to be paid for their undercover work. Although the trial judge ruled that the contracts would not have affected the outcome because the principal witnesses testified primarily concerning the firearms charges on which Bagley was acquitted, the court of appeals disagreed. The Supreme Court agreed with the trial judge and found that nondisclosure of impeachment evidence, like nondisclosure of other exculpatory evidence, requires reversal only if the evidence was material in the sense that it might have affected the outcome of the trial. No such showing was made on the facts of this case.

Justice Blackmun's opinion set forth a single "standard of materiality" applicable to nondisclosed exculpatory evidence:

> [Suppressed evidence] is material only if there is a reasonable probability that, had the evidence been disclosed to the defense, the result of the proceeding would have been different. A reasonable probability is a probability sufficient to undermine confidence in the outcome.

Justice Blackmun noted that this test was "sufficiently flexible" to cover no request, general request, and specific request cases. In a part of the opinion joined only by Justice O'Connor, Justice Blackmun reasoned that "the more specifically the defense requests certain evidence * * * the more reasonable it is for the defense to assume from the nondisclosure that the evidence does not exist and to make pretrial and trial decisions on the basis of this assumption." Thus, specific request cases present special considerations in applying the single "reasonable probability" standard of materiality. The more specific the request, the more likely the suppression will be "material" in the *Brady* sense.

Justice White, joined by Chief Justice Burger and Justice Rehnquist, concurred in the judgment in *Bagley*. Although he expressed agreement with the single materiality standard developed by Justice Blackmun, he saw "no reason to attempt to elaborate on the relevance to the inquiry of the specificity of the defense's request for disclosure."

Justice Marshall, joined by Justice Brennan, dissented and argued that "when the Government withholds from a defendant evidence that might impeach the prosecution's *only witnesses,* that failure to disclose cannot be deemed harmless error." Justice Stevens, who authored *Agurs,* also dissented. He argued that, unlike *Agurs,* the instant case involved a specific request and that *Brady* requires reversal for failure to disclose evidence favorable to an accused upon a specific request if the evidence is material either to guilt or punishment. Thus, he would have remanded for a determination of whether there was "any reasonable likelihood" that the nondisclosure could have affected the judgment of the trier of fact.

3. *Comments on* Brady–Agurs–Bagley

Professor Stacy, in *The Search for the Truth in Constitutional Criminal Procedure,* 91 Colum. L. Rev. 1369, 1392 (1991), has this to say about the *Bagley* standard of materiality:

> The *Bagley* standard, which focuses on the likely impact of evidence on the ultimate result in the case, suffers from two interrelated deficiencies. The first problem is that the standard will frequently be misapplied. A prosecutor's lack of information about the planned defense and partisan inclinations impede her from making an accurate and objective assessment of the evidence's effect on the outcome. The second problem is that many misapplications of the *Bagley* standard will never be detected and remedied. Because the prosecution has exclusive possession of the evidence subject to the duty to disclose and a clear incentive to withhold it, the defense or a court will sometimes never learn of evidence wrongly withheld.
>
> In short, the Court has interpreted the prosecution's duty to disclose exculpatory evidence more narrowly than a true concern for accurate factfinding implies. For a Court genuinely interested in the search for the truth, neither the adversarial system, prosecutorial burdens, nor the constitutional text can justify the *Bagley* standard, which will result in important exculpatory evidence not being disclosed in a significant number of cases.

As a prosecutor, would you now be entitled to refuse to turn over evidence that appears to be exculpatory but not sufficiently so to require a new trial under *Brady–Agurs–Bagley?* Should prosecutors be trusted with this authority? What would be wrong with requiring the prosecutor to turn over all evidence that a defense counsel would conclude *might tend* to exculpate the defendant?

FYI

Professor Capra, in *Access to Exculpatory Evidence: Avoiding the Agurs Problems of Prosecutorial Discretion and Retrospective Review,* 53 Fordham L. Rev. 391 (1984), argues that a per se right to an in camera hearing, at which the court would examine a prosecutor's files for *Brady* material, would be more effective than retrospective review of claims that exculpatory evidence was suppressed.

H. Applying the Brady Rule

1. *Fact–Intensive Application:* Kyles v. Whitley

The Court reaffirmed its *Brady–Agurs–Bagley* line of cases in *Kyles v. Whitley*, 514 U.S. 419 (1995), and applied those cases in an intensely fact-specific manner to reverse a conviction and death sentence. Kyles was convicted (after his first trial ended in a hung jury) of murdering a woman during the course of a robbery outside Schwegmann's grocery store. There was evidence that the killer left his car in the parking lot and drove away in the victim's car. The prosecution presented four eyewitnesses who identified Kyles unequivocally both before and at the trial. Kyles argued that an acquaintance, Beanie, committed the murders and framed him by planting the murder weapon (a gun) and the victim's purse and other items at Kyles's house. Beanie had originally approached the police with information that Kyles was the killer, and received a reward for his information. Beanie was not called by either side to testify at Kyles's trial. The prosecution suppressed many pieces of evidence, including: 1. pretrial statements from two of the eyewitnesses, which were markedly inconsistent with their later identifications, and one of which appeared to point to Beanie rather than Kyles as the perpetrator; 2. a series of statements by Beanie that were inconsistent, and which inconsistencies were ignored by the investigating officer; and 3. a police report indicating that Kyles's car was not on the list of cars found at the Schwegmann's shortly after the murder.

Justice Souter, writing for five Justices, made the following general points about the Court's *Brady–Agurs–Bagley* materiality standard:

> Four aspects of materiality under *Bagley* bear emphasis. * * * *Bagley's* touchstone of materiality is a "reasonable probability" of a different result, and the adjective is important. The question is not whether the defendant would more likely than not have received a different verdict with the evidence, but whether in its absence he received a fair trial, understood as a trial resulting in a verdict worthy of confidence. A "reasonable probability" of a different result is accordingly shown when the Government's evidentiary suppression "undermines confidence in the outcome of the trial."

> The second aspect of *Bagley* materiality bearing emphasis here is that it is not a sufficiency of evidence test. * * * The possibility of an acquittal on a criminal charge does not imply an insufficient evidentiary basis to convict. One does not show a *Brady* violation by demonstrating that some of the inculpatory evidence should have been excluded, but by showing that the favorable evidence could reasonably be taken to put the whole case in such a different light as to undermine confidence in the verdict.

Third, we note that * * * once a reviewing court applying *Bagley* has found constitutional error there is no need for further harmless-error review. Assuming arguendo that a harmless error enquiry were to apply, a *Bagley* error could not be treated as harmless, since "a reasonable probability that, had the evidence been disclosed to the defense, the result of the proceeding would have been different," necessarily entails the conclusion that the suppression must have had "substantial and injurious effect or influence in determining the jury's verdict." * * *

The fourth and final aspect of *Bagley* materiality to be stressed here is its definition in terms of suppressed evidence considered collectively, not item-by-item. * * * [T]he Constitution is not violated every time the government fails or chooses not to disclose evidence that might prove helpful to the defense. We have never held that the Constitution demands an open file policy * * *.

Justice Souter stressed that suppression of exculpatory evidence implicates *Brady* rights *even if the suppression is by police officers and the prosecutor is unaware of it.* He explained this point as follows:

* * * In the State's favor it may be said that no one doubts that police investigators sometimes fail to inform a prosecutor of all they know. But neither is there any serious doubt that procedures and regulations can be established to carry the prosecutor's burden and to insure communication of all relevant information on each case to every lawyer who deals with it. Since, then, the prosecutor has the means to discharge the government's *Brady* responsibility if he will, any argument for excusing a prosecutor from disclosing what he does not happen to know about boils down to a plea to substitute the police for the prosecutor, and even for the courts themselves, as the final arbiters of the government's obligation to ensure fair trials.

The State in *Kyles* argued that the *Brady-Bagley* standard of materiality should be made more rigorous (i.e., harder for the defendant to meet) because the current standard places a prosecutor in the uncomfortable position of having to predict the materiality of evidence before the trial. The State asked for "a certain amount of leeway in making a judgment call" as to the disclosure of any given piece of evidence. But the majority rejected the State's argument, and adhered to the *Brady-Bagley* standard of materiality, in the following analysis:

[W]ith or without more leeway, the prosecution cannot be subject to any disclosure obligation without at some point having the responsibility to determine when it must act. Indeed, even if due process were thought to be violated by every failure to disclose an item of exculpatory or impeachment evidence (leaving harmless error as the government's only fallback), the prosecutor would still be forced to make judgment calls about what would count as favorable evidence, owing to the very fact that the character of a piece of evidence as favorable will often turn on the context of the existing or potential evidentiary record. Since the prosecutor would have to exercise some judgment even if the State were subject to this most stringent disclosure obligation, it is hard to find merit in the State's complaint over the responsibility for judgment under the existing system, which does not tax the prosecutor with error for any failure to disclose, absent a further showing of materiality. * * *

This means, naturally, that a prosecutor anxious about tacking too close to the wind will disclose a favorable piece of evidence. This is as it should be. Such disclosure will serve to justify trust in the prosecutor * * * [and] will tend to preserve the criminal trial, as distinct from the prosecutor's private deliberations, as the chosen forum for ascertaining the truth about criminal accusations. The prudence of the careful prosecutor should not therefore be discouraged.

Applying all these principles to the case, Justice Souter concluded that the cumulative effect of the suppressed evidence satisfied the materiality standard of *Brady–Agurs–Bagley*. In the majority's view, the suppressed evidence would have caused the jury to doubt the statements of two eyewitnesses, due to their inconsistent prior statements, and would further have caused the jury to doubt the integrity of the lead investigator, who trusted Beanie completely and never considered him as a suspect, even though Beanie's statements were often inconsistent and implausible. The majority concluded:

> [T]he question is not whether the State would have had a case to go to the jury if it had disclosed the favorable evidence, but whether we can be confident that the jury's verdict would have been the same. Confidence that it would have been cannot survive a recap of the suppressed evidence and its significance for the prosecution. The jury would have been entitled to find
>
> > (a) that the investigation was limited by the police's uncritical readiness to accept the story and suggestions of an informant [Beanie] whose accounts were inconsistent to the point, for example, of including four different versions of the discovery of the victim's purse, and whose own behavior was enough to raise suspicions of guilt;

(b) that the lead police detective who testified was either less than wholly candid or less than fully informed;

(c) that the informant's behavior raised suspicions that he had planted both the murder weapon and the victim's purse in the places they were found;

(d) that one of the four eyewitnesses crucial to the State's case had given a description that did not match the defendant and better described the informant;

(e) that another eyewitness had been coached, since he had first stated that he had not seen the killer outside the getaway car, or the killing itself, whereas at trial he claimed to have seen the shooting, described the murder weapon exactly, and omitted portions of his initial description that would have been troublesome for the case;

(f) that there was no consistency to eyewitness descriptions of the killer's height, build, age, facial hair, or hair length.

Since all of these possible findings were precluded by the prosecution's failure to disclose the evidence that would have supported them, "fairness" cannot be stretched to the point of calling this a fair trial. Perhaps, confidence that the verdict would have been the same could survive the evidence impeaching even two eyewitnesses if the discoveries of gun and purse were above suspicion. * * * But confidence that the verdict would have been unaffected cannot survive when suppressed evidence would have entitled a jury to find that the eyewitnesses were not consistent in describing the killer, that two out of the four eyewitnesses testifying were unreliable, that the most damning physical evidence was subject to suspicion [of having been planted], that the investigation that produced it was insufficiently probing, and that the principal police witness was insufficiently informed or candid.

Justice Scalia, joined by Chief Justice Rehnquist and Justices Kennedy and Thomas, dissented in *Kyles*. The dissenters did not disagree with the majority's restatement of the principles derived from *Brady*, *Agurs* and *Bagley*. Rather, they argued that reversal was unwarranted because the suppressed evidence, even considered cumulatively, was not materially exculpatory. Justice Scalia stated that even with the suppressed evidence, Kyles could not have overcome the implausibility of his own defense, which was that the witnesses misidentified him and that Beanie framed him. Justice Scalia explained as follows:

[P]etitioner's theory was that he was the victim of a quadruple coincidence, in which four eyewitnesses to the crime mistakenly identified him as the murderer—three picking him out of a photo-array without hesitation, and all four affirming their identification in open court after comparing him with Beanie. The extraordinary mistake petitioner had to persuade the jury these four witnesses made was not simply to mistake the real killer, Beanie, for the very same innocent third party (hard enough to believe), but in addition to mistake him for the very man Beanie had chosen to frame—the last and most incredible level of coincidence. However small the chance that the jury would believe any one of those improbable scenarios, the likelihood that it would believe them all together is far smaller. The Court concludes that it is "reasonably probable" the undisclosed witness interviews would have persuaded the jury of petitioner's implausible theory of mistaken eyewitness testimony, and then argues that it is "reasonably probable" the undisclosed information regarding Beanie would have persuaded the jury of petitioner's implausible theory regarding the incriminating physical evidence [i.e., that Beanie had planted it in Kyles' house]. I think neither of those conclusions is remotely true, but even if they were the Court would still be guilty of a fallacy in declaring victory on each implausibility in turn, and thus victory on the whole, without considering the infinitesimal probability of the jury's swallowing the entire concoction of implausibility squared.

[Question 3]

A defendant has been charged with murder. The government's case is based mainly on the testimony of an eyewitness. The prosecutor and defense enter into plea negotiations. At that time, the prosecutor knows --- but the defendant does not --- that the eyewitness has died. If the prosecutor keeps this information secret, it is probable that the defendant will plead guilty to a crime with significant jail time. If the defendant is told about the death of the eyewitness, the prosecutor will be unlikely to get a plea to a crime with jail time.

Is the prosecutor constitutionally or ethically required to disclose the death of the eyewitness?

(A) Yes

(B) No

> A student Note argues that, although *People v. Jones*, 375 N.E.2d 41, 43 (N.Y. 1978), found no constitutional duty to provide such information, a prosecutor's duty to "do justice" implies an ethical duty of disclosure in this situation. David Aaron, Note, *Ethics, Law Enforcement, and Fair Dealing: A Prosecutor's Duty to Disclose Nonevidentiary Information*, 67 Fordham L. Rev. 3005 (1999).

2. Brady *and Guilty Pleas:* United States v. Ruiz

If the prosecutor has materially exculpatory evidence, must it be disclosed before the defendant enters into a guilty plea? Or is the *Brady* right simply a trial right? The question arises in the following procedural context: the defendant pleads guilty, later learns of exculpatory evidence that was suppressed, and moves to vacate his guilty plea as insufficiently knowing and voluntary.

In *United States v. Ruiz,* 536 U.S. 622 (2002), the Court held that during guilty plea negotiations the government is not required to disclose information that could impeach government witnesses, nor information that could be used by the defendant to prove an affirmative defense.

Justice Breyer, writing for a unanimous Court, noted that "impeachment information is special in relation to the *fairness of a trial,* not in respect to whether a plea is *voluntary.*" Justice Breyer expressed concern that requiring disclosure of impeachment information during guilty plea negotiations "could seriously interfere with the Government's interest in securing those guilty pleas that are factually justified, desired by defendants, and help to secure the efficient administration of justice." Specifically, early disclosure of impeachment evidence "could disrupt ongoing investigations and expose prospective witnesses to serious harm."

As to required disclosure of impeachment evidence, Justice Breyer concluded that it

> could force the Government to abandon its general practice of not disclosing to a defendant pleading guilty information that would reveal the identities of cooperating informants, undercover investigators, or other prospective witnesses. It could require the Government to devote substantially more resources to trial preparation prior to plea bargaining, thereby depriving the plea-bargaining process of its main resource-saving advantages. Or it could lead the Government instead to abandon its heavy reliance upon plea bargaining in a vast number—90% or more—of federal criminal cases. We cannot say that the Constitution's due process requirement demands so radical a change in the criminal justice process in order to achieve so comparatively small a constitutional benefit.

As to required disclosure of information bearing on an affirmative defense, the Court concluded as follows:

> We do not believe the Constitution here requires provision of this information to the defendant prior to plea bargaining—for most (though not all) of the reasons previously stated. That is to say, in the context of this agreement, the need for this information is more closely related to the

fairness of a trial than to the *voluntariness* of the plea; the value in terms of the defendant's added awareness of relevant circumstances is ordinarily limited; yet the added burden imposed upon the Government by requiring its provision well in advance of trial (often before trial preparation begins) can be serious, thereby significantly interfering with the administration of the plea bargaining process.

The Court in *Ruiz* recognized the government's duty to disclose information bearing on the defendant's "factual innocence" during guilty plea negotiations, as well as a continuing duty to disclose such information throughout the plea proceedings. Indeed, the government recognized this obligation by including it in the plea agreement in *Ruiz*. *See also Sanchez v. United States*, 50 F.3d 1448 (9th Cir. 1995) (guilty plea vacated because evidence material to innocence was suppressed, noting that otherwise "prosecutors may be tempted to deliberately withhold exculpatory information as part of an attempt to elicit guilty pleas").

What is the test of materiality in a guilty plea context? The court in *Sanchez, supra*, declared that suppressed evidence is material if "there is a reasonable probability that but for the failure to disclose the *Brady* material, the defendant would have refused to plead and would have gone to trial." How is a court to determine this question? Does it rely on the defendant's assertions? On the power of the suppressed evidence? On a comparison between the deal that the defendant received and the sentence that he would have faced if convicted? *See Miller v. Angliker*, 848 F.2d 1312 (2d Cir. 1988) (test of materiality, in the guilty plea context, is an objective one that centers on "the likely persuasiveness of the withheld information").

For a discussion of the relationship between *Brady* material and guilty pleas, *see* Corinna Barrett Lain, *Accuracy Where It Matters:* Brady v. Maryland *in the Plea Bargaining Context*, 80 Wash. U. L.Q. 1 (2002) (noting that "*Brady's* importance in the plea bargaining context is clear in part just because so many cases are resolved there"); *see also* John G. Douglass, *Fatal Attraction? The Uneasy Courtship of* Brady *and Plea Bargaining*, 50 Emory L.J. 437 (2001) ("If we are serious about better-informed guilty pleas, then we should address the problem when it matters most: before the plea.").

I. Rule-Based Requirements

Brady does *not* require prosecutors to turn over every piece of evidence that might be considered favorable to the defense. The duty is to turn over "materially exculpatory" evidence. But is it a problem that the determination of what is "materially exculpatory" is left to the prosecutor? Wouldn't even a fair-minded prosecutor have a tendency to downplay the importance of evidence favorable to the defendant? For example, in *Muhammad v. Kelly*, 575 F.3d 359 (4th Cir.

2009), the prosecution of the D.C. sniper, the government suppressed a number of documents favorable to the defense, such as an FBI analyst's report that the sniper committing the shootings was likely acting alone. The court found that the report, while favorable, was not materially exculpatory because the language in the report was tentative and "did not definitively conclude that the killings were the work of a single shooter." Other favorable evidence that was suppressed was also found "cumulative" of evidence the defendant presented at trial and therefore not materially exculpatory. The court noted, however, that

> we by no means condone the action of the Commonwealth in this case. As a matter of practice, the prosecution should err on the side of disclosure, especially when a defendant is facing the specter of execution. When questioned at oral argument regarding why this information was withheld or why the Commonwealth did not take the step of instituting an open-file policy, the Commonwealth had no explanation. Yet, at this stage of the process, we deal only with actions that were clear violations of the Constitution. While not admirable, the Commonwealth's actions did not violate the Constitution.

Many lawyers, judges, and academics have argued for a discovery rule requiring the prosecutor to disclose all information that a *defense counsel might consider favorable* to the defense. That is, the prosecutor reviewing the evidence in the file should put on the defense counsel's hat and, from that perspective, disclose all the information that the defense counsel would find helpful.

The push toward a broader rule of disclosure—mandated by rule, beyond the constitutional minimum set by *Brady*—was spurred by revelations that prosecutors in the corruption trial of Senator Ted Stevens had suppressed evidence about the star witness in the case. Prosecutors apparently acknowledged that the evidence might have helped the defense in attacking the witness's credibility, but didn't think that the evidence was important enough to be "materially exculpatory" under *Brady*. The presiding judge, Emmett Sullivan, was so frustrated by the prosecutor's conduct that he wrote a letter to the Judicial Conference Advisory Committee on Criminal Rules, asking the Committee to amend Fed. R. Crim. P. 16—the non-constitutionally-based rule governing discovery in criminal cases—to require the government to produce all favorable information to the defense. In an interview, Judge Sullivan stated that "whether, when and how much exculpatory evidence the defendant receives should not depend on the prosecutor, the judge, or any other circumstances."

The Department of Justice is opposed to amending Criminal Rule 16 to require the production of all favorable evidence. Assistant Attorney General Lanny Breuer, speaking in opposition to any rule amendment, stated that, despite the high profile nature of the Stevens case, improper suppression by the government is minimal. He noted that an internal DOJ review uncovered only 15 cases of misconduct over a nine-year period. He argued that eliminating the materiality standard "seriously comes into conflict" with victim rights, witness security and, in some cases, national security. In response, Senator Stevens' defense counsel, Brendan Sullivan, said in a statement that the materiality limitation "allows prosecutors to play games with their constitutional duties" and that "criminal trials are supposed to be a search for the truth, and there is no justification whatsoever for concealing any exculpatory information from the defense."

At the time of this writing, the Judicial Conference Advisory Committee on Criminal Rules is still considering the proposal to amend Rule 16 to require the prosecutor to disclose all favorable information to the defense.

Rule 3.8(d)

Rule 3.8 establishes an independent ethical duty on the part of the prosecutor to disclose favorable evidence to the defense:

> The prosecutor in a criminal case shall make timely disclosure to the defense of all evidence or information known to the prosecutor that tends to negate the guilt of the accused or mitigates the offense, and, in connection with sentencing, disclose to the defense and to the tribunal all unprivileged mitigating information known to the prosecutor, except when the prosecutor is relieved of this responsibility by a protective order of the tribunal[.]

In Formal Opinion 09-454 analyzing the Rule, the ABA Standing Committee on Ethics and Professional Responsibility indicated that ethics rules are more stringent than constitutional requirements in the context of prosecutors revealing to defendants information that might help them fight criminal charges. ABA Comm. on Ethics and Prof'l Responsibility, Formal Op. 09-454 (2009). Although the ABA adopted rule 3.8 against the background of *Brady v. Maryland*, the ethics committee explained that "most understand that the rule did not simply codify existing constitutional law but imposed a more demanding disclosure obligation," and that "Rule 3.8(d) does not implicitly include the materiality limitation recognized in the constitutional case law."

The opinion explains that the principal difference between the constitutional obligation and Rule 3.8 is that Rule 3.8(d) "requires the disclosure of evidence or information favorable to the defense without regard to the anticipated impact of the evidence or information on a trial's outcome." This evidence and information "includes both that which tends to exculpate the accused when viewed independently and that which tends to be exculpatory when viewed in light of other evidence or information known to the prosecutor." Thus, Rule 3.8 provides a standard much like that sought by some judges and commentators for an amendment to Fed. R. Crim. P. 16, discussed immediately above.

Under Rule 3.8, the information a prosecutor must disclose is not limited to admissible evidence. The opinion states that inadmissible evidence may aid a defendant by leading a defendant's attorney "to admissible testimony or other evidence or assist him in other ways, such as in plea negotiations." The defendant's lawyers must consider any legally cognizable defenses in determining what information to reveal, not only defenses that the defendant or his or her attorney express an interest in raising.

The ABA compares through the following hypothetical the obligations of prosecutors under the constitution and Rule 3.8(d):

> A grand jury has charged a defendant in a multi-count indictment based on allegations that the defendant assaulted a woman and stole her purse. The victim and one bystander, both of whom were previously unacquainted with the defendant, identified him in a photo array and then picked him out of a line-up. Before deciding to bring charges, the prosecutor learned from the police that two other eyewitnesses

> FYI

> Despite the imposition by Rule 3.8 of relatively higher ethical obligations on prosecutors, the courts and disciplinary authorities give these obligations "comparatively little recognition." Eileen Libby, *A Higher Law*, A.B.A. J., Oct. 2009, at 28. Disciplinary actions taken against prosecutors found to have committed *Brady* violations range from censure (*People v. Steele*, 65 N.Y.S.2d 214 (Gen. Sess. 1946)), to suspension (*Price v. State Bar*, 30 Cal. 3d 537 (1982)), to disbarment, as in the highly publicized case involving rape charges filed by Durham County, North Carolina, District Attorney Michael Nifong, against members of Duke University's lacrosse team. In that egregious case, Nifong failed to inform the defendants that their DNA samples did not match the DNA found on the victim's body, instructed the investigating doctor to exclude this information from the doctor's report, and lied to the court regarding the existence of the DNA evidence. *See* Bennett L. Gershman & Joel Cohen, *No Gatekeeper of Justice*, Nat'l L. J., Feb. 2007, at 1-2. Ultimately, the charges against the defendants were dismissed and Nifong was disbarred by the North Carolina State Bar.

> However, the case of Mr. Nifong is generally considered an exception to the general practice of courts to give the ethical obligations imposed by Rule 3.8 "comparatively little recognition." *See* Libby, *supra*, at 28; Richard A. Rosen, *Disciplinary Sanctions Against Prosecutors For Brady Violations: A Paper Tiger*, 65 N.C. L. Rev. 693 (1987).

viewed the same line-up but stated that they did not see the perpetrator, and that a confidential informant attributed the assault to someone else. The prosecutor interviewed the other two eyewitnesses and concluded that they did not get a good enough look at the perpetrator to testify reliably. In addition, he interviewed the confidential informant and concluded that he is not credible.

Does Rule 3.8(d) require the prosecutor to disclose to defense counsel that two bystanders failed to identify the defendant and that an informant implicated someone other than the defendant? If so, when must the prosecutor disclose this information? Would the defendant's consent to the prosecutor's noncompliance with the ethical duty eliminate the prosecutor's disclosure obligation?

The Committee concludes that, in the hypothetical, information the prosecutor knows would be favorable, but not necessarily material under constitutional law, must be given to the defense.

J. Trial Conduct

1. Voir Dire

CLAUSELL v. MONTANA

106 P.3d 1175 (Mont. 2005)

Justice BRIAN MORRIS delivered the Opinion of the Court.

Amuir Sekou Clausell (Clausell) appeals from the denial of his Petition for Postconviction Relief by the Thirteenth Judicial District Court, Yellowstone County. We affirm.

Clausell raises the following issues on appeal: 1. Whether the District Court erred in denying Clausell's Petition for Postconviction Relief based upon prosecutorial misconduct. * * *

* * *

Misconduct by a prosecutor may form the basis for granting a new trial where the prosecutor's actions have deprived the defendant of a fair and impartial trial.

* * *

Clausell argues that the prosecutor improperly attacked [Clausell's attorney] Gillen by stating during *voir dire* and closing statement that Gillen was "hiding the ball," thereby implying Gillen lied during the presentation of Clausell's case. The context of the prosecutor's "hide the ball" comments reveals that the prosecutor used the term to remind the jurors of his point during *voir dire* that jurors should use their common sense when deciding this matter. After analogizing about using common sense to make decisions when crossing a street, the prosecutor stated:

> [T]he books, the movies we watch, all hide the ball. . . . That is what you see in the movies. We hide the ball until the last minute when the butler in the back jumps up and screams, I did it.

> I just want to make sure we can all use our common sense. Can we all agree on that?

The prosecutor revisited his *voir dire* comments about common sense during his closing statement: "Counsel, ladies and gentlemen, you have heard a masterful job by a very eloquent attorney at attempting to hide the ball. . . . Now we agreed we could use our common sense in accordance with the Judge's instructions." He then related a story about his child's friend lying to him in order to focus the jury's attention on Clausell's conflicting stories. The record confirms that the prosecutor's comments did not constitute prosecutorial misconduct as they were not meant to impugn Gillen's credibility, but to keep the jury focused on the evidence presented.

Clausell next argues that the prosecutor improperly commented on Clausell's credibility and inferred he was lying when, during closing statement, the prosecutor related the story about his child's friend lying to him and immediately tied that story to Clausell's defense theory. The State points out, however, that Clausell takes these comments out of context. Indeed, the record shows that this story formed part of the same example Clausell used to allege that the prosecutor improperly attacked Gillen. The State contends that the prosecutor referred to Clausell's conflicting statements and, through the use of analogy, illustrated how a decision-maker weighs the inconsistent statements against the physical evidence in order to find the truth. We agree.

2. Argument During Trial

BERGER v. UNITED STATES

295 U.S. 78 (1935)

Mr. Justice SUTHERLAND delivered the opinion of the Court.

Petitioner was indicted in a federal district court charged with having conspired with seven other persons named in the indictment to utter counterfeit notes purporting to be issued by designated federal reserve banks, with knowledge that they had been counterfeited. The indictment contained eight additional counts alleging substantive offenses. Among the persons named in the indictment were Katz, Rice, and Jones. Rice and Jones were convicted by the jury upon two of the substantive counts and the conspiracy count. Petitioner was convicted upon the conspiracy count only. Katz pleaded guilty to the conspiracy count, and testified for the government upon an arrangement that a nolle prosequi as to the substantive counts would be entered. It is not necessary now to refer to the evidence further than to say that it tended to establish not a single conspiracy as charged, but two conspiracies-one between Rice and Katz and another between Berger, Jones and Katz. The only connecting link between the two was that Katz was in both conspiracies and the same counterfeit money had to do with both. There was no evidence that Berger was a party to the conspiracy between Rice and Katz. During the trial, the United States attorney who prosecuted the case for the government was guilty of misconduct, both in connection with his cross-examination of witnesses and in his argument to the jury, the particulars of which we consider at a later point in this opinion. At the conclusion of the evidence, Berger moved to dismiss the indictment as to the conspiracy count, on the ground that the evidence was insufficient to support the charge. That motion was denied. Petitioner, Rice, Katz, and Jones were sentenced to terms of imprisonment.

[*Ed.'s Note:* In part one of the opinion, the Court considers the substance of the conspiracy conviction before addressing the prosecutor's misconduct during the trial.]

* * *

2. That the United States prosecuting attorney overstepped the bounds of that propriety and fairness which should characterize the conduct of such an officer in the prosecution of a criminal offense is clearly shown by the record. He was guilty of misstating the facts in his cross-examination of witnesses; of putting into the mouths of such witnesses things which they had not said; of suggesting by his questions that statements had been made to him personally out of court, in respect of which no proof was offered; of pretending to understand that a witness had said something which he had not said and persistently cross-examining the witness upon that basis; of assuming prejudicial facts not in evidence; of bullying and arguing with witnesses; and, in general, of conducting himself in a thoroughly indecorous and improper manner. We reproduce in the margin[FN*] a few excerpts from the record illustrating some of the various points of the foregoing summary. It is impossible, however, without reading the testimony at some length, and thereby obtaining a knowledge of the setting in which the objectionable matter occurred, to appreciate fully the extent of the misconduct. The trial judge, it is true, sustained objections to some of the questions, insinuations and misstatements, and instructed the jury to disregard them. But the situation was one which called for stern rebuke and repressive measures and, perhaps, if these were not successful, for the granting of a mistrial. It is impossible to say that the evil influence upon the jury of these acts of misconduct was removed by such mild judicial action as was taken.

The defendant (petitioner) was on the stand; cross-examination by the United States attorney:

'Q. The man who didn't have his pants on and was running around the apartment, he wasn't there? A. No, Mr. Singer. Mr. Godby told me about this, he told me, as long as you ask me about it, if you want it, I will tell you, he told me 'If you give this man's name out, I will give you the works.'

'Q. Give me the works? A. No, Mr. Godby told me that.

'Q. You are going to give me the works? A. Mr. Singer, you are a gentleman, I have got nothing against you. You are doing your duty.

'Mr. Wegman: You are not going to give Mr. Singer the works. Apparently Mr. Singer misunderstood you. Who made that statement?

'The Witness: Mr. Godby says that.

'Q. Wait a minute. Are you going to give me the works? A. Mr. Singer, you are absolutely a gentleman, in my opinion, you are doing your duty here.

'Q. Thank you very much. But I am only asking you are you going to give me the works? A. I do not give anybody such things, I never said it.

'Q. All right. Then do not make the statement.

'Mr. Wegman: The witness said that Mr. Godby said that.

'The Court: The jury heard what was said. It is not for you or me to interpret the testimony.

'Q. I asked you whether the man who was running around this apartment * * *, was he there in the Secret Service office on the morning that you were arrested? A. I didn't see him.

'Q. I wasn't in that apartment, was I? A. No, Mr. Singer.

'Q. I didn't pull the gun on you and stick you up against the wall? A. No.

'Q. I wasn't up in this apartment at any time, as far as you know, was I? A. As far as I know, you weren't.

'Q. You might have an idea that I may have been there? A. No, I should say not.

'Q. I just want to get that part of it straight. * * *

'Q. Was I in that apartment that night? A. No, but Mr. Godby-

'Q. Was Mr. Godby in that apartment? A. No, but he has been there. * * *

'Q. Do you include as those who may have been there the Court and all the jurymen and your own counsel? A. Mr. Singer, you ask me a question. May I answer it?

'Mr. Wegman: I object to the question.

'The Witness: Are you serious about that?

'The Court: I am not going to stop him because the question includes the Court. I will let him answer it.

'Mr. Singer: I would like to have an answer to it.

'The Witness: Mr. Singer, you asked me the question before-

'The Court: You answer this question. (Question repeated by the reporter.) A. I should say not; that is ridiculous. * * *

'Q. Now Mr. Berger, do you remember yesterday when the court recessed for a few minutes and you saw me out in the hall; do you remember that? A. I do, Mr. Singer.

'Q. You talked to me out in the hall? A. I talked to you?

'Q. Yes. A. No.

'Q. You say you didn't say to me out in the hall yesterday, 'You wait until I take the stand and I will take care of you'? You didn't say that yesterday? A. No; I didn't, Mr. Singer; you are lying.

'Q. I am lying, you are right. You didn't say that at all? A. No.

'Q. You didn't speak to me out in the hall? A. I never did speak to you outside since this case started, except the day I was in your office, when you questioned me.

'Q. I said yesterday. A. No, Mr. Singer.

'Q. Do you mean that seriously? A. I said no.

'Q. That never happened? A. No, Mr. Singer, it did not.

'Q. You did not say that to me? A. I did not.

'Q. Of course, I have just made that up? A. What do you want me to answer you?

'Q. I want you to tell me I am lying, is that so? * * *

(No effort was later made to prove that any such statement had ever been made.) * * *

'Q. Did she say she was going to meet me for anything except business purposes? A. No.

'Q. If she was to meet me? A. Just told me that you gave her your home telephone number and told her to call you up after nine o'clock in the evening if she found out anything about the case that you could help me with, that is what she told me.

'Q. Even if that is so, what is wrong about that, that you have been squawking about all morning.'

The prosecuting attorney's argument to the jury was undignified and intemperate, containing improper insinuations and assertions calculated to mislead the jury. A reading of the entire argument is necessary to an appreciation of these objectionable features. The following is an illustration: A witness by the name of Goldie Goldstein had been called by the prosecution to identify the petitioner. She apparently had difficulty in doing so. The prosecuting attorney, in the course of his argument, said

'Mrs. Goldie Goldstein takes the stand. She says she knows Jones, and you can bet your bottom dollar she knew Berger. She stood right where I am now and looked at him and was afraid to go over there, and when I waved my arm everybody started to holler, 'Don't point at him.' You know the rules of law. Well, it is the most complicated game in the world. I was examining a woman that I knew knew Berger and could identify him, she was standing right here looking at him, and I couldn't say, 'Isn't that the man?' Now, imagine that! But that is the rules of the game, and I have to play within those rules.'

The jury was thus invited to conclude that the witness Goldstein knew Berger well but pretended otherwise; and that this was within the personal knowledge of the prosecuting attorney.

Again, at another point in his argument, after suggesting that defendants' counsel had the advantage of being able to charge the district attorney with being unfair 'of trying to twist a witness,' he said:

But, oh, they can twist the questions, * * * they can sit up in their offices and devise ways to pass counterfeit money; "but don't let the Government touch me, that is unfair; please leave my client alone."

The United States Attorney is the representative not of an ordinary party to a controversy, but of a sovereignty whose obligation to govern impartially is as compelling as its obligation to govern at all; and whose interest, therefore, in a criminal prosecution is not that it shall win a case, but that justice shall be done. As such, he is in a peculiar and very definite sense the servant of the law, the twofold aim of which is that guilt shall not escape or innocence suffer. He may prosecute with earnestness and vigor-indeed, he should do so. But, while he may strike hard blows, he is not at liberty to strike foul ones. It is as much his duty to refrain from improper methods calculated to produce a wrongful conviction as it is to use every legitimate means to bring about a just one.

It is fair to say that the average jury, in a greater or less degree, has confidence that these obligations, which so plainly rest upon the prosecuting attorney, will be faithfully observed. Consequently, improper suggestions, insinuations, and, especially, assertions of personal knowledge are apt to carry much weight against the accused when they should properly carry none. The court below said that the case against Berger was not strong; and from a careful examination of the record we agree. Indeed, the case against Berger, who was convicted only of conspiracy and not of any substantive offense as were the other defendants, we think may properly be characterized as weak—depending, as it did, upon the testimony of Katz, an accomplice with a long criminal record.

In these circumstances prejudice to the cause of the accused is so highly probable that we are not justified in assuming its nonexistence. If the case against Berger had been strong, or, as some courts have said, the evidence of his guilt "overwhelming," a different conclusion might be reached. Moreover, we have not here a case where the misconduct of the prosecuting attorney was slight or confined to a single instance, but one where such misconduct was pronounced and persistent, with a probable cumulative effect upon the jury which cannot be disregarded as inconsequential. A new trial must be awarded.

* * *

Judgment reversed.

3. Inconsistent Prosecutions

STUMPF v. MITCHELL

367 F.3d 594 (6th Cir. 2004)

DAUGHTREY, Circuit Judge

The petitioner, John David Stumpf, is a state prisoner incarcerated on Ohio's death row. He appeals the district court's dismissal of his habeas corpus petition * * * . Specifically, Stumpf alleges * * * that his due process rights were violated by the state's use of inconsistent theories to secure convictions against both Stumpf and his accomplice, Clyde Wesley * * * .

We conclude * * * that Stumpf's due process rights were violated by the state's deliberate action in securing convictions of both Stumpf and Wesley for the same crime, using inconsistent theories. * * *

I. PROCEDURAL AND FACTUAL BACKGROUND

A. The District Court's Factual Findings

On May 14, 1984, Stumpf, Clyde Daniel Wesley, and Norman Leroy Edmonds, after visiting a bar in Washington, Pennsylvania, got on Interstate 70 and headed west toward Ohio. By sundown, they had reached Guernsey County. They stopped their car along I-70 and, leaving Edmonds in the car, Stumpf and Wesley walked to a nearby house under the pretense of needing to make a phone call. The house they chose was owned and occupied by Norman and Mary Jane Stout. Stout admitted Stumpf and Wesley into his home and allowed them to use the phone. When they had completed the call, both Stumpf and Wesley produced pistols and announced a robbery. Stumpf held the Stouts at gunpoint in a back bedroom while Wesley searched the house for items to steal.

At some point, Stout moved toward Stumpf, and Stumpf shot him between the eyes with his pistol. The shot was not fatal, and Stout subsequently pushed Stumpf into the next room. During this altercation, Stout was struck on the head with a pistol and shot in the head a second time. These actions were enough to render him semi-conscious but not to kill him. While lying on the floor in the other room, Stout heard four gunshots. There is no dispute that Mary Jane Stout was shot and killed during the course of this robbery, although there is a dispute as to whether Stumpf or Wesley fired the fatal shots. After Mrs. Stout was killed, Stumpf and Wesley stole the Stout's car and fled. Stumpf was arrested several days later, and after initially denying any knowledge about these crimes and then being told that Stout had survived, he confessed to being involved.

At the time the trial court proceedings occurred, Wesley had not yet been extradited from Texas. However, subsequent to Stumpf's having pleaded guilty and having been sentenced to death, Wesley was convicted of aggravated murder by a jury and received a sentence of life imprisonment without the possibility of parole for 20 years. The State introduced evidence at Wesley's trial that Wesley and not Stumpf fired the shots that killed Mrs. Stout. Edmonds was not charged in the Stout murder and robbery, but was charged for other offenses committed during this crime spree, and he agreed to and did testify against both Stumpf and Wesley concerning the murder of Mary Jane Stout.

B. Additional Facts Regarding Ballistics Evidence

Of the two bullets that struck Stout, only pieces of each were recovered. Part of the bullet that struck him between the eyes was recovered during surgery, while a second fragment was found in the second bedroom. A portion of the bullet that struck Stout in the top of the head was recovered during surgery, but part of it had to be left in place. Another bullet was recovered from the mattress of the second bedroom.

Stout's wife was shot four times in the first bedroom. She died from three gunshots to the left side of her head. The fourth bullet went through her left wrist and struck her chest without penetrating the skin of her chest. A fifth bullet was recovered from the wall of that bedroom, above the headboard of the bed.

* * *

At Stumpf's plea proceeding, the prosecutor argued that the ballistics evidence supported the conclusion that Stumpf had shot Mrs. Stout, since she was apparently shot with the same weapon used against her husband, saying, "There's ample evidence to conclude that this defendant fired all shots that hit anybody, because the same gun fired all of those shots." However, during Wesley's trial, the same prosecutor put Eastman, Wesley's cellmate, on the witness stand, to repeat Wesley's confession to him. According to Eastman, Wesley told him that after Stumpf had shot Stout in the face, he dropped the [gun] and ran, at which point Wesley picked up the pistol and shot Mrs. Stout. This version of the crime was also supported by the ballistics evidence that the [other] pistol had a tendency to jam after firing just one round, which may have led Wesley to discard it after shooting it only once.

C. The Guilty Plea

Stumpf and Wesley could not be tried together because Wesley contested his extradition from Texas, where he had been apprehended. As a result, while Wesley was still detained in Texas, Stumpf pleaded guilty to the aggravated murder of Mary Jane Stout* * * and to the capital specification * * * that the murder was committed for the purpose of escaping detection, apprehension, trial or punishment for the offenses of the aggravated robbery of the Stouts. He also pleaded guilty to the attempted aggravated murder of Norman Stout and to a firearms specification for each count. * * *

II.

* * *

III.

* * *

IV.

* * *

B. The Due Process Violation

At the time of Stumpf's post-plea evidentiary hearing and his mitigation-or sentencing-hearing, his accomplice, Wesley, was still in Texas, fighting extradition. During both Stumpf's plea hearing * * * and his sentencing hearing, the prosecutor argued, and the three-judge panel ultimately found, that Stumpf was the principal offender, responsible for actually shooting Mary Jane Stout. After Stumpf's sentencing in the fall of 1984, the state tried Clyde Wesley before a jury in the spring of 1985. Wesley was also charged with aggravated murder with capital specifications, and during his trial, the state argued that Wesley, not Stumpf, was the shooter. To support this argument, the state presented testimony from Eastman, Wesley's cellmate, about statements Wesley had made to Eastman concerning details about the murder. Wesley took the stand and denied that he was the shooter, but the jury convicted him of the aggravated murder of Mrs. Stout. At the sentencing phase of Wesley's trial, the same jury then recommended a sentence of 20 years to life, rather than the death penalty.

Stumpf argues that the prosecutor's use of two conflicting theories concerning the identity of the shooter to convict both him and Wesley constitutes a due process violation.

Drawing on the principle that the Constitution's "overriding concern [is] with the justice of the finding of guilt," several of our sister circuits have found, or implied, that the use of inconsistent, irreconcilable theories to secure convictions against more than one defendant in prosecutions for the same crime violates the due process clause. On this issue of first impression in this court, we now join our sister circuits in finding that the use of inconsistent, irreconcilable theories to convict two defendants for the same crime is a due process violation.

In *Smith v. Groose,* the Eighth Circuit considered a case in which a prosecutor had used two different, conflicting statements by a co-defendant at successive trials to convict the petitioner at the first trial and a second individual at a second trial. That case involved a group of four young men who were looking for homes to burglarize one evening. In the course of their search, they saw another group of burglars breaking into a home. They realized they knew these men and decided to help them break into the house. The residents were murdered in the course of the burglary. The primary issue at trial was whether the murders took place before or after the four young men began participating in the offense. One of the four men first told the police that the other group had committed the murders without the participation of the group of four. Two days later, he told police that he had seen one of the four men from his group stabbing the victims with a pocketknife; he later recanted this story. The prosecutor then used both statements to obtain convictions against men in each of the two groups.

Examining the record before it, the Eighth Circuit held that "[t]he use of inherently factually contradictory theories violates the principles of due process." The court found that in order to amount to a due process violation, an inconsistency in the prosecutor's theories "must exist at the core of the prosecutor's case against defendants for the same crime." *Id.* This constitutes a due process violation because it renders convictions unreliable, given that "[the s]tate's duty to its citizens does not allow it to pursue as many convictions as possible without regard to fairness and the search for truth."

In finding a due process violation under these circumstances, the Eighth Circuit in *Smith v. Groose* was careful to distinguish the facts in its case from those in the Fifth Circuit's opinion in *Nichols v. Scott,* 69 F.3d 1255 (5th Cir. 1995), where the court did not reach the due process question in a case in which the prosecutor argued in two separate cases that different defendants had each shot the one bullet that killed the victim. The distinction in the *Nichols* case was that both perpetrators had fired shots at the victim, and both could have been convicted under a felony murder theory. Therefore, the prosecutor's arguments were not factually inconsistent, because both defendants could have been convicted even if the prosecutor had used the identical argument in both cases.

Finally, the Ninth Circuit considered a similar situation in *Thompson*. In that case, the prosecutor argued at one trial that, based on jailhouse informant testimony, one defendant had committed a rape and murder. At a second trial, the prosecutor used different jailhouse informants to argue that the second defendant had the motive and disposition to commit the crimes. A plurality of the en banc Ninth Circuit,[7] specifically excluding situations where new evidence comes to light, found that a prosecutor cannot use inconsistent theories of the same crime in order to secure multiple convictions. The court echoed Judge Clark's concurrence in an Eleventh Circuit case which, although it granted habeas relief on alternate grounds, also involved inconsistent theories:

> The prosecutor's theories of the same crime in the two different trials negate one another. They are totally inconsistent. This flip flopping of theories of the offense was inherently unfair. Under the peculiar facts of this case the actions by the prosecutor violate the fundamental fairness essential to the very concept of justice ... The state cannot divide and conquer in this manner. Such actions reduce criminal trials to mere gamesmanship and rob them of their supposed search for the truth.

In this case, the state clearly used inconsistent, irreconcilable theories at Stumpf's hearings and Wesley's trial. At each proceeding, the prosecutor argued that the defendant had been the one to pull the trigger, resulting in the fatal shots to Mary Jane Stout. At Wesley's trial, the prosecutor relied on Eastman's testimony and on the gun-switching scenario argued by Stumpf, to secure Wesley's conviction. The prosecutor asserted:

> Believing he had killed Mr. Stout, [Stumpf] pitched the gun aside and left the immediate area back the hallway down the steps to the basement. At that point [Wesley,] whose own gun was jammed, picked that chrome colored Raven up and as Mrs. Stout sat helplessly on her bed, shot her four times in order to leave no witnesses to the crime.

These statements are irreconcilably inconsistent with those made by the very same prosecutor at Stumpf's plea hearing, when he told the trial court:

---

7. The majority opinion rested on an ineffective assistance of counsel claim. However, despite the fact that a majority of judges did not join in the portion of the opinion finding a due process violation, several of the concurring and dissenting judges indicated that they would find a due process violation for the use of wholly inconsistent theories to convict separate defendants. *See, e.g., id.* at 1063-64 (Tashima, J., concurring, joined by Thomas, J.) (agreeing with the premise that "due process is violated when a prosecutor pursues wholly inconsistent theories of a case at separate trials" but arguing that, in order to find prejudice, the court must decide which of the two theories is true) (quotation omitted); *Id.* at 1066-73 (Kozinski, J., dissenting, joined by Nelson, J.)("In the case of mutually inconsistent verdict, which I am not sure is the case here, I believe that the state is required to take the necessary steps to set aside or modify at least one of the verdicts." *Id.* at 1071.)

> Believing that he had killed Mr. Stout, Stumpf [then] turned the same
> chrome colored Raven automatic pistol upon Mary Jane Stout as she sat
> on the bed and shot her four times. Three times in the left side of the
> head and neck and one time in the writs; obviously in order not to leave
> anyone available to identify him.

The state claims that, because Eastman's testimony was not available at the time of
Stumpf's guilty plea, Stumpf is really asserting Wesley's due process claim in the
guise of his own. The state also argues that "it was of no import to the charge of
capital murder against Stumpf which of the two [defendants] killed the witness
[Mrs. Stout]" since the capital specification was that Mrs. Stout was killed because
she was a witness to the crime, and not that the defendant had been the shooter.
Finally, the state asserts that inconsistent, irreconcilable theories were not used in
these two cases, because the prosecution did not rely on Eastman's testimony at
Wesley's trial. None of these arguments is persuasive.

First, Stumpf clearly has a due process claim even though Eastman's testimony
was not available at the time of his trial. It is true that this is not a case where the
prosecutor selectively presented evidence in Stumpf's case to support the theory
of the murder he was arguing in that case. However, the due process challenge
to the use of inconsistent theories is based on the notion of fundamental fairness. Because inconsistent theories render convictions unreliable, they constitute
a violation of the due process rights of any defendant in whose trial they are
used. * * * Furthermore, it is disingenuous of the state to argue that there is no
violation of Stumpf's rights because the prosecutor had no knowledge of Eastman's
testimony at the time of Stumpf's plea. The state learned of Eastman's testimony
soon after Stumpf's plea and sentencing and yet continued to maintain that the
convictions of both Stumpf and Wesley, each of which was obtained by arguing
that a different individual was the shooter, were sound and reliable.[8] Indeed * * *
the state maintained that Eastman's testimony was unreliable during a hearing on
Stumpf's motion to vacate his plea and/or his sentence. To this day, there has been
no suggestion of corrective action by the state.

The state's second argument * * * is that the identity of the shooter was not the
critical issue in either trial and that therefore the use of different theories did not
violate Stumpf's due process rights. By pleading guilty to capital murder, the state's
argument goes, Stumpf admitted concerted action with Wesley in causing the
death of Mary Jane Stout for the purposes of avoiding detection. All that was left
for the prosecution then to prove, under this theory, was that Mrs. Stout was killed
so that the defendant could escape detection for other crimes. But this argument

---

8. In fact, Wesley's counsel wanted to inform the jury that the prosecutor had previously argued that
   Stumpf, and not Wesley, was the shooter. The prosecutor argued that Stumpf had never admitted
   to firing the shots, and that his own argument was irrelevant. The trial court did not allow Wesley's
   counsel to discuss Stumpf's proceedings in front of the jury.

ignores the fact that, as the aggravated murder statute existed in 1984, specific intent was a necessary element of the crime. Because Stumpf never confessed to specific intent to kill Mrs. Stout, the prosecution bore the burden of proving beyond a reasonable doubt that Stumpf was guilty of the charge.

Finally, the state argues that irreconcilable theories were not used because Eastman's testimony was completely unreliable. State's counsel even asserted at oral argument that the state did not rely on Eastman's testimony in order to prosecute Wesley. This argument is just short of astounding, given the fact that in seeking to convict Wesley of aggravated murder, the prosecution offered no proof of the element of specific intent other than the theory that Wesley was the actual shooter. That the state relied on Eastman's testimony is evident from the fact that it presented his testimony to the jury, and from the fact that it prevented Wesley's counsel from presenting evidence of Stumpf's guilty plea. Had the state presented a theory of the crime consistent with the theory it asserted at Stumpf's evidentiary hearing, it would have had no need to keep that information from Wesley's jury.

* * *

Finally, the state presses an argument that Eastman's testimony was not credible because it relied on "the same type of implausible gun switching and gun juggling that Stumpf told."[10] This, of course, is beside the point. The pertinent fact for Stumpf's due process claim is not whether Eastman's gun-switching story is plausible, but whether the prosecution relied on that story to secure Wesley's conviction. The prosecution found Eastman's testimony credible enough to present the "implausible gun switching" theory to Wesley's jury and obtain his conviction on that theory.

In holding that a constitutional violation occurred in this case, we recognize that at least one circuit has suggested that a due process violation for the use of conflicting theories may be obviated when the second of two inconsistent theories results from the discovery of new evidence. *See Thompson*, 120 F.3d at 1058 ("when no new significant evidence comes to light a prosecutor cannot, in order to convict two defendants at separate trials, offer inconsistent theories and facts regarding the same crime"). We have no quarrel with this proposition, to the extent that it is meant to acknowledge a state's need to continue to investigate crimes and to present all available evidence in court. However, in this case, although Eastman's testimony did not come to light until after Stumpf had been convicted and sentenced to death, the state had many opportunities to correct its use of conflicting theories. Stumpf, upon learning of the state's reliance on the theory

---

10   Eastman testified at Wesley's trial that Wesley told him that after Stumpf had shot Mr. Stout, Stumpf panicked and dropped the .25 caliber Raven. Wesley then picked up the Raven and shot Mrs. Stout a few times. When Mrs. Stout moaned, Wesley shot her again to make sure she was dead.

that Wesley was actually the shooter, timely filed a motion to vacate his guilty plea and/or his sentence. The two judges hearing this motion expressed some concern over whether there was evidence that Stumpf was not in fact the shooter, but the state did not take that opportunity to advocate that all the available evidence be presented to the sentencing panel.

* * *

Measured against this standard, the state's due process violation mandates that both Stumpf's plea and his sentence be set aside. First, there is a reasonable probability that, had the prosecution not pursued conflicting theories concerning who was the actual shooter, Stumpf either would not have pleaded guilty or the three-judge panel would not have found a factual basis for the specific intent element of aggravated murder. Second, and perhaps more likely, there is a reasonable probability that, had the prosecution not pursued inconsistent theories, Stumpf would not have been sentenced to death.

* * *

Boggs, Chief Judge, dissenting

* * * The majority cites three cases from other circuits to buttress its theory that Ohio's prosecution of Wesley, which took place in April 1985, some seven months after Stumpf pleaded guilty and was sentenced to death, somehow violates Stumpf's due process rights. None of the three are germane to this case.

In *Thompson v. Calderon,* a celebrated California death penalty case, the court vacated a death sentence because the prosecutor presented two mutually incompatible theories for the rape-murder during contemporaneous trials of two defendants, Thompson and Leitch. During the pre-trial proceedings for both men, and in Leitch's trial, the prosecutor's theory was that Leitch killed the victim, his girlfriend, because he wanted to get back together with his ex-wife; Thompson assisted him in the crime. In Thompson's trial, however, the prosecutor argued that Thompson had raped the victim and then killed her to cover up his act. He presented different jail house informants at each trial to bolster each contradictory theory. The Ninth Circuit held that this shift in arguments violated a prosecutor's duty to discover the truth and that he was improperly trying to secure convictions for their own sake. It also found that Thompson, who was tried first, was prejudiced due that the fact that "[o]nly in Thompson's trial did the prosecutor change the theory and the arguments [from those presented in the pre-trial hearing], and offer facts that directly conflicted with the underlying premise of the charges he brought."

Distinguishing *Thompson* from the case before us is not difficult, however. First of all, the prosecutor in *Thompson* pursued the two mutually incompatible theories of the murder at contemporaneous trials after joint pre-trial proceedings, and deliberately chose witnesses who would tell the conflicting story that he needed to convict each defendant. Knowingly putting on false evidence is prosecutorial misconduct that violates the Due Process Clause. Nothing in this case indicates that the prosecutors deliberately presented false evidence: Stumpf pleaded guilty to aggravated murder with the specification of killing a witness and attempted aggravated murder with a firearm. The State had every reason to believe his overall admission of responsibility. It was under no obligation, however, to accept at face value his assertion that he did not actually pull the trigger, especially in light of contradictory forensic evidence, such as the fact that a .25-caliber weapon killed Mrs. Stout, the same caliber as Stumpf's gun.

Nor did the prosecutor in *Thompson* collect new evidence between trials; he simply manipulated the facts that he had. In contrast, Wesley's trial took place seven months after Stumpf pleaded guilty, during which time informant Eastman told prosecutors that Wesley confessed that he murdered Mrs. Stout. However, Wesley denied having confessed to Eastman, and the forensic evidence suggested that Eastman's statement was not airtight. A cursory comparison of the facts to those in *Thompson* therefore reveals that the California case has little application to our case.[1]

In *Drake v. Kemp,* an Eleventh Circuit case, the majority remanded for a new trial because the burden of proof was improperly shifted to the defendant and the prosecutor violated the defendant's rights during his closing arguments in the sentencing phase. A single concurring judge argued that Drake's Fourteenth Amendment rights had been violated. The prosecutor, in trials that were a year apart, argued in one instance that a co-defendant must have committed the murder alone and, after having secured a conviction, argued that same person was not strong enough to commit the crime, and therefore Drake must have helped. The concurring judge concluded that it "seems inescapable that the prosecutor obtained Henry Drake's conviction through the use of testimony he did not believe; bringing this case under the logical if not actual factual framework of . . . *Napue.*" (Clark, J. specially concurring). *Drake* therefore does not further Stumpf's case either: a concurring opinion that turns on the prosecutor's inferred knowledge that he was presenting false evidence does not comport with the facts in this case.

The last case cited by the majority, is equally unconvincing. That case involved two groups of robbers, the first of which, when preparing to burglarize a house,

---

1. It is worth noting that constitutional claim made in *Thompson* ultimately did not prevent the defendant's execution on July 14, 1998. *Calderon v. Thompson,* <u>523 U.S. 538, 566, 118 S.Ct. 1489, 140 L.Ed.2d 728 (1998)</u> (reinstating the mandate denying habeas relief).

discovered the second already in the process of stealing the homeowner's posses-sions. The two groups joined forces, and at some point during the crime the hom-eowners were murdered. The leader of the first group, Anthony Lytle, provided varying accounts of what happened, alternately claiming that the head of the second group, Michael Cunningham, killed the couple and that one of his (Lytle's) cohorts, James Bowman, was the murderer. The state convicted Jon Keith Smith, another member of Lytle's group, for felony-murder based on his association with purported fellow gang member Bowman, who was argued to be the actual killer. Four months later, the state then successfully prosecuted Cunningham for the same murders, based on Lytle's other story that Cunningham had already killed the couple when Lytle and his friends entered the house.

The Eighth Circuit ultimately granted Smith a writ of habeas corpus because the state's prosecution of Cunningham violated Smith's due process rights. Again, the crux of the case was the deliberate presentation of false evidence: "In short, what the State claimed to be true in Smith's case it rejected in Cunningham's case, and vice versa." Only a showing of this kind of prosecutorial misconduct could support a claim, dubious as it might be, that Stumpf's constitutional rights were retroactively violated.

* * * It is undisputed that the prosecution did not know of Eastman's statement at the time of Stumpf's conviction and sentencing. Nothing indicates that the prosecution cherry-picked facts in order to confirm Stumpf's guilty plea in the evi-dentiary hearing. The majority does not argue that the prosecution was under any obligation to confess error in Stumpf's post-conviction proceedings or appeals, nor even to bring Eastman's statement to Stumpf's attention. There is simply no prosecutorial misconduct in this case that could retroactively implicate Stumpf's due process rights.

Groose does not hold that prosecutors must present precisely the same evidence and theories in trials for different defendants. Rather it holds only that the use of inherently factually contradictory theories violates principles of due process. The majority remarkably expands this holding to conclude that *evidence* in a second case that contradicts a *guilty plea* in an earlier case can implicate due process rights. * * * Therefore, I do not see any grounds on which to base an allegation that the prosecution skewed the same set of facts in two different trials in order achieve two mutually incompatible guilty verdicts. This case has little or no similarity with the facts of *Thompson, Drake,* and *Groose.*

Far more instructive is the Ninth Circuit's quite recent decision in *Shaw v. Terhune,* 353 F.3d 697 (9th Cir. 2003). The court held that imposing sentence enhance-ments on two defendants for personal use of a firearm during an attempted rob-bery and assault on a restaurant manager was not a violation of due process, although the testimony clearly indicated that only one perpetrator had held a gun to the manager's head. * * *

However, the *Shaw* court distinguished its case from *Thompson,* pointing to the fact that the prosecutor did not manipulate evidence-the same crucial distinction that is present in our case. Ambiguous evidence is not false evidence; "regrettable" tactics are not necessarily unconstitutional. The fact of the matter is that no one but Wesley and Stumpf know who shot Mrs. Stout. The State is entitled to put on the available evidence to convince the finder of fact of guilt. As long as it does so in a good faith manner, without manipulating or selecting out critical evidence, due process is not violated.

The *Shaw* court also speculated that if there were a constitutional violation, that Watts, the second defendant, rather than Shaw, would be the one who could argue the point. Similarly, I could understand a court accepting Wesley's claim that the prosecution could not honestly present evidence in *his* case that contradicted what the government had relied upon previously (a type of "prosecutorial estoppel"), or even that it could not present evidence that contradicted a position it was taking elsewhere. However, none of those theories can retroactively render unfair the fundamentally fair proceedings that Stumpf received.

> For discussion of the legal and ethical issues raised when prosecutor's present inconsistent factual theories in separate proceedings, *see* Michael Q. English, Note, *A Prosecutor's Use of Inconsistent Factual Theories of a Crime in Successive Trials: Zealous Advocacy or a Due Process Violation?,* 68 Fordham L. Rev. 525, 547 (1999); Anne Bowen Poulin, *Prosecutorial Inconsistency, Estoppel, and Due Process: Making the Prosecution Get Its Story Straight,* 89 Cal. L. Rev. 1423, 1423 (2001).

* * *

K. Sentencing

ABA Standards, The Prosecution Function

Standard 3-6.1 Role in Sentencing

(a) The prosecutor should not make the severity of sentences the index of his or her effectiveness. To the extent that the prosecutor becomes involved in the sentencing process, he or she should seek to assure that a fair and informed judgment is made on the sentence and to avoid unfair sentence disparities.

(b) Where sentence is fixed by the court without jury participation, the prosecutor should be afforded the opportunity to address the court at sentencing and to offer a sentencing recommendation.

(c) Where sentence is fixed by the jury, the prosecutor should present evidence on the issue within the limits permitted in the jurisdiction, but the prosecutor should avoid introducing evidence bearing on sentence which will prejudice the jury's determination of the issue of guilt.

Standard 3-6.2 Information Relevant to Sentencing

(a) The prosecutor should assist the court in basing its sentence on complete and accurate information for use in the presentence report. The prosecutor should disclose to the court any information in the prosecutor's files relevant to the sentence. If incompleteness or inaccurateness in the presentence report comes to the prosecutor's attention, the prosecutor should take steps to present the complete and correct information to the court and to defense counsel.

(b) The prosecutor should disclose to the defense and to the court at or prior to the sentencing proceeding all unprivileged mitigating information known to the prosecutor, except when the prosecutor is relieved of this responsibility by a protective order of the tribunal.

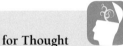

Food for Thought

Though a prosecutor's responsibility is to be "neutral" and objectively make sentencing recommendations, what role, if any, should a prosecutor's personal feelings regarding the appropriateness of a sentence play? What ethical rules, if any, would a prosecutor who is ethically opposed to the death penalty be violating if he refused to pursue the death penalty in a capital punishment case?

PENNSYLVANIA v. DEJESUS

580 Pa. 303, 860 A.2d 102 (2004)

Justice CASTILLE.

This is a direct appeal from a sentence of death imposed by the Philadelphia County Court of Common Pleas. Following a capital jury trial, which commenced on September 10, 1999, appellant was convicted of first-degree murder, carrying firearms on a public street, and possession of an instrument of crime. At the penalty phase, the jury found two aggravating circumstances and two mitigating circumstances. The jury found that the aggravating circumstances outweighed the mitigating circumstances, and accordingly, imposed a sentence of death for appellant's first-degree murder conviction. On October 28, 1999, the trial court formally imposed the death sentence and, in addition, imposed two consecutive sentences of one to two years' incarceration for appellant's remaining convictions. Appellant did not file post-sentence motions. This appeal followed. For the reasons set forth below, we affirm appellant's convictions, but reverse the sentence of death and remand the matter for a new penalty hearing.

We begin, as we do in all death penalty direct appeals, by independently reviewing the evidence to ensure that it is sufficient to support the first-degree murder conviction. * * * [The Court affirmed appellant's convictions upon a finding that the evidence was sufficient to support jury's conviction for first-degree murder.]

* * *

Appellant argues, *inter alia,* that the prosecutor ignored enumerated statutory mitigating/aggravating factors and undermined the jury's ability to render a fair verdict when he urged the jury to "send a message" by sentencing appellant to death:

> He has shown you again and again that he hurts people because he likes to and he want to, and he has earned the right to be on death row. **When you think of the death penalty, there are messages to be sent. There's a message on the street saying, look at that, he got death, you see that, honey, that's why you live by the rules, so you don't end up like that. Because they're in these bad neighborhoods. . . . You also send a message in prisons.** When you peep in that bus and talk and whisper, you can say, death penalty. Maybe you've got just one inmate sitting there going, well, he got death, this is serious, I don't want to end up like that. Maybe your penalty you'll save one guy, to scare him straight.

When the prosecutor completed his closing argument, appellant moved for a mistrial arguing, among other things, that the prosecutor's "send a message" statement was prejudicial. The trial court denied the motion. Counsel then asked the trial court to "tell the jury they should disregard everything [the prosecutor] said." Appellant did not request a specific cautionary instruction regarding the prosecutor's "send a message" argument, and the trial court issued no such instruction; however, in its charge concerning the jury's weighing of aggravating circumstances, the trial court adverted to the argument as follows:

> It's terribly important that you also understand that in your evaluation of aggravators, that's those things that the Commonwealth says are aggravating circumstances, you should follow the law and you should not

base your findings on the possibility of any future crimes that might be committed, and **you should not sentence him because one might feel that there is a need to send a message to the community, nor should you sentence him just because the other prisoners need some message.**

The Commonwealth argues that the prosecutor was merely employing oratorical license and impassioned argument and notes that a prosecutor is afforded more latitude in doing so at the penalty phase. The Commonwealth also cites two cases in which this Court held that a prosecutor's "send a message" exhortation was within the bounds of permissible oratorical flair. Finally, the Commonwealth argues that any prejudice to appellant was cured by the trial court's instructions warning the jury that they should not sentence appellant in order to send a message.

Our adversary system permits the prosecutor to "prosecute with earnestness and vigor." Nevertheless, the arguments advanced must be confined to the evidence and the legitimate inferences to be drawn therefrom. "Deliberate attempts to destroy the objectivity and impartiality of the finder of fact so as to cause the verdict to be a product of the emotion rather than reflective judgment will not be tolerated."

Although there is sometimes a "gray zone" separating acceptable from improper advocacy, this Court has categorically prohibited certain prosecutorial arguments that we have deemed extremely and inherently prejudicial. Thus, in *Chambers*, this Court held that a prosecutor's reliance upon the Bible or other religious writings as an independent source of law supporting the imposition of a death penalty is reversible error *per se*. In so holding, the *Chambers* Court noted that such an appeal to Biblical bases for returning a death verdict constituted a deliberate attempt to destroy the objectivity and impartiality of the jury which could not be cured. Moreover, we noted that in invoking a religious reference in support of the death penalty, the prosecutor reached outside the law of the Commonwealth:

> Our courts are not ecclesiastical courts and, therefore, there is no reason to refer to religious rules or commandments to support the imposition of a death penalty. Our Legislature has enacted a Death Penalty Statute which carefully categorizes all the factors that a jury should consider in determining whether the death penalty is an appropriate punishment and, if a penalty of death is meted out by a jury, it must be because the jury was satisfied that the substantive law of the Commonwealth requires its imposition, not because of some other source of law.

It is notable that the *Chambers per se* holding followed upon a series of cases in which this Court "narrowly tolerated" Biblical references, deeming them to be on the limits of oratorical flair but cautioning that such references were "a dangerous practice which we strongly discourage." In *Chambers*, we noted that, our cautionary teaching having been ignored, we would no longer tolerate such references, and indeed, would deem such references "reversible error *per se*" and might also "subject violators to disciplinary action."

This Court has expressed similar concerns regarding prosecutorial arguments that exhort the jury to return a sentence of death in order to "send a message." Although until now we have not explicitly adopted a *per se* prescription similar to that set forth in *Chambers*, it is fair to say that we have been in the "narrow toleration" and close scrutiny stage for some time. This Court has repeatedly reminded the bench and bar that "send a message" exhortations in criminal trials are particularly prejudicial and should be avoided.

As the Commonwealth correctly notes, in some of our older cases, this Court determined that, in some contexts, "send a message" arguments may be tolerable. In *DeHart*, we denied relief where the prosecutor stressed the general "deterrent effect" of the death penalty. *DeHart* relied upon this Court's decision in *Zettlemoyer*, which reasoned that a prosecutor's reference to the deterrent effect of the death penalty was not prejudicial because it was a matter of public knowledge based on ordinary human experience:

> We do not believe that the impact of this statement, which is a "matter of common public knowledge based on ordinary human experience," would have biased or prejudiced the jury or hindered an objective weighing of the evidence, especially considering the district attorney's explicit directions to the jury to return a verdict of death "solely and exclusively as the law indicates it may be [imposed], based on the circumstances of this case, that it involved a premeditated, intentional killing of a witness to a serious crime, a felony."

Similarly, in *Peterkin* this Court concluded that, while a prosecutor may not exhort a jury to send a message to the judicial system, he may urge them to send a direct message to the defendant. There, the prosecutor asked the jury to "[s]end out a message about the conduct engaged in by [the defendant] as he sits passively at that table, [that his conduct] cannot be condoned among civilized men." In distinguishing this remark from similar "send a message" arguments that this Court had deemed improper, * * *we noted that the prosecutor's comments, viewed in context, had merely asked the jury to send a message to the defendant. Indeed, we noted that in his very next sentence the prosecutor said, "[t]ell [the defendant] what you did, when you did it, how you did and for the reason that you did it you must die."

The *Peterkin* issue is not presented in the case *sub judice*: the prosecutor here did not exhort the jury to send a message to appellant. Arguably, the *Zettlemoyer/DeHart* situation also is not strictly at issue, as this was not an argument concerning the general "deterrent effect" of the death penalty. We would not overstate this distinction, however. We acknowledge that "send a message" and "deterrent effect" arguments are related in that they suggest that such an external factor may properly play a role in the jury's determination of life or death.

In any event, in the many years since *Zettlemoyer* and *DeHart* were decided, this Court has strongly admonished prosecutors to refrain from exhorting jurors to use their verdict to "send a message" to the community or the judicial system. This admonishment has particular significance when the sentence of death is at stake. In contrast to the determination of guilt, which usually depends on relatively objective findings, the decision as to whether to impose a sentence of death depends upon the weighing of specific aggravating and mitigating circumstances that may involve subjective considerations. Indeed, in *Crawley*, this Court noted that a prosecutor's argument asking the jury to send a message to the judicial system by returning a sentence of death is "extremely prejudicial" because a jury's determination must be based solely upon the evidence of aggravating and mitigating circumstances, and not upon an external emotional appeal.

* * *

In this instance, * * * the prosecutor inexplicably and directly exhorted the jury to impose the death penalty in order to send a message to people on the street and to people in prisons. The plea to such an external irrelevancy was so direct that it culminated in the prosecutor inviting the jury to sentence this appellant to death so as to "scare straight" others who might be considering murder. There was no role for such an argument here. The prosecutor's improper comments effectively invited jurors to ignore their sworn duty to decide the matter exclusively upon the facts presented concerning the weighing of specific statutory aggravating and mitigating circumstances.

This Court well appreciates the pressures and challenges of trying criminal cases, and particularly cases where the ultimate penalty is involved. We also recognize that there are many things that occur in the course of a trial which are beyond the control or anticipation of counsel and the trial judge—such as witnesses, jurors or spectators acting inappropriately. But one aspect of a trial which is far more subject to rational control is the behavior of attorneys—officers of this Court whose professionalism is absolutely indispensable to the fair administration of justice in this Commonwealth. * * *

We are aware that the trial judge in this case ultimately informed the jury that it "should not" sentence appellant in order to send a message. But we have little confidence that such a charge was adequate to remove the prejudice resulting from the prosecutor's decision to employ an inherently prejudicial argument that had specifically been deemed off-limits. The jury in this case ultimately found two aggravating circumstances and two mitigating circumstances, and thus was required to weigh the competing factors to determine which ones predominated. In such an instance, the fact that the prosecutor had argued that a collateral external effect of a death verdict would be to send a message to others which might prevent future crimes-a factor which does not exist as a proper statutory aggravating circumstance-may well have played a role, direct or indirect, in at least one juror's balancing process. In this regard, it is also significant that the trial court's cautionary charge could be read as having inadvertently validated the prosecutor's non-record-based assumptions that a verdict of death indeed would send a message both to the community at large or other prisoners. In instructing the jury, the court did not question the accuracy or legitimacy of those assumptions, but instead directed that the jury should not base its verdict upon them. On such a record, we conclude that the ability of the sentencing jury to weigh the evidence objectively was fatally compromised and, accordingly, appellant is entitled to a new sentencing proceeding.

More importantly, we conclude here, as we did in *Chambers* when confronted with a similar challenge to this Court's directives concerning what comprises appropriate argument in the penalty phase of a capital trial, that penalty phase arguments requesting that the jury send a message with its verdict are prejudicial *per se*. We reach this conclusion in part because of the inherently prejudicial nature of the remarks, and in part as a matter of our supervisory authority over Pennsylvania attorneys. We do not reach the conclusion lightly. * * * The argument goes to the very core of the penalty phase jury's task, injecting an improper external element in favor of death. As this Court has made clear in the decisions culminating in *Chambers* and *LaCava,* it is essential that arguments made in favor of the ultimate penalty be confined to those statutory aggravating circumstances which are specifically charged and which thereby serve as the only appropriate basis for a verdict of death. Given the critical balancing process required of the penalty phase jury, the important individual role of jurors in this assessment, the inherently prejudicial nature of the argument, and the fact that the content of a lawyer's argument is easily within his control, we will no longer proceed with case-by-case assessments in this area. Such arguments are to be avoided and the peril of defiance is to fall upon the party who would flout the rule.

Accordingly, for the foregoing reasons, this Court affirms appellant's convictions, but vacates the sentence of death and remands this matter for a new sentencing hearing. * * *

L. Post-Conviction Evidence of Innocence

Rule 3.8

* * *

(g) When a prosecutor knows of new, credible and material evidence creating reasonable likelihood that a convicted defendant did not commit an offense of which the defendant was convicted, the prosecutor shall:

(1) promptly disclose that evidence to an appropriate court or authority, and

(2) if the conviction was obtained in the prosecutor's jurisdiction,

(A) promptly disclose that evidence to the defendant unless a court authorizes delay, and

(B) undertake further investigation, or make reasonable efforts to cause an investigation, to determine whether the defendant was convicted of an offense that the defendant did not commit.

(h) When a prosecutor knows of clear and convincing evidence establishing that a defendant in the prosecutor's jurisdiction was convicted of an offense that the defendant did not commit, the prosecutor shall seek to remedy the conviction.

Niki Kuckes, in *The State of Rule 3.8: Prosecutorial Ethics Reform Since Ethics 2000*, 22 Geo. J. Legal Ethics 427 (2009), discusses the background to these provisions, which she regards as among the most important in Rule 3.8:

A host of recent cases initiated by Innocence Projects involving exonerations based on DNA evidence demonstrated the fallibility of the system, and the very real possibility that innocent defendants had been wrongfully convicted. Several influential newspaper exposes, based on studies of thousands of criminal cases, similarly highlighted the problem of prosecutorial misconduct, including a number of cases in which innocent defendants were later found to have been wrongfully convicted. A comprehensive study by the Center for Public Integrity in 2003 revealed, similarly, that prosecutorial misconduct was endemic, and that the most common form of prosecutorial misconduct was the failure to disclose exculpatory evidence. These studies made clear that the problem of wrongful convictions of innocent persons was very real, and highlighted the responsibility of prosecutors, as "ministers of justice," to help remedy such miscarriages of justice.

> **FYI**
>
> The first five states to adopt versions of one or both of these provisions were Delaware, Wisconsin, Colorado, Idaho, and Tennessee. Delaware adopted Rule 3.8(g) but not Rule 3.8(h). Wisconsin has adopted a slightly revised version of these provisions, available here. Colorado's version of Rule 3.8(g) omits the duty to investigate new evidence.

II. Ethical Standards for Judges

A. Introduction[1]

When presiding over judicial proceedings, judges are required to be neutral and impartial.[2] To insure an impartial judiciary, judges' extrajudicial conduct and relationships are subject to various bodies of regulation. These include the Constitution's Due Process Clause, federal and state statutes, and codes of judicial ethics. Together, these are intended to promote public confidence in the integrity of the judicial system.

Constitutional Requirements. As interpreted by the Supreme Court and other courts, the Due Process Clause sometimes requires judges to "recuse themselves when they face possible temptations to be biased, even when they exhibit no actual bias against a party or a case."[3] Although the common law rule was that a judge would be "disqualified for direct pecuniary interest and nothing else,"[4] the constitutional rule goes somewhat further. The Due Process Clause requires disqualification where the judge has a direct pecuniary or other interest in the outcome of the case, so that there is a significant incentive for a judge to favor one side.[5] The constitutional provision does not require recusal, however, where there are other conceivable reasons for a judge to be biased. For example, even

---

1   This introduction is adapted from Bruce A. Green, *May Judges Attend Privately Funded Educational Programs? Should Judicial Education Be Privatized?: Questions of Judicial Ethics and Policy*, 29 Fordham Urb. L.J. 941 (2002).

2   *See, e.g., Ward v. Village of Monroeville*, 409 U.S. 57, 62 (1972); *In re Murchison*, 349 U.S. 133, 136 (1955).

3   *Del Vecchio v. Illinois Dep't of Corrections*, 31 F.3d 1363, 1372 (7th Cir. 1994).

4   *See* John P. Frank, *Disqualification of Judges*, 56 Yale L.J. 605, 609, 618-19 (1947).

5   *See, e.g., Aetna Life Ins. Co. v. Lavoie*, 475 U.S. 813 (1986) (decision in case would set legal precedent bearing directly on two pending cases filed by judge as plaintiff); *Ward v. Village of Monroeville*, 409 U.S. 57, 60 (1972) (city mayor could not sit as traffic court judge because responsibility for town finances provided incentive to find against defendants to "maintain the high level of contribution from the mayor's court"); *Mayberry v. Pennsylvania*, 400 U.S. 455, 466 (1971) (judge could not try defendant for contempt of court based on defendant's insults during previous trial, because defendant's insults were "apt to strike 'at the most vulnerable and human qualities of a judge's temperament'"); *Tumey v. Ohio*, 273 U.S. 510 (1927) (judge in criminal case was paid only if defendant was convicted).

though they may offer a "possible temptation" to be biased, "[m]atters of kinship [or] personal bias . . . would generally be matters of legislative discretion."[6] As one court has explained:

> This merely recognizes, at least implicitly, that in the real world, "possible temptations" to be biased abound. Judges are human; like all humans, their outlooks are shaped by their lives' experiences. It would be unrealistic to suppose that judges do not bring to the bench those experiences and attendant biases they may create. A person could find something in the background of most judges which in many cases would lead that person to conclude that the judge has a "possible temptation" to be biased. But not all temptations are created equal. We expect—even demand—that judges rise above these potential biasing influences, and in most cases we presume judges do.
>
> * * *
>
> As the common law recognized, and as experience teaches, the lure of lucre is a particularly strong motivation, and therefore judges ought to be prohibited from presiding over cases in whose outcomes they have a direct financial interest. Of course, the Supreme Court has held that the due process clause requires disqualification for interests besides pecuniary interests. But the constitutional standard the Supreme Court has applied in determining when disqualification is necessary recognizes the same reality the common law recognized: judges are subject to a myriad of biasing influences; judges for the most part are presumptively capable of overcoming those influences and rendering evenhanded justice; and only a strong, direct interest in the outcome of a case is sufficient to overcome that presumption of evenhandedness.[7]

Thus, for the most part, the Constitution leaves questions of judicial disqualification, and judicial ethics generally, to be decided by legislators through the enactment of relevant statutes, by the judiciary through the adoption and interpretation of codes of judicial ethics, and by judges individually.

Statutory Requirements. Various federal and state statutes impose restrictions beyond the constitutional ones.[8] Of course, criminal law forbids judges from seeking or accepting a bribe.[9] Of more frequent relevance are statutes requiring

---

6   *Aetna Life Ins.*, <u>475 U.S. at 820</u>; *see also Tumey*, <u>273 U.S. at 523</u>.
7   *Del Vecchio*, <u>31 F.3d at 1372-73</u>.
8   *See, e.g.*, <u>5 U.S.C.A., app. 4, §§ 101-111 (West 2001)</u> (requiring judges to make certain financial disclosures); Mass. Ann. Laws ch. <u>268B, § 5 (Law. Co-op 1992)</u> (same).
9   For example, a federal criminal statute makes it a crime for a federal judge to seek or accept compensation in relation to any proceeding, request for a ruling, or other determination or matter involving the United States. <u>18 U.S.C. § 203(a) (2000)</u>.

judges to recuse themselves in circumstances where they have, or appear to have, a bias or interest that would influence their decisions. For example, 28 U.S.C. § 455, the federal disqualification statute, which dates back to 1911,[10] requires a judge to disqualify himself in any proceeding where his impartiality might reasonably be questioned. The statute also identifies particular circumstances in which a judge must disqualify himself, including "[w]here he has a personal bias or prejudice concerning a party, or personal knowledge of disputed evidentiary facts concerning the proceeding"; where he worked on the matter while in private practice or as a government employee; and where he or a close family member has a financial interest or other interest or involvement in the controversy. The federal disqualification statute requires a judge to "inform himself about his personal and fiduciary financial interests," 28 U.S.C. § 455(c), in order to decide whether disqualification is required.

Various state and federal laws also require judges to disclose certain financial information.[11] For example, federal law, 5 U.S.C.A., app. 4, §§ 101-111 (West 2001), requires federal judges to file annual financial disclosure forms. These forms identify and describe all gifts of more than a minimal amount received in the prior year (except when received from a relative or, in the case of food, lodging, or entertainment, as "personal hospitality"), and all reimbursements in more than minimal amounts received in the prior year. Additionally, certain state laws applicable to government officials generally, or to judges in particular, impose further restrictions on state judges.

Codes of Conduct. Finally, judges are regulated by judicial codes of conduct adopted by state and federal judiciaries to govern the conduct of judges. The federal judiciary and most state judiciaries have adopted, with different degrees of variation, a code of conduct drafted by the American Bar Association. The earliest judicial code, the ABA Canons of Judicial Conduct, was drafted by a committee under the direction of Chief Justice Taft and approved by the ABA in 1924.[12] This early code was comprehensively reviewed from 1969 to 1972 by an ABA committee chaired by retired Chief Justice Roger J. Traynor of the California Supreme Court and comprised of thirteen members, including Supreme Court Justice Potter Stewart and five other state or federal judges. The committee produced the Code of Judicial Conduct that was approved by the ABA in August 1972.[13] The Code was substantially amended in 1990 and again in 2007. Most states have judicial commissions, typically comprised of both judges and lawyers, who have

---

10 *See generally* Seth E. Bloom, *Judicial Bias and Financial Interest as Grounds for Disqualification of Federal Judges*, 35 Case W. Res. L. Rev. 662, 663-80 (1985) (describing federal disqualification statutes and their history); Randall J. Litteneker, *Disqualification of Federal Judges for Bias or Prejudice*, 46 U. Chi. L. Rev. 236, 236 n.4 (1978).

11 *See, e.g.,* FLA. CONST. ART. 2, § 8; 5 U.S.C., §§ 101-111, app. 4; MASS. ANN. LAWS CH. 268B, § 5 (LAW. CO-OP 1992); OKLA. STAT. ANN. tit. 5, ch. 1, app. 4 (West 2001); PA. CONS. STAT. ANN. §§ 1104-1105 (West 2000).

12 *See* Lisa L. Milord, *The Development of the ABA Judicial Code* (1992).

13 *See* E. Wayne Thode, *Reporter's Notes to Code of Judicial Conduct* (1973).

authority to investigate violations of the state's judicial code and to sanction judges who are found to have engaged in violations.

B. Performing the Duties of the Judicial Office

For Additional Research

For treatises on judicial ethics, *see* James J. Alfini et al., *Judicial Conduct and Ethics* (4th ed. 2007); Richard E. Flamm, *Judicial Disqualification* (2d ed. 2007).

Judicial independence and impartiality are dominant principles running through the Model Code of Judicial Conduct. Judges must act independently from, and without partiality toward, third parties—be they friends and family, parties and their lawyers, or government officials. Judges must also maintain the appearance of independence and impartiality in order to promote public confidence in the particular judge and the judiciary as a whole.

Some Model Code provisions express these principles in fairly general terms. For example, Rule 2.4 requires judges to avoid external influences on their conduct: they may not be "swayed by public clamor or fear of criticism," may not "permit family, social, political, financial, or other interests or relationships to influence

Food for Thought

Suppose that you serve as an intern or law clerk for a judge. If the judge is pleased with your work, may the judge write a reference letter on judicial letterhead to help you obtain employment with a law firm, or would doing so improperly "abuse the prestige" of the judicial office for the benefit of a third party, namely, you? The Comment to Rule 1.3 clarifies that this use of judicial letterhead is permissible as long as the judge does not appear to be exerting pressure on the letter's recipient by virtue of the judicial office. Where is the line between a permissible and impermissible letter of reference? And where is the line between other permissible and impermissible uses of judicial letterhead and credentials? May a judge telephone a restaurant and request a reservation for "*Judge* Jones"?

[their] judicial conduct or judgment," and may not "convey or permit others to convey the impression that any person or organization is in a position to influence" them. Similarly, Rule 1.3 forbids a lawyer to "abuse the prestige of judicial office to advance the personal or economic interests of the judge or others, or allow others to do so."

To some extent, the accompanying Comments illustrate these general prohibitions, and opinions build on them. For example, judges may be disciplined for abusing the prestige of their judicial office to advance private interests when they use their judicial letterhead or credentials for their personal benefit—e.g., to attempt to persuade the police not to give them speedy tickets or to obtain other favorable treatment by government authorities.

[Question 1]

A trial court judge had instructed his court clerk and his secretary that one of them should be present in the office during working hours to answer the telephone. One day, however, the secretary was out sick. The judge was in his office when his court clerk was at lunch, and when the telephone rang, the judge answered it. The call was from a lawyer in a case presently pending before the judge. The lawyer was calling to attempt to reschedule a pretrial conference set for the next day because of a sudden family emergency. The lawyer had tried to call opposing counsel on the case, but she was not answering his calls. The judge agreed to reschedule the pretrial conference for the following week. When the judge's court clerk returned from lunch, the judge instructed the clerk to contact opposing counsel to inform her of the telephone call and the fact that the pretrial conference had been rescheduled.

Did the judge act properly?

  (A) No, because the judge participated in an ex parte communication.

  (B) No, because there was still time for the calling lawyer to notify opposing counsel in order to reach agreement on rescheduling the pretrial conference.

  (C) Yes, because the ex parte communication was for scheduling purposes only and did not deal with substantive matters or issues.

  (D) Yes, because there was no one else in the office to take the lawyer's call.

[Question 2]

A judge has served on a trial court of general jurisdiction for almost three years. During that time, he was assigned criminal cases almost exclusively. Several months ago, however, the judge was assigned an interesting case involving a constitutional challenge to a statute recently passed by the state legislature. The statute permitted any local public school district with an overcrowding problem to purchase educational services for its students in any other public or private school within fifteen miles.

Although the briefs submitted by the parties were excellent, the judge was not confident that he had a good grasp of the issues in the case. Accordingly, he took one of his more experienced colleagues on the trial court out to lunch and discussed the case with her in great detail. The colleague was far more conservative than the judge, but he agreed with her and eventually ruled in accord with her views. The case is now on appeal.

Is the judge subject to discipline?

(A) Yes, because the judge sought an ex parte communication on the merits of a case pending before him.

(B) Yes, because the judge initiated a discussion with a colleague that may have influenced his judgment in the case.

(C) No, because the judge is permitted to obtain the advice of a disinterested expert on the law.

(D) No, because the judge was permitted to consult about a pending case with another judge.

An important provision of the judicial code promoting judicial fairness is Rule 2.9, governing ex parte communications. In general, Rule 2.9(A) prohibits the judge from communicating with anyone—including, but not limited to, a lawyer or party to a proceeding—"concerning a pending or impending matter" if the communication occurs "outside the presence of the parties or their lawyers." For example, the judge may not communicate about the case with one of the lawyers outside the presence of the other lawyers; nor may the judge talk about the case with a friend. But there are exceptions contained in Rule 2.9(A), including that, in specified circumstances, the judge may engage in "ex parte communication for scheduling, administrative, or emergency purposes, which does not address substantive applications." Also, under specified circumstances, "[a] judge may obtain written advice of a disinterested expert on the law applicable to a proceeding before the judge," talk about the case with another judge (but not *any* other judge), or confer separately with the parties in order to promote a settlement. Of course, the judge may consult with court staff—e.g., the judge's law clerks—and with court officials. And the judge may communicate ex parte when authorized by law to do so—for example, when they law allows a party to make an emergency application outside the presence of the opposing party.

> **Keep in Mind**
>
> Remember that lawyers have corresponding obligations. ABA Rule 3.5(b) forbids a lawyer from communicating ex parte with a judge "unless authorized to do so by law or court order." To the extent that a lawyer engages in permissible ex parte communications—e.g., for scheduling or administrative purposes or to make an emergency application—it is ordinarily expected or required that the lawyer give notice to the other side afterward. Additionally, ABA Rule 3.3(d) imposes a heightened duty of candor on lawyers in ex parte proceedings.

Also important is Rule 2.9(C), forbidding the judge from conducting an independent factual investigation or considering facts outside the record other than where the evidence rules allow "judicial notice" of an undisputed fact. This means that a technology-savvy judge must avoid the temptation to get on the internet and seek publicly available information about a case or party. Rule 2.9(D) requires the judge to impose the same restraint on judicial staff.

C. Judicial Disqualification

[Question 3]

Judge, a state court judge, has presided over the pretrial proceedings in a case involving a novel contract question under the Uniform Commercial Code. During the pretrial proceedings, Judge has acquired considerable background knowledge of the facts and law of the matter and, therefore, is particularly well qualified to preside at the trial.

Shortly before the trial date, Judge discovered that his brother owns a substantial block of stock in the defendant corporation. He determined that his brother's financial interests would be substantially affected by the outcome of the case. Although Judge believed he would be impartial, he disclosed to the parties, on the record, his brother's interest.

Is it proper for Judge to hear the case?

Food for Thought

Rule 2.8(B) requires a judge to "be patient, dignified, and courteous" to parties, their lawyers, and others with whom the judge interacts. Bruce A. Green and Rebecca Roiphe criticize the courtesy rule in *Regulating Discourtesy on the Bench: A Study in the Evolution of Judicial Independence,* 64 N.Y.U. Ann. Surv. Am. L. 497 (2009), on the ground that judges should be free to be a bit impatient or discourteous and that, in any event, being human, judges sometimes cannot help it. They argue that judges should be able to bring their full personalities to the task of judging, even at risk of treating parties and lawyers impatiently, particularly in the context of problem-solving courts where judges are not supposed to be the equivalent of umpires, calling balls and strikes, as Chief Justice John Roberts characterized the judge's role in his confirmation hearings. They suggest that the courtesy rule ultimately encroaches on judicial independence: by putting judges at risk of discipline for rudeness, the rule discourages judges from engaging in legitimate judicial techniques.

(A) Yes, because Judge is particularly well qualified to preside at the trial.

(B) Yes, because Judge believes his judgment wilt not be affected by his brother's stockholding.

(C) No, because disqualification based on a relative's financial interest cannot be waived.

(D) No, unless after proper proceedings in which Judge did not participate all parties and their lawyers consent in writing that Judge may hear the case.

<u>Rule 2.11</u> addresses judicial disqualification. Rule 2.11(A) requires a judge to "disqualify himself or herself in any proceeding in which the judge's impartiality might reasonably be questioned," and provides a non-exclusive list of circumstances where disqualification is required. These include where:

- The judge "has a personal bias or prejudice concerning a party or a party's lawyer."

- The judge has personal knowledge of facts that are in dispute in the case (i.e., knowledge that comes from outside the judicial proceedings).

- The judge or a family member of the judge is a party to the proceeding or a lawyer in the proceeding.

- The judge or a family member of the judge, has a "more than de minimis interest that could be substantially affected by the proceeding."

- The judge or a family member of the judge is "likely to be a material witness in the proceeding."

- The judge previously served as a lawyer in the matter or as a judge in the matter in another court.

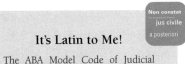

> ### It's Latin to Me!
>
> The ABA Model Code of Judicial Conduct includes a section on Terminology, which defines "de minimis" for purposes of Rule 2.11 to mean "an insignificant interest that could not raise a reasonable question regarding the lawyer's impartiality."

Among the other specified grounds for disqualification under Rule 2.11 of the ABA Model Code of Judicial Conduct is one directed at elected judges. Rule 2.11(A)(4) provides for disqualification when a party or a party's lawyer contributed more than a designated amount to the judge's campaign. However, few states have adopted this model provision. Consequently, elected judges lack specific guidance about when they must disqualify (or "recuse") themselves when a campaign contributor appears in a case. That is the problem that led to the following decision.

CAPERTON v. A.T. MASSEY COAL CO., INC.

<u>129 S. Ct. 2252 (2009)</u>

Justice KENNEDY delivered the opinion of the Court.

In this case the Supreme Court of Appeals of West Virginia reversed a trial court judgment, which had entered a jury verdict of $50 million. Five justices heard the case, and the vote to reverse was 3 to 2. The question presented is whether the Due Process Clause of the Fourteenth Amendment was violated when one of the justices in the majority denied a recusal motion. The basis for the motion was that the justice had received campaign contributions in an extraordinary amount from, and through the efforts of, the board chairman and principal officer of the corporation found liable for the damages.

Under our precedents there are objective standards that require recusal when "the probability of actual bias on the part of the judge or decisionmaker is too high to be constitutionally tolerable." Applying those precedents, we find that, in all the circumstances of this case, due process requires recusal.

I

In August 2002 a West Virginia jury returned a verdict that found respondents A.T. Massey Coal Co. and its affiliates (hereinafter Massey) liable for fraudulent misrepresentation, concealment, and tortious interference with existing contractual relations. The jury awarded petitioners Hugh Caperton, Harman Development Corp., Harman Mining Corp., and Sovereign Coal Sales (hereinafter Caperton) the sum of $50 million in compensatory and punitive damages.

In June 2004 the state trial court denied Massey's post-trial motions challenging the verdict and the damages award, finding that Massey "intentionally acted in utter disregard of [Caperton's] rights and ultimately destroyed [Caperton's] businesses because, after conducting cost-benefit analyses, [Massey] concluded it was in its financial interest to do so." In March 2005 the trial court denied Massey's motion for judgment as a matter of law.

Don Blankenship is Massey's chairman, chief executive officer, and president. After the verdict but before the appeal, West Virginia held its 2004 judicial elections. Knowing the Supreme Court of Appeals of West Virginia would consider the appeal in the case, Blankenship decided to support an attorney who sought to replace Justice McGraw. Justice McGraw was a candidate for reelection to that court. The attorney who sought to replace him was Brent Benjamin.

In addition to contributing the $1,000 statutory maximum to Benjamin's campaign committee, Blankenship donated almost $2.5 million to "And For The Sake Of The Kids," a political organization formed under 26 U.S.C. § 527. The § 527 organization opposed McGraw and supported Benjamin. Blankenship's donations accounted for more than two-thirds of the total funds it raised. This was not all. Blankenship spent, in addition, just over $500,000 on independent expenditures-for direct mailings and letters soliciting donations as well as television and newspaper advertisements-"to support ... Brent Benjamin.'"

To provide some perspective, Blankenship's $3 million in contributions were more than the total amount spent by all other Benjamin supporters and three times the amount spent by Benjamin's own committee. Caperton contends that Blankenship spent $1 million more than the total amount spent by the campaign committees of both candidates combined.

Benjamin won. He received 382,036 votes (53.3%), and McGraw received 334,301 votes (46.7%).

In October 2005, before Massey filed its petition for appeal in West Virginia's highest court, Caperton moved to disqualify now-Justice Benjamin under the Due Process Clause and the West Virginia Code of Judicial Conduct, based on the conflict caused by Blankenship's campaign involvement. Justice Benjamin denied the motion in April 2006. He indicated that he "carefully considered the bases and accompanying exhibits proffered by the movants." But he found "no objective information ... to show that this Justice has a bias for or against any litigant, that this Justice has prejudged the matters which comprise this litigation, or that this Justice will be anything but fair and impartial." In December 2006 Massey filed its petition for appeal to challenge the adverse jury verdict. The West Virginia Supreme Court of Appeals granted review.

In November 2007 that court reversed the $50 million verdict against Massey. The majority opinion, authored by then-Chief Justice Davis and joined by Justices Benjamin and Maynard, found that "Massey's conduct warranted the type of judgment rendered in this case." It reversed, nevertheless, based on two independent grounds-first, that a forum-selection clause contained in a contract to which Massey was not a party barred the suit in West Virginia, and, second, that res judicata barred the suit due to an out-of-state judgment to which Massey was not a party. Justice Starcher dissented, stating that the "majority's opinion is morally and legally wrong." Justice Albright also dissented, accusing the majority of "misapplying the law and introducing sweeping 'new law' into our jurisprudence that may well come back to haunt us."

Caperton sought rehearing, and the parties moved for disqualification of three of the five justices who decided the appeal. Photos had surfaced of Justice Maynard vacationing with Blankenship in the French Riviera while the case was pending. Justice Maynard granted Caperton's recusal motion. On the other side Justice Starcher granted Massey's recusal motion, apparently based on his public criticism of Blankenship's role in the 2004 elections. In his recusal memorandum Justice Starcher urged Justice Benjamin to recuse himself as well. He noted that "Blankenship's bestowal of his personal wealth, political tactics, and 'friendship' have created a cancer in the affairs of this Court." Justice Benjamin declined Justice Starcher's suggestion and denied Caperton's recusal motion.

The court granted rehearing. Justice Benjamin, now in the capacity of acting chief justice, selected Judges Cookman and Fox to replace the recused justices. Caperton moved a third time for disqualification, arguing that Justice Benjamin had failed to apply the correct standard under West Virginia law-*i.e.,* whether "a reasonable and prudent person, knowing these objective facts, would harbor doubts about Justice Benjamin's ability to be fair and impartial." Caperton also included the results of a public opinion poll, which indicated that over 67% of West Virginians doubted Justice Benjamin would be fair and impartial. Justice Benjamin again refused to withdraw, noting that the "push poll" was "neither credible nor sufficiently reliable to serve as the basis for an elected judge's disqualification."

In April 2008 a divided court again reversed the jury verdict, and again it was a 3-to-2 decision. Justice Davis filed a modified version of his prior opinion, repeating the two earlier holdings. She was joined by Justice Benjamin and Judge Fox. Justice Albright, joined by Judge Cookman, dissented: "Not only is the majority opinion unsupported by the facts and existing case law, but it is also fundamentally unfair. Sadly, justice was neither honored nor served by the majority.". The dissent also noted "genuine due process implications arising under federal law" with respect to Justice Benjamin's failure to recuse himself.

Four months later-a month after the petition for writ of certiorari was filed in this Court-Justice Benjamin filed a concurring opinion. He defended the merits of the majority opinion as well as his decision not to recuse. He rejected Caperton's challenge to his participation in the case under both the Due Process Clause and West Virginia law. Justice Benjamin reiterated that he had no "'direct, personal, substantial, pecuniary interest' in this case.'" Adopting "a standard merely of 'appearances,'" he concluded, "seems little more than an invitation to subject West Virginia's justice system to the vagaries of the day-a framework in which predictability and stability yield to supposition, innuendo, half-truths, and partisan manipulations."

* * *

III

Caperton contends that Blankenship's pivotal role in getting Justice Benjamin elected created a constitutionally intolerable probability of actual bias. Though not a bribe or criminal influence, Justice Benjamin would nevertheless feel a debt of gratitude to Blankenship for his extraordinary efforts to get him elected. * * *

Justice Benjamin was careful to address the recusal motions and explain his reasons why, on his view of the controlling standard, disqualification was not in order. In four separate opinions issued during the course of the appeal, he explained why no actual bias had been established. He found no basis for recusal because Caperton failed to provide "objective evidence" or "objective information," but merely "subjective belief" of bias. Nor could anyone "point to any actual conduct or activity on [his] part which could be termed 'improper.' " In other words, based on the facts presented by Caperton, Justice Benjamin conducted a probing search into his actual motives and inclinations; and he found none to be improper. We do not question his subjective findings of impartiality and propriety. Nor do we determine whether there was actual bias.

Following accepted principles of our legal tradition respecting the proper performance of judicial functions, judges often inquire into their subjective motives and purposes in the ordinary course of deciding a case. This does not mean the inquiry is a simple one. "The work of deciding cases goes on every day in hundreds of courts throughout the land. Any judge, one might suppose, would find it easy to describe the process which he had followed a thousand times and more. Nothing could be farther from the truth." B. Cardozo, *The Nature of the Judicial Process* 9 (1921).

The judge inquires into reasons that seem to be leading to a particular result. Precedent and *stare decisis* and the text and purpose of the law and the Constitution; logic and scholarship and experience and common sense; and fairness and disinterest and neutrality are among the factors at work. To bring coherence to the process, and to seek respect for the resulting judgment, judges often explain the reasons for their conclusions and rulings. There are instances when the introspection that often attends this process may reveal that what the judge had assumed to be a proper, controlling factor is not the real one at work. If the judge discovers that some personal bias or improper consideration seems to be the actuating cause of the decision or to be an influence so difficult to dispel that there is a real possibility of undermining neutrality, the judge may think it necessary to consider withdrawing from the case.

The difficulties of inquiring into actual bias, and the fact that the inquiry is often a private one, simply underscore the need for objective rules. Otherwise there may be no adequate protection against a judge who simply misreads or misapprehends the real motives at work in deciding the case. The judge's own inquiry into actual bias, then, is not one that the law can easily superintend or review, though actual bias, if disclosed, no doubt would be grounds for appropriate relief. In lieu of exclusive reliance on that personal inquiry, or on appellate review of the judge's determination respecting actual bias, the Due Process Clause has been implemented by objective standards that do not require proof of actual bias. In defining these standards the Court has asked whether, "under a realistic appraisal of psychological tendencies and human weakness," the interest "poses such a risk of actual bias or prejudgment that the practice must be forbidden if the guarantee of due process is to be adequately implemented."

We turn to the influence at issue in this case. Not every campaign contribution by a litigant or attorney creates a probability of bias that requires a judge's recusal, but this is an exceptional case. We conclude that there is a serious risk of actual bias-based on objective and reasonable perceptions-when a person with a personal stake in a particular case had a significant and disproportionate influence in placing the judge on the case by raising funds or directing the judge's election campaign when the case was pending or imminent. The inquiry centers on the contribution's relative size in comparison to the total amount of money contributed to the campaign, the total amount spent in the election, and the apparent effect such contribution had on the outcome of the election.

Applying this principle, we conclude that Blankenship's campaign efforts had a significant and disproportionate influence in placing Justice Benjamin on the case. Blankenship contributed some $3 million to unseat the incumbent and replace him with Benjamin. His contributions eclipsed the total amount spent by all other Benjamin supporters and exceeded by 300% the amount spent by Benjamin's campaign committee. Caperton claims Blankenship spent $1 million more than the total amount spent by the campaign committees of both candidates combined.

Massey responds that Blankenship's support, while significant, did not cause Benjamin's victory. In the end the people of West Virginia elected him, and they did so based on many reasons other than Blankenship's efforts. Massey points out that every major state newspaper, but one, endorsed Benjamin. It also contends that then-Justice McGraw cost himself the election by giving a speech during the campaign, a speech the opposition seized upon for its own advantage.

Justice Benjamin raised similar arguments. He asserted that "the outcome of the 2004 election was due primarily to [his own] campaign's message," as well as McGraw's "devastat[ing]" speech in which he "made a number of controversial claims which became a matter of statewide discussion in the media, on the internet, and elsewhere."

Whether Blankenship's campaign contributions were a necessary and sufficient cause of Benjamin's victory is not the proper inquiry. Much like determining whether a judge is actually biased, proving what ultimately drives the electorate to choose a particular candidate is a difficult endeavor, not likely to lend itself to a certain conclusion. This is particularly true where, as here, there is no procedure for judicial factfinding and the sole trier of fact is the one accused of bias. Due process requires an objective inquiry into whether the contributor's influence on the election under all the circumstances "would offer a possible temptation to the average . . . judge to . . . lead him not to hold the balance nice, clear and true." Blankenship's campaign contributions-in comparison to the total amount contributed to the campaign, as well as the total amount spent in the election-had a significant and disproportionate influence on the electoral outcome. And the risk that Blankenship's influence engendered actual bias is sufficiently substantial that it "must be forbidden if the guarantee of due process is to be adequately implemented."

The temporal relationship between the campaign contributions, the justice's election, and the pendency of the case is also critical. It was reasonably foreseeable, when the campaign contributions were made, that the pending case would be before the newly elected justice. The $50 million adverse jury verdict had been entered before the election, and the Supreme Court of Appeals was the next step once the state trial court dealt with post-trial motions. So it became at once apparent that, absent recusal, Justice Benjamin would review a judgment that cost his biggest donor's company $50 million. Although there is no allegation of a *quid pro quo* agreement, the fact remains that Blankenship's extraordinary contributions were made at a time when he had a vested stake in the outcome. Just as no man is allowed to be a judge in his own cause, similar fears of bias can arise when-without the consent of the other parties-a man chooses the judge in his own cause. And applying this principle to the judicial election process, there was here a serious, objective risk of actual bias that required Justice Benjamin's recusal.

Justice Benjamin did undertake an extensive search for actual bias. But, as we have indicated, that is just one step in the judicial process; objective standards may also require recusal whether or not actual bias exists or can be proved. Due process "may sometimes bar trial by judges who have no actual bias and who would do their very best to weigh the scales of justice equally between contending parties." failure to consider objective standards requiring recusal is not consistent with the imperatives of due process. We find that Blankenship's significant and disproportionate influence-coupled with the temporal relationship between the election and the pending case—""offer a possible temptation to the average . . . judge to . . . lead him not to hold the balance nice, clear and true."" On these extreme facts the probability of actual bias rises to an unconstitutional level.

IV

Our decision today addresses an extraordinary situation where the Constitution requires recusal. Massey and its *amici* predict that various adverse consequences will follow from recognizing a constitutional violation here-ranging from a flood of recusal motions to unnecessary interference with judicial elections. We disagree. The facts now before us are extreme by any measure. The parties point to no other instance involving judicial campaign contributions that presents a potential for bias comparable to the circumstances in this case.

* * *

One must also take into account the judicial reforms the States have implemented to eliminate even the appearance of partiality. Almost every State-West Virginia included-has adopted the American Bar Association's objective standard: "A judge shall avoid impropriety and the appearance of impropriety." ABA Annotated Model Code of Judicial Conduct, Canon 2 (2004). The ABA Model Code's test for appearance of impropriety is "whether the conduct would create in reasonable minds a perception that the judge's ability to carry out judicial responsibilities with integrity, impartiality and competence is impaired." Canon 2A, Commentary.

The West Virginia Code of Judicial Conduct also requires a judge to "disqualify himself or herself in a proceeding in which the judge's impartiality might reasonably be questioned." Canon 3E(1); *see also* 28 U.S.C. § 455(a) ("Any justice, judge, or magistrate judge of the United States shall disqualify himself in any proceeding in which his impartiality might reasonably be questioned"). Under Canon 3E(1), " '[t]he question of disqualification focuses on whether an objective assessment of the judge's conduct produces a reasonable question about impartiality, not on the judge's subjective perception of the ability to act fairly.' " Indeed, some States require recusal based on campaign contributions similar to those in this case.

These codes of conduct serve to maintain the integrity of the judiciary and the rule of law. The Conference of the Chief Justices has underscored that the codes are "[t]he principal safeguard against judicial campaign abuses" that threaten to imperil "public confidence in the fairness and integrity of the nation's elected judges." This is a vital state interest:

> "Courts, in our system, elaborate principles of law in the course of resolving disputes. The power and the prerogative of a court to perform this function rest, in the end, upon the respect accorded to its judgments. The citizen's respect for judgments depends in turn upon the issuing court's absolute probity. Judicial integrity is, in consequence, a state interest of the highest order."

It is for this reason that States may choose to "adopt recusal standards more rigorous than due process requires."

"The Due Process Clause demarks only the outer boundaries of judicial disqualifications. Congress and the states, of course, remain free to impose more rigorous standards for judicial disqualification than those we find mandated here today." Because the codes of judicial conduct provide more protection than due process requires, most disputes over disqualification will be resolved without resort to the Constitution. Application of the constitutional standard implicated in this case will thus be confined to rare instances.

* * *

The judgment of the Supreme Court of Appeals of West Virginia is reversed, and the case is remanded for further proceedings not inconsistent with this opinion.

It is so ordered.

Chief Justice ROBERTS, with whom Justice SCALIA, Justice THOMAS, and Justice ALITO join, dissenting.

I, of course, share the majority's sincere concerns about the need to maintain a fair, independent, and impartial judiciary-and one that appears to be such. But I fear that the Court's decision will undermine rather than promote these values.

Until today, we have recognized exactly two situations in which the Federal Due Process Clause requires disqualification of a judge: when the judge has a financial interest in the outcome of the case, and when the judge is trying a defendant for certain criminal contempts. Vaguer notions of bias or the appearance of bias were never a basis for disqualification, either at common law or under our constitutional precedents. Those issues were instead addressed by legislation or court rules.

Today, however, the Court enlists the Due Process Clause to overturn a judge's failure to recuse because of a "probability of bias." Unlike the established grounds for disqualification, a "probability of bias" cannot be defined in any limited way. The Court's new "rule" provides no guidance to judges and litigants about when recusal will be constitutionally required. This will inevitably lead to an increase in allegations that judges are biased, however groundless those charges may be. The end result will do far more to erode public confidence in judicial impartiality than an isolated failure to recuse in a particular case.

I

There is a "presumption of honesty and integrity in those serving as adjudicators." All judges take an oath to uphold the Constitution and apply the law impartially, and we trust that they will live up to this promise. We have thus identified only *two* situations in which the Due Process Clause requires disqualification of a judge: when the judge has a financial interest in the outcome of the case, and when the judge is presiding over certain types of criminal contempt proceedings.

It is well established that a judge may not preside over a case in which he has a "direct, personal, substantial pecuniary interest." This principle is relatively straightforward, and largely tracks the longstanding common-law rule regarding judicial recusal. *See* Frank, *Disqualification of Judges*, 56 Yale L.J. 605, 609 (1947) ("The common law of disqualification ... was clear and simple: a judge was disqualified for direct pecuniary interest and for nothing else"). For example, a defendant's due process rights are violated when he is tried before a judge who is "paid for his service only when he convicts the defendant."

It may also violate due process when a judge presides over a criminal contempt case that resulted from the defendant's hostility towards the judge. In *Mayberry v. Pennsylvania,* 400 U.S. 455, 91 S.Ct. 499, 27 L.Ed.2d 532 (1971), the defendant directed a steady stream of expletives and *ad hominem* attacks at the judge throughout the trial. When that defendant was subsequently charged with criminal contempt, we concluded that he "should be given a public trial before a judge other than the one reviled by the contemnor."

Our decisions in this area have also emphasized when the Due Process Clause does *not* require recusal:

> "All questions of judicial qualification may not involve constitutional validity. Thus matters of kinship, personal bias, state policy, remoteness of interest, would seem generally to be matters merely of legislative discretion."

Subject to the two well-established exceptions described above, questions of judicial recusal are regulated by "common law, statute, or the professional standards of the bench and bar."

In any given case, there are a number of factors that could give rise to a "probability" or "appearance" of bias: friendship with a party or lawyer, prior employment experience, membership in clubs or associations, prior speeches and writings, religious affiliation, and countless other considerations. We have never held that the Due Process Clause requires recusal for any of these reasons, even though they could be viewed as presenting a "probability of bias." Many state *statutes* require recusal based on a probability or appearance of bias, but "that alone would not be sufficient basis for imposing a *constitutional* requirement under the Due Process Clause." States are, of course, free to adopt broader recusal rules than the Constitution requires-and every State has-but these developments are not continuously incorporated into the Due Process Clause.

II

In departing from this clear line between when recusal is constitutionally required and when it is not, the majority repeatedly emphasizes the need for an "objective" standard. The majority's analysis is "objective" in that it does not inquire into Justice Benjamin's motives or decisionmaking process. But the standard the majority articulates-"probability of bias"-fails to provide clear, workable guidance for future cases. At the most basic level, it is unclear whether the new probability of bias standard is somehow limited to financial support in judicial elections, or applies to judicial recusal questions more generally.

But there are other fundamental questions as well. With little help from the majority, courts will now have to determine:

1. How much money is too much money? What level of contribution or expenditure gives rise to a "probability of bias"?

2. How do we determine whether a given expenditure is "disproportionate"? Disproportionate *to what* ?

3. Are independent, non-coordinated expenditures treated the same as direct contributions to a candidate's campaign? What about contributions to independent outside groups supporting a candidate?

4. Does it matter whether the litigant has contributed to other candidates or made large expenditures in connection with other elections?

5. Does the amount at issue in the case matter? What if this case were an employment dispute with only $10,000 at stake? What if the plaintiffs only sought non-monetary relief such as an injunction or declaratory judgment?

6. Does the analysis change depending on whether the judge whose disqualification is sought sits on a trial court, appeals court, or state supreme court?

7. How long does the probability of bias last? Does the probability of bias diminish over time as the election recedes? Does it matter whether the judge plans to run for reelection?

8. What if the "disproportionately" large expenditure is made by an industry association, trade union, physicians' group, or the plaintiffs' bar? Must the judge recuse in all cases that affect the association's interests? Must the judge recuse in all cases in which a party or lawyer is a member of that group? Does it matter how much the litigant contributed to the association?

9. What if the case involves a social or ideological issue rather than a financial one? Must a judge recuse from cases involving, say, abortion rights if he has received "disproportionate" support from individuals who feel strongly about either side of that issue? If the supporter wants to help elect judges who are "tough on crime," must the judge recuse in all criminal cases?

10. What if the candidate draws "disproportionate" support from a particular racial, religious, ethnic, or other group, and the case involves an issue of particular importance to that group?

11. What if the supporter is not a party to the pending or imminent case, but his interests will be affected by the decision? Does the Court's analysis apply if the supporter "chooses the judge" not in *his* case, but in someone else's?

12. What if the case implicates a regulatory issue that is of great importance to the party making the expenditures, even though he has no direct financial interest in the outcome (*e.g.,* a facial challenge to an agency rulemaking or a suit seeking to limit an agency's jurisdiction)?

13. Must the judge's vote be outcome determinative in order for his non-recusal to constitute a due process violation?

14. Does the due process analysis consider the underlying merits of the suit? Does it matter whether the decision is clearly right (or wrong) as a matter of state law?

15. What if a lower court decision in favor of the supporter is affirmed on the merits on appeal, by a panel with no "debt of gratitude" to the supporter? Does that "moot" the due process claim?

16. What if the judge voted against the supporter in many other cases?

17. What if the judge disagrees with the supporter's message or tactics? What if the judge expressly *disclaims* the support of this person?

18. Should we assume that elected judges feel a "debt of hostility" towards major *opponents* of their candidacies? Must the judge recuse in cases involving individuals or groups who spent large amounts of money trying unsuccessfully to defeat him?

19. If there is independent review of a judge's recusal decision, *e.g.,* by a panel of other judges, does this completely foreclose a due process claim?

20. Does a debt of gratitude for endorsements by newspapers, interest groups, politicians, or celebrities also give rise to a constitutionally unacceptable probability of bias? How would we measure whether such support is disproportionate?

21. Does close personal friendship between a judge and a party or lawyer now give rise to a probability of bias?

22. Does it matter whether the campaign expenditures come from a party or the party's attorney? If from a lawyer, must the judge recuse in every case involving that attorney?

23. Does what is unconstitutional vary from State to State? What if particular States have a history of expensive judicial elections?

24. Under the majority's "objective" test, do we analyze the due process issue through the lens of a reasonable person, a reasonable lawyer, or a reasonable judge?

25. What role does causation play in this analysis? The Court sends conflicting signals on this point. The majority asserts that "[w]hether Blankenship's campaign contributions were a necessary and sufficient cause of Benjamin's victory is not the proper inquiry." But elsewhere in the opinion, the majority considers "the apparent effect such contribution had on the outcome of the election," and whether the litigant has been able to "choos[e] the judge in his own cause." If causation is a pertinent factor, how do we know whether the contribution or expenditure had any effect on the outcome of the election? What if the judge won in a landslide? What if the judge won primarily because of his opponent's missteps?

26. Is the due process analysis less probing for incumbent judges-who typically have a great advantage in elections-than for challengers?

27. How final must the pending case be with respect to the contributor's interest? What if, for example, the only issue on appeal is whether the court should certify a class of plaintiffs? Is recusal required just as if the issue in the pending case were ultimate liability?

28. Which cases are implicated by this doctrine? Must the case be pending at the time of the election? Reasonably likely to be brought? What about an important but unanticipated case filed shortly after the election?

29. When do we impute a probability of bias from one party to another? Does a contribution from a corporation get imputed to its executives, and vice-versa? Does a contribution or expenditure by one family member get imputed to other family members?

30. What if the election is nonpartisan? What if the election is just a yes-or-no vote about whether to retain an incumbent?

31. What type of support is disqualifying? What if the supporter's expenditures are used to fund voter registration or get-out-the-vote efforts rather than television advertisements?

32. Are contributions or expenditures in connection with a primary aggregated with those in the general election? What if the contributor supported a different candidate in the primary? Does that dilute the debt of gratitude?

33. What procedures must be followed to challenge a state judge's failure to recuse? May *Caperton* claims only be raised on direct review? Or may such claims also be brought in federal district court under 42 U.S.C. § 1983, which allows a person deprived of a federal right by a state official to sue for damages? If § 1983 claims are available, who are the proper defendants? The judge? The whole court? The clerk of court?

34. What about state-court cases that are already closed? Can the losing parties in those cases now seek collateral relief in federal district court under § 1983? What statutes of limitation should be applied to such suits?

35. What is the proper remedy? After a successful *Caperton* motion, must the parties start from scratch before the lower courts? Is any part of the lower court judgment retained?

36. Does a litigant waive his due process claim if he waits until after decision to raise it? Or would the claim only be ripe after decision, when the judge's actions or vote suggest a probability of bias?

37. Are the parties entitled to discovery with respect to the judge's recusal decision?

38. If a judge erroneously fails to recuse, do we apply harmless-error review?

39. Does the *judge* get to respond to the allegation that he is probably biased, or is his reputation solely in the hands of the parties to the case?

40. What if the parties settle a *Caperton* claim as part of a broader settlement of the case? Does that leave the judge with no way to salvage his reputation?

These are only a few uncertainties that quickly come to mind. Judges and litigants will surely encounter others when they are forced to, or wish to, apply the majority's decision in different circumstances. Today's opinion requires state and federal judges simultaneously to act as political scientists (why did candidate X win the election?), economists (was the financial support disproportionate?), and psychologists (is there likely to be a debt of gratitude?).

The Court's inability to formulate a "judicially discernible and manageable standard" strongly counsels against the recognition of a novel constitutional right. The need to consider these and countless other questions helps explain why the common law and this Court's constitutional jurisprudence have never required disqualification on such vague grounds as "probability" or "appearance" of bias.

III

A

To its credit, the Court seems to recognize that the inherently boundless nature of its new rule poses a problem. But the majority's only answer is that the present case is an "extreme" one, so there is no need to worry about other cases. The Court repeats this point over and over.

But this is just so much whistling past the graveyard. Claims that have little chance of success are nonetheless frequently filed. The success rate for certiorari petitions before this Court is approximately 1.1%, and yet the previous Term some 8,241 were filed. Every one of the "*Caperton* motions" or appeals or § 1983 actions will claim that the judge is biased, or probably biased, bringing the judge and the judicial system into disrepute. And all future litigants will assert that their case is *really* the most extreme thus far.

Extreme cases often test the bounds of established legal principles. There is a cost to yielding to the desire to correct the extreme case, rather than adhering to the legal principle. That cost has been demonstrated so often that it is captured in a legal aphorism: "Hard cases make bad law."

* * *

It is an old cliché, but sometimes the cure is worse than the disease. I am sure there are cases where a "probability of bias" should lead the prudent judge to step aside, but the judge fails to do so. Maybe this is one of them. But I believe that opening the door to recusal claims under the Due Process Clause, for an amorphous "probability of bias," will itself bring our judicial system into undeserved disrepute, and diminish the confidence of the American people in the fairness and integrity of their courts. I hope I am wrong.

I respectfully dissent.

[Justice Scalia's dissenting opinion is omitted.]

Go Online

The respondent, Massey Coal, was the operator of a West Virginia mine where, in 2010, an explosion killed 29 in the United States's worst mine disaster in forty years. Click here for more details.

Do you agree with the dissenting Justices' prediction in *Caperton* that elected judges who previously received campaign contributions from a lawyer or party (and who do not disqualify themselves on their own initiative) will be flooded by disqualification motions? Would you predict that if lawyers begin to file frequent *Caperton* motions, the public will become aware of the practice, will perceive that the lawyers are involved in litigation gamesmanship, and will lose respect for the judicial process as a result?

Food for Thought

At least initially, *Caperton* did not appear to unleash a flood of disqualification motions as the dissenting Justices foresaw, but it did unleash a flood of law review articles. For a skeptical view of the dissenting opinions' prediction that *Caperton* would breed litigation gamesmanship and public respect, *see* Bruce A. Green, *Fear of the Unknown: Judicial Ethics After* Caperton, 60 Syracuse L. Rev. 229 (2010). Jeffrey W. Stempel also criticizes the dissent. In his article, *Playing Forty Questions: Responding to Justice Roberts's Concerns in* Caperton *and some Tentative Answers About Operationalizing Judicial Recusal and Due Process*, 39 Sw. L. Rev. 1 (2009), Stempel argue that there are adequate answers to the questions posed by Justice Roberts's dissent.

For a small sample of the many other writings on *Caperton*, *see, e.g.*, Bert Brandenburg, *Big Money and Impartial Justice: Can They Live Together?*, 52 Ariz. L. Rev. 207 (2010); Gerard J. Clark, Caperton's *New Right to Independence in Judges*, 58 Drake L. Rev. 661 (2010); Pamela Karlan, *Electing Judges, Judging Elections, and the Lessons of* Caperton, 123 Harv. L. Rev. 80 (2009); Kenneth L. Karst, Caperton's *Amici*, 33 Seattle U. L. Rev. 633 (2010); Ronald D. Rotunda, *Judicial Disqualification in the Aftermath of* Caperton v. A.T. Massey, 60 Syracuse L. Rev. 247 (2010); James Sample, *Court Reform Enters the Post-*Caperton *Era*, 58 Drake L. Rev. 787 (2010); Jed Handelsman Shugerman, *In Defense of Appearances: What* Caperton v. Massey *Should Have Said*, 59 DePaul L. Rev. 529 (2010); Jeffrey W. Stempel, *Completing* Caperton *and Clarifying Common Sense Through Using the Right Standard for Constitutional Judicial Recusal*, 29 Rev. Litig. 249 (2010); Jeffrey W. Stempel, *Impeach Brent Benjamin Now!? Giving Adequate Attention to Failings of Judicial Impartiality*, 47 San Diego L. Rev. 1 (2010); Hon. Catherine Stone & Wendy Martinez, Caperton v. A.T. Massey Coal Co.: *The Texas Implications*, 41 St. Mary's L.J. 621 (2010); Nancy A. Welsh, *What is (Im)Partial Enough in a World of Embedded Neutrals?*, 52 Ariz. L. Rev. 395 (2010).

According to *Caperton*, one of the state court Justices recused himself "apparently based on his public criticism of Blankenship's role in the 2004 elections." Should he have refrained from making this criticism? Several provisions of the judicial code limit judges' ability to speak off the bench or require their recusal when they have done so. Rule 2.11(A)(4) requires a judge's disqualification when "[t]he judge . . . has made a public statement, other than in a court proceeding, judicial decision, or opinion, that commits or appears to commit the judge to reach a particular result or rule in a particular way in the proceeding or controversy." Rule 2.10 generally forbids a judge from making public statements about a pending or impending case outside the context of the judicial proceedings if the statements might affect the outcome or impair the fairness of the litigation.

> ### Food for Thought
>
> Should there be an exception to the restriction on judicial speech to enable judges to correct public misunderstandings about pending proceedings or to respond to unfair criticism (equivalent to the fair comment provision of ABA Model Rule 3.6(c), which allows litigators to make otherwise impermissible public comments "to protect a client from the substantial undue prejudicial effect of recent publicity")? In 2007, the ABA considered, but rejected, a proposed addition to Rule 2.10 to allow a judge to respond "to allegations in the media or elsewhere concerning the judge's conduct in a matter." U.S. District Judge Nancy Gertner argued in favor of the exception in *"Tradeoffs of Candor: Does Judicial Transparency Erode Legitimacy?" Symposium: Remarks of Hon. Nancy Gertner,* 64 N.Y.U. Ann. Surv. Am. L. 449 (2009), based on her experience in a school desegregation case. In response to a newspaper article which erroneously criticized her for denying certification of the lawsuit as a class action, she wrote to the newspaper to explain that she had simply postponed ruling on the motion for class certification pending further discovery and she enclosed a copy of her order. In a divided decision, the court of appeals subsequently disqualified her from continuing to preside in the case, based on what it found to be an impermissible communication with the press. For additional writings on this subject, *see* Nancy Gertner, *To Speak or Not to Speak: Musings on Judicial Silence,* 32 Hofstra L. Rev. 1147 (2004); Mark I. Harrison & Keith Swisher, *When Judges Should Be Seen, Not Heard: Extrajudicial Comments Concerning Pending Cases and the Controversial Self-Defense Exception in the New Code of Judicial Conduct,* 64 N.Y.U. Ann. Surv. Am. L. 559 (2009).

Another West Virginia Justice in *Caperton* recused himself after photos surfaced of him vacationing with Blankenship, the chairman of the appellant company, "in the French Riviera while the case was pending." Was the Justice's disqualification ("recusal") required, or was the Justice being unduly cautious? Is the risk of judicial partiality diminished because Blankenship was not himself a party but was simply the chairman of a corporate party? Imagine a judge in a small rural community who know his or her neighbors, especially the community's lawyers, and considers many of them friends. Is it necessary for the judge to be disqualified when a friend or acquaintance is a lawyer or party, because the judge may be partial or have knowledge of the case gained outside the courtroom? Jeremy M. Miller argues in *Judicial Recusal and Disqualification: The Need for a Per Se Rule* on *Friendship (Not Acquaintance)*, 33 Pepp. L. Rev. 575 (2006) that the existing provisions of the judicial code do not adequately deal with the problems raised by judges' friendships.

In West Virginia, there was a process for replacing Justices who recused themselves, but that is not true in all jurisdictions. If a Justice of the U.S. Supreme Court recuses himself, the other eight Justices decide the case. Sometimes, the Justices divide 4-4, with the result that no majority decision is issued and the lower court opinion is affirmed "by an equally divided court." Under these circumstances, should a Justice be more hesitant than a lower-court judge to disqualify himself or herself?

CHENEY v. UNITED STATES DISTRICT COURT FOR THE DISTRICT OF COLUMBIA

541 U.S. 913 (2004)

Memorandum of Justice SCALIA.

I have before me a motion to recuse in these cases consolidated below. The motion is filed on behalf of respondent Sierra Club. The other private respondent, Judicial Watch, Inc., does not join the motion and has publicly stated that it "does not believe the presently-known facts about the hunting trip satisfy the legal standards requiring recusal." (The District Court, a nominal party in this mandamus action, has of course made no appearance.) Since the cases have been consolidated, however, recusal in the one would entail recusal in the other.

I

The decision whether a judge's impartiality can "'reasonably be questioned'" is to be made in light of the facts as they existed, and not as they were surmised or reported. The facts here were as follows:

For five years or so, I have been going to Louisiana during the Court's long December-January recess, to the duck-hunting camp of a friend whom I met through two hunting companions from Baton Rouge, one a dentist and the other a worker in the field of handicapped rehabilitation. The last three years, I have been accompanied on this trip by a son-in-law who lives near me. Our friend and host, Wallace Carline, has never, as far as I know, had business before this Court. He is not, as some reports have described him, an "energy industry executive" in the sense that summons up boardrooms of ExxonMobil or Con Edison. He runs his own company that provides services and equipment rental to oil rigs in the Gulf of Mexico.

During my December 2002 visit, I learned that Mr. Carline was an admirer of Vice President Cheney. Knowing that the Vice President, with whom I am well acquainted (from our years serving together in the Ford administration), is an enthusiastic duck-hunter, I asked whether Mr. Carline would like to invite him to our next year's hunt. The answer was yes; I conveyed the invitation (with my own warm recommendation) in the spring of 2003 and received an acceptance (subject, of course, to any superseding demands on the Vice President's time) in the summer. The Vice President said that if he did go, I would be welcome to fly down to Louisiana with him. (Because of national security requirements, of course, he must fly in a Government plane.) That invitation was later extended—if space was available—to my son-in-law and to a son who was joining the hunt for the first time; they accepted. The trip was set long before the Court granted certiorari in the present case, and indeed before the petition for certiorari had even been filed.

We departed from Andrews Air Force Base at about 10 a.m. on Monday, January 5, flying in a Gulfstream jet owned by the Government. We landed in Patterson, Louisiana, and went by car to a dock where Mr. Carline met us, to take us on the 20-minute boat trip to his hunting camp. We arrived at about 2 pm., the 5 of us joining about 8 other hunters, making about 13 hunters in all; also present during our time there were about 3 members of Mr. Carline's staff, and, of course, the Vice President's staff and security detail. It was not an intimate setting. The group hunted that afternoon and Tuesday and Wednesday mornings; it fished (in two boats) Tuesday afternoon. All meals were in common. Sleeping was in rooms of two or three, except for the Vice President, who had his own quarters. Hunting was in two- or three-man blinds. As it turned out, I never hunted in the same blind with the Vice President. Nor was I alone with him at any time during the trip, except, perhaps, for instances so brief and unintentional that I would not recall them—walking to or from a boat, perhaps, or going to or from dinner. Of course we said not a word about the present case. The Vice President left the camp Wednesday afternoon, about two days after our arrival. I stayed on to hunt (with my son and son-in-law) until late Friday morning, when the three of us returned to Washington on a commercial flight from New Orleans.

II

Let me respond, at the outset, to Sierra Club's suggestion that I should "resolve any doubts in favor of recusal." That might be sound advice if I were sitting on a Court of Appeals. There, my place would be taken by another judge, and the case would proceed normally. On the Supreme Court, however, the consequence is different: The Court proceeds with eight Justices, raising the possibility that, by reason of a tie vote, it will find itself unable to resolve the significant legal issue presented by the case. Thus, as Justices stated in their 1993 Statement of Recusal Policy: "[W]e do not think it would serve the public interest to go beyond the requirements of the statute, and to recuse ourselves, out of an excess of caution, whenever a relative is a partner in the firm before us or acted as a lawyer at an earlier stage. Even one unnecessary recusal impairs the functioning of the Court." Moreover, granting the motion is (insofar as the outcome of the particular case is concerned) effectively the same as casting a vote against the petitioner. The petitioner needs five votes to overturn the judgment below, and it makes no difference whether the needed fifth vote is missing because it has been cast for the other side, or because it has not been cast at all.

Even so, recusal is the course I must take—and will take—when, on the basis of established principles and practices, I have said or done something which requires that course. I have recused for such a reason this very Term. I believe, however, that established principles and practices do not require (and thus do not permit) recusal in the present case.

A

My recusal is required if, by reason of the actions described above, my "impartiality might reasonably be questioned." Why would that result follow from my being in a sizable group of persons, in a hunting camp with the Vice President, where I never hunted with him in the same blind or had other opportunity for private conversation? The only possibility is that it would suggest I am a friend of his. But while friendship is a ground for recusal of a Justice where the personal fortune or the personal freedom of the friend is at issue, it has traditionally *not* been a ground for recusal where *official action* is at issue, no matter how important the official action was to the ambitions or the reputation of the Government officer.

A rule that required Members of this Court to remove themselves from cases in which the official actions of friends were at issue would be utterly disabling. Many Justices have reached this Court precisely because they were friends of the incumbent President or other senior officials--and from the earliest days down to modern times Justices have had close personal relationships with the President and other officers of the Executive. John Quincy Adams hosted dinner parties featuring such luminaries as Chief Justice Marshall, Justices Johnson, Story, and Todd, Attorney General Wirt, and Daniel Webster. Justice Harlan and his wife often "'stopped in'" at the White House to see the Hayes family and pass a Sunday evening in a small group, visiting and singing hymns. Justice Stone tossed around a medicine ball with members of the Hoover administration mornings outside the White House. Justice Douglas was a regular at President Franklin Roosevelt's poker parties; Chief Justice Vinson played poker with President Truman. A no-friends rule would have disqualified much of the Court in *Youngstown Sheet & Tube Co. v. Sawyer*, 343 U.S. 579 (1952), the case that challenged President Truman's seizure of the steel mills. Most of the Justices knew Truman well, and four had been appointed by him. * * *

It is said, however, that this case is different because the federal officer (Vice President Cheney) is actually a *named party*. That is by no means a rarity. At the beginning of the current Term, there were before the Court (excluding habeas actions) no fewer than 83 cases in which high-level federal Executive officers were named in their official capacity—more than 1 in every 10 federal civil cases then pending. That an officer is named has traditionally made no difference to the proposition that friendship is not considered to affect impartiality in official-action suits. Regardless of whom they name, such suits, when the officer is the plaintiff, seek relief not for him personally but for the Government; and, when the officer is the defendant, seek relief not against him personally, but against the Government. That is why federal law provides for *automatic substitution* of the new officer when the originally named officer has been replaced. * * *

To be sure, there could be political consequences from disclosure of the fact (if it be so) that the Vice President favored business interests, and especially a sector of business with which he was formerly connected. But political consequences are not my concern, and the possibility of them does not convert an official suit into a private one. That possibility exists to a greater or lesser degree in virtually all suits involving agency action. To expect judges to take account of political consequences—and to assess the high or low degree of them—is to ask judges to do precisely what they should not do. It seems to me quite wrong (and quite impossible) to make recusal depend upon what degree of political damage a particular case can be expected to inflict.

In sum, I see nothing about this case which takes it out of the category of normal official-action litigation, where my friendship, or the appearance of my friendship, with one of the named officers does not require recusal.

B

The recusal motion claims that "the fact that Justice Scalia and his daughter [sic] were the Vice President's guest on Air Force Two on the flight down to Louisiana" means that I "accepted a sizable gift from a party in a pending case," a gift "measured in the thousands of dollars."

Let me speak first to the value, though that is not the principal point. Our flight down cost the Government nothing, since space-available was the condition of our invitation. And, though our flight down on the Vice President's plane was indeed free, since we were not returning with him we purchased (because they were least expensive) round-trip tickets that cost precisely what we would have paid if we had gone both down and back on commercial flights. In other words, none of us saved a cent by flying on the Vice President's plane. The purpose of going with him was not saving money, but avoiding some inconvenience to ourselves (being taken by car from New Orleans to Morgan City) and considerable inconvenience to our friends, who would have had to meet our plane in New Orleans, and schedule separate boat trips to the hunting camp, for us and for the Vice President's party. * * *

The principal point, however, is that social courtesies, provided at Government expense by officials whose only business before the Court is business in their official capacity, have not hitherto been thought prohibited.

Members of Congress and others are frequently invited to accompany Executive Branch officials on Government planes, where space is available. * * * I daresay that, at a hypothetical charity auction, much more would be bid for dinner for two at the White House than for a one-way flight to Louisiana on the Vice President's jet. Justices accept the former with regularity. While this matter was pending, Justices and their spouses were invited (*all* of them, I believe) to a December 11, 2003, Christmas reception at the residence of the Vice President—which included an opportunity for a photograph with the Vice President and Mrs. Cheney. Several of the Justices attended, and in doing so they were fully in accord with the proprieties.

* * *

As the newspaper editorials appended to the motion make clear, I have received a good deal of embarrassing criticism and adverse publicity in connection with the matters at issue here—even to the point of becoming (as the motion cruelly but accurately states) "fodder for late-night comedians." If I could have done so in good conscience, I would have been pleased to demonstrate my integrity, and immediately silence the criticism, by getting off the case. Since I believe there is no basis for recusal, I cannot. The motion is denied.

Go Online

For an example, click here to view a Jon Stewart segment titled "Duck Duck Recuse".

The judicial canons on disqualification potentially put judges in a bit of a bind, because they are not permitted to disqualify themselves simply to avoid criticism. Rule 2.7 requires a judge to "hear and decide matters assigned to the judge, except when disqualification is required by Rule 2.11 or other law." Thus, judges have to get it exactly right: they may not disqualify themselves when disqualification is not required, but they must disqualify themselves when it is. Shouldn't judges have some wiggle room in close cases? As a practical matter, they do: Judicial commissions are unlikely to sanction judges who make honest mistakes on close calls.

In limited circumstances, the parties may "waive" a judge's disqualification: Rule 2.7(C) provides that when the judge's disqualification is based on the judge's "personal bias or prejudice concerning a party or a party's lawyer" or is based on the judge's "personal knowledge of facts that are in dispute in the proceeding," the judge may disclose the basis for disqualification and ask the parties and their lawyers to consider, outside the judge's presence, whether to waive disqualification. The judge and his or her staff may not participate in these discussions. Note that disqualifications based on other grounds may not be waived.

D. Judges' Extrajudicial Activities

[Question 4]

Judge is a judge of the trial court in City. Judge has served for many years as a director of a charitable organization that maintains a camp for disadvantaged children. The organization has never been involved in litigation. Judge has not received any compensation for her services. The charity has decided to sponsor a public testimonial dinner in Judge's honor. As part of the occasion, the local bar association intends to commission and present to Judge her portrait at a cost of $4,000. The money to pay for the portrait will come from a "public testimonial fund" that will be raised by the City Bar Association from contributions of lawyers who are members of the association and who practice in the courts of City.

Is it proper for Judge to accept the gift of the portrait?

(A) Yes, because the gift is incident to a public testimonial for Judge.

(B) Yes, because Judge did not receive compensation for her services to the charitable organization.

(C) No, because the cost of the gift exceeds $1,000.

(D) No, because the funds for the gift are contributed by lawyers who practice in the courts of City.

[Question 5]

The state bar association has offered Judge and her spouse free transportation and lodging to attend its institute on judicial reform. Judge is expected to deliver a banquet speech.

Is it proper for Judge to accept this offer?

(A) Yes, unless the value of the transportation and lodging exceeds $500.

(B) Yes, because the activity is devoted to the improvement of law.

(C) No, if members of the bar association regularly appear in Judge's court.

(D) No, because the bar association is offering free transportation to Judge's spouse.

Judges cannot reasonably be expected to cloister themselves; they have to live in the world. But at the same time, there is a public interest in discouraging judges from activities that might undermine their impartiality. Where should the line be drawn? Robert B. McKay, then Dean of New York University School of Law, observed in *The Judiciary and Nonjudicial Activities*, 25 Law & Contemp. Probs. 9, 12 (1970):

> It would be easy, but intellectually lazy, to hold that the sole business of judges is judging, that all else is at least distracting, and that accordingly a judge should avoid all nonjudicial activities that might either be time-consuming or influence his opinion on matters that come before him. The argument proves too much. If a judge is to live in *this* world and not in the isolation of a sequestered juror, he is constantly shaping his views on all kinds of matters that may come before him. The perceptions of a judge are influenced by conversations with family, friends, and colleagues; by his choices among the competing news media; his preferences in recreational activities; and even his tastes in clothes and hair styles (the long and short of it).

> Skeptics may well charge overkill at this point, for of course no one suggests that judges cut themselves off from family, friends, and colleagues. But anything short of that impossible dream is unlikely to accomplish the objectives of those who seek immunization of the judiciary from all the opinion-shaping forces that surround them. It is at least arguable—and I for one would so argue—that a judge is likely to be a better dispenser of justice if he is aware of the currents and passions of the time, the developments of technology, and the sweep of events. To judge in the real world a judge must live, breathe, think, and partake of opinions in the real world.

Canon 3 of the ABA Model Code of Judicial Conduct calls upon a judge to "conduct the judge's personal and extrajudicial activities to minimize the risk of conflict with the obligations of judicial office," and brings together rules that are intended to restrict judges' activities that might undermine judicial impartiality without going overboard. Rule 3.1 establishes the general principle: Judges generally may engage in extrajudicial activities, but not those activities that will interfere with the judge's work, lead to frequent disqualification, or appear to undermine the judge's independence, integrity or impartiality. Other rules provide more specific guidance. For example:

- Rule 3.6 forbids a judge from being a member of an organization that invidiously discriminates on the basis of race, sex, gender, religion, national origin, ethnicity or sexual orientation. It also forbids a judge from using the facilities of such an organization (although it allows the judge to attend an isolated event when doing so does not appear to endorse the organization's practices).

- Rule 3.7(A) provides that, subject to the limitation of Rule 3.1, a judge may participate in activities "sponsored by organizations or governmental entities concerned with the law, the legal system, or the administration of justice, and those sponsored by or on behalf of educational, religious, charitable, fraternal, or civic organizations not conducted for profit." The rule provides a non-exclusive list of permissible activities, including assisting such an organization in *planning* relating to fund-raising (but not in actually requesting contributions other than from members of the judge's family and other judges whom the judge does not supervise); appearing or speaking at the organization's program; or serving as an officer or director of the organization (as long as the organization does not engage in frequent litigation or have a matter likely to come before the judge). The rule is more liberal in permitting the judge's affiliation with organizations (such as bar associations) whose activities involve the law, the legal system or the administration of justice.

- Rule 3.7(B) allows a judge to encourage lawyers to provide pro bono legal services.

- Rule 3.9 forbids a judge from serving as a mediator or arbitrator or performing other judicial functions apart from the judge's official duties, whether or not for pay. (Of course, as part of the judge's official duties, a judge may participate in settlement conferences or attempt to mediate a dispute.)

- Rule 3.12 allows a judge to receive reasonable compensation for extrajudicial activities that are permitted—e.g., for teaching law as an adjunct professor or for writing a book—as long as being compensated does not appear to undermine the judge's independence, integrity or impartiality.

- Rule 3.13 forbids a judge from accepting "any gifts, loans, bequests, benefits, or other things of value,, if acceptance is prohibited by law or would appear to a reasonable person to undermine the judge's independence, integrity or impartiality." The rule specifically permits the judge to accept certain items (in some cases, subject to a reporting requirement). These include "items with little intrinsic value," such as greeting cards; gifts, loans and other things of value from friends, relatives and others whose relationship would require the judge to be disqualified if they appeared before the judge; publications provided by the publisher for the judge's official use; and "ordinary social hospitality."

- Rule 3.14 generally allows the judge to be reimbursed for expenses in connection with permissible extracurricular activities, such as travel costs to speak at a bar association program.

E. Seeking Judicial Election

REPUBLICAN PARTY OF MINNESOTA v. WHITE

536 U.S. 765 (2002)

Justice SCALIA delivered the opinion of the Court.

The question presented in this case is whether the First Amendment permits the Minnesota Supreme Court to prohibit candidates for judicial election in that State from announcing their views on disputed legal and political issues.

I

Since Minnesota's admission to the Union in 1858, the State's Constitution has provided for the selection of all state judges by popular election. Since 1912, those elections have been nonpartisan. Since 1974, they have been subject to a legal restriction which states that a "candidate for a judicial office, including an incumbent judge," shall not "announce his or her views on disputed legal or political issues."This prohibition, promulgated by the Minnesota Supreme Court and based on Canon 7(B) of the 1972 American Bar Association (ABA) Model Code of Judicial Conduct, is known as the "announce clause." Incumbent judges who violate it are subject to discipline, including removal, censure, civil penalties, and suspension without pay. Lawyers who run for judicial office also must comply with the announce clause. Those who violate it are subject to, *inter alia,* disbarment, suspension, and probation.

In 1996, one of the petitioners, Gregory Wersal, ran for associate justice of the Minnesota Supreme Court. In the course of the campaign, he distributed literature criticizing several Minnesota Supreme Court decisions on issues such as crime, welfare, and abortion. A complaint against Wersal challenging, among other things, the propriety of this literature was filed with the Office of Lawyers

Professional Responsibility, the agency which, under the direction of the Minnesota Lawyers Professional Responsibility Board, investigates and prosecutes ethical violations of lawyer candidates for judicial office. The Lawyers Board dismissed the complaint; with regard to the charges that his campaign materials violated the announce clause, it expressed doubt whether the clause could constitutionally be enforced. Nonetheless, fearing that further ethical complaints would jeopardize his ability to practice law, Wersal withdrew from the election. In 1998, Wersal ran again for the same office. Early in that race, he sought an advisory opinion from the Lawyers Board with regard to whether it planned to enforce the announce clause. The Lawyers Board responded equivocally, stating that, although it had significant doubts about the constitutionality of the provision, it was unable to answer his question because he had not submitted a list of the announcements he wished to make.

Shortly thereafter, Wersal filed this lawsuit in Federal District Court against respondents [officers of the Lawyers Board and of the Minnesota Board on Judicial Standards (Judicial Board), which enforces the ethical rules applicable to judges], seeking, *inter alia,* a declaration that the announce clause violates the First Amendment and an injunction against its enforcement. Wersal alleged that he was forced to refrain from announcing his views on disputed issues during the 1998 campaign, to the point where he declined response to questions put to him by the press and public, out of concern that he might run afoul of the announce clause. Other plaintiffs in the suit, including the Minnesota Republican Party, alleged that, because the clause kept Wersal from announcing his views, they were unable to learn those views and support or oppose his candidacy accordingly. * * *

II

Before considering the constitutionality of the announce clause, we must be clear about its meaning. Its text says that a candidate for judicial office shall not "announce his or her views on disputed legal or political issues."

We know that "announc[ing] . . . views" on an issue covers much more than *promising* to decide an issue a particular way. The prohibition extends to the candidate's mere statement of his current position, even if he does not bind himself to maintain that position after election. All the parties agree this is the case, because the Minnesota Code contains a so-called "pledges or promises" clause, which *separately* prohibits judicial candidates from making "pledges or promises of conduct in office other than the faithful and impartial performance of the duties of the office," *ibid.*-a prohibition that is not challenged here and on which we express no view.

There are, however, some limitations that the Minnesota Supreme Court has placed upon the scope of the announce clause that are not (to put it politely) immediately apparent from its text. The statements that formed the basis of the complaint against Wersal in 1996 included criticism of past decisions of the Minnesota Supreme Court. One piece of campaign literature stated that "[t]he Minnesota Supreme Court has issued decisions which are marked by their disregard for the Legislature and a lack of common sense." It went on to criticize a decision excluding from evidence confessions by criminal defendants that were not tape-recorded, asking "[s]hould we conclude that because the Supreme Court does not trust police, it allows confessed criminals to go free?" It criticized a decision striking down a state law restricting welfare benefits, asserting that "[i]t's the Legislature which should set our spending policies." And it criticized a decision requiring public financing of abortions for poor women as "unprecedented" and a "pro-abortion stance." Although one would think that all of these statements touched on disputed legal or political issues, they did not (or at least do not now) fall within the scope of the announce clause. The Judicial Board issued an opinion stating that judicial candidates may criticize past decisions, and the Lawyers Board refused to discipline Wersal for the foregoing statements because, in part, it thought they did not violate the announce clause. The Eighth Circuit relied on the Judicial Board's opinion in upholding the announce clause, and the Minnesota Supreme Court recently embraced the Eighth Circuit's interpretation.

There are yet further limitations upon the apparent plain meaning of the announce clause: In light of the constitutional concerns, the District Court construed the clause to reach only disputed issues that are likely to come before the candidate if he is elected judge. The Eighth Circuit accepted this limiting interpretation by the District Court, and in addition construed the clause to allow general discussions of case law and judicial philosophy. The Supreme Court of Minnesota adopted these interpretations as well when it ordered enforcement of the announce clause in accordance with the Eighth Circuit's opinion.

It seems to us, however, that-like the text of the announce clause itself-these limitations upon the text of the announce clause are not all that they appear to be. First, respondents acknowledged at oral argument that statements critical of past judicial decisions are *not* permissible if the candidate also states that he is against *stare decisis*. Thus, candidates must choose between stating their views critical of past decisions and stating their views in opposition to *stare decisis*. Or, to look at it more concretely, they may state their view that prior decisions were erroneous only if they do not assert that they, if elected, have any power to eliminate erroneous decisions. Second, limiting the scope of the clause to issues likely to come before a court is not much of a limitation at all. One would hardly expect the "disputed legal or political issues" raised in the course of a state judicial election to include such matters as whether the Federal Government should end the embargo of Cuba. Quite obviously, they will be those legal or political disputes that are the proper (or by past decisions have been made the improper) business of the state courts. And within that relevant category, "[t]here is almost no legal or political issue that is unlikely to come before a judge of an American court, state or federal, of general jurisdiction." Third, construing the clause to allow "general" discussions of case law and judicial philosophy turns out to be of little help in an election campaign. At oral argument, respondents gave, as an example of this exception, that a candidate is free to assert that he is a "'strict constructionist.'" But that, like most other philosophical generalities, has little meaningful content for the electorate unless it is exemplified by application to a particular issue of construction likely to come before a court-for example, whether a particular statute runs afoul of any provision of the Constitution. Respondents conceded that the announce clause would prohibit the candidate from exemplifying his philosophy in this fashion. Without such application to real-life issues, all candidates can claim to be "strict constructionists" with equal (and unhelpful) plausibility.

In any event, it is clear that the announce clause prohibits a judicial candidate from stating his views on any specific nonfanciful legal question within the province of the court for which he is running, except in the context of discussing past decisions-and in the latter context as well, if he expresses the view that he is not bound by *stare decisis.*

Respondents contend that this still leaves plenty of topics for discussion on the campaign trail. These include a candidate's "character," "education," "work habits," and "how [he] would handle administrative duties if elected." Indeed, the Judicial Board has printed a list of preapproved questions which judicial candidates are allowed to answer. These include how the candidate feels about cameras in the courtroom, how he would go about reducing the caseload, how the costs of judicial administration can be reduced, and how he proposes to ensure that minorities and women are treated more fairly by the court system. Whether this list of preapproved subjects, and other topics not prohibited by the announce clause, adequately fulfill the First Amendment's guarantee of freedom of speech is the question to which we now turn.

III

* * *

The Court of Appeals concluded that respondents had established two interests as sufficiently compelling to justify the announce clause: preserving the impartiality of the state judiciary and preserving the appearance of the impartiality of the state judiciary. Respondents reassert these two interests before us, arguing that the first is compelling because it protects the due process rights of litigants, and that the second is compelling because it preserves public confidence in the judiciary. Respondents are rather vague, however, about what they mean by "impartiality." * * *

A

One meaning of "impartiality" in the judicial context-and of course its root mean-ing-is the lack of bias for or against either *party* to the proceeding. Impartiality in this sense assures equal application of the law. That is, it guarantees a party that the judge who hears his case will apply the law to him in the same way he applies it to any other party. This is the traditional sense in which the term is used. * * *

We think it plain that the announce clause is not narrowly tailored to serve impar-tiality (or the appearance of impartiality) in this sense. Indeed, the clause is barely tailored to serve that interest *at all,* inasmuch as it does not restrict speech for or against particular *parties,* but rather speech for or against particular *issues.* To be sure, when a case arises that turns on a legal issue on which the judge (as a candidate) had taken a particular stand, the party taking the opposite stand is likely to lose. But not because of any bias against that party, or favoritism toward the other party. *Any* party taking that position is just as likely to lose. The judge is applying the law (as he sees it) evenhandedly.

B

It is perhaps possible to use the term "impartiality" in the judicial context (though this is certainly not a common usage) to mean lack of preconception in favor of or against a particular *legal view.* This sort of impartiality would be concerned, not with guaranteeing litigants equal application of the law, but rather with guarantee-ing them an equal chance to persuade the court on the legal points in their case. Impartiality in this sense may well be an interest served by the announce clause, but it is not a *compelling* state interest, as strict scrutiny requires. A judge's lack of predisposition regarding the relevant legal issues in a case has never been thought a necessary component of equal justice, and with good reason. For one thing, it is virtually impossible to find a judge who does not have preconceptions about the law. As then-Justice REHNQUIST observed of our own Court: "Since most Justices come to this bench no earlier than their middle years, it would be unusual if they had not by that time formulated at least some tentative notions that would influence them in their interpretation of the sweeping clauses of the Constitu-tion and their interaction with one another. It would be not merely unusual, but extraordinary, if they had not at least given opinions as to constitutional issues in their previous legal careers." Indeed, even if it were possible to select judges who did not have preconceived views on legal issues, it would hardly be desirable to do so. "Proof that a Justice's mind at the time he joined the Court was a complete *tabula rasa* in the area of constitutional adjudication would be evidence of lack of qualification, not lack of bias." The Minnesota Constitution positively forbids the selection to courts of general jurisdiction of judges who are impartial in the sense of having no views on the law. And since avoiding judicial preconceptions on legal issues is neither possible nor desirable, pretending otherwise by attempting to preserve the "appearance" of that type of impartiality can hardly be a compelling state interest either.

C

A third possible meaning of "impartiality" (again not a common one) might be described as open-mindedness. This quality in a judge demands, not that he have no preconceptions on legal issues, but that he be willing to consider views that oppose his preconceptions, and remain open to persuasion, when the issues arise in a pending case. This sort of impartiality seeks to guarantee each litigant, not an *equal* chance to win the legal points in the case, but at least *some* chance of doing so. It may well be that impartiality in this sense, and the appearance of it, are desirable in the judiciary, but we need not pursue that inquiry, since we do not believe the Minnesota Supreme Court adopted the announce clause for that purpose.

Respondents argue that the announce clause serves the interest in open-mindedness, or at least in the appearance of openmindedness, because it relieves a judge from pressure to rule a certain way in order to maintain consistency with statements the judge has previously made. The problem is, however, that statements in election campaigns are such an infinitesimal portion of the public commitments to legal positions that judges (or judges-to-be) undertake, that this object of the prohibition is implausible. Before they arrive on the bench (whether by election or otherwise) judges have often committed themselves on legal issues that they must later rule upon. More common still is a judge's confronting a legal issue on which he has expressed an opinion while on the bench. Most frequently, of course, that prior expression will have occurred in ruling on an earlier case. But judges often state their views on disputed legal issues outside the context of adjudication-in classes that they conduct, and in books and speeches. Like the ABA Codes of Judicial Conduct, the Minnesota Code not only permits but encourages this. That is quite incompatible with the notion that the need for open-mindedness (or for the appearance of open-mindedness) lies behind the prohibition at issue here. * * *

IV

To sustain the announce clause, the Eighth Circuit relied heavily on the fact that a pervasive practice of prohibiting judicial candidates from discussing disputed legal and political issues developed during the last half of the 20th century. It is true that a "universal and long-established" tradition of prohibiting certain conduct creates "a strong presumption" that the prohibition is constitutional: "Principles of liberty fundamental enough to have been embodied within constitutional guarantees are not readily erased from the Nation's consciousness." The practice of prohibiting speech by judicial candidates on disputed issues, however, is neither long nor universal.

At the time of the founding, only Vermont (before it became a State) selected any of its judges by election. Starting with Georgia in 1812, States began to provide for judicial election, a development rapidly accelerated by Jacksonian democracy. By the time of the Civil War, the great majority of States elected their judges. We know of no restrictions upon statements that could be made by judicial candidates (including judges) throughout the 19th and the first quarter of the 20th century. Indeed, judicial elections were generally partisan during this period, the movement toward nonpartisan judicial elections not even beginning until the 1870's. Thus, not only were judicial candidates (including judges) discussing disputed legal and political issues on the campaign trail, but they were touting party affiliations and angling for party nominations all the while.

The first code regulating judicial conduct was adopted by the ABA in 1924. It contained a provision akin to the announce clause: "A candidate for judicial position . . . should not announce in advance his conclusions of law on disputed issues to secure class support . . . ." ABA Canon of Judicial Ethics 30 (1924). The States were slow to adopt the canons, however. "By the end of World War II, the canons . . . were binding by the bar associations or supreme courts of only eleven states." Even today, although a majority of States have adopted either the announce clause or its 1990 ABA successor, adoption is not unanimous. Of the 31 States that select some or all of their appellate and general-jurisdiction judges by election, 4 have adopted no candidate-speech restriction comparable to the announce clause, and 1 prohibits only the discussion of "pending litigation." This practice, relatively new to judicial elections and still not universally adopted, does not compare well with the traditions deemed worthy of our attention in prior cases.

* * *

There is an obvious tension between the article of Minnesota's popularly approved Constitution which provides that judges shall be elected, and the Minnesota Supreme Court's announce clause which places most subjects of interest to the voters off limits. (The candidate-speech restrictions of all the other States that have them are also the product of judicial fiat.) The disparity is perhaps unsurprising, since the ABA, which originated the announce clause, has long been an opponent of judicial elections. That opposition may be well taken (it certainly had the support of the Founders of the Federal Government), but the First Amendment does not permit it to achieve its goal by leaving the principle of elections in place while preventing candidates from discussing what the elections are about. "[T]he greater power to dispense with elections altogether does not include the lesser power to conduct elections under conditions of state-imposed voter ignorance. If the State chooses to tap the energy and the legitimizing power of the democratic process, it must accord the participants in that process . . . the First Amendment rights that attach to their roles."

The Minnesota Supreme Court's canon of judicial conduct prohibiting candidates for judicial election from announcing their views on disputed legal and political issues violates the First Amendment. Accordingly, we reverse the grant of summary judgment to respondents and remand the case for proceedings consistent with this opinion.

Justice O'CONNOR, concurring.

I join the opinion of the Court but write separately to express my concerns about judicial elections generally. Respondents claim that "[t]he Announce Clause is necessary . . . to protect the State's compelling governmental interes[t] in an actual and perceived . . . impartial judiciary." I am concerned that, even aside from what judicial candidates may say while campaigning, the very practice of electing judges undermines this interest.

We of course want judges to be impartial, in the sense of being free from any personal stake in the outcome of the cases to which they are assigned. But if judges are subject to regular elections they are likely to feel that they have at least some personal stake in the outcome of every publicized case. Elected judges cannot help being aware that if the public is not satisfied with the outcome of a particular case, it could hurt their reelection prospects. * * * Even if judges were able to suppress their awareness of the potential electoral consequences of their decisions and refrain from acting on it, the public's confidence in the judiciary could be undermined simply by the possibility that judges would be unable to do so.

Moreover, contested elections generally entail campaigning. And campaigning for a judicial post today can require substantial funds. Unless the pool of judicial candidates is limited to those wealthy enough to independently fund their campaigns, a limitation unrelated to judicial skill, the cost of campaigning requires judicial candidates to engage in fundraising. Yet relying on campaign donations may leave judges feeling indebted to certain parties or interest groups. Even if judges were able to refrain from favoring donors, the mere possibility that judges' decisions may be motivated by the desire to repay campaign contributors is likely to undermine the public's confidence in the judiciary.

Despite these significant problems, 39 States currently employ some form of judicial elections for their appellate courts, general jurisdiction trial courts, or both. Judicial elections were not always so prevalent. The first 29 States of the Union adopted methods for selecting judges that did not involve popular elections. As the Court explains, however, beginning with Georgia in 1812, States began adopting systems for judicial elections. From the 1830's until the 1850's, as part of the Jacksonian movement toward greater popular control of public office, this trend accelerated, and by the Civil War, 22 of the 34 States elected their judges. By the beginning of the 20th century, however, elected judiciaries increasingly came to be viewed as incompetent and corrupt, and criticism of partisan judicial elections mounted. In 1906, Roscoe Pound gave a speech to the American Bar Association in which he claimed that "compelling judges to become politicians, in many jurisdictions has almost destroyed the traditional respect for the bench."

In response to such concerns, some States adopted a modified system of judicial selection that became known as the Missouri Plan (because Missouri was the first State to adopt it for most of its judicial posts). Under the Missouri Plan, judges are appointed by a high elected official, generally from a list of nominees put together by a nonpartisan nominating commission, and then subsequently stand for unopposed retention elections in which voters are asked whether the judges should be recalled. If a judge is recalled, the vacancy is filled through a new nomination and appointment. This system obviously reduces threats to judicial impartiality, even if it does not eliminate all popular pressure on judges. The Missouri Plan is currently used to fill at least some judicial offices in 15 States.

Thirty-one States, however, still use popular elections to select some or all of their appellate and/or general jurisdiction trial court judges, who thereafter run for reelection periodically. Of these, slightly more than half use nonpartisan elections, and the rest use partisan elections. Most of the States that do not have any form of judicial elections choose judges through executive nomination and legislative confirmation.

Minnesota has chosen to select its judges through contested popular elections instead of through an appointment system or a combined appointment and retention election system along the lines of the Missouri Plan. In doing so the State has voluntarily taken on the risks to judicial bias described above. As a result, the State's claim that it needs to significantly restrict judges' speech in order to protect judicial impartiality is particularly troubling. If the State has a problem with judicial impartiality, it is largely one the State brought upon itself by continuing the practice of popularly electing judges.

Justice KENNEDY, concurring.

* * *

Here, Minnesota has sought to justify its speech restriction as one necessary to maintain the integrity of its judiciary. Nothing in the Court's opinion should be read to cast doubt on the vital importance of this state interest. Courts, in our system, elaborate principles of law in the course of resolving disputes. The power and the prerogative of a court to perform this function rest, in the end, upon the respect accorded to its judgments. The citizen's respect for judgments depends in turn upon the issuing court's absolute probity. Judicial integrity is, in consequence, a state interest of the highest order.

Articulated standards of judicial conduct may advance this interest. To comprehend, then to codify, the essence of judicial integrity is a hard task, however. "The work of deciding cases goes on every day in hundreds of courts throughout the land. Any judge, one might suppose, would find it easy to describe the process which he had followed a thousand times and more. Nothing could be farther from the truth." B. Cardozo, *The Nature of the Judicial Process* 9 (1921). Much the same can be said of explicit standards to ensure judicial integrity. To strive for judicial integrity is the work of a lifetime. That should not dissuade the profession. The difficulty of the undertaking does not mean we should refrain from the attempt. Explicit standards of judicial conduct provide essential guidance for judges in the proper discharge of their duties and the honorable conduct of their office. The legislative bodies, judicial committees, and professional associations that promulgate those standards perform a vital public service. Yet these standards may not be used by the State to abridge the speech of aspiring judges in a judicial campaign.

Minnesota may choose to have an elected judiciary. It may strive to define those characteristics that exemplify judicial excellence. It may enshrine its definitions in a code of judicial conduct. It may adopt recusal standards more rigorous than due process requires, and censure judges who violate these standards. What Minnesota may not do, however, is censor what the people hear as they undertake to decide for themselves which candidate is most likely to be an exemplary judicial officer. Deciding the relevance of candidate speech is the right of the voters, not the State. The law in question here contradicts the principle that unabridged speech is the foundation of political freedom.

* * *

If Minnesota believes that certain sorts of candidate speech disclose flaws in the candidate's credentials, democracy and free speech are their own correctives. The legal profession, the legal academy, the press, voluntary groups, political and civic leaders, and all interested citizens can use their own First Amendment freedoms to protest statements inconsistent with standards of judicial neutrality and judicial excellence. Indeed, if democracy is to fulfill its promise, they must do so. They must reach voters who are uninterested or uninformed or blinded by partisanship, and they must urge upon the voters a higher and better understanding of the judicial function and a stronger commitment to preserving its finest traditions. Free elections and free speech are a powerful combination: Together they may advance our understanding of the rule of law and further a commitment to its precepts.

* * *

Justice STEVENS, with whom Justices SOUTER, GINSBURG, and BREYER join, dissenting.

* * *

There is a critical difference between the work of the judge and the work of other public officials. In a democracy, issues of policy are properly decided by majority vote; it is the business of legislators and executives to be popular. But in litigation, issues of law or fact should not be determined by popular vote; it is the business of judges to be indifferent to unpopularity. Sir Matthew Hale pointedly described this essential attribute of the judicial office in words which have retained their integrity for centuries:

> "'11. That popular or court applause or distaste have no influence in anything I do, in point of distribution of justice.'"

> "'12. Not to be solicitous what men will say or think, so long as I keep myself exactly according to the rule of justice.'"

Consistent with that fundamental attribute of the office, countless judges in countless cases routinely make rulings that are unpopular and surely disliked by at least 50 percent of the litigants who appear before them. It is equally common for them to enforce rules that they think unwise, or that are contrary to their personal predilections. For this reason, opinions that a lawyer may have expressed before becoming a judge, or a judicial candidate, do not disqualify anyone for judicial service because every good judge is fully aware of the distinction between the law and a personal point of view. It is equally clear, however, that such expressions after a lawyer has been nominated to judicial office shed little, if any, light on his capacity for judicial service. Indeed, to the extent that such statements seek to enhance the popularity of the candidate by indicating how he would rule in specific cases if elected, they evidence a lack of fitness for the office.

Of course, any judge who faces reelection may believe that he retains his office only so long as his decisions are popular. Nevertheless, the elected judge, like the lifetime appointee, does not serve a constituency while holding that office. He has a duty to uphold the law and to follow the dictates of the Constitution. If he is not a judge on the highest court in the State, he has an obligation to follow the precedent of that court, not his personal views or public opinion polls. He may make common law, but judged on the merits of individual cases, not as a mandate from the voters.

By recognizing a conflict between the demands of electoral politics and the distinct characteristics of the judiciary, we do not have to put States to an all or nothing choice of abandoning judicial elections or having elections in which anything goes. As a practical matter, we cannot know for sure whether an elected judge's decisions are based on his interpretation of the law or political expediency. In the absence of reliable evidence one way or the other, a State may reasonably presume that elected judges are motivated by the highest aspirations of their office. But we do know that a judicial candidate, who announces his views in the context of a campaign, is effectively telling the electorate: "Vote for me because I believe X, and I will judge cases accordingly." Once elected, he may feel free to disregard his campaign statements, but that does not change the fact that the judge announced his position on an issue likely to come before him *as a reason to vote for him*. Minnesota has a compelling interest in sanctioning such statements.

* * *

The Court boldly asserts that respondents have failed to carry their burden of demonstrating "that campaign statements are uniquely destructive of open-mindedness." But the very purpose of most statements prohibited by the announce clause is to convey the message that the candidate's mind is not open on a particular issue. The lawyer who writes an article advocating harsher penalties for polluters surely does not commit to that position to the same degree as the candidate who says "vote for me because I believe all polluters deserve harsher penalties." At the very least, such statements obscure the appearance of open-mindedness. More importantly, like the reasoning in the Court's opinion, they create the false impression that the standards for the election of political candidates apply equally to candidates for judicial office.

* * *

Justice GINSBURG, with whom Justices STEVENS, SOUTER and BREYER join, dissenting.

* * *

II

Proper resolution of this case requires correction of the Court's distorted construction of the provision before us for review. According to the Court, the Announce Clause "prohibits a judicial candidate from stating his views on any specific non-fanciful legal question within the province of the court for which he is running, except in the context of discussing past decisions-and in the latter context as well, if he expresses the view that he is not bound by *stare decisis*." In two key respects, that construction misrepresents the meaning of the Announce Clause as interpreted by the Eighth Circuit and embraced by the Minnesota Supreme Court, which has the final word on this matter.

First and most important, the Court ignores a crucial limiting construction placed on the Announce Clause by the courts below. The provision does not bar a candidate from generally "stating [her] views" on legal questions; it prevents her from "publicly making known how [she] would *decide*" disputed issues. That limitation places beyond the scope of the Announce Clause a wide range of comments that may be highly informative to voters. Consistent with the Eighth Circuit's construction, such comments may include, for example, statements of historical fact ("As a prosecutor, I obtained 15 drunk driving convictions"); qualified statements ("Judges should use *sparingly* their discretion to grant lenient sentences to drunk drivers"); and statements framed at a sufficient level of generality ("Drunk drivers are a threat to the safety of every driver"). What remains within the Announce Clause is the category of statements that essentially commit the candidate to a position on a specific issue, such as "I think all drunk drivers should receive the maximum sentence permitted by law." See Tr. of Oral Arg. 45 (candidate may not say "'I'm going to decide this particular issue this way in the future'").

Second, the Court misportrays the scope of the Clause as applied to a candidate's discussion of past decisions. Citing an apparent concession by respondents at argument, the Court concludes that "statements critical of past judicial decisions are not permissible if the candidate also states that he is against *stare decisis*." That conclusion, however, draws no force from the meaning attributed to the Announce Clause by the Eighth Circuit. In line with the Minnesota Board on Judicial Standards, the Court of Appeals stated without qualification that the Clause "does not prohibit candidates from discussing appellate court decisions." The Eighth Circuit's controlling construction should not be modified by respondents' on the spot answers to fast-paced hypothetical questions at oral argument.

The Announce Clause is thus more tightly bounded, and campaigns conducted under that provision more robust, than the Court acknowledges. Judicial candidates in Minnesota may not only convey general information about themselves, they may also describe their conception of the role of a judge and their views on a wide range of subjects of interest to the voters. Further, they may discuss, criticize, or defend past decisions of interest to voters. What candidates may not do-simply or with sophistication-is remove themselves from the constraints characteristic of the judicial office and declare how they would decide an issue, without regard to the particular context in which it is presented, *sans* briefs, oral argument, and, as to an appellate bench, the benefit of one's colleagues' analyses. Properly construed, the Announce Clause prohibits only a discrete subcategory of the statements the Court's misinterpretation encompasses.

* * *

III

Even as it exaggerates the reach of the Announce Clause, the Court ignores the significance of that provision to the integrated system of judicial campaign regulation Minnesota has developed. Coupled with the Announce Clause in Minnesota's Code of Judicial Conduct is a provision that prohibits candidates from "mak[ing] pledges or promises of conduct in office other than the faithful and impartial performance of the duties of the office." Although the Court is correct that this "pledges or promises" provision is not directly at issue in this case, the Court errs in overlooking the interdependence of that prohibition and the one before us. In my view, the constitutionality of the Announce Clause cannot be resolved without an examination of that interaction in light of the interests the pledges or promises provision serves.

A

All parties to this case agree that, whatever the validity of the Announce Clause, the State may constitutionally prohibit judicial candidates from pledging or promising certain results.

The reasons for this agreement are apparent. Pledges or promises of conduct in office, however commonplace in races for the political branches, are inconsistent "with the judge's obligation to decide cases in accordance with his or her role." This judicial obligation to avoid prejudgment corresponds to the litigant's right, protected by the Due Process Clause of the Fourteenth Amendment, to "an impartial and disinterested tribunal in both civil and criminal cases." The proscription against pledges or promises thus represents an accommodation of "constitutionally protected interests [that] lie on both sides of the legal equation." Balanced against the candidate's interest in free expression is the litigant's "powerful and independent constitutional interest in fair adjudicative procedure."

* * *

* * * When a judicial candidate promises to rule a certain way on an issue that may later reach the courts, the potential for due process violations is grave and manifest. If successful in her bid for office, the judicial candidate will become a judge, and in that capacity she will be under pressure to resist the pleas of litigants who advance positions contrary to her pledges on the campaign trail. If the judge fails to honor her campaign promises, she will not only face abandonment by supporters of her professed views; she will also "ris[k] being assailed as a dissembler," willing to say one thing to win an election and to do the opposite once in office.

* * *

Prohibiting a judicial candidate from pledging or promising certain results if elected directly promotes the State's interest in preserving public faith in the bench. When a candidate makes such a promise during a campaign, the public will no doubt perceive that she is doing so in the hope of garnering votes. And the public will in turn likely conclude that when the candidate decides an issue in accord with that promise, she does so at least in part to discharge her undertaking to the voters in the previous election and to prevent voter abandonment in the next. The perception of that unseemly *quid pro quo*-a judicial candidate's promises on issues in return for the electorate's votes at the polls-inevitably diminishes the public's faith in the ability of judges to administer the law without regard to personal or political self-interest.[1] Then-Justice REHNQUIST's observations about the federal system apply with equal if not greater force in the context of Minnesota's elective judiciary: Regarding the appearance of judicial integrity,

> "[one must] distinguish quite sharply between a public statement made prior to nomination for the bench, on the one hand, and a public statement made by a nominee to the bench. For the latter to express any but the most general observation about the law would suggest that, in order to obtain favorable consideration of his nomination, he deliberately was announcing in advance, without benefit of judicial oath, briefs, or argument, how he would decide a particular question that might come before him as a judge."

B

The constitutionality of the pledges or promises clause is thus amply supported; the provision not only advances due process of law for litigants in Minnesota courts, it also reinforces the authority of the Minnesota judiciary by promoting public confidence in the State's judges. The Announce Clause, however, is equally vital to achieving these compelling ends, for without it, the pledges or promises provision would be feeble, an arid form, a matter of no real importance.

Uncoupled from the Announce Clause, the ban on pledges or promises is easily circumvented. By prefacing a campaign commitment with the caveat, "although I cannot promise anything," or by simply avoiding the language of promises

---

1   [footnote 4 in original – ed.] The author of the Court's opinion declined on precisely these grounds to tell the Senate whether he would overrule a particular case:

"Let us assume that I have people arguing before me to do it or not to do it. I think it is quite a thing to be arguing to somebody who you know has made a representation in the course of his confirmation hearings, and that is, by way of condition to his being confirmed, that he will do this or do that. I think I would be in a very bad position to adjudicate the case without being accused of having a less than impartial view of the matter." 13 R. Mersky & J. Jacobstein, The Supreme Court of the United States: Hearings and Reports on Successful and Unsuccessful Nominations of Supreme Court Justices by the Senate Judiciary Committee, 1916-1986, p. 131 (1989) (hearings before the Senate Judiciary Committee on the nomination of then-Judge Scalia).

or pledges altogether, a candidate could declare with impunity how she would decide specific issues. Semantic sanitizing of the candidate's commitment would not, however, diminish its pernicious effects on actual and perceived judicial impartiality. To use the Court's example, a candidate who campaigns by saying, "If elected, I will vote to uphold the legislature's power to prohibit same-sex marriages," will feel scarcely more pressure to honor that statement than the candidate who stands behind a podium and tells a throng of cheering supporters: "I think it is constitutional for the legislature to prohibit same-sex marriages." Made during a campaign, both statements contemplate a *quid pro quo* between candidate and voter. Both effectively "bind [the candidate] to maintain that position after election." And both convey the impression of a candidate prejudging an issue to win votes. Contrary to the Court's assertion, the "nonpromissory" statement averts none of the dangers posed by the "promissory" one.

By targeting statements that do not technically constitute pledges or promises but nevertheless "publicly mak[e] known how [the candidate] would decide" legal issues, the Announce Clause prevents this end run around the letter and spirit of its companion provision.[2] No less than the pledges or promises clause itself, the Announce Clause is an indispensable part of Minnesota's effort to maintain the health of its judiciary, and is therefore constitutional for the same reasons.

* * *

This Court has recognized in the past, as Justice O'CONNOR does today, a "fundamental tension between the ideal character of the judicial office and the real world of electoral politics." We have no warrant to resolve that tension, however, by forcing States to choose one pole or the other. Judges are not politicians, and the First Amendment does not require that they be treated as politicians simply because they are chosen by popular vote. Nor does the First Amendment command States that wish to promote the integrity of their judges in fact and appearance to abandon systems of judicial selection that the people, in the exercise of their sovereign prerogatives, have devised.

For more than three-quarters of a century, States like Minnesota have endeavored,

---

2 [footnote 5 in original – ed.] In the absence of the Announce Clause, other components of the Minnesota Code of Judicial Conduct designed to maintain the nonpartisan character of the State's judicial elections would similarly unravel. A candidate would have no need to "attend political gatherings" or "make speeches on behalf of a political organization," for she could simply state her views elsewhere, counting on her supporters to carry those views to the party faithful. And although candidates would remain barred from "seek [ing], accept[ing,] or us[ing] endorsements from a political organization," parties might well provide such endorsements unsolicited upon hearing candidates' views on specific issues. Those unsolicited endorsements, in turn, would render ineffective the prohibition against candidates "identify[ing] themselves as members of a political organization," "Indeed, it is not too much to say that the entire fabric of Minnesota's non[p]artisan elections hangs by the Announce clause thread."

through experiment tested by experience, to balance the constitutional interests in judicial integrity and free expression within the unique setting of an elected judiciary. The Announce Clause, borne of this long effort, "comes to this Court bearing a weighty title of respect." I would uphold it as an essential component in Minnesota's accommodation of the complex and competing concerns in this sensitive area.

The decision in *Minnesota v. White* led to a wide range of reactions and reflections. For a small sample, *see* Richard Briffault, *Judicial Campaign Codes After Republican Party of* Minnesota v. White, 153 U. Pa. L. Rev. 181 (2004); Rachel Paine Caufield, *In the Wake of* White: *How States are Responding to Republican Party of* Minnesota v. White *and How Judicial Elections are Changing*, 38 Akron L. Rev. 625 (2005); Michael Richard Dimino, Sr., *Counter-Majoritarian Power and Judges' Political Speech*, 58 Fla. L. Rev. 53 (2005); Michelle T. Friedland, *Disqualification or Suppression: Due Process and the Response to Judicial Campaign Speech*, 104 Colum. L. Rev. 563 (2004); Charles Gardner Geyh, *Why Judicial Elections Stink,* 64 Ohio St. L.J. 43 (2003); Sherrilyn A. Ifill, *Through the Lens of Diversity: The Fight for Judicial Elections After Republican Party of* Minnesota v. White, 10 Mich. J. Race & L. 55 (2004); Hon. Rick A. Johnson, *Judicial Campaign Speech in Kentucky after Republican Party of* Minnesota v. White, 30 N. Ky. L. Rev. 347 (2003); Andrew L. Kaufman, *Judicial Correctness Meets Constitutional Correctness: Section 2C of the Code of Judicial Conduct*, 32 Hofstra L. Rev. 1293 (2004); David Schultz, Minnesota Republican Party v. White *and the Future of Federal Judicial Selection*, 69 Alb. L. Rev. 985 (2006); Nat Stern, *The Looming Collapse of Restrictions on Judicial Campaign Speech*, 38 Seton Hall L. Rev. 63 (2008); Kathleen M. Sullivan, Republican Party of Minnesota v. White: *What Are the Alternatives?*, 21 Geo. J. Legal Ethics 1327 (2008).

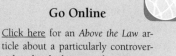

Go Online

Click here for an *Above the Law* article about a particularly controversial judicial election advertisement that led to a deadlock in the Wisconsin State Supreme Court. To see the advertisement itself, click here.

F. Moving From Judging (or Arbitrating) to Private Practice

[Question 6]

An attorney's law firm regularly represented a large company in its international business transactions. The company became involved in a contractual dispute with a foreign government. The company invoked a mandatory arbitration procedure contained in the contract. Under the arbitration clause, each party was allowed to choose a partisan arbitrator and the partisan arbitrators were to choose an additional arbitrator to sit on the panel. The company selected the attorney to be on the arbitration panel. Neither the attorney nor his law firm had represented the company in connection with the contract with the foreign government. The arbitration was completed, and the company was awarded the sum of $100,000. The company then hired the attorney to enforce the award. The attorney obtained the consent of the other arbitrators before accepting the representation. He was successful in enforcing the award.

Is the attorney subject to discipline?

(A) Yes, because the attorney should not have represented the company in a matter in which the attorney had been an arbitrator.

(B) Yes, because the attorney should have declined the arbitration assignment in view of his law firm's regular representation of the company.

(C) No, because the attorney obtained the consent of the other arbitrators before accepting the representation.

(D) No, because the attorney was appointed to the arbitration panel as a partisan arbitrator.

Rule 1.12

(a) Except as stated in paragraph (d), a lawyer shall not represent anyone in connection with a matter in which the lawyer participated personally and substantially as a judge or other adjudicative officer or law clerk to such a person or as an arbitrator, mediator or other third-party neutral, unless all parties to the proceeding give informed consent, confirmed in writing.

(b) A lawyer shall not negotiate for employment with any person who is involved as a party or as lawyer for a party in a matter in which the lawyer is participating personally and substantially as a judge or other adjudicative officer or as an arbitrator, mediator or other third-party neutral. A lawyer serving as a law clerk to a judge or other adjudicative officer may negotiate for employment with a party or lawyer involved in a matter in which the clerk is participating personally and substantially, but only after the lawyer has notified the judge or other adjudicative officer.

(c) If a lawyer is disqualified by paragraph (a), no lawyer in a firm with which that lawyer is associated may knowingly undertake or continue representation in the matter unless:

(1) the disqualified lawyer is timely screened from any participation in the matter and is apportioned no part of the fee therefrom; and

(2) written notice is promptly given to the parties and any appropriate tribunal to enable them to ascertain compliance with the provisions of this rule.

(d) An arbitrator selected as a partisan of a party in a multimember arbitration panel is not prohibited from subsequently representing that party.

Rule 1.12 is intended to preserve judges' impartiality by removing the incentive for judges to make determinations with an eye toward future employment. Note that Rule 1.12 applies to judges' law clerks as well as to judges. Rule 1.12(b) does not forbid a law clerk from negotiating future employment with a party or lawyer involved in a matter on which the clerk is working, as it forbids the judge from doing so. But it does require a judge's law clerk to notify the judge, who may then decide to take the law clerk off the case.

Rule 1.12 is the only provision of the ABA Model Rules of Professional Conduct that specifically addresses the obligations of lawyers functioning as arbitrators or other third-party neutrals. The ABA Model Code of Judicial Conduct also does not apply to lawyer-arbitrators. That is a subject for other law and standards.

Organizations administering arbitrations may develop and enforce principles of self-governance to avoid appearances of impropriety and, thereby, to promote the confidence of parties and the public in the fairness and neutrality of the arbitration process. For example, the ABA and the American Arbitration Association have approved "The Code of Ethics for Arbitrators in Commercial Disputes," http://www.abanet.org/dispute/commercial_disputes.pdf, containing various provisions directed at avoiding an appearance of partiality, bias or other impropriety. Additionally, courts may refuse to confirm arbitrators' awards when the arbitrator was biased. For example, under Section 10(a)(2) of the Federal Arbitration Act, 9 U.S.C. § 10 (1988 & Supp. V 1993), as well as under similar or identical state laws, a court reviewing an arbitration award may vacate the award where there was "evident partiality" on the part of one or more arbitrators. The case law dealing with arbitrators' bias fleshes out the legal standard. In general, what courts expect of arbitrators by way of impartiality is not nearly as stringent as what they expect of judges. For example, it is not uncommon for arbitrators to be selected precisely because of their relationship or familiarity with the parties or the relevant industry.

CHAPTER **8**

What is the Proper Role of a Lawyer?

I. Introduction

Today, the dominant understanding of the lawyer's role is that of the neutral partisan, commonly described as the hired gun. This Chapter will explore the justifications for, and criticisms of, the neutral partisan role. It will also describe alternative proposals—the lawyer as civics teacher, moral activist, religious person, feminist, and racial justice advocate. At the end of the Chapter, you will be asked to choose the role of the lawyer with which you most identify.

II. The Role Morality of the Neutral Partisan

A. The Buried Bodies Case

Many, if not most, lawyers are familiar with the so-called "Buried Bodies" case, one of the classic legal ethics dilemmas. After a well-publicized manhunt, the police arrested Robert Garrow for the murder of teenager Phillip Domblewski in upstate New York. The court asked Frank Armani to defend him. A lawyer from Syracuse, Armani had previously represented Garrow in another matter. Armani, in turn, asked Francis Belge, an experienced criminal defense lawyer, to join him as counsel.

Garrow was also suspected of kidnapping two young women, Alicia Hauck and Susan Petz. Garrow told his lawyers that he had murdered Hauck and Petz and told them where to find the bodies. The lawyers went to the locations, found the bodies, and photographed them. But they kept the death of the young women confidential, even when the parents of Hauck and Petz begged the lawyers for information about their missing daughters. The lawyers did not disclose any information to the parents.

Professor Heidi L. Feldman describes a television interview where Armani explained his thinking:

> *"All we went by at the time was our oath of office to keep inviolate the secrets of our clients." In a later segment of the interview, Armani describes the issue*

as involving a conflict, a question of "which is the higher moral good." On the one hand, Armani felt that his duty to defend Garrow required him to keep silent. "It's a question of the Constitution, a question of whether a bastard like [Garrow] having a proper defense, having adequate representation, being able to trust his lawyer as to what he says . . . " On the other hand, Armani knew that the information he held could ease the pain of the grieving family. Armani balanced his duty to defend Garrow "against the breaking hearts of a parent." In the end, Armani judged that the families' suffering did not outweigh his duty to Garrow: "[t]heir suffering was not worth jeopardizing my sworn duty or my oath of office or the Constitution." The extent to which Armani felt a moral conflict is suggested by a later segment of the interview in which Armani discusses his inability to answer a letter from one of Garrow's victims' sister. Armani states, "I caused them pain . . . What do you say? Nothing I could say would justify it in their minds. You couldn't justify it to me."[1]

The lawyers offered the prosecution a plea bargain. They would provide information regarding the Hauk and Petz disappearances in exchange for an agreement to place Garrow in a mental hospital. The prosecution refused.

As part of an insanity defense at trial, Garrow admitted to the killings of Hauk and Petz. The public was outraged. Professor Lisa Lerman explains:

> At that point it became apparent that the two lawyers had known and concealed this information for some time. The parents of the victims and the community where they were practicing law were furious with the lawyers. Their colleagues deserted them. Their practices dried up. Their families had to leave town for their own protection. There were death threats against the lawyers and their families.[2]

Garrow was convicted. The prosecutors began an investigation of Armani and Belge. They obtained an indictment of Belge, but not Armani, for violating a public health law provisions relating to a decent burial and to report a death "occurring without medical attendance." The courts dismissed the indictment on the ground that the "[attorney-client] privilege effectively shielded the defendant-attorney from his actions which would otherwise have violated the Public Health Law." *People v. Belge*, 50 A.D.2d 1088 (1975), *aff'd*, 41 N.Y.2d 60 (1976).

A few years later, Armani was featured in the public television documentary, *Ethics on Trial*. As a result, Frank Armani, an ordinary small city lawyer, became a hero to a generation of law professors, lawyers, and law students.[3]

---

1 Heidi Li Feldman, *Codes and Virtues: Can Good Lawyers Be Good Ethical Deliberators?*, 69 S. Cal. L. Rev. 885, 900 (1996).

2 Lisa G. Lerman, Frank H. Armani, Thomas D. Morgan, & Monroe H. Freedman, *The Buried Bodies Case: Alive and Well After Thirty Years*, 2007 Prof. Law. 19-20.

3 Id. at 31.

Before answering the following questions, read the text materials below. For purposes of this course, the morality questions throughout this Chapter have no right answer. For purposes of your life as a lawyer, you determine the correct answers to those questions.

[Question 1]

In plea bargaining, did Armani and Belge violate the Rules?

(A) Yes

(B) No

[Question 2]

Armani and Belge behaved morally by plea bargaining.

(A) True

(B) False

Food for Thought

We recommend that you watch the approximately twenty-five minute segment of the documentary that features an journalist Fred Graham's interview of Frank Armani. If your professor does not have a copy available, you may be able to obtain one from your library. Otherwise, your library should be able to obtain a copy from WETA, Washington, DC. You may also want to read Tom Alibrandi and Frank Armani's riveting account of the case, PRIVILEGED INFORMATION (1984).

[Question 3]

Under the Rules, Armani and Belge:

(A) had to disclose the existence and location of the buried bodies.

(B) had discretion to disclose the existence and location of the buried bodies.

(C) had to keep confidential the existence and location of the buried bodies.

[Question 4]

Armani and Belge behaved morally in keeping confidential the existence and location of the bodies.

(A) True

(B) False

[Question 5]

Role morality requires lawyers to take actions that are immoral under ordinary morality.

(A) True

(B) False

[Question 6]

Which of the following is NOT a justification for the hired gun role?

(A) **The adversary system.**

(B) **The traditional understanding of professionalism.**

(C) **Client autonomy.**

(D) **Democracy and access to law.**

Review the materials on Professionalism in Chapter 1 and Rule 1.6.

N.Y. STATE BAR ASS'N COMM. ON PROF'L ETHICS

Op. No. 479 (1978)

Preliminary Statement

The following opinion, incorporating only minor editorial changes unrelated to substance, was prepared in 1974. Its publication was withheld until, as we have recently learned, all proceedings relating to the matter were concluded. Reported proceedings are discussed in *People v. Belge,* 83 Misc. 2d 186 (1975), *aff'd* 50 App. Div. 2d, 1088 (4th Dept. 1975), *aff'd* 41 N.Y. 2d 60 (1976).

The allegations on which our opinion was based may be summarized as follows:

A client charged with homicide tells his lawyer during the course of representation that he had previously killed two other persons in homicides totally unrelated to that for which he has been indicted. The lawyer makes a record of his client's conversation containing this incriminating information. At the lawyer's request, the client also informs him of the location of the corpses, which was indicated on a diagram.

Following such disclosure, the lawyer goes to this location, discovers the bodies and photographs them. Before doing so, he moves parts of a body which had been dismembered to bring it within range of his camera. No attempt is made to conceal either body in any way.

At a later date, the lawyer destroys the photographs, the record of his conversation with his client and the diagram of the location of the bodies. He does not disclose to the authorities or to anyone else any of the information so obtained. Thereafter, during discussions with the District Attorney concerning the crime charged in the indictment, the lawyer, in discussing the possibility of an appropriate plea disposition, suggests that he is in a position to provide information concerning two unsolved murders still under investigation by the authorities.

QUESTIONS

1. Under the circumstances alleged, would a lawyer be acting improperly in failing to disclose to the authorities his knowledge of the two prior murders and the location of the bodies?

2. Under the circumstances alleged, would a lawyer be acting improperly in withholding and destroying (a) the records of his conversation with the client, (b) the photographs taken by him of the bodies of the victims and (c) the diagram showing the physical location of the bodies?

3. Under the circumstances alleged, would a lawyer be acting improperly in moving parts of one of the bodies prior to taking photographs?

4. Under the circumstances alleged, would a lawyer be acting improperly, in his attempt to negotiate a plea disposition, in suggesting to the District Attorney that he had information concerning two unsolved murders?

OPINION

The questions raised are complex and difficult. Legal issues, upon which we do not pass, may be inextricably interwoven with ethical considerations. Illegal conduct involving moral turpitude is per se unethical. DR1-102(A) (3).

1. The lawyer's failure to disclose his knowledge of the two unrelated homicides was not improper, assuming, as the facts given us indicate, that the information came to the lawyer during the course of his employment. Furthermore, the requirements of Canon 4 that "a lawyer should preserve the confidences and secrets of a client" * * * [and] DR 4-101(B) would have been violated if such disclosure had been made.

DR 4-101(B) provides:

"Except when permitted under DR 4-101(C), a lawyer shall not knowingly:

(1) Reveal a confidence or secret of his client.

(2) Use a confidence or secret of his client to the disadvantage of the client.

(3) Use a confidence or secret of his client for the advantage of himself or of a third person, unless the client consents after full disclosure."

Proper representation of a client calls for full disclosure by the client to his lawyer of all possibly relevant facts, even though such facts may reveal the client's commission of prior crimes. To encourage full disclosure, the client must be assured of confidentiality, a requirement embodied by law in the attorney-client privilege and broadly incorporated into Canon 4 of the Code and the EC's and DR's thereunder.

Frequently clients have a disposition to withhold information from lawyers. If the client suspects that his confidences will not be adequately protected or may in some way be used against him, he will be far more likely to withhold information which he believes may be to his detriment or which he does not want generally known. The client who withholds information from his lawyer runs a substantial risk of not being accorded his full legal rights. At the same time, the lawyer from whom such information is withheld may well be required to assert, in complete good faith and with no violation of EC 7-26 or DR 7-102(A), totally meritless or frivolous claims or defenses to which his client has no legal right. Thus, the interests served by the strict rule of confidentiality are far broader than merely those of the client, but include the interests of the public generally and of effective judicial administration.

Narrow and limited exceptions to the rule of confidentiality have been incorporated in DR 4-101(C) and DR 7-102(B)(1), the most important of which relate to information involving the intention of the client to commit a crime in the future or the perpetration of a fraud during the course of the lawyer's representation of the client, or where the client consents following full disclosure. * * * None of the specified narrow exceptions appear to apply to the situation here presented.

* * *

Moreover, if a lawyer were compelled to reveal information inculpating a client, the lawyer would, in effect become his client's adversary in violation of the mandate of EC 4-5 and DR 4-101(B).

Thus, the lawyer was under an injunction not to disclose to the authorities his knowledge of the two prior murders, and was duty-bound not to reveal to the authorities the location of the bodies. The lawyer's knowledge with respect to the location of the bodies was obtained solely from the client in confidence and in secret. Without the client's revelation in secret and in confidence, he would not have been in a position to assist the authorities in this regard. Thus, his personal knowledge is a link solidly welded to the chain of privileged communications and, without the client's express permission, must not be disclosed. The relationship between lawyer and client is in many respects like that between priest and penitent. Both lawyer and priest are bound by the bond of silence.

* * *

2. A lawyer's obligation to hold a client's confidences and secrets inviolate extends beyond information imparted orally and embraces written material from the client "coming into existence merely as a communication to the attorney." * * * The memorialization by a lawyer of statements, information and documents received from a client, whether by shorthand or longhand notes, dictated and typed memoranda, speedwriting, electronic or magnetic recording, xerox, photostat, photograph or other form of recordation or reproduction does not alter the fact that the communication from the client is privileged. Such memorialization may be useful in facilitating the handling of a matter by the lawyer and is part of the lawyer's work product. When the lawyer's purpose is served, the work product may be destroyed without violation of ethical standards.

Similarly, written material prepared by the client for his lawyer is a form of written communication and falls within the attorney-client privilege. Such documents are not instruments or fruits of the crime, which under certain circumstances the lawyer might be obliged to turn over to authorities. * * * Accordingly, neither the lawyer nor his client was obliged to reveal an incriminating diagram, whether prepared by the client for his lawyer or by the lawyer on the basis of information gained by him during the course of the client's representation, under EC 7-27 and DR 7-102. Provided it was not contrary to his client's wishes for him to do so, there was no ethical inhibition against its destruction by the lawyer.

3. This Committee does not pass upon the legality of alleged conduct, but if such conduct is illegal, it would of course be unethical, with rare exceptions of inadvertent violations involving no moral turpitude. Thus, any tampering, concealment or destruction of physical evidence in violation of <u>N.Y. Penal Law § 215.40</u> would also be violative of the Code. Even in this absence of any violation of law and in the absence of an intention on the part of the lawyer to tamper, conceal or destroy evidence, there could be an appearance of impropriety in violation of Canon 9 in moving a part of one of the bodies. Such conduct should be avoided to prevent even the appearance that there might have been an intent to tamper with or suppress evidence.

4. There is no ethical impropriety in the lawyer's discussing with the District Attorney the possibility of an appropriate plea disposition, provided that the lawyer had the express consent of his client before making such disclosure. Plea bargaining is an accepted part of our criminal procedures today. A lawyer engaged or attempting to engage in it with his client's consent would be properly serving his client. Thus, the lawyer's suggestion to the District Attorney that he might be in a position to assist the authorities in resolving open cases during such a discussion would appear to involve no violation of proper professional standards. One can conceive of a variety of circumstances in which such a disclosure might be helpful to a client. For example, the disclosure of the client's commission of prior crimes of violence might very well establish the client's need for confinement for medical treatment rather than imprisonment.

David Luban, Lawyers and Justice: An Ethical Study xx (1988)

The theory of role morality takes off from a distinction between universal moral duties that binds us all because we are all moral agents and special duties that go with various roles or "stations in life. * * * This notion, at the level of general ethical theory, explains how people in certain social roles may be morally required to do things that seem immoral.

[T]he standard conception of the lawyer's role [consists] of (1) a role obligation (the "principle of partnership") that identifies professionalism with extreme partisan zeal on behalf of the client and (2) the "principle of nonaccountaiblity," which insists that the lawyer bears no moral responsibility for the client's goals or the means.

Lord Brougham

In 1820, Lord Henry Brougham led the defense of Queen Caroline against King George IV's charges of adultery. Brougham learned "that the King had secretly married a Roman Catholic before assuming the throne and, therefore, was ineligible to rule."[5] If the King's marriage were revealed, turmoil and perhaps even civil war would have resulted. Intent on sending a message to the King and his allies, Brougham claimed he would reveal the King's prior marriage if the matter was not settled in favor of Queen Caroline.

On the floor of the House of Lords, Brougham declared that:

> An advocate, in the discharge of his duty knows but one person in <u>all</u> the world, and that person is his client. To save that client by all means and expedients, and at all hazards to other persons, and among them to himself, is his first and only duty; and in performing this duty he must not regard the alarm, the torments, the destruction he may bring upon others. Separating the duty of a patriot from that of advocate, he must go on, reckless of the consequences: though it should be his unhappy lot to involve his country in confusion.[6]

Professor Geoffrey Hazard has described Lord Brougham's famous statement of the advocate's duty as the "classic statement' of the lawyer's role. Geoffry C. Hazard, Jr., *The Future of Legal Ethics*, <u>100 Yale L.J. 1239, 1280 (1991)</u>.

Monroe H. Freedman & Abbe Smith, Understanding Lawyers' Ethics 13, 62-63 (3d ed. 2004)[6]

In its simplest terms, an adversary system resolves disputes by presenting conflicting views of fact and law to an impartial and relatively passive arbiter, who decides

---

5   Russell G. Pearce, *Lawyers as America's Governing Class: The Formation and Dissoluton of the Original Understanding of the American Lawyer's Role*, <u>8 U. Chi. Sch. Roundtable 381, 394 (2001)</u>.

6   *Id.*

6   Please note that a new edition of Freedman and Smith's book should be available by the time that this casebook is published.

which side wins what. In the United States [,] the phrase adversary system is synonymous with the American system for administration of justice[.] * * * [I]t consist of a core of basic rights that recognize, and protect, the dignity of the individual in a free society. * * * An essential function of the adversary system, therefore, is to maintain a free society in which individual rights are central.

* * *

One of the essential values of a just society is respect for the dignity of each member of that society. Essential to each individual's dignity is the free exercise of his autonomy. Toward that end, each person is entitled to know his rights with respect to society and other individuals, and to decide whether to seek fulfillment of those rights through due processes of law.

The lawyer, by virtue of her training and skills, has a legal and practical monopoly over access to the legal system and knowledge about the law. The lawyer's advice and assistance are often indispensable, therefore, to the effective exercise of individual autonomy.

[Question 7]

Under the Rules, Zimmerman's lawyers had:

   (A) a duty to keep confidential Spaulding's medical condition.

   (B) a duty to disclose Spaulding's medical condition.

   (C) discretion to choose whether to keep confidential or disclose Spaulding's medical condition.

[Question 8]

Zimmerman's lawyers behaved morally.

   (A) True

   (B) False

TIMOTHY W. FLOYD & JOHN GALLAGHER, *LEGAL ETHICS, NARRATIVE, AND PROFESSIONAL IDENTITY: THE STORY OF DAVID SPAULDING,*
59 Mercer L. Rev. 941, 944-47 (2008)

* * * David Spaulding was twenty years old in 1956. He lived in Elbow Lake, a town just twenty-two miles west of Brandon, in west-central Minnesota with his

parents, his brothers, and his sister. Fifty years later, it's still possible to hear in his voice the neighbor he was reared to be—patient and respectful of others.

When Mr. Spaulding tells about what happened in August of that year and about the years that followed, he steps with caution around the spaces occupied by the other people in his story. In his very quiet, rasping voice, he doesn't blame, he describes.

* * *

In those days, David Spaulding, his oldest brother, Alan, and his friend, Howard Lerpas, found work in the small road construction company owned by Ed Zimmerman. For David, this was a summer job. Come fall, he would be returning to the University of North Dakota.

* * *

On Friday, August 23, 1956, on a farm outside of Brandon, the Lederman family had plans to go to the county fair about fifteen miles away in Alexandria. All six family members—John, Pauline, and their four kids, Elaine, twelve, her fifteen-year-old brother Florian, and the two younger brothers, Ben and Phil—climbed into their 1950 Ford. * * * their farm and headed south on one of the county roads that sectioned the many farms of Douglas County.

On the other side of the county, a little before seven o'clock, Ed Zimmerman's road construction crew had decided to pack it in. Zimmerman often gave the Spauldings a ride to Elbow Lake before he headed to his own home in Barnett, a few miles away. They typically packed their gear and squeezed themselves into Zimmerman's 1956 Plymouth Fury, six men bone-tired from working under the sun all day long, covered in dust and smelling of macadam.

* * *

On every side the flat Minnesota road, corn was planted to the very edge of the fields, rising well above the height of these young men.

* * *

The two cars, one driven by fifteen-year-old Florian Lederman and the other by nineteen-year-old Jack Zimmerman, reached the four-way intersection on Old Highway Number 3, just outside Brandon, at precisely the same moment that evening. Neither driver would have thought to stop at the crossing because there were no stop signs. Neither driver could have easily seen the other approach because of the wall of corn limiting their sight lines.

In that one brief moment, when they did see each other, it must have seemed like an apparition. Another car appearing out of nowhere, as if out of the field of corn. At fifty miles an hour, they struck. The Zimmerman car rolled for 140 feet and finally landed in the cornfield. Its front end was compacted in two feet, and the roof was flattened to the level of the passenger seats.

Nine of the ten passengers were strewn over the road. Zimmerman's oldest son, Jimmy, was killed instantly. David Spaulding recalled, "The Lederman girl, you know, the one that died, my oldest brother said she was out on the road that night picking up billfolds. But the next morning she just keeled over."

John Lederman was in critical condition with a crushed chest and an arm so badly injured that he would never be able to work his farm again. Forty-four years later, Florian Lederman said that his father "did live to the age of eighty-nine, and he had a lot of pain through those years. It is something that's there all the time, the loss of your daughter."

Ed Zimmerman's neck was broken. And young David Spaulding was unconscious for three days with a severe brain concussion, two broken clavicles, multiple rib fractures, and a crushed chest.

* * *

In rural Minnesota in the 1950s, filing lawsuits against friends and neighbors was almost unthinkable. Being a good neighbor was important around Brandon, a kind of measure of a person's worth, where a man would be judged by how his acts affected his community. (The radio station most listened to in those days in rural Minnesota was WCCO, "Your Good Neighbor Station.") A good neighbor minded his own business, worked toward his own self-sufficiency and respected yours, but noticed when you needed help. It made little sense to be adversaries or competitors because they all needed each other to face acts of fate and God: the tractor that wouldn't start, the broken arm at harvest time, a death in the family.

But while suing friends and neighbors went against the grain, reaching into the resources of an insurance company was something else. Although the typical policy limit in those days was $50,000, and the state law capped a wrongful death award at $15,000, there was surely enough in the Zimmerman and Lederman policies to cover the medical bills and funeral costs for all of the families.

David's father hired a young lawyer in Elbow Lake to represent the claim he was making on his son's behalf. Richard "Dick" Roberts was twenty-five years old, recently out of the St. Paul School of Law. David Spaulding remembers Dick Roberts as "an aggressive young lawyer." There was only one other lawyer in town. "An old lawyer. He was a kind of income tax man. And this whippersnapper Dick Roberts came along, you know, and so I guess I didn't have a question about him."

The situation seemed fairly straightforward, just a matter of filing the appropriate claim forms and sending along the documentation of David's medical bills. David was still in the hospital when the claims were being processed.

* * *

Three months after the accident, Dick Roberts brought a suit against Florian Lederman, John Zimmerman, and their parents who owned the vehicles. Under the terms of the Zimmerman and Lederman insurance policies, the insurance companies were required to pay for lawyers to defend the case; the insurance companies also had the right to select those lawyers. The Zimmermans' insurer selected Norman Arveson, an experienced trial lawyer from a Fergus Falls law firm. The Lederman's insurance company chose Chester Rosengren, whose law firm was also located in Fergus Falls. * * *

SPAULDING v. ZIMMERMAN

116 N.W.2d 704 (Minn. 1962)

THOMAS GALLAGHER, Justice.

Appeal from an order of the District Court of Douglas County vacating and setting aside a prior order of such court dated May 8, 1957, approving a settlement made on behalf of David Spaulding on March 5, 1957, at which time he was a minor of the age of 20 years; and in connection therewith, vacating and setting aside releases executed by him and his parents, a stipulation of dismissal, an order for dismissal with prejudice, and a judgment entered pursuant thereto.

The prior action was brought against defendants by Theodore Spaulding, as father and natural guardian of David Spaulding, for injuries sustained by David in an automobile accident, arising out of a collision which occurred August 24, 1956, between an automobile driven by John Zimmerman, in which David was a passenger, and one owned by John Ledermann and driven by Florian Ledermann.

On appeal defendants contend that the court was without jurisdiction to vacate the settlement solely because their counsel then possessed information, unknown to plaintiff herein, that at the time he was suffering from an aorta aneurysm which may have resulted from the accident, because (1) no mutual mistake of fact was involved; (2) no duty rested upon them to disclose information to plaintiff which they could assume had been disclosed to him by his own physicians;

* * *

After the accident, David's injuries were diagnosed by his family physician, Dr. James H. Cain, as a severe crushing injury of the chest with multiple rib fractures; a severe cerebral concussion, probably with petechial hemorrhages of the brain; and bilateral fractures of the clavicles. At Dr. Cain's suggestion, on January 3, 1957, David was examined by Dr. John F. Pohl, an orthopedic specialist, who made X-ray studies of his chest. Dr. Pohl's detailed report of this examination included the following:

'* * * The lung fields are clear. The heart and aorta are normal.'

Nothing in such report indicated the aorta aneurysm with which David was then suffering. On March 1, 1957, at the suggestion of Dr. Pohl, David was examined from a neurological viewpoint by Dr. Paul S. Blake, and in the report of this examination there was no finding of the aorta aneurysm.

In the meantime, on February 22, 1957, at defendants' request, David was examined by Dr. Hewitt Hannah, a neurologist. On February 26, 1957, the latter reported to Messrs. Field, Arveson, & Donoho, attorneys for defendant John Zimmerman, as follows:

'The one feature of the case which bothers me more than any other part of the case is the fact that this boy of 20 years of age has an aneurysm, which means a dilatation of the aorta and the arch of the aorta. Whether this came out of this accident I cannot say with any degree of certainty and I have discussed it with the Roentgenologist and a couple of Internists. * * * Of course an aneurysm or dilatation of the aorta in a boy of this age is a serious matter as far as his life. This aneurysm may dilate further and it might rupture with further dilatation and this would cause his death.

'It would be interesting also to know whether the X-ray of his lungs, taken immediately following the accident, shows this dilatation or not. If it was not present immediately following the accident and is now present, then we could be sure that it came out of the accident.'

Prior to the negotiations for settlement, the contents of the above report were made known to counsel for defendants Florian and John Ledermann.

The case was called for trial on March 4, 1957, at which time the respective parties and their counsel possessed such information as to David's physical condition as was revealed to them by their respective medical examiners as above described. It is thus apparent that neither David nor his father, the nominal plaintiff in the prior action, was then aware that David was suffering the aorta aneurysm but on the contrary believed that he was recovering from the injuries sustained in the accident.

On the following day an agreement for settlement was reached wherein, in consideration of the payment of $6,500, David and his father agreed to settle in full for all claims arising out of the accident.

Richard S. Roberts, counsel for David, thereafter presented to the court a petition for approval of the settlement, wherein David's injuries were described as:

'* * * severe crushing of the chest, with multiple rib fractures, severe cerebral concussion, with petechial hemorrhages of the brain, bilateral fractures of the clavicles.'

Attached to the petition were affidavits of David's physicians, Drs. James H. Cain and Paul S. Blake, wherein they set forth the same diagnoses they had made upon completion of their respective examinations of David as above described. At no time was there information disclosed to the court that David was then suffering from an aorta aneurysm which may have been the result of the accident. Based upon the petition for settlement and such affidavits of Drs. Cain and Blake, the court on May 8, 1957, made its order approving the settlement.

Early in 1959, David was required by the army reserve, of which he was a member, to have a physical checkup. For this, he again engaged the services of Dr. Cain. In this checkup, the latter discovered the aorta aneurysm. He then reexamined the X rays which had been taken shortly after the accident and at this time discovered that they disclosed the beginning of the process which produced the aneurysm. He promptly sent David to Dr. Jerome Grismer for an examination and opinion. The latter confirmed the finding of the aorta aneurysm and recommended immediate surgery therefor. This was performed by him at Mount Sinai Hospital in Minneapolis on March 10, 1959.

Shortly thereafter, David, having attained his majority, instituted the present action for additional damages due to the more serious injuries including the aorta aneurysm which he alleges proximately resulted from the accident. As indicated above, the prior order for settlement was vacated. In a memorandum made a part of the order vacating the settlement, the court stated:

'The facts material to a determination of the motion are without substantial dispute. The only disputed facts appear to be whether * * * Mr. Roberts, former counsel for plaintiff, discussed plaintiff's injuries with Mr. Arvesen, counsel for defendant Zimmerman, immediately before the settlement agreement, and, further, whether or not there is a causal relationship between the accident and the aneurysm.

'Contrary to the * * * suggestion in the affidavit of Mr. Roberts that he discussed the minor's injuries with Mr. Arvesen, the Court finds that no such discussion of the specific injuries claimed occurred prior to the settlement agreement on March 5, 1957.

'* * * [T]he Court finds that although the aneurysm now existing is causally related to the accident, such finding is for the purpose of the motions only and is based solely upon the opinion expressed by Dr. Cain * * * which, so far as the Court can find from the numerous affidavits and statements of fact by counsel, stands without dispute.

'The mistake concerning the existence of the aneurysm was not mutual. For reasons which do not appear, plaintiff's doctor failed to ascertain its existence. By reason of the failure of plaintiff's counsel to use available rules of discovery, plaintiff's doctor and all his representatives did not learn that defendants and their agents knew of its existence and possible serious consequences. Except for the character of the concealment in the light of plaintiff's minority, the Court would, I believe, be justified in denying plaintiff's motion to vacate, leaving him to whatever questionable remedy he may have against his doctor and against his lawyer.

'That defendants' counsel concealed the knowledge they had is not disputed. The essence of the application of the above rule is the character of the concealment. Was it done under circumstances that defendants must be charged with knowledge that plaintiff did not know of the injury? If so, an enriching advantage was gained for defendants at plaintiff's expense. There is no doubt of the good faith of both defendants' counsel. There is no doubt that during the course of the negotiations, when the parties were in an adversary relationship, no rule required or duty rested upon defendants or their representatives to disclose this knowledge. However, once the agreement to settle was reached, it is difficult to characterize the parties' relationship as adverse. At this point all parties were interested in securing Court approval.

* * *

'But it is not possible to escape the inference that defendants' representatives knew, or must be here charged with knowing, that plaintiff under all the circumstances would not accept the sum of $6500.00 if he or his representatives knew of the aneurysm and its possible serious consequences. Moreover, there is no showing by defendants that would support an inference that plaintiff and his representatives knew of the existence of the aneurysm but concluded that it was not causally related to the accident.

'When the adversary nature of the negotiations concluded in a settlement, the procedure took on the posture of a joint application to the Court, at least so far as the facts upon which the Court could and must approve settlement is concerned. It is here that the true nature of the concealment appears, and defendants' failure to act affirmatively, after having been given a copy of the application for approval, can only be defendants' decision to take a calculated risk that the settlement would be final.

* * *

'To hold that the concealment was not of such character as to result in an unconscionable advantage over plaintiff's ignorance or mistake, would be to penalize innocence and incompetence and reward less than full performance of an officer of the Court's duty to make full disclosure to the Court when applying for approval in minor settlement proceedings.'

1. The principals applicable to the court's authority to vacate settlements made on behalf of minors and approved by it appear well established. With reference thereto, we have held that the court in its discretion may vacate such a settlement, even though it is not induced by fraud or bad faith, where it is shown that in the accident the minor sustained separate and distinct injuries which were not known or considered by the court at the time settlement was approved; and even though the releases furnished therein purported to cover both known and unknown injuries resulting from the accident. The court may vacate such a settlement for mistake even though the mistake was not mutual in the sense that both parties were similarly mistaken as to the nature and extent of the minor's injuries, but where it is shown that one of the parties had additional knowledge with respect thereto and was aware that neither the court nor the adversary party possessed such knowledge when the settlement was approved * * * at the other's expense.'

2. From the foregoing it is clear that in the instant case the court did not abuse its discretion in setting aside the settlement which it had approved on plaintiff's behalf while he was still a minor. It is undisputed that neither he nor his counsel nor his medical attendants were aware that at the time settlement was made he was suffering from an aorta aneurysm which may have resulted from the accident. The seriousness of this disability is indicated by Dr. Hannah's report indicating the imminent danger of death therefrom. This was known by counsel for both defendants but was not disclosed to the court at the time it was petitioned to approve the settlement. While no canon of ethics or legal obligation may have required them to inform plaintiff or his counsel with respect thereto, or to advise the court therein, it did become obvious to them at the time, that the settlement then made did not contemplate or take into consideration the disability described. This fact opened the way for the court to later exercise its discretion in vacating the settlement and under the circumstances described we cannot say that there was any abuse of discretion on the part of the court in so doing under Rule 60.02(6) of Rules of Civil Procedure.

3. Defendants contend that, since plaintiff's counsel also had information with respect to plaintiff's injuries which was not disclosed to the court at the time settlement was made and which might have caused the court to withhold approval thereof, plaintiff cannot in good conscience now seek to have the settlement set aside. Without determining whether a minor would be thus bound by his counsel's actions, we find no basis for defendants' contentions in this respect. Their claim has reference to a letter of Dr. Paul S. Blake to plaintiff's counsel dated March 1, 1957, wherein he stated:

'* * * There may be some permanent brain injury in association with such a condition (cerebral concussion and contusion).

* * *

'I think I can say that he has a post-concussion syndrome, moderately severe and that these symptoms will probably improve gradually over the next 6 to 12 months. * * * I would recommend that this case not be settled for at least a year or so that these findings can be definitely assessed and so that we can guard against any unforeseen complications developing.'

While this letter was not submitted to the court at the time it approved the settlement, it does appear that an affidavit of Dr. Blake attached to the petition asking approval of the settlement was submitted to it. Therein the following appears:

'* * * That your affiant conclude(s) on that date (February 22, 1957,) that David Spaulding had had a cerebral concussion and contusion and probably had some post-concussion cerebral edema. That there may be some permanent brain injury in association with such a condition, and that he is probably having a post-concussion syndrome and that these symptoms will probably improve gradually over the next six to twelve months.'

It is clear therefrom that all essential and basic information as to plaintiff's concussion with the possibility of some permanent brain injury was fully disclosed to the court before it approved the settlement; and that this factual situation would not be sufficient to estop plaintiff from seeking to have the settlement vacated because the aorta aneurysm had not been disclosed to the court or taken into consideration at the time such settlement was approved.

* * *

Affirmed.

FLOYD & GALLAGHER, *LEGAL ETHICS, NARRATIVE, AND PROFESSIONAL IDENTITY: THE STORY OF DAVID SPAULDING*

supra <u>p. 775, at 948-50</u>

* * * Dr. Cain sent him down to Minneapolis for immediate surgery. The operation was performed in Mount Sinai Hospital under the direction of five doctors and was originally scheduled to last five hours. Spaulding remembers:

Back in those days, I think it was the second operation of its kind in Minneapolis at Mount Sinai Hospital. They laid me on my side and took my left arm, put it over my head, and cut a rib out. And then they went in from the left side. When they got in there, the aneurysm was so big that they had to sacrifice what they called the recurrent laryngeal nerve. The original plan was to snip the aorta, remove the damaged section, and then sew it together around a piece of nylon tubing. But after the heart was uncovered, this plan had to be revised. It was decided that the weakened portion had to be removed and sewn up without the benefit of a plastic insert. This far riskier and more difficult procedure lasted almost ten hours. Even more important to David was that, following his surgery, his speech was permanently and irrevocably affected. "After the operation, I always talked with a very high pitch, sounded kind of feminine." David would speak with that voice for another ten years.

The doctors believed that the aneurysm had been caused by the injuries sustained in the car accident, and the Spauldings decided to reopen the suit to recover the medical costs. Dick Roberts went up to Fergus Falls where Norman Arveson was practicing and mentioned to him that they had just found out that one of the boys who had been involved in the accident had an aortic aneurysm. According to David Spaulding, Arveson responded, "Oh hell. We knew that from the very beginning." In the subsequent legal proceedings, it was discovered that in the examination that took place in February 1957, Dr. Hewlitt Hannah, the neurologist who had been retained by Norman Arveson, had seen the aneurysm.

* * *

Roberts filed a motion for the trial court to set aside the earlier settlement, alleging that the defendants had fraudulently concealed the existence of the aneurysm. The trial judge granted the motion and reopened the case. The insurance company appealed the judge's ruling, claiming that nothing improper had taken place in 1957.

The appeal was headed for the Minnesota Supreme Court. Dick Roberts bowed out, suggesting that the Spauldings hire a lawyer with experience appearing in front of the state supreme court. They hired the firm of Gislason, Gislason and O'Brien. David Spaulding remembers that "they had a young lawyer, Bob Gislason, who wanted to argue the case." So they agreed to take on the suit.

Norman Arveson and Chester Rosengren also did not appear. They selected Richard Pemberton, a new young lawyer from Rosengren's law firm to argue the case on their behalf. According to Pemberton, neither Arveson nor Rosengren wanted to face the justices and explain their behavior, having made no attempt to protect the boy.

Pemberton stated,

> It was a distasteful case, and I figured that I was going to get buffeted around by the justices. But I think they knew that I had been sent down to do this thing. They could see that my senior partner and Arveson, who were good friends as well as professional colleagues, had sent this young guy to handle this case.

Pemberton, however, had deep misgivings about defending what his senior partner had done.

At the time, I had a year-and-a-half old son, my wife was pregnant or [had] just given birth to our second son. If I had a few more years of maturity, I would have refused to argue this case. I would have said, 'Find somebody else.' Of course, it would have meant that I would have had to find some other place to practice law, too.

> **FYI**
>
> Timothy Floyd and John Gallagher's article helps bring the *Spaulding* issues to life. Another way to do so is to watch a story on the television series *The Practice*, featuring facts roughly analogous to those in *Spaulding*. You can find this story in *The Practice: Honor Code* (ABC television broadcast Nov. 18, 2001) and *The Practice: Suffer the Little Children* (ABC television broadcast Nov. 25, 2001).

* * *

Review the materials for Questions 1-6, *supra*.

B. The Neutral Partisan in Historical and Philosophical Context

[Question 9]

The Preambles to the Canons and the Code emphasize the lawyer's responsibilities to his or her client.

(A) True

(B) False

[Question 10]

The original understanding of the lawyer's role in the United States was that of the European guild.

(A) True

(B) False

[Question 11]

The Rules:

(A) require lawyers to be neutral partisans.

(B) prohibit lawyers from being neutral partisans.

(C) permit lawyers discretion to choose whether to be morally responsible or a neutral partisan.

[Question 12]

The Tennessee ethics opinion advises a lawyer opposed to abortion that his ethical obligations require him, in representing a minor seeking judicial consent for an abortion:

(A) to suggest that she consider talking to her parents.

(B) to suggest that she consider alternatives to abortion.

(C) to suggest that she consider the moral pros and cons of her decision.

(D) none of the above.

[Question 13]

The Tennessee ethics opinion is consistent with Rule 2.1.

(A) True

(B) False

[Question 14]

The Legal Profession as a Blue State reading argues that the ascendance of the hired gun approach and the decline of lawyers' commitment to good results from:

(A) increasing business-like behavior by lawyers.

(B) law schools' disdain of law practice and legal ethics.

(C) the trend toward greater emphasis on individualism.

(D) the increasing diversity of the legal profession.

[Question 15]

The adversary system approach to justice resembles market theory in that it:

(A) rejects moral relativism.

(B) distributes justice equally.

(C) always favors the wealthy.

(D) assumes that facilitating the pursuit of individual self-interest is best for society.

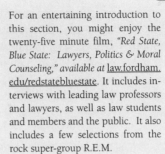

Go Online

For an entertaining introduction to this section, you might enjoy the twenty-five minute film, *"Red State, Blue State: Lawyers, Politics & Moral Counseling," available at* law.fordham. edu/redstatebluestate. It includes interviews with leading law professors and lawyers, as well as law students and members and the public. It also includes a few selections from the rock super-group R.E.M.

Review the materials on Role Morality, at pages 778-79, *supra*, where Monroe Freedman and Abbe Smith explain the grounding of the neutral partisan role in the adversary system.

Judge Richard Posner has noted the connection between the adversary system and the market. He asserts that the adversary system "resembles the market in its impersonality, its subordination of distributive considerations. The invisible hand of the market has its counterpart in the aloof disinterest of the judge." Richard A. Posner, Economic Analysis of Law 322 (1972). For further consideration of the analogy between the adversary system and the market, *see* Russell G. Pearce, *Redressing Inequality in the Market for Justice: Why Access to Lawyers Will Never Solve the Problem and Why Rethinking the Role of Judges Will Help*, 73 Fordham L. Rev. 969, 970-72 (2004) and sources collected at n.12 of that article.

Preamble, Canons of Professional Ethics (1908)

In America, where the stability of Courts and of all departments of government rests upon the approval of the people, it is peculiarly essential that the system for establishing and dispensing Justice be developed to a high point of efficiency and so maintained that the public shall have absolute confidence in the integrity and impartiality of its administration. The future of the Republic, to a great extent, depends upon our maintenance of Justice pure and unsullied. It cannot be so maintained unless the conduct and the motives of the members of our profession are such as to merit the approval of all just men.

Preamble, Model Code of Professional Responsibility (1970)

The continued existence of a free and democratic society depends upon recognition of the concept that justice is based upon the rule of law grounded in respect for the individual and his capacity through reason for enlightened self-government. Law so grounded makes justice possible, for only through such law does the dignity of the individual attain respect and protection. Without it, individual rights become subject to unrestrained power, respect for the law is destroyed, and rational self-government is impossible. Lawyers, as guardians of the law, play a vital role in the preservation of society. The fulfillment of this role requires an understanding by lawyers of their relationship with and function in our legal system. A consequent obligation of lawyers is to maintain the highest standards of ethical conduct.

Preamble, Rules

[1] A lawyer, as a member of the legal profession, is a representative of clients, an officer of the legal system and a public citizen having special responsibility for the quality of justice. * * *

 [6] As a public citizen, a lawyer should seek improvement of the law, access to the legal system, the administration of justice and the quality of service rendered by the legal profession. As a member of a learned profession, a lawyer should cultivate knowledge of the law beyond its use for clients, employ that knowledge in reform of the law and work to strengthen legal education. In addition, a lawyer should further the public's understanding of and confidence in the rule of law and the justice system because legal institutions in a constitutional democracy depend on popular participation and support to maintain their authority. A lawyer should be mindful of deficiencies in the administration of justice and of the fact that the poor, and sometimes persons who are not poor, cannot afford adequate legal assistance. Therefore, all lawyers should devote professional time and resources and use civic influence to ensure equal access to our system of justice for all those who because of economic or social barriers cannot afford or secure adequate legal counsel. A lawyer should aid the legal profession in pursuing these objectives and should help the bar regulate itself in the public interest.

[7] Many of a lawyer's professional responsibilities are prescribed in the Rules of Professional Conduct, as well as substantive and procedural law. However, a lawyer is also guided by personal conscience and the approbation of professional peers. A lawyer should strive to attain the highest level of skill, to improve the law and the legal profession and to exemplify the legal profession's ideals of public service. * * *

[12] The legal profession's relative autonomy carries with it special responsibilities of self-government. The profession has a responsibility to assure that its regulations are conceived in the public interest and not in furtherance of parochial or self-interested concerns of the bar. Every lawyer is responsible for observance of the Rules of Professional Conduct. A lawyer should also aid in securing their observance by other lawyers. Neglect of these responsibilities compromises the independence of the profession and the public interest which it serves. * * *

[13] Lawyers play a vital role in the preservation of society. * * * *

Review <u>Rules 1.2(b)</u>, <u>1.6(b)</u>, and <u>1.16(b)</u>, and <u>2.1</u>.

BOARD OF PROFESSIONAL RESPONSIBILITY OF THE SUPREME COURT OF TENNESSEE

<u>Formal Ethics Op. 96-F-140, 1996 WL 340719 (1996)</u>

[A lawyer who is morally opposed to abortion has been appointed to represent a minor seeking judicial permission for an abortion without the consent of her parents. The lawyer asks for ethical advice on a number of questions, including whether he could "advise the minor seeking an abortion about alternatives and/or advise her to speak with her parents or legal guardian about the potential abortion[.]" * * *

Make the Connection

The next case will look familiar. In Chapter 2, we explored the Tennessee lawyer's question of whether he could ethically seek to withdraw. Review that material. Here we will consider whether he can ethically counsel the client on alternatives to abortion.

If the appointed attorney represents only the minor (as we believe), then counsel has a duty to "explain a matter to the extent reasonably necessary to permit the client to make informed decisions regarding the representation." DR 7-101(A)(3). Whether informing the minor about alternatives to abortion and suggesting that she discuss the potential procedure with her parents or legal guardian is ethically appropriate may depend on a case-by-case analysis. If the minor is truly mature and well-informed enough to go forward and make the decision on her own, then counsel's hesitation and advice for the client to consult with others could possibly implicate a lack of zealous representation under DR 7-101(A)(4)(a) and (c) (a lawyer shall not intentionally fail to seek the client's lawful objectives, or prejudice or damage his client during the course of the professional relationship). Counsel also has a duty of undivided loyalty to his client, and should not allow any other persons or entities to regulate, direct, compromise, control or interfere with his professional judgment. * * * To the extent that counsel strongly recommends that his client discuss the potential abortion with her parents or with other individuals or entities which are known to oppose such a choice, compliance with Canon 5 is called into question. * * *

RUSSELL G. PEARCE, *THE LEGAL PROFESSION AS A BLUE STATE: REFLECTIONS ON PUBLIC PHILOSOPHY, JURISPRUDENCE, AND LEGAL ETHICS,*

<u>75 Fordham L. Rev. 1339, 1339-62 (2006)</u>

Many conservative commentators view the legal profession as a Blue State--as a captive of the Democratic Party and political liberalism. They assert that most lawyers vote for Democratic presidential candidates. They attack the American Bar Association for supporting abortion rights and equal rights for lesbians and gays and argue that it gives preferred treatment to Democratic nominees to the federal courts. Many opposed the nomination of Harriet Miers to the Supreme Court on the ground that she lacks "'the spine and steel necessary to resist the pressures that constantly bend the American legal system toward the left.'" They create law schools affiliated with religious conservatives to create lawyers free of the politically liberal taint.

I would like to suggest that this affinity between the legal profession and a Blue State, which often manifests itself in differences on substantive issues of policy and law, has its roots in conceptions of public philosophy, jurisprudence, and legal ethics. In particular, I would like to focus on the way that people who express a priority for moral values are far more likely to be part of Red State America. Although this distinction undoubtedly glosses over some nuances, such as the Republican allegiance of economic libertarians and the strong values commitments of religious liberals and secular humanists, it does offer a reasonably accurate description of what Michael Barone has described as "two Americas . . . of different faiths." Indeed, as a general matter, Blue State voters are less friendly to the promotion of moral values through the public sphere. In contrast to Red State voters, they are more likely to embrace a liberal public philosophy that emphasizes a conception of individual freedom grounded in the "basic principle of human dignity, [that] no person or group has the right deliberately to impose personal ethical values . . . on anyone else."

The dominant—although not exclusive—modern conception of the lawyer as a hired gun tracks this commitment to removing personal ethical values from politics. It asserts that the proper functioning of the legal system requires lawyers to remove personal ethical values from their work. Their role is to function as extreme partisans without moral accountability for their own conduct or even that of their clients so long as both have not definitively crossed the bounds of the law. In this role, they are to be morally neutral. As Sanford Levinson has observed, the dominant conception requires "'bleaching' out of [the] merely contingent aspects of the self, including the residue of particularistic socialization that we refer to as our 'conscience.'"

A powerful illustration of the confluence between the conception of the lawyer's role and the Blue State approach to values is a recent decision of the Tennessee Supreme Court's Board of Professional Responsibility. A Catholic lawyer who believed that abortion was murder sought to avoid a court appointment to represent a teenage girl seeking court permission to obtain an abortion without her parents' consent or, in the alternative, to recommend to his client that it would be better for her to seek parental consent and explore alternatives to abortion. Even though a literal reading of the applicable rules would appear to have permitted, though not endorsed, either course of action, the Board found that if the lawyer were to make a recommendation to his client based upon his personal beliefs, or even if he were to withdraw representation, his conduct would improperly create the risk of imposing his values upon the client or upon the legal system. Even in the Red State of Tennessee, the legal profession felt bound to follow a Blue State approach to values.

This approach to values was not always the dominant approach of the legal profession. * * *

I. From Guild to Governing Class

A. The English Guild

In colonial America, the legal profession largely borrowed from the English guild model. Society trusted guilds to rise above self-interest and to police themselves. In turn, the government permitted the guilds autonomy in membership, production, and marketing. Although English craft guilds had largely lost their authority by the eighteenth century, the guild continued to provide the organizational basis for the professions. In the legal profession, this meant that lawyers would perform their obligations to the legal system with excellence and integrity.

But English lawyers were not the governing class. Their commitment was to what H.L.A. Hart termed an "internal point of view," faithfulness to the secondary rules that society maintained for resolving disputes, not to maintaining the public good. Although lawyers came from the social class of "gentlemen," possessed of "good behavior, well bred, amiable, [and] high-minded," the task of governing fell to aristocrats and their oldest sons who assumed their place, not their younger sons who might become lawyers. Accordingly, although Blackstone's natural law jurisprudence included an expansive commitment to the public good that lawyers would have to understand, the primary responsibility for identifying and pursuing the good for society fell to the gentry and not to the community of lawyers. As Perry Miller observed, "Blackstone tailored his masterpiece to the needs on an eighteenth-century England, wherein the gentry still ruled as justices of the peace, with the House of Commons as their club."

B. The Original American Understanding

["Beginning with Perry Miller, and continuing through the tremendously influential work of Gordon Wood * * * historians have identified the period following the Revolution as the moment of creation of a uniquely American understanding of lawyers as a necessary governing class in a democracy."] * * * The experience of republican government after the American Revolution shattered the elite's faith in the ability of individuals and majorities to overcome their selfish interests. "[P] rivate interest," they concluded, "ruled most social relationships," and the expectation that "most people [would] sacrifice their private interests for the sake of the public good was utopian." Observing that legislatures disregarded property and individual rights in expropriating land and in making biased or corrupt decisions, the elite no longer believed that deliberative democracy would result in virtuous government for the benefit of the public good.   Instead, they came to fear that unchecked majority rule would result in tyranny of the majority.

They turned instead to a public political philosophy that combined both liberal and republican impulses. Retaining the republican goal of government as promoting the public good, they tended to define that good in liberal terms, such as "security, justice, prosperity and liberty." At the same time, they maintained the republican distrust of commerce and of self-interested factions. They embraced checks and balances as a roadblock to tyranny of the majority and concluded that majority rule would only coincide with the public good, including rule of law and protection of minority rights, so long as an elite governing class provided leadership to the majority. In the view of the framers, professionals, as the sector of society that pursued the public good and not self-interest, were best suited to this role.

Antebellum jurisprudence assigned this vital governing class role to lawyers on account of their virtue and their central role in governance. Virtue inhered in lawyers both in their status as professionals and in the nature of legal practice. Americans transformed the English notion of lawyers as gentlemen by class into a conception of lawyers as gentlemen as a moral badge of their ability to rise above self-interest, whatever their class origin. Ensuring lawyers' virtue was the practical wisdom necessary to succeed in their work of representing clients. This work required an ability to master both natural law and empirical knowledge. As Joseph Story wrote, "'The Law of Nature . . . lies at the foundation of all other laws, and constitutes the first step in the science of jurisprudence.'" Nonetheless, the appropriate methodology for applying this science to a particular case was "instrumental and pragmatic," grounded ultimately in "experience" that reflected "social context," and not "jurisprudential theory" alone. Story viewed the common law as "'constantly expanding . . . with the exigencies of society,'" such as its "commercial needs."

 As the custodians of the formal and informal institutions of governance, lawyers applied their ability to identify and promote the public good to providing the leadership necessary to ensure that laws would be consistent with the public good and that the majority would respect the rule of law. Within the formal government, lawyers "controlled the judicial branch and dominated the legislature and the executive." Equally important, as representatives of clients and as members of the community, they also served as intermediaries between the formal institutions of government and the people. In "counsel[ing] clients, making arguments in court to judge[s] and jur[ies]," and participating in civic life, they "sought to gain the confidence of and 'to diffuse sound principles among the people.'"

The governing class conception embraced a necessary connection between lawyers' ethics and the public good. Commentators agreed that legal ethics required moral counseling, moral considerations in deciding who to represent, respect for court and colleagues, and personal integrity. Beyond these axioms, the two leading American ethicists disagreed on how to reconcile republican and adversarial obligations. David Hoffman urged lawyers not to pursue a defense or claim that they believed "cannot, or rather ought not, to be sustained," including the Statute of Limitations when based on the "mere efflux of time." In a criminal case "of the deepest dye," where the lawyer believed the client guilty, Hoffman argued that it would be unprofessional to apply "ingenuity . . . beyond securing to them a fair and dispassionate investigation of the facts of their cause." In contrast, George Sharswood urged lawyers to zealously put the prosecution to its proof in order to protect the defendant's liberty interests, even where the crime was heinous. In civil matters too, Sharswood, in contrast to Hoffman, believed that liberty and property rights of defendants required lawyers to defend an "unrighteous claim." Nonetheless, Sharswood limited advocacy of that claim "to assuring the defendant 'a fair trial'" and advised lawyers to refrain from assisting a client in "frustrat[ing] legitimate property rights, such as . . . the 'just demands of creditors.'"

The commitment to the public good in legal ethics, grounded in jurisprudence and public political philosophy, withstood pressures from both inside and outside the legal profession. Throughout the antebellum period, some argued that lawyers were business people. Still others argued for a hired gun perspective. They endorsed Lord Brougham's well-known maxim that "an advocate, in the discharge of his duty, knows but one person in all the world, and that person is his client." Hoffman and Sharswood expressly rejected these approaches.

During the Jacksonian era, prevailing public sentiment rejected the notion that lawyers, or any other elite group, had a superior ability to identify and pursue the public good. As a result of this egalitarian impulse, many states abolished or minimized the qualifications for becoming a lawyer. Rather than accept these critiques, the dominant thinkers in the bar continued to rely on the teaching of natural law jurisprudence and elite political philosophy. Indeed, the Jacksonian era was the time when Hoffman and Sharswood published their legal ethics treatises articulating the governing class approach to the lawyer's role.

II. Redefining and Limiting the Duty to the Public Good

In the period from the Civil War through the 1960s, the duty of lawyers to the public good narrowed both in terms of defining the public good and in terms of lawyers' capacity for pursuing the good. Promoting this redefinition was the shift in the dominant jurisprudence from natural law to empiricism, a shift that reflected the increasing influence of liberalism in the larger society.

A. The Decline of the Public Good in Elite Public Political Philosophy

After the Civil War, the increasing influence of liberalism undermined the republican faith in an organic community that promoted the public good. While liberalism encompassed a variety of particular political prescriptions, its fundamental emphasis was promoting freedom of the individual. At its core, liberalism conceived of the individual as fundamentally self-interested and viewed the role of government as permitting individuals the greatest freedom possible. When individuals maximized freedom, they would also maximize what was best for society through the invisible hand of the market or through the democratic electoral process. As a political philosophy, liberalism did not, at its core, include a conception of the public good independent of individual freedom.

This absence permitted the development of hybrid public political philosophies that combined liberalism with conceptions of the public good that were not apparently inconsistent with the logic of liberalism. Prior to liberalism, dominant philosophies tended to view society as having an organic component that was more than the compilation of individual self-interest and as having a goal of promoting the public good. As liberalism advanced, some public political philosophies sought to accommodate the reality of individual self-interest that liberalism identified with the goal of promoting the public good. For example, as discussed above, liberal republicanism in the antebellum period derived a conception of the good from natural law that included the liberal commitment to individual freedom, a conception of justice that transcended individual self-interest, and an elite governing class that placed the public good above self-interest.

Nonetheless, the logic of liberalism made individual freedom primary. As liberalism extended its influence, hybrid approaches like liberal republicanism were less persuasive. First, they were inconsistent with the core of liberalism. The insistence on a public good independent of the pursuit of individual self-interest prevented the maximization of individual freedom. Second, they were unnecessary. Although liberalism may have needed justifications grounded in natural law when it was a less powerful force, as it became dominant it no longer needed external sources of support.

The two most significant changes in public political philosophy that would influence the understanding of the function of lawyers related to knowledge of truth and faith in majority rule. In the antebellum period, access to truth required both virtue and empirical knowledge. Following the Civil War and continuing through the 1960s, empirical knowledge became by far the more dominant way of establishing the truth, at least in elite culture, and the influence of ethics grounded in virtue diminished considerably. Higher education, for example, shifted from a primary emphasis on moral development of the student to a primary—and later almost exclusive—emphasis on empirical knowledge.

As belief in virtue as the source of knowledge declined, the trends in public political philosophy following the Civil War minimized or eliminated surviving republican notions. A more liberal and democratic sense of capacity for self-rule challenged the belief that a particular class in society was qualified to provide elite political leadership. If an elite class was not better able to identify the truth, majority rule shifted from a source of mistrust to grounds for celebration. Indeed, majority rule offered a way, roughly analogous to the market, for self-interested individuals to exercise their political freedom in a way that reconciled their preferences. Where the elite's liberal republicanism had required an elite governing class to make democracy function properly, in the period following the Civil War and continuing through today, the dominant understanding, even among the elite, was that majority rule was an unqualified good and that arguments for limiting majority rule faced a heavy burden.

Ironically, the increasing influence of liberalism in promoting empiricism and belief in majority rule coincided with a declining commitment to the vision of maximizing economic freedom through laissez-faire economics. By the late nineteenth century, the prevailing conception of natural law enshrined the "ideal that government should not interfere in the natural workings of the market." Proponents rejected government regulation of "property rights and the right to contract." Incorporating a strong conception of individual self-reliance and construing contract solely as an individual right, they condemned labor unions as interfering with natural law and urged courts to employ natural law conceptions to strike down legislation regulating business or empowering unions. By undermining the existence of a public good independent of self-interest and embracing deference to majority rule, the emerging dominant liberal approach either permitted these types of government intervention in the name of limiting judicial discretion or encouraged them in order to pursue an empirically justified social good.

B. The Diminishing Role of Lawyers in Jurisprudence

Reflecting these shifts, jurisprudential commentators redefined the role of lawyers in a way so as to minimize—or in some cases eliminate—their role as the governing class. The natural law-based jurisprudence of James Kent and Joseph Story gave way to empirically grounded approaches like the pragmatism of Oliver Wendell Holmes, the formalism of Christopher Columbus Langdell, and the sociological jurisprudence of Roscoe Pound. As they rejected the natural law basis of antebellum jurisprudence, they also rejected its suspicion of majority rule. Indeed, the empirical schools strongly embraced majority rule.

The change from natural law to empiricism as the dominant basis for jurisprudence was not seamless. Judges who had been educated in the natural law approach persisted in employing substantive due process to strike down progressive legislation despite the increasing influence of empirical jurisprudence as the dominant jurisprudence of the twentieth century. Even Lon Fuller, the most influential of the twentieth century natural law scholars, adopted a largely procedural version of natural law that embraced majority rule in the same way as did the empirically grounded jurisprudential commentators.

In these approaches to jurisprudence, lawyers were no longer central actors. If the majority could be trusted, threats to the rule of law were the exception and not the rule. As virtue became marginal to jurisprudence, so did the need for lawyers as a virtuous leadership class to maintain the public good and rule of law. As the role of lawyers diminished, or disappeared altogether, jurisprudence no longer focused on how the lawyer should combine virtue with empirical knowledge to ascertain the law. Instead, the dominant subject became law as "what the judges say it is."

Lawyers played a supporting role as technicians whose task was to study and anticipate the decisions of judges, a role that required no particular commitment to the public good in either Langdell's formalism or Holmes's pragmatism. Pound's sociological jurisprudence nonetheless continued to afford lawyers some important public responsibilities. While judges played the lead role, lawyers who applied scientific methods to legal structures could provide them with beneficial support.

These trends continued through the early 1960s. Empirical approaches to jurisprudence, such as the legal realist, legal process, and positivist perspectives, continued to focus on judges and to minimize the significance of the lawyer's role. Even legal process, which highlighted the contribution of lawyers as problem solvers, limited the scope of this function to the technical resolution of challenges facing individuals and not the engineering of societal structures.

Fuller's natural law jurisprudence continued to place lawyers in a governing class role, but a far narrower one than that proposed by antebellum thinkers. Embracing majority rule and lacking a broad conception of lawyers' virtue, Fuller largely found the public good in the "internal morality of the law" and lawyers' roles in protecting process. This was far less ambitious than the antebellum understanding that lawyers identified and promoted the substantive, as well as the procedural, public good and guided majority rule.

C. Professionalism Both Preserves and Narrows Lawyers' Obligation to the Public Good

With these changes in public political philosophy and jurisprudence, lawyers had to rethink their connection to the public good. Like all professionals, in the late nineteenth century they faced a challenge to their status grounded in the assertion that they were just as self-interested as business people and therefore deserving of no special authority. Resentment of the privileges of professionals in general and lawyers in particular became widespread. Robert Wiebe observed that "[w]ith the exception of bankers, no group late in the nineteenth century stood in lower public repute [than lawyers]."

In contrast to the Jacksonian era, lawyers could no longer mobilize jurisprudence and elite public political philosophy to justify their claim to serving as a virtuous governing class. As a result many lawyers joined the public in bemoaning lawyers' failure to deserve the professional status they claimed. Robert Gordon has described "the extraordinary outpouring of rhetoric, from all the public pulpits of the ideal—bar association and law school commencement addresses, memorial speeches on colleagues, articles and books—on the theme of the profession's decline from a profession to a business."

In the face of this challenge, lawyers turned to the Progressive Era's ideological embrace of professionalism. Professionalism posited "a bargain between the profession and society." Society would permit the profession autonomy in exchange for the promise to use its skills for the good of its clients and the public. Justifying this bargain were two factors. One, the esoteric knowledge of lawyers made it difficult, if not impossible, for lay people to evaluate their services and to regulate them. Two, the altruism of lawyers—the fact that they worked primarily for the public good in contrast to business people who worked for self interest—guaranteed that society could trust lawyers to regulate themselves.

While continuing to find importance in lawyers' commitment to the public good, professionalism nonetheless offered a more circumscribed understanding both of lawyers' capacity and their societal function. Where Hoffman and Sharswood had identified lawyers' innate virtue as the source of their superior ability to identify and pursue the public good, professionalism made the empirically grounded claim that these characteristics derived from lawyers' training and experience. Professionalism also had less confidence in the commitment of the individual lawyer. In contrast to the republican faith in the individual lawyer and the policing power of reputation, the rhetoric of commentators like Brandeis conceded that the standards of the profession had fallen and sought to restore them. Professionalism recognized that lawyers' commitment to the public good could only be guaranteed through self-regulating bar associations that controlled admission to the bar, educated lawyers to their ethical duties, and enforced proper conduct through discipline.

Like the conception of lawyers' capacity for the public good, the conceptions of lawyers' function also narrowed. The antebellum notion that lawyers were a governing class responsible for maintaining the public good and the rule of law gave way to a perspective that defined a more limited scope for the governing class role. Pound's view of lawyers as "social engineers" retained the aspiration that "lawyers [should] lead the people . . . instead of giving up their legitimate hegemony in legislation and politics to engineers and naturalists and economists." But where the antebellum view understood leadership as defining the public good for the people, Pound viewed it as an "adjustment of the relations of men to each other and to society as conforms to the moral sense of the community." Brandeis articulated a similar notion that retained lawyers as a governing class charged with balancing the competing interests of rich and poor in order to maintain a fair and stable social order. At the same time that Brandeis and Pound articulated a narrower, but still robust, conception, Holmes appeared to abandon the governing class project altogether in describing the entire role of lawyers as predicting legal consequences for their clients.

While a view consistent with that of Holmes would ultimately prevail, the bar of his time preferred the governing class vision that Brandeis and Pound articulated. In 1908, the American Bar Association promulgated the Canons of Ethics, the first national code of ethics for lawyers. The preamble to the Canons stated expressly that "[t]he future of the republic, to a great extent, depend[ed] upon [lawyers'] maintenance of Justice pure and unsullied" through "conduct and the motives [that] merit the approval of all just men." Although the promulgation of the Canons as a formal code of ethics reflected a lesser degree of confidence in the individual lawyer than that of Sharswood's general guidance, the Canons themselves largely adopted Sharswood's approach to balancing duties to clients and the public. The Canons stated that "The Lawyer's Duty in Its Last Analysis" was "the countermajoritarian obligation of loyalty to the law and the judicial system despite the contrary urging of any 'client, corporate or individual, however powerful, nor any cause, civil or political, however important . . . .'" At the same time, they urged "'entire devotion to the interests of the client, warm zeal in the maintenance and defense of his rights and the exertion of his utmost learning and ability.'" The Canons expressly stated that this zealousness did not require the "lawyer to do whatever may enable him to succeed in winning his client's cause." Indeed, the Canons provided that "[t]he responsibility for advising as to questionable transactions, for bringing questionable suits, for urging questionable defenses, is the lawyer's responsibility. He cannot escape it by urging as an excuse that he is only following his client's instructions." The lawyer "must obey his own conscience and not that of the client."

In the period from the early twentieth century through the 1960s, the rhetoric of aspiring to the public good remained consistent, while the understanding of lawyers' function continued to narrow. Toward the end of this period, growing support for the hired gun role led the American Bar Association to restate the profession's commitment to the public good. In 1958, the Joint Conference on Professional Responsibility of the American Bar Association and the Association of American Law Schools, for which Fuller served as co-reporter, declared the "lawyer's role" as a "trusteeship for the integrity of those fundamental processes of government and self-government upon which the successful functioning of our society depends." Erwin Smigel's study of Wall Street lawyers, published in 1964, confirmed that elite lawyers endorsed a similar understanding. The lawyers Smigel interviewed described themselves to be "guardians of the law," urging their clients to adopt "proper and moral legal positions." Although the Joint Conference did describe a narrower obligation to the public good than that of the early twentieth century, Smigel's Wall Street lawyers kept alive the broader construction of Brandeis.

III. The Rise of the Hired Gun

As the influence of liberalism continued inexorably to expand, even this less ambitious commitment of lawyers to the public good would fade. Following the 1960s, while bar leaders retained a rhetoric of professionalism that was necessary to maintain self-regulation, most lawyers abandoned the notion that they had any special obligation to the public good, and, if they acknowledged it at all, they limited it to the margins of practice.

The 1960s represented a watershed in American culture. While proponents of philosophical liberalism, whether identified politically as liberal or conservative, had been dominant in elite culture since the late nineteenth century, certain pre-liberal conceptions, such as the public good, had continued to coexist in a less ambitious form. The 1960s marked the ascendance of purer forms of liberalism that questioned even a rhetorical commitment to the public good.

On the right, Milton Friedman's libertarianism eventually eclipsed traditional conservatism as the engine for elite conservative political philosophy. While traditional conservatism had valued both economic freedom and the public good, Friedman rejected the public good as subversive of individual freedom. People were fundamentally self-interested. Claims of a public good were false and only interfered with individuals' freedom to maximize their self-interest. Conservative commitment to the public good did not disappear entirely. Traditional conservatism survived, especially among religious conservatives whose views would eventually become very influential among the public. But at the level of elite culture, those views were hard to find. Conservative perspectives that emulated Friedman's gained ascendance in the academy and the larger intellectual community, such as through the rise of the law and economics movement.

On the left, the dominant strains of liberalism also found every individual to be self-interested and applied skepticism to claims of values derived from the public good. The protest movements of the 1960s cast doubt on the legitimacy of established authority, while making the broader claim that no person or group was better able to ascertain and pursue the public good. The liberal goal was a public square that maximized individual freedom by remaining neutral with regard to "competing visions of the good life." Persons should have the freedom to live their life without others, especially the government, imposing values upon them. Conceptions of the public good should remain in the private realm. Critics of liberalism from the left often went even further. Not content to restrict the pursuit of the public good to the home, they labeled it a subterfuge for the naked exercise of power and sought to banish it entirely.

The dominant trends in jurisprudence reflected those in elite political philosophy. Whether law and economics on the right, liberal jurisprudence in the middle, or critical theory on the left, they either rejected outright the legitimacy of a public good independent of individual freedom or sought to make the concept as thin and private as possible. The rejection of virtue and the acceptance of majoritarianism became so complete that the diminished role lawyers played in earlier jurisprudences, like those of Fuller and of the legal process school, gave way to the dominance of the Holmesian perception that lawyers were mere technicians. Lawyers largely disappeared from jurisprudence altogether as the focus on judges became even more pronounced. For example, in contrast to the significant attention Fuller gave lawyers, even natural law scholars such as Robert George, no longer found it necessary to maintain a virtuous legal elite. The only exceptions to this approach were individual scholars of both jurisprudence and the legal profession, such as David Luban and Anthony Kronman, whose works had little impact on prevailing jurisprudential perspectives.

Not surprisingly, consistent with these developments in jurisprudence and public political philosophy, survey data and anecdotal impressions revealed that the hired gun perspective had become dominant among lawyers. If the concept of the public good did not exist, then lawyers could claim no special relationship to it. If all people were self-interested, lawyers could not claim to be above self-interest. If majority rule could be trusted, society did not require lawyers to serve as an elite leadership class.

The hired gun conception rejected an obligation to the public good and privileged individual autonomy. It required lawyers to advocate zealously for their client's self-interest and to disregard their own values in order to avoid interfering with their client's autonomy. Lawyers' role prescribed extreme partisanship on behalf of clients within the bounds of the law and without moral accountability for their actions or those of their clients.

The bar faced a dilemma. According to professionalism, lawyers' commitment to the public good was a precondition to self-regulation. The bar responded in two ways. First, it continued to employ the rhetoric of allegiance to the public good. When it became undeniable that most lawyers were devoting themselves to their own self-interest and that of their clients, bar leaders declared a crisis of professionalism. They implemented commissions and mandatory classes to remind lawyers of their public obligation. Second, the bar redefined legal ethics and the public good to legitimize the hired gun view.

In its ethical codes, the bar minimized the centrality of the public good and expanded the commitment to promote the client's interests. While the 1970 Code of Professional Responsibility echoed the 1908 Canons in proudly declaring that "[l]awyers, as the guardians of the law, play a vital role in the preservation of society," the 1983 Model Rules of Professional Conduct identified the lawyer's first role as "a representative of clients" and only after that "a public citizen having special responsibility for the quality of justice," a less ambitious role than that of a leadership class upon which the very "preservation of society" depended.

Moreover, both the Code and the Rules accommodated the hired gun by elevating the lawyer's duty to the client. The Code directed lawyers to "represent a client zealously" within the bounds of the law and required a lawyer "to seek the lawful objectives of his clients through reasonably available means permitted by law and the disciplinary rules." While this language could have been read to permit lawyers broad discretion, lawyers understood it as a command to serve the client as a hired gun. The Model Rules continued to privilege this vision. Indeed, for the first time in an ethical code, the ABA identified client representation, and not commitment to the public good, as lawyers' primary obligation.

The bar further accommodated the hired gun ideal by shifting responsibility for the public good from the average lawyer to the public interest practitioner. In the 1960s, public interest law emerged as a separate field of practice. It expanded from a few, small groups, such as the NAACP and the ACLU, to include significant numbers of lawyers engaged in a variety of causes. The bar came to embrace public interest work and to identify public interest lawyers as role models. In doing so, the bar located responsibility for the public good in the aptly named public interest bar and discarded it from its historical place in ordinary practice.

The bar also encouraged lawyers to remove any remaining personal obligation they felt to the public good from their everyday work and place it in the limited confines of the new ethical duty of pro bono. Although free legal services for those who could not afford them had long been one part of the larger governing class ideal, the idea of the pro bono duty as a separate ethical obligation arose in the 1970s. In 1970, the Code of Professional Responsibility became the first legal ethics code to articulate a separate, though aspirational, ethical duty to provide pro bono legal services. While the duty remained aspirational, it received greater attention and more detailed consideration in the Model Rules. Commitment to provide a minimum number of pro bono hours, often in conjunction with public interest firms, became a major preoccupation of the bar's professionalism campaign, thereby compartmentalizing the public good into the few hours a lawyer devoted to pro bono and further legitimizing the hired gun approach to representing clients.

Food for Thought

Many commentators have offered alternative explanations for the perceived decline in lawyers' commitment to the public good. As noted in Chapter 1, "[b]ar leaders like to blame [this decline as manifested in the crisis of professionalism on] changes in the market for legal services, increased diversity in the profession, and changes in legal education that devalued practice and ethics."[7] To read more about these perspectives, see the sources cited in Russell G. Pearce, *Lawyers as America's Governing Class: The Formation and Dissolution of the Original Understanding of the American Lawyer's Role*, 8 U. Chi. L. Sch. Roundtable 381, 410-15 (2001).

C. Competing Visions of Professional Morality

Not surprisingly, as the neutral partisan role became ascendant in the early 1970s, alternative perspectives emerged. We have selected examples from four different areas to introduce you the voluminous literature that has developed. William Simon[8] and David Luban[9] offered different approaches to viewing lawyers as morally responsible. Tom Shaffer,[10] in his work on being a Christian lawyer, inspired lawyers of all faiths to consider whether their religion could offer a guide for their work. Carrie Menkel-Meadow[11] suggested the potential of feminism, while Derek Bell,[12] David Wilkins,[13] and Margaret Russell[14] asked whether racial identity could provide a lawyering ethic. The original understanding of lawyers as a governing class has reemerged in the guise of lawyer as civics teacher. At the

---

7 Russell G. Pearce, Brian Danitz & Romelia Leach, *Revitalizing the Lawyer-Poet: What Lawyers Can Learn From Rock and Roll*, 14 Widener L.J. 907, 910 (2005).
8   *See infra* p. 804.
9   *See infra* p. 804.
10 Thomas L. Shaffer, On Being a Christian and a Lawyer (1981)
11 *See infra* p. 816.
12 Derrick A. Bell, *Racial Realism*, 24 Conn. L. Rev. 363 (1992).
13 *See infra* p. 867.
14 Margaret M. Russell, *Beyond "Sellouts" and "Race Cards": Black Attorneys and the Straitjacket of Legal Practice*, 95 Mich. L. Rev. 766, 792 (1997).

conclusion of the section, you will have to choose whether the neutral partisan or any of these alternative roles is the role you choose for yourself.

1. Moral Responsibility

[Question 1]

Which of the following statements is true?

    (A) The Rules prohibit morally responsible lawyering.

    (B) The Rules require morally responsible lawyering.

    (C) The Rules permit a lawyer's discretion to be morally responsible in deciding whether to represent a client, counsel a client, and deciding whether to withdraw from representing a client.

[Question 2]

Which of the following statements is true?

    (A) Both David Luban and William Simon urge lawyers to bring extralegal morality into their work.

    (B) Neither David Luban nor William Simon urge lawyers to bring extra-legal morality into their work.

    (C) David Luban urges lawyers to bring extralegal morality into their work.

    (D) William Simon urges lawyers to bring extralegal morality into their work.

[Question 3]

Which author expressly suggests that evading the spirit of the law might be more appropriate in representing a low income person than a wealthy corporation?

    (A) David Luban.

    (B) William Simon.

    (C) Both David Luban and William Simon.

    (D) Neither David Luban nor William Simon.

David Luban, Lawyers and Justice: An Ethical Study 173-74 (1988)

Moral activism * * * involves law reform—explicitly putting one's *phronesis*, one's savvy, to work for the common weal—and client counseling. The latter activity, I think is ultimately more important, because it is available even to lawyers whose humble practices and whose distaste for public life make law reform as remote and unattractive a vocation as it is for most of us. And client counseling, in turn,

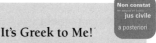

It's Greek to Me!

phronesis – prudence; practical wisdom could include a portion of Nicomachean Ethics. Aristotle considered this the highest of the virtues and the cornerstone of his thesis of the "unity of the virtues"

means discussing with the client the rightness or wrongness of her projects, and the possible impact of those projects on "the people," in the same matter-of-fact and (one hopes) unmoralistic manner that one discusses the financial aspects of a representation. It may involve considerable negotiation about what will and won't be done in the course of a representation; it may eventuate in a lawyer's accepting a case only on condition that it takes a certain shape, or threatening to withdraw from a case if a client insists on pursuing a project that the lawyer finds unworthy. Crucially, moral activism envisions the possibility that it is the lawyer rather than the client who will eventually modify her moral stance. If it is a mistake to take the client's ends as preset and inflexible, it is also a mistake to assume that the lawyer is incapable of learning from the client what justice really requires. But, ultimately, the encounter may result in a parting of ways or even a betrayal by the lawyer of a client's projects, if the lawyer persists in the conviction that they are immoral or unjust. Unlike the standard conception of the lawyer's role, moral activism accepts these possibilities without flinching. Without flinching much, at any rate.

WILLIAM H. SIMON, *ETHICAL DISCRETION IN LAWYERING*,

101 Harv. L. Rev. 1083 (1988)

* * * I. CONVENTIONAL DISCOURSE: TWO MODELS

Consider two crude models designed to evoke some familiar tendencies of lawyers' discussions of ethical decisionmaking. The first model emphasizes the lawyer's role as advocate and her duty of loyalty to the client; the second emphasizes the lawyer's role as officer of the court and her duty of loyalty to the public.

The first might be called the libertarian approach. Its basic maxim is that the lawyer is obliged—or at least authorized—to pursue any goal of the client through any arguably legal course of action and to assert any nonfrivolous legal claim. In this approach, the only ethical duty distinctive to the lawyer's role is loyalty to the client. Legal ethics impose no direct responsibilities to third parties or the public other than those the system imposes on citizens generally.

The libertarian approach privileges procedure over substance. It legitimates conduct that is authorized by procedural rules but undercuts substantive rules—for example, pleading the statute of frauds to defeat the enforcement of a contract or invoking litigation rules that create delay and expense in order to encumber the enforcement of a substantively valid claim. The libertarian approach also privileges form over purpose by authorizing appeals to interpretations of rules that frustrate the purposes of the rules.

* * *

The second model can be called the regulatory approach. Its basic maxim is that the lawyer should facilitate informed resolution of the substantive issues by the responsible officials. The regulatory model privileges substance over procedure. It sees the lawyer's basic function as contributing to the enforcement of the substantive law, and it inclines toward forbidding her to use procedural rules in ways that frustrate the enforcement of substantive norms. The most important way it does so is by giving the lawyer strong responsibilities as a distiller and transmitter of information. Her basic duty is to clarify the issues in ways that contribute to a decision on the merits, not to manipulate information to serve the client's goals. The job still involves advising the client on ways to advance her interests and presenting the client's case, but it also involves a duty to develop and disclose adverse information that would be important to the responsible official. The duty applies in negotiation as well on the theory that disclosure is likely to move settlements closer to the resolution that the responsible officials would have imposed.

The regulatory approach tends to privilege purpose over form. It understands the enforcement task in terms of the purposes expressed in the articulated law. And it tends to privilege broad ways of framing issues over narrow ones. It refuses to exempt the lawyer from responsibility for circumstances that impede enforcement merely because her conduct has not affirmatively contributed to them. In particular, it imposes affirmative duties to share information and to correct misunderstanding.

Despite their opposed perspectives, the libertarian and regulatory models share a common style of reasoning. The style might be called categorical, by which I mean simply the practice of restrictively specifying the factors that a decisionmaker may consider when she confronts a particular problem. In the categorical style, a rigid rule dictates a particular response in the presence of a small number of factors. The decisionmaker has no discretion to consider factors she encounters that are not specified or to evaluate specified factors in any way other than that given in the rule.

* * *

II. THE DISCRETIONARY APPROACH

The basic maxim of the approach I propose is this: The lawyer should take those actions that, considering the relevant circumstances of the particular case, seem most likely to promote justice. This 'seek justice' maxim suggests a kind of non-categorical judgment that might be called pragmatist, and hoc, or dialectical, but that I will call discretionary. 'Discretionary' is not an entirely satisfactory term; I do not mean to invoke its connotations of arbitrariness or nonaccountability, but rather its connotations of flexibility and complexity. Unlike the private norms of the *Code* and *Model Rules*, discretionary norms, as I define them, do not connote standardlessness and nonreviewability. I use the term in what Ronald Dworkin call 'a weak sense' to indicate that the relevant norms 'cannot be applied mechanically but demand the use of judgment.'

In the context of professional responsibility, lawyers tend to be skeptical that judgments applying abstract ideals to particular cases could be anything but arbitrary. Yet lawyers also tend to regard discretionary judgment as plausible in the context of the judicial role. The kind of complex, flexible judgment proposed here has been extensively defended against more categorical styles in some of the best-known literature of judicial decisionmaking. Although this portrayal has been challenged, it has gained wide acceptance, even among lawyers hostile to this style of decision in legal ethics. The preference for categorical reasoning in the lawyering context reflects nothing more than a failure to carry through to the lawyering role the critique of formalism, mechanical jurisprudence, and categorical reasoning that has been applied to the judicial role throughout this century.

Another pertinent context in which lawyers have been relatively willing to accept the posibility of meaningful discretionary judgment is that of the public prosecutor. Indeed, my formulation of the basic maxim of the discretionary approach has been partly inspired by the maxim the *Code* prescribes for the prosecutor: 'The responsibility of a public prosecutor differs from that of the usual advocate; his duty is to seek justice, not merely to convict.'

To propose a style of ethical judgment for private lawyers analogous to that familiarly associated with judges or prosecutors is not to say that lawyers should act as if they were judges or prosecutors. The analogy is to the style of judgment, not necessarily to the particular decisions that judges and prosecutors make. The discretionary approach incorporates much of the traditional lawyer role, including the notion that lawyers can serve justice through zealous pursuit of clients' goals. Although it assumes a public dimension to the lawyer's role as well, that dimension is grounded in the lawyer's age-old claim to be an 'officer of the court' and in notions about the most effective integration of the lawyering role with other roles in the legal system.

There are two dimensions to the judgment that the discretionary approach requires of the lawyer. The first is an assessment of the relative merits of the client's goals and claims and the goals and claims of others whom the lawyer might serve. The second is an effort to confront and resolve the competing factors that bear on the internal merits of the client's goals and claims.

A. Relative Merit

Neither of the dominant approaches adequately confronts a central fact about the legal system: most people are unable to enforce most of their rights most of the time. An important reason is that enforcement requires resources, and the most important resource is professional assistance. The problem is not simply the bar's failure to live up to its professed commitment to provide assistance to those who cannot afford it. At any plausible level of expanded pro bono activity, the problem would remain, because hardly anyone in the society would want to devote the resources needed to bring us even close to a state in which rights could be generally enforced. Thus, legal services are necessarily a scarce resource.

The legal system cannot be indifferent to the distribution of this resource. First, our legal ideals presume a high degree of continuity between the prescriptions of legal norms and the conduct of citizens and officials.

* * *

Second, some rights or interests are more important than others.

* * *

Third, the distribution of legal resources is important because the practical value of some rights depends more on the relative than on the absolute amount of the citizen's enforcement resources.

* * *

 The proper standard requires not only a threshold judgment, but also a relative one. In deciding whether to commit herself to a client's claims and goals, a lawyer should assess their merits in relation to the merits of the claims and goals of others whom she might serve. The criteria the lawyer should employ in making this assessment are suggested by the bases of legal concern about the distribution of services: the extent to which the claims and goals are grounded in the law, the importance of the interests involved, and the extent to which the representation would contribute to the equalization of access to the legal system.

Of course, merit cannot be the only consideration to determine how the lawyer allocates her efforts. The lawyer's financial interests are also necessarily important. But the financial considerations that tacitly determine the distribution of legal services under the dominant approaches are substantially arbitrary in relation to the most basic goals of the legal system—those concerning legal merit. Lawyers can mitigate the tendency of the market to produce an inappropriate distribution of legal services by integrating considerations of relative merit into their decisions about whom to represent and how to do so. In making such judgments, lawyers will have to balance their legitimate financial concerns with their commitment to a just distribution of legal services. A lawyer who cannot refuse to assist a particular client without impairing her ability to earn a reasonable income may have to compromise her judgments of relative merit more than one who can say no without great financial sacrifice. It may or may not be desirable for the bar to prescribe collectively how individual lawyers should strike this balance. The minimum that the discretionary approach requires is that the lawyer try in good faith to take account of relative merit in her decisions.

The type of consideration urged here simply extends to conventional practice the kind of judgments many lawyers now make in pro bono practice. Lawyers who do pro bono work usually choose cases in accordance with some estimate of the relative merits of the claims competing for their services. The judgments made in pro bono practice illustrate the possibility of judgments of relative merit, and they show that financial considerations do not invariably swamp ethical ones in practice. However, the limitation of this type of ethical discretion to the pro bono sphere is arbitrary. A client's ability to pay is not an irrelevant consideration, but there is no reason why it should preclude all assessment of relative merit.

* * *

B. Internal Merit

The second aspect of the lawyer's assessment of merit involves an attempt to reconcile the conflicting legal values implicated directly in the client's claim or goal. These conflicts usually arise in the form of the overlapping tensions between substance and procedure, purpose and form, and broad and narrow framing.

By tending to privilege one or the other of the conflicting elements, the conventional approaches discourage the lawyer from confronting these tensions. In doing so, they authorize or require the lawyer to act in a way that she would concede, were the encouraged to make a judgment on the issue, frustrates the most legally appropriate resolution of the matter. By contrast, the discretionary approach requires that the lawyer make her best effort to achieve the most appropriate resolution in each case.

The discretionary approach does not ignore considerations of institutional competence. It does not assume that the full responsibility for a proper resolution rests on the lawyer alone. It is compatible with the conventional understanding of the role of judicial and administrative officials in law enforcement. The discretionary approach is distinctive, first, in treating the premises of that understanding as rebuttable presumptions that do not warrant reliance when they do not apply, and second, in imposing a more flexible and demanding duty on the lawyer to facilitate official decision when the premises do apply.

1. Substance Versus Procedure—One manifestation of the substance versus procedure tension is the lawyer's sense of the limitations both of her individual judgment of the substantive merits of the dispute on the one hand and of the established procedures for resolving it on the other. We could tell the lawyer to work only to advance claims and goals that she determined were entitled to prevail. The most important objection to this precept is not that the lawyer's decisions about the merits would be controversial—the decisions of judges, juries, and executive officials may also the controversial. Instead, the most important objection is that judges, juries, and executive officials acting within the relevant public procedures are generally able to make more reliable determinations on the merits than the individual lawyer. But the qualification 'generally' is crucial. The lawyer will often have good reason to recognize that the standard procedure is not reliably constructed to respond to the problem at hand, and she will often be in a position to contribute to its improvement.

The basic response of the discretionary approach to the substance-procedure tension is this: the more reliable the relevant procedures and institutions, the less direct responsibility the lawyer need assume for the substantive justice of the resolution; the less reliable the procedures and institutions, the more direct responsibility she need assume for substantive justice. * * *

2. Purpose Versus Form.—Part of the substance versus procedure tension could be considered a special variation of the purpose versus form tension. When the lawyer impeaches a witness she knows to be truthful, when she objects to hearsay she knows to be accurate, when she puts the opposing party to proof on a matter the client has no legitimate interest in disputing, she takes advantage of procedural rules designed to promote accurate, efficient decisionmaking in a way that frustrates this purpose. When judges apply rules, we expect them to take account of the purposes underlying the rules. But the judge often lacks sufficient knowledge to determine whether the relevant purposes would be served by applying the rules. The lawyer, however, often does have sufficient knowledge to do so.

* * *

The argument so far suggests that a lawyer's choice between a purposive or formal approach to procedural rules should depend on which approach seems better calculated to vindicate the relevant legal merits. In most contexts, considerations of merit favor a purposive approach. Yet the discretionary approach also requires the lawyer to remain alert for indications that a purposive approach might not further consideration on the merits. This point merely summarizes the substance versus procedure discussion in terms of purpose versus form. It will be useful, however, to consider the purpose versus form tension more generally because in many situations, especially those in which the lawyer must take direct responsibility for considerations of substantive merit, purpose versus form considerations are distinctively troubling.

Part of the reason for regarding law as legitimate in our culture is that it embodies the purposes adopted by authoritative lawmakers: parties to a contract, legislators enacting a statute, judges pronouncing a common law rule, the people adopting a constitution. But the legitimacy of law also depends on these intentions being embodied in the form of rules. By mediating between legislative intention and coercive application to specific cases, the rule form distinguishes law from a regime of direct personal subordination to the legislator. The rules cannot be applied sensibly without considering their underlying purposes, but the purposes can only be implemented appropriately by referring to their formal expression as rules.

* * *

Now consider a case in which the relevant purpose is less clear and more problematic. The client is a public assistance recipient under the Aid to Families with Dependent Children program. She and her child live, rent-free, in a home owned by her cousin. Under the applicable regulations, the receipt of lodging 'at no cost' is considered 'income in kind' that requires a reduction of about $150 in the welfare grant. The lawyer has to decide whether to recommend that the client make a nominal payment of, say, five dollars to the cousin so that she would no longer be receiving lodging 'at no cost,' and thus avoid the $150 reduction in her grant.

Again, assume that some institutional failure requires that the lawyer take some responsibility for the substantive merits. Upon examination, she is unable to come up with a sense of legislative purpose as clear and coherent as the one involved in the tax case. On the one hand, the benefit reduction seems designed to reflect the lesser needs of people who live rent free, and the fact that the provision could be effectively nullified by the type of financial planning in question suggests that such planning was not contemplated. On the other hand, nothing in the language of the regulation suggests an intention to preclude such planning, although it would have been simple enough to do so by providing for a benefit reduction in cases of low rent payments of the difference between the rent payment and the $150 implicit shelter allowance in the grant.

* * *

Suppose that background case law and legislative history suggest that the regulation is in part a compromise between the principle that grants should reflect the lesser needs of people with low rent expense and the competing 'flat grant' principle that need determinations should consider only the basic and easily determinable factors of cash income and family size. The 'flat grant' principle is animated by solicitude for recipient autonomy and privacy as well as administrative efficiency concerns. In addition, the regulations seem to reflect a rough compromise between a half-hearted effort by the federal government (which subsidizes the program) to push the states to raise grant levels generally and efforts by the states to retain flexibility to lower them in some circumstances. In this situation, the lawyer has no clear sense of which course of action would be most consistent with legislative purpose. It is thus proper for her to treat the regulation formally.

Even if the lawyer found stronger indication of a purpose to preclude strategic planning, she might be justified in disregarding it if she thought it problematic. A purpose is problematic to the extent that it endangers fundamental values. The lawyer might decide that the claimant's interest in a minimally adequate income is a value of exceptional legal importance, that the AFDC grant levels provide considerably less than a minimally adequate income, and that the plan in question would move her closer to one. Thus, the lawyer might conclude that a purpose to preclude such a plan should not be assumed without an explicit legislative statement of it. In doing so, she might apply the presumption against a problematic purpose that the Supreme Court seemed to apply in *Kent v. Dulles*, a presumption reflecting both a judgment regarding probable legislative intent and a substantive policy disfavoring certain purposes by requiring more explicit articulation of them.

3. Broad Versus Narrow Framing.—This tension arises as ethical issues are defined. If we define an issue narrowly in terms of a small number of characteristics of the parties and their dispute, it will often look different than if we define it to encompass the parties' identities, relationship, and social circumstances. On the one hand, legal ideals encourage narrow definition of legal disputes in order to limit the scope of state intrusion into the lives of private citizens and to conserve scarce legal resources. On the other hand, making rights enforcement effective and meaningful often seems to require broadening the definition of disputes. When disputes are narrowly defined, their resolution is often influenced by factors such as wealth and power that, when we are forced to confront them, often seem arbitrary. Moreover, the growth of government regulation and civil rights enforcement has produced a large number of legal norms that regulate broadly the structures of relationships and organizations. Thus, large scale public institutional reform or antitrust litigation often challenges and seeks to transform the basic identity of the defendant.

The broad versus narrow definition tension substantially overlaps the other tensions. For example, in debates that I characterized in terms of substance versus procedure, Monroe Freedman responds to regulatory arguments by hypothesizing situations in which candor and openness may impede the appropriate substantive resolution because of some procedural deficiency. A famous example concerns whether a criminal defense lawyer should cross-examine a prosecution witness who accurately places the defendant near the scene of the crime about her defective vision. In Freedman's scenario, although the testimony is accurate and thus the contemplated impeachment seems irrelevant, the defendant is in fact innocent but lacks an alibi and is the victim of some unlucky circumstantial evidence. So the proper resolution—acquittal—may depend on the willingness to impeach the truthful witness. * * * What Freedman does in these examples is to broaden the frame. The issue initially posed is one of candor about a specific piece of information. He insists that the matter be viewed in the context of the other evidence and in terms of the likely incremental influence of disclosure on the resolution. Nevertheless, broad framing has no place in Freedman's view of individual lawyer decisionmaking. At that level, he adopts the general libertarian practice of narrow framing. He favors a categorical duty of aggressive impeachment of vulnerable witnesses regardless of the surrounding context. Freedman adopts the broader perspective only when he takes the point of view of the rulemaker deciding whether to mandate cross-examination in this context.

In contrast, the discretionary approach gives individual lawyers substantial responsibility for determining whether broad or narrow framing is appropriate in the particular case. It suggests that the lawyer should frame ethical issues in accordance with three general standards of relevance. First, a consideration is relevant if it is implicated by the most plausible interpretation of the applicable law. Issues tend to be defined more narrowly under legal norms that regulate narrowly. For example, traffic laws suggest narrower framing than family laws. Second, a consideration is relevant if it is likely to have a substantial practical influence on the resolution. Issues tend to be defined more narrowly to the extent that the parties are situated so that substantively irrelevant factors are not likely to influence the resolution. Equality of resources and of access to information are among the more important factors weighing toward narrow definition under this second standard. Third, knowledge and institutional competence will affect the appropriate framing. More broadly framed issues tend to require more knowledge and more difficult judgments. When the lawyer lacks needed knowledge or competence, narrow framing becomes more appropriate.

* * *

C. The Limits of Role and Legality

The discretionary approach is grounded in the lawyer's professional commitments to legal values. It rejects the common tendency to attribute the tensions of legal ethics to a conflict between the demands of legality on the one hand and those of nonlegal, personal or ordinary morality on the other. Although critics of conventional legal ethics discourse often adopt the law versus morality characterization, its strongest influence is to bias discussion in favor of conventional, especially libertarian, responses. Typically the conventional response is portrayed as the 'legal' one; the unconventional response is portrayed as a 'moral' alternative. This rhetoric connotes that the 'legal' option is objective and integral to the professional role, whereas the 'moral' alternative is subjective and peripheral. Even when the rhetoric expresses respect for the 'moral' alternative, it implies that the lawyer who adopts it is on her own and vulnerable both intellectually and practically. The usual effect is to make it psychologically harder for lawyers and law students to argue for the 'moral' alternative. In many such situations, however, both alternatives could readily be portrayed as competing *legal* values.

The specious law-versus-morality characterization is used most frequently to privilege client loyalty. For example, in the hypothetical discussed above involving a personal injury negotiation in which the plaintiff's lawyer underestimated the value of the claim because of a mistake about the law, the defense counsel's client loyalty option is often seen as the 'legal' one and the disclosure option as a 'moral' alternative. In fact, of course, concern for the plaintiff is strongly grounded in the belief that without disclosure the plaintiff will be deprived of a substantive legal entitlement to recover for negligently inflicted losses. Thus, both options are equally 'legal' in the sense that they are grounded in important legal values.

The discretionary approach does not deny that some issues are best understood as involving conflicts between legal and nonlegal moral commitments. In fact, the distinction between legal and nonlegal commitments has some importance in delimiting the sphere of the discretionary approach, since the approach does not address decisionmaking involving nonlegal commitments. There are currently no generally accepted guidelines for making such distinctions, and I am not prepared to offer any here. However, it may be helpful to emphasize that such distinctions depend on important issues of legal theory that all lawyers need to resolve (though not necessarily self-consciously) in formulating their understandings of their role. In particular, such distinctions depend first on the relationship between institutional competence norms and fundamental substantive norms, and second, on the scope of lawyer discretion within the scheme of institutional competence. Whether it makes sense to view ethical conflict in terms of 'law versus morals' or the lawyer's problems as functions of 'role differentiation' depends on how these issues are resolved.

* * *

Almost all lawyers will give weight to clear legislative expression, and many would regard it as dispositive of their obligations. However, a 'natural law lawyer' in the style of, say, Lon Fuller would have to consider whether the decisions of the legislature were so plainly wrong and the values they affronted so fundamental that the lawyer should disregard the decisions. The natural law lawyer cannot divorce 'his duty of fidelity to law' from 'his responsibility for making law what it ought to be.' Such a lawyer believes that a legal system must meet certain normative preconditions to be entitled to respect and compliance, and perhaps even to be considered a system of law. Thus, legal ideals may require that a person repudiate norms that violate such preconditions even when promulgated by otherwise legally authoritative institutions. Such repudiation is the opposite of lawlessness; it moves the system closer to being worthy of respect as lawful.

A lawyer in the welfare case who accepted this natural law theory of legal order would have to consider whether the norm of minimal subsistence income is so fundamental that it amounts to a precondition of legal legitimacy. Such a lawyer might reason that a core value of legality is the autonomy of the individual and that a person who lacked minimal material subsistence would be so dependent and debilitated that she would be incapable of exercising the autonomy that legality aspires to safeguard. In this way, the lawyer might conclude that this value is fundamental and hence that norms that violate it are not entitled to respect.

Even when a lawyer regards the decisions of authoritative institutions as conclusive, she needs to consider the scope of her own authority within the scheme of legal institutions. In particular, she needs to consider whether the lawyering role allows her nullifying powers of the sort commonly imputed to the roles of prosecutor, jury, and judge, and—less commonly—private citizen (to the extent that civil disobedience is justified in terms of, rather than in opposition to, legal values).

* * *

The discretionary approach does not require that the issues of the relation of institutional and substantive norms and of the lawyer's range of autonomy within the scheme of institutional competence be resolved in any particular way. But how a lawyer resolves these issues will affect how she draws the distinction between professional and private ethics. In some situations, the lawyer will feel that she has a professional obligation to some legally authoritative norm that conflicts with her private, nonlegal commitments. In other situations, she may feel that her private commitment outweighs the professional one. But she will feel such a conflict only when she is reasonably certain that the legal system fails to acknowledge some value to which she is committed or that the system has conclusively rejected such a value. Only at this point is it appropriate to talk of her problem in terms of the limits of 'role morality' or 'role differentiation.' Until then, the problem remains one of the most appropriate performance of her role within the legal system. * * *

2. Feminist

[Question 1]

Which of the following is true?

(A) Catherine MacKinnon and Carrie Menkel-Meadow define a feminist lawyer as primarily a supporter of women's causes.

(B) Catherine MacKinnon defines a feminist lawyer as primarily a supporter of women's causes

(C) Carrie Menkel-Meadow defines a feminist lawyer as primarily a supporter of women's causes

(D) Neither Catherine MacKinnon nor Carrie Menkel-Meadow define a feminist lawyer as primarily a supporter of women's causes

[Question 2]

Carrie Menkel-Meadow's approach to feminist lawyering relies primarily upon:

(A) women's rights

(B) women's support for individualism

(C) women's understanding of relationships

(D) women's superiority to men

[Question 3]

Under Menkel-Meadow's approach, a man could be a feminist lawyer.

(A) True

(B) False

[Question 4]

Menkel-Meadow suggests that feminist lawyering has implications for:

(A) the lawyer-client relationship

(B) ethics rules

(C) the legal workplace

(D) none of the above

Food for Thought

Should there be an aspirational rule stating that "lawyers are morally accountable for their conduct at law?" Professor Russell Pearce has made this argument. He suggests that this rule would be neutral between perspectives, like those of David Luban, Deborah Simon, and Deborah Rhode, that understand moral responsibility as potentially limiting the lawyer's zealousness and those similar to Monroe Freedman's, who asserts that moral responsibility requires unbounded zealousness. It would exclude only lawyering perspectives grounded in an amoral rationale. Pearce suggests a rule requiring moral responsibility would move debates regarding the lawyer's role "to a more prominent place in the bar's official deliberations and continuing legal education courses, as well as in the efforts of the conscientious lawyer to explore her own moral accountability." Pearce further asserts that the Rule would improve the bar's public image. He writes that "[b]y compelling [all lawyers, including] zealous advocates or other representatives of the unpopular to explain their conduct on moral grounds, Rule 1.0 will not undermine their arguments and may make them more effective. The public--and other lawyers and judges--are much more likely to be persuaded (or at least less offended) by a moral justification of the advocate's role, like that proposed by Freedman, than by the bald assertion that "[a]s a lawyer, I am not morally accountable." Russell G. Pearce, *Model Rule 1.0: Lawyers Are Morally Accountable*, 70 Fordham L. Rev. 1805 (2002). What do you think?

CARRIE MENKEL-MEADOW, *PORTIA IN A DIFFERENT VOICE: SPECULATIONS ON A WOMEN'S LAWYERING PROCESS,*

1 Berkeley Women's L.J. 39, 41-60 (1985)

* * *

I find persuasive, though not unproblematic, the notion that values, consciousness, attributes, and behavior are gendered, i.e., that some are identified as belonging to women and others to men. The attachment of gender labels is a product of both present empirical research[1] and social process. Thus, we may label the quality of caring a female quality, but note its presence in many men. Further, a man who exhibits many feminine qualities may be perceived as feminine, *e.g.* "He's too sensitive to be a good trial lawyer," or alternatively, an assertive woman may be met with remarks such as, "She's as sharp as any of the men on the team." Attributing behavior characteristics to a particular gender is problematic, because even as we observe such generalizations to be valid in many cases, we risk perpetuating the conventional stereotypes that prevent us from seeing the qualities as qualities without their gendered context. * * *

Several recent studies and books in psychological development have traced the implications of gender differences in psychological development for personality, moral development, child rearing, and ultimately, the very structure of major social institutions. The common theme that unites this body of work by psychologists such as Chodorow, Dinnerstein, Miller, Schaef, and most recently, Gilligan, is that women experience themselves through connections and relationships to others while men see themselves as separately identified individuals. * * *

In her book, *In a Different Voice: Psychological Theory and Women's Development,* Gilligan observes that much of what has been written about human psychological development has been based on studies of male subjects exclusively. As a consequence, girls and women have either not been described, or they are said to have "failed" to develop on measurement scales based on male norms. * * *

An example drawn from Gilligan's work best illustrates the duality of girls' and boys' moral development. In one of the three studies on which her book is based, a group of children are asked to solve Heinz's dilemma, a hypothetical moral reasoning problem used by Kohlberg to rate moral development on his six-stage scale. The dilemma is that Heinz's wife is dying of cancer and requires a drug which the local pharmacist has priced beyond Heinz's means. The question is posed: should Heinz steal the drug?

To illustrate and explain the differences between the ways boys and girls approached this problem, Gilligan quotes from two members of her sample, Jake and Amy.

Jake, an eleven-year-old boy, sees the problem as one of "balancing rights," like a judge who must make a decision or a mathematician who must solve an algebraic equation. Life is worth more than property, therefore Heinz should steal the drug. For Amy, an eleven-year-old girl, the problem is different. Like a "bad" law student she "fights the hypo"; she wants to know more facts: Have Heinz and the druggist explored other possibilities, like a loan or credit transaction? Why couldn't Heinz and the druggist simply sit down and talk it out so that the druggist would come to see the importance of Heinz's wife's life? In Gilligan's terms, Jake explores the Heinz dilemma with "the logic of justice" while Amy uses the "ethic of care." Amy scores lower on the Kohlberg scale because she sees the problem rooted in the persons involved rather than in the larger universal issues posed by the dilemma.

In conventional terms Jake would make a good lawyer because he spots the legal issues of excuse and justification, balances the rights, and reaches a decision, while considering implicitly, if not explicitly, the precedential effect of his decision. But as Gilligan argues, and as I develop more fully below, Amy's approach is also plausible and legitimate, both as a style of moral reasoning and as a style of lawyering. Amy seeks to keep the people engaged; she holds the needs of the parties and their relationships constant and hopes to satisfy them all (as in a negotiation), rather than selecting a winner (as in a lawsuit). If one must be hurt, she attempts to find a resolution that will hurt least the one who can least bear the hurt. (Is she engaged in a "deep pocket" policy analysis?) She looks beyond the "immediate lawsuit" to see how the "judgment" will affect the parties. If Heinz steals the drug and goes to jail, who will take care of his wife? Furthermore, Amy is concerned with *how* the dilemma is resolved: the process by which the parties communicate may be crucial to the outcome. (Amy cares as much about procedure as about substance.) And she is being a good lawyer when she inquires whether all of the facts have been discovered and considered.

The point here is not that Amy's method of moral reasoning is better than Jake's, nor that she is a better lawyer than Jake. (Some have read Gilligan to argue that the women's voice is better. I don't read her that way.) The point is that Amy does some things differently from Jake when she resolves this dilemma, and these things have useful analogies to lawyering and may not have been sufficiently credited as useful lawyering skills. Jake and Amy have something to learn from one another.

Thus, although a "choice of rights" conception (life vs. property) of solving human problems may be important, it is not the only or the best way. Responsibilities to self and to others may be equally important in measuring moral, as well as legal decision making, but have thus far been largely ignored. For example, a lawyer who feels responsible for the decisions she makes with her client may be more inclined to think about how those decisions will hurt other people and how the lawyer and client feel about making such decisions. (Amy thinks about Heinz, the druggist, and Heinz's wife at all times in reaching her decision; Jake makes a choice in abstract terms without worrying as much about the people it affects.)

In tracing through the sources of these different approaches to moral reasoning, Gilligan's analysis tracks that of Chodorow, Dinnerstein and Noddings. Men, who have had to separate from their differently gendered mother in order to grow, tend to see moral dilemmas as problems of separateness and individual rights, problems in which choices must be made and priorities must be ordered. Women, who need not completely separate from their same gendered mother in order to grow, see the world in terms of connections and relationships. "While women thus try to change the rules in order to preserve relationships, men, in abiding by these rules, depict relationships as easily replaced." Where men see danger in too much connection or intimacy, in being engulfed and losing their own identity, women see danger in the loss of connection, in not having an identity through caring for others and by being abandoned and isolated.

Both Gilligan and Noddings see differences in the ethics men and women derive from their different experiences of the world. Men focus on universal abstract principles like justice, equality and fairness so that their world is safe, predictable and constant. Women solve problems by seeking to understand the context and relationships involved and understand that universal rules may be impossible.

The two different voices Gilligan describes articulate two different developmental processes. To the extent that we all have both of these voices within us and they are not exclusively gender based, a mature person will develop the ability to consider the implications of both an abstract rights analysis and a contextualized responsibilities analysis. For women, this kind of mature emotional and intellectual synthesis may require taking greater account of self and less account of the other; for men, the process may be the reverse. Such an integration will not resolve all issues of personal development. Those who seek interdependence will not necessarily find it by the individualistic integration and reciprocity of reasoning styles proposed above. And if this integration fosters equality between the sexes, there still remains the problem of equity. As one of Gilligan's subjects observed: "People have real emotional needs to be attached to something and equality doesn't give you attachment. Equality fractures society and places on every person the burden of standing on his own two feet." The different paths toward mature moral development for men and women may give us more than one road to take to the same place, or we may find that there is more than one interesting place to go. * * *

The basic structure of our legal system is premised on the adversarial model, which involves two advocates who present their cases to a disinterested third party who listens to evidence and argument and declares one party a winner. In this simplified description of the Anglo-American model of litigation, we can identify some of the basic concepts and values which underlie this choice of arrangements: advocacy, persuasion, hierarchy, competition, and binary results (win/lose). The conduct of litigation is relatively similar (not coincidentally, I suspect) to a sporting event—there are rules, a referee, an object to the game, and a winner is declared after the play is over. As I have argued elsewhere, this conception of the dispute resolution process is applied more broadly than just in the conventional courtroom. The adversarial model affects the way in which lawyers advise their clients ("get as much as you can"), negotiate disputes ("we can really get them on that") and plan transactions ("let's be sure to draft this to your advantage"). All of these activities in lawyering assume competition over the same limited and equally valued items (usually money) and assume that success is measured by maximizing individual gain. Would Gilligan's Amy create a different model?

By returning to Heinz's dilemma we see some hints about what Amy might do. Instead of concluding that a choice must be made between life and property, in resolving the conflict between parties as Jake does, Amy sees no need to hierarchically order the claims. Instead, she tries to account for all the parties' needs, and searches for a way to find a solution that satisfies the needs of both. In her view, Heinz should be able to obtain the drug for his wife and the pharmacist should still receive payment. So Amy suggests a loan, a credit arrangement, or a discussion of other ways to structure the transaction. In short, she won't play by the adversarial rules. She searches outside the system for a way to solve the problem, trying to keep both parties in mind. Her methods substantiate Gilligan's observations that women will try to change the rules to preserve the relationships.

Furthermore, in addition to looking for more substantive solutions to the problem (i.e., not accepting the binary win/lose conception of the problem), Amy also wants to change the process. Amy sees no reason why she must act as a neutral arbiter of a dispute and make a decision based only on the information she has. She "belie[ves] in communication as the mode of conflict resolution and [is convinced] that the solution to the dilemma will follow from its compelling representation. . . ," If the parties talk directly to each other, they will be more likely to appreciate the importance of each other's needs. Thus, she believes direct communication, rather than third party mediated debate, might solve the problem, recognizing that two apparently conflicting positions can both be simultaneously legitimate, and there need not be a single victor.

The notion that women might have more difficulty with full-commitment-to-one-side model of the adversary system is graphically illustrated by Hilary, one of the women lawyers in Gilligan's study. This lawyer finds herself in one of the classic moral dilemmas of the adversary system: she sees that her opponent has failed to make use of a document that is helpful to his case and harmful to hers. In deciding not to tell him about the document because of what she sees as her "professional vulnerability" in the male adversary system, she concludes that "the adversary system of justice impedes not only the supposed search for truth (the conventional criticism), but also *the expression of concern for the person on the other side.*" Gilligan describes Hilary's tension between her concept of rights (learned through legal training) and her female ethic of care as a sign of her socialization in the male world of lawyering. Thus, the advocacy model, with its commitment to one-sided advocacy, seems somehow contrary to "apprehending the reality of the other" which lawyers like Hilary experience. Even the continental inquisitorial model, frequently offered as an alternative to the adversarial model, includes most of these elements of the male system—hierarchy, advocacy, competition and binary results.

So what kind of legal system would Amy and Hilary create if left to their own devices? They might look for ways to alter the harshness of win/lose results; they might alter the rules of the game (or make it less like a game); and they might alter the very structures and forms themselves. Thus, in a sense Amy and Hilary's approach can already be found in some of the current alternatives to the adversary model such as mediation. Much of the current interest in alternative dispute resolution is an attempt to modify the harshness of the adversarial process and expand the kinds of solutions available, in order to respond better to the varied needs of the parties. Amy's desire to engage the parties in direct communication with each other is reflected in mediation models where the parties talk directly to each other and forge their own solutions. The work of Gilligan and Noddings, demonstrating an ethic of care and a heightened sense of empathy in women, suggests that women lawyers may be particularly interested in mediation as an alternative to litigation as a method of resolving disputes.

Even within the present adversarial model, Amy and Hilary might, in their concern for others, want to provide for a broader conception of interested parties, permitting participation by those who might be affected by the dispute (an ethic of inclusion). In addition, like judges who increasingly are managing more of the details of their cases, Amy and Hilary might seek a more active role in settlement processes and rely less on court-ordered relief. Amy and Hilary might look for other ways to construct their lawsuits and remedies in much the same way as courts of equity mitigated the harshness of the law courts' very limited array of remedies by expanding the conception of what was possible.

The process and rules of the adversary system itself might look different if there were more female voices in the legal profession.   If Amy is less likely than Jake to make assertive, rights-based statements, is she less likely to adapt to the male-created advocacy mode? In my experience as a trial lawyer, I observed that some women had difficulty with the "macho" ethic of the courtroom battle. Even those who did successfully adapt to the male model often confronted a dilemma because women were less likely to be perceived as behaving properly when engaged in according to the stereotypic conception of appropriate trial behavior. The woman who conforms to the female stereotype by being "soft" or "weak" is a bad trial lawyer; but if a woman is "tough" or "strong" in the courtroom, she is seen as acting inappropriately for a woman. Note, however, that this stereotyping is contextual: the same woman acting as a "strong" or "tough" mother with difficult children would be praised for that conduct. Women's strength is approved of with the proviso that it be exerted in appropriately female spheres.

Amy and Hilary might create a different form of advocacy, one resembling a "conversation" with the fact finder, relying on the creation of a relationship with the jury for its effectiveness, rather than on persuasive intimidation. There is some anecdotal evidence that this is happening already. Recently, several women prosecutors described their styles of trial advocacy as the creation of a personal relationship with the jury in which they urge the jurors to examine their own perceptions and values and encourage them to think for themselves, rather than "buying" the arguments of one of the advocates. This is a conception of the relationship between the lawyer and the fact-finder which is based on trust and mutual respect rather than on dramatics, intimidation and power, the male mode in which these women had been trained and which they found unsatisfactory.

In sum, the growing strength of women's voice in the legal profession may change the adversarial system into a more cooperative, less war-like system of communication between disputants in which solutions are mutually agreed upon rather than dictated by an outsider, won by the victor, and imposed upon the loser. Some seeds of change may already be found in existing alternatives to the litigation model, such as mediation. It remains to be seen what further changes Portia's voice may make. * * *

Does the female voice of relationship, care and connection lead to a different form of law practice? Although the present adversarial system may limit the ways in which concern for others may be expressed toward adversaries, the values of relationship and care may be expressed with one's work partners. * * *

While hierarchy produces efficiency and individual achievement, as lawyers, Amy and Hilary might chose to emphasize other values such as collectivity and interpersonal connection. This attempt to work in a different way not only affects relationships within the working unit, but is also apparent in the work of feminists who seek to demystify law and the legal profession by working with clients on lay advocacy projects or self-representation.

To illustrate the issues involved in a women's way of practicing law, consider the following example. My colleague Grace Blumberg, an expert in marital property law, was asked to write the first draft of an amicus brief in a case involving the legal treatment of a professional degree in a community property regime. * * *

The story of this brief-writing exercise also reveals another aspect of the women's lawyering process—concern for the interconnection of personal and professional life. In the "interstices of work," the lawyers engaged in this project shared information about their personal lives and brought sustenance to each other (intellectually, emotionally and nutritionally). Virtually every report of women lawyers discusses the impact of personal lives on professional lives and vice versa, where one finds almost no such reports in the descriptions and ethnographies of male lawyers. The concern for the quality of life and the relation between one's work and one's personal life is consistent with the ethic of care and relationship exhibited by Gilligan's female subjects. To Jake, who can separate life and property, the division between work and the rest of one's life is easier. * * *

Perhaps the most salient feature of Portia's different voice is in the lawyer-client relationship, where the values of care and responsibility for others seem most directly applicable. Amy and Hilary, with their ability to "take the part of the other and submerge the self," may be able to enter the world of the client, thereby understanding more fully what the client desires and why, without the domination of what the lawyer perceives to be "in the client's best interest." More fully developed sensitivities to empathy and altruism, as reported by Gilligan and Noddings, may enable women lawyers to understand a fuller range of client needs and objectives. As we increasingly become aware that lawyers and clients may not have the same view of the world or what they want from that world, the ability to examine *all* of the client's perspective becomes even more significant. Where the Jakes of this world may make assumptions about the primacy of economic and efficiency considerations of their cases, the Amys and Hilarys may see a greater number of issues in the social, psychological and moral aspects. Of course, in a fully mature and integrated vision of lawyering all of these aspects of the case would be considered important, as noted by one of Gilligan's subjects:

> It is taking the time and energy to consider everything. To decide carelessly or quickly or on the basis of one or two factors when you know that there are other things that are important and that will be affected, that's immoral. The moral way to make decisions is by considering as much as you possibly can, as much as you know.

* * * [T]he tendency to personalize and contextualize problems may incline women lawyers to ask for more information on a broader range of subjects and thereby develop a fuller understanding of the context of the client's life. This, in turn, may make women better lawyers, especially in their relationships with clients and in their ability to see the human complexities of some legal problems. * * *

If Amy and Hilary use different considerations in their moral reasoning, would they create different ethical codes for the profession based on their different ways of engaging in moral reasoning? We have some evidence that Hilary would not place the same emphasis on the adversarial model of placing one's own client above the other if the result might be to hurt the other side (as well as to defeat a meritorious claim). Would Amy and Hilary have adopted the original Kutak Commission's proposal to increase the duty of a lawyer to reveal a client's wrongdoing if it caused harm to another? Would Amy and Hilary create rules about relationships between lawyers, based on mutual affiliation in the same profession, and requiring greater candor and fairness in dealing with each other? Would the conflict of interest rules or withdrawal from representation rules be different because of an ethic of care and affiliation that would lead to a different conception of client loyalty? Might a broader conception of the legal problem and its causes lead to less concern about the unauthorized practice of law and more toleration, if not encouragement, of work with other professionals and laypersons to solve those problems?

These are only a few of the available speculations about how our adversarial system might be affected by Portia's different voice. * * *

CATHERINE A. MACKINNON, *FEMINISM UNMODIFIED: DISCOURSES ON LIFE AND LAW* 205 (1987)

Why are women lawyers, feminists, siding with the pornographers? To be a lawyer orients you to power, probably sexually as well as in every other way. The law has a historical hostility to new ideas, hurt women, and social change. But more than that, we were let into this profession on the implicit condition that we would enforce the real rules: women kept out and down, sexual access to women enforced. These remain the rules whether you are in and up, and whether you practice it or have it practiced on you. It keeps the value of the most exceptional women high to keep other women out and down and on their backs with their legs spread. I may be missing something, but I don't see a lot of women lawyers, feminist or otherwise, selling their asses on the street or looking for a pornographer with a camera in order to fulfill their sexual agency and I don't think it is because they are sexually repressed. What law school does for you is this: it tells you that to become a lawyer means to forget your feelings, forget your community, most of all, if you are a woman, forget your experience. Become a maze-bright rat. Women lawyers as a group have not been much of an exception to this, except that they go dead in the eyes like ghetto children, unlike the men, who come out of law school glowing in the dark. Women who defend the pornographers are defending a source of their relatively high position among women under male supremacy, keeping all women, including them, an inferior class on the basis of sex, enforced by sexual force.

I really want you to stop your lies and misrepresentations of our position. * * * I want you to remember your own lives. I also really want you on our side. But, failing that, I want you to stop claiming that your liberalism, with its elitism, and your Freudianism, with its sexualized misogyny, has anything in common with feminism.

3. Religious Lawyering

[Question 1]

According to Professor Sanford Levinson, the dominant understanding of professionalism requires a lawyer to "bleach out" all personal characteristics, including religion, morality, race, gender, and other forms of identity.

(A) True

(B) False

[Question 2]

Under all of Professor Allegretti's models, a Christian lawyer must bring her religious values into her work as a lawyer.

(A) True

(B) False

[Question 3]

In her work at a large law firm, Professor Azizah al-Hibri found which area of practice most consistent with her values as a Muslim?

(A) Litigation

(B) Corporate transactions

(C) Securities regulation

(D) Trust and estates

[Question 4]

According to Professor Russell Pearce, all the streams of Judaism:

(A) agree that a Jew must bring her religion into her work.

(B) agree that a Jew must bring her religion into her work but only to the extent of observing Jewish holidays.

(C) reject the notion that a Jew must bring her religion into her work.

(D) take different positions with regard to the basic principle that a Jew must bring her religion into her work.

[Question 5]

Professor Robert Vischer identifies the following as irrefutable objections to religious lawyering:

(A) The threat to client autonomy.

(B) The threat to publicly accessible norms.

(C) The threat of illiberal communities.

(D) None of the above.

RUSSELL G. PEARCE, *THE JEWISH LAWYER'S QUESTION*,

27 Tex. Tech L. Rev. 1259, 1259-70 (1996)

* * * Religious identification is problematic for all lawyers as a result of the "professional project," or the process of creating and maintaining professional role. Sanford Levinson has described how the "professional project [of law] . . . 'bleach[es] out' . . . merely contingent aspects of the self, including the residue of particularistic socialization that we refer to as our 'conscience.'" As I have noted elsewhere, "rule of law implies that the quality of lawyering and of justice an individual receives does not depend on the group identity of the lawyer or judge." Lawyers are to take a neutral approach to their work, free of external group identifications, including their religion. Under the professional project, lawyers are fungible. No distinction exists among Christian, Jewish, Moslem, Hindu, and Buddhist lawyers who are not to permit their religion to intrude on their professional role. Indeed, injecting religion into the lawyer's work contravenes the professional project. Professionalism suggests that "Jewishness play no role" in a lawyer's work. * * *

ROBERT K. VISCHER, *HERETICS IN THE TEMPLE OF THE LAW: THE PROMISE AND PERIL OF THE RELIGIOUS LAWYERING MOVEMENT*,

19 J.L. & Religion 427, 427-33 (2004)

* * * [The professional project views lawyers as secular priests.] Not surprisingly, this * * * paradigm is not without its detractors, both inside and outside the legal profession. Among the most pressing challenges to its continued supremacy is an emerging awareness among many lawyers that their primary loyalty is not to the profession's stated vision of the good lawyer, but to their own faith tradition's stated vision of the good person. For many religious lawyers grappling with the all-encompassing reach and explanatory power of faith, the presumption that

they can or should bracket the dictates of their devotion when they are operating within the temple of law is a non-starter.

That the presumption is meeting resistance is evidenced by the tension accompanying the frequent overlap between the compulsions of faith and the compulsions of the profession. The tension is unmistakable when a state ethics board, requiring a devout Christian lawyer to represent a minor seeking an abortion without parental consent, reasons that religious beliefs are not a legitimate basis for declining a court appointment. It is also unmistakable when a lawyer who opposes capital punishment for religious reasons is faced with a death row client who wishes to forego all court challenges to the imposition of his sentence, when a Muslim litigator is expected to make an opposing witness look like a liar on the stand, even if she believes that the witness is testifying truthfully, or when a lawyer whose faith compels her to stand up for the oppressed is told by her client to initiate eviction proceedings against low-income tenants who lack alternative shelter. And on a broader stage, the tension is unmistakable when the leader of the Catholic Church seems to suggest publicly that Catholic divorce lawyers can remain Catholic, or can remain divorce lawyers, but cannot persist in both identities.

Such anecdotes, however, do not begin to capture the depth of many lawyers' faith-based resistance to the presumption of the priesthood paradigm. The increasingly visible resistance has an impact not only on the clients and causes lawyers take on, but also the means they employ in serving clients and the shaping they attempt to undertake of their clients' objectives. The pervasiveness of these lawyers' resistance can be seen in the legal academy's emerging cognizance of the "religious lawyering movement" as evidenced by an ever-expanding array of law review articles, books, conferences, and even entire law school institutes devoted to the subject. The movement directly challenges the notion, embodied in the priesthood of lawyers paradigm, that a lawyer's personal allegiances and affiliations should be irrelevant to her representation of clients.

* * * Religious lawyers do not function as atomistic conscientious objectors opposing the unitary leviathan of the profession. Increasingly, the profession itself seems more properly viewed as a host of competing and contrasting subcommunities of lawyers, and many of these subcommunities are explicitly religious in nature. By way of illustration:

> • The Christian Legal Society is a rapidly expanding organization "committed to loving and serving Jesus Christ and advocating justice and religious freedom." More than 4000 CLS members meet in local chapters designed as a "forum for Christian attorneys to have fellowship and to encourage one another in the faith and in the profession." Membership requires signing a statement of faith that entails a belief in the Bible as the inspired word of God, and belief in the deity, resurrection and personal return of Christ, among other tenets.

- The International Association of Jewish Lawyers and Jurists (IAJLJ) is "an international membership association of lawyers, judges, professors and students who join the organization because they share a commitment to its stated principles: justice, human rights and the rule of law as informed by Jewish ethics and Jewish values that come from the Jewish tradition." There are IAJLJ members in thirty countries, and six chapters in the United States. The organization wants "our members to feel that, not only are they supporting an organization that tries to do some good by joining, but they are enriching themselves by being able to affiliate in a way that combines their Jewish heritage, identity, in whatever way they define that, and their professionalism."

- The National Association of Muslim Lawyers was founded "to be the national representative of the Muslim legal profession," seeking to promote "the long-term well-being and successful integration of Muslims into American society."

- The Catholic Lawyers Guild and the St. Thomas More Society both consist of relatively independent local chapters of Catholic lawyers organized within a particular diocese. They provide a forum for fellowship and are responsible for organizing various events, most notably the annual Red Mass to mark the opening of the courts and the bestowing of the St. Thomas More Award. * * *

JOSEPH ALLEGRETTI, _CHRIST AND THE CODE: THE DILEMMA OF THE CHRISTIAN ATTORNEY_,

34 Cath. Law. 131 (1991)

In "Christ and Culture," a classic work on Christian ethics, H. Richard Niebuhr identified and evaluated a number of typical approaches that Christians have taken towards culture in society at large, ranging from the absolute rejection of secular culture in the name of Christ, to the whole-hearted embrace of secular culture on behalf of Christ. This essay is intended to adapt Niebuhr's typology and examine a number of approaches open to the Christian attorney as he or she seeks to balance the loyalty to God with the professional duties owed to courts, clients, and the public. How is the Christian attorney to render to Christ what is Christ's and to the Code what is the Code's? The word "Code" is used herein as shorthand to signify the basic principles of professional ethics that govern the attorney's work in our legal system. * * *

I. CHRIST AGAINST THE CODE

To be explored first is an adaption of Niebuhr's first model, what he called "Christ against culture." The first letter of John is a good example of the application of this model. It views the world as an evil place that the Christian must avoid. Secular society is rejected for the sake of Christ. This approach to culture is represented in some strands of monasticism, in groups like the Mennonites, and in the works of Tertullian and Leo Tolstoy.

When applied to the legal profession, the analogous model might be termed "Christ against the Code." Let me illustrate it with a story. I had been at divinity school only a few weeks when I met another student who was also a lawyer. She told me that she had quit the practice of law because she could not square it with her Christian beliefs. She had grown tired of being a "hired gun" whose job was to help clients avoid their moral obligations. "I couldn't be both a lawyer and a Christian," she told me. She even purported to have Biblical grounds for her view, in 1 Corinthians 6, where Paul expressed his dismay that Christians were bringing lawsuits against each other. Paul wrote that Christians should not bring each other before pagan courts, but should suffer wrong rather than seek a legal remedy.

There are other ways to read this passage, of course, in light of particular pastoral problems confronting Paul at Corinth. Few observers would adopt this student's reading, and fewer, if any, would consider the practice of law "off limits" to Christians. Nevertheless, the story illustrates one model of the relationship between Christ and the Code. This model bluntly insists that a Christian cannot be a lawyer. Christians are to have as little to do with the structures and institutions of secular society as possible. Between Christ and the Code is a gulf that cannot be bridged. In its more moderate form, this model may motivate those who seek to establish Christian tribunals, divorced from the normal legal process, in which Christians can resolve disputes between themselves through mediation and fraternal correction. This model deserves respect for its single-minded devotion to following Christ. At the same time, however, it risks forgetting that sin resides not just in social structures but also in the human heart, and that God is at work redeeming not only individuals but of all creation. It forgets that Christ came to reconcile all things to God, and that Christians are called to follow Him into the world and make disciples of all nations. Still, even for those of us who do not advocate this model, it can serve as a cautionary note. Have we been too quick to accommodate our religious beliefs to the dictates of our culture and our Codes? Have we sold out? Have we bought in?

II. CHRIST IN HARMONY WITH THE CODE

This leads the reader to a second model. Niebuhr writes about the "Christ of culture." According to this view, there is no tension at all between the Gospel and the world. Instead, Christian values are thought to be identical with the highest values of civilization. In the life and teachings of Jesus, we see the ultimate goal toward which the world is directed. Perhaps this model reached its culmination in nineteenth century liberal Protestantism, which so often saw Jesus as a Victorian gentlemen who came preaching liberty, tolerance, and evolutionary optimism. The values of democratic society were equated with the Gospel's central message.

As applied to the legal profession, one might call the analogous model "Christ in harmony with the Code." Its adherents see no conflict between their work as lawyers and their lives as Christians. When lawyers act in accordance with the standard paradigm, they not only avoid legal trouble, but they act in a manner that is "fundamentally right." The Code itself embodies a morally appropriate vision of the lawyer's role. Thus, it seems to raise no ethical problem if a lawyer makes an honest witness look like a liar, or reveals only that portion of the truth favorable to the lawyer's client, or defends what he or she knows to be an unjust cause. Under these principles, what the Code says you can do, you can do, and what the Code says you must do, you must do, so to speak. It is this understanding that underlies the model of "Christ in harmony with the Code." There is no tension between Christian values and professional life, because the practice of law serves noble ends, or is noble in and of itself. By fulfilling the lawyer's role in the adversary system, the attorney can be confident that he or she is in fact doing what is "good and right" in the eyes of God.

This interpretation has its own strengths. Initially, it reminds us that the whole world is the arena in which God's kingdom is being realized. It recognizes that God is at work in institutions as well as in individuals. Concurrently, however, it gives rise to a risk that whatever is acceptable to the wider culture will come to be perceived as "God's will." No longer would it be presumed that Christ sits in judgment upon culture. The end result may be that "loyalty to contemporary culture [will have] so far qualified the loyalty to Christ that he [will have] been abandoned in favor of an idol called by [H]is name."

This model presents risks for the Christian lawyer as well. It can lead the attorney to abdicate moral responsibility for his or her actions, which in turn can lead to the collapse of the lawyer's moral universe. It is suspected that society's recognition of this moral abdication results in much of the criticism levied at the legal profession and to the scathing attacks on lawyers as "prostitutes," "mouthpieces," or "hired guns."

III. CHRIST IN TENSION WITH THE CODE

Cynics and skeptics might assume that all lawyers fit the description of this second model. But the author's experience is that many attorneys are aware of the unavoidable tension between Christ and the Code. They wish to be both good people and good lawyers, and come to realize that the two may not be identical. It is suggested that once an attorney begins to reflect upon the problem of serving two masters, the attorney no longer fits within this second model. Instead, a third model needs to be considered, based upon what Niebuhr called "Christ and culture in paradox."

This third paradigm lies between the first two. The first, the reader will recall, rejects the secular world as incompatible with Christian values. The second accepts the secular world as embodying Christian values. Our third model avoids this "either/or" for a "both/and" approach, but it does have some similarities to each. Like the first model, it admits that human culture is sinful, and to be involved with it leads to sin. Like the second, it insists that our sinful world is sustained and redeemed by a loving God. Christian theologians who favor this model are fond of paradoxical language. They juxtapose law and grace, God's wrath and God's mercy. They describe the individual as simultaneously both saint and sinner. This supposition can be seen variously in the theology of Augustine, Martin Luther and Reinhold Niebuhr. Christians inhabit two worlds, a private realm in which they relate to God as individuals and are bound by the teachings of Christ, and a public realm in which they live and work and must make accommodations to the sinfulness of the human condition. Christ and culture are in conflict, yet each must be obeyed. Hence, the Christian is subject to two moralities, and must live "precariously and sinfully in the hope of a justification which lies beyond history."

This model has its own advantages. It is frank about the moral ambiguities and the interwoven joys and tragedies of everyday life. It captures the central insight of the Reformers-that nothing we can do can make us right with God. That, however, is the whole point. While we were yet sinners, Christ died for us and reconciled us to God. As applied to the legal profession, one might call the analogous model "Christ in tension with the Code." Here, the attorney admits that sometimes he or she does things that a nonlawyer should not do. The attorney admits that "ordinary" morality would sometimes condemn the attorney's actions. The lawyer argues, however, that everyday morality is not applicable to professional life. The attorney's professional obligations give rise to a unique set of concerns. As an agent of the client, the lawyer should be judged solely by the rules of legal ethics embodied in the Code. According to Richard Wasserstrom, the result is that the lawyer becomes, in essence, an "amoral technician," who inhabits a moral world far simpler and less ambiguous than the moral world of everyday life. It becomes easy to "turn aside so many ostensibly difficult moral dilemmas and decisions with the reply: but that is not my concern; my job as a lawyer is not to judge the rights and wrong[s] of the client or the cause; it is to defend as best I can my client's interests."

As in our second model, the appeal to the principles of zealousness and nonaccountability remain. But there is a difference. The individual in the second model has no doubts that a good lawyer can also be a good Christian, while the lawyer in the third model hopes that it is possible to be both, fears that it is not, and knows no way out of the dilemma. The result can be a kind of "moral schizophrenia." The attorney compartmentalizes his or her life. The public and private dimensions of life are separated and the attorney concludes that his or her Christian values apply only to the private. On the professional side of life the lawyer insists that he or she be judged only by the rules of the legal profession.

Such a situation is inherently unstable. Something has to give, and it is no surprise that studies indicate that if a lawyer argues positions that conflict with personal values, over time those values will change. * * *

IV. CHRIST TRANSFORMING THE CODE

As a final model, Niebuhr writes of "Christ transforming culture." In some ways this resembles our third model. It also recognizes that culture is sinful, yet acknowledges that Christians have obligations to culture. Unlike the third model, however, this one claims that the Christian need not be immobilized between the demands of Christ and the demands of culture. The Christian is one under the power of Christ, and Christ is the one who redirects and reinvigorates our world. The Gospel is seen as penetrating all of life, converting both people and institutions.

This model is exemplified in Christian theology in the philosophies of Augustine and John Calvin. It is suggested that this model has a strong Biblical foundation as well. Jesus teaches that the kingdom of God has arrived. "It is presently in our midst, growing like a mustard seed, penetrating all of life. It is here, but it is not yet fully realized." Lawyers who maintain analogous views conform to the model I will call "Christ transforming the Code." Such talk is admittedly imprecise. Critics of Niebuhr have commented at length on the slipperiness of terms like "transformation" and "conversion." Vital questions remain unanswered. What does it mean to say that Christ is at work transforming culture? What counts as evidence? And how would this apply to the work of lawyers?

Despite these difficulties, this model at least recognizes that Christ is the Lord of all, even those in the legal profession, and that Christians are called to serve Him in their private and professional lives. Moreover, this model has the great advantage of rejecting the artificial separation of life into private and public realms, with religion limited to the former. The Christian attorney is to bring his or her values into the workplace, with the hope and trust that these values might revitalize and transform the lawyer's relationships and, ultimately, the profession itself. The lawyer is not a "hired gun," or an "amoral technician," and cannot avoid moral responsibility for his or her actions by resorting to professional rules and roles. The attorney is a "moral agent," whose actions have moral consequences for which the attorney is responsible, not just personally and to others, but ultimately to God.

This model is unfamiliar to most attorneys. Its implications are uncertain. It seems to threaten traditional attorney-client relations. Let me try to advance the discussion by briefly sketching three avenues for reflection. Each is an attempt to realize the goal of a legal profession transformed by the saving power of Christ.

A. The Lawyer's Vocation

First, it is suggested that we need to take a fresh look at the concept of "vocation." A "professional" is what one professes to be, but a vocation is what one is called to be, what God calls one to be. Luther and Calvin were aware that any occupation can be a calling if its primary motive is to serve God and neighbor. In an insightful article, Charles Kammer has argued that the concept of vocation can serve as a check upon the tendency of professionals like doctors and lawyers to prefer their own self-interest to the public good." According to Kammer, a profession that understands itself as a vocation "can escape many of the problems generated by . . . narrow self-interest because it is governed by a higher vision of the purposes the profession is intended to serve.'" As the professional is liberated from self-interest, he or she is set free to serve others. Work becomes an avenue of discipleship to Christ. "Our vocation becomes that of loving our neighbor through our occupation."

Still, several questions come to mind. Does it make sense to talk of a "lawyer's vocation"? In what ways can a lawyer's work be a vehicle of service to God and neighbor? More concretely, how would viewing law as a vocation affect the attorney's relationship to clients, courts, and adversaries? What would be the impact on the standard paradigm of legal ethics and the principles of zealousness and nonaccountability?

B. The Lawyer as Prophet

A second approach would be to focus on the traditional Biblical notions of priest and prophet. Sociologists have been quick to point out that the legal system plays a cultic role in society. It is the mechanism by which society resolves conflicts that threaten the social fabric. It has its own myths and rituals, its own language, its own garb. To the layperson, the legal system can be a mysterious dispenser of blind justice. In the "temple" of the law, the courthouse, lawyers and judges are the priests. Yet we know from the Scripture—from Jeremiah, Ezekiel, and Jesus—that priests can also be prophets. Lawyering can be seen not only as a priestly profession, but as an avenue for prophetic ministry. Generally speaking, a prophet interprets the signs of the time in the light of faith, and speaks God's word for that time and place. The prophet criticizes people and institutions, but not as an outsider. The prophet stands with the sinful as one of the sinful, confronting the terrible majesty of God's justice. At the same time, the prophet holds out a vision of God's mercy and faithfulness, and of the new life possible on the other side of judgment.

The task of the prophet "is to bring to expression the new realities against the more visible area of the old order.'" "The prophet offers an alternative vision of reality based upon God's freedom and God's will for justice." What would it mean to claim a prophetic role for lawyers? What is the alternative perception of reality to which they might point? First and foremost, the acceptance of a prophetic role would mean a new commitment by lawyers to the just distribution of legal services. In today's America, the poor have little access to legal counsel, and the middle-class is finding it increasingly difficult to afford legal assistance. As long as legal representation is a commodity to be purchased like any other, those who can afford lawyers will have them, and those who cannot will be left without the means to assert their legal rights. As the old law school adage goes, a right without a remedy is no right at all. Legal rights without the means to enforce them are a sham.

Although there have been a few notable exceptions, by and large, lawyers in America have served as defenders of wealth, power, and entrenched privilege. An appreciation of their prophetic role would spark a new concern for the weak and poor, those who have little voice in today's system. It would lead lawyers to question the prevailing assumption that pro bono work is a deed of charity rather than a duty of justice. Furthermore, this prophetic role shines new light on the ethical problems that lawyers confront in their daily practice. A heightened sense of social justice, for example, would force attorneys to reexamine their cherished commitment to the standard paradigm. Perhaps unqualified loyalty to the client produces injustice and social harm. Perhaps attorneys should no longer be immune from moral criticism for the ends they achieve or the means they employ. The prophetic dimension raises disturbing questions about the social and personal costs of the principles of zealousness and nonaccountability.

A prophetic role for Christian attorneys would build upon the rich legacy of the Hebrew prophets. Amos, Isaiah, and the others refused to separate worship of God from the duty to help those who could not help themselves. They attacked all who trampled the poor, turned aside the needy, exploited the weak, and corrupted the legal process. Indeed, the plea of Isaiah could almost serve as a credo for the Christian attorney: "Make justice your aim; redress the wronged, hear the orphan's plea, defend the widow." Jeremiah put it succinctly—to know God is to do justice to the poor and needy.

C. An Ethic of Care

Finally, one might follow the lead of Thomas Shaffer, and begin to explore a vision of lawyering which puts less stress on the dictates of position and more on the duty to care. The conventional wisdom too often views lawyers as possessing only two options when they have moral qualms about their client's case. The lawyer must commit to do everything legally possible to win for the client or withdraw from the case. This view of the lawyer-client relationship assumes that lawyers and clients are morally isolated from each other, and do not influence each other. Neither is open to change. Reality is quite to the contrary. An ethic of care recognizes that lawyers and clients are not morally autonomous. They are not islands unto themselves.

As they come together they become mutually dependent. In their dependence each is open to change. Conversion is possible. What Buber called the "I-Thou" relation can emerge. Openness, risk and vulnerability characterize such a relationship. The recognition of an ethic of care would produce an epochal shift in lawyering, away from the amoral provision of technical assistance, towards service to the client as a person. Shaffer writes:

> The broader professional consequences could be revolutionary: Lawyers would have to become morally attentive, attending, that is, to the persons of their clients as much as to the problems clients bring to them. Law students would come to insist on education which trains them in the skills of sincerity, congruence, and acceptance. Every level of the legal enterprise would come again to think of moral development as part of its task, all toward a professional ethic of receiving as well as giving-of unfurling rather than imposing, to use Buber's phrase.

Such an ethic ultimately rests upon the conviction that God is at work in all human relationships, and therefore all things are possible. God is the "invisible third party" in every human encounter. Again, we need to consider the impact of such a view on traditional attorney-client relationships. Would an ethic of care intrude upon client autonomy? How would it inform the attorney's approach to particular ethical duties like confidentiality? Would lawyers who adopted an ethic of care become more or less committed to the principles of zealousness and nonaccountability? Is an ethic of care even possible? Perhaps an attorney can have a relationship of openness and vulnerability with a flesh-and- blood client, but what about the attorney who represents a corporation, a union, a pension board? An ethic of care is inherently tentative and open-ended. It provides no definitive answers to ethical questions, because only in the give-and-take of the relationship can the morally responsible course of action be discerned. Nevertheless, it deserves further exploration by those who seek an integration of the personal values and professional life of the attorney.

Is it actually an attempt to bring the force of the Gospel message to bear upon the lawyer-client relationship? Here, perhaps, is the seed for a new understanding of the Christian lawyer, a hired gun no longer, but (dare I say it?) a minister to his or her clients.

* * *

AZIZAH AL-HIBRI, *ON BEING A MUSLIM CORPORATE LAWYER*,

27 Tex. Tech L. Rev. 947 (1996)

It is not easy for me to discern the ways in which my faith has informed my professional life. I have been shielded from this awareness for most of my adult life by thick layers of subconscious denial. The interesting antecedent question thus becomes: "Why did I feel the need to deny, to shield myself from a recognition of the relationship between my faith and my profession?" Upon reflection, the puzzling answer I settle upon is: "Because I am trying to be a good American Muslim."

Clearly, this paradoxical answer needs some elaboration. I have denied the impact of my faith on my professional life because I am a good American Muslim. Yet, as every religious person will readily admit, being religious is central to one's life. You cannot, for example, decide to be dishonest in the office and a good Muslim, Christian or Jew at home. Religion just does not work that way. It provides you with a worldview, complete with a set of moral and other rules that are supposed to permeate every aspect of your life and inform your daily practices.

In particular, my religion requires me to be a law-abiding citizen. To do so in the United States, I have to abide by the constitutional principle of the separation of Church and State. I have been told that this principle requires me to drive a wedge between my public activities and my faith. Consequently, to be a good American Muslim, I have had to be less of a person of faith, at least less publicly so.

This is the existential paradox I and other people of faith find ourselves in. For example, Archbishop John Hughes made the following statement at Saint Patrick's day over a hundred years ago: "Well, there is but one rule for a Catholic wherever he is, and that is to do his duty there as a citizen." At the time he made that statement, the good archbishop was no doubt aware of the potential tensions between being a good Catholic and being a good citizen in a secular state. Some Christians have even found the very ideology of nationalism as objectionable on religious grounds. Nevertheless, religious people in this country seem to have somehow reached an acceptable *modus operandi*.

Recognizing one aspect of this paradox, Stephen Carter writes: "We have created a political and legal culture that presses the religiously faithful to be other than themselves, to act publicly, and sometimes privately as well, as though their faith does not matter to them." His view echoes a statement by De Tocqueville who pointed out as early as the Nineteenth Century, that "[i]n America religion is a distinct sphere, in which the priest is sovereign, but out of which he takes care never to go." Thus, compartmentalization of faith into private life has been a basic feature of this society for a long time. In this Symposium I, an immigrant who came to the United States from Lebanon three decades ago, am being asked to describe the ways in which I have failed to compartmentalize my faith.

A First Level of Analysis

Glancing quickly at my recent past, I notice that when I practiced corporate law on Wall Street, I did not assess it from an Islamic vantage point, whatever that might be. Similarly, I do not offer today a religious critique of the subject when I teach it. I teach about the legal aspects of modern business in America; I do not judge these aspects. I take them as I find them. In other words, as an American citizen, I have thoroughly internalized the demand to compartmentalize the religious aspects of my life. I have not failed in being a good citizen.

Yet now that the door of recollection and reflection has been opened on this subject, I look back for the first time at my days as a practitioner with greater compassion and understanding. I begin discerning many levels of analysis regarding that experience. I start with the most obvious one which relies on the basic religious principles of fairness and hard work. I recall the first agreement I drafted. I had looked at all the precedents and found them lacking. The document related to a big deal and time was of the essence. I therefore felt that drafting a fair agreement that took into account the interests of both parties would get us to the finish line faster. That was of course the first big strategic mistake. The other was to make certain language in the agreement clear and precise.

I was soon reminded that our legal system is based on an adversarial way of doing things. Consequently, I should have looked out solely for the interests of my client and let the other lawyer look after the interest of hers. If she failed to do so adequately, then that only meant that our client had the better lawyers. I also learned that I should have left the ambiguity in the language where such ambiguity worked in favor of my client. I was reminded that these were the rules of the game, but they still did not come to me naturally.

Upon reflection, I now realize that subconsciously I was playing by different rules. As a person of faith I had already internalized my own religious values, which demanded fairness. The Qur'an is replete with statements asking us to deal with others fairly. Some verses refer specifically to commercial contexts. For example, one verse states: "And O my people! give just measure and weight, Nor withhold from the people the things that are their due . . . ." Another enjoins us to "[g]ive just measure, and cause no loss (to others by fraud). And weigh with scales true and upright. And withhold not things justly due to [people], nor do evil in the land, working mischief."

Notice that the last verse mentions commercial injustice in the same passage as doing evil in the land and working mischief. Also, notice that the verse does not permit one to shift the responsibility for achieving justice to others, such as the other person's lawyer. Being just is one's own burden. Now as I already said, I wanted to be a good citizen. Subconsciously, I did not want to be party to an injustice in my country which is akin to working mischief. Sure, I was being paid handsomely by my law firm. Yes, the firm was not being unethical by professional standards. To the contrary, it would have been remiss if it did not zealously represent the interests of its client. Yes, zealous representation has been interpreted by the profession to mean, in the context of corporate law, drafting a document which tilts scales and measures in one's own client's favor. Still, I had problems.

I had difficulty with the common understanding of the concept of zealous representation. I had difficulty with the adversarial system. I had difficulty with common negotiation tactics, starting from those that keep the other side waiting for hours and ending with those that start serious negotiations only when the other side is ready to go to bed. All of these appeared to derive from a worldview based on domination and manipulation which was foreign to my religious beliefs. I know that I am not alone in my aversion. Many lawyers have pondered these issues. Some have found a way to adjust to secular legal realities. Others continue to resist in various ways.

As for my job security at the firm, the Qur'an says that it is God who determines our financial destinies and that we should not give up our principles for money. Sound like the Bible? You bet; same God, same principles. So how is it that I was surrounded at the law firm with Christians and Jews who appeared not to be conflicted about this matter? I do not know, but I have to say that the turn-over rate is high at these firms despite the great financial rewards. Could it be the subconscious of some of these lawyers is at work? Is that why the term "hired gun" evokes such negative reactions in us?

I wanted to be in corporate law because I believe in private enterprise. Private enterprise fits nicely with my religious beliefs. The Qur'an recognizes legitimate profit and the fact that people have different levels of wealth. In fact, it discusses business in several places. The Prophet himself, as well as his wife Khadija, were successful business people. What the Qur'an warns against, however, is making a profit by taking unfair advantage of others. It also denounces elevating the profit motive above faith. For this reason, it tells Muslims that it is better for them to pray when it is time for prayer, than to do business. God's "business," it notes, is much more profitable.

Working on Wall Street, it was "business" eighteen to twenty four hours a day. It was the height of market activity, and law firms were leveraging their human resources to the hilt. Driven by the Qur'anic injunction to do my job well, I put in long hours. But my firm and I were not quite on the same page. The firm wanted to maximize its profits, while offering quality services. I wanted to oblige. Yet, I was hampered in my efforts by my ambivalence about the system. I also had no time to do God's "business." There was no time to perform my five daily prayers, even in a corner of my office. It was not possible to fast the month of Ramadan or even celebrate my holidays. How could I when I had to work and bill every working moment of my long days and nights? I couldn't even get sick!

There was, however, one bright spot in my law firm experience. There was one area of the law that (subconsciously) suited my values quite well, that of securities regulation. This area of the law came into existence in order to protect public interest. For this end, full and adequate disclosure (in religious terms, telling the truth) by issuers of securities was required. I therefore launched into this difficult area of the law with a great deal of zest. In fulfilling the injunction of doing my work well, I spent long careful hours conducting due diligence and drafting documents, so that the public interest would be properly protected. I flourished doing that kind of work, I withered doing deals.

In due course, however, I concluded that the world of law firms had something fundamentally wrong with it. It was based on a system of substantive hierarchy or domination (as opposed to a merely formal one). Combined with the principle of maximizing profit to partners (at the top of the hierarchy), the system created a great deal of misery among aspiring lawyers.

The issue of hierarchy is a very significant issue for me as a Muslim feminist. Let me take the time to discuss it. In the story of the fall of Satan, we are told that God asked Satan and the angels to bow to Adam. The angels did, but Satan refused. He objected saying: "I am better than he, [you created] me from fire and [created him] from clay." This Satanic arrogance which led to challenging the Divine Will resulted in God cursing Satan.

The story has become an important symbol of what is wrong with arrogance and hierarchy. Al-Ghazali, a major Muslim jurist from the Tenth Century, states that in Islam, the rich are not better than the poor, nor are the white better than the black. These categories, he argues, are all irrelevant in the eyes of God, but they can imbue a person with a feeling of false power and arrogance, leading him to disobey God and to posit himself or another entity as a false deity. This is why wealth has often been referred to in the Qur'an as a trial or a temptation (as well as a blessing). In another passage, the Qur'an tells the story of two friends. One of them became quite arrogant about his wealth. He told his poor friend: "[I have more wealth] than you, and more honour and power in my following of [people]." God destroyed his wealth overnight.

These kinds of stories are hard to ignore. They are part of one's religious consciousness. Yet, with few exceptions among the old guard, there is increasingly no room for modesty on Wall Street. In fact, arrogance is an important indication of one's stature. A partner for example is less likely to return your greeting than an associate. Indeed, that is one way to tell the two apart. Yet the Prophet encouraged us to greet each other. He also encouraged us to return the greeting with an even better one.

It is dehumanizing to be in an oppressive hierarchy, regardless of your level within the corporation. But it is most dehumanizing for those at the lower end. After several years of practice, I felt that my mind was slipping. I no longer knew whether the mind which had produced many works in the area of philosophy was capable of any further original thinking. I felt drained, saddened and oppressed. When I returned to academia, I felt engulfed by sublime sunshine. I celebrated my liberation with several articles. I knew in a very fundamental way how much of a blessing it was to be free again.

My religious beliefs worked (again subconsciously) to my advantage in academia. There, I could pursue the prophetic injunction that learning is the duty of every Muslim, female and male. So, I tried to keep abreast of all legal developments and do my best toward all my students. Significantly, I was able to do so without being conflicted. I derive great pleasure out of teaching securities regulation and imbuing in my students the ethical values important for a lawyer in this area. I also enjoy teaching corporate law and encouraging my students to take private enterprise seriously. I stay away from teaching negotiating tactics.

I have been uplifted by my school's commitment to diversity. This too springs from my commitment to the principle of fundamental human equality which is another lesson of the story about Satan. Satan thought that being made from fire made him superior to Adam, who was made from clay. His belief was so unshakable that he was willing to risk God's wrath. But there is only one God. Everyone else is God's creature. To forget that is to move away from the true essence of monotheism and fall into Satanic logic. Thus, I celebrate diversity in the classroom by treating it as a very average thing. I treat my students with respect and concern, because they are God's creatures too. I have never consciously tried to place a substantive hierarchal relation between us. The results have been good for all.

I have also been finally able to do my job as well as my religion requires of me. I know I work harder than my students in preparing for each class meeting, regardless of how many times before I have taught the subject matter. I pay special attention to women in my class who take the course not because they want to, but because they need it for the bar exam. They often come to my office and shyly reveal their secret. They really have no interest or prior experience in corporate law. They would rather "help people." I think, on the other hand, that perhaps we can help people by placing more of these concerned and compassionate individuals in corporate America. So, I reveal to them that I knew nothing about corporations when I took my first course in law school, and that I ended up working in that area for many years in major law firms. I ask them to give the subject a real chance. My personal revelation almost invariably imbues them with confidence. Many do very well. Some get the top grades.

Two other principles inform my classroom teaching. The first principle is that a Muslim scholar may not hide her knowledge from others. I do not, and in doing so I can finally draft lectures (and articles) that embrace clarity with vengeance. Free at last! I have never subscribed (even as a philosopher) to the school of mystification of knowledge. Not only do I prepare lectures that are as clear as I can make them, but I also tailor the lectures to the special interests of the student group. Consequently, while the same material is covered every term, the lectures and class discussion can be quite different.

Furthermore, abiding by this principle of clarity works well for students, especially those who are either hostile towards or intimidated by the subject. It helps them develop their business intuitions. I also tell them repeatedly that "profit" is not a bad word. It enables one to help others. It works.

The second principle is that of modesty. I had learned that principle from my faith, and had it reaffirmed during my life as a philosophy professor. There is nothing shameful about being wrong. Only God is right every time. What is shameful is to hide the fact that you are wrong or refuse to be corrected. One famous Muslim jurist, Imam Malik Bin Anas, made this point with endearing modesty. He said: "I am only human. At times I am right, at others I am wrong. So, look into my opinion critically . . . ." Khalifah 'Umar wrote his appointed judge Abu Musa al-Ash'ari advising him not to be bound even by the judge's own precedent, once the judge has concluded that it was erroneous. 'Umar added in the same letter, "correcting oneself is better than persevering in the wrong." In short, there is no such thing as incorrigible human knowledge.

This view of the human condition, as well as my commitment to the principle of fundamental human equality, has helped me act in a democratic fashion in my classes. I am always good for a serious argument. I am always willing to be convinced that the other point of view is better. But the student had better work hard at making her point and making it well, after all she is arguing with a logician. This approach has brought life into the classroom and reduced the level of alienation inherent in the role of being a student. Obviously, teaching works much better for me than practice, and it shows.

A Second Level of Analysis

Despite the rewards and pleasures of academia, the tension between my faith and profession is not totally eliminated. Certain problems remain. These relate more to the substance of what I am teaching, rather than the surrounding working conditions.

I go back to corporate law. In that course, I teach my students about a system of financial organization which is primarily driven by the profit motive. I emphasize to them that a corporation is not a welfare institution. If profitability is down, then serious reexamination should follow. Perhaps a restructuring is in order. In that case many employees may lose their jobs. Here, I inject some discussion about the possible rights of stakeholders in a company, I even introduce the views of progressive corporate law advocates. Thus, I try to open the students' thinking to alternative ways of looking at the corporate structure, without distorting the basic facts about that structure as it operates today.

But how do people of faith feel about the fact that profit is the primary driving force in corporate America today? They have mixed feelings. Walter Wink, a respected Christian theologian, has addressed this issue. In his award-winning book *Engaging the Powers,* he notes that what characterizes our society is the unique value ascribed to money. He is very troubled by that fact, which he views as part of a "domination system." That domination system, he observes, consists of an entire network of powers becoming integrated around idolatrous values. He concludes that Satan is the presiding spirit of the domination system. This kind of language is reminiscent of al-Ghazali's analysis of the story of the fall of Satan. The singular commitment to the pursuit of wealth posits an alternative god with a whole different morality.

Clearly, the worship of wealth is idolatry, but the pursuit of wealth need not be synonymous with its worship. Consequently, what is needed is not a rejection of wealth, but a rejection of values that make it possible for a human being to regard wealth as an end in itself. We need to regain a worldview which sees society as an integral whole in which the wealthy have a duty to share part of their resources with the less privileged. We need a system which does not dehumanize workers. But such a refinement in values will require significant changes in the existing legal system itself. It will not, however, require a total rejection of the legal and business status quo.

It is important to note that in seeking such changes, religionists are not alone. Many lawyers and economists have presented humanist secular reasons for the modification of the existing system. These arguments are usually based on the high social costs of the present arrangements and the false or arbitrary assumptions on which they rest.

The Qur'an tells us that God extends wealth to whomever God pleases. God also warns us against accumulating wealth in our coffers instead of helping others. The Qur'an repeatedly states that those who are needy and deprived have a "recognized right" (*haqq ma'lum*) in the wealth of a Muslim. Under this Qur'anic view, to be rich is a blessing (and a temptation) which affords a person the opportunity to do good deeds.

Coming from a religious family which has engaged in business for centuries, I have respect for both religion and business. I also understand that it was profit earned from this business which enabled my family to establish charitable institutions. These institutions continue to exist to this day and have benefitted countless people over the years. Thus my religious beliefs do not conflict with my worldly belief in profitable business.

Consequently, I view this debate about profit as akin to that other debate about whether technology is good or bad. It is not the technology. It is human values. Similarly, it is not the money, it is how you view it, as a means to help others or as an end in itself. Both attitudes are consistent with a general corporate goal of maximizing profits within certain acceptable parameters, but they lead to drastically different consequences. So, it is not the substantive aspects of corporate law that trouble me. These may need some further refinement and development, but they are not fundamentally problematic. It is the student learning this body of law who needs to have her values straight.

Are there other troublesome points in corporate law? At this point of the discussion I am inclined to submerge any further thoughts on this issue. Subconsciously, I am concerned that opening this theological Pandora's box could make it impossible for me to teach a traditional introductory class on corporations. If I end up having problems with basic assumptions on which corporate law rests, where do I go from there? So, I tend to shut down my critical powers. Like the law firms, I opt for lack of clarity as the solution. So do many other people of faith in this country.

But this approach does not work. The door to my subconscious has been opened and ideas keep rushing out. So, I turn to this example. I teach about interest and how it works. Am I teaching my students how to engage in *riba* (usury), or is interest a different concept? This issue is not unique to Muslim Americans. It also is familiar to Christians and Jews. Also, since many modern Muslim countries have adopted the same financial and legal structures we have in the United States, what have they done about interest? Have Christians and Muslims succumbed to secularist practices on this issue and abdicated their religious responsibility, or have they resolved matters satisfactorily?

While some thinkers may be said to have abdicated their religious responsibility in the pursuit of secular modernity, others have made a serious attempt at a reconciliation. On the particular question of interest, debate was heated in Muslim communities for quite a while. Finally, some jurisprudentially acceptable solutions were worked out, which were consistent with the over-all global business and legal structures.

Certain jurists distinguished between the concept of *riba* and the modern concept of interest. Others defined new financial instruments or relations having a similar financial effect as the ones involving an interest-bearing loan. For example, Muhammad Anwar, a Muslim economist, describes many alternative ways which Muslim banks devised in order to do business without falling into *riba.* These include *musharaka,* where the bank is an active partner with the borrower and shares in the profit and loss of his enterprise; *murabaha,* where the bank buys the goods and resells them to the borrower at cost plus an agreed upon profit; and *qard hassanah,* which is a straight forward interest-free loan.

At the same time, other thinkers have found jurisprudential bases for permitting Muslims in the West to become parties to agreements involving interest-bearing instruments. They did so by relying on well-established Islamic principles, such as the principle of necessity. This principle permits a Muslim to even consume pork if that is the only available food. It is founded on express statements in the Qur'an and, more generally, on the fundamental principle of jurisprudence that the Law Giver's intent (*makasid al-shari'*) in prescribing laws is public interest (the "Public Interest Principle").

For some Muslims, some or all of these solutions remain questionable, for others they are acceptable articulations of Islamic law under existing circumstances. The concept of "existing circumstances" is itself an important concept which is broadly defined. Existing circumstances in Muslim countries are usually understood to include not only the need of the local Islamic monetary system to interact with the global one, but more importantly, a variety of internal conditions within the country itself.

In particular, the Islamic financial system is supposed to be an integral part of an overarching social and political order characterized at minimum by the principles of *takaful* and *shura.* The first principle asserts the collective responsibility of the community in meeting the basic needs of every one of its members. The second principle insures the basic right of every citizen to a democratic government. In the absence of one or both of these principles, the application of certain Islamic laws may well result in undue hardship to many. But, when conditions distort or reverse the intended outcome, a modification is permissible under the Public Interest Principle, so long as such conditions persist.

The position of a Muslim in a non-Muslim country is complicated by additional or different considerations for various other issues. An American Muslim recognizes the fact that she lives in a society that has in some areas a set of rules that she may disagree with. What should a Muslim do about that? Actually, no more than what any other person (religious or not) is expected to do. If these different rules are patently unfair, discriminatory or otherwise impose a hardship on the person in the exercise of her own religion, then she should try to change these rules. If every possibility of meaningful change is rejected by the majority, then the Muslim is encouraged to move to a community which is more in tune with her values. After all, many prophets of the past left their homeland for similar reasons. If there is no such community to be found or if it is not possible for the Muslim to relocate, then the principle of necessity may apply.

Living by one's religious beliefs turns out, however, not to be a problem for the American Muslim. An American Muslim lives in a society which shares the basic principles taught by Islam. It is a society which believes in and practices democratic governance. It is a society which believes in *takaful,* although it has not settled yet the question of whether such social responsibility should be the domain of the government or the private sector. Finally, it is a society which has constitutional guarantees for the freedom of worship. Ideally, a person of faith does not have to leave this country in order to avoid religiously oppressive laws. She only needs to go to court. A Muslim can thus be quite comfortable in this religiously diverse society because she has a place at the table like everyone else and, furthermore, she likes the table manners.

But what about the difficult question of interest? Muslims who hold the view that financial institutions in the United States violate their religious rules, can remedy the situation by establishing their own interest-free financial institutions, or by extending *qard hasanah* to each other. In fact, such developments have taken place within the community, although I am not clear about their extent. But the practice does not seem to represent a significant enough development to cover in my main stream course about finance. Furthermore, all students, Muslim and non-Muslim alike, need to understand the basic financial structure in this country in order to function in the business world successfully. They do not have to like the system, they do not have to borrow on terms that offend them, but they do need to know about it. So, I have no religious problem to teach about how interest works in our society.

From this vantage point, corporate law generally becomes a collection of rules to manage the marketplace in a presumably faith-neutral way. It provides a wide umbrella under which people of faith and secularists can come and do business together. I can thus teach it without being conflicted. I can also refuse, in practice, to avail myself of those aspects of corporate law that I find troubling. The latter, however, is a personal decision, not a matter of instruction.

Furthermore, had I been teaching a course in international business and finance, I would probably find it interesting to include some lectures on Islamic banking which is now in existence in many parts of the world. I would, for example, inform my students that the number of Islamic banks around the world has grown fifty folds within the last ten years, with Malaysia leading the way. Since 1993, Malaysia has increased its Islamic institutions from three to thirty-nine.

During that same period, banking deposits increased from 249 million Ringgits to one billing, 700 million Ringgits. It appears that Islamic banking works and that depositors are pleased with the results.

The Third Level of Analysis

The first level of analysis focused on principles involved in the practice and teaching of corporate law. The second level of analysis focused on substantive issues in corporate law. But the third level of analysis goes beyond the previous two by focusing on the way in which a belief system or worldview invariably transmutes the "raw data" received. The argument in this third level is that regardless of anyone's best efforts, it is simply not possible to experience the world "objectively," that there is no such thing as "objectivity" and that consequently, neither our laws nor our interpretation of them are "objective." Therefore, the whole project of separation of Church and State is in a very important sense metaphysically flawed and epistemically impossible.

This is not a ground-breaking claim, except perhaps in its application to corporate law. Many scientists, philosophers, feminists and others have argued repeatedly and convincingly, that there is no such thing as purely objective data. In particular, feminists initially had difficulty supporting their claim that science was "infected" with a male-perspective. This claim was extremely questionable because it was intended as an attack on that branch of knowledge that is considered to be the epitome of "objectivity." The scientific method, we all thought, allowed no room for bias. It simply calculated and reflected what was out there. In time, however, feminists succeeded in developing a very enlightening critique in support of their thesis. In the words of Nancy Tuana, a philosophy professor,

By practicing the scientific method, scientists are believed to be detached from their personal motives or expectations, and simply report facts. Given this model of science, the idea that knowledge or reason could be gendered was nonsense.

Feminists, in company with other theorists, have rejected this image of science. Science is a cultural institution and as such is structured by the political, social, and economic values of the culture within which it is practiced.

This argument is perhaps even more urgent in the realm of law and corporations. Recently, several legal authors have written along these lines. Of these I single out the contributions of Jonathan Stubbs, who attempted to support a similar claim with his theory of perceptual prisms, and Mark Roe who argued that corporate structures (both legal and nonlegal), as we know them today, are in considerable part the result of political decisions and compromises. The latter I mention for the benefit of those who believe that corporate structures are purely the result of "objective" market forces and principles.

Much work needs to be done in this area to uncover the systematic secular bias in our corporate law. To deny the existence of such a bias is to espouse the myth of "objectivity." We have been led to believe that laws that do not reflect a religious perspective are "neutral" laws. We hold this belief because we live in a culture where the dominant ideology is that of secularism. But the values of a dominant culture are invariably invisible, because they are always perceived as "objective," "the way things are." It is only when the dominant ideology is questioned that its systematic shaping of our lives and laws become visible. This essay has led me to start that questioning in my field and I can already discern the outlines of the secular "invisible hand."

We live in a country where religious freedom is guaranteed to all, and no religion may be oppressed by another. Yet, in the name of achieving those goals we have abandoned *all* religious perspective and replaced it with a secular one. Such an unfortunate approach denies the very truth and authenticity of the religious perspective *per se,* and thus oppresses all religions. That was not, I believe, what the Founding Fathers intended.

So, at this third level of the analysis, I conclude that to be a good American, I need to participate in unveiling the multi-layered secularist ideology which has systematically shaped our very legal model and reasoning. I believe that our democratic system, with its guarantees, would be better served with laws that accommodate all individuals, secular and religious, without requiring capitulation from either in the name of a national compromise.

Religious consciousness has certain distinctive characteristics that set it apart from the dominant paradigm of secularist consciousness. Foremost among these differences are matters essential to the definition of one's own self. For example, are we creatures of a superior being or are we the *ubermensche* himself? Are moral values objective and transcendental or can we put any values into question? These two matters alone point to fundamental structural differences that could arise between the secularist and the religionist. They could also easily inform the development of our legal model.

Our nation has been engaging in collective self-denial by pretending that these differences do not exist and that our laws reflect a neutral, objective compromise. Such claims make it difficult for the average person to recognize the roots of her dissatisfaction and produces a malaise that has a high cost to society. A more rational approach to this problem would be to revisit the matter, uncover the "invisible" assumptions and try to reach a compromise which is better tailored to the needs of both secularists and religionists.

Conclusion

It appears to me that religion subconsciously informs our individual professional practice and that a non-humanitarian form of secularism has quietly shaped our corporate laws. The attendant dissonance causes severe dissatisfaction, and at times even disfunction, in our society. The claim that our present corporate laws are imbued with a non-humanist secularist perspective deserves closer examination from a religious vantage point. Given our constitutional guarantees, our present legal structure appears to place undue burdens on persons of faith in this country. A more just balance between religious and various forms of secular perspectives is, I submit, a worthy goal for us all.

RUSSELL G. PEARCE, *THE JEWISH LAWYER'S QUESTION,*

27 Tex. Tech L. Rev. 1259, 1259-70 (1996)

* * *

As a lawyer and a teacher of lawyers and law students, my experience has been that Jewish lawyers are even more uncomfortable than Christian lawyers with the possibility that their legal practice might have a religious dimension. Last Spring, for example, I had the opportunity to help lead an Auburn Theological Seminary program for Jewish and Christian lawyers on the role of religion in a lawyer's work. At the first session, the lawyers received text sources and heard talks from a leading Christian theologian and a prominent Rabbi on religious perspectives on professional role. I then separated the lawyers into a Christian group and a Jewish group and asked them to construct a religious concept of the lawyer's professional role. The Christian lawyers debated whether the concepts of vocation and calling applied to their work. Despite explicit guidance from the Rabbinic speaker, the Jewish lawyers ignored the religious implications of their practice. Instead, they focused on how their minority status and the resulting experience of discrimination influenced their approach to lawyering, including their commitment to rule of law and social justice.

* * *

When I began to reflect on these differences, I realized that I too for many years had avoided confronting the consequence of my religious belief for my legal work. As a law clerk, associate at a Wall Street firm, legal services lawyer, and general counsel to a governmental civil rights agency, I had only a vague sense of the connection between my Judaism, my pro bono and public interest choices, my integrity, and my treatment of coworkers and adversaries. Despite my belief that Judaism entered all areas of my life, I did not begin to think systematically or in depth about the implications of Judaism for law practice until I became a law professor and I read Joseph Allegretti's and Thomas Shaffer's scholarship on Christian lawyering.

Although a major reason for this distinction is the very existence of a readily perceived Jewish, and not a Christian, ethnic identity, I suspect that this factor is only part of a complex set of reasons why Jewish lawyers find appealing a concept of professional role which excludes or drastically limits the influence of religious identity on professional conduct. These include minority status, a history of discrimination, and the existence of modern Jewish religious and ethnic perspectives which would interfere little, if at all, with professional obligations.

A. The Professional Project's Liberating Appeal to a Religious Minority

* * * The professional project's promise of neutrality affords Jews great comfort because of our minority status and history of discrimination. We are 2.5% of the United States population. In a legal system where the participants acted on their personal affiliations, rather than their duty to the legal system, we would be losers. We would only obtain justice at the majority's sufferance, not as a matter of right.

Equally important to Jewish lawyers is the professional project's promise of equal treatment to all individual lawyers. During the twentieth century, leaders of the bar and members of the public have stereotyped Jewish lawyers as "overly aggressive hired guns," adopting unethical "gutter" tactics, lacking in character, and "Oriental in their fidelity to the minutiae of the subject without regard to any controlling rule or reason." Extensive hiring discrimination against Jewish lawyers was documented as late as the 1960s and stereotypes of Jewish lawyers, both positive and negative, persist today.

While stereotypes and discrimination have coexisted with the professional project, the project offers as an ideal a vision of a profession where individuals are judged solely on their merits, not by virtue of their group identification. The project promised to liberate us from stereotypes and discrimination. Indeed, today, despite the persistence of some stereotypes, this promise seems to have been largely realized. The number of Jewish lawyers significantly exceeds our percentage of the population and many Jewish lawyers are among the profession's elite. Jerold S. Auerbach, the historian who has most thoroughly documented the history of antisemitism in the legal profession, recently noted "the astonishing success story of Jewish lawyers, as they erased the stigma of professional ostracism . . . ."

Auerbach suggests yet another explanation for the attachment of Jewish lawyers to the ideas embodied in the professional project. He suggests that "[e]specially for Jews, American law offered enticing rewards, beyond financial security and professional status." For immigrant Jews, the practice of law was the ultimate opportunity for assimilation as an American. In some sense, lawyers were the definitive "good Americans." They "interpret the traditions and explicate the rules of American society," and serve as the "respected custodians of American culture." Auerbach further asserts that in service of assimilation Jewish lawyers "replaced . . . their own sacred law tradition . . . with the rule of American law."

Each of these perspectives may help explain why on some levels the professional project and its promise of a nonreligious role morality offers attractions to Jewish lawyers beyond those offered majority Christian lawyers.

B. The Availability of Jewish Identities Compatible with Professional Role

Complementing the appeal of the professional project is the ready availability of Jewish identities that interfere little, if at all, with professional role. They offer the Jewish lawyer the opportunity to identify as both a Jew and a good professional.

Although the absolutist version of the professional project excludes all extraprofessional identifications, a more nuanced version permits commitments which do not interfere significantly with the substantive obligations of professional role. Sanford Levinson's use of the example of Sandy Koufax's refusal to pitch in the World Series on Yom Kippur is instructive on this point. If the influence of Koufax's religion was limited to when he pitched and not how he pitched, it only interfered with his professional role to a limited extent. A pitcher who does not pitch on one day when the interests of his team would otherwise require it breaches his professional obligations, but far less so than if his religion required him to depart from professional norms on a daytoday basis.

A Jewish lawyer could similarly be Jewish in ways which would not disturb the core of professionalism. One way is nonreligious. In part, this could stem from Jewishness as an ethnic, rather than religious, identification. Louis Brandeis chose to advocate on behalf of Jewish communal interests and economic justice, and Jack Greenberg to advocate for the rights of AfricanAmericans, from commitments derived from a desire not only to end the oppression of Jews but to realize a world where equal justice was available to all. The Jewish lawyers at the Auburn Theological Seminary program I described above similarly attributed the commitment of Jewish lawyers to rule of law and equal justice to their experience of discrimination and not to their religious beliefs.

These ethnic Jewish identifications may influence the causes Jewish lawyers adopt, but do not otherwise influence how a lawyer engages in practice. Ethnicity could of course have broader implications, much the same way some commentators have suggested a feminist style of lawyering. But excluding stereotypes, the only ethnically Jewish approaches to lawyering thus far suggested have been the limited ones described here.

A parallel variety of Jewish religious approaches to lawyering similarly interfere minimally with the professional project. While Helen Neuborne and Joseph Rauh join Brandeis and Greenberg in viewing their lawyering for social justice as the product of their Jewishness, Neuborne and Rauh recognize the Jewish religious content of their commitment. As with Jewish ethnicity, the choice of causes on religious grounds would not interfere with how one practiced law. A similarly limited conception of religious lawyering would involve observing Jewish holy days or other ritual, like Sandy Koufax, "but leaving the internal norms of legal practice untouched."

C. Religious Influences Facilitating the Professional Project

The absence of express religious authority on the lawyer's role and the presence of religious perspectives compatible with the project also facilitate the Jewish lawyer's adherence to the professional project.

While Judaism does have a tradition of great judges who have a duty to develop a full and fair record, it lacks a developed or formal ethic for the specific role of a lawyer. Parties generally represented themselves before a Jewish court. Levinson observes that the opposition of the great medieval Jewish scholar Maimonides to the practice of law resulted from his view that a lawyer was "a legal manipulator an artful 'arranger' concerned less with absolute fidelity to the law than with crafting ostensibly legal arguments that would enable the client to prevail against an adversary." A seventeenth century rabbi similarly condemned lawyers for "leading to argumentation and strife, deception and the adoption of false argumentation to justify the wicked and defame the righteous." Although Jewish courts have permitted lawyers since the middle ages, only in 1960 did the Israeli rabbinate "formally accept 'practices permitting legal counsel to argue on behalf of either litigant. . . .'

The Jewish tradition's general hostility to an adversarial role appears to have an ironic result. The tradition offers little specific guidance for the modern lawyer who practices in an adversarial system. Absent a developed or formal code of Jewish legal ethics, a Jewish lawyer may therefore adopt the values of the professional project without confronting any contrary religious authority directly on point to the lawyer's role.

At the same time, two common modern versions of Judaism facilitate observance of the professional project. One version separates the public from the religious. Martin Buber describes how "[m]odern thinking" results in versions of religion where "one participates in religious services without hearing the message commanding him to go out into the world." One manifestation of this trend in Judaism has been "the development of a pure ritualism" which accepts "observance of certain prescribed forms" as the fulfillment of the covenant. The modern versions of Judaism which emphasize "pure ritualism" or other forms which reject the command "to go out into the world" permit the Jewish lawyer to subscribe to the professional project or some limited religiosity compatible with the project.

Another very different version of Judaism identifies the religious with the public. This version involves going "out into the world," but in so doing identifies

American values, including the professional project, as being identical with Jewish values. Jerold Auerbach argues that as leaders of the American Jewish community, lawyers such as Louis Brandeis, Felix Frankfurter, and Louis Marshall helped create a "synthesis of Judaism and Americanism." This synthesis "identified Judaism with Americanism, within a common tradition that emphasized the rule of law and the quest for social justice."

II. JUDAISM DEMANDS A PLACE IN PROFESSIONAL PRACTICE

In his essay The Holy Way: A Word to the Jews and to the Nations, Martin Buber declares the "modern thinking" embodied in professionalism's separation of the religious self from the professional self to be "totally unJewish." In contrast to the professional ideal, "the world of true Judaism is the world of a unified life on earth." Buber observes that "man can do justice to the relation to God that has been given to him only by actualizing God in the world in accordance with his ability and the measure of each day, daily." The separation of work from religion, like the separation of "holinessthroughworks from holiness by grace," is "alien" to Judaism.

In this regard, Buber's observation has roots in traditional Jewish thinking. Godly actions have been a necessary part of being a religious Jew. The portion of the Torah called The Life of Holiness enjoins Jews to be holy as God is holy, and requires, among other things, that you leave "the gleanings of your harvest . . . for the poor and the stranger," "love your neighbor as yourself," and treat "the stranger who resides with you . . . as one of your citizens." Similarly, the prophets remind us that faith and prayer alone are not sufficient service to God. The Prophet Isaiah, for example, told the people that God would not listen to their prayers until they began to "devote yourselves to justice; aid the wronged; uphold the rights of the orphan; and defend the cause of the widow."

The understanding of Judaism as a way of life is common to the diverse strains of modern Jewish thought. According to eminent Reform Jewish theologian Rabbi Leo Baeck, a Jew "directs him[or her] self toward God in such a way that no part of his [or her] life is without this center, without this contact." The great Conservative theologian Rabbi Abraham Joshua Heschel similarly taught that "the meaning of redemption is to reveal the holy that is concealed, to disclose the divine that is suppressed. Every person is called upon to be a redeemer, and redemption takes place every moment, every day." The eminent Orthodox scholar Rabbi Joseph B. Soloveitchik also instructed that the Halakhah "penetrates into every nook and cranny of life. The marketplace, the street, the factory, the house, the meeting place, the banquet hall, all constitute the backdrop for the religious life."

Jewish tradition therefore contains the framework for a version of Jewish lawyering radically different in premise from that underlying the professional project.

III. ANSWERING THE JEWISH QUESTION

Within the Jewish community, I take an expressly pluralist perspective. As a Reform Jew, I respect "the right of individual Jews to make the final decision as to what constitutes Jewish belief and practice for them." In that spirit, and following the teaching that Judaism is a way of life, I offer my own answerinprogress to the Jewish question. The answer is at once both directly contrary to, and substantially compatible with, the prevailing conception of the lawyer's role.

* * * [T]he Baal Shem Tov reproache[d] his student the Maggid of Mezeritch for reading without "soul." If one can read with soul, one can surely lawyer with "soul." As Abraham Joshua Heschel taught, "[i]t is not enough to do the mitzvah; one must live what he does. . . . When the soul is dull, the mitzvah is a shell." Heschel describes the integration of soul into act as Kavvanah, "direction to God. . . . It is the act of bringing together the scattered forces of the self; the participation of heart and soul, not only of will and mind." Interestingly, Heschel expressly calls for us to bring God into the legal system. He writes that "God will return to us when we shall be willing to let Him into all parts of our lives, including into our courts."

Such a kavvanah of lawyering demands a rejection of the professional project's separation of the professional from the religious self. As a Jewish lawyer, I would direct my heart toward God in every moment of my legal practice. This task requires study and prayer, but it also requires conduct. As Rabbi Leib, son of Sarah, taught, a Jewish lawyer (like all Jews) "should see to it that all his [or her] actions are a Torah."

But how exactly to fulfill this goal is far from clear. As discussed above, this lack of clarity results in part from Jewish tradition's hostility to a lawyer's zealous representation of a client. As a result, those who try to derive a Jewish ethic for a modern lawyer have to look beyond legal ethics to construct explanations of why adversarial legal conduct is appropriate. For example, in two of the few articles discussing Jewish approaches to legal ethics, Rabbis Alfred Cohen and Gordon Tucker examined the extent of a professional's duty of confidentiality when a client poses threat of harm to a nonclient. Both applied the principle that halakhah requires putting the interests of the community above that of the individual. In the application of this principle to the problem of confidentiality, their analysis diverged. Rabbi Tucker argued that the good of the community requires revealing confidences to protect a nonclient from physical or financial harm even though the individual client will suffer detriment. In contrast, while advising consultation with halakhic authority, Rabbi Cohen asserted that "it may be that maintaining professional secrecy is so absolutely integral to the proper function of that profession and the profession so essential to the welfare of society that the halacha would decide that the practitioner must maintain his professional secrets."

In legal ethics, therefore, as in many modern moral questions, the Jewish response is not selfevident. For the Jewish lawyer, legal ethics becomes a subject for Jewish study and reflection. But while recognizing the vital importance of further study, we can find in our tradition foundational principles that on their face not only harmonize with, but require dedication to, the best aspirations of our legal system. Recognizing the risk of oversimplifying our often complicated and sometimes contradictory tradition, I will tentatively suggest two such principles.

One principle is equal justice under law. The Torah's command "[j]ustice, justice, shall you pursue" requires the creation of a just legal system. While the Torah was not speaking of a political system like our own, it does suggest attributes of justice that are applicable today. One such principle is equal justice under law. Decisions should "not favor the poor or show deference to the rich." The "stranger who resides with you shall be to you as one of your citizens." Another such principle is concern for the poor and powerless. Proverbs instructs judges to "open thy mouth for the dumb" and "plead the cause of the poor and needy."

These principles suggest that the conduct of the Jewish lawyer in upholding the rule of law and in serving the poor could be quite consistent with professional ideals. What differentiates this perspective from the simple equation of Jewish and professional values is that its foundation is Jewish values which may overlap with professional values, but will not necessarily do so.

So long as the Jewish lawyer seeks equal justice under law from a religious perspective, she will reject the professional project but not equal justice under law. As I have argued elsewhere, religious lawyering's rejection of the professional project does not necessarily undermine rule of law. Acceptance of personal identity rather than a professionally neutral role suggests a different way to think about realizing the goal. Instead of trying to "bleach out" difference, we should try to "create community" by speaking frankly about how to realize a legal system which results in equal justice given our differences and our similarities. This indeed is very much the task of the Jewish lawyer. As Buber teaches, "holiness is true community with God and true community with human beings, both in one."

Conclusion

After the Baal Shem reproached the Maggid of Mezeritch for reading without soul, the Baal Shem began to read. At that point, "the room filled with light and the Maggid stood at Sinai again." Through understanding Judaism as a way of life, we may be able to answer the "Jewish question" in a way that furthers both our legal system's commitment to equal justice and enhances the spirituality of our actions. While it is far from clear how to fulfill these goals, our task begins with practicing mitzvot, acting with kavannah, and following the instruction of the eminent sage Rabbi Hillel to go and study.

ROBERT K. VISCHER, HERETICS IN THE TEMPLE OF THE LAW: THE PROMISE AND PERIL OF THE RELIGIOUS LAWYERING MOVEMENT,

19 J.L. & Religion 427, 461-88 (2004)

* * * The widespread resistance to the prospect of a greater role for religion in a lawyer's provision of professional services is not, of course, unfounded. The potential benefits described above notwithstanding, the religious lawyering movement represents, to many observers, a direct affront to the most fundamental presumptions of the American legal system. * * *

A. The Threat to Publicly Accessible Norms

Much of the resistance to the integration of a lawyer's religious and professional identities mirrors the broader and pervasive debate over religion's role in our liberal democracy. As state-licensed gatekeepers to our society's system of legal rights and privileges, lawyers are seen as operating within the public sphere, and thus subject to a degree of personal-professional demarcation that would not apply, for example, to the services provided by butchers or novelists. * * * If a lawyer * * * seeks to convert a client to her own faith tradition, red flags immediately appear. The skepticism many feel toward the lawyer's conduct tracks the skepticism many feel whenever public officials blur the line between personal faith and public function. * * *

[T]he broader consideration underlying much of the theorists' work in this area * * * is public accessibility. That is, the legitimacy of an individual's participation in the conversation over public norms hinges on her ability to translate private views into arguments capable of being engaged by a reasonable person's exercise of rationality. This sentiment has been applied widely to the legal profession, as reflected in comments by Leslie Griffin:

> The legal profession must be governed by standards of "public reason," by legal and constitutional standards that all lawyers can reasonably be expected to endorse. In a public reason theory of legal ethics, lawyers must translate their theological convictions whenever they seek to influence the profession's norms. Theological objectors should phrase their criticism in the language of public reason. Some theologies cannot make this translation, and their adherents will "opt out" of the profession; but other religious believers can so translate. Religious beliefs should not become the profession's norms as long as they are expressed theologically, in the language of one tradition.

The impact that a lawyer's faith might legitimately have on the collective endeavor to construct binding profession-wide norms is thus not negated, but it is narrowed: the lawyer must translate her theological convictions into publicly accessible language before injecting her views into the collective endeavor. Absent such translation, religious argument is seen as playing a marginal, possibly unhealthy role in the public discourse.

On some issues, there is very little need for translation, for the relevant religious convictions are humanistic to the extent that their epistemological validity does not depend on the truth of divine revelation—most obviously, in religion's pervasive concern for the poor. Further, in these areas, there tends to be such overlap among religious traditions that there is little potential for divisiveness stemming from religion's entry into the debate. * * *

The prerequisite of (or, in its softer versions, the preference for) translated religious convictions suggests that liberal, enlightened groups can participate, but not theologically conservative groups, who do not accept fallibilism. Restricting access in this way, while by no means evenhanded, seems essential, for when political discourse is open religious argument that "rejects the claims of reason and relies on a source of truth that is beyond challenge or debate," such argument attends to undermine a basic tenet of our democratic system—that legal policies should be formulated on the basis of a dialogic decision-making process, a process requiring an openness of mind that religious fundamentalism does not allow. This impulse to condition the standing of religious arguments within political discourse on their public accessibility or intelligibility may be functionally prudent, but it also is at odds with much that is fundamental to our understanding of faith. Kierkegaard eloquently points out that faith, at its core, is inherently inaccessible to the surrounding community. He portrays faith as "precisely the paradox that the single individual as the single individual is higher than the universal, is justified before it, not as inferior to it but as superior," because "the single individual as the single individual stands in an absolute relation to the absolute." * * * Faith, consequently, "cannot be mediated into the universal, for thereby it is cancelled." This paradox means that the person of faith "simply cannot make himself understandable to anyone."

Whether or not one finds Kierkegaard's portrayal of faith to bear any resemblance to the predominant portrayal of faith in modern America, it is undeniable that there is a significant component—or perhaps to the most jaded observers of politically driven American religion, at least a residue—that is left behind whenever faith is forced to translate itself into concepts understandable to non-believers. Such translation does not facilitate meaningful community in this regard, for it is only through "the subjective commitment of the individual, through a mode of consciousness and of communication extending beyond purely intellectual-manipulative types of relationship," that community is possible. The disconnect resulting from the required translation makes the subjective commitment of the individual highly unlikely, especially where the individual's motivation to commit stems from her faith. The alternative, where a sense of belonging is "built upon intellectual commitment, organization, and the manipulations of democratic, industrial mass society," results in a future that Kierkegaard saw, somewhat dramatically, as "dread, despair, and anxiety" for the affected individuals.

Accordingly, on one hand we are told that religious argument must be rendered publicly accessible before it can gain entry into the political discourse. On the other hand, we are told that such rendering is practically impossible, or at least that it transforms the argument of faith, not simply by matters of degree, but into something else entirely. For the individual religious lawyer, this seems to be a lose-lose proposition. If she resists the translation of her deeply-held beliefs into publicly accessible language, her beliefs will have no bearing whatsoever on the construction of profession-wide norms. But if she submits to the translation, she will emerge with publicly accessible language that has only a tenuous connection with her faith. Either way, her faith convictions have little or no bearing beyond her individual conscience.

* * * But what happens if we introduce multiple, divergent subcommunities into the professional paradigm? How, if at all, does that change the accessibility requirement?

Put simply, accessibility is no longer a concern when the target audience is made up of individuals who share the speaker's faith commitment. Certainly Kierkegaard contemplates that there is a core element of faith that is not expressible to anyone outside the individual, even those within the faith community, but there is a vast middle ground between that core irreducible kernel and the faith-informed arguments that cannot be expressed to the wider society. It is within this vast middle ground that the capacity for individual empowerment of groups like the Christian Legal Society becomes obvious. Such groups equip religious lawyers with the ability to apply their faith—as faith, not as secularly intelligible byproducts—in real-world settings that go beyond their own consciences. The broad, almost vacuous framework of the Model Rules leaves ample room for the crafting of supplemental ethical norms by voluntary associations of lawyers, enforced not as prerequisites for practicing law, but perhaps as conditions of membership in the particular association. By participating in the communal dialogue and distillation that would accompany such an endeavor, the lawyer's religious convictions may actually serve as the basis for community-wide ethical norms, something that can never occur as long as the only purportedly relevant community is the legal profession in its entirety.

Religious lawyering thus provides an avenue around the faith-marginalizing requirement of public accessibility which does not negate the prudence underlying the accessibility requirement. By providing a forum in which lawyers' most deeply held beliefs can not only be expressed, but potentially brought to bear on their surroundings, religious lawyering groups serve a mediating function in the purest sense. The "untranslated" communal expression of religious beliefs not only brings coherence and a sense of efficacy to the individual lawyer, but also can enrich the wider profession to the extent that it is exposed to the resulting norms, as they are implemented by the community and its members.

This becomes especially apparent when one realizes that, as a practical matter, much of the crafting of ethical norms within a religious community will necessarily be casuistic. To the extent that religious lawyering communities were to promulgate ethics codes consisting solely of broad principles or overarching admonitions drawn from the words of Jesus or Mohammed, the potential to engage the wider profession would understandably seem limited. But a practical, professional system of ethics will entail substantial reliance on contextual, case-by-case judgments. Simply reading the Sermon on the Mount will not spawn an obvious or remotely comprehensive response to the everyday ethical scenarios with which lawyers must grapple. To a certain degree, the religious lawyer, like the ethical philosopher, "must wait on facts."

* * *

Casuistry is not currently a meaningful option for lawyers to pursue on a profession-wide basis, of course, because shared norms—at least the shared norms that matter most to many religious lawyers—are absent. Casuistry pursued within the community of faith, however, can not only bridge the gap between broad religious principles or prohibitions and fact-specific professional dilemmas, but can also produce a system of ethical judgments that may actually prove to be accessible to the wider profession. That is, even if the underlying motivation for choosing one course of conduct over another is not accessible to those outside the faith community, the choice of conduct dictated by these motivations are accessible, and by making those choices on a day-to-day basis, lawyers within that community are exposing other lawyers to that course of conduct. By giving religious lawyers space to distill their convictions into practical judgments, religious lawyering communities give real-world relevance to their members' most deeply held beliefs without sacrificing the notion that profession-wide ethical norms should be intelligible throughout the profession.

B. The Threat to Client Autonomy

Making religious lawyers' ethical norms accessible to the profession is not the only obstacle faced by the religious lawyering movement. The most central, sensitive, and potentially problematic relationship implicated by a lawyer's integration of faith and practice is not the one with her colleagues, but the one with her client. At the attorney-client level, the accessibility problem is even starker, for it is not a question of simply making the lawyer's motivations intelligible to her client, but making them agreeable to her client. Indeed, many would argue that the lawyer's personal convictions, religious or not, are entirely irrelevant to the relationship with the client. And even those who seek to hold the lawyer morally accountable for "both the ends chosen and the means chosen to reach those ends" within a given representation, the accountability is conceived of in terms of "society's shared set of moral commitments." Thus, there must be, on the lawyer's part, "a willingness to provide publicly intelligible reasons for one's actions, a commitment to be held accountable to others for one's conduct." So what happens when the lawyer's reasons for acting (or not acting) emanate from the lawyer's own religious convictions?

* * *

A lawyer who defies role-differentiation is feared to be engaging in paternalism, which is seen as "a grave violation of individual rights" because our system's guarantee of freedom spawns "the privilege of the individual to be the sole judge of the moral legitimacy of her actions." Consequently,

> [l]awyers in a liberal system must take care not to frustrate their clients' pursuit of their own conception of the good life by appealing to a moral principle that is unique to the lawyer's conception of the good. In this regard, "[t]he foundational moral principle of the regulatory model is that the lawyer should defer to her client's instructions and seek to carry them out through any lawful means."

But in its more extreme versions, this focus on client autonomy reflects a "monistic account[] of professional responsibility," and as we know from [Bradley] Wendel's work,

> [t]he central tradition of evaluative monism has been challenged by a considerable body of philosophy which maintains that human values cannot be reduced to a single common unit of value, nor can they be compared with one another in every case. These insights are especially valuable in our approach to client autonomy, which is fettered to some degree by strictly practical considerations, of course, but also, in the views of many commentators, impoverishes the practice of law when its value is extolled in absolute terms, outside the context of a meaningful attorney-client dialogue.

Such dialogue is aimed not simply at the protection of interests external to the client, but at the well-being of the client herself. Tom Shaffer, for example, traces the scope of our devotion to individual autonomy, observing that, "[i]n moral discourse, as in political and legal discourse, we don't talk about good people, we talk about rights," and we assume "that what citizens want for one another, or lawyers for their clients, is not goodness but isolation and independence." * * * A dialogical relationship allows lawyers to help their clients decide what it is they really want, to help them make up their minds as to what their ends should be, a function that differs importantly from the instrumental servicing of preestablished goals. Such morally active legal practice presumes that "the lawyer who disagrees with the morality or justice of a client's ends does not simply terminate the relationship, but tries to influence the client for the better."

Even among religious lawyers, the tendency is to view one's self as the passive recipient of morally significant requests, responding to them with amoral techniques. But from the religious lawyer's point of view, the problems of role-differentiation are especially pronounced. * * * [F]or most religious lawyers, a belief in absolute truth is inescapable. Requiring such a lawyer to ignore her conception of truth in formulating or pursuing her client's objectives is to ask her to deny her own moral agency, to have her act as a mere tool of technique without moral standing, and to treat her client as an object of servitude incapable of moral reflection.

But while unfettered client autonomy is undoubtedly a bad idea, few would dispute the understanding that a lawyer should aim to serve the client's interests, not her own, in a given matter. Absolute truth or not, a lawyer cannot be empowered to hijack the representation to further her own conception of the good, perhaps even in a way that goes undetected by the client. This compels a clear limitation on the religious lawyering movement: the client-directed quality of legal representation must be honored. Role-differentiation is not to be replaced by the trump of the lawyer's morality, but by moral dialogue in which both the lawyer and client treat each other as agents capable of meaningful moral thought and reflection. Lawyers must be vigilant against overreaching or subtle coercion when it comes to any contact with the client, and morality-driven conversations are no exception.

This vigilance is not just defensive, but requires a proactive mindset on the part of the religious lawyer, for we will have to rely on the lawyer to initiate conversations regarding the paths by which the lawyer's identity may impact the representation. One fear common to those troubled by the religious lawyering movement is the prospect of unknowing clients being swept along in service of the lawyer's overarching religious commitment. For example, if a religious lawyer makes a point of never lying in a negotiation on behalf of her client, the client may never be aware of the fact that the Model Rules permit certain misrepresentations in negotiation, or realize the strategic advantage that could have accrued to the client's cause if such misrepresentations were made. The attorney must bring up this limitation in consultation with the client—the earlier the better—even though such a conversation will be awkward at best, and at worst will result in a loss of business.

This does not necessarily mean that religious lawyers should emblazon their religious affiliation on their letterhead, for such overt self-categorization will not tell prospective clients much about the likely relationship between the lawyer's identity and the course of the representation. Moreover, it may have the unintended and unwelcome consequence of functioning as a signal that individuals who do not share the lawyer's identity should look elsewhere for counsel. But a lawyer is obligated to keep the client apprised to the extent that the lawyer recognizes the bearing her own religious convictions and inclinations will have on the decisions presented by the matter. Often, the identity-representation interplay will be obvious at the initial lawyer-client conversation as the lawyer learns of the client's objectives, such as a lawyer asked by a minor to help her procure court permission for an abortion. At other times, the lawyer's own identity will remain relatively immaterial pending unforeseen developments over the course of the representation, such as a discovery dispute in which the client expects the lawyer to engage in "hardball" tactics. Whatever the timing, a lawyer bold enough to bring her personal values into her provision of legal services must also be bold enough to ensure that her client is aware of those values and approves of their entry into the representation.

But * * * religious lawyering should not be seen as essentially deontological, affording little room for compromise, but it should be more focused on character, intention, and practical judgment. In other words, the focus of religious lawyers should be not so much on whether the lawyer's deeply held beliefs are ultimately reflected in the outcome of the representation, but whether the values emanating from those beliefs, once implicated by the representation, were offered for consideration. Of course, often a fully informed client will take issue either with the lawyer's values, or, more likely, with the specific way in which the values are brought to bear on the pursuit of the client's lawful objectives. When there is an irreconcilable conflict between the lawyer's religious identity and the client's wishes, the lawyer must give way, either by acceding to the client's wishes or by stepping aside in favor of another lawyer.

This raises the other key component of informed choice by consumers of legal services: informed choice not only presumes adequate information, but also viable alternatives. This should not be much of a problem in the legal profession. Membership in religious communities of lawyers makes up a small fraction of the profession; there is no shortage of non-religious lawyers, and many religious lawyers do not seem to chafe under the priesthood paradigm's belief/conduct disconnect. And of course, many religious lawyers inclined to integrate their beliefs with their practice are not willing to pursue such integration at the cost of lost business. In short, there is no reason to believe that a wider embrace of pluralism within the profession will erode the availability of legal services offered under the traditional presumptions of the [secular] priesthood paradigm.

Significantly, the communal focus of religious lawyering should give further reassurance to those who question the compatibility of client-directed representation with the premises of religious lawyering. Even within the priesthood paradigm, we have no real assurances that individual lawyers leave their religious or moral convictions at home. The fact that a lawyer's values are left unstated does not mean they are left out of the representation—they may simply be driven underground, inaccessible to the client, unexamined by the lawyer, and untested by a community of peers. As Joseph Allegretti observes, "A lawyer's conscious or unconscious moral and religious misgivings do not disappear merely because the lawyer decides to keep them to herself." Often the alternative to moral dialogue between lawyer and client is an unspoken undercurrent of morality driving the lawyer's approach to the case.

Communities of religious lawyers can bring individual convictions into the open, subjecting them to review by fellow believers, and requiring the individual to express and examine her own views, thereby separating motivations of faith from personal predilections that may have found a convenient, but untested, faith cover. By placing individual convictions within a communal framework, the intra-community dialogue not only helps the lawyer strengthen and sort her convictions, but it protects the client by increasing the likelihood that the convictions will be knowable by the client. By facilitating the distillation of lawyers' religious convictions into professional norms, the community engages in a sort of translation that makes the convictions more accessible to the client. Further, to the extent that the norms are implemented on a community-wide basis—either as obligations of conduct or aspirations of character—the vague leanings of an individual lawyer's conscience are fleshed out and made explicit, enhancing the likelihood that the norms will be communicated in some fashion to the client.

Communication to the client of a lawyer's faith-based ethical norms is key, for some clients will want no part in the lawyer's integration of faith and legal practice under any circumstances. Such inclinations should be recognized and addressed as early in the representation as possible, if just for the purpose of deciding that other counsel may be a better fit. There is nothing unethical about declining representation, or withdrawing from ongoing representation, for moral reasons, as has been made explicit in recent versions of the Model Rules. To extrapolate from the possibility of client discomfort to a conclusion that the lawyer's personal beliefs should be excluded from the representation not only disregards the lawyer's moral agency and diminishes the client's moral capacity, but it also defies the reality of human experience. The Model Rules already recognize that moral considerations are a legitimate part of the attorney-client dialogue. As long as the attorney is upfront with her client about the content of the faith-based norms that she proposes to bring to bear on the conduct of the representation, and as long as the client has alternative legal service providers from which to choose, client autonomy is not significantly threatened by the religious lawyering movement, especially when the religious convictions emerge not simply from the individual lawyer's own conscience, but are filtered, tested, and implemented within the community of faith.

C. The Threat of the Illiberal Community

It is tempting to paint a uniformly rosy picture of religious lawyering and its potentially uplifting impact on the wider profession, especially if we portray religious lawyering groups as mainstream Jews, Christians and Muslims dedicated to the humble pursuit of peace, justice and ecumenical dialogue. But under a meaningful vision of pluralism, religion is not so easily contained. We not only have to address lawyers motivated by faith to open a legal aid office, but lawyers motivated by faith to pursue racial purity. Matthew Hale and his white-supremacist sect, World Church of the Creator, would gladly take up the flag of the religious lawyering movement alongside the mainstream groups mentioned above. When the Illinois Supreme Court denied Hale's admission to the bar on the grounds that his racially discriminatory ideology was incompatible with membership in the legal profession, was the court unwisely propping up the priesthood paradigm? What does the religious lawyering movement do with groups that defy the bedrock principles of the liberal project?

Any defender of religious lawyering groups must readily concede that granting any community of lawyers an unfettered license to conduct their professional lives as they see fit would court disaster. As commentators like Wendel have pointed out, "there is no guarantee in the concept of a community that the community's norms will be those that ethically ought to be endorsed," and that "[u]nless informal social norms are kept in check by extra-community criticism, nothing prevents the community's values from moving toward vice instead of virtue." For quasi-public agents like lawyers, communal vice can arise not simply from explicitly illiberal beliefs like white supremacy, but from a broader set of attitudes that are usually captured (albeit imperfectly and pejoratively) under the label "fundamentalism." As Habermas explains [,] We call "fundamentalist" those religious movements which, given the cognitive limits of modern life, nevertheless persist in practicing or promoting a return to the exclusivity of premodern religious attitudes. * * * [F]undamentalism's legitimacy in the liberal public discourse is foreclosed by its failure to display the attitudes of fallibilism and pluralism. * * * From the vantage point of many religious individuals, though, the problem with liberal theorists' insistence that every community embrace fallibilism and moral pluralism—especially when coupled with the uncompromising emphasis on individual autonomy—is that they effectively "refuse to give people the option to live in a community of obedience." Liberalism's espousal of pluralism is not all-encompassing: there must be at least a modicum of mutual toleration, if not respect, among groups occupying the liberal public square. Conservative Southern Baptists, for example, defy the fallibilism and pluralism norms by virtue of their belief in the veracity and the uniqueness of the divine revelation to which they adhere, and thus their overt presence in political discourse exerts pressure on liberalism's inclusiveness norm—i.e., they are sufficiently illiberal to trigger exclusion. The exclusiveness of liberal inclusiveness is a tension underlying many of the religious liberty debates today.

For lawyers, the issue is even more complicated. There is something disconcerting about an avowed white supremacist serving as a gatekeeper to the legal system, even if we do not object to the white supremacist spouting his views freely on a street corner. The discomfort would be heightened were an entire group of lawyers to organize for the purpose of deepening their racist beliefs and furthering the white supremacist cause through the conduct of their professional lives. Groups of lawyers staking out communal opposition to gay rights, by way of a hot-button example, provoke discomfort that varies in degree, but not in nature, from Matthew Hale and his ilk. Pursuing such causes under the banner of religion poses an acute challenge to liberalism, for two fundamental reasons: first, in defiance of value pluralism, the substance of the group's cause is inconsistent with liberalism's devotion to equality, which is seen as essential to safeguarding individuals' autonomy over the choices impacting their own lives; second, in defiance of fallibilism, the group's cause is grounded in divine revelation, and thus is not subject to revision or retraction via rational discourse or shifting societal norms.

And within the legal profession, such communal causes are problematic for an additional reason: objectives that emanate from religious beliefs understood in absolute terms by the believer are accessible neither to other lawyers nor to clients who do not share those religious beliefs. Thus, the causes threaten not only the ideological unity of the profession (a unity that probably has been a fiction all along, in any event), but the epistemological unity—that is, subcommunities of lawyers are pursuing causes that the liberal system opposes, and they do so for reasons that are by definition incapable of rational engagement. And the causes threaten the autonomy of the client by subjecting her to the trump of the lawyer's inaccessible and illiberal views.

Tracing the problem of the illiberal community helps demarcate the prudent limits of the religious lawyering movement, and further underscores the benefits of channeling individual lawyers' religious convictions into a communal forum. First, the illiberal beliefs of religious lawyers should not be a pressing concern for the profession when they are explored within a group of lawyers sharing the same beliefs, but such beliefs are problematic, for the reasons stated above, when they are explicitly invoked in an effort to sway the norms that bind non-believing lawyers. For example, a legal profession committed to value pluralism will make space for the Christian Legal Society to discuss methods for halting the perceived advance of a gay rights agenda in light of St. Paul's admonitions against homosexual conduct. Value pluralism understood against the background of liberalism, however, does not require the profession to stand idly by were the Christian Legal

Society to attempt to convince the ABA's House of Delegates to incorporate St. Paul's admonitions into the Model Rules of Professional Conduct as a basis for forbidding lawyers from seeking to advance the cause of gay rights.

Second, the illiberal beliefs of religious lawyers should not be a pressing concern for the profession when they are expressed openly within the attorney-client dialogue, provided that the client is given the options of declining advice borne of religious conviction, or else seeking new counsel. The profession should take steps to ensure that lawyers do not use their position to bring their clients' objectives into closer alignment with the lawyer's beliefs without a conscious decision by the client to do so.

The faith community of lawyers helps guard these boundaries, even if unintentionally, by facilitating the distillation of religious beliefs into practical professional norms and guiding the implementation of such norms within the broad regulatory framework of the profession. To the extent that the beliefs are not susceptible to communal distillation or implementation within the profession's framework, a lawyer may indeed need to think twice before seeking to shape her legal practice according to such beliefs. * * *

As an example of implementation within the regulatory framework, an individual religious lawyer may believe that homosexuality is a sin and a perversion of God's creation, and thus she may have an aversion to representing gay causes, gay clients, or even working with gay lawyers. If she is left alone to integrate her beliefs with her practice, and thereby is required to verbalize the path of integration or expose it to the views of peers, the result is more likely to be inconsistent with lawyers' gatekeeping function. If a community of Christian lawyers engages the task of formulating coherent and explicit ethical norms, they are likely to have a moderating influence, both because as a group they are more likely to have a broader and richer exposure to gay individuals, and because even if they share the lawyer's beliefs on homosexuality, they are more likely to feel constrained by professional norms. This is not to say that conservative religious groups will encourage an open embrace of causes like gay rights, but simply that they are more likely to differentiate between stances that diverge from those of the wider profession—e.g., declining to represent causes seeking to advance gay rights—and those that defy the profession—e.g., declining to represent gay individuals.

But not all groups will exert a moderating influence, of course, which brings us to * * * Matthew Hale[. A]ssuming that he had been admitted to the Illinois bar, would have held racist views as an individual, and there is no reason to believe that, if he were able to assemble a group of lawyers under his World Church of the Creator, this community would have been any less racist than he is. After all, where a group is expressly dedicated to an illiberal cause, there is little reason to join it if one does not share those illiberal views. Certainly communal distillation would still be possible: Hale may hold broadly racist views, and his community may aid him in integrating racism with his practice by exploring practical ideas of, for example, declining representation of racial minorities. But such a norm is incapable of implementation within the profession's regulatory framework. One of the few core principles on which the gatekeeping function depends is that representation may not be denied based on an individual's immutable characteristics as opposed to the objective the client seeks to pursue (or her inability to pay for the services, of course). To allow lawyers—religious or not—to avoid this limitation threatens the ability of disfavored groups to access the legal system, and could turn the pluralist profession into a vehicle by which society itself becomes further balkanized.

The priesthood paradigm wisely recognizes this anti-discrimination limitation, but unwisely expands it into the broader position that lawyers should not bring their own religious identities to bear on any representation decisions. The paradigm elevates the gatekeeping function to an absolute, monistic theory of value, ignoring countervailing values such as the moral elements of legal practice, especially the need for coherence and meaningful dialogue. However, to allow Hale and his ilk to pursue their own worldview at the cost of individuals denied representation based on who they are, rather than on the goals they seek to pursue, is to proceed too far in the opposite direction. The religious lawyering movement need not be resisted for fear of the slippery slope; distinctions can and must be made between those who seek to integrate their faith with the functions they serve as professionals, and those who seek to follow their faith in ways that render their professional role unrecognizable.

Admittedly, even mainstream religious views may not always be compatible with certain core, irreducible gatekeeping functions of the legal profession. Certainly the predominant religious affiliations of American lawyers—Christianity, Judaism, and Islam—do not seem to threaten the gatekeeping function in the same way that avowed racists like Hale would, given their orientations toward social justice and service to the "other." But other conflicts are readily apparent. Especially in family law or criminal law, many religious lawyers may face a sharp conflict between their moral convictions and their clients' objectives. And unlike the contexts discussed above, the conflict is not amenable to moral dialogue, as often the conflict consists of the very reason that the client retained the lawyer. Religious lawyering is not cost-free to the lawyer. If she is being honest with herself and her clients about the impact her faith has on her professional identity, there likely will be practice areas that she is unsuited to enter, and there will undoubtedly be cases, in an otherwise suitable practice area, that she is unfit to take on.

An even broader point bears emphasis. Properly conceived, value pluralism in the legal profession makes room for religious values. But value pluralism does not call into question the supremacy of the temporal law. Lawyers are sworn to uphold the law, and religious convictions cannot be exempted from this core function. This does not mean that a religious lawyer will never encounter circumstances where her convictions and the law stand in tension with each other (just as nonreligious lawyers encounter such circumstances). Rather, it simply means that the gatekeeping function of lawyers would be significantly impeded were religious lawyers granted an exemption from following the law every time their faith-based beliefs ran afoul of the law. Within the myriad areas in which the governing ethics regime grants lawyers decision-making discretion, religious lawyers should feel free to exercise their discretion in ways that are deliberately consistent with—indeed, expressly grounded in—their religious beliefs, even their illiberal religious beliefs. But if religious lawyers, either standing alone or in community, feel compelled by their faith to defy the minimal constraints of the ethics regime, they must face the consequences, as does any individual or group engaged in civil disobedience. The embrace of religious lawyering does not entail supporting an exemption from any laws or professional regulations that impede on the lawyer's faith. It simply means that the lawyers must be given space to craft their own ethical norms within the wide latitude granted them by the largely vacuous regulatory framework. * * *

4. Racial Justice

An extensive literature discusses the relationship between race and lawyering. David Wilkins analyzes a number of these perspectives in explaining his own.

[Question 1]

Anthony Griffin argues that:

   (A) **as an African-American he had an obligation to represent the Klan.**

   (B) **as an African-American he had an obligation to refuse to represent the Klan.**

   (C) **his being African-American was irrelevant to his decision to represent the Klan.**

[Question 2]

According to David Wilkins, African-American lawyers:

   (A) **should place their professional obligations above their racial obligation.**

   (B) **should place their racial obligation above their professional obligation.**

   (C) **should reconcile their professional and racial obligations.**

   (D) **have no legitimate racial obligation.**

[Question 3]

David Wilkins argues that in the O.J. Simpson trial:

(A) Johnnie Cochran appropriately navigated racial and professional obligations.

(B) Christopher Darden appropriately navigated racial and professional obligations.

(C) both Cochran and Darden appropriately navigated racial and professional obligations.

(D) neither Cochran nor Darden appropriately navigated racial and professional obligations.

[Question 4]

David Wilkins concludes that Robert Johnson managed his opposition to the death penalty:

(A) more appropriately than Robert Morgenthau.

(B) just as appropriately as Robert Morgenthau.

(C) less appropriately than Robert Morgenthau.

DAVID B. WILKINS, *IDENTITIES AND ROLES: RACE, RECOGNITION, AND PROFESSIONAL RESPONSIBILITY,*

57 Md. L. Rev. 1502 (1998)

* * * Consider the following cases:

1. Anthony Griffin, a black lawyer affiliated with the ACLU, agrees to defend the Grand Dragon of the Ku Klux Klan. The case involves the State of Texas's attempt to subpoena the Klan's membership list in order to assist a probe into Klan violence against black residents in a newly integrated housing project. The African American head of the Port Arthur branch of the NAACP subsequently fires Griffin from his position as the unpaid general counsel for that organization when Griffin refuses to withdraw from representing the Klan.

2. Robert Johnson, the elected black district attorney representing the Bronx, announces that he will refuse to seek the state's newly enacted death penalty in any case in part because he believes it will inevitably be applied in a racially discriminatory manner. Subsequently, Governor Pataki removes Johnson from considering whether to seek the death penalty in a highly publicized case involving three young black youths accused of shooting a white police officer. Pataki replaces the black DA with a white lawyer who is a committed death penalty hawk.

3. Gil Garcetti assigns Christopher Darden as one of the lead prosecutors in the racially charged Simpson prosecution. During the course of the trial, Darden seeks to bar the defense from questioning Mark Fuhrman about whether he used racial epitaphs in the past. Subsequently, Johnnie Cochran, the black lead defense lawyer, argues to the predominately black jury that they should acquit his client in part as a means of "sending a message" that police racism and misconduct will not be tolerated.

Each of these high-profile cases has become a part of America's great conversation- -or more accurately "angry polemic" on race. At one time or another, each of the major black protagonists—Griffin, the head of the Port Arthur branch of the NAACP, Johnson, Darden, and Cochran—has been accused of racial "crimes" ranging from "selling out" to "playing the race card." Other equally vociferous combatants retort that one or the other of these attorneys has in fact served the cause of racial justice by upholding the highest standards of professionalism. These high profile cases, therefore, provide useful vehicles for examining the relationship between racial identity and professional role.

* * *

Bleached out professionalism is the dominant narrative through which most observers have examined the conduct of the attorneys in the three cases cited [above.] * * * Indeed, most participants in these cases, including virtually all of the black lawyers, have been careful to pay allegiance to bleached out professionalism as a core professional ideal. Thus, Anthony Griffin sometimes claimed that race had "nothing to do" with his decision to represent the Klan, branding as "racist" both "'those black folks who told me I should have let a white lawyer take th[e] case'" and "'Anglos, who regarded me as some kind of oddity because I was a black man who represented the Klan.'" Similarly, Christopher Darden flatly states that "'if I thought I was being assigned to the case primarily because I was black, I would've rejected it.'" Nevertheless, Darden believes that for many Americans, he "'was a black prosecutor, nothing more.'"

* * * In practice * * * bleached out professionalism has been closely linked to particular normative and empirical claims that are themselves importantly bleached. Specifically, the idea that lawyers should not consider their racial identities when acting in their professional role is closely linked to the understanding that the legal rules and procedures that lawyers interpret and implement are also unaffected by issues of race. The claim that "our constitution"—and indeed justice itself—"is color-blind" is taken by many to be a bedrock principle of our legal order. Lawyers who either explicitly or implicitly call attention to racial issues are frequently viewed as undermining this ideal.

This charge—that a lawyer who interjects race or racism into a legal proceeding has "played the race card" in a manner that undermines "colorblind" justice—is itself formally colorblind, but in practice, color conscious. The charge is formally colorblind in the sense that it can be leveled against any lawyer regardless of that lawyer's race. * * * When a black lawyer adopts an explicitly race-conscious strategy, however, the charge of "playing the race card" is likely to be closely linked to the related charge of group-based loyalty in violation of the norms of bleached out professionalism. [T]he Simpson case is instructive. When critics accused Johnnie Cochran of "playing the race card," they frequently linked Cochran's explicitly race-conscious lawyering strategy with his identity as an African American. * * *

Finally, the practical link between bleached out professionalism and colorblindness has been strengthened by the implicit empirical claim that the American legal system is in fact largely, if not completely, colorblind. Once again, there is no necessary connection between the normative and the empirical sides of the colorblindness debate. One can subscribe to colorblindness as a normative ideal without also believing that our legal institutions fully, or even largely, live up to this ideal in practice. * * * The practical effect of bleached out professionalism * * * is to push all lawyers in the direction of accepting colorblindness as both a normative ideal and a factual reality in our contemporary culture.

* * *

Just as bleached out professionalism provides the dominant narrative through which most Americans have come to understand the three cases described [above], representing race theories have supplied the counternarrative that has helped to give these events much of their saliency. Thus, the country's fascination with Darden and Griffin is fueled in part by the charge, sometimes explicit, often merely implicit, that these two black attorneys have "betrayed" their race—in Darden's case by working on behalf of a "hostile white society to bring a strong black man down," and in Griffin's, by representing an organization that has brutalized and intimidated African-Americans for more than a century. The general perception of Cochran and Johnson has been similarly influenced by the counternarrative of representing race theories, albeit in the opposite direction. With respect to these lawyers, the charge is that they have represented their racial interests all too well—Cochran by "playing the race card" to free Simpson and Johnson by opposing the death penalty on the basis of his loyalty to his predominately black and Latino constituents—all at the expense of their professional obligations.

* * * The representing race model of lawyering, like the bleached out professionalism it challenges, underscores important goals that are central to our system of justice. * * * For black Americans, however, race continues to pose a substantial obstacle to obtaining anything like equal access to the benefits and protections of the law. Representing race accounts of lawyering, by focusing attention on this disparity and by directing lawyers to identify and to work against race prejudice, arguably help America move closer to its legitimating ideals. * * * It is this feature of the representing race model—its connection to the social justice claims of the entire black community—that provides the strongest justification for transforming a general critique of colorblindness into a repudiation of bleached out professionalism. The claim that blacks who obtain positions of power and influence in American society have an obligation to "give back" to their community is an old and venerable one. * * * The application of this maxim of race-based obligations to lawyers can be traced to Charles Hamilton Houston. In the 1930s, Houston argued that black lawyers should be trained to be social engineers "'prepared to anticipate, guide and interpret group advancement.'" Over the next twenty years, Houston and his protégé Thurgood Marshall created a new model for achieving social justice through law and the nation's first public interest law firm, the NAACP Legal Defense and Education Fund, with the skill and commitment to put that strategy into action. By calling on black lawyers to pay particular attention to the manner in which their professional activities are likely to affect the interests of the black community as a whole, representing race accounts of lawyering continue this Houstonian tradition.

The benefits of Houston's social engineering model for the justice claims of black Americans in the period leading up to Brown v. Board of Education cannot seriously be challenged. Perhaps it is possible to imagine that Brown would have eventually occurred without Houston's black social engineers, but it hardly seems worth the effort. Like virtually every other group that has ever attempted to overcome bigotry and oppression, black Americans in the pre-Brown period understood that their fate depended in large measure upon their own efforts to achieve liberation. Although black lawyers were certainly not the only participants in the civil rights movement—many whites also fought valiantly for the cause of equal rights—the fact that Houston's social engineers were prepared to self-consciously and forthrightly represent their race in the corridors of legal and political power has substantially improved the status of every black American, including those who continue to suffer in poverty and degradation.

Moreover, by dismantling de jure segregation, Houston and Marshall removed a powerful blight on the legal profession's age-old claim that lawyers are connected to justice. It is now common for liberals and conservatives alike to point to the crusade leading up to Brown as definitive proof that the legal profession, notwithstanding all of its connections to power and the status quo, in fact stands on the side of justice for all citizens. As a result, Houston's race-conscious lawyering strategy has ironically become a key element in the defense of the bleached out professional norm that "[l]awyers, as guardians of the law, play a vital role in the preservation of society."

* * * In theory, representing race accounts need not require the level of total commitment to racial issues that Houston sometimes seemed to suggest was required of the black lawyers in his day. For example, none of the theorists cited above suggest that the only appropriate role for black lawyers is the kind of full-time civil rights practice for which Houston prepared his social engineers. Nor must representing race advocates completely reject the moral force of the profession's traditional bleached out norms. Both Houston and Marshall, for example, consistently demonstrated respect for the profession's rules and practices even as they pursued their explicitly race-conscious strategy for social change.

In practice, however, representing race models tend to treat race as the central feature in the lives of black lawyers—a feature that overwhelms other professional commitments. This is clearly true in the popular debate about the obligations of black lawyers. In that debate, racial loyalty is often presented as an "either/or proposition—you're either for us or against us, a race man or a sellout." In such a world, as the popular portrayal of the Darden Dilemma amply demonstrates, when a black lawyer conforms his conduct to the profession's bleached out values, he "risk[s] his status as an authentic black man—and in the race man ideology, to be an authentic black man is to put the black race first."

Academic supporters of representing race models reject this sharp dichotomy. For example, in an important essay, Margaret Russell argues that black lawyers must move beyond the "false dichotomies" of "sellouts" and "race cards" in order to find meaningful ways of representing their clients and their communities.

Nevertheless, a good deal, although by no means all, of the scholarship in this area tends to minimize the importance of a black lawyer's professional obligations relative to those connected to her racial identity. * * * Even Margaret Russell's analysis of Darden and Simpson, although rejecting the popular dichotomy between sellouts and race men, suggests that race is the most important factor in the professional lives of black attorneys. Thus, Russell argues that given pervasive and systematic racism in the American justice system, every case involving a black lawyer "is at some level a 'race case.'" As a result, Russell concludes, race is often the defining feature of a black lawyer's professional identity. Nor does Russell believe that existing professional norms are likely to play much of a role in helping black lawyers resolve issues such as those that confronted Darden and Cochran. Instead, Russell proposes "community-based reflection" within the black community as the method for determining what it means for a black lawyer to represent her race.

* * *

If bleached out professionalism and representing race theory provide the narrative and counternarrative * * * , personal morality accounts of the lawyer's role constitute a seldom articulated but nevertheless pervasive subtext. On some occasions, this subtext is deployed as an indictment of conduct that allegedly undermines the norms of bleached out professionalism. For example, in a letter to Johnson concerning his decision not to seek the death penalty in any case, Governor Pataki stated, "'I cannot permit any District Attorney's personal opposition to a law to stand in the way of its enforcement . . . . No one . . . can substitute his or her sense of right and wrong for that of the Legislature.'" On other occasions, black lawyers invoke personal moral commitments as a defense to what are often perceived to be the all-encompassing demands of either race or role. For example, in responding to pleas from his NAACP colleagues that he "defer to another lawyer to handle matters involving the Klan," Anthony Griffin repeatedly emphasized his personal commitment to a near-absolutist interpretation of the First Amendment. Similarly, Darden defends his angry exchanges with Johnnie Cochran on the ground that he had "'responsibilities as a human being that were just as important as the responsibilities of being an African American.'"

* * * As the statements by Griffin and Darden * * * underscore, one way that black professionals have sought to escape the stark dilemma of the "sellout or race man" trope is to insist that questions such as this are primarily a matter of personal moral commitment. Thus, as I noted at the outset, Stephen Carter argues that the question whether a black lawyer has fulfilled his obligations to the black community "is something personal"; a choice that is "insulated from the cruel suggestions that we have left our people behind, because only we know that."

* * *

[F]or black Americans, the relationship between race and identity is a series of seemingly unending paradoxes. Race constitutes a significant aspect of our identity without there being any consistent set of narratives that constitute black identity. It affects other aspects of identity without determining them. Black Americans—like all Americans—have multiple and intersecting identities. Some are chosen for us—e.g., race, nationality, and family. Others we choose—e.g., politics, friends, and jobs. * * * Moreover, the line between chosen and choice is both difficult to see and subject to change. [F]or African Americans at the end of the millennium, race continues to be one of those rooted aspects of identity that helps to make us who we are.

Finally, as I indicated at the outset, for many blacks, their racial identity carries moral as well as practical significance. For many blacks, membership in the black community is an important source of human flourishing. As Stephen Carter has observed: "[r]acial solidarity, in the sense of self-love, is the key to our survival in a frustratingly segregated integrated professional world, just as it is the key to our survival in a frustratingly oppressive nation." But even those blacks who view racial identity as an unjust burden that must constantly be challenged have moral reasons for caring about the collective welfare of other blacks. Given the link between individual opportunity and collective advancement, even those blacks who care only about their own moral right to be free from racist constraints ought to recognize a moral responsibility to participate in collective projects to end racist oppression.

It is this complex sense of identity that black Americans bring to their roles as lawyers. None of the three models we have been discussing—bleached out professionalism, representing race theory, or personal morality lawyering—sufficiently accounts for this complexity. * * * Once we view racial identity as relatively rooted and salient in the lives of black Americans—in part as a result of the salience that this identity continues to have in the eyes of those who are not black—neither of these propositions is plausible. Black lawyers, even those who are strongly committed to their roles as lawyers, will have a difficult time "checking" their identities at the door. Christopher Darden is a perfect case in point. Darden repeatedly emphasized that he became a prosecutor in part so that he could "embolden my black brothers and sisters, show them that this was their system as well, that we were making progress." Racial identity, in other words, played a crucial role in shaping Darden's sense of his own professional identity. But, as Darden soon found out, the framing of the intersection of his racial and professional identities was not exclusively, or even primarily, within his control. "[I]nstead," Darden laments, "I was branded an Uncle Tom, a traitor used by The Man." Nor, in Darden's view, were whites able to look beyond "'the pigmentation of my skin.'" Race, in other words, defined the way that others saw him as much or more than it defined his own self image.

Given the saliency of race in our contemporary culture, none of this should be particularly surprising. The claim that lawyers and those with whom they interact can ignore race even if they wanted to requires believing that there is an "essential" core of rationality free from the pervasiveness of racial imagery, or that individuals can "construct" such a self out of existing cultural materials. Neither belief is warranted. Bleached out professionalism does not tell us how to come to terms with this reality.

Representing race theory constitutes one plausible method for filling this void. These theories rightly call attention to the importance of race in the lives of black Americans. By stressing the extent to which race dominates the lives of black lawyers, however, strong representing race accounts tend to undervalue the degree to which the decision to become a lawyer inevitably shapes a black lawyer's moral identity.

The Simpson case is again instructive. As I noted earlier, Margaret Russell divorces her examination of the manner in which race structured the famous exchanges between Christopher Darden and Johnnie Cochran from the legal and ethical merits of the lawyering strategies these two men employed. This way of framing the issue, however, obscures the moral weight of voluntarily assumed professional commitments. Unlike ordinary black citizens, both Darden and Cochran made an express commitment to abide by the rules of legal ethics. Consequently, in order to determine whether Christopher Darden "sold out" the interests of the black community by opposing the introduction of Fuhrman's alleged racism, or whether Johnnie Cochran "played the race card" in urging jurors to "send a message" that police racism and deception would no longer be tolerated, it is necessary to examine the legal and ethical merits of the arguments they employed. * * *

The consumer protection critique underscores that the public—judges, clients, victims—depend upon black lawyers, as they depend upon all lawyers, to honor their professional commitments. Black lawyers, therefore, cannot lightly dismiss professional norms that seek to protect the interests of defendants—particularly black defendants—accused of racially sensitive crimes. Nor should one disregard the professional norms that intend to protect the victims and potential victims—most of whom will also be African American—of black defendants accused of non-violent crimes. Strong versions of representing race ethics run the risk of subordinating all of these individual interests to the greater good of the black community.

Nor is there a credible argument that the legitimate constraining force of these voluntarily assumed professional commitments has been nullified by racism. * * * Indeed, it is precisely because of the racism that pervades American society that black lawyers have an acute interest in being recognized as free and equal moral actors capable of honoring their chosen commitments. As the opportunity critique underscores, the perception that black lawyers consider themselves exempt from ordinary role obligations threatens this status. To see the danger that strong versions of representing race theory pose to this crucial value, one need only imagine the likely effects of Paul Butler's proposal for black jury nullification. * * *

It is not inconceivable, for example, that if courts believe that black jurors are engaged in widespread race-based nullification, they might relax or perhaps even abrogate recent judicially imposed restrictions on using race as a proxy for jury selection. Even if courts refrain from taking this drastic step, prosecutors would certainly increase their covert efforts to accomplish this unlawful, but extremely difficult to detect, result. Equally important, the legitimacy of the determinations of those blacks who do manage to serve on juries would undoubtedly be called into question even more frequently than they are today.

Personal morality accounts of the lawyer's role paradoxically reinforce these problems. By emphasizing the importance of lawyers' getting in touch with their own "authentic" moral commitments, personal morality theories validate the element of choice in a black lawyer's moral personality that representing race theories tend to slight. The purpose behind this recognition, however, is to put individuals in touch with the moral commitments that they had before becoming lawyers and to help them learn to recognize circumstances where these commitments modify (or, in extreme cases, trump) what otherwise would be considered binding professional commitments. Once again, this formulation gives too little weight to collectively defined professional values. * * * As I have already indicated, lawyers are more than ordinary citizens; they have been given a monopoly by the state to occupy a position of trust both with respect to the interests of their clients and the public purposes of the legal framework. This status is a part of the moral identity of black lawyers.

Moreover, the rhetoric of individual reflection and personal values used by many personal morality theorists implies that moral decisionmaking is the product of "'the unencumbered self,'" free from any "'aims and attachments it does not choose for itself.'" It is this "self" that cultivates values and makes commitments that must ultimately be assimilated into one's professional role.

The view that moral commitments are the product of individual moral choice underestimates the important role that communal attachments--including attachments that are created without our express consent—play in the development of our moral personalities and in human flourishing more generally. As David Luban argues, "at bottom, moral deliberation takes place within communities—communities that can include friends and families, religious congregations, coworkers, or professional groups." For black lawyers, the black community is an important source of moral community.

* * * Bleached out professionalism, representing race theory, and personal morality lawyering all privilege one form of identity in a manner that distorts the proper significance of racial identity in the lives of black lawyers. * * * [T]he three models make a similar mistake about the lawyer's role. * * * Bleached out

professionalism, representing race theory, and personal morality lawyering all seek to simplify a black lawyer's moral universe by privileging one set of moral considerations—professionalism, racial solidarity, personal moral reflection—over other arguably relevant considerations. A full understanding of the integration of identity and role must begin by rejecting this kind of simplification. Black lawyers simultaneously inhabit all three of these moral domains: the "professional," representing the legitimate demands that accompany their professional status as lawyers; the "obligation thesis," representing the legitimate moral commitments that black lawyers owe to the African American community; and, for want of a better term, the "personal" universe, representing the inherent right of every black lawyer to pursue her own unique projects and commitments. * * * [I]n principle racial obligations are morally justified provided that black lawyers who seek to honor this commitment can do so in a manner consistent with the legitimate constraints imposed by the consumer protection and opportunity critiques. * * * The ethical life of a black attorney involves learning how to evaluate and balance these three moral domains—the professional, the obligation thesis, and the personal—within the confines of our common moral commitments. This is clearly a complex task. * * *

First, it is important to emphasize that the demands of the three moral worlds will not always be in conflict. * * * Second, even in circumstances where two or more of the moral spheres appear to be in conflict, a careful examination of the issues at stake can often reduce, although perhaps not eliminate, the scope of disagreement. Two standard interpretive tools should help black attorneys narrow the range of conflict. [L]awyers should employ the "principle of charity" to define the reasonable scope of each sphere. Under this principle, the lawyer should give professional norms, racial obligations, and personal commitments the best plausible interpretation that is consistent with the fact that each is bounded by the legitimate demands of the others, and ultimately, by common morality. [B]lack lawyers should utilize conventionalist theories of interpretation, which attempt to find coherence in the practices and conventions of a given interpretive community. * * * Third, in the event of a direct conflict—and such conflicts, I believe, are inevitable—black lawyers should choose the course of action that best supports the social purposes of the lawyering role in question. By "social purposes," I mean those aspects of a given lawyer's role that disinterested social actors would describe as necessary to achieve the social function for which the specific legal task at issue is designed to achieve. * * *

Finally, even if black lawyers were scrupulously to follow the method of reasoning I propose, it will still frequently be impossible for them to account for the legitimate demands of each moral sphere in every case. In particular cases, the legitimate moral demands of professionalism, group obligations, and personal commitments will conflict in ways that no overarching decisionmaking criteria can resolve. As a result, even the best thought-out and executed moral plan is likely to produce what the noted philosopher Bernard Williams refers to as "a moral remainder:" the moral residue from the competing moral positions that simply could not be accommodated in the final action. * * * Black lawyers must develop methods for accounting for this moral residue in future actions.

* * *

Let us return to the three cases with which we began: the black lawyer who represents the Ku Klux Klan, the black district attorney who refused to seek the death penalty, and the Simpson prosecution. The first step in applying the framework I propose is to recharacterize each case in terms of a clash among the lawyer in question's professional, race-related, and personal moral commitments. Thus, Anthony Griffin's decision to represent the Klan is solidly grounded in both a long-standing professional commitment to provide legal representation for even the most repugnant clients and Griffin's strong personal commitment to his colleagues at the ACLU and, more generally, to a robust interpretation of the First Amendment. These professional and personal commitments, however, appear (at least on first blush) to conflict with Griffin's obligation to protect the black community's interest in combating racist oppression, or, at a minimum, not to assist those who victimize blacks from escaping prosecution.

Robert Johnson's situation exemplifies a somewhat different configuration of interests. Johnson's race-based obligation to refrain from participating in a form of punishment that, in his view, will inevitably be applied in a racially discriminatory manner appears to conflict with his professional obligation to enforce the law as written. Johnson also appears to be personally opposed to the death penalty.

The now infamous Darden-Cochran exchanges highlight additional alignments. As one of the lead prosecutors, Darden had a strong professional obligation to present all reasonable arguments pointing to Simpson's guilt. Moreover, this role-related obligation coincided with Darden's personal belief that Simpson was guilty and, more generally, with his commitment to vigorous law enforcement. In the eyes of many blacks and some whites, however, Darden's efforts to suppress Fuhrman's prior racist statements—and his prosecution of Simpson generally—are emblematic of the manner in which the criminal justice system fails to respect the rights of African Americans. Many of these same blacks and whites viewed Cochran's infamous call for the jury to "send a message" that police racism and incompetence should not be tolerated as speaking directly to this race-related obligation. Like Darden, Cochran's advocacy tracked his personal beliefs, both about Simpson's guilt (i.e., that Simpson was innocent) and about law enforcement generally (i.e., that the police frequently mistreat, and not infrequently attempt to frame, African American defendants). Although these race-based and personal commitments were consistent with Cochran's duty to provide Simpson a zealous defense, many assert that they led him to exceed the legitimate professional boundaries of such a defense by unethically injecting race into the trial.

The first thing to notice about this recharacterization of these three cases is that it demonstrates that adherents of bleached out professionalism exaggerate the danger of allowing lawyers to incorporate their identity into their professional roles. In each of these cases, one important consequence of integrating identity and role is to reinforce, at great personal cost, professional norms. Thus, Anthony Griffin's strong suspicion of state power is rooted in his experience as a black man growing up in the South. This suspicion, in turn, underlies his personal commitment to the ACLU and its strong support of First Amendment rights, which in turn motivates Griffin to uphold one of bleached out professionalism's highest aspirational goals: making legal counsel available to clients with unpopular views. Similarly, Robert Johnson's opposition to the death penalty, rooted in his experience in and commitment to the black community, was the motivating force behind his willingness to risk his career in an effort to prevent the State from pursuing a course of action that threatens the legal profession's central bleached out maxim: the promise of equal justice under law. Finally, both Darden and Cochran directly called on their experiences as African American men to support their professional obligation to zealously advocate their respective clients' positions regarding the admission of Fuhrman's prior racist statements * * *.

That being said, all three of these cases also appear to present a classic conflict among the competing demands of race, individual autonomy, and professional role. In order to determine whether there is such a conflict, however, it is necessary to look more closely at the claims that have been made about the content and scope of the obligations emanating from each of these moral domains.

A. Charity and Conventionalism: Narrowing the Gap

Consider the case of the black lawyer and the Ku Klux Klan. Many media commentators—and even Griffin himself—discussed this case as if Griffin had an ethical obligation to represent the Klan. Current bleached out professional norms, however, impose no such requirement. Instead, the rules of professional responsibility expressly grant lawyers the permission to turn down cases for virtually any reason, including that the lawyer has a sincere moral disagreement with the client or the client's cause. As William Kunstler, who for more than four decades was perhaps America's foremost advocate for unpopular clients, once stated when explaining why he would not represent the Klan: "Everyone has a right to a lawyer, that's true. But they don't have a right to me."

* * *

To note that the professional sphere's demands on Griffin are not as capacious as some have portrayed, however, does not mean that they are unimportant. The rules of professional responsibility urge lawyers not to turn away unpopular clients or causes. * * * As a loyal member of the ACLU, Griffin was committed to defending First Amendment principles regardless of his personal opposition to his client's views. This strongly held personal conviction is crucial to any evaluation of Griffin's actions. Nevertheless, it is important to see that Griffin was not compelled to represent the Klan by the profession's norms. Nor should he have been, given our respect for the very moral autonomy that, in the last analysis, makes me support his decision to represent the Klan in this case.

* * * [In the Johnson case,] Governor Pataki and many critics in the media claimed that Johnson put himself "above the law" when he refused to drop his opposition to the death penalty after the legislature enacted New York's first capital statute. This characterization, however, fails to acknowledge sufficiently those aspects of Johnson's role as district attorney that provide space for at least some of Johnson's actions. For example, in addition to being an "advocate," Johnson is also an administrator. In that capacity, he is responsible for allocating the scarce resources of the prosecutor's office in the most efficient manner possible. Johnson argued that one reason he did not intend to seek the death penalty is that death cases were not an efficient use of the office's resources compared with the alternative of seeking life without parole. * * * Moreover, in addition to being an administrator, Johnson is also an elected official. * * *

Although these role-related considerations help us to place Johnson's decision in its proper context, they do not justify his blanket refusal to seek the death penalty in all cases. Although the statute expressly grants Johnson discretion, a fair reading requires a district attorney to exercise that discretion on a case-by-case basis consistent with the legislature's determination that the death penalty is at least presumptively cost justified. Similarly, although Johnson is responsible to his constituents, he does not have the authority to exempt his jurisdiction from laws enacted by a higher sovereign authority. * * * Johnson, therefore, had a professional obligation to seek the death penalty in cases where, in his professional judgment, the punishment was warranted under the statute. Assuming that the death penalty is not per se immoral, Johnson was morally bound by this commitment. * * *

When faced with a direct conflict between or among the legitimate demands of two or more moral spheres, black lawyers must learn to recognize and give regard to the legitimate social purposes underlying the particular lawyering role in question. * * * Consider, for example, the prosecution's strategy in the Simpson case. Both Garcetti and Darden stated repeatedly that race was not an issue in the case. To the extent that these statements were intended to convey the impression that race was irrelevant, they were clearly wrong. Long before Fuhrman's racism or the racial composition of the jury surfaced as issues in the case, the simple fact that a black man was accused of murdering his white (blond, no less) former wife and her handsome white friend ensured that race was likely to play an important role in how people viewed the case. Nevertheless, the prosecution's statements captured an important aspirational norm fundamental to the social purpose of our justice system: that race should not affect the determination of the accused's guilt or innocence. To honor this norm, however, prosecutors are sometimes justified in engaging in race-conscious lawyering strategies.

Viewed from this perspective, Garcetti's decision to prosecute Simpson in Los Angeles County rather than in Santa Monica County and his addition of Darden to the prosecution team support, rather than undermine, the legitimate aspirations of the criminal justice system. Given the composition of the respective jury pools, a Los Angeles jury would likely include several blacks. A Santa Monica jury would not. In light of the racially charged atmosphere in L.A. at the time of the Simpson trial, and the long history of the demonization of black male sexuality, trying the case before a jury that included at least some blacks arguably made it more likely that the legal system would honor—and just as important, be seen as honoring—its commitment that race should not affect the determination of Simpson's guilt. Similarly, Garcetti's race-conscious decision to add a black prosecutor to the team—particularly one with a history of uncovering and prosecuting police misconduct—plausibly increased the chance that Simpson's allegations of official bias and corruption would receive—and, once again, be perceived as receiving—a fair hearing.

The argument that these race-conscious lawyering strategies support, rather than undermine, the legitimate social purposes of the criminal justice system presumes that those black participants included in the proceeding will honor their legitimate role obligations and will not simply become racial patriots. This does not require that they subscribe to bleached out professionalism. Thus, black jurors were entitled to bring their experience and understanding of racism and official corruption into the jury room. At the end of the day, however, they were obligated to acquit or convict Simpson on the basis of the evidence and arguments presented during the trial. * * *

Similar arguments constrained Darden and Cochran. As I have already indicated, Darden's argument in favor of suppressing Fuhrman's racist statements was expressly color-conscious. Given that he was one of the lead prosecutors on the case, however, Darden was obligated to deploy this color-conscious strategy for the purpose of keeping Fuhrman's statements away from the jury. As a black man, and a strong opponent of racism within the police department, Darden may well have believed that exposing Fuhrman's racism would advance the black community's interests by highlighting the problems with the police that African Americans encounter on a daily basis. Nevertheless, as a prosecutor, Darden had an ethical obligation to make all reasonable arguments in favor of Simpson's guilt. Darden had good grounds under the applicable rules of evidence for seeking to exclude Fuhrman's statements during his initial appearance on the witness stand. To honor the legitimate social purpose that the strength of the State's case should not be affected by the race of the prosecutor, Darden was obligated to present this argument.

One can apply the same analysis to Cochran's "send a message" statement during his closing argument. Once again, Cochran's argument was race-conscious to the extent that it directed the jury's attention to the defense's claim that police racism infected the investigatory process. However, Cochran's argument may not have exceeded the bounds of legitimate advocacy in a criminal case. "Send a message" arguments are a standard part of the trope of both prosecutors and defense lawyers in criminal cases. Although controversial, this rhetorical device arguably is not a call for nullification. Unlike Butler's proposal, Cochran's argument was based on the alleged existence of racism and corruption in the Simpson prosecution itself. Nor did Cochran limit his appeal to black jurors; instead, he emphasized that all Americans have a stake in ensuring that police racism does not taint the trial process. Regardless of whether one finds these arguments convincing, as Simpson's defense lawyer, Cochran was ethically obligated to present all reasonable arguments in favor of his client.

* * *

The social purposes underlying criminal defense do not license any and all conduct that might advance the client's cause. Arguments designed to appeal to the racial prejudice of black jurors, for example by suggesting that beating a white man is morally acceptable because of the existence of widespread racism among whites, undermine, rather than support, the legitimate social purposes of criminal defense advocacy. * * * Even in circumstances where a black lawyer feels compelled to violate an express professional command, considerations of social purposes dictate that she do so in a manner that respects the moral force of existing norms. One can see the value of this requirement by contrasting Robert Johnson's actions in death penalty cases with those of Robert Morganthau, the respected District Attorney for the Borough of Manhattan. Johnson publicly announced his intention not to seek the death penalty and carefully explained his reasons for not doing so. By all accounts, Morganthau shares Johnson's view that the death penalty is administratively inefficient and morally reprehensible. Unlike Johnson, however, Morganthau has consistently taken the position that "he would enforce the will of the people but privately did as little as possible to actually prepare a death-penalty case."

Although Morganthau has largely escaped criticism by covertly submerging his opposition to the death penalty into case-by-case decisionmaking, Johnson, not Morganthau, has demonstrated the appropriate respect for the social purposes of his role as prosecutor. As David Luban argues, lawyers who conscientiously object to unjust laws can play an important role in educating the public about the pernicious effects of legal rules. Given their express authority to interpret legal rules, prosecutors are in a particularly strong position to accomplish this objective. To do so, however, prosecutors must make their objections public and open to review and criticism. By so doing, they both foster public debate and reaffirm respect for the law. The fact that this form of conscientious objection might not be effective—as it was not in Johnson's case—is simply the predictable price of life in a morally complex world. This brings us to the issue of the moral remainder.

* * *

Let us return to the challenge with which we began. Is it possible to define a role for race-based moral obligations that neither undermines the legitimate rights of consumers nor unduly constrains the opportunities of black lawyers? I submit that we can now answer this question with a qualified "yes."

The analysis I propose offers consumers four interlocking safeguards that their legitimate interests will be protected. First, the model insists that professional obligations carry independent moral weight. Black lawyers, like all lawyers, must take these obligations seriously. Second, all legitimate racial obligations must be derived from, and ultimately be subservient to, common morality. Racial obligations are therefore no excuse for race-based oppression. Third, in cases where there is an unavoidable conflict between a black lawyer's racial obligations and her professional commitments, it is the legitimate social purposes underlying her professional obligations that must eventually carry the day. Racial solidarity, in other words, can never undermine the legitimate (as opposed to the self-interested) demands of professionalism. Fourth, to the extent that a black lawyer finds it impossible to conform to these demands, she must, like Robert Johnson, express her disagreement in ways that ultimately support the moral force of the professional norm.

These safeguards should, in turn, help to protect black lawyers from the claim that they are not "real" lawyers because they have commitments based on contingent features of their identity. As a preliminary matter, these commitments will often reinforce, rather than undermine, a black lawyer's willingness to uphold the legal profession's articulated standards. But even in circumstances where professional and group-based concerns conflict, it is far from clear that the profession or those it serves would be better off if these conflicts were always resolved in favor of existing norms or practices. By branding all outside ideas as illegitimate, bleached out professionalism tends to discourage innovation in the delivery of legal services.

* * *

Of course, the fact that black lawyers committed to the obligation thesis may confer certain benefits on clients and the profession will not prevent them from being stigmatized as less than "real" lawyers. This danger, of course, must be put in the context of the kind of demonizing of black lawyers that currently goes on under the banner of bleached out professionalism. It is possible, perhaps even likely, that any move by black lawyers to embrace the obligation thesis more fully will only serve to exacerbate these affronts.

The real question, therefore, is not whether the obligation thesis can ever completely escape the opportunity critique; it cannot. Instead, the question that must be asked is whether the benefits of black lawyers' embracing this moral commitment outweigh its costs. These costs and benefits cannot be measured solely, or even primarily, from the perspective of those black women and men who are fortunate enough to become lawyers. Black lawyers have already benefited from the obligation thesis. Without the dedicated actions of Charles Hamilton Houston and Thurgood Marshall, the current generation of black lawyers would have few of the advantages that they currently enjoy. Instead, calculations concerning the benefits of the obligation thesis, like any other moral obligation, must be evaluated primarily from the perspective of those the thesis is intended to benefit: the black women and men who continue to suffer in poverty and degradation in the midst of this land of plenty. This community desperately needs the support and commitment of those of us who have managed to stake out a tenuous, but nevertheless important, toehold on the American dream. Providing that help inevitably involves risks, but those risks (at least as I have defined them) pale in comparison with the chance to finally make progress on ending America's legacy of racial oppression. * * *

5. *Civics Teacher*

Today, the original understanding of lawyers as America's governing class has little traction with law students and lawyers who consider this view elitist and anti-democratic. Proponents of the civics teacher approach offersa different way to revive the values of the original understanding without the assumptions that critics find elitist and antidemocratic. Do they succeed?

[Question 1]

In the 1960s, Erwin Smigel found that big firm lawyers viewed their role as closer to that of the:

  (A) civics teacher.

  (B) hired gun.

[Question 2]

Proponents of the lawyer as civics teacher argue that lawyers are properly civics teachers because they are necessarily more virtuous than nonlawyers?

  (A) Yes

  (B) No

[Question 3]

Proponents argue that lawyers are civics teachers:

(A) because descriptively they serve that function.

(B) because normatively they should serve that function.

(C) both A and B.

(D) neither A nor B.

[Question 4]

A lawyer acting as civics teacher would always:

(A) spy on her client for the government.

(B) be a hired gun because the system requires it.

(C) explain the spirit of the law as well as the letter.

(D) impose her values on the client.

[Question 5]

Both perspectives on the lawyer as teacher require moral counseling.

(A) True

(B) False

[Question 6]

If clients generally shared the view of Ben W. Heineman, Jr., former Senior Vice-President for Law and Public Affairs for General Electric, they would:

(A) object to the lawyer as civics teacher.

(B) welcome the lawyer as civics teacher.

(C) be indifferent to the lawyer as civics teacher.

RUSSELL G. PEARCE, *THE LEGAL PROFESSION AS A BLUE STATE:
REFLECTIONS ON PUBLIC PHILOSOPHY, JURISPRUDENCE, AND LEGAL ETHICS,*
75 Fordham L. Rev. 1339, 1362-65 (2006)

* * * But the bar's strategy of combining the rhetoric of the public good with the hired gun perspective took a toll on lawyers and society. Professionalism's promise that lawyers' work contributed to the public good had provided earlier generations of lawyers with a coherent understanding of why their work was important. As lawyers came to view themselves as largely self-interested, the rhetoric of professionalism rang false. Absent an alternative approach to finding fulfillment in their stressful practices, lawyers had difficulty finding reward in their work. Their rates of job dissatisfaction, substance abuse, and anxiety-related mental illness exceeded those for other occupations.

Lawyers also failed their obligation to society. Even though the hired gun ideal denied it, lawyers continued to serve as the governing class. Aside from their continued overrepresentation in the formal institutions of government, they remained the primary intermediaries between the people and the law through their representation of clients and their community leadership. In that role, lawyers brought disrespect to the law and the legal system when they pursued self-interest at the same time as they claimed to serve the public good. To the public and to themselves, lawyers appeared to be "hypocrites, cynics, or fools."

Moreover, as hired guns who denied moral accountability, lawyers taught clients to view the law instrumentally and to devalue obligations to conscience and community. This approach only benefited society under a rather pure libertarian view, like that of Milton Friedman, which defined a just society as one where individuals pursue their own self-interest within the bounds of the letter of the law and reject the existence of moral obligations derived from a public good. Most Americans, even those who employed Blue State rhetoric, did not actually accept individual freedom as the complete measure of a just society. To them, the hired gun's amorality undermined the responsibilities a community rightfully demanded from its members.

Even within the legal system itself, the hired gun approach failed to satisfy lawyers' responsibilities. The adversarial legal system delivers justice and truth when each party has an equal opportunity to promote its interests to the court. This can only occur if each party has equal access to * * * the same quality of legal services. Otherwise, unequal justice will result. In our current system, where access to legal services is pervasively unequal, the hired gun exacerbates injustices that a commitment to the public good could possibly mitigate. * * *

In a society where deep divisions exist regarding fundamental value questions, lawyers have failed to provide leadership in healing those divisions. A legal profession identified with the Blue State vision of excluding values from the public square has little to contribute if the public square is inevitably full of value conflict and debate. Indeed, even those in the Blue State camp have begun to recognize this dilemma. An increasing number of politically liberal commentators are acknowledging what conservative and progressive critics of liberalism have long argued: that the asserted effort to prevent the "impos[ition of] personal ethical values" actually conceals value judgments grounded in specific visions of the public good. The legal profession, too, must abandon the Blue State rhetoric if it is to play a leading role in helping transform value conflicts from culture wars to civil and respectful disagreement.

All people, lawyers or not, are morally accountable for their work at the same time as they balance their duty to the public good with their self-interest. What makes lawyers different is not their superior moral capacity, as lawyers have historically claimed. Rather, it is their work. As the intermediaries between the law and the people, lawyers have both an individual and collective responsibility for the health of the legal system and society. Unless lawyers believe, like Milton Friedman, that the public good consists of nothing more than maximizing individual freedom, they must find a way to translate their public responsibility into their everyday work. That would not require dictating to clients or overriding their choices. It would require counseling clients on the moral implications of their choices.

To effectively perform that role, lawyers would have to revive their capacity to serve as a political leadership class. Engaging clients in moral counseling would require lawyers to develop the ability to promote dialogue among and between people of differing values. If lawyers incorporated this ethic into their role as intermediaries between the people and the law, they would better serve their governing class function and make a valuable contribution to healing the Blue State-Red State divide.

BRUCE A. GREEN & RUSSELL G. PEARCE, "PUBLIC SERVICE MUST BEGIN AT HOME": THE LAWYER AS CIVICS TEACHER IN EVERYDAY PRACTICE,
50 Wm. & Mary L. Rev. 1207 (2009)

Fifty years ago, the leading national representatives of the American legal profession, the American Bar Association (ABA), and the Association of American Law Schools (AALS), issued a joint report (the Report) on the nature of lawyers' professional responsibility in the context of the adversary system. Principally authored by legal philosopher Lon Fuller, who co-chaired the joint conference that issued it, the Report's premise was that the legal profession's inherited traditions provided only indirect guidance to lawyers in light of their changing roles, and that a "true sense of professional responsibility" must derive from an understanding of the "special services" that the legal profession "renders to society and the services it might render if its full capacities were realized." A decade later, the Report was quoted throughout the footnotes to the Preamble and Ethical Considerations of the ABA Code of Professional Responsibility, suggesting that the Report captured or influenced understandings that continued at least through the early 1970s.

* * *

The conception of the lawyer as civics teacher directly addresses the lawyer's role as client counselor in the daily private practice of law, regardless of whether the matter relates to a transaction or to litigation. It emphasizes that when lawyers counsel clients about their legal rights and obligations, and about how to act within the framework of the law, lawyers invariably teach clients not only about the law and legal institutions, but also, for better or worse, about rights and obligations in a civil society that may not be established by enforceable law-including ideas about fair dealing, respect for others, and, generally, concern for the public good. This conception also addresses aspects of lawyers' work aside from client counseling, because lawyers teach clients by example, especially when lawyers address their own legal obligations in the course of a representation. Adopting and elaborating upon the idea of the lawyer's role as civics teacher, we suggest, would lead lawyers to perform this function more self-consciously and, therefore, more often for the better.

* * *

I. The Idea of the Lawyer as Civics Teacher

In his dissenting opinion in Olmstead v. United States, Justice Brandeis wrote that: "Our Government is the potent, the omnipresent teacher. For good or for ill, it teaches the whole people by its example." * * *

Borrowing Justice Brandeis's phrase, we would describe lawyers also as potent and omnipresent teachers, particularly on the subject of civic norms and values.   In part, our claim is descriptive. In society, lawyers in fact teach their fellow citizens how to understand their rights and responsibilities as members of a community-their obligations to obey the law, aspirations to fulfill the spirit of the law, and responsibilities to the good of their neighbors and the general public. Lawyers teach civics both directly in the course of counseling clients and indirectly by example. They do so through what they say and do, and through their silence and inaction, whether or not they are self-conscious about the role, and, if they are self-conscious, whether they consider this function to be central or incidental to their work. Like the government, lawyers teach for good or for ill and whether or not they intend to do so.

A few examples will help illustrate this idea.

When lawyers counsel clients about how to act within the law, especially when the meaning of the law is unclear, they explicitly or implicitly teach their clients about civic obligations both under the law and beyond the law. Advising the client to stay comfortably within the law (or to comply with the imperfectly expressed spirit or purpose of the law) teaches one conception of civic obligation. Encouraging the client to exploit legal loopholes or to test legal limits teaches a different conception. Similar lessons are taught by example. When litigators decide how to comply with uncertain discovery and procedural obligations—whether to implement the spirit of the law or to exploit the law's inexactitude-they teach by example, conveying to clients how the lawyer regards her own civic responsibility in addressing legal boundaries.

When transactional lawyers advise clients about what to disclose to those with whom their clients are doing business, independently of legal disclosure obligations, lawyers convey their understandings about mutual obligation among those who engage in commerce within the civic community. Lawyers teach similar lessons by example when clients observe the lawyer's own negotiations and the extent to which the lawyer is candid or unforthcoming.

When a lawyer concludes that the client has only a weak legal claim or defense in litigation, the lawyer's advice (or lack of advice) about whether to proceed in litigation teaches a lesson. The client has a legal right to exploit the proceedings if the claim or defense is not frivolous, and doing so may enable the client to pressure the opposing party to settle on favorable terms. Whether the lawyer encourages this, admonishes that this is not a proper use of the courts or not a proper attitude toward legal rights and obligations, or, indeed, refuses to represent the client in court, teaches the client not only about legal rights but also about the role of the courts and attitudes toward the law and legal institutions. Of course, additional counseling considerations apply where a case raises issues of systemic or distributive justice, such as when a party seeks law reform to promote a broader view of justice, where significant imbalances in power exist between the power of the parties, or where a party's fundamental needs (such as food or shelter) are at stake.

Similar lessons are taught when a lawyer counsels a client whose claim or defense, although legally sound, is inequitable. Two examples are traditionally given. In the first, a debtor client with the financial ability to pay a just debt must decide whether to repay the debt or invoke the statute of limitations to bar the creditor from recovering. In the second, a client who agreed orally to convey property and received money for it, but then received a better offer, might decide whether to convey the property or attempt to defeat a claim for transfer of the property by arguing that a writing was necessary to establish a binding agreement. Whether the lawyer advises the first client to pay the debt or advises the second client to convey the property, as a matter of civic obligation, or instead accepts the representation and invokes the legal defense, teaches the client, for better or worse, about how to regard legally unenforceable agreements made to others in the community. Here, too, questions of systemic or distributive justice may also complicate the counseling challenge.

Although our focus is on everyday private practice, we note also that lawyers unavoidably teach civics by example outside their professional work. When lawyers serve on juries, they make an implicit public statement about the significance of this civic obligation. When they seek to avoid jury service, claiming that they lack the time or suggesting that they know too much to be fair, they teach the opposite lesson, whether or not intentionally.

* * * The lawyer as civics teacher is an ordinary, contemporary American lawyer whose sense of civic obligation influences his or her daily private practice, and most especially his or her approach to counseling clients.

This means that the lawyer does not rest on the claim that ordinary legal practice plays a significant role in civic life for reasons that are intrinsic to law practice-for example, as may be true, that lawyers promote a just society whenever they advocate for clients within the bounds of the law and that they promote the rule of law whenever they advise clients about the law's limits. The civic teaching role we envision involves a more robust idea of "civics" and a more self-conscious idea of teaching. At a minimum, this includes educating clients about civic obligations that are not legally enforceable and that may be found in the "spirit" of the law. Further, and perhaps even less precisely, our concept includes counseling clients about general concepts (equality, respect for others, fairness, civility) that are not captured by either the law's letter or spirit, but that reflect ideas of civic obligation that influence people's voluntary conduct as an ordinary matter and that may therefore bear on the client's or lawyer's conduct in a legal representation.

Three additional observations: First, we would not limit the lawyer-client conversation about the public good to situations where the clients' proposed conduct is patently antisocial. Lawyers assist clients in making fully informed decisions. This requires consideration of all relevant considerations, not just legal considerations. Considerations of civic obligation are relevant even when it is far from clear which way they point or when they point in conflicting directions.

Second, and relatedly, civic obligations can mean different things to different lawyers and at different moments in history. The nineteenth-century legal elite had a notion of civic obligation that was typically aligned with that of their clients, that gave primacy to property interests, and that was inconsistent in many ways with contemporary notions. Lawyers today may have ideas of civic obligation that are far less closely aligned with their clients' civic intuitions. Thus, we do not suggest that lawyers' civic teachings must have any prescribed content, other than that the "hired gun approach, focusing exclusively on compliance with the "letter of the law," reflects too narrow a view. Generally speaking, as Deborah Rhode has previously observed, the lawyer's role requires counseling about and consideration for "the letter of the law, and . . . core principles of honesty, fairness, and social responsibility."

Finally, it follows from this that our emphasis is on opening up a lawyer-client conversation about civic obligation and the public good. We are not proposing that lawyers demand that the client act in any particular way or that lawyers generally decline or terminate a representation when the client's lawful conduct strikes the lawyer as antisocial, although there may be situations that warrant doing so. Some nineteenth-century writers took that stronger view of lawyers' obligation to integrate civic considerations into their practice, insisting that certain objectives, although lawful, should not be furthered, and certain means, although lawful, should not be employed. Some commentators today take a similar view. We do not do so, in part because we think that discerning obligations of citizenship, beyond maintaining a commitment to compliance with the law, is complicated, and in part because we believe that good "teaching" means having a mutually respectful conversation in which the teacher does not compel adherence to her views.

II. Why Lawyers Should Teach Civics Well

Besides making a descriptive claim, we make a prescriptive claim: that lawyers should consider their role as civics teachers to be central to their work and should strive to teach it well. We offer two arguments. The first, which echoes Brandeis's observation in Olmstead, might be summed up as follows: "As long as lawyers are unavoidably teaching ethics, they ought to try to do a good job of it, if only out of a sense of public obligation." The second, which derives from the ABA/AALS Report and from other writings before and since, reflects an affirmative understanding of the lawyer's responsibilities.

A. Teaching Civics Well as a Public Service

Lawyers should teach civics self-consciously and for the better because lawyers are potent and invariable teachers of the subject, the subject is important, and teaching it well is a public service that lawyers can provide with no special effort.

To begin with, the need for civics education is plain. In a collection of writings on the "citizen lawyer," it is most appropriate to cite no less a source than Thomas

Jefferson, who wrote: "I know of no safe depository of the ultimate powers of society but the people themselves; and if we think them not enlightened enough to exercise their control with a wholesome discretion, the remedy is not to take it from them but to inform their discretion." To put it more prosaically, people need to understand their rights, responsibilities, and roles in a civil society. The effective functioning of our society presupposes that they do. Each new generation must be taught.

It is also well-acknowledged that schools do not always do the job successfully and thoroughly, and people have too few other effective opportunities to learn. People can learn indirectly through observation of others, but those whom they observe may not be adequate role models or, in observing, people may infer the wrong lessons.

A legal representation, on the other hand, is an obvious context in which to teach civics to clients and to the community. Understandings about how to regard the law and how to interact with legal institutions and fellow citizens are implicitly or explicitly implicated in virtually all representations. We have noted that clients can learn indirectly by observing their lawyers, or they can learn directly in the civics tutorial that we ordinarily call client counseling. But beyond that, clients can "learn by doing," which is one of the most effective ways to learn. That is the case when the legal representation calls on the client to give effect to, or to ignore, his understanding of his own civic obligations. Neither form of education is limited to clients alone. Friends, family, coworkers, employees, employers, adversaries, community members-all who learn of the matter through word of mouth or the press and all whose lives are affected directly and indirectly-will receive a lesson in civic responsibility.

One can argue that the government, in licensing lawyers, might fairly demand that lawyers shoulder this responsibility. Or one might argue, as we do below in Section B, that promoting clients' sound understandings of civic responsibility is intrinsic to the lawyer's role, properly understood. But those are separate claims. Our point here is simply that, if teaching civics by word and deed is unavoidable, lawyers' commitment to the public good compels the conclusion that lawyers should take this function seriously and strive to teach well. Lawyers who teach civics well serve an important public function, while those who teach poorly undermine the public interest in having civically disposed and informed citizens.

B. Teaching Civics Well as Intrinsic to the Lawyer's Social Function

Fuller's Report does not refer to lawyers as "civics teachers." But it does describe the lawyer's role in a manner that * * * gives significant weight to the lawyer's duty to serve the public in ordinary private practice and that, in particular, takes note of the lawyer's pedagogic role in doing so. The ABA/AALS Report's conception had antecedents in earlier writings on the legal profession and it was carried over into subsequent writings

1. The ABA/AALS Report's Idea of Lawyers' Pedagogic Role as Derived from Their Social Function

To begin with, Fuller's Report takes the view that a lawyer's "work must find its direction within a larger frame" than simply "the faithful discharge of duties assigned to him by others." That larger framework is provided by an understanding of the lawyer's societal role. The Report recognizes that "[p]rivate practice is a form of public service when it is conducted with appreciation of, and a respect for, the larger framework of government of which it forms a part, including under the term government . . . voluntary forms of self-regulation."

That lawyers in private practice serve a quasi-governmental function is a pervasive concept in the Report, which refers to the lawyer's position as an "office," suggesting that the lawyer serves as more, or other, than simply an agent of private clients. This conception is set forth explicitly by the Report's pronouncement that "[t]he lawyer's highest loyalty" is not to the client "but to procedures and institutions"—an implicit repudiation of the "hired gun" conception that is often attributed to Henry Lord Brougham. The Report describes the lawyer as a trustee "for the integrity of those fundamental processes of government and self-government upon which the successful functioning of our society depends," and observes that "democratic and constitutional government is tragically dependent on voluntary . . . co-operation in the maintenance of its fundamental processes and forms." The Report sketches out the significance of this conception of the private practitioner's role in the context of three functions that lawyers perform: advocacy, negotiating and drafting, and counseling.

Not surprisingly, the Report envisions adjudication as serving a crucial governmental function: the impartial resolution of disputes. It describes adjudication within an adversary setting in particular as crucial to just resolutions. Without adversary presentations, the judge would be required to serve not only as neutral arbiter but as both parties' representatives, going back and forth between a sympathetic identification with the parties and a neutral role, with the likelihood of judging prematurely. "Partisan advocacy," which relieves the judge of these multiple roles, thus "plays a vital and essential role in one of the most fundamental procedures of a democratic society. . . . The institution of advocacy is . . . an expression of human insight in the design of a social framework within which man's capacity for impartial judgment can attain its fullest realization." Partisan advocacy, however, does not invariably serve the prescribed social function. Partisanship must be restricted in accordance with these general principles. On one hand, "[t]he advocate plays his role well when zeal for his client's cause promotes a wise and informed decision of the case. . . . Thus, partisan advocacy is a form of public service so long as it aids the process of adjudication." On the other hand, partisan advocacy ceases to serve the public "when it hinders that process, when it misleads, distorts and obfuscates, when it renders the task of the deciding tribunal not easier, but more difficult."

Although the lawyer's role in negotiating and drafting takes place outside the setting of government institutions and processes, the Report situates that role in the context of voluntary self-governance, which it regards as playing an equally important role in a democracy. It notes that most "human relations are set" in our society "by the voluntary action of the affected parties," who "collaborate and . . . arrange their relations" by, for example, "forming corporations [and] partnerships," contracting and leasing, and transacting in other large and small ways "by which their rights and duties toward one another are defined." "[S]uccessful . . . collaboration" requires "a framework for the parties' future dealings," comparable to a formal charter, and in our society, the lawyer is "the natural architect of this framework." In this role, the lawyer "advances the public interest when he facilitates the processes of voluntary self-government" but "works against the public interest when he obstructs the channels of collaborative effort, when he seeks petty advantages to the detriment of the larger processes in which he participates." As in advocacy, the lawyer's duty is not solely to the client: "[T]he good lawyer does not serve merely as a legal conduit for his client's desires, but as a wise counselor, experienced in the art of devising arrangements that will put in workable order the entangled affairs and interests of human beings."

Finally, as counselor, the lawyer "contributes to the administration of the law" and "effective realization of the law's aims" by advising clients about the outcome of potential litigation and about compliance with the law. The Report observes that by reminding clients of the "long-run costs" of proposed conduct, "the lawyer often deters his client from a course of conduct technically permissible under existing law, though inconsistent with its underlying spirit and purpose." And it cautions that "[t]he reasons that justify and even require partisan advocacy . . . do not grant any license to the lawyer to participate as legal advisor in a line of conduct that is immoral, unfair, or of doubtful legality."

The Report envisions the lawyer's responsibility to promote governance and self-governance as including a pedagogic role. For example, it observes that the lawyer has a duty to preserve voluntary cooperation "by imparting the understanding necessary to give it direction and effectiveness"—"a duty that attaches [both] to his private practice [and] to his relations with the public." Further, the lawyer "has an affirmative duty to help shape the growth and development of public attitudes toward fair procedures and due process;" otherwise, "there is an inevitable tendency for practice to drift downward to the level of those . . . whose experience of life has not taught them the vital importance of preserving just and proper forms of procedure."

* * *

[T]he Report expresses a conception of the citizen-lawyer that has been largely overwhelmed by two other ideas. One is the popular conception of the zealous advocate that has leached into virtually all aspects of law practice. The other is the idea that public service takes place largely outside the private practice of law on behalf of ordinary clients: through public office, law reform activities, pro bono representation, and the "representation of unpopular causes."

2. Antecedents to the ABA/AALS Report's Idea of Lawyers' Pedagogic Role

The Report's conception that lawyers in ordinary law practice should serve the public good in part by teaching clients about cooperative relationships and fair dealings has its roots in earlier understandings. Both David Hoffman and George Sharswood, two of the first major American legal ethicists, saw the everyday work of lawyers instructing clients as vital to the proper functioning of society. They believed that without lawyers' guidance people would undermine "order, liberty, and property" as they sought to "promote their interests at the expense of the rights and interests of others." The function of lawyers was to persuade clients to understand and respect the rule of law and the public good. In contrast to their self-interested clients, lawyers possessed a greater virtue that enabled them to identify and pursue the public good. This virtue enabled lawyers both to "gain the confidence of" clients and to persuade them of "'sound principles'" that went beyond the letter of the law. As Sharswood noted, "[a] very important part of the advocate's duty is to moderate the passions of the party, and, where the case is of a character to justify it, to encourage an amicable compromise of the controversy." Counsel to a client should consider not only what was legal but what was just. Clients should not pursue the letter of the law at the expense of its spirit. Sharswood advised, "confine not yourself in your transactions with your fellow-men to giving them simply the strict measure of their legal rights, give them all that is honestly theirs as far as you have ability, whether the law affords them a remedy or not."

Both Hoffman and Sharswood took a strong view of lawyers' civic obligations. Although differing between themselves, both took the view that the lawyer's civic obligation in private representations went beyond the lawyer's counseling function. Each called on the lawyer to refrain in some cases either from engaging in lawful but antisocial conduct or from engaging in lawful conduct that would serve antisocial ends. For example, each asserted that lawyers should refuse to pursue an unjust claim on behalf of plaintiffs. Hoffman urged lawyers not to use defenses that "ought not[] to be sustained," such as "the Statute of Limitations, when based on the mere efflux of time." Sharswood was less categorical, maintaining that lawyers should not assist debtors of "'ample means'" in harassing or taking advantage of a creditor. In defense of a criminal defendant accused of an egregious crime such as a parricide, Hoffman said a lawyer should not provide "'special exertions,'" only the efforts needed to "'secur[e] to them a fair and dispassionate investigation of the facts of their cause, and the due application of the law.'"

As corporate legal practice developed in the late nineteenth century, Louis Brandeis extended this perspective to the corporate lawyer. In an essay that is more famous today for its discussion of the lawyer's responsibility in the area of law reform, Brandeis observed that representing corporations implicated the wisdom and skill required for "diplomacy" and "statesmanship." With "training . . . [that] leads to the development of judgment," lawyers had achieved the societal "position of the adviser of men." In the business arena, "lawyers are needed, not only because of the legal questions involved, but because [of] the particular mental attributes and attainments which the legal profession develops." Applying good judgment to the representation of businesses was a form of public service. Brandeis observed that:

The relations between rival railroad systems are like the relations between neighboring kingdoms. The relations of the great trusts to the consumers or to their employees is like that of feudal lords to commoners or dependents. The relations of public-service corporations to the people raise questions not unlike those presented by the monopolies of old.

A well-known incident from Brandeis's own practice offers an example of how the civics teacher role requires lawyers to think beyond the material self-interest of the client and to advise the client on the implications of its actions on others. Representing United Shoe against its employees who complained that their employment should be annual rather than seasonal, Brandeis "determined that these claims were legitimate and worked with his client to revamp the plants' manufacturing schedule in a manner Brandeis believed to be in the best interest of both his client and the employees."

In 1908, when the ABA promulgated its first code of ethics, it wholeheartedly embraced the notion that the civic responsibility of lawyers was fundamental to their work. According to the Preamble to the Canons of Professional Ethics ("Canons"), "The future of the republic, to a great extent, depends upon [lawyers'] maintenance of justice pure and unsullied." To fulfill this obligation, lawyers must reject the "false claim ... that it is the duty of the lawyer to do whatever may enable him to succeed in winning his client's cause." While providing "entire devotion to the interest of the client, warm zeal in the maintenance and defense of his rights," civic responsibility required the lawyer to "advis[e]" the client to avoid pursuing "questionable transactions, . . . bringing questionable suits, [and undertaking] questionable defenses. . . ." According to the Canons, in the

"'Last Analysis[,] . . . despite the contrary urging of any 'client, corporate or individual, however powerful, nor any cause, civil or political, however important . . .,' [t]he lawyer 'will find his highest honor in a deserved reputation for fidelity to private trust and to public duty, as an honest man and as a patriotic and loyal citizen.'"

3. The Perpetuation of the ABA/AALS Report's Idea of Lawyers' Pedagogic Role

The Report's conception of civic responsibility continued in professional discourse through the 1970s. In the early 1960s, according to Erwin Smigel, Wall Street lawyers described their role as a "buffer between the illegitimate desires of . . . clients and the social interest." Lawyers representing corporations would "serve . . . as the conscience of big business." They urged their clients to consider not only the letter of the law but its spirit and the good of the community, based "upon not only what is permissible but also what is desirable." Smigel found that big firm "[l]awyers often use their positions as advisors to guide their clients into what they believe to be proper and moral legal positions," applying this view both to litigation and to transactional work.

As previously noted, the 1970 ABA Model Code of Professional Responsibility cited repeatedly to Fuller's Report. Among other things, it expressed the understanding that "[l]awyers, as guardians of the law, play a vital role in the preservation of society, [such as through the maintenance of] the rule of law grounded in respect for the dignity of the individual and his capacity through reason for enlightened self-government." Similarly, the 1983 Model Rules of Professional Conduct described the lawyer as a "public citizen having a special responsibility for the quality of justice" and permitted the lawyer to counsel clients on civic responsibility under a rule authorizing the lawyer to refer to "moral, economic, social and political factors." But in general, after the 1960s, professional discourse about lawyers' civic role, their contributions to governance even as private practitioners, and their obligation to temper their own advocacy and to counsel clients in light of a broader sense of social responsibility was filtered out of the professional discourse. By 1985, for example, most elite lawyers no longer claimed that the public good played a major role in their everyday practice.

In the past year, a consortium of corporate law firms issued a statement of "shared values" that illustrates how far the corporate bar's ideology now departs from Fuller's conception. The statement posits that as a matter of principle a lawyer must "vindicate the values of the client-up to the limits of the law," without regard for countervailing "values currently important to the general public" or to "the amorphous concept of 'common good.'" Indeed, the statement advises that lawyers must embrace their clients' values and perceived interests with what it calls principled enthusiasm, as "[c]lients pay their lawyers not just for results, but for attitude as well." Although noting that lawyers should be "publicly engaged and committed participants in the political and social processes," the statement conceives of this function of "'engaged' citizenship," like that of pro bono services, as extrinsic from the representation of private clients.

III. The Significance of the Concept in Professional and Academic Discourse

The concept of lawyers as civics teachers in everyday law practice offers a different way of thinking about at least four important subjects: the lawyer's commitment to the public good; the lawyer's role in a contemporary democracy; the lawyer's counseling function; and lawyers' relationships with each other.

A. Serving the Public Good

First, the civics teacher concept offers a view of the lawyer's role that is somewhat different from that found in the conventional conversation regarding the lawyer's commitment to the public good. As a general matter, the contemporary conversation does not focus on lawyers' everyday practice. The conversation ordinarily concerns the duties of lawyers to provide pro bono assistance, to defend civil rights and civil liberties. and, * * * to promote law reform. To the extent that the conversation about serving the public good touches on everyday practice, it has sought to set boundaries that would prevent lawyers from assisting in client wrongdoing or has identified lawyers as role models in exemplifying obedience to law.

As civics teachers, lawyers have a far broader responsibility for incorporating an understanding of the public good into their practice. Doing so is quotidian, not exceptional. In almost every aspect of practice, whether providing advice, negotiating with an adversary, appearing in court, or in other capacities, lawyers affect how clients and, in many cases, third parties, conceive of their rights and responsibilities. In this work, lawyers have great discretion. They may choose to teach that the only guide to appropriate conduct is maximizing individual conduct within the bounds of the enforceable law-that one's civic responsibility is only to oneself and to respect the law only as a boundary on self-interest. On the other hand, lawyers may choose to teach that appropriate conduct requires taking into account not only one's self-interest but also one's obligations to one's fellows and one's community. Lawyers primarily teach these lessons through their conversations with clients, but they also teach them when they interact with others on a client's behalf.

B. The Lawyer's Role in a Democracy

Second, the concept adds to the broader discussion of the lawyer's role in a democracy. Although this discussion was historically prominent in the United States, today it takes place largely with respect to transitional and developing democracies, where our own bar ascribes to lawyers an important role in promoting and sustaining democratic legal and institutional reform, largely through work outside the everyday representation of private clients. This ascribed democratic role may also include educating the public about its legal rights and how to assert them as well as educating the public about legal obligations and restrictions. The idea of the American lawyer as civics teacher underscores that promoting and sustaining a democracy is not just a job for foreign lawyers and invites us to engage in exchanges with professional colleagues in developing democracies about our comparative roles and challenges.

C. The Lawyer's Counseling Function

The concept also offers a different way of discussing the lawyer's counseling function. The ABA acknowledges the legitimacy of discussing nonlegal considerations with clients, including relevant "moral, economic, social and political factors," and many have argued for the importance of providing "wise counsel," rather than more narrow, technical, and exclusive focus on explaining the meaning and application of the law. But many lawyers feel uncomfortable counseling clients with respect to moral, as distinct from business, considerations out of skepticism about the legitimacy of their own values or out of concern that their values are not shared by the client. The idea of the lawyer as civics teacher suggests a particular class of nonlegal considerations to which the lawyer might refer-namely, those relating to the expectations and obligations of citizenry. In their particulars, civic values may not be universally shared. Nonetheless, ideas of civic obligation and virtue should be regarded as legitimate subjects of discussion and, at the general level, as shared values, in a way that other beliefs and ideas may not be.

Although some lawyers are reluctant to discuss these concerns, clients may welcome such guidance. Ben W. Heineman, Jr., General Electric's former senior vice president and general counsel, has explained how he sought in outside counsel both "an outstanding technical lawyer" and "a wise counselor," who could offer "thoughtful insights into all the nonlegal issues-ethical, reputational, and commercial." Heineman similarly understood his own role as general counsel as including "establishing global values and standards beyond what financial and legal rules require; shaping the company's . . . role as a corporate citizen[,] and . . . addressing questions of how to balance the company's private interests with the public interests affected by the corporation's actions."

Discussions about civics may ultimately point clients in the same direction as discussions of morality or other nonlegal considerations, but the discussion will sound different and may resonate with the client in a different way. Both lawyer and client may find it easier to engage in conversation regarding civic responsibility, and both may perceive that lawyers have a stronger claim of expertise when it comes to civic considerations, such as the value of concern for the "spirit" of the law.

D. The Lawyer's Relationship with Professional Colleagues

Finally, the idea that a lawyer should model good citizenship within the context of client representation offers a different way of thinking about relations among lawyers. Within the adversary process, for example, lawyers are in relationships with their counterparts, just as clients are in relationships with their own. Lawyers might think of each other as "opposing counsel" or "adversaries," but they might also think of each other as professional brethren. This is the conception suggested by the title of a recent centennial history of the New York County Lawyers' Association. They might construct uncivil, even hostile relationships. Or they might strive, to the extent possible, to create relationships of civility and mutual trust within which they advocate for their clients zealously and perhaps even more effectively than if they were so-called "hardball litigators."

Thinking about professional relationships as an expression of one's civic understandings provides a different way of thinking about recurring subjects of professional conduct in the adversary process. Among these are whether one comports with civility codes, whether one extends professional courtesy, how one deals with inadvertent disclosures, whether lawyers make and adhere to handshake deals, whether one makes true but intentionally misleading representations, whether one takes an aggressive approach to discovery obligations and other legal and ethical obligations, and the like. Further, the idea of the lawyer as civics teacher may provide a different kind of rationale for resolving these kinds of questions. The preference, where possible, for developing relationships of trust, for treating others fairly, for complying with the spirit of the law, and for negotiation and compromise may serve as a rationale for improving professional relationships when calls for "professionalism" are not sufficiently compelling.

Conclusion

At times, lawyers have been asked to serve as societal role models, and particularly as "citizen-lawyers." One aspect of the lawyer's role as citizen-lawyer might be characterized as that of a civics teacher. This conception draws on concepts and discourse going back to the American legal profession's earliest days but finds especially full expression and justification in a Report authored by Lon Fuller a half-century ago. * * * [W]e offer a vision of everyday lawyers who incorporate public service by word and deed into their everyday private law practices, including the manner in which they counsel clients, interact with other lawyers, and regard their own legal obligations. Teaching civics, we suggest, is an unavoidable role for such lawyers. The only question is how well they fulfill it.

Summary

Food for Thought

How would each of the perspectives on the lawyer's role—neutral partisan, morally responsible, feminist, religious, racial justice, and civics teacher—resolve the following issues:

1. Should a lawyer represent:
   (a) Osama bin Laden?
   (b) a tobacco company?
   (c) a Swiss bank accused of hiding accounts from holocaust survivors?

2. If the lawyer decided to represent any of the clients, how would the perspective on the lawyer's role influence the representation?

3. How would the lawyer's perspective influence representation in the following situations:
   (a) Bigco has accidentally dumped ToxicTox in Smalltown's water supply. A few residents may die soon; a larger number are likely to develop cancer.
   (b) Lincoln Motors is deciding whether to make a design change in the LS Model not required by law this year but required next year. The change would save 100 lives a year but raise the price of each car $5000.[15]
   (c) Popular Clothing is negotiating a contract with a foreign manufacturer that pays employees 25 cents an hour, forbids union representation, and disregards basic workplace safety standards.[16]
   (d) After 9/11, the President asks you to advise on whether intelligence agents can legally use torture to gain vital national security information from terrorists.[17]

In considering how to counsel the clients in the hypotheticals presented above, keep in mind Professor Katherine Kruse's admonition to avoid seeing clients as "one dimensional figures interested only in maximizing their legal and financial interests." Katherine R. Kruse, *Beyond Cardboard Clients in Legal Ethics*, 23 Geo. J. Legal Ethics 103 (2010).

---

15 To read more about the Ford Pinto case, upon which this hypothetical is based, see the contrasting perspectives in David Luban, Lawyers and Justice 210, 214 (1988) (criticizing the lawyers for Ford); Gary T. Schwartz, *The Myth of the Ford Pinto Case*, 43 Rutgers L. Rev. 1013, 1032-33 (1991) (defending Ford's safety record).

16 Amelia J. Uelmen, *Can A Religious Person Be A Big Firm Litigator?*, 26 Fordham Urb. L. J. 1069 (1999).

17 *See, e.g.*, Michael Hatfield, *Professionalizing Moral Deference*, 104 Nw. U. L. Rev. Colloquy 1 (2009); Robert K. Vischer, *Professionalizing Moral Engagement (A Response to Michael Hatfield)*, 104 Nw. U. L. Rev. Colloquy 33 (2009); W. Bradley Wendel & Michael Hatfield, *The Effect of Legal Professionalization on Moral Reasoning: A Reply to Professor Vischer and Professor Wendel*, 104 Nw. U. L. Rev. Colloquy 300 (2010).

[Question 7]

If I had to choose one perspective for my role as lawyer, I would choose:

(A) hired gun.

(B) moral advocate.

(C) feminist lawyer.

(D) racial justice lawyer.

(E) religious lawyer.

(F) civics teacher.

CHAPTER 9

Why Do Lawyers Have Special Privileges and Responsibilities?

This Chapter will explore in detail the privileges and responsibilities that professionalism has traditionally mandated. Today, commentators both inside and outside the legal profession question whether lawyers continue to deserve the exclusive privilege to provide legal services and whether lawyers continue to fulfill their responsibilities to society. The criticism from within the bar has been that law practice has become a business and is no longer a profession; and that a result lawyers have failed to uphold their responsibilities as stewards of a legal system that provides equal justice under law for people regardless of their income or identity. The criticism from outside the bar has been that lawyers are seeking to preserve their privileges to enrich themselves, and includes the claim that with the knowledge available on the internet nonlawyers have just as much access to legal expertise as lawyers. But even a minority of lawyers have joined in urging some modification of lawyer's privileges to permit limited nonlawyer practice to provide greater access to justice for low and middle income persons or to permit collaborations between lawyers and nonlawyers in order to provide services more effectively and efficiently.

This Chapter will provide you with the tools to make your own decisions regarding these issues. It will ask you to evaluate whether the requirements for admission to the bar and the procedures for disciplining lawyers justify giving lawyers the exclusive privilege to provide legal services under unauthorized practice laws. It will then revisit the debates regarding allowing nonlawyers to provide some, or all, legal services. Next, the Chapter examines proposals that seek to encourage lawyers to be more responsible for equal justice in the legal system and equal opportunity in the legal profession.

In doing so, the Chapter brings together themes and issues raised throughout the course. In conclusion, it returns to the questions with which the course began. How do you understand your life as a lawyer? Will you be entering a business or a profession? Or do you have a different understanding of what it means to practice law?

I. The Professional Privilege

A. Review of Professionalism & Unauthorized Practice

Professionalism traditionally rested on a dichotomy between a profession and a business. Traditional lawyer professionalism had three core elements. First, lawyers have expertise in understanding the law that lay people are unable to evaluate. Second, lawyers work to primarily to promote the public good in contrast to business people who work primarily to maximize their self-interest. Third, as a result of lawyer's inaccessible expertise and commitment to the public good, society permits lawyers greater autonomy to regulate themselves than it permits businesses.

While professionalism provides the basis for lawyers' exclusive privilege to practice law, its broad claims are not necessary to justify the prohibition on nonlawyer practice. These prohibitions require two elements: one, that state licensing is necessary to protect consumers of legal services from unqualified and unethical providers, and two, that the existing procedures for regulating lawyers are both necessary and adequate to protect those consumers.

Review the material in Chapter 1 on Professionalism and Chapter 2 on Unauthorized Practice of Law.

B. Do the Standards for Bar Admission and Discipline Guarantee that Lawyers Meet the Standards Necessary to Justify Unauthorized Practice of Law Prohibitions?

This section will ask whether the requirements for admission and procedures for discipline fulfill the consumer protection goals of the unauthorized practice of law statutes. It will examine the contention that consumers can rely on lawyers being more skilled, more ethical, and more easily policed than nonlawyers.

1. Can Consumers Rely on Lawyers to be Competent?

[Question 1]

Law school training ensures that most lawyers are competent providers of legal services.

(A) True

(B) False

[Question 2]

People without law school training are unable to provide competent legal services.

   (A) True

   (B) False

[Question 3]

Consumer protection requires that legal services providers graduate from law school.

   (A) True

   (B) False

[Question 4]

The bar exam ensures that lawyers are competent to provide legal services.

   (A) True

   (B) False

[Question 5]

People who have not passed the bar exam are unable to provide competent legal services.

   (A) True

   (B) False

[Question 6]

Consumer protection requires that lawyers pass the bar exam.

   (A) True

   (B) False

[Question 7]

The requirements of law school education and the bar exam together ensure that lawyers can provide competent legal services.

(A) True

(B) False

[Question 8]

People who have not both graduated from law school and passed the bar exam cannot provide competent legal services.

(A) True

(B) False

[Question 9]

Consumer protection requires that lawyers both graduate from law school and pass the bar exam.

(A) True

(B) False

Review the materials on competence in Chapter 2 at Part V, especially the Food for Thought entry on page 86.

Two recent influential and controversial studies of legal education are William M. Sullivan et al., Educating Lawyers: Preparation for the Profession of Law (2007) (popularly known as the "Carnegie Report" because of the Carnegie Foundation's sponsorship) and Roy E. Stuckey, Best Practices for Legal Education: A Vision and a Road Map (2007) (popularly known as "Best Practices" and sponsored by the Clinical Legal Education Association). Following are comments from the primary authors of those books.

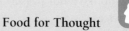

Food for Thought

Would any of your answers be different if you substituted "professionalism" for "consumer protection" in Questions 3, 6, and 9? Why or why not?

TRANSCRIPT --- MORNING SESSION, SYMPOSIUM: *THE OPPORTUNITY FOR LEGAL EDUCATION*,

59 Mercer L. Rev. 821 (2007)

* * *

PROFESSOR [JUDITH] WEGNER: * * * *One of the touchstones for legal education in the last century has been our commitment to teaching students to think like lawyers, particularly during the first year of law school. In our field work, we asked law students and faculty what they meant by "thinking like a lawyer." We asked this question so we could understand what it was that seemed like the "center of gravity" that shapes the current system of legal education. We asked both first year and advanced students, what they understood about this business of thinking like a lawyer. How do you learn it? What does it mean to you? What we learned over the course of our field work was that there are many dimensions to thinking like a lawyer.

First of all, there is thinking in a very structured and organized way. That is a crucial dimension and a powerful goal we embrace in preparing law students to become lawyers. Indeed, I think lawyers often forget that they lacked these abilities by the time they have graduated. For the law students among us, I hope that you still remember that fundamental first year experience of feeling your mind changing, your capacity to understand shifting. * * *

"Thinking like a lawyer" has multiple dimensions, however. There is the structured reasoning part of it, without doubt. But we need to recognize that there is also an effort to help students understand what we mean by "law" and the "rule of law." There is also an introduction to lawyers and the language that they use.

Most of all, there is emphatically a change in the appreciation of the nature of knowledge and the nature of learning. Some of you are first year students. When you come to law school from your prior experience in education, you may have thought that studying law would involve mastering a set of rules. You wanted to know the code book, where to find it, and how to unlock all the secrets found there. And yet, what you are really up against is finding a different way to think about authority, where authority comes from, how authority bears on the nature of truth, the work you hope to do, and people's lives.

There is very interesting research on this subject. People who are in their teens and twenties often have the impression that authority and knowledge is "out there" somewhere. It is as though they think they need to turn their heads to the side and ask that the knowledge be poured straight into their ears. In law school, however, the rules are very different. Instead of just memorizing rules, you are asked to "domesticate doubt." You are really learning to deal with uncertainty in ways that make people very uncomfortable. Dealing with uncertainty is likewise part of the fundamental process that we reference when we talk about thinking like a lawyer.

Dealing with uncertainty also lies at the heart of development for professionals in other fields. Dealing with uncertainty is inherent in the work of those who are professionals. They are people who are charged by society, educated, and prepared to deal with ill-defined problems of those who seek their assistance. They therefore need to be comfortable in working within the zone of uncertainty, mapping its contours, and learning the entrance and exit ramps.

So, the first "opportunity for legal education" we face is how to help students learn more readily how to "think like lawyers" by domesticating doubt and learning to navigate uncertainty. That is a powerful thing to do, but it is oftentimes not very visible to either faculty or students. We need to confront this reality and help students embrace it as they begin to walk down their professional paths.

Another "opportunity for legal education" concerns how we teach students to "think like lawyers." How do we as faculty members engage with that challenge? As I think Bill Sullivan will mention later, one of the findings across the Carnegie set of studies on the professions has to do with what Carnegie calls "signature pedagogies," distinctive ways in which faculty teach in the different professional fields. These are the distinctive tools or approaches to teaching and learning that seem to resonate with specific forms of professional education. * * *

For legal education, I would call the signature pedagogy the "case-dialogue" method, a very powerful approach that we use in the first year. I do not call it "Socratic" because I do not think it involves a search for the philosophical "good" through dialogue in the way that Socrates proceeded. Nonetheless, in legal education, we do take distilled cases and use them as a template useful in instructing students about legal language, professional roles, and analysis in a new field. I am sure that the students here today will remember occasions in which your friends and family have caught you asking them structured questions when they describe a problem or speaking in legalese, which they find disconcerting. Sometimes people want you just to listen, not to engage in problem solving. Sometimes, you will start using your new terminology before realizing you need to switch to plain English at least every now and again. At least I hope that is the case.

* * * Having a set of structured cases lends itself to building legal literacy (speaking, reading, and writing) to developing a crucial capacity to work through problems in a careful analytical way. * * * The "case-dialogue" method takes students through these cognitive moves in rapid and demanding fashion. It is a very powerful strategy that prepares students to take on the intellectual challenges that lawyers face. Nonlawyer colleagues who observed law classes during our field work were incredibly impressed by how quickly law students develop analytical stances, a capacity to use language, and things of that sort.

Strikingly, however, across our very diverse set of schools, the approaches were not altogether uniform. First year faculty generally used the "case-dialogue" method as their basic approach, but the details varied from one school to the next depending on who the students were and what their prior background might have been. For a school with a fairly wide range of students, a substantial portion of whom were first generation college or law students, professors appeared to use a range of teaching approaches on top of the "case-dialogue" foundation. Some used concept maps or visual displays, while others incorporated problem-based scenarios rather than simple case reading to draw their differing students into the conversation. Some used teams or small group breakouts to modulate the instruction and engage the abilities of all the students in the class in ways that complemented the students' differences.

In more elite schools, it was still possible to see techniques more reminiscent of movies. Some of you may remember Professor Kingsfield in The Paper Chase who used a very different approach to the "case-dialogue" method. He did some things that we did not see anywhere, for * * * example communicating to students that "I have the power and you don't." We did not see anyone trying to pepper students with questions in order to embarrass them. * * *

That is the second observation I would offer. We have a very powerful signature "case-dialogue" pedagogy that does a good deal of good. The downside is that we love this approach and find it so powerful that we do not want to give it up after it has run its course. * * *

We also need to think about another opportunity, one that would compensate for a shortcoming in the "case-dialogue" method that we have not really taken to heart. One downside of the "case-dialogue" method is the way in which it tends to remove questions about professional skills and strategies from the conversation since the focus is generally on appellate decisions. It is also not a particularly useful way to teach students to deal with statutes in the regulatory state, and it is definitely not a particularly useful approach to deal with teaching people about the identity of lawyers and the values of lawyers.

* * * My third observation is about assessment. We are not very good at assessment. * * * The Carnegie study said that legal educators need to be doing more with what is called "formative assessment" by giving people feedback in various ways that will allow them to really see where they are and continue building up their capacity. However, I think we need to do more than that. We have conflated some of what we do with our grading curves and approaches to grading. We are telling students about their comparative standing when that does not make much sense to them and does not help them build expertise, which is really the point. We confuse students because we do not give them meaningful benchmarks about the progress they are making toward the goal of being effective, talented lawyers. We need to do more about that.

* * * A fourth "opportunity for legal education" relates to the potential to build more progression into the second and third year curriculum and pedagogy. We are very good at embracing the "case-dialogue" method, but we are not good at what happens after that. Should not the second year be different? That is where things go off-track. Typically, by the third year, students think about taking clinical offerings, seminars, or advanced offerings after they have developed a certain level of expertise and gained experience in subject matter that interests them. They are lucky if they grasp the opportunity to focus and embrace a particular career path at this point, but many students are left adrift.

The Carnegie Report suggests that legal education has an opportunity to work more concertedly on educational progression. One way we might do that would be to help students develop a more considered understanding of their personal goals, professional identity, and values at an early stage in their education. If we did that, they might be better able to navigate the progression that is needed beyond the first year.

* * * Such an approach might be linked to more intensive and integrated advising that integrates academic. We need to work intentionally with individual students to help them understand that they need to take their lives in their own hands and choose what they want to study with an eye upon what they want to do in the future. There are now many more opportunities than when President Underwood, Dean Floyd, and I were in law school, and many more opportunities to develop professional skills. Students are often left in a wilderness without knowing how to shape their professional lives.

A fifth area of "opportunity for legal education" lies in our ability to address the development of professional identity and values. * * * [P]rofessional values play a central role in every profession. I think students know that they need to develop a set of values and a sense of professional identity. They do their best to explore what it means to be a professional, often by participating in a host of extracurricular activities. Unfortunately their pursuit of such opportunities (and the sense of self-worth that they hope to find by doing so) pulls them away from the day-to-day academic work. * * *

DR. [WILLIAM] SULLIVAN:

* * * "Legal Education: The Academy, the Practice, and the Public," describes the focus of my remarks. I am concerned with how to understand legal education so as to do justice to the three interests it is pledged to serve: that of the academy, that of the community of practitioners, and that of the public that depends for much of its well-being on the workings of the rule of law. I suspect few will dispute the fact that there is real tension among these three interests, especially tension due to their expecting and valuing different things. * * *

* * * The Metaphor of Apprenticeship

* * * [F]rom the students' point of view, entrance into the professional school is still the beginning of apprenticeship, but one now decomposed into three largely separate dimensions. Students encounter a cognitive or intellectual apprenticeship, the practical or apprenticeship of skill, and the apprenticeship of identity formation. Professional education in the university context falls roughly into three large chunks each based in different facets of professional expertise as the particular school teaches these and each guided by differing pedagogical intentions.

The first apprenticeship could be called intellectual or cognitive. Of the three, it is most at home in the university context since it embodies that institution's great investment in quality of analytical reasoning, argument, and research. Here, students must meet the standards that define the academy's interest in legal education. In professional schools, the intellectual training is focused upon the academic knowledge base of the domain including the habits of mind which the faculty judge most important to the profession. This apprenticeship is driven by the question of what a competent member of the profession should know.

The students' second apprenticeship is to the often tacit body of skills shared by competent practitioners. Students encounter this skills-based kind of learning through quite different pedagogies, often from different faculty members than those through which they are introduced to the first, the intellectual apprenticeship. In this second apprenticeship, students learn to take part in imagined or simulated practice situations, as in case studies or actual "clinical" experience with real clients. This apprenticeship is guided by the issue of what to do as a competent practitioner. Its expectations embody the practitioner community's interest in the preparation of competent lawyers.

The third apprenticeship introduces students to the values and attitudes shared by the professional community, aiming to develop dispositions essential to professional identity and purpose. Like the second apprenticeship of practice, it is ideally taught through dramatic pedagogies of performance. In some fields, however, such efforts are primarily didactic, while in others more participatory. The essential goal is to teach the skills and traits, along with the ethical standards, social roles, and responsibilities which mark the professional in that field. Through learning about these and beginning to practice them, however, the novice is also being introduced to the meaning of an integrated practice of all dimensions of the profession, grounded in the profession's fundamental purposes. Here, the student encounters the expectations of clients and the public for legal professionalism. If professional education is to introduce students to the full range of professional demands, it has to initiate learners into all three apprenticeships. But it is the third apprenticeship through which the student's professional self can be most broadly explored and developed. The guiding theme here is how to act and what to be as a competent practitioner.

These three types of apprenticeship provide a metaphor, an analytical lens through which to see more clearly how the business of professional training gets carried on in different fields and schools. They represent more than three elements in the curriculum served by different kinds of pedagogy. These dimensions of apprenticeship also reflect contending emphases within all professional education, a conflict of values which has deep roots in the history and organization of professional training in the university. That is why obtaining a balance among them is so often a challenge and the achievement of integration of the three is always a significant achievement.

The academic setting, however, clearly tilts the balance toward the cognitive. In as much as professionals require facility in deploying abstract, analytic representations—symbolic analysis—school-like settings are very good environments for professional learning. At the same time, however, professionals must also be able to integrate, or re-integrate, this kind of knowledge within on-going practical contexts. But in this area students learn mostly by living transmission through pedagogy of modeling and coaching. For all professional schools, it is this re-integration of the separated parts which provides the great challenge. * * *

What might this mean for legal education? As a start toward an answer, I want to draw directly from Educating Lawyers, the Carnegie Foundation for the Advancement of Teaching's 2007 study of legal education. Large-scale changes in the conditions of practice have washed away many of the institutional pilings that supported the ideals still expressed in the American Bar Association's Model Rules of Professional Conduct. Lawyer professionalism is still importantly defined with reference to ideals first annunciated by leaders of the bar in the early part of the twentieth century. These ideals include independent service of the public and requiring and supporting counsel to clients that would also be independent of possible benefit to the attorney or law firm. Over the last several decades, however, the relatively stable and secure relationships that characterized at least the upper levels of the bar in the mid-twentieth century have altered radically. Decades of major economic restructuring, along with social changes that have brought significant numbers of previously underrepresented groups into the legal profession, have disrupted the old patterns beyond recovery.

We are currently in an era marked by a growing body of lawyers, trained by an increasing number of law schools, who enter unstable and highly competitive domains of practice. Under these conditions, it has proven hard to make the old ideals of independent public service the basis of everyday legal practice. The result has been confusion and uncertainty about what goals and values should guide professional judgment in practice, leaving many lawyers, in Mary Ann Glendon's words, "wandering amidst the ruins of those [past] understandings." one professor we spoke with in our research put it: "There is no one distinct role that is appropriate for lawyers. It all depends on the type of lawyering you do. There are many lawyers who do many things. Torts is basically litigation oriented. It would focus on questions like 'if you were a judge or in the legislature, how would you resolve or answer the question.' In contract drafting, it would be helping people draft documents to represent the agreement. It is concerned with avoiding litigation rather than creating it. So it would be a totally different perspective on what lawyers do." Students at least need to be made aware not only of the various sorts of lawyer they might become but also of the various kinds of approach they can take toward lawyering itself.

Not in spite of, but precisely because of these complexities in the many roles lawyers must take on today, legal education needs to attend very seriously to its formative potentials. The challenge is to deploy its formative power in the authentic interests of the profession and the students as future professionals. Under today's conditions, students' great need is to begin to develop the knowledge and abilities that can enable them to understand and manage the tensions inherent in practice so that they will sustain their professional commitment and personal integrity over the course of their careers. In a time of professional disorientation, the law schools have an opportunity to provide direction. Law schools can help the profession become smarter and more reflective about strengthening its slipping legitimacy by finding new ways to advance its enduring commitments.

To do this, however, law schools need to further deepen their knowledge of how the formative dimension of their curriculum—both manifest and hidden—actually works. That is, they must improve their understanding of their own formative capacity, including learning from their own strengths as well as those of other professions. Further, schools need to attend more systematically to the pedagogical practices that foster the formation of integrated, responsible lawyers.

* * *

TRANSCRIPT – AFTERNOON SESSION, SYMPOSIUM: *THE OPPORTUNITY FOR LEGAL EDUCATION,*

59 Mercer L. Rev. 859 (2007)

* * * PROFESSOR [ROY] STUCKEY: This is a wonderful time to be a law teacher. For the first time in a long time, there is a lot of excitement and energy about new directions we might take in our curriculums and in our individual courses. There may not have been another time in history when there was more hope for the future of legal education. * * *

I am almost sixty years old. I have been a law teacher since I was twenty-five, more than thirty-four years ago. I am retiring in January, at least for a while. This might be the last presentation I make before my retirement, so I would like to use my time with you to share some reflections about legal education.

When I started teaching, I taught in-house clinical courses. Nothing else. We practiced law with our students. One thing you learn very quickly when you teach in a clinic is that third year law students are not ready to practice law without supervision—not even close to ready. Go spend a semester teaching a clinic. The level of your third year students' preparation for practice will scare you, and it might inspire you to do something about it.

I did not make a career decision to study legal education and become an advocate for change. It just worked out that way. I was fortunate to have opportunities over the course of many years to participate in the work of the American Bar Association's Section of Legal Education and Admissions to the Bar. I began by serving on various committees. Then I spent six years on the Council of the Section, which is the official accrediting body for law schools in the United States.

In 1987 while I was on the Council, I chaired a national conference for the Section on Professional Skills and Legal Education. The chair of the section, the Honorable Rosalie Wahl, was disheartened by what she learned at the conference about the state of professional skills instruction in American law schools. Consequently, she created a special task force on law schools and the profession and persuaded former ABA President Bob MacCrate to chair it. I served on the MacCrate Task Force during the three years that it took to produce its report.

Through my work with the ABA, I began to see what was wrong with legal education. I also learned how difficult it is to address those problems in meaningful ways.

I have also been involved in some international projects involving legal education, working with ABA-CEELI and other organizations. * * * No system of legal education is perfect, and countries all over the world are searching to find the best ways to transform lay people into professionals.

In 2001 I was given an opportunity to put some of these experiences to use. I was asked to chair the Steering Committee for the Best Practices Project of the Clinical Legal Education Association (the "CLEA"). Our charge was simply stated: "develop a statement of best practices." It was easy to say but difficult to accomplish. We did not know what to do or even how to begin. In the end, however, over six years later in March 2007, we published Best Practices for Legal Education.

* * * As you know, the Carnegie Report and the Best Practices book call for significant, fundamental changes in what law schools teach and how they teach it. Of course, nothing in these books will have any real value unless they lead to positive changes in legal education. A growing number of law teachers agree with many of the recommendations in these books. Some law teachers, however, perhaps a majority, are not convinced that it is necessary to make substantial changes to legal education. Is it? Let me pose some questions to you.

Do you agree with the Carnegie authors that attention to clients and values is largely missing from the first year curriculum? That the experience of students during the first year can be characterized as a "moral lobotomy"?

Surely, these findings require the close attention of every law school teacher, not just first year teachers.

Do you agree with the authors of the Carnegie Foundation's report that our students' intellectual development stagnates after the first year because we continue teaching the same lessons using the same methods of instruction?

If so, what are you going to do about that at your school and in your classes?

Do you agree with the authors of the Carnegie Foundation's report that law schools focus too much on teaching legal doctrine and too little on teaching students how to think and act like members of the legal profession?

If so, what are you, personally, planning to do to change this?

Do you agree that most law school graduates are not adequately prepared to represent clients without supervision and that the licensing process is not adequately protecting the public from incompetent new lawyers?

How can anybody tolerate this? Even if law schools do a much better job of preparing students for practice, and they should, licensing authorities should not continue giving novice lawyers unrestricted licenses to practice law. Why are law school teachers and bar examiners not constantly communicating to figure out what to do about this?

Do you understand that every expert who has studied the way we test our students has concluded that the traditional assessment methods of law schools are not valid, they are not reliable, and they are not fair? This means that the students who make the best grades and get the top jobs may not be the students who deserve those grades and jobs. Do you think our students do not know that our assessment methods are indefensible?

How can we know this and still look our students in their eyes? What are we going to do to fix this absolutely unacceptable situation?

Are you aware of the studies and do you accept the data showing that legal education is harmful to the emotional and psychological well-being of many law students? And, most importantly, that this harm is unnecessary? Have you asked your students how they feel about their law school experience?

Let me read you something that appeared in a student newsletter at a southeastern university's law school—not South Carolina or Mercer. I think it captures the mind set of more of our students than we want to admit.

I freely confess to absolutely hating law school. I loathe it with every fiber of my being. Law school is everything it shouldn't be, with a little extra needless pain and suffering heaped on top. After a year spent in these hallowed halls, I understand even less about law school's purpose than I did as a 1L. I began my study of the law full of ambition, respect, and inspiration. A year later, I'm laughing at my notions of classes that would be applicable to real life, of teachers that would have a firm grasp on what the hell they were lecturing about, and of grades that would be representative of my worth as a student and future legal practitioner. I came to law school having aced the LSAT and stunned my previous legal employers with my aptitude for the study of law. I present myself to you now, bitter, disillusioned, and apathetic. Now I chalk up my dismal grades to the ineffective teaching style of certain foreign faculty members and ineptly continue about my business.

Does the fact that many law students are damaged by what we do deeply concern you? Do you not feel a sense of personal responsibility for so many students hating law school? Why have we not fixed this? Is there any good reason why law school cannot be a positive, enriching experience for all of our students?

If you have read the Carnegie Report and the Best Practices book, you know I could go on and on. If you agree with the findings I have just reviewed, or any of them, how can you deny that significant, fundamental changes are needed?

Would you not expect that every law teacher in the country would be very troubled by their students' negative feelings about legal education and by the findings of the Carnegie Foundation that we are doing a poor job of preparing our students for the legal profession?

Would you not expect to find the faculty at every law school working furiously to resolve as many of these very serious problems as possible? Do we not have an ethical obligation and a fiduciary duty to give our students the best possible legal education?

Perhaps that would be the expectation of most outsiders, but what we find among law teachers is widespread indifference. First, you have to find law teachers who have actually read either book. Then, if you ask them why they are not actively working to change the way they do business, you get answers like "I am too busy producing scholarship," "It would take too much work," "We have a committee looking into that, I think," or "That's why we have clinics." It is enough to make you crazy.

Fortunately, some schools began trying to change their students' law school experiences even before the Carnegie Report or the Best Practices book were published. Mercer is one example, and there are others. Today, many more law schools are reconsidering their educational programs, and new initiatives seem to be appearing every day. There is reason to have hope.

Let me share with you a vision of what the future of legal education could be, if we want it badly enough. Let's take a look into the future. * * *

* * *

Lawyers are very competent, and their collective reputation for integrity, fair dealing, and public consciousness makes them more highly esteemed than members of any other profession. Not many lawyers have high incomes, and those that do have high incomes donate most of their money to charity. The major complaint of lawyers is that there are not enough pro bono cases to go around.

Law schools are largely responsible for the competence and public spirit of lawyers. No one is hired to teach in a law school with less than ten years of practice experience. Especially highly prized in job searches are lawyers who actually represented people in practice, not corporate or governmental attorneys. New teachers are required to attend teacher training programs to obtain teaching certificates by the end of their first year, if they do not have one when hired. Teacher training programs include extensive instruction about assessing student learning.

Members of the faculty collaborate with groups of practitioners to remain current on trends in law practice. They are encouraged to continue practicing law, particularly through the schools' clinical programs which represent both indigent and paying clients in large, modern law offices. Any income that is generated from practicing law or writing textbooks is shared with the school. This income, combined with the faculty's law salaries, helps keep tuition quite low.

The program of instruction is very student-centered. Students are treated with kindness and respect inside and outside of class, and their workloads are carefully coordinated to ensure that they are kept busy, but not overworked. The curriculum is designed to develop students' professional knowledge, skills, and values in a progressive manner throughout their law school careers. Emphasis is placed on reflective learning, client-centered practice, compassion, and personal responsibility.

From their first day in law school, students spend time with practicing lawyers, observe transactional and dispute resolution law practice, work in teams, grapple with solving simulated legal problems in context, and eventually participate in the representation of actual clients, including the representation of corporations and government agencies, as well as individuals.

A committee consisting of lawyers, judges, law teachers, and students is responsible for tracking the effectiveness of the curriculum and reviewing new course proposals. Another committee trains its members to visit and evaluate the classes of all teachers, with special attention to members of the faculty who receive below average student evaluations.

Students' strict adherence to the honor code and to the school's code of professionalism ensure that no cheating occurs. The academic and professional support program not only helps the faculty assist students who are having academic problems, but it also tries to rehabilitate students who are exhibiting signs of irresponsible or unprofessional behavior. Students who continue to have academic or professionalism problems are dismissed from school. This rarely occurs, however, because the strict admissions screening process and the culture of professionalism at the school make it unlikely that any student would engage in personal or professional misconduct. The faculty and staff are also subject to discipline, including dismissal, if they violate the code of professionalism.

All students must pass comprehensive competency exams to graduate. These exams are developed by testing experts working with practitioners and law teachers. Law schools are committed to ensuring that no student graduates who is not prepared for practice. If students are not able to pass the competency exams, they have the option of continuing to go to law school at no expense until they achieve the requisite levels of proficiency.

Students are admitted directly into practice from law school. There is no bar examination nor even a character and fitness check. The licensing authorities are confident that the law schools prepare all students adequately for the practice of law and weed out potentially unscrupulous lawyers. Of course, new lawyers are not fully licensed to practice law; they must work for a qualified lawyer long enough to demonstrate the ability to represent clients without supervision.

This may seem like a whimsical vision of legal education. And it is, at least for now. But if more of us refuse to tolerate the worst practices of legal education and commit ourselves to promoting best practices in the future, who knows what might happen?

* * *

POSTING OF MONROE H. FREEDMAN, *ON TEACHING AND TESTING IN LAW SCHOOL*, TO LEGAL ETHICS FORUM: THE PURPOSE OF LAW SCHOOL CLASSES?,

http://www.legalethicsforum.com/blog/2006/10/the_purpose_of_.html (Oct. 11, 2006)

I start with the premise that the job of law professors is to train students in the kinds of skills that they need to practice law. These skills include, among others, the following:

• Assimilating facts presented by a client's matter and identifying those that are relevant;

• Identifying potential ways of serving the client's interests, including counseling, drafting, negotiating, and litigating;

• Identifying the legal issues that might be important in serving the client's interests;

• Analyzing the strengths and weaknesses of the client's legal position, including reading and interpreting the language of statutes, contracts, and other legal documents;

• Creating the most effective ways of advancing the strengths and countering the weaknesses in the client's matter, including developing and making persuasive arguments;

• Making judgments about how best to proceed on the client's behalf;

• Determining how to carry out those judgments, through effective counseling, drafting, negotiating, and/or litigation;

• Being able to do the same things on behalf of the other party in the event that that party were your client; and

• Doing all of the above informed by an understanding of the nature of the judicial process, including the practical importance of differing jurisprudential views among judges.

Students tend to think that class discussion, and particularly the colloquies between the professor and students, are a waste of time, because those colloquies don't give them "the rule of the case," the "black-letter law," or "the answer" that they will need to take an exam. As a law professor once said, we should give the students, at the end of the class, "a summary of what the class session has been about," or a "take-away point." I have two objections to this. One is that giving students an end-of-class take-away point encourages them to play video games or do their email during class, secure in the knowledge that nothing they need to know is happening in the class discussions between the professor and other students, and that everything they need to know will come in the last few minutes.

On the contrary, however, the primary purpose of the discussion is the discussion itself, that is, the give and take, the pros and cons, the creative thinking, and the ability to think around and beyond the facts of the case at hand. That is, the entire process of thinking through and arguing out the issues is itself the take-away point. What I believe we should test for in exams, therefore, is not some "right" answer but, rather, the students' ability to do the very kind of analysis that is involved in class discussions, particularly their ability to think through the pros and cons of the issues presented by the cases and statutes, and to exercise their own judgment about them. * * *

Society of American Law Teachers Statement on the Bar Exam,

52 J. Legal Educ. 446 (2002)

* * *

Bar examinations, as currently administered,

- fail to adequately measure professional competence to practice law,

- negatively affect law school curricular development and the law school admission process,

- and are a significant barrier to achieving a more diverse bench and bar.

Recent efforts in some states to raise the requisite passing scores only serve to aggravate these problems. In response to these and other concerns outlined below, the Society of American Law Teachers (SALT),* the largest membership organization of law teachers in the nation, strongly urges states to consider alternative ways to measure professional competence and license new attorneys.

The current bar exam inaccurately measures professional competence to practice law.

Although the history of the bar examination extends back to the mid-1800s, when law school attendance was not a prerequisite for a law license, the present bar exam format—a 200-question, multiple-choice, multistate exam (the MBE), combined with a set of essay questions on state law—dates only from the early 1970s. In creating the MBE, the National Conference of Bar Examiners was responding to states' desires to find a time-and cost-efficient alternative to administering their own comprehensive essay exams. More recently, some states have adopted a written "performance" test in addition to the MBE, state essay exam questions, and the multiple-choice ethics exam (MPRE).

The stated purpose of the bar examination is to ensure that new lawyers are minimally competent to practice law. There are many reasons why the current bar exam fails to achieve its purpose. First, despite the inclusion of multiple sections, the exam attempts to measure only a few of the many skills new lawyers need in order to competently practice law. A blue-ribbon commission of lawyers, judges, and academics issued a report (the MacCrate Report) detailing the skills and values that competent lawyers should possess. The bar examination does not even attempt to screen for many of the skills identified in the MacCrate Report, including key skills such as the ability to perform legal research, conduct factual investigations, communicate orally, counsel clients, and negotiate. Nor does it attempt to measure other qualities important to the profession, such as empathy for the client, problem-solving skills,

---

*   [*Ed.'s Note*—The Society of American Law Teachers (SALT) describes itself as "a community of progressive law teachers working for justice, diversity, and academic excellence." http://www. saltlaw.org/.]

the bar applicant's commitment to public service work, or the likelihood that the applicant will work with underserved communities.

* * *

Second, the examination overemphasizes the importance of memorizing legal doctrine. Memorizing legal rules in order to pass the bar examination does not guarantee that what is memorized will actually be retained for any length of time after the exam. Memorization of legal principles so that one can answer multiple-choice questions or spot issues on an essay exam does not mean that one actually understands the law, its intricacies and nuances. In fact, practicing lawyers who rely upon their memory of the law, rather than upon legal research, may be subject to judicial sanctions and malpractice claims. Yet a large part of successfully taking the bar examination depends upon the bar applicant's ability to memorize hundreds of legal rules. The ability to memorize the law in order to pass the bar examination is simply not a measure of one's ability to practice law.

Third, the exam assesses bar applicants' ability to apply the law in artificial ways that are unrelated to the practice of law. In most states, up to one-half of the total bar examination score is based upon the MBE, a multiple-choice test that covers the majority/minority rules in six complex, substantive legal areas. In answering the questions, the examinee must choose the "most correct," or in some cases the "least wrong" of four answers. No practicing lawyer is faced with the need to apply a memorized legal principle to a set of facts she has never seen before and then choose, in 1.8 minutes, the "most correct" of four given answers. No lawyer can competently make decisions without more context for the case and without the opportunity to ask more questions or to clarify issues. Yet if a bar applicant cannot successfully take multiple-choice tests, the applicant may never have the opportunity to practice law.

Fourth, a substantial portion of the examination does not test the law of the administering state. The MBE questions are based upon the majority/minority rules of law that may, or may not, be the same as the law in the administering state. In addition, many states have now adopted the Multistate Essay Examination (MEE), which is also based upon majority rules rather than the administering state's law. In all states, up to one-half of the examination is not based upon the administering state's own laws; in some states, the entire exam requires no knowledge of the particular administering state's governing law. Thus, even if one believes that memorizing the law equates to "knowing" the law, the existing examination does not test how well the applicant knows the law that he or she will actually use in practice.

Fifth, the examination covers a very wide range of substantive areas, thus failing to recognize that today's practitioners are, by and large, specialists not generalists. Although some basic knowledge of a broad range of fields is important, the current examination does not test for basic knowledge, but instead often tests relatively obscure rules of law. In the modern legal world it is virtually impossible, even for the most diligent, skilled, and experienced lawyer, to remain truly current in more than one or two related fields. The examination thus fails to test for competence as it is really reflected in today's market—a market in which lawyers need expertise in their specific area of practice, rather than a broad but shallow knowledge of a wide range of legal rules.

Sixth, most law students take a ten-week bar review course, and some take an additional course on essay writing or on how to take multiple-choice questions, in order to pass the bar examination. These review courses, which may cost as much as $3,000, drill bar applicants on the black letter law and "tricks" to answering bar exam questions. They are not geared toward fostering an in-depth understanding of important legal concepts, nor do they focus on synthesizing rules from various substantive areas. The content of the review courses, and the necessity of taking the courses in order to pass, belie the argument that the bar examination is geared toward testing professional competence or aptitude in any meaningful way.

The current bar exam has a negative impact on law school curricular development and the law school admission process.

In addition to failing to measure professional competence in any meaningful way, the bar examination has a pernicious effect on both law school curricular development and the law school admission process. From the moment they enter law school through graduation, students realize that unless they pass the bar examination, their substantial financial commitment and their years of hard work will be wasted. As a result, many students concentrate on learning primarily what they need to know in order to pass the bar exam, which often translates into high student attendance in courses that address the substantive law tested on the bar examination and reduced participation in clinical courses—the courses designed to introduce students to the skills required for the actual practice of law—and in courses such as environmental law, poverty law, civil rights litigation, law and economics, and race and the law. As a result, the students fail to fully engage in a law school experience that will give them both the practical skills and the jurisprudential perspective that will make them better lawyers.

In addition to being a driving force in the law school curriculum, the bar examination inevitably influences law school admission decisions. Schools want to admit students who will pass the bar exam. A high bar pass rate bodes well for alumni contributions, is perceived to play an important role in U.S. News and World Report rankings, brings a sense of satisfaction to the faculty, eases students' fears about their own ability to pass the examination, and makes it easier to attract new students. Since there is some correlation between LSAT scores and bar exam scores, law school admission officers may be overly reliant on LSAT scores in admitting students. As Kristin Booth Glen notes, "If you take students who know how to take a test almost exactly like the bar examination and know how to take it successfully, as the LSAC study tells us is the case with the LSAT, you don't actually have to do much with those students in law school to assure their success on the bar examination." Thus, many schools may overemphasize the value of the LSAT, at the expense of admitting students who will bring a broader perspective into the student body, into law school classes, and ultimately into practice.

Finally, the bar examination has a negative impact on how law schools assess students. Like the bar exam, most law school grades are based upon a one-time make-or-break examination that focuses on only a very few of the many skills that competent lawyers need. If the bar exam assessed a broader range of skills, or assessed skills in various ways, law schools might also adjust their assessment modalities so that they were not all geared toward rewarding just one type of skill or intelligence. In sum, from the admission process through curriculum choices and law school assessment modalities, the bar examination has a far-reaching negative pedagogical effect.

The current bar exam negatively affects states' ability to create a more diverse bench and bar.

In the 1980s and 1990s, many states and federal circuits established commissions on racial and gender equality. After extensive study, many of these commissions concluded that people of color were underrepresented in the legal profession on both the state and the national level, that there is a perception of racial and ethnic bias in the court system, and that there is evidence that the perception is based upon reality. To begin to achieve a more racially and ethnically balanced justice system, many commissions recommended that states take affirmative steps to increase minority representation in the bench and bar.

There are many reasons for states to want a more diverse bench and bar. A diverse bench and bar improves public perceptions about the justice system. It also increases the availability of legal services for underserved segments of our population. Additionally, a more diverse bar is likely to be a more public-minded bar. A University of Michigan study found that, among graduates who enter private practice, "minority alumni tend to do more pro bono work, sit on the boards of more community organizations, and do more mentoring of younger attorneys than white alumni do."

The failure of the current bench and bar to be as diverse as they could be is partly attributable to the existing bar exam. The current examination disproportionately delays entry of people of color into, or excludes them from, the practice of law. A six-year study commissioned by the Law School Admission Council indicates that first-time bar examination pass rates are 92 percent for whites, 61 percent for African-Americans, 66 percent for Native Americans, 75 percent for Latino/Latinas, and 81 percent for Asian-Americans. Although the disparity between pass rates narrowed when applicants retook the bar examination, a substantial number of applicants who failed on the first attempt did not retake the exam. And for those who did retake it, the psychological and financial cost of doing so was extremely high.

Despite the disparate impact that the bar examination has on people of color, numerous states have raised, or are considering raising, the passing scores on their bar exams. Many states have hired Stephen P. Klein, the National Conference of Bar Examiners' chief psychometric consultant, to help them set a new passing score and to help them determine the effect of the higher score on minority passing rates. Klein has concluded that raising the passing score on the bar examination will not disproportionately affect minority bar applicants. But serious flaws appear to exist both in the methodology Klein uses to set new passing scores and in his contention that higher passing scores will not disproportionately affect people of color. In fact, one commentator has found that not only will raising the passing score have a disparate impact on the bar passage rate for people of color; the decision to raise bar passing scores also correlates with admission officers' putting more weight on the LSAT, rather than on undergraduate GPAs, thereby widening the law school admission gap between white students and students of color.

Even if the bar examination were a valid screening device, one would have to ask whether its disproportionate impact on people of color could be justified. Given that the bar exam is not a good measure for determining professional competency, it is simply wrong to retain it without trying to find a better assessment tool.

What are the alternatives?

We cannot hope to exhaust all the possible alternatives to the bar exam in this brief document. But, preliminarily, SALT recommends that states begin to explore one or more of the following alternatives.

> 1. The diploma privilege. This method of licensure, currently used in Wisconsin, grants a law license to all graduates of the state's ABA-accredited law schools.
>
> 2. A practical-skills-teaching term. Using this method of licensure, states could require satisfactory completion of a ten-week teaching term, similar to one phase of the licensing requirements in some Canadian provinces. During the Canadian teaching term, bar applicants must pass two three-hour tests which assess their knowledge of basic principles in ten substantive areas. They also receive training—and must receive a passing grade on assessments—in interviewing, advocacy, legal writing, and legal drafting skills.
>
> 3. The public service alternative to the bar exam. States could adopt the pilot project proposed by Kristin Glen, in which bar applicants are given the option of either taking the existing bar exam or working for 350 hours over ten weeks within the court system and satisfactorily completing a variety of assignments in which competence on all of the MacCrate Report skills is evaluated by trained court personnel and law school clinical teachers.

4. Computer-based testing. States also should begin exploring the use of computer-based testing as another potential way to assess a broader range of skills and to measure the skills in ways that better reflect the practice of law.

These alternatives, and others that might be developed, can provide states with options other than the current examination to measure the competence of nascent lawyers. SALT recommends that states begin to study and experiment with these and other alternatives to the existing bar exam so as to ameliorate the pernicious effects of the existing examination structure.

* * *

The bar examination, by testing a narrow range of skills and testing them in a way unrelated to the practice of law, fails to measure in any meaningful way whether those who pass the exam will be competent lawyers. In addition to not measuring what it purports to measure, the examination negatively affects the law school admission process, as well as the curriculum and course content, and impedes the attainment of a more diverse bench and bar. Raising the passing score on the bar examination exacerbates these negative effects. Thus, SALT strongly opposes the move to increase the passing score on the bar examination. Maintaining the status quo is not enough. SALT recommends that states make a concerted, systematic effort to explore better ways of measuring lawyer competency without perpetuating the negative effects elaborated above.

SUZANNE DARROW-KLEINHAUS, *RESPONSE TO THE SOCIETY OF AMERICAN LAW TEACHERS STATEMENT ON THE BAR EXAM,*

54 J. Legal Educ. 442 (2004)

In a perfect world there would be no tests, and a test like the bar exam would probably be outlawed instead of required for the practice of law. But not for the reasons the Society of American Law Teachers would have us believe. The bar exam—or any exam—would be unnecessary because we would all be born with superior intellects, abilities, and capacities, and the assessment of individual competencies would be irrelevant. But in our world competence matters, as it does in the case of a lawyer's ability to engage in critical analysis. The bar examination, by testing competency in the most basic and essential analytical skills required for the practice of law, serves a necessary function. * * *

The Bar Exam's Role in Assessing Competency

The bar examination seeks only to test the fundamental skills that should have been learned in law school. SALT faults the bar exam for not addressing the concerns of its Bar Exam Committee, concerns that might well be appropriate for the goals of the profession but not for the goals of the bar exam. It appears to have lost sight of two very important aspects of the bar exam: first, that bar passage is only one of a number of jurisdictionally set criteria candidates must meet before gaining admission to the practice of law, and second, that the bar exam does not purport to test more than the basic analytical skills required for legal practice. Still, the exam has become the most analyzed, criticized, and contested part of the bar admission process. Perhaps that is because it stands as one of the final hurdles to admission; perhaps it is simply because bar exam failures are visible for all to see.

I submit that the bar examination

- seeks to measure the analytical skills required for the practice of law, which requires an understanding of the rules and not just the ability to memorize.

- tests the ability to act and not react under pressure.

- requires a sound mastery of legal principles and basic knowledge of core substance for which tricks or techniques cannot be substituted.

- covers the subjects students should have learned in law school in preparation for the general practice of law.

- neither demands nor requires the sacrifice of skills-based courses for substantive courses.

The bar exam adequately assesses competency in the basic analytical skills required for the practice of law.

The bar exam is designed to see whether the law graduate has mastered the legal skills and general knowledge that a first-year practicing attorney should have. While this means a firm grasp of black letter law, it also means a solid grounding in basic analytical, reading, and writing skills. A candidate must demonstrate mastery of the fundamentals of IRAC (the Issue-Rule-Application-Conclusion structure of legal analysis), must read carefully, and must communicate in the language of the law. * * *

While bar exams vary by jurisdiction, each one tests the candidate's ability to write. * * * The essence of lawyering is communication. Essays afford the bar examiners a basis for evaluating a candidate's ability to communicate knowledge of the substantive law in an organized and articulate way. * * * Bar examiners rely on essays for the same reason that law teachers do: writing a well-constructed legal essay is a learned skill that requires mastery of the law and the nature of logical argument. In working with candidates preparing to retake the bar exam, what I found perhaps most incomprehensible was that after three and sometimes four years of law school, and presumably after reading hundreds of cases, these candidates sounded nothing like lawyers. The language of Holmes, Cardozo, Brennan, and Blackmun had not made the slightest impression on them. In their essays, there was not a scintilla of evidence that they had even attended law school. The "problem" was not in the bar exam questions but in the way they approached and answered the questions. The concept of an issue-based analysis had eluded them; it was absent from their essays and, more important, from their thought process. These are core legal skills. A licensing process that fails to assess the candidate's ability to write, analyze, and reason logically would be not only inadequate but suspect.

The bar exam tests understanding of the rules of law, not simply the ability to memorize.

The bar exam requires one to know the rules of law with precision and specificity; it also requires a solid understanding of those rules. Memorization plays a part, but no more nor less than it does throughout the educational process. We have all had to memorize the elements of the intentional torts, the rule against perpetuities, the types of jurisdiction, and the standard for summary judgment. The same principle applies here. While the process may begin with rote memorization, the end result is knowledge of the material, for the bar exam and for law practice.

If the bar exam were solely a test of memory skills, the students I worked with surely would have passed on their first attempt; they had memorized the rules of law. But because they did not really understand them, they could not recognize a rule when it assumed a different form or appeared in language different from what they had memorized. They needed to know when a particular rule was implicated by the facts. By failing to identify the issue, they failed to recognize when a particular rule was in controversy. Then it did not matter whether they knew the rule or not. They never got to apply it because they did not see the issue.

In working with students in academic difficulty, I have learned that deficiencies in these areas are as typical of poorly performing law students as of those graduates who fail the bar exam. Both groups have the same weaknesses: the inability to identify the legal issues, the failure to separate relevant from irrelevant material, and the absence of a reasoned, organized analysis which demonstrates an understanding of the relevant legal principles. If these deficiencies are not corrected by the time students graduate, it should come as no surprise if they fail the bar exam.

A solid knowledge of the rules of law is required to write bar exam essays and answer objective short-answer questions. Unfortunately, too many candidates walk into the bar exam without truly understanding enough black letter law. A candidate could spend hours studying intentional torts, presumably "know" the elements of a battery, and nevertheless answer questions incorrectly if this knowledge was based solely on memorization without genuine understanding. This is because the bar exam, like a typical law school exam, does not test a candidate's superficial knowledge of the law. * * *

The MBE is meant to weed out those candidates possessing anything less than mastery of the black letter law with a level of detailed sophistication. This is not to say that a candidate must walk into the exam knowing every single rule of law and its fine distinctions. Considering that a candidate can pass the bar exam despite answering almost 80 out of 200 questions incorrectly (depending on the weight accorded the MBE in a particular jurisdiction), it is evident that one need not know every rule to be deemed "minimally competent" to practice law.

Still, SALT objects to the MBE, claiming that these short-answer questions require candidates to apply the law in artificial ways unrelated to the practice of law: "No lawyer can competently make decisions without more context for the case and without the opportunity to ask more questions or to clarify issues" * * * . While this is a true statement, it is not relevant to the bar exam. The point of the exam question is to create a hypothetical universe and test the candidate's knowledge and thought process within that limited universe. The MBE question is crafted to contain all the facts relevant to resolving the issue. There is no need to go outside the question. The ability to read carefully and rely only on the facts presented and the reasonable inferences that can be drawn from them is a critical legal skill—one that the MBE seeks to test.

While it certainly might be improved, the MBE is a means of testing a range of substantive law while keeping the grading process manageable. Multiple-choice tests can be graded objectively, free from the possibility of human inconsistencies. Some candidates actually prefer multiple-choice questions because they find it easier to select the correct answer than to articulate one of their own in an essay.

The bar exam tests the ability to act and not react under pressure.

The bar exam requires a candidate to "think like a lawyer." In law school we teach our students that lawyers act; they do not react. They think deliberately and respond accordingly. The bar exam tests the candidate's ability to "think precisely, to analyze coldly." Bar passage requires that a candidate respond to questions with an orderly thought process. The exam demands that a candidate remain calm under pressure and not panic.

Clearly the bar exam is anxiety-producing, but a certain level of anxiety is a good thing. Anxiety is a very real part of the lawyer's everyday world of deadlines, conferences, and trials. A lawyer cannot afford to lose control because of pressure but must remain focused.

The bar exam requires a mastery of legal principles and core substance; tricks or techniques are no substitute.

When I work with candidates preparing for the bar, especially those who are retaking the exam, I do not teach tricks or strategies for bar passage, unless

- it is a trick to write an issue-based analysis.

- it is a trick to distinguish between legally relevant and irrelevant facts.

- it is a trick to include a solid discussion of the relevant rule of law before applying it to the facts.

- it is a trick to read carefully and thoughtfully and comprehend what you have read.

- it is a trick to organize one's thoughts before writing.

- it is a trick to use language carefully to convey precisely what you mean.

One of the most serious misconceptions about the bar exam is that passing it depends on tricks and techniques. There are no tricks to be learned, only the law, as any retaker will unfortunately be able to tell you. This does not mean, however, that a candidate can afford to be unfamiliar with the exam itself. One must know what to expect.

We tell our students that the key to success is preparation—preparation for class and for exams in law school, preparation for clients and for court in practice. Still, SALT condemns the bar exam because it requires preparation.

Not only do law students prepare for exams by studying from past exams, but practitioners regularly consult previously written complaints, memos, and briefs when drafting new motions. This is especially true of new associates in their first year of practice. Sometimes the only guidance on a project a new associate receives is a file of similar documents showing what the firm expects in terms of format, composition, style, and even specific language. Preparing for the bar exam by working with released exam questions is no different.

Admittedly, bar review courses have come to play a role in the process. But the course will be insufficient for bar passage if the student comes to it without the fundamental skills that should have been acquired in law school. The course simply puts all the rules tested in the jurisdiction in a structured, cohesive package; it does not teach anyone how to analyze a question, write an essay, or think through a problem. It assumes that the candidate learned these skills in law school.

The bar exam tests the subjects students should have learned in law school in preparation for the general practice of law.

The bar exam seeks to test a wide range of substantive law but focuses on the areas important to a beginning lawyer. It tests general topics because most law school graduates become sole or small-firm practitioners and need the basic bread-and-butter knowledge. It tests general subjects and not boutique areas because law students do not graduate as experts in a particular field, although most eventually specialize and practice in one or a few areas. The six subjects tested by the MBE are required courses in virtually every law school; they represent the core substance of a legal education.

Perhaps more important, the bar exam acknowledges our dual system of government and recognizes the lawyer's need to know both federal and state law. Still, the bar exam remains pretty much a creature of the state. Except for the MBE, it is state-specific. Presumably it reflects the interests of the jurisdiction, as determined by that jurisdiction. Different states may test different subjects—a diversity that reflects the complexities of our form of government and, more particularly, state sovereignty in such matters.

The bar exam neither demands nor requires the sacrifice of skills-based courses for substantive courses.

Unfortunately, SALT's assertion that the bar exam has become a "driving force in the law school curriculum" * * * is accurate, at least in some law schools. But the problem is not the exam; it is the schools' misunderstanding of the skills required for bar passage. A school need not design a curriculum around the specific topics tested on the bar exam. Most if not all of the skills that the exam tests are already being taught routinely in law classes—both substantive and practice-based courses. Whether the course is Civil Procedure or Pretrial Litigation, students have to read, think logically about what they have read, and produce a written work product in one form or another. Every course requires legal reasoning. Any distinction between the so-called bar courses and clinical courses is a false one. Students can take both substantive and clinical courses without jeopardizing their bar passage.

SALT contends that concern with bar passage has so influenced law school admission decisions that schools seek "to admit students who will pass the bar exam" at the expense of other criteria, with the effect of reducing the number of students—and graduates—"who will be more likely to serve underserved legal communities * * *. As a member of my school's Admissions Committee, I can say that we look at the sum total of the application package and admit students we believe are capable of learning the law. Our rationale is that if they have the ability to learn the law, they will have the ability to pass the bar exam. This approach rightly places the burden on the institution to fulfill its obligation to the student, instead of the other way around.

Testing What Law School Teaches

Learning to think like a lawyer is the key to passing the bar. The fiction that success on the bar exam depends mainly on proficiency in taking standardized tests such as the LSAT is just that—a myth that does not survive scrutiny. According to a comparison between incoming law students and law graduates from the same law schools, who had virtually identical average LSAT scores, "the highest MBE score earned by the novices was lower than the lowest score earned by any of the graduates. A logical conclusion is that "if general intellectual ability and test-wiseness were the major factors influencing MBE scores, both groups should have had very similar MBE scores." Additional research indicates that MBE scores "are highly correlated with other measures of legal skills and knowledge, such as scores on state essay examinations and law school grades." After controlling for law school quality, test reliability, subject matter and test type, time limits, and the ability to take tests, researchers concluded that "the higher the law school grade point average (LGPA), the greater the likelihood the applicant will pass. No other measured variable really mattered once there was control for LGPA."

Problems with SALT's Suggested Alternatives to the Bar Exam

It would be unwise to abandon the bar exam in favor of any of SALT's suggested alternatives. The proposals either fail to adequately address the need for a uniform measure of minimum competency in the basic analytical skills required for law practice or risk the creation of a legal hierarchy based on the licensing process. Neither the proposed "diploma privilege" nor a licensing measure that relies on public service alternatives would properly serve the interests of the profession as a whole.

First, one goal of an exam that almost every U.S. law school graduate has to pass must be to ensure some measure of uniformity and consistency among test takers who attended widely varying law schools. The requirement of bar passage compensates to some extent for the differences between law schools and individual faculty.

Second, SALT's proposed ten-week practical skills component as a substitute for the bar exam is not only inappropriate but unnecessary. Basic legal education includes assessment of interviewing, advocacy, legal writing, and legal drafting skills. Passing such courses should be sufficient evidence of competency.

Third, SALT's proposal to adopt the teaching-term model of some Canadian provinces would eliminate neither the testing of substantive law nor the need for preparation. The Canadian licensing process relies heavily on both. For example, admission to the bar in British Columbia requires the candidate to complete the ten-week Professional Legal Training Course and pass a two-part qualification examination, which covers substantive law in eight areas and includes multiple-choice, true/false, and short-essay questions. Similarly, Upper Canada requires the candidate to successfully complete an eighteen-week academic phase and pass licensing exams in eight substantive courses before being called to the bar. The Law Society of Upper Canada offers candidates exam-writing tips similar to those provided by the NCBE and such states as New York and New Jersey—for example, "set yourself time deadlines for the exam questions and abide by those deadlines"; "[e]xtraneous information may change a correct answer into an incorrect answer." Apparently there is unanimity not only in what bar examiners expect, but in what bar candidates produce to inspire such advice.

Fourth, the proposal for an alternative licensing system that would rely on a term of public service could create a tiered structure in the profession. Perhaps there are tiers of law schools (as in the *U.S. News and World Report* rankings), but the equality among licensed attorneys is recognized by the general population and the profession. An alternative licensing program could lead to a schism in the profession and create a legal caste system, one caste including those who sat for the bar exam, the other consisting of those who chose public service instead.

While SALT does not specifically advocate oral examinations in place of written ones, it suggests such a move when it faults the bar exam for not testing a candidate's ability to "communicate orally, counsel clients, and negotiate" * * *. Oral exams are problematic for two reasons: first, there is neither time nor resources for a one-on-one dialog with each candidate; and second, the inherent nature of dialog would make such a testing device ineffective and unreliable.

Besides being expensive and impractical, a system based on oral examinations would be inappropriate for evaluation purposes. Oral exams are inherently subjective and generally fail to assess a student's true knowledge. The dynamics of dialog necessarily intrude into the test situation; the questioner may unintentionally give the examinee clues as to the desired response. If you have ever conversed with a student who you thought knew the material and then been astonished by a dreadful final exam, then you know what I mean: there is often a profound difference between an oral presentation and a written one. In oral exchanges the student is as much led by the questioner's subliminal prompts as the questioner is led to fill in gaps in the dialog with her own perception of what the student "intends" to say. The natural prompting that occurs in dialog is entirely absent when the student is left alone to write. Written words stand on their own, and their meaning must be clear without interpretation or question.

SALT's Misunderstanding of the Bar Exam

When the SALT statement is examined in its entirety, it becomes apparent that what SALT blames on the bar exam is not properly attributable to the exam. SALT holds it responsible for everything from the type of exams administered in law schools to the career choices of law graduates and ultimately to the composition of the profession. But the bar exam simply is not the engine behind every aspect of the law school experience.

In a classic case of the tail wagging the dog, SALT faults the bar exam for the type of exams administered in law schools: "If the bar exam assessed a broader range of skills, or assessed skills in various ways, law schools might also adjust their assessment modalities so that they were not all geared toward rewarding just one type of skill or intelligence" * * *. Surely a law teacher would not adopt the same testing devices as a national or statewide exam unless he believed that essays and multiple-choice questions were appropriate devices to test the skills and substantive knowledge students should have acquired in his course.

It is also inappropriate for SALT to fault the bar exam for the typical law school practice of basing grades on a single final examination. A teacher can certainly choose to use midterms, quizzes, and writing assignments. This creates far more work for the teacher, but the bar exam does not dictate how she chooses to evaluate her students.

Not only does the bar exam impose no particular type of test on law schools, it imposes no requirement on where the candidate will practice, nor does it recognize any difference in areas of law. * * * [T]hese skills are as fundamental to the practice of public interest law as they are for the practice of criminal law. If a law school admits students who plan to represent underserved legal communities, the school and the individual students make those choices, not the bar exam.

* * * Day-to-day participation in the law school culture is responsible for a huge change in the well-being, values, and beliefs of the first-year law student. While SALT claims that law students pass up clinical classes and courses such as environmental law, poverty law, civil rights litigation, law and economics, and race and the law because of concerns with bar passage * * *, it is the institutional culture of law school that influences these decisions.

While it might be appropriate for SALT to urge law schools to inculcate certain values and suggest particular career paths to their students in an effort to guide the profession toward the achievement of specific goals, it is wholly inappropriate to place this burden on the bar exam. Since bar admission in nearly all jurisdictions requires a law degree, any requirements that law schools decide to impose on students would become de facto requirements for a law license.

Finally, while SALT concludes that the bar exam has a "disparate impact on people of color" * * *, it offers no justification to support such a claim aside from a single bar passage rate. Unfortunately, such inflammatory and harmful misconceptions about the bar exam persist, including the myth that it discriminates against minority applicants. The fact is that "the MBE neither widens nor narrows the gap in performance levels between minority applicants and other applicants." Research indicates that "differences in mean scores among racial and ethnic groups correspond closely to differences in those groups' mean LSAT scores, law school grade point averages, and scores on other measures of ability to practice law, such as bar examination essay scores or performance test scores."

Perhaps it is most telling that SALT has failed to mention such studies, especially those which indicate a strong correlation between higher grades in law school and success in passing the bar. That link clearly supports the argument that the bar exam tests the skills learned in law school. It further supports the claim that success on the bar exam is not a mere reflection of test-taking abilities but a measure of the skills and knowledge acquired through a legal education.

If there are differences between groups, the disparities existed before and during law school. While bar exam results may reflect differences between groups to some degree, the exam does not create these differences. SALT's statement that "the failure of the bench and bar to be as diverse as they could be is partly attributable to the existing bar exam" because it "disproportionately delays entry of people of color into, or excludes them from, the practice of law" * * * is unsupportable. If it has been difficult to increase the diversity of the bar as much as we would like, the bar exam is not the source of our frustration. * * *

VIJAY SEKHON, OVER-EDUCATION OF AMERICAN LAWYERS: AN ECONOMIC AND ETHICAL ANALYSIS OF THE REQUIREMENTS FOR PRACTICING LAW IN THE UNITED STATES,

14 Geo. Mason L. Rev. 769, 771-788 (2007)

* * *

* * * The Law School Prerequisite

* * * [U]ntil 1923, no state required any lawyer to have graduated from law school. Individuals could become lawyers by clerking for a certain period of time and then sitting for the state's bar examination. However, due to lobbying efforts by the ABA during the Great Depression, by 1935, nine states required graduation from an ABA-approved law school in order to sit for the state's bar examination, and twenty-three states had imposed this requirement by 1938. Today, almost all states require graduation from an accredited law school in order to sit for the state bar examination.

* * * [M]andating law school graduation requires a compelling justification due to the significant cost of attending law school. According to John A. Sebert, the average tuition at private law schools in 2003 was $25,584. The average tuition for public law schools was $20,171 for non-residents and $10,820 for residents. Assuming graduation from law school in three years, the average cost of a law degree for a private law student in 2003 was approximately $76,752; for a non-resident public law student, $60,513; and for a resident public law student, $32,460. This great expense requires a compelling justification.

*** Justifications for the Law School Requirement

There are four main justifications for requiring lawyers to graduate from law school before taking the state bar examination. First, many lawyers and legal scholars contend that law school teaches students to "think like a lawyer." As Benjamin Barton notes, law schools teach lawyers a "specialized bundle of thought processes and heuristics" that allow them to "learn[] the operative facts, discern[] the law, and apply[] one to the other," which they can sell on the market to individuals in need of legal assistance. Law schools, the argument goes, help teach lawyers these skills through the Socratic method, reading cases, writing briefs, writing legal memoranda, and taking law school examinations with hypothetical fact-patterns that require law students to apply an abundance of case law in a particular subject to a new set of facts.

These skills are imperative to effective advocacy in the American legal system. But law school may not be the most efficient and most effective way of teaching lawyers these skills. Law firms, for example, could develop training methods to teach their employees the socially optimal quantity and content of the skills currently taught by law schools. Private markets for courses teaching these skills would develop if these skills were desired by legal employers in the absence of the law school requirement to practicing law. Such courses would more effectively provide the socially optimal quantity and content of these skills due to the market forces certain to be imposed on firms providing such legal education services. In short, it is not obvious that law schools are the cheapest and most effective places to teach prospective attorneys the "specialized bundle of thought processes and heuristics" that are imperative to effective advocacy in the United States.

Second, many argue that law school is needed to teach prospective attorneys the basic legal principles and doctrines of the American legal system. Law schools, through teaching law students the primary legal courses such as constitutional law, torts, contracts, and criminal law as well as more advanced courses, give students a basic understanding of the law that prepares them for their professional responsibilities upon graduation.

But again, law school may not be the most efficient or effective means teaching law. Law students recognize this. Before taking the bar examination, most law students enroll in preparatory courses, such as BarBri and PMBR, in order to learn material tested on the state bar examination and to review material already taught in law school. Also, most law school graduates are not adequately prepared to practice in any particular area, and require substantial additional training in order to effectively represent clients by themselves.

Furthermore, as discussed below, attorneys probably do not need to know the basic legal doctrines in all of the subjects taught in law school in order to be effective advocates. A transactional attorney closing an acquisition of a public corporation will be little helped by having memorized the requirements for a prima facie case of conversion of property, and a criminal defense attorney will never be required to know the nuances of the rule against perpetuities. And if law school was eliminated as a requirement to practice law in the United States, attorneys could research the relevant legal doctrines and learn on the job, as most attorneys do when presented with novel or arcane legal issues. In short, it is difficult to argue that the benefits of three years of law school justify its significant economic cost.

Third, many argue that law schools promote legal scholarship, which is a public good that would otherwise be under-produced relative to its socially optimal level. Nevertheless, the fact that legal scholarship is a public good does not promote the argument that such legal scholarship should be provided in law schools. Given the substantial inefficiencies of law school illustrated above, it is not difficult to imagine alternative methods of producing legal scholarship that are more efficient and focused than that currently provided by contemporary American law schools. For example, the government could require licensed attorneys to contribute a fixed sum annually, which would be used to pay full-time legal scholars and sponsor writing competitions tailored towards identified areas of need in legal scholarship. Furthermore, such programs could be supplemented by private donations that are currently provided by law school graduates to their law schools. Finally, it is unlikely that the elimination of the law school requirement will terminate the existence of law schools; legal scholarship would almost certainly continue to be produced by law professors employed by the law schools still in existence following an elimination of the law school requirement to practice law in the United States. In other words, the fact that legal scholarship is a public good does not substantiate requiring graduation from law school as a prerequisite to practicing law.

Fourth, another argument posited in favor of requiring law schools for practicing attorneys is that the grading systems of law schools serve as a signaling mechanism for legal employers to distinguish applicants. The fact that law schools can serve as an effective signal of applicant quality is an insufficient justification to require prospective attorneys to spend tens or even sometimes hundreds of thousands of dollars. Again, it is not difficult to imagine alternative signals for legal employers that are more efficient and focused than that currently provided by contemporary American law schools. For example, SAT and LSAT scores, undergraduate academic records, scored bar examinations tailored to specific areas of law and other examinations developed by the private market for legal employers (as well as tests administered by legal employers themselves) would surely be more efficient and narrowly tailored signaling mechanisms than those currently provided by American law schools. In short, the fact that law schools provide a signal to legal employers is insufficient justification to impose the substantial cost of law school on prospective attorneys.

* * * The Economics of the Law School Rquirement

* * * Beyond the weak arguments that support the law school requirement, significant economic and ethical considerations argue against it. * * * The average cost of law school tuition for three years of law school ranges from about $32,460 to $76,752. Assuming for the sake of argument that half of all law students attended private law schools and half attended public law schools as residents, requiring America's approximately one million lawyers to obtain law school degrees would cost over $57 billion at today's prices. This is a steep cost to impose on lawyers and, by extension, consumers of legal services, and it is not clear that it is justified.

That figure does not include the opportunity costs, imposed on lawyers and society, of attending law school. Law students could engage in a multitude of activities rather than attend law school. These activities could include working, vacationing, and performing community service.

Consumers of legal services foot some of the bill for the law school requirement. The cost of law school is a barrier to entry to the legal profession, dissuading many prospective lawyers from becoming attorneys. With fewer lawyers, legal services are more expensive than they would otherwise be. Taken as a whole, these factors once again impose a deadweight loss on society focused upon consumers of legal services.

Finally, * * * American taxpayers also foot the bill of the law school requirement through the enormous sums that taxpayers pay to fund federal and state loan programs, grant programs, and tax breaks that subsidize legal education.

* * * The Ethical Issues Surrounding the Law School Requirement

* * * First, the law school requirement prevents many individuals from lower income families from attending law school and hence becoming lawyers. From a societal standpoint, this is unethical because it unnecessarily prevents members of society from entering a profession based upon happenstance of birth or financial circumstance. Second, the law school requirement deters many prospective public interest attorneys from entering the profession due to the high costs of law school and the low income of public interest lawyers. Third, it does not seem ethical to require individuals to spend three years of their lives studying and paying for law school when it has not been shown that the economic costs of law school are outweighed by its benefits. Such a great cost to an individual, in terms of money and years, requires more justification than has been demonstrated. Finally, law schools discriminate against prospective attorneys who test poorly, which has almost nothing to do with most forms of legal practice. Prohibiting prospective attorneys who test poorly from practicing law is unethical, especially given the fact that there is substantial evidence that law school is inadequately tailored towards teaching law students what they need to know when they enter the legal profession.

Therefore, the two primary justifications for law school prerequisite to becoming a lawyer in the United States, teaching students to "think like a lawyer" and the basic legal doctrines of the American legal system, are open to significant criticism and are insufficient to outweigh the economic and ethical considerations that arise from the requirement.

* * * The Bar Examination Prerequisite

State supreme courts govern the regulation of lawyers in all fifty states. In almost every state, lawyers must take and pass a state bar examination before being admitted into the state bar association and practicing law in the state. Generally, law school graduates must pass the bar examination of the state in which they intend to practice. According to the American Bar Association, seventeen states require experienced, licensed attorneys from other states to retake some or all of the state bar examination in order to gain admission to the state bar association. Other states allow attorneys from other states to "waive into" the state bar association upon demonstration of a sufficient bar examination score or demonstration of good standing in the state bar association for a period of time, generally five to seven years.

According to the National Conference of Bar Examiners, the nationwide pass rate for first-time test-takers was 76% in 2005. Thirty-one states had first-time passage rates of 80% or above. Research shows that 96% of bar candidates eventually pass the examination and go on to practice law. Although these passage rates seem high, it should be noted that prospective attorneys spend an enormous amount of time and money on studying for these examinations.

The bar examination was not always this way. Through the 1920s, bar examinations were "casual, local, and undemanding." Over the next few decades, as the ABA grew in clout and began to effectively regulate the field of law for the benefit of existing lawyers, state bar examinations became more rigid and difficult, and passage rates steadily declined to the rates observed today. The bar examination's evolution may not have been for the better.

* * * Justifications for the Bar Examination Requirement

There are two non-monopolistic justifications given for why American attorneys are required to pass a state bar examination before being admitted into the state bar association and allowed to practice law.

First, some argue that bar examinations ensure that all practicing attorneys have a basic understanding of the law, reducing the incidence of poor legal representation. The state bar examinations, especially the Multistate Bar Examination ("MBE") component of most state bar examinations, tests a general understanding of basic legal doctrines in such areas as torts, criminal law, criminal procedure, civil procedure, constitutional law, and contracts. General knowledge of these subjects, however, may not be necessary for, or even relevant to, effective representation. Once again, a criminal defense attorney has no need to know about the nuances of the rule against perpetuities, and a corporate attorney will gain little from a detailed understanding of family law and criminal procedure. States have no compelling reason to require attorneys to have a general understanding of so many legal subjects before being admitted to practice.

Second, some argue that the bar examination requirement helps legal consumers to obtain good representation by reducing the information asymmetry between lawyers and prospective clients. The argument is that the bar examination requirement permits only capable attorneys to remain in the profession, mitigating the lemon problem in the market for legal services. The lemon problem dictates that only low-quality, incapable attorneys will remain in the profession when consumers cannot readily distinguish between high- and low-quality attorneys because the expected value of a high-quality attorney's services is diminished by the probability that the attorney is of low quality. Because high-quality attorneys will not enter a market in which their services are not adequately compensated, they will leave the market, and the market will be left with low-quality attorneys. The bar examination, it is argued, mitigates this problem by eliminating low-quality attorneys from the legal services market, permitting high-quality attorneys to remain in the market and receive appropriate compensation.

Although knowing that an attorney has passed the bar examination might be useful for clients who rarely deal with the legal system, who lack independent resources for checking qualifications, or who have relatively small or routine matters that do not justify significant investigation, there are two significant negative aspects of the bar examination as a signaling mechanism that may eliminate its benefits. First, licensed attorneys may have done well on portions of the bar examination unrelated to their area of practice and still either performed poorly or were not even tested on subjects of relevance to their area of practice, reducing the utility of the bar examination to signal quality to consumers of legal services. Second, other mechanisms, such as attorney advertising and reputation, educational certifications, etc., could be and currently are adequate to provide consumers with information—perhaps better information—about legal service providers than the bar examination.

In short, there are significant holes in the argument that the bar examination ensures that all practicing attorneys have a basic understanding of the law or that the bar examination provides much information to prospective clients. As shown below, these weak arguments are insufficient to justify the substantial costs of the bar examination requirement.

* * * The Economics of the Bar Examination Requirement

There are a plethora of costs associated with taking a state bar examination. First, the bar examination itself is quite expensive, ranging from $250 to $815. Assuming, for the sake of argument, that the average lawyer's bar examination fee is $400, America's one million lawyers would have to spend $400 million to take the bar examination at today's prices. In addition, most law students opt to take bar examination preparatory courses such as BarBri, PMBR, and The Writing Edge. The prices of these courses range from $1,695 to $3,995. Although minor in comparison to the costs of college and law school, the monetary costs of the bar examination are still substantial.

Second, * * * bar examinations exact opportunity costs on those who take them, to their detriment and society's. Generally, first-time test takers study from the end of their last semester in mid-May until the state bar examination in late July, a period of two-and-one-half months. Repeat test-takers and practicing attorneys attempting to become licensed to practice in another state generally work during the day and study at night, or take a period of time off of work and study for the bar examination. Rather than study for the bar examination, those preparing for the test could either work or engage in recreational activities.

Third, American consumers of legal services foot part of the bill of the cost of the bar examination. The bar examination is a barrier to entry to the legal profession, dissuading prospective lawyers or repeat test takers from taking the examination and becoming attorneys. This increases the cost of legal services and creates a deadweight loss to American society. These economic effects are similar to the economic effects of college and law school on the supply (and consequently price) of lawyers in the United States.

* * * The Ethical Issues Surrounding the Bar Examination Requirement

* * * First, the bar examination requirement prevents individuals from lower income families from becoming lawyers. Second, the bar examination requirement deters prospective public interest attorneys from entering the profession. Third, it does not seem fair to require individuals to study for and take the bar examination when its value is empirically unproven and it may not accomplish the goals that its supporters claim for it. Fourth, the bar exam provides a false sense of security to consumers of legal services, providing an imprimatur that misleads consumers who rely on bar passage as a valuable signaling mechanism when the reliability of the bar examination as an effective signaling mechanism to differentiate competent from incompetent attorneys is dubious at best. Finally, as with law schools, the bar examination discriminates against prospective attorneys who test poorly, which has almost nothing to do with most forms of legal practice. Prohibiting law school graduates who test poorly from practicing law is unethical, especially given the fact that there is substantial evidence that the bar examination is a poor measure of attorney competency.

Thus, the two primary justifications for requiring American lawyers to take the state bar examination are open to numerous critiques that raise doubt as to whether the bar examination requirement is sufficiently justified to warrant the economic and ethical costs that it imposes on prospective lawyers and society. * * *

2. Can Consumers Rely on Lawyers to be Ethical?

[Question 1]

A required law school professional responsibility course ensures that lawyers are ethical providers of legal services.

(A) True

(B) False

[Question 2]

People who have not passed a Professional Responsibility course cannot ethically provide legal services.

(A) True

(B) False

[Question 3]

Consumer protection requires that legal services providers pass a Professional Responsibility course.

(A) True

(B) False

[Question 4]

The MPRE ensures that most lawyers are ethical providers of legal services.

(A) True

(B) False

[Question 5]

People who have not passed the MPRE cannot ethically provide legal services.

(A) True

(B) False

[Question 6]

Consumer protection requires that legal services providers pass the MPRE.

(A) True

(B) False

[Question 7]

A law graduate who has failed to repay student loans should be admitted to the bar.

(A) True

(B) False

[Question 8]

A law graduate with a prior conviction for selling marijuana should be admitted to practice law.

(A) True

(B) False

[Question 9]

A law graduate who served a sentence for manslaughter before beginning law school should be admitted to the bar.

(A) True

(B) False

[Question 12]

An adulterer should be admitted to the bar.

(A) True

(B) False

[Question 10]

An alcoholic should be admitted to the bar.

    (A) True

    (B) False

[Question 11]

A Nazi should be admitted to the bar.

    (A) True

    (B) False

[Question 12]

The character and fitness requirement ensures that lawyers are ethical providers of legal services.

    (A) True

    (B) False

[Question 13]

People who do not pass the character and fitness requirement are not ethical providers of legal services.

    (A) True

    (B) False

[Question 14]

Consumer protection requires that legal services providers pass a character and fitness test.

    (A) True

    (B) False

[Question 15]

Consumer protection requires that legal services providers:

   (A) **pass a Professional Responsibility course, the MPRE, and the character and fitness test.**

   (B) **pass a Professional Responsibility course and the MPRE.**

   (C) **pass the MPRE and the character and fitness test.**

   (D) **pass a Professional Responsibility course and the character and fitness test.**

   (E) **None of the above.**

Review the materials on teaching legal ethics in Chapter 1, Part C.

NATIONAL CONFERENCE OF BAR EXAMINERS, *DESCRIPTION OF THE MPRE,*

http://www.ncbex.org/multistate-tests/mpre/mpre-faqs/description0/

The purpose of the NCBE Multistate Professional Responsibility Examination (MPRE) is to measure the examinee's knowledge and understanding of established standards related to a lawyer's professional conduct; thus, the MPRE is not a test to determine an individual's personal ethical values. Lawyers serve in many capacities: for example, as judges, as advocates, as counselors, and in other roles. The law governing the conduct of lawyers in these roles is applied in disciplinary and bar admission procedures, and by courts in dealing with issues of appearance, representation, privilege, disqualification, contempt, or other censure, and in lawsuits seeking to establish liability for malpractice and other civil or criminal wrongs committed by a lawyer while acting in a professional capacity.

The law governing the conduct of lawyers is based on the disciplinary rules of professional conduct currently articulated in the American Bar Association (ABA) Model Rules of Professional Conduct and the ABA Model Code of Judicial Conduct, as well as controlling constitutional decisions and generally accepted principles established in leading federal and state cases and in procedural and evidentiary rules.

The MPRE consists of 60 multiple-choice test items. These test items are followed by 10 Test Center Review items that request the examinee's reactions to the testing conditions. The examination is two hours and five minutes in length.

Test items covering judicial ethics measure applications of the ABA Model Code of Judicial Conduct (CJC). Other items will deal with discipline of lawyers by state disciplinary authorities; in these items, the correct answer will be governed by the current ABA Model Rules of Professional Conduct (MRPC). The remaining items, outside the disciplinary context, are designed to measure an understanding of the generally accepted rules, principles, and common law regulating the legal profession in the United States; in these items, the correct answer will be governed by the view reflected in a majority of cases, statutes, or regulations on the subject. To the extent that questions of professional responsibility arise in the context of procedural or evidentiary issues, such as the availability of litigation sanctions or the scope of the attorney-client evidentiary privilege, the Federal Rules of Civil Procedure and the Federal Rules of Evidence will be assumed to apply, unless otherwise stated.

DEBORAH L. RHODE, *ETHICS BY THE PERVASIVE METHOD*,

42. J. Legal Educ. 31, 40-41 (1992)

* * * Ironically enough, bar examiners' determination to treat ethics issues more seriously has undermined law school efforts to do the same. In the wake of Watergate, states began requiring more examination on professional responsibility issues, and most eventually moved to the multistate multiple-choice format developed for other core subjects. The rationale for this change, as its national administrator once explained to me, is that essay questions had been impossible to evaluate; virtually all bar applicants chose the moral highroad. With an objective test, examiners could construct curves. In practice, however, that is accomplished by including ambiguous questions, choices between unsatisfying answers, and a focus on relatively obscure provisions of ethics codes.

This strategy tends both to trivialize the subject matter and to encourage law school courses to focus on bar exam preparation. In one typical case, a student was overheard advising a friend to avoid taking professional responsibility with a certain faculty member who "asks a lot of uncomfortable questions about what you think is right, and never spends any time teaching you the rules for the exam." Many of us who specialize in the area attempt to resist such pressure by making clear that law school courses are unnecessary to pass multiple-choice tests. It is often enough to take a brief bar preparation class and, when in doubt, pick the second most ethical course of conduct. Yet in many institutions, professional responsibility has found its identity as a course in statutory analysis of ABA codes. As William Simon argues, this rule-bound conception of legal ethics has little to do with ethics. * * *

CAIT MURPHY, *"YALE'S MARKOVITS REDEFINES 21ST CENTURY LEGAL ETHICS,"* INTERVIEW WITH DANIEL MARKOVITS, PROFESSOR, YALE LAW SCHOOL,

Mod. Ethical Law., http://modernethicallawyer.com/articles.php?id=7

* * *

I don't think ethics training makes people better; there is no direct relationship between intellectual thought and ethical behavior. If there were, moral philosophers would be better people than others, but in fact they are not better. The same is true for priests, rabbis and imams.

The goal of intellectual work in these fields is to understand what our practices are, to interpret what we have. I am trying to show students what they are doing when they are lawyering; to make them more reflective. But they are going to have to be self-disciplined and morally creative on their own; this is not something you can teach.

* * *

CAIT MURPHY, *"STANFORD'S RHODE LEGAL ETHICS ROCK STAR,"* INTERVIEW WITH DEBORAH RHODE, PROFESSOR, STANFORD LAW SCHOOL,

Mod. Ethical Law., http://modernethicallawyer.com/articles.php?id=2.

* * *

Do you think more ethics teaching results in lawyer who are more ethical?

I'm a realist in terms of how much classroom experience can affect real-world behavior in any area where strong self interest pulls in the opposite direction. But what we know from decades of research is that well-designed ethics classes can improve students' skills in ethical reasoning. These course can make future practitioners more aware of the rules—where the lines are before they are in a position to cross one—and can give them some sense of the social pressures and organizational dynamics that underpin misconduct. Students become more aware of flaws in the legal system, and develop a better understanding of the enormous gap between our rhetorical commitment to equal justice under law and what passes for justice among the have nots. It's worth noting that when you survey lawyers, most think law schools should do more ethics training, not less.

* * *

DEBORAH L. RHODE, *MORAL CHARACTER AS A PROFESSIONAL CREDENTIAL*,

94 Yale L.J. 491 (1985)

* * *

Those involved in the character certification process have almost uniformly identified its central justification as protecting the public. * * * In response to open-ended questions concerning their objectives in character review, bar examiners generally stressed a need to safeguard the public from the 'morally unfit' lawyer; their goal was both to exclude individuals with 'unsavory characters' or traits 'not appropriate' for practitioners, and to deter those with 'obvious' problems from seeking a license.

More specifically, courts and commentators have traditionally identified two prophylactic objectives for the certification process. The first is shielding clients from potential abuses, such as misrepresentation, misappropriation of funds, or betrayal of confidences. Since the 'technical nature of law' and the attorney's 'peculiar position of trust' place clients in a vulnerable position, individuals whom the state certifies as fit to practice should be worthy of the confidence reposed in them. A second concern involves safeguarding the administration of justice from those who might subvert it through subornation of perjury, misrepresentation, bribery, or the like. * * *

A second, although less frequently articulated, rationale for character screening rests on the bar's own interest in maintaining a professional community and public image. * * *

As the most recent Bar Examiners' Handbook candidly concedes: 'No definition of what constitutes grounds for denial of admission on the basis of faulty character exists. On the whole, judicial attempts to give content to the standard have been infrequent and unilluminating. * * * More specifically, in *Konigsberg v. State Bar of California*, the Court focused on whether a 'reasonable man could fairly find that there were substantial doubts about [the applicant's] 'honesty, fairness and respect for the rights of others and for the laws of the state and nation." Following , a number of courts have applied analogous standards. The difficulty, of course, is that reasonable men can readily disagree about what conduct would raise substantial doubts, a point amply demonstrated by the divergence of views among judges, bar examiners, and law school administrators.

Nor have alternative legislative and judicial formulations added greater determinacy to the character requirement. The most facially precise approach is to catalogue relevant traits such as honesty, candor, trustworthiness, and respect for law. * * * Even greater indeterminacies characterize the most common alternative approach, which is to invoke some broad conclusory definition of virtue. For example, the Oregon Supreme Court demands 'ethically cognizant and mature individuals [able] to withstand . . . temptation[ ].' * * *

At an abstract level, courts and bar committees have similar convictions about what traits are undesirable in candidates for their profession. Conduct evidencing dishonesty, disrespect for law, disregard for financial obligations, or psychological instability triggers serious concern. Yet, at a more concrete level, there is considerable divergence of views as to what prior acts are sufficiently probative to warrant delaying or withholding certification. From a public policy perspective, the justifications for certain of the bar's concerns are less than convincing. * * *

With few exceptions, courts and committees have developed no categorical policies toward particular offenses. Although a few jurisdictions have formally stated or informally determined that certain conduct will not be a matter for concern (e.g., sexual relationships, a single misdemeanor marijuana charge, conduct 'in the nature of horseplay'), most examiners indicated that their decisions would depend on a broad range of factors, including the nature, number, and proximity of offenses, the applicant's age when they were committed, and evidence of rehabilitation. But while agreeing on those common criteria, courts and committees have arrived at quite different conclusions regarding comparable attitudes and activities. * * *

A threshold difficulty in applying character standards stems from the inclusiveness of 'disrespect for law' as a ground for excluding applicants. The conventional view has been that certain illegal acts—regardless of the likelihood of their repetition in a lawyer-client relationship—evidence attitudes toward law that cannot be countenanced among its practitioners; to hold otherwise would demean the profession's reputation and reduce the character requirement to a meaningless pretense. The difficulty, of course, is that this logic licenses inquiry into any illegal activity, no matter how remote or minor, and could justify excluding individuals convicted of any offense that affronted the sensibilities of a particular court or character committee. In fact, bar inquiry frequently extends to juvenile offenses and parking violations, and conduct warranting exclusion has been thought to include traffic convictions and cohabitation.

* * * Decisions concerning drug and alcohol offenses have proven particularly inconsistent. Convictions for marijuana are taken seriously in some jurisdictions and overlooked in others; much may depend on whether the examiner has, as one put it, grown more 'mellow' towards 'kids smoking pot.' * * * Attitudes toward sexual conduct such as cohabitation or homosexuality reflect similar diversity. Some bar examiners do not regard that activity as 'within their purview,' unless it becomes a 'public nuisance' or results in criminal charges. * * *

Other major areas of concern to courts and bar committees have been psychological instability, financial irresponsibility, and radical political involvement, although again attitudes vary widely as to the significance of particular conduct. For example, * * * the bar applications of some jurisdictions make no inquiries as to mental health; others require a psychiatrist's certificate and in some cases an examination for candidates who have a history of treatment. * * *

Financial mismanagement provokes comparable disagreement. Most jurisdictions (73%) make no inquiries concerning debts past due, while others demand detailed information ranging from parking fines to child support obligations. * * * Attitudes toward bankruptcies also varied. Some respondents appeared to assume that applicants who 'don't have a conscience when it comes to paying their own bills . . . may not have a conscience when it comes to their fiduciary responsibilities to their clients.' Discharges to avoid student loans have resulted in denial in some jurisdictions. Yet about a third of all state bar applications made no inquiries in the area, and some examiners, particularly those who handle bankruptcies in private practice, felt that individuals had a right to such remedies. * * * Judicial decisions regarding bankruptcy have yielded equally inconsistent results. For example, applicants who discharged student loans have been admitted or excluded depending on a highly selective assessment of whether 'undue hardship' justified the default. * * *

A third area in which the bar has shown interest is the ideology of its applicants. Religious fanatics, suspected subversives, and 'rabble rousers' have been delayed, deterred, and occasionally excluded under both admission and disciplinary standards. Although existing caselaw constrains states' ability to deny entry solely for political associations, it has done little to curb investigation into political offenses. * * * Denying or delaying admission is typically justified not in terms of the likely risk to the public, but rather by reference to vague generalities about respect for law. Yet in many instances, the appearance of such respect seems to assume greater significance than the values it is designed to reflect. * * *

Food for Thought

Later in her article, Professor Rhode argues that the character and fitness evaluations lack predictive value, drain resources needed for professional discipline, and create problems in terms of First Amendment and Due Process values. If you agree with her, how could the bar continue to claim that lawyers have higher moral character than nonlawyers? Does a passing grade on the MPRE provide an alternative? What do you think?

A final context in which decisionmaking has proven particularly idiosyncratic involves candidates' apparent attitudes toward their prior conduct and committee oversight. Arrogance, 'argumentativeness,' 'rudeness,' 'excessive immatur[ity],' 'lackadaisical' responses, or intimations that a candidate is 'not interested in correcting himself' can significantly color character assessments. * * * The ultimate sin in many jurisdictions is a failure to seem 'up front' with the committee. Nondisclosure, even about relatively trivial matters, may evidence the wrong 'mental attitude,' and 'glib, equivocal responses,' even if technically accurate, may prove more damning than the conduct at issue. * * *

In some, particularly criminal, cases, the applicant's efforts to atone for prior conduct are of equal concern. * * * Yet what evidence will suffice to establish redemption varies considerably. * * *

JAMES C. GALLAGHER, *DRUGS, ALCOHOL, MENTAL HEALTH, AND THE VERMONT LAWYER,*

Vt. Bar J. & L. Dig., Spring 2006, at 5.

* * * [T]he state bars of California, Minnesota, and New Jersey estimate that two-thirds of disciplinary complaints in those states result from substance abuse. A report prepared by the ABA Young Lawyers Division Commission on Impaired Attorneys says "[s]tudies from the Washington State Bar Association found that 21% of lawyers in that state are addicted to alcohol or other drugs as compared to 10% of the general population, based on figures from the National Institute on Alcohol and Drug Abuse. Findings from California and Georgia estimate that 60% to 80% of lawyer discipline cases are the result of addiction. * * *

> **FYI**
>
> Legal developments since the publication of Professor Rhode's article in 1985 have changed some potential character and fitness inquiries. In *Lawrence v. Texas*, 539 U.S. 558 (2003) decriminalized homosexual sodomy removing it as a possible character and fitness issue. In addition, courts have applied disability rights protections to mental health inquiries regarding the mental health of bar applicants. *See, e.g.*, Mariam Alikhan, Note, *The ADA is Narrowing Mental Health Inquiries on Bar Applications: Looking to the Medical Profession to Decide Where to Go From Here*, 14 Geo. J. Legal Ethics 159 (2000).

DECISION OF INQUIRY OF THE COMMITTEE ON CHARACTER AND FITNESS OF THE SUPREME COURT OF ILLINOIS FOR THE THIRD APPELLATE DISTRICT * * * IN THE MATTER OF: THE APPLICATION FOR ADMISSION TO THE BAR OF MATTHEW F. HALE

Decision of Inquiry Panel (1998), *aff'd*, Committee on Character and Fitness of Illinois for the Third Judicial District (1999), *aff'd*, 723 N.E.2d 206 (Ill., 1999)

* * * Introduction

Matthew F. Hale has applied for admission to the Bar of Illinois after having passed its examination conducted in the summer of 1998. * * * [T]he Chairperson of the Third District Committee assigned the application to this Inquiry Panel for further review and examination. * * * In declining to certify the applicant and thereby causing the matter to be referred to a Hearing Panel, we are setting forth our reasons for this decision in some detail.

* * * [T]he Rules of Procedure places the burden on the applicant to prove by clear and convincing evidence that he has the requisite character and fitness for admission to the practice of law. Nonetheless, the denial of a request for admission results

in serious adverse consequences for the applicant, as noted by the *United States Supreme Court in Konigsberg v. State Bar of California*, <u>353 U.S. 252, 257-258 (1957)</u>:

The Committee's action prevents him from earning a living by practicing law. This deprivation has grave consequences for a man who has spent years of study and a great deal of money in preparing to be a lawyer.

Additionally, as discussion will demonstrate, the reasons for our decision relate to the applicant's active advocacy of his core beliefs. When an issue of that type is injected into the reasons for denial of certification, "a heavy burden lies" upon the State to demonstrate that "a legitimate state interest" is sought to be protected. *Baird v. Arizona*, <u>401 U.S. 1, 6-7 (1971)</u>. Under these circumstances, the reasons for voting to deny certification should be carefully explained. * * *

Matthew F. Hale is 27 years old, attended undergraduate school at Bradley University in Peoria and received a J.D. degree in 1998 from Southern Illinois University School of Law at Carbondale. By his frank admission he is an avowed racist who, since his teenage days, has been actively involved in promoting white supremacy through organizations and by the distribution of literature. This literature portrays blacks, Jews, and other minorities in an extreme negative light. * * *

Mr. Hale is currently the head of an organization called the World Church of the Creator which is claimed to be a religious organization. His title as head of this church is Pontifex Maximus (Supreme Leader). * * * Mr. Hale has stated that "he would dedicate his life to Creativity," referring to the World Church of the Creator. This religion, according to its founder, Ben Klassen, has as one of its major tenets the hatred of Jews, blacks and other colored people.

Mr. Hale's church admires Adolph Hitler and the National Socialism movement as practiced in Germany, except that it holds Hitler was mistaken in promoting only German nationalism. Instead, his church believes that Hitler's ideas relating to racial superiority should have been applied for the benefit of the entire "white race as opposed to just Germans."

Mr. Hale and his church disavow violence and an intention to seek the forcible overthrow of the United States Government. However, Mr. Hale stated in his interview with us that if his organization would gain power by peaceable means it would call for the deportation of Jews, blacks and others whom his church refers to as "mud races." The United States would then become a country for members of the "white race" only.

[During the] Inquiry Panel's interview[,] * * * Mr. Hale was extremely polite and answered all questions quite candidly. He is intelligent and articulate. He stated that after becoming a lawyer he would continue his activities as leader of his church, including his distribution of racist literature. He also plans to be active on the Internet to promote his church's racist views. * * *

On the issue of moral character, he argued that his frank and open admission of the advocacy of racism shows greater moral character than do lawyers and others who are in fact racist but who utter such thoughts only in privacy.

Mr. Hale was asked whether or not he could take the oath to support the United States Constitution and the Constitution of the State of Illinois in good conscience. * * *

He unhesitatingly answered that he would have no difficulty even though, based on his beliefs, he obviously would be in substantial disagreement with current interpretations of the constitutions. He likened his situation to that of a judge or jury whose duty it is to follow the law even though they may disagree with it.

In connection with the oath, he was shown Article 1, § 20 of the Constitution of the State of Illinois which condemns "communications that portray criminality, depravity or lack of virtue in, or that incite violence, hatred, abuse or hostility toward, a person or group of persons by reason of or by reference to religious, racial, ethnic, national or regional affiliation." In response, Mr. Hale said that to the extent this Illinois constitutional provision limited "communications," it would run afoul of the First Amendment to the Constitution of the United States and therefore would not be binding on him.

Additionally, [Professional Conduct] Rule 8.4(a)(5) * * * was brought to his attention. Mr. Hale was asked if he could abide by that rule if admitted to the Bar. The rule, in part, states that a lawyer shall not engage in conduct that is prejudicial to the administration of justice. In relation thereto, a lawyer shall not engage in adverse discriminatory treatment of litigants, jurors, witnesses, lawyers, and others, based on race, sex, religion, or national origin.

Again, Mr. Hale stated that he would have no problem with following this rule, reaffirming his statements that he would follow the law until such time as he could have it changed by peaceful means. He also said that in a recent employment in Champaign where he worked as a law clerk for a few months, he dealt with black clients and engaged in no acts of racism toward them. The accuracy of this statement was confirmed by independent inquiry.

Analysis Of Moral Character

As noted, the applicant must establish his "good moral character and general fitness to practice law" "by clear and convincing evidence." * * * If these requisites may be established by simply showing an absence of criminal conduct in the past and having one or more persons vouch for one's character, Mr. Hale has established these requisites by clear and convincing evidence?

On the other hand, if the lack of good moral character and general fitness to practice law may be judged on the basis of active advocacy that attempts to incite hatred of members of various groups by vilifying and portraying them as inferior and robbing them of human dignity, Mr. Hale has not established good moral character or general fitness to practice law. As indicated, Mr. Hale's life mission is to bring about peaceable change in the United States in order to deny the equal protection of the laws to all Americans except perhaps those that his church determines to be of the "white race." Under any civilized standards of decency, the incitement of racial hatred for the ultimate purpose of depriving selected groups of their legal rights shows a gross deficiency in moral character, particularly for lawyers who have a special responsibility to uphold the rule of law for all persons.

However, even if the Illinois standards for considering moral character and general fitness to practice law allows the Committee to make a determination in this manner, the question remains as to whether or not denying certification for admission to the Bar is constitutional on that basis.

The Constitutional Analysis

At an earlier time the Committee on Character and Fitness might have desired to disqualify Mr. Hale on the ground that, despite his statements to the contrary, his views make it impossible for him to take the required oath "in good conscience." * * * Moreover, the Membership Manual for his church * * * [states that a church member] "puts loyalty towards his own race above every other loyalty." * * * A reasonable question for the applicant is what happens when that loyalty conflicts with his oath to support the United States and Illinois Constitutions?

Additionally, even though Mr. Hale claimed to be able to abide by the Rules of Professional Conduct relating to non-discriminatory treatment, his activities in this regard arguably cast doubt on these representations. For example, in 1995, only a few weeks before he started law school, he wrote a letter to a woman who apparently had made comments in the Peoria Journal Star on racial issues that were contrary to his. In this letter he referred to "the nigger race" as "inferior in intellectual capacity" and condemned the "misbegotten equality myth" as "garbage" that was "destroying" "our whole country." * * * He also suggested that this woman's rape or murder by a "nigger beast" might enlighten her.

With the applicant capable of such outrageous and intemperate conduct, one might have concluded that he was insincere when he said he could comply with the Rules of Professional Conduct and conscientiously take the oath. However, later cases of the United States Supreme Court suggest that these very real questions about the applicant might be a frail reed upon which to deny certification. *See, e.g., Bond v. Floyd,* 385 U.S. 116 (1966) and *Law Students Research Counsel v. Wadmond,* 401 U.S. 154, 163-164 (1971), which appear to hold that once an oath to support the Constitution is taken, others cannot urge that it was not taken sincerely.

Finally, an applicant cannot be denied admission to the Bar on a ground formerly announced by the Illinois Supreme Court—"that the practice of law is a privilege, not a right."

In Re Anastaplo, 3 Ill.2d 471,482 (1954). On the contrary, the United States Supreme Court later stated that "the practice of law is not a matter of grace, but of right for one who is qualified by his learning and his moral character." *Baird v. Arizona, supra,* 401 U.S. 1 at 8.

Absolute First Amendment Rights vs. A Balancing Test

The easiest resolution of Mr. Hale's application would be to certify him. This would be in accord with the view that the First Amendment is virtually absolute. By adhering to such a view, line drawing problems and degree questions are avoided, and as the dissenting opinion makes clear, the analysis for reaching a decision can be simple and direct.

Certainly statements found in some Supreme Court opinions, taken in isolation and without regard to the specific facts of the cases, might support this view. For example, in the bar admission case of *Re Stolar,* 401 U.S. 23, 28-29 (1971), it was stated that the State cannot "penalize petitioner solely because he personally... 'espouses illegal aims.'"

Nonetheless, on balance, a majority of the Inquiry Panel bas concluded that the constitutional issues involving a case precisely like this one are open, and that the Illinois requirement for moral character and general fitness to practice law precludes the applicant from being certified.

The latest United States Supreme Court decisions relating to bar admissions located by the Inquiry Panel are over 25 years old. In 1971, the year of its most recent cases on this subject, the Court characterized its earlier opinions as containing "confusing formulas, refined reasonings, and puzzling holdings." *Baird v. Arizona,* 401 U.S. 1, (1971).

In that case, the Court, in a 5 to 4 split decision, he'd that "a State may not inquire about a man's views or associations solely for the purpose of withholding a right or benefit because of what he believes." * * * The Court also said in that case:

> While First Amendment issues in this case are difficult and The First Amendment's protection of association prohibits a State from excluding a person from a profession or punishing him solely because he is a member of a particular political organization or because he holds certain beliefs. * * *

> A similar result in another 5 to 4 decision was reached on the same day in 1971 in the case of *Re Stolar,* 401 U.S. (1971).

> Neither of those decisions involved individuals who were actively involved in inciting racial hatred and who had dedicated their lives to destroying equal rights under law that all Americans currently enjoy. On

the contrary, the applicants in those cases refused to reveal their views. But in this case Matthew Hale has no interest in keeping his views a secret. In a 1997 interview that appears on the Internet, he said that "we have several websites going now. . . . We are . . . , hoping to expand all these operations . . . to give people full knowledge of Creativity. * * * And his * * * autobiography proclaims "that he looks forward to leading Creativity to worldwide White Victory!"

The case of *Elrod v. Burns*, <u>427 U.S. 347, 362 (1976)</u>, laid down the following formula for evaluating whether or not a public employee may have his First Amendment rights curtailed:

It is firmly established that a significant impairment of First Amendment rights must survive exacting scrutiny. . . . The interest advanced must be paramount, one of vital importance, and the burden is on the government to show the existence of such an interest.

> Assuming that the courts would apply the stringent Elrod formula for public employees to bar admission cases, we believe that the impairment of First Amendment rights that the Panel's decision affects does survive exacting scrutiny and that the interest advanced with respect to the role of the legal profession, hereafter to be explained, is paramount. * * *

The Commitment Of The Bar To Fundamental Truths

The balance that the majority chooses requires that a lawyer cannot, as his life's mission, do all in his power to incite racial and religious hatred among the populace so that it will peaceably abolish the rule of law for all persons save those of the "white race." Instead, and by rejecting Matthew Hale's application, let it be said that the Bar and our courts stand committed to these fundamental truths:

- All persons are possessed of individual dignity.

- As a result, every person is to be judged on the basis of his or her own individuality and conduct, not by reference to skin color, race, ethnicity, religion or national origin.

- The enforcement and application of these timeless values to specific cases have, by history and constitutional development, been entrusted to our courts and its officers—the lawyers—a trust that lies at the heart of our system of government.

- Therefore, the guardians of that trust—the judges and lawyers, or one or more of them—cannot have as their mission in life the incitement of racial hatred in order to destroy those values.

Commencing with Jefferson's ringing declaration that all men are created equal, and continuing with the adoption of our Constitution, the Emancipation Proclamation and the Fourteenth Amendment, the moral, ethical and legal strugglefor the precious values contained in those writings has been costly, difficult and long. The Bar and our courts, charged with the duty of preserving those values, cannot allow Mr. Hale or any other applicant the use of a law license to attempt their destruction.

Finally, and this is the heart of our analysis, the majority's judgment is that to the extent its decision limits the First Amendment activities of lawyers, the fundamental truths identified above are so basic to the legal professionthat, in the context of this case, they must be preferred over the values found in the First Amendment. The relationship of the profession to those truths was eloquently described in *Schware v. Board of Bar Examiners*, 353 U.S. 232, 246 (1957), by the late Justice Felix Frankfurter in a concurring opinion:

> . . . all the interests of man that are comprised under the constitutional guarantees given to "life, liberty and property" are in the professional keeping of lawyers.

The balance of values that we strike leaves Matthew Hale free, as the First Amendment allows, to incite as much racial hatred as he desires and to attempt to carry out his life's mission of depriving those he dislikes of their legal rights. But in our view he cannot do this as an officer of the court.

A preference for antidiscriminatory values over the First Amendment would not be new to Supreme Court decision making. Only five years ago the Court unanimously rejected First Amendment claims that "hate crimes" penalty enhancement statutes were invalid. The * * * Supreme Court had no difficulty in finding the statute constitutional because "hate crimes" are "thought to inflict greater individual and societal harm." * * * Arguably, the rationale in this case for preventing the applicant from becoming an officer of the Court is stronger than it was in the "hate crimes" case.

CONCLUSION

America's chief war crimes prosecutor at Nuremberg, wrote during World War II in *West Virginia Board of Education v. Barnette*, 319 U.S. 624, 638 (1943):

> The very purpose of a Bill of Rights was to withdraw certain subjects from the vicissitudes of political controversy, to place them beyond the reach of majorities and officials and to establish them as legal principles to be applied by the courts. One's right to life, liberty, and property, to free speech, a free press, freedom of worship and assembly, and other fundamental rights may not be submitted to vote; they depend on the outcome of no elections.

Jackson's statement that the immutable principles of the Bill of Rights are to be "applied by the courts" has significance because "[t]here ... comes from the [legal] profession the judiciary." *In re Anastaplo*, 3 Ill.2d 471,479. Mr. Hale's life mission, the destruction of the Bill of Rights, is inherently incompatible with service as a lawyer or judge who is charged with safeguarding those rights.

The quotation from Barnette is important for another reason. Justice Jackson concluded that "fundamental rights may not be submitted to vote." But Mr. Hale wants to do exactly that, and it is a chilling thought indeed, considering that he and his church are admirers of Adolph Hitler, who acquired his absolute power peacefully, "quite legally" and "in a perfectly constitutional manner."

* * *

While Matthew Hale has not yet threatened to exterminate anyone, history tells us that extermination is sometimes not far behind when governmental power is held by persons of his racial views. The Bar of Illinois cannot certify someone as having good moral character and general fitness to practice law who has dedicated his life to inciting racial hatred for the purpose of implementing those views.

Respectfully submitted * * *.

Judge Gregory McClintock, Chairperson of Inquiry Panel
Stuart Lefstein, Member of Inquiry Panel

RICHARD L. SLOANE, NOTE, *BARBARIAN AT THE GATES: REVISITING THE CASE OF MATTHEW F. HALE TO REAFFIRM THAT CHARACTER AND FITNESS EVALUATIONS APPROPRIATE PRECLUDE RACISTS FROM THE PRACTICE OF LAW*, 15 Geo. J. Legal Ethics 397, 425 (2002)

* * * On June 30, 1999, the Illinois Committee on Character and Fitness issued its decision to deny Hale certification to practice law. The next day, Benjamin Smith, a former member of Hale's church, went on a vicious shooting spree. Smith began his rampage in West Rogers Park in Chicago by shooting six Orthodox Jewish men after they had attended an evening synagogue service. He then drove to Skokie, a suburb of Chicago, where he shot and killed former Northwestern University basketball coach Ricky Byrdsong. Later that night, Smith traveled to another Chicago suburb, where he shot at an Asian couple in their car. The following day, Smith injured an African-American man in Springfield, Illinois, and an African-American minister in Decatur, Illinois. Later that night, Smith fired at six Asian students from the University of Illinois, in Urbana, injuring one. The next day, Smith shot at a group of Koreans exiting church in Bloomington, Indiana, killing a 26-year old

Korean graduate student named Won-Joon Yoon, who had been studying at Indiana University. In total, Smith shot at twenty minorities. Smith stole a car, which led to a police chase ending with Smith taking his own life. Nine people were wounded in these events, all of them Orthodox Jews or African-Americans.

Following the incident, Hale cited the acts of his character witness Benjamin Smith as "an example of what happens when people at least perceive their freedom of speech is being disrupted."
Similarly, following the issuance of the Findings and Conclusions of the Committee and the Smith shooting rampage, Hale was quoted as saying: "If people can't speak, violence automatically results in society."

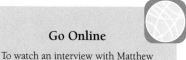

Go Online

To watch an interview with Matthew Hale, click here.

Even in light of the Smith rampage, Hale has consistently argued that he is opposed to violence. * * *

3. Can Consumers Trust that Practicing Lawyers Are Well-Regulated for Competence and Ethics?

[Question 1]

According to professionalism, lawyer discipline functions adequately only if lawyers snitch on each other.

   (A) True

   (B) False

[Question 2]

The snitch rule works at law school because almost all students inform the law school administration when they believe that another student has cheated.

   (A) True

   (B) False

[Question 3]

Lawyers reliably report disciplinary violations by other lawyers.

   (A) True

   (B) False

[Question 4]

The Arkansas disciplinary regulators received a complaint that William Jefferson Clinton: 1) provided false, misleading, and evasive deposition answers; 2) intentionally provided false testimony regarding sexual relations with Monica Lewinsky; and 3) misled the American people in a televised address regarding plaintiff's lawyers' questions. If true, what sanction should President Clinton have received?

(A) Disbarment

(B) Suspension

(C) Censure

(D) No punishment

[Question 5]

The disciplinary system protects consumers from legal services providers who are either incompetent or unethical.

(A) True

(B) False

Review the materials on competence in Chapter 2, Part V.

TIMOTHY K. MCPIKE & MARK I. HARRISON, *THE TRUE STORY ON LAWYER DISCIPLINE*,

70 A.B.A. J., Sept. 1984, at 92

Like a stain from a tar brush, the old accusation that the legal profession isn't doing enough to discipline unethical lawyers hasn't faded away.

It came up in a rhetorical question from Chief Justice Burger last February at the ABA midyear meeting. It is the perennial complaint leveled by the public and the press.

The criticism is unfair, unjustified by the record and unsupported by the facts.

Lawyer disciplinary practices have been transformed in the last 14 years from what was called in 1970 a "scandalous situation" to a sophisticated, effective system of self-regulation today.

Consider the facts:

- Disciplinary agency budgets for all states total almost $23 million in 1982 and states reporting to the American Bar Association had more than $8 million in funds to reimburse clients wronged by unethical lawyers.

- The number of sanctions imposed for ethics violations has increased nationally in all categories by 73 percent from 1978 to 1982.

- The ABA Standards for Lawyer Discipline and Disability Procedures provide a detailed set of guidelines for state disciplinary systems; 47 states revised their disciplinary rules after the standards were published in 1979.

- The ABA National Disciplinary Data Bank has been distributing names of lawyers for 13 years to prevent a lawyer who was disbarred in one state from moving to another state to practice law.

Of primary importance, however, is the attitude that has developed among lawyers about lawyer discipline. Twenty-nine states have public members on their disciplinary boards. Of those states, 11 have been evaluated by the ABA, and it turns out that the lawyer members of the boards are more likely to find misconduct and to vote for a stronger sanction than nonlawyer members.

From 17 evaluations and hundreds of interviews with lawyers, clients, judges and others, it is clear that there is a new understanding about professional discipline. It is understood to be fundamental to the profession's duty to the public. Any tolerance for misconduct is in retreat.

NEAL v. CLINTON

2001 WL 34355768 (Ark. Cir. 2001)

Agreed Order of Discipline

* * * Come now the parties hereto and agree to the following Order of this Court in settlement of the pending action:

The formal charges of misconduct upon which this Order is based arose out of information referred to the Committee on Professional Conduct ("the Committee") by the Honorable Susan Webber Wright, Chief United States District Judge for the Eastern District of Arkansas. The information pertained to William Jefferson Clinton's deposition testimony in a civil case brought by Ms. Paula Jones in which he was a defendant * * * .

Mr. Clinton was admitted to the Arkansas bar on September 7, 1973. On June 30, 1990, he requested that his Arkansas license be placed on inactive status for continuing legal education purposes, and this request was granted. The conduct at issue here does not arise out of Mr. Clinton's practice of law. At all times material to this case, Mr. Clinton resided in Washington, D.C., but he remained subject to the Model Rules of Professional Conduct for the State of Arkansas.

On April 1, 1998, Judge Wright granted summary judgment to Mr. Clinton, but she subsequently found him in Civil contempt * * * , ruling that he had "deliberately violated this Court's discovery orders and thereby undermined the integrity of the judicial system." * * * Judge Wright found that Mr. Clinton had "responded to plaintiff's questions by giving false, misleading and evasive answers that were designed to obstruct the judicial process . . . . [concerning] whether he and Ms. [Monica] Lewinsky had ever been alone together and whether he had ever engaged in sexual relations with Ms. Lewinsky." * * * Judge Wright offered Mr. Clinton a hearing, which he declined * * * . Mr. Clinton was subsequently ordered to pay, and did pay, over $90,000, pursuant to the Court's contempt findings. Judge Wright also referred the matter to the Committee "for review and any action it deems appropriate." * * *

Mr. Clinton's actions which are the subject of this Agreed Order have subjected him to a great deal of public criticism. Twice elected President of the United States, he became only the second President ever impeached and tried by the Senate, where he was acquitted. After Ms. Jones took an appeal of the dismissal of her case, Mr. Clinton settled with her for $850,000, a sum greater than her initial in her complaint. As already indicated, Mr. Clinton was held in civil contempt and fined over $90,000.

Prior to Judge Wright's referral, Mr. Clinton had no prior disciplinary record with the Committee, including any private warnings. He had been a member in good standing of the Arkansas Bar for over twenty-five years. He has cooperated fully with the Committee in its investigation of this matter and has furnished information to the Committee in a timely fashion.

Mr. Clinton's conduct, as described in the Order, caused the court and counsel for the parties to expend unnecessary time, effort, and resources. It set a poor example for other litigants, and this damaging effect was magnified by the fact that at the time of his deposition testimony, Mr. Clinton was serving as President of the United States.

Judge Wright ruled that the testimony concerning Ms. Lewinsky "was not essential to the core issues in this case and, in fact, that some of this evidence might even be inadmissible . . . ." * * * Judge Wright dismissed the case on the merits by granting Mr. Clinton summary judgment, declaring that the case was "lacking in merit-a decision that would not have changed even had the President been truthful with respect to his relationship with Ms. Lewinsky." * * * As Judge Wright also observed, as a result of Mr. Clinton's paying $850,000 in settlement, "plaintiff was made whole, having agreed to a settlement in excess of that prayed for in the complaint." * * * Mr. Clinton also paid to plaintiff $89,484 as the "reasonable expenses, including attorney's fees, caused by his willful failure to obey the Court's discovery orders." * * *

On May 22, 2000, after receiving complaints from Judge Wright and the Southeastern Legal Foundation, the Committee voted to initiate disbarment proceedings against Mr. Clinton. On June 30, 2000, counsel for the Committee filed a complaint seeking disbarment in Pulaski County Circuit Court, Civ. No.2000-5677. Mr. Clinton filed an answer on August 29, 2000, and the case is in the early stages of discovery.

In this Agreed Order Mr. Clinton admits and acknowledges, and the Court, therefore, finds that:

> A. That he knowingly gave evasive and misleading answers, in violation of Judge Wright's discovery orders, concerning his relationship with Ms. Lewinsky, in an attempt to conceal from plaintiff Jones' lawyers the true facts about his improper relationship with Ms. Lewinsky, which had ended almost a year earlier.

> B. That by knowingly giving evasive and misleading answers, in violation of Judge Wright's discovery orders, he engaged in conduct that is prejudicial to the administration of justice in that his discovery responses interfered with the conduct of the case by causing the court and counsel for the parties to expend unnecessary time, effort, and resources, setting a poor example for other litigants, and causing the court to issue a thirty-two page Order civilly sanctioning Mr. Clinton.

Upon consideration of the proposed Agreed Order, the entire record before the Court, the advice of counsel, and the Arkansas [Rules] * * * , the Court finds:

> 1. That Mr. Clinton's conduct, heretofore set forth, in the case violated * * * Rule 8.4(d), when he gave knowingly evasive and misleading discovery responses concerning his relationship with Ms. Lewinsky, in violation of Judge Wright's discovery orders. * * * Rule 8.4(d) states that it is professional misconduct for a lawyer to "engage in conduct that is prejudicial to the administration of justice."

WHEREFORE, it is the decision and order of this Court that William Jefferson Clinton, * * * be, and hereby is, SUSPENDED for FIVE YEARS for his conduct in this matter, and the payment of fine in the amount of $ 25,000. The suspension shall become effective as of the date of January 19, 2001.

IT IS SO ORDERED.

PATRICK J. SCHILTZ, *LEGAL ETHICS IN DECLINE: THE ELITE LAW FIRM, THE ELITE LAW SCHOOL, AND THE MORAL FORMATION OF THE NOVICE ATTORNEY,*

82 Minn. L. Rev. 705 (1998)

* * * First, whether law is practiced ethically in any particular community depends not upon the community's formal rules, but upon its culture. Second, the culture of a legal community does not reflect "big" decisions that members of the community make about "big" problems, as much as it reflects the dozens of ordinary, mundane decisions that every attorney makes—and makes intuitively—every day. And finally, the intuition that guides these decisions is in large part a product of the mentoring received by the attorney. In sum, conduct is influenced by culture, culture by intuition, and intuition by mentoring. * * *

TANINA ROSTAIN, *ETHICS LOST: LIMITATIONS OF CURRENT APPROACHES TO LAWYER REGULATION,*

71 S. Cal. L. Rev. 1273 (1998)

* * * [T]he success of a regulatory project depends on an unacknowledged supporting frame: an infrastructure of shared commitments to law and legal institutions among lawyers and regulators that cannot be sustained through external incentives. * * *

Typically, people obey laws not primarily because they fear sanctions but because they have internalized commitments to legal institutions and values. Political regimes that have sought to maintain themselves through external social controls have proven highly unstable. * * *

While rules are undoubtedly important, the focus of legal ethics cannot be limited to debates about their content or the schemes through which they are enforced. For regulation to be effective, it needs to be undergirded by widespread commitments among lawyers to the values reflected in the regulatory enterprise. * * *

RICHARD W. PAINTER, *RULES LAWYERS PLAY BY,*

76 N.Y.U. L. Rev. 665, 739 (2001)

* * * Bar disciplinary boards give practicing lawyers very little feedback on how ethically and competently they are practicing law. Few lawyers, particularly large-firm lawyers, are ever brought before disciplinary boards. Furthermore, because the discipline process is inherently adversarial, it calls upon a lawyer to justify her

conduct, thus enhancing the lawyer's already strong motivation to find confirmation for her prior decisions. * * *

Much of the feedback that lawyers get about ethics thus takes place not in bar disciplinary proceedings, but in law practice. In dealing with other lawyers, lawyers presumably receive feedback from the reputational paradigm when they learn that "what goes around, comes around." Unethical lawyers presumably are taught to be ethical, or are discharged by their firms, and the fact that disciplinary cases often involve solo practitioners suggests that intrafirm feedback is somewhat effective at helping lawyers avoid discipline. * * *

HALT, *2006 LAWYER DISCIPLINE REPORT CARD,*

http://www.halt.org/reform_projects/lawyer_accountability/report_card_2006/index_2.php

HALT[*] graded lawyer discipline systems in six categories:

Adequacy of Discipline --- The most critical category produced the weakest grades. Analyzing the ABA's most recent statistics, HALT found that only six states - Maine, Massachusetts, Nevada, New Hampshire, West Virginia and Wisconsin - review every grievance, while the average state investigates only 58 percent of the complaints it receives. And unfortunately, investigations rarely result in discipline. A whopping 24 states impose formal public sanctions—disbarments, suspensions and public reprimands—in just five percent of investigated cases. In the average jurisdiction, only 7.8 percent of investigations yield public discipline. Almost half of the sanctions take the form of private discipline, rendered behind closed doors. "A secret reprimand amounts to little more than a slap on the wrist," explained HALT Associate Counsel Suzanne Blonder. "Because it is so lenient, it fails to deter unethical conduct and because it is done in secret, it fails to warn consumers about which attorneys to avoid."

Publicity and Responsiveness --- While disciplinary bodies are not publicized in courthouses and local media as much as they were four years ago, their online resources have dramatically improved since 2002. Today, most disciplinary Web sites offer downloadable complaint forms, information about upcoming hearings and clear explanations about the disciplinary process—features that most states

---

[*]   [*Ed.'s Note*—According to its web site, "HALT (Help Abolish Legal Tyranny) * * * was founded in 1978. * * * In the three decades since then HALT has matured into the nation's largest legal reform organization, a nonprofit, nonpartisan public interest group of more than 20,000 members. Dedicated to providing simple, affordable, accountable justice for all, HALT's Reform Projects challenge the legal establishment to improve access and reduce costs in our civil justice system at both the state and federal levels." http://www.halt.org/about_halt/.]

lacked four years ago. Unfortunately, telephone services have not seen as much progress. California is one of the nation's worst offenders, forcing consumers to wade through a complex and time-consuming automated system before they can obtain information from Bar staff.

Openness --- Attorney discipline continues to be shrouded in secrecy. Nine states—Alabama, Delaware, Hawaii, Idaho, Iowa, Maryland, Nevada, Utah and Wyoming—prohibit the public from attending disciplinary hearings. Hamstrung by rules that require them to keep the process secret, officials in the vast majority of states refuse to release information about attorneys' discipline histories. Oregon and Arizona have always been the exceptions to the rule, providing consumers with complete records, including whether a grievance was ever filed against a lawyer. After HALT submitted comments to New Hampshire in 2004, the state adopted new rules which now allow disciplinary officials in that state to release complete disciplinary histories.

Fairness --- Disciplinary systems still utilize biased procedures. The most egregious—Alabama, Arkansas, Delaware, Iowa, Mississippi, South Dakota, Texas and Utah—prohibit consumers from disclosing information until the disciplinary body imposes public discipline in the case. New Jersey and Tennessee are the only two states that significantly improved in this area. At HALT's urging, supreme courts in both states struck down their gag rules as unconstitutional.

Public Participation --- On most hearing panels just one out of every three members is a nonlawyer. Six states—California, Hawaii, Kansas, Mississippi, South Carolina and Tennessee—do not allow a single layperson to hear evidence in disciplinary proceedings. Idaho is the only jurisdiction in the country where nonlawyers comprise the majority on hearing committees.

Promptness --- Shamefully, 18 states—Alaska, Arkansas, the District of Columbia, Hawaii, Idaho, Illinois, Indiana, Michigan, Minnesota, Missouri, New Hampshire, New Jersey, North Carolina, South Carolina, Vermont, Virginia, Washington and Wisconsin—stonewalled, refusing to release information about their timeliness to the ABA. Of the states that did report on the pace of their case processing, the average jurisdiction took nine months just to bring charges against an attorney and an additional five months to impose sanctions. Louisiana, the nation's most inefficient disciplinary body, took an astonishing 45 months—nearly four years!—to file formal charges in the average case.

"American legal consumers deserve a system that investigates promptly, deliberates openly, and weeds out unethical or incompetent attorneys," stated [James C.] Turner, [Executive Director of HALT]. "Until there is meaningful reform, the legal profession has only itself to blame for the widespread public mistrust that mars every attorney's reputation."

C. Who Should Be Permitted to Provide Legal Services?

[Question 1]

Who should provide legal services?

(A) Only lawyers should provide legal services.

(B) Generally lawyers should provide legal services but independent paralegals should also be allowed to provide simple legal services.

(C) Anyone should be able to provide legal services but only lawyers should be able to hold use the term "lawyers" to identify themselves.

[Question 2]

Should multidisciplinary practice be permitted?

(A) Yes

(B) No

> **FYI**
>
> An excellent introduction to this section is the portion of the documentary, "The Future Just Happened," on Marcus Arnold and changes in the legal profession. To watch on-line, click here.

1. Nonlawyer Practice

Marcus Arnold

In his book Next: The Future Just Happened (2002), Michael Lewis includes the story of Marcus Arnold, the 15 year old buy who became one of the highest rated legal advisors on the internet. The following description of Marcus Arnold's story, including quotations, is based on a New York Times Magazine article Lewis wrote based on stories from his book. Michael Lewis, *Faking It: The Internet Revolution has Nothing to Do With the NASDAQ*, N.Y. Times Mag., July 15, 2001.

In the early 2000s, www.AskMe.com emerged as an internet message board. The way the site worked was quite simple—someone posted a question on the site and then another person posted a response. The site ranked responses and identified resident experts based on those ranking. In June 2000, the 10th highest ranked legal expert on AskMe.com was LawGuy1975, aka Justin Anthony Wyrick, Jr., who fielded countless legal questions, often numbering in the hundreds per day, and provided aswers to his satisfied "clients." LawGuy1975 was Marcus Arnold, a fifteen-year-old boy. Arnold was not an attorney. He had not yet finished high school.

In general, Marcus Arnold's clients posed simple questions, and Marcus responded with simple, direct answers:

Q: What amount of money must a person steal or gain through fraud before it is considered a felony in Illinois?

A: In Illinois you must have gained $5,001+ in an illegal fashion in order to constitute fraud. If you need anything else please write back! Sincerely, Justin Anthony Wyrick Jr.

Q: Can a parole officer prevent a parolee from marrying?

A: Hey! Unless the parolee has "no marriage" under the special conditions in which he is released, he can marry. If you have any questions, please write back. Sincerely, Justin Anthony Wyrick Jr.

When Lewis asked Arnold how he knew the answers to these questions, Arnold stated that he "'just did,'" from watching television and browsing on the Internet. Arnold claimed never to have independently researched the answer to a single question.

Eventually, Arnold decided to update his profile on www.AskMe.com to reflect the fact that was a fifteen-year-old boy. Immediately, other "legal experts" on the site began to send him emails ranging from admonishments to threats and even gave Arnold intentionally low rankings on his legal advice to lower his high-ranking.

Aside from his critics, however, Arnold also received overwhelming support from what might well be called his client based. As Lewis notes, "[a] lot of people seemed to believe that any 15-year-old who had risen so high in the ranks of AskMe.com legal experts must be some kind of wizard. They began to seek him out more than ever before; they wanted his, and only his, advice."

Go Online

To view a picture of Marcus Arnold click here

Two weeks after Arnold admitted he was only fifteen, he was the single-highest ranked legal expert on AskMe.com.

Lewis suggests that Arnold symbolizes the descent of the legal field from a profession to an business that is simply the sum of its parts; one of its parts being information. He writes that, "Once the law became a business, it was on its way to becoming a commodity. Reduce the law to the sum of its information, and, by implication, anyone can supply it." Even a fifteen-year-old boy.

AskMe.com continues to include nonlawyers as legal experts. See http://www.askmehelpdesk.com/ .

AMERICAN BAR ASSOCIATION COMMISSION ON PROFESSIONALISM,
". . . IN THE SPIRIT OF PUBLIC SERVICE:" A BLUEPRINT FOR THE REKIN-
DLING OF LAWYER PROFESSIONALISM

112 F.R.D. 243, 301 (1986)

* * * One of the most intractable problems confronting the legal profession today is the lack of access by the middle class to affordable legal services. While there may be some evidence of overlawyering in our society, there is certainly evidence of the under-representation of middle class persons. * * * [T]he limited licensing of paralegals to perform certain functions seems to be a desirable step. Possible areas for the provision of such limited services include certain real estate closings, the drafting of simple wills, and selected tax services now being performed by lawyers. That is not to say that lawyers should not perform these services in the future. But, they should have to compete with properly licensed paraprofessionals. The continuing high cost of legal services requires that such approaches be considered if clients of ordinary means are to be served at all.

Care must be exercised in having paraprofessionals enter these areas and in making sure that the training, supervision and testing required is comprehensive. No doubt, many wills and real estate closings require the services of a lawyer. However, it can no longer be claimed that lawyers have the exclusive possession of the esoteric knowledge required and are therefore the only ones able to advise clients on any matter concerning the law. Inroads on lawyer exclusivity have been made and will continue to be made. Lawyer resistance to such inroads for selfish reasons only brings discredit on the profession.

Still, licensing standards must be rigorous because abuses by paraprofessionals do occur. An Hispanic member of the Florida Bar testified before the Commission that underground networks of 'notarios' (notaries public) at one time sprang up in sections of Miami and elsewhere, giving incorrect legal advice to immigrants who did not speak English. Where such abuses of clients occur, unauthorized practice committees of bar associations have a place.

In the past, both the public and some segments of the Bar have viewed state bar unauthorized practice of law committees as existing to protect lawyers' economic interests. Today, most bar associations recognize that such committees' sole obligation should be to protect the public from incompetent and unqualified legal service providers. However, in doing so, innovative approaches to the distribution of legal services should not be stifled, but instead should be encouraged. * * *

POSTING OF LARRY RIBSTEIN, *IS LAWYER LICENSING REALLY NECESSARY?*
TO IDEOBLOG,

http://busmovie.typepad.com/ideoblog/2006/05/is_lawyer_licen.html   (May   6,
2006)

Brian Woods sued the Akron school board to get an education for his autistic son.
He won, his relief including about $160,000.

So what's the problem? He didn't have a lawyer. So as discussed in today's NYT,
the Cleveland Bar Association sued Mr. Woods, seeking a $10,000 fine and other
relief. The Ohio Supreme Court indicated its skepticism, and the bar association
backed down. The US Supreme Court may get the issue of whether nonlawyer
parents can represent their children under the Individuals With Disabilities Education Act. The Cleveland Bar may resume its action after the Supreme Court acts
on this issue.

Is something wrong with this picture?

As I have discussed here, and in *Lawyers' Property Rights in State Law* (published
as *Lawyers as Lawmakers: A Theory of Lawyer Licensing,* 69 Mo. L. Rev. 299 (2004))
there is scant justification for lawyer licensing laws. My limited defense of licensing is based on encouraging lawyers to participate in lawmaking. My theory would
sharply reduce the scope of licensing requirements.

I am beginning to wonder whether it's worth preserving any piece of lawyers'
monopoly on legal representation. Cases like the one the NYT discusses make me
wonder more. Clearly there was no client-protection justification. Since Mr. Woods
could have acted as his own lawyer, and for his son in finding a lawyer, there's obviously no reason not to let him decide to dispense with the lawyer rather than paying
the huge fee a lawyer would have asked or having to drop the case.

One might argue that we need licensing laws to preserve order in the court—that
is, ensure only those inculcated with lawyer knowledge and norms enter the
courtroom. But we already let nonlawyers represent themselves. How much do
we gain from keeping dads out of court.

Now let's take this further. If people can decide to bring cases on behalf themselves or their children, to make myriad other legal judgments without lawyers, to
choose among the wide variety of licensed lawyers about whom all the licensing
requirement tells us is that they passed a bar exam sometime in the distant past
and spent three years in a law school, perhaps taking courses on the law of the
horse or whatever, and to make the zillions of other decisions adults make about
their lives, why should we not let people decide to be represented by somebody
who is not certified as a lawyer?

Note that I said "certified"—nothing would prevent bar groups from providing the service of certifying people to practice law, or aspects of law, should these people want to do so. Then nonlawyers could decide whether they want to be represented by one of these folks.

Just asking.

Jonathan B. Wilson, Is Lawyer Licensing Necessary?, PointofLaw.com,

http://www.pointoflaw.com/feature/archives/002514.php (May 19, 2006)

Recently, Larry Ribstein and I kicked off a debate on the necessity of lawyer licensing. * * *

The topic must have touched a nerve, as a number of the leading blawgs chimed in and even the Wall Street Journal conducted an online poll on the topic. (Smug aside: As of Friday afternoon the "yes" votes commanded a 59%/41% lead.) * * *

What is Lawyer Licensing?

By defending lawyer licensing, I am defending a system whereby, in order to legally practice law, an individual must receive a license at the state level. In nearly every state, this license takes the form of admission to the bar, usually following successful completion of an ABA-approved course of study and passage of the state's bar exam.

Most state bars also require an applicant to complete a "moral fitness" examination. In my home state of Georgia that entails a detailed personal application, identifying every place of residence, job, and course of study taken by the applicant since the age of 18. The moral fitness exam in Georgia also includes an investigation of the applicant by the bar's examiners (many of whom are former FBI agents) and contacting the applicant's relatives, friends and neighbors to validate the applicant's claims.

So what is it, exactly, that lawyer licensing is supposed to achieve?

Lawyer Licensing Ensures Competency and Moral Fitness

* * * The chief purpose of lawyer licensing is to ensure technical competence and at least the minimum level of moral character required to perform as an attorney. This aim supports a number of public policy goals:

> 1. The public is protected by the state mandate that only licensed attorneys can hold themselves out to the public as qualified, both technically and morally, to practice law.

2. The state is protected by ensuring that attorneys who appear in its courts have a sufficient level of competence. (An excessive number of incompetent practitioners could clog the courts with inappropriate or excessive process. * * *

The moral examination, at least in Georgia, is quite rigorous and includes questions and third party validation of the following points for each applicant:

> unlawful conduct; academic misconduct, including plagiarism; making of a false statement, including omission of relevant facts in the fitness process; misconduct in employment; acts involving dishonesty, fraud, deceit or misrepresentation; abuse of legal process; neglect of financial responsibilities, especially failure to repay student loans; neglect of professional obligations; violation of an order of a court, especially failure to pay child support; evidence of mental or emotional instability; evidence of drug or alcohol dependency; denial of admission to the bar in another jurisdiction on character and fitness grounds; disciplinary action by a lawyer disciplinary agency or other professional disciplinary agency of any jurisdiction

So, at its heart, the issue of lawyer licensing is one of protecting the public from the baneful effects of incompetent or immoral lawyers.

But the Current System is Flawed!

Readers of these pages know that our litigation system is flawed and at least some measure of responsibility for those flaws rests with attorneys, the bar associations that license and police the attorneys and the judges who began their careers as attorneys. Supporting the continued licensing of lawyers does not necessarily entail blindness to the shortcomings of the current system.

Indeed, the flaws in the status quo suggest that lawyer licensing should be improved and strengthened, rather than eliminated.

The Laissez-Faire Argument

Of course all students of the school of law and economics prefer a market solution where one exists. In his paper on the subject, Professor Ribstein suggests that lawyer licensing is unnecessary, except to the extent that it facilitates the involvement of attorneys in the law-making process.

Without addressing the professor's theory of lawyers' property rights in the law of their home states, I think a more direct justification for lawyer licensing is that laissez-faire simply doesn't work when it comes to the market for legal services.

In classical economic theory, a free market works efficiently to set prices among competing goods when there is ubiquitous and accurate information concerning the relative merits of competitors.

As I describe in *Out of Balance: Prescriptions for Reforming the American Litigation System*, in the market for apples, there is exactly this kind of information. Everyone knows what they like (or don't like) about apples. A consumer who wishes to compare the apples from producer A and producer B, for minimal cost, can sample both and choose the one that presents the preferred qualities and price.

Legal services are utterly unlike apples. Consumers are ill-equipped to evaluate the skills of competing attorneys and the cost of "sampling" attorneys is very high. Indeed, the cost of sampling an attorney's services (and the possible consequential damages if the attorney proves to be unskilled) could be disastrously high. An *ex post facto* analysis of the quality of the service will, in nearly all cases, be completely inadequate.

Bad Facts Make Bad Law

Professor Ribstein began this debate by recounting a particularly ugly story in which Brian Woods represented his autistic son in litigation against the Akron school board involving the son's access to educational facilities. After successfully obtaining a remedy, Mr. Woods was rewarded by an unauthorized practice of law prosecution, initiated by the Cleveland Bar Association. Professor Ribstein connected this case to lawyer licensing when he wrote:

> Since Mr. Woods could have acted as his own lawyer, and for his son in finding a lawyer, there's obviously no reason not to let him decide to dispense with the lawyer rather than paying the huge fee a lawyer would have asked or having to drop the case.

The Ohio Supreme Court was right to have chastised the Cleveland bar and there seems to be widespread agreement that the bar should not have gone after Woods. I would even be amenable to a more general rule that permits close family members who are unlicensed to represent each other in non-criminal cases. The family relationships in those situations generally eliminate the client-protection rationales for lawyer licensing.

But Brian Woods' good fortune as a *pro se* litigant does not mean that every Tom, Dick and Harry should be permitted to hang out his (or her) own shingle.

In-house practitioners like myself quickly amass a treasure chest of war stories involving *pro se* litigants. Litigating against a pro se plaintiff, in many situations, is more costly than litigating against a well-heeled attorney. The plaintiff who represents himself will often get "velvet glove" treatment from the judge (who fears looking like a lout on appeal) and the professionally-represented defendant will be forced (via the American rule of attorneys' fees) to literally pay for the plaintiff's education on the finer points of law.

Rather than the somewhat orderly pre-trial and discovery process that results when professional lawyers practice their craft, the self-represented plaintiff will force his professional opponent to respond to out-of-order motions and arguments, helter-skelter, in an inefficient and lengthy march towards the likely conclusion of a defense victory.

So, while I applaud the individual merits of parents like Brian Woods and am somewhat embarrassed when bar associations create this kind of bad publicity for themselves, stories like this one do not justify the wholesale elimination of lawyer licensing. At most, they may suggest the need for limited exceptions to the general rule that attorneys must be licensed.

What Would an Unlicensed Bar Look Like?

Perhaps the best argument against eliminating lawyer licensing is asking the question, "what would our litigation system look like if lawyers were not required to be licensed?"

Do you think our courts have too many weak or unjustified cases?

An unlicensed bar would compound that problem as individuals with no legal training would be free to make up whatever legal theories they wish. With the American rule of attorneys' fees, defendants will bear the costs of disproving every harebrained theory that comes along.

Do you think our courts are two willing to consider unscientific legal theories and novel theories of liability?

If every citizen were free to hold himself out to the public as a legal advocate for hire there would be no end to the novel legal theories these hired guns would be able to pursue. Perhaps judges might be prompted to clamp down on novel claims in a post-licensing era, but the past offers little reason for optimism.

Licensed attorneys have enough difficulty applying the Daubert rule to their cases in the current regime. Do you think that unlicensed attorneys would have a better chance of getting it right?

Are the existing limitations on lawyers' ability to pursue weak or frivolous cases toothless and ineffective?

Imagine how toothless and utterly irrelevant they will become when unlicensed lawyers can defend themselves against Rule 11 sanctions by complaining that they had never heard of Rule 11. If any person could act as an attorney, why even bother having principles (like Fed. R. Civ. P. 11) that hold some persons to a higher standard than others? How could an unlicensed attorney, perhaps with no legal training whatsoever, distinguish between those arguments that are valid and those that are not?

Conclusion

Criticizing the legal profession for protecting its turf via UPL prosecutions is fair game. Lawyers are often their own worst enemies when it comes to their public reputations and their share of the public trust. When the legal profession allows its sense of professionalism to atrophy and when the state bars become little more than trade associations for a guild that protects its own, its entirely understandable for sensible persons to question why the state bars should hold a monopoly on the licensing of lawyers.

But this criticism ought to remind us why lawyer licensing is necessary and the flaws in the status quo should give us reason to preach reform, rather than deregulation.

Lawyers behaving badly is a far too common occurrence. The solution is to tighten the rules of ethics and to empower prosecutors to pursue lawyers who breach those rules.

A related solution for the problem of a profession that has lost its sense of professionalism is to reform those laws that tend to encourage lawyers to think of their craft as just another good in the marketplace. If our sense of civil justice is offended by "complaint mill" plaintiffs who churn out hundreds of filings in the hope that a handful will result in a lucrative payday we should reform the laws that permit this practice, rather than empowering the general citizenry to engage in the practice.

Deregulating lawyers as punishment or retribution for a profession that has lost its way would be a recipe for disaster. Deregulating the practice of law would open the floodgates to fraud of every conceivable variety and would only compound the problems that the readers of these pages see in our civil justice system.

LARRY RIBSTEIN, *FINAL THOUGHTS ON LAWYER LICENSING*, POINTOFLAW.COM, http://www.pointoflaw.com/feature/archives/002536.php (May 25, 2006)

* * * In my last post, I listed supposed problems in the legal marketplace that lawyer licensing is supposed to deal with, and summarized why it is at best a flawed response to these problems.

Jonathan persists in his claims that mandatory licensing would work better than the market, but has no support for those claims other than repetition. I can only again point to my lengthy article on the subject cited in early posts and repeat that the absence of mandatory regulation does NOT mean that there would be no mechanisms for dealing with these problems, but only that they would be dealt with through a competitive market rather than by the lawyer's cartel.

Jonathan asserts in response to my argument that licensing inflates the price of legal services that, in fact, lawyers charge a wide variety of prices, and it's not clear lawyers are "overpriced;" that legal services "don't seem to be that expensive;" that "I often see a line at the counter at McDonald's. I've never seen a line outside a lawyer's office. I would be interested to see alternative data but my experience tells me there is no shortage of legal services in the marketplace and therefore no effective cartel created by lawyer licensing;" and that "I can see no evidence that lawyer licensing is driving up the cost of legal services. Legal services of the kind often purchased by the poor and the middle-class seem to be readily available at more-or-less reasonable prices."

I would prefer a more scientific approach to the problem. I don't know what the "right" price for lawyers is. We have markets for that. What is the "length of line" test supposed to prove? Those who can't afford a lawyer are not waiting at the lawyer's office—they're doing without the advice.

I do know that reducing the supply of something usually raises the price. Ideally this would invite more supply, unless it's restricted by a licensing law. The law of supply and demand suggests that the price is higher given licensing than it would be without regulation. I suspect that an unregulated market would look very different at the lower end, maybe not so different at the higher end. The big question is whether the higher prices are worth it, which gets back to the value of licensing.

As for evidence, the best measure of the economic effect of lawyer licensing that I'm aware of is Dean Lueck et al., *Market and Regulatory Forces in the Pricing of Legal Services*, 7 J. Reg. Econ. 63 (1995). They show no correlation between barriers to entry (e.g., bar passage rates) and the price of legal services, but they do show a correlation between sets of regulatory barriers and lawyer earnings. A detailed analysis of this paper is in my article.

There is a lot of analysis of the discriminatory effects of licensing laws: Milton Friedman, *Occupational Licensure*, in Capitalism and Freedom 137, 150-51 (1962); S. David Young, *The Rule of Experts: Occupational Licensing in America*, 75-80 (1987); Richard B. Freeman, *The Effect of Occupational Licensure on Black Occupational Attainment*, in Occupational Licensure and Regulation 1 (Simon Rottenberg ed., 1980) at 165; Benjamin Hoorn Barton, *Why Do We Regulate Lawyers?: An Economic Analysis of the Justifications for Entry and Conduct Regulation*, 33 Ariz. St. L.J. 429, 444 (2001); Walter Gellhorn, *The Abuse of Occupational Licensing*, 44 U. Chi. L. Rev. 6, 18 (1976).

Josh Wright, over at Truth on the Market asks:

> "I am curious as to the state of the empirical evidence with respect to lawyer licensing and its impact on consumers. If I recall, the Federal Trade Commission has recently been involved in some advocacy efforts in favor of limiting the scope of unauthorized practice of law statutes. My sense is that a number of states must have relaxed unauthorized practice of law restrictions (I think Arizona is one), or similarly relaxed restrictions on lawyer licensing, such that one could directly test the impact of these restrictions on consumers in terms of prices and quality of service. There must be work on this somewhere. My quick Google search did not return anything right away, but does anybody know of empirical work in this area?"

Good questions. Joyce Palomar, *The War Between Attorneys and Lay Conveyancers—Empirical Evidence Says "Cease Fire!"*, 31 Conn. L. Rev. 423 (1999) found little evidence of risk to the public from lay providers of real estate settlement services. But there's obviously a lot more work to be done. Fred. S. McChesney & Timothy I. Muris, *The Effect of Advertising on the Quality of Legal Services*, 65 A.B.A. J. 1503 (1979) and *Advertising and the Price and Quality of Legal Services: The Case for Legal Clinics*, 1979 Am. B. Found. Res. J. 179 found that a legal clinic using advertising in high-volume practice reduced costs without compromising quality.

There's obviously a lot more empirical work to be done.

This gets to Jonathan's question about "transition" to a market regime. Actually, it would be a fairly simple matter for states to simply decide to allow people to do what they previously couldn't do. Most of the adjustment would be for the previously protected class of lawyers.

But that doesn't mean we shouldn't proceed carefully, and our federal system allows us to do just that. Jonathan decries the fact that "With 50 separate state regimes to manage, policy-makers would either have to endure a decades-long transition in which some states deregulated and others didn't or there would have to be some kind of nationwide, federally-mandated deregulation that trumped state law. How would that work? How could it work?"

In fact, these separate regimes are a blessing, not a curse. With 50 (actually, 51) different regulators we have an opportunity to test how reforms actually work, as Josh Wright suggests. This sort of test doesn't have to wait—and indeed shouldn't wait—for some "blue ribbon commission" to complete its work. I don't see a problem with such a commission, as I said before, but the best possible commission is the formidable laboratory enabled by our federal system. The time to start is now.

2. Multidisciplinary Practice

WRITTEN REMARKS OF LAWRENCE J. FOX, *YOU'VE GOT THE SOUL OF THE PROFESSION IN YOUR HANDS,*

http://www.abanet.org/cpr/mdp/fox1.html

Dear Commissioners:

Thank you for the chance to appear before you and to follow up my testimony with these written remarks. * * * Along the way to this presentation I * * * had nightmares. It was five years from now, the ABA was in steep decline and I had fallen into the annual meeting of the National Association of Multi-Disciplinary Professional Firms. Well-dressed individuals with badges scurried about, and the hail-fellow-

Food for Thought

Should customer satisfaction make a difference? In the Brumbaugh case, Chapter 1, *supra,* the court notes that the allegations of unauthorized practice "did not arise from a complaint by any of Ms. Brumbaugh's customers as to improper advice or unethical conduct–[The action] has been initiated by members of the Florida Bar[.]" Professor Deborah Rhode has observed that "Surveys of federal administrative agencies, consumer regulatory organizations, reported judicial decisions, and bar enforcement committees generally reveal no significant incidence of customer injury from lay practice. So too, the only research on customer satisfaction finds higher approval ratings for nonlawyer specialists than for lawyers." Deborah L. Rhode, *Institutionalizing Ethics,* 44 Case W. Res. L. Rev. 665, 727 (1994).

well-met greetings in the corridors had a familiar ring, but after an exhaustive search no programs on pro bono were to be found, the crisis in death penalty representation went unnoticed, free speech only referred to the charge for attending the programs, not the cherished civil liberty, and no one was worrying about the independence of the judiciary despite President Quayle's recent call for the impeachment of seventeen federal judges who granted habeas petitions in the last twelve months. In their place I found programs featuring "Medicine: the Next Multi-disciplinary Frontier," "Leveraging Your Audit Services into Profits in Legal Services" and "Eliminating Confidentiality: Improving Society." Then I woke up and realized I had to persuade you here and now why you should reaffirm our values and ethical commitments to our clients.

The issue before you is the independence of our profession. Though this critical value finds its expression in Rule 5.4's prohibition on sharing fees with nonlawyers, an interdiction that sounds strangely as if it is designed to protect our profession's turf, the rule in fact embodies the only prohibition that is likely to be effective in maintaining our professional independence. If for President Clinton it was "It's the economy, stupid," for our profession the watchword is "It's the money." Follow the money and you'll follow the power. Follow the power and you'll know whose in control. And as soon as the power rests with nonlawyers not trained in, not dedicated to, and not subject to discipline for our ethical principles, you will see the independence of the profession fall away.

"Oh no," shout the Philistines at our gates. "Even if lawyers are controlled by nonlawyers the results will be the same." Who should you believe? The hysterics like I who see the destruction of the profession? Or the wing-tipped shod accountants who call us alarmists and proponents of antiquated notions of professional responsibility?

The great news is that your Commission need not decide which side's rhetorical excess is more charming. Nor need you rely on idle speculation. No, the real world has already offered us a laboratory where you can learn just how fragile a value professional independence is and how assiduously we all must work to defend it.

To what do I refer? Where have these experiments been going on unnoticed by the profession? The answer: right in front of our very eyes. First, look at our colleagues in the medical profession. A decade ago they relaxed the rules on physicians working for non-physicians. Suddenly a floodgate of pseudo-prosperity opened up and a tidal wave of cash spread across the land, offering the docs thousands, even millions for their practices. I remember myself looking longingly at my physician friends as they cashed out their patient lists. Why did I decide I hated the sight of blood, I thought.

But where are the physicians today? Can you find a happy doc? Of course not and why would one expect to? Having sold out to Mammon they now find themselves acting as supplicants in endless phone calls with high school clerks who decide for the physicians which medicine to prescribe, which procedures to undertake and how soon their patients are thrown out of their hospital beds. If this is what happens to a vulnerable value—professional independence—when literally matters of life and death are on the line, can we expect a different result when the issue is the preservation of important, if less cosmic values like loyalty, confidentiality and client autonomy?

Nevertheless, some might argue that all that organic chemistry and ninety hour weeks as residents have left the medical professional more likely than tough lawyers to lose their independence. To them I point to my second example: lawyers hired by insurance companies to represent the insureds. Nowhere to date have we seen more interference with independent professional judgment than what has occurred as these economic behemoths have retained counsel, on a take it or leave it basis, to undertake these important engagements. Here its not billing clerks but claims adjusters working on compensation incentives that have nothing to do with effective representation and everything to do with minimizing costs on a macro basis who tell lawyers if and when they can take depositions, whether they can engage experts, what motions to file and whether they can bill for in-house conferences. Some insurance companies even insist that lawyers misrepresent their status to their insured clients by establishing fake law firm names, letterhead and office décor to hide the fact that these "independent" lawyers work full-time for the insurance companies. The drive to interfere with professional independence went so far that when the august American Law Institute sought to address the role of the lawyers hired by the insurance companies to represent the insured in drafting the Restatement of the Law Governing Lawyers, the insurance industry's representative (a most articulate and independent lawyer himself) fought to have the words "professional independence" removed from the applicable provision, § 215!

While I would disagree, some might assert that insurance is also a special case. What happens there is unlikely to be a precedent for what would happen if lawyers went to work for a prestigious professional service firm like Arthur Anderson. Which brings me to the third example and the one the proves the point. We don't have to speculate on whether lawyer's would lose their professional independence if they became a part of KPMG. The lawyers have already done so. While we slept the Big Five have systematically hired thousands of our best and brightest. Look at that result, Honorable Members of the Commission, and you will find all the proof you need that this road leads to perdition.

First, these lawyers are violating Rule 5.4 by sharing fees with nonlawyers. Recognizing the impediments presented by Rule 5.4, the accounting firms argue these lawyers are not practicing law—no, they are practicing tax or investigations or mergers and acquisitions. But not law. The argument that these lawyers are not engaged in the practice of law has as much merit as President Clinton's that he did not engage in sex. The contention relied upon—that a law degree is not required to do the things these lawyers are doing—in some cases is simply false and in others irrelevant. There are many activities lawyers undertake that nonlawyers are free to do. But, this does not mean that when lawyers do them they are not the practice of law. The construct invented by the accountants is worse than fallacious—it is cynical, insensitive and speaks volumes about the attitude those in control of accounting firms take toward the precious commodity we call being a lawyer. To compound the error these firms tout these individuals as lawyers in all their advertisements and promotional literature, the lawyers turned Big 5[3] employees maintain their bar membership and a visit to their offices reveals their bar admission plaques proudly displayed on the walls. But, remember, they are

---

3 [Ed.] Today, the Big 5 have become the Big 4. In the aftermath of the Enron scandal, and after a conviction which was later overturned, Arthur Anderson collapsed. Jonathan D. Glater, *Life after Enron for Anderson's Ex-staffers*, N.Y. Times, Feb. 21, 2006, *available at* http://www.nytimes.com/2006/02/21/business/worldbusiness/21iht-account.html?_r=1&scp=5&sq=arthur%20anderson%20demise%20verdict%202002&st=cse

not practicing law. They cling to the valuable designation as lawyers: they simply ignore the concomitant ethical responsibility that gives that status real meaning.

The fact that many talented lawyers would erect such a disingenuous argument to rationalize their unethical conduct should alone demonstrate how quickly lawyers who work for nonlawyers become beholden to their masters. But there is more, so much more. While a Kathryn Oberly may appear before your Commission to declaim that the Big 5 seek to preserve our core values, one learns on even a quick examination that in fact the accounting firms are a one profession wrecking crew, destroying any ethical rules that stand in their path.

Take confidentiality. Our rules preserve confidential treatment for all information learned in the course of a representation. What an uncomfortable notion that must be when a lawyer works at an accounting firm. By definition the core value of the attest function of an accounting firm is the public disclosure of material information. While the accounting firms grate at the strictures this audit role places on their ability to grow, since providing too many consulting services, to say nothing of legal services, to their audit clients will undoubtedly compromise their independence, the Big 5 don't want to give up auditing entirely. Because of the oligopoly power, the entire world of public companies must hire one of the Big 5 as auditors, which of course provides these firms with their wedge into this cohort of the biggest enterprises and permits them to leverage that presence into a vast array of other engagements.

But in the legal arena the attest function presents special problems. Just when a legal client may most want to preserve a confidence, lawyers working at these accounting firms will be compelled to disclose it—running directly afoul of our most cherished professional value. Recognizing the fact that their lawyers really are practicing law and the inherent conflict in roles and rules, the Big 5 responds by explaining that they receive waivers of confidentiality from their clients before each engagement. But this is no cure. A lawyers duty of confidentiality is not waiveable for the benefit of the lawyer and, even if it were, a prospective waiver would be void since by definition it could never be knowing and intelligent.

Demonstrating both the weakness of their waiver argument and their callous disregard for our values, the auditors then argue that confidentiality is really no big deal. After all, if a public company has a duty to disclose, all that Big 5 lawyers are getting their clients to agree to is the disclosure by the lawyer of information to the auditors that the client would be obliged to tell the auditors anyway.

The argument is as outrageous as it is indifferent to our core values. All lawyers know that in order to be effective at what we do a client must know that the lawyer-client relationship is sacrosanct. One need look no further than how we viewed Ken Starr's attack on the deceased Vince Foster's privileged communications to understand how fragile our assurances of confidentiality can be and how jealously we must guard them. The profession rightly rose as one to argue that our clients will be inhibited even by knowing that disclosure of their confidences will only follow death. Here the possibility of disclosure is more likely, guaranteed to be timely, and obviously something that the client will be forced to live with.

Moreover, information is ambiguous and materiality a term of art, not a mathematical formula. To place a lawyer in a trap between a duty to a client and a duty to his nonlawyer auditing masters creates an impossible dilemma whose only product can be second-rate legal services and a compromise of ethical principles. Advocates (and by that term I include all lawyers, transactional and trial), and auditors, as in that old Sesame Street song, don't "go together," especially when the topic is preserving confidences.

The Big 5's response to our other core value—loyalty—is even more troubling, in part because it affects every representation. Quite simply the accounting firms don't recognize, clear or care about conflicts of interest. This is so because in their view all conflicts are personal, limited to the individuals working on an engagement. And could it be any other way if they are to divide the entire corporate world in cinque partem? Which is fine, one would suppose, (or at least none of our business) if the services being offered are in the audit arena. But when it comes to lawyering, we promise and deliver far more. We impute one lawyer's conflicts to all lawyers in the lawyer's firm. Our clients need not worry that while we are suing A on behalf of B that our tax department is developing a new pension plan for A, unless B is told of the representation of A and consents to waive the conflict.

A recent personal example should dramatize the problem. I was representing an organization in a tax dispute with one of its partners. The organization had been audited by a Big 5 accounting firm for a decade or more, though its tax returns were prepared by a smaller firm. Right before trial we learned for the first time that this same Big 5 firm was providing litigation assistance to the other side. The accounting firm defended the conduct saying different personnel were involved in each engagement!

Kathryn Oberly, before this Commission, defended this loosey-goosey approach to conflicts of interest by arguing that "firewalls" erected by the accounting firms would guarantee that no confidential information from one client would infect another. Of course, I do not need to explain to this Commission how this assertion does not solve the loyalty problem. But, even if it did, her use of the word "firewall" does not mean that anything like that exists. There are no firewalls at any law or accounting firm. In fact, our profession's word, "screens," is much more apt since it refers to those items we install in the spring to let in light, air and sound.

The truth is the only protection against the misuse of information is the integrity and diligence of the individuals involved. They have to be honest and they have to remember that they are screened, in an office setting in which there might be hundreds or thousands of screens over long periods of time. As you consider how sanguine you would be in endorsing screens to provide any protection for clients, I ask you to think of the most scoundrel law firm you know and then ask yourself how you would feel if they told you "Don't worry. We have erected a screen."

The truth is that accountants, in order to guarantee their ability to hire and retain lawyers to work for their firms, actually have the chutzpah to ask us to destroy what they refer to as our "antiquated notions" of loyalty, to eliminate imputation and embrace their more "enlightened" views on this topic, views that have made it possible for them to employ more lawyers than our largest law firms. As a reward for their blatant violation of Rule 5.4, we should now accommodate them further by repealing Rule 1.10!

This Commission, this profession, must not fall into this trap. It is the fact that some have argued "why should I, a lawyer in the D.C. office of a 500-lawyer twelve-office law firm, be restrained by representations in our Hong Kong office? I've never been there, I've never met most of the lawyers there and what do I care what representations they undertake. They wouldn't compromise me."

But those who advocate this position are wrong and the answer to this too-clever- by-half assertion must be delivered loud and clear. So long as lawyers hold themselves out as one firm, tout to their clients the vast resources of their far-flung offices and the ability to call on anyone in any office to assist with the client's representation, and share fees among all, then it is the firm, not individual partners, that must deliver complete loyalty to the firm's clients.

The Big 5 retorts that, more important than loyalty, we give the clients freedom of choice. If they don't like the fact that we undertake conflicting representations they can take their business elsewhere. Has there ever been an argument that more sublimated client protection to business expansion? If they ever tell the client of the conflicting representation at all (something the accounting firms do not even attempt to assure) examine carefully the choice of the Big 5 Offers. A client hires a lawyer at the Big 5. The lawyer performs services for eighteen months. The client is now told the auditing firm is taking on the client's adverse party in a (let us hope) unrelated matter. What is the choice? The client can accept the fact that its multi-disciplinary provider is working for the other side and worry how many punches will be pulled to assure that the new offending representation stays put. Or the client can fire the Big 5 firm, waste the fees, time and learning curve the firm provided, and look for another firm to represent the client. The only choice presented is the one our friend Hobson was given. Yet the Big 5 proudly proclaim this choice as a preservation of our core values. Ladies and Gentlemen of the Commission: Orwell lives.

On the other hand, we lawyers provide our clients with real choice. We disclose all potential conflicts before the representation, and if we think they will not interfere with the representation (and only then), we may ask for a waiver. But if the prospective client rejects the proffer, that is the end. If the conflict arises after the representation begins, we still provide full information to the client. And if the client states that the lawyer may not take on the new representation, the lawyer does not take it on. That is real choice and reflects a truly enlightened system in which the client is in control, granting waivers when the client chooses, withholding them when the client determines its interests are not served.

Some have suggested, including an esteemed member of the Commission (one of my heroes) that we should abolish imputation, at least in the non-litigation arena. Permit me to give this accommodating argument the respectful interment it deserves. Nothing would be more divisive for our profession than two different imputation rules. It would make partnerships between litigators and business lawyers economically disadvantageous for the latter. Why associate with trial lawyers if they burden you with their conflicts. Second, it would be impossible to administer. When does a matter transmogrify into one that must be imputed? When nasty letters are sent? When mediation is tried? Third, law firms would lose representations mid-stream as a conflict that was allowed to be ignored in a transactional context suddenly had to be identified and acted upon with the filing of a complaint. Fourth, the whole concept confuses adverseness of interests with decibel level. Clients often care just as much, if not more, about a sale, merger, loan or new contract than they do about a small litigated matter that may be just a cost of doing business: for example, product liability suits for manufacturers of heavy equipment. In other words, the worries about a lawyer's loyalty and protection of confidential information that imputation is supposed to put to rest are just as likely to arise in a non-litigation context as in a contested civil proceeding.

Another major problem with the relaxation of imputation is that it creates a division of our professional standards based on firm size. Sole practitioners must live with all their conflicts and must turn away every conflicting representation. But under the Brave New World envisioned by the fans of MDP's, as firms get larger and establish more offices or separate practice departments, conflicts within the enterprise can be ignored, while all happily share the fees, prestige and name recognition a giant firm conveys. What such a construct conveys in terms of elitism and large firm bias is too unflattering and unseemly to contemplate.

The frontal attacks on our core values of confidentiality and loyalty are not the end of what we find occurring at the laboratory of the Big 5 accounting firms. Far from it.

1. Non-competition Agreements. Professionals at the accounting firms are asked to sign agreements not to compete after they leave the firms. An American Express-owned accounting firm is seeking to enforce one of these against a former employee lawyer right now. The seeking or providing of such a restriction on the right to practice law is an assault on client autonomy that our ethical rules to not tolerate. The accountants apparently don't care.

2. Steering. The power of the Big 5 cannot be overstated. Without their unqualified opinion, companies cannot go public, have difficulty raising money and often cannot survive. Only these five entities can provide the Good Housekeeping Seal of Approval, and without the seal. . . . well, nobody wants to find out. This entrée into the rarefied world of the world's largest enterprises has been the fuel behind the vast expansion the Big 5 has enjoyed. While auditing is a slow-growth line of endeavor, the Big 5 have increased their non-audit services in consulting to the point that the Chief Accountant of the SEC has expressed the Commission's concern that the independence of the audit function may be compromised. Yet we learned in a MDP forum in Toronto at the ABA Annual Meeting that the Big 5 in Europe are using their audit power to steer clients to hire their lawyers as well. Such a steering strategy is quite troublesome, certainly flying in the face of our rules about paying anyone something of value for referring business to lawyers.

3. Advertising. Our profession has so carefully circumscribed what advertising of legal services is permissible. We may not promise results. We may not tout past success. We may not use the identity and experience of our clients. It will come as no surprise to the members of the Commission, who cannot miss what the Big 5's awesome ad budgets buy as you flip the channels or race through airport concourses, that those firm's advertisements violate all these principles. Slick. For sure. Ethical for lawyers. Certainly not.

4. Business with Clients. My reference to the Big 5 entering the medical service field may have been facetious. But there are few areas of financial endeavor the Big 5 don't think they can enter. We have learned how the Big 5 now seeks to sell insurance, annuities and other investment "opportunities" to their accounting clients. The rules governing lawyers doing business with their clients are elaborate, designed to provide meaningful safeguards if lawyers dare to enter this fray. The Stanley Commission, in examining professionalism, argued that the one of the greatest threats to this value was lawyers engaging in business with their clients. Lawyers working for accounting firms, for whom doing business with clients is an ever-expanding profit center of the firm, are confronted with grave ethical questions under Rule 1.8.

The Big 5 approach to the evisceration of our ethics rules relies in part on the notion that anything that occurs between consenting adults is perfectly OK. The

Big 5 can ask for anything, the argument goes. If they get it from a sophisticated client, why should we bother prying into their bedroom? This commission is far too smart to accept such glib nonsense. The bedrock foundation of our profession is that there are some things lawyers may not seek. Clients cannot be asked to waive the protections of confidentiality or of Rule 4.2, contacts with represented persons. Some conflicts of interest are unwaivable, including those that no reasonable lawyer would pursue. Lawyers may not avoid malpractice liability nor limit their personal liability for their misconduct in any way. Do these rules make us less profitable? Less flexible? Less able to achieve the maximum amount of business? Of course they do. But that is a small price to pay to deliver the quality of representation that makes us lawyers, not just vendors of services.

One final note on the Big 5 entering the law world, if you will. Some, including one member of your Commission has argued that there is no difference between the conduct of the Big 5 in hiring lawyers and the movement by corporations to hire in-house counsel. In each case the lawyers are employed by nonlawyers, so the syllogism apparently goes.

To which I say balderdash. In one case a client hires a fulltime lawyer to represent the client. While it is true that this lawyer, in order to exercise the ultimate act of professional independence—withdrawal—must lose her job. But that lawyer deals with no conflicts (she only has one client), has no need to compromise the client's confidentiality, and does not represent a profit center for its employer, but rather a cost. On the other hand, when lawyers are employed by nonlawyers to deliver services to third party clients all of the issues on imputation, confidentiality and independence of professional judgment arise.

You remember I began this discussion about what was happening at the accounting firms as proof that professional independence was fragile and that when nonlawyers were in control the lawyers not only might but would lose independence. And after listening to this litany—from the willingness to argue they are not practicing law to the catalogue of ethical violations those lawyers routinely engage in -- the point cannot be disputed. It's a sad story, the discussion of our lapsed brethren and sisters, but it is not speculation, it is fact.

It is the Big 5 that has triggered your Commission's activities, but as you confront the issues raised by their assault on our ethical rules, you must remember we are not crafting rules for five globe-girdling accounting firms. If we say lawyers can share fees with nonlawyers we cannot, despite Kathryn Oberly's attempts otherwise, limit that fee sharing to the very prestigious partnerships of these so-called MDP's whose principles dress like us, have names like law firm names, employ cushy stationery and feature hunting prints on their walls. I have remarked in the past the only difference between KPMG and my firm DB&R is an ampersand

and $4,000,000,000 in revenues. The rule would have to be that anyone and any entity, regardless of its purposes or area of endeavor, could employ lawyers and offer their services to clients at a profit. The same broad side destructive result obtains if we permit the accountants to perpetuate their current nullification of imputation. If the Big 5 need not impute conflicts among their professional personnel, no other entity that employs lawyers could be shackled with a contrary result. Even existing law firms would suddenly be free to erect "firewalls" between every lawyer's office in the law firm!

This last point demonstrates why the accounting firms are particularly inappropriate stalking horses for the untimely demise of our professional independence. While they certainly seem high-faluting enough, only the accounting firms, among the potential employers of lawyers, have a public disclosure obligation that conflicts with the lawyers' ethical duty of confidentiality. Similarly, though many possible owners of legal service firms might like to destroy our rules of loyalty in order to make their businesses expand faster by never turning away business (heaven forefend!), only the Big 5, of necessity, must ignore our ethical mandate on conflicts of interest because they are so big and perform services for such a vast array of individuals, companies and organizations. This is not an invitation, needless to say, to destroy our ethical fabric for nonlawyers other than the Big 5, but simply to note with irony how bizarre it really is to have these firms leading the charge.

As you consider the attempts by the Visigoths to simply reduce lawyers and lawyering to their lowest common denominator—just another set of service providers providing just another service all to be offered at a one stop shop—I ask you to cast your eyes toward the ballroom at the Mayflower Hotel in Washington, D.C. Recall with me, if you will, the ten years the august American Law Institute has spent considering the Restatement of the Law Governing Lawyers, a project now nearing completion. Tens of thousands of hours, thousands of pages, thirty drafts to achieve a codification of the special law that governs lawyer conduct and lawyer responsibility. You cannot find better "proof" that lawyers are anything but generic service providers and that what is in peril here is so much more important and worth preserving than any benefits that could possibly be achieved by destroying our ethical foundations. Yet all of that work is trivialized by those who would treat us like a stockbrokers, insurance salesmen and business consultants to our "customers."

Before I appeared before your Commission, I had always defended our Model Rules and particularly Rule 5.4 in the name of clients. And I remain convinced that client protection alone provides more than enough justification for our present regulatory framework. Not one of the ethical rules I have discussed is designed to protect lawyers. We would all be far better off economically if each of them was discarded. But it is for the clients that they were crafted and it is for the clients that they should remain in place.

There is another important argument, however, which deserves great weight. The independence of our profession has significant institutional value for our American society. Whatever may be the role of lawyers in these other countries where the Big 5 have swallowed law firms with nary a whimper, our profession in America is different. Each of us is an officer of the court, each of us is licensed with power to start law suits, subpoena witnesses, opine regarding transactions, stand between our clients and the awesome power of the state. It is we who are charged with undertaking pro bono services, defending the independence of the judiciary, accepting court appointments, providing volunteer services for our bar associations, recommending discipline of our own, teaching continuing legal education courses, explaining our system to the public and working to improve the laws and legal institutions. What will happen to these values when lawyers work for others in for-profit enterprises providing legal services to the world? Can we expect Arthur Andersen to take a tolerant attitude toward a death penalty representation? Or Sears to be pleased its lawyer employees are supporting the Legal Services Corporation, the funder of consumer complaints on behalf of the indigent?

This is not, like the destruction of our ethics rules, a cataclysmic point. This one reflects more likely a slow death. It reminds me of what happens when the biggest company in a town gets purchased by folks from far way. The new buyer may give lip service to giving back to the community. But the reality is the town will soon learn it has lost its soul.

Members of the Commission, you have a golden opportunity to reaffirm our professional values and assure that the profession does not simultaneously lose both its independence and its soul. Don't miss this chance. For you should issue the clarion call, to our disciplinary officials to enforce Rule 5.4, to our profession to defend our ethical integrity, to the clients of America to understand how much is really at stake. One stop shopping, you must announce, is just a benign way of describing the destruction of everything lawyers should and must stand for.

JOHN S. DZIENKOWSKI & ROBERT J. PERONI, *MULTIDISCIPLINARY
PRACTICE AND THE AMERICAN LEGAL PROFESSION: A MARKET APPROACH
TO REGULATING THE DELIVERY OF LEGAL SERVICES IN THE TWENTY-FIRST
CENTURY*,

69 Fordham L. Rev. 83 (2000)

* * *

The American legal profession has * * * embraced the concept that nonlawyers
should not become partners or owners in a law firm or other entity delivering
legal services for a pecuniary gain. The 1908 Canons of Professional Ethics did
not contain any restrictions on nonlawyer ownership of law firms. In 1928, however, the ABA amended the Canons of Professional Ethics to urge that lawyers not
create partnerships with members of other professions if any part of the business
is to consist of the practice of law. In 1969, the ABA strengthened this ban,
making it mandatory in the Model Code of Professional Responsibility. The ABA
restated this position in 1983 by adopting Model Rule 5.4(a), which prohibits
partnerships between lawyers and nonlawyers.

In 1928, the ABA completed the ban on nonlawyer involvement in the practice of
law by adopting Canon 34 of the Canons of Professional Ethics that prohibited any
sharing of legal fees with nonlawyers. Canon 35 also prohibited third party interference with the professional independence of the lawyer. The ABA later adopted
similar prohibitions in the Model Code and the Model Rules. * * *

In 1982, however, during the drafting of the Model Rules, the Kutak Commission
proposed a rule that would have significantly changed the ABA's position on nonlawyer involvement in the practice of law. A proposed model rule on the "Professional Independence of a Firm" provided that a lawyer could be employed by an
organization in which nonlawyers held a financial or managerial interest as long as
the professional independence of the lawyer was preserved. This rule, however,
was completely rejected on the floor of the ABA House of Delegates meeting, and
rewritten and replaced with the current version of Model Rule 5.4. Ironically,
the 1999 proposals of the ABA Commission on Multidisciplinary Practice came
almost "full circle" back to the Kutak position.

In 1988, both the District of Columbia bar and North Dakota bar proposed that
their respective versions of Model Rule 5.4 be modified to allow lawyers and nonlawyers to hold ownership interests in a law firm. The District of Columbia bar
sought to change the rule in order to allow nonlawyers to contribute to the legal
services provided to clients. This proposal was in part a reaction to the non-law
divisions of lobbying, real estate, and investment banking that some District of
Columbia law firms had begun to develop as subsidiaries. The North Dakota rule
sought to allow lawyers and nonlawyers to offer combined services. Ultimately,

after much debate and controversy, the District of Columbia rule passed, but the
North Dakota rule was withdrawn by the state supreme court.

In reaction to a perceived commercialization of the legal profession that allegedly
threatened the ability of lawyers to render independent advice, the ABA began to
consider an ethics rule on ancillary business services. Some in the ABA thought
that the ABA needed to provide the states with an alternative rule to D.C. Rule 5.4
so that states would have an option when their lawyers pushed for modifying the
codes of conduct to accommodate non-legal services. In 1991, the ABA House of
Delegates adopted new Model Rule 5.7, "Responsibilities Regarding Law-Related
Services." The 1991 version of this rule was very strict as to lawyer involvement in
law-related services provided to law firm clients. It required that such services ancillary to the practice of law be provided only to the clients of the law firm, and only by
employees of the law firm, not of a subsidiary. Also, the rule required that the lawyer
make appropriate disclosure to the client, and required that the law firm not hold
itself out to the public as engaging in any non-legal activities. The comments to the
rule make clear that the ABA sought to restrict "the ability of law firms to provide
ancillary non-legal services through affiliates to non-client customers and clients
alike, the rendition of which raises serious ethical and professionalism concerns."

The severe restrictions of the 1991 Model Rule 5.7 were contrary to many practices within state bars regarding the provision of lawyer-owned non-legal services.
In many states, lawyers owned title companies that were marketed to the general
public as well as to firm clients. Thus, in 1992, the ABA House of Delegates deleted
the 1991 version of Rule 5.7. In 1994, the ABA considered a different approach
to lawyer provision of ancillary business services and adopted a revised version of
Model Rule 5.7. The revised version of Model Rule 5.7 does not address the ethical
or professional consequences of lawyers and law firms providing ancillary business
services. Instead, it focuses on the client expectations that may arise when ancillary
business services are provided by a law firm. Essentially, under revised Model Rule
5.7, a law firm's ancillary business services may or may not be included under the
protection of the rules of ethics. To avoid application of the ethics rules, a law firm
must provide the services in a manner distinct from the delivery of legal services.
Additionally, the client must be informed that the services are not legal services and
that the protections of the attorney-client relationship do not apply.

Although the ABA properly identified one key issue in the provision of ancillary business services--whether the attorney-client relationship attaches to those
services--the new version of Model Rule 5.7 blatantly ignored all of the concerns
that the ABA addressed in 1991. This exhibits the "politics of regulating the bar"
within the ABA. Although nothing was done to alleviate the professional concerns
in the provision of ancillary business services, the revised rule accommodated the
practices throughout the country whereby lawyers provided non-legal services to
clients and non-clients for significant profits, in some cases without disclosing the
lawyers' ownership interests in the non-law business.

* * * As mentioned above, one major area in which nonlawyers and lawyers in accounting firms have been involved in the delivery of legal services is in the practice of tax law. State unauthorized-practice-of-law statutes and case law must be read in conjunction with the federal system of authorizing lawyers and non-lawyers to practice in certain areas in the federal system. Under the Supremacy Clause, Congress and the Executive Branch can preempt state regulation of the unauthorized practice of law. Although the federal system has often deferred to the state bar system of lawyer regulation, one major area of federal preemption is federal tax practice. The federal scheme authorized by Congress allows lawyers and certain nonlawyers to practice in the area of federal tax.

In recent years, the Big Five accounting firms, as well as mid-sized accounting firms, have hired thousands of tax lawyers for their growing domestic and international tax planning practices (including well-known partners from major law firms in cities throughout the country). These efforts have been met with great concern and suspicion by state bar authorities and lawyers in general. In fact, several state bars have investigated the activities of the "Big Five" firms for violations of the unauthorized-practice-of-law statutes, but to date no unauthorized-practice-of-law complaints have been successfully maintained against such firms.

The Big Five accounting firms have argued that they are not engaged in the practice of law, but instead are engaged in tax consulting, something somehow different than tax law practice even though it involves interpretation and application of tax law. This argument appears to have no substance. A better argument by the Big Five accounting firms would be that to the extent they are engaged in the practice of tax law, at least at the federal level, the preemption doctrine prevents state bar authorities from successfully maintaining unauthorized-practice actions against them.

Federal law clearly preempts unauthorized-practice-of-law complaints by state bar authorities if and to the extent that the accounting firms' activities fall within the federal scheme of preemption. A federal statute, Treasury Circular 230, and the Tax Court Rules specifically authorize accountants and lawyers to practice in the area of federal taxation. Further, this federal authority does not limit partnerships or associations between lawyers and accountants working in this area. * * *

There is, however, one collateral aspect of tax practice that could involve the unauthorized practice of law. If a nonlawyer or a lawyer in an accounting firm provides tax services about a future transaction, and the client decides to adopt the advice, that client will often need non-tax services to implement the tax plan. Such services may include drafting of a will, transferring title to a property, or drafting the documents for a family limited partnership. Providing these services could arguably constitute the unauthorized practice of law.

There is no doubt that if a nonlawyer or a lawyer practicing in an accounting firm drafted an entire agreement and had the client execute the agreement in the accounting office, this activity would constitute the practice of law and could be enjoined by the state bar under the current ethical rules. A nonlawyer or a lawyer practicing in an accounting firm should, however, be able to propose language for inclusion in a legal document and draft such language without violating the unauthorized-practice-of-law rules. Such language could be provided to a client with the instruction that the client should take the language to an independent lawyer and have the lawyer include it in the legal documents only after review. Furthermore, an accounting firm could also draft an entire document for review by the client's lawyer. Although this comes closer to the practice of law, if the accounting firm sent this draft directly to the client's lawyer, that would arguably still be authorized by federal tax law. For the accounting firm to provide the draft directly to the client raises more serious liability concerns. On a case-by-case basis, it is unlikely that giving the draft to the client would trigger unauthorized-practice-of-law restrictions if the accounting firm makes it clear that the client needs to engage a separate lawyer to review the document before it is executed. There is always a risk, however, that a client could attempt to execute a complete document without review by a lawyer. Thus, an improperly executed will, for example, could be invalid and could subject the accounting firm to liability.

* * * In August of 1998, then ABA President Phillip Anderson appointed a commission to study the concept of multidisciplinary services and what changes, if any, should be made to the ABA Model Rules of Professional Conduct. * * *

The ABA Commission issued its Final Report on June 8, 1999, as part of a submission to the ABA House of Delegates for the August 1999 meeting. The Commission recommended that the ABA House of Delegates amend the Model Rules to permit lawyers to offer legal services through an MDP. The Report ultimately suggested that the ABA not constrain the type of entity that lawyers could use in offering multidisciplinary services. In other words, lawyers could offer legal services through any of the five models, even in the form of a fully integrated MDP. The Commission acknowledged, however, that the delivery of legal services through an MDP could threaten the core values of the legal profession. Thus, if the Commission's recommendations were adopted, MDPs would be required to follow the same rules that law firms followed and would have to certify their compliance with that requirement to the state bar. MDPs controlled by nonlawyers would be subject to an annual state bar audit to determine whether the certification was in fact true. Failure to comply with the certification could result in the firm's disbarment from MDP status. Moreover, nonlawyer controlled MDPs would have to pay the cost of the annual state bar audit. In addition, the Report recommended that the definition of an MDP be expanded to include any entity that employs lawyers for providing legal services. Thus, under the Commission's recommendations, in exchange for permission to deliver legal services through an MDP, all entities hiring lawyers for the performance of quasi-legal services would have to agree to be bound by the lawyer's rules of conduct and to be subject to a state bar audit.

* * * The vigorous debate at the August 1999 ABA meeting led the Commission on Multidisciplinary Practice to withdraw its proposal and to support further study. The ABA House of Delegates adopted a resolution proposed initially by the Florida delegates. * * * In March of 2000, the Commission issued recommendations to the House of Delegates, scaling back its 1999 recommendations to the following:

> 1. Lawyers should be permitted to share fees and join with nonlawyer professionals in a practice that delivers both legal and nonlegal profes-sional services (Multidisciplinary Practice), provided that the lawyers have the control and authority necessary to assure lawyer independence in the rendering of legal services. "Nonlawyer professionals" means mem-bers of recognized professions or other disciplines that are governed by ethical standards.

> 2. This Recommendation must be implemented in a manner that pro-tects the public and preserves the core values of the legal profession, including competence, independence of professional judgment, protec-tion of confidential client information, loyalty to the client through the avoidance of conflicts of interest, and pro bono publico obligations.

> 3. To protect the public interest, regulatory authorities should enforce existing rules and adopt such additional enforcement procedures as are needed to implement the principles identified in this Recommendation.

> 4. This Recommendation does not alter the prohibition on nonlawyers delivering legal services and the obligations of all lawyers to observe the rules of professional conduct. Nor does it authorize passive investment in a Multidisciplinary Practice.

The ABA Commission presented this recommendation to the House of Delegates in July of 2000, and the House of Delegates rejected it. * * *

PAUL D. PATON, *MULTIDISCIPLINARY PRACTICE REDUX: GLOBALIZATION, CORE VALUES, AND REVIVING THE MDP DEBATE IN AMERICA,*
78 Fordham L. Rev. 2193 (2010)

* * * When in August 2000 the American Bar Association's House of Delegates rejected the recommendations of its own Commission on Multidisciplinary Prac-tice that the Model Rules of Professional Conduct be amended to permit inte-grated multidisciplinary practices (MDPs) involving lawyers and other profession-als, it did so with a vengeance. The passage of Resolution 10F followed a nearly three-year investigation and rancorous debate within the ABA. The Resolution emphatically rejected fee sharing with nonlawyers and nonlawyer ownership and control of law firms as "inconsistent with the core values of the legal profession" and proposed that rules barring such alternative service delivery innovations be preserved. The Resolution provided a nonexhaustive list of "core values" and urged that each jurisdiction responsible for lawyer regulation implement the "principles" set out in the resolution, all of which would function as a bulwark against encroachment on the traditional law firm model. For all intents and purposes, the MDP was dead, buried in "core values" rhetoric. That rhetoric served to preserve a regime for the delivery of legal services, which, while anchored in legitimate concerns about conflicts of interest, independence, and preserving privilege, also functioned to prevent competition and to protect lawyers' turf.

But the MDP may have new life in America. In August 2009, the ABA created its new Ethics 20/20 Commission and gave it explicit instructions to "review lawyer ethics rules and regulation across the United States in the context of a global legal services marketplace." This means that the ABA will need to assess how "alternative business structures" for the delivery of legal services adopted in the intervening decade since Resolution 10F—including the MDP—are now functioning in other major common-law jurisdictions, including England, Australia, and Canada. In announcing the creation of the Commission, ABA President Carolyn Lamm signaled that the Commission should consider how regulatory structures can enable U.S. legal providers to compete with those in other countries while continuing to protect the public and—again—the "core values" of the profession. She subsequently signaled that MDPs "may well be" one of the topics of consideration for the Commission.

* * * As a December 2009 Law Society of Upper Canada (LSUC) Task Force report neatly summarized, "[t]here is now a worldwide market for legal services, driven by clients seeking to operate globally," clients are "looking for lawyers who are tapped in to the global market and are able to provide seamless service," "[t]he legal profession is facing increasing competition from other service providers," the "business structure of the profession is shifting," and the "profession's ability to maintain self-regulation has been eroded." Some of the myriad challenges facing the profession as a result of globalization are also identified in the ABA Ethics 20/20 Preliminary Issues Outline released on November 19, 2009. As the introduction to that document notes, "already the profession is encountering the competitive and ethical implications of U.S. lawyers and law firms seeking to represent American and foreign clients abroad and foreign lawyers seeking access to the U.S. legal market"; this "increase in globalized law practice raise[s] serious questions about whether existing ethical rules and regulatory structures adequately address the realities and challenges of 21st Century law practice."

Indeed, in confronting the issue of "alternative business structures," including MDPs, the Ethics 20/20 Commission notes that such structures "raise ethical and regulatory questions for U.S. lawyers and law firms of all sizes employed, associated, or otherwise doing business with these entities and their clients." The

Issues Outline asks whether the Model Rules of Professional Conduct need to be amended to take account of those structures, and frames the "core values" discussion this way: "How can core principles of client and public protection be satisfied while simultaneously permitting U.S. lawyers and law firms to participate on a level playing field in a global legal services marketplace that includes the increased use of one or more forms of alternative business structures?"

Revisiting both the tenor and the substance of the MDP debates of a decade ago is therefore both timely and necessary in order to assess various questions: When national bar association commissions in both the United States and Canada in the late 1990s had recommended the adoption of rules permitting MDPs, why did the governing bodies responsible for the ultimate decisions so forcefully reject them? Were the recommendations fundamentally flawed, or was the political and economic context within the profession at the time such that domestic adoption of liberal rules was impossible? What happened in the intervening period internationally to change the competitive environment in which U.S. firms must now operate? Is the search for new revenue by firms dealing with the impact of the 2008-2009 economic downturn, combined with the pressures of globalization, sufficient to propel a different outcome if the MDP comes before the ABA House of Delegates again? Now that England has adopted legislation permitting alternative business structures (including the MDP) in order to encourage competition and consumer choice in legal services provision, how have authorities there managed to address the ethical, "core values" challenges posed by the MDP and reconcile that with a government-driven agenda to reform the profession in the public interest?

* * * In Australia, the multidisciplinary practice, nonlawyer ownership, and even public ownership of shares in law firms is a new reality. Certain Canadian regulations adopted after 2000 permit a modified form of MDP as well as an "affiliated law firm" model in which law firms establish relationships with other professional services firms for the joint marketing, promotion, and delivery of legal and other services to clients. In England, the 2007 Legal Services Act, which transformed and effectively ended the self-regulation of the legal profession in that country, was the direct result of political debate and direct government involvement. That Act provides specific authorization for the establishment of alternative business structures for the delivery of legal services by lawyers and nonlawyers together. In the United States, a California State Bar Long Range Strategic Plan in 2002 had recommended continuing assessment of the "feasibility and ethical implications of permitting lawyers to join with nonlawyer professionals in a practice where both legal and non-legal professional services are offered to the public." A 2001 California State Bar Task Force report found that a fully integrated professional services firm would permit the "'core values' of the legal profession not only [to] be maintained, but [to] be reaffirmed." A Demonstration Project was proposed to translate Task Force recommendations into reality. But the MDP still does not exist in the United States in a form that would be recognized elsewhere; in all U.S.

jurisdictions except for the District of Columbia, firms cannot be organized for the
practice of law if nonlawyers have ownership interests in them.

The changed economic reality for law firms in the United States in the aftermath
of the economic downturn of 2008-2009 and the dramatic lawyer and staff job
losses of early 2009 may mean a new imperative—self-serving or otherwise—to
reconsider whether "core values" rhetoric needs to be viewed through a new lens
and new forms of business models including the MDP need to be permitted. The
profession is continuing to experience "growing internal political dissension at
the very moment when it also confronts the profound and permanent external
challenges of the new economy." Looking to the history of the MDP debate can
therefore provide signs not only about the way forward for legal service delivery,
but also for the profession's own conception of how its essential values and principles can be sustained in this "brave new world."

* * *

As the Ethics 20/20 Commission deeply engages the challenges emerging from
globalization of the profession, it will have to squarely address not whether, but
how, alternative business structures like the multidisciplinary practice will be part
of the American regulatory landscape in the future. The English and Australian
experiences, in particular, demonstrate that thinking about the profession as a
business does not have to mean the abandonment of "core values" as the profession evolves. Rather, the challenge is to ensure that the dialogue and debate is
broad ranging, not beholden to a politically powerful segment or segments of the
bar, and that consumer interests are kept front and center.

This will require a different sort of debate than what went on in North America
roughly a decade ago. Yet at both the ABA and at the CBA, Commissions charged
with deep study recommended fundamental change; the failure to act came when
the issue came to a vote and "core values" rhetoric was invoked to sustain the status
quo. Even regulators in Canada and those responsible for regulating the profession in the United States in the public interest demonstrated greater fealty to guild
protection. In that respect, "core values" was used as a "veto over change." This
time, however, the opportunities presented by alternative business structures such
as the MDP, and the economic threats coming not from accounting firms but from
globalization of legal services and law firms in England and Australia means that the
subtext--and likely the outcome--will be different. Further, from an access to justice
perspective, permitting alternative delivery structures such as MDPs will have a far
broader impact on ordinary citizens' ability to purchase legal services than the Big
Five accounting firm initiatives about which the ABA, CBA, and regulators were so
concerned a decade ago. There is also a greater risk if the bar fails to appropriately
and credibly consider the public interest in assessing the merits of MDPs and to act
accordingly: attracting a legislative response that not only implements rules with
which the profession itself is not satisfied, but using that to justify further encroach-

ments on lawyer self-regulation. In the aftermath of Enron, Congress demonstrated that it was prepared to legislate rules for lawyers appearing before the Securities and Exchange Commission, despite fierce resistance from the ABA. The fundamental transformation of regulation in England resulted when the profession was moving towards action, just not quickly or dramatically enough.

Getting across the threshold of accepting change, not just "peering over the ethical precipice" can then lead to a deeper engagement of how to reconcile traditional "core values" questions with new models of service delivery. Thinking about how to regulate the firm rather than just the individual lawyers practicing within it, for example, will require a paradigm shift, but the foundation for that was laid in the United States nearly twenty years ago. Current economic challenges and the changed global legal environment present the opportunity for the profession in North America to once again consider the MDP, economic self-interests of the profession, a consumer welfare perspective, and how these forces might align. Reviewing the lessons from the previous MDP debate is a place to start. Reaffirming that lawyers' ethical identities and professional values transcend models of business delivery, and ensuring that both the profession and the public recognize that in an era of increased globalization, is a daunting task but one that will be fundamental to both this next MDP debate, and the future of the profession as a whole.

DZIENKOWSKI & PERONI, *MULTIDISCIPLINARY PRACTICE AND THE AMERICAN LEGAL PROFESSION: A MARKET APPROACH TO REGULATING THE DELIVERY OF LEGAL SERVICES IN THE TWENTY-FIRST CENTURY*,

69 Fordham L. Rev. 83, 205-07 (2000)

* * * If the United States is to remain a center of global commerce, the legal profession must accommodate the demand for multidisciplinary services. The state bars now have a unique opportunity to develop a regulatory structure that protects the core values of the legal profession while accommodating consumer demand for integrated services. A decision by the organized bar attempting to reinforce the status quo ultimately will lead to the American legal profession's inability to play a key role in shaping the delivery of multidisciplinary services.

The states should modify their rules of professional conduct as follows. First, Model Rule 5.4 should be modified to allow fee-sharing between lawyers and non-lawyers providing professional services to a client. No pure referral fees should be permitted to nonlawyers. Second, the rules should be amended to permit lawyer participation in the delivery of multidisciplinary services. Although a structure that permitted all models of multidisciplinary services, including the fully integrated MDP, is optimal, such a step may be too radical for many states. Thus, states should strongly consider adopting rules that would permit contractual and joint venture MDPs to exist to offer legal and non-legal services in a coordinated manner. Both contractual and joint venture MDPs would offer experimentation in how conflicts of interest would be handled in the two separate kinds of firms. The organized bar could evolve the rules on conflicts in response to the experience with such arrangements. The contractual and entity joint ventures will afford many of the benefits of multidisciplinary practice with few of the costs.

The optimal approach for allowing lawyer participation in MDPs would involve removing the ban against nonlawyer partners and shareholders in business entities that provide legal services. Lawyers and nonlawyers should be able to form a single entity to offer both legal and non-legal services to clients. The delivery of legal services must conform to the same professional responsibility rules and standards as would apply if a law firm provided the services. The delivery of legal services would need to be controlled by lawyers, although there should be no requirement that lawyers have voting control in the fully integrated, single entity MDP. In order to facilitate lawyer control over legal services, lawyers in a single entity MDP should be organized in a legal department with checks and balances similar to those implemented in a corporate counsel context. There should be no requirement that the nonlawyers in an MDP be only those from a licensed profession because such a requirement is both vague and theoretically indefensible.

The states should also promulgate professional responsibility rules and standards that apply to all MDPs. MDPs should be permitted to litigate in the federal and state courts. Passive investments should be permitted in both law firms and MDPs; if, however, rules governing law firms are not liberalized to allow such passive investment, then the rules for MDPs on this issue must remain consistent with those for law firms. When a client is receiving legal services, a lawyer must supervise all aspects of work falling within the legal umbrella. Nonlawyer partners and managers must agree not to interfere in the delivery of legal services and must also require that all lawyers in the firm follow the rules of professional conduct. Additionally, the profession should implement peer review for law firms and other entities, including MDPs, that are delivering legal services to clients.

The question is not whether MDPs will exist and thrive in the future or whether lawyers in ever greater numbers will choose to work for MDPs. The trends in favor of MDPs are pronounced and unstoppable. Nothing the ABA or the state bars do can change that fact of economic life. The question is whether the ABA and state bars will have any significant role in regulating lawyers who work in MDPs, thereby protecting client interests and ensuring that lawyers' participation in multidisciplinary practice does not undercut the core values of the profession.

* * *

Client protection and protection of the core values of the legal profession should be the primary basis for regulation of MDPs. The rules of professional conduct for lawyers should permit innovation in the professional service marketplace. Unneeded and overbroad regulation, often motivated by economic protectionism, should be discarded. The state bar authorities should design their regulation of MDPs in the manner this Article suggests and thereby protect the public interest without unnecessarily interfering with the operation of market forces in the professional services arena.

II. Special Responsibilities

In a sense, the entire book explores lawyers' responsibilities flowing from lawyers' special privileges to practice law. In this section, we will examine in more depth the general responsibility for equal justice under law found in the Preambles to the Canons, the Model Code, and the Rules. For the text of these Preambles, *see* Chapter 8, pp. 787-88. In particular, this Section will examine lawyers' responsibilities with regard to equal access to justice, for rich and poor, or depending on identity.

A. Pro Bono

[Question 1]

Should Pro Bono service be mandatory for law students?

(A) Yes

(B) No

[Question 2]

Should Pro Bono service be mandatory for lawyers?

(A) Yes

(B) No

Rule 6.1 provides that "[a] lawyer should aspire to render at least (50) hours of pro bono publico legal services per year." It further advises that:

the lawyer should:

(a) provide a substantial majority of the (50) hours of legal services without fee or expectation of fee to:

(1) persons of limited means or

(2) charitable, religious, civic, community, governmental and educational organizations in matters that are designed primarily to address the needs of persons of limited means; and

(b) provide any additional services through:

(1) delivery of legal services at no fee or substantially reduced fee to individuals, groups or organizations seeking to secure or protect civil rights, civil liberties or public rights, or charitable, religious, civic, community, governmental and educational organizations in matters in furtherance of their organizational purposes, where the payment of standard legal fees would significantly deplete the organization's economic resources or would be otherwise inappropriate;

(2) delivery of legal services at a substantially reduced fee to persons of limited means; or

(3) participation in activities for improving the law, the legal system or the legal profession.

In addition, a lawyer should voluntarily contribute financial support to organizations that provide legal services to persons of limited means.

Go Online

To view the documentary "So Goes A Nation: Lawyers and Low Income Communities," click here.

DEBORAH L. RHODE, *CULTURES OF COMMITMENT: PRO BONO FOR LAWYERS AND LAW STUDENTS*,

67 Fordham L. Rev. 2415 (1999)

Nowhere is the gap between professional ideals and professional practice more apparent than on issues of pro bono responsibility. For decades, bar leaders, ethical codes, and countless commissions and committees have proclaimed that all lawyers have obligations to assist individuals who cannot afford counsel. And for decades, the percentage of lawyers who actually do so has remained dispiritingly small. Recent estimates suggest that most attorneys do not perform significant pro bono work, and that only between ten and twenty percent of those who do are assisting low-income clients. The average for the profession as a whole is less than a half an hour per week. Few lawyers come close to satisfying the American Bar Association's Model Rules, which provide that "[a] lawyer should aspire to render at least [fifty] hours of pro bono publico legal services per year" primarily to "persons of limited means" or to "organizations in matters which are designed primarily to address the needs of [such] persons."

The bar's failure to secure broader participation in pro bono work is all the more disappointing when measured against the extraordinary successes that such work has yielded. Many of the nation's landmark public-interest cases have grown out of lawyers' voluntary contributions. Moreover, particularly over the last decade, growing numbers of attorneys have donated time and talents to less visible but no less critical poverty law programs. For children with disabilities, victims of domestic violence, elderly citizens without medical care, and other low-income clients, these pro bono programs are crucial in meeting basic human needs. For lawyers themselves, such work is similarly important in giving purpose and meaning to their professional lives. Our inability to enlist more attorneys in pro bono service represents a significant lost opportunity for them as well as for the public.

How best to narrow the gap between professional ideals and professional practice has been a matter of considerable controversy. Proposals for mandatory pro bono requirements have come and gone, but mainly gone. The bar generally has resisted mandatory service, although a few jurisdictions require lawyers to accept judicial appointments for limited categories of cases, and one state, Florida, requires lawyers to report their annual pro bono contributions.

This resistance to required contributions, coupled with the limited success of voluntary efforts, has encouraged more pro bono initiatives in law schools. By enlisting students early in their legal careers, these initiatives attempt to inspire an enduring commitment to public service. The hope is that, over time, a greater sense of moral obligation will "trickle up" to practitioners. With that objective, an increasing number of schools have instituted pro bono requirements for students. So too, in 1996, the American Bar Association amended its accreditation standards to call on schools to "encourage . . . students to participate in pro bono activities and provide opportunities for them to do so." These revised ABA standards also encourage schools to address the obligations of faculty to the public, including participation in pro bono activities.

Despite such initiatives, pro bono still occupies a relatively marginal place in legal education. Only about ten percent of schools require any service by students and only a handful impose specific requirements on faculty. At some of these schools, the amounts demanded are quite minimal: less than twenty hours by the time of graduation. Over ninety percent of institutions offer voluntary programs, but their scope and quality varies considerably. About one-third of schools have no law-related pro bono projects or projects involving a few dozen participants. The majority of students have no legal pro bono work as part of their educational experience.

What legal education could or should do to expand such public-service commitments is subject to increasing debate. While law school administrators overwhelmingly support pro bono participation, they are divided about whether current programs are adequate and whether required service is desirable. * * *

This Essay attempts to place the debate over pro bono initiatives in legal education in broader perspective. Although much has been written about the value of public service and the merits of requiring it, relatively little attention has focused on the factors that encourage support for either voluntary or mandatory programs. Even less effort has centered on evaluating the effectiveness of law school programs. The effort here is to increase our understanding of what can build a culture of commitment to pro bono service.

To that end, discussion begins with the rationale for pro bono involvement by lawyers. * * * The primary rationale for pro bono contributions rests on two premises: first, that access to legal services is a fundamental need, and second, that lawyers have some responsibility to help make those services available. The first claim is widely acknowledged. As the Supreme Court has recognized in other contexts, the right to sue and defend is the right that protects all other rights. Access to the justice system is particularly critical for the poor, who often depend on legal entitlements to meet basic needs such as food, housing, and medical care. Moreover, in a democratic social order, equality before the law is central to the rule of law and to the legitimacy of the state. Social science research confirms what political theorists have long argued: Public confidence in legal processes depends heavily on opportunities for direct participation.

In most circumstances, those opportunities are meaningless without access to legal assistance. Our justice system is designed by and for lawyers, and lay participants who attempt to navigate without counsel are generally at a disadvantage. Those disadvantages are particularly great among the poor, who typically lack the education and experience necessary for effective self-representation. For example, studies of eviction proceedings find that tenants with attorneys usually prevail; tenants without attorneys almost always lose. Inequalities in legal representation compound other social inequalities and undermine our commitments to procedural fairness and social justice. As a New York judicial report noted: "Our justice system cannot proclaim in the bold letters of the law that it is just, but then block access to justice. We cannot promise due process, but raise insurmountable odds for those who seek it."

While most lawyers acknowledge that access to legal assistance is a fundamental interest, they are divided over whether the profession has some special responsibility to help provide that assistance, and if so, whether the responsibility should be mandatory. One contested issue is whether attorneys have obligations to meet fundamental needs that other occupations do not share. According to some lawyers, if equal justice under law is a societal value, society as a whole should bear its cost. The poor have fundamental needs for food and medical care, but we do not require grocers or physicians to donate their help in meeting those needs. Why should lawyers' responsibilities be greater?

One answer is that the legal profession has a monopoly on the provision of essential services. Lawyers have special privileges that entail special obligations. In the United States, attorneys have a much more extensive and exclusive right to provide legal assistance than attorneys in other countries. The American bar has closely guarded those prerogatives and its success in restricting lay competition has helped to price services out of the reach of many consumers. Under these circumstances, it is not unreasonable to expect lawyers to make some pro bono contributions in return for their privileged status. Nor would it be inappropriate to expect comparable contributions from other professionals who have similar monopolies over the provision of critical services.

An alternative justification for imposing special obligations on lawyers stems from their special role in our governance structure. As the New York Report explained, much of what lawyers do

> is about providing justice, [which is] . . . nearer to the heart of our way of life . . . than services provided by other professionals. The legal profession serves as indispensable guardians of our lives, liberties and governing principles. . . . Like no other professionals, lawyers are charged with the responsibility for systemic improvement of not only their own profession, but of the law and society itself.

Because lawyers occupy such a central role in our governance system, there is also particular value in exposing them to how that system functions, or fails to function, for the have nots. Pro bono work offers many attorneys their only direct contact with what passes for justice among the poor. To give broad segments of the bar some experience with poverty-related problems and public-interest causes may lay critical foundations for change. Pro bono programs have often launched leading social reform initiatives and strengthened support for government subsidies of legal services.

A final justification for pro bono work involves its benefits to lawyers individually and collectively. Those benefits extend beyond the intrinsic satisfactions that accompany public service. Particularly for young attorneys, such work can provide valuable training, trial experience, and professional contacts. Through pro bono assistance, lawyers can develop capacities to communicate with diverse audiences and build problem-solving skills. Involvement in community groups, charitable organizations, and public-interest activities is a way for attorneys to expand their perspectives, enhance their reputations, and attract paying clients. It is also a way for the bar to improve the public standing of lawyers as a group. In one representative ABA poll, nearly half of nonlawyers believed that providing free legal services would improve the profession's image.

For all these reasons, the vast majority of surveyed lawyers believe that the bar should provide pro bono services. However, as noted earlier, only a minority in fact provide significant assistance and few of their efforts aid low-income clients. The reasons for this shortfall do not involve a lack of need. A wide gap remains between the rhetoric and reality of America's commitment to equal justice. Studies of low-income groups find that over three-quarters of their legal needs remain unmet. Studies cutting across income groups estimate that individuals do not obtain lawyers' help for between thirty to forty percent of their personal legal needs. Moreover, these legal needs studies do not include many collective problems where attorneys' services are often crucial, such as environmental risks or consumer product safety.

The bar's response to inadequate access alternates between confession and avoidance. Some lawyers simply deny the data. Unburdened by factual support, they insist that no worthy cause goes unassisted, thanks to voluntary pro bono efforts, legal-aid programs, and contingent fee representation. A more common approach is to acknowledge the problem of unmet needs but to deny that mandatory pro bono service is the solution. In one representative survey, about sixty percent of California attorneys believed that poor people's access to legal assistance would continue to decline, but an equal number opposed minimum pro bono requirements.

Opponents raise both moral and practical objections. As a matter of principle, some lawyers insist that compulsory charity is a contradiction in terms. From their perspective, requiring service would undermine its moral significance and compromise altruistic commitments.

There are several problems with this claim, beginning with its assumption that pro bono service is "charity." As the preceding discussion suggested, pro bono work is not simply a philanthropic exercise; it is also a professional responsibility. Moreover, in the small number of jurisdictions where courts now appoint lawyers to provide uncompensated representation, no evidence indicates that voluntary assistance has declined as a result. Nor is it self-evident that most lawyers who currently make public-service contributions would cease to do so simply because others were required to join them. As to lawyers who do not volunteer but claim that required service would lack moral value, David Luban has it right: "You can't appeal to the moral significance of a gift you have no intention of giving."

Opponents' other moral objection to mandatory pro bono contributions involves the infringement of lawyers' own rights. From critics' vantage, conscripting attorneys undermines the fundamental rights of due process and just compensation; it is a form of "latent fascism" and "involuntary servitude."

The legal basis for such objections is unconvincing. A well-established line of precedent holds that Thirteenth Amendment prohibitions extend only to physical restraint or a threat of legal confinement. They do not apply if individuals may choose freedom at a price. Since sanctions for refusing pro bono work would not include incarceration, most courts have rejected involuntary servitude challenges.

Leading decisions have also dismissed objections based on the takings clause. Their reasoning is that "the Fifth Amendment does not require that the Government pay for the performance of a public duty [if] it is already owed." As long as the required amount of service is not unreasonable, takings claims generally have failed. * * *

Not only are lawyers' takings and involuntary-servitude objections unpersuasive as a legal matter, they are unconvincing as a moral claim. Requiring the equivalent of an hour a week of uncompensated assistance hardly seems like slavery. * * *

The stronger arguments against pro bono obligations involve pragmatic rather than moral concerns. Many opponents who support such obligations in principle worry that they would prove ineffective in practice. A threshold problem involves defining the services that would satisfy a pro bono requirement. If the definition is broad, and encompasses any charitable work for a nonprofit organization or needy individual, then experience suggests that poor people will not be the major beneficiaries. Most lawyers have targeted their pro bono efforts at friends, relatives, or matters designed to attract or accommodate paying clients. A loosely defined requirement is likely to assist predominately middle-class individuals and organizations such as hospitals, museums, and churches. By contrast, limiting a pro bono requirement to low-income clients who have been given preferred status in the ABA's current rule would exclude many crucial public-interest contributions, such as work for environmental, women's rights, or civil rights organizations. Any compromise effort to permit some but not all charitable groups to qualify for pro bono credit would bump up against charges of political bias.

A related objection to mandatory pro bono requirements is that lawyers who lack expertise or motivation to serve under-represented groups will not provide cost-effective assistance. In opponents' view, having corporate lawyers dabble in poverty cases will provide unduly expensive, often incompetent services. The performance of attorneys required to accept uncompensated appointments in criminal cases does not inspire confidence that unwillingly conscripted practitioners would provide acceptable representation. Critics also worry that some lawyers' inexperience and insensitivity in dealing with low-income clients will compromise the objectives that pro bono requirements seek to advance.

Requiring all attorneys to contribute minimal services of largely unverifiable quality cannot begin to satisfy this nation's unmet legal needs. Worse still, opponents argue, token responses to unequal access may deflect public attention from the fundamental problems that remain and from more productive ways of addressing them. Preferable strategies might include simplification of legal procedures, expanded subsidies for poverty law programs, and elimination of the professional monopoly over routine legal services.

Those arguments have considerable force, but they are not as conclusive as critics often assume. It is certainly true that some practitioners lack the skills and motivation necessary to serve those most in need of assistance. * * * To be sure, hiring additional poverty law specialists would be a more efficient way of increasing services than relying on reluctant dilettantes. Unfortunately, the funding increase that would be necessary to meet existing demands does not appear plausible in this political climate. Nor is it likely, as critics claim, that requiring pro bono contributions would divert attention from the problem of unmet needs. Whose attention? Conservatives who have succeeded in curtailing legal-aid funds do not appear much interested in increasing representation for poor people, whether through pro bono service or government-subsidized programs. As earlier discussion suggested, exposing more lawyers to the needs of poverty communities might also increase support for crucial reform efforts.

Moreover, mandatory pro bono programs could address concerns of cost-effectiveness through various strategies. One option is to allow lawyers to buy out of their required service by making a specified financial contribution to a legal-aid program. Another possibility is to give credit for time spent in training. Many voluntary pro bono projects have effectively equipped participants to provide limited poverty-law services through relatively brief educational workshops, coupled with well-designed manuals and accessible backup assistance.

A final objection to pro bono requirements involves the costs of enforcing them. Opponents often worry about the "Burgeoning Bureaucratic Boondoggle" that they assume would be necessary to monitor compliance. Even with a substantial expenditure of resources, it would be extremely difficult to verify the amount of time that practitioners reported for pro bono work or the quality of assistance that they provided.

Supporters of mandatory pro bono programs have responded with low-cost enforcement proposals that would rely heavily on the honor system. In the absence of experience with such proposals, their effectiveness is difficult to assess. There is, however, a strong argument for attempting to impose pro bono requirements even if they cannot be fully enforced. At the very least, such requirements would support lawyers who want to participate in public-interest projects but work in organizations that have failed to provide adequate resources or credit for these efforts. Many of the nation's most profitable law firms and leading corporate employers fall into that category. They could readily afford a greater pro bono commitment and a formal requirement might nudge them in that direction. As to lawyers who have no interest in public-interest work, a rule that allowed financial contributions to substitute for direct service could materially assist underfunded legal-aid organizations.

However the controversy over mandatory pro bono service is resolved, there is ample reason to encourage greater voluntary contributions. Lawyers who want to participate in public-interest work are likely to do so more effectively than those who are fulfilling an irksome obligation. How best to encourage a voluntary commitment to pro bono service demands closer scrutiny.

* * *

The primary justifications for pro bono service by law students parallel the justifications for pro bono service by lawyers. Most leaders in legal education agree that such service is a professional responsibility and that their institutions should prepare future practitioners to assume it. Ninety-five percent of deans responding to the AALS survey agreed that "[i]t is an important goal of law schools to instill in students a sense of obligation to perform pro bono work during their later careers." During the formative stages of their professional identity, future lawyers need to develop the skills and values that will sustain commitments to public service.

So too, many law faculties share the enthusiasm for school-based public-service programs that are gaining support among other educators. Such programs share a common premise: that students benefit in unique and valuable ways from community involvement, particularly if it is coordinated with their academic experience. On that assumption, a growing number of secondary schools are requiring community service, and many colleges and graduate schools are expanding support for such service as part of their curricular and extracurricular offerings. Supporters of these requirements believe that public-interest experiences encourage future public service and that they have independent educational value.

Among law students, evidence for the first assertion is thin but consistent. At Tulane, the first school to impose pro bono requirements, two-thirds of graduates reported that participation in public service had increased their willingness to participate in the future, and about three-quarters agreed that they had gained confidence in their ability to represent indigent clients. At other schools, between three-fourths and four-fifths of students who participated in mandatory pro bono programs also indicated that their experience had increased the likelihood that they would engage in similar work as practicing attorneys. * * *

Evidence concerning community-service programs outside of law schools is similarly limited. Surveys of participants generally find an increase in students' reported sense of social responsibility and their willingness to continue working for equal opportunity or helping those in need. But no research has tested those claims by analyzing postgraduate public service. All we know is that youthful involvement in volunteer activity increases the likelihood of adult participation. * * *

From the limited evidence available, the safest generalization seems to be that positive experience with pro bono work as a student will at least increase the likelihood of similar work later in life. Such experience can also break down the rigid distinctions that prevail in many law schools between students who are preparing for public-interest careers and those who are not. These "on-the-boat or off-the-boat" dichotomies send the wrong message about integrating private practice and public service.

The rationale for pro bono programs in law school does not, however, rest solely on these benefits. Whatever their effects on later public service, such programs have independent educational value. Like other forms of clinical and experiential learning, participation in public service helps bridge the gap between theory and practice, and enriches understanding of how law relates to life. For students as well as beginning lawyers, pro bono work often provides valuable training in interviewing, negotiating, drafting, problem solving, and working with individuals from diverse backgrounds. Aid to clients of limited means exposes students to the urgency of unmet needs and the law's capacity to cope with social problems. As former Tulane Law School Dean John Kramer notes, pro bono work can help "sensitize professionals to worlds they usually ignore." It also can increase their awareness of ethical issues and the human costs of professional inattention or incompetence.

So too, pro bono programs can provide other practical benefits to law students and law schools. For many participants, public service offers valuable career information and contacts. Students can get a better sense of their interests and talents, as well as a focus for further coursework and placement efforts. Pro bono experience also may encourage more individuals to press potential employers for information about their public-interest opportunities. Too many students who report interest in such opportunities now lack an adequate basis for comparison.

For law schools, pro bono programs can prove beneficial in several respects apart from their educational value. Most obviously, such programs demonstrate a tangible commitment to the community. Each year, at schools with well-developed programs, students provide as much as 16,000 hours of free legal assistance to underserved groups. Such assistance offers opportunities for cooperation with local bar organizations and for outreach to alumni who can become sources, sponsors, and supervisors for student projects. Successful projects can contribute to law school efforts in student recruitment, public relations, and development. In the AALS survey, over ninety percent of deans agreed that pro bono activities had provided valuable goodwill in the community, and two-thirds felt that such work had proven similarly valuable with alumni.

Given this range of benefits, it is hard to find anyone who opposes law school pro bono programs, at least in principle. In practice, however, considerable disagreement centers on the form these programs should take and on the priority they should assume in a world of scarce institutional resources.

* * *

Law schools support a broad variety of pro bono activities. To gain information about current programs, the AALS Commission asked deans whether their schools offered any opportunities, apart from in-house faculty-staffed clinics, for students to "provide uncompensated legal or other services to individuals or groups or participate in public policy matters or initiatives." By that definition, ninety-two percent of law schools had pro bono programs.

Such programs vary considerably in scope and structure. As noted earlier, about ten percent of schools make pro bono service mandatory, although they differ widely in what counts as service and how much is required. At one end of the spectrum are schools with fairly minimal demands, such as ten or twenty hours, which can include nonlegal as well as legal assistance. At the other end are schools that demand about forty to sixty hours of law-related service.

Schools also have different policies toward allowing externships or clinical courses to help satisfy the pro bono requirement. Some policies exclude any work done for academic credit on the theory that pro bono means uncompensated assistance. Other policies define all public-service placements as pro bono on the theory that no work done to meet a graduation requirement is uncompensated in a pure sense and that students should not be deterred from activities that are integrated with academic coursework.

Schools also differ in the kinds of substantive work that complies with mandatory pro bono policies. Some use an expansive definition, and include any services for nonprofit, public-interest, or government organizations. Other policies are more restrictive and require that the work assist indigent individuals. A third group of mandatory programs fall somewhere in between, and specify a variety of public-service placements from which students can choose.

Voluntary pro bono programs are equally varied. Some are highly structured, generously financed, and relatively well subscribed. Schools with these programs typically have a broad array of clinical courses and externships, as well as an active public-service office. Fordham Law School is an example. Its Public Interest Resource Center assists eleven student-run organizations providing legal and non-legal services. Clinics and externships offer community-service placements, and a fellowship program assists students who are preparing for public-service careers. By contrast, other schools provide relatively little support for pro bono work.

Student involvement is often limited to traditional charitable activities requiring fairly minimal time commitments and few legal skills. Common examples include blood or food drives, tutoring programs, food kitchens, and fundraising events for local community organizations or for the school's own summer public-interest fellowships.

Most schools fall somewhere in the middle. Even where administrative support is limited, many students display extraordinary initiative and commitment. Despite heavy demands from school, work, and family, law students devote thousands of unpaid hours to a wide range of projects. They assist low-income clients on issues including immigration, domestic violence, capital punishment, unemployment compensation, welfare, bankruptcy, wills, health care, social security, and juvenile justice. Law schools contribute to virtually all of the leading public-interest organizations in areas such as civil rights, civil liberties, environmental law, women's rights, and gay/lesbian rights.

Yet, considerable talent remains untapped. * * * Administrators who participated in the AALS Commission interviews estimated that only about one-quarter to one-third of the law students at their schools volunteered for service, and average time commitments were quite modest. Some student involvement remains at token levels and seems intended primarily as resume padding.

Not all faculty seem interested in setting a better example. In the AALS law school survey, only about half of the administrators of pro bono programs agreed that "[m]any of the faculty [at their] school provide good role models to the students by engaging in uncompensated public-service work themselves." About one-fifth disagreed and one-third were unsure. As some administrators added in followup interviews, if they were ignorant about professors' involvement, most students probably were as well. Even administrators who had reported that "many" faculty were good role models also believed that many faculty were not. This should come as no surprise in light of the limited institutional incentives for pro bono service, particularly for clients of limited means. Most law schools do not even have a policy requiring or encouraging faculty to engage in such work.

Nor does expanding pro bono participation appear to be a priority at most institutions. About two-thirds of the deans responding to the AALS survey were satisfied with the level of pro bono participation by faculty and students at their schools. Given the absence of involvement among most students and the absence of data concerning faculty, that level of satisfaction is itself somewhat unsatisfying. It is, however, scarcely surprising. Why should deans see a problem if no one else does?

And at most institutions, no one is complaining. Nor is the extent of any problem plainly visible. Neither ABA accreditors nor AALS membership-review teams ask for specific information on pro bono contributions by students and faculty. As noted earlier, there appears little institutional interest in collecting it. The absence of data on nonparticipation makes it easy to draw unduly positive generalizations from examples of involvement that are easily visible and especially vivid. High-profile cases by faculty or student clinics, or widespread participation in fundraising events for public-interest activities are likely to skew perceptions in positive directions. That tendency is reinforced by natural cognitive biases. When an event is particularly vivid, individuals generally overestimate its frequency, especially when it reflects well on themselves. Memorable pro bono work may lead faculty and students to magnify their involvement, particularly if they are not asked to keep records of the time spent.

Moreover, good pro bono programs require substantial administrative resources. In a world of significant funding constraints, such programs simply may not rank high enough in any constituency's pecking order to become an institutional priority. Professors have their own research and teaching needs to consider, and while many are deeply committed to personal pro bono work, few have been similarly concerned about creating cultures of commitment. According to a recent survey of 172 of the 177 law schools approved by the ABA, only three have imposed a pro bono requirement on professors, and the hours demanded have been minimal.

For most students, the tradeoffs have been similar. Although many might like to see additional administrative support for pro bono work, their resource priorities are likely to involve more pressing concerns, such as financial aid or loan forgiveness. Few student bodies have voted in favor of pro bono requirements, and one that did, Columbia, opted to exclude itself and to bind only future classes. * * *

So too, although most alumni and central university administrators undoubtedly support public service in principle, they have not translated rhetorical support into resource commitments. In the AALS survey, a majority of law school deans indicated that they would like to expand pro bono programs but lacked the necessary funds. For many law school and central university administrators, public-service initiatives seem less pressing than other budget items more directly linked to daily needs and national reputations. For example, U.S. News & World Report rankings of law schools have become increasingly important. Not only are pro bono opportunities excluded from the factors that determine a school's rank, they compete for resources with programs that do affect its position.

* * * If the principal goal of law school pro bono programs is to maximize future contributions by lawyers, it makes sense to maximize current contributions by students. The obvious way to accomplish that is to require service. Such a requirement sends the message that pro bono work is a professional obligation. A mandatory program generally increases resources for public-service programs and

reaches individuals who would not voluntarily participate. By their own accounts, some of these individuals become converts to the cause, and most students report a greater interest in future pro bono service as a result of required participation. Virtually all administrators of mandatory programs can point to individual success stories. For example, a Loyola student specializing in corporate tax insisted that he had no skills relevant to poverty communities and objected to being forced into service. After gaining a tax refund for his first low-income client, though, the student became one of the pro bono program's strongest supporters. Some of these supporters maintain continued involvement after graduation by supervising students and providing financial support.

Yet, as noted earlier, current research is insufficient to determine whether mandatory programs yield greater pro bono contributions than well-supported optional alternatives. * * * Students who see pro bono work simply as one more graduation requirement are missing the message that program supporters intend.

When participants are unmotivated or end up in unsuitable placements, the results can be counterproductive for all concerned. Program administrators do not lack for examples of students who feel ignored, bored, and unchallenged by routine tasks. For these reluctant participants, client contact often served to confirm adverse stereotypes of poverty communities. For example, one Pennsylvania student's work on welfare appeals left him with disgust for undeserving "able bodied" claimants who were abusing the system. Experiencebwith such participants can, in turn, discourage overburdened supervising lawyers from accepting further placements or from spending the time necessary to structure and monitor assignments. They prefer working with motivated pro bono volunteers and students doing externships or clinical coursework.

Supervisors' preferences compound the challenges of finding appropriate placements for mandatory service. Some administrators report difficulties identifying sufficient positions to accommodate students' time constraints, academic schedules, and skill levels. The extent of these difficulties depends primarily on the school's definition of pro bono work and its local network of service providers. Some schools, like Tulane, have solved their placement problems only by hiring supervising lawyers, which adds significantly to program costs.

Pro bono requirements pose other challenges apart from expense. One involves the definition of public service. Should it include only legal work or assistance targeted to the poor? Expansive definitions pose fewest problems in securing student placements, and provide many participants with a broader perspective on their legal work. On the other hand, inclusive programs also offer fewest opportunities for training students to meet the legal needs of underserved communities. Restrictive definitions serve that goal but bump up against shortages in supervised positions and accusations of ideological bias. Groups such as the Washington Legal Foundation have criticized law schools' public-interest placements for being skewed in favor of liberal causes. Related problems involve enforcing pro bono requirements and assuring the quality of client service provided. The difficulties of monitoring students and their supervisors have led some experts to prefer voluntary over mandatory programs, and others to advocate faculty-run clinics.

A final concern with pro bono requirements involves the appropriateness of exempting professors. "Do as I say, not as I do" is the position of faculty at all but a few schools, and its limitations have not gone unnoticed. As one Washington Post reporter noted, mandatory pro bono programs confront professors with the expectation that they should "take on the same responsibilities as, God forbid, the practicing bar and even their own students." Of course, pro bono requirements serve educational values apart from reinforcing a service ethic and these provide some basis for including only students. However, if the primary goal of a mandatory program is to create a culture of commitment to public service, then exempting faculty role models is counterproductive. As research on giving behavior makes clear, individuals learn more by example than exhortation. Unless and until faculty are willing to include themselves in any mandatory program, a voluntary alternative has obvious advantages.

Other benefits of an elective system involve its reinforcement of student initiative and altruistic commitment. At schools like Fordham, students do not simply participate in public service; they also learn how to run a public-service program. Participants develop the fundraising, recruitment, and community-outreach skills necessary to sustain pro bono involvement. They also experience the personal satisfaction that accompanies voluntary service. Because an elective program involves only committed participants, it generally is cheaper and easier to administer than a mandatory system.

Yet, some of these advantages are double-edged. Voluntary approaches fail to reach some individuals who might benefit most, and are especially likely to lack adequate resources and quality control. Also, insufficient clinical opportunities may seriously compromise students' educational experience. Unless and until more institutions make support for voluntary service a priority, a mandatory alternative has much to commend it.

In short, the single most important insight from law school pro bono efforts is that no single model is clearly preferable. Different approaches create different tradeoffs, which vary from institution to institution. Designing an appropriate program requires schools to assess their own priorities, resources, community networks, faculty support, and student culture. Whatever structure schools choose, they can benefit from the experiences of other institutions. Recent efforts to encourage pro bono service suggest the following strategies, which are likely to prove beneficial no matter what kind of program is in place. * * *

HEATHER MACDONALD, *WHAT GOOD IS PRO BONO?*,

10 City J., Spring, 2000, at 14

For most of its history, the organized bar in America has been conservatism incarnate, standing foursquare for the sanctity of property rights and the rule of law. Today, there is hardly a cause too left-wing to receive its patronage. Do you advocate expanding entitlements, blocking welfare reform, multiplying the victim classes, or promoting homosexual rights? The bar wants to help, and its most elite members want to help most of all. The whitest-shoe corporate law firms will shower you with funding, provide million-dollar attorneys to sit on your board, and maybe even furnish a $600-an-hour litigator to prosecute your case for free.

The bar has hardly forsworn its intimate relationship with corporate America, of course. But even as it earns billions of dollars a year in fees from its business clients, it pursues a variety of causes that would have astounded the bar's early leaders. It does so in the name of a venerable legal tradition: pro bono publico law, or legal service undertaken "for the public good." Pro bono publico law went through a radical transformation in the 1960s; ever since, it has been the vehicle through which elite corporate lawyers could participate in the entitlements revolution, in the litigation revolution that turned lawyers and judges into unelected legislators, and in the cultural revolution that turned America into a nation of victims. * * *

Starting in the 1970s, the ABA and local bar associations began furiously cranking out position papers on pro bono work and revising relevant codes of professional responsibility to further the bar's involvement in the advocacy agenda. Over a decade ago, the Ford Foundation created the ABA's Law Firm Pro Bono Project, which pressures elite firms to commit 3 to 5 percent of their total billable hours to hands-on pro bono work, in addition to donating money to legal groups that represent the poor. The pressure has been effective. Many large firms now have full-time pro bono coordinators or partners, complete with staff; almost as many regularly place associates with advocacy and legal services groups on a rotating basis. The organized bars and the advocacy groups together have created an elaborate infrastructure to link big firms with the ever-proliferating public interest law outfits.

This infrastructure urges firms to take on big, politically charged cases. The results: in just the last several years, titans of the corporate bar have sued to dissolve anti-gang injunctions in gang-infested southern California areas; to fight quality-of-life law enforcement in San Francisco; to saddle prisons with court orders; to allow felons to vote; to block the death penalty in hundreds of cases, including for a woman who kidnapped and sexually abused a 13-year-old girl, injected the girl with drain cleaner, then shot her in the back when she didn't die; to force gun manufacturers to pay potentially millions in damages to crime victims; to defend minority set-asides and preferential admissions policies; to require bilingual education for Haitians; to make the Virginia Military Institute and the Citadel admit girl cadets; to declare the busty waitresses at the Hooters restaurant chain victims of gender discrimination; to compel the Boy Scouts to accept homosexual scoutmasters; to block the classification of AIDS as a sexually transmitted, or even communicable, disease; to enact homosexual marriage; and to challenge industrial facilities on grounds of "environmental racism." In New York City alone, big-firm panjandrums have sued to force the city to pay union-scale wages to workfare workers; to enjoin aggressive crime-fighting in high-crime neighborhoods; to force the city to spend even more on the HIV-infected than the mind-boggling amount it already disburses; to wring $600 million from the city in a sex discrimination case (successfully prosecuted); to require the Saint Patrick's Day Parade to accept homosexual-rights marchers; and to force New York City to create special foster-care programs for children who "question their sexuality." And this is just a sampling of cases undertaken in the name of the public good.

* * * Pro bono work provides many other opportunities for showering taxpayer dollars on favorite charities. To understand how this works, first jettison the biggest misconception about contemporary pro bono litigation: that it is done for free. In fact, firms purporting to be fulfilling their public service obligations sometimes rake in thousands, even millions, of dollars in fees, usually from the government. The firms cash in under statutes that allow winning plaintiffs in rights cases to collect their attorneys' fees from the defendant (though the rationale that firms wouldn't otherwise take such cases breaks down in a pro bono context). The Silicon Valley powerhouse firm of Wilson Sonsini Goodrich & Rosati demanded $8.3 million in fees from defendant California in a prison litigation suit, then magnanimously settled for $3.5 million. San Francisco's Morrison & Foerster collected $1.24 million from California for invalidating a parental notification requirement for minors seeking abortions.

Having collected fees for something they claim to be doing charitably, a remarkable 30 percent of big firms pocket the entire sum without apology. The rest make an enormous show of donating some or all of the money—fresh from taxpayers' pockets—to their favorite public interest group. Often the recipient is the very advocacy group with which the firm just co-litigated, and the money goes to finance more suits against the public treasury. Thus is the litigation machine kept ever stoked with taxpayer dollars.

* * *

Many big-firm lawyers today sound like Marxist academics when they discuss pro bono work. Take John Kiernan, a $600-an-hour litigation partner at Debevoise & Plimpton, who is also director of Legal Services for New York and the Lawyers Committee for Civil Rights Under the Law. Scorning the homely small-town tradition of pro bono work, he defines pro bono for "us big-city litigators" as the "process of committing resources for the legal representation of the disenfranchised."

"Disenfranchised" is pretty strong stuff, calling up images of a racist South trampling on voting rights. Asked for an example of the disenfranchised today, Kiernan cites blacks allegedly targeted by the New York City police for stop-and-frisks. Are their legislators not representing them? "I mean disempowered, not disenfranchised literally," he says.

But disempowered? Consider that Kiernan's firm, spurred on by the Amadou Diallo shooting, is suing the New York City Police Department, charging that its Street Crimes Unit illegally singles out blacks for street stops. In the wake of that shooting, black leaders in New York City and beyond focused unprecedented international attention on the NYPD; they persuaded the president, the First Lady, the Justice Department, the U.S. Civil Rights Commission, the New York attorney general, and a host of lesser political entities to denounce the department. Given that political muscle, it strains credulity to claim that blacks in Harlem and the Bronx lack political power.

But wait, there is one group that is literally disenfranchised today—felons—and Debevoise & Plimpton has sued to change that, too. Kiernan claims that the law that disenfranchises felons violates blacks' voting rights, because so many blacks are in prison. Kiernan has no problem taking away white felons' voting rights, but "you worry when [the disenfranchisement laws] have a racial impact." Isn't the real problem the black crime rate? No, because the drug sentencing laws discriminate, too, he says—a dodge that ignores the very real problem of crime and violence in minority neighborhoods.

* * *

Fortunately, pro bono work has broadened in the last several years beyond adversarial suits against government and claims of discrimination. Now, corporate attorneys from Paul Weiss and Winthrop Stimson, among other firms, help small businesses, many of them located in minority areas or empowerment zones, with their legal needs. Milbank Tweed lawyers counsel individuals seeking to adopt children and help elderly homeowners trapped in foreclosure proceedings. Cleary Gottlieb attorneys mentor inner-city high school students. The Volunteers of Legal Services, a New York City pro bono clearinghouse, finds attorneys for poor elderly people needing legal help. There has even been a slight counter-movement to include more "conservative" cases in support of personal responsibility, assimilation, and color-blindness. In a landmark for conservative pro bono work, Los Angeles-based Gibson, Dunn & Crutcher represented Cheryl Hopwood in her successful challenge to racial preferences at the University of Texas Law School. Davis Polk has defended the eviction of drug dealers from public housing and recently supported a family member's request to medicate a severely psychotic sibling without her consent. Skadden, Arps, Slate, Meagher & Flom defended California's ballot initiative banning bilingual education against a court challenge, albeit anonymously.

Still, at least Skadden Arps took the case—unlike the prestigious Manhattan firm where two partners wanted to argue against racial gerrymandering several years ago, also without using their firm's name on the legal papers. They were forbidden, on the grounds that fighting for color-blind legislative districting would tar the firm as "racist" at law schools. "I became discouraged," one of the partners recalls. "To take a high-profile conservative case—too many people here think it's disgusting."

Overall, getting prestigious firms to accept conservative cases pro bono remains an uphill struggle. Top-scoring Chinese-American students, barred by racial quotas from San Francisco's prestigious Lowell High School, were turned away by every big San Francisco firm they solicited for pro bono representation. Dennis Saffran of the mildly conservative Center for the Community Interest, an advocate for public safety and quality of life, says that finding pro bono counsel for every case is "a fight." By contrast, when the ABA sent out a call for additional firms to represent homosexual scoutmaster James Dale against the Boy Scouts, Morrison & Foerster's pro bono coordinator Kathi Pugh had a Mo Foe attorney lined up "within an hour," she says. Other firms, such as Kramer Levin Naftalis & Frankel, signed up as well.

It is time for firms to ask whether their pro bono programs in fact serve the public good. The problems of the long-term poor today cannot be solved with litigation; attorneys would accomplish far more acting as Big Brothers and Big Sisters, scoutmasters, and tutors. Though the pro bono industry pushes for bigger and bigger cases, what the most troubled poor need is on the micro level—an understanding of work, the commitment to stay in school, a stable family. If benefits and more government spending could solve juvenile delinquency, non-work, or illegitimacy, we would have solved them long ago.

* * *

B. Should the Rules Mandate Equal Opportunity?

New York Rule 8.4(g)

A lawyer or law firm shall not:

* * *

(g) unlawfully discriminate in the practice of law, including in hiring, promoting or otherwise determining conditions of employment on the basis of age, race, creed, color, national origin, sex, disability, marital status or sexual orientation. Where there is a tribunal with jurisdiction to hear a complaint, if timely brought, other than a Departmental Disciplinary Committee, a complaint based on unlawful discrimination shall be brought before such tribunal in the first instance. A certified copy of a determination by such a tribunal, which has become final and enforceable and as to which the right to judicial or appellate review has been exhausted, finding that the lawyer has engaged in an unlawful discriminatory practice shall constitute prima facie evidence of professional misconduct in a disciplinary proceeding[.]

AM. BAR ASS'N PRESIDENTIAL INITIATIVE COMM'N ON DIVERSITY, *2009 ABA STUDY OF THE STATE OF DIVERSITY IN THE LEGAL PROFESSION,*

http://new.abanet.org/centers/diversity/PublicDocuments/Diversity_Summary_Report.pdf

Several racial and ethnic groups, sexual and gender minorities, and lawyers with disabilities continue to be vastly underrepresented in the legal profession. From a racial/ethnic perspective, Whites constitute about 70% of working people over age 16, yet they represent 89% of all lawyers and 90% of all judges, according to 2009 census data. Each year, the numbers of lawyers with disabilities and openly lesbian, gay, bisexual or transgendered (LGBT) lawyers increase slightly, but their respective representation remains less than 1%. For example, in 2009 NALP (Directory of Legal Employers) reported that only about 47% of reporting law offices had even one openly LGBT lawyer, and most are clustered in just four large coastal cities. Most law offices do not collect data on disabilities, but the 18% that do report data (about 110,000 lawyers) identified only 255 lawyers with a disability.

This Report devotes its pages to specific recommendations for increasing diversity in the different sectors of the profession, namely law firms and corporations, the judiciary and government, law schools and the academy, and bar associations.

* * * The overarching message is that a diverse legal profession is more just, productive and intelligent because diversity, both cognitive and cultural, often leads

to better questions, analyses, solutions, and processes. To provide a conceptual and normative context, the Report articulates and re-emphasizes four rationales for creating greater diversity within the legal profession and draws attention to similar diversity efforts and reporting in the medical profession. Compelling arguments for diversity in the legal profession include:

The Democracy Argument: Lawyers and judges have a unique responsibility for sustaining a political system with broad participation by all its citizens. A diverse bar and bench create greater trust in the mechanisms of government and the rule of law.

The Business Argument: Business entities are rapidly responding to the needs of global customers, suppliers, and competitors by creating workforces from many different backgrounds, perspectives, skill sets, and tastes. Ever more frequently, clients expect and sometimes demand lawyers who are culturally and linguistically proficient.

The Leadership Argument. Individuals with law degrees often possess the communication and interpersonal skills and the social networks to rise into civic leadership positions, both in and out of politics. Justice Sandra Day O'Connor recognized this when she noted in Grutter v. Bollinger that law schools serve as the training ground for such leadership and therefore access to the profession must be broadly inclusive.

The Demographic Argument. The U.S. is becoming diverse along many dimensions and we expect (and hope) that the profile of GLBT lawyers and lawyers with disabilities will increase more rapidly. With respect to the nation's racial/ethnic populations, the Census Bureau projects that by 2042 the U.S. will be a "majority minority" country.

Nicole Lancia, Note, New Rule, New York: A Bifocal Approach to Discipline and Discrimination,

22 Geo. J. Legal Ethics 949 (2009)

* * *

The special responsibilities and ethical duties of lawyers to clients, the public, and the legal profession support the need for specific disciplinary rules prohibiting discrimination by lawyers and law firms. Those in the legal profession charged with upholding principles of fairness and justice are and should be held to higher ethical standards.

* * *

The ABA heavily debated the adoption of an anti-discrimination amendment to * * * Rule 8.4, but failed to reach a consensus on the appropriate language to amend the text and therefore, never officially adopted a rule prohibiting discrimination in the legal profession. Article 8 of the ABA * * * Rules of Professional Conduct prescribes five black-letter rules on "[m]aintaining the [i]ntegrity of the [p]rofession." * * * Rule 8.4 addresses general instances of professional misconduct, one of which is * * * Rule 8.4(d), which states that it is professional misconduct for a lawyer to "engage in conduct that is prejudicial to the administration of justice . . . ." Comment 3 provides illustrative guidance on the intended application of Model Rule 8.4(d) to knowing manifestations of bias or prejudice by attorneys in the course of representing a client.

* * * Although the ABA never adopted a black-letter rule prohibiting discrimination by lawyers, several state bars currently have some version of an anti-discrimination rule, but some do not. This section will textually compare five approaches to prohibiting anti-discrimination, exemplified by the District of Columbia, Florida, California, Minnesota, and New York. These five rules represent a continuum of categorical approaches to addressing discrimination within the legal profession, ranging from limited, under-inclusive rules in the District of Columbia, Florida and California, to Minnesota's broad, over-inclusive rule, and finally, to New York's sufficiently-inclusive bifocal rule as a means to maintaining the integrity of the legal profession as a whole. * * *

The anti-discrimination rules of the District of Columbia, Florida, and California prohibit discrimination in determining conditions of employment only, the practice of law only, and in determining the conditions of employment and accepting or terminating client representation, respectively.

Since 1991, the District of Columbia's Rules of Professional Conduct have included non-discrimination Rule 9.1. This Rule states: "A lawyer shall not discriminate against any individual in conditions of employment because of the individual's race, color, religion, national origin, sex, age, marital status, sexual orientation, family responsibility, or physical handicap." The District of Columbia did not intend Rule 9.1 "to create ethical obligations that exceed those imposed on a lawyer by applicable law." For example, if a member of the District of Columbia bar refuses to hire homosexuals in his Virginia office, he does not violate Rule 9.1 because "neither Virginia nor Maryland, nor the Federal law, expressly forbid discrimination in employment based on sexual orientation." Rule 9.1 is limited for two reasons: first, it does not address discrimination in the practice of law, but only in conditions of employment; second, since the rule expressly intends to avoid overstepping the laws of states where the conduct occurred, its enforcement of non-discrimination in conditions of employment relies on whether a particular form of discrimination is unlawful in the state where the conduct occurs.

In 1993, the Supreme Court of Florida approved the Florida Bar's petition to amend Rule 4-8.4(d) relating to misconduct, which states that a lawyer shall not:

> engage in conduct in connection with the practice of law that is prejudicial to the administration of justice, including to knowingly, or through callous indifference, disparage, humiliate, or discriminate against litigants, jurors, witnesses, court personnel, or other lawyers on any basis, including, but not limited to, on account of race, ethnicity, gender, religion, national origin, disability, marital status, sexual orientation, age, socioeconomic status, employment, or physical characteristics.

Florida's rule "made diversity a component of its Rules of Professional Conduct" in the adoption of this rule, which was proposed "because studies by the Florida Supreme Court Racial and Ethnic Bias Study Commission and the Florida Supreme Court Gender Bias Study Commission identified a number of problems faced by minorities and women in the legal profession." The Florida Bar proposed rules specifically dealing with discrimination in employment, but the Florida Supreme Court did not adopt them because "[the] Court's constitutional authority over the courts of Florida and attorney admission and discipline does not extend to the employment practices of lawyers." Florida's Rule 4-8.4(d) is thus limited in scope similar to D.C.'s Rule 9.1, but Rule 4-8.4(d) applies only to conduct connected with the practice of law, not conditions of employment.

California adopted Rule 2-400 in 1993 after eight years of discussion and debate by the Board Committee on Professional Standards about adding a new rule to prohibit discriminatory conduct by attorneys. This rule, like New York's DR 1-102(A)(6), applies to law firms as well as lawyers, but unsuccessfully attempts to extend to both employment practices and the practice of law. Rule 2-400(B) (1)-(2) states:

In the management or operation of a law practice, a member shall not unlawfully discriminate or knowingly permit unlawful discrimination on the basis of race, national origin, sex, sexual orientation, religion, age or disability in: (1) hiring, promoting, discharging of otherwise determining the conditions of employment of any person; or (2) accepting or terminating representation of any client.

Under Rule 2-400(B)(2), a lawyer or law firm cannot discriminate when accepting or terminating representation, but this provision does not include discrimination during representation of a client. California has various state discrimination laws, most of which prohibit discrimination in employment by any person or business establishment. A lawyer may only be subject to professional discipline for discriminating in the practice of law under other California laws, such as

California Business & Professions Code § 125.6, concerning discrimination in the "performance of a licensed activity," in this case, the practice of law. Rule 2-400(B) specifically addresses workplace discrimination in determining conditions of employment, but does not extend to, and provides no discipline for, discrimination during the representation of a client.

Taken together, these three rules address discrimination in multiple aspects of a lawyer's professional activities: However, each individual rule ignores discrimination either in the practice of law or determining conditions of employment. * * *

Minnesota's anti-discrimination rule broadly applies to all of a lawyer's activities, even those done in an extra-professional capacity. Minnesota's Rule 8.4(h) makes it professional misconduct for a lawyer to:

> commit a discriminatory act, prohibited by federal, state, or local statute or ordinance that reflects adversely on the lawyer's fitness as a lawyer. Whether a discriminatory act reflects adversely on a lawyer's fitness as a lawyer shall be determined after consideration of all the circumstances, including: (1) the seriousness of the act, (2) whether the lawyer knew that it was prohibited by statute or ordinance, (3) whether the act was part of a pattern of prohibited conduct, and (4) whether the act was committed in connection with the lawyer's professional activities[.]

Rule 8.4(h) was developed after the Minnesota Supreme Court Task Force for Gender Fairness in the Courts, established in 1987, found that participants in the courtroom were subjected to discriminatory treatment based on gender and that sexual harassment was highly common in the legal profession. This subcommittee convened initially to consider amending the Rules of Professional Conduct to prohibit discrimination in the attorney's professional capacity, but eventually drafted an over-inclusive rule covering all acts by lawyers, professionally and extra-professionally. Moreover, the effectiveness of Rule 8.4(h) is questionable in light of its requirement that the unlawful discriminatory act reflect adversely on the lawyer's fitness to practice law. * * *

New York Code of Professional Responsibility DR 1-102(A)(6)[4] is the only state ethics rule implementing a bifocal approach, as it explicitly prohibits lawyers and law firms from discriminating both in the practice of law *and* determining conditions of employment. DR 1-102(A)(6) provides that a lawyer or "law firm" shall not: "Unlawfully discriminate in the practice of law, including in hiring, promoting or otherwise determining conditions of employment, on the basis of age, race, creed, color, national origin, sex, disability, marital status, or sexual orientation . . . ."

---

4   This provision has been recodified as Rule 8.4(g), *supra*.

Furthermore, the rule states that any complaint based on unlawful discrimination must be brought before a tribunal before being submitted to a disciplinary committee and that a finding of unlawful discriminatory practice constitutes *prima facie* evidence of professional misconduct in a disciplinary proceeding. Thus, it provides procedural safeguards against an influx of meritless claims by requiring that the conduct violate existing anti-discrimination laws and that a complaint be brought to a tribunal before a disciplinary committee.

DR 1-102(A)(6) allows for disciplinary action to be taken for discrimination both in the practice of law and determining conditions of employment. It therefore simultaneously avoids limiting the focus to only one aspect of a lawyer's duties and overreaching into a lawyer's private activities.

* * * The legal profession should not be narrowly confined to the practice of law and the role of lawyers as client representatives in courtrooms, but should necessarily include the relationship between lawyers and the ethical duties that lawyers owe to each other as administrators of justice. Anti-discrimination rules should envision and acknowledge the legal profession as encompassing both sets of duties. DR 1-102(A)(6) encompasses both realms of the legal profession, recognizing the importance of the attorney-client relationship and attorney-attorney relations in maintaining "public trust and confidence" in the profession. State bar associations should adopt New York's bifocal approach to combat discrimination in the legal profession as a whole, governing lawyers and law firms in their conduct towards clients and other lawyers. * * *

Lawyers should conduct themselves professionally and personally in accordance with the requirements of the law. First, state Rules of Professional Conduct governing lawyers should prohibit discrimination in the practice of law because of the lawyer's duty to her client, the public and ultimately, the profession. Second, in light of recent studies on diversity in law firms, including partnership and turnover rates of racial minorities and women in law firms, state rules should also prohibit discrimination in determining conditions of employment to fully effectuate a policy of increasing diversity in the legal profession, thereby improving the profession. * * *

Public trust and confidence in the legal system is necessarily related to and predicated upon trust and confidence in the legal profession generally and in the ethical standards by which lawyers govern themselves and are governed within the profession. Therefore, it is essential that disciplinary rules prohibit discrimination in the practice of law. The lawyer's professional obligation to perform these duties can only be fulfilled by promoting an ethics of equality and impartiality in the legal profession.

State bar associations have a legitimate interest in prohibiting discrimination in "hiring, promoting, or otherwise determining conditions of employment." A disciplinary rule prohibiting discrimination in this capacity would arguably motivate law firms to continue their efforts to increase diversity in recruitment, promotions, and development, which in turn would positively influence the public image of the profession. By working to promote diversity, law firms, in turn, consciously aim to prevent employment discrimination, thereby maintaining the integrity of the profession.

In 2006, the ABA urged all state and territorial bar associations to increase diversity in the legal profession through collaborating with state or territory bar examiners, accredited law schools, colleges and universities, and elementary and secondary schools. Despite efforts to increase diversity in the profession, an examination of partnership and turnover rates in law firms by race and gender reveals only a slight improvement for racial and ethnic minorities and women.

In 2007, minorities at major law firms comprised 18.07.% of associates and 5.4% of partners, up from 2.55% in 1993 Among the New York offices of major law firms, in 2006 minorities accounted for 15.2% of all attorneys, the same percentage as in 2004. Minorities comprised 5% of partners and 7.4% of new partner promotions in 2006, as compared with 4.7% of partners and 7% of new partner promotions in 2004. Racial and ethnic minority associates across the board have an attrition rate of 29.6% while the rate for their white counterparts is 26.9%. "While partner turnover is quite low even for minorities, the racial gap is still a cause for concern given the low representation of minorities in the partnership overall . . . ." The stagnation of minorities in partnership positions, high minority attrition rate, and overall underrepresentation of minorities and women in law firms indicate the need for law firms to create more inclusive, diverse workplaces to retain and develop minority attorneys.

NALP 2007 figures report an increase in women partners overall at 18.4%, compared with 12.27% in 1993. The New York offices of major law firms lagged somewhat behind this nationwide percentage—16.6% in 2006. However, in January 2006, women in New York offices represented 29% of the most recent partner promotions, increasing from 20.3% in 2004. Women associates have a higher turnover rate than men associates, but at the partnership level, the attrition rate for women is 7.2%, compared with 8.1% for men. Men and women of color account for 5.1% of total partners in New York offices, with men of color comprising 3.4% and women of color comprising 1.7%. NALP 2007 figures showed that only 1.65% of partners and 10.07% of associates at major firms were women of color. Collectively, men and women of color have higher turnover rates at all firm levels. Men of color have the highest partner turnover rate. However, women of color have the highest attrition rates at all levels other than partnership.

The women of color turnover rate can be attributed to their unique perception of the lack of diversity in law firms as both racial and ethnic minorities and women. Also, women of color are not only more likely to experience discrimination, but they are also less likely to report it.

There is considerable diversity across race and gender in associate ranks in New York firms, but that is not yet reflected in partnership ranks. Though law firms may hire or attempt to hire diverse incoming associate classes, minority and women attrition accounts for the relative representational invisibility of these groups. Firms are making progress with regard to women attorneys generally, but should make stronger efforts to "attract, retain, and advance" women of color and implement anti-discrimination policies. A disciplinary rule prohibiting discrimination in conditions of employment would arguably motivate firms to implement such a policy, and promote diversity in law firms and the legal profession.

* * * DR 1-102(A)(6) has been generally effective in shaping policies of anti-discrimination, justice, and respect for the profession. However, it has only been implemented to impose disciplinary action and sanctions on lawyers who violate the rule in the practice of law, and has not yet been used as a basis for law firm discipline for discriminating in conditions of employment.

New York courts have found violations of DR 1-102(A)(6) and consequently taken disciplinary action and imposed sanctions on attorneys for gender and race discrimination against other attorneys. In 1992, the state supreme court ordered financial sanctions against an attorney for calling opposing counsel "little girl" and repeatedly demeaning her on account of her gender. The court noted that such offensive language is "not proper professional conduct" and "tarnishes *963 the image of the legal profession." In 2002, New York Appellate Division's Second Department publicly censured an attorney for his race-based abuse of opposing counsel in violation of DR 1-102(A)(6). The attorney harangued the opposing counsel, a black woman, for her pronunciation of the words "establish" and "especially." After disciplinary action by a federal court and an order to pay fines and costs in a separate hearing, the attorney sent a formal letter of apology conceding that his conduct violated DR 1-102(A)(6) and the opposing counsel and prosecuting attorney determined that public censure was appropriate, with which the Second Department agreed. As these cases demonstrate, DR 1-102(A)(6) successfully enables courts to discipline lawyers for discrimination in the practice of law.

However, DR 1-102(A)(6) has not proven effective in disciplining law firms for discriminatory practices in hiring, promoting, or otherwise determining conditions of employment. In general, law firm discipline is infrequent and virtually non-existent in any jurisdiction, and in New York, "there has been no public enforcement and only two 'private admonitions' of firms." Allegations of discrimination by law firms in conditions of employment may arise, but ultimately settle privately. More often, perceptions of discrimination in the workplace are unreported.

New York has only found law firms liable for discrimination in conditions of employment under existing state laws. In 1993, the Division of Human Rights found that a law firm discriminated against the complainant by terminating his employment because he had the AIDS virus, in violation of the state Human Rights Law. The Division awarded compensatory damages of $500,000 and back pay from the date of the complainant's termination to the date of his death.

DR 1-102(A)(6) effectively provides a means to discipline lawyers for violations of the first prong of the rule--discrimination in the practice of law--but has failed to discipline law firms for discrimination in conditions of employment. With respect to the second prong, DR 1-102(A)(6) is aspirational at best. In light of the ineffectiveness of DR 1-102(A)(6) in imposing disciplinary action for discrimination in conditions of employment, the New York State Bar Association should consider ways to ensure that the rule is actually enforced, not theoretically available.

State bar associations should and must be able to discipline lawyers, as members of the legal profession, for discrimination in the practice of law and conditions of employment. State bars should adopt New York's bifocal approach to instill in its members a sense of commitment to the multiple responsibilities and duties lawyers are expected to fulfill and also, to contribute to state and national efforts to increase diversity in the profession. The adoption of a rule with this type of bifocal approach inevitably garners public trust and confidence in the legal justice system because it exemplifies the integrity of the legal profession and the profession's adherence to ethical and moral foundations of justice.

* * *

AKSHAT TEWARY, *LEGAL ETHICS AS A MEANS TO ADDRESS THE PROBLEM OF ELITE LAW FIRM NON-DIVERSITY*,

12 Asian L.J. 1 (2005)

* * *

Several important commentators have recognized the significant lack of diversity in the field of law, and have called for action to resolve it. To address this issue, the ABA created a Task Force on Minorities in the Legal Profession, which issued a set of recommendations and best practices that would improve law firm diversity. In Miles to Go 2000: Progress of Minorities in the Legal Profession, the ABA's Commission on Racial and Ethnic Diversity in the Profession reported numerous disturbing statistics that demonstrate the gravity of the diversity situation.

The field of law is already one of the least integrated professions in the country. In fact, the ABA found that only two professions, the natural sciences and dentistry, feature less diversity than law. For example, whereas African Americans and Hispanics comprised 14.3% of all accountants, 9.7% of physicians, and 9.4% of university professors in 1998, they made up a mere 7.5% of all lawyers. Another report indicates that, in 1996-1997, African Americans received 7.36% of all law degrees granted for that school year, even though they comprised almost 13% of the U.S. population at that time. The case of Asian American representation in the law is somewhat special in that Asian Americans are actually slightly overrepresented, but an analysis of Asian American representation across the professions still suggests a relatively lower presence in the law. The Asian American population according to the U.S. Census 2000 was 4.2% of the national population. According to statistics compiled by the U.S. Department of Education, in 1999-2000, Asian Americans received 10.7% of all professional degrees granted that year, including 18.8% of dentistry degrees, 17.3% of medicine degrees, 20.1% of pharmacy degrees, but only 6.4% of law degrees. Thus, although Asian Americans were overrepresented in virtually every profession, such overrepresentation was smallest in the law.

These statistics are an already troubling disapprobation of commitment to diversity in the legal profession as a whole. Unfortunately, the nation's elite law firms, in particular, suffer even more acutely from non-integration than the legal profession at large. Indeed, the Law School Admissions Council's research confirms that the number of minorities in private practice is disproportionately lower than their number in law schools. According to a survey conducted by David B. Wilkins and G. Mitu Gulati, minorities constitute 17.2% of the lawyers employed by government agencies in the Chicago area. By contrast, they found that minorities make up a mere 3.6% of the large Chicago firms. The disparity is starker at managerial levels: they found that minority lawyers make up 19.5% of supervisors in the government agencies, but only 1.6% of the partners in the elite law firms they had surveyed. Unless one is prepared to assume that the government's lawyers are of a lower caliber, these numbers demonstrate that qualified minority lawyers are "out there," but are underutilized. These statistics are confirmed by more recent research conducted by the National Association for Law Placement (NALP), an organization that surveys the nation's largest law firms annually. The research indicates that, although almost 30% of the country is minority, attorneys of color comprise 15.06% of associate positions and a mere 4.32% of partner positions at major law firms. In fact, 43% of the offices of surveyed firms had no minority partners at all.

It is true that some progress has been made in firm diversity in recent times as compared to years ago. However, there is evidence that this progress can oftentimes be ephemeral; as minorities take one step forward, they seem to take another one back. For example, a 2003 NALP study on associate retention found that 29.6% of male minority associates left within 28 months of starting, as compared to 21.6% of men overall, and 68% of minority males left within 55 months, as compared to 52.3% of men overall. Similarly, 64.4% of female minority associates left within 55 months, as compared to 54.9% of women overall. The ABA confirmed this trend by finding that over 50% of minority associates at law firms leave within three years. There is evidence that minorities suffer such high attrition rates partly because they feel social and professional isolation, and because they are not given quality work assignments. Thus, there is a real risk that, recent gains in hiring notwithstanding, a significant number of minorities at elite firms face difficulty in achieving something more than token advancement. This puts the contrast between the 15.06% figure for minority associates and 4.32% for minority partners, cited above, in startling perspective. These problems are more pronounced for female attorneys of color, who are even less likely than their male counterparts to begin their careers in private practice.

Numerous other commentators have echoed these observations, finding that problems of diversity are especially distressing among elite law firms.

* * *

If one were to accept * * * that elite law firms unconsciously discriminate against minorities, thereby leading to disproportionately fewer minority attorneys working in these firms, a logical conclusion might be that federal employment discrimination law should be utilized to counteract and penalize these practices. However, Title VII has been largely unhelpful in combating non-overt forms of discrimination, both in general and with respect to law firms in particular. There is little reason to believe it could be of much utility to the cause for elite law firm diversity.

Title VII of the Civil Rights Act of 1964 prohibits employment discrimination on the basis of race (and other characteristics). A Title VII case can be brought on the basis of two theories: disparate impact or disparate treatment. Under a disparate treatment claim, the plaintiff seeks to prove that the employer intentionally discriminated against him on the basis of race, color, religion, sex, or national origin. The plaintiff has the burden of ultimately proving this discriminatory intent, although in some cases it can be established inferentially. By contrast, a disparate impact claim is (theoretically) easier to prove since it only requires a plaintiff to show that a facially neutral practice has a disproportionately adverse impact on a protected group (such as a racial group, a religious group, etc.). However, much of the usefulness of this doctrine has been eviscerated by recent cases that have required something akin to proof of discriminatory intent in disparate impact cases.

It has been exceedingly difficult to prove discriminatory intent in cases where employment decisions involve subjective decision-making. * * * [A]side from the usage of (ostensibly) objective signals to screen applicants, law firms make their hiring decisions largely based upon whether the candidate would make a good "fit" for the firm. This is necessarily an amorphous and subjective determination. * * *

Title VII is especially ineffective because it is burdened by what Alan David Freeman has term the "perpetrator perspective." In his view, antidiscrimination law perceives discrimination not as a continuing, psychological process, but rather as an atomistic action or series of actions whereby perpetrators inflict harm upon victims. By focusing solely on inappropriate conduct (malevolent, overt racism), the antidiscrimination regime does little to address the underlying conditions of racial discrimination, such as disparities in money, housing, and in the case of elite law firms, jobs. Freeman would prefer if antidiscrimination law adopted a victim perspective, which would require affirmative efforts to change these discriminatory conditions directly.

The perpetrator perspective is also problematic because it is undergirded by the principle of formal equality. The implication of the formal equality principle is that all people have equal opportunities to succeed in society, regardless of race, and that compensating those few individuals who are discriminated against by blatantly racist acts will ensure that society remains equal. Under this thinking, members of each race are all placed on an even level, and any distributive inequalities that ensue are attributable to merit and worth. * * *

Antidiscrimination law, shackled by the perpetrator perspective, is unable to look beyond the simplistic formal equality doctrine, and is therefore of little use in combating unconscious institutional racism in law firm hiring. Both disparate treatment and disparate impact claims are inherently compensatory and reactionary in that they focus on redressing obvious wrongs and not on effecting positive change.

* * * Not surprisingly, courts have been averse to finding discrimination in the subjective decision-making of firms. The case of Lawrence Mungin serves as an excellent example of antidiscrimination law's inability to correct discriminatory practices at law firms.

Mungin was raised by a single mother in a Queens housing project, and eventually worked his way to Harvard College and Harvard Law School. After working at other firms, Mungin was hired as a lateral by the Washington, D.C. office of Katten, Muchin & Zavis as a senior bankruptcy associate. Mungin claimed that while working at Katten, he was mistreated on a frequent and continual basis.

For example, he was excluded from the bankruptcy practice group's meetings even though he was a senior bankruptcy associate. In one instance, the firm called in a white associate from another office to speak with a client about the firm's bankruptcy practice, even though Mungin had had experience dealing with complex bankruptcy transactions at prior firms. Despite being a seventh year associate with extensive experience in bankruptcy, Mungin was consistently given work at a second or third year associate level, and at times at a paralegal level. In fact, Mungin was once called for an important meeting with a client, and was notified that his only role at the meeting would be to carry the overheard projector for a presentation.

Mungin did not receive performance reviews on schedule, but the ones he did receive were generally approbatory. Understandably, Mungin became dissatisfied with his treatment at Katten, and after being passed up for partner, he sued the firm on the basis of Title VII employment discrimination. At the district court level, a jury trial was held, and the jury found that the firm had indeed discriminated against Mungin, and awarded him $1 million in compensatory damages and another $1.5 million in punitive damages. After interpreting the evidence, the jurors admitted that the defense had an extremely weak case, and that they had decided to award punitive damages in order to make sure that it did not discriminate against other attorneys in the way it had against Mungin.

However, two white judges on the D.C. Court of Appeals voted over a single dissent to overturn this decision, holding that no reasonable jury could have found that Mungin had been discriminated against in violation of Title VII. The court held that Mungin had indeed been mistreated, but that this was no different from the kind of mistreatment that some other white associates also experienced. For example, both Mungin and Stuart Soberman, a white bankruptcy associate, had failed to receive raises. Using this reasoning, the court held that the firm had legitimate, nondiscriminatory reasons for its treatment of Mungin, and he could proffer no countervailing evidence to render these reasons to be pretextual. This holding was clearly short-sighted because, given that most firms are likely to be majority-white, the mere fact that some whites were also mistreated says nothing about whether Mungin was or was not mistreated on the basis of race. For instance, Soberman may have been denied a raise for any number of reasons—such as his work ethic, his dedication to the firm, or the quality of his work—but those reasons would probably have no bearing on whether Mungin's failure to receive a raise was discriminatory in nature. This legal sidestepping by the court highlights one of the basic flaws of Title VII burden shifting. Once a defendant has offered any plausible business reason for the mistreatment (e.g., many associates were treated the same way), the onus is on the plaintiff to essentially prove that the defendant's offered reason was not the one that actually applied, which is an exceedingly difficult task unless there is an overt and obvious act of discrimination.

Another interesting part of the Mungin holding has to do with the question of whether Mungin was qualified. Mungin clearly had done complex bankruptcy work at his prior firms, and received good reviews for the work that he did at Katten. However, the work that he received at Katten was at the junior associate level or lower. Eventually, his hourly billing rate was even reduced from $185 to $125. Mungin was overqualified for the work he was doing, and the fact that his hourly rate was reduced should suggest that he was treated unfairly. Interestingly, the judge in the appellate court used this fact to draw the opposite conclusion. In the judge's view, Mungin's former rate of $185 "imperfectly" reflected his capabilities. This point further highlights the vagaries involved in a Title VII analysis, under which evidence can often be interpreted to reach opposite conclusions. Since the plaintiff in Title VII actions bears the ultimate burden of proof, only the most incontrovertible pieces of evidence will suffice to surpass this evidentiary manipulation.

Thus, where there is no "smoking gun" piece of evidence of discriminatory intent, Title VII claims are difficult to prove. In this respect, Title VII suffers from the perpetrator perspective, since only overt and obvious acts of racism end up being actionable. In the context of highly subjective law firm hiring decisions, Title VII's perpetrator perspective precludes its availability as a tool to integrate elite firms.

* * *

In order to improve diversity in elite law firms, principles of legal ethics should be utilized instead of either mere advocacy/exhortation, or the conventional anti-discrimination regime. There are some questions as to whether business organizations need concern themselves with moral or ethical considerations, as long as their actions are legal. However, unlike many other professions, the field of law requires its members to uphold rigid ethical standards in their professional lives. As we have seen, law firm non-diversity can be explained primarily by hiring processes that unfairly disadvantage minorities due to the structural effects of the hiring process and rational economic decisionmaking. In this section I argue that such practices are clearly in contravention of principles of ethical lawyering, and that the ABA and state ethics boards should incorporate these considerations into currently inadequate ethics rules. By doing so, these entities would transform legal ethics into an effecting agent that would impel law firms to act beyond mere tokenism or rhetoric within the realm of firm diversity. Legal ethics could be used to accomplish internally and organically what Title VII and mere exhortation cannot: the integration of elite law firms.

* * *

Typically, state legislatures act in concert with the ABA when it comes to the promulgation of legal ethics rules that bind members of the bar of particular states. Although each state is certainly free to adopt and modify its own state ethics rules, the ABA holds inordinate influence in codifying ethical guidelines and in broaching dialogue on new issues of interest. In 1970, the ABA promulgated the Model Code of Professional Responsibility ("Model Code"), and almost all the states eventually adopted their basic form. The Code comprised of three parts: Canons, Ethical Considerations, and Disciplinary Rules. The Disciplinary Rules were meant to be a basis for disciplinary action, while the Canons and Ethical Considerations were an "inspirational guide to the members of the profession." In the early 1980s, the ABA worked on a new set of model rules that would replace the Model Code's confusing tripartite structure with one with obligatory and discretionary rules, accompanied by explanatory comments. This effort culminated in the Model Rules of Professional Conduct ("Model Rules"), which has been adopted by a majority of the states.

State ethics codes, whether based on the Model Rules or Model Code, barely touch on issues of race in the legal profession in their current form. To the extent that they do, the focus is on acts of discrimination; none address firm diversity. Some state rules of lawyer professional responsibility expressly prohibit discriminatory practices in hiring and in employment. Unlike these state rules, neither the Model Code nor the Model Rules explicitly forbids discrimination in employment by lawyers. Certain commentators have criticized the ABA for not incorporating discrimination into the Model Rules, yet the criticism has gone unheeded. Model Rule 8.4(d) does prohibit "conduct that is prejudicial to the administration of justice." However, the comments to this rule impose burdensome limitations on the applicability of this Rule to the context of discrimination. The knowing manifestation of bias or prejudice by a lawyer, on the basis of race, sex, religion, national origin, disability, age, sexual orientation or socioeconomic status is a violation of 8.4(d) if it occurs "in the course of representing a client" and if "such actions are prejudicial to the administration of justice." It is somewhat unfortunate that the Model Rules did not make a more sweeping prohibition against discrimination in lawyering. Under the comment's current form, it is unlikely that law firm hiring, a purely internal "non-billable" matter, would qualify as being "in the course of representing" a particular client.

In any case, even if the Model Rules adopted a broad prohibition of discrimination (as have states like New York and California), it is unlikely that the rule would be very useful in ameliorating law firm non-diversity for the same reasons that make Title VII ineffective. Indeed, if Title VII, which features a gargantuan amount of caselaw precedent, is poorly suited to address firm diversity, trying to effect change through the hodgepodge of state anti-discrimination ethics rules in their current form smacks of folly. Not surprisingly, there is no case of a firm being disciplined for a lack of diversity under any of the state codes that mirror Model Rule 8.4(d), or any of the stronger state anti-discrimination ethics rules either, and no ethics opinion of any state addresses the issue. Even if the ABA were bold enough to add a disciplinary rule barring discrimination in law firm practice at-large, a case under such a rule would likely suffer the same doomed fate as one under Title VII.

C. What does it mean to be a lawyer?

We conclude the course by asking you to reflect on a theme that has been constant throughout the course. Based on what you have learned, do you believe law is a profession, a business, or both? What does it mean to be a profession? A business? Do you understand your career through a different lens, such as a thinking of it as vocation?

[Question 23]

Legal practice is a:

(A) profession.

(B) business.

(C) vocation.

(D) other.

Index

✝